THE HANDBOOK OF NEOLIBERALISM

Neoliberalism is easily one of the most powerful concepts to emerge within the social sciences in the last two decades, and the number of scholars who write about this dynamic and unfolding process of socio-spatial transformation is astonishing. Even more surprising is that there has, until now, not been an attempt to provide a broad volume that engages with the multiple registers in which neoliberalism has evolved.

The Handbook of Neoliberalism seeks to offer a wide-ranging overview of the phenomenon of neoliberalism by examining a number of ways that it has been theorized, promoted, critiqued, and put into practice in a variety of geographical locations and institutional frameworks. With contributions from over 50 leading authors working at institutions around the world, the volume's seven parts provide a systematic overview of neoliberalism's origins, political implications, social tensions, knowledge productions, spaces, natures and environments, and aftermaths in addressing ongoing and emerging debates.

The volume aims to provide the first comprehensive overview of the field and to advance the established and emergent debates in a field that has grown exponentially over the past two decades, coinciding with the meteoric rise of neoliberalism as a hegemonic ideology, state form, policy and programme, and governmentality. It includes a substantive introductory chapter and will serve as an invaluable resource for undergraduates, graduate students and professional scholars alike.

Simon Springer is an Associate Professor in the Department of Geography at University of Victoria, Canada.

Kean Birch is an Associate Professor in the Department of Social Science at York University, Canada.

Julie MacLeavy is a Senior Lecturer in Human Geography at the University of Bristol, UK.

THE HANDBOOK OF NEOLIBERALISM

*Edited by Simon Springer,
Kean Birch and Julie MacLeavy*

Routledge
Taylor & Francis Group

NEW YORK AND LONDON

First published 2016
by Routledge
2 Park Square, Milton Park, Abingdon, Oxon OX14 4RN

and by Routledge
711 Third Avenue, New York, NY 10017

Routledge is an imprint of the Taylor & Francis Group, an informa business

British Library Cataloguing in Publication Data
A catalogue record for this book is available from the British Library

Library of Congress Cataloging in Publication Data
Names: Springer, Simon, editor. | Birch, Kean, editor. | MacLeavy, Julie, editor.
Title: The handbook of neoliberalism / edited by Simon Springer, Kean Birch and Julie MacLeavy.
Description: New York, NY: Routledge, 2016.
Identifiers: LCCN 2015050383 | ISBN 9781138844001 (hardback: alk. paper) ISBN 9781315730660 (ebook)
Subjects: LCSH: Neoliberalism.
Classification: LCC HB95 .H335 2016 | DDC 330.1–dc23
LC record available at http://lccn.loc.gov/2015050383

ISBN: 978-1-138-84400-1 (hbk)
ISBN: 978-1-315-73066-0 (ebk)

Typeset in Bembo
by Cenveo Publisher Services, India

Printed and bound in Great Britain by
TJ International Ltd, Padstow, Cornwall

CONTENTS

Contents

FIGURES

TABLES

CONTRIBUTORS

Manuel B. Aalbers, a human geographer, sociologist and urban planner, is Associate Professor of Geography at KU Leuven/University of Leuven, Belgium, where he leads an ERC project and research group on the intersection of real estate, finance and states [http://ees.kuleuven.be/refcom]. Previously, he was at the University of Amsterdam and Columbia University. He has published on financialization, redlining, social and financial exclusion, neoliberalism, mortgage markets, the privatization of social housing, neighbourhood decline, gentrification and the Anglo-American hegemony in academic research and writing. He is the author of *Place, Exclusion, and Mortgage Markets* (Wiley-Blackwell, 2011) and *The Financialization of Housing: A Political Economy Approach* (Routledge, 2016) and the editor of *Subprime Cities: The Political Economy of Mortgage Markets* (Wiley-Blackwell, 2012). He is also the associate editor of the *Encyclopedia of Urban Studies* (Sage, 2010) and of geography journal *TESG*, and has served as the guest editor for seven different journals.

Kean Birch is an Associate Professor in the Department of Social Science at York University, Canada. His research focuses on the changing political economy of science, innovation and environment. His book *We Have Never Been Neoliberal* was published by Zero in 2015. His website can be found at http://www.keanbirch.net/.

Ulrich Brand teaches and does research as Professor of International Politics at the Department of Political Science at the University of Vienna, Austria. His interests lie in critical state and governance studies, regulation and hegemony theory, political ecology, international resource and environmental politics, and social-ecological transformation; his regional focus is Latin America. He has published in journals like *Review of International Political Economy, Antipode, Geoforum, Law, Environment and Development Journal, Austrian Journal of Development Studies, Politische Vierteljahresschrift, Prokla, Österreichische Zeitschrift für Politikwissenschaft* and recently co-edited books on regulation theory, political ecology and Latin America. He received his PhD at Frankfurt am Main University, Germany, and his habilitation at Kassel University, Germany (www.univie.ac.at/intpol).

Ian Bruff is Lecturer in European Politics at the University of Manchester, UK. He has published widely on capitalist diversity, neoliberalism, and social theory. He recently completed a large cross-country project on the diversity of contemporary capitalism(s) with Matthias Ebenau, Christian May and Andreas Nölke, which produced two German-language collections in 2013 (with Westfälisches Dampfboot and the journal *Peripherie*), plus an English-language special issue in 2014 (the journal *Capital & Class*) and an English-language volume in 2015 (with Palgrave Macmillan). He is currently researching the political economy of authoritarian neoliberalism in Europe, and is the Managing Editor of the Transforming Capitalism book series published by Rowman & Littlefield International.

Jessica Budds is Senior Lecturer in Geography and International Development at the University of East Anglia, Norwich, UK. Her research examines the political economy of access to water among low-income groups in the global South, focusing on the application of economic and market principles to water management, as well as the effects of the expansion of water-related economic sectors, including agribusiness, mining and hydropower.

William K. Carroll's research interests are in the areas of the political economy of corporate capitalism, social movements and social change, and critical social theory and method. A member of the Sociology Department at the University of Victoria since 1981, he established the Interdisciplinary Program in Social Justice Studies at the University of Victoria in 2008 and served as its director from 2008 to 2012. His books include *The Making of a Transnational Capitalist Class, Corporate Power in a Globalizing World, Corporate Power and Canadian Capitalism, Remaking Media* (with Bob Hackett), *Critical Strategies for Social Research, Challenges and Perils: Social Democracy in Neoliberal Times* (with R.S. Ratner) and *Organizing Dissent*. His current project, 'Mapping the power of the carbon-extractive corporate resource sector', is an interdisciplinary partnership of several universities and civil-society organizations, tracing modalities of corporate power within the global political economy, and focusing particularly on carboniferous capitalism in western Canada.

Sealing Cheng is Associate Professor in the Department of Anthropology, the Chinese University of Hong Kong. Before that, she was Associate Professor in Women's and Gender Studies at Wellesley College, USA. Her research is focused on sexuality with reference to sex work, migration, asylum-seeking, and human trafficking. Her book, *On the Move for Love: Migrant Entertainers and the US Military in South Korea* (University of Pennsylvania Press, 2010) received the Distinguished Book Award of the Sexualities Section of the American Sociological Association in 2012.

Rosemary-Claire Collard is an Assistant Professor in the Department of Geography, Planning and Environment at Concordia University in Montreal, Canada. Her main research interest is in the relationship between capitalism and biological – especially animal – life. She is co-editor of *Critical Animal Geographies* (Routledge, 2015) and is working on her own book *Zoo-fetishism and the Politics of Commodity Life in the Global Exotic Pet Trade* (under contract with Duke University Press).

Julie Cupples is Reader in Human Geography and Co-director of the Global Development Academy at the University of Edinburgh, UK. She is the author of *Latin American Development* (Routledge, 2013), the co-editor of *Mediated Geographies and Geographies of Media* (Springer, 2015) and the co-author of *Media/Communications/Geographies* (forthcoming, Routledge). Her work has appeared in journals such as *Annals of the Association of American Geographers, Antipode, Feminist Media Studies, Gender, Place and Culture, Television and New Media* and *Transactions of the*

Institute of British Geographers. She is a principal investigator on a research project entitled Geographies of Media Convergence, funded by the Marsden Fund of the Royal Society of the New Zealand. For the past few years, she has been working with indigenous and Afro-descendant broadcasters in both Aotearoa New Zealand and Central America and exploring the geopolitical dimensions of entertainment television within a rapidly changing media environment.

Jessica Dempsey is an Assistant Professor in the Department of Geography at the University of British Columbia, Canada. Her research focuses on the political ecologies of biodiversity conservation and her book *Enterprising Nature* is forthcoming from the *Antipode* book series (Wiley-Blackwell).

Rae Dufty-Jones is a Senior Lecturer in Geography and Urban Studies at Western Sydney University. Rae is an economic and social geographer who researches mobility, housing, neoliberal governance and urban and regional development. Her work includes the 2015 edited collection *Housing in 21st Century Australia* (Ashgate) and articles in *Housing Studies* and *Dialogues in Human Geography*.

Gérard Duménil was born in 1942. He graduated from the École des Hautes Études Commerciale (HEC) and has a PhD in Economics; he was formerly Research Director at the Centre National de la Recherche Scientifique. He is the author of *Le concept de loi économique dans 'Le Capital', avant-propos de L. Althusser* (Maspero, 1978). With Dominique Lévy: *The Economics of the Profit Rate: Competition, Crises, and Historical Tendencies in Capitalism* (Edward Elgar, 1993); *Capital Resurgent: Roots of the Neoliberal Revolution* (2004) and *The Crisis of Neoliberalism* (2011, both Harvard University Press). With Jacques Bidet: *Altermarxisme: Un autre marxisme pour un autre monde* (Presses Universitaires de France, 2007). With Michaël Löwy and Emmanuel Renault: *Lire Marx* and *Les cent mots du marxisme* (both Presses Universitaires de France, 2009).

Matthew Eagleton-Pierce is a Lecturer (Assistant Professor) in International Political Economy at the School of Oriental and African Studies (SOAS), University of London. His primary research interests concern the history and contemporary analysis of neoliberalism, and the political economy of world trade. Such research has a particular focus on the relations between power and processes of legitimation in capitalism. He is the author of *Neoliberalism: The Key Concepts* (Routledge, 2016) and *Symbolic Power in the World Trade Organization* (Oxford, 2013). His journal publications have featured in *New Political Economy* and *Millennium*. He has taught at the University of Oxford, the London School of Economics, and the University of Exeter. He holds a DPhil (PhD) in International Relations from the University of Oxford.

Kim England is Professor of Geography and Adjunct Professor of Gender, Women and Sexuality Studies at the University of Washington. She is an urban, social and feminist geographer whose research focuses on care work, critical social policy analysis, economic restructuring, and urban inequalities, primarily in North America.

Jamey Essex is Associate Professor in the Department of Political Science at the University of Windsor, in Windsor, Ontario, Canada. His research examines the geopolitics and geoeconomics of development, focusing on official development institutions and aid strategies; the political and economic geographies of globalization, focusing on changes in governance and the state; and the restructuring of agriculture and food systems at multiple scales, focusing on food security and hunger.

Maria Fannin is Senior Lecturer in Human Geography in the School of Geographical Sciences, University of Bristol, UK. Her research focuses on the social and economic dimensions of health, medicine and technology, particularly in relation to reproduction. She has conducted research on the use of contracts in commercial cord blood banking and theories of hoarding in relation to the human tissue economy. Her most recent project examined the creation and maintenance of a regional placenta biobank in the UK. Her work has appeared in *Body & Society*, *Feminist Theory* and *New Genetics & Society*.

Michael R. Glass is a Lecturer in the Urban Studies Program at the University of Pittsburgh, Pennsylvania, USA. His research focuses on city-region development and neighbourhood change. He is co-editor of *Performativity, Politics, and the Production of Social Space*, published with Routledge in 2014, and co-author of *Priced Out: Stuyvesant Town and the Loss of Middle-Class Neighborhoods*, published with NYU Press in 2016.

Kevin Glynn teaches Media Studies at Massey University in Wellington, New Zealand. He is author of *Tabloid Culture: Trash Taste, Popular Power and the Transformation of American Television* (Duke University Press, 2000) and co-author of *Communications / Media / Geographies* (Routledge, 2015). His work has also appeared in anthologies and many leading international journals, including *Cultural Studies, Camera Obscura: Feminism, Culture and Media Studies, International Journal of Cultural Studies, Television and New Media, Gender, Place and Culture, Comparative American Studies, Antipode, Annals of the Association of American Geographers*, and others. He is a principal investigator on a research project entitled 'Geographies of Media Convergence', which is funded by the Marsden Fund of the Royal Society of the New Zealand. His recent publications have examined television and media convergence; decolonial struggles in the new media environment; and intersections between popular culture, politics, cultural citizenship and the media.

Peter Graefe is an Associate Professor in the Department of Political Science at McMaster University, Canada. His research seeks to apply political economy analysis to the study of social development policies in Canada, and to the study of Quebec nationalism.

Tess Guiney, PhD, is a graduate of the Geography and Tourism Departments of the University of Otago, Dunedin, New Zealand. Her research focuses on untangling perceptions of place, the popularization of particular humanitarian forms, impacts on host communities, and resistance to these development trends. Her doctoral research utilized orphanage tourism in Cambodia to unravel these issues within a specific setting.

Max Haiven is a writer, teacher, organizer, and Assistant Professor in the Division of Art History and Critical Studies at the Nova Scotia College of Art and Design in K'jipuktuk in Mi'kma'ki (Halifax, Canada). He is author of the books *Crises of Imagination, Crises of Power: Capitalism, Creativity and the Commons* (Zed Books, 2014), *The Radical Imagination: Social Movement Research in the Age of Austerity* (with Alex Khasnabish, Zed Books, 2014) and *Cultures of Financialization: Fictitious Capital in Popular Culture and Everyday Life* (Palgrave Macmillan, 2014).

Reijer Hendrikse is a researcher based at the Department of Geography, Planning and International Development Studies at the University of Amsterdam, Netherlands. His interests include the linkages between neoliberalization and financialization, and the intricacies constituting what David Harvey labels 'the state-finance nexus'. His PhD (University of

Amsterdam, 2015) was entitled 'The long arm of finance'. It explored the relatively neglected financialization of governments, public institutions (including universities) and the state itself. His most recent work focuses on the financialization of Apple Inc. (with Rodrigo Fernandez). Working on the duplicitous liberal divide between states and markets, he is currently exploring and theorizing the global ascent of financialized corporations couched in sovereign powers.

Jason Hickel is an anthropologist at the London School of Economics, UK. He specializes in democracy, development, globalization, and finance, and his work has been supported by grants from Fulbright-Hays, the National Science Foundation, and the Leverhulme Trust. He has published two books, including *Democracy as Death: The Moral Order of Anti-Liberal Politics in South Africa* (University of California Press, 2015). In addition to his academic work, Jason contributes regularly to the *Guardian*, Al Jazeera, and other outlets.

Douglas Hill, PhD, is a Senior Lecturer in Development Studies in the Geography Department of the University of Otago, Dunedin, New Zealand. He has published widely on development issues related to India and elsewhere in Asia, including issues related to migrant labour and urban restructuring, India politics, rural development and environmental management. His most recent work is concerned with transboundary water resources in South Asia.

Matthew Huber is Associate Professor of Geography at Syracuse University, New York. He teaches on energy, environment and the political economy of capitalism. His research looks at the relationship between energy systems and the larger social, cultural and political forces. His 2013 book *Lifeblood: Oil, Freedom and the Forces of Capital* (University of Minnesota Press) examines the role of oil in shaping suburbanization and the rightward turn of American politics in the 1970s and beyond.

Ben Jackson is Associate Professor of Modern History at Oxford University, UK, and a Fellow of University College. He is the author of *Equality and the British Left* (Manchester University Press, 2007) and co-editor of *Making Thatcher's Britain* (Cambridge University Press, 2012). He is currently working on the intellectual history of neoliberalism, on the dissemination of neoliberal ideas into British politics, and on the history and politics of Scottish nationalism.

Bob Jessop is Distinguished Professor of Sociology and Co-Director of the Cultural Political Economy Research Centre, Lancaster University, UK. He is best known for his contributions to state theory, critical political economy, and, most recently, cultural political economy. He has been critiquing neoliberalism since the 1980s and this has interacted with the development of his broader theoretical approach. His latest book is *The State: Past, Present, Future* (Polity, 2015) and his personal archive is at www.bobjessop.org.

Cristóbal Kay is Emeritus Professor in the International Institute of Social Studies (ISS) of Erasmus University Rotterdam in The Hague, Netherlands; Professorial Research Associate in the Department of Development Studies of the School of Oriental and African Studies (SOAS), University of London, and Visiting Professor at the Facultad Latinoamericana de Ciencias Sociales (FLACSO) in Quito, Ecuador. He is an editor of the *Journal of Agrarian Change* and a member of the international advisory board of the *Journal of Peasant Studies*.

Roger Keil is York Research Chair in Global Sub/Urban Studies in the Faculty of Environmental Studies at York University in Toronto, Canada. A former director of York University's City

Institute, he researches global suburbanization, urban political ecology, cities and infectious disease, and regional governance, and is Principal Investigator of a major collaborative research initiative on 'Global Suburbanisms: Governance, Land and Infrastructure in the 21st Century' (2010–17). He is the editor of *Suburban Constellations* (Jovis, 2013) and co-editor (with Pierre Hamel) of *Suburban Governance: A Global View* (University of Toronto Press, 2015).

Nicholas Kiersey is Associate Professor in Political Science at Ohio University, USA. His work focuses on the place of subjectivity and crisis in the reproduction of capitalist power. Recently published articles of his can be found in the *Journal of Critical Globalization Studies*, *Global Society*, and *Global Discourse*. He recently co-edited the volume *Battlestar Galactica and International Relations* with Iver Neumann (Routledge, 2013). His current book project, entitled *Negotiating Crisis: Neoliberal Power in Austerity Ireland*, is set to be published by Rowman & Littlefield in 2016.

Sonja Killoran-McKibbin is a PhD student in the Faculty of Environmental Studies at York University, Canada.

Nick Lewis is an Associate Professor in the School of Geography, Geology and Environmental Science at the University of Auckland, New Zealand.

Dominique Lévy was born in 1945. He graduated from the École Polytechnique and has a PhD in Physics; he was formerly Research Director at the Centre National de la Recherche Scientifique. With Gérard Duménil, he is the author of *The Economics of the Profit Rate: Competition, Crises, and Historical Tendencies in Capitalism* (Edward Elgar, 1993); *Capital Resurgent: Roots of the Neoliberal Revolution* (2004) and *The Crisis of Neoliberalism* (2011, both Harvard University Press).

Alex Loftus teaches and researches in the Department of Geography at King's College London. He is the author of *Everyday Environmentalism: Creating an Urban Political Ecology* (University of Minnesota Press, 2012) and co-editor of *Gramsci: Space, Nature, Politics* (Wiley-Blackwell, 2013).

Larry Lohmann is an activist working with The Corner House, a research and advocacy organization based in the UK. He has contributed to scholarly journals in sociology, politics, development, science studies, law, social policy, environment, accounting and Asian studies. His last book was *Mercados de Carbono: La Neoliberalizacion del Clima* (Quito, 2012).

Julie MacLeavy is a Senior Lecturer in Human Geography at the University of Bristol, UK. Her research contributes to the study of neoliberalism as real-world phenomena and as a theoretical object by providing empirically grounded and critically engaged analysis of labour market regulation, welfare provision and urban renewal in the UK and elsewhere. She has published in a number of scholarly journals including *Environment and Planning A*, *Geoforum*, *Urban Studies*, *Cambridge Review of Regions, Economy and Society* and *Gender, Place and Culture: A Journal of Feminist Geography*. She is the lead editor of a special issue of *Antipode* on new state spatialities and has recently co-edited a special issue of *Social Politics* on gendered transformations of governance, economy and citizenship.

Sheila L. Macrine, PhD, is an Associate Professor at the University of Massachusetts Dartmouth, USA. Her research focuses on two areas: (1) connecting the cultural, political, and institutional contexts of pedagogy as they relate to the public sphere, democratic education and social imagination and (2) developing alternative assessments for students with differences, including the culturally and linguistically diverse (CLD) population. She has published numerous articles and a number of books on critical pedagogy.

Katharyne Mitchell is a Professor of Geography at the University of Washington, USA, specializing in transnationalism, humanitarianism, and urban governance. She has published over 75 refereed articles and chapters and authored or edited nine books and guest edited journals, including *Crossing the Neoliberal Line: Pacific Rim Migration and the Metropolis* (Temple University Press, 2004), and *Practising Public Scholarship: Experiences and Possibilities Beyond the Academy* (Wiley-Blackwell, 2008). Mitchell served as Simpson Professor of the Public Humanities at the University of Washington from 2004–7 and Department Chair from 2008–13. She is the recipient of grants from the MacArthur Foundation, the Spencer Foundation, and the National Science Foundation.

Stephanie L. Mudge is an Assistant Professor of Sociology at the University of California-Davis, USA, who specializes in the study of western politics and expertise. Her work has appeared in journals including *Socio-economic Review*, *American Journal of Sociology*, *Annual Review of Sociology* and *European Journal of Sociology*. Her chapter updates and expands on her previous work on neoliberalism, drawing partly from a manuscript-in-process that is tentatively titled Neoliberal Politics.

Warwick E. Murray is Professor of Human Geography and Development Studies at Victoria University of Wellington, New Zealand. He has held university positions in the UK and Fiji and has been a visiting professor at universities in Europe and South America. He is President of the Australasian Iberian and Latin American Studies Association. He has served as editor on a number of journals including *Asia Pacific Viewpoint* and *Journal of Rural Studies*. His regional expertise covers the Pacific Islands, Oceania, and Latin America.

Vlad Mykhnenko is a Lecturer in Human Geography (Urban Adaptation and Resilience), School of Geography, Earth, and Environmental Sciences, University of Birmingham, UK. Previous appointments were at the University of Nottingham, a Research Fellow at the University of Glasgow, and an International Policy Fellow at the Centre for Policy Studies at Central European University, Budapest, Hungary. His research interests are economic geography, political geography, and qualitative comparative analysis, including currently the study of urban and regional economies; local government finance, fiscal federalism, and devolution; regional development, spatial policy and governance; and geopolitics and critical cartography.

Joseph Nevins is an associate professor in the Department of Earth Science and Geography at Vassar College in Poughkeepsie, New York, USA. His research interests include socio-territorial boundaries and mobility, violence and inequality, and political ecology. Among his books are *Operation Gatekeeper and Beyond: The War On 'Illegals' and the Remaking of the US–Mexico Boundary* (Routledge, 2010); *Taking Southeast Asia to Market: Commodities, Nature, and People in the Neoliberal Age* (co-edited with Nancy Peluso, Cornell University Press, 2008); and *A Not-so-distant Horror: Mass Violence in East Timor* (Cornell University Press, 2005).

Edward Nik-Khah is an Associate Professor of Economics at Roanoke College, New York, USA. He has completed research on interactions between the Chicago School of Economics, the pharmaceutical industry, and pharmaceutical science; the neoliberal origins of economics imperialism; the distinctive role of George Stigler as architect of the Chicago School; and the tensions emerging from economists' assumption of a professional identity as designers of markets. His forthcoming book on the history of knowledge and information in economics (with Philip Mirowski) is entitled *The Knowledge We Have Lost in Information*.

Phillip O'Neill is Professorial Research Fellow in Economic Geography at the Western Sydney University, Australia. He is also the Director of its Centre for Western Sydney. The Centre is the university's portal for policy and research dissemination for the Western Sydney region. Phillip's current research focus is on infrastructure, its privatization, and the implications of private financing for the functioning of cities. His research historically has focused on the regional impacts of industrial change, the role of the state in economic transitions, and the relationships between corporate capital and productive investment.

John Overton is Professor of Development Studies and Human Geography at Victoria University of Wellington, New Zealand. He has held university positions at four other institutions including the Australian National University. He is past President of the New Zealand Geographical Society and former Director of the Commonwealth Geographical Bureau. He has served as an editor for a range of journals including *Asia Pacific Viewpoint*. His regional expertise covers the Pacific Islands, Oceania, South East Asia, and Southern Africa.

Michael A. Peters is Professor of Education at the University of Waikato, New Zealand, and Emeritus at the University of Illinois, Urbana-Champaign. His is Executive Editor of *Educational Philosophy and Theory* and the author of *Neoliberalism and After? Education, Social Policy, and the Crisis of Western Capitalism* (Peter Lang, 2011) and editor of *The Global Financial Crisis and Educational Restructuring* (Peter Lang, 2015) with T. Besley and J. Paraskeva.

Dieter Plehwe is a Senior Fellow in the Department Inequality and Social Policy at the Berlin Social Science Center. His research is located at the interface of comparative capitalism, political sociology, and intellectual history. He co-edited *The Road from Mont Pèlerin* with Philip Mirowski (Harvard University Press, 2009), is a member of the editorial board of *Critical Policy Studies*, and started the think tank network research initiative (www.thinktanknetworkresearch.net). More information can be found on his website: https://www.wzb.eu/de/personen/dieter-plehwe

Russell Prince is Senior Lecturer in Human Geography at Massey University in New Zealand. His research focuses on policy formation and mobility and the geography of expertise. His work has been published in *Transactions of the Institute of Human Geographers*, *Sociology*, and *Environment and Planning A*. His website can be found at: http://www.researchgate.net/profile/Russell_Prince

Mark Purcell is a Professor in the Department of Urban Design and Planning at the University of Washington, USA, where he studies cities, political theory, and democracy. He is the author of *Recapturing Democracy* (Routledge, 2008), *The Down-Deep Delight of Democracy* (Wiley-Blackwell, 2013), and numerous articles in journals including *International Journal of Urban and Regional Research*, *Urban Geography*, *Antipode*, *Urban Studies*, and *Planning Theory*. His blog can be found at http://pathtothepossible.wordpress.com, and his professional webpage at http://faculty.washington.edu/mpurcell

David J. Roberts is an Assistant Professor, Teaching Stream in the Urban Studies Program at the University of Toronto, Canada. His interests include the study of race and geography, mega-events, urban infrastructure and public–private partnerships, and popular culture. His recent scholarship includes articles published in the journals *Dialogues in Human Geography*, *Environment and Planning C*, *Sport in Society*, and *Antipode*.

Susan M. Roberts is Associate Dean for International Affairs in the College of Arts and Sciences at the University of Kentucky, USA, where she is also Director of the International Studies Program and Professor of Geography. She is interested in political economy, feminist thought, and questions of inequality and development. Sue's recently published research includes papers on the rise of development contractors executing development assistance projects for USAID, and the political economy of geospatial intelligence. She teaches economic and political geography as well as courses on neoliberalism and development thinking.

James Rowe is an Assistant Professor in the School of Environmental Studies at the University of Victoria, Canada. His research is currently centred on the role of micropolitics in macropolitical change, with a particular focus on mind/body practices. His website can be found at: http://www.jameskrowe.com/

J.P. Sapinski, University of Oregon, USA. He earned his PhD from the University of Victoria, BC. His research maps out the relations between the global corporate elite and the field of climate politics, with a special focus on policy-planning organizations located at the interface between corporations and politics. His most recent project looks at climate geoengineering in the context of the relationship between the state, scientific knowledge, and the reproduction of global capitalism through the climate crisis. He also did work on global networks of corporate power and on counter-hegemonic networks of knowledge production and mobilization.

Christina Scharff is a Senior Lecturer at the Department of Culture, Media and Creative Industries, King's College London, UK. Her research interests include gender, media and culture and she is author of *Repudiating Feminism: Young Women in a Neoliberal World* (Ashgate, 2012) and, with Rosalind Gill, co-editor of *New Femininities: Postfeminism, Neoliberalism and Subjectivity* (Palgrave Macmillan, 2011). She has researched engagements with feminism in Germany and Britain and her publications have appeared in various international journals, including *Theory, Culture & Society*, *Sociology*, *Feminism & Psychology*, *Feminist Media Studies*, and *The European Journal of Women's Studies*. She is currently holding an ESRC Future Research Leaders grant to conduct research on gender, cultural work and entrepreneurial subjectivities. Her second monograph *Music, Gender and Entrepreneurialism* is forthcoming with Routledge.

James D. Sidaway is Professor of Political Geography at the National University of Singapore. His recent fieldwork and publications have been on security and space in Cambodia, Iraqi Kurdistan and Mozambique (with Till Paasche), the geography of diplomacy (with Virginie Mamadouh and other colleagues in Amsterdam) and about migrant lives in Persian Gulf cities (with Robina Mohammad). His most recent book is a seventh edition of *Geography and Geographers: Anglo-American Human Geography since 1945* (with Ron Johnston, Taylor & Francis, 2015).

Tom Slater, PhD is Reader in Urban Geography at the University of Edinburgh. His research centres on the relations between market processes and state structures in producing and reinforcing urban inequalities. He has written extensively on gentrification (notably the co-authored books, *Gentrification*, 2008, and *The Gentrification Reader*, 2010, both Routledge), displacement from urban space, territorial stigmatization, welfare reform, and social movements. He is currently working on a long-term study of the role of free market think tanks in manufacturing ignorance of the causes of urban inequalities. For more information, including many downloadable papers, see: http://www.geos.ed.ac.uk/homes/tslater

Matthew Sparke is Professor of Geography, International Studies and Global Health at the University of Washington, USA, where he also serves as the Director of Integrated Social Sciences. He is the author of *Introducing Globalization: Ties, Tensions and Uneven Integration* (Wiley-Blackwell, 2013), and *In the Space of Theory: Post-foundational Geographies of the Nation-State* (University of Minnesota Press, 2005). Based on grants from the National Science Foundation, the Mellon Foundation, and other foundations, his research is focused on the uneven geographies of globalization, including, most recently, the epidemiologies of inequality embodied in global biological citizenship and its others.

Simon Springer is an Associate Professor in the Department of Geography at the University of Victoria, Canada. His research agenda explores the political, social, and geographical exclusions that neoliberalization has engendered in post-transitional Cambodia, emphasizing the spatialities of violence and power. He cultivates a cutting-edge theoretical approach to his scholarship by foregrounding both poststructuralist critique and a radical revival of anarchist philosophy. Simon's books include *The Discourse of Neoliberalism: An Anatomy of a Powerful Idea* (Rowman & Littlefield, 2016), *The Anarchist Roots of Geography: Towards Spatial Emancipation* (University of Minnesota Press, 2016), *Violent Neoliberalism: Development, Discourse and Dispossession in Cambodia* (Palgrave Macmillan, 2015), and *Cambodia's Neoliberal Order: Violence, Authoritarianism, and the Contestation of Public Space* (Routledge, 2010). Simon serves as an editor of *ACME: An International E-Journal for Critical Geographies* and the Transforming Capitalism book series published by Rowman & Littlefield. His website can be found at: http://uvic.academia.edu/SimonSpringer.

David Tyfield is a Reader in the Lancaster Environment Centre at Lancaster University, UK, and Director of the International Research and Innovation Centre for the Environment, Guangzhou, China. His research focuses on the interaction of political economy, social change and developments in science, technology and innovation. His book *The Economics of Science* (2 volumes) was published by Routledge in 2012.

Robert Van Horn is Associate Professor of Economics at University of Rhode Island, USA. His research has primarily focused on the history of the post-war Chicago School. He is co-editor of *Building Chicago Economics* (Cambridge University Press, 2011). *History of Political Economy* and *Journal of the History of the Behavioral Sciences*, among others, have published his work. More information can be found at: http://www.uri.edu/faculty/vanhorn/index.htm.

Nave Wald, PhD, is a graduate of the Geography Department of the University of Otago, Dunedin, New Zealand. His work focuses on issues of rural development, food politics, radical politics and civil society. His doctoral research focused on grassroots peasant–indigenous organizations in northwest Argentina, the challenges they face and their responses.

Kevin Ward is a Professor in Human Geography in the School of Education, Environment and Development and Director of cities@manchester (www.cities.manchester.ac.uk) at the University of Manchester. He is a geographical political economist by training, with interests in comparative urbanism, economic and social governance, the financing of infrastructure and urban politics and policy.

Sally Weller is an economic geographer and an Australian Research Council Future Fellow at Monash University in Melbourne, Australia. Her research, which focuses on developing a spatialized interpretation of the ongoing restructuring of the Australian economy, includes studies of labour market and industrial restructuring, cultural industries, regional economies, globalization and the processes of socio-economic change. Her Fellowship project (2012–16) is a comparative study of the politics of transition in two vulnerable regions.

Richard J. White is a Reader in Human Geography at Sheffield Hallam University, UK. Greatly influenced by anarchism and anarchist geographies, Richard's main research and teaching interests address a range of ethical and economic landscapes rooted in the context of social justice and total liberation movements. His research has been published in key international interdisciplinary journals, and he has recently co-edited *Anarchism and Animal Liberation* (McFarland Press, 2015) and contributed chapters to *Critical Animal Geographies* (Routledge, 2014) and *Defining Critical Animal Studies* (Peter Lang, 2014).

Heather Whiteside is Assistant Professor of Political Science at the University of Waterloo and Fellow at the Balsillie School of International Affairs, Canada. Her research interests centre on the political economy of privatization, financialization, and fiscal austerity. She has published on these themes in journals such as *Economic Geography*, *Studies in Political Economy* and *Health Sociology Review*, in her latest book *Purchase for Profit: Public–Private Partnerships and Canada's Public Health Care System* (University of Toronto Press, 2015), and in her 2011 co-authored book *Private Affluence, Public Austerity: Economic Crisis and Democratic Malaise in Canada* (with Stephen McBride, Fernwood).

Colin C. Williams, Professor, is Director of the Centre for Regional Economic and Enterprise Development (CREED) in the Management School at the University of Sheffield, UK. His research interests are in work organization, the informal economy and post-capitalist economic practices, subjects on which he has published some 20 books and 350 journal articles over the past 25 years.

Japhy Wilson, University of Manchester, UK. He is Research Coordinator at the National Strategic Centre for the Right to Territory (CENEDET), a research institute directed by David Harvey and based in Quito, Ecuador. His research explores the relationship between space, power and ideology in the politics of development. He is the author of *Jeffrey Sachs: the Strange Case of Dr Shock and Mr Aid* (Verso, 2014), and co-editor (with Erik Swyngedouw) of *The Post-Political and Its Discontents: Spaces of Depoliticisation, Spectres of Radical Politics* (Edinburgh University Press, 2014).

Anna Zalik is Associate Professor in the Faculty of Environmental Studies at York University. Her research concerns the political economy and ecology of extraction. More information on her work is available at: http://azalik.apps01.yorku.ca/publications/blog/.

ACKNOWLEDGEMENTS

Simon, Kean and Julie would like to acknowledge the following people for their help and support in the development, writing and production of this volume. Andrew Mould at Routledge for approaching Simon with the idea and correctly believing he, Kean and Julie were gullible enough to take on the challenge of bringing *The Handbook of Neoliberalism* to fruition! Sarah Gilkes for negotiating the use of the brilliant artwork by Tony Taylor on the cover and, together with Egle Zigaite, providing editorial assistance for the duration of this project. All of the authors who contributed to this volume and inspired us by writing lots of cool stuff, which was fun to read. Huge thanks are due to Jennifer Mateer for being a sucker for punishment and fearlessly taking on the job of formatting this massive volume on our behalf.

We would also like to pay tribute to our families for their unwavering support and encouragement. Simon would like to thank his partner, Marni, and their kids for their patience in letting him send a billion and one emails at all hours of the day and night to get things organized! Kean would like to thank Sheila and Maple for making his evenings and his life generally that much more fulfilling. And Julie would like to thank Columba, Cillian, Darragh and Aisling for allowing her the time and space to work on this project as well as providing a ready source of light relief.

AN INTRODUCTION TO NEOLIBERALISM

Simon Springer, Kean Birch and Julie MacLeavy

Welcome to *The Handbook of Neoliberalism*, a volume that offers the most complete overview of the field to date. The compiled chapters explore the phenomenon of neoliberalism by examining the range of ways that it has been theorized, promoted, critiqued, and put into practice in a variety of geographical locations and institutional frameworks. Neoliberalism is easily one of the most powerful concepts to emerge within the social sciences in the last two decades, and the number of scholars who are now writing about this dynamic and unfolding process of socio-spatial transformation is nothing short of astonishing. Even more surprising, though, is that there has, until now, not been an attempt to provide a wide-ranging volume that engages with the multiple registers in which neoliberalism has evolved. *The Handbook of Neoliberalism* was assembled with the specific goal of changing that, and accordingly it intends to serve as an essential guide to this vast intellectual landscape.

With contributions from over 60 leading authors, this handbook offers a systematic overview of neoliberalism by addressing ongoing and emerging debates, as well as charting new trajectories for future research. With this volume we have sought to bring the diverse scope and wide-ranging coverage of neoliberalism under a single roof by incorporating an expansive agenda. Most of the edited volumes and monographs on neoliberalism that have been published to date have a very specific thematic focus, either on particular empirical case studies, or by attempting to wrestle with a specific theoretical concern. In contrast, *The Handbook of Neoliberalism* aims to provide a comprehensive survey of the field by offering an interdisciplinary and global perspective. Our authors are working in multiple domains at institutions all around the world, which enables a thorough examination of how neoliberalism has been taken up in diverse contexts and how it is understood by social scientists working from different theoretical perspectives. Our goal for this volume is to advance the established and emergent debates surrounding neoliberalism. As a field of study, neoliberalism has grown exponentially over the past two decades, coinciding with the meteoric rise of this phenomenon as a hegemonic ideology, a state form, a policy and programme, an epistemology, and a version of governmentality.

Neoliberalism is a slippery concept, meaning different things to different people. Scholars have examined the relationships between neoliberalism and a vast array of conceptual categories, including cities (Hackworth 2007; MacLeavy 2008a), gender (Brown 2004; MacLeavy 2011; Oza 2006), citizenship (Ong 2006; Sparke 2006), discourse (Springer 2012, 2016), biotechnology (Birch 2006, 2008), sexualities (Oswin 2007; Richardson 2005), labour (Aguiar and Herod 2006;

Peck 2002), development (Hart 2002; Peet 2007), migration (Lawson 1999; Mitchell 2004), nature (Bakker 2005; McCarthy and Prudham 2004), race (Goldberg 2009; Haylett 2001), homelessness (Klodawsky 2009; May *et al.* 2005), and violence (Springer 2009, 2015) to name but a few. Beyond the academy, activist circles have also seen neoliberalism replace earlier labels that referred to specific politicians and/or political projects (Larner 2009). The term entered global circulation following the Zapatistas' 'encounters' with neoliberalism in Chiapas, Mexico, beginning with the signing of the North American Free Trade Agreement in 1994. Neoliberalism has since become a means of identifying a seemingly ubiquitous set of market-oriented policies as being largely responsible for a wide range of social, political, ecological and economic problems. Given the diversity of domains in which neoliberalism can be found, the term is frequently used somewhat indiscriminately and quite pejoratively to mean anything 'bad', characterizing different social processes (e.g. privatization), institutions (e.g. free markets), and social actors (e.g. corporate power) (Boas and Gans-Morse 2009). While there is a strategic reason for such usage, particularly in terms of mobilizing it as a 'radical political slogan' (Peck 2004), such lack of specificity reduces its capacity as an analytic frame. If neoliberalism is to serve as a way of understanding the transformation of society over the last few decades then the concept is in need of unpacking.

At a very base level we can say that when we make reference to 'neoliberalism', we are generally referring to the new political, economic, and social arrangements within society that emphasize market relations, re-tasking the role of the state, and individual responsibility. Most scholars tend to agree that neoliberalism is broadly defined as the extension of competitive markets into all areas of life, including the economy, politics, and society (see Amable 2011; Bourdieu 1998; Cerny 2008; Crouch 2011; Davies 2014; Dean 2012; Harvey 2005; Mirowski 2013; Mudge 2008; Styhre 2014). Key to this process is an attempt to instill a series of values and social practices in subjects (MacLeavy 2008b). This process can have lasting effects by virtue of being embedded in practices of governance at the local level, which often leads to a sense of neoliberalism being everywhere (Peck and Tickell 2002). It is nonetheless important to attune our analysis to the ways in which neoliberal ideas resonate with a diverse range of state projects, policy objects, and socio-political imaginaries. Contra the prevailing view of neoliberalism as a pure and static end-state, geographical enquiry has sought to illuminate neoliberalism as a dynamic and unfolding process (Peck and Tickell 2002; Brenner *et al.* 2010; England and Ward 2007; Springer 2010). The concept of 'neoliberalization' is thus seen as more appropriate to geographical theorizations inasmuch as it acknowledges the mutated and mongrelized forms of neoliberalism as it travels around our world. Yet by recognizing that there is no pure or paradigmatic version of neoliberalism, and instead a series of geopolitically distinct hybrids (Peck 2004), we contribute once more to the difficulty of achieving consensus on a conceptual definition of what 'neoliberalism' actually means. In many ways, this is the crux of the matter when it comes to scholarship on neoliberalism. There is no shortage of writing on the topic, but how can we be entirely certain that we are engaging in the same conversation?

One could argue that the concept of neoliberalism is simply too amorphous to pin down as the contradictions between paradigm and particularities can perhaps never be fully reconciled (Barnett 2005; Castree 2006). Yet rather than ending the discussion on what neoliberalism means, particularly in terms of its embodied effects and lived realities, commentaries to this effect have instead given rise to some very different, yet also necessarily overlapping, conceptualizations of neoliberalism as scholars have attempted to overcome the conceptual impasse. In this very vein, Stephanie Mudge (2008) has attempted a synthesis of the various perspectives on neoliberalism, as she considers it as a *sui generis* ideological system born of historical processes of struggle and collaboration in three worlds: intellectual, bureaucratic, and political. These three formations of neoliberalism correspond with Wendy Larner's (2000) earlier inquiry that looks to ideology, policy, and governmentality as the three prongs of neoliberalism's theorization. More recently Ward and England (2007) have expanded upon Larner's reading by separating the category of 'policy' into 'policy and programme' and 'state form'. Meanwhile, Simon Springer (2012) has attempted to merge these various understandings, and particularly the divisions between Marxist and Foucauldian readings, through a notion of neoliberalism as a discourse. While it will take time to see whether these attempts prove theoretically useful, for now we can say that the successful mobilization of neoliberalism as a research analytic requires us to emphasize its various roles in shaping state strategies, innovative modes of governance, and new forms of political subjectivity. It demands that we be alert to neoliberalism's different yet somehow unified effects in different spaces and at different times. In seeking to understand neoliberalism as emergent in and through a spectrum of connectivity we ought not to assume that there are implied subject-effects of its programmes of rule. Instead, we can problematize how subjects are being (re)made through neoliberal politics and the discourses that have come to be associated with its 'messy actualities' (Larner 2000: 14). We could even go further in examining the processes through which the concept of the human subject as 'an autonomous, individualized, self-directing, decision-making agent at the heart of policy-making' (Bondi 2005: 499) has been called into being by neoliberalism. Attempting to understand how far this vision of neoliberal subject-making is recognized and assimilated, as well as exploring levels of resistance and refraction, is now one of the key goals of scholarship on neoliberalism.

Although subject formation has arisen as a primary concern, it is not to be taken for granted. Indeed, through a geographical lens of articulation and variegation neoliberalism suddenly seems less assured (Brenner *et al.* 2010; Springer 2011). Historically speaking, there are also limitations to the contemporary view of neoliberalism as a monolithic and complete project. We can start by appreciating that neoliberalism actually started life as a fringe utopian idea (Peck 2008), where it was only over the course of a number of false starts and setbacks that it eventually emerged as an orthodox doctrine. The ideas and policies that are now standard practice in the contemporary neoliberal toolkit surely seemed incomprehensible 60 years ago as the dust settled in the aftermath of World War II. At that time, the global North was enamoured with Keynesian economics, while the ideologies of the right, thanks to the Nazis, became completely anathema to the spirit of the time. This makes the contemporary dominance of neoliberalism all the more surprising. So what happened in the intervening years to allow neoliberalism to become the contemporary 'planetary vulgate' (Bourdieu and Wacquant 2001)? Scholars like George (1999), Duménil and Lévy (2004), and Harvey (2005) have all sketched the unfolding of neoliberalism, while Peck (2008) has provided a detailed analysis of the 'prehistories' of 'protoneoliberalism'. The common theme among all of these accounts is an acceptance of a historical lineage to the development of neoliberalism, that it came from somewhere and that its trajectories were largely purposeful. It is for this very reason that neoliberalism is typically associated with a specific group of influential thinkers, politicians, and policy-makers from the last century, including Friedrich Hayek, Milton Friedman, James Buchanan, Margaret Thatcher, Ronald Reagan, and Alan Greenspan. The claims advanced by this group insist that the market is the most efficient and moral institution for the organization of human affairs, which seems to suggest that it could and perhaps even should replace all other institutions (e.g. family, state, community, and society) as the primary mechanism for producing, promoting, and preserving social order. In particular, neoliberals have argued that the market should replace any collectivist forms of planning, where socialist and redistributive policies are seen as key impediments (Hayek 1944/2001; Friedman 1962). Consequently, neoliberalism entails both positive assumptions (i.e. the market is more efficient than other institutions) and normative assumptions (i.e. the market should replace other institutions because it is both more efficient and liberating).

Understanding neoliberalism necessarily requires unravelling its complex geographies, diverse intellectual histories, and multifarious political implications, rather than simply equating it with one particular school of thought (e.g. Austrian, Freiburg, or Chicago schools), or with neoclassical economics more generally (Birch 2015; Mirowski 2013). There is a complexity to neoliberalism that has sustained it as an area of scholarship for well over a decade now. Throughout this volume we attempt to make greater sense of the ways in which it has been taken up in various registers and the effects that have been and are continuing to be produced as a result of its particular brand of marked-based logic. The assembled chapters will, we hope, afford greater conceptual clarity into what neoliberalism is all about. Our intention is to provide a better sense of the field for those who are new to the study of neoliberalism, but also to offer sufficient depth and new insights for those who are already well immersed. We have organized the discussion around seven key themes: 1) origins; 2) political implications; 3) social tensions; 4) knowledge productions; 5) spaces; 6) natures and environments; and 7) aftermaths. While this offers an organizing principle for the volume, attentive readers will recognize that there are a multitude of important connections to be found between the various sections. The book could be read cover to cover, but we actually encourage readers to jump in wherever they feel inclined, and, from there, to chart their own unique paths through the chapters. Doing so will, we suspect, enable new insights and connections to be drawn.

Starting at the beginning, in the first section on 'Origins', we hope to guide readers through a discussion of how something called 'neoliberalism' came to be, detailing its early formation and eventual uptake across a diverse range of economic matrixes, social contexts, policy environments, and institutional settings. Matthew Eagleton-Pierce kicks things off by asking 'What is new about neoliberalism?', where he takes us through an argument that positions neoliberalism as the latest ideological 'spirit' in the history of capitalism. By interpreting neoliberalism as an ethos of sorts, Eagleton-Pierce is able to caution us on imputing neoliberalism as a bounded concept with historical coherence by dissecting the contradictions between theory and practice. Edward Nik-Khah and Robert Van Horn then trace the rise of the Chicago School of Economics and the inordinate influence it has had on post-World War II economics in the USA. The chapter isn't exclusively concerned with the US setting, though, as it examines the relationship and rich interplay that existed between the Chicago School and their European counterparts in the Mont Pelerin Society. Nik-Khah and Van Horn highlight three crucial figures – Milton Friedman, Aaron Director, and George Stigler – in their analysis, illustrating the views of these pivotal neoliberals and particularly their thinking on the appropriate role of the economist. William K. Carroll and J.P. Sapinski then expand the lens by focusing their attention on the transnational capitalist class, and particularly its intersections with neoliberalism and the deep lineages between the two. Their chapter traces the development of capitalist internationalism, initially within the International Chamber of Commerce, then within the Mont Pelerin Society, and later within the World Economic Forum, as sites for establishing a neoliberal consensus in a transnational process of policy-planning. In their chapter, Kim England and Kevin Ward reflect on the diversity of approaches to theorizing neoliberalism, focusing on the work of scholars from two main traditions: political economy approaches emphasizing a 'process' perspective and post-structuralists emphasizing a 'contingency' perspective. Both traditions illustrate the need for hybridity in any account of neoliberalism. In the following chapter, Dieter Plehwe provides another way to analyse neoliberalism as discourse, in this case as hegemony. Here Plehwe stresses studying the evolution of neoliberal ideas and discourses in their historical context so that scholars avoid crude forms of reductionism whereby neoliberalism is equated with one policy or another. A similar set of concerns arise in Nick Lewis's chapter, in which he theorizes neoliberalism in terms of the Foucauldian notion of governmentality. In his chapter, Lewis is particularly interested in deploying governmentality in the conceptualization of a 'poststructuralist political economy' that can grapple with neoliberalism as a rationality and technology that informs, shapes and disciplines individual subjectivities. Following this, Phillip O'Neill and Sally Weller present a critique of the construction and use of the idea of neoliberalism. Their title 'Neoliberalism in question' echoes Andrew Sayer's (1989) critique of post-Fordism to suggest that the idea is overly flexible and insufficiently specialized. They argue that the range and fluidity of definitions of neoliberalism tend to dull academic argument and advocate a more robust examination of and debate about the nature of contemporary socio-economic change and the issues at stake in explaining continuity and change. Stephanie Mudge concludes this section with a consideration of how best to conceptualize neoliberalism for social scientific purposes. There is, she argues, no completely satisfactory alternative for this term in the social sciences at present. And for this reason, she makes the case for a relational, meso-level approach to studying neoliberalism as a multifaceted social fact.

The second section draws the reader's attention to the variety of 'Political implications' attendant to neoliberal reform. Ian Bruff begins by assessing the connections between neoliberalism and authoritarianism, recalling that state-directed coercion insulated from democratic pressures is central to the creation and maintenance of this politico-economic order, defending it against impulses towards greater equality and democratization. While neoliberalism has long contained authoritarian tendencies, Bruff argues that this character has become significantly more prominent since the outbreak of global capitalist crisis in 2008, particularly in the European Union, where neoliberalizing processes have intensified in recent years. In the next chapter Katharyne Mitchell brings questions of citizenship to centre stage, where she recalls it as processual, formative, and relational. She argues that the speed associated with fast and mobile citizenship often entails the slow-down or stoppage of movement for others, and her main objective is accordingly to identify the ways in which the spatial effects of neoliberalization impact citizenship formation and the relations between individuals and populations around the globe. Douglas Hill, Nave Wald, and Tess Guiney tackle the question of development and neoliberalism, examining the changes that have taken place in the post-World War II era, where neoliberal ideas have come to pervade in every nook and cranny of how mainstream development is currently practised. Jason Hickel then looks to so-called 'free trade' and the limits of democracy, questioning how both are situated under neoliberalism, given the demonstrable lack of freedoms that exist for individuals. While corporate freedoms are now firmly entrenched, the rhetoric of 'free trade' debases the very things that promote real human freedoms – such as the right of workers to organize, equal access to decent public services, and safeguards for a healthy environment. Hickel argues that these are cast as somehow anti-democratic, having been reframed as 'red tape' or as 'barriers to investment', thus positioning neoliberalism's banner of 'freedom' as an assault on democracy. In the following chapter Simon Springer argues that neoliberalism exhibits a distinct relational connection with violence, so much so that we might actually productively consider neoliberalism itself as a particular form of violence. Promises of a free market utopia are confronted with the stark dystopian realities that exist in a growing number of countries where Springer demonstrates how neoliberalization has not resulted in greater peace and prosperity, but in a profound and unmistakable encounter with violence. Nicholas Kiersey then surveys the concept of biopolitics and its situation within ongoing processes of sociological transformation. To explore these issues, his chapter contends that we should bring an innovative attitude to our reading of Foucault's few rudimentary remarks on neoliberal capitalist subjectivity, integrating more fine-grained methods of 'postliberal' economic analysis from Autonomist Marxism, among other sources. In the next chapter, Julie Cupples and Kevin Glynn look to the conjuncture between neoliberalism and the emergence of a highly elaborated and complex convergent media environment marked by rapid technological development, digitalization, miniaturization, and mobilization. Their chapter explores the clash between top-down and bottom-up forces within this complex moment, wherein citizens, activists and conventionally marginalized populations are forging new modes of media consumption/production and devising more democratic ways to communicate, express their views and challenge hegemonic and neoliberal structures of power. In the final chapter of this section, Vlad Mykhnenko looks at resilience in relation to neoliberalism. While he adopts a sceptical perspective on the implications of this discourse and its capacity to recapitulate neoliberal ideas rather than offer a systemic break from them, he also recognizes that resilience theory's insistence on the value of redundant capacities for shock absorption and stress resistance has progressive potential.

Next we turn our attention towards 'Social tensions'. Although cognizant of the false dichotomy that separating the social from the political implies, we nonetheless felt it was a useful organizing principle to try to tease out societal strains as distinct from political effects. In this third section of the volume we set out to cover major identity categories such as race, gender, class and sexuality, while also focusing on neoliberal consequences for health, welfare, and patterns of punitive reform. David J. Roberts begins this section with an examination of the co-constitution of race and neoliberalism. His chapter re-articulates an argument he made (with Mahtani) that early approaches to race and neoliberalism were problematic insofar as they tended to focus on the racialized outcomes of neoliberal reforms (Roberts and Mahtani 2010). While neoliberalism is saturated with race, it also modifies the way that race and racism is understood and experienced in contemporary society. Recognition of this, he suggests, has enabled recent moves beyond the treatment of race as a set of fixed immutable categories and an emergent focus on racialization as an ongoing and evolving process. The manner through which gender comes to have meaning and is experienced is the focus of the next chapter by Christina Scharff. Scharff considers what kind of gendered subjects are compatible with the free, self-sufficient, and self-advancing subjects of neoliberalism. Honing in on the constitution of young women as ideal neoliberal subjects in contemporary western societies, she explores the contradictions, exclusions and politics of neoliberal gendered subjectivity using case study research with female classical musicians. Sealing Cheng follows this with a discussion of how neoliberal governance and subject-making are contested in the realm of sexuality. While scholars generally agree that neoliberalism varies across locations, examining sexuality as a 'dense transfer point for relations of power' (Foucault 1990: 130) illuminates the paradoxes and contradictions of neoliberalism. Cheng asks 'What kind of sexuality does neoliberalism endorse, let be, or penalize?' and seeks to identify what she calls 'the sexual limits of neoliberalism' through analysis of the culture wars and policy debates around sex, ranging from gay marriage to sex trafficking. In the next chapter, Matthew Sparke considers the way in which both macro forms of neoliberal governance and micro practices of neoliberal governmentality come together in context-contingent ways to shape health policies, health systems and embodied health outcomes. He argues that neoliberalization is leading to extremely unequal but interconnected regimes of biopolitics and necropolitics globally. In drawing attention to the connections between these different regimes, Sparke takes us beyond static statistical accounts of how inequality maps onto ill-health in particular data-set defined populations. He illuminates how neoliberal governance comes to have ill-effects on health, as well as how efforts to respond to ill-health remain dominated by neoliberal market logics and language. Julie MacLeavy's chapter follows this and examines the neoliberal impulses underlying the restructuring of contemporary welfare states across the developed world, and elsewhere. Her particular focus is on how a neoliberalized approach to the broader political economy has been translated in an age of austerity and used to legitimate cuts to central and local government budgets, welfare services and benefits, and the privatization of public resources. Using the UK as an illustrative case, MacLeavy traces the rise of a more punitive policy approach in which self-sufficiency and individual requirements to work are emphasized, and points towards the consequences of the neoliberalization of welfare for different social groups. Ben Jackson then turns our attention to labour, which has been central to the concerns of neoliberalism from its ideological inception to the roll-out of neoliberal policies in government in the late twentieth and early twenty-first centuries. His chapter focuses, in particular, on the way in which neoliberal theory has sought to treat labour as a commodity to be bought and sold like any other on the market. A distinctive feature of neoliberal thinking is the view that there is no such thing as market-based coercion in labour relations, only coercive interventions into the market sponsored by the state and by powerful, state-backed unions. The chapter investigates the ideological foundations and policy implications of this stance, which has led neoliberals to adopt a sceptical pose towards labour market regulation and collective bargaining. In the next chapter, Max Haiven explores the relationship of the commons to neoliberalism. He traces both neoliberalism and the idea of the commons as stemming from the crisis of post-war Keynesianism and outlines the ways in which, over the past twenty years, neoliberalism has come to adopt and co-opt certain aspects of the reality and the idea of the commons in an effort to reproduce itself. Turning to a new generation of radical theorizations (and practices) of the commons, including Stefano Harney and Fred Moten's (2013) concept of the 'undercommons' and Silvia Federici's (2012) historically informed conceptualization of the commons as the fabric of a struggle over social reproduction, Haiven suggests that we must hold fast to the conceptual and actual power of the commons to resist and confront neoliberalism, but in ways that attend to the potential for co-optation and the need to retain a broader analysis of capitalism. Peter Graefe then concludes the section. His chapter provides an account of how the social economy translates or relates to a broader neoliberal project or programme. Are we witnessing the roll-out of new institutions and governmentalities so as to extend market metrics deeper into social provisions, and, indeed, into organizations previously marked by non-market cultures and rationalities, or is the attention to the social economy more akin to creating flanking mechanisms to compensate for problems in social reproduction that might hobble the neoliberal project? Considering both Foucauldian and regulationist accounts of the development of the social economy, Graefe argues that there is a tendency to overstate processes that reproduce neoliberalism, and to ignore the potential for the social economy to serve as an element of a settlement that might break with neoliberalism. This is not so much a strategy of introducing agency so as to then adopt an excessive voluntarism, but, he suggests, one of keeping an analytical door open to possibilities of change.

The fourth section explores both the implications of neoliberalism to 'Knowledge productions' (Tyfield 2012) and neoliberalism as a particular epistemological order (Mirowski 2013). A recent book by Dardot and Laval (2014), for example, argues that neoliberalism has entailed the reshaping of our subjectivities through the promotion of particular ways of thinking about ourselves 'economically'; that is, we are encouraged to think of ourselves as business enterprises. It starts with Michael A. Peters discussing the implications of human capital theory to education, especially in relation to Foucault's notion of *homo economicus* as being the 'entrepreneur of the self'. In this chapter, Peters turns to the 2012 discussion between Gary Becker – proponent of human capital theory – and François Ewald about the work of Foucault, especially the contentious claim that Foucault was sympathetic to neoliberalism. Next, Sheila L. Macrine provides a detailed overview of a wider set of 'pedagogies of neoliberalism', or ideas promoted by neoliberals ranging from deregulation through the rule of law to economic education, thereby going beyond a narrow focus on economics. She outlines the different neoliberal pedagogies, with the aim of providing readers with the means to critically unpack the assumptions underpinning neoliberalism as a pedagogy. In his chapter, Kean Birch focuses on a specific form of economic knowledge – financial economics – and its site of reproduction – the business school. Birch notes an ambiguity between critiques of neoliberalism, which tend to focus on markets, and the dominant business form in the neoliberal era, namely the monopolistic or oligopolistic corporation. As such, he posits an important role for the business school in the reproduction of neoliberalism through the production and dissemination of economic knowledge that legitimates corporate monopoly, an issue that is often left out of critical analyses of neoliberalism. The following chapter by Russell Prince deals with broader notions of neoliberal knowledge dissemination, focusing specifically on neoliberal policy transfer. In the chapter, Prince discusses three perspectives of such policy transfer: first, as the result of coercion or consent among policy elites; second, as the result of newly established policy parameters; and third, as the result of assemblages of neoliberal technologies. Neoliberalism has significant implications for other forms of knowledge production, including science and innovation as David Tyfield illustrates in his chapter. Tyfield argues that science and innovation are integral to the emergence of neoliberalism by providing legitimation for political economic restructuring (one example being claims about knowledge-based economies replacing manufacturing-based ones). At the same time, neoliberalism has led to the wholesale transformation of science and innovation through new practices of knowledge enclosure, commodification and asset creation. This entanglement of knowledge and practice is central to Michael R. Glass's chapter, in which he discusses the concept of performativity; specifically, how neoliberal ideas are performed as neoliberal practices. As Glass argues, neoliberalism is always (necessarily) incomplete and in the process of being performed, meaning that there is always an opportunity for alternatives to arise. In a similar although theoretically distinct vein, Heather Whiteside charts the co-evolution of conceptions of austerity and policy manifestations of this theory of fiscal restraint since the 1970s, but with a particular focus on the period following the global financial crisis. Whiteside shows how knowledge (in this instance, theories of austerity and fiscal restraint) has a particular temporality, spatiality and institutional dimension. The final chapter in this section is by Tom Slater, who adopts a focus on the production of 'ignorance' rather than knowledge, or *agnotology*. In order to do this, Slater analyses recent debates on the UK housing crisis, especially the policy discourses emanating from right-wing think tanks. He argues that the dominance of neoliberalism can be explained partly by the right-wing think tank mastery of 'decision-based evidence making', which requires exposure and critical analysis. With this section our intention is to demonstrate how neoliberalism operates through various frames and framings of knowledge, and draw attention to the wider capillaries of power in neoliberalism. Processes of education and the impact on the university and pedagogy are perhaps the most obvious domains, but we also seek to understand how things like innovation, policy ideas, and economic knowledges are produced, disseminated and performed, coming to constitute specific forms of neoliberalism. More embodied forms of knowledge are also covered by thinking through performativity, while the role of ignorance in relation to neoliberalization is highlighted as an important concept to consider.

The fifth section highlights the material implications of neoliberalism. It is at this point that we look specifically at the 'Spaces' in which the phenomenon operates. Given that human geography has been one of the most important disciplinary players in the articulation of critiques against neoliberalism, we wanted to devote specific attention to the spatial patterns of neoliberalism. Such a focus is critically important in understanding both its operation and ongoing power. We look first to the urban and rural frames to tease out similarities and discontinuities, before then considering the notion of heartlands and peripheries at a more global scale. Roger Keil begins this section. His chapter demonstrates that the current 'urban age' – often portrayed as an almost natural demographic, morphological and economic force – has, in many ways, been a product of, and has been productive of, neoliberalization. While 'urbanism' and 'neoliberalism' are mostly open-ended ideological formations, Keil describes how urbanization and neoliberalization are material and discursive processes that lead to real (and imagined) constellations through which modern capitalist societies are being reproduced. Cristóbal Kay follows with an account of neoliberalism as related to rural development. He describes how the neoliberal paradigm has resulted in a profound restructuring of the agricultural sector and rural spaces. This transformation of the countryside has not gone uncontested and Kay also discusses some rural counter-movements contesting neoliberalism. Bob Jessop's chapter then adopts a regulation- and state-theoretical variegated capitalism approach to the genealogy and subsequent development of neoliberalism. He distinguishes four kinds of neoliberal project: post-socialist system transformation, principled neoliberal regime shifts, pragmatic neoliberal policy adjustment, and neoliberal structural adjustment regimes. The heartlands of neoliberalism, Jessop suggests, are characterized by principled neoliberal regime shifts, typified by the USA and UK but with variations in Canada, Éire, Australia, New Zealand, and Iceland. Warwick E. Murray and John Overton follow with a consideration of how the peripheries of the global economy have been deeply engaged in, and affected by, neoliberalism. Their chapter details how neoliberal reforms were encouraged and often forced on countries removed from the centres of global power, including peripheral developing economies, as in sub-Saharan Africa or Latin America, as well as more affluent New World economies, for example Australia and New Zealand, and the consequences in terms of uneven development. Having considered the implications of neoliberalism for core–periphery relations, we then look to geopolitics and territorial borders as particularly salient expressions of the complementary processes that reflect and reproduce a world of gross inequalities. Susan M. Roberts sketches a picture of neoliberal geopolitics, reviewing the ways in which geographers and others have considered the relations between neoliberalism and geopolitical power relations. The chapter considers the recent US-led wars in Afghanistan and Iraq and the ongoing use of drone strikes by the USA as examples, where, broadly speaking, the emphasis is on the relations between the generalization of the logics of the market and ways of viewing and engaging the world premised on the use of force. In the following chapter, Joseph Nevins observes that while the neoliberal era has seen a marked increase in transboundary mobility by the relatively affluent, it has also seen a simultaneous hardening of territorial boundaries for those deemed less than desirable migrants by receiving countries. Rae Dufty-Jones concludes the section in a more intimate frame with a consideration of the domesticating implications of neoliberalism in terms of its penetration of the home. Her account reflects on housing as not just a static tool in neoliberal governing strategies, but also an arena in which the movements of neoliberalism can be witnessed and even potentially subverted.

How neoliberalism is entangled with 'Natures and environments' is the focus of the sixth section. The burgeoning literature on the neoliberalization of nature and environment (e.g. Castree 2008, 2010; McCarthy and Prudham 2004; Moore 2015; etc.), as it has come to be known, forms part of broader debates about the idea that we are living through a geological era best described as the 'Anthropocene' – that is, an era shaped by human action, especially human industrial development. To start this section, Rosemary-Claire Collard, Jessica Dempsey and James Rowe unpack the relationship between neoliberalism and the environment, especially as this relates to shifting regulatory frameworks instituted to govern both access to and use of natural resources. According to Collard *et al.*, this involves environmental re-regulation rather than deregulation, covering new regulations that enable greater exploitation of the environment, innovation in private and voluntary governance, and development of market-based solutions to environmental problems. One key example of a market-based solution is climate emissions trading, the starting point for Larry Lohmann's chapter. However, Lohmann does more than focus on emissions trading; more importantly, he considers how the climate is understood in the neoliberal era and how this differs from previous periods. Consequently, he is able to show how the 'environment' is constructed in contrast to 'society', and the reasons for this and for changing conceptions. Following this, Matthew Huber highlights how neoliberalism is correlated to a particular political economy of energy, especially in the entanglement of neoliberalism and the 'energy crisis' in the 1970s. By means of extension, Huber also argues that neoliberalism is implicated in broader energy developments like the regulation of oil drilling (e.g. Deepwater Horizon) and household energy consumption. A related set of issues arise with other natural resources, as Alex Loftus and Jessica Budds highlight with water and Jamey Essex with agriculture. Starting with water, Loftus and Budds argue that the neoliberalization of water has four different moments involving privatization, corporatization, financialization and marketization of this vital resource. With agriculture and food, Essex discusses how neoliberalism has profoundly impacted agricultural systems since the 1970s. In particular, he highlights the emergence of a new 'neoliberal-corporate' food regime. The section finishes with two chapters concerned with different forms of commodification. First, Maria Fannin discusses the emerging 'bioeconomy' involving the transformation of human bodies and their tissues into commodities through new biotechnologies. As she points out, this bioeconomy entails the alignment of neoliberal political economic structures with scientific epistemologies based on the flexibility, competitiveness and promissory nature of biological processes. Second, Sonja Killoran-McKibbin and Anna Zalik discuss the extractive industries, and a specific 'extractive' form of neoliberalism. In so doing, they highlight the distinctiveness of the extraction of 'nature' and its commodification from other 'productive' activities. In this way, Killoran-McKibbin and Zalik seek to problematize the notion of a 'resource curse', emphasizing that this curse is not environmental, as commonly conceived, but social and capitalist.

In the last section we look towards the future by exploring the 'Aftermaths' of neoliberalism and the possible ways in which we might enable an exit from this now orthodox political economic idea towards more heterodox and alternative modes of organizing our collective lived realities. Neoliberalism continues to have resonant effects in the aftermath of a global financial crisis (Birch and Mykhnenko 2010), reverberations that have been framed in a variety of ways, including 'zombification' and by applying a 'post' to the concept of neoliberalism. Crucially, though, there is also resistance to neoliberalism and a desire to move on. This section begins with Gérard Duménil and Dominique Lévy's unpacking the crisis of neoliberalism. In particular, they trace the failings of neoliberalism both historically and geographically, before focusing in on the latest major crisis culminating in 2008 in the old centres, namely the USA and Europe. They argue that the process of financialization and globalization (and specifically their intersection as financial globalization) led to the construction of a fragile and unwieldy edifice that largely accounts for the crisis of neoliberalism. Manuel B. Aalbers also looks to the financial, but the focus of his chapter is on the complex relation between financial regulation and neoliberalism, where he argues that the label 'deregulation' is somewhat misleading. His contention is that actually existing regulation and neoliberalism are not so much market-oriented as they are devoted to the dominance of markets and public life by financialized corporations. James D. Sidaway and Reijer Hendrikse shift gears slightly, by returning our attention to the recent financial crisis, but recognizing diagnoses of the end of neoliberalism as premature. They chart the reformulation of neoliberalism since the crisis, positing that a 3.0 version is now in effect. In a similar vein, Ulrich Brand looks explicitly to the idea of 'postneoliberalism'. Recognizing that there are multiple conceptualizations of differing scope, complexity, and depth with respect to what might be meant by 'post', he traces the origin of the concept to 1990s Latin America in an attempt to find a common ground in terms of some form of break with specific aspects of 'neoliberalism'. For some, the recent crisis has meant that any calls for postneoliberalism must account for neoliberalism's afterlives, where a zombified version has arisen. Japhy Wilson takes this line of critique even further. By tracing the literature on the phenomenon of so-called 'zombie neoliberalism', he envisions an even deeper sense of morbidity at the centre of neoliberal philosophy, which he refers to as the 'neoliberal gothic'. Richard J. White and Colin C. Williams then help us to see how such latent energy for change might be released by looking at the present situation with a new set of eyes, wherein the presence of diverse alternative economic practices suggests alternatives to neoliberalism already exist. Their chapter demonstrates the pervasive nature of alternative (non-commodified) spaces of work and organization within contemporary capitalist society. By highlighting the shallow purchase of capitalism in everyday coping strategies, they focus on ways to harness an economic future that breaks with neoliberalism. Our final chapter in the volume comes from Mark Purcell, who pulls no punches in asking what use we even have for a volume on neoliberalism. Purcell has had enough of neoliberalism, and compels us to think through what it might mean to do away with this discussion and instead focus on what we do want. When we fixate on neoliberalism, on injustice, on inequality, on exploitation, on enclosure, he argues, we ignore justice, equality, free activity, and the common. Our own power must come back into view, so Purcell says 'no' to neoliberalism, urging us to realize that we have got better things to do.

While we are certain this volume will not be the final word, we tend to agree with Purcell that neoliberalism has become too dominant a discourse. It is a powerful and thus enchanting logic, where even those of us who oppose its effects have been captivated by its spell and caught up in its web. *The Handbook of Neoliberalism* seeks to intervene by outlining how theorizations of neoliberalism have evolved over time and by exploring new research agendas, which we hope will inform policy-making and activism moving forward. We acknowledge the important work of existing scholarship on neoliberalism in all its guises, but we want to end by opening up rather than closing down debate on what neoliberalism means and how we deploy this concept in academia, activism, politics, and beyond. A literature is emerging that is critical of the current uses of neoliberalism, both analytically and empirically. In a similar vein to Purcell, Boas and Gans-Morse (2009) have noted the way in which neoliberalism is used to denote very different things, from policies and development models to ideologies and academic paradigms. Similarly, Rajesh Venugopal (2015: 169) has recently argued that neoliberalism is now shouldering 'an inordinate descriptive and analytical burden in the social sciences'. It is an adjective that can be added to almost anything (e.g. state, space, logic, technologies, discourse, agenda, project, development, governance, regulation). From a slightly different perspective, Barnett (2009) has argued that neoliberalism is a useful 'straw man' – or even 'bogeyman' – for critical scholars; while others like Terry Flew (2014), Carolyn Hardin (2014), Sean Phelan (2014), Sally Weller and Phillip O'Neill (2014), and Kean Birch (2015) agree that neoliberalism risks ending up as some sort of totalizing rhetorical signifier or trope, rather than a concept we can use to reflect the specificity and particularity of human social life.

By presenting a comprehensive examination of the field, we hope that you will find this edited volume useful as you explore the difficult questions of neoliberalism and its multifarious effects, but most of all we hope it inspires you to find the courage to live differently, to speak out, to chart a new path, to resist, to organize, to refuse, and to always remember that there most definitely are alternatives. We must allow our political imaginations to dream beyond the confines of neoliberalism, to embrace the very real possibility of meaningful transformation and lasting change. Indeed, we present this volume to you in the sincere hope that very soon it will be irrelevant. What we mean by this is that we too desire a world free from the chains of neoliberal ideas, and the sooner this book becomes a historical curiosity the better.

References

Aguiar, L.L.M., and Herod, A. eds. 2006. *The Dirty Work of Neoliberalism: Cleaners in the Global Economy.* Oxford: Blackwell.

Amable, B. 2011. Morals and Politics in the Ideology of Neo-Liberalism. *Socio-economic Review*, 9.1: 3–30.

Bakker, K. 2005. Neoliberalizing Nature? Market Environmentalism in Water Supply in England and Wales. *Annals of the Association of American Geographers*, 95.3: 542–65.

Barnett, C. 2005. The Consolations of 'Neoliberalism'. *Geoforum*, 36.1: 7–12.

—. 2009. Publics and Markets: What's Wrong with Neoliberalism? In Smith S.J., Pain, R., Marston, S.A., and Jones, J.P. III, eds. *The SAGE Handbook of Social Geographies*. London: Sage: 271.

Birch, K. 2006. The Neoliberal Underpinnings of the Bioeconomy: The Ideological Discourses and Practices of Economic Competitiveness. *Life Sciences, Society and Policy*, 2.3: 1.

—. 2008. Neoliberalising Bioethics: Bias, Enhancement and Economistic Ethics. *Life Sciences, Society and Policy*, 4.2: 1.

—. 2015. *We Have Never Been Neoliberal.* Winchester: Zero Books.

Birch, K., and Mykhnenko, V. eds. 2010. *The Rise and Fall of Neoliberalism: The Collapse of an Economic Order?* London: Zed Books.

Boas, T.C., and Gans-Morse, J. 2009. Neoliberalism: From New Liberal Philosophy to Anti-Liberal Slogan. *Studies in Comparative International Development*, 44.2: 137–61.

Bondi, L. 2005. Working the Spaces of Neoliberal Subjectivity: Psychotherapeutic Technologies, Professionalisation and Counselling. *Antipode*, 37.3: 497–514.

Bourdieu, P. 1998. The Essence of Neoliberalism. *Le Monde Diplomatique*, 3.

Bourdieu, P., and Wacquant, L. 2001. NewLiberalSpeak: Notes on the New Planetary Vulgate. *Radical Philosophy*, 105.January/February: 2–5.

Brenner, N., Peck, J., and Theodore, N. 2010. Variegated Neoliberalization: Geographies, Modalities, Pathways. *Global Networks*, 10: 182–222.

Brown, M. 2004. Between Neoliberalism and Cultural Conservatism: Spatial Divisions and Multiplications of Hospice Labor in the United States. *Gender, Place and Culture: A Journal of Feminist Geography*, 11.1: 67–82.

Castree, N. 2006. From Neoliberalism to Neoliberalisation: Consolations, Confusions, and Necessary Illusions. *Environment and Planning A: International Journal of Urban and Regional Research*, 38.1: 1–6.

—. 2008. Neoliberalising Nature: The Logics of Deregulation and Reregulation. *Environment and Planning A: International Journal of Urban and Regional Research*, 40.1: 131.

—. 2010. Neoliberalism and the Biophysical Environment 1: What 'Neoliberalism' is, and What Difference Nature Makes to it. *Geography Compass*, 4.12: 1725–33.

Cerny, P.G. 2008. Embedding Neoliberalism: The Evolution of a Hegemonic Paradigm. *The Journal of International Trade and Diplomacy*, 2.1: 1–46.

Crouch, C. 2011. *The Strange Non-Death of Neo-Liberalism.* London: Polity Press.

Dardot, P., and Laval, C. 2014. *The New Way of the World: On Neoliberal Society.* London: Verso Books.

Davies, W. 2014. *The Limits of Neoliberalism: Authority, Sovereignty and the Logic of Competition.* London: Sage.

Dean, M. 2012. Free Economy, Strong State, in Cahill, D., Edwards, F., and Stilwell, F., eds. *Neoliberalism: Beyond the Free Market.* Cheltenham: Edward Elgar: 69–89.

Duménil, G., and Lévy, D. 2004. *Capital Resurgent: Roots of the Neoliberal Revolution.* Cambridge: Harvard University Press.

England, K., and Ward, K. eds. 2007. *Neoliberalization: States, Networks, Peoples.* Malden: Blackwell.

Federici, S. 2012. *Revolution at Point Zero: Housework, Reproduction, and Feminist Struggle.* Oakland: PM Press.

Flew, T. 2014. Six Theories of Neoliberalism. *Thesis Eleven*, 122.1: 49–71.

Foucault, M. 1990. *The History of Sexuality: An Introduction.* New York: Vintage.

Friedman, M. 1962. *Capitalism and Freedom.* Chicago: University of Chicago Press.

George, S. 1999. A Short History of Neo-Liberalism: Twenty Years of Elite Economics and Emerging Opportunities for Structural Change. Paper presented at the Economic Sovereignty in a Globalising World conference, Bangkok, 24–26 March.

Goldberg, D.T. 2009. *The Threat of Race: Reflections on Racial Neoliberalism.* Malden: Blackwell.

Hackworth, J. 2007. *The Neoliberal City: Governance, Ideology, and Development in American Urbanism.* Ithica: Cornell University Press.

Hardin, C. 2014. Finding the 'Neo' in Neoliberalism. *Cultural Studies*, 28.2: 199–221.

Harney, S., and Moten, F. 2013. *The Undercommons: Fugitive Planning and Black Study*. New York: Minor Compositions Press.

Hart, G. 2002. Geography and Development: Development/s Beyond Neoliberalism? Power, Culture, Political Economy. *Progress In Human Geography*, 26.6: 812–22.

Harvey, D. 2005. *A Brief History of Neoliberalism*. New York: Oxford University Press.

Hayek, F.A. 1944/2001. *The Road to Serfdom*. Routledge Classics edition. New York: Routledge.

Haylett, C. 2001. Illegitimate Subjects?: Abject Whites, Neoliberal Modernisation, and Middle-Class Multiculturalism. *Environment and Planning D: Society and Space*, 19.3: 351–70.

Klodawsky, F. 2009. Home Spaces and Rights to the City: Thinking Social Justice for Chronically Homeless Women. *Urban Geography*, 30.6: 591–610.

Larner, W. 2000. Neo-Liberalism: Policy, Ideology, Governmentality. *Studies in Political Economy*, 63: 5–25.

—. 2009. Neoliberalism, in Kitchen, R., and Thrift, N., eds. *International Encyclopedia of Human Geography*. Amsterdam: Elsevier: 374–8.

Lawson, V. 1999. Questions of Migration and Belonging: Understandings of Migration Under Neoliberalism in Ecuador. *International Journal of Population Geography*, 4.5: 261–76.

MacLeavy, J. 2008a. Managing Diversity? 'Community Cohesion' and its Limits in Neoliberal Urban Policy. *Geography Compass*, 2.2: 538–58.

—. 2008b. Neoliberalising Subjects: The Legacy of New Labour's Construction of Social Exclusion in Local Governance. *Geoforum*, 39.5: 1657–66.

—. 2011. Reconfiguring Work and Welfare in the New Economy: Regulatory Geographies of Welfare-to-Work at the Local Level. *Gender, Place and Culture*, 18.5: 611–33.

May, J., Cloke, P., and Johnsen, S. 2005. Re-Phasing Neoliberalism: New Labour and Britain's Crisis of Street Homelessness. *Antipode*, 37.4: 703–30.

McCarthy, J., and Prudham, S. 2004. Neoliberal Nature and the Nature of Neoliberalism. *Geoforum*, 35.3: 275–83.

Mirowski, P. 2013. *Never Let a Serious Crisis go to Waste: How Neoliberalism Survived the Financial Meltdown*. London: Verso Books.

Mitchell, K. 2004. *Crossing the Neoliberal Line: Pacific Rim Migration and the Metropolis*. Philadelphia: Temple University Press.

Moore, J.W. 2015. *Capitalism in the Web of Life: Ecology and the Accumulation of Capital*. London: Verso.

Mudge, S.L. 2008. What is Neo-Liberalism? *Socio-Economic Review*, 6.4: 703–31.

Ong, A. 2006. *Neoliberalism as Exception: Mutations in Citizenship and Sovereignty*. London: Duke University Press.

Oswin, N. 2007. Producing Homonormativity in Neoliberal South Africa: Recognition, Redistribution, and the Equality Project. *Signs: Journal of Women in Culture and Society*, 32.3: 649–69.

Oza, R. 2006. *The Making of Neoliberal India: Nationalism, Gender, and the Paradoxes of Globalization*. New York: Routledge.

Peck, J. 2002. Political Economies of Scale: Fast Policy, Interscalar Relations, and Neoliberal Workfare. *Economic Geography*, 78.3: 331–60.

—. 2004. Geography and Public Policy: Constructions of Neoliberalism. *Progress in Human Geography*, 28: 392–405.

—. 2008. Remaking Laissez-Faire. *Progress in Human Geography*, 32.1: 3–43.

Peck, J., and Tickell, A. 2002. Neoliberalizing Space. *Antipode*, 34: 380–404.

Peet, R. 2007. *Geography of Power: Making Global Economic Policy*. London: Zed Books.

Phelan, S. 2014. Critiquing Neoliberalism: Three Interrogations and a Defense, in Lievrouw, L.A., ed. *Challenging Communication Research*. Pieterlen: Peter Lang: 27–41.

Richardson, D. 2005. Desiring Sameness? The Rise of a Neoliberal Politics of Normalization. *Antipode*, 37.3: 515–35.

Roberts, D., and Mahtani, M. 2010. Neoliberalizing Race, Racing Neoliberalism: Representations of Immigration in the Globe and Mail. *Antipode*, 42.2: 248–57.

Sayer, A. 1989. Postfordism in Question. *International Journal of Urban and Regional Research*, 13: 666–95.

Sparke, M. 2006. A Neoliberal Nexus: Economy, Security and the Biopolitics of Citizenship on the Border. *Political Geography*, 25.2: 151–80.

Springer, S. 2009. The Neoliberalization of Security and Violence in Cambodia's Transition, in Peou, S., ed. *Human Security in East Asia: Challenges for Collaborative Action*. New York: Routledge: 125–41.

—. 2010. Neoliberalism and Geography: Expansions, Variegations, Formations. *Geography Compass*, 4.8: 1025–38.

—. 2011. Articulated Neoliberalism: The Specificity of Patronage, Kleptocracy, and Violence in Cambodia's Neoliberalization. *Environment and Planning A*, 43.11: 2554–70.

—. 2012. Neoliberalism as Discourse: Between Foucauldian Political Economy and Marxian Poststructuralism. *Critical Discourse Studies*, 9.2: 133–47.

—. 2015. *Violent Neoliberalism: Development, Discourse and Dispossession in Cambodia*. New York: Palgrave Macmillan.

—. 2016. *The Discourse of Neoliberalism: An Anatomy of a Powerful Idea*. Lanham: Rowman & Littlefield.

Styhre, A. 2014. *Management and Neoliberalism: Connecting Policies and Practices*. New York: Routledge.

Tyfield, D. 2012. *The Economics of Science*. London: Routledge.

Venugopal, R. 2015. Neoliberalism as Concept. *Economy and Society*, 44.2: 165–87.

Ward, K., and England, K. 2007. Introduction: Reading Neoliberalization, in England, K., and Ward, K., eds. *Neoliberalization: States, Networks, Peoples*. Malden: Blackwell: 1–22.

Weller, S., and O'Neill, P. 2014. An Argument with Neoliberalism: Australia's Place in a Global Imaginary. *Dialogues in Human Geography*, 4.2: 105–30.

PART I

Origins

1

HISTORICIZING THE NEOLIBERAL SPIRIT OF CAPITALISM

Matthew Eagleton-Pierce

What is new about neoliberalism? Such a question immediately implies that certain objects and processes can be defined as 'neoliberal' and, importantly, that the contents of the 'neo' can be explained by reference to a larger phenomenon called liberalism. A veritable galaxy of things are now attached to the term 'neoliberalism', if not as some primary identifying marker then at least as one descriptive property among others. This chapter seeks to offer a window through which to problematize and analyse this core, if recalcitrant, question. In keeping with other debates in the social sciences, it proposes that the frame of neoliberalism tries to capture something about developments in capitalism since the 1970s, with commodification, financialization, and general moves towards 'market-based' modes of regulation or governmentality being major debates in the literature (Harvey 2005; Brenner *et al.* 2010; Peck *et al.* 2012; Springer 2010, 2012). While accepting this temporal frame as a starting point, the chapter seeks to contextualize the history of neoliberalism in two ways. First, the chapter sheds a sharper light on the relationship between capitalism and its mechanisms of legitimation, particularly at the level of everyday experience. Second, within the inevitable space constraints, the argument traces certain threads of meaning that connect the history of the liberal tradition to the present, specifically the themes of individualism, universalism, and meliorism. Thus, the chapter aims to reveal how justifications for neoliberal capitalist practices are the product of a long history of social struggles that are, moreover, often confusing, multifarious, and even contradictory. Ironically, once this perspective is recognized, the task of deciphering contemporary neoliberalism arguably becomes harder, particularly concerning efforts to understand where certain ideas and values tied to neoliberalism acquire their commonsensical power. If neoliberalism is a moving concept then scholarship needs to be equally adept at moving with it.

The spirit of capitalism

The justifications advanced for the maintenance of the capitalist system can often appear unconvincing, fragile, or even absurd. From the nineteenth century, with its growth of industrial organization, capitalism has been shadowed by different forms of critique. Some of the most common reasons given for opposition against capitalism have included arguments that the system fosters inequalities in material wealth, oligopolistic market structures, excessively close relations between political and commercial elites, and dehumanizing social effects. Within this complex history, across many institutional settings, people are yoked into commercial pursuits that can be mundane, distasteful, or even dangerous to their health. Most workers are confronted with limited options throughout their lives: with respect to accessing labour markets, the reliability of paid employment, and the basic activities of the working day. Even where forms of social security have been politically constructed, such as in developed societies since the Second World War, a large population is only two or three pay cheques away from poverty, if they do not already experience such conditions. For capitalists and managers, a class fraction who have power over the means of production, enhanced positions of relative security are cultivated. Yet even among these groups, life is often marked by an anxious and seemingly insatiable struggle for competitive advantage, of which luxury consumption represents one major avenue for social distinction.

Despite these tendencies, the capacity for capitalism to renew itself in the face of tensions, crises, and contradictions has surprised many of its most prominent supporters and detractors. To survive and reconfigure, capitalism requires reasons for encouraging people to commit to particular accumulation processes. The degree to which this commitment is accepted varies, not only across time and territories, but also with respect to the moral values of each participant. Commitment could range from the zealous embrace of business promoted by management gurus, through to moderate levels of contentment and, at the other end of the spectrum, a quiet frustration or resignation that refrains from spilling over into outright hostility against the prevailing order. Remuneration is one tool for ensuring commitment, but is often insufficient on it own. Thus, many critical writers have been preoccupied with trying to understand how certain social mechanisms contribute to the justification of capitalist practices. For instance, in the Marxist tradition, ideology has occupied a major conceptual space, often depicted as an elite-led 'cloaking' instrument that aims to secure the legitimation of business. From this viewpoint, the emphasis is placed on how methods of legitimation are used by capitalists and state officials to maintain particular social relations and how conflict is reduced or 'masked' through seemingly consensual means (Marx and Engels 1970; Gramsci 1971; for an introduction to ideological analysis, see Freeden 1996). Elsewhere, in a similar way, Pierre Bourdieu (1991, 2005) devised the notion of symbolic power to explore how the naturalization of authority, including economic agendas, can become sedimented into the mental frameworks of both dominant and dominated agents (see Springer this volume).

The conceptual framing of this chapter stems from these long-standing scholarly enquiries into the necessity of capitalism to justify itself to different audiences. A specific inspiration here comes from Luc Boltanski and Ève Chiapello's *The New Spirit of Capitalism* (2007), a book which dissects a range of French management texts in order to elucidate the processes through which neoliberalism, conceived as the current stage of capitalism, has sustained itself through the selective alteration of critiques derived from the 1960s and 1970s (also see Chiapello 2003; Boltanski and Chiapello 2007; Boltanski and Thévenot 2006). By referencing 'spirit', Boltanski and Chiapello follow the classic proposition from Max Weber (2001[1930]: 17) that capitalism has fostered a 'peculiar ethic', one that is 'not mere business astuteness', but a broader 'ethos' or 'duty' around the ambition of unlimited capital accumulation. Boltanski and Chiapello invoke ideology as a way to study the changing properties of this spirit, but their definition departs from the frequently perceived reductionist Marxist sense of the 'dominant ideology', a presumed coherent 'regime' engineered by Machiavellian elites in order to conceal material interests. Rather, they draw attention to the practical, everyday making and consumption of ideology beyond the world of elites. In other words, following Paul Ricoeur (1986), Boltanski and Chiapello try to offer a broader 'culturalist' perspective, one which is attuned to how ideology performs not only a distorting and legitimating function, but is also directed towards the social integration and organization of populations.

What does the concept of the spirit of capitalism offer to the study of neoliberalism? Three possibilities can be suggested. First, by foregrounding capitalism as the larger object of analysis, it helps to situate historically phenomena associated with neoliberalism and, therefore, guard against any propensity to reify or exaggerate recent events since the 1970s as being necessarily 'unique' or 'distinctive'. Even worse is the general predilection seen in some scholarly agendas to gravitate towards claiming the 'new' in order to attract attention, even if such labels may not in themselves have merit. The spotlight on capitalist practices also sharpens the analytical optic on political economy, with its attendant links to questions of distribution, a focus not always seen in the wider literature on neoliberalism which sidelines the master concept of capitalism (on the reasons for the academic and popular decline in the use of the term 'capitalism', see Eagleton-Pierce 2016). Second, through this attention to history, one can better grasp how the neoliberal spirit both incorporates and rejects other ideological properties from earlier periods of capitalism. This benefit is often overlooked and is worthy of investigation, particularly for explaining the relative 'stability' of theories, narratives, and agendas that are claimed to carry a neoliberal stamp. Thus, how a neoliberal viewpoint resonates as 'coherent' – that is, treated as 'normal' or 'natural' – can often be explained through tracing the genealogy of such opinions through a longer liberal tradition. Third, the focus on the looser category of ideological spirit also helps to relax certain presumptions on what ideas filter in and out of neoliberal justificatory schemas. In other words, my argument is that the potency of neoliberalism rests not simply on 'scientific' theories, notably neoclassical economics, but also on a range of commonly held norms, ethical values, and aspirations that become integrated into a neoliberal cosmos. Indeed, the variety of these types of justification – composed for different audiences with specific vocabularies, customs, and rules, yet still capitalist in orientation – is precisely what helps to give practices tied to neoliberalism a hegemonic-like appearance.

Three themes in the liberal tradition

Like a prism that refracts light into different wavelengths, the study and practice of liberalism has spawned a rich variety of forms. The complexity of this history – which spans socialist to conservative theories, nationally specific mutations and ruptures, and many different societal applications – resists easy summation. A single unchanging essence of liberalism cannot be captured and pinned down. At the same time, there is no attempt here to offer an exhaustive survey of all the potential properties within the neoliberal spirit of capitalism. Rather, the discussion highlights some enduring themes within the history of liberal thought which, in turn, have been rediscovered in neoliberal revisions and articulations. Following John Gray (1995), these family resemblances help to grant liberalism the quality of a 'tradition' – that is, a patterned or inherited way of thinking. Three themes are examined: (1) individualism, whereby the individual tends to acquire ontological priority over the collective; (2) universalism, such as seen in the expansionary moves towards a world market; and (3) meliorism, whereby humans, it is claimed, have the potential to improve and remake themselves. Gray (ibid.) also examines the theme of egalitarianism, but that is not explicitly debated here. The discussion therefore seeks to selectively contextualize how such themes – often read as emblematic of contemporary neoliberalism – should be situated in relation to a longer incorporated history of social struggles.

Individualism

Prior to the eighteenth century, the modern notion of seeing oneself as 'an individual', a person endowed with a distinctive set of qualities, was probably not a common conception. Obligation to family, religion, empire, or king often superseded any claims to individual subjectivity. From the eighteenth century, classical liberal writers began to construct an argument around the individual as a moral figure. This line of reasoning did not necessarily deny the significance of collectives – such as the state, society, or community – but, rather, sought to promote the abstract individual as a normative baseline. Thus, in Adam Smith's writing, commercial society was defined as the aggregate of individual decisions, although Smith was particularly interested in the emotional content of such actions (such as empathy, sloth, indulgence etc.) (Smith 1776[1993]). From the late nineteenth century, in a departure from this latter appeal to emotions, neoclassical economists redefined the concept of the individual. The neoclassical theorization of the individual suggested that only human beings are 'real' and can be measured. In terms of its disciplinary and political impact, this formulation has generated profound consequences. Social entities and institutions still matter for neoclassical economics, but such forms can only be explained in relation to the beliefs and choices of individuals (Hausman and McPherson 2008). In turn, this principle often slips comfortably into a second feature: the individual as a character driven by private tastes who, significantly, acts as a 'rational' decision-maker in crafting choices. The ideal individual surfaces here as a calculating animal who is or, more prescriptively, *should be*, attentive to his or her material efficiency (Robbins 1935; also see Jevons 1875; for a critique, see Davis 2003).

Inspired in part by the Romantic movement, the idea of individualism takes off in the nineteenth century. As charted by Lukes (1973), individualism has an elaborate semantic history with a range of meanings informed by national contexts. In the USA, for instance, it became 'a symbolic catchword of immense ideological significance, expressing all that has at various times been implied in the philosophy of natural rights, the belief in free enterprise, and the American Dream' (ibid.: 26). By contrast, in France in particular, but also elsewhere, individualism has carried a pejorative tone, with the implication that to become too focused on the individual jeopardizes the presumed higher interests of society. This latter connotation has, therefore, made individualism a useful concept for critics of capitalism, as illustrated by Marx's argument that individuals are not born free and rational, but struggle to make their own history 'under circumstances existing already, given and transmitted from the past' (Marx 1852[2000]: 329). Thus, since the notion of individualism is mobilized both in defence and opposition to capitalism, it is not surprising that the term has become a point of struggle. For instance, Friedrich Hayek (1948), often considered an early neoliberal thinker, argued for a 'true' theory of individualism, one which set its face against socialist approaches to society, but at the same time did not treat individuals as either isolated or infallible beings removed from larger forces (see also Stedman Jones 2012). In sum, by the mid-twentieth century, prior to the mainstream adoption of policy-making linked to neoliberalism, the idea of individualism was already diffused into everyday discourse.

How, therefore, has the notion of individualism been recast in relation to the neoliberal spirit of capitalism? Among many illustrations, developments in consumerism can be noted. In advertising, the nurturing of the self, through the purchase of commodities, is frequently offered as being both desirable and necessary. The neoliberal twist on 'individual' is distinctive in at least two ways. First, the category of the 'consumer' has now extended into other fields, such as politics, education, and health. While 'consumer' has always carried an unfavourable tone, initially meaning to destroy and to waste, one could argue that the popularization of the term beyond purely commercial settings is helping to neutralize this criticism. Second, with the valorization of choice and competitiveness as guiding principles for societal organization, the appeal to personalization and customization offers further extensions of neoliberal thinking. From the late 1980s, these latter expressions became concerns for many businesses, with marketing theory helping to craft, and implement, such agendas. The rise of 'mass customization' systems was made financially viable by new flexible manufacturing processes, such as seen in the automotive industry (Davis 1989; Kotler 1989; Alford *et al.* 2000). In this sense, therefore, the marketing of individualized choice to larger populations – a visible phenomenon by the turn of the century – required the development of an elaborate infrastructure, with respect to manufacturing, processing, and trade.

Yet the concept of the 'individual' remains a difficult notion to understand in the neoliberal period, not least because of gaps that often appear between the ideology of individualism and how social agents actually behave or desire to behave. Many critics have argued that neoliberalism is 'causing' a more individualistic and, by implication, privatized world. Margaret Thatcher's famous remark – that there is 'no such thing as society, only individual men and women' – is often quoted to support such claims (as in Harvey 2005: 23). Since the 1980s, across a number of industries, there is no question that the erosion of certain collective structures, notably trade unions, has weakened ties of solidarity that proved beneficial for worker rights (Gumbrell-McCormick and Hyman 2013). In turn, this trend has fuelled a corresponding emphasis by conservative voices on 'moral individualism' and 'responsibility', with a particular focus on the alleged personal inadequacies of poorer citizens who require state welfare (rather than exploring, for instance, class politics or other historical legacies that structure inequalities) (Wacquant 2009). The recent rise of the notion of 'individual resilience' has only served to underscore this general argument that the redistributive social state model is considered out of date. Such debates are important for shedding light on the power struggles that intersect between forms of capitalism, state structures, and citizenship.

However, as perceptively suggested by Clive Barnett (2005), this analysis potentially risks creating a polarized opposition between individualism (as bad) and collectivism (as good). Barnett proposes that a different research agenda would uncover the 'new and innovative forms of individualized collective action' operating in the modern period (ibid.: 11). For instance, many forms of advertising promote an ambiguous tension between, on the one hand, the aspiration to fulfil personal individuality and, on the other, the social comfort of fitting into larger collectives or fashions (peer groups, social classes, nations, environmentalism etc.). Again, as argued by cultural historians such as Trentmann (2005, 2012, 2016), these advertising strategies are not new, but have been tested and refined over decades or even centuries. One can debate the extent to which such notions of 'individualized collective action' are 'real' or how they may conflict with other identities of the self, but it is difficult to deny that consumerism in the neoliberal period pulls many levers at the same time. Another problem in this area concerns the common association of 'collective' with movements on the political left that seek to critique capitalism when, in reality, the term 'collective' would also aptly describe agendas that seek to mobilize capitalist opinion, such as the World Economic Forum. In short, through these ways, the larger liberal theme of individualism can be further problematized in relation to concrete capitalist practices.

Universalism

In the *Grundrisse* (1993[1939]), Marx speaks about how capitalism cannot abide by limits of any kind: '[t]he tendency to create the *world market* is directly given in the concept of capital itself. Every limit appears as a barrier to be overcome' (ibid.: 408, italics in original). This unceasing effort to bypass or transcend limits – which may take physical, financial, political, or cultural forms – gives capitalism its familiar expansionary logic. New opportunities for reinvesting surplus capital matter not only for generating fresh sources of profit, but also for containing potential contradictions and crises within larger accumulation processes. In this respect, as Harvey

(2006) argues, capitalism always needs to improvise and create 'spatial fixes' to manage its problems, such as through the search for faster transportation and communication technologies, new sources of labour, or alternative consumer markets. Through these expansionary patterns, both real and desired, capitalism strives to 'nestle everywhere, settle everywhere, and establish connections everywhere' (Marx and Engels (1998[1848]: 39).

This tendency towards capitalist expansion has been examined and, indeed, normatively justified by many writers in the liberal tradition. Enlightenment thinkers and, earlier, the Stoics in Greek philosophy have been among the major sources of inspiration for such debates. From Locke and Kant, through to Mill and Hayek, convergence around a presumed rational and cosmopolitan universal civilization has often appeared as a *telos* (Gray 1989, 1995). For some authors, appeals to Divine Providence have implicitly or explicitly informed such conceptions. For instance, as Kant expressed it, 'the spirit of commerce sooner or later takes hold of every people, and it cannot exist side by side with war' (Kant 2003[1795]: 114). The notion of progress, which implies a stage theory of history, has always been important for enhancing the social and political potency of universalist arguments. From the eighteenth century, in the context of imperialism, the construction of the 'inferior', non-Western 'Other' was intimately related to this ideology. By the twentieth century, under the influence of the 'new science' of development and the work of the United Nations, the narrative of progress was repackaged into modernization theory (Rostow 1960). In this sense, variation in development levels is accepted, but all actors are still assumed to benefit from the defence of an enlarged commercial order.

There are many ways to unpick universalist justifications in the spirit of capitalism. With a view to shedding light on how this theme continues to inform conceptions of, and practices within, neoliberalism, one can highlight here the master notion of the market. From the sixteenth century, 'market' began to be imagined in a more abstract sense as not only reflecting a particular geographical space, but also as a general process for buying and selling. In turn, this extension allowed the market to be metaphorically re-conceived as a flexible category (Dilley 1992). However, although the term was commonly invoked during this period, the major conceptual advance took place in the context of the industrial revolution. Defining the trading of intangible assets as markets (stocks, foreign exchange etc.) was coined during the nineteenth century, along with the popular imagining of entire countries and, ultimately, the world, under the same label. Thus, part of the commonsense appeal of the concept lies in how it is *not* inspected, but rather assumes a non-institutionalized quality. In the most profound doxic sense, 'market' sometimes appears constitutive of some divine order or of human nature itself (Carrier 1997). As one Nobel prize-winning economist once quipped, in a line that encapsulates this logic of apparently timeless application seen in much neoclassical economics literature, 'in the beginning, there were markets' (Williamson: 1983: 20).

Neoliberalism is often summarized as 'rule', 'discipline', or 'tyranny' by world markets (Bourdieu 1998, 2003; Harvey 2005; Brenner *et al.* 2010; Peck *et al.* 2012; Springer 2010). However, similar to the deep-rooted theme of individualism, one can question the extent to which the appeal to universal markets has undergone substantial change in the neoliberal period. Two issues can be touched on here. First, the concept of the market has arguably become more pervasive and taken-for-granted, serving as a kind of metaphorical oxygen supply for the neoliberal body. In explaining this discursive circulation, the end of the Cold War is particularly significant. For instance, in the *Financial Times*, prior to 1990, the phrase 'global economy' was invoked only 18 times. During the 1990s, the expression is found in 175 stories, and by the first decade of this century, 809 uses are recorded. With the collapse of the Soviet Union, the notion of forming a global business or, perhaps more precisely in many instances, *aspiring to be seen as global*, became a possibility for many corporate entities. A similar conceptual evolution is seen with 'emerging markets', an expression coined by a World Bank economist to encourage Wall Street banks to make investments in developing countries (van Agtmael 2007). For those looking at emerging markets from the outside (that is, the West), the phrase carries with it an imagery of discovery and opportunity. It is no surprise, therefore, that the concept helps to convey an impression that all countries should orientate themselves to a market-based vision as a universal goal.

Second, although the term 'market' is frequently treated as an ordinary phrase, it also offers a focal point for scepticism on the enduring impacts of capitalist practices, or even if the system should exist. Again, the basic tone of this criticism is not radically new (for example, see the Counter-Enlightenment movement or, by the twentieth century, Polanyi 2001[1944]). In Boltanski and Chiapello's (2007) analysis, social critique plays a significant role in constraining capitalist accumulation processes, although the 'effectiveness' of such actions is often limited, disorganized, and beset by setbacks. In short, critics of capitalism are frequently critics of the ideology of universalism preached in its name. According to such arguments, the aspiration for a world market has a quasi-mythical form that, rather than satisfying all, tends to benefit only select groups. Among the most familiar critiques of capitalism is the claim that the system can suffocate the potential plurality of human identities. This core criticism resurfaces in the neoliberal period in many forms and guises. For instance, from the 1990s, with respect to international development policy, critics began arguing that 'market fundamentalism' had gone too far and, as a consequence, more attention needed to be devoted to particular social actors, domestic institutions, 'governance', and country 'ownership' agendas. As Dani Rodrik (2007) has argued, the early twentieth-first-century orthodoxy on development policy is a kind of 'augmented Washington Consensus', one which still contains the core 'Victorian virtue' of 'free markets and sound money' (Krugman 1995: 29), but now incorporates a range of 'second generation reforms' (Serra and Stiglitz 2008). In sum, at the heart of many policy struggles over the notion of the market is this inherent tension between recognizing socio-political diversity and advocating global prescriptions.

Meliorism

If individualism and universalism are commonly recognized themes in the liberal tradition, the explicit notion of meliorism has attracted less attention. This feature is defined by Gray (1993) in the following terms:

> [e]ven if human institutions are imperfectible, they are nonetheless open to indefinite improvement by the judicious use of critical reason. To say this is to say that, though no contemporary liberalism can credibly presuppose historical laws guaranteeing inevitable human improvement, equally, no liberalism can do without some idea of progress, however attenuated.
>
> *(Ibid.: 286)*

Thus, the notion of meliorism tries to capture how many voices associated with liberalism, particularly linked to the world of professional politics, adopt a 'reformist' mindset, one which is often not bound to a sentimental faith or excessive optimism but a pragmatic adaptability in the face of change. To this extent, the melioristic attitude – with its core focus on improvability through intelligent labour – fits comfortably with the historical appeal to progress through universalism (Hildebrand 2013).

Meliorism can be viewed as one of the ace cards for sustaining commitment to a capitalist ethic, although it should not be read as exclusively tied to capitalism. In other words, the spirit of capitalism cannot exist as a fantasy that is never concretely realized: the system must, at least partially, follow through on its promises. It is this potential to hold up tangible illustrations of 'success', along with cultivating the hope that others may enhance themselves in ways that achieve similar success, which enables a refreshing of confidence in the melioristic disposition. For instance, in most countries, the term 'middle class' carries culturally favourable meanings, associated with the aspiration to achieve socio-economic distinction (on the contested and often confusing history of the category, including its relationship to 'bourgeoisie', see Moretti 2013). The desire to appear as middle class (even if one may not have the means) remains extra-ordinarily attractive and, as a consequence, is often invoked or exploited by politicians who seek votes and legitimacy. In a related sense, at the international level, the commercial prominence of countries such as China and India is on many occasions held up as proof that 'globalization works' and that the Global South need not be 'lost' in the world economy (Bhagwati 2004; Wolf 2004). Thus, even the apparently innocent phrase of 'rising powers' carries the traces of a melioristic fetish – that is, a presumption of movement from an 'immature' to a 'mature' status whereby an ideal model can be achieved (Williams 1985[1976]: 121).

The value of this attitude is particularly visible when the spirit of capitalism is placed under renewed scrutiny and, as a result, the defenders of the spirit are forced to improve the veracity and persuasiveness of their claims. It is here where the neoliberal spirit has encountered some problems in mobilizing constituents around a commitment to meliorism. For example, in the USA, the link between productivity and wages has decoupled since the 1970s, meaning that many Americans today are striving harder to maintain a standard of living that is perceived to be middle class (Erickson 2014). In opinion polls, when compared to other countries, Americans have historically expressed greater tolerance for societal inequality. However, since the financial crisis and rise of the super rich, social perceptions are drawing closer to the material reality of the class system described by social scientists (Gilbert 2014). In 2008, 53 per cent of Americans self-identified themselves as being middle class, with another 25 per cent associating themselves with the lower-class category. But by 2014, the former figure had dropped to 44 per cent, while the latter rose to 40 per cent (Pew Research Center 2014). Combined with a visceral apathy directed towards Congress, such indicators give a flavour of how many Americans are losing faith in institutions to either elevate or maintain their position in the class system.

Conclusion

Inspired by Boltanski and Chiapello (2007), this chapter has sought to offer a particular framing of neoliberalism as the latest ideological 'spirit' in the history of capitalism. My aim has been to showcase how this sociological perspective, which is attentive to material forces and the means by which such phenomena are symbolically justified, can enhance our understanding of how the commercial world takes its objectified forms, not least at the quotidian or consumer level. Through widening the historical optic, one can explore how the themes of individualism, uni-versalism, and meliorism are connecting tendencies found throughout the liberal tradition. The chapter has not tried to imply, in any kind of pre-emptive mode of analysis, that nothing new can be found in practices tied to neoliberalism, nor that all actions defined as neoliberal always carry the imprint of such themes. The discussion has also been alert to the perennial problem of gaps emerging between ideological expressions and how human behaviour is con-cretely realized or desired. Rather, the more limited task has been to provide a window through which to shed some new light on core enquiries related to scholarship on neoliberalism.

By attending to the deeper webs of meaning that form an apparent coherence to the neoliberal spirit, a concern which is developed in Eagleton-Pierce (2016) in reference to a vocabulary of terms that have acquired a commonsensical neoliberal twist, one can better grasp questions of continuity and change in dominant ideas and practices.

References

Alford, D., Sackett, P., and Nelder, G. 2000. Mass Customisation: An Automotive Perspective. *International Journal of Production Economics*, 65.1: 99–100.

Barnett, C. 2005. The Consolations of 'Neoliberalism'. *Geoforum*, 36.1: 7–12.

Bhagwati, J. 2004. *In Defense of Globalization*. Oxford: Oxford University Press.

Boltanski, L. and Chiapello, E. 2007. *The New Spirit of Capitalism*. London: Verso.

Boltanski, L. and Thévenot, L. 2006. *On Justification: Economies of Worth*. Princeton, NJ: Princeton University Press.

Bourdieu, P. 1991. *Language and Symbolic Power*. Cambridge: Polity Press.

—. 1998. *Acts of Resistance: Against the New Myths of Our Time*. Cambridge: Polity Press.

—. 2003. *Firing Back: Against the Tyranny of the Market 2*. London: Verso.

—. 2005. *The Social Structures of the Economy*. Cambridge: Polity Press.

Brenner, N., Peck, J., and Theodore, N. 2010. Variegated Neoliberalization: Geographies, Modalities, Pathways. *Global Networks*, 10.2: 182–222.

Carrier, J.G. 1997. Introduction, in Carrier, J.G. ed. *Meanings of the Market: The Free Market in Western Culture*. Oxford: Berg.

Chiapello, E. 2003. Reconciling the Two Principal Meanings of the Notion of Ideology: The Example of the Concept of the 'Spirit of Capitalism'. *European Journal of Social Theory*, 6.2: 155–71.

Davis, J.B. 2003. *The Theory of the Individual in Economics*. London: Routledge.

Davis, S. 1989. From Future Perfect: Mass Customizing. *Planning Review*, 17.2: 16–21.

Dilley, R. 1992. Contesting Markets: A General Introduction to Market Ideology, Imagery and Discourse, in Dilley, R., ed. *Contesting Markets: Analyses of Ideology, Discourse and Practice*. Edinburgh: Edinburgh University Press: 1–34.

Eagleton-Pierce, M. 2016. *Neoliberalism: The Key Concepts*. Abingdon: Routledge.

Erickson, J. 2014. *The Middle-Class Squeeze: A Picture of Stagnant Incomes, Rising Costs, and What We Can Do to Strengthen America's Middle Class*. Washington, DC: Center for American Progress.

Freeden, M. 1996. *Ideologies and Political Theory: A Conceptual Approach*. Oxford: Oxford University Press.

Gilbert, D. 2014. *The American Class Structure in an Age of Growing Inequality*. London: Sage.

Gramsci, A. 1971. *Selections from the Prison Notebooks*. London: Lawrence and Wishart.

Gray, J. 1989. *Liberalisms: Essays in Political Philosophy*. London: Routledge.

—. 1993. *Post-Liberalism: Studies in Political Thought*. London: Routledge.

—. 1995. *Liberalism*. Buckingham: Open University Press.

Gumbrell-McCormick, R., and Hyman, R. 2013. *Trade Unions in Western Europe: Hard Times, Hard Choices*. Oxford: Oxford University Press.

Harvey, D. 2005. *A Brief History of Neoliberalism*. Oxford: Oxford University Press.

—. 2006. *The Limits to Capital*. London: Verso.

Hausman, D.M., and McPherson, M.S. 2008. The Philosophical Foundations of Mainstream Normative Economics, in Hausman, D.M. ed., *The Philosophy of Economics: An Anthology*. Cambridge: Cambridge University Press.

Hayek, F.A. 1948. *Individualism and Economic Order*. Chicago: University of Chicago Press.

Hildebrand, D. 2013. Dewey's Pragmatism: Instrumentalism and Meliorism, in Malachowski, A. ed., *The Cambridge Companion to Pragmatism*. Cambridge: Cambridge University Press.

Jevons, W.S. (1875). *The Progress of the Mathematical Theory of Political Economy: With an Explanation of the Principles of the Theory*. New York: Sentry Press.

Kant, I. 2003. Perpetual Peace: A Philosophical Sketch [1795], in Reiss, H.S. ed., *Kant: Political Writings*. Cambridge: Cambridge University Press.

Kotler, P. 1989. From Mass Marketing to Mass Customization. *Planning Review*, 17.5: 10–47.

Krugman, P. 1995. Dutch Tulips and Emerging Markets: Another Bubble Bursts. *Foreign Affairs*, July/August: 28–44.

Lukes, S. 1973. *Individualism*. Oxford: Basil Blackwell.

Marx, K. 1852[2000]. The Eighteenth Brumaire of Louis Napoleon, in McLellan, D. ed., *Karl Marx: Selected Writings*. Oxford: Oxford University Press.

—. 1993[1939]. *Grundrisse: Foundations of the Critique of Political Economy*. London: Penguin.

Marx, K., and Engels, F. 1970. *The German Ideology*. London: Lawrence and Wishart.

—. 1998[1848]. *The Communist Manifesto: A Modern Edition*. London: Verso.

Moretti, F. 2013. *The Bourgeois: Between History and Literature*. London: Verso.

Peck, J., Theodore, N., and Brenner, N. 2012. Neoliberalism Resurgent? Market Rule after the Great Recession. *The South Atlantic Quarterly*, 111. 2: 265–88.

Pew Research Center. 2014. *Despite Recovery, Fewer Americans Identify as Middle Class*. 27 January.

Polanyi, K. 2001[1944]. *The Great Transformation: The Political and Economic Origins of Our Time*. Boston: Beacon Press.

Ricoeur, P. 1986. *Lectures on Ideology and Utopia*. New York: Columbia University Press.

Robbins, L. 1935. *An Essay on the Nature and Significance of Economic Science*. London: Macmillan and Co.

Rodrik, D. 2007. *One Economics, Many Recipes: Globalization, Institutions, and Economic Growth*. Princeton, NJ: Princeton University Press.

Rostow, W.W. 1960. *The Stages of Economic Growth: A Non-Communist Manifesto*. Cambridge: Cambridge University Press.

Serra, N., and Stiglitz, J.E. 2008. *The Washington Consensus Reconsidered: Towards a New Global Governance*. Oxford: Oxford University Press.

Smith, A. 1776[1993]. *An Inquiry into the Nature and Causes of the Wealth of Nations*. Oxford: Oxford University Press.

Springer, S. 2010. Neoliberalism and Geography: Expansions, Variegations, Formations. *Geography Compass*, 4. 8: 1025–38.

—. 2012. Neoliberalism as Discourse: Between Foucauldian Political Economy and Marxian Poststructuralism. *Critical Discourse Studies*, 9.2: 133–47.

Stedman Jones, D. 2012. *Masters of the Universe: Hayek, Friedman, and the Birth of Neoliberal Politics*. Princeton, NJ: Princeton University Press.

Trentmann, F. ed. 2005. *The Making of the Consumer: Knowledge, Power and Identity in the Modern World*. Oxford: Berg.

—. ed. 2012. *The Oxford Handbook of the History of Consumption*. Oxford: Oxford University Press.

—. 2016. *Empire of Things. How We Became a World of Consumers, from the Fifteenth Century to the Twenty-First*. London: Allen Lane.

van Agtmael, A. 2007. *The Emerging Markets Century: How a New Breed of World-Class Companies is Overtaking the World*. New York: Free Press.

Wacquant, L. 2009. *Punishing the Poor: The Neoliberal Government of Social Insecurity*. Durham, NC: Duke University Press.

Weber, M. 2001[1930]. *The Protestant Ethic and the Spirit of Capitalism*. London: Routledge.

Williams, R. 1985[1976]. *Keywords: A Vocabulary of Culture and Society*. London: Fontana.

Williamson, O.E. 1983. *Markets and Hierarchies: Analysis and Antitrust Implications*. New York: Macmillan.

Wolf, M. 2004. *Why Globalization Works*. New Haven: Yale University Press.

2

THE ASCENDANCY OF CHICAGO NEOLIBERALISM

Edward Nik-Khah and Robert Van Horn

The Chicago School of Economics emerged as one of the primary intellectual formations in the US economics orthodoxy in the post-World War II Era.[1] Not only is it America's most influential school of economic thought, but it has also exerted demonstrable influence across the disciplines.

Many non-economists (as well as a fair share of economists) mistakenly equate Chicago with neoclassical economics, and they hold certain images about Chicago, which are oversimplified, shortsighted, and ahistorical. The first misperception concerns 'economics imperialism': Chicago economists have purposively and successfully claimed portions of the terrain of other disciplines by applying their understanding of economics in those disciplines. Chicago is not, however, coextensive with orthodoxy. Chicago neoliberals are not merely exponents of the logic of economics; they expound neoliberal ideas via economic language. A second misperception is that Milton Friedman is the quintessential icon of Chicago Economics, and played the most fundamental role in its ascendancy. This overlooks that Friedman by no means represents the whole of Chicago. Moreover, there were numerous factors beyond the individual scholarly achievements of Chicago's icons that contributed to its ascendancy. The lesser-explored methods of Chicago's ascendance, developed by Chicago's other icons and put into practice through assiduous efforts, compose the substance of this chapter.

The MPS and the birth of Chicago neoliberalism

One of the most crucial facts to grasp about the Chicago School is that it is not coterminous with those housed within Chicago's Department of Economics.[2] Although there has been an economics department at the University of Chicago since the days of Thorstein Veblen (at that time it was called the 'Department of Political Economy'), the 'Chicago School of Economics' came into being only after World War II. Hence, it is distinct from the work of an earlier generation of scholars, including Frank Knight, Jacob Viner, and Henry Simons (Van Horn 2011). As noted by George Stigler (1988: 148), there was no 'Chicago School' in the current sense of the term prior to the first meeting of the Mont Pèlerin Society (MPS). Following World War II, Stigler, Friedman, Aaron Director, and others worked to construct one.

The fact that the MPS and the Chicago School were joined at the hip from birth is attested by the presence of most of the major protagonists at the creation of both: Director, Friedman, and Allen Wallis.[3] When the MPS was legally constituted, it was registered as a non-profit corporation in Illinois, with offices formally listed as the University of Chicago Law School. A transnational institutional project, the MPS sought to reinvent a liberalism that had some prospect of challenging collectivist doctrines ascendant in the immediate postwar period. It enabled its members – liberals from America, most of whom represented the Chicago School, and Europe – to debate and offer each other mutual support.

To appreciate how the MPS and the Chicago School came to be conjoined at birth, it is necessary to briefly examine the role of F.A. Hayek in the founding of both. In April 1945, when on tour in the USA promoting his recently published *The Road to Serfdom*, Hayek met with Harold Luhnow, head of the Volker Fund and anti-New Deal conservative. Luhnow wanted Hayek to write an American version of *The Road to Serfdom* and offered him Volker money to do so. The two men agreed that the Volker Fund would finance an investigation of the legal foundations of capitalism and that a product of this investigation would be an American *Road to Serfdom*. The two also agreed that Hayek could outsource the investigation.

Hayek considered his proposal to be of great importance. Hayek, who positioned himself as an opponent of laissez-faire liberalism in *The Road to Serfdom*, championed the creation of an institutional framework, or what he later called a 'competitive order', so that effective competition would flourish. Hayek did not oppose all forms of planning, only those that undermined effective competition. He advocated planning *for* competition – that is, a properly designed competitive order. In general, the competitive order necessitated well-organized institutions, but, in particular, and most importantly according to Hayek, it required a well-crafted legal framework. He suggested that an in-depth study of the competitive order had regrettably never occurred. He also suggested that the task for the future would be to succeed where nineteenth-century liberals had failed. As a prerequisite, twentieth-century liberals would need to thoroughly investigate and understand the competitive order to thereby reconstitute the liberal doctrine.[4] Thus, when he made his counter-offer to Luhnow, Hayek hoped that the Volker Fund would provide the means to enable the building of a reinvigorated and robust liberalism.

To outsource the investigation, Hayek approached Simons and his colleagues at the University of Chicago. Liking Hayek's proposal, Simons lobbied in support of the investigation – or the 'Hayek Project', as Simons and his colleagues referred to it. Since Simons viewed the liberal doctrine as withering and the collectivist doctrine as prevailing and burgeoning, he envisioned the Hayek Project as an endeavour to reinvigorate the liberal doctrine in order to countervail collectivist doctrine. Moreover, Simons endorsed Aaron Director as the leader of the project. Simons feared that without an organized effort to revive liberalism, it would 'be lost', and he believed that Director's leadership would help to engender a liberal stronghold at the University of Chicago.

Director responded favourably to the proposed Hayek Project. Director also drafted a proposal for the project, called the 'Free Market Study' (FMS). Director's proposal delineated the benefits and limitations of the free market and enumerated the departures from the free market at the close of World War II – including barriers to entry and government controls. In keeping with Hayek's vision for a twentieth-century liberalism, Director also listed numerous policies that needed to be examined to return to a free market economy, including antitrust policy and corporate policy. For example, Director called for considering limitations on corporate size and for federal incorporation to be required, investigations into the successes and failures of antitrust law, and a reconsideration of patent policy.

In sum, as the efforts to organize the study at Chicago got underway, the principals involved in its organization, such as Simons and Aaron Director, considered it Hayek's endeavour and even explicitly referred to it as the 'Hayek Project'. Furthermore, Hayek believed that the study would fulfil his own objectives. Indeed, in a letter to a fellow liberal, Walter Eucken, Hayek stated that he considered the project a 'positive complement' to his *Road to Serfdom*.

After many trials and tribulations that have been detailed elsewhere (see Van Horn and Mirowski 2009), by May 1946, Hayek had successfully arranged for the FMS to be housed at the Chicago Law School and for Director to head the project. Once FMS got underway in the autumn of 1946, its members – which included Friedman and Edward Levi (Law School) – convened regularly in order to debate how to reconstitute liberalism and create a competitive order. By empirically investigating the facts taken for granted by both liberals and collectivists, they sought to develop a more robust liberal policy to counter collectivism and thereby reorient policy in the USA. Indeed, in a *New York Times* interview, Director indicated that one criterion for assessing the success of the FMS was its ability to exert political pressure in order to engender policy change.[5]

After the 1947 MPS meeting, the work of the FMS proceeded apace. It undertook a couple of empirical studies geared towards countervailing collectivism and reinvigorating liberalism. One was Warren Nutter's evaluation of the extent of industrial monopoly in the USA. Nutter argued that there had been no significant increase in business monopoly since 1900. Director noted that Nutter's finding challenged the collectivist claim that the efficiency of large-scale industry would inevitably give rise to more and more business monopoly, thereby resulting in less and less competition and necessitating socialist economic planning. Since collectivists hinged their argument on the premise that industrial monopoly had been significantly increasing, and since, as Director pointed out, a widespread belief in the inevitability thesis gave rise to collectivist policies, Nutter's investigation dealt a blow to collectivism.

From 1950–2, in their efforts to combat collectivism, Director and other members of the FMS sharply departed from the classical liberal concern about the negative implications of concentrations of business power.[6] (See Henry Simons's position in the following section for the classical liberal perspective.) For example, in 1951, Director claimed that large corporations no longer should be considered a threat to competition because of their concentrated power, but should be considered another feature of a competitive market since corporations approximated the impersonal ideal of the market. In short, the FMS came to maintain that concentrated markets tended to be efficient.

In sum, because of its determination to reconstitute liberalism in order to attack collectivism and because of its departure from the classical liberal opposition to concentrations of business power, the FMS served as an incubator for a new form of liberalism, 'Chicago neoliberalism'. Furthermore, because of its shared concern with the MPS – that is, what legal foundations were necessary for effective competition – because both sought to countervail collectivism, and because Hayek played a sine-qua-non role in creating both, the FMS and MPS should be viewed as inextricably connected and ineluctably symbiotic.

Imperial Chicago

Some of the most significant activities contributing to Chicago's ascendance were undertaken outside the discipline of economics. The Chicago Law School and the Graduate School of Business became important staging grounds for imperialistic excursions into disciplines adjacent to economics.

The Chicago Law School: the Antitrust Project

On the heels of the FMS, Director organized and led the Volker-funded Antitrust Project and Edward Levi (then Dean of the Chicago Law School) assisted with it.[7] Other members included later luminaries of Chicago law and economics, such as Robert Bork and Ward Bowman.

The Antitrust Project focused on issues of monopoly, select areas of antitrust law, and the history of the Sherman Act.[8] It investigated these topics in the light of the conclusions of FMS. Moreover, in the spirit of the study's attempt to influence policy, it investigated these topics with a critical eye towards US antitrust law precedent, and many of the conclusions of the Antitrust Project contravened the conclusions of the courts. The Antitrust Project attacked the conventional wisdom of the legal profession in a number of ways – too many to summarize here, hence it is necessary to look at a sample. First, Bork claimed that vertical mergers did not enhance monopoly power. He therefore suggested that vertical mergers should always be legal. Consequently, Bork implied that one aspect of antitrust law precedent, requiring an investigation of the motives of a vertical merger in order to make a determination of its legality, was erroneous. Second, Ward Bowman maintained that the conventional legal wisdom – as represented by the *Report of the Attorney General's National Committee to Study the Antitrust Laws* (1954) – grossly exaggerated the effects of a tying arrangement.[9] The *Report* deemed the purpose of such arrangements to be monopolistic exploitation. In contrast, Bowman suggested that in most cases a tying contact was merely a means of effectively utilizing monopoly power that was already possessed, not a means of extending it.

Significantly, like the FMS, the Antitrust Project should also be viewed as an attempt to oppose collectivism. First, the Antitrust Project continued the mission of the FMS – that is, to create and advocate the competitive order. Second, during the time of the Antitrust Project, Director emphasized the importance of countering collectivism (Director ([1953]1964). Third, the Chicago neoliberal conclusions of the FMS – particularly those concerning concentrations of business power – influenced the conclusions of the Antitrust Project.[10] For these three reasons, the Antitrust Project represented much more than simply the application of Chicago price theory to areas of antitrust law.

It would be many years before the US courts and legal community would take the work of Director and the Antitrust Project seriously. With hindsight, Friedman suggested that it was unrealistic to expect immediate change. He saw his work, as well as that of his colleagues, to be that of: '[developing] alternatives to existing policies, to keep them alive and available until the politically impossible becomes the politically inevitable' (1962: xiv). Here, Friedman echoed Hayek's 1947 Mont Pèlerin address. Hayek had stated:

> Public opinion … is the work of men like ourselves, the economists and political philosophers of the past few generations, who have created the political climate in which the politicians of our time must move … It is from [a] long-run point of view that we must look at our task. It is the beliefs which must spread, if a free society is to be preserved, or restored, not what is practicable at the moment, which must be our concern.
>
> *(1948: 108)*

In a way, therefore, the study, the Antitrust Project, and later the Law and Economics Program acted as incubators for Chicago neoliberalism and thereby kept its core insights 'alive and available' for later use.

The impact of this later use should not be underestimated. About 30 years after the emergence of Chicago neoliberalism, the Reagan administration's appointees to the Antitrust Division of the Department of Justice echoed the arguments in Bowman's *Patent and Antitrust Law*, including his analysis of patent tie-ins.[11] The Antitrust Division staked out a broad area in which it would not challenge patent licensing agreements, including patent tie-ins. Thus, firms, without fear of prosecution, used patent tie-ins. More recently, in 2007, the US Department of Justice and the Federal Trade Commission (the two federal agencies that enforce antitrust laws in the USA), as well as the Antitrust Modernization Commission, endorsed a fundamental idea of the Antitrust Project. The federal agencies and the Commission espoused a rule of reason approach in those cases in which patent rights conflicted with the objectives of antitrust law. Thus, all three opposed the per se illegality of patent tie-ins, and all three suggested that the claim that patents created and extended business monopoly should be viewed with scepticism.

The Graduate School of Business: The Governmental Control Project

George Stigler's arrival at Chicago in 1958 completed the formation of the Chicago School.[12] Upon his arrival, Stigler was already viewed as a leading member of the Chicago School. He had been associated with the School through his friendships with Friedman, and Director, and Chicago economists were quite familiar with his existing body of work. Importantly, Stigler's stature at Chicago was bolstered by the Walgreen Foundation, which had been established by a grant from the drugstore magnate Charles Walgreen and was placed under Stigler's control by Allen Wallis (now dean of Chicago's Graduate School of Business), with the consent of Charles Walgreen, Jr, and his advisor (and founding MPS member) Leonard Read.

Shortly after his arrival at Chicago, Stigler announced his intention to devote the Walgreen resources to a study of the 'causes and effects of governmental control over economic life'.[13] He hired a full-time research assistant (Claire Friedland), established the famous Industrial Organization Workshop, and funded research he deemed relevant to the study of governmental control. Stigler himself contributed studies of the regulation of electricity and securities and of the enforcement of antitrust laws (Stigler and Friedland 1962; Stigler 1964, 1966), and financed through Walgreen several others. Stigler motivated the 'governmental control' project by appealing to the need to counteract collectivism: 'If it can be shown that in important areas of economic life substantial and unnecessary invasions of personal freedom are already operative, the case for caution and restraint in invoking new political controls will acquire content and conviction' (Stigler 1975a: 18).

Stigler used his Walgreen funds to recruit to Chicago a handful of leading economists (Gary Becker from Columbia University, Sam Peltzman from UCLA, Robert Lucas from Carnegie) and to finance short stays for other economists sympathetic to his efforts. Stigler's efforts set the tone at Chicago, not only through his published work, but also through his ability to shape the composition of the faculty and to finance their work on governmental control. The effort would later expand as a result of the establishment the Center for the Study of the Economy and the State (CSES), which Stigler founded in 1977 with an initial roster that included Becker, Richard Posner, Peltzman, Peter Linneman, and George Borjas (Stigler assumed the directorship).

The research produced by Stigler's governmental control project deviated from that of the previous generation of Chicago scholars. As Stigler noted elsewhere (1983: 529), providing economic explanations of politics marked a profound break with the approach of his teacher Frank Knight, who was deeply sceptical of discovering the principles governing political life. Not only did Stigler call for the exploration of a new subject matter, he also called for new methods to do so: 'it is reasonably certain that new theories and new methods will be required to unravel some of the major problems we have encountered [in understanding public regulation]' (1988: xvii). And whereas Jacob Viner refused to participate in political discussions, Stigler's research was produced to counter collectivism.

According to Stigler, the problem with existing studies of the government was that they presented an unrealistic view of the capacities of democracy, and thereby provided poor guides for legislative and administrative decision-making. He viewed these studies as uncritically adhering to the belief that regulation was sought for the public interest, whereas Stigler was intent on persuading that such problems were *endemic* to regulation. Stigler believed that political scientists, along with economists, were the main culprits. Hence, Stigler's project carried a rationale for imperialism similar to that of Director's project: the theories of political scientists and economists needed to be countervailed with a reconstituted liberalism, and that one needed to advance on other disciplines to do so.

Stigler called for two types of studies. The first would study the effects of past economic policies, to develop techniques for auditing and guiding, and thereby controlling, administrative bodies. The second would study and test hypotheses on the nature of the political process, for the purpose of counteracting the attitudes of political scientists and economists within those academic disciplines. Although only the second type of studies corresponds to the sort one often has in mind when thinking of economics imperialism – the development and application of an economic logic to address phenomena outside the traditional domain of economics – the first sought to displace the standing of other scientific fields in guiding regulation, a less-noticed form of economics imperialism.

To understand how this form of imperialism worked, it is helpful to peruse an influential example, Sam Peltzman's (1973) critical examination of the US Food and Drug Administration (FDA). Peltzman's primary complaint about the FDA was that while it was supposed to have reduced the costs of producing information about drugs (by substituting FDA-sanctioned information for drug company advertisements and doctors' experience with medicines), it had actually decreased the value of information available to consumers: FDA restrictions on pharmaceutical companies' claims would decrease the amount of information on non-sanctioned uses of drugs, while any reduction in marketing for a drug of a particular brand would reduce information about the drug type in general. Peltzman then connected the decrease in information to social welfare by attributing a decline in the demand for new drugs to the decrease in information, and therefore a decrease in the consumer surplus associated with consuming drugs. In this study the intended target was *clinical science*. Peltzman never actually engaged clinical science (a fact that was not lost on those clinical scientists who read Peltzman's piece); instead, he attempted to undermine the entire enterprise of using clinical science to guide regulation, and thereby to displace one set of goals (efficacy) with another set (consumer surplus or, in other cases, 'innovation') (Nik-Khah 2014). The study was immensely influential: the enabling legislation of the FDA would eventually be amended, to instruct it to reduce the burden of regulation and speed drug approval.

The three pillars of the Chicago School

By the close of the 1950s, the iconic personages of Chicago neoliberalism – Aaron Director, Milton Friedman, and George Stigler – were in place at Chicago. They agreed that it was of the utmost importance to promote freedom, but they touted a specific expression of freedom that actually entailed curbing the economic and political influence of democratic discussion.[14]

Milton Friedman

Friedman's conception of freedom and democracy can be appreciated by briefly contrasting Henry Simons's *Economic Policy for a Free Society* (1948) and Friedman's *Capitalism and Freedom* (1962). Simons extensively and explicitly discussed the importance of democracy and freedom, and he basically used these two terms interchangeably. He called monopoly in all its forms 'the great enemy of democracy'. In his book, he provided policy recommendations, such as limiting corporate size and federal incorporation, to ensure effective competition and thereby stave off the threat of concentrations of business power to freedom and democracy. Simons indicated that a democracy depended upon extensive discussion:

> The democratic process rests proximately upon representative, deliberative assemblies. It contemplates agitation, discussion of problems, proposals for dealing with them, examination of such proposals, continuous compromise and revision of bills, and eventual enactments of legislation. At best, such final enactments will mainly not involve close votes or sharp dissent; discussion and compromise should usually eventuate in substantial legislative consensus.... With good government, the discussion of problems is more important than the action to which it immediately leads. It tends to define areas of large agreement (if only by neglecting or ignoring) as well as of small disagreement and thus to enlarge or deepen that consensus which is the moral basis of order.
>
> *(1948: 8–9)*

Hence, Simons suggested the importance of an educated citizenry by advocating for discussion as the linchpin of democracy and freedom.

Friedman, however, ignored democracy in his analysis. Perhaps this is why he used the term 'freedom' and not 'democracy' in his title for *Capitalism and Freedom*. Indeed, to the best of our knowledge, he used the term 'democracy' nowhere in his book. Friedman later shed light on why he emphasized freedom and not democracy. He stated:

> Let's be clear, I don't believe in democracy in one sense. You don't believe in democracy. Nobody believes in democracy. You will find it hard to find anybody who will say that if ... democracy is interpreted as majority rule. You will find it hard to find anybody who will say that [if] 55% of the people believe the other 45% of the people should be shot. That's an appropriate exercise of democracy. What I believe in is not a democracy but in individual freedom in a society in which individuals cooperate with one another. And in which there is an absence of coercion and violence. Now it turns out that democracy in the sense of majority voting is an effective means for achieving agreement on some things. On things which are not very important.[15]

Because Friedman's conception of freedom did not hinge on discussion, he, unlike Simons, did not imply an intelligent citizenry is needed.

But if Friedman held a dim view of public discussion, then why did he expend such considerable effort at popularizing his views – namely through his bestselling books, his television series, or his *Newsweek* column? Basically, it provided a means to construct the conditions needed for the success of Chicago neoliberalism. According to Friedman, the dependence of scholars on government (e.g. the National Science Foundation, state legislatures for those housed at state universities) produced a 'chilling effect' on academic speech directed at the activities of the government (Friedman and Friedman 1980: 68–9; Friedman 1981). Friedman sought to overcome this distortion by linking neoclassical economics to neoliberal ideas, and thereby alert people to the costs of government intervention.[16] In doing so, he ultimately sought to encourage the public to accept neoliberal ideas, not empower its members to participate in robust public discourse (although at times it did appear that way) and thereby contribute to the policy-making process. In short, Friedman wanted to limit public discussion – at least as Simons defined it.

Aaron Director

Like Friedman, Director viewed democracy as a necessary evil.[17] The clearest expression of this view is found in his address entitled 'The Parity of the Economic Market Place' (Director [1953]1964). If political discussion and decision increasingly governed the functioning of the economy, then, according to Director, individual choice would be dramatically curbed. For him, freedom meant 'freedom to choose one's ends as well as means for attaining them', and a crucial component of that choice meant individuals being able to engage in choice in the market (ibid.: 8–9). Director maintained that because most people devoted a substantial amount of their time to economic activity, they greatly valued freedom of choice in employment, investment, and consumption.

One of Director's central concerns was ensuring that minority voices were not stifled by the majority. Director placed his faith in what he held to be the proper division of labour between the political and economic realms. Hence Director's remark that 'the proponents of the priority of the market place for ideas … must of necessity rely on exhortation and on the fragile support of self-denying ordinances in constitutions' (ibid.: 9). If the state became the principal employer, 'we may expect great hesitation in advocating unpopular opinions, and serious obstacles put before those who overcome these hesitations', according to Director. In other words, only when the division of labour between political and economic institutions had been properly preserved could those on the margins of society freely voice their opinions without fear of retaliation by society.

For Director, the market system should be utilized to address economic and social problems, such as inequality or the organization of education, *unless* it could be clearly shown that the market system did an inadequate job addressing these problems. He called this the 'presumption-of-error doctrine' (ibid.: 3). However, he thought a deficiency in the free market system was rare.

Director suggested that the majority rule of democracy was a necessary evil that needed to be minimized, especially when it came to economic and social policy-making. He expressed deep scepticism of economic policies based on consensus, where the voices of all perspectives had been taken into account, unless the 'presumption of error test' had been met. Director suggested that he did not trust the government or the populace to make collective decisions on policy matters. Hence, Director suggested that the legal framework necessary for effective competition, such as antitrust policy, should not be based on a mature consensus through democratic discussion, but rather on economic analysis, particularly of the Chicago neoliberal hue.

George Stigler

Stigler shared Friedman's and Director's scepticism towards democratic discussion. And, as with Director, Stigler appealed to the operation of the marketplace of ideas to encourage intellectuals to reconsider their support for democratic discussion. But Stigler also devoted considerable attention to the principles underlying its operation, leading him to become the standard-bearer for the positions that (a) the same forces operate in trade, politics and intellectual life alike, and (b) the extent of market failure in any one of these domains is much exaggerated.[18]

Stigler held that voters collect the individually rational amount of information. But democracy would neither make the best use of social science, nor was it generally a good way to organize intellectual life:

> Affairs of science, and intellectual life generally, are not to be conducted on democratic procedures. One cannot establish a mathematical theorem by a vote, even a vote of

mathematicians. [Therefore] an elite must emerge and instill higher standards than the public or the profession instinctively desire.

The best econ[omics] in the US is not the one the public would elect: a science must impose the standards of an elite upon a profession.[19]

Stigler argued that democratic results such as the public's willingness to countenance an expansion of government regulation were due to its instinctual revulsion towards markets.[20]

Such considerations led Stigler to take exception with an image of the marketplace of ideas he believed to be implicit in *Capitalism and Freedom*.[21] If Friedman's popularizations of Chicago neoclassical economics were effective, this would imply that the public 'underinvests' in knowledge, a market failure. But if agents maximized in collecting information, they will already have gathered all the information that it was appropriate for them to have. Friedman's efforts at popularization would be of no use to them. For Stigler, economists were truly influential only when they worked on technical matters for an audience of technical economists and not when they spoke directly to society. Society needed Friedman's *A Monetary History of the United States* (Schwartz and Friedman 1963), not his *Capitalism and Freedom*.

Rather than call for the public to rethink its views and support measures to eliminate regulation, as did Friedman, Stigler sought to immunize government policy from the public – for example, by developing for regulators a set of 'intelligent guides', and subjecting regulators to performance audits conducted by scientific bodies purged of their public interest attitudes (see Stigler 1975a). Therefore, Stigler's programme to study the 'capacities' of democracy was informed by a profoundly negative view of the instincts of the vast majority of people. For example, Peltzman's performance audits (discussed in the previous section) were devised for the express purpose of preventing the calls of public interest and consumer welfare groups for tightening the FDA's drug approval process from having any effect.

Concluding observations

One question suggested by considering the methods of Chicago's ascendance is: what accounts for their success? Although we cannot cover all the conditions, we focus on two suggested by the preceding analysis.

First, Chicago's simultaneous espousal of distinct and to some extent contradictory positions, far from being a weakness, proved to be a source of strength. Director's programme addressed itself to judges and lawyers, and ultimately to the construction of the legal foundations of the 'competitive order'; Stigler's programme addressed economists and political scientists, and ultimately produced guidance for regulatory bodies and for the social organization of knowledge. In popularizing elements of these programmes, Friedman helped gain popular acceptance for measures to limit the reach of democratic discussion. Having one message for the masses, and another for the elite, contributed to the advancement of (Chicago) neoliberal ideals.

Second, Chicago participated in a larger epistemic community that not only spanned national and disciplinary boundaries, but also included non-academics, often located at think tanks (Plehwe and Walpen 2006; Weller and Singleton 2006). Think tanks operate between politics, academia, and the media. Their location within this 'hybrid and interstitial position' gives them their capacity for effective public intervention (Eyal and Buchholz 2010; Medvetz 2010).[22] For example, Chicago neoliberals staffed think tanks such as the American Enterprise Institute, and they also founded think tank-type institutions on Chicago's campus, such as the Stigler CSES and the Becker–Friedman Institute.[23] When compared with rival economics programmes, the features of Chicago's epistemic community – originally coordinated by the MPS and eventually with multifarious institutions participating – offered its scholars more opportunity to leverage ideas for world-changing action.

Acknowledgements

We wish to thank Stephen Stigler for his permission to access the George J. Stigler Papers. Archival materials from the George J. Stigler Papers (Special Collections Research Center, Regenstein Library, University of Chicago) are quoted with permission.

Notes

1 The others are the MIT School of Paul Samuelson and Robert Solow, and the Cowles Commission School of Kenneth Arrow and Leonid Hurwicz. See Mirowski (2002).
2 This section draws extensively from Van Horn (2013) and Van Horn and Klaes (2011).
3 George Stigler, who would only later accept a position at Chicago in 1958, was also present. Wallis was not a founding member, but joined immediately thereafter and served as its treasurer during its initial phase (Hartwell 1995: 45).
4 For a detailed look at Hayek's understanding of the competitive order and its significance at this juncture, see Van Horn (2013). Simons considered Hayek his intellectual comrade in arms, and Hayek considered Simons a 'great friend'.
5 Chicago University to Scan Free Market, 1946, *The New York Times*, 2 November: 31.
6 For a detailed look at this position shift, see Van Horn (2011) and Van Horn and Klaes (2011).
7 This section depends heavily on Nik-Khah and Van Horn (2012).
8 For a list of the articles and books that the Antitrust Project published and that it caused to be published, see Van Horn (2009).
9 A tying arrangement is one form of vertical integration. Tying takes place when a seller stipulates that a buyer must purchase the 'tied' product in order to obtain the 'tying' product, the one the buyer wants. A tying arrangement is almost always imposed by the seller on the buyer. For example, if a retailer, a small business owner, runs a fishing boat business, and if a manufacturer that commands a monopoly in the fishing boat motor market demands that the retailer purchase the manufacturer's motor oil in order to purchase its motors, then the manufacturer has tied its fishing motors (tying product) to its oil (tied product).
10 For example, Bork maintained that '[vertical mergers added] nothing to monopoly power' (1954: 195), and his claim assumed that increased concentration resulting from a vertical merger was necessarily benign.
11 This paragraph draws from Scherer (2008: 37–9).
12 The following discussion of Stigler's project is taken from Nik-Khah and Van Horn (2012).
13 Letter of Stigler to Walgreen, 28 December 1959 (GSRL Box 13, File: Walgreen Correspondence).
14 Given space constraints, it is not possible to thoroughly explore the views of each.
15 Milton Friedman, in an interview transcript posted at http://hellocoolworld.ca/media/TheCorporation/Democracy.pdf (accessed 4 March 2015).
16 It was not merely courage that would enable Friedman to escape the chill of government finance, but also the identification and courting of new sources of funding: pro-market advocacy foundations and corporations.
17 This paragraph draws extensively from Van Horn and Emmett (2014).
18 The remainder of this section draws from Nik-Khah (2011a).
19 GSRL Box 26, File Mont Pèlerin Society 10th Anniversary Meeting.
20 See also Stigler (1963: 95): 'I cannot believe that any amount of economic training would wholly eliminate the instinctive dislike for a system of organizing economic life through the search of profits'.
21 'As I mentally review Milton's work, I recall no important occasion on which he has told businessmen how to behave… Yet Milton has shown no comparable reticence in advising Congress and public on [a variety of policies] … Why should businessmen – and customers and lenders and other economic agents – know and foster their own interests, but voters and political coalitions be so much in need of his and our lucid and enlightened instruction?' (Stigler 1975b: 312).

22 Think tanks such as the American Enterprise Institute also housed what Michel Foucault (2008: 246–7) called 'permanent criticism' of the state. Think tanks would audit regulatory bodies according to market principles; Chicago articulated the principles.
23 On the neoliberal orientation of these institutes, see Nik-Khah (2011a, 2011b).

References

Bork, R. 1954. Vertical Integration and the Sherman Act: The Legal History of an Economic Misconception. *University of Chicago Law Review*, 22: 157–201.

Director, A. [1953]1964. The Parity of the Economic Market Place. *Journal of Law and Economics*, 7: 1–10.

Eyal, G., and L. Buchholz. 2010. From the Sociology of Intellectuals to the Sociology of Interventions. *Annual Review of Sociology*, 36: 117–37.

Foucault, M. 2008. *The Birth of Biopolitics*. New York: Palgrave Macmillan.

Friedman, M. 1962. *Capitalism and Freedom*. Chicago: University of Chicago Press.

Friedman, M., and Schwartz, A., 1963. *A Monetary History of the United States*. Princeton, NJ: Princeton University Press.

—. 1981. An Open Letter on Grants. *Newsweek*, 18 May: 99.

Friedman, M., and Friedman, R. 1980. *Free to Choose*. New York: Harcourt Brace Jovanovich.

Hartwell, M. 1995. *A History of the Mont Pelerin Society*. Indianapolis: Liberty Fund.

Hayek, F. 1948. 'Free' Enterprise and Competitive Order, in Hayek, F.A. ed., *Individualism and Economic Order*. Chicago: University of Chicago Press: 107–18.

Medvetz, T. 2010. *Think Tanks in America*. New York: Oxford University Press.

Mirowski, P. 2002. *Machine Dreams*. New York: Cambridge University Press.

Nik-Khah, E. 2011a. George Stigler, the Graduate School of Business, and the Pillars of the Chicago School, in Van Horn, R., Mirowski, P., and Stapleford, T. eds., *Building Chicago Economics*. New York: Cambridge University Press: 116–47.

—. 2011b. Chicago Neoliberalism and the Genesis of the Milton Friedman Institute (2006–2009), in Van Horn, R., Mirowski, P., and Stapleford, T. eds., *Building Chicago Economics*. New York: Cambridge University Press: 368–88.

—. 2014. Neoliberal Pharmaceutical Science and the Chicago School of Economics. *Social Studies of Science*, 44.4: 489–517.

Nik-Khah, E., and Van Horn, R. 2012. Inland Empire: Economics Imperialism as an Imperative of Chicago Neoliberalism. *Journal of Economic Methodology*, 19.3: 259–82.

Peltzman, S. 1973. The Benefits and Costs of New Drug Regulation, in Landau, R. ed., *Regulating New Drugs*. Chicago: University of Chicago Center for Policy Studies: 113–211.

Plehwe, D., and Walpen, B. 2006. Between Network and Complex Organization: The Making of Neoliberal Knowledge and Hegemony, in Plehwe, D., Walpen, B., and Neunhöffer, G. eds., *Neoliberal Hegemony: A Global Critique*. New York: Routledge: 27–50.

Scherer, F. 2008. Conservative Economics and Antitrust: A Variety of Influences, in Pitofsky, R. ed., *How the Chicago School Overshot the Mark*. New York: Oxford University Press.

Simons, H. 1948. *Economic Policy for a Free Society*. Chicago: University of Chicago Press.

Stigler, G. 1963. *The Intellectual and the Market Place, and Other Essays*. New York: Free Press.

—. 1964. Public Regulation of the Securities Markets. *Journal of Business*, 37.2: 117–42.

—. 1966. The Economic Effects of the Anti-Trust Laws. *Journal of Law & Economics*, 9: 225–58.

—. 1975a. *The Citizen and the State*. Chicago: University of Chicago Press.

—. 1975b. The Intellectual and His Society, in Selden, R. ed., *Capitalism and Freedom: Problems and Prospects*. Charlottesville: University Press of Virginia: 311–21.

—. 1983. The Process and Progress of Economics. *Journal of Political Economy*, 91.4: 529–45.

—. 1986. George J. Stigler, in Breit, W., and Spencer, R.W. eds., *Lives of the Laureates: Seven Nobel Economists*. Cambridge: MIT Press: 79–93.

—. 1988. *Chicago Studies in Political Economy*. Chicago: University of Chicago Press.

Stigler, G., and Friedland, C. 1962. What Can Regulators Regulate? The Case of Electricity. *Journal of Law and Economics*, 5: 1–16.

Van Horn, R. 2009. Reinventing Monopoly and the Role of Corporations, in Mirowski, P., and Plehwe, D., eds. *The Road from Mont Pèlerin: The Making of the Neoliberal Thought Collective*. Cambridge, MA: Harvard University Press: 204–37.

—. 2011. Jacob Viner's Critique of Chicago Neoliberalism, in Van Horn, R., Mirowski, P., and Stapleford, T. eds., *Building Chicago Economics*. New York: Cambridge University Press: 279–300.

—. 2013. Hayek's Unacknowledged Disciple. *Journal of History of Economic Thought*, 35. 3: 271–90.

Van Horn, R., and Emmett, R. 2014. Two Trajectories of Democratic Capitalism in the Post-War Chicago School. *Cambridge Journal of Economics*, 39.5: 1443–55.

Van Horn, R., and Klaes, M. 2011. Intervening in Laissez-Faire Liberalism: Chicago's Shift on Patents, in Van Horn, R., Mirowski, P., and Stapleford, T. eds., *Building Chicago Economics*. New York: Cambridge University Press: 180–207.

Van Horn, R., and Mirowski, P. 2009. The Rise of the Chicago School of Economics and the Birth of Neoliberalism, in Mirowski, P., and Plehwe, D. eds., *The Road from Mont Pèlerin: The Making of the Neoliberal Thought Collective*. Cambridge, MA: Harvard University Press.

Weller, C. and Singleton, L. 2006. Peddling Reform: The Role of Think Tanks in Shaping the Neoliberal Policy Agenda for the World Bank and International Monetary Fund, in Plehwe, D., Walpen, B., and Neunhöffer, G. eds., *Neoliberal Hegemony: A Global Critique*. New York: Routledge: 70–86.

Archival source

GSRL = George J. Stigler Papers, Regenstein Library, University of Chicago.

3

NEOLIBERALISM AND THE TRANSNATIONAL CAPITALIST CLASS

William K. Carroll and J.P. Sapinski

Although a literature on the transnational capitalist class (TCC) began to form in the 1970s, along with the first stirrings of neoliberal public policy, these intersecting phenomena have deeper lineages in elite capitalist networks, transnationalizing investment, and the interaction between the two. This chapter explores those lineages and interactions.

First, two matters of definition. As doctrine, neoliberalism asserts that 'free' markets 'are the most moral and the most efficient means for producing and distributing goods and services' (Cahill 2012: 111). As for the TCC, this concept is closely identified with the globalization of capitalism. Capital has been internationalizing for over half a millennium, but the twentieth century witnessed a more fully fledged process of capitalist globalization. Particularly after World War II, this involved two interrelated developments: 'an increase in the mobility of capital and an expansion of its geographical reach' (Kotz and McDonough 2010: 99). To invoke the classical Marxist distinction, these provided the structural basis – in capital accumulation – for a transnational capitalist *class-in-itself*. Concomitantly, however, the TCC developed the capacities to act as a *class-for-itself*, defining and pursuing its interests within a more transnationalized political field. Both aspects of TCC formation are tied to neoliberalism as a distinct form of advanced capitalism. We focus on the latter, but begin with an account of how the globalization of capital provided structural underpinnings for both neoliberalism and a TCC-in-itself.

In the decades following World War II economic globalization brought an enormous increase in cross-border investment and by the late twentieth century, the global financial market was awash with stateless money capital. Already in 1974, Hymer noted the class implications of these developments: 'an international capitalist class is emerging whose interests lie in the world economy as a whole and a system of international private property which allows free movement of capital between countries' (Hymer 1974: unpaginated).

The subsequent proliferation of transnational capital circuits saw worldwide export of goods multiply by a factor of 6.9 between 1970 and 2008, global foreign direct investment flows multiply by a factor of 48 between the 1970s and 2000s, and international bank loans multiply by a factor of 52 from 1977 to the peak level in 2008 (Duménil and Lévy 2012: 37). A TCC-in-itself, centred in the corporate owners and managers subtending the accumulation of capital on a transnational basis, developed in step with the internationalization of capital.

Our first cut at the relation between the TCC and neoliberalism considers the TCC as a class-in-itself. What is most significant in this context is that capital's enhanced mobility and transnational reach have conferred upon it an unprecedented 'structural power' (Gill and Law 1989). In the later decades of the twentieth century, as capitalist globalization ruptured the territorial coincidence of mass production and mass consumption, the conditions in advanced capitalist nation-states for high-wage, Fordist capitalism and an expansive welfare state weakened. With increased international mobility and reach, transnational capital gained prominence, as investments deserted certain high-wage regions (e.g. 'rust-belt' cities like Detroit and Cleveland) in favour of locations in the global South offering low wages and high productivity. Quite apart from the collective agency of a TCC-for-itself, an increasingly internationalized economic circuitry has posed the threat of capital withdrawal for any jurisdiction whose policies stray very far from an investor-friendly policy paradigm prioritizing 'supply-side' issues (i.e. attracting and retaining an ever-increasing stock of private investment to fuel 'economic growth') over 'demand-side' concerns (the maintaining of collective purchasing power of local populations) (Carroll 2003). Financialization – 'the growing weight of finance' in the economy (Krippner 2005: 174) – has further magnified capital's structural power, increasing the volume of capital that can move across national borders at the click of a mouse, as in currency speculation. As a class-in-itself, the TCC – those who own and/or control (the flow of) capital within an expanding transnational field – exercises structural power molecularly, in a multitude of market-mediated, profit-maximizing decisions that add up to a (shifting) verdict on particular places, states and industries. Once capital has attained unparalleled mobility and transnational reach, capitalists can play one national workforce, or local government off against another, bidding-down wages, taxes, labour standards, regulations and social programmes in what can be described as a 'race to the bottom'. It is no coincidence that these are the stuff of neoliberal policy.

Thus, capitalist internationalization, and the closely linked formation of a TCC-in-itself, created a structural basis for neoliberal policy. In international competition, the state's predominant role shifted from that of promoting 'its' *capitalists* as leading agents of a national economy requiring robust effective demand (as in Keynesian and social-democratic industrial strategies), to that of promoting its *territory* as an attractive site for transnationally mobile investment intent on cutting its costs of production to the bone. This shift also meant a re-articulation of nationalist discourse. In organizing consent within a world-system of divided sovereignties, nationalist appeals to shared values and culture establish 'a supra-class identity' which, when aligned with the state, appears to transcend class struggle. The state seems to act 'in the interest of the national body' (Atkins 1986: 30). In the late twentieth century, the neoliberal re-articulation of national identity mobilized a 'national interest' around the ideology of *international competitiveness*, presenting 'international class dominance as national economic necessity' (Bryan 1995: 190). In short, the internationalization of capital and formation of a TCC-in-itself provided impetus for a paradigm shift in policy, and in the discourse of policy within imagined national communities. At the global level, the neoliberal shift has sought 'to harmonize a wide range of fiscal, monetary, industrial, and commercial policies among multiple nations, as a requirement for fully mobile transnational capital to move simultaneously, and often instantaneously, across numerous national borders' (Robinson and Harris 2000: 41).

Yet the narrative of a class-in-itself, amassing greater structural power as it subtends increasingly transnational capital circuits, only gives us the broadest outline of the relationship between the TCC and the development of neoliberalism, without highlighting the forms of collective agency through which the TCC became a leading protagonist in the political construction of neoliberalism. In the remainder of this chapter, we take up the roles that the TCC has played as a nascent class-for-itself, in the development of neoliberalism. In the next section we sketch the developing social-organizational basis for a TCC-for-itself: the formation in the late twentieth century of a global corporate elite with extensive ties to a growing panoply of transnational policy groups dedicated to fashioning and promoting neoliberal initiatives. This social-organizational basis inheres in several key transnational sites of class leadership and consensus formation, which have developed in a century-long process, as well as in an elite network of transnational capitalists and the organic intellectuals that advise and support them. We next consider the question of fractions and distinct neoliberal projects within the TCC, showing that, although cumulatively integrated, the TCC is not an economically and politically homogeneous entity, just as neoliberalism itself is a variegated and evolving set of processes (Brenner *et al.* 2010). Finally, we take up the relationship between neoliberalism and the TCC in the context of the former's 'second life', after the financial meltdown of 2008.

Policy-planning and elite networks

Three transnational policy-planning bodies have been, since their inception, key sites of TCC agency and have played a crucial role in promoting a neoliberal globalizing outlook. Each has mobilized the agency of transnational capitalists, ultimately leading to the consolidation of transnational neoliberalism from the 1970s onward. Funded by corporations and private foundations, these groups elaborate the general neoliberal worldview shared by transnational capitalists and diffuse it to constituencies beyond the TCC, a process Domhoff (2014) calls policy-planning. Concomitantly, they act as nodes of class cohesion among TCC members, creating solidarity among the owners/managers of capital and various aligned social forces. These two hegemonic mechanisms have amplified the TCC's capacity to act as a class-for-itself while strengthening its structural power through policy initiatives that favour investor rights and the free flow of capital.

International Chamber of Commerce

The International Chamber of Commerce (ICC) was an early promoter of capitalist internationalism and of the free trade agenda embodied in what later came to be called neoliberalism. It was founded in 1919, in the wake of World War I, by a group of investment bankers portraying themselves as 'merchants of peace', who saw international trade as a means to avoid wars between nations. Today, the ICC boasts 'hundreds of thousands of member companies and associations in over 130 countries'.[1] It has pursued a free market agenda since its inception, advocating market deregulation and opposing any form of governmental intervention in trade (Carroll and Carson 2003: 72). Beginning in the late 1980s, the ICC brought this outlook to global environmental politics, especially through its involvement in the 1992 Rio Earth Summit, which culminated in the creation of the World Business Council for Sustainable Development (WBCSD). Since the mid-1990s, it has promoted corporate self-regulation, and collaborated with the UN and the WBCSD to create the Global Compact in 2000.

In accordance with its globalist outlook, the ICC has played a major role in organizing the TCC as a class-for-itself. Its executive board functions as a high-level forum where politically active transnational capitalists can meet, resolve disputes, and forge strategic consensus and a common international policy framework (ibid.). Participation in the ICC board and other activities also works to integrate global capitalists located outside the capitalist core (Van der Pijl 1998), organizing the corporate elite on a truly global level. In the 1990s, the ICC adopted the explicit mandate to create solidarity among 'business' more generally, re-branding itself the 'World Business Organization'. It functions as a global network whose tentacles reach down to local chambers of commerce around the world, through its World Chambers Federation. While the ICC's executive board creates a 'horizontal' link among elite transnational capitalists, its multi-tiered organizational structure creates a 'vertical link' between the transnational capitalist interests of its TNC membership and its broad membership of locally and regionally anchored small and medium-sized enterprises (Carroll and Carson 2003: 73).

Mont Pèlerin Society

The Mont Pèlerin Society (MPS) was founded by Friederich von Hayek in 1947, in reaction to the emergent post-World War II state interventionist regime. It regrouped intellectuals supportive of the free market paradigm who were dissatisfied with Keynesian economic policy and sought to develop the neoliberal economic paradigm founded on free market ideals. The MPS played a different role than the ICC in the rise of neoliberalism and the rise of the TCC as a class-for-itself. Instead of regrouping elite capitalists, the MPS initially brought together a group of organic intellectuals organized around a core of common ideas and belief in the free market as the most efficient way to organize social life (Plehwe 2009). It thus constituted a conscious effort by militant intellectuals to solidify and disseminate the political ideas foundational to neoliberalism, so as to create 'a hegemonic project that could ultimately contribute to a neoliberal counter-revolution' (Carroll 2007: 43). The MPS quickly expanded its intellectual reach by organizing a global network of think tanks, later regrouped under the aegis of the Atlas Network, committed to furthering neoliberal free market thought and disseminating it among national policy networks around the globe.

Whereas the ICC supports an infrastructure that fosters direct interaction of transnational capitalists, the MPS builds long-term capacity for the development and diffusion of a 'neoliberal culture' to which its members are ideologically committed (Van der Pijl 1998). It does so by bringing together intellectuals, (mainly economists), as well as a smaller number of 'practical men' – corporate elites, politicians, journalists – committed to neoliberal principles (Carroll 2007: 44). Contrary to the ICC, the MPS was not established as a forum for discussion of different strategic options, but rather to propagate among policy circles what its members understood as unquestioned truth (Van der Pijl 1998). Such intellectual networking created a knowledge base around which the TCC mobilized as a class-for-itself when the Keynesian regime started to falter during the 1970s. An important elaboration of the MPS network is the Atlas Economic Research Foundation Network, founded in 1981 and comprising more than 400 market-oriented think tanks, most of them initiated and run with help from at least one MPS member (Plehwe 2009: 35). In great part through the work of the MPS and its associated groups, the idea of a society organized solely around the market migrated from marginality in the post-World War II period to become part of the TCC's abiding common sense.

World Economic Forum

Established in 1971 by business policy expert Klaus Schwab, the World Economic Forum (WEF) was initially an informal gathering of European CEOs dedicated to discussing European corporate strategy in the world market (Carroll and Carson 2003: 74). It grew into a large-scale gathering of 'world economic leaders' in the early 1980s, including top transnational capitalists but also high-ranking politicians and heads of key international governmental organizations (IGOs) that manage the neoliberal regime at the global level, such as the International Monetary Fund (IMF) and the World Bank. The WEF's core is organized around a group of elite capitalists, the 'Foundation Members', who are limited to 'the 1,000 foremost companies around the world' (WEF 2013: 7). From this core membership, the WEF extends to a broad array of satellite 'constituents' – scientists, academics, media leaders, public figures, artists and NGO heads – who attend its yearly meetings in Davos, Switzerland.

In similar fashion to the ICC, the WEF integrates capitalists from around the world. Originally mostly restricted to capitalists from core countries, the WEF gradually expanded its reach to include TCC members from all regions, and now holds regional meetings in China, India and Africa. The distinguishing characteristics of the WEF are two-fold. First, the breadth of the constituents invited to Davos helps diffuse the hegemony of the TCC across the political as well as the cultural realm of globalized society. Hence, beyond politicians, academics, and media figures, the WEF also seeks to establish the TCC's cultural leadership through the involvement of 'thought leaders' in Forum activities. It thereby seeks 'to integrate top level cultural leaders, with a proven track record of social activity and impact'.[2]

Second, the WEF uses its broad reach to set the agenda for global governance. Its Network of Global Agenda Councils, created in 2008, attempts to define the agenda on many topics relevant to the TCC, from global economic growth to health, and to corporate social responsibility and environmental issues. The network regroups 'more than 1,500 of the world's most relevant experts from academia, business, civil society, government and international organizations', hierarchically organized into 80 individual-issue councils and six 'metacouncils'. The various councils interact extensively, monitoring trends, identifying global risks, discussing ideas and interconnections between issues, and developing recommendations that are integrated into WEF activities 'as well as into global decision-making processes'.[3]

The integrative role of corporate-elite networks

The sprawling transnational networks of the ICC, MPS and WEF are complemented by a configuration that links many of the world's major capitalists to each other and to leading sites of neoliberal political agency. Indeed, the ICC, MPS and WEF represent just three nodes within a much broader network that rests on multiple types of links – corporate board interlocks created by directors sitting on the boards of other corporations and policy groups, direct corporate funding of policy groups, and intercorporate ownership webs – all of which help integrate the TCC. Since the early 1970s, the consolidation of a transnational network of interlocking corporate boards, centred in the North Atlantic region formed 'a kind of superstructure bridging national corporate communities' (Carroll 2010: 225). Board interlocks that tie the largest global corporations together operate at two levels. First, they create an inter-organizational network that provides a loose mechanism for the coordination of money flows, forming an infrastructure for the exercise of the TCC's allocative power. Second, they form an inter-personal network of interlocking directors who serve on common boards, thus strengthening class cohesion and contributing towards a shared worldview and sense of community – prerequisites for collective political action (Domhoff 2014).

Policy-planning groups such as the ICC and WEF have been linked into the transnational corporate network as leading corporate directors sit on their governance boards. They provide places for elite capitalists to plan political strategy, while enhancing the overall cohesion of the TCC as a class-for-itself. Carroll and Sapinski (2010) find that as the corporate-interlock networks have been thinning since the mid-1990s, 'policy boards have become more integrative nodes in the global corporate power structure' (530). Although the policy-planning network is centred upon the North Atlantic zone, groups like the Trilateral Commission and the WBCSD include directors of corporations based in Japan and (more recently) high-growth countries of the global South, creating 'a complex organizational ecology, unified by a neoliberal consensus yet differentiated by regional and other issues and interests' (ibid.).

The organizations and networks discussed in this section furnish crucial mechanisms in the formation of a TCC-in-itself, and underline the close relationship between that formation and the neoliberal paradigm shift. However, despite all this, the TCC is far from a unified entity, but is transected by multiple fractionations and competing strategic visions. These will be discussed in the next section.

Fractions and projects

The notion of a TCC-for-itself implies, as we have seen, the development of institutional forms through which collective interests can be articulated and collective agency exercised. However, since capital itself is divided – into many competing units and (despite global governance frameworks) within an international system of divided sovereignties – the issue of how fractional divisions within capital bear upon the relationship between the TCC and neoliberalism merits further scrutiny.

As early as 1983, Kees van der Pijl offered a theoretically grounded analysis of capitalist class fractions in the formation of a neoliberal hegemonic project. In his initial formulation, Van der Pijl (1983, 1984) noted that projects like Fordist-Keynesianism or neoliberalism take shape on the basis of distinct vantage points or fractional perspectives which the structural division of capital between production and circulation makes available: those of productive capital and money capital. Intrinsic to production are the technical issues surrounding the creation of use value – in a word, planning. Intrinsic to circulation is the free movement of goods and capital, especially in money form, and thus the convertibility of currencies. The *money-capital* perspective posits 'a system of harmony and progress as long as through the price mechanism, the rate of profit remains the exclusive regulatory device' (Van der Pijl 1983: 22). The *productive-capital* perspective constructs an interest from the position of the industrialist, who is willing 'to subordinate the orthodoxy of the market mechanism to a strategy better suited to the real socialization of the productive forces' (ibid.: 28).

These fractional standpoints underpin definite political projects that take shape through the efforts of organic intellectuals in universities, government commissions, and policy-planning groups (ibid.: 14, 20). It is in making a fractional perspective comprehensive – 'an effective vector of class formation within and beyond the bourgeoisie' (Van der Pijl 1984: 12) – that a project becomes hegemonic as fractional interests are transcended and a general interest constructed.

Beginning with the Pinochet dictatorship in Chile (1973–90), and continuing through the Thatcher and Reagan initiatives in the 1980s, neoliberalism was consolidated as a hegemonic project. In positing 'sound money', free labour, and unimpeded international circulation (and in marginalizing the productive-capital concern with planning), neoliberalism presented the perspective of money capital as a general interest around which the sectoral interests of different capital fractions could be assembled (Van der Pijl 1986: 3). Its subsequent expansion, from the Chilean beachhead and the Lockean heartland of anglophone capitalism to a transnational hegemonic project for global capitalism and the TCC, was facilitated by financialization (itself a product of neoliberal policy that cumulatively skewed profit distribution in favour of short-term financial assets as opposed to fixed-capital industrial investment), by the consolidation of global governance around the so-called Washington Consensus promoting investor rights as 'free trade' and mandating austerity programmes in the debt-ridden global South, and by the collective agency of a TCC centred in the North Atlantic and including many strata of organic intellectuals and a growing assemblage of policy-planning groups (Van der Pijl 1998).

A significant chapter in this process has been the neoliberalization of continental Europe and the closely associated making of a European TCC. Indeed, more than anywhere else, Europe has witnessed the deepest process of TCC formation over the past three decades. Van Apeldoorn has documented the leading role of European capitalists in 'the creation of a transnational space for capital in which the latter's rule is established precisely by preserving the formal sovereignty of member states while subordinating their democratic governance to the dictates of the single market' (2013: 189). Interestingly, this project has been championed by the European Round Table of Industrialists (ERT), which after its founding in 1983 became the premier policy-planning body of Europe's TCC. This apparent anomaly shows how, as neoliberalism gained ideological hegemony the money-capital perspective was taken up as a general point of view within (and beyond) the capitalist class.

As the global financial crisis unfolded from 2007 onward, the spatialized contradictions of neoliberal Europe surfaced, particularly in the austerity programmes imposed upon Europe's debt-ridden southern periphery, a strategy for shoring up financial institutions and accumulation in Europe's affluent north while shrinking the economies of the south (and rendering their debt reduction 'ever more elusive' (ibid.: 198)). The challenges to neoliberal hegemony (in Europe and more generally) and the tendency for that hegemony to give way to 'a new authoritarian neoliberalism in which democracy is hollowed out' (ibid.: 199) are taken up in the last section of this chapter.

Another major contribution to scholarship on neoliberalism and the TCC is William Robinson's 'theory of global capital' (Robinson 2004, 2012). Robinson identifies globalization with the formation of a TCC and transnational state, in opposition to 'national' fractions of capital. The key statement of this position was made in Robinson and Harris's 2000 article, which sees capitalist globalization as replicating, on a world-scale, the nation-building stage of early capitalism: constructing an integrated market with common laws, currency, taxes, 'and political consolidation around a common state', in this case a transnational state apparatus constituting 'a new legal and economic superstructure for the global economy' (2000: 42). This article distinguishes three neoliberal strategic ('factional') positions within the TCC, described as free market conservative, neoliberal structuralist, and neoliberal regulationist. The first position ideologically opposes any state intervention in economic relationships beyond upholding private property rights, whereas the last supports state intervention to reduce the worst economic and social contradictions of neoliberalism, so as to thwart political contestation and stabilize the regime. In between them, the neoliberal structuralist faction, dominant among the TCC according to Robinson and Harris, favours minimal economic intervention to contain crises, for example through bail-outs for banks when their collapse would threaten the neoliberal regime itself.

Robinson's reading of globalization as transnational political consolidation posits a major fractional division between national capitalists, whose business practices are largely contained within national borders, and the TCC. Robinson (2012) holds that, within countries, transnational capitalist fractions were successful in the 1980s and 1990s in wresting state power from national fractions, and that neoliberal globalization has proceeded under their direction. Such a zero-sum scenario may fit with some experiences, but it encounters problems as a general account, particularly when we consider that it has often been local and national capital that has pressed, through chambers of commerce and other market-oriented groupings, for low tax, laissez-faire regimes to limit their wage costs (Carroll 2012). Our earlier discussion showed how the TCC has long been a key participant in developing global neoliberal policy networks. Yet this does not discount the extensive role national fractions of capital have played in bolstering neoliberalism through their support of nationally based think tanks and political parties, as exemplified by the MPS-supported Atlas Network, mentioned earlier.

In practice, the distinction between 'national' capitalists and 'transnational' capitalists is blurry. Van Apeldoorn and De Graaff's (2012) analysis of the corporate affiliations of key cabinet-ranking and senior advisors in the Clinton, Bush and Obama administrations revealed not only a remarkable number of connections into the 'national' American corporate community, but also a strong presence of US-based transnational capital. For them the overwhelming predominance of the latter, *at once national and transnational*, at the heart of the US capital-state nexus, helps explain the strong US commitment to transnational neoliberalism within a 'grand strategy' that in fact 'reflects the interests of US transnational capital' (ibid.: 600).

Thus, despite tendencies towards becoming a class-for-itself, the TCC does not express a single unified volition. Contradictory dynamics still issue from the fractional perspectives of money capital and industrial capital, and neoliberal thought harbours multiple approaches to the best strategy for maintaining TCC dominance. Certain national dynamics may also come into contradiction with now globalized circuits of accumulation, though the prominence of these tensions is not as clear-cut as first suggested by Robinson and Harris (Carroll 2013). The next section discusses how these processes have played out since the last major crisis to have rocked the neoliberal regime.

Second life: the 2008 financial meltdown and beyond

The global economic crisis – cascading from the massive devaluation of bundled assets tied to the US mortgage market in 2007 to insolvent investment banks, crashing stock markets and, by late 2008, a 'frozen' international financial system threatening worldwide depression – was greeted by many as a sign of neoliberalism's demise. Although, in the aftermath of the financial meltdown, some observers announced this demise, instead of 'post-neoliberalism' the crisis actually granted neoliberalism a second life (Mirowski 2013; Bruff 2014; Springer 2015). Here, we first consider the changes in the TCC associated with the mutation of transnational neoliberalism in the years surrounding the global crisis, and then we examine implications of neoliberalism's post-2008 second life for the TCC as a class-for-itself.

On the first point, Van der Pijl and Yurchenko (2014) offer an interpretation that adds nuance to the former's analysis of the connection between neoliberalism and TCC formation. They periodize the neoliberal era not in terms of policy content (the familiar 'rolling back' and 'rolling out' phases – see Peck and Tickell 2002), but in terms of the social class complexes and circuits of accumulation favoured by each version. In neoliberalism's prehistory, during the era of Fordist-Keynesian class compromise, capitalism's 'lead circuit' was that of productive capital, furnishing the basis in the global North for a general interest in robust national economies. But in the 1970s, as productivity gains in the world-system's core fell behind wage increases, depressing profits, corporations shifted production to low-wage zones. Concurrently, the circuit of money capital gained global sweep and the swelling volume of internationally mobile money capital fed inflation. The Volcker Shock of 1979, which inaugurated the neoliberal roll-back by putting brakes on the expansion of money (thus forcing up interest rates), was aimed at restoring the discipline of capital at home while obliging indebted states to avoid default by privatizing assets. It thereby 'widened the sphere of capital accumulation under the auspices of interest-bearing money capital' (Van der Pijl and Yurchenko 2014: 8).

The objective in this 'systemic' phase of neoliberalism was to restore profitability via real accumulation, in no small measure through attacks on organized labour for which the Reagan and Thatcher regimes became notorious. But as financialization created an ever-expanding volume of derivatives, neoliberalism 'slowly mutated into a "*predatory*" version in which real capital accumulation becomes a secondary consideration altogether' (ibid.: 9, emphasis added).

In neoliberalism's predatory phase, it is money-dealing capital, claiming profit through speculative arbitrage, which dominates the accumulation process. As shown in the crisis of 2007–9, state authorities are deeply implicated in this process: when the crash comes, their bail-outs refuel the bubble economy, indicating an alignment between predatory neoliberalism and ascendant money-dealing capital. Yet socializing bank losses turns a crisis of money-dealing capital into a crisis of public finance. 'Austerity, the asset-stripping of entire societies, thus becomes the downside of refueling speculative money-dealing capital' (ibid.: 18).

For the TCC, the transition, in neoliberalism's predatory phase, to a fully financialized capitalism brought a weakening of corporate-interlock networks, both national and transnational, as relationship-based financing via interest-bearing bank loans gave way to transaction-based finance through securitized financial paper (Carroll 2010). In the emergent form of neoliberal capitalism, the TCC continues to be well-organized politically, through its core policy-planning organs, but the corporate-interlock network thins, as corporate governance becomes a matter of speculative capital market control rather than corporate self-regulation (ibid.). As we have seen, the continuing proliferation of transnational policy groups and neoliberal think tanks offers a more directly political form of TCC social organization, useful in constructing and championing pro-market policies.

Predatory neoliberalism, however, faces a thinning basis for popular consent. Van der Pijl and Yurchenko (ibid.) describe a move from a (narrow) class compromise, under systemic neoliberalism, between capital and the asset-owning middle classes to an exclusivist, oligarchic order. As neoliberalism becomes more predatory, it also becomes more authoritarian (Bruff 2014): societal asset-stripping – the project of 'total privatization' (Albo and Fanelli 2014) – can provoke intense resistance, requiring a ratcheting-up of the free market/strong state relation that was already deeply inscribed in the Thatcherite version of neoliberalism (Gamble 1988). Surveillance, the criminalization of dissent, the militarization of policing and the framing by neoliberal governments of 'protestors, and political opposition in general, as a threat to economic recovery and competitiveness' (Albo and Fanelli 2014: 21–2) become the order of the day.

Yet a more predatory and authoritarian neoliberalism does not negate the need for the dominant class to win a modicum of consent from subaltern groups (see e.g. Springer 2009). Indeed, the weakening of neoliberal hegemony needs to be viewed in conjunction with 'full-spectrum' neoliberalism as it has matured in the think tanks and related groups supported by the TCC: a spectrum of short-, middle- and long-term initiatives organized around 'the immutable solidity of the market' (Mirowski 2013: 342). These various strategies do not fit seamlessly into a monolithic programme – they may even contradict each other on the surface; and, we might add, they attract different factions and fractions of the TCC as their sponsors and champions.

For instance, 'the phenomena of "science denialism," "carbon permit trading," and the nascent science of "geoengineering" are not three unrelated or rival panaceas, but together constitute the full-spectrum neoliberal response to the challenge of global warming' (ibid.: 337). Transnational capitalists like the billionaire Koch brothers (inventors of oil derivatives, heavily invested in Alberta's tar sands and bankrollers of the US Tea Party) trumpet climate-change denial and laissez-faire conservatism, defending the sanctity of the market and of business-as-usual in the short term.[4] Carbon trading finds favour within the financial sector, as a mid-range strategy, aligned with neoliberal structuralism, which creates new instruments of financialization. Geoengineering (sponsored by such billionaires as Bill Gates and Richard Branson and implying in its global scale some degree of neoliberal regulation) mobilizes science and industry for longer-term investments in absorbing/sequestrating carbon or in reflecting sunlight away from the Earth.[5] Here we can see how, in full-spectrum neoliberalism, the TCC's laissez-faire conservative, structural and regulationist factions, and its financial and industrial fractions, mobilize around variegated initiatives that have in common the reproduction of neoliberal capitalism on an expanding scale. The relationship between neoliberalism and the TCC, whether in its formative era, its heyday or now its second life, has been both complex and fateful.

Notes

1 Source: www.iccwbo.org/global-influence/icc-network/ (retrieved 12 December 2014).
2 Source: https://web.archive.org/web/20141006212146/http://www.weforum.org/issues/thought-leadership-through-art-culture-and-sport (retrieved 12 December 2014).
3 Source: http://www.weforum.org/community/global-agenda-councils (retrieved 5 January 2015).
4 See the investigative reports and related material at the International Forum on Globalization's site http://kochcash.org
5 The World Business Council on Sustainable Development, including CEOs of financial and industrial TNCs, is an important site for mediating across this spectrum. A longstanding advocate of voluntary corporate guidelines, it has in the past decade elaborated principles for carbon pricing and trading, and in September 2014 announced its support of carbon capture and storage. See http://www.wbcsd.org/changing-pace/business-perspectives/energyandpower.aspx and http://www.wbcsd.org/Pages/eNews/eNewsDetails.aspx?ID=16323 (retrieved 8 January 2015).
6 Published posthumously.

References

Albo, G., and Fanelli, C. 2014. *Austerity Against Democracy: An Authoritarian Phase of Neoliberalism?* Toronto: Socialist Project. www.socialistproject.ca/documents/AusterityAgainstDemocracy.pdf (last accessed 2 January 2015).

Atkins, F. 1986. Thatcherism, Populist Authoritarianism and the Search for a New Left Political Strategy. *Capital & Class*, 28: 25–48.

Brenner, N., Peck, J., and Theodore, N. 2010. Variegated Neoliberalization: Geographies, Modalities, Pathways. *Global Networks*, 10: 182–222.

Bruff, I. 2014. The Rise of Authoritarian Neoliberalism. *Rethinking Marxism*, 26: 113–29.

Bryan, D. 1995. *The Chase Across the Globe: International Accumulation and the Contradictions for Nation States.* Boulder, CO: Westview Press.

Cahill, D. 2012. The Embedded Neoliberal Economy, in Cahill, D., Edwards, L., and Stilwell, F., eds. *Neoliberalism: Beyond the Free Market.* Cheltenham, UK: Edward Elgar: 110–27.

Carroll, W.K. 2003. Undoing the End of History: Canada-Centred Reflections on the Challenge of Globalization, in Atasoy, Y., and Carroll, W.K., eds. *Global Shaping and its Alternatives.* Aurora, Ontario: Garamond Press: 33–55.

—. 2007. Hegemony and Counter-Hegemony in a Global Field. *Studies in Social Justice*, 1.1: 36–66.

—. 2010. *The Making of a Transnational Capitalist Class: Corporate Power in the 21st Century.* London and New York: Zed Books.

—. 2012. Global, Transnational, Regional, National: The Need for Nuance in Theorizing Global Capitalism. *Critical Sociology*, 38.3: 365–71.

—. 2013. Whither the Transnational Capitalist Class? *Socialist Register*, 50: 162–88.

Carroll, W.K., and Carson, C. 2003. Forging a New Hegemony? The Role of Transnational Policy Groups in the Network and Discourse of Global Corporate Governance. *Journal of World-Systems Research*, 9.1: 67–102.

Carroll, W.K., and Sapinski, J.P. 2010. The Global Corporate Elite and the Transnational Policy-Planning Network, 1996–2006: A Structural Analysis. *International Sociology*, 25.4: 501–38.

Domhoff, G.W. 2014. *Who Rules America? The Triumph of the Corporate Rich.* 7th edn. New York: McGraw-Hill.

Duménil, G., and Lévy, D. 2012. The Crisis of Neoliberalism as a Stepwise Process: From the Great Contraction to the Crisis of Sovereign Debts, in Cahill, D., Edwards, L., and Stilwell, F., eds. *Neoliberalism: Beyond the Free Market.* Cheltenham, UK: Edward Elgar: 31–53.

Gamble, A. 1988. *The Free Economy and the Strong State.* London: Macmillan.

Gill, S.R., and Law, D. 1989. Global Hegemony and the Structural Power of Capital. *International Studies Quarterly*, 33.4: 475.

Hymer, S. 1974. International Politics and International Economics: A Radical Approach (mimeographed). *Monthly Review*,[6] 29.1.

Kotz, D.M., and McDonough, T. 2010. Global Neoliberalism and the Contemporary Social Structure of Accumulation, in McNonough, T., Reich, M., and Kotz, D.M., eds. *Contemporary Capitalism and its Crises*. New York: Cambridge University Press: 93–120.

Krippner, G.R. 2005. The Financialization of the American Economy. *Socio-Economic Review*, 3: 173–208.

Mirowski, P. 2013. *Never Let a Serious Crisis Go to Waste: How Neoliberalism Survived the Financial Meltdown*. London: Verso.

Peck, J., and Tickell, A. 2002. Neoliberalizing Space. *Antipode*, 34.3: 380–404.

Plehwe, D. 2009. Introduction, in Mirowski, P., and Plehwe, D., eds. *The Road from Mont Pèlerin: The Making of the Neoliberal Thought Collective*. Cambridge, MA: Harvard University Press.

Robinson, W.I. 2004. *A Theory of Global Capitalism*. Baltimore, MD: Johns Hopkins University Press.

—. 2012. Global Capitalism Theory and the Emergence of Transnational Elites. *Critical Sociology*, 38.3: 349–63.

Robinson, W.I., and Harris, J. 2000. Towards a Global Ruling Class? Globalisation and the Transnational Capitalist Class. *Science & Society*, 64.1: 11–54.

Springer, S. 2009. Renewed Authoritarianism in Southeast Asia: Undermining Democracy through Neoliberal Reform. *Asia Pacific Viewpoint*, 50.3: 271–6.

—. 2015. Post-neoliberalism? *Review of Radical Political Economics*, 47.1: 5–17.

Van Apeldoorn, B. 2013. The European Capitalist Class and the Crisis of Its Hegemonic Project. *Socialist Register*, 50: 189–206.

Van Apeldoorn, B., and de Graaff, N. 2012. The Limits of Open Door Imperialism and the US State-Capital Nexus. *Globalizations*, 9.4: 593–608.

Van der Pijl, K. 1983. Imperialism and Class Formation in the North Atlantic Area. Doctoral dissertation, University of Amsterdam.

—. 1984. *The Making of an Atlantic Ruling Class*. London: Verso.

—. 1986. Neoliberalism vs Planned Interdependence: Concepts of Control in the Struggle for Hegemony. Paper presented at the Conference on Interdependence and Conflict in the International System, Polemologisch Instituut, Groningen, 19–21 November.

—. 1998. *Transnational Classes and International Relations*. London: Routledge.

Van der Pijl, K., and Yurchenko, Y. 2014. Neoliberal Entrenchment of North Atlantic Capital: From Corporate Self-Regulation to State Capture. *New Political Economy*, 20.4: 1–23.

World Economic Forum (WEF). 2013. *Annual Report 2012–2013*. Geneva: World Economic Forum.

4

THEORIZING NEOLIBERALIZATION

Kim England and Kevin Ward

Neoliberalism is the defining political economic paradigm of our time.

(McChesney 1999: 7)

There has everywhere been an emphatic turn towards neoliberalism in political-economic practices and thinking since the 1970s.

(Harvey 2005: 2)

Neoliberalism defines a certain existential norm.

(Dardot and Laval 2014: 3)

So, here we are again then! Plus ça change, plus c'est la même chose! Over ten years ago the two of us were brought together by an early attempt to construct an infrastructure to support the internationalization agenda that is now such an important element of higher educational reform in many counties around the world. The Worldwide Universities Network (WUN) now claims to be 'a leading global higher education and research network made up of 19 universities, spanning 11 countries on five continents' (WUN 2015: n.p.). Back in the early 2000s it was an altogether smaller operation. When WUN was just starting out, one of its flagship initiatives was a seminar series involving human geography graduate students and faculty. We met in 2002 at the first WUN sponsored faculty workshop on neoliberalism, and, after that, organized sessions at the annual conferences of the American Association of Geographers (AAG) and Royal Geographical Society (with the Institute of British Geographers) (RGS-IBG). For a few years a broader group from the universities of Bristol, Leeds, Manchester, Sheffield and Southampton in the UK and from the universities of Illinois at Urbana-Champaign Madison-Wisconsin, Penn State and Washington in the USA convened to discuss contemporary issues in the sub-discipline under the designation *Horizons in Human Geography*. In badly lit rooms of varying sizes, often via slightly sketchy connections, presentations would be given, questions asked and geographically distant parts of the world would be brought closer together, albeit temporally.

While *Horizons in Human Geography* only lasted a few years (brought down by institutional politics in a number of participating universities), together with a couple of associated face-to-face meetings, it provided the impetus for a series of academic endeavours around neoliberalism (Leitner *et al.* 2007; Tickell *et al.* 2007), including our own *Neoliberalization: States, Networks,*

Peoples (England and Ward 2007). The aim of our book was to bring together some of those writing from a number of disciplines on what was then referred to as 'neoliberalism'. It was one of a number of authored and edited monographs at the time and in subsequent years that spoke to the ongoing intellectual project of theorizing neoliberalism (Harvey 2005; Macdonald and Ruckert 2009; Mirowski and Plehwe 2009; Birch and Mykhnenko 2010; Peck 2010).

Fast-forward to 2016. For almost two decades, human geographers and other social scientists have been naming and writing about something called 'neoliberalism', working on a range of substantive topics – citizenship, climate change, crime, drugs, education, labour markets, migration, security, the environment, urban redevelopment, welfare reform – and from across the spectrum of epistemological, methodological and theoretical stances, to which we turn later in this chapter. Such has been the growth in the use of the term and the work it has been asked to do that it has become something of a 'rascal concept' (Smith 1987; Peck *et al.* 2009). For some, the focus has been on exploring its policy and programmatic implications. For others, the challenge has been to reveal the etymology of the word: its histories and its geographies. Still others have sought to unpack it, to consider whether it should be regarded as something that does the explaining of something – an explanatory concept – or that needs explaining – a descriptive concept. In these examples, and there are very many, studies of, for instance, environmental politics, or urban renewal are useful on their own terms as well as saying something about the wider processes of neoliberalization. And here our choice of words is deliberate. We use the term 'neoliberalization', emphasizing the processual, relational and variegated nature of regulatory restructuring and subject-making (Brenner *et al.* 2010a, 2010b). This distinction matters. Why? Well, because, as Springer (2015: 7) argues:

> In utilizing this dynamic conception of neoliberalism-as-a-verb over static notions of neoliberalism-as-a-noun we arrive at the conclusion that while particular social spaces, regulatory networks, sectoral fields, local formations, and so forth will frequently be hampered by crises, this does not necessarily imply that they will resonate throughout an entire aggregation of neoliberalism. In other words, because 'neoliberalism' indeed does not exist as a coherent and fixed edifice, as an equilibrial complex, or as a finite end-state, it is consequently unlikely to fail in a totalizing moment of collapse.

Whether you understand the world as witnessing some version of post-neoliberalism (Brand and Sekler 2009; Springer 2015), or its unfolding 'zombie' condition (Peck 2014), attempting to review the ways that neoliberalism/neoliberalization has been defined and theorized is a daunting task. Some might even suggest it is a foolhardy one. Over a decade ago McCarthy and Prudham (2004: 276) noted that 'defining neo-liberalism is no straightforward task'. In the ten years since we began working on *Neoliberalization: States, Networks, Peoples* it is a task that has probably got harder, not easier. And that is despite the continuously growing volume of words dedicated to its defining and analysis. Or, perhaps it is precisely because of the generation of so many words that agreement and clarity have been in relatively short supply (Brenner *et al.* 2010a). You don't have to be 'in denial' (Springer 2014: 154) to acknowledge the different uses of the term 'neoliberalism'. Moving away from the most basic text book-like definitions, as most social scientists have over the last decade, it becomes quickly apparent that there is very little agreement on a number of fairly fundamental matters.

For example, what is meant by 'neoliberalism', where did it start, where does it stop, has it ended, what are its edges, what status does 'neoliberalism' have in the intellectual-cum-theoretical vocabulary and what extra-theoretical purchase do academics gain (or lose) when using the term 'neoliberalism'? In the years in which we have worked together and individually on grappling with the politics, processes and practices of neoliberalization it is clear to us that as the use of the term has escalated, so have the number of ways it is used and the meanings invested in it. It has become 'oft-invoked but ill-defined' (Mudge 2008: 703), its upsurge in usage accompanied 'by considerable imprecision, confusion and controversy' (Brenner *et al.* 2010a: 328). There remains disagreement over what is meant by the term 'neoliberalism' and how best to conceptualize and to study 'it', even if 'it' can be thought of as an 'it'. Is it a cultural, economic, political or social formation, or all four and more besides? Is it a hegemonic 'big picture' project? Or is it a set of experiments, without a common objective, largely disconnected, and malleable in the extreme? Does it constitute less, more or a new form of state regulation? What gets included or seen in its usage and what does not and what are the consequences for the imagining and realising of potential futures?

Despite all the complexity that exists around the intellectual genealogy of neoliberalism/ neoliberalization, the focus of the remainder of this chapter is quite simple. First, it outlines the two dominant approaches to theorizing neoliberalization: those from political economy and post-structural approaches. While both act as a short-hand for more internally heterogeneous contributions, there are, nevertheless, some commonalities around which contributions in the two approaches coalesce. Second, the chapter turns to four ways in which the term has been used to refer to particular 'formations' (Larner 2003). These are an ideological hegemonic project, as policy and programme, as statecraft and as governmentality. This builds upon our earlier work.

In conclusion, and as if to reinforce the plus ça change, plus c'est la même chose sentiment with which we began our chapter, we make a similar set of points to those we made almost a decade ago. For, while it may have been 'on the ropes' (Peck *et al.* 2009: 94), those with a stake in neoliberalization have, to continue with the boxing analogy, come out swinging. The onset of the financial crisis in late 2008 appeared to at least pose the question: are we about to witness the slow and geographically uneven unravelling of neoliberalization? Not overnight and not everywhere at once. For neoliberalization is not 'an all-encompassing global totality' (Brenner *et al.* 2010a: 342) and hence evidence of any 'ending' was always likely to be incremental and partial. However, while the financial crisis has led to more mature and nuanced theorizations of neoliberalization, particularly those which situate contestation and resistance as a co-presence in its origins, the emergences, the circulations and the consolidations (Featherstone *et al.* 2015), in many countries of the world its presence remains. What we have witnessed is the emergence of what Hendrikse and Sidaway (2010: 2037) have termed 'neoliberalism 3.0'. While there may be future arguments to be had with neoliberalism (Weller and O'Neill 2014), for now at least any alternative political futures are going to be forged along with it, not instead of it.

Conceptualizing neoliberalization: political economy, post-structuralism, or both?

There is no shortage of those who would take on the intellectual challenge of conceptualizing neoliberalization (Harvey 2005; Macdonald and Ruckert 2009; Mirowski and Plehwe 2009; Birch and Mykhnenko 2010; Peck 2010; Springer 2015). From across the social sciences, the last two decades has witnessed a quickening of the pace of theoretical offerings. While this literature has a number of discernible characteristics, in this chapter we want briefly to focus on the two conceptual approaches that have contributed most to contemporary understandings of neoliberalization. These are those from a political economy and from a post-structural approach. We do not wish to overdraw this division (a binary even) between these two 'camps' by counter-posing one against the other, not least because these camps themselves are far from unified and mono-lithic, but instead consist of several co-existing (and not always comfortable) approaches. Instead we outline each one's defining features.

So, for those working within the broadly political economy tradition, grappling with neolib-eralization can be characterized as part of a longer-term intellectual programme examining the ongoing and qualitative restructuring of the spatial, scalar and temporal co-ordinates of the state. The focus is on its macro-political, contextual and inter-institutional logic (Brenner and Theo-dore 2002; Peck and Tickell 2002). Proponents of this position would likely deny they are arguing for a monolithic conceptualization of neoliberalization that suggests the processes are the same everywhere, undifferentiated, or even that there is a universal convergence of histori-cally different state formations and models of capitalism. Rather the emphasis is, nevertheless, on *shared* features, on *generic* characteristics and on *family* resemblances. The essence of this approach is nicely laid out in the following quote:

> In our conceptualization, neoliberalization is not an all-encompassing global totality but an unevenly developed *pattern* of restructuring that has been produced through a succession of path-dependent collisions between emergent, market-disciplinary regu-latory projects and inherited landscapes across places, territories and scales.
>
> *(Brenner et al. 2010a: 342, original emphasis)*

It is possible to further disaggregate this formulation into three analytical dimensions (Brenner *et al.* 2010a: 335): (1) *regulatory experiments* which consist of 'place-, territory- and scale-specific projects designed to impose, intensify or reproduce market-disciplinary modalities of gover-nance'; (2) *systems of inter-jurisdictional policy transfer* through which 'neoliberal policy prototypes are circulated across places, territories, and scales, generally transnationally, for redeployment elsewhere'; and (3) transnational rule regimes which 'impose determinate 'rules of the game' on contextually specific forms of policy experimentation and regulatory reorganization, thereby enframing the activities of actors and institutions within specific politico-institutional parame-ters.' Taken together, a variegated notion of neoliberalization with 'regulatory uneven develop-ment' (Brenner *et al.* 2010b: 217) at its explanatory core underscores the political economy approach.

For those working primarily from post-colonial/post-structural perspectives (and we acknowledge significant differences between the two), the focus is on the junking of 'grand nar-ratives'. Instead attention is on situated experiences, meanings and representations and explora-tions of neoliberalism as a cultural project (Ferguson and Gupta 2002; Hall and Lamont 2013). Power is understood 'as a *relational* concept that has repressive *and* productive consequences' (Prince and Dufty 2009: 1746). Drawing on interdisciplinary work on classic and advanced lib-eralism, the project, subjects and techniques involved in neoliberalization are theorized as a means to highlight complexities, tensions and contradictions. This approach to conceptualizing neoliberalization owes an intellectual debt to the far wider critique of political economy, and its proponents argue for a more situated analysis of contemporary geo-economical and geo-politi-cal processes, rationalities and technologies.

Neoliberalization is theorized as culturally produced and spatially contextual, constituted with a range of social relations and materialized through socio-spatial processes and practices in a range of scales, sites and spaces (Larner 2000, 2003; Kingfisher 2013; Springer 2012). An aspect of this approach is challenging the notion of the state as autonomous from society, and emphasiz-ing the *active* remaking and redeployment of the state in creating the political subjectivities and enabling the conditions for marketization. It includes Foucauldian tracings of the specificities of elements associated with neoliberalisms such as the technologies of the enrolment and regulation of subjectivities, and the calculative and self-enterprising forms of conduct (Dardot and Laval 2014).

Neoliberalizations (in the plural) are conceptualized as sets of hybrid processes and situated meanings, with the emphasis on exploring their *different* features, *distinctive* characteristics and veritable *uniqueness*. Neoliberalizations involve actually existing people engaged in situated, grounded practices and governmental technologies that produce particular places and particular outcomes in those places. By extension, neoliberalism is spatially varied, playing out differently in different places in articulation with the particular cultural, economic and political trajectories in those places.

While there appears to remain an intellectual appetite for 'the potential reconcilability of the different approaches' (Springer 2012: 143), these differences persist. For us, the most fruitful intellectual manoeuvre is to acknowledge the power of neoliberalization without re-inscribing 'it' as a unitary hegemonic project. J.K. Gibson-Graham's (2006: 1) caution about the efforts to understand capitalism as an object of analysis can also be applied to neoliberalism: be alert, because all too easily 'the project of understanding the beast has itself produced a beast'. We therefore agree with Sparke (2006: 11) that the way foreword is 'to nuance rather than abandon our analyses of neoliberalism'. While there is, of course, much that distinguishes the two bodies of work – their intellectual referents, ontological categories, and epistemological assumptions to name but three – we still see many points of connection that mean the two can be held in productive tension. For instance, Larner *et al.* (2013: 21) offer the following provocative observation regarding gendered transformations of governance, economy, and citizenship:

> juxtaposing states and subjectivities, production and social reproduction, market, and culture, we can reveal not only more about how new gendered formations are emerging but also underline the need for a wider conceptual repertoire than has often previously been the case.

A process of dialogues, engagements and reflections is, in and of itself, incredibly useful, even if there remain some irreconcilable differences. Debates and disagreements are intellectually fruitful. Indeed, our current understanding of neoliberalization would not have been generated, we would argue, were it not for the intellectual differences that continue to characterize the writings in this field. Contributions and counter-contributions have proved academically nourishing and stimulating and we hope to see the lively discussions about the complexities and contingencies of neoliberalization continue.

Understandings of neoliberalization

It is almost a cliché to claim that neoliberalism is a difficult concept to pin down. Despite the work that has been spent apparently doing just that – pinning it down – only recently Weller and O'Neill (2014: 107) were still compelled to ask 'What is neoliberalism?' Of course, their question was not asked from a neutral standpoint. Questions rarely are. Rather, Weller and O'Neill's query came out of a concern to challenge whether Australia had ever been neoliberal, as had been claimed by some. Leaving aside the rights or wrongs of this particular 'argument' and its potentially more significant implications for the relationship between 'theory' and the 'world', the 'meteoric' (Springer 2012: 135) expansion of work on neoliberalism/neoliberalization has not yet led to the emergence of a consensus on its meaning. Rather, a cursory scanning of the pages of blogs, books, journals and websites reveals the myriad ways that neoliberalism/neoliberalization continues to be used. Some of these reflect disciplinary differences (such as that between economics and human geography, for example), while other differences are born out of some combination of the geographic location of authors (that is, from where on the map work is being generated) and the particular geographies about which are being written. The slipperiness of neoliberalism/neoliberalization's defining and usage means that it is frequently used as a proxy for a dizzying range of outcomes, processes and things. Bundled together and objectified, given a sense of coherence, the important distinctions between processes of state-market entanglements such as marketization and privatization have sometimes tended to be lost or subsumed in the rush to identify patterns and regularities (Larner 2003; Birch and Siemiatycki 2015).

In this light, the focus of this section is to unbundle and to reflect upon the different understandings of neoliberalization. Our identification of them rested on a method of aggregation. That is looking for similarities in the range of ways in which human geographers and others were defining and using at first the term 'neoliberalism' and then, as an outcome of some of this work, more latterly, the term 'neoliberalization' (Peck and Tickell 2002; Tickell and Peck 2003). These intellectual exercises often say as much about those undertaking them as they do about the fields they purport to represent. That was a charge that could have been levied against us a decade ago (but it wasn't!). It is one against which our defence would be weak today. Nevertheless, in the absence of a consensus on 'What is neoliberalism?', there thus remain important variations in the using of the verb 'neoliberalization'. Four, in particular, stand out.

Neoliberalization as an ideological hegemonic project

This understanding refers to the places and the peoples behind its origins and that are involved in its apparent uptake in geographically discrete but socially connected parts of the world. So, around differing views of neoliberalizations are 'homelands' of connections and relations between countries in the global North and South and chronologies of 'shock' and 'therapy'. An important strand in the more general growth in social science work on neoliberalism/neoliberalization has been on its genealogies, geographies and histories (and pre-histories). These are multiple and relational. Some are known, others less so. Substantive contributions by Harvey (2005), Mirowski and Plehwe (2009) and Peck (2010) have taken aim directly at those involved and the work they have done in the emergence of neoliberalization. This includes detailing agencies and institutions of differing geographical reach and their roles. This has generated an understanding of a landscape consisting of a criss-crossing and overlapping lattice of differently headquartered consultants, lobbyists, state actors and think tanks. Experimental, incremental, opportunistic, as likely to fail as to succeed, this is an image of a 'project' that emerged over decades without a blueprint, without a map.

In much of this work, political dominance is often seen to emerge and be exercised through the formation of class-based alliances – elite actors, institutions and other representatives of capital – at a variety of spatial scales, who produce and circulate what appear to be a reasonably coherent programme of ideas and images about the world, its problems and how these are best addressed. All of these are, of course, deeply interwoven with ageist, gendered and racialized power hierarchies (Gibson-Graham 2006; Kofman 2007). Certainly, hegemony is not only political and economic control, it is also the capacity of the dominant class to project its own way of seeing onto the world so that those who are subordinated by it view it as 'common sense', even 'natural' (see Plehwe 2016). For example, the notion of the 'free market' is represented as naturally occurring. This is not just about imposition, but also about the willing 'consent' by those being subordinated, so that 'common sense' becomes how the subordinate class lives its subordination (Harvey 2005). Among the 'definitional families' of neoliberal analysis, Weller and O'Neill (2014: 107) argue that the neoliberalization as ideology perspective is the 'most stable' and they label it as 'neoliberalism-in-theory'.

Neoliberalization as policy, practice and programme

This understanding refers to the transfer of ownership from the public or state sector to the private or corporate sector, and in the process often involves a reworking of what these categories might mean (including what they mean for the communities and households left to fill the gaps, again all of which is over-determined by social relations of difference). It is possible to distinguish between four elements of this use: the context to which the policy is a response, the logic underpinning the policy, the agencies and institutions involved in the doing and evaluation of policy, and the intended audiences for the policy (see Slater 2016). Generally, policies involve replacing state ownership with private ownership, the logic underpinning this transformation being that transferring ownership to the market creates a more efficient system. However, evidence suggests that matters are rarely this straightforward.

Ownership is rendered more complicated through the various types of contractual relationships in which are located states and markets. Moreover, while in legal terms ownership may, in some cases, remain unchanged, governance and management (sometimes at a distance) challenges the logics, norms and understandings around notions of the 'public' and the 'private'. What emerges is a sense of engagements and entanglements. Examples include policies pursued under the banners of 'de-regulation', 'liberalization', 'marketization' and 'privatization'. These have taken place in a number of fields of policy-making, including in crime, drugs, economic development, education, and transportation.

In the words of Hendrikse and Sidaway (2010: 39) the relationship between states and markets becomes reconfigured so that 'they become more thoroughly intermeshed'. Those involved in authoring and orchestrating this shift include a range of socially and spatially situated actors – nation-states and their various agencies and branches, as well as a whole range of others such as community groups, consultants, labour unions, NGOs and think tanks. This reflects the work that argues for the co-constitution of neoliberalization involving the presence of those seeking to make and unmake policy. For Mudge (2008: 704) this is the 'bureaucratic face' of neoliberalism, while for Weller and O'Neill (2014: 108) it might usefully be labelled as 'neoliberalism-in-general', in reference to a 'globally interconnected and constantly reworked set of policies and practices'.

Neoliberalization as statecraft

This understanding refers to the quantitative and qualitative restructuring of nation-states, involving redrawing the boundaries between civil society, market and state, and sometimes their territorial borders (Brenner *et al.* 2010a, 2010b; also see Jessop 2016). Most often this has involved fiscal austerity efforts by the state to 'solve' the tensions between commitments to a territorialized political system and remaining economically competitive in a globalizing economy (Cowen and Smith 2009). Neoliberalization as statecraft involves an agenda aimed at reducing government spending while increasing economic efficiency and competitiveness, an agenda steeped in the rhetoric of free markets, privatization and marketization, along with 'the multidimensional rooting of the neoliberal state in the global economy' (ibid.: 41). The state is transformed into a model of governance underpinned by economic liberalism that calls for privileging the market and limiting government spending, especially on social welfare programmes, but perhaps not on the military.

This understanding of neoliberalism involves the 'rolling back' and the 'rolling out' (Peck and Tickell 2002) of state formations, with the reconfiguration of the scalar, spatial and temporal selectivities. Included here is a redrawing of where the state starts and stops – its edges – as well as a reorganization of its internal spaces and its institutional architecture. The 'rolling back' mantra of 'less government' translates into stemming the growth of the state (especially social programmes), limiting taxes, and 'the destruction and discrediting of Keynesian welfarist and social-collectivist institutions (broadly defined)' (MacLeavy 2012: 251). This unfolds alongside a qualitative shift to active state-building, often of an authoritarian penal sort, via rolling out new institutions and new (de)regulatory reforms around, for instance, social assistance, immigration, international investment and foreign policy. In fact, neoliberalization often means more not less state intervention and, as Julie MacLeavy remarks (ibid.: 252), 'rather than simply encouraging the withering away of the state, neoliberal programmes of government have instead entailed reconstitution of state capacities and political subjectivities across different spatial contexts'.

This redrawing and reorganization of the state is associated with different implications according to hierarchies of gender, race and so on, because the state is a set of gendered (as well as ableist, heterosexed and raced) institutions with spatialized social practices that differently situate and impact women compared with men (Kofman 2007; Kingfisher 2013). Neoliberalization as statecraft includes recasting the state's responsibilities to civil society, for the collective well-being of its citizens and, as such, there is a shift in the responsibilities between the state, the market, communities and families. In the process, the parameters of the role of the state, citizenship and popular understandings about the public/private and collective/individual relations have altered significantly.

Neoliberalization as governmentality

Taking its cue from Foucault (1980), this understanding pivots on neoliberalism as processual, and, as Weller and O'Neill (20014: 109) describe, 'operates through a range of practices and processes that combine social, cultural and economic domains to constitute new spaces and subjects' (also see Lewis 2016). This gets at the ways in which the relations among and between peoples and things might be imagined, assembled and translated (and, indeed, reimagined, reassembled and retranslated) that induce self-regulating subjectivities, thus enabling a form of power that governs at a distance (Larner 2000, 2003; Sparke 2006). Neoliberalization as governmentality means that the state, rather than being something 'out there' acting upon society and individuals, is mutually constituted in and through an assortment of social relations and materialized through innumerable socio-spatial practices in innumerable spaces (Larner, 2000; Crampton 2012; Kingfisher, 2013).

In this framing both the economy and the state are involved in economic calculative practices that construct autonomous, responsibilized 'neoliberal subjects'. For instance, in the global North, social policy has been rebuilt to encourage a culture of surveillance and self-regulation. The individual is 'responsibilized' as a self-sufficient moral agent and social problems become failures of the individual, which require individual, 'private' solutions, not collective, public solutions like public assistance and social insurance (Kingfisher 2013; also see Peters 2016).

For Wendy Brown (2005: 40), neoliberalization as a form of governmentality involves 'extending and disseminating market values to all institutions and social action'. The market is not merely self-perpetuating but a normative outcome of particular sorts of social policies. Market-logic rationalities of efficiency, choice and possessive individualism permeate multiple aspects of life and become the normative criteria for valuing people. Elizabeth Povinelli (2011: 22) takes this further, arguing:

Any form of life that (can) not produce values according to market logic would not merely be allowed to die, but, in situations in which the security of the market (and since the market was now the raison d'être of the state) seemed at stake, ferreted out and strangled.

In addition, viewing governmentality conceptualizations of neoliberalism as a spatial imaginary – in and through which peoples and places are understood in particular ways – opens up room to address neoliberalization's possible regressive *and* progressive elements. Understanding neoliberalism as a process involves acknowledging successes and failures, intended and unintended consequences and that the end results of policies and programmes are not defined by design, nor enviable, but are open to all manner of manipulations.

While there is much that distinguishes these four definitions and understandings of neoliberalism, in epistemological, methodological and ontological terms, there are also points of overlap and of connection. Our attempt to unpack and 'pin down' the multiple meanings and understandings of neoliberalization may raise analytical and conceptual problems for some. But our goal is not to merely describe neoliberalism, but also to identify the factors that systemically bring it into being, be that as an intellectual project or as a governing philosophy.

Conclusion

Hindsight is a wonderful thing. In part it depends on who you are and where you are. Armed with a processual and relational understanding of neoliberalization, did we ever really think that the financial crisis of the late 2000s would mark the end of neoliberalism? Probably not! However, what was already a lively field of intellectual endeavour was given an extra academic frisson with the significant changes in the real urban and national economies of the world. Not only was the notion of 'post'-neoliberalism considered, but understandings of the constitution of neoliberalism were reconsidered, offering a tantalising glimpse of a 'very different political cartography of the present' (Featherstone 2015: 5). For some 'its [i.e. neoliberalism's] growing inability to deal with the upcoming contradictions and crises' (Brand and Sekler 2009: 6) did constitute a space to imagine alternatives. Not because it was believed that it would suddenly cease to exist. Rather, because 'moments of crisis always reveal a great deal about the nature of neoliberalization as an adaptive regime of socioeconomic governance' (Peck *et al.* 2009: 95). Almost a decade on from the first signs of the financial crisis in late 2007, and in much of the world, neoliberalization continues to cast a long shadow over matters of economic and social justice. That is certainly not to say there are not visions of another future being imagined and put to work. There are. Rather, it is to underscore the incredible adaptability and durability of neoliberalization.

Given this context, we discussed two quite different ontological positions on neoliberalization. The political economy and post-structural orientations are those that have been present in the field since the upsurge of interest in the phenomenon by human geographers almost two decades ago. A rapprochement shows no sign of emerging, despite some attempts to 'destabilize the ostensible incompatibility that some scholars undertaking their separate usage seem keen to assume' (Springer 2012: 143). Whether one is possible is a moot point. Whether one is preferable is also questionable. Some of the insights that have been generated, particularly over the last decade, have come about, we would argue, precisely because of foundational disagreements. An attempt to bring dissenters together would have run the risk of closing down matters. Our chapter has also focused on the different understandings and theorizations of neoliberalization. These, we hope, will be picked up on and extended, stretched and transformed over the course of this collection. Four were outlined that we believe continue to characterize much of the still growing literature from across the social sciences. A method of simplification and aggregation underpins their generation, with some work transcending any single 'formation' (Springer 2012: 1031). Others might disagree with our assessment, but then our view is that continued constructive disagreement and engagement promises to be both fruitful and to continue to reveal much about neoliberalization's past, its presents and its various possible futures.

References

Birch, K., and Mykhnenko, V. eds. 2010. *The Rise and Fall of Neoliberalism: The Collapse of an Economic Order.* London: Zed Books.

Birch, K., and Siemiatycki, M. 2015. Neoliberalism and the Geographies of Marketization: The Entanglements of State and Markets. *Progress in Human Geography*, doi:0309132515570512.

Brand, U., and Sekler, N. eds. 2009. Postneoliberalism: Catch-All Word or Valuable Analytical and Political Concept? *Development Dialogue*, 51: 5–13.

Brenner, N., and Theodore, N. 2002. Cities and the Geographies of 'Actually Existing Neoliberalism'. *Antipode*, 33: 349–79.

Brenner, N., Peck, J., and Theodore, N. 2010a. After Neoliberalization? *Globalizations*, 7: 327–45.

—. 2010b. Variegated Neoliberalization. *Global Networks*, 10: 182–222.

Brown, W. 2005. *Edgework: Essays on Knowledge and Politics* Princeton, NJ: Princeton University Press.

Cowen, D., and Smith, N. 2009. After Geopolitics? From the Geopolitical Social to Geoeconomics *Antipode*, 41: 22–48.

Crampton, J.W. 2012. Foucault and Space, Territory, Geography, in Falzon, C., O'Leary, T., and Sawicki, J., eds. *A Companion to Foucault*. Oxford: Blackwell.

Dardot, P., and Laval, C. 2014. *The New Way of the World: On Neoliberal Society*. Brooklyn: Verso.

England, K., and Ward, K. 2007. *Neoliberalization: States, Networks, Peoples*. Malden, MA: Blackwell.

Featherstone, D. 2015. Thinking the Crisis Politically: Lineages of Resistance to Neo-liberalism and the Politics of the Present Conjuncture. *Space and Polity*, 19: 12–30.

Featherstone, D., Strauss, K., and MacKinnon, D. 2015, in, Against and Beyond Neo-liberalism: The 'Crisis' and Alternative Political Futures. *Space and Polity*, 19: 1–11.

Ferguson J., and Gupta, A. 2002. Spatializing States: Towards an Ethnography of Neoliberal Governmentality. *American Ethnologist*, 29: 981–1002.

Foucault, M. 1980. *Power/Knowledge: Selected Interviews and Other Writings 1972–1977*. Gordon, C., ed. Brighton: Harvester.

Gibson-Graham, J.-K. 2006. *The End of Capitalism (As We Knew It): A Feminist Critique of Political Economy.* Cambridge: Blackwell.

Hall, P.A., and Lamont, M. 2013. *Social Resilience in the Neoliberal Era*. Cambridge: Cambridge University Press.

Hall, S. 2011. The Neo-liberal Revolution. *Cultural Studies*, 25: 705–28.

Harvey, D. 2005. *A Brief History of Neoliberalism*. Oxford: Oxford University Press.

Hendrikse, R.P., and Sidaway, J. 2010. Neoliberalism 3.0. *Environment and Planning A*, 42: 37–42.

Jessop, B. 2016. The Heartlands of Neoliberalism and the Rise of the Austerity State, in Springer, S., Birch, K., and MacLeavy, J., eds. *The Handbook of Neoliberalism*. London: Routledge, 396–407.

Kingfisher, C. 2013. *A Policy Travelogue: Tracing Welfare Reform in Aotearoa/New Zealand and Canada.* Oxford: Berghahn.

Kofman, E. 2007. Feminist Transformations of Political Geography, in Cox, K., Lowe, M., and Robinson, J., eds. *Handbook of Political Geography*. Thousand Oaks, CA: Sage: Chapter 4.

Larner, W. 2000. Neo-liberalism: Policy, Ideology, Governmentality. *Studies in Political Economy*, 63: 5–26.

—. 2003. Neoliberalism? *Environment and Planning A: Society and Space*, 21: 509–12.

Larner, W., Fannin, M., MacLeavy, J., and Wang, W.W. 2013. New Times, New Spaces: Gendered Transformations of *Governance*, Economy, and Citizenship. *Social Politics*, 20.2: 157–64.

Leitner, H., Peck, J., and Sheppard, E.S. 2007. *Contesting Neoliberalism: Urban Frontiers*. London: Guilford Press.

Lewis, N. 2016. Governmentality at Work in Shaping a Critical Geographical Politics, in Springer, S., Birch, K., and MacLeavy, J., eds. *The Handbook of Neoliberalism*. London: Routledge, 59–69.

Macdonald, L., and Ruckert, A. eds. 2009. *Post-neoliberalism in the Americas*. New York: Palgrave.

MacLeavy, J. 2012. The Lore of the Jungle: Neoliberalism and Statecraft in the Global Local Disorder. *Area*, 44: 250–3.

McCarthy, J., and Prudham, S. 2004. Neoliberal Nature and the Nature of Neoliberalism. *Geoforum*, 35: 275–83.

McChesney, R. 1999. Foreword. *Profit over People: Neoliberalism and Global Order*. New York: Seven Stories Press.

Mirowski, P., and Plehwe, D. eds. 2009. *The Road from Mont Pelerin: The Making of the Neoliberal Thought Collective*. Cambridge: Harvard University Press.

Mudge, S.L. 2008. What is Neo-liberalism? *Socio-Economic Review*, 4: 703–31.

Peck, J. 2010. *Constructions of Neoliberal Reason*. Oxford: Oxford University Press.

—. 2014. Zombie Neoliberalism and the Ambidextrous State. *Theoretical Criminology*, 14: 104–10.

Peck, J., and Tickell, A. 2002. Neoliberalizing Space. *Antipode*, 34: 380–404.

Peck, J., Theodore, N., and Brenner, N. 2009. Postneoliberalism and its Malcontents. *Antipode*, 41: 94–116.

Peters, M. 2016. Education, neoliberalism, and Human Capital: *Homo Economicus* as 'Entrepreneur of Himself', in Springer, S., Birch, K., and MacLeavy, J., eds. *The Handbook of Neoliberalism*. London: Routledge, 283–93.

Plehwe, D. 2016. Neoliberal Hegemony, in Springer, S., Birch, K., and MacLeavy, J., eds. *The Handbook of Neoliberalism*. London: Routledge, 47–58.

Povinelli, E.A. 2011. *Economies of Abandonment: Social Belonging and Endurance in Late Liberalism*. Durham, NC: Duke University Press.

Prince, R., and Dufty, R. 2009. Assembling the Space Economy: Governmentality and Economic Geography. *Geography Compass*, 3: 1744–56.

Slater, T. 2016. The Housing Crisis in Neoliberal Britain: Free Market Think Tanks and the Production of Ignorance, in Springer, S., Birch, K., and MacLeavy, J., eds. *The Handbook of Neoliberalism*. London: Routledge, 356–68.

Smith, N. 1987. Rascal Concepts, Minimalizing Discourse, and the Politics of Geography. *Environment and Planning D: Society and Space*, 5: 377–83.

Sparke, M. 2006. Political Geography: Political Geographies of Globalization (2) – Governance. *Progress in Human Geography*, 30: 1–16.

Springer, S. 2012. Neoliberalism as Discourse: Between Foucauldian Political Economy and Marxian Poststructuralism. *Critical Discourse Studies*, 9: 133–47.

—. 2014. Neoliberalism in Denial. *Dialogues in Human Geography*, 4: 154–60.

—. 2015. Postneoliberalism? *Review of Radical Political Economy*, 47: 5–17.

Tickell, A., and Peck, J. 2003. Making Global Rules: Globalization or Neoliberalization? In Peck, J., and Yeung, H.W.C., eds. *Remaking The Global Economy: Economic-Geographical Perspectives*. London: Sage: Chapter 10.

Tickell, A., Sheppard, E., Peck, J., and Barnes, T. 2007. *Politics and Practice in Economic Geography*. London: Sage.

Weller, S., and O'Neill, P. 2014. An Argument with Neoliberalism: Australia's Place in a Global Imaginary. *Dialogues in Human Geography*, 4: 105–30.

Worldwide Universities Network (WUN) [website]. 2015. About Us. Retrieved from http://www.wun.ac.uk/about.html

5

NEOLIBERAL HEGEMONY

Dieter Plehwe

Confusing neoliberalism and hegemony

Back in the 1990s, Social Democratic politicians and many observers proclaimed the end of the neoliberal era when New Labour, New Democrats and New Social Democrats in the UK, USA and Germany, respectively, defeated the heirs of Thatcher and Reagan. A few years later, however, Tony Blair, Bill Clinton and Gerhard Schröder became famous mostly due to their efforts to extend neoliberal ideas to the public sector in general and to the sphere of social and labour market policy in particular. New types of marketization like public private partnership and new public management, cross-border financial liberalization and welfare state retrenchment became cornerstones of new social democratic reforms (Birch and Siemiatycki 2015; Helleiner 2014; Svalfors and Taylor-Gooby 1999). Conversely, few efforts were made to reverse previous neoliberal agendas, and disillusioned voters eventually abandoned Social Democracy, and politics in general, in droves (Marlière 2008; Mair 2013; Plehwe *et al.* 2006).

Fast forward to 2008, and once again politicians and commentators, even a number of economists, declared the end of neoliberalism. The global financial crisis ushered in a return to Keynesian economic policies across the OECD world. Deregulation and cross-border liberalization, many now argued, had gone too far. Yet only two years later, governments in the European Union, for example, have changed course to prescribe austerity regimes, which have reinforced public sector and welfare state retrenchment in many countries (Blyth 2013; Streeck 2013). Moreover, North America and the EU have started pushing for unprecedented free trade agreements to further advance cross-border liberalization. Although it is rare to hear outspoken advocates of radical neoliberal messages nowadays, there is no shortage of neoliberal programming and policy-making, and neoliberal resilience in general (Cahill 2014; Crouch 2011; Mirowski 2014).

In order to address questions and issues around this continuing neoliberal hegemony, it is necessary to clarify the understanding of both neoliberalism and hegemony. Neoliberalism has been associated with specific historical periods: for example, UK and US politics during the Thatcher and Reagan eras, military dictatorship in Latin America, 'Washington Consensus politics' in the global South of the 1990s, or 'shock therapy' in different regions. Yet neoliberal influence was quite strong in countries like Germany or Switzerland right after World War II; neoliberals already had bridgeheads in many Latin American states and in Japan during the 1950s and 1960s; and neoliberal politicians and scholars played a significant role in the early history of the European Community (e.g. with regard to competition law) and the Global Agreement on Tariffs and Trade (GATT, e.g. Gottfried Haberler 1958 report, Baldwin 1982). In order to clarify if, to what extent, and how historical configurations are actually 'neoliberal', the study of neoliberal ideas and activities has to be taken seriously. Even more so as neoliberal ideas, much like other ideas, have been evolving, and have been advanced in gradual manner in many places, frequently compromised and as a result of compromise rather than pristine and in confrontation.

Instead of looking for the one comprehensive neoliberal system or regime, students of neoliberalism really need to look both at neoliberal ideas carefully and at social, political and ideological power relations.

Studying neoliberal ideas: historical social network analysis and group biography (prosopography)

Beyond neoliberalism as a swear word, the discussion of neoliberal ideas, concepts, policies and instruments can be analytically distinguished from the discussion of varieties of neoliberal capitalism, regimes, and political configurations. Neoliberal influence can be conceptualized and examined in two ways. It can be a) a historical instantiation of an ideology carried by social forces in particular power relations. It can be b) an instance of successful (if restricted) institutionalization of social relations according to neoliberal perspectives. In consideration of these dimensions we can perceive of a sufficiently broad research programme designed to establish both a large set of examples and varieties of neoliberal ideas on the one hand, and their relevance in countries and policy or issue areas over time on the other hand.

Neoliberal hegemony in such an understanding differs from a more general notion of bourgeois or capitalist class hegemony and requires specifying the neoliberal (or right-wing liberal) content and meaning of political leadership and institutions. Closer attention needs to be paid to intellectual history. Neoliberalism can be traced to its origin in the 1930s in opposition to both laissez-faire liberalism and socialism or collectivism (Walpen 2004; Plickert 2008). From there we can follow the subsequent evolution, and also try to note if sufficiently clear demarcations can be observed vis-á-vis social liberalism and the revival of free market radicalism (e.g. anarcho-capitalism, conservative libertarianism etc.).[1] Roots of neoliberalism precede the history of neoliberalism, of course. But the works of later neoliberals in the course of the 1920s, for example, does not yet entail a clearly perceived distance from classical liberalism. In the eyes of 1920s liberals, the advance of Soviet socialism and organized interests in Western capitalism posed a threat, but the belief in the viability of capitalism was not yet shaken by the Great Depression, which really started liberals to think of and define neoliberalism as a space between classical liberalism and collectivism; or, as a third way in competition to the other neoliberalism, (British) new liberalism. It is problematic, therefore, to date the first period of neoliberalism back to the 1920s, as Stedman Jones (2012) does, without offering a convincing reason. Ordoliberalism, which Stedman Jones mentions, was created during the 1930s rather than 1920s (Ptak 2009), even though key members of the German-Swiss ordo-/neoliberal community like Röpke or Rüstow were active intellectuals in the Weimar Republic. The social reform programme of or akin to British new liberals flourished in the 1920s in various countries, of course, but only in the course of the 1930s can we distinguish the opening of explicit neoliberal space in the battle over the future of capitalism and the 'good society' (Lippmann 1937).

Historical ideas centred analysis of neoliberalism has been originally conceived and developed to study intellectuals and scholars organized in the Mont Pèlerin Society (MPS), and related think tank networks (Plehwe *et al.* 2006). The MPS has been conceived (by Hayek) as a right-wing, yet global counterpart to Fabian elite socialists (Walpen 2004). A focus on the MPS does not imply exclusiveness, of course, but can be considered initially helpful to capture the related varieties of neoliberal ideas and the role they played in a great many countries over time since World War II (Walpen 2004; Plickert 2008; Plehwe and Mirowski 2009).

Prominent elements studied so far include Austrian Economics, German-Swiss Ordoliberalism, American Chicago-School, and Public Choice traditions, for example. But the neoliberal 'style of thought' and 'thought collective' (Mannheim 1922) has many more pillars like Italy's Bocconi School, British development economics, and Scandinavian trade theory. Neoliberal intellectuals worked inter alia in Mexico, Australia, Japan and South Africa. Even if the MPS is too small a world to study the whole of the neoliberal ideas' universe, it is a good antidote to common reductionism to European, German and British varieties of neoliberalism in particular, or to American components of the history of neoliberal ideas. Burgin's (2012) effort to describe a shift from Hayek to Friedman provides some additional information on US neoliberals, but sadly fails to broaden the understanding of the history of neoliberal ideas and neoliberal influence. The Italian Bocconi School impact on public finance, for example, recently became highly relevant beyond Italy through arguments around 'expansionary austerity' (i.e. spending cuts as good to both consolidate budgets and stimulate growth), which have been used to legitimate much of the European crisis management since 2010 (Blyth 2013). We still know almost nothing about neoliberals in Japan, where numerous members of the MPS held high-ranking positions in government, central banking, business associations etc. The dominant focus on Anglo-American neoliberals reinforces an existing bias in academic knowledge regimes, but does not really improve the study of the international and transnational dimensions of neoliberal ideas and influence.

Studying varieties of neoliberalism: hegemonic constellations

A broader view of comparative capitalism in the age of neoliberal hegemonic constellations acknowledges a large-scale transformation from social (or embedded) liberalism to neoliberalism, which is always embedded in certain ways as well, of course (Cahill 2014), but often does not look closely at the history of ideas dimension. The hitherto best example of the study of the diversity of neoliberal economic and political institutions is the work of Bohle and Greskovitch (2012). In the tradition of comparative capitalism, Bohle and Greskovitch examine the configuration and diversity of neoliberal economic and political institutions in Central Europe after the collapse of the Soviet Union. They argued that only Slovenia evolved in ways that did not fit well into a framework based on neoliberal institutions and social relations. But the study also identifies variations in the primarily neoliberal configurations in the Baltic States, in the Czech Republic and Slovakia, and Poland. Hegemonic constellations in Central Europe find expression in a variety of neoliberal institutional configurations even if the ideologies of leading parties would not always fit easily with the neoliberal universe of ideas. Some countries have been governed at times by post-socialist parties that are members of the Social Democratic party alliance; some have been governed by conservative parties. The shift from socialism and social liberalism to neo- or right-wing liberalism is nevertheless important in each of the non-neoliberal or anti-neoliberal camps. New social democracy has embraced market solutions to most problems and conservatives have embraced a somewhat more tolerant individualist outlook.

If neoliberalism is a complicated concept due to its polyvalence in terms of ideas and *Realpolitik*, hegemony is an exacting term due to its multiple theoretical underpinnings. Antonio Gramsci developed a sociological and relational understanding of hegemony which focused mostly on agency dimensions of leadership, although Gramsci also referred to structural proportions (Anderson 1976). Most frequently scholars associate hegemony with Gramsci's notion of consensus politics (Gill 1986), which must be distinguished from straightforward coercion. Consensus, at the same time, cannot be reached without integrating significant parts of marginalized strata of society, which otherwise would have to be repressed. In any case, intellectuals and ideas are credited for the architecture of hegemony whereas repressive police and military functions are central to politics of constraint.

Gramsci's key concern was socialist strategy in the face of defeat and the victory of fascism: unlike Bolshevism in Russia, socialist strategy in Italy and Western Europe could not rely on capturing power and the state in a 'war of movement'. Civil society in support of the bourgeoisie and capitalist order was too strong to overturn the rulers in one stroke. Instead, Gramsci clearly perceived of a need to engage in a long-lasting 'war of position' covering many different political, economic and cultural spheres. Here we can also appreciate his link between agency and structure: Gramsci was aware of structural change, which can be driven by different forces. He no longer considered superstructures as simply (and fully) determined by economic structures. Accordingly, a class position rooted in economic power only is insufficient to achieve a hegemonic position. Political and cultural spheres have to be considered realms and sources of social power in their own right, which does not mean they can be studied in isolation from economic power relations (Opratko 2014). Studying neoliberal networks through think tanks, for example, enables the tracing of links between (corporate) funding and other constituencies of neoliberal intellectual life, which also helps avoiding a pure and apolitical history of ideas.

The 1970s and 1980s witnessed a revival of Gramscian thought, which also extended to international relations (Cox 1983). But the use of the term 'hegemony' in relation to welfare state capitalism, to the role of intellectuals, and to comprehensiveness came at a price.

First, hegemony has been equated to post-war Fordism and the welfare state, which Gramsci certainly did not (and could not) have in mind in his writing on hegemony. Gramsci could only draw on examples of the late nineteenth and early twentieth centuries due to his premature death in 1937. Hegemony as rule based on consent in addition to constraint arguably referred simply to countries and circumstances of 'normal' functioning of political democracy: no civil war, no revolution, and no state of extraordinary rebellion. The extent to which such normal functioning of the political system required social integration should not be judged by the standards of a fully developed welfare state.

Second, the role of intellectuals as architects of hegemony does not require them to be interested in compromise in general. While hegemony cannot be achieved by way of unilateral imposition of a specific world view, a new compromise between relevant classes and factions can necessitate fighting against the former architecture of compromise. Neoliberals, much like marginalized segments of society, have refused 'passive revolution', or adaptation to the dominant order. Hayek and the other MPS neoliberals were convinced of the need to develop their own (original) perspective, instead of prematurely fighting on the turf of social liberalism. The compromise function of intellectuals does, in any case, not preclude other avant-garde and leadership roles.

Third, hegemony is sometimes stated to be near universal, which hardly conforms to Gramsci's notion of war of position, and his primary focus on national configurations. Sometimes hegemony is held to be impossible to achieve by neoliberal forces simply because they do not want to and cannot integrate the social underclasses. Yet classical liberalism arguably obtained hegemonic status in certain countries at times despite relegating social matters to the church and private charity.

Fourth, in neo-Gramscian perspective, the analysis of hegemony requires asking how social forces can move in the direction of socialism. Neoliberal hegemony instead is perceived in paradoxical ways. Some analysts draw a coherent picture of an iron cage, other (e.g. post-neoliberalism) analysts seem to believe that neoliberal hegemony can simply collapse (like the implosion of the Soviet Union), but refrain from carefully analysing and demonstrating the reach and the limits of neoliberalism in time and space.

A productive alternative to general notions of neoliberal hegemony is asking for comparative analyses of neoliberal hegemonic constellations, which need to combine national and transnational dimensions in the contemporary era of globalized capitalism and to allow differentiation according to different social spheres and political matters. If the era of social-liberal hegemonic constellations lasted up until Thatcher and Reagan in general, a careful analysis will observe that the roll back started earlier: in Chile after competing economic policy orientations were replaced within the dictatorship (Fischer 2009), in the USA with the U-turn under Carter (Harrison and Bluestone 1988), in the UK with IMF-imposed cut-backs. Institutions of a previous age are not easily and entirely dismantled, of course. The resilience of the welfare state has been an important topic in the comparative welfare regime research (Pierson 1996). Defending public health systems, for example, may limit neoliberal hegemony in some countries and policy areas at the same time that neoliberal hegemony advances in financial affairs and economic regulations. Latin America's increasing investments in a basic welfare state co-exists with advanced liberalization vis-à-vis North America and the WTO. Notions of hegemony thus have to be comprehensive without becoming monolithic, and compromise architectures may require more or fewer doses of constraint in addition to active or, possibly more important, passive consent.

I will go through the three major phases of the manifestation of neoliberalism next, and distinguish origins, movement building and momentum, consolidation and defensive stages. I only consider the later stages to be mostly neoliberal hegemonic constellations due to overall architecture of economic and social policy-making and the evolution of social relations. The concluding section will address the perspective of counter-hegemony, which cannot be restricted to emancipatory movements, unfortunately.

Studying neoliberalism before, during and towards the end of neoliberal hegemonic constellations

Origins and early manifestations

Neoliberalism was born after the Great Depression. Contrary to the frequent reduction of neoliberalism to anti-state/pro-market ideology since the Thatcher and Reagan years (e.g. Crouch, 2011), a wide range of right-wing liberals started to think about the limits of laissez-faire capitalism and the market-state dichotomy in classical liberal theories when the Great Depression undermined the very existence of capitalism and private property. Henceforth, neoliberals confronted a double threat of socialism (or collectivism) and the insufficient framework of classical liberalism. Neoliberals competed with social and political (new) liberalism for ideas and leadership as to how to stabilize the capitalist order. Both with regard to ends and to means the neoliberal right differed from the liberal mainstream and left, even if there was a convergence with regard to recognizing the need of the state to secure economic and social stability.

At the end of World War II, neoliberal ideas did not enjoy widespread support. War-related planning and social integration on the premises of macro-economic (Keynesian) management under reliance on public sector investment was widely considered to offer the most promising solution for the post-war period. The Bretton Woods order secured the road towards a new social order, which materialized as a variety of capitalist welfare states (Esping-Andersen 1990). John Ruggie (1982) described the new order in Polanyian-terms as 'embedded liberalism'.

Hegemony by and large was social liberal in the OECD world during the heyday of the 'social democratic century' (Dahrendorf 1983), under pressure from consolidated Soviet Union socialism and the rising developmental states of the global South (Hobsbawm 1994). But during the 1950s, right-wing liberals nevertheless enjoyed powerful positions in several countries and specific policy areas. While Friedrich Hayek and other neoliberals who founded the MPS in 1947 maintained a posture of marginalized minority surrounded by socialism (compare Hartwell 1995), in a number of countries and policy areas early neoliberals were contributing significantly to the social order. For example, and, contrary to widespread beliefs, Germany's social market economy was conceived by neoliberal scholars and politicians around Ludwig Erhard, even though real-world policies were not identical to the ideas of Alfred Müller-Armack, who coined the term, or Wilhelm Röpke, who was a key adviser to Erhard (Ptak 2009). Germany's post-war neoliberals had to struggle with the other wings of Christian Democracy and the labour movement. The German ordo-neoliberals opposed the significant power of trade unions and the emerging configuration of welfare capitalism in Germany much like the neoliberals rein-forced the corporate opposition against the New Deal in the USA. Right-wing German and Swiss leaders inspired by the ordoliberal ideas even opposed the economic growth models because they objected to the expansion of both big business and big unions. They wanted to control the increasing concentration of economic activity and wanted to limit 'proletarianiza-tion' of social structures. Ideas about the economic order centred on anti-trust and competition, on the one hand, and around small and medium-sized family enterprise, on the other hand. A mix of industrial and agricultural work was considered as ideal for social integration, not socialist planning or the big welfare state (Slobodian 2014). But Ludwig Erhard and his Mont Pèlerin circles lost some of their critical battles – for example, the fight against the public pension system (Erhard preferred private insurance).

It is interesting to note that the difference between Hayek and Keynes in regard to social policy and welfare provision was, arguably, not that great. We can only speculate if the endorse-ment of social minimum standards by both Keynes and Hayek were unambiguous or contextu-ally specific to the late 1940s.[2] Right-wing liberals, in any case, lost many of the decisive battles of the 1950s and 1960s to trade union-backed Social Democracy and popular (Christian) Conservatism. In the USA, the Great Society programme and new social regulation manifested itself less in generous welfare provisions beyond social security, but more in powerful regulatory agencies like the Organization of Safety and Health Administration or the Environmental Policy Agency. In more or less comprehensive ways, public pension systems, public health systems and progressive tax and transfer regimes ushered in the era of welfare state capitalism based on productivity growth and rapid wage increases compared to previous times.

But neoliberals during this 'defensive era' were not merely 'saving the books' (Hartwell 1995). They managed to build bases and bridgeheads in many countries and policy areas, and consolidated a leading position in a few rather important policy areas like competition policy and international trade (Walpen 2004; Plehwe *et al.* 2006; Plehwe and Mirowski 2009). A lot of work still remains to be done on neoliberal circles in many countries, academic fields and policy areas to understand better the configuration of neoliberal positions in the era of social liberalism. The subsequent movement and momentum towards neoliberal hegemony can be much better explained if the actor networks and agencies are tracked and traced across time. Scholars who insist on structural transformation as major explanation for the rise of the neoliberal age (e.g. Harvey 2005; Doering-Manteuffel and Lutz 2010) tend to obscure the lineages and heri-tage of early neoliberalism as well as the contributions of neoliberals to the shaping of critical battles and to the capacity building for neoliberal political leadership. This is most important to better understand the 'movement phase' of the neoliberal attack on welfare capitalism during the 1970s.

Movement phase: an alternative perspective of the 1970s and 1980s

In contemporary histories of capitalist democracies, the late 1960s and 1970s are frequently seen in the light of student rebellion and the advance of progressive movements in many countries. National liberation movements around the world defined progressive nationalism and restricted Western interest spheres. Socialist and non-aligned countries forged a strong alliance in economic policy areas culminating in the demands for a new world economic order (Bair 2009). In the advanced industrialized countries, old and new social movements also advanced during this period of time. For example, social and environmental regulations were extended during these decades. The Club of Rome members added momentum to this new agenda with their worries about the natural limits of capitalism, thereby establishing legitimacy for environmental activism. Under the umbrella of the United Nations, the ecological policy agenda added a new layer of national and international environmental state institutions. Precautionary environmental agendas and climate change politics, in particular, were considered to require increasing state and planning capacities (Bernstein 2001).

Yet, at the same time, the neoliberal counter-movement moved from its mostly defensive posture, with regard to the rise of welfare capitalism, and expanded its capacities and policy influence in many areas way beyond trade and competition politics. The dissolution of the Bretton Woods regime followed a script written by a group of neoliberal advisers around Fritz Machlup, Gottfried Haberler and Milton Friedman who exerted a new authority with regard to the international monetary regime of flexible exchange rates long before monetarism became an authority in national central banks. MPS members focused on the preservation of capital mobility as prime concern during this rocky period (Schmelzer 2010). Rational choice-based scholarship formed the basis of an increasingly vigorous attack on traditional welfare economics (e.g. market failure) and shifted the focus on problems of government (e.g. public choice, state failure theory). In practical terms, the neoliberal research agenda fuelled the deregulation and privatization movements that took shape in the 1970s (Canedo 2008). While social regulation expanded to health and environmental matters in many OECD countries, economic regulation was pushed back at the same time.

The most violent counter attacks came in the global South. Dictatorships in Chile and Argentina served as the earliest models of privatization of social welfare regimes, anticipating the developments of the 1980s and 1990s in the global North (Fischer 2009; Plehwe 2013). Obviously, this would not be an example of hegemony in Gramsci's terminology since brutal force was required, and consent was rather limited. Yet it is also clear that social democratic liberalism and socialism had lost an opportunity to consolidate progressive hegemony, and neoliberal approaches had gained a very serious advantage in addressing the major issues of economic and social policy-making under conditions of military dictatorships. Authoritarian neoliberalism was ambivalent (Dussel-Peters 2006), however, because it threatened to undermine the magic of the liberty concept which was still needed in ideological competition with the socialist empire. As long as human civil rights abuses could be blamed on Northern supporters of Southern dictatorships, the Western campaign for freedom and democracy remained shackled and marred in contradictions.

The great crisis of Fordism eventually prepared the shift in the balance of power towards neoliberalism in many countries (Yergin and Stanislaw 2008). Economic stagnation, combined with rising unemployment and rising inflation, suggested limits to Keynesian economic wisdom in the OECD world. The French experiment in left-wing Keynesianism under Mitterrand in the early 1980s shows that neoliberal approaches to deal with the stagflation crisis were not the only game in town. But the failure of the French strategy demonstrated the very limited room to manoeuvre for socialist or social-liberal alternatives to neoliberalism after the shift of global hegemonic constellations in the direction of the latter. When it was clear that there cannot be liberal socialism in one republic, French Socialists – under additional pressure from German central banders –became the key architects of Europe's economic and monetary union, and the larger world of global finance (Abdelal 2007). The debt crisis of the early 1980s and near collapse of many developing countries in the global South signalled an end to import substitution and state-led development paradigms at the same time the French experiment failed. The 1980s witnessed the collapse of authoritarian neoliberalism, yet also paved the way for the so called 'Washington Consensus', which is widely regarded as a period of neoliberal convergence. While many, if not most, countries moved in a similar direction, there are important differences between Argentina's radical currency board neoliberalism and more pragmatic varieties (and continuities) in Chile, for example, let alone between the Eastern European transformation countries. Varieties of neoliberal (austerity) capitalism emerged in confrontations between weaker social democratic and stronger neoliberal and conservative forces, not least within the capitalist classes.

By the 1970s, the preparation of the networks of intellectuals and think tanks during the 1950s and 1960s provided neoliberalism with great capacities to fully exploit the problems and contradictions of the opponents even if neoliberals continued to fight an uphill battle in some areas (e.g. with regard to defending Pinochet, with regard to environmental activism, etc.). It is important to realize that Thatcher and Reagan, or Helmut Kohl in Germany and many other leaders who were orchestrating the political shift of the 1980s leaning towards neoliberal approaches, did not come out of the blue in terms of political thought and epistemic authority. All of the new centre-right governments relied to no small degree on the capacities developed in civil society by privately financed, more or less business-related neoliberal networks. Sprawling civil society networks in turn enabled the intellectual leadership to point in a neoliberal direction. After the Heritage Foundation presented a new government programme to Reagan, the social technology of administration programming was imitated across the world. Transnational networks of neoliberal think tanks provided excellent channels for the diffusion of ideas, policy instruments and PR techniques (Wedel 2009; Dinan and Miller 2007). The political power shifts of the late 1970s, 1980s and early 1990s allowed neoliberals to greatly expand their networks (compare Plehwe and Walpen 2006), which was a prerequisite of the successful consolidation of neoliberal hegemonic constellations.

Consolidation: 1989 until ?

The broad story of consolidation of neoliberal hegemonies from the 1990s is easily related: Europe deepened and widened the single market after the collapse of socialism in Central and Eastern Europe as well as in large parts of Asia. There was no talk of a third way or market socialism in the former Soviet empire (Bohle and Neunhöffer 2006); there was no alternative to neoliberal (globalized) capitalism at this point in time. North America reacted to European regionalism by way of pursuing NAFTA and eventually continental free trade across the Americas. The shift towards export (and import!) orientation had removed the long-standing reservations vis-à-vis the power of the USA in particular. The book title *The Poverty of 'Development Economics'* (Lal 2000[1983]) signalled the unification of neoliberal market economic ideas. This was not simply neoclassical orthodoxy, but the replacement of the synthesis of neoclassical economics and Keynesianism by combinations of neoliberal and neoclassical traditions, which still need to be better understood. The shift towards micro-economics and information economics, for example, represents the profound influences of Austrian economics in general and Hayek in particular on neoclassical macro-economics. Behavioural and experimental economics even broke with the rationality assumptions of the neoclassical tradition; bounded rationality underlines the key neoliberal insight according to which markets need to be constructed and secured (Ptak 2009; Peck 2012).

The term 'consolidation' might seem awkward for an era that also witnessed some of the greatest crises of neoliberal capitalism (e.g. Russia, Argentina, South East Asia). Consolidation should definitely not be considered smooth and harmonious. Consolidating neoliberalism, in fact, meant pushing back countervailing forces and limiting the extent to which compromises were needed to integrate disaffected members of society. The reduction and market-oriented reorientation of the welfare state (e.g. retrenchment, individual asset-based welfare) certainly produced conflicts that advanced neoliberalism in society. The main point to be made is that the contradictions of neoliberal capitalism and its crises did not lead to a comprehensive move towards an alternative. Latin American countries went further than others in the search for alternatives when backed by state oil revenues (e.g. Venezuela), but neither Argentina nor Brazil, for example, were able to push for an alternative to free trade and free capital movement with the North. The evolution of the varieties of welfare capitalism in the southern hemisphere suggests thinking of a shared perspective of limited welfare states rather than of a countermovement against neoliberal hegemonic constellations.

When it came, the North Atlantic financial crisis demonstrated the systemic fragility of neoliberal globalization and financialization. The key insight that capitalism has to be stabilized by the state had been violated with financialization, and the post-hoc stabilization came at the steep price of significantly increasing public and private debt (Streeck 2013). Neoliberal resilience and strategic reform capacities were demonstrated by way of temporary reliance on fiscal stimulus combined with monetary easing, and a quick return to more severe versions of austerity capitalism in Europe, in particular. Reform neoliberalism displays a greater propensity to re-regulate on neoliberal terms, relying on the insights of behavioural economics and the original recognition of neoliberal statehood. No better title than the paradoxical formula of libertarian paternalism (Sunstein and Thaler 2003) could be found to demonstrate the distance to traditional socialist and social-liberal concepts of solidarity and social citizenship.

Conclusions: prospects of counter-hegemonic forces

Since the lingering great recession and the approaches and capacities of neoliberal statehood to cope with the contradiction of neoliberal austerity capitalism have not led to a shift reminiscent of the 1970s, we may need to consider the contemporary dynamics of really existing neoliberalism (Brenner and Theodore 2002), more or less hegemonic, as indicative of a still ongoing great transformation. This would be the third after the original birth of liberal capitalism and the second transformation towards the welfare state capitalism Polanyi analysed before it was 'complete'. The beginning of the third transformation would be dated back to the earliest instances of authoritarian neoliberalism from where it was extended to the OECD and eventually to the 'second world' of Soviet socialism. The 'strange non-death of neoliberalism' (Crouch 2011) and neoliberal resilience are one side of the coin: the entrenched power of neoliberal social social forces, enhanced corporate, technocratic and epistemic authorities. But the other side of the coin would be the contradictions, movements and transformations, including the building of pockets and bridgeheads of counter-hegemonic forces.

The consolidation of varieties of neoliberal capitalism currently seems to suffer from stagflation 2.0 problems; namely the combination of stagnation and deflation rather than inflation. If reflation is not successfully orchestrated by way of neoliberal leadership, its contradictions and limits will be more visible in the future than they have been in the past. But would-be counter-hegemonic forces still need to become clearer about their own perspectives. Neoliberalism has proven capable of a considerable amount of problem-solving capacity, integration and innovation, which is partly due to an intelligent and quite plural intellectual conversation within neoliberal confines. Those wings of neoliberalism that try to rewrite liberal history as linear (classical) or even break away from Mont Pèlerin essentials like the freedom and property society inspired by von Mises's descendants do not belong to the realm of neoliberalism, in fact. The new and positive programme of neoliberalism of the 1930s and 1940s understood the need to break with orthodoxy; contemporary free market right-wingers do not. Neoliberals did indeed compete with social liberals and socialists. They did and will do better, arguably, as long as there was and will be a significant other. The neoliberal history of social movement and counter-movements still needs to be written, though.

Comprehensive moves against right-wing liberal perspectives need to clarify an alternative to competitive federalism, individualism, and the iron cage of profit maximization that is inherent to capitalist socialization processes. There are many types of non-liberal and anti-liberal objections, but many of those can be considered quite compatible with overall neoliberal hegemonic constellations. Authoritarian neoliberalism and communitarian islands of limited solidarity are not obstacles to continuity. Universal social citizenship, transnational solidarity and a confrontation with profitability concerns are not. While cultural spheres and the state at all levels are critical areas to contemporary wars of position, the counterattack needs to reach into the private sector. Unless inroads are made in this direction, the main source of right-wing liberal hegemony cannot be curtailed. It has not been an accident that corporate citizenship rose when social citizenship declined. Corporate social responsibility in combination with nudging of market citizens (consumers) provide for an alternative neoliberal frame that has yet to be challenged in a comprehensive and decisive way.

Notes

1 The Mont Pélerin Society has been the home for a variety of liberalism since 1947. Some radical wings around von Mises were never fully at ease with the spectrum of Mont Pèlerin neoliberalism. In 2006, the property and freedom society was founded to finally offer an alternative home for 'Austian libertarianism' (http://propertyandfreedom.org/about/).
2 Ben Jackson (2010) emphasizes the diversity of early neoliberal perspectives and quotes Henry Simons and Walter Lippmann in particular with regard to neoliberal acceptance of welfare provisions. While he suggests Lippmann to be on the far left of the neoliberal spectrum, Simons did not make it to the Mont Pèlerin meeting in 1947 due to his premature death. The Mont Pèlerin formula of 'social minimum standards not inimical to the market' in any case qualifies welfare provision agendas.

References

Abdelal, R. 2007. *Capital Rules: The Construction of Global Finance*. Cambridge: Harvard University Press.
Anderson, P. 1976. The Antinomies of Antonio Gramsci. *New Left Review*, 100: 5–78.
Bair, J. 2009. Taking Aim at the New International Economic Order, in Mirowski, P., and Plehwe, D. eds. *The Road from Mont Pèlerin: The Making of the Neoliberal Thought Collective*. Cambridge, MA, and London: Harvard University Press: 347–85.
Baldwin, R.E. 1982. Gottfried Haberler's Contributions to International Trade Theory and Policy. *Quarterly Journal of Economics*, 97.1: 141–8.

Bernstein, S. 2001. *The Compromise of Liberal Environmentalism*. New York: Columbia University Press.

Birch, K., and Siemiatycki, M. 2015. Neoliberalism and the Geographies of Marketization: The Entangling of State and Markets. *Progress in Human Geography*, 0309132515570512: 1–22.

Blyth, M. 2013. *Austerity: The History of a Dangerous Idea*. New York: Routledge.

Bohle, D., and Greskovitch, B. 2012. *Capitalist Diversity on Europe's Periphery*. Ithaca: Cornell University Press.

Bohle, D. and Neunhöffer, G. 2006. Why is There no Third Way? The Role of Neoliberal Ideology, Networks and Think Tanks in Combating Market Socialism and Shaping Transformation in Poland, in Plehwe, D., Walpen, B., and Neunhöffer, G., eds. *Neoliberal Hegemony: A Global Critique*. London: Routledge: 89–104.

Brenner, N., and Theodore, N. 2002. Cities and the Geographies of 'Actually Existing Neoliberalism'. *Antipode*, 34.3: 349–79.

Burgin, A. 2012. *The Great Persuasion: Reinventing Free Markets Since the Depression*. Cambridge: Harvard University Press.

Cahill, D. 2014. *The End of Laisser Faire?: On the Durability of Embedded Neoliberalism*. Cheltenham: Edward Elgar.

Canedo, E. 2008. *The Rise of the Deregulation Movement in Modern America, 1957–1980*. Doctoral Dissertation, Department of History, Columbia University.

Cox, R.W. 1983. Gramsci, Hegemony and International Relations: An Essay in Method. *Journal of International Studies*, 12: 162–75.

Crouch, C. 2011. *The Strange Non-Death of Neoliberalism*. Cambridge: Polity.

Dahrendorf, R. 1983. *Die Chancen der Krise. Über die Zukunft des Liberalismus*. Stuttgart: DVA.

Dinan, W., and Miller, D. eds. 2007. *Thinker, Faker, Spinner, Spy: Corporate PR and the Assault on Democracy*. London: Pluto Press.

Doering-Manteuffel, A., and Lutz, R. 2010. *Nach dem Boom: Brüche und Kontinuitäten der Industriemoderne seit 1970*. Göttingen: Vandenhoeck & Ruprecht.

Dussel-Peters, E. 2006. The Mexican Economy Since NAFTA: Socioeconomic Integration or Disintegration? In Plehwe, D., Walpen, B., and Neunhöffer, G., eds. *Neoliberal Hegemony: A Global Critique*. London: Routledge: 120–38.

Esping-Andersen, G. 1990. *Three Worlds of Welfare*. Cambridge: Polity Press.

Fischer, K. 2009. The Influence of Neoliberals in Chile Before, During and After the Pinochet, in Mirowski, P., and Plehwe, D., eds. *The Road from Mont Pelerin: The Making of the Neoliberal Thought Collective*. Cambridge and London: Harvard University Press: 305–46.

Gerber, D. J. 1994. Constitutionalizing the Economy: German Neo-Liberalism, Competition Law and the 'New Europe'. *The American Journal of Comparative Law*, 42: 25–84.

Gill, S. 1986. Hegemony, Consensus and Trilateralism. *Review of International Studies*, 12: 205–22.

Harrison, B., and Bluestone, B. 1988. *The Great U-turn: Corporate Restructuring and Polarizing of America*. New York: Basic Books.

Hartwell, R.M. 1995. *A History of the Mont Pelerin Society*. Indianapolis: Liberty Fund.

Harvey, D. 2005. *A Brief History of Neoliberalism*. New York: Oxford University Press.

Helleiner, E. 2014. *The Status Quo Crisis: Global Financial Governance After the 2008 Meltdown*. Oxford: Oxford University Press.

Hobsbawm, E. 1994. *The Age of Extremes: The Short Twentieth Century, 1914–1991*. London: Abacus.

Jackson, B. 2010. At the Origins of Neo-liberalism: The Free Economy and the Strong State, 1930–47. *Historical Journal*, 53.1: 129–51.

Lal, D. 2000[1983]. *The Poverty of 'Development Economics'*. Cambridge: MIT Press.

Lippmann, W. 1937. *The Good Society*. New Jersey: Transaction.

Mair, P. 2013. *Ruling the Void? The Hollowing out of Western Democracy*. London: Verso.

Mannheim, K. 1922. Über die Eigenart Kultursoziologischer Erkenntnis, in Kettler, D., Meja, V., and Stehr N., eds. *Strukturen des Denkens*. Frankfurt: Suhrkamp: 33–154.

Marlière P. 2008. *La Social-démocratie Domestiquée. La Voie Blairiste*. Brussels: Aden.

Mirowski, P. 2014. *Never Let a Serious Crisis go to Waste*. London: Verso.

Opratko, B. 2014. *Hegemonie*. Münster: Westfälisches Dampfboot.

Peck, J. 2012. *Constructions of Neoliberal Reason*. Oxford: Oxford University Press.

Pierson, P. 1996. The New Politics of the Welfare State. *World Politics*, 48: 143–79.

Plehwe, D. 2013. *Converging on Strike Revisited: Deregulation and the Rise of Low Cost Employment Regimes in the European Airline Industry*. WZB Discussion Paper, No.SP III 2013-502. Retrieved from: http://hdl.handle.net/10419/90435

Plehwe, D., and Mirowski, P. eds. 2009. *The Road from Mont Pelerin: The Making of the Neoliberal Thought Collective*. Cambridge and London: Harvard University Press.

Plehwe, D., and Walpen, B. 2006. Between Network and Complex Organization, in Plehwe, D., Walpen, B., and Neunhöffer, G., eds. *Neoliberal Hegemony: A Global Critique*. London: Routledge.

Plehwe, D., and Walpen, B., and Neunhöffer, G. 2006. Introduction: Reconsidering Neoliberal Hegemony, in Plehwe, D., Walpen, B., and Neunhöffer, G., eds. *Neoliberal Hegemony: A Global Critique*. London: Routledge: 1–25.

Plickert, P. 2008. *Wandlungen des Neoliberalismus*. Stuttgart: Lucius und Lucius.

Ptak, R. 2009. Neoliberalism in Germany: Revisiting the Ordoliberal Foundations of the Social Market Economy, in Mirowski, P., and Plehwe, D., eds. *The Road from Mont Pelerin: The Making of the Neoliberal Thought Collective*. Cambridge and London: Harvard University Press: 98–138.

Ruggie, J.G. 1982. International Regimes, Transactions, and Change: Embedded Liberalism in the Postwar Economic Order. *International Organization*, 36:2: 379–415.

Schmelzer, M. 2010. *Freiheit für Wechselkurse und Kapital. Die Ursprünge neoliberaler Währungspolitik und die Mont Pèlerin Society*. Marburg: Metropolis.

Schmidt, V., and Thatcher, M. 2013. *Resilient Liberalism in Europe's Political Economy*. Cambridge: Cambridge University Press.

Slobodian, Q. 2014. The World Economy and the Color Line: Wilhelm Röpke, Apartheid and the White Atlantic. *German Historical Bulletin Supplement*, 10: 61–87.

Stedman Jones, D. 2012. *Masters of the Universe*. Princeton, NJ: Princeton University Press.

Streeck, W. 2013. *Gekaufte Zeit. Die Vertagte Krise des Demokratischen Kapitalismus*. Berlin: Suhrkamp.

Sunstein, C. and Thaler, R. 2003. Libertarian Paternalism is Not an Oxymoron. *University of Chicago Law Review*, 70.4: 1159–202.

Svalvors, S., and Taylor-Gooby, P. 1999. *The End of Welfare*. London: Routledge.

Walpen, B. 2004. *Die offenen Feinde und ihre Gesellschaft. Eine hegemonietheoretische Studie zur Mont Pèlerin Society*. Hamburg: VSA.

Wedel, J. R. 2009. *Shadow Elite: How the World's New Power Brokers Undermine Democracy, Government, and the Free Market*. New York: Basic Books.

Williamson, J. 2003. From Reform Agenda to Damaged Brand Name: A Short History of the Washington Consensus and Suggestions for What to do Next. *Finance & Development*, 10.13: 1.

Yergin, D., and Stanislaw, J. 2008. *The Commanding Heights: The Battle Between Government and the Marketplace that is Remaking the Modern World*. New York: Free Press.

6

GOVERNMENTALITY AT WORK IN SHAPING A CRITICAL GEOGRAPHICAL POLITICS

Nick Lewis

> Governmentality. The very word makes some scholars tremble with anticipation and leaves others cold at the thought of inscrutable text and a high level of abstraction.
>
> (Rutherford 2007: 291)

The concept of governmentality focuses attention on the practices of governing, or, as Nikolas Rose (1999) puts it, the 'how' of government. In short, a *governmentality* configures forms of governmental knowledge, expertise, and practice into a particular 'politics' or 'regime' of truth (Lemke 2002; Rose 1999). The concept has become prominent in the critique of neoliberalism, particularly in terms of the coupling 'neoliberal governmentalities'. In my own discipline, while geographers were relatively slow to pick up on the concept (Prince and Dufty 2009), it became an important analytical frame from the early 2000s and began to stimulate the passage of insights and political sensitivities across sub-disciplinary, geographical and epistemological boundaries within the discipline (see, for example, MacKinnon 2000, Uitermark 2005, Painter 2006, Sparke 2006, Rose-Redwood 2006, Rutherford 2007, Elden 2007, Huxley 2008, Dowling 2010). The notion of governmentality was used more or less explicitly to bridge conceptual separations between strategy or ideology and the practice of governing, the political and the cultural, the material and the discursive, the ideological and the technological, and the politics of the subject and the politics of the state, or at least to hold them in creative tension (Ettlinger 2011; Larner and Walters 2004). How effective the approach has proven in connecting these different knowledge terrains is uncertain, but I argue in this chapter that it has, at least in one academic setting, served to foster a distinctive critical geography, what Larner and Le Heron (2002) have termed 'post-structuralist political economy' (PSPE).

The chapter traces the ways in which governmentality has been deployed in a particular field, economic geography. I examine how it has led a particular group of economic geographers to build a project of knowledge production from a long-term critical engagement with the changing nature, form and work of neoliberal governmentalities in the antipodes. In this way the chapter weaves together an abbreviated genealogy of governmentality analysis in economic geography with a reflection on my own situated engagement with it as a New Zealand geographer. This engagement has involved seeking to account for the work of neoliberal governmentalities in structuring a particular neoliberal social formation and to shape a political response as an academic economic geographer. The chapter, therefore, provides a situated reading of the conceptual work of governmentality in shaping PSPE as a positioned, constructively critical accounting of neoliberalism. Two points are crucial here. First, in keeping with the emphasis on practice and the particular in governmentality thinking itself, the chapter is very much an explicitly situated reading of governmentality, one that is set, as is all knowledge production, in time, place, and discipline. Second, it is offered as a humble and partial response to Ferguson's (2011) call for a very different and genuinely 'left' art of government, which he suggests demands of us a commitment to different political practices. Inspiration for such a commitment, he argues, might be better found in an experimental materialist application of Foucault than in continued distantiated denunciation of neoliberalism.

Governmentality

Governmentality refers to the interplay of the mentalities and practices of rule that guide the production of governable subjects and spaces. In Huxley's terms (2008: 142–3) terms, it can be seen as a 'composite' of government, 'practices, programmes and projects that aspire to bring about certain aims for the government of individuals', and mentality, 'the discursive 'truths' that serve as rationales for the aims of government of others and the self'. The concept directs attention to the links between technologies of power (governing, or the exercise of power) and the political rationalities (modes of thought) that underpin them and take elaborated forms around them. For Foucault, the object of contemporary government is the population, which is ruled through a biopolitics embedded in 'the administration of life itself' (McKee 2009). Government is interpreted as the 'conduct of conduct', a set of calculated strategies and related interventions that encourage individuals to act upon themselves (Foucault 2003). Government brings the self into a productive relationship with its own subjectivity through technologies of self-control. Power is, in this sense, understood as productive and to work through the subject via the conduct of conduct. Lemke (2002) suggests that Foucault developed the concept of governmentality to examine how all this works; that is, how technologies and programmes of political rule and economic exploitation mobilize the capacity of the self-governing subject to govern itself, and how technologies of the self are aligned to technologies of domination. Governmentality offers an analytical framework for a critique of the assemblage of rationalities and micro-practices of governance and techniques of control that we have come to term 'neoliberalism'.

For state theorists, governmentality allows us to grasp the implications of how 'neoliberalism re-codes the locus of the state in the discourse of politics' (Rose and Miller 1992: 199). It helps us to extend the more familiar observations that: markets have displaced planning as 'regulators of economic activity'; market principles have displaced government responsibilities for welfare; and economic competition and entrepreneurship have displaced self-discipline, passivity and dependence in relation to regulation as a basis for self-optimization. Rather than rendering neoliberalism intelligible by 'counterposing a non-interveniontist state to an interventionist state', governmentality analysis reads it as 'a reorganisation of political rationalities that brings them into a kind of alignment with contemporary technologies of government' (ibid.). Neoliberalism renders contemporary economies and nation-states governable by mobilizing markets to achieve a 'congruence' between 'a responsible and moral individual and an economic-rational actor' (Lemke 2001: 203). As Lemke (ibid.) argues:

> the theoretical strength of the concept of governmentality consists of the fact that it construes neo-liberalism not just as ideological rhetoric, as a political-economic reality or as a practical anti-humanism, but above all as a political project that endeavors to create a social reality that it suggests already exists.

A focus on governmentality, then, directs attention to technologies of control as much as the political programmes that materialized them. It is a framework of thought for examining the interplay between political agency and neoliberal ideology (and its agents), in a context set by Foucault's conception of power, 'government', and 'biopolitics'. In these terms, Walters (2006) suggests that governmentality accounts offer both more and less than alternative theoretical positions – more sensitivity to micro-politics and discursive political formulations than the position taken by political economy, yet a recognition that there is always more than the discursive at work. Both Walters (ibid.) and Lemke (2002) refer, for example, to the way that such a recognition should encourage a genealogy of the state rather than a theory of the state. For Li (2007: 277), this focus on governmentality highlights the political potential that lies in critique of detail and the recognition that 'politics is not external to government, it is constitutive of it'. For geographers interested in the spatiality of power (see, for example, Allen 2003), the creative agonism at the heart of governmentality between the governance of a population and the governance of the self (Ettlinger 2011: 540) challenges the analytical value and ontological status of scalar hierarchies of power in a productive way.

Together these critical insights borne of governmentality thinking highlight three trajectories of scholarship that have been pivotal to the development and practice of PSPE, which I outline below. The first is that any actualized neoliberalism and any critique of it as a political project cannot help but be situated, not only in place-specific political economy but also within the context of particular institutions of knowledge production. Second, as rationalities grounded in practice and thereby in place, governmentalities presuppose connection to political projects. They may stimulate, provoke, become attached to or emerge from grounded political projects scaled at levels from the subject to the household, community, neighbourhood, city, nation-state or even the global (Larner *et al.* 2007). An exploration of neoliberalism's governmentalities should thus point to particular *placed neoliberal assemblages* of political programmes, ideologies, rationalities, and technologies. And, third, as Li emphasizes, the fissures created by the inevitable contradictions within governmentalities, the inability to map technologies of the self seamlessly onto those of population control or domination, the routine failures of the self to be efficiently self-governing, and the failures in coordination across all these different technologies and their alignments with political programmes, all promise to open up opportunities for politics. If a governmentality critique of neoliberalism therefore points to grounded political geographies and multiple spaces for politics, then it also issues an intellectual or moral imperative to treat explorations of different neoliberalisms and examinations of experiences of them as resources for political possibility. This is what those working with PSPE are increasingly labelling 'enactive critique' (Lewis *et al.* 2016). What's required, however, to see in governmentality what Ferguson terms a potentially new political 'art' of the Left are projects of knowledge production that transcend an interest in the mentalities of rule or a disengaged denouncement of governmental projects as neoliberal (Ferguson 2011). This will necessitate new, possibly ethnographic ways of doing scholarship and critique that address 'how subjects subjectify' (McKee 2009; Prince and Dufty 2009; Barnett *et al.* 2008).

Governmentality in economic geography

Lemke (2002) suggests that the critique of neoliberalism across the critical social sciences is characterized by an assault on: its 'manipulative promotion of a "wrong knowledge" of society and economy'; its materialization in new political regimes that enable and foster a global, corporate capitalism; and its destructive impacts on particular individuals and social groups. Political economy is counterposed as 'a right or emancipatory knowledge' the triumph of which will somehow overthrow the neoliberal political order. While political economy in geography has typically been more grounded and nuanced, it has nonetheless largely eschewed the finer-grained critique of neoliberal government and statecraft offered by governmentality analyses and, in turn, the practice of an engaged politics that might ensue (see Keil 2009). Prince and Dufty (2009) point to a governmentality-influenced economic geography exploring the mobilities of neoliberal ideas, policy and actors. Arguably, however, as is the case with other governmentality critiques of the neoliberal state, even this literature has tended to draw evidence from the 'discursive' realm rather than material practice, thereby concentrating on the rationales of governing as manifest in key (government) documents, rather than more specific and concrete 'arts of governing' (McKee 2009: 473). McKee suggests that governmentality analysis ought also to consider the 'extent to which these political ambitions have been realized in practice' and confront why it is that the imagined governable subject does not appear in practice (ibid.: 475).

This must lead us to question whether, with exceptions (see Murdoch and Ward 1997), economic geographers have yet to realize the full political potential of governmentality approaches to examine material practices and subject formation in economies (be they in the realm of regulation, production, consumption, finance or otherwise). This gap was certainly true for my own work with neoliberal governmentality in models of parental choice in schooling, where I imagined but did not explore the choosing and responsibilized parental subjectivities of quasi-markets in state schooling (Lewis 2004a). The example illustrates how this early work in geography, to quote McKee again, risked not only promoting an 'overly abstract view of governing in which politics is reduced to rationality', but also of representing neoliberalism 'as omnipresent and totalizing' and thereby negating agency and the possibility of politics. Such accounts use governmentality to perform a more incisive deconstruction of its ideological centre and market-centric rationalities of rule that Springer (2010: 1033) suggests is a necessary first step to mount a constructive opposition to neoliberalism. While yet to perform such a politics, they have occasionally recognized its possibility.

The recent interventions of Nancy Ettlinger (2011, 2014), however, suggest that more is to come as economic geographers seek to deal with the empirical messiness of economy (Ettlinger and Hartmann 2015). So too do the turns to practice (see Jones and Murphy 2010) and market-making (Berndt and Boeckler 2011) in economic geography, and the promise of a complementary turn to ethnography. Combined with the new interest in economy-making, such an approach may lead economic geographers to a long-overdue engagement with economic subjectivity and real economic subjects going about their experimentation in economy-making in mundane daily settings. Other examples of untapped possibility here include the grounded community economies project to 'take back' the economy led by Gibson-Graham *et al.* (2013) and the vital materialities emphases of the biological economies project (Lewis *et al.* 2013; Lewis *et al.* 2016).

The work of Wendy Larner has been particularly influential on this trajectory. In the late 1990s, influenced by the Carleton School of Foucauldian scholars and the New Zealand experience of neoliberalism, Larner developed two arguments about neoliberalism that were later refined in her highly influential 2003 paper. She argued that, rather than a singular reprogramming of social life rolled out across space and through time, neoliberalism ought to be understood as a multiple, emergent and always situated and co-constitutive assemblage of ideology, political programmes and governmentality (Larner 1998). Thus understood, neoliberalism has had multiple origin points as political subjects have encountered, explored and reworked its conditions of possibility (Larner 2000). In bringing 'governmentality' to political-economic geography in this way, Larner privileged it as an analytical frame for considering the interplay of strategic projects and routine micro-practices of the state, and for considering the work of neoliberalism in reworking both subject and state simultaneously. Both moves offered economic geographers a lens for seeing the co-constitutiveness of what Peck and Tickell (2002) were later to term the 'roll-back' and 'roll-out' moments of neoliberalism. Intriguingly, in another governmentality inspired account, Ettlinger and Hartmann (2015: 37) have recently suggested that these apparently contradictory trajectories of disentanglement and re-engagement by which the state was relocated in politics under neoliberalism are better understood 'in relational terms relative to principles not time periods' and as 'mutually entangled' in the context of neoliberal practices rather than sequential.

Treating neoliberalism as governmentality rather than an impenetrable coupling of ideology and political programme opens up a realm of politics unreachable through orthodox political economy. Where political economists have struggled to develop a politics that might assist communities, publics, politicians or state officials to deliver something different, governmentality analysts have highlighted the micro-politics, practices and technologies of control at play. Even if guilty, as charged by McKee (2009), of over-concentrating on policy documents and political discourses, or, as charged by Barnett *et al.* (2008), of failing to identify and examine neoliberal subjects empirically, the focus on the practical identifies sites of struggle and/or reform. Even if the political potentiality of this focus is as yet far from fully realized, holding political economy and questions of subject and community formation in simultaneous focus raises the possibility of performing politics by engaging with neoliberal subjects theoretically and in the moments and places of their agency. By holding ideology and practice in creative tension, governmentality accounts complement political economy interests in sameness, trajectories, and structurings with an interest in the mutabilities, cracks and weak points in neoliberalism (see Carolan 2016). There are two important observations to be drawn from this reflection. First, when it comes to neoliberalism, a turn towards a governmentality reading of the significance of practice, the conception of power as constructive, and the discursive construction of social realities suggests that there is still a politics to be played within and through the state. And second, as Larner (2003) and many others writing about neoliberalism beyond the North Atlantic axis insist, there are multiple origins, trajectories, and actualized expressions of neoliberalism.

For those who embrace either or both of these reflections, the co-constitutive situatedness of knowledge, action and experience is crucial. It means that neoliberalism cannot be reduced to a universalist account globalizing ideology or political programme spreading out from its centres tempered by a recognition of the consequences of frictions generated by encounters with a material, social and economic topography (Lewis 2012). Rather, different actualized neoliberalisms reflect the incompleteness and internal contradictions of neoliberalism itself as well as local political projects and institutions. Antipodean geographers have also emphasized the significance of how we have come to know neoliberalism on what it is that we now observe and know as neoliberalism (Wray *et al.* 2013).

Like Larner, and often alongside her, I have built my knowledge of neoliberalism from New Zealand (Lewis 2004b, Larner *et al.* 2007, 2009), which experienced new public management reforms that went further and faster than most other places in driving neoliberalism into social formation through the state. It was, as Kelsey (1995) suggests, a remarkable 'experiment'. There is much in the socio-spatial context responsible for the nature and speed of this experiment and its successful completion, including smallness and institutional thinness (Lewis 2012). One of the consequences of New Zealand's smallness is a cross-disciplinary academic community that fed, first, neoliberalism and, then, governmentality into the mincing wheel that is geographical thought earlier than elsewhere. As a knowable assemblage of agency, practice, and discourse and an object for critique by geographers, neoliberalism was brought into being differently and earlier in New Zealand as a result of cross-disciplinary exposure to the work of Power (1994), Rose (1999), Clarke and Newman (1997) and others. New Zealand geography's engagement with neoliberalism was also different (see Lewis 2004b). A tradition of academic engagement with state actors in debates about spatial efficiency and equity in fields from regional development to urban transport, environmental management, health, education and so on (see Lewis *et al.* 2013), left geographers struggling to find a new audience and politics of engagement at precisely the time when they were developing a critique of the neoliberal political project. A path of disengaged and distanced critique of the 'neoliberalism of it all' from the sanctuary of elite institutions was not available to New Zealand geographers as a way out, even if it were desired. The challenge was to find new tools for thinking and engaging.

From governmentality towards a post-structuralist political economy in New Zealand

Governmentality analysis provided such a platform for Larner and Le Heron. In the early 2000s, they secured a blue skies grant that allowed them to develop the ideas of PSPE first signalled in Larner's doctoral dissertation. This project was built on a critique of neoliberalism in which governmentality was not only the object of analysis and epistemology, but also a key instrument in a political project of knowledge-making. Together, and in what was a unique intervention in global scholarship, Larner and Le Heron ran four cross-disciplinary workshops in Auckland, Canberra, Seattle and Bristol under the title Beyond Globalisation: Subjectification and Governmentality. I participated in the Auckland and Bristol workshops.

The workshops were purposefully dialogical. Each assembled up to 25 established, new generation, and graduate student scholars for one to two days (Le Heron 2007); and each focused debate on subjectification and/or spatiality in relation to a reinterpretation of globalization as governmentality. While populated largely by geographers, scholars were assembled from across disciplines and epistemological divides. Le Heron (ibid.: 35) describes the workshops as spaces of 'release' ('where participants were free to think with and also outside disciplinary norms') and engagement, where, despite whatever political economy or post-structural ideas participants brought with them, 'everyone was able to engage'. Rather than meetings of the converted, the workshops used 'governmentality' to generate boundary-crossing conversations.

The workshops had a number of effects. Most notably, in Le Heron's terms, they held up academic subjectivities to scrutiny, asking 'how we cultivate ourselves as thinking subjects' (ibid.: 36). In so doing, they enlarged the intellectual commons, enriching the quality of geographical scholarship on the neoliberal state and the neoliberalism of everyday life and catalysing some of the growth of interest in both the critique of neoliberalism and the rise of governmentality analysis in geography. The workshops demonstrated that all this might be achieved and that knowledge might be made performatively and unexpectedly political. They created debates between political economy and post-structuralism in what were safe spaces by comparison to major conferences or the journals, and spaces where no one had straightforward answers. And they put these various effects and governmentality insights about the constitutiveness of practices and relations in terms of both affect and effects (*the how of what is*) at the heart of a new political turn in the form of a PSPE, the shape of which they themselves enacted into being.

The Canberra workshop established new conversations between the PSPE that was beginning to develop in Gibson-Graham's work and that which was nascent in Larner and Le Heron's governmentality project. The prologue to Gibson-Graham's *A Post-Capitalist Politics* (2006), for example, discusses her shift from Marxism to feminism and post-structuralism, and more as a set of productive inflections than rejections. While not labelled PSPE, this intellectual journey, together with her community economies project, her rejection of capitalocentrism and essentialist conceptions of 'the economy', weak theory, engaged politics, and the political projects of diverse and community economies looked, from New Zealand, very much like a version of PSPE. In this, the economy is denaturalized as a categorization of material activities brought into being by a complex set of technologies and practices (ibid.: xiii); and 'loses its character as an asocial body... [to become instead] a space of recognition and negotiation' (ibid.: xxx).

As Larner and Le Heron continued to develop PSPE, governmentality insights themselves remained central to their own work on the neoliberal university (Larner and Le Heron 2005), the local state (Le Heron 2009; Wetzstein and Le Heron 2010), globalizing networks of economic and political practice (Larner 2007; Larner and Laurie 2010); and the notion of after-neoliberalism as post-structuralist antidote to the homogenizing accounts of 'roll-out' and 'roll-back' neoliberalism and their effects on geographic knowledge of neoliberalism (Larner *et al.* 2007; Lewis 2009). In what follows, I point to how these insights became entangled in the genealogy of what a group of New Zealand and Australian economic geographers have come to label PSPE (see Larner and Le Heron 2002; Le Heron 2007; Lewis *et al.* 2013).

Post-structuralist political economy: crafting a political project of knowledge production from a productive critique of neoliberalism

The particular PSPE fashioned in Auckland built on a critique of political economy accounts of economy and its central categories of knowledge, which we portray as macro, abstracted, disembodied and disembedded, agentless, and politically blunt (Lewis *et al.* under revision). Without rejecting the central place played in the production of space by investment trajectories and their structuring, we sought a sharper and more political critique of neoliberalism and an understanding of economy capable of capturing its messiness. Readily observable yet obscured by political economy, this messiness included the presence of many more economic actors beyond capital and labour, a sense of the mundane and the everyday, the presence of economic subjectivity (especially in consumption), other ordering practices such as calculation, experimentation, and performativity, and the possibilities of moral economy. To understand investment trajectories, then, we figured that we needed new objects of analysis, a 'theorization away' from messy empirics, and new methodological schema. Further if investments and institutions were embodiments of alterable practices and contingent/uncertain agency, not only must economy be re-visioned but so too must politics (see Lewis *et al.* 2016). We began to seek an economic scholarship more attuned to the messy, agentic practice of economy, and one that asked how academics might 'do the politics of knowledge' (Le Heron 2009).

What then do we mean by PSPE? Its core propositions begin with a recognition that investment processes shape our worlds and our different places in them, and that they are shaped by actors, institutions, and micro-politics that take situated, geographical forms and exert agency. The list goes on: economies exceed capital-market-firm-labour configurations and are messy and emergent; economic agency is relational; the economic categories that structure economic knowledge are made and make the world; and structuring work is performed amid this messiness by political projects. Far from being prefigured, despite the structuring work of knowledge categories and political projects, the economies that emerge are open relational assemblages (Lewis *et al.* 2016). The upshot is that politics is possible and needs to take the form of challenging knowledge categories and destabilizing political projects. This implies a certain wildness of approach that asks alternative questions, emphasizes the making of economies rather than discerning their structural forms, engages with unlikely actors and initiatives, works through encounters rather than projects, mirrors the messiness of social reality, and challenges scholars to break away from existing approaches.

To practise such a politics requires, and can be practised by, assembling political projects of knowledge-making that make visible the invisible, give voice to the silent, theorize weakly away from messy empirics, involve a wildness of research, work with other agents in making the world otherwise, and above all commit to enactive knowledge-making practices in multiple situated settings. At core is precisely the call made by Ferguson (2011) to do more than denounce, and to recognize that this may take all manner of humble as well as heroic forms. For Gibson-Graham, this is the community economies project; for the group of antipodean economic geographers, of which I form a part, it is intervening alongside institutional actors to ask different questions and trouble assumed knowledge in the theorized 'hope' that state–capital relations might conceivably be enacted differently at some scale in neighbourhood or city planning, environmental practice, regional development initiatives and so on. This is what Carolan (2016) and Lewis *et al.* (2016) are calling a turn towards a more constructive critical moment or an enactive politics of critical research.

My argument here, however, is not that PSPE is a readily distinctive, fully formed, or self-contained approach or that it represents a decisive assault on extant paradigms; it is more that PSPE issues a licence and imperative to ask different, more agent-centric questions in new ways. My point in this chapter is to suggest that it stands as a demonstration of the productive force of governmentality thinking. The points of entanglement of governmentality analysis and PSPE include deconstructing and denaturalizing taken-for-granted arrangements of power, denaturalizing the categories of economy by which we come to know these arrangements and perform them into being, rethinking economy as a messy, embodied and social space of government, recognizing the state to be only one of multiple authorities and formations of expertise involved in rule, grasping the productive nature of power, and glimpsing a politics of both incomplete reach and contradictions among technologies of the self and domination under neoliberalism.

Governmentality analysis also points to the scales of practice and micro-technologies required to understand power and social formation, and to the influence of the discursive realm that contains, represents and leads us to perform the common sense of the economy. In so doing, it identifies a wider range of the relationalities that matter than critical economic knowledge received from political economy, and also highlights their situatedness in contested power-knowledge relations and resultant unevenness, instability, partiality, and incompleteness. It suggests at least a partial open-endedness, and while pointing to the omni-presence of power and its configuration into powerful programmes of rationalities and practices, it also suggests the possibility of politics in the departure of the actual effects of any programme from its aims and a history characterized by the permanent 'failure' of programmes.

The turn to an enactive politics was foreshadowed in both the aims and demonstrated effects of the governmentality workshops, which went on to encourage Le Heron and Lewis to participate fully in New Zealand's Building Research Capability in the Social Science experiment and influence how it was practised (see Le Heron *et al.* 2011). It also resonated in Larner's work with David Craig and others in negotiating local and national welfare state rationalities with local government partners (Larner and Craig 2005), and in the engagement of McGuirk, Dowling and O'Neill with institutional actors in Sydney (McGuirk and Dowling 2009; McGuirk and O'Neill 2012). Our governmentality-influenced counter to the 'neoliberalism of it all' was assembled in a Special Issue of *Asia Pacific Viewpoint* titled provocatively Progressive Spaces of Neoliberalism? (Lewis 2009). Significant in this work, and in the theorizing of after-neoliberalism, was the governmentality inflected notion of *political project* (Larner *et al.* 2007), a situated and unstable alignment of political narratives, material interests, and technologies of government into a project that both explained and sought governmental force (knowledge economy, global warming, sustainable development, globalization and so on).

These features of PSPE take in more post-structuralist influences than just governmental-ity. Indeed, PSPE drew on Callon ('performativity', 'research in the wild'), Mitchell ('rethink-ing economy'), Barry ('anti-political economy'), Ferguson ('anti-politics machine'), Carolan ('I do therefore there is', 'experimentation', 'difference power'), Thrift ('non-representational theory'), Mol ('multiple ontologies'), Law and Urry ('enactment'), and Deleuze ('assem-blage') (see Lewis *et al.* 2013). However, governmentality was the point (in time–place and epistemology) where Larner, Le Heron and Lewis started their journey as economic geogra-phers concerned with neoliberal restructuring but increasingly sceptical of the merits of political economy as it was practised. And there is little doubt that it performed as a disrup-tive knowledge project, which was given particular embodied and socialized forms in the governmentality workshops. It encouraged the Auckland-based geographers to use work-shops to facilitate a politics of knowledge production with actors beyond the academy (see Le Heron *et al.* 2011), and gave them confidence to challenge the political effects and affect of political economy.

Conclusion

This chapter questions the productivity of governmentality thinking in economic geography. At stake is a need to rethink the political spatiality of economy in a way that sustains economic geography's epistemological usefulness over other critical economic analyses. Governmental-ity helps it escape the weight of lumpy categories on its explanatory powers and political potential to address new audiences in ways that allow for it to roll disruptively with neoliber-alism (see Keil 2009) in the search for a politics and meaningful intervention. My colleagues in agri-food scholarship have been grappling creatively with this challenge for some time. They observe that the 'very idea of 'post structural… political economy' speaks to paradig-matic disciplinary struggles. In geography it points to the struggles faced by political economists working with realist critiques of capitalist social transformation to grasp the incisive and deconstructive analytics of Foucualdian and actor network ideas. On the one hand, there lie the materialist categories of investment, accumulation, labour and the corporation, and scalar hierarchies of nation, region, neighbourhood, community that defined geography's approaches; and, on the other, the deconstructive impulse that recognizes them to be analyti-cal and/or constructed rather than ontological. PSPE attempts to find a critical creativity in the collisions between a political economy critique and the deconstructive critique of post-structuralism.

In this chapter I suggest that governmentality analysis has catalysed the turn to a particular PSPE in New Zealand economic geography. It taught us that the messiness and complexity involved in the struggles around subjectivity offer a more nuanced and finely grained analysis of governing and economy than accounts of the 'neoliberalism of it all'. It also taught us that it is hard to properly grasp political-economic structures without understanding how they are constituted, co-created, and enacted. This chapter is, however, more a story of the genera-tive capacity of governmentality in a particular place at a particular time than an advocacy for further governmentality-inspired deconstructions of the power relations of economic initiatives. It demonstrates the potential creativity residing in the tensions across which gov-ernmentality analysis is put to work (Ettlinger 2011). It is this creativity that future govern-mentality analysis ought to seek to uncover, particularly its potential to be political. In McKee's (2009) terms, it is precisely this potential that might allow us 'to put back in' the concerns with the role of the state, politics and social difference that governmentality analysis is accused of ignoring.

References

Allen, J. 2003. *Lost Geographies of Power.* Oxford: Blackwell.

Barnett, C., Clarke, N., Cloke, P., and Malpass, A. 2008. The Elusive Subjects of Neo-liberalism: Beyond the Analytics of Governmentality. *Cultural Studies*, 22: 624–53.

Berndt, C., and Boeckler, M. 2011. Geographies of Markets: Materials, Morals and Monsters in Motion. *Progress in Human Geography*, 35: 559–67.

Carolan, M. 2016. The Very Public Nature of Agrifood Scholarship, and its Problems and Possibilities, in Le Heron, R., Campbell, H., Lewis, N., and Carolan, M., eds. *Biological Economies: Experimentation and the Politics of Agrifood Frontiers.* London: Routledge: 225–39.

Clarke, J., and Newman, J. 1997. *The Managerial State: Power, Politics and Ideology in the Remaking of Social Welfare.* London: Sage.

Dowling, R. 2010. Geographies of Identity: Climate Change, Governmentality and Activism. *Progress in Human Geography*, 34: 488–95.

Elden, S. 2007. Rethinking Governmentality. *Political Geography*, 26: 29–33.

Ettlinger, N. 2011. Governmentality as Epistemology. *Annals of the Association of American Geographers*, 101: 537–60.

—. 2014. Delivering on Poststructural Ontologies: Epistemological Challenges and Strategies. *ACME: An International E-Journal for Critical Geographies*, 13: 589–98.

Ettlinger, N., and Hartmann, C. 2015. Post/neo/liberalism in Relational Perspective. *Political Geography*, 48: 37–48.

Ferguson, J. 2011. Toward a Left Art of Government: From 'Foucauldian Critique'to Foucauldian Politics. *History of the Human Sciences*, 24: 61–8.

Foucault, M. 2003. Governmentality, in Rabinow, P., and Rose, N., eds. *The Essential Foucault: Selections from Essential Works of Foucault 1954–1984.* London: The New Press: 229–45.

Gibson-Graham, J.K. 2006. *A Post-Capitalist Politics.* Minneapolis: University of Minnesota Press.

Gibson-Graham, J.K., Cameron, J., and Healy, S. 2013. *Take Back the Economy: An Ethical Guide for Transforming our Communities.* Minneapolis: University of Minnesota Press.

Huxley, M. 2008. Space and Government: Governmentality and Geography. *Geography Compass*, 2: 1635–58.

Jones, A., and Murphy, J. 2010. Theorizing Practice in Economic Geography: Foundations, Challenges, and Possibilities. *Progress in Human Geography*, 35: 366–92.

Keil, R. 2009. The Urban Politics of Roll-with-it Neoliberalization. *City*, 13: 230–45.

Kelsey, J. 1995. *The New Zealand Experiment: A World Model for Structural Adjustment?* Auckland: Auckland University Press.

Larner, W. 1998. Sociologies of Neo-liberalism: Theorising the New Zealand Experiment, *Sites*, 36: 5–21.

—. 2000. Neo-liberalism: Policy, Ideology, Governmentality. *Studies in Political Economy*, 63: 5–25.

—. 2003. Neoliberalism? *Environment and Planning D Abstract*, 21: 509–12.

—. 2007. Expatriate Experts and Globalising Governmentalities: The New Zealand Diaspora Strategy. *Transactions of the Institute of British Geographers*, 32: 331–45.

Larner, W., and Craig, D. 2005. After Neoliberalism? Community Activism and Local Partnerships in Aotearoa New Zealand. *Antipode*, 37: 402–24.

Larner, W., and Laurie, N. 2010. Travelling Technocrats, Embodied Knowledges: Globalising Privatisation in Telecoms and Water. *Geoforum*, 41: 218–26.

Larner, W., and Le Heron, R. 2002. The Spaces and Subjects of a Globalising Economy: A Situated Exploration of Method. *Environment and Planning D: Society and Space*, 20: 753–74.

—. 2005. Neo-liberalizing Spaces and Subjectivities: Reinventing New Zealand Universities. *Organization*, 12: 843–62.

Larner, W., and Walters, W. 2004. Globalization as Governmentality. *Alternatives*, 29: 494–514.

Larner, W., Le Heron, R., and Lewis, N. 2007. Co-Constituting Neoliberalism: Globalising Governmentalities and Political Projects in Aotearoa New Zealand, in England, K., and Ward, K., eds. *Neoliberalisation: States, Networks and People.* London: Routledge: 233–47.

Larner, W., Lewis, N., and Le Heron, R. 2009. State Spaces of 'After Neoliberalism': Co-constituting the New Zealand Designer Fashion Industry, in Keil, R., and Mahon, R., eds. *Leviathan Undone? Towards a Political Economy of Scale.* Vancouver: UBC Press: 177–94.

Le Heron, E., Le Heron, R., and Lewis, N. 2011. Performing Research Capability Building in New Zealand's Social Sciences: Capacity-capability Insights from Exploring the Work of BRCSS's 'Sustainability' Theme. *Environment and Planning A*, 43: 140–2.

Le Heron, R. 2007. Globalisation, Governance and Post-structural Political Economy: Perspectives from Australasia. *Asia Pacific Viewpoint*, 48: 26–40.

—. 2009. 'Rooms and Moments' in Neoliberalising Policy Trajectories of Metropolitan Auckland, New Zealand: Towards Constituting Progressive Spaces Through Post-structural Political Economy. *Asia Pacific Viewpoint*, 50: 135–53.

Lemke, T. 2001. 'The Birth of Bio-politics': Michel Foucault's Lecture at the Collège de France on Neo-liberal Governmentality. *Economy and Society*, 30: 190–207.

—. 2002. Foucault, Governmentality, and Critique. *Rethinking Marxism: A Journal of Economics, Culture & Society*, 14: 49–64.

Lewis, N. 2004a. Embedding the Reforms in New Zealand Schooling: After Neo-liberalism? *GeoJournal*, 59: 149–60.

—. 2004b. Geographies of the 'New Zealand Experiment'. *GeoJournal*, 59: 161–6.

—. 2009. Progressive Spaces of Neoliberalism? *Asia Pacific Viewpoint*, 50: 113–19.

—. 2012. Splitting a Northern Account of New Zealand's Neoliberalism. *New Zealand Geographer*, 68: 168–74.

Lewis, N., Le Heron, R., Campbell, H., Henry, M., Le Heron, E., Pawson, E., Perkins, H., Roche, M., and Rosin, C. 2013. Assembling Biological Economies: Region Shaping Initiatives in Making and Retaining Value. *New Zealand Geographer*, 69: 180–96.

Lewis, N., Le Heron R., Carolan M., Campbell, H., and Marsden, T. 2016. Assembling Generative Approaches in Agrifood Research, in Le Heron, R., Campbell, H., Lewis, N., and Carolan, M., eds. *Biological Economies: Experimentation and the Politics of Agrifood Frontiers*. London: Routledge: 1–20.

Lewis, N., McGuirk, P., and Le Heron, R. under revision. Practicing Generative Economic Geography: A Post-structural Political Economy Approach. *Progress in Human Geography*.

Li, T. 2007. Governmentality. *Anthropologica*, 49: 275–81.

MacKinnon, D. 2000. Managerialism, Governmentality and the State: A Neo-Foucauldian Approach to Local Economic Governance. *Political Geography*, 19: 293–314.

McGuirk, P., and Dowling, R. 2009. Master-planned Residential Developments: Beyond Iconic Spaces of Neoliberalism? *Asia Pacific Viewpoint*, 50: 120–34.

McGuirk, P., and O'Neill, P. 2012. Critical Geographies with the State: The Problem of Social Vulnerability and the Politics of Engaged Research. *Antipode*, 44: 1374–94.

McKee, K. 2009. Post-Foucauldian Governmentality: What Does it Offer Critical Social Policy Analysis? *Critical Social Policy*, 29: 465–86.

Murdoch, J., and Ward, N. 1997. Governmentality and Territoriality: The Statistical Manufacture of Britain's 'National Farm'. *Political Geography*, 16: 307–24.

Painter, J. 2006. Prosaic Geographies of Stateness. *Political Geography*, 25: 752–74.

Peck, J., and Tickell, A. 2002. Neoliberalizing Space. *Antipode*, 34: 380–404.

Power, M. 1994. *The Audit Explosion*. London: Demos.

Prince, R., and Dufty, R. 2009. Assembling the Space Economy: Governmentality and Economic Geography. *Geography Compass*, 3: 1744–56.

Rose, N. 1999. *Powers of Freedom: Reframing Political Thought*. Cambridge: Cambridge University Press.

Rose, N., and Miller, P. 1992. Political Power Beyond the State: Problematics of Government. *British Journal of Sociology*, 43.2: 173–205.

Rose-Redwood, R. 2006. Governmentality, Geography, and the Geo-coded World. *Progress in Human Geography*, 30: 469–86.

Rutherford, S. 2007. Green Governmentality: Insights and Opportunities in the Study of Nature's Rule. *Progress in Human Geography*, 31: 291–307.

Sparke, M. 2006. A Neoliberal Nexus: Economy, Security and the Biopolitics of Citizenship on the Border. *Political Geography*, 25: 151–80.

Springer, S. 2010. Neoliberalism and Geography: Expansions, Variegations, Formations. *Geography Compass*, 4: 1025–38.

Uitermark, J. 2005. The Genesis and Evolution of Urban Policy: A Confrontation of Regulationist and Governmentality Approaches. *Political Geography*, 24: 137–63.

Walters, W. 2006. Border/control. *European Journal of Social Theory*, 9: 187–203.

Wetzstein, S., and Le Heron, R. 2010. Regional Economic Policy In-the-Making: Imaginaries, Political Projects and Institutions for Auckland's Economic Transformation. *Environment and Planning A*, 42: 1902–24.

Wray, F., Dufty-Jones, R., Gibson, C., Larner, W., Beer, A., Le Heron, R., and O'Neill, P. 2013. Neither Here nor There or Always Here and There? Antipodean Reflections on Economic Geography. *Dialogues in Human Geography*, 3: 179–99.

7

NEOLIBERALISM IN QUESTION

Phillip O'Neill and Sally Weller

> Faced with the bewildering variety of changes which are taking place, it is tempting to seize upon simple polemical contrasts... Inevitably we risk ending up with... overly elastic concepts. Worse, we invite a consequent diminution in the richness – and therefore the power – of our conceptual equipment.
>
> (Sayer 1989: 666)

The question is: what is this neoliberalism? This book abounds with definitions – a motivating spirit, a theoretical approach, an internationalized policy framework, a mobile policy knowledge, a complex of regimes, a set of practices, a cultural orientation infiltrating contemporary life, and so on. This chapter, which takes its title from Andrew Sayer's (1989) critique Post-Fordism in Question, challenges the usefulness of calling so many different ideas and practices neoliberalism. Our objective is to question the usefulness of the concept as a framework for explaining contemporary capitalism and the politics surrounding it, and to ask whether neoliberalism's power to shape contemporary societies is overstated.

The next section fleshes out our central argument that definitions of neoliberalism have become so broad, so fluid and so multifaceted that the word may have become an obstacle to quality academic argument. It has become, for some, a crutch holding up weak analysis or a vague, insufficiently argued-for, one-size-fits-all explanation for a diverse range of events and circumstances. Its readily made assumptions press all manner of events into a single template and avoid detailed scrutiny of the real forces and processes driving economic, cultural and social change. Abstractions that better address and explain observed commonalities and differences, we argue, would enhance understandings and open up opportunities to develop more desirable alternative policies and practices. In a world of evidence-based policy, more rigorous analysis might also attract policy-maker interest and expose mainstream politicians to policy alternatives. Going beyond these broad criticisms, section three identifies three varieties of neoliberalism. While distinctions between these types are not always clear in practice, our classification helps us analyse the diverse components of the idea. First are approaches defining neoliberalism as a set of theoretical propositions capable of enactment, with varying degrees of success, in actual contexts. We call these approaches 'neoliberalism-in-theory'. Second are approaches that build the idea of neoliberalism from observed similarities in actual practices. We call these approaches 'neoliberalism-in-general'.

Third are approaches that conceive of neoliberalism as a form of governmentality or a set of logics and practices that infiltrate everyday life. We call these 'neoliberal governmentality'. We then examine the practical reunification of the three forms. The penultimate section advocates greater self-consciousness in the use of the term 'neoliberalism'. Querying whether the idea of neoliberalism is the best way to pursue robust and inquisitive analysis of contemporary capitalism, and assessing the political utility of the term, are matters we discuss in our conclusion.

Questioning neoliberalisms

The term 'neoliberalism' refers to different types of phenomena from abstract ideas and ideologies to categories of occurrences, to sets of practices, and to forms of governmentality. It is sometimes positioned as a causal force, sometimes a process, sometimes a change agent, and sometimes an effect or outcome. Some see this multiplicity as a distinguishing characteristic of the concept. Springer (2015: 7), for example, rejects conferring a 'thing-like' status, insisting instead that neoliberalism 'does not exist as a coherent and fixed edifice'. Yet can we afford to give such a mercurial position to an idea that purports to be a dominant societal force? Some authors have concerns. Collier (2015: n.p.), for instance, wonders about the ontological status of neoliberalism, about 'how it can be constituted as an object of inquiry: How it can be made into something about which we can discover something new and unexpected?' For Larner (2014: n.p.) neoliberalism has become a 'preconstituted theoretical explanation and self-evident descriptor of contemporary forms of economic, political, social and environmental change'.

Our concern is that the word stands for too many things. Weiss (2012: 28) says that neoliberalism's many definitions risk creating 'one of those giant omnibus words that threaten to capsize with overstretched capacity'. Like other giant words – including, for example, 'globalization', 'modernization' and 'sustainability' – it presages important processes, and ideas that must be taken seriously, but is non-specific enough to mean different things to different audiences. Conflating multiple meanings in a single word makes precise analysis and quality debate difficult. Moreover, assigning the tag 'neoliberal' too often replaces close study of the relationships among state policies, economies, societies and developmental trajectories. Using one word to describe so many processes effectively flattens the ontological landscape in a way that disregards the important effects of interactions among scales of activity.

Some view the idea of neoliberalism as a frame or lens that captures sight of particular ideas and events and exposes them to scrutiny. This can have advantages, of course, if there is generated a 'critical opening through which it becomes possible to see certain kinds of relationships and formations that were previously difficult to discern' (Collier 2014: 20). But there are risks. On the one hand, overarching narratives can generate intellectual blind spots. Privileging the idea of neoliberalism as the driver of contemporary political thought and action tends to marginalize or exclude or de-value the examination of processes and events that merit analysis but are not seen as associated with neoliberalism. On the other hand, many observations seen as neoliberal tend to self-enroll as core elements of the political process, with new studies valued for how they confirm (rather than question) the narrative. What emerges is a patterned empiricism reinforcing the narrative of neoliberalism; it becomes omnipotent and increasingly impervious to criticism. Block and Somers (2014: 156–8) argue that inherently persuasive ideas gain a sort of 'epistemic privilege' that make them immune from refutation; they 'come equipped with their own internal claims to veracity'. We think we need to be alert to a tendency to see everything as a facet of, or as evidence of, neoliberalism; indeed there may well be events taken as examples of neoliberalism which, by careful research, are revealed as having different or even opposing motivations (see Larner and Craig 2005).

We worry too about the way accounts of neoliberalism focus on similarities and overlook differences. Differences are too easily dismissed as anomalies of historical context, diminished as matters of lesser empirical substance, or excluded as being the result of some unusual circumstance. Yet neoliberalism scholarship can't account adequately for the diverse ways things play out in different places; and can't decide how much difference is tolerable before the label 'neoliberal' is abandoned (Collier 2012: 191). Elsewhere we (O'Neill and Weller 2013; Weller and O'Neill 2014) take up this question of difference in interrogating the case of Australia's post-Keynesian economic trajectory and conclude that there are insufficient grounds to warrant the claim of neoliberalist ascendancy or neoliberal regime. While some disagree with this assessment (Argent 2014), others raise similar doubts in relation to their national contexts (Challies 2014; Benediktsson 2014; Hayter 2014). Such dissent, we think, shows two things: first, that the search for commonalities across a global neoliberal project has so far compiled incomplete evidence; and, second, that a neoliberalist framework of analysis lacks the means for accounting for difference across domains.

We also raise concern about neoliberalism's relationship to notions of contemporary globalization and contemporary capitalism. We query the benefits of discussing varieties of neoliberalism rather than varieties of capitalism. Perhaps past discussions focused on capitalism have over-emphasized the economic dimension, making neoliberalism's attention to social, political and governmental matters a much-needed corrective. But while accounts of neoliberalism bring in policy and social concerns, they often leave out detailed analysis of the economic relations and events that shape public policy and stimulate social change. And, often, these relationships are best analysed by frameworks that don't call on the precepts of neoliberalism. For example, contrasting capitalist economic and social policy platforms – national interventionism, developmental statecraft, city-state projects or Scandinavian-style corporatism – warrant explicit analysis to determine the type of capitalism they create. These might contain elements of neoliberalism while not ever being defined by it (see also Hart-Landsberg 2006).

Varieties of neoliberalism

This section identifies and examines three ways neoliberalism is used in the literature to better understand the concept and better assess its usefulness as an explanatory and political mobilization device. Following Weller and O'Neill (2014), we call the three varieties neoliberalism-in-theory, neoliberalism-in-general, and neoliberal governmentality. It is important to emphasize that these varieties are abstractions created to isolate partial aspects of the concept (see Sayer 1984), and are not intended as a typology able to be mapped directly onto actual examples. In practice, accounts of neoliberalism often combine the elements of all three varieties, bleeding one into the others, sometimes culminating in a pervasive neoliberal universe (e.g. Hilgers 2011). Recognizing that neoliberalism is presented and interpreted in many different ways puts a brake on the omnibus use of the word and steers us instead towards more precise analyses and more useful interventions.

Neoliberalism-in-theory

Neoliberalism-in-theory begins with a set of propositions that together create a normative vision of the conduct of human society and a blueprint for governance (see Harvey 2005). Neoliberalism-in-theory is motivated by, and made coherent by, a set of ideological or philosophical propositions about human nature, freedom, individuality and reward. These seemingly universal truths animate neoliberal ideas, imbuing them with an evangelistic spirit in a manner akin to the *pneuma* (breath) animating some versions of Christian faith (see Carroll 2001). As a set of higher-order ideas or abstractions, this neoliberalism can be spoken about in ways removed from the complexities and histories of the actually existing world. The advantage of this detachment is that it enables the concept to have a clear definition open to comparison with other world views and ideologies, and therefore able to be discussed, and criticized, and proselytized relatively freely.

Six principal dimensions can be derived from these motivating ideas. First, the preference for private forms of property ownership over mutual, common or public forms of ownership enables self-interested behaviour to become society's driving force. All manner of things and activities are commodified to feed the accumulation of private wealth. Second, market-based mechanisms of exchange and for-profit transactions are promoted as the most efficient means of allocating resources, and for distributing the income generated by production. Third, economic growth proceeds by intensifying and extending the reach of markets, especially by promoting the global integration of trade and the free movement of capital, goods, people and ideas. Fifth, market logics are extended to human behaviours, insisting that the interests of workers are best served when labour arrangements are individualized and transacted in markets, and when collective forms of labour organization are suppressed. Fifth, individuals and their immediate households acting in their own interests become the primary subjects of social organization: society becomes no more than an aggregate of individuals and their partisan interests. Sixth, state-led attempts to steer productive resources into particular areas, or to redistribute incomes in favour of particular groups, are deemed counterproductive because they pervert the economic signals governing markets. The overarching assumption is that, when all actors act self-interestedly in the exchange of private property, the collective interest is also secured. Fortuitously, as market-based processes shift costs and economic value among actors, they also resolve society-wide economic crises. Like them or not, it is easy to see the consistency of the market logic working across these six dimensions.

This form of neoliberalism offers a set of ideas available for propagation and adoption. The propositions are relatively easy to understand and identify with, which, in large part, explains the popularity of neoliberalism's foundational texts, at least among those with private property to defend (see Hayek 1944, 1960; Friedman and Friedman, 1980). However, enunciating a set of propositions does not guarantee their translation into material existence in actual observable political and economic circumstances. While its tenets translate into a coherent logic that can underpin policy development, the capacity of neoliberalism-in-theory to guide economic systems and shape events is indeterminate. There is no guarantee that actualizations will resemble the theoretical shape or intent. Neoliberalism's founding texts are vague about what drives its installation in the material world, save that implementation requires some sort of transformative agent and perhaps some motivating vision. Not surprisingly, empirical studies show that enactments are invariably partial and incomplete; they occur through processes of experiment, learning and knowledge exchanges in which idealized objectives are inevitably transformed or mutated by their confrontations with historically produced realities (Peck 2011). The point to be made here is that an abstraction can never anticipate or determine the actual form of a thing or an event. Reality is always the play-out of contingent things.

Neoliberalism-in-general

The approach we call neoliberalism-in-general takes a different view of how neoliberalism is constituted and how its actual world existences are produced. In this grounded form, the word 'neoliberalism' stands for a category produced by observed commonalities among policies and events. The word thus becomes a summary, uniting a variety of policies and practices that have sufficient qualities in common to allow them to be grouped; like the category 'furniture' refers rather neatly to a class of constructed items inside homes and offices; or 'emotions' refers to a set of physiological, behavioural and psychological responses and feelings. The point is that furniture and emotions only have meaning in so far as they capture essential or general features of observed phenomena. The major benefit of thinking in generalized rather than in theoretical categories is that the absence of a theory of furniture or emotion does not prevent the tagging of actual, existing things as pieces of furniture or as emotions. They are what they are seen to be.

From this approach, we can identify economic and political changes to capitalism since the 1970s that have many things in common – including being undesirable socially – that are not necessarily connected to the marketization or individualizing logics of neoliberalism-in-theory. These might include: a technological and communications revolution; the expansion of money credit, the empowerment of financial services, and accelerated financial flows; a new spatial organization of production and the expansion of transnational firms; the containment of wages, the suppression of organized labour and the retrenchment of welfare entitlements; the emergence of multi-scalar forms of governance; invigorated capitalist competition and the recovery of the rate of profit; and, increased tolerance of inequality, both within and between national jurisdictions. These developments could be incorporated into neoliberalism-in-general, regardless of theoretical match, as it transforms its identity by absorbing emerging innovations.

Neoliberalism-in-general, then, constructs neoliberalism not as a set of principles in abstract but as observed *commonalities* across collections of practices and strategies. The things, events or circumstances it embraces are capable of existing independently, and are not necessarily dependent on attempts to implement a set of ideological principles. In neoliberalism-in-general there are only observable practices in the first instance. Their grouping into a general category and its assignment to a portfolio we might call neoliberalism occurs subsequently. This definition of neoliberalism is agile, able to identify emerging policy initiatives that enact or extend neoliberal ideas in novel ways. It lends neoliberalism a tendential rather than a deterministic character (Peck 2006).

But things get difficult when neoliberalism-in-general includes events or activities that could not be anticipated from neoliberalism-in-theory. We readily understand what it is that makes a chair a piece of furniture, because the definition of furniture is stable and clear. It is more difficult to categorize events and practices as neoliberal, however, because neoliberal-in-general definitions are necessarily fluid. What is missing is a criterion for inclusion and exclusion. Two examples highlight the problem. Suppose, on the one hand, that a novel reform rewards wealthy people over ordinary people and is classified as neoliberal, even though the particular policy is foreign to the family of interventions familiar to the neoliberalism-in-theory repertoire. Is the classification correct? We can only trust the classifier, and that may not be enough. On the other hand, suppose a government assisted the trade position of a friendly nation by making a regulatory change that contained identifiably neoliberal elements, but did so without any recognizably neoliberal motivation. Is this neoliberalism? Perhaps to qualify a policy or response needs to emerge and be observed in multiple sites independently? But would that criterion exclude policies that for local reasons only emerge in one location? These difficulties arise because of the way neoliberalism-in-general often relies on the presence of narrow and shallow commonalities; for example, noting the common existence of markets (rather than making detailed comparison of their competitive structure). The merits of comparative political analyses are clear, but the strongest and most enduring generalizations are produced when the range of investigative questions is wide, the approach open to unanticipated answers and observations, and the analysis deep enough to be alert to the unspoken assumptions, values and beliefs motivating actual events and practices (see Castree 2015). We worry when the category of occurrences identified by neolib-eralism-in-general is elevated to the status of a hybrid, variegated theoretical construct when the construct is based on chaotic collections of only partially similar things.

Neoliberalism as governmentality

When neoliberalism is understood as a form of governmentality, definitions take a different tack again. The concept of governmentality draws on Foucault's studies of discipline and biopolitics to link neoliberalism's celebration of individuality to the self-disciplining internalization of iden-tifiably neoliberal logics and rationalities. Here the word neoliberalism describes an amalgam of social, economic and cultural technologies that seek to govern everyday lives. Neoliberalism as governmentality infiltrates the practices and technologies of living, especially those that produce and reproduce autonomous beings capable of strategizing for success and accumulating rewards. Neoliberal logics become so ingrained they become ordinary common sense. The logics build legitimacy for disciplining those who resist and for dismantling institutions established for col-lective ends. These acts are made possible by imposing surveillance, imaginings, calculative devices and micro-scale technologies that control space at a distance to create complex patterns of inclusion and exclusion. The strength of the governmentality approach, as we see it, is its recognition that neoliberalism has to play out in everyday, observable practices; which means, inevitably, that acceptance can never be guaranteed. There is no outside pervasive force levering neoliberal logics into daily life, but nor is there a docile human population; people are endlessly capable of resistance or creative diversion.

We see two problems with neoliberalism as governmentality. The first is that many of the practices this version of neoliberalism describes have been made possible by, or are the effects of, changes that have revolutionized human behaviour, especially those associated with digitiza-tion and high-speed telecommunications. Human creativity, not 'neoliberalism', assembled the communications and surveillance capacities needed to produce the outcomes described in neo-liberalism as governmentality approaches. The idea of hands-off government at a distance, for example, might be explained simply as a response to complexity. The point is that these changes are not necessarily associated with any particular form of social or economic organization and are likely to appear – with greater or lesser intensity – in all locations reached by technology. This is not to deny the importance of governmentality research or to sanction the oppressive ways institutions and governments use the digital traces of human behaviour for nefarious ends. Our argument is that governmentality, as a heuristic device to guide analysis of such oppressions, isn't added to by modifying it with the word 'neoliberalism'. The second problem is rather straightforward: that the meaning of the word, when used in its governmentality sense, does not refer to the same things as in neoliberalism's other forms.

Enactments

Our approach to varieties of neoliberalism produces three separate abstractions: the first derives neoliberalism from philosophical arguments, the second imputes neoliberalism from observed practices and the third deduces neoliberalism from Foucauldian analyses of power. Collier (2014: 5) understands neoliberalism as a 'style and practice of thinking', but here we have three different styles of thinking. In practice, the three are generally conflated, concealing the different understandings they produce.

We think the relationship between neoliberalism-in-theory and neoliberalism-in-general is best understood by their different orientations with respect to the periodization of history.

The logics and propositions of neoliberalism-in-theory can be identified with regimes that have attempted, with various degrees of success, to implement a neoliberal vision. Thatcherism is an obvious example (see Peck and Tickell 2002). Following a broadly regulationist understanding of political-economic change, it can be argued that regimes guided by the foundational principles of neoliberalism-in-theory endured because they offered workable solutions to the contradictions that disabled Keynesian forms of organization from the 1970s. Like all regimes of accumulation, however, neoliberal regimes contain contradictions that become the seeds of regime downfall. Hence we saw debates about whether the global financial crisis would destabilize neoliberalism and trigger the dawn of a post-neoliberal era. Neoliberalism-in-theory invites this sort of episodic thinking. But this is not the case with the more agile orientation of neoliberalism-in-general, given its limitless capacity to incorporate emerging conditions. This approach dissolves the need to declare a crisis for neoliberalism and denies the possibility of a post-neoliberal outcome. Broader mutations of the typology of government (Collier 2014) are, in fact, out of sight. Moreover, here, a regime might be adjudged to be neoliberal – by virtue of evolving similarities to other regimes – without any local political will to pursue neoliberal ideals. In practice, we think, this isn't possible: neoliberalism-in-general cannot be endlessly pragmatic and must continue to be guided by the durable tenets of neoliberalism-in-theory (contrast Peck and Theodore 2012).

The theoretical and practical aspects of neoliberalism can be united using Gramsci's notion of hegemony. Gramsci posited that theory and practice are inextricably intertwined, and that principles drawn from an ideology are enacted and reproduced in daily practices so they become naturalized, a common sense. For neoliberalism to achieve hegemonic status would require, therefore, the widespread social acceptance of, and compliance with, recognizably neoliberal ideas, logics and expectations, as anticipated by neoliberal governmentality. Jackson Lears (1985) doubts that could be possible, since it would require ordinary people to agree with arrangements that are contrary to their own self-interest (which would be contrary to neoliberal thought). Still, Margaret Thatcher was an elected prime minister, so the possibility of acting contrary to self-interest needs explaining. Dean (2014: 154) usefully observes that neoliberalism is a 'doctrine of double truths', constructing one truth – about freedom, self-expression, self-reliance, and so on – for general public consumption; and another truth – about the means to expand capital at the expense of working people – for its privileged knowledge community. This duality enables authoritarianism to thrive in the name of freedom. Another plausible proposition is to assert a partial hegemony, whereby the penetration of neoliberal ideas and logics is limited to elites in business, government and social institutions.

Beyond hegemony, however, there are also instances where the different aspects of neoliberalism are rolled into a single, multifaceted, and multi-scalar 'explanatory repertoire' (Hilgers 2011: 361). Neoliberalism thus solidifies into an entity or power, becoming the driving causal force of major political, social and economic change, empowered to reach into all facets of governance and policy. When category mutates into power, its imagined affectivity blurs the boundaries between practices that are identifiably neoliberal and practices that are not recognizable as such. It is only a short step then for neoliberalism to become the totality, the major determinant of nearly everything. Needless to say, we are not impressed by such brave accounts of the world.

Conclusion: be wary of undifferentiated neoliberalism

The analysis of neoliberalism and its effects is important. But rather than treating neoliberalism as many undifferentiated things simultaneously, we aspire to clarity about what is being looked for and how it can be explained. The core of our argument is that we need to be wary of what sort of neoliberalism we are talking about and to be careful about shifting among meanings inadvertently. For example, carefully defining neoliberalism at the outset enabled Sheppard and Leitner (2010) to bring clarity to their subsequent evidence and argument. In many other cases, where the word is used without clear definition, we think that removing it from the analyses might help to produce more careful explanations. Following Sayer (1984), research targeting realities, like the spatial influences on the relationship between markets and monopolies, is more likely to create knowledge than research focused on stretching the boundaries of a construct.

Still, given the contemporary pervasiveness of this way of seeing the world, we think it worthwhile to ask if something is neoliberal or not. We should be arguing about which aspects of neoliberalism are influential at particular places and times, in what way, and why difference persists. As social researchers, we recognize that facts are laden with politics and with values that influence what evidence counts and how much it counts. That means we need to be more conscious of how we build descriptions, abstractions and generalizations about the observed world. We need to take differences across political territories seriously and into account, cognizant of the fact that ideologies or ways of governing cannot simply migrate, colonize and occupy. We need to recognize both the interdependence and independence of multiple forces, allowing the possibility of both mutually reinforcing tendencies and incontrovertible incompatibilities. We need to be open to possibilities: to appreciate that some times and places produce hybrids and mutant forms, or create completely new effects, but other times and places seem impervious to both the ideas and their practices. We need to spend more time studying these exceptions; they hold the clues to our liberation. We need to think more about the vast domains of human activity where neoliberalism remains largely irrelevant: where the idea's expansionary energy flags and expires.

We conclude by recognizing the relationship between research into neoliberalism and the propagation of disruptive political projects. But we baulk at the elevation of opposition to neoliberalism into an (the) object of protest, to its establishment as the enemy, as the thing we are fighting against, as the political project that overwhelms all others. Effective political activism must target actual events and occurrences that affect ordinary people's lives, and engage in ways that mobilize their interests, preferably in opposition to solid things that you can metaphorically throw a rock at, not imaginary things that defy definition. Even when ideas, processes and events are recognizably neoliberal, it may be more politically efficacious to afford them provisional status, to view them as trial-and-error experiments riven with contradictions, and to work at opening up their spaces in ways that create more desirable outcomes.

Acknowledgements

We thank the editors for their helpful comments. Phillip O'Neill would like to thank the Bartlett School of Planning at University College London for its generosity during the time this chapter was written.

References

Argent, N. 2014. The 'N' word: Australian Particularism, Taxonomies of Development and Epistemology. *Dialogues in Human Geography*, 4: 147–9.

Benediktsson, K. 2014. Nature in the 'Neoliberal Laboratory'. *Dialogues in Human Geography*, 4: 141–6.

Block, F., and Somers, M. 2014. *The Power of Market Fundamentalism*. Boston, MA: Harvard University Press.

Carroll, S. 2001. *The Western Dreaming*. Sydney: HarperCollins.

Castree, N. 2015. Geography and Global Change Science: Relationships Necessary, Absent, and Possible. *Geographical Research*, 53.1: 1–15.

Challies, E. 2014. Reining in Rascal Geographies of Neoliberalism in the Periphery? *Dialogues in Human Geography*, 4: 131–6.

Collier, S. 2012. Neoliberalism as Big Leviathan, or… ? A Response to Wacquant and Hilgers. *Social Anthropology/Anthropologie Sociale*, 20.2: 186–95.

—. 2014. *Second Thoughts on 'The Death of the Social?': Neoliberalism as Critique*. Retrieved from: http://www.stephenjcollier.com

—. 2015. *Neoliberalism*. Retrieved from: http://stephenjcollier.com/neoliberalism.htm

Dean, M. 2014. Rethinking Neoliberalism. *Journal of Sociology*, 50.2: 150–63.

Friedman, M., and Friedman, R. 1980. *Free to Choose*. New York: Harcourt.

Hart-Landsberg, M. 2006. Neoliberalism: Myths and Realities. *Monthly Review*, 57.11.

Harvey, D. 2005. *A Brief History of Neoliberalism*. Oxford: Oxford University Press.

Hayek, F. 1944. *The Road to Serfdom*. London: Routledge & Kegan Paul.

—. 1960. *The Constitution of Liberty*. Chicago: University of Chicago Press.

Hayter, R. 2014. Recognizing (Geographic) Limits/Alternatives to Neoliberalism. *Dialogues in Human Geography*, 4: 150–3.

Hilgers, M. 2011. The Three Anthropological Approaches of Neoliberalism. *International Social Science Journal*, 61: 351–64.

Jackson Lears, T.J. 1985. The Concept of Cultural Hegemony: Problems and Possibilities. *The American Historical Review*, 90: 567–93.

Larner, W. 2014. Heterogeneity of Neoliberalism and its Diverse Impacts. Paper presented at the UNRISD Conference New Directions in Social Policy: Alternatives from and for the Global South. Geneva, 7–8 April. Retrieved from: http://www.unrisd.org/publications.htm

Larner, W., and Craig, D. 2005. After Neoliberalism? Community Activism and Local Partnerships in Aotearoa New Zealand. *Antipode*, 37.3: 402–24.

O'Neill, P., and Weller, S. 2013. To What Extent has Australia's Development Trajectory been Neoliberalist? *Human Geography*, 6: 69–84.

Peck, J. 2006. Response: Countering Neoliberalism. *Urban Geography*, 27.8: 729–33.

—. 2011. Geographies of Policy from Transfer-Diffusion to Mobility-Mutation. *Progress in Human Geography*, 35.6: 773–97.

Peck, J., and Theodore, N. 2012. Reanimating Neoliberalism: Process Geographies of Neoliberalisation. *Social Anthropology*, 20.2: 177–85.

Peck, J., and Tickell, A. 2002. Neoliberalizing Space. *Antipode*, 34.3: 380–404.

Sayer, A. 1984. *Method in Social Science: A Realist Approach*. London: Hutchinson.

—. 1989. Postfordism in Question. *International Journal of Urban and Regional Research*, 13: 666–95.

Sheppard, E., and Leitner, H. 2010. Quo Vadis Neoliberalism? The Remaking of Global Capitalist Governance after the Washington Consensus. *Geoforum*, 41.2: 185–94.

Springer, S. 2015. Postneoliberalism? *Review of Radical Political Economics*, 47: 5–17.

Weiss, L. 2012. The Myth of the Neoliberal State, in Kyung-Sup, C., Weiss, L., and Fine, B., eds. *Developmental Politics in Transition: The Neoliberal Era and Beyond*. Basingstoke: Palgrave Macmillan: 27–41.

Weller, S., and O'Neill, P. 2014. An Argument with Neoliberalism: Australia's Place in a Global Imaginary. *Dialogues in Human Geography*, 4: 105–30.

8

NEOLIBERALISM, ACCOMPLISHED AND ONGOING

Stephanie L. Mudge

'Neoliberalism' is now a commonplace, if contentious, term in the human sciences. It generally refers to three phenomena. The first is an effort that began in the late 1930s of primarily intellectual elites to reconfigure and re-legitimate free market beliefs. Second, neoliberalism refers to a complex of political logics, calculative techniques, policies, and organizations that facilitated a remaking of social spheres in the image of markets. Third, neoliberalism refers to a global conjuncture in which the rise of post-Cold War American hegemony and the uncorking of international finance, along with the two aforementioned phenomena, changed the world as we knew it. In the first case, neoliberalism is a cultural project; in the second, it is a phenomenon of politics and government; in the last, it is a period in capitalist and geopolitical development. Like Keynesianism and socialism, neoliberalism qualifies as an 'ism' because it is irreducibly all of these things.

Every modern era is punctuated by political-economic crisis, and neoliberalism is no exception. Born of recessions, monetary turbulence, political unrest, and energy price shocks between the late 1960s and early 1970s, the neoliberal era reached its apogee around the turn of the twenty-first century. It then destabilized – or so some think – with the financial crisis of 2007–8. Whether the situation since signals a 'post-neoliberal' phase or neoliberalism's 'strange non-death' remains an open question (Brenner *et al.* 2010; Crouch 2011; Calhoun and Derlugian 2011; Comaroff 2011; Mirowski 2013). Regardless, there is work to be done.

This chapter assesses neoliberalism as a category and a social fact. A background motivation is to underline the continuing importance of the term itself. Because 'neoliberalism' is politically laden, some avoid it – but no satisfactory alternative exists. 'Globalization' lacks the attention to knowledge and ideology and, by extension, the critical edge that neoliberalism calls forth. 'Advanced capitalism' (or 'third-wave marketization'[1]) evokes concerns with class interests and modes of capital accumulation, but renders the neoliberal era merely the next phase of something always *en train*. 'Financialization' and 'American hegemony' refer to economic developments and geopolitical power arrangements (respectively) that are connected to, but not coterminous with, neoliberalism. 'Neo-conservatism' refers to only one side of the political spectrum, offering a partial view of the wholesale political transformation that neoliberalism entailed. In the end, none can fill neoliberalism's conceptual shoes.

Taking neoliberalism as a fuzzy and politicized, but as-yet *irreplaceable*, concept, this chapter also updates an earlier contribution on the topic (Mudge 2008). There, I attempted to conceptualize neoliberalism in a historically grounded way, without vacating its critical edge or placing arbitrary limits on it. Invoking the concept of field as a way of separating out neoliberalism's different faces, I also pointed out a tendency in early scholarship *not* to focus on its political expressions. Here I called for more attention to the left, and for a reflexive gaze on the relationship between politics and expertise.

In this chapter I update these themes and extend them in two ways: developing a brief historical genealogy of 'neoliberalism' as a category, and making the case for a relational, meso-level approach to studying it as a social fact. This discussion – which reflects my disciplinary location (American sociology) and focal areas of study (Western politics and expertise), which does not imply that mine is the best or only perspective from which neoliberalism can be understood – proceeds as follows. The second part tracks neoliberalism as a category and a social fact, concluding with a specific historical quandary: Western politics neoliberalized since the 1970s, and yet it is largely bereft of 'neoliberals'. In the third part I consider how to deal with the problem, revisiting my original conceptualization of neoliberalism and arguing for a field-theoretic approach that can accommodate first-person accounts. The fourth part briefly concludes.

Neoliberalism as a category and social fact

How 'neoliberalism' moved to the USA, to economics, and to the right

The meaning of 'neoliberalism' has changed significantly in the last few decades. Rooted in the Latin *liber* ('free man'), from the late 1700s 'liberal' was associated with an egalitarian, Western politics that tilted left, being linked with opposition to aristocratic and monarchical rule.[2] In the late 1800s, as socialist and workers' movements changed the political landscape and generalized demands for protection clashed with gold standard constraints, the term 'New Liberalism' emerged to denote British Liberal politicians' embrace of social reformism (Powell 1986). In the USA neither 'liberal' nor its variants had particular left–right associations in the late 1800s (Mudge unpublished manuscript), but liberalism then became 'left' with the rise of the Democratic Party's New Deal era labour–liberal faction (Disalvo 2010; Mudge forthcoming). Decades later, in the early 1980s, 'neo-liberal' then was re-born in the vernacular of the Democratic intelligentsia, referring to younger-generation critics of unreconstructed New Deal liberalism (Schlesinger 1980; Peters 1983; Farrell 1984; Kaus 1984). In all cases 'neoliberal' modified things and people on the left.

With the 1973 *coup d'état* of Augusto Pinochet in Chile, followed by the Thatcher government in Britain and Reagan presidency in the USA, 'neoliberalism' went right. Each of these figures were associated in some way with the Mont Pelerin Society (MPS, established 1947), which originated as a loose gathering of continental European, American and British intellectuals with shared worries about the fate of liberalism (Hartwell 1995; Mirowski and Plehwe 2009; Phillips-Fein 2009; Jones 2012; Burgin 2012; Bourne 2013). Over time the MPS and affiliates built organizational bases in professional economics, international networks of free market foundations and think tanks, and some branches of the legal profession, reaching into the political and intellectual life of many countries, and into the offices of international financial institutions (IFIs – especially the International Monetary Fund [IMF]), by the 1980s (Cockett 1994; Valdés 1995; Blyth 2001; Speth 2004; Mudge 2008; Teles 2008; Gross *et al*. 2011). With Friedrich Hayek, Milton Friedman, and other prominent economists in the lead, MPS members and associates were arguably the only real 'neoliberals' in today's sense of the term. Interpreting liberalism in a particular way that rendered free markets both the means and ends of good government (Foucault 1978–9[2008]), neoliberals counselled aggressive liberalizing, privatizing, monetarist, anti-union, and deregulatory policies. On the Western centre-lefts, meanwhile, 'neoliberalism' came to mean something roughly akin to going right by the 1990s, with special reference to the third-way agenda associated with the Clinton–Blair axis (Mudge 2011; Centeno and Cohen 2012). In Latin America 'neoliberalism' was closely linked with the US-backed, IMF-led imposition of structural adjustment reforms that were famously identified by the economist John Williamson (1990[2002]) as the 'Washington Consensus'.

'Neoliberalism' thence denoted a new brand of pro-market people, policies, and ways of thinking that were grounded in neoclassical economics, associated with the right, and linked with American hegemony. At the same time – no doubt in connection with anti-globalization protests (Brenner and Theodore 2002; Evans 2005) – its geographic range expanded: newspaper coverage moved from the USA towards Latin America and Europe in the 1990s, and to all regions of the world in the 2000s.[3] As for the social sciences, before the 1990s relatively few English-language works dealt with neoliberalism in its new sense; a handful of articles on German ordoliberalism (e.g. Friedrich 1955; Megay 1970) and Foucault's (1978–9[2008]) lectures on biopolitics at the Collège de France were rare exceptions. But neoliberalism scholarship took off from the 1990s, first in geography and then across the human sciences (in particular, anthropology and sociology).[4] By the early 2000s useful disciplinary overviews were easy to find (e.g. Harvey 2005[2009]; Peck 2011; Hilgers 2011 [*cf.* Wacquant 2012]; Centeno and Cohen 2012).

This does not mean that the social scientific disciplines have either converged on a shared definition of, or taken a uniform interest in, neoliberalism. What some call neoliberalism is globalization for others, with emphasis on the expansion of world trade and, with it, a less critical sense of uncontrollable forces 'out there'. Attention in economics has been particularly limited: after Joseph Stiglitz, a former World Bank vice-president and 2001 Nobel Prize winner in economics, published his remarkable critique of the IMF and its 'market fundamentalists' in *Globalization and its Discontents* (2002), the question of whether the 'age of Milton Friedman' – that is, what others would call the neoliberal era – was, on balance, good or bad became a matter of limited debate (e.g. Shleifer 2009). To date neoliberalism is not a mainstream topic in economics, appearing mainly in neo-Keynesian, institutionalist, and heterodox political economy journals.[5]

One interpretation is that – depending on whether heterodox economics, geography, sociology, and anthropology can be fairly characterized as more left than orthodox economics[6] – 'neoliberalism' became a category used by the left, referring to things on the right. This has its downsides: Evans and Sewell, Jr (2013: 36), for instance, comment on the 'strong left-leaning political inflection' of neoliberalism, 'used far more often by those who criticize the current economic order than by those who favor it' and 'all too often' used 'more as an epithet than as an analytically productive concept'. Hartwich (2009) argues that 'neoliberal' is rarely a label people apply to themselves.

This genealogy provides some sense of neoliberalism's distinctiveness as a social fact and the reasons for its contentiousness. As liberalism's mantle moved right and into the jurisdiction of economics from the 1970s, Keynesianism, socialism, and social democracy were more easily cast as defunct leftist ideologies. Neoliberalism scholarship was arguably an expression of this very marginalization. Defying Polanyi's (1944[2001]) assertion that market-making would call forth a double movement, decades of financialization and accelerating economic inequality prompted no cross-national resurgence of mainstream political opposition until after the 2007–8 financial crisis. As neoliberalism became a mainstream social scientific concept in the early 2000s, it thus named something at once familiar yet radically new.

Accomplished, and ongoing

Anyone who tries to explain neoliberalism to, say, a college student encounters problems of concision. Some simplify by giving neoliberalism actorhood: *it* seeks 'to dismantle or suppress extramarket forms of economic coordination'; *it* bears policies aimed at undoing redistributive taxation, deficit spending, exchange controls, and welfare provisions (Centeno and Cohen 2012: 318). For many students of neoliberalism (myself included) this usage is perfectly reasonable, but it can be confusing. The anthropologist John Comaroff, for instance, argues that the noun form incorrectly renders neoliberalism 'an accomplished object' (2011: 142).

Yet, in some respects, neoliberalism *is* accomplished – for instance, as the 'global ideological project' (in Comaroff's words (2011)) outlined above, and as a set of policies. The post-1970s, cross-national spread of liberalizing, market-making, and market-supporting policies is beyond doubt (Simmons *et al.* 2006; Henisz *et al.* 2005; Quinn and Toyoda 2007), not to mention the shift to inflation-control over unemployment-minimization, and to more independent central banks (Polillo and Guillén 2005). The interventions and mandates of IFIs played an important causal role here (Simmons *et al.* 2006). On the urban scale, the post-Fordist remaking of Western cities kicked off a series of very real reform projects that Neil Brenner and Nik Theodore (2002: 2) call 'actually existing neoliberalism'. Here the mid-1970s crisis and economic restructuring of New York City was a landmark event (Krinsky 2011; Harvey 2005[2009]).

Neoliberalism is also an important effect in itself, rooted not just in the thinking of a gaggle of intellectuals, but also in geopolitical conflict, economic crisis, and political struggle. Things started to unravel in the late 1960s, when the difficulties of managing exchange rates via Bretton Woods institutions intensified in a context of rapidly escalating American expenditures during the Vietnam War. This led to Nixon's 1971 decision (inevitable, some argue – although Nixon's adviser, the economist Arthur Burns, says otherwise (Ferrell 2010)) to break the link between gold and the dollar, ushering in a world of market-determined exchange rates.[7] Then came the Organization of the Petroleum Exporting Countries (OPEC) price shocks of 1973, also linked to American military engagements (specifically, its support for Israel during the Arab–Israeli war). The rise of new social movements, labour unrest, and the onset of 'stagflation' (in which inflation and unemployment rates accelerated apace) mobilized conservative opposition, called Keynesian management (and managers) into question, and unsettled existing governing coalitions.

Out of this emerged a whole new political-economic order, and a corresponding contraction of 'embedded liberalism' (Ruggie 1982). Among other things, the period witnessed the growing power of public and private financial institutions over domestic politics and governments. In Europe this was partly accomplished with the remaking of the European Union into a single market with a unified currency between 1985 and 1999, administered by the remarkably independent European Central Bank (ECB). A related phenomenon was the declining power of organized labour, not always in quantitative terms but certainly in terms of political strength (Ebbinghaus and Visser 1999; Howell 2001). Last, but not least, was the post-1970s proliferation of domestic policies that changed welfare provisioning and education systems by reducing benefits, strengthening income-contingency and work conditionality and introducing markets and market mechanisms into heretofore insulated spheres. In the USA especially, this was accompanied by a radical expansion of incarceration and punishment (Western 2007, Wacquant 2009).

And yet, this story is too tidy. Saying that neoliberalism was accomplished does not mean that 'neoliberals' did the accomplishing; that pre-existing institutional arrangements and cross-contextual variations were immaterial; or that neoliberalism took hold all of a sudden after 1971. Nor does it mean that we fully understand neoliberalism's origins, trajectories, and implications.

For instance, Aaron Major (2014) argues that neoliberalism has earlier roots than is commonly assumed: as governments relaxed restrictions on capital movements in the 1950s and 1960s, authority over money transnationalized and classical liberal orthodoxies took hold in financial and banking circles well *before* the neoliberal era. Johanna Bockman (2011) shows that neoliberal economics had definite socialist origins. In my research on left parties in Sweden, Germany, the USA, and Britain, I find that that relationships between professional economics, governments and centre-left political parties built between the 1930s and the 1960s conditioned neoliberalism's cross-national trajectories (Mudge forthcoming). Turning to the period since the 2007–8 financial crisis, others argue that neoliberal transformations are still very much unfolding, particularly in the form of social-psychological, community-level, and cultural effects (e.g. Hall and Lamont 2013). Neoliberalism's lasting imprint on states, cities, and geographical space (e.g. Peck 2001; Peck and Tickell 2002) remain important research frontiers. And last, but not least, there is the question of neoliberalism's imprint on politics.

Neoliberal politics

The neoliberal era was marked by a shift in political commonsense, in which free markets became the primary lever of good government (Babb 2004; Campbell and Pedersen 2001; Dezalay and Garth 2002; Fourcade-Gourinchas and Babb 2002; Massey *et al.* 2006; Mudge 2008). Elsewhere I have argued that this was a traceable, and consequential, shift in the self-presentation of mainstream parties across the Western political spectrum (Mudge 2011). It was not a simple shift to the right, but rather a wholesale collapse of familiar left–right distinctions, along with what some argue was a narrowing of the political field itself.

This changed political landscape featured a decline of partisan identities in rich democracies, a rise of professionalized politics divorced from grassroots publics, and the waning significance of partisan government as a predictor of macroeconomic policy choices (Boix 2000; Dalton and Wattenberg 2002; Fiorina 2002; Katz and Mair 1995, 2009). Recent scholarship on the USA documents a divorce between polarized partisan activists and a politically alienated general public (Baldassarri and Gelman 2008; Pacewicz 2015). With mainstream parties increasingly 'ruling the void', populist, anti-political and extreme politics returned to the West (Mair 2006).

The causal pathways here are not obvious. The post-1970s divorce of activist- and elite-dominated political parties from a demobilized general public – essentially, an electoral collapse in 'demand' – casts doubt on the possibility that changes in politics were driven by the preferences of the electorate. An alternative 'articulation' perspective, in which parties drive political identities and the formation of socio-political blocs (e.g. De Leon *et al.* 2015), is helpful, but only if the problematic is reversed: arguably neoliberal politics in Western democracies was more about *de*articulation than anything else.

Recent research on civic, urban and partisan political contention in the USA, and the situation of professionals and economic interests within it, makes important explanatory inroads (e.g. McQuarrie 2013; Walker 2014; Walker and Rea 2014; Pacewicz 2013a, 2013b; Laurison 2014; Lee 2015; Lee *et al.* 2015). Taking the study of professionalized politics in a new direction (Agranoff 1976; Sabato 1981; Swanson and Mancini 1996; Mayhew 1997; Thurber and Nelson 2000; Farrell *et al.* 2001; Grossman 2009), these works show how changes in federal policy, the rise of political consultants and participatory professionals, and transformations in civic culture have blurred the lines between civic action and profit-seeking, narrowed the focus of community advocacy to homeownership and property values, constrained authentic political engagement, and imposed structural limits on democratic contestation. They thus offer insight into neoliberal politics' institutional underpinnings, at least in the USA.

But there is a catch: these works are not about 'neoliberals', and some are only tangentially about neoliberalism. Do they really speak to something called neoliberal politics? I would argue that the answer is 'yes', but that understanding how and why requires dealing with the perennial problematic of studies of hegemony: consent.

Neoliberalism without neoliberals

More than half a century ago Antonio Gramsci pinpointed civil society as politics' key Western power base, since it was through civic institutions that political blocs built and sustained hegemony (Gramsci 1929–35[1971]). Western political authority involved an unthinking acceptance of the' rules', even by groups whose interests were not well served by the powers-that-be. In fact, the stability of a hegemonic order requires the willing participation of social actors who see themselves as either neutral about, or *actively opposed* to, that order.

Gramsci's insights are apt: many people with no particular connection to, awareness of, or overt sympathies with free market-touting elites have nonetheless participated in neoliberalizing projects (that is, they made the world look more like a market). What scholars call 'neoliberalism' is a cumulative effect of a whole series of struggles in settings in which the MPS is unknown, free markets are not at issue, and the category 'neoliberal' is meaningless. This makes the analytical task tricky, but no less necessary: few topics in the present-day historical social sciences weigh more heavily on the current conjuncture. How do we analyse neoliberalism, absent *neoliberals*? One answer can be found in the recent resurgence in relational and field-theoretic thinking in the social sciences.

Conceptualizing neoliberalism

In an earlier essay I argued that neoliberalism is built on a worldview in which markets are morally superior to politics and hierarchies (Mudge 2008). Here, I did not mean to argue that neoliberalism is analytically prior to interests, economic processes, international institutions, or anything else. Rather, I was asserting simply that neoliberalism is grounded in deeply held moral convictions about markets, and that there are historical figures – some powerful, some not – who think about things in this way (Fourcade and Healy 2007). This conceptualization is rooted in the venerable insight that, under certain conditions, worldviews have within them a capacity to make themselves true (Thomas and Thomas 1928; Merton 1948).

But neoliberalism's definition cannot stop there, devoid of history and context. There were institutions in place by the 1970s, and not before, that made neoliberalism 'neo'. Drawing from Bourdieu's language of field and the Weberian thinking behind it, I have thus argued for a historically and institutionally grounded definition of neoliberalism as:

> an ideological system that holds the 'market' sacred, born within the 'human' or social sciences and refined in a network of Anglo-American-centric knowledge producers, expressed in different ways within the institutions of the postwar nation-state and their political fields.
>
> *(Mudge 2008)*

On the one hand, this definition has affinities with a Polanyian view that takes neoliberalism's predecessor – the 'liberal creed' – as a semi-religious vision, borne by utopian intellectual and political prophets (Polanyi 1944[2001]; Mudge 2008: 12). On the other hand, it is also reconcilable with Foucault's argument that neoliberalism is not just old wine in new bottles.[8] But, most importantly, this definition aims to retain a notion of neoliberalism as a worldview while also keeping it historically grounded, separating its origins from worlds in which it found indirect expressions and elective affinities.

Behind this way of thinking is a whole set of orientations rooted in a meso-level, field-theoretic approach (Weber 1904[1949], 1915[1958]; Bourdieu 1990, 1991[1968], 1993; Martin 2003; Fligstein and McAdam 2012). Here 'field' is roughly analogous to a game: a bounded social space in which unequally resourced social actors are invested in shared stakes, but have limited control over the rules and cumulative effects of their actions. More than just jargon, the term imports an emphasis on thinking relationally as opposed to mechanistically, and a sensitivity to actors as strategic and reasonable, but not all-knowing and rational, players. It also imports cognizance of the connections between what actors do, how they see the world, and their positions *viz* one another, allowing for explanations that might make sense not just to social scientists, but also to the players themselves (Martin 2011).

To drive home the point, I will turn briefly to a particular instance of neoliberalism without neoliberals: that of John Williamson, the economist who, at most vaguely aware of this thing called 'neoliberalism', nonetheless helped to crystallize it with his famous articulation of the 'Washington Consensus'.

A partial application

The phrase 'Washington Consensus' originated in 1989 when Williamson, an economist at the Institute of International Economics (IIE), wrote an article in preparation for a small conference about government debt in Latin America. The article identified a list of commonsense reforms including fiscal discipline, the reorganization of public spending, and the liberalization of trade and finance (Williamson 1990[2002], 1993). All of them, so Williamson thought, were scientifically grounded, consensual policies that rightfully stood beyond partisan concerns (Williamson 1993: 1330; Williamson 2003: 10). But Williamson's article lent a new name to a set of policies that were increasingly targets of political protest, and soon found himself grouped among the 'neoliberals'.

Hardly the dogmatic free marketeer, bearer of capitalist interests, or right-wing conspirator that might, for some, be invoked by the label 'neoliberal', Williamson was, at the time, an accomplished mainstream economist, based at an officially nonpartisan think tank known for its Democrat-friendliness (Passell 1992). In keeping with the historical tendencies of the economics profession writ large, Williamson self-identified as 'left of center' (Williamson 1993: 1330; Williamson 2003). Once he looked into the MPS he explicitly distanced himself from it, characterizing it as 'a scholarly group founded after World War II to promote the most right-wing version of a liberal agenda' (Williamson 2003: 11). Unwillingly identified with neoliberalism, he later ruefully commented that he wrote his article 'never dreaming that I was coining a term that would become a war cry in ideological debates for more than a decade' (ibid.: 10).

What made it possible for an expert, doing what experts routinely do, to unwittingly play a significant role in the crystallization of a worldview that he himself disclaimed? An important part of the answer is that, by the time Williamson was putting pen to paper, professional economics had become a privileged point of entry into government and politics (Markoff and Montecinos 1993). To understand this, we have to consider the history of Keynesianism (not neoliberalism), and the position of economists in political and public life that it brought forth (Mudge forthcoming). By 1989 economics was globalized, internationalized (with hierarchies structured by, for instance, a Nobel Prize, quantification, and a convergence on English), and imbricated with politics and policy-making authority on the one hand, and with business and finance on the other (Coats 1986, 2000; Dezalay and Garth 2002; Fourcade 2006; Lebaron 2006; Barder 2013; Fourcade and Khurana 2013; Mudge 2015). This became especially clear in the Reagan and Thatcher years, by which time the profession was an important tool of justification and a site of political struggle unto itself. Economics' dual status in the post-1970s period – that is, as a political tool and a site of struggle – was itself an effect of its *pre*-1970s colonization of governments, political parties, research departments of organized labour, and international organizations, which made the profession a terrain worth fighting on, and over.

In short, by the 1990s figures like John Williamson were situated in a two-sited battle of which any particular player could not have been completely aware: political struggles in economics, and expert struggles in politics. A similar dynamic played out in many countries, but never in the same way: the economics–politics relationship in Germany, for instance, has featured an exceptional historical unpopularity of Keynesianism and strong ordoliberal alliance with the centre-right; in Sweden, meanwhile, professional economics has had a particularly tight relationship with social democratic policy-making (James 1989; Sandelin *et al.* 2000; Mudge forthcoming). Complicating things further, by the 1990s many economists in policy-making circles probably perceived, correctly, that their influence was increasingly mediated by think tank 'wonks' and political professionals.

In short, understanding how Williamson was central to neoliberalism's crystallization, and yet taken by surprise by the association, requires placing him not only in the geopolitical moment but also in his immediate national, political, and professional world. Perhaps, by doing things in this way, we could cultivate a broader analytical and historical conversation about neoliberalism.

Conclusions

The story of Williamson, like all stories about the neoliberal era, deserves a careful telling, lest we should fall back on accounts that are so simplistic as to be plainly wrong (e.g. 'neoliberal economists caused neoliberalism'). A final step – not taken here, but crucial nonetheless – is to get down to Williamson himself, situating him in time and place, and linking the historical and contextual factors just described with his particular trajectory. Such an approach would take us some way towards grasping neoliberalism, both accomplished and ongoing, as a cumulative effect of many kinds of field struggles.

Notes

1 This is Michael Burawoy's phrase (Harris 2013).
2 The birth of left and right, and the placement of liberal on that spectrum, was born of the spatial organization of the Estates General during the French Revolutionary period (Lipset 1960: 132).
3 Source: Lexis-Nexis search, world newspapers, for "neoliberal*" and variants, 3 July 2013.
4 A search in the *Web of Science* returns 126 articles on neoliberalism between 1990 and 1999, but 1,021 between 2000 and 2009. The single largest percentage (40%) was in geography.
5 A JSTOR search returns 127 articles in economics (from 925 journals) with the word 'neoliberal' or some variant in the title, in such journals as the *Review of African Political Economy*, *Review of International Political Economy*, the *Journal of Economic Issues*, *Challenge*, the *International Journal of Political Economy*, and *Economic Geography*.
6 On the politics of academics, see Gross *et al.* 2011; Gross 2013.
7 For a fascinating account, see Graeber 2011[2012]: 361–92.
8 In Foucault's words: '[n]eo-liberalism is not Adam Smith; neo-liberalism is not market society' (Foucault 1978–9[2008]: 131).

References

Agranoff, R. 1976. *The New Style in Election Campaigning?* 2nd edn. Boston: Halbrook.

Babb, S. 2004. *Managing Mexico: Economists from Nationalism to Neoliberalism.* Princeton, NJ: Princeton University Press.

Baldassarri, D., and Gelman, A. 2008. Partisans Without Constraint: Political Polarization and Trends in American Public Opinion. *American Journal of Sociology*, 114.2: 408–46.

Barder, A. 2013. American Hegemony Comes Home: The Chilean Laboratory and the Neoliberalization of the United States. *Alternatives: Global, Local, Political*, 38.2: 103–21.

Blyth, M. 2001. The Transformation of the Swedish Model: Economic Ideas, Distributional Conflict, and Institutional Change. *World Politics*, 54 October: 1–26.

Bockman, J. 2011. *Markets in the Name of Socialism: The Left-Wing Origins of Neoliberalism.* Stanford, CA: Stanford University Press.

Boix, C. 2000. Partisan Governments, the International Economy, and Macroeconomic Policies in Advanced Nations, 1960–93. *World Politics*, 53: 38–73.

Bourdieu, P. 1990. *In Other Words: Essays Towards a Reflexive Sociology.* Stanford, CA: Stanford University Press.

—. 1991[1968]. *The Craft of Sociology: Epistemological Preliminaries.* Berlin: Walter de Gruyter.

—. 1993. *The Logic of Practice.* Cambridge: Polity Press.

Bourne, R. 2013. *Lady Thatcher's Relationship with Friedrich Hayek and Milton Friedman.* Retrieved from www.pieria.co.uk

Brenner, N., and Theodore, N. eds. 2002. *Spaces of Neoliberalism: Urban Restructuring in North America and Western Europe.* Oxford: Blackwell.

Brenner, N., Peck, J., and Theodore, N. 2010. Variegated Neoliberalization: Geographies, Modalities, Pathways. *Global Networks*, 10.2: 182–222.

Burgin, A. 2012. *The Great Persuasion: Reinventing Free Markets since the Great Depression.* Cambridge, MA: Harvard University Press.

Calhoun, C., and Derlugian, G. 2011. *Aftermath: A New Global Economic Order.* New York: New York University Press.

Campbell, J., and Pedersen, O. eds. 2001. *The Rise of Neoliberalism and Institutional Analysis.* Princeton, NJ: Princeton University Press.

Centeno, M., and Cohen, J. 2012. The Arc of Neoliberalism. *Annual Review of Sociology*, 38: 317–40.

Coats, A.W. 1986. The Role of Economists in Government and International Agencies: A Fresh Look at the Field. *History of Economics Review*, 34 Summer: 19–32.

—. ed. 2000. *The Development of Economics in Western Europe Since 1945.* London: Routledge.

Cockett, R. 1994. *Thinking the Unthinkable: Think-Tanks and the Economic Counter-Revolution, 1931–1983.* London: HarperCollins.

Comaroff, J. 2011. The End of Neoliberalism? What is Left of the Left. *Annals of the American Academy of Political and Social Science*, 637.1: 141–7.

Crouch, C. 2011. *The Strange Non-Death of Neo-liberalism.* Cambridge: Polity Press.

Dalton, R.J., and Wattenberg, M.P. eds. 2002. *Parties Without Partisans: Political Change in Advanced Industrial Democracies.* Oxford: Oxford University Press.

De Leon, C., Desai, M., and Tu al, C. eds. 2015. *Building Blocs: How Parties Organize Society.* Stanford, CA: Stanford University Press.

Dezalay, Y., and Garth, B. 2002. *The Internationalization of Palace Wars: Lawyers, Economists, and the Contest to Transform Latin American States.* Chicago, IL: University of Chicago Press.

Disalvo, D. 2010. The Politics of a Party Faction: The Liberal–Labor Alliance in the Democratic Party, 1948–1972. *The Journal of Policy History*, 22.3: 269–99.

Ebbinghaus, B., and Visser, J. 1999. When Institutions Matter: Union Growth and Decline in Western Europe, 1950–1995. *European Sociological Review*, 15.2: 135–58.

Evans, P.B. 2005. Counter-Hegemonic Globalization: Transnational Social Movements in the Contemporary Global Political Economy, in Janoski, T., Alford, R., Hicks, A., and Schwartz, M.A., eds. *The Handbook of Political Sociology.* Cambridge: Cambridge University Press: 655–70.

Evans, P.B., and Sewell Jr, W.H. 2013. Neoliberalism: Policy Regimes, International Regimes, and Social Effects, in Hall, P., and Lamont, M., eds. *Social Resilience in the Neoliberal Era.* Cambridge: Cambridge University Press: 35–68.

Farrell, D.M., Kolodny, R., and Medvic, S. 2001. Parties and Campaign Professionals in a Digital Age: Political Consultants in the United States and their Counterparts Overseas. *International Journal of Press/Politics*, 6.4: 11–30.

Farrell, W. 1984. 'Neoliberals' in Need of Constituents. *The New York Times*, October: B8.

Ferrell, R.H. ed. 2010. *Inside the Nixon Administration: The Secret Diary of Arthur Burns, 1969–1974.* Lawrence: Kansas University Press.

Fiorina, M.P. 2002. Parties and Partisanship: A 40-year Retrospective. *Political Behavior*, 24: 93–115.

Fligstein, N., and McAdam, D. 2012. *A Theory of Fields*. Oxford: Oxford University Press.

Foucault, M. 1978–9[2008]. *The Birth of Biopolitics: Lectures at the Collège de France, 1978–1979.* New York: Palgrave Macmillan.

Fourcade, M. 2006. The Construction of a Global Profession: The Transnationalization of Economics. *American Journal of Sociology*, 112: 145–94.

Fourcade, M., and Healy, K. 2007. Moral Views of Market Society. *Annual Review of Sociology*, 33: 285–311.

Fourcade, M., and Khurana, R. 2013. From Social Control to Financial Economics: The Linked Ecologies of Economics and Business in Twentieth Century America. *Theory and Society*, 42: 121–59.

Fourcade-Gourinchas, M., and Babb, S. 2002. The Rebirth of the Liberal Creed: Paths to Neoliberalism in Four Countries. *American Journal of Sociology*, 108.3: 533–79.

Friedrich, C.J. 1955. The Political Thought of Neo-liberalism. *American Political Science Review*, 49: 509–25.

Graeber, D. 2011[2012]. *Debt: The First 5,000 Years*. Brooklyn: Melville House.

Gramsci, A. 1929–35[1971]. *Selections from the Prison Notebooks*. New York: International.

Gross, N. 2013. *Why are Professors Liberal and Why do Conservatives Care?* Cambridge, MA: Harvard University Press.

Gross, N., Medvetz, T., and Russell, R. 2011. The Contemporary American Conservative Movement. *Annual Review of Sociology*, 37: 325–54.

Grossmann, M. 2009. Going Pro? Political Campaign Consulting and the Professional Model. *Journal of Political Marketing*, 8.2: 81–104.

Hall, P., and Lamont, M. 2013. *Social Resilience in the Neoliberal Era*. Cambridge: Cambridge University Press.

Harris, K. 2013. *Michael Burawoy and Immanuel Wallerstein: Answering Crisis*. Retrieved from http://kevan-harris.princeton.edu/blog/2013/03/michael-burawoy-and-immanuel-wallerstein-answering-crisis

Hartwell, R.M. 1995. *A History of the Mont Pelerin Society*. Indianapolis: Liberty Fund.

Hartwich, O.M. 2009. Neoliberalism: The Genesis of a Political Swearword. *CIS Occasional Paper*, 114. Centre for Independent Studies.

Harvey, D. 2005[2009]. *A Brief History of Neoliberalism*. Oxford: Oxford University Press.

Henisz, W.J., Zelner, B.A., and Guillén, M.F. 2005. The Worldwide Diffusion of Market-Oriented Infrastructure Reform, 1977–1999. *American Sociological Review*, 70: 871–97.

Hilgers, M. 2011. The Three Anthropological Approaches to Neoliberalism. *International Social Science Journal*, 61.202: 351–64.

Howell, C. 2001. The End of the Relationship Between Social Democratic Parties and Trade Unions? *Studies in Political Economy*, 65: 7–37.

James, H. 1989. What is Keynesian about Deficit Financing? The Case of Interwar Germany, in Hall, P., ed. *The Political Power of Economic Ideas: Keynesianism Across Nations*. Princeton, NJ: Princeton University Press: 231–62.

Jones, D.S. 2012. *Masters of the Universe: Hayek, Friedman, and the Birth of Neoliberal Politics*. Princeton, NJ: Princeton University Press.

Katz, R.S., and Mair, P. 1995. Changing Models of Party Organization and Party Democracy: The Emergence of the Cartel Party. *Party Politics*, 1.1: 5–28.

—. 2009. The Cartel Party Thesis: A Restatement. *Perspectives on Politics*, 7.4: 753–66.

Kaus, M. 1984. Too Much Technology, Not Enough Soul: The Gospel According to Randall Rothenberg. *The Washington Monthly*, September: 48–54.

Krinsky, J. 2011. Neoliberal Times: Intersecting Temporalities and the Neoliberalization of New York City's Public-Sector Labor Relations. *Social Science History*, 35.3: 381–422.

Laurison, D. 2014. Positions and Position-Takings Among Political Producers: The Field of Political Consultants, in Grenfell, M., and Lebaron, F., eds. *Bourdieu and Data Analysis: Methodological Principles and Practice*. Bern: Peter Lang: 253–72.

Lebaron, F. 2006. 'Nobel' Economists as Public Intellectuals: The Circulation of Symbolic Capital. *International Journal of Contemporary Sociology*, 43.1: 87–101.

Lee, C. 2015. *Do-it-Yourself Democracy*. Oxford: Oxford University Press.

Lee, C., McQuarrie, M., and Walker, E. 2015. *Democratizing Inequalities: Dilemmas of the New Public Participation*. New York: New York University Press.

Lipset, S.M. 1960. *Political Man*. London: Heinemann.

Mair, P. 2006. Ruling the Void: The Hollowing of Western Democracy. *New Left Review*, 42 November–December: 25–51.

Major, A. 2014. *Architects of Austerity: International Finance and the Politics of Growth*. Stanford, CA: Stanford University Press.

Markoff, J., and Montecinos, V. 1993. The Ubiquitous Rise of Economists. *Journal of Public Policy*, 13.1: 37–68.

Martin, J.L. 2003. What is Field Theory? *American Journal of Sociology*, 109.1: 1–49.

—. 2011. *The Explanation of Social Action*. Oxford: Oxford University Press.

Massey, D.S., Sanchez, R.M., and Behrman, J.R. 2006. Of Myths and Markets. *The Annals of the American Academy of Political and Social Science*, 606: 8–31.

Mayhew, L.H. 1997. *The New Public: Professional Communication and the Means of Social Influence*. Cambridge: Cambridge University Press.

McQuarrie, M. 2013. Community Organizations in the Foreclosure Crisis: The Failure of Neoliberal Civil Society. *Politics and Society*, 41.1: 73–101.

Megay, E.N. 1970. Anti-Pluralist Liberalism: The German Neoliberals. *Political Science Quarterly*, 85.3: 422–42.

Merton, R.K. 1948. The Self-Fulfilling Prophecy. *The Antioch Review*, 8.2: 193–210.

Mirowski, P. 2013. *Never Let a Serious Crisis Go to Waste*. London: Verso.

Mirowski, P., and Plehwe, D. 2009. *The Road from Mont Pelerin: The Making of the Neoliberal Thought Collective*. Cambridge, MA: Harvard University Press.

Mudge, S.L. 2008. What is Neo-liberalism? *Socio-Economic Review*, 8: 703–31.

—. 2011. What's Left of Leftism? Neoliberal Politics in Western Party Systems, 1945–2006. *Social Science History*, 35.3: 337–79.

—. 2015. Explaining Political Tunnel Vision: Politics and Economics in Crisis-Ridden Europe, Then and Now. *European Journal of Sociology*, 56.1: 63–91.

—. Forthcoming. Reinventing Leftism. Cambridge, MA: Harvard University Press.

Pacewicz, J. 2013a. Tax Increment Financing, Economic Development Professionals and the Financialization of Urban Politics. *Socio-economic Review*, 11: 413–40.

—. 2013b. Regulatory Rescaling in Neoliberal Markets. *Social Problems*, 60.4: 433–56.

—. 2015. Playing the Neoliberal Game: Why Community Leaders Left Party Politics to Partisan Activists. *American Journal of Sociology*, 121, 3:826–81.

Passell, P. 1992. Economic Scene: More Advisers, Less Council? *The New York Times, Business Day*. Retrieved from http://www.nytimes.com/1992/12/17/business/economic-scene-more-advisers-less-council.html

Peck, J. 2001. Neoliberalizing States: Thin Policies/Hard Outcomes. *Progress in Human Geography*, 25: 445–55.

—. 2011. *Constructions of Neoliberal Reason*. Oxford: Oxford University Press.

Peck, J., and Tickell, A. 2002. Neoliberalizing Space. *Antipode*, 34: 380–404.

Peters, C. 1983. A Neoliberal's Manifesto. *Washington Monthly*, May: 8–18.

Phillips-Fein, K. 2009. *Invisible Hands: The Businessmen's Crusade Against the New Deal*. New York and London: Norton.

Polanyi, K. 1944[2001]. *The Great Transformation*. Boston, MA: Beacon Press.

Polillo, S., and Guillén, M.F. 2005. Globalization Pressures and the State: The Worldwide Spread of Central Bank Independence. *American Journal of Sociology*, 110.6: 1764–802.

Powell, D. 1986. The New Liberalism and the Rise of Labour, 1886–1906. *The Historical Journal*, 29.2: 369–93.

Quinn, D., and Toyoda, A.M. 2007. Ideology and Voter Preferences as Determinants of Financial Globalization. *American Journal of Political Science*, 51: 344–63.

Ruggie, J. 1982. International Regimes, Transactions, and Change: Embedded Liberalism in the Postwar Economic Order. *International Organization*, 36.2: 379–415.

Sabato, L.J. 1981. *The Rise of Political Consultants: New Ways of Winning Elections*. New York: Basic Books.

Sandelin, B., Sarafoglou, N., and Veiderpass, A. 2000. The Post-1945 Development of Economics and Economists in Sweden, in Coats, A.W., ed. *The Development of Economics in Western Europe Since 1945*. London: Routledge: 42–66.

Schlesinger, A. 1980. The End of an Era? *Wall Street Journal*, 20 November: 26.

Shleifer, A. 2009. The Age of Milton Friedman. *Journal of Economic Literature*, 47.1: 123–35.

Simmons, B.A., Dobbin, F., and Garrett, G. 2006. Introduction: The International Diffusion of Liberalism. *International Organization*, 60: 781–810.

Speth, R. 2004. *Die Politischen Strategien der Initiative Neue Soziale Marktwirtschaft*. Düsseldorf: Hans Böckler Stiftung.

Stiglitz, J.E. 2002. *Globalization and its Discontents*. New York: W.W. Norton and Co.

Swanson, D., and Mancini, P. 1996. *Politics, Media and Modern Democracy: An International Study of Innovations in Electoral Campaigning and their Consequences*. Westport: Praeger.

Teles, S. 2008. *The Rise of the Conservative Legal Movement: The Battle for Control of the Law*. Princeton, NJ: Princeton University Press.

Thomas, W.I., and Thomas, D.S. 1928. *The Child in America*. New York: Knopf.

Thurber, J.A., and Nelson, C. eds. 2000. *Campaign Warriors: Political Consultants in Elections*. Washington, DC: Brookings.

Valdés, J.G. 1995. *Pinochet's Economists: The Chicago School in Chile*. Cambridge: Cambridge University Press.

Wacquant, L. 2009. *Punishing the Poor: The Neoliberal Government of Social Insecurity*. Durham, NC: Duke University Press.

—. 2012. Three Steps to a Historical Anthropology of Actually Existing Neoliberalism. *Social Anthropology*, 20.1: 66–79.

Walker, E. 2014. *Grassroots for Hire: Public Affairs Consultants in American Democracy*. Cambridge: Cambridge University Press.

Walker, E., and Rea, C.M. 2014. The Political Mobilization of Firms and Industries. *Annual Review of Sociology*, 40: 281–304.

Weber, M. 1904[1949]. *The Methodology of the Social Sciences*. New York: Free Press.

—. 1915[1958]. Religious Rejections of the World and their Directions, in Gerth, H.H., and Mills, C.W., eds. *From Max Weber*. Oxford: Oxford University Press: 323–59.

Western, B. 2007. *Punishment and Inequality in America*. New York: Russell Sage.

Williamson, J. 1990[2002]. What Washington Means by Policy Reform, in Williamson, J., ed. *Latin American Adjustment: How Much Has Happened?* Washington, DC: Peterson Institute for International Economics.

—. 1993. Democracy and the 'Washington Consensus'. *World Development*, 21: 1329–36.

—. 2003. From Reform Agenda to Damaged Brand Name. *Finance and Development*, September: 10–13.

PART II

Political implications

PART II

Political Implications

9

NEOLIBERALISM AND AUTHORITARIANISM

Ian Bruff

Neoliberalism and authoritarianism have often been mentioned in the same breath. There are good reasons for this: one can think of the post-coup developments in Pinochet-era Chile, the attacks on national self-determination embodied in structural adjustment programmes for countries in sub-Saharan Africa, and the co-existence of 'free market' policies and strengthened security apparatuses in countries such as the USA and China. However, for the most part this connection between neoliberalism and authoritarianism has been articulated in problematic ways. Principally, neoliberalism's valorization of the 'free market' by way of an ostensibly anti-statist outlook continues to receive respect (implicitly or explicitly) in even critical literatures. In consequence, authoritarianism tends to be portrayed as an outcome of the contradictions between 'pure' neoliberal ideology and 'messy' neoliberalizing practices which result in a larger role for the state than anticipated.

Unfortunately, this misses the point of the neoliberal agenda, which *from the beginning* has been less interested in giving free rein to markets than in engineering and managing the markets that it wishes to see. Moreover, state-directed coercion insulated from democratic pressures is central to the creation and maintenance of this politico-economic order, defending it against impulses towards greater equality and democratization. Nevertheless, although neoliberalism, along with more classical strands of 'free market' thought, has always contained authoritarian tendencies, this has become significantly more prominent since the outbreak of global capitalist crisis in 2008. This has two consequences for our understanding of neoliberalism: refrain from offering implicit or explicit respect to its anti-statist rhetoric; and expand more traditional conceptualizations of authoritarianism in order to capture more appropriately contemporary processes. As I have argued elsewhere, 'one should not view 'authoritarianism' as merely the exercise of brute coercive force (for instance, policing of demonstrations, racist political rhetoric, etc.). Authoritarianism can also be observed in the reconfiguring of state and institutional power in an attempt to insulate certain policies and institutional practices from social and political dissent' (Bruff 2014: 115).

In order to illustrate most effectively this approach to neoliberalism, the chapter discusses the post-2008 and, especially, the post-2010 period in the European Union (EU), and particularly for the countries in the Eurozone. This is a useful exercise because, more than anywhere else in the world, Europe's self-image is that of a socially aware, more generous and more inclusive form of capitalism than in other world regions. The notion of 'social Europe' is a powerful trope which is regularly invoked to justify painful restructuring and austerity, yet a key contemporary aspect of these discourses is the argument that such forms of capitalism can survive only if 'social' institutions such as the welfare state prove able to adapt to change (for instance, through the growing emphasis on the responsibility of individuals to work rather than the collective entitlement to protection from socio-economic restructuring). Recent years have seen the dramatic intensification of neoliberalizing processes that were already taking place, bearing witness to the reconceptualization of the European state as increasingly non-democratic through its subordination to (often supranational) constitutional and legal rules that are portrayed as 'necessary' for prosperity to be achieved. This even extends to the deliberate violation of EU law by the very institutions charged with upholding it, as a means of removing the accountability of the institutions to the European and national parliaments. In addition, protests and resistance against such rules – rules that have in some cases led to drastic forms of austerity – have provoked growing levels of coercive response. These include the increasingly violent forms of policing against alleged 'extremists' in the anti-austerity camp in an attempt to prevent alternatives to neoliberalism from emerging, and most recently (writing in August 2015) the crushing of the Syriza programme and ignorance of the referendum against austerity in Greece.

Despite the highly pessimistic nature of this picture, I view authoritarian neoliberalism as a response both to wider capitalist crisis and more specific legitimation crises of capitalist states. Hence, the apparent strengthening of the state simultaneously entails its growing fragility, for it is becoming an increasingly direct target of a range of popular struggles, demands, and discontent by way of the pressures emanating from this strengthening. It should be kept in mind that, as with neoliberalism's authoritarian tendencies, examples of state strengthening/weakening are not confined to just the contemporary period. Nevertheless, there have been considerably more visible and significant crises of legitimation across a number of countries since 2008. As a result, the attempted 'authoritarian fix' is potentially more of a sticking plaster than anything more epochal. The question, then, is whether the contradictions inherent to authoritarian neoliberalism – especially with regard to the strengthening/weakening of the state – have created conditions in which progressive and radical politics can begin to reverse the tide of the last three decades.

The chapter is structured into three main parts, all elaborating upon the above comments. First, in line with the critiques of classical political economy articulated in Michael Perelman's *The Invention of Capitalism* (2000), I compare and contrast the underlying respect for neoliberalism's anti-statist rhetoric with the central focus of neoliberal ideology on the *reconceptualization* of the capitalist state towards a more coercive, anti-democratic social purpose. Second, I discuss the EU in order to demonstrate that, even in a world region which would theoretically be the most resistant to such a reconceptualization, the steady drum beat of neoliberalization has dramatically intensified since 2008, often via the explicit mobilization of juridical power to both constitutionalize austerity and selectively violate EU law. Third, I explore whether the increasingly coercive levels of response to protest and resistance against these developments – mirroring examples elsewhere in the world, which will also be commented on – have the potential to actually make it *more* and not less possible that new, more equitable modes of living can emerge and flourish. Finally, I conclude with reflections on the broader implications of my argument and suggestions for further research.

Neoliberalism: marketing the market, reconceptualizing the state

Neoliberalism's genesis during a period bearing witness to the growing role of social democracy, organized labour, welfare programmes, and so on, in capitalist political economies, means that its worldview has from the beginning covered all areas of social life. Hence Jamie Peck's argument that neoliberal ideology has always been 'preoccupied with the necessary evils of governmental rule' and 'framed by the distinctively post-laissez-faire question of appropriate forms and fields of state intervention in the socioeconomic sphere' (Peck 2008: 7). In consequence, the virtually innumerable aspects of social life that could, in an ideal world, be reformed in the name of the 'market' makes it relatively simple for neoliberalism to be rhetorically deployed against all manner of intellectual, political, and social enemies. As Peck (2010: 7–8) further notes, '[e]ven after decades of neoliberal reconstruction, it is remarkable how many present-day policy failures are still being tagged to intransigent unions, to invasive regulation, to inept bureaucrats, and to scare-mongering advocacy groups'.

This means that it is commonplace for a critique of neoliberalism to focus on the contradictions between 'pure' neoliberal ideology and 'messy' neoliberalizing practices, whereby the role for the state is larger than anticipated in neoliberal ideology due to the socio-historical conditions in which neoliberalism emerged and rose to prominence (in addition to Peck, see also Harvey 2005; Mirowski and Plehwe 2009; Cahill 2014). Examples include the enforcement of the neoliberal agenda through vigilance against 'distortions' of the market by groups such as trade unions, and the maintenance of 'law and order' in times of economic crisis and/or protests against a smaller economic and social role for the state. However, as argued by Martijn Konings (2010), there is an enduring tendency to view neoliberalism as fundamentally about the 'free market': the disembedding of the market from state and other forms of institutional regulation in the name of the mythical invisible hand. Hence, the neoliberal/neoliberalizing contradiction should only be the beginning and not the core of our critique.

Such an acknowledgement encourages us to take further steps, and ask whether the relentless focus on 'marketing the market' (Desai 1994: 48) has masked underlying philosophical commitments immanent to neoliberalism. To give one example, Friedrich Hayek, one of the key neoliberal intellectuals, argued in the 1970s that 'the political institutions prevailing in the Western world necessarily produce a drift [towards the destruction of the market] which can be halted or prevented only by changing these institution' (Hayek 1973: 9). Note here that Hayek is seeking to change rather than do away with the state, a point which he then elaborates on by attacking conceptions of democracy that are, in his view, incompatible with capitalism (ibid.). Yet many forms of democratic participation and governance would fall foul of this categorization, as shown by his subsequent argument that there is a need to restrict strongly the power of elected parliaments in favour of the creation of institutional safeguards. Such safeguards make it possible for the executive part of the state to coercively enforce obedience to general rules that are applicable to all:

> The root of the evil is thus the unlimited power of the legislature in modern democracies, a power which the majority will be constantly forced to use in a manner that most of its members may not desire. What we call the will of the majority is thus really an artifact of the existing institutions, and particularly of the omnipotence of the sovereign legislature, which by the mechanics of the political process will be driven to do things that most of its members do not really want, simply because there are no formal limits to its powers.
>
> *(Ibid.: 11; see also Hayek 1944, 1960)*

In other words, the conditions for neoliberal order are *not* realized through the unleashing of market forces alone, as per neoliberal rhetoric; nor is the state significant only in periods of transition towards the utopia of a market order, as per 'pragmatic' interpretations of this ideology. Instead, we should see the state as a *permanent* and *necessary* part of neoliberal ideology, institutionalization and practice. For it is state-directed coercion insulated from democratic pressures that is central to the creation and maintenance of a politico-economic order which actively defends itself against impulses towards greater equality and democratization (see also Klein 2007; Springer 2015).

None of this should come as a surprise when one considers the fact that this has always been a hallmark of so-called 'free market' worldviews. Michael Perelman (2007: 44) argues that although classical political economists such as Adam Smith and David Ricardo 'generally attempted to show [in their core theoretical writings] how market forces could benefit people… they understood that market society required strong measures in order to coerce large numbers of people to join the market revolution'. This often entailed their (sometimes private) support for widespread legal restrictions on self-provisioning in the countryside, especially regarding food, and for enclosures of the land which drove agricultural workers into factories and mills (Perelman 2000: 5–6). Such a position, which contradicted their more public and principled avowal of laissez-faire economics, was merely a continuation of early democratic theory, which declared a clear preference for the liberty of the owners of private property over the collective democratic rights of the populace as a whole. Hence depriving people of a means of living was justified on the grounds that the land should be owned and used by 'the industrious and rational… [not] the fancy or covetousness of the quarrelsome and contentious' (Locke 1947[1689]: 137).

This means that the classic early capitalist state, the British, did not live up to its image of a minimal, liberal set of institutions. Partly inspired by the interventions of classical political economists and political theorists on the need for enclosures and wage dependence to 'improve' the economy, the lot of the people and especially the lot of the poor, 'the taking of game [became] tantamount to challenging [private] property rights' (Perelman 2007: 52; see also Perelman 2000: 38–58). Indeed, poaching – that is, traditional self-provisioning for sustenance – was seen as such a serious crime 'that it was, on occasion, even equated with treason… several poachers were actually executed' (Perelman 2007: 52; see also Thompson 1977). As a result, Britain during the eighteenth and nineteenth centuries exhibited 'levels of state violence that would have been unthinkable' in countries such as Prussia, one of the traditional examples cited of an 'authoritarian', non-democratic transition to capitalism (Clark 2007: 465). Clark notes that 'the number of persons executed… exceeded the Prussian figure by a factor of sixteen-to-one' in the 1816–35 period, taking differences in overall population into account (ibid.: 466). Moreover, 'the great majority of English and Welsh capital sentences were passed for property crimes (including quite minor ones)' (ibid.), which would have included offences such as stealing farm animals from enclosed land as well as attacks on property by desperate, starving people (see also Thompson 1977, 1991).

Therefore, if we can find little evidence during the so-called 'classical' era of capitalist development and politico-economic thought of a 'free market' in theory or in practice, then why should this be the case in more modern times? (See also Bruff 2011a, 2011b.) Furthermore, if there is plenty of evidence during this period of authoritarian state practices in the dedicated pursuit of liberty for the owners of private property at the expense of the collective democratic rights of the populace as a whole, then why should neoliberalism not also be fully supportive of such practices today?

'Social Europe' and the post-2008 rise of authoritarian neoliberalism

As noted in the introduction, it is a useful exercise to focus on the EU when discussing neoliberalism and authoritarianism because, more than anywhere else in the world, Europe's self-image is that of a socially aware, more generous and more inclusive form of capitalism than in other world regions. Principally, three features are generally held to have distinguished Western Europe after 1945 from other middle- to high-income capitalist countries (see Albert 1993; Hay *et al.* 1999; Esping-Andersen 1990). These are relatively low levels of socio-economic inequality, generous welfare states and a significant role for organized labour in the workplace and in policy-making – all of which were underpinned by a supportive political consensus that gave a prominent role to 'non-market' institutions in the political economy. Of course, this varied across different countries, but Western European political economies appeared after 1945 to combine economic success and social cohesion in a way not observed in other 'developed' parts of the world. This unity in diversity increasingly became, with the ongoing broadening and deepening of the European integration project, a point around which a wide range of social and political actors and opinions could rally, not least with the rise of discourses on 'globalization' in the 1990s. During this decade, the idea of a pan-European social model (i.e. inclusive of post-socialist states) was so prominent that it became a dominant trope when talking about political economy issues (Jepsen and Pascual 2005; European Commission 1994; Vaughan-Whitehead 2003).

Nevertheless, despite the attachment to 'social Europe', Europe has in reality been neoliberalizing *through*, not against, 'social' institutions of governance since the 1980s. One could observe, even before 2008: the growing use of collective bargaining negotiations to explicitly discipline labour rather than treat unions as an equal partner; increased welfare retrenchment and the broader shift from welfare to workfare; and the decline of 'catch-all' political parties and the rise of narrower social and political coalitions (sometimes in tandem with a resurgent far-Right) (Bruff 2014; see also Bruff 2015 on Germany, the proclaimed 'model' for other countries to emulate). Furthermore, the growing importance of the EU has tended to reinforce these developments, with initiatives such as the Single Market, Economic and Monetary Union (EMU) plus the Lisbon Agenda promoting social cohesion only insofar as it is 'defined in terms of the adaptation of labour to the exigencies of global competition' (van Apeldoorn and Hager 2010: 227).

This all laid the foundations for the rise of a distinctly European form of authoritarian neoliberalism after 2008. I have argued elsewhere that the rise of authoritarian neoliberalism is centred on a three-fold reconfiguring of state and institutional power:

> (1) the more immediate appeal to material circumstances as a reason for the state being unable, despite 'the best will in the world', to reverse processes such as greater socio-economic inequality and dislocation; (2) the deeper and longer-term recalibration of the kinds of activity that are feasible and appropriate for nonmarket institutions to engage in, diminishing expectations in the process; and (3) the reconceptualization of the state as increasingly nondemocratic through its subordination to constitutional and legal rules that are deemed necessary for prosperity to be achieved.
>
> *(Bruff 2014: 115–16)*

While such developments can be observed across the world, the most compelling example of this shift can be found in the EU because of Europe's aforementioned self-image. For example, in the late 2000s European and especially German elites were vocal in their criticisms of 'Anglo-Saxon' capitalism, which, via the implosion of the American sub-prime market and the violent chain reaction culminating in the massive global crisis in late 2008, was portrayed as promoting excesses that would not be permitted by the more socially responsible European capitalisms. However, the large fiscal deficits created across Europe by the massive bailouts and recapitalizations of numerous financial institutions, plus the sharp falls in GDP in 2008–9, were portrayed as a clear sign that European states had been living beyond their means.

This built on the dominant argument, both politically and academically, in the 1990s and especially the 2000s: 'social Europe' could continue to exist, but only if 'social' institutions proved able to adapt to change (*cf.* Blair and Schröder 1999; Sapir 2006; Kitschelt and Streeck 2004; Ferrera *et al.* 2001). By and large, labour market flexibilization, welfare retrenchment, and the reduction of trade union power were viewed as central to any successful adaptation. As a result, the curious case of cognitive dissonance from before 2008 – laud the superiority of 'social' models of capitalism while simultaneously seeking to dilute precisely these 'social' elements – continued in increasingly strident forms after 2008. This means that, even today (August 2015), it is still asserted by those responsible for promoting and imposing drastic neoliberalizing changes that a type of capitalism distinctive from the Anglo-Saxons is the goal. The catch is that the overwhelming focus has been on ensuring that the relevant 'social' institutions and policies are reformed 'appropriately'.

The acceleration and intensification of neoliberalizing processes can be divided into two main components: the content of the proposed reforms; and the means by which the reforms are implemented and enforced. On the content, the thrust is towards: often drastic austerity in the rush towards balanced budgets and possibly even fiscal surpluses, primarily through the reduction in the size of the welfare state and the public sector; the significant loosening of labour market regulations to promote the growth of atypical employment – that is, not of full-time and/or permanent jobs; and reductions in unit labour costs in the name of greater 'competitive-ness', achieved primarily through austerity, atypical jobs, but also legally mandated wage freezes or reductions. None of this could be said to reflect the values embodied in traditional notions of 'social Europe'. Moreover, the disastrous economic performance in the Eurozone since 2008 – by 2014, EU GDP was no higher than the pre-recession peak (EuroMemo Group 2015: 8) – means that one cannot argue that the changes have 'worked' even when assessed against a narrow set of criteria for 'success'.

For both of these reasons – the abandonment of traditional notions of 'social Europe' and the invisibility of any benefits to wider society accruing from the measures – the task of gaining societal consent for such changes has been and is likely to be, at best, only partially successful. Hence the widespread development of (supra)national constitutional and legal mechanisms since 2008 to impose these changes and also restrict significantly the scope for future generations to overturn them. This emerged initially in Germany, which only months after the collapse of Lehman Brothers passed a constitutional amendment mandating the achievement of a balanced budget from 2016 onwards (in the name of avoiding Anglo-Saxon excess, of course). Following on from this, in the aftermath of the Greek crisis in 2010 a whole raft of measures were proposed and agreed on at the EU level. These new 'economic governance' regulations seek to construct a permanent, continent-wide conditionality regime that is aimed at all states, regardless of their economic performance. In contrast to 'traditional' structural adjustment programmes in Africa, Latin America and Asia (where some of the connections between neoliberalism and authoritari-anism were made prior to 2008), which were reactively imposed on specific crisis-hit countries, in the EU the attempt is to *pre-emptively self-impose* such measures.

There is not the space here to investigate the specificities of the different agreements, pacts and treaties – such as the Euro Plus Pact, the Six-Pack, the Two-Pack, and the Treaty on Stabil-ity, Coordination and Governance – and I direct interested readers to the outstanding work of Lukas Oberndorfer on the various legal provisions (Oberndorfer 2012, 2014, 2015). Neverthe-less, five points can be made. First, the aim of EU economic governance is, in the words of the European Commission, to 'detect, prevent, and correct problematic economic trends'.[1] Second, problematic economic trends are defined primarily in terms of 'excessive' budget deficits and 'high' unit labour costs that must be reduced in the name of competitiveness. Third, the executive authority of the European Commission has been strengthened to not only monitor closely member states, but also propose/impose sanctions on them such as fines of up to 0.2 per cent of GDP.

Fourth, the 'Reverse Majority Rule' states that Commission proposals are accepted as valid if they are not prevented within ten days by the European Council's veto with a simple majority, and member states are expected to respond to Commission suggestions for budget consolidation (which overwhelmingly focus on austerity measures) before their respective national parliament is consulted. Fifth, as noted by Oberndorfer and other critical legal scholars, many of these changes are in violation of EU law. Examples include the very limited consultative role for the European Parliament in the new regime, despite its oversight function ('co-decision') in the EU's institutional architecture, and the illegality of the 'Reverse Majority Rule'. I will return to this point below.

Finally for this section, the EU's economic governance regime is implemented via the European Semester, which is organized according to an annual cycle. The European Semester is also the declared institutional mechanism for promoting 'social Europe' as part of the 'Europe 2020' agenda. In other words, despite all of the above – the drastic changes required and the anti-democratic violation of EU law that their implementation entails – the EU is still claiming to uphold the values embodied in the notion of 'social Europe'. For instance, even in the highly punitive Euro Summit 'agreement' of 2015 (more details below), it is asserted that Greek labour market policies should be 'in line with the relevant EU directive... along the timetable and the approach agreed with [IB: read 'imposed by'] the Institutions [the European Commission, the European Central Bank, and the International Monetary Fund]... with the goals of promoting sustainable and *inclusive* growth' (Euro Summit 2015: 3; emphasis added). The question, then, is what can be done in response to both increasingly authoritarian modes of governance and the ongoing attempts to cloak such developments with legitimizing tropes such as 'social Europe'.

The fragility of the 'authoritarian fix'

Lukas Oberndorfer (2015) argues that whereas before 2008 neoliberalization proceeded primarily via an erosion of *substantive* democracy, since 2008 we have seen various breaks with *formal* democracy. Hence, the scope of neoliberalization has widened from the reversal of social and economic gains made during the twentieth century, via the presentation by neoliberals in the late twentieth and early twenty-first centuries of *alternatives* to the current mode of governance at elections and through other forms of political participation, to *alternations* of different neoliberal governments as the only choice seemingly on offer (for a prescient discussion, see Poulantzas 1978: 231–40). But it is this apparent strengthening of capitalist state formations which leaves them as more fragile and delegitimated entities, by way of the more visible role for coercion in both the legal and repressive senses and the relative absence of material benefits for the majority of the population.

This sheds light on the aforementioned Euro Summit 'agreement' of 12 July 2015. Here, despite the election of the anti-austerity Syriza government in Greece in January 2015, and the resounding Greek referendum result in June 2015 against further rounds of austerity and neo-liberalization, the European institutions imposed perhaps the harshest terms yet on the Greek population since 2010 (see Euro Summit 2015 for details). The measures were preceded by a dramatic development in the role of the Eurogroup of finance ministers for the Eurozone countries, which is responsible for managing EMU affairs outside the monetary policy controlled by the legally independent European Central Bank (ECB). On the one hand, numerous ministers led by Germany's Wolfgang Schäuble openly supported Greece's ejection from the Eurozone; on the other, a remarkable legal somersault was performed. As noted earlier, many aspects of the new EU regime are in violation of EU law – meaning that various declarations after January 2015 that European law prevented Greece from revisiting earlier bailout terms were rather ironic. But this acquired a farcical dimension in late June 2015, when Greek finance minister Yanis Varoufakis was expelled from the Eurogroup meeting because his presence would make a unanimous agreement on Greece impossible. When he queried this, the justification was that the Eurogroup does not exist in European law as it is an informal group and thus is not bound by any legal statutes or regulations (Lambert 2015). As such, the Eurogroup possesses highly significant legal powers when it suits the European institutions (potentially forcing a 'Grexit'), and it does not exist when it suits the European institutions (when the basis for a 'Grexit' is challenged). Conveniently forgotten in all of this is the formal legal basis for the Eurogroup, as mandated by the 2009 Lisbon Treaty.

This is merely the most recent example of the increasingly flagrant breaches of formal democratic procedures and rights one can observe around the world. Take, for instance, the 'gag' laws introduced in Spain in summer 2015, which significantly restrict and to a degree criminalize the freedom of assembly and protest. This includes being disrespectful to police officers and trying to prevent an eviction from taking place, i.e. far removed from more traditional notions of 'public disorder' (see also, for a similar set of legal provisions and restrictions, Canada's C51 Bill passed in 2015). In addition, consider the routine practices of police violence and the illegal mobilizations of juridical power across the globe, be it the repression of the Occupy movement in the US in 2011, the massacre of striking miners in South Africa in 2012, or the violent crackdown on the Gezi Park protests in Turkey in 2013. Consider also how the protests, strikes and resistances have been framed: as an 'extremist' attack on 'democracy', thus justifying the coercive reaction. Hence my argument that one should not view 'authoritarianism' as merely the exercise of brute coercive force: it can also be observed in the reconfiguring of state and institutional power in an attempt to insulate certain policies and institutional practices from social and political dissent.

Nevertheless, despite the highly pessimistic nature of this picture, we must always keep in mind that authoritarian responses to capitalist crises are 'partially responsible for new forms of popular struggle' which seek to create and live in a different kind of world to the one being imposed on them (Poulantzas 1978: 246). In other words, the capitalist state is currently evolving into a stronger and more authoritarian but also a more fragile and delegitimated entity. As a result, the attempted 'authoritarian fix' is potentially more of a sticking plaster than anything more epochal. The question, then, is whether the contradictions inherent to authoritarian neoliberalism – especially with regard to the strengthening/weakening of the state – have created conditions in which progressive and radical politics can begin to reverse the tide of the last three decades.

As in the past (for example, the 1918–39 period), the current conjuncture has ambiguous implications for radical/progressive politics of the Left, not least because of the success of radical Right movements and parties in narrating the post-2008 period for rather different political ends. In Europe, one can find examples across the continent, be it the FN in France, the PVV in the Netherlands or Golden Dawn in Greece. However, one can find more positive examples, too. These include the widespread growth of self-organization in countries hit hardest by crisis and crisis response – for instance, the formation of citizen health centres and community kitchens in Greece and the creation of the Spanish *Plataforma de Afectados por la Hipoteca* (Platform of Those Affected by Mortgage Debt, PAH) to fight against widespread evictions and promote housing as a human right. Furthermore, there has been the delegitimation of large parts of the political establishment in some countries, opening up space for the growth of parties of the Left (such as Sinn Fein in Ireland and Syriza in Greece) which reject the neoliberalized social democracy of the traditional party (the latter arguably being the case even after the August 2015 formation of the Popular Unity party, created by Syriza opponents of the party leadership's strategy since entering office, in advance of the national election on 20 September 2015). And, finally, even if this appears an optimistic spin on the Euro Summit 'agreement' of July 2015, the protracted negotiations after the election of the Syriza government opened real splits in the pro-austerity camp in Europe and also between the European institutions and the International Monetary Fund, with the latter admitting belatedly that the shock therapy of the last five years has not worked and that a programme of debt relief for Greece is now needed (the likelihood of which is now growing).

These developments are significant, because all of them – the rise of self-organized communities, the emergence of new parties of the Left, the growing splits in the pro-austerity camp – challenge ingrained assumptions about the state, the law, and 'social' values. 'Left' politics has frequently been guilty of taking the law and 'social' institutions in capitalism to be somehow neutral, ignoring in the process how 'non-market' social forms have often been central to, not resistant against, the rise of neoliberalism. The approach I have put forward in this chapter alerts us in a more expansive way to how inequalities of power are produced and reproduced in capitalist societies, which in turn enables us to consider how other, more emancipatory and progressive, worlds are possible through this enhanced awareness. More to the point, it helps bring to the forefront an emancipatory anti-statism that is both at a distance from the state and potentially transformative of it through new forms of democratic struggle.

Certainly, while the current conjuncture can look bleak, it has confirmed three things: talk of the 'free market' no longer masks the centrality of the state to the (re)production of massive inequalities; rhetoric about 'social' values is hollow when it is accompanied by the erosion of precisely such values; and the defence of authoritarianism with recourse to the language of economic necessity often indicates a violation of formal and substantive rights. We cannot say that we were oblivious, not least because there are plenty of examples of protest and resistance that explicitly recognize what the state of play is.

Conclusion

This chapter has argued that, unlike many understandings of neoliberalism, and 'free market' thought more generally, the state is central to such understandings and their implementation in practice. Neoliberalism is fundamentally about the creation and management of markets that it wishes to see, meaning that the state has a permanent and necessary role to play in this process. Moreover, present-day Europe is an excellent example of the rise of authoritarian neoliberalism, whereby the response to capitalist crisis has facilitated a substantial investment of state and juridical power in the intensification of the attack on formal and substantive rights. Finally, the belated recognition that the state is imbricated in and not protective of neoliberal practices might, in the longer-term, create more propitious conditions for the emergence of new, more equitable modes of living which are the outcome of the rethinking of traditional assumptions about the role of the 'non-market' in capitalism.

Inevitably, there are still under-explored areas surrounding the relationship between neoliberalism and authoritarianism that future research could explore (although see Tansel 2016). They include a serious examination of 'classical' neoliberal writings regarding the role of the state, which goes beyond the otherwise laudable efforts of Peck and others to expose the contradictions between neoliberal thought and practice. Moreover, a much more sustained engagement with feminist work on social reproduction, the household and the gendered effects of austerity is needed for a richer picture to be constructed of the pernicious impacts of authoritarian neoliberalism and the transformative possibilities this potentially entails – that is, beyond the 'public' sites of capitalist society such as the state (although see Bruff and Wöhl 2016). Finally, the notion of the 'non-market' should be developed further to encompass more fully the multi-faceted aspects of life, which form part of neoliberal society today and could also form the basis for an alternative society in the future (see White and Williams this volume). There are surely more areas, too, but, whatever they are, it is essential that they take seriously the need to reject out of hand the notion that neoliberalism has anything to do with the 'free market' or with democracy.

Note

1 See European Commission [webpage] (n.d) for more information.

References

Albert, M. 1993. *Capitalism Against Capitalism*. Haviland, P., trans. London: Whurr.

Blair, T., and Schröder, G. 1999. *Europe: The Third Way/Die Neue Mitte*. London and Berlin: Labour Party/ Sozialdemokratische Partei Deutschlands.

Bruff, I. 2011a. Overcoming the State/Market Dichotomy, in Shields, S., Bruff, I. and Macartney, H., eds. *Critical International Political Economy: Dialogue, Debate and Dissensus*. Basingstoke: Palgrave Macmillan: 80–98.

—. 2011b. What About the Elephant in the Room? Varieties of Capitalism, Varieties in Capitalism. *New Political Economy*, 16.4: 481–500.

—. 2014. The Rise of Authoritarian Neoliberalism. *Rethinking Marxism*, 26.1: 113–29.

—. 2015. Germany and the Crisis: Steady as She Goes? In Westra, R., Badeen, D., and Albritton, R., eds. *The Future of Capitalism After the Financial Crisis: The Varieties of Capitalism Debate in the Age of Austerity*. Abingdon: Routledge: 114–31.

Bruff, I., and Wöhl, S. 2016. Constitutionalizing Austerity, Disciplining the Household: Masculine Norms of Competitiveness and the Crisis of Social Reproduction in the Eurozone, in True, J., and Hozic, A., eds. *Scandalous Economics: Gender and the Politics of Financial Crises*. Oxford: Oxford University Press.

Cahill, D. 2014. *The End of Laissez-Faire? On the Durability of Embedded Neoliberalism*. Cheltenham: Edward Elgar.

Clark, C. 2007. *Iron Kingdom: The Rise and Downfall of Prussia, 1600–1947*. London: Penguin.

Desai, R. 1994. Second-hand Dealers in Ideas: Think-tanks and Thatcherite Hegemony. *New Left Review*, 1.203: 27–64.

Esping-Andersen, G. 1990. *The Three Worlds of Welfare Capitalism*. Princeton, NJ: Princeton University Press.

EuroMemo Group. 2015. *EuroMemorandum 2015: What Future for the European Union – Stagnation and Polarisation or New Foundations?* Retrieved from http://www.euromemo.eu/euromemorandum/ euromemorandum_2015/

European Commission. 1994. *European Social Policy: A Way Forward for the Union*. Brussels: European Commission.

European Commission [webpage]. n.d. EU Economic Governance. Retrieved from http://ec.europa.eu/ economy_finance/economic_governance/index_en.htm

Euro Summit. 2015. *Euro Summit Statement*, 12 July. Brussels: European Union.

Ferrera, M., Hemerijck, A. and Rhodes. M. 2001. The future of the 'European social model' in the global economy. *Journal of Comparative Policy Analysis*, 3.2: 163–90.

Harvey, D. 2005. *A Brief History of Neoliberalism*. Oxford: Oxford University Press.

Hay, C., Watson, M., and Wincott, D. 1999. Globalisation, European Integration and the Persistence of European Social Models. *Working Paper 3/99*. Birmingham: ESRC One Europe or Several Research Programme.

Hayek, F.A. 1944. *The Road to Serfdom*. Chicago, IL: University of Chicago Press.

—. 1960. *The Constitution of Liberty*. London: Routledge & Kegan Paul.

—. 1973. Economic Freedom and Representative Government. *Institute of Economic Affairs*, Fourth Wincott Memorial Lecture, Occasional Papers no. 39.

Jepsen, M., and Pascual, A.S. 2005. The European Social Model: An Exercise in Deconstruction. *Journal of European Social Policy*, 15.3: 231–45.

Kitschelt, H., and Streeck, W. eds. 2004. *Germany: Beyond the Stable State*. London: Frank Cass.

Klein, N. 2007. *The Shock Doctrine: The Rise of Disaster Capitalism*. New York: Picador.

Konings, M. 2010. Neoliberalism and the American State. *Critical Sociology*, 36.5: 741–65.

Lambert, H. 2015. Yanis Varoufakis Full Transcript: Our Battle to Save Greece. *New Statesman*, 13 July. Retrieved from http://www.newstatesman.com/world-affairs/2015/07/yanis-varoufakis-full-transcript-our-battle-save-greece

Locke, J. 1947[1689]. *Two Treatises of Government*. Cook, T.I, ed. New York: Hafner Press.

Mirowski, P., and Plehwe, D. eds. 2009. *The Road from Mont Pelerin: The Making of the Neoliberal Thought Collective*. Cambridge, MA: Harvard University Press.

Oberndorfer, L. 2012. Hegemoniekrise in Europa – Auf dem Weg zu Einem Autoritären Wettbewerbsetatismus? In Forschungsgruppe 'Staatsprojekt Europa', eds. *Die EU in der Krise: Zwischen Autoritärem Etatismus und Europäische Frühling*. Münster: Westfälisches Dampfboot: 49–71.

—. 2014. A New Economic Governance Through Secondary Legislation? Analysis and Constitutional Assessment: From New Constitutionalism, via Authoritarian Constitutionalism to Progressive Constitutionalism, in Bruun, N., Lörcher, K., and Schömann, I., eds. *The Economic and Financial Crisis and Collective Labour Law in Europe*. Cheltenham: Edward Elgar: 25–54.

—. 2015. From New Constitutionalism to Authoritarian Constitutionalism: New Economic Governance and the State of European Democracy, in Jäger, J., and Springler, E., eds. *Asymmetric Governance and Possible Futures: Critical Political Economy and Post-Keynesian Perspectives*. Abingdon: Routledge: 186–207.

Peck, J. 2008. Remaking Laissez-faire. *Progress in Human Geography*, 32.1: 3–43.

—. 2010. *Constructions of Neoliberal Reason*. Oxford: Oxford University Press.

Perelman, M. 2000. *The Invention of Capitalism: Classical Political Economy and the Secret History of Primitive Accumulation*. Durham, NC, and London: Duke University Press.

—. 2007. Primitive Accumulation from Feudalism to Neoliberalism. *Capitalism Nature Socialism*, 18.2: 44–61.

Poulantzas, N. 1978. *State, Power, Socialism*. Camiller, P., trans. London: New Left Books.

Sapir, A. 2006. Globalization and the Reform of European Social Models. *Journal of Common Market Studies*, 44.2: 369–90.

Springer, S. 2015. *Violent Neoliberalism: Development, Discourse, and Dispossession in Cambodia*. New York: Palgrave Macmillan.

Tansel, C.B. ed. 2016. *States of Discipline: Authoritarian Neoliberalism and the Crises of Capitalism*. London: Rowman & Littlefield International.

Thompson, E.P. 1977. *Whigs and Hunters: The Origin of the Black Act*. revised edn. London: Penguin.

—. 1991. *Customs in Common*. London: Merlin Press.

van Apeldoorn, B., and Hager, S.B. 2010. The Social Purpose of New Governance: Lisbon and the Limits to Legitimacy. *Journal of International Relations and Development*, 13.3: 209–38.

Vaughan-Whitehead, D. 2003. *EU Enlargement versus Social Europe? The Uncertain Future of the European Social Model*. Cheltenham: Edward Elgar.

10

NEOLIBERALISM AND CITIZENSHIP[1]

Katharyne Mitchell

Citizenship is most often conceptualized with respect to theories of political rights and duties of membership in a defined community. *Modern* citizenship in western democracies begins with the nation-state scale as the defined community of greatest relevance. The codification and institutionalization of individual freedoms at the national level was one of the key components of the growth of citizenship as it originated in Britain in the seventeenth century. It reflected a shift from local, communal relations and social rights rooted in village membership into a sense of a national community and of individual rights guaranteed by a state.

Citizenship is also conceptualized vis-à-vis forms of status and feelings of belonging or alienation, sometimes referred to as cultural citizenship (Ong 2003). It is also often theorized as encompassing behaviour, or citizenship 'acts' – the demonstrative practices of community members that indicate acceptance and support of the community or a willingness and desire to make changes to it (Nielson and Isin 2008). Additionally, the idea of governing *through* citizenship in the sense of regulating and managing individual and community behaviour via liberal citizenship rationalities and practices is an important subject of scholarly attention (Hindess 2002; Ong 2006).

In all of these conceptualizations citizenship must be understood first and foremost as a process, as something that mutates and transforms through time and in place (Marston and Mitchell 2005). Signifying the mutable quality of citizenship, the British sociologist T.H. Marshall famously delineated three different periods of citizenship formation (Marshall and Bottomore 1992). In Marshall's view, citizenship was seen to follow a positive trajectory of ever-greater inclusiveness and expansiveness with respect to individual rights and entitlements. Hence the first period of citizenship, in the eighteenth century, encompassed forms of entitlements such as *habeas corpus* and trial by jury; the second era in the nineteenth century saw the institutionalization of parliamentary rights and the enfranchisement of working men; and the third (mid-twentieth century) included welfare supports and subsidies in the arenas of health and education.

While Marshall's insights have been helpful vis-à-vis his recognition of the mutability of citizenship, his theory was also limited in scope. In addition to his neglect of gender, he maintained a fundamentally blinkered desire to trace what he saw as the fulfilment of the promise of liberalism over time (a scholarly position critiqued by many, see, e.g. Vogel 1991; Barbalet 1988; Turner 1986). Writing from his own position in post-war Great Britain and the height of Keynesian ideals and welfare state expansion, he theorized a seemingly natural progression between economic development and the growth of civil society.

Numerous scholars have discussed the lack of any necessary link between economic development and the growth of civil society, or the expansion of political space as a logical outcome of capitalist development (see, e.g. Mann 1987). Indeed, historical research indicates that the frontiers of citizenship can contract as well as expand under different circumstances (Turner 1986). Despite these critiques, Marshall's conception of the transformative nature of citizenship remains useful vis-à-vis understanding the ever-present but also ever-changing connections between citizenship formation and capitalism, and between liberalism, capitalism, and nationalism. His theoretical framework is also useful as a backdrop and foil for further examinations of the constitution of neoliberal citizenship in the contemporary moment.

Marshall's assumption of a necessary progression from a citizenship based primarily on economic status to a more open and democratic one established liberalism as a political formation inherently compatible with both nation-building and capitalist development. For Marshall this was an intersection of processes that he believed could only improve on the emancipatory promise of liberalism through time. Instead, many scholars have noted how the relationship between capitalism and liberalism in recent years has been marked rather by an aggressive assault on Keynesian redistributive models – a distinctly *regressive* rolling back of welfare social protections over the past three to four decades (Peck 2001; Peck and Tickell 2002). At the same time, the chummy, naturalized connections between the spaces of the territorial nation-state and the experiences of a citizenship 'community' have likewise been torn asunder.

In this chapter I investigate and critique the assumption of the benign and ultimately progressive nature of liberalism by focusing on current struggles over citizenship formation within the last few decades. I do this through an examination of some of the transformations in financial markets, spaces of nationalism, and forms of liberal governance in juxtaposition with changes in the policies and practices of citizenship in western democracies. Specific transformations I examine include the rise of liberalized markets and more flexible and financially based regimes of capital accumulation; the global flows and disarticulation of citizenship and national territory; and systems of governance involving the growth of entrepreneurialism and constitution of universal 'free' subjects – juxtaposed with forms of enclaving and exclusion in which the 'ungovernable' are forever rendered as surplus populations. I look in detail at these broad and interlinked changes and struggles as they impact citizenship – drawing attention, in particular, to the spatial component of each transformative process.

Flexible regimes of capital accumulation and flexible citizenship

We are now in an era of intensified market liberalization, with increasingly unhindered and accelerated flows of capital, commodities, and information across the globe. The greater flexibility of financial systems and increasing mobility of finance is strongly connected with the movements of people both within states and also across international borders (Castles and Miller 2014). The greater speed of capital, its developing and dislocating effects and increased pressures on livelihoods and the mobility of people, all have a strong impact on why, where, and how people move, who moves, and what happens in the process. In this section I investigate three features of the rise of liberalized markets and more flexible regimes of capital accumulation on citizenship: these are transnationalism and flow; mobility and differential speed; and place-based vs free-floating identities.

Transnationalism and flow

The increased flexibility of financial systems under neoliberalism has led to an increased amount of foreign direct investment (FDI) originating in wealthier countries and directed to less developed nations (Dicken 2015). With increased capital investment and decreased forms of state regulation there is frequently an increase in wealth polarization and loss of livelihoods for populations at the bottom of the economic pyramid (Sparke 2013). Moreover, as capital rapidly enters into circulation it often disrupts traditional means of support, uproots and dislocates poor and primarily rural populations, and often forces them into motion (Sassen 1990).

This type of forced mobility is evident historically, especially in the era of rapid industrialization in the nineteenth century; it is also apparent in recent years. Over the last few decades, with the (re)liberalization of finance and global FDI in the neoliberal era, we can observe another period of major economic migration, one encompassing new migration regions and hotspots as well as different forms of movement both domestically and across international borders (Salt 1989; Castles and Miller 2014). As in the past, these economic migrations operate in relation to the flows of capital as well as to migration policy regimes that are in place in various nation-states.

One of the most important developments in this recent migration stream as it impacts citizenship formation is the rise of transnational migration. This is a pattern of migration involving frequent communication, journeys, and often flows of money and goods between communities located in sending and receiving societies. Transnational movement has been aided by technological advances in transportation and communication. As in the case of earlier eras, however, it is a process that also remains profoundly connected to market expansion and rapid flows of investment into new geographical regions.

While, historically, migrants have often moved back and forth between their leaving society and host society, the neoliberal period has seen an accelerated and intensified version of this phenomenon, where the connections are maintained between cross-border communities in a deep and almost simultaneous manner. Indeed, researchers have observed that contemporary migrants often participate with equal interest and intensity in both sending and receiving societies. The migrants create ties and allegiances to more than one national community and nourish 'multi-stranded social relations (linking) together their societies of origin and settlement' (Basch *et al.* 1994: 6; Faist and Ozveren 2004; Levitt 2001).

A number of scholars have explored the shifting meanings of citizenship in the context of these new forms of transnational migration and transnational governance (Smith 2003; van Bochove *et al.* 2010). For example, the rights and responsibilities of migrants have become increasingly complex, where a migrant may obtain the right to vote in a local election or participate in a discussion about the provision of local services beyond territorial membership but at the same time be denied formal citizenship rights at the national scale (Bauböck 2005). Additionally, the supranational state system of the European Union (EU) complicates matters even further, as membership rights can become blurred in the context of 'post-national' or multi-level systems of governance (Soysal 1994; Olsen 2012).

Transnationalism is intricately connected to the rise of these kinds of differential regimes of citizenship, and also to the changing relationship of the state to its most mobile citizens and denizens. How can the state control the finances and maintain the allegiance of its citizens who may be living across one or more national borders? Some states have offered the prospect of dual citizenship while others rely on more punitive sanctions and regulations, particularly around property ownership and inheritance laws. But in almost all cases these laws or policies are never set in stone but rather are characterized by expedient transitions from one form of citizenship formation to another depending on the larger political and economic context in which actors are operating.

The flexible nature of the current regime of capital accumulation and the state's highly contextual response in terms of legal rights and policies has been matched by flexible citizenship strategies by many migrants. Ong (1999), for example, has documented the strategies through which some diasporic Chinese migrants locate family members in multiple nation-states in order to obtain citizenship and greater protections in the face of potential harm or adversity. Additionally, the flexible citizenship strategy adopted by migrants can aid in business dealings in which information and personal ties are used to advantage in multiple locales.

Mobility and differential speed

Another effect of market liberalization has to do with speed and the nature of contemporary mobility. In investigating both the rules and the opportunities related to cross-border movements under neoliberalism it becomes apparent that differential speed is a significant ramification of the financial and technological changes of the past few decades. Neoliberal policy related to cross-border movement, manifested in free trade agreements such as NAFTA, for example, enables expedited forms of movement for some, but significantly slower movement (or no movement) for others.

Business elites and the wealthy become 'super' citizens, who are able to move faster and with greater mobility across borders with the aid of various kinds of expedited border-crossing programmes and passes; these include mundane, yet influential programmes such as first- and business-class passage on flights, TSA (Transportation Security Administration) 'pre-check' lines, and preferred flyer arrangements at airport terminals worldwide; they also include Smart Border programmes such as the Nexus lane at the US–Canada border. In contrast, second-class citizens, third-country nationals, denizens, and irregular migrants are the 'sub' citizen masses, who are constrained and forced to move more and more slowly across borders, if at all. Thus the values and benefits of citizenship can be considered in relation to the lack of those values and benefits for others.

Sparke (2006, 2004) has written extensively about the relational nature of expedited border-crossing programmes for the elite business classes, and the slowdowns related to increased securitization and anti-immigrant sentiment in the USA for others. Indeed, during the immediate post-2001 era, the exclusions related to nationalist sentiment and to the fear of terrorist attack included not just decreased mobility for the 'sub' classes, but also what he terms a kind of 'carceral cosmopolitanism': anti-immigrant forms of forced movement such as expedited removal and extraordinary rendition. He notes how this 'neoliberal nexus' of national securitization vis-à-vis the movement of immigrants and the poor should always be seen in relation to the expedition of transnational movement for capital and the elite.

The biopolitical nature of this altered terrain of political citizenship is likewise evident at many borders around the globe. On an individual basis it occurs with respect to the many forms of monitoring and surveillance that occur directly *on the body*; these include iris scans, heat detectors (for fevers ostensibly caused by flu pandemics), full body scans, and required thumb-printing in the USA and many other societies worldwide. Additionally, the broader regimes of biopolitical control of the type discussed by Foucault (2010) are manifested in the norms of mobility management that pervade every aspect of citizenship as it plays out at the border and beyond; these include the assumptions of value and self-care that marks the responsible and moral individual as an 'economic-rational actor' (Lemke 2001: 197). The fast-moving business-man is thus seen to deserve the perks of unfettered movement as he embodies (quite literally) the values of the entrepreneurial market society.

Place-based versus free-floating actors

The economic-rational actors of contemporary citizenship regimes are not just fast and efficient as they move across borders, they are also inherently free-floating. The preferred neoliberal subject lacks deep allegiance to a single locale, operating rather as an entity responsible to the networks and flows of the system itself. Flexible regimes of capital accumulation act to erode the sticky particularity of place-bound actors in favour of transnational subjects operating above and beyond any one locale. These newly formed transnational spaces and actors have ramifications for citizenship vis-à-vis attitudes and practices in the arenas of culture, health, and responsibility for the care of others and the planet itself.

The economic value placed on the free-floating subject simultaneously vaunts the seeming neutrality of the mobile elite and erodes the respect and dignity of those seen as bound to specific cultural traditions and locales. This often has a gendered component to it, where women are represented as hindered by the sticky particularities of place-bound ascriptions and practices, whereas businessmen are constituted as free-floating and universalist. Additionally, these divergent cultural norms are frequently portrayed in spatial terms, where the culturally bound woman harkens back to a pre-modern, rural location, whereas the liberal and secular male is represented as modern precisely because he lacks any specific grounding in place or tradition (Gökariksel and Mitchell 2005).

Another major implication of the free-floating subject of neoliberal citizenship is in the attitudes towards the care of people and the environment. The responsibility to the environment is frequently diminished with a loss of allegiance to specific locales (Mason 2009). And with respect to the care of people, forms of social reproduction that necessarily take place *in place* such as education and elder care are also greatly affected by the peripatetic nature of elite movement and the greater value placed on flow and a free-floating orientation (Mitchell *et al.* 2004; Strauss and Meehan 2015).

The disarticulations of nation, citizenship, and territory

The greater flexibility of financial systems and global flows characteristic of neoliberalism is paralleled by a disarticulation of citizenship from national territory. The result of both geopolitical and geoeconomic forces, this has implications for the production of ideas and institutions that extend the reach of the state and its sovereign will beyond territorial boundaries. It is also implicated in the rise of supra state and sub-state entities and actors and the actions of those both enabling and contesting the simultaneous expansion and contraction of state practices.

Sovereignty across borders

In one study of the expanded reach of the sovereign state across international borders and protocols Elden (2009) examined how the concept of territorial integrity was disrupted following the attacks of 9/11 and the aggressive ensuing stance by the Bush administration. Although the relationship between territory and sovereignty was considered inviolate since the modern formation of nations, this notion was called into question by the war on terror. Open military intervention into the sovereign affairs of other nations could be legitimized as long as the proper justifications were offered up to the global community.

This leads us to a number of interesting questions vis-à-vis the functioning of citizenship across borders. If sovereignty is increasingly unconstrained by national territory in the war on terror era, what does this mean for citizenship? How do western states seek to administer their populations – as well as those of so-called 'failed states' – outside of territorial borders? What are the new strategies and tactics employed by individuals and populations that operate in liminal and transnational sites, both inside and outside the spaces of liberal governance?

With respect to state regimes of governance and political attitudes on transnational practices, these are ultimately dependent on context. In some situations states want to capture migrant remittances and allegiances and thus encourage dual citizenship and transnational lifestyles; in others, states frown on the loss of loyalty perceived in dual citizenship claims and cross-border practices. Meanwhile, both state actors and non-state actors seek to gain advantages within the systems in which they are imbricated. For the transnational elite, cross-border movements occur in many directions and take many forms, but the relative lack of friction at the border distinguishes their mobility from the movements of the less privileged.

The movements of this transnational class are critical to study as this elite group often has an outsized impact on the communities in which they operate. They might head up research and design teams in Singapore or Hong Kong, oversee factory production in China, and be involved with their children's education in Canada; in each setting their views on education, culture, or democratic citizenship can be significant. In a study of Hong Kong migrants in Vancouver, BC, for example, Mitchell (2004) showed how the Chinese immigrants' presumed tastes in homes influenced the types of house styles and gardens built by developers hoping to make money from this wealthy and highly kinetic population. When the new aesthetics became part of a fractious public debate, the existing democratic system and practices of local governance emerged as another important topic of discussion. Thus, in addition to debates about landscapes and lifestyles, the norms and practices of participatory citizenship were also impacted by this encounter.

The rise of supra state and sub-state citizenship formations

The disarticulation of national territory and citizenship is also manifested in the growth of multiple institutions at scales other than that of the nation-state. These include supra state formations such as the EU as well as sub-state organizations at regional and urban scales of governance. They also include systems of transnational governance that are largely orchestrated around and through non-state actors such as transnational social and environmental movements and solidarity organizations.

Transnational governance is a critical feature of contemporary society as it involves policy coordination across national borders, primarily by non-state actors and non-governmental organizations (NGOs). This form of transnationalism is distinct from supranational governance (such as the International Criminal Court) because it does not subsume national institutions but rather operates more informally to address specific problems impacting more than one area of jurisdiction. It has become particularly important to study in the era of global climate change and other profound cross-border problems as new actors and networks have emerged alongside more traditional national, international, and intergovernmental organizations.

Some of the key questions that arise with the institutionalization of transnational concepts of membership in late welfare states have to do with the quality and meaning of social citizenship in these formulations as well as the development of civil society and the practices of democracy. A number of scholars have argued that the social citizenship rights and entitlements that were won through the Keynesian era have been eroded through scale bending or 'jumping scale' to supra and sub-national governance levels (e.g. Swyngedouw 1996; Smith 2004). With the reconfiguration of national governance and citizenship entitlements and claims under neoliberal globalization, ensuing forms of restructuring often result in the production of alternative scales and sites that are ultimately exclusionary and authoritative. In this view, rescaling practices have given rise to new global *and* local or 'glocal' forms of governance, many of which lead to the loss of various social and economic protections for previously marginalized social groups.

Others argue, however, that it remains important to interrogate specific cases of glocalization, as some may exhibit positive or 'complementary' spaces of citizenship at different scales. Faist (2001), for example, examines citizenship as a 'nested membership' category in supranational entities such as the EU. He argues that European citizenship at different scales of governance can function in complementary ways – in some cases upholding the entitlements of social citizenship in specific contextually dependent situations. However, outside of the EU context most examples of scale-jumping in the neoliberal era have been shown to occur mainly at the expense of welfare protections or the environment.

Securitization and shifting regimes of migration policy

The changing nature of the nation-state with respect to citizenship regimes is also evident in new forms of securitization and the rise of so-called fortress enclaves and security states. This is nowhere more apparent than in policies related to migration control and asylum claims in Europe. Huysman (2000, 2006) and Bigo (2002) have shown how new forms of securitization in Europe in the 1980s and 1990s involved the formation of a fortified EU 'inside' space, through the conflation of different forms of perceived illegality on the outside. These were those cross-border processes and movements deemed a threat to the community. The blurred and conflated outside forces that were frequently combined into one giant perception of 'risk' included immigrants, drug-runners, asylum claimants, refugees, terrorists, and criminals.

In this context, new kinds of barriers to access and to claims to citizenship have proliferated and taken new forms as nation-states use multiple technologies to defer and defeat irregular migrants and asylum-seekers in their quest for entry. Mountz (2011: 118), for example, has investigated the ways in which many advanced industrial nation-states employ new techniques of migration control that involve deflecting or capturing migrants offshore and keeping them from ever reaching sovereign national territory. (Other tactics include payment by wealthy societies for the refugee 'problem' to be handled by poorer neighbours.) The new 'enforcement archipelago' described by Mountz operates through the use of islands at the periphery of nation-states, where migrants are pre-emptively picked up and detained in remote sites far from the possibilities of asylum claims, judicial review, citizenship opportunities, or even humanitarian aid.

In this work Mountz demonstrates how states are often able to avoid the dictates of international conventions (such as the 1951 Convention relating to the Status of Refugees), as well as human rights claims at all scales, through hiding asylum-seekers from public view and keeping human rights monitors away from certain geographical sites. States thus use space – the geography of the islands – and sub-national jurisdictional status to manage their borders and self-perceived rights to administer sovereign territory as they deem fit, creating distinctive 'graduated zones of sovereignty' in the process (Ong 2006). These actions take place within the wider war on terror and national justifications for deferred or denied civil rights on the basis of security.

New regimes of securitization that have been put in place during the 'war on terror' can thus be seen to have impacted citizenship in innumerable ways. In addition to the new forms of geographical deferral and outsourced detention indicated above, the body of the migrant is increasingly subjected to suspicion and exclusion within nation-states as well. For example, the prior efforts to integrate immigrants through various forms of policies promoting liberal tolerance towards 'difference' – particularly the strong multicultural stances taken in countries such as the Netherlands and the UK, have either been ended or transformed into more assimilative platforms over the past decade (Vertovec and Wessendorf 2010). This shift indicates a move away from the socially liberal era of the incorporation of difference and encouragement of cultural diversity within the nation to a harsher period of citizenship formation dependent on acclimation and assimilation to the dominant culture.

The aggressively anti-multicultural positions taken by conservative politicians such as David Cameron and Angela Merkel, both of whom have derided multiculturalism as a 'failure', reflects the rise of concerns about national security in the wake of Islamic fundamentalism post 9/11 as well the sharpening neoliberal imperative for individuals to evolve and adjust to new circumstances – including both labour market changes and cultural shifts. This push manifests the increasing devolution of responsibility for immigrant integration to the individual, absolving the state of responsibility at the same time as making assimilation imperative. If immigrants are unable to or refuse to assimilate they are coded as security threats. Politically they join the ranks of the monitored margins, those ungovernable subjects inhabiting the liminal spaces on the edges of society; economically they become part of the surplus population, threatening by virtue of their inability to function as *homo economicus* in the neoliberal nation (Bigo 2005).

While the conceptualization of the threatening, unassimilable Other is often constituted in relation to immigrants and security fears, it is also evident in everyday encounters involving forms of difference based on class, race, sexuality, and other manifestations of alterity. And, mirroring the attempted enclaving of national space through border security, fortification, and containment, interior spaces within the nation are also formed into enclaves and similarly policed. These kinds of enclaves take many forms, including monitored residential neighbourhoods and gated communities, clubs, societies, and elite universities – all of which manifest a type of dominant or privileged citizenship existing in relation to the sub-citizenship of the masses. Race, as well as economic standing, often plays a key role in the categorization of who it is that is worthy or not worthy of this privileged citizenship status.

The citizens of the enclave can thus be found at all scales and always express a spatial relation to those *outside* the protected community. Whether this be at the supranational, national, urban, neighbourhood, or club scale, these enclaves work on the basis of exclusion and exclusivity; they are formed in relation to Others who are secondary or surplus populations within the economic formations and formulations of neoliberalism. Elite citizenship is thus paradoxically about both the capacity to be mobile and free-floating *and* the ability to form and inhabit an enclave. These spaces can thus be configured as nodes in a larger constellation of a citizenship archipelago – where the privileged are connected through transnational travel and yet can land in protected and pleasurable zones around the globe.

Neoliberal citizenship: subjectivity and governance

Heretofore I have been mainly concerned with the multiple ways that individuals and populations have been detained, deferred, demoted, excluded, or rendered as surplus from the citizenship norms, rights, and sense of cultural belonging in western democracies under neoliberalism. In this section I look at a seemingly opposite yet parallel condition in which states actively promote citizenship – but in very specific forms. Citizenship is considered here as something that is formative of new ways of being – as a process that helps to constitute subjects in specific contexts. How are subjects constituted and governed *as* citizens in the neoliberal era? In this section I examine some of the myriad ways in which subjects are both formed as and governed through the discourse and practices of liberal citizenship.

Constituting the strategic cosmopolitan and lifelong learner

One of the key institutions through which subjects are formed as citizens is education. Over the past several decades the national systems of education in many advanced western democracies have mirrored broader changes in society. These include a declining rhetoric on the importance of multiculturalism and an increasing interest in the cultivation of young citizens who are nimble, flexible and adaptable learners. These young learners are trained to rely on themselves and to be less oriented towards tolerance of difference, and more towards a kind of competitive or strategic cosmopolitanism.

The cultivation of these new strategic citizens takes place in the broader context of flexible regimes of accumulation and the disarticulation of nation and territory. As the nation–state has ceased to function as the normative back-stop for democratic practices and understandings, educational imperatives have arisen that serve to reconfigure the child and the student. From what was once the individual citizen prefigured to live and labour for a lifetime in a national community under Fordism, the neoliberal moment has led us to flexible, globally oriented actors, who must strategically learn and re-learn, train and re-train in order to adapt to a flowing and unstable set of living and working environments (Mitchell 2003).

Educational systems strain to keep up with these changes, offering new mission statements, mantras, and curricula on an evolving basis. International schools have skyrocketed in number (Parker 2011). School mission statements – even at the elementary level – rarely miss the opportunity to herald their global curricula, which will help children to be competitive 'global citizens' in a rapidly 'globalizing economy'. Meanwhile, 'lifelong learning' is an ongoing favourite catchphrase, appearing in documents promoting citizenship at multiple scales, educational outreach brochures, and primary school curricula in many advanced industrial societies worldwide. Rather than the original conceptualization of lifelong learning as benefiting the ongoing constitution of a thoughtful democratic citizen over the course of a lifetime, the contemporary rendering reflects the imperative to adapt to rapidly changing work environments (Mitchell 2006).

With a declining sense that working with difference is an important strategy of national unification, many nations now tolerate or even encourage the separation out of different ethnic, religious or gender-based groups from the public education system. Parents are encouraged to choose the educational model that will work best for their child, again reflecting the devolution of state-based responsibility and authority (for education in this case) to the individual level. If the parent chooses badly and the child does not succeed, the fault and the ensuing problems are laid squarely on the head of the individual.

In this educational scenario we can see the promotion of freedom as a necessary condition for subjects. In other words, as Rose (1999) has pointed out, freedom is a form of governance in advanced liberalism, one that requires subjects to be free. Parental choice in American schools, now a rallying cry for both conservatives and liberals, both opens the way to the increasing privatization of national systems of public education and simultaneously recruits and inculcates parents into neoliberal assumptions about how to help their children become good global citizens (Mitchell and Lizotte 2014).

Citizenship and governance worldwide

In addition to choice-making and freedom in advanced liberal societies, citizenship is also conducted as a liberal tool of governance in many developing parts of the globe. We can see the positioning and promotion of citizenship as something that operates within and through market norms in developing societies. This promotion is part of a broader liberal project in which advanced western societies shape the actions of developing societies through universalist understandings of democratic practice and good governance. As Hindess (2002: 127–8) succinctly puts it: 'where the liberal government of non-western populations was once predicated on a denial of citizenship, contemporary liberal attempts to govern the people of the non-western world are increasingly channeled through citizenship itself'.

The channelling that Hindess alludes to incorporates not just the system of states, but also a broader supranational regime. This includes transnational corporations and agencies, non-governmental organizations, and other non-profit or non-political bodies. In other words, citizenship governance casts a wide net, and does so in terms of compliance to the norms of liberalism, including assumptions about individual autonomy, good governance and political and economic freedom. Within these norms and buried in plain sight is the image of the market, which serves as the 'exemplary form of free interaction' (ibid.: 134). It is the free market that must be encouraged in order for the civilization process to be completed and the residents of the community to be accorded full citizenship status as free and autonomous actors. 'The ideal image of the market, in effect, provides liberal political reason with a model of the governmental uses of freedom' (ibid.: 135).

It is also the market that regulates and defines improvement, and thus the liberal project of progress – the progressive development of poorer societies – is administered through the assumptions and practices of freedom. Those perceived as unable or unwilling to be governed through technologies of freedom, such as participation in systems of self-improvement and democratic self-governance, are relegated outside the liberal project. The creation of an outside to the liberal project is reserved for those not worthy of being governed, who are increasingly left as remainders – surplus populations indigestible by the liberal project of citizenship governance.

In her work on development projects in Indonesia Tania Li (2007) has investigated the consistent and ongoing 'will to improve' that has shaped colonial and post-colonial relations for centuries. While highlighting the ways in which outside 'experts' have set liberal reform projects in motion, she also brings out the multiple ways in which the targets of reform – the people and institutions of the highlands of Sulawesi – negotiate liberal governance regimes. Thus citizenship governance is not all one-way, but involves the various interactions of actors with the specific practices and tools that are brought to bear in the name of the improvement of populations.

Some scholars, such as Ashutosh and Mountz (2011), have interrogated the role of non-state actors in normalizing and entrenching a global liberal citizenship agenda – one that repeatedly returns to the hierarchical power relations between nation-states. Their work investigates, in particular, the work of the International Organization for Migration, showing how this agency represents itself in terms of normative understandings of global humanitarian assistance and human rights yet frequently operates on behalf of nation-states in the promulgation of a wider vision of sovereign control over borders and regimes of governance. These types of international institutions act to regulate and constrain the actions of post-colonial states and their often unwieldy or 'ungoverned' populations within the parameters of advanced state norms of good governance; this good governance, moreover, is that in which the free market operates 'freely' – often to the advantage of western societies (see also Hindess 2002; Springer 2010).

Conclusion

In this chapter I examined the development and expression of neoliberal citizenship in the context of changes in the workings of capitalism, transformations in nation-state relations, and shifts in forms of governing. Beginning with the important yet limited insights of citizenship scholar T.H. Marshall, I addressed citizenship as a formation – one that is constantly evolving and always constituted in relation to spatial and temporal processes and effects. While Marshall imagined a progressive future of increasing openness and inclusion, the actual workings of neoliberal citizenship indicate more complicated patterns. For some populations contemporary citizenship norms and practices have reflected and in some cases deepened forms of inequity and exclusion. In other cases the freedoms of liberal citizenship have encouraged and facilitated universalist assumptions about rational behaviour and good governance – freedoms that ultimately direct included individuals and populations to market-oriented choices and ways of being.

Ultimately, it is important to foreground the relationality of neoliberal citizenship. For all those who are constituted as legal citizens in the modern era there are others who are deliberately excluded from legality. The speed associated with fast and mobile citizenship often entails the slow-down or obstruction of movement for others. The formation of certain kinds of positive identities and feelings of security vis-à-vis urban, national, or supranational enclaves frequently corresponds with feelings of alienation and fear for those outside these bordered communities. Likewise, healthy bodies and well-educated minds for some citizens are achieved through the ill health and ignorance of others. Space is formative in all of these relational processes – through enclaving, targeting, deterritorialization, and other geographical forms of exclusion and inclusion.

Note

1 Portions of this chapter have been adapted from the following sources: Marston and Mitchell, Citizens and the State: Contextualizing Citizenship Formations in Space and Time, in Clive Barnett and Murray Low (eds), *Spaces of Democracy*. London: Sage, 2002; Mitchell, 2016. Transnationalism. In Richardson, D., Castree, N., Goodchild, M., Liu, W., Kobayashi, A., and Marston, R. eds. *The International Encyclopedia of Geography*. Hoboken, NJ: Wiley-Blackwell..

References

Ashutosh, I., and Mountz, A. 2011. Migration Management for the Benefit of Whom? Interrogating the Work of the International Organization for Migration. *Citizenship Studies*, 15: 21–38.

Barbalet, J.M. 1988. *Citizenship: Rights, Struggle and Class Inequality*. Minneapolis: University of Minnesota Press.

Basch, L., Glick Schiller, N., and Szanton Blanc, C. eds. 1994. *Nations Unbound: Transnational Projects, Postcolonial Predicaments and Deterritorialized Nation-states*. New York: Routledge.

Bauböck, R. 2005. Expansive Citizenship: Voting Beyond Territory and Membership. *Political Science and Politics*, 38: 683–87.

Bigo, D. 2002. Security and Immigration: Toward a Critique of the Governmentality of Unease. *Alternatives*, 27: 63–92.

—. 2005. Globalized (in)Security: The Field of the Professionals of Unease Management and the Ban-opticon, in Solmon, J., and Sakai, N., eds. *Translation, Philosophy, Colonial Difference*. Hong Kong: University of Hong Kong Press: 109–57.

Castles, S., and Miller, M. 2014. *The Age of Migration: International Population Movements in the Modern World*. New York: Guilford Press.

Dicken, P. 2015. *Global Shift: Mapping the Changing Contours of the World Economy*. New York: Guilford Press.

Elden, S. 2009. *Terror and Territory: The Spatial Extent of Sovereignty*. Minneapolis: University of Minnesota Press.

Faist, T. 2001. Social Citizenship in the European Union: Nested Membership. *Journal of Common Market Studies*, 39: 37–58.

Faist, T., and Ozveren, E. eds. 2004. *Transnational Social Spaces: Agents, Networks and Institutions*. London: Ashgate.

Foucault, M. 2010. *The Birth of Biopolitics: Lectures at the Collège de France, 1978–1979*. London: Picador.

Gökariksel, B., and Mitchell, K. 2005. Veiling, Secularism and the Neoliberal Subject: National Narratives and Supranational Desires in Turkey and France. *Global Networks*, 5: 147–65.

Hindess, B. 2002. Neo-liberal Citizenship. *Citizenship Studies*, 6: 127–43.

Huysman, J. 2000. The European Union and the Securitization of Migration. *Journal of Common Market Studies*, 38: 751–77.

—. 2006. *The Politics of Insecurity: Fear, Migration and Asylum in the EU*. London and New York: Routledge.

Lemke, T. 2001. 'The Birth of Bio-politics': Michel Foucault's Lecture at the Collège de France on Neo-liberal Governmentality. *Economy and Society*, 30: 190–207.

Levitt, P. 2001. *The Transnational Villagers*. Berkeley: University of California Press.

Li, T. 2007. *The Will to Improve: Governmentality, Development, and the Practice of Politics*. Durham, NC: Duke University Press.

Mann, M. 1987. Ruling Class Strategies and Citizenship. *Sociology*, 21: 339–54.

Marshall, T.H., and Bottomore, T. 1992. *Citizenship and Social Class*. London: Pluto Press.

Marston, S., and Mitchell, K. 2005. Citizens and the State: Contextualizing Citizenship Formation in Space and Time, in Low, M., and Barnett, C., eds. *Spaces of Democracy*. London: Sage: 124–44.

Mason, A. 2009. Environmental Obligations and the Limits of Transnational Citizenship. *Political Studies*, 57: 280–97.

Mitchell, K. 2003. Educating the National Citizen in Neoliberal Times: From the Multicultural Self to the Strategic Cosmopolitan. *Transactions of the Institute of British Geographers*, 28: 387–403.

—. 2004. *Crossing the NeoLiberal Line: Pacific Rim Migration and the Metropolis*, Philadelphia, PA: Temple University Press.

—. 2006. Neoliberal Governmentality in the European Union: Education, Training and Technologies of Citizenship. *Environment and Planning D: Society and Space*, 24: 389–407.

Mitchell, K., and Lizotte, C. 2014. The Grassroots and the Gift: Moral Authority, American Philanthropy, and Activism in Education. *Foucault Studies*, 18: 66–89.

Mitchell, K., Marston, S., and Katz, C. 2004. Introduction, in Mitchell, K., Marston, S., and Katz, C., eds. *Life's Work: Geographies of Social Reproduction*. London: Blackwell: 1–26.

Mountz, A. 2011. The Enforcement Archipelago: Detention, Haunting, and Asylum on Islands. *Political Geography*, 30: 118–28.

Nielsen, G., and Isin, E. 2008. *Acts of Citizenship*. New York: Zed Books.

Olsen, E. 2012. *Transnational Citizenship in the European Union: Past, Present, and Future*. London and New York: Continuum International.

Ong. A. 1999. *Flexible Citizenship: The Cultural Logics of Transnationality*. Durham, NC: Duke University Press.

—. 2003. *Buddha is Hiding: Refugees, Citizenship, the New America*. Berkeley: University of California Press.

—. 2006. Mutations in Citizenship. *Theory, Culture & Society*, 23: 499–531.

Parker, W. 2011. International Education in US Public Schools. *Globalisation, Societies, and Education*, 9: 487–501.

Peck, J. 2001. *Workfare States*. New York: Guilford Press.

Peck, J., and Tickell, A. 2002. Neoliberalizing Space. *Antipode*, 34: 380–404.

Rose, N. 1999. *Powers of Freedom: Reframing Political Thought*. Cambridge: Cambridge University Press.

Salt, J. 1989. A Comparative Overview of International Trends and Types, 1950–80. *International Migration Review*, 23: 431–56.

Sassen, S. 1990. *The Mobility of Labor and Capital: A Study in International Investment and Labor Flow*. Cambridge: Cambridge University Press.

Smith, M.P. 2003. Transnationalism, the State, and the Extraterritorial Citizen. *Politics & Society*, 31: 467–502.

Smith, N. 2004. Scale Bending and the Fate of the National, in Sheppard, E., and McMaster, R., eds. *Scale and Geographic Inquiry: Nature, Society, and Method*. Oxford: Wiley Blackwell.

Soysal, Y. 1994. *Limits of Citizenship: Migrants and Postnational Membership in Europe*. Chicago, IL: University of Chicago Press.

Sparke, M. 2004. Passports into Credit Cards: On the Borders and Spaces of Neoliberal Citizenship, in Migdal, J., ed. *Boundaries and Belonging*. Cambridge: Cambridge University Press: 251–83.

—. 2006. The Neoliberal Nexus: Economy, Security, and the Biopolitics of Citizenship on the Border. *Political Geography*, 25: 155–80.

—. 2013. *Introducing Globalization: Ties, Tensions, and Uneven Integration*. New York: Wiley Blackwell.

Strauss, K., and Meehan, K. 2015. *Precarious Worlds: Contested Geographies of Social Reproduction*. Athens: University of Georgia Press.

Springer, S. 2010. Neoliberal Discursive Formations: On the Contours of Subjectivation, Good Governance, and Symbolic Violence in Posttransitional Cambodia. *Environment and Planning D: Society and Space*, 28: 931–50.

Swyngedouw, E. 1996. Restructuring and Welfare State Regimes. *Urban Studies*, 33: 1407–30.

Turner, B. 1986. *Citizenship and Capitalism*. London: Allen and Unwin.

van Bochove, M., Rusinovic, K., and Engbersen, G. 2010. The Multiplicity of Citizenship: Transnational and Local Practices and Identifications of Middle-Class Migrants. *Global Networks*, 10: 344–64.

Vertovec, S., and Wessendorf, S. eds. 2010. *The Multiculturalism Backlash: European Discourses, Policies and Practices*. London and New York: Routledge.

Vogel, U. 1991. Is Citizenship Gender-specific? In Vogel, U., and Moran, M., eds. *The Frontiers of Citizenship*. New York: St Martin's Press: 58–85.

11

DEVELOPMENT AND NEOLIBERALISM

Douglas Hill, Nave Wald and Tess Guiney

This chapter provides an overview of the various issues related to neoliberalism and development. We will see that thinking about what development is and how it can be achieved has gone through tremendous shifts in the post-World War II era. Indeed, while a neoliberal orthodoxy now predominates in how mainstream development institutions think about economic policies in many countries of the global South, this has not always been the case, nor have the contours of what neoliberal policy meant always been consistent or discursively stable. In fact, in the years immediately after World War II, development was synonymous with economic policy led and directed by the state and those who adhered to an economic philosophy that emphasized the need to rely upon the market to allocate resources for development purposes were marginalized. However, just as neoliberalism began to assume ascendancy in the latter part of the twentieth century in the global North, so too did the 'retreat of the state' and associated policy prescriptions become the norm for countries of the global South after the debt crisis of the 1970s.

Thus, as we will see, from the 1980s onwards, neoliberalism became the orthodoxy for countries aligned to the Western powers, particularly through the imposition of structural adjustment programmes (SAPs). The 'new world order' envisioned by neoconservative think tanks and implemented through the Washington Consensus included a dual shift, one towards political liberalization and democracy, and another towards neoliberal macroeconomic policy. The emerging neoliberal state had to be (at least nominally) democratic, open for foreign investment and trade, and withdrawn from the provision of welfare (Petras and Veltmeyer 2011). Although the exact requirements of this neoliberal economic policy package varied from one country to another, there was undoubtedly a commonality in terms of what was usually prescribed by major donors such as the World Bank and the IMF, and this came to be known as the Washington Consensus. Significantly, at the same time that this neoliberal political-economic model rolled back the state and removed existing subsidies and social programmes, it also created a space for civil society to re-emerge and expand, in some countries after decades of military rule and civil wars.

While the contours of neoliberalism in the so-called developing world are a significant theme of this chapter, it also explores the way that the imposition of this doctrine has been challenged in different kinds of ways. Indeed, the implementation and outcomes of SAP according to the Washington Consensus in different parts of the world have been a subject of much debate and commentary. So, after outlining the role of SAPs in intensifying the neoliberalization of different parts of the globe in the early part of the chapter, the next section examines how the consensus came to be challenged in various ways in the early 1990s and beyond. Indeed, there was significant opposition arising against the imposition of these neoliberal policies in countries of the global South, and there have been a variety of shifts in development policy orthodoxy as a consequence.

The chapter focuses on three major challenges to the neoliberalization of development. First, from the 1990s onwards there was increased attention on those East Asian countries that appeared to have done very well economically despite following policies which had a more active role for the state than that prescribed under the Washington Consensus. Second, it examines how it is in this milieu that various kinds of social movements and manifestations of civil society have begun operating in an emergent political space. La Vía Campesina (The Peasant Way – LVC), one of the world's largest networks of NGOs and people's movements, is highlighted here as an example of the challenges to neoliberalism that can be engendered by the opening of this emergent political space. What comes out clearly from this section is that, as a consequence of these various popular and discursive challenges to neoliberalism, development orthodoxy in the 2000s has again shifted. The third of these challenges comes from the growing embrace of what has come to be known as a 'post-development critique', which has arisen from within the academy as a consequence of the utilization of post-colonial and post-structuralist approaches to development.

The final section of the chapter explores how neoliberalism has shaped the attitude of people in the global North to development issues in the global South. In so doing, it will investigate the notion of neoliberal subjectivities through volunteer tourism, which is a relatively recent but growing phenomena whereby growing numbers of people, particularly young people from the global North, are volunteering to undertake development-related activities in the global South for short- and medium-term periods. To some people, this represents a welcome democratization of the ethics of care and demonstrates new forms of solidarity being forged across old divides between the 'West' and 'the rest'. Others, however, are more sceptical of this movement and suggest that its emphasis on the individual as having the capacity to significantly alter global injustices is naive and simply reinforces old imaginaries that resonate with ideas about the white man's burden. To those critics, the reproduction of celebrity humanitarianism that has become so widespread in the contemporary era has the effect of eliding the deeper structural issues of global injustice.

Defining development

'Development' is a notoriously difficult term to define, carrying with it what some people believe is an undue emphasis upon replicating the lifestyles, values and economic systems of the Western world (Haynes 2008). The early thinkers on development in the post-World War II era, most famously Rostow, believed that it was self-evident that countries that were previously colonies of the Western powers needed to imitate the countries of the West in these matters if they were to have any hope of catching up with the more advanced states. Over time, this view has come to be contested in a variety of different ways, with many people arguing that this Eurocentric perspective overlooks the tremendous diversity found throughout the globe in terms of people's way of understanding themselves, their relationship to nature, and their priorities for what constitutes a good life (Escobar 2000).

In the immediate era of decolonization that took place after World War II and beyond, there was a belief that the state had an important role to play as the engine of economic development. The source for this belief was twofold: in the Western world, the experience of Keynesianism and planning had demonstrated to many people that the state was important in creating an appropriate allocation of resources while also ensuring the social welfare of its citizens. In the Soviet bloc, centrally planned economies were ostensibly producing high growth rates and enabling industrialization in countries that historically had been based around agriculture. At the Bretton Woods conference in 1944 an international institutional architecture was put in place that was to become incredibly important in how development was understood and enacted in the post-World War II era. Indeed the World Bank and the IMF, as well as regional banks such as the Asian Development Bank and the Inter-American Bank, became the primary conduits for finance and expertise to flow between the global North and the global South in the name of development.

It is certainly the case that during this period there are examples in the global South where the state accomplished a great deal to increase economic growth, although it is also the case that much violence, displacement and disruption of livelihoods was carried out in the name of the national interest in many places as well. A great deal of money was lent by Western powers to the leaders of some countries in the global South because they were important allies in a geopolitical sense rather than because they always had the best interests of their citizens in mind. Unsurprisingly, perhaps, by the 1970s many countries found themselves deeply in debt and, with the 1973 oil crisis and the rise of OPEC, many countries in the global South were functionally bankrupt (Martinussen 1997; McMichael 2012).

It was at this stage that neoliberalism began to become the standard orthodoxy in the policy prescriptions meted out by multilateral donors such as the World Bank and the IMF through SAPs. The election of Reagan and Thatcher in the USA and UK respectively added tremendous impetus to the growth of neoliberal orthodoxy in the global South, aided by now influential think tanks which provided the intellectual backing for their political agendas (George 1999; Harvey 2005). In the case of development economics, which has always provided the discursive framework by which development policies discussed and enacted, this meant that hitherto marginalized figures such as P.T. Bauer and Bella Balassa became central to debates that emphasized the importance of the market in most efficiently allocating resources and the necessity to reduce the role of the state, which was seen as inevitably compromised by rent-seeking behaviour.

There are essentially two phases to SAPs: a short-term adjustment period that brings the economy back under control, reduces its levels of inflation and appreciates its currency. This is followed by a longer-term recovery period when the fundamentals of the economy are changed, with the idea that this will eventually lead to the economy of the country being able to grow in a more sustainable manner (Mohan *et al.* 2000). These changes were more often than not incredibly controversial in the countries where they were enacted because they often withdrew subsidies and the provision of public goods that were disproportionately aimed towards helping the poor. Opposition to these policies took the form of food riots in some parts of South America for example, where people protested about the withdrawal of state-subsidized food grain programmes.

One of the most common ways to understand the form of neoliberalization that took place during this period is the term 'the Washington Consensus' that was coined to describe the set of measures prescribed by the World Bank and the IMF to countries of Latin America in the wake of their economic and financial crisis during the 1980s. These measures consisted of ten specific policy recommendations outlined below:

1 Fiscal policy discipline
2 Removal of public subsidies, particularly those viewed as politically motivated and indiscriminate
3 Tax reform

4   Introduction of market-based interest rates
5   Competitive exchange rates
6   Trade liberalization
7   Liberalization of foreign direct investment
8   Privatization of state-owned enterprises and a move away from import substitution
9   Deregulation
10 Introduction of private property rights.

(Williamson 2004)

With the implosion of the Soviet bloc after 1991, the neoliberal policy orthodoxy began to spread to many countries that had previously been classified as belonging to the so-called 'second world', including, for example, countries of Eastern Europe and Central Asia. However, as we shall see in the next two sections, the hegemony of the Washington Consensus was subsequently challenged from a range of different sources.

The East Asian miracle and its challenge to neoliberalism

Beyond the significant opposition and protest in both the global North and the global South against neoliberalism in development policy, another significant intellectual battle against this form began to arise from a closer examination of the experience of the so-called Asian Tigers – that is, countries such as Japan, South Korea and Taiwan that, during the post-World War II period, had managed to successfully industrialize, develop a significant export economy and create a standard of living for their citizens that was broadly comparable with that experienced by people in the Western world. Initially, writers advocating for neoliberalism claimed that the success of these countries vindicated the prescriptions of the Washington Consensus and proved that by following these kinds of policies it was, indeed, possible for countries to grow rapidly and compete in the global economy. This perspective became solidified with the publication of a World Bank report in 1993 called *The East Asian Miracle*, which argued that the success of the Tiger economies 'proved' the case for neoliberalism.

However, this position was quickly and effectively challenged by a number of influential scholars that asserted a close reading of the experience of these countries, including their institutional frameworks, their economic policies and the role that they gave to the state, pointed to exactly the opposite conclusions – that is, these East Asian countries had become successful precisely because they had not adopted Washington Consensus-style policies (Chang 2006; Wade 1996). Some important points to note here include that each of these countries had a significant role for what became known as the development state – that is, a state which was able to create the conditions for industrialization, including through the provision of highly targeted credit to specific economic entities which they wanted to foster; an initial period of import substitution during which time local business houses could become strong and able to compete globally; and, subsequently, a sympathetic trade environment that gave the products of these countries an entry into Western markets largely as a consequence of their geopolitical importance (Amsden 1989; Chang 2006).

Towards a post-neoliberal era of development? Or deepening the neoliberalization of everyday life?

Unsurprisingly, the combination of widespread popular opposition to the difficulties imposed upon everyday people by neoliberal development policies in the global South has meant that the neoliberal orthodoxy as it came to be understood during the 1980s and early 1990s has increasingly been contested. Matched by empirical evidence, à la the East Asian miracle, the question was not whether the state should be involved but what the appropriate role of the state should be. It is certainly the case that the multilateral institutions have shifted away from such a narrowly focused policy agenda and argue that their prescriptions are no longer able to be characterized as market fundamentalism in the way that they were in the past. Certainly it is the case that the development community now places a much stronger and more central place for mechanisms that increase the inclusion of previously marginalized people. Decentralization, participation and increased attention to ways to increase the legitimacy of development among the community have become part of the policy packages of donors throughout the globe (Williams 2004; Wong 2003). However, there is a great deal of contention about the extent to which the so-called post-Washington Consensus, with its emphasis upon 'getting the institutions right', is a departure from neoliberal orthodoxy or is instead a deepening of this orthodoxy into realms that were previously untouched by development (Cammack 2004; Fine 2009; Ruckert 2006). Certainly we can say that the World Bank has shifted a considerable way from its early position in many respects, and has diverged in important ways from the IMF. The Bank now has poverty at the centre of its agenda; it places a great deal more emphasis upon the state and has funds available for programmes devoted to the removal of social inequalities, such as those around gender or micro-finance, that were not part of its thinking two or more decades before. In that respect, the IMF is much closer to the US Treasury in terms of the narrowness of its policy prescriptions.

An important question to ask at this juncture is whether or not the shifts in development policy that we have seen in the last decade reject many elements of neoliberalism (Jomo and Fine 2005). The case of social capital may be illustrative in that sense since it has become a prominent part of development thinking during this period and the promotion of social capital is an aim of many development policies around the world (Harriss 2001). To its advocates, the promotion of social capital is part of a long overdue recognition of the importance of social relations in fostering the conditions for development and as such demonstrates that development orthodoxy has moved beyond the narrow economism that characterized earlier neoliberal policy prescriptions. To its critics, in contrast, the focus upon social capital is an attempt to extend neoliberal categories of understanding the world into areas that are far more complex than such thinking would allow. Thus, for example, Ben Fine (1999) suggests that social capital – as it is promoted by the World Bank – is influenced by the thinking of scholars such as Robert Putnam and, as such, largely ignores issues of power at a variety of scales. Indeed, his broader critique is that these institutions believe that by promoting social capital ultimately market allocation will become more efficient as information asymmetries will be reduced. To Fine, then, the increasing emphasis upon the social aspects of development has not reduced the predominance of neoliberalism in the theory and practice of development, but is, rather, reflective of what advocates view as an increasingly sophisticated understanding of the conditions which need to be created in order for neoliberalism to flourish.

A further challenge to neoliberalism has arisen in the growing interest in and embrace of an approach to development called post-development. Rather than a single theory of development, post-development began as a critique of the epistemological and ontological closures of mainstream development, drawing extensively from post-structuralist and post-colonial work, particularly, at least initially, from Michel Foucault (Escobar 1995) and Edward Said (McEwan 2008). Post-development argues that development is inherently limited because of its teleological assumptions about progress drawn from Western categories of thought and historical experience, that privilege white, male heteronormative understandings of the world (Ziai 2004). To scholars working in this tradition, the imposition of neoliberal development delegitimizes the experiences and knowledges of 'others' who do not conform to this worldview. To them, effectively, resistance to neoliberalism must necessarily include a question of the foundations of development thought and practice (McKinnon 2007).

Development civil society actors under neoliberalism

The effects of these neoliberal shifts on the agency of people in the global South is contentious for a variety of reasons. On the one hand, neoliberalism deprived the poor and marginalized from at least some state assistance, while, on the other hand, it created a political space for communities to get involved in decision-making over development directions (Jackson and Warren 2005). The development vacuum that was created and the space for civil society to mobilize and organize prompted a proliferation of NGOs and social movements. This proliferation, however, was not unintentional. In the 1980s, the World Bank and other international aid donors made a strategic decision to make NGOs prominent partners in development projects. NGOs were perceived by these bodies as more reliable than governments and as more in touch with and committed to those in need of assistance (Parpart and Veltmeyer 2004). Donor agencies began to pursue a 'New Policy Agenda' which positioned civil society as a prominent force in development efforts. According to Edwards and Hulme (1996) the New Policy Agenda rested on two main pillars, one economic and the other political. The economic pillar rested on a foundational belief in the market and the private sector as the most efficient mechanisms for realizing economic growth and therefore poverty alleviation and development. The political pillar reflected a belief in a good democratic governance as being essential for creating and maintaining an efficient economy. Some development NGOs, therefore, enjoined substantial financial support from Western governments, private foundations and international institutions, and were seen as the new agents of decentralized and participatory development.

In general terms, NGOs were often seen as important players in strengthening liberal democracy by pluralizing the socio-political arena, by facilitating the activities of grassroots organizations of the poor and marginalized, and by scrutinizing state power and pressing for change. NGOs, therefore, were heralded by official agencies and the wider public as important catalysts of a positive democratic development and a 'healthy' and 'vibrant' civil society (Mercer 2002). NGOs have had a progressive promise and the ability to devise and implement innovative programmes (Klees 1998). NGOs were not, however, an invention of neoliberalism, as they already have had a long history of providing health and social services in places where governments lacked the capacity to do so. But under this New Policy Agenda NGOs became the preferred agents for delivering social welfare, and that was a fundamental strategic shift (Edwards and Hulme 1996).

This reliance on civil society, and particularly on NGOs, has been widely questioned and critiqued. The neoliberal theoretical underpinning of the New Policy Agenda may have struck a chord with donors and members of the public, but the empirical evidence was very mixed. There was, and still is, a plethora of NGOs employing a myriad of measures and pursuing a great number of objectives. Not all of them, therefore, are progressive and 'good'. While some were believed to have fulfilled their efficiency and other potentials, that was not always the case and the 'poorest-of-the-poor', for instance, were not always reached. However, as argued by Wallace (2004: 202), 'Evidence-based research does not noticeably shape this analysis, which appears to be influenced more by changing macroeconomic ideologies'. In other words, the 'NGOzation' of development efforts rested more on a neoliberal ideology than on empirical evidence. This does not to imply that NGOs inherently have a neoliberal agenda, although that could sometimes be the case. Nevertheless, the system of pursuing and delivering development through civil society organizations created a high level of dependency, where NGOs need to compete for funding, which in turn comes with conditionalities attached. This has arguably made NGOs propagators, even if reluctantly, of neoliberal agendas in different parts of the world (Hickey and Mohan 2005; Wallace 2004).

Notwithstanding the complex and contested role of development NGOs, it is also the case that they often form associations with progressive social movements, which constitute another element of civil society that is generally more dissenting and combative towards neoliberalism and its various economic, social and political effects. Like NGOs, social movements are not inherently progressive or transformative, but those who are deemed 'progressive' (promoting social justice, equitable wealth distribution, human rights, environmental sustainability and so forth) have been identified by development theorists as having the potential for realizing radical change. As noted by Escobar (1992: 29), 'For many it is in relation to social movements that questions about daily life, democracy, the state, political practice, and the redefinition of develop-ment can be most fruitfully pursued'. Thus, while NGOs have often been criticized for depoliti-cizing development and promoting neoliberal ideas, progressive social movements have represented for many a hopeful political space where individuals and groups challenge and resist different forms of exclusion and exploitation, some historic and others resulting from processes of global neoliberal capitalism.

One of the most notable and celebrated social movements of this kind is the transnational peasant movement La Vía Campesina (The Peasant Way – LVC). This movement has positioned itself in direct and radical opposition to the neoliberal model of global capitalism, with a particular emphasis on food politics. LVC is a worldwide coalition of 164 organizations from 73 countries that brings together some 200 million producers from a range of rural groups, including peasants, small to medium-size farmers, rural indigenous communities, landless workers, rural women and more. The movement was officially established in 1993 as a response to neoliberal restructuring of agricultural policies that favoured large-scale agribusiness corporations and marginalized small-scale family producers. LVC was thus created out of a common vision that family farmers and peasants from the North and South are being threatened by similar processes of neoliberal globalization, albeit facing different local realities and challenges. LVC promotes a grassroots participatory model of agriculture and rural development which aims to generate an encompassing social, political and economic change through the democratic control of communities over productive resources. As the movement grew and consolidated internally, it also reached out and formed alliances with other social movements and NGOs with common interests and visions (Desmarais 2008; Martínez-Torres and Rosset 2010).

In comparison to some other notable global social movements such as the alter-globalization movement or the environmental movement, LVC has a much clearer structure and mechanisms for decision-making. And while democracy has been of rhetorical importance to neoliberal ideology, LVC practices and promotes a far more radical model of a direct democratic participation, where decisions require deliberation and consensus. This horizontal organizational structure, although not without challenges, seeks to promote equality, transparency and solidarity within the movement and among its member organizations and communities. This structure also facilitates the integration of and dialogue between groups of different socio-cultural backgrounds and ideological inclinations (Martínez-Torres and Rosset 2014).

LVC is particularly known for developing and popularizing the concept of food sovereignty. First discussed by LVC in 1996, food sovereignty represents an alternative framework of food production and consumption that is based on:

> the right of peoples to healthy and culturally appropriate food produced through
> ecologically sound and sustainable methods, and their right to define their own food

and agriculture systems… [and that] puts those who produce, distribute and consume food at the heart of food systems and policies rather than the demands of markets and corporations.

(Nyéléni 2007: 9)

This concept, therefore, is positioned in direct opposition to the 'corporate food regime', which is governed by and organized according to neoliberal policies that idealize the market economy (McMichael 2009). This concept has received substantial academic attention in recent years, some more critical and some more sympathetic, but it is worth noting the collaborative and participatory way in which the conceptualization of food sovereignty has evolved over time. And while some aspects may be less clear, such as international trade and the role of the state, food sovereignty remains an important anti-neoliberal framework that engages with one of the most sensitive issues even within neoliberal free trade agreements – agriculture.

LVC and its key framework of food sovereignty are not, therefore, merely a critique of a global neoliberal political economy of agriculture and food production, but a much broader political project. This project explicitly rejects the neoliberal model of rural development and aims to bring about social, economic and political change by opening up democratic spaces and empowering people to actively participate in them and influence political and development processes. In short, LVC 'believes that this kind of change can occur only when local communities gain greater access to and control over local productive resources, and gain more social and political power' (La Vía Campesina 2009: 41).

Individual subjectivities within neoliberalism

Along with the rise of new political actors to resist global injustice, the increased dominance of neoliberalism has also changed the subjectivities of individuals, including those residing in the global North. A significant manifestation of this is an increasing acceptance and embrace of popular humanitarianism with young people becoming particularly mobilized behind humanitarian causes. Celebrity humanitarianism and the iconography of aid present so-called 'developing' nations as places devoid of carers or individuals working towards development (Conradson 2011) and promote a view that Westerners are needed to fill this void. Such acts are heralded for their virtue, with Bornstein (2012) arguing that what makes liberal humanitarian acts heroic is precisely because they are for the 'distant other' rather than for a family member, which is simply expected behaviour. Therefore, although we may feel responsible for providing support and care to these nations, our complicity in their suffering is ignored. Humanitarianism towards people they have no previous connection with is predicated upon 'liberal assumptions about how to perform moral "good"' (ibid.: 151). Yet this ignores the structural violence within the neoliberal capitalist system, with the consequence that people fail to consider how such band-aid solutions dissuade guilt while failing to enact real change (Daley 2013; Vrasti 2013; Vrasti and Montsion 2014).

It has been widely noted that with the roll-back of the state under neoliberalism, volunteering has become increasingly popular as a response to the increased individualization of previously state services and a cultural shift towards moral consumption (Baillie Smith and Laurie 2011; Kapoor 2012; Vrasti 2013; Vrasti and Montsion 2014). Individualized forms of development have become prolific in the neoliberal present with volunteer tourism at the forefront of tourism development agendas (Brown and Morrison 2003; Harlow and Pomfret 2007; McIntosh and Zahra 2007; Mostafanezhad 2014b). Such individualized responses to global inequality are generally by unskilled, young volunteers and for a short-term duration, rather than by traditional development actors trained in specific fields (Chouliaraki 2012; Daley 2013; Kapoor 2012; Mostafanezhad 2013; Wilson and Brown 2009). To Guiney (2015), the growing popularity of these kinds of activities for those from the global North is also indicative of larger processes surrounding the responsibility that Western nations feel towards the global South and the neoliberalization of aid and volunteering. As Vrasti (2013: 2) puts it:

> Phrases like 'giving back to the community' and 'making a difference in the world' that litter the brochure discourse are meant to tickle the post-materialist and anti-modernist sensibilities of the Western ethical consumer looking to demonstrate their superior social capital by 'travelling with a purpose'.

From this perspective, it becomes clear that volunteer tourism is not a spontaneous trend, but rather one steeped in moral and cultural notions of what it means to be an active and moral global citizen and illustrates the importance of an individualized neoliberal subjectivity within the international system (Vrasti 2013; Vrasti and Montsion 2014).

Although initial examinations of volunteer tourism were overwhelmingly positive (Stoddart and Rogerson 2004; Wearing 2001, 2004; Wearing and Neil 2000; Zahra and McIntosh 2007), negative critiques are becoming pronounced (Guttentag 2009, 2011; McGehee and Andereck 2009; Simpson 2004). Increasingly, these critiques are focused upon the ironic juxtaposition of neoliberal actors seeking to address inequality in the neoliberal system by ignoring these structural conditions. Thus, many commentators have argued that the consumer demand for volunteer experiences has emerged partly as a consequence of the rise of celebrity humanitarianism, which celebrates the capacity of the individual to 'make a difference' while simultaneously not seeking to alter the dynamics of the capitalist system (Daley 2013; Guiney 2015; Mostafanezhad 2014a). Biccum (2011) directly links celebrity advocacy with youth mobilization and global citizenship – neoliberalism's solution to inequality and injustice. As Brown and Hall (2008: 845) argue:

> it reduces development to individual acts of charity which seek to work round rather than transform the relationship of poor, rural societies to the natural world. The use of volunteers, who often have little knowledge or experience of the work they are undertaking (an attraction for the volunteers), also calls into question their effectiveness and raises the spectre of neo-colonialism in the tacit assumption that even ignorant Westerners can improve the lot of people in the South.

Such tourism development forms are predicated upon notions of making a difference through travel; however, the impact of these experiences may not actually address poverty and inequality at an adequate or systemic level. Volunteer tourism could ironically be distracting volunteers and visitors from wider social issues, issues that are responsible for inequality within the global system. Such examples alert us to the reality of contemporary neoliberalization of development; namely, that the advancement of these discourses serves to discursively delimit what is discussed and how it is discussed. On the one hand, the processes of global capitalism continue to be responsible for significant social, environmental and ecological injustice. On the other hand, the promotion of neoliberal subjectivities, through tropes such as celebrity humanitarianism, has the effect of enabling those from more privileged parts of the globe to absolve themselves of complicity in the perpetuation of these injustices through the performance of volunteer acts in the global South.

Conclusion

The chapter has outlined the contours of the shifts in development policy and practice over time, so that the reader is placed to assess the position of neoliberalism in the contemporary era of development. Are we now entering an era of a post-Washington Consensus that has seen a lessening of neoliberalism in development policy and practice? Certainly, there is a greater acceptance among some institutions that there is a role for the state in creating the conditions for development to occur, albeit the kind of development linked to the flourishing of markets. It also seems that there is a greater emphasis now put upon issues such as decentralization, participation, gender and the generation of social capital that are much more focused on mechanisms of inclusion than the previously very narrowly focused era of structural adjustment. However, as this chapter has demonstrated, opinion is starkly divided about the extent to which these shifts in development orthodoxy represent a significant *departure* from the neoliberal policies or whether they are instead a *deepening* of neoliberalism in the global South.

The latter part of the chapter has utilized examples of challenges to neoliberalism within development. For those in the global North, the increasing neoliberal subjectivities demonstrated in the rise of celebrity humanitarianism and volunteer tourism illustrate an elision of the ongoing structural biases of global capitalism. However, the rise of global justice movements demonstrates the range of alternatives beyond neoliberal development; while the success of alternative worldviews and practices is always contingent and subject to co-option, it is clear that development will remain a vital battleground in policy and practice for the ongoing spread of neoliberalism throughout the globe.

References

Amsden, A.H. 1989. *Asia's Next Giant: South Korea and Late Industrialization*. Oxford: Oxford University Press.

Baillie Smith, M., and Laurie, N. 2011. International Volunteering and Development: Global Citizenship and Neoliberal Professionalisation Today. *Transactions of the Institute of British Geographers*, 36.4: 545–59.

Biccum, A. 2011. Marketing Development: Celebrity Politics and the 'New' Development Advocacy. *Third World Quarterly*, 32.7: 1331–46.

Bornstein, E. 2012. *Disquieting Gifts: Humanitarianism in New Delhi*. Stanford, CA: Stanford University Press.

Brown, F., and Hall, D. 2008. Tourism and Development in the Global South: The Issues. *Third World Quarterly*, 29.5: 839–49.

Brown, S., and Morrison, A.M. 2003. Expanding Volunteer Vacation Participation: An Exploratory Study on the Mini-Mission Concept. *Tourism Recreation Research*, 28.3: 73–82.

Cammack, P. 2004. What the World Bank Means by Poverty Reduction, and Why it Matters. *New Political Economy*, 9.2: 189–211.

Chang, H.-J. 2006. *The East Asian Development Experience: The Miracle, the Crisis and the Future*. London: Zed Books.

Chouliaraki, L. 2012. The Theatricality of Humanitarianism: A Critique of Celebrity Advocacy. *Communication and Critical/Cultural Studies*, 9.1: 1–21.

Conradson, D. 2011. Care and Caring, in Del Casino, V.J., Thomas, M.E., Cloke, P., and Panelli, R., eds. *A Companion to Social Geography*. Oxford: Wiley-Blackwell: 454–71.

Daley, P. 2013. Rescuing African Bodies: Celebrities, Consumerism and Neoliberal Humanitarianism. *Review of African Political Economy*, 40.137: 375–93.

Desmarais, A.A. 2008. The Power of Peasants: Reflections on the Meanings of La Vía Campesina. *Journal of Rural Studies*, 24.2: 138–49.

Edwards, M., and Hulme, D. 1996. Too Close for Comfort? The Impact of Official Aid on Nongovernmental Organizations. *World Development*, 24.6: 961–73.

Escobar, A. 1992. Imagining a Post-Development Era? Critical Thought, Development and Social Movements. *Social Text*, 31/2: 20–56.

—. 1995. *Encountering Development: The Making and Unmaking of the Third World.* Princeton, NJ: Princeton University Press.

—. 2000. Beyond the Search for a Paradigm? Post-Development and Beyond. *Development*, 43.4: 11–14.

Fine, B. 1999. The Developmental State is Dead: Long Live Social Capital? *Development and Change*, 30.1: 1–19.

—. 2009. Development as Zombieconomics in the age of Neoliberalism. *Third World Quarterly*, 30.5: 885–904.

George, S. 1999. A Short History of Neoliberalism. Paper presented at the Conference on Economic Sovereignty in a Globalising World, Bangkok, Thailand, 24–26 March. Retrieved from https://www.tni.org/en/article/short-history-neoliberalism

Guiney, T.C. 2015. Orphanage Tourism in Cambodia: The Complexities of 'Doing Good' in Popular Humanitarianism. Doctoral dissertation. Geography Department, University of Otago, Dunedin, New Zealand.

Guttentag, D. 2009. The Possible Negative Impacts of Volunteer Tourism. *International Journal of Tourism Research*, 11.6: 537–51.

—. 2011. Volunteer Tourism: As Good as it Seems? *Tourism Recreation Research*, 36.1: 69–74.

Harlow, S., and Pomfret, G. 2007. Evolving Environmental Tourism Experiences in Zambia. *Journal of Ecotourism*, 6.3: 184–209.

Harriss, J. 2001. *Depoliticizing Development: The World Bank and Social Capital.* New Delhi: LeftWord Books.

Harvey, D. 2005. *A Brief History of Neoliberalism.* Oxford: Oxford University Press.

Haynes, J. 2008. *Development Studies: Short Introduction.* Cambridge: Polity.

Hickey, S., and Mohan, G. 2005. Relocating Participation within a Radical Politics of Development. *Development and Change*, 36.2: 237–62.

Jackson, J.E., and Warren, K.B. 2005. Indigenous Movements in Latin America, 1992–2004: Controversies, Ironies, New Directions. *Annual Review of Anthropology*, 34.1: 549–73.

Jomo, K.S., and Fine, B. eds. 2005. *The New Development Economics: After the Washington Consensus.* New Delhi: Tulika Books.

Kapoor, I. 2012. *Celebrity Humanitarianism: The Ideology of Global Charity.* New York: Routledge.

Klees, S. 1998. NGOs: Progressive Force or Neoliberal Tool? *Current Issues in Comparative Education*, 1.1: 49–54.

La Vía Campesina. 2009. La Vía Campesina Policy Documents. Paper presented at the 5th Organizational Meeting and Conference, Mozambique, 16–23 October. Retrieved from http://viacampesina.org/en/index.php/publications-mainmenu-30

Martínez-Torres, M.E., and Rosset, P.M. 2010. La Vía Campesina: The Birth and Evolution of a Transnational Social Movement. *Journal of Peasant Studies*, 37.1: 149–75.

—. 2014. Diálogo de Saberes in La Vía Campesina: Food Sovereignty and Agroecology. *Journal of Peasant Studies*, 41.6: 979–97.

Martinussen, J. 1997. *Society, State and Market: A Guide to Competing Theories of Development.* London: Zed Books.

McEwan, C. 2008. *Postcolonialism and Development.* New York: Routledge.

McGehee, N.G., and Andereck, K. 2009. Volunteer Tourism and the 'Voluntoured': The Case of Tijuana, Mexico. *Journal of Sustainable Tourism*, 17.1: 39–51.

McIntosh, A.J., and Zahra, A. 2007. A Cultural Encounter Through Volunteer Tourism: Towards the Ideals of Sustainable Tourism? *Journal of Sustainable Tourism*, 15.5: 541–56.

McKinnon, K. 2007. Postdevelopment, Professionalism, and the Politics of Participation. *Annals of the Association of American Geographers*, 97.4: 772–85.

McMichael, P. 2009. A Food Regime Analysis of the 'World Food Crisis'. *Agriculture and Human Values*, 26.4: 281–95.

—. 2012. *Development and Social Change: A Global Perspective.* 5th edn. Thousand Oaks, CA: Sage.

Mercer, C. 2002. NGOs, Civil Society and Democratization: A Critical Review of the Literature. *Progress in Development Studies*, 2.1: 5–22.

Mohan, G., Brown, E., Milward, B., and Zack-Williams, A.B. 2000. *Structural Adjustment: Theory, Practice and Impacts.* London: Routledge.

Mostafanezhad, M. 2013. Getting in Touch with your Inner Angelina: Celebrity Humanitarianism and the Cultural Politics of Gendered Generosity in Volunteer Tourism. *Third World Quarterly*, 34.3: 485–99.

—. 2014a. Volunteer Tourism and the Popular Humanitarian Gaze. *Geoforum*, 54 July: 111–18.

—. 2014b. *Volunteer Tourism: Popular Humanitarianism in Neoliberal Times.* Farnham: Ashgate.

Nyéléni. 2007. Nyéléni 2007: Forum for Food Sovereignty. Retrieved from http://nyeleni.org/DOWNLOADS/Nyelni_EN.pdf

Parpart, J.L., and Veltmeyer, H. 2004. The Development Project in Theory and Practice: A Review of its Shifting Dynamics. *Canadian Journal of Development Studies*, 25.1: 39–59.

Petras, J., and Veltmeyer, H. 2011. *Social Movements in Latin America: Neoliberalism and Popular Resistance.* New York: Palgrave Macmillan.

Ruckert, A. 2006. Towards an Inclusive-Neoliberal Regime of Development: From the Washington to the Post-Washington Consensus. *Labour, Capital and Society*, 39.1: 34–67.

Simpson, K. 2004. 'Doing Development': The Gap Year, Volunteer-Tourists and a Popular Practice of Development, *Journal of International Development*, 16.5: 681–92.

Stoddart, H., and Rogerson, C.M. 2004. Volunteer Tourism: The Case of Habitat for Humanity South Africa. *GeoJournal*, 60.3: 311–18.

Vrasti, W. 2013. *Volunteer Tourism in the Global South: Giving Back in Neoliberal Times.* New York: Routledge.

Vrasti, W., and Montsion, J.M. 2014. No Good Deed Goes Unrewarded: The Values/Virtues of Transnational Volunteerism in Neoliberal Capital. *Global Society*, 28.3: 336–55.

Wade, R. 1996. Japan, the World Bank, and the Art of Paradigm Maintenance: The East Asian Miracle in Political Perspective. *New Left Review*, 217: 3–36.

Wallace, T. 2004. NGO Dilemmas: Trojan Horses for Global Neoliberalism? *Socialist Register*, 40: 202–19.

Wearing, S. 2001. *Volunteer Tourism: Experiences That Make a Difference.* New York: CABI.

—. 2004. Examining Best Practice in Volunteer Tourism, in Stebbings, R.A., and Graham, M., eds. *Volunteering as Leisure/Leisure as Volunteering: An International Assessment.* Cambridge: CABI: 209–24.

Wearing, S., and Neil, J. 2000. Refiguring Self and Identity Through Volunteer Tourism. *Society and Leisure*, 23.2: 389–419.

Williams, G. 2004. Evaluating Participatory Development: Tyranny, Power and (re) Politicisation. *Third World Quarterly*, 25.3: 557–78.

Williamson, J. 2004. A Short History of the Washington Consensus. Paper presented at the conference From the Washington Consensus towards a new Global Governance, Barcelona, Spain, 24–25 September. Retrieved from http://www.iie.com/publications/papers/williamson0904-2.pdf

Wilson, R.A., and Brown, R.D. 2009. *Humanitarianism and Suffering: The Mobilization of Empathy.* Cambridge: Cambridge University Press.

Wong, K.-F. 2003. Empowerment as a Panacea for Poverty: Old Wine in New Bottles? Reflections on the World Bank's Conception of Power. *Progress in Development Studies*, 3.4: 307–22.

Zahra, A., and McIntosh, A.J. 2007. Volunteer Tourism: Evidence of Cathartic Tourist Experiences. *Tourism Recreation Research*, 32.1: 115–19.

Ziai, A. 2004. The Ambivalence of Post-Development: Between Reactionary Populism and Radical Democracy. *Third World Quarterly*, 25.6: 1045–60.

12

NEOLIBERALISM AND THE END OF DEMOCRACY

Jason Hickel

A contradiction lies at the very centre of the neoliberal project. On a theoretical level, neoliberalism promises to bring about a purer form of democracy, unsullied by the tyranny of the state. Indeed, this claim serves as the moral lodestar for neoliberal ideology – the banner under which it justifies radical market deregulation. But, in practice, it becomes clear that the opposite is true: that neoliberalism tends to *undermine* democracy and political freedom (see Bruff 2014; Springer 2009). More than 40 years of experimentation with neoliberalism shows that it erodes the power of voters to decide the rules that govern the economic systems they inhabit. It allows for the colonization of existing political forums by elite interests – a process known as political capture – and sets up new political forums, such as the World Bank, the IMF, and the WTO, that preclude democratic representation from the outset. Neoliberalism also tends to undermine national sovereignty, to the point where the parliaments of putatively independent nations no longer have power over their own policy decisions, but are governed instead by foreign banks, the US Treasury, trade agreements, and undemocratic international institutions, all of which exercise a kind of invisible, remote-control power.

On the face of it, this may seem like an accident – as though the erosion of democracy were an unfortunate outcome of an otherwise well-intended theory. And to be fair, we might grant that many of the policy-makers who have been won over by the rhetoric of neoliberal ideology – and perhaps even the think tanks that promote it – sincerely believe its claims. But the history of the past 40 years suggests a different story, namely, that the erosion of democracy has been a necessary political precondition for the implementation of neoliberal economic policy. In other words, radical market deregulation has required the dismantling or circumvention of the very democratic mechanisms that neoliberal ideology claims in theory to support and protect.

In the name of freedom

To understand the tendency of neoliberalism to undermine democracy, it helps to understand the political context from which it emerged. The Keynesian revolution that followed the Great Depression and World War II dramatically transformed the distribution of wealth and power between classes, closing the inequality gap that had become so pronounced from the late nineteenth century through to the 1920s. In the USA, Franklin Roosevelt's New Deal had brought in higher tax rates on the very rich and full employment through state spending, while the union movement – which had built up unprecedented strength – was keeping workers' wages high and rising with productivity. In Britain, Clement Atlee's Labour government had nationalized public utilities and the commanding heights of industry, and was rolling out a robust welfare state that included free healthcare and higher education for all. In the global South, many regions had been swept by democratic elections that brought in pro-poor candidates who sought to restrict the power of Western multinational corporations in favour of 'developmentalist' policies that promised land reforms and supported national industries with subsidies and tariff protections. Not only were these measures popular among voters, they also delivered remarkably high rates of economic growth and had a substantial impact against poverty. This was the age of what David Harvey (2005) has called 'embedded liberalism', in a gesture to Karl Polanyi (1944). It was a form of market capitalism that was embedded in society, devoted to social welfare, and responsive to democratic processes.

But this system had its enemies. While embedded liberalism delivered high rates of growth, the very rich – whose economic and political power had been curtailed during the post-war decades – were taking home a smaller proportion of the overall pie. In the USA, the share of national income going to the richest 1 per cent fell from 16 per cent to 8 per cent. And it was even worse for the richest 0.1 per cent, the very elite. In the USA, Britain, and France, their share of national income fell from more than 10 per cent to less than 2 per cent (Piketty and Saez 2003). The elite class knew that the only way to restore their power was to roll back the economic regulations that had been brought in by the Keynesian consensus, following the prescriptions of economists like Friedrich von Hayek and Milton Friedman, who argued for the abolition of nearly all forms of state intervention in the economy. There was only one problem: the voters who had benefited so much from the Keynesian revolution would never be willing to support such a regressive move. Because it was impossible to acquire the political capital necessary to accomplish this in the USA or Britain, or in any country with a functioning democracy, the first experiments in neoliberalism had to be imposed by force.

Chile provided an ideal crucible for this experiment. In 1973, the CIA backed a coup that toppled the democratically elected government of Salvador Allende, who had angered the USA by implementing a popular programme of nationalization. The coup replaced Allende with a military junta led by Augusto Pinochet, who proceeded to impose a battery of economic policies that were designed by Friedman and economists who had studied under him at the University of Chicago, the hub of neoliberal thought at the time. The Pinochet regime knew that these measures – the privatization of state companies, banks, education, and social security; the elimination of tariff barriers, subsidies, and price controls; and deep cuts to government spending on social services – would lead to mass unemployment, impoverishment, and economic contraction. The only way to push them through was to do so quickly and without any democratic debate, and then to clamp down on political dissent – what Friedman himself referred to as 'shock treatment'. According to declassified CIA documents, the Pinochet regime arrested and imprisoned between 80,000 and 100,000 political dissidents, most of them peasants and workers. Some 3,200 people were disappeared or executed, many of them in sports stadiums that were used as mass death camps. Another 200,000 were exiled or fled as political refugees (Klein 2007:76).

Chile was not the only early experiment in forced market liberalization. Friedman and his students served as advisors to the Brazilian government in the 1970s as it presided over similar economic reforms. In Uruguay, a US-backed military junta took power in 1973 and applied Chicago School principles under the direction of Arnold Harberger. In Argentina, a US-backed junta seized power in 1976 and applied the same measures: banning strikes, lifting price controls, privatizing state companies, and using torture to suppress political resistance. The important point to take from this history is that the imposition of neoliberal economic policies required the abolition of democratic government, and a state terror programme that was robust enough to disable resistance wherever it emerged. In other words, the political sphere had to be *regulated* – and heavily so – in order to *deregulate* the economy to the extent that neoliberal ideology demanded. Total market freedom required total political unfreedom, even to the extent of mass imprisonment and concentration camps.

In the West, where coups were not an option, this battle had to be fought at the level of ideology. The proponents of neoliberalism had to convince voters that market deregulation would bolster freedom and democracy. Hayek and Friedman were instrumental in building this argument, which was a new addition to the rhetoric of free-market capitalism. Hayek's 1944 book, *The Road to Serfdom*, argued that government interference with the economy – such as the Keynesian policies that dominated the USA and Britain at the time – would lead inevitably to totalitarianism, and that the push to secure the welfare of the masses through socialism would end up demolishing the political freedoms that socialists claimed to revere. True freedom could only be secured by unfettered market capitalism, he claimed. Friedman took this argument further in his 1962 book, *Capitalism and Freedom*, which proposed specific economic policies and advocated for the complete elimination of trade barriers, currency controls, public education, labour regulation, and graduated taxes. These ideas were picked up and pushed by lobbying groups such as the conservative Heritage Foundation, the Business Roundtable, and later the Cato Institute, which sought to build up the association between neoliberalism and democracy in the public consciousness.

This argument proved to be incredibly appealing to Western voters, particularly as the Cold War gathered steam and as anti-state, anti-union, and anti-bureaucracy sentiment gained traction after 1968. The argument was given fresh credence when Hayek and Friedman each won the Sveriges Riksbank Prize in the 1970s, which is commonly, but incorrectly, known as the Nobel Prize in Economics. So when economic crisis hit in the 1970s, voters were primed to accept the alternative economic model that Hayek and Friedman had proposed. The Reagan and Thatcher administrations eventually came to power on platforms that promised to enhance individual freedoms by liberating capitalism from the 'shackles' of the state – reducing taxes on the rich, cutting state spending, privatizing utilities, deregulating financial markets, and curbing the power of unions. After Reagan and Thatcher, these policies were carried forward even by putatively progressive administrations such as Clinton's in the USA and Blair's in Britain, thus sealing the new economic consensus across party lines.

A creeping tyranny

The claim was that these radical free-market policies would increase economic growth and that the yields would 'trickle down' to the people, but in reality the opposite happened. Per capita income growth rates fell from 3.2 per cent to 2.1 per cent, beginning in the 1980s (Chang 2007: 26), and inequality increased at an alarming rate: in the USA, the proportion of national income going to the richest 1 per cent more than doubled, from 8 per cent to 18 per cent, while in Britain it jumped from 6.5 per cent to 13 per cent, restoring levels not seen since the Gilded Age. It bears pointing out that the people who benefited most from this upward redistribution of wealth were not necessarily the same people – or even the same class – who lost it during the post-war decades. This was particularly true in Britain, where Thatcher's policies eroded the power of the old aristocracy and handed it instead to corporate executives. In the USA, CEO salaries increased by an average of 400 per cent during the 1990s (Anderson *et al.* 2006). Meanwhile, median household incomes stagnated, and wages declined in real terms. The deregulation of the financial sector (marked in Britain by the 'Big Bang' of 1986 and in the USA by the abolition of the Glass-Steagall Act in 1999) paved the way for trends in risky market speculation that led, in the end, to the 2008 financial crisis, massive economic contraction, and long-term unemployment (Stiglitz 2010).

The growing economic power of the richest percentiles translated directly into increased political power, as they gained new influence over elections. In the USA, the collapse of the unions as a result of neoliberal reforms has meant that corporations are able to outcompete labour in campaign financing. Their position was further strengthened in 2010, when the Supreme Court ruled in Citizens United vs FEC that corporations have a constitutional right to spend unlimited amounts of money on political advertising as an exercise of 'free speech'. In a 2014 case known as McCutcheon vs FEC, the Court went a step further and struck down all government restrictions on individual contributions to political parties. These measures – justified according to the principle of corporate personhood – have made it difficult for candidates to win elections without direct corporate support, placing politicians under pressure to eschew policy positions that might be unpalatable to economic elites.

This elite political capture has been furthered by the rise of the lobbying industry: $3.55 billion was spent on federal lobbying in the USA in 2010, up from $1.45 billion in 1998 (Center for Responsive Politics 2014). A 2009 study found that corporations that invested in lobbying the US Congress earlier in the decade earned returns of up to 22,000 per cent in the form of tax breaks and profits from preferential treatment (Alexander *et al.* 2009). Yet another expression of political capture can be seen in the 'revolving door' phenomenon, whereby government regulators of key industries are drawn from the very industries they are supposed to regulate. One striking recent example is Henry Paulson, who served as the CEO of Goldman Sachs before becoming the US Treasury Secretary and orchestrating the Wall Street bailout of 2008.

As a result of political capture, the interests of economic elites in the USA almost always prevail in government policy decisions even when the vast majority of citizens disagree. A 2014 study by scholars at Princeton and Northwestern universities confirmed this with evidence from 1981 to 2002, leading the authors to conclude that the USA resembles an oligarchy more than a democracy (Gilens and Page 2014). Britain exhibits similar tendencies, albeit for different (and older) reasons. Britain's financial hub and economic powerhouse, the City of London, has long been immune from many of the nation's democratic laws and remains free of parliamentary oversight. Voting power in the City of London council is allocated not only to residents, but also to businesses, taking corporate personhood to another level. And the bigger the business, the more votes it gets, with the largest firms getting 79 votes each. In the British Parliament, the House of Lords is filled not by election but by appointment, with 92 seats inherited by aristocratic families, 26 set aside for the Church of England, and many others 'sold' to rich individuals in return for large campaign donations (Hope and Swinford 2013).

In both the USA and Britain, political dissent is managed by a combination of mass surveillance (as Edward Snowden and Julian Assange have revealed), an increasingly militarized police force (on display during the Occupy protests of 2011 and the Ferguson protests of 2014), and the consolidation of media ownership. In the USA, the Telecommunications Act of 1996 largely deregulated the media industry, allowing for cross-ownership which has since led to significant mergers. In the early 1980s, 50 companies controlled 90 per cent of all American media; by 2011, that same 90 per cent share was controlled by only six companies. In Britain, the Thatcher administration allowed unprecedented consolidation in the newspaper industry, so that today only three companies control 70 per cent of the market, with Rupert Murdoch's empire controlling more than a third (Media Reform Coalition 2014).

Remote-control power

The above illustrates how democracy in the USA and Britain has been undermined by economic policies that have shifted political power to elites and corporations. But outside the West democracy has faced a different kind of threat – one that has to do with the structure of international debt. During the 1970s, Wall Street investment banks peddled large loans to the governments of capital-starved developing countries, confident that this would be a safe investment as governments would be unlikely to default. But when interest rates shot up in the early 1980s as a result of the Volcker Shock in the USA, indebted countries slid to the brink of default in what became known as the Third World Debt Crisis. Intent on protecting Wall Street from collapse, the US government stepped in to ensure that developing countries would repay their debts. They used the IMF to roll over the debts on the condition that developing countries would agree to a series of 'structural adjustment programmes', or SAPs. Development countries could technically refuse and proceed with default, but if they did so they risked US military invasion. SAPs included three broad policies: cuts to social spending, privatization of public assets, and liberalization of trade and finance. Beginning in the 1980s, these same principles were set as preconditions for new development loans from the World Bank.

In other words, debt became a powerful mechanism for imposing neoliberalism around the world, and for rolling back the developmentalist agenda that Washington found so threatening – more powerful, even, than the coups that had been used in the past. The promise, once again, was that neoliberal reform would improve economic growth and reduce poverty, but instead it did exactly the opposite. Per capita income growth rates in developing countries plunged to half their previous levels, falling from more than 3 per cent to 1.7 per cent. In Sub-Saharan Africa the GNP of the average country *shrank* by around 10 per cent during the 1980s and 1990s (Chang 2007: 27–8). All told, developing countries lost roughly $480 billion per year in potential GDP (Pollin 2003). It would be difficult to overestimate the scale of human suffering that these numbers represent. Yet multinational corporations, for their part, benefited tremendously from the opportunity to enter new markets, access cheap labour and raw materials, and buy up state assets at fire-sale prices.

Structural adjustment represented a serious attack on democracy in the global South. It meant that key decisions over economic policy were made not by national parliaments, but rather by bankers and technocrats in Washington and New York. It operated as a new kind of coup: a way for Washington to impose its economic agenda without the bloodshed, torture, and overt dictatorship that marked the Chile experiment. Furthermore, most citizens would never know it happened; they would continue to believe that their elected representatives held power, when, in fact, power – at least over some policy portfolios – had been shifted abroad. If given the chance, citizens probably would have voted against the harmful economic policies imposed through structural adjustment, but they were never afforded that opportunity. When adjustment caused unemployment to rise, wages to decline, and food prices to skyrocket, people took to the streets with protests and riots. These 'IMF riots', as they were called, swept across the global South in the 1980s and 1990s, but they had little effect: the ultimate targets of their discontent were in Washington, and had no reason to listen to them. It is interesting to consider the significance of this. Structural adjustment marked the end of meaningful national sovereignty only a few decades after global South countries gained their independence from colonialism.

Another key problem is that the international institutions that impose structural adjustment, and govern global economic policy more broadly, are themselves profoundly undemocratic. Voting power in the IMF and World Bank is apportioned according to each nation's share of financial ownership, just as in corporations. Major decisions require 85 per cent of the vote, and the US Treasury, which holds about 16 per cent of the shares in both institutions, wields de facto veto power. Middle- and low-income countries, which constitute some 85 per cent of the population, have only about 40 per cent of the vote. This is ironic, given that both institutions – and particularly the World Bank – require 'democratic governance' of borrowers as a condition for loans. What is more, the leaders of these institutions are not elected, but appointed by the USA and Europe: according to a longstanding gentleman's agreement, the president of the World Bank is always an American (and almost always a Wall Street executive or a US military boss), while the president of the IMF is always a European. There have been repeated calls by developing countries to democratize the World Bank and the IMF. In 2010 a reform package was finally introduced, but it amounted to little more than window dressing: only 3 per cent of voting power shifted from rich countries to poor countries (about half of that going to China), and the USA retained its veto power.

The World Trade Organization, too, has come under scrutiny for its democratic deficit. Founded in 1994, the WTO is technically governed according to a one-country, one-vote process, and all major decisions are supposed to be made on a consensus basis. But, in practice, market size determines bargaining power: large economies like the USA grant access to their consumer markets in exchange for tariff reductions and special concessions for their corporations, which can be devastating to local industries in poorer countries. On top of this, rich countries negotiate key decisions in special 'green room' meetings from which developing countries are generally excluded – a tactic that allows them to circumvent the consensus process. Finally, rich countries can afford to maintain a permanent contingent of staff at the WTO headquarters in Geneva, and send hundreds of people to the bargaining meetings; poorer countries that cannot afford such staff have little say, even in decisions that affect them directly. As a result of these imbalances, the international trade system is skewed heavily in favour of rich countries. And this order is protected by the WTO's private courts: if poor countries choose to disobey trade rules that hurt their economies, rich countries can retaliate with crushing sanctions.

But perhaps the most profound threat to democratic sovereignty comes from financial liberalization, which has created what some scholars have called a 'virtual senate' (Chomsky 2010). This requires a bit of explanation. The Bretton Woods system designed by Keynes was intended to grant states the power to control capital flows across their borders. If foreign investors wanted to pull their money out, they had to go through a rigorous application process. This helped prevent sudden outflows of capital, which can be very damaging particularly to smaller economies. But neoliberal reforms have gradually dismantled these capital controls, giving investors the ability to move capital whenever they please. This has granted them an enormous amount of political power. If a country decides to increase its minimum wage or regulate pollution, thus reducing corporate profit margins, then investors can quickly pull their money out and send it somewhere else. This means that investors can conduct moment-by-moment referendums on decisions made by voters or governments around the world, bestowing their favor on countries that facilitate profit maximization while punishing those that prioritize other concerns, like decent wages or a healthy environment, by pulling their capital. And when investors decide to punish, it hurts – for poor countries that rely on foreign investment just to stay afloat, it can push them to the brink of crisis. In this sense, investors operate as a virtual senate. Sitting in their high-rise offices somewhere out there, they are the ones with ultimate power over economic policy. Voters dare not cross them. The work of the virtual senate is lubricated by the World Bank's 'Doing Business Report', which ranks countries each year according to their friendliness to foreign investment. Investors use the rankings to decide how to move their money. As a result, countries must compete to deregulate in order to rise in the rankings and attract the favor of foreign investors (Hickel 2014).

The growing power of the virtual senate and the rise of global governance organizations like the World Bank, the IMF, and the WTO pose a conundrum for neoliberal theory. People commonly think of neoliberalism as an ideology that promotes totally free markets, where the state retreats from the scene and abandons interventionist policies. But in reality the extension of neoliberalism has entailed powerful new forms of state intervention. The creation of a global 'free market' required not only violent coups and dictatorships backed by Western governments, but also the invention of a totalizing global bureaucracy with reams of new laws, backed up by the military power of the USA (Graeber 2009). In other words, an unprecedented expansion of state power has been necessary to force countries around the world to liberalize their markets against their will. This process has not enhanced political freedom and democracy, as its proponents claimed it would; rather, it has shifted political power away from democratically elected decision-making bodies and placed it in the hands of remote, unelected bureaucrats.

The 'free trade' fallacy

Neoliberal policies are promoted around the world not only by international financial institutions and the WTO, but also by free trade agreements, or FTAs. The first major FTA was the North American Free Trade Agreement between Canada, Mexico, and the USA, which came into effect in 1994. NAFTA, like other FTAs, focused on removing trade barriers, legalizing capital flight, and ending 'market distortions' like price controls. Not surprisingly, NAFTA was highly controversial and widely resisted by voters. In Mexico, hundreds of thousands of farmers took to the streets of the capital with their tractors. In Canada, the general elections in 1988 and 1993 were fought almost exclusively on the issue of NAFTA. A majority of Canadians voted for parties that promised to stop NAFTA in both elections; nonetheless, the governments that assumed power each time ended up accepting the agreement. In the USA, however, the agreement was more or less successfully marketed under the banner of 'freedom'. Indeed, the term 'free trade' itself proved capable of neutralizing opposition: to take a stand against free trade appeared as taking a stand against freedom itself, which is not a tenable position in American politics.

Yet, in reality, agreements like NAFTA have nothing to do with enhancing human freedom. Rather, they are designed primarily to enhance *corporate* freedom: the freedom for corporations to move around the world at will, to access new export markets and investment opportunities, and to make use of cheaper labour. By stripping away Mexico's tariff barriers, NAFTA allowed US agricultural companies to dump cheap, heavily subsidized corn over the border. This caused the local market to collapse and some 2 million farmers were forced to abandon their land, much of which was then snapped up by American companies. And because NAFTA deregulated food prices, the cost of tortillas shot up by 279 per cent in the first decade. According to a recent report by *The New York Times*, as a result of NAFTA 'Twenty-five percent of the population does not have access to basic food and one-fifth of Mexicans suffer from malnutrition' (Carlson 2013). NAFTA has also taken a heavy toll on workers. Today, the income of a farm worker in Mexico is one-third what it was before NAFTA, real wages across the board are lower, and the minimum wage is worth 24 per cent less (Public Citizen n.d.). In the USA, NAFTA displaced a total of 682,900 jobs, most of which were high-paying and unionized, further eroding the labour movement and contributing to downward pressure on wages (Scott 2011).

But the most interesting of NAFTA's provisions, for the purpose of this chapter, was the inclusion of Chapter 11, which focused on 'investor state dispute settlement', or ISDS. ISDS allows investors to sue their host states for laws that might reduce their 'expected future profits'. For example, imagine that Mexican voters elect politicians who promise to roll out new worker safety standards for garment sweatshops, or new limits on the toxic chemical dyes that sweatshops dump into local rivers. And imagine that these new rules are ratified by the national parliament with unanimous support. If the multinational corporations that run those sweatshops – say, Nike or Gap – believe that their profits will be negatively affected by these rules, they have the power to sue the Mexican government to stop their implementation, subverting the will of the people and overriding the power of their elected representatives.

There have been many such cases filed under NAFTA's Chapter 11. Metalclad, a US corporation, sued the state of Mexico for refusing to award a construction permit for the hazardous waste landfill it had proposed to develop, on the basis that it would be harmful to the environment. Mexico was forced to pay $16.7 million to Metalclad in damages.[1] In Canada, Dow Agrosciences, a US corporation, is suing the government for banning the use of its pesticides on the basis that they may cause cancer in humans.[2] All of these cases follow the same pattern: corporations sue the state for laws that limit their potential profits in the interest of human rights, public health, or the environment. These lawsuits have the power to force states to back down from regulatory legislation. It is worth pausing to consider the implications of this. ISDS effectively grants corporations the power to strike down the laws of sovereign nations. In other words, corporations are empowered to regulate democratic states, rather than the other way around – a frontal assault on the ideas of sovereignty and democracy, and one that is, ironically, being conducted under the banner of freedom. Even when lawsuits are not filed, the mere threat of them can act as a powerful disciplining force that curtails the latitude that elected representatives have over policy space.

What is perhaps most troubling about ISDS mechanisms is that they are intrinsically imbalanced. Investors have the right to sue states, but states do not have a corresponding right to sue foreign investors. The most a state can hope to win out of an ISDS settlement is the nullification of the suit; a state cannot claim damages from foreign corporations. In other words, ISDS grants special new powers and freedoms to undemocratic corporate investors while eroding those of sovereign, democratic states. Furthermore, ISDS hearings are conducted in secret tribunals that have none of the checks and balances and transparency that characterize normal public courts. The judges in these hearings are corporate lawyers – a practice that persists despite the obvious conflict of interest – and the proceedings are conducted in secret (Perry 2012).[3] The citizens and communities that are negatively affected by the investors are not represented in the hearings. And yet the investors have the power to overthrow the decisions of parliaments and the rulings of national courts. This arrangement is so shocking that one arbiter from Spain has said:

> When I wake up at night and think about arbitration, it never ceases to amaze me that sovereign states have agreed to investment arbitration at all… Three private individuals are entrusted with the power to review, without any restriction or appeal procedure, all actions of the government, all decisions of the courts, and all laws and regulations emanating from parliament.
>
> *(Cited in ibid.)*

NAFTA has served as a blueprint for similar FTAs elsewhere around the world, and there are now dozens of them. CAFTA, for example, was passed in 2005, also under controversial circumstances: voting was held open nearly two hours longer than normal in the US House of Representatives in order to get some members to change their votes, which yielded a final margin of 217–215. Like NAFTA, CAFTA includes an ISDS mechanism, and it has already been brought into use on a number of occasions. In El Salvador, citizens recently voted to ban a gold mine planned by Pacific Rim, a Canadian corporation, because it threatened to destroy part of the national river system. Pacific Rim is now suing El Salvador for $315 million-worth of lost potential profits (Kosich 2013).

As of 2015, there are two new FTAs that are under negotiation: the Transatlantic Trade and Investment Partnership (TTIP), which will govern trade between the USA and the European Union, and the Trans-Pacific Partnership (TPP), which will govern trade between the USA and Pacific Rim countries. These trade deals go much further than earlier deals, which seem almost quaint by comparison. The primary aim of TTIP, for instance, is not to reduce trade tariffs, as these are already at minimal levels, but rather to reduce any 'barriers' to corporate profit maximization: labour laws, digital privacy laws, environmental protections, food safety standards, and financial regulations. TTIP could make it illegal for governments to stop commercial banks from engaging in securities trading, which was one of the main causes of the 2008 financial crisis. It will also prevent governments from limiting the size of banks, and will prohibit the proposed Robin Hood Tax on financial transactions – two measures that are considered essential to preventing another financial crisis. And, perhaps most worryingly of all, it will restrict governments from limiting the extraction and consumption of fossil fuels. If it is passed, elected politicians will find themselves stripped of their power to defend the interests of their people and the planet against economic crisis and climate change.

The TPP, for its part, includes a chapter that would seriously curtail internet freedoms (it includes much of the text of SOPA, a controversial bill that was rejected by the US Congress), and extends the duration of monopoly patents – even for life-saving medicines and seeds. We only know about these provisions because of whistleblowers who have leaked draft chapters of the TTIP and TPP to the public.[4] At the time of writing the rest of the chapters remain shrouded in secrecy. Not even the parliaments of the signatory nations have been allowed to read the draft agreement, much less the voting public. Only the negotiators – which include advisors to 605 corporations – have full access.

These new FTAs amount to something like a corporate coup d'état on an international scale. They create an avenue for legislation that completely bypasses national parliaments and any form of democratic discussion, pouring scorn on the idea of elected government. In this sense, it appears that the ideology of 'free trade' has overplayed its hand, and exposed itself as farce. TTIP and TPP make it clear that free trade was never meant to be about freedom in the first place. Indeed, the very things that *do* promote real human freedoms – such as the rights of workers to organize, equal access to decent public services, and safeguards for a healthy environment – are being cast as somehow anti-democratic, or even totalitarian. These freedoms are reframed as 'red tape' or as 'market barriers', even when, as is almost always the case, they have been won by popular grassroots movements exercising their democratic franchise. In this paradigm, democracy itself is targeted, bizarrely, as anti-democratic, inasmuch as it grants voters control over the economic policies that affect their lives.

Democratic backlash

News media commonly celebrate the fact that an increasing number of countries are run by democratic governments. Indeed, today the majority of people on the planet live under some kind of democracy. But this claim becomes questionable when we consider the reality of political capture and media monopolies, and the shift of sovereign power away from elected governments and into the hands of global governance institutions, free trade agreements, and financial centres. Democracy, it appears, is thriving in name only.

People are beginning to recognize this fact. In 1994, a group of the indigenous Mexican farmers harmed most by NAFTA opted to withdraw from the political system altogether and established their own autonomous zone. The Zapatistas, as they are called, persist to this day, and have inspired similar movements for democratic sovereignty across Latin America (Zibechi 2005). In 1999, tens of thousands of anti-globalization activists from around the world succeeded in shutting down the WTO meetings in Seattle, in what was the most highly publicized act of resistance to neoliberalism up to that point. In 2011, the Occupy movement in New York and the Indignados in Spain sparked global protests against financial liberalization, the outsized power of big banks, and the austerity measures imposed as a form of structural adjustment in Western states as a supposed 'solution' to economic crisis. Tellingly, in all of these protests resistance against neoliberal capitalism has come not as a demand for socialism – as one might have expected a few decades ago – but as a demand for democracy. A prominent banner in the Occupy London camp proclaimed 'Real democracy reborn here'. Resistance is now also appearing in the sphere of electoral politics. In 2014, a referendum in Scotland saw nearly half the population vote to leave the United Kingdom, in a bold rebuke of remote-control power from Westminster and Washington. In 2015, Syriza won national elections in Greece with their call to reclaim democratic sovereignty and liberate the country from the overbearing power of external creditors. A number of similar movements have emerged across southern Europe as austerity continues to take its toll.

Neoliberal reforms have undermined democratic sovereignty over the past 40 years, but they have also set off a popular backlash that is growing bold enough to make demands for new and more radical forms of democracy (Juris 2008; Maeckelbergh 2009). It is still too early to tell, but the end of democracy as we knew it might also mark the beginning of something else.

Notes

1 See *Metalclad Corp. vs United Mexican States.*
2 See *Dow AgroSciences LLC vs Government of Canada.*
3 Secrecy provisions in many ISDS tribunals are now changing, in the face of public pressure.
4 A full draft of the TTIP text was leaked to the BBC in February 2015. Two chapters of the TPP have been leaked to Wikileaks: a chapter on intellectual property was leaked in November 2013, and a chapter on ISDS was leaked in March 2015.

References

Alexander, R.M., Mazza, S.W., and Scholz, S. 2009. Measuring Rates of Return for Lobbying Expenditures: An Empirical Case Study of Tax Breaks for Multinational Corporations. *Journal of Law and Politics*, 25.401.

Anderson, S., Cavanagh, J., Collins, C., and Benjamin, E. 2006. Executive Excess 2006: 13th Annual CEO Compensation Survey. Pizzigati, S., ed. *Institute for Policy Studies and United for a Fair Economy*. Retrieved from http://s3.amazonaws.com/corpwatch.org/downloads/ExecutiveExcess2006.pdf

Bruff, I. 2014. The Rise of Authoritarian Neoliberalism. *Rethinking Marxism: A Journal of Economics, Culture, and Society*, 26.1: 113–29.

Carlson, L. 2013. Under NAFTA, Mexico Suffered, and the United States Felt its Pain. *The New York Times*, 24 November. Retrieved from http://www.nytimes.com/roomfordebate/2013/11/24/what-weve-learned-from-nafta/under-nafta-mexico-suffered-and-the-united-states-felt-its-pain

Center for Responsive Politics. 2014. *Lobbying Database*. Retrieved from https://www.opensecrets.org/lobby/

Chang, H. 2007. *Bad Samaritans: The Guilty Secrets of Rich Nations and the Threat to Global Prosperity*. London: Random House.

Chomsky, N. 2010. *Hopes and Prospects*. Chicago: Haymarket.

Friedman, M. 1962. *Capitalism and Freedom*. Chicago: University of Chicago Press.

Gilens, M., and Page, B.I. 2014. Testing Theories of American Politics: Elites, Interest Groups, and Average Citizens. *Perspectives on Politics*, 12.3: 564–81.

Graeber, D. 2009. *Direct Action: An Ethnography*. Oakland: AK Press.

Harvey, D. 2005. *A Brief History of Neoliberalism*. Oxford: Oxford University Press.

Hayek, F. 1944. *The Road to Serfdom*. Chicago: University of Chicago Press.

Hickel, J. 2014. The New Shock Doctrine: 'Doing Business' with the World Bank. *Al Jazeera English*. Retrieved from http://www.aljazeera.com/indepth/opinion/2014/04/new-shock-doctrine-doing-busines-20144473715915842.html

Hope, C., and Swinford, S. 2013. Peerages for Multi-millionaires. *The Telegraph*, 1 August. Retrieved from http://www.telegraph.co.uk/news/politics/10217409/Peerages-for-multi-millionaires-who-donated-their-way-into-the-Lords.html

Juris, J. S. 2008. *Networking Futures: The Movements Against Corporate Globalization*. Durham, NC: Duke University Press.

Klein, N. 2007. *The Shock Doctrine: The Rise of Disaster Capitalism*. New York: Metropolitan.

Kosich, D. 2013. Pacific Rim Mining Files $315m Claim Against El Salvador. *Mineweb*, 2 April. Retrieved from http://www.mineweb.com/archive/pacific-rim-mining-files-us315m-claim-against-el-salvador/

Maeckelbergh, M. 2009. *The Will of the Many: How the Alterglobalisation Movement is Changing the Face of Democracy*. New York: Pluto Press.

Media Reform Coalition. 2014. The Elephant in the Room: A Survey of Media Ownership and Plurality in the United Kingdom. Retrieved from http://www.mediareform.org.uk/wp-content/uploads/2014/04/ElephantintheroomFinalfinal.pdf

Perry, S. 2012. Arbitrator and Counsel: The Double-Hat Syndrome. *Global Arbitration Review*, 7.2. Retrieved from: http://globalarbitrationreview.com/journal/article/30399/stockholm-arbitrator-counsel-double-hat-syndrome

Piketty, T., and Saez, E. 2003. Income Inequality in the United States, 1913–1998. *Quarterly Journal of Economics*, 118: 1–39.

Polanyi, K. 1944. *The Great Transformation*. Boston: Beacon Press.

Pollin, R. 2003. *Contours of Descent: US Economic Fractures and the Landscape of Global Austerity*. New York: Verso.

Public Citizen. n.d. NAFTA's Legacy for Mexico. *Public Citizen*. Retrieved from https://www.citizen.org/documents/ImpactsonMexicoMemoOnePager.pdf

Scott, R. 2011. Heading South: US–Mexico Trade and Job Displacement after NAFTA. *Economic Policy Institute*, May 3. Retrieved from http://www.epi.org/publication/heading_south_u-s-mexico_trade_and_job_displacement_after_nafta1/

Springer, S. 2009. Renewed Authoritarianism in Southeast Asia: Undermining Democracy Through Neoliberal Reform. *Asia Pacific Viewpoint*, 50: 271–6.

Stiglitz, J. 2010. *Freefall*. New York: W.W. Norton & Co.

Zibechi, R. 2005. Subterranean Echos: Resistance and Politics 'Desde el Sotano'. *Socialism and Democracy*, 19: 13–39.

13

THE VIOLENCE OF NEOLIBERALISM

Simon Springer

The ascent of neoliberalism can be understood as a particular form of anxiety, a disquiet born in the wake of the Second World War when the atrocities of Nazi Germany, Fascist Italy, and the Soviet Union fostered a belief that government intervention trampled personal freedoms and thereby unleashed indescribable slaughter (Mirowski and Plehwe 2009). There is some truth to be found in this concern, but the response that followed has exhibited its own violent tendencies. The Mont Pelerin Society, the originary neoliberal think tank, responded by resurrecting classical liberalism's three basic tenets. First, a concentrated focus on the individual, who was viewed as the most qualified to communicate his or her desires, whereby society should be reoriented towards removing obstacles that hinder this goal. Second, free markets were considered the most proficient means for advancing self-reliance, whereby individuals could pursue their needs through the mechanism of price. Finally, a faith in a non-interventionist state that would emphasize and maintain competitive markets and guarantee individual rights shaped around a property regime (Hackworth 2007; Plehwe and Walpen 2006). From the geopolitical context of the war's aftermath, the origins of neoliberalism as a political ideology can be understood as reactionary to violence. In short, neoliberals conceived that violence could be curbed by a return to Enlightenment thinking and its explicit basis in advancing the merits of individualism.

This historical context is ironic insofar as structural adjustment, fiscal austerity, and free trade, the basic principles of neoliberalism, are now 'augmented by the direct use of military force' (Roberts *et al.* 2003), where the 'invisible hand' of the global free market is increasingly clenched into the 'visible fist' of the US military. The relationship between capital accumulation and war is of course longstanding (Harvey 1985), and the peaceful division that early neoliberals pursued for their economic agenda demonstrated a certain naivety. While not all wars are decidedly capitalist, it is difficult to envisage conditions wherein an economic ideology like neoliberalism could not come attendant to violence insofar as it seeks a global domain, supports universal assumptions, and suppresses heterogeneity as individuals are remade according to the normative image of 'neoliberal proper personhood' (Kingfisher 2007). Either the lessons of colonialism were entirely overlooked by the Mont Pelerin Society, or they uncritically embraced its narrative appeal to the supposed higher purpose of the 'white man's burden'. Just as colonialism paved a road to hell with ostensibly good intentions, the neoliberal imagination of an eventual harmonious global village now demonstrates much the same. Embedded within such promises of utopia are the dystopian realities that exist in a number of countries, where neoliberalization has not produced greater peace, but a profound and often ruinous encounter with violence.

The historical record indicates that the years under neoliberalism have been characterized by recurrent crises and deepening divisions between and within the world's nations on ethno-religious grounds. Although in some instances poverty has arguably been alleviated, or at least not got any worse under neoliberalism, in many more contexts poverty remains painfully acute, while inequality has undeniably increased both within and between cities, states, and regions (Wade 2003; Harvey 2005). There is a nascent literature that is quickly gathering momentum, which attempts to make these connections between neoliberalism and violence more explicit (Auyero 2000; Borras and Ross 2007; Chatterjee 2009; Coleman 2007; Collier 2008; Goldstein 2005; Marchand 2004). From this growing concern comes increasing recognition for the idea that the imposition of neoliberal austerity measures may actually promote conditions of increased impoverishment that subsequently provide multiple opportunities for violent conflict (Bourdieu 1998; Bourgois 2001; Farmer 2004; Uvin 2003; Wacquant 2009). Within my own work I have attempted to demonstrate an urgent need to build linkages between the violence occurring in various sites undergoing neoliberalization, and to identify threads of commonality within these diverse spaces so that an emancipatory agenda of transnational scope may potentially begin to emerge (Springer 2015).

Although acknowledgement for the violence of neoliberalism continues to grow, it is important to recognize how simplistic and problematic it is to assume uniformity across the various constellations of violent geographies that are occurring in neoliberalizing contexts. Such an approach serves to reinforce the authority of neoliberal discourse by continuing to circulate the idea that neoliberalism as a particular model of statecraft is unavoidable, a criticism Gibson-Graham (1996) make more generally with regard to capitalism. Likewise, to treat the material expression of violence only through its directly observable manifestation is a reductionist appraisal. This view disregards the complexity of the endless entanglements of social relations, and further ignores the future possibilities of violence (Nordstrom 2004). When we bear witness to violence, what we are seeing is not a 'thing', but a moment with a past, present, and future that is determined by its elaborate relations with other moments of social process (Springer 2011). The material 'act' of violence itself is merely a confluence in the flows of oppressive social relations, and one that is persistently marked with absolutist accounts of space and time, when instead violence should be recognized as being temporally dispersed through a whole series of 'troubling geographies' (Gregory 2006). Nonetheless, understanding the resonances of violence within the now orthodox political economic model of neoliberalism – however disparate, protean, and variegated – is of critical importance to social justice. Only through a conceptualization of fluidity and process can we begin to recognize how violence and neoliberalism might actually converge.

I begin this chapter by identifying how processes of othering coincide and become a central component of neoliberal logic by providing it with the discursive tools to realize its heterogeneous ideals. In the following section I describe how attention to the relationality of space and time allows us to recognize neoliberalism and violence as mutually reinforcing moments of social process where it becomes very difficult to disentangle these two phenomena. I then turn my attention towards the exclusions of neoliberalism, where I consider how the exceptional violence of this process comes to form the rule. Here I identify neoliberalism as having produced a state of exception through its particular version of sovereign authority and the dire consequences this results in for the downtrodden and dispossessed. I then conclude on a hopeful note by insisting that collectively we are powerful actors who have the radical potential to resist, transform, and ultimately undo neoliberalism.

Neoliberal othering

Although mainstream examinations of conflict theory have a tendency to focus on 'local' origins by invoking the idea of 'backward' cultural practices as the most suitable explanations for violence (see Huntington 1996; Kaplan 2000), this reading problematically overlooks the influence of ideology and economics. The geographical imagination of violence vis-à-vis neoliberalism treats violence as an externality, a wrong-headed vision that engenders Orientalist ideas. Such othering discourses insidiously posit 'local' cultures as being wholly responsible for any ensuing bloodshed following neoliberalization, thus ignoring the mutability and relationality of the 'global' political economy of violence. Here we can look for guidance to the influence of Said (2003), who has made significant contributions to a broader interest in how geographical representations and practices produced notions of 'us' and 'them', or 'Self' and 'Other'. In a contemporary sense, othering licenses further neoliberal reforms, as neoliberalization is positioned as a 'civilizing' enterprise in the face of any purported 'savagery' (Springer 2015). Neoliberalism is rarely interrogated and is typically either openly endorsed (see Fukuyama 1992) or tacitly accepted (see Sen 1999) as both the sine qua non of human development and the cure-all for violence. Such othering places neoliberalism 'under erasure', where we are encouraged to approach neoliberal ideas without a critical lens.

Popular geopolitics has repeatedly imagined 'African', 'Asian' and 'Islamic' cultures as being somehow ingrained with a supposedly 'natural' inclination towards violence, a tendency that has intensified in the context of the ongoing 'war on terror'. The public performance of such ideas feeds into particular geostrategic aims, thus allowing them to gather momentum and develop a certain form of 'commonsense' validity. The imaginative geographies of such Orientalism are creations that meld difference and distance through a sequence of spatializations that not only assign particular people as 'Other', but also construct 'our' space of the familiar as distinct and separate from 'their' unfamiliar space that lies beyond (Gregory 2004; Said 2003). This is the exact discourse that colonialism rallied to erect its authority in the past, and in the current conjuncture, Orientalism can be considered as neoliberalism's latitude insofar as othering enables a powerful discursive space for promoting the ideals of the free market. Such a connection between neoliberalism and Orientalism may appear counter-intuitive when neoliberalism is accepted at face value. After all, the neoliberal doctrine envisages itself as the champion of a liberal internationalism centred around the vision of a single human race peacefully united by a common code of conduct featuring deregulated markets, free trade, shared legal norms and states that feature civic liberties, electoral processes, and representative institutions (Gowen 2001). Nonetheless, an appreciation for neoliberalization's capacity to promote inequality, exacerbate poverty, license authoritarianism, and advance a litany of other social ills is growing (Bourdieu 1998; Duménil and Lévy 2011; Giroux 2004; Goldberg 2009; MacEwan 1999; Springer 2008). Such recognition hints at the numerous 'erasures' neoliberal ideologues have attempted to engage through neoliberalism's discursive concealment.

Klein (2007) has persuasively argued that natural disasters have been used as opportunities to push through unpopular neoliberal reforms on peoples and societies too disoriented to protect their interests. In their absence, othering lays the necessary foundation for manufactured 'shocks' in procuring openings for neoliberalism. Similar to the originary state-level neoliberal trial run in Chile (Challies and Murray 2008), the current sequence of imperialism-cum-neoliberalization in the Middle East is exemplary of American geopolitical intervention and a variety of militarism rooted in the Orientalist idea of folding distance into difference. Would the mere presence of ISIS, as problematic as this organization is, have been enough to galvanize America's authorization of air strikes had their fragmented activities and threats occurred on Canadian soil rather than in

Iraq and Syria? We can only speculate, but, given the wholesale devastation that ensues, without a significant dose of Orientalism the idea of launching missiles and dropping bombs on a country in all probability would not get off the ground and a different strategy would be devised to ensure minimal civilian casualties. Similarly, it was 'unknown/faraway' Santiago and not 'familiar/nearby' Ottawa that played host to Washington's subversions in the lead up to the 'other 9/11' in 1973, when the neoliberal experiment was first realized with the installation of Pinochet.

Attention to how particular geographies, including imaginative ones, are 'produced by multiple, often unnoticed, space-making and space-changing processes' is of critical importance (Sparke 2007: 338, 2005). Sparke (2007) argues that such appreciation is itself an ethical commitment to consider the *exclusions* – which can be read in the double sense of 'under erasure' and 'othering' – in the production of any given geographical truth claims. The geography of neoliberalism involves recognizing its variegated expressions (Peck and Tickell 2002), imperialist impulses (Escobar 2004; Hart 2006), and authoritarian responses (Canterbury 2005; Springer 2009), all of which dispel the theoretical tall-tales of a smooth-space, flat-earth where neoliberalism rolls-out across the globe without friction or resistance. To deal with the inconsistencies between these material interpretations and a doctrine allegedly premised on peace, othering practices are employed to indemnify 'aberrant', 'violent', and 'local' cultures in explaining away any failings of neoliberalism, thereby leaving its class project unscathed (Springer 2015). Orientalism is used to legitimize the doublespeak neoliberal proponents invoke in the global distribution of violence (Sparke 2007), to code the violence of anti-neoliberal resistance, and to geographically allocate and place the blame for violence by asserting that violence sits in particular, 'Oriental' places (Springer 2011). The responsibility of critical theory under this 'new imperialism' (Harvey 2003) is thus to illuminate such erasures so that the othering of neoliberalism is laid bare and therein may be refused.

Momentous violence

In my attempt to link neoliberalism to violence one might be inclined to ask if the former actually causes the latter and how that could be proven. My response is that the question itself is largely irrelevant. The empirical record reveals a noticeable upswing in inequality under neoliberalism (Wade 2003), which Harvey (2005) regards as neoliberalism's principal substantive achievement. Inequality alone is about measuring disparity, however qualified, while the link between inequality and violence is typically considered as an appraisal of the 'validity' of a causal relationship, where the link may or may not be understood to take on multiple dimensions including temporally, spatiality, economics, politics, culture and so forth. The point is that violence and inequality are mutually constitutive. Inequality precipitates violence, and violence gives rise to further inequalities. Accordingly, if we wish to attenuate the devastating and disaffecting effects of either, we need to rid ourselves of a calculative model and instead consider violence and inequality as an integral system or particular *moment*. 'Thinking in terms of moments', Hartsock (2006: 176) argues, can allow scholars 'to take account of discontinuities and incommensurabilities without losing sight of the presence of a social system within which these features are embedded'. Although the enduring phenomenon of violence is fragmented by variations, strains and aberrations as part of its processual nature, within the current moment of neoliberalism, violence is all too often a reflection of the chaotic landscapes of globalized capitalism.

At different moments capitalism creates particular kinds of agents who become capable of certain kinds of violence dependent upon both their distinctive geohistorical milieu and their situation within its hierarchy. It is in this distinction of *moments* that we can come to understand the correlations between violence and neoliberalism. By exploring the particular histories and distinctive geographies that define individual neoliberalizations, scholars can begin to shed light on the phantasmagoria of violence that is projected within neoliberalism's wider rationality of power. In other words, it is important to recognize and start working through how the *moment* of neoliberalism and the *moment* of violence converge. The intention here is not to produce a Cartesian map, wherein the same interpretation is replicated in each and every context of neo-liberalization. Neoliberalism should not be read as an all-powerful and self-reproducing logic. Lending such an infallible appearance serves to empower the idea that neoliberalism is beyond reproach. It is imperative to contest the neoliberalism-as-monolithism argument for failing to recognize space and time as open and always becoming (Springer 2014). In focusing solely on an externally constructed neoliberalism we neglect the local geographies of existing political economic circumstances and institutional frameworks, wherein the vagaries of societal influences and individual agency play a key role in the circulation and (re)production of neoliberalism. In short, to focus exclusively on external forces is to risk producing over-generalized accounts of a singular and omnipresent neoliberalism.

While acknowledging the problematics of a monolithic reading of neoliberalism it is also critically important to acknowledge that an intensive focus on internal phenomena is also limit-ing. Without attention to the relational connections of neoliberalism across space we cannot adequately addresses the essential features and important connections of neoliberalism as a global project (Peck and Tickell 2002). This 'larger conversation' of neoliberalism is considered impor-tant in relating similar constellations of experiences across various locations as a potential basis for emancipation (Brand and Wissen 2005; Featherstone 2005; Routledge 2003; Springer 2008; Willis *et al.* 2008). Retaining the abstraction of a 'global' neoliberalism allows phenomena like inequality and poverty, which are experienced across multiple sites, to find a point of similarity, a *moment*. In contrast, a refusal of the global scope of neoliberalism hinders attempts at developing and maintaining solidarity beyond the micro-politics of the 'local'. For that reason, conceptual-izing neoliberalism requires awareness for the complex connections between local and extralocal forces functioning within the global political economy (Brenner and Theodore 2002; Peck 2001). To understand the violence of neoliberalism then, we must be willing to sift through and account for the traction of violence in the contexts of its particular hybridized and modified instances of neoliberalization, while at the same time preserving the notion of neoliberalism as a 'radical theoretical slogan' (Peck 2004: 403). The latter can be employed as a reference point in opposing violence and bringing together distinct struggles against the controlling, abusive, and punishing structures of capitalism.

It was only over the course of a succession of setbacks, interruptions, and false starts that neoliberalism as a marginal utopian idea began to emerge as an established doctrine that has congealed as a diverse yet related series of neoliberalizations (Peck 2010; England and Ward 2007). Part of the 'success' of neoliberalism as the common language of global discourse is that it is based on a series of nostrums that, once employed, foretell that free market forces will lead to a thriving future, where all of the world's peoples will be unified in an equitable and harmo-nious 'global village'. Put differently, the neoliberal apostles are false prophets of emancipation, proselytizing peace as they wage war. So while I want to argue that understanding neoliberal violence requires attention to particular specificities that are conditional and context dependent, the violence of neoliberalism also has a relational character that extends across multiple sites, having been entwined within particular discourses and (re)productions of space (Lefebvre 1991). Acknowledgement of this dialectic *moment* brings a broader significance to neoliberalism's encounter with violence, where contextually specific patterns of violence that are associated with unique social events, political circumstances, cultural processes, and spatial transformations can also be read more broadly across an array of sites undertaking neoliberalizing processes all across the globe. While the inflections, cadences, and pulses of neoliberalism will always have some measure of idiosyncrasy in different contexts, from moment to moment the funeral march remains the same. Concealed beneath the allure of sirens, neoliberalism is actually a cacophony of violence and conflict, where there is profound dissonance between what it promises and what it ultimately delivers.

The neoliberal state of exception

The continuing exclusions of neoliberalism should motivate us to get involved and galvanize our collective strength to stand in opposition. But beyond the desire for compassion, an affinity that never takes for granted our shared humanity (Day 2005), lurks the threat of complacency, the shadow of indifference, and the menace of detachment among those of us who have not *yet* been subjected to our homes being forcibly taken by armed bandits known as police, to our children's curiosity languishing because a basic education is an expense we cannot shoulder, or to our spouses dying in our arms having been denied adequate healthcare. The examples are not mere abstractions. Each of these scenarios has been revealed to me with disturbing regularity during the course of my ongoing research in Cambodia (Springer 2010, 2013, 2015). What those of us still on the winning side of neoliberalism do not anticipate or account for – and let there be no mistake that this is a system that unquestionably produces winners and losers – is that in this *aban*donment of our 'Others', we produce a state of exception (Ong 2006). The relation of the ban is nothing if not ambiguous, and to abandon someone is not simply to ignore or forsake them. As Agamben (1998: 72) explains, 'What has been banned is delivered over to its own separateness and, at the same time, consigned to the mercy of the one who abandons it – at once excluded and included, removed and at the same time captured'. In other words, to ban is to create a *state of exception*, wherein the 'exception does not subtract itself from the rule; rather, the rule, suspending itself, gives rise to the exception and, maintaining itself in relation to the exception, first constitutes itself as a rule' (ibid.: 14). Consequently, it is through the construction of a new neoliberal normative frame – wherein malice and malevolence become the rule – that the exceptional violence of neoliberalism is transformed into exemplary violence.

Exceptional violence always runs the risk of becoming exemplary, or so routinized, quotidian, ordinary, and banal that we no longer feel an emotional response to its appearance precisely because it is the norm. We may recognize it as violence, but we remain indifferent. Exemplary violence is most effective when it is no longer recognized as violence at all, a destructive form of unconsciousness that Bourdieu (2001) referred to as 'symbolic violence'. It is in this mundanity of the everyday that we find meaning in Arendt's (1963) 'banality of evil'. History's profoundest moments of iniquity are not performed by extremists or psychopaths, but by ordinary people – potentially you and me – as we come to accept the premises of the existing order. The banality of evil is thus an erasure that deprives us of our ability to recognize violence as a *moment* that is at once both exceptional and exemplary. As Agamben (1998: 14) explains, an exception,

> does not limit itself to distinguishing what is inside from what is outside but instead traces a threshold (the state of exception) between the two, on the basis of which outside and inside, the normal situation and chaos, enter into those complex topological relations.

The exception and the example accordingly always exist in a dialectic relationship, and it is for this reason that the ongoing abandonment of the 'Other' under neoliberalism comes to define the sovereign authority of neoliberalism as a political economic order.

As our political capacities knowingly and unknowingly embrace the social disarticulation and anomie of neoliberalism's dystopia of individualism, the violence of this process deepens. Within neoliberalism's imaginative geographies of an affluent global village, what is not spoken is the desire for a certain and particular homogeneity, an impulse to remake the 'Other' in 'our' image, whereby the space of 'the peculiar', 'the exotic', 'the bizarre' is continually (re)produced through the relation of the ban. But this is a relation that Agamben (ibid.: 21) knows well to be one where 'outside and inside, become indistinguishable', and thus, as with all fantasies and desires, at the heart of neoliberalism's chimera of strength and confidence lurks a profound sense of anxiety (Gregory 1995). This is not a disquiet without consequence, but one that licenses particular violent geographies in ensuring that the 'tableau of queerness' (Said 2003) never disrupts the neoliberal vision of global sovereignty. The ominous specter of the banality of evil is signalled by the juxtaposition between a panacean fantasy of a 'new world order' and the sheer magnitude of violence that permeates our contemporary world. This is a routinized, clichéd, hackneyed, and mundane force, an evil whose potential resides within each and every one of us, and whose hostility is nurtured, accumulated, and consumed through the othering of neoliberalism.

Fantasy and reality collide under neoliberalization, and our involvement in this process allows for the normative entrenchment of violence against the marginalized, the dispossessed, the poor, the downtrodden, the homeless, the unemployed, the disaffected, and the 'Other'. Yet this necropolitics of violence is not the conclusion of neoliberalism's violent fantasy; rather, it is its genesis. The violence of neoliberalism is continuing to unravel the world. In this grave realization, and in echoing Marx, critical scholarship must not merely seek to *interpret* the world; it must seek to *change* it by aligning its theory and practice on all occasions and in all instances to the service of social justice. By seeking to shine a light on the variety of ways in which the processes of neoliberalization are saturated with both exceptional and exemplary violence, we open our geographical imaginations to the possibility of (re)producing space in ways that make possible a transformative and emancipatory politics. This *moment* of 'Empire' (Hardt and Negri 2000) demands such courage of our scholarship. As members of the assemblage we call humanity, we each have a moral obligation to stand up and speak out as an act of solidarity with those whom the violence of neoliberalism has targeted, and those who have been silenced by the complacency of a stifled collective imagination wherein neoliberalism is considered an inexorable force.

Conclusion

The rolling-back of the state is a rationale of neoliberal governance, not an informed choice of the autonomous agents that comprise the nation. Thus, resistance to neoliberalism often provokes a more despotic outlook as states move to ensure that reforms are pushed through, particularly if the changes are rapid and a legitimizing discourse for neoliberalization has not already become widely circulated. This is why effective subjectification to neoliberal ideals and the production of 'othering' discourses become a hallmark of neoliberalization. Yet complete acquiescence to neoliberalism is improbable for two reasons. First, every single member of a given society is never going to completely accept or agree with the dominant discourses. Thus, we so often find that those marginalized by neoliberal reforms are actively engaged in continuous struggles to have their voices heard, which is unfortunately just as frequently met with state violence in response. Second, social processes have an essential temporality, meaning that they continue to unfold. While notions of temporal stasis and spatial uniformity pervade popular accounts of a fully integrated 'global village' (see Friedman 1999), these ideas are fundamentally reliant upon a problematic assignment of monolithism and inevitability to neoliberalism, as though space–time has only one possible trajectory (Massey 2005). In the popular imagination, there is little acknowledgement of the discursive work that goes into the (re)production and distribution of neoliberal ideas in a diverse range of contexts (Plehwe and Walpen 2006). As the utopian discourse of neoliberalism rubs up against empirical realities – such as heightened inequality and ongoing poverty – citizens are more likely to express discontent with particular characteristics of neoliberalization, most obviously the reduction of essential social provisions such as healthcare and education. Resorting to violence accordingly becomes one of the few disciplinary options available to governments transformed by neoliberalization as they attempt to retain legitimacy, where 'othering' becomes a primary mechanism in the articulation of power. In short, those who don't fit the mould of a proper neoliberal subject are treated as enemies.

The rising tide against neoliberalism and the geographically dispersed protests that signify and support such a movement necessarily occur in terrains that always exceed neoliberalism (Hart 2008; Leitner *et al.* 2007). Consequently, we can never attribute neoliberalism to a direct calculable expression. Although the idea of a distinct singular form of neoliberalism is prominent in the popular imagination, such a formulaic interpretation of a pure neoliberalism is an untenable idea that has been altogether dismissed by geographers (Peck and Tickell 2002). Neoliberalism is a theoretical abstraction that rubs up against geographical limits, and consequently its 'actually existing' circumstances are never paradigmatic. Yet it is nonetheless enormously important to recognize how the evolving geographies of protest, resistance, and contestation can be interpreted as a shared sense of betrayal with what can be broadly defined as 'neoliberal policy goals'. The implication of this reading is a growing recognition for transnational solidarity as being inseparable from 'local' movements, which prompts a relational understanding of both resistance to and the violence of neoliberalism (Featherstone 2005; Wainwright and Kim 2008). Some of the most noticeable outcomes of neoliberalization are increased class tensions, intensified policing, expanded surveillance, and heightened security measures, which inevitably arise from strained relations. So while there are variegations and mutations to account for in neoliberalism's travels, there is also a need to appreciate the similar deleterious outcomes that all too frequently arise.

The relationship between neoliberalism and violence is directly related to the system of rule that neoliberalism constructs, justifies, and defends in advancing its hegemonies of ideology, of policy and programme, of state form, of governmentality, and, ultimately, of discourse (Springer 2012). Neoliberalism is a context in which the establishment, maintenance, and extension of hierarchical orderings of social relations are re-created, sustained, and intensified, where processes of 'othering' loom large. Accordingly, neoliberalization should be regarded as integral to violence inasmuch as it generates social divisions within and across space. Yet the world as we see it today where the violence of neoliberalism proceeds with a careless lack of restraint is neither necessary nor inevitable. By increasing our shared understanding for the cruelty that neoliberalism engenders we set in motion a process of awakening from the allure of market logic, a process that shatters the influence of anomie and sounds a death knell for neoliberal ideas. As exceptional violence comes to form the rule, people around the world are becoming more acutely aware that something is not right, and consequently we are becoming more willing to stand up for our communities, for ourselves, and for 'Others'. Every time we refuse to sit idle before would-be evictors speculating on land, have the courage to protest exclusion from democratic process, strike against an exploitative employer who denies a fair wage, or resist being framed as violent savages incapable of agency, the rhizomes of emancipation grow stronger. There is a world to be won, and as long as we can come to recognize the reflection of 'Others' within ourselves, we will prevail.

Acknowledgement

A SSHRC Insight Development Grant (Award Number 430-2014-00644) provided support.

References

Agamben, G. 1998. *Homo Sacer: Sovereign Power and Bare Life*. Stanford, CA: Stanford University Press.

Arendt, H. 1963. *Eichmann in Jerusalem: A Report on the Banality of Evil*. New York: Viking.

Auyero, J. 2000. The Hyper-shantytown: Neo-liberal Violence(s) in the Argentine Slum. *Ehtnography*, 1: 93–116.

Borras, S., and Ross, E. 2007. Land Rights, Conflict, and Violence Amid Neo-liberal Globalization. *Peace Review: A Journal of Social Justice*, 19: 1–4.

Bourdieu, P. 1998. Utopia of Endless Exploitation: The Essence of Neoliberalism. *Le Monde Diplomatique*, December: 1–5.

—. *Masculine Domination*. Stanford, CA: Stanford University Press.

Bourgois, P. 2001. The Power of Violence in War and Peace: Post-Cold War Lessons from El Salvador. *Ethnography*, 2: 5–34.

Brand, U., and Wissen, M. 2005. Neoliberal Globalization and the Internationalization of Protest: European Perspective. *Antipode*, 37: 9–17.

Brenner, N., and Theodore, N. 2002. Cities and the Geographies of 'Actually Existing Neoliberalism'. *Antipode*, 34: 349–79.

Canterbury, D.C. 2005. *Neoliberal Democratization and New Authoritarianism*. Burlington, VT: Ashgate.

Challies, E., and Murray, W. 2008. Towards Post-neoliberalism? The Comparative Politico-Economic Transition of New Zealand and Chile. *Asia Pacific Viewpoint*, 49: 228–43.

Chatterjee, I. 2009. Social Conflict and the Neoliberal City: A Case of Hindu–Muslim Violence in India. *Transactions of the Institute of British Geographers*, 34: 143–60.

Coleman, L. 2007. The Gendered Violence of Development: Imaginative Geographies of Exclusion in the Imposition of Neo-liberal Capitalism. *The British Journal of Politics and International Relations*, 9: 204–19.

Collier, C. 2008. Neoliberalism and Violence Against Women: Can Retrenchment Convergence Explain the Path of Provincial Anti-violence Policy, 1985–2005? *Canadian Journal of Political Science*, 41: 19–42.

Day, R. 2005. *Gramsci is Dead: Anarchist Currents in the Newest Social Movements*. London: Pluto.

Duménil, G., and Lévy, D. 2011. *The Crisis of Neoliberalism*. Cambridge: Harvard University Press.

England, K., and Ward, K. eds. 2007. *Neoliberalization: States, Networks, Peoples*. Malden, MA: Blackwell.

Escobar, A. 2004. Development, Violence and the New Imperial Order. *Development*, 47: 15–21.

Farmer, P. 2004. An Anthropology of Structural Violence. *Current Anthropology*, 45: 305–25.

Featherstone, D. 2005. Towards the Relational Construction of Militant Particularisms: Or Why the Geographies of Past Struggles Matter for Resistance to Neoliberal Globalization. *Antipode*, 37: 250–71.

Friedman, T. 1999. *The Lexus and the Olive Tree: Understanding Globalization*. New York: Farrar, Strauss and Giroux.

Fukuyama, F. 1992. *The End of History and the Last Man*. New York: The Free Press.

Gibson-Graham, J.K. 1996. *The End of Capitalism (As We Knew It): A Feminist Critique of Political Economy*. Cambridge: Blackwell.

Giroux, H.A. 2004. *The Terror of Neoliberalism: Authoritarianism and the Eclipse of Democracy*. Boulder, NC: Paradigm.

Goldberg, D.T. 2009. *The Threat of Race: Reflections on Racial Neoliberalism*. Malden, MA: Blackwell.

Goldstein, D. 2005. Flexible Justice: Neoliberal Violence and 'Self-Help' Security in Bolivia. *Critique of Anthropology*, 25: 389–411.

Gowen, P. 2001. Neoliberal Cosmopolitanism. *New Left Review*, September–October: 79–94.

Gregory, D. 1995. Imaginative Geographies. *Progress in Human Geography*, 19: 447–85.

—. 2004. *The Colonial Present: Afghanistan, Palestine, Iraq*. Malden, MA: Blackwell.

—. 2006. Introduction: Troubling Geographies, in Castree, N., and Gregory, D., eds. *David Harvey: A Critical Reader*. Malden, MA: Blackwell: 1–25.

Hackworth, J. 2007. *The Neoliberal City: Governance, Ideology, and Development in American Urbanism*. Ithaca: Cornell University Press.

Hardt, M., and Negri, A. 2000. *Empire*. Cambridge: Harvard University Press.

Hart, G. 2006. Denaturalizing Dispossession: Critical Ethnography in the Age of Resurgent Imperialism. *Antipode*, 38: 977–1004.

—. 2008. The Provocations of Neoliberalism: Contesting the Nation and Liberation After Apartheid. *Antipode*, 40: 678–705.

Hartsock, N. 2006. Globalization and Primitive Accumulation: The Contributions of David Harvey's Dialectical Marxism, in Castree, N., and Gregory, D., eds. *David Harvey: A Critical Reader*. Malden, MA: Blackwell: 167–90.

Harvey, D. 1985. The Geopolitics of Capitalism, in Gregory, D., and Urry, J., eds. *Social Relations and Spatial Structures*. London: Macmillan: 128–63.

—. 2003. *The New Imperialism*. Oxford: Oxford University Press.

—. 2005. *A Brief History of Neoliberalism*. Oxford: Oxford University Press.

Huntington, S.P. 1996. *The Clash of Civilizations and the Remaking of World Order*. New York: Simon & Schuster.

Kaplan, R. 2000. *The Coming Anarchy*. New York: Random House.

Kingfisher, C. 2007. Spatializing Neoliberalism: Articulations, Recapitulations (A Very Few) Alternatives, in England, K., and Ward, K., eds. *Neoliberalization: States, Networks, Peoples*. Malden, MA: Blackwell: 195–222.

Klein, N. 2007. *The Shock Doctrine: The Rise of Disaster Capitalism*. Toronto: A.A. Knopf.

Lefebvre, H. 1991. *The Production of Space*. Oxford: Blackwell.

Leitner, H., Peck, J., and Sheppard, E.S. eds. 2007. *Contesting Neoliberalism: Urban Frontiers*. New York: Guilford.

MacEwan, A. 1999. *Neoliberalism as Democracy? Economic Strategy, Markets, and Alternatives for the 21st Century*. New York: Zed Books.

Marchand, M. 2004. Neo-Liberal Disciplining, Violence and Transnational Organizing: The Struggle for Women's Rights in Ciudad Juárez. *Development*, 47: 88–93.

Massey, D. 2005. *For Space*. London: Sage.

Mirowski, P., and Plehwe, D. eds. 2009. *The Road from Mont Pelerin: The Making of the Neoliberal Thought Collective*. Cambridge: Harvard University Press.

Nordstrom, C. 2004. The Tomorrow of Violence, in Whitehead N.L., ed. *Violence*. Santa Fe: School of American Research Press: 223–42.

Ong, A. 2006. *Neoliberalism as Exception: Mutations in Citizenship and Sovereignty*. London: Duke University Press.

Peck, J. 2001. Neoliberalizing States: Thin Policies/Hard Outcomes. *Progress in Human Geography*, 25: 445–55.

—. 2004. Geography and Public Policy: Constructions of Neoliberalism. *Progress in Human Geography*, 28: 392–405.

—. 2010. *Constructions of Neoliberal Reason*. Oxford: Oxford University Press.

Peck, J., and Tickell, A. 2002. Neoliberalizing Space. *Antipode*, 34: 380–404.

Plehwe, D., and Walpen, B. 2006. Between Network and Complex Organization: The Making of Neoliberal Knowledge and Hegemony, in Plehwe, D., Walpen, B., and Neunhoffer, G., eds. *Neoliberal Hegemony: A Global Critique*. London: Routledge: 27–50.

Roberts, S., Secor, A., and Sparke, M. 2003. Neoliberal Geopolitics. *Antipode*, 35: 886–97.

Routledge, P. 2003. Anti-geopolitics, in Agnew, J., Mitchell, K., and Toal, G., eds. *A Companion to Political Geography*. Oxford: Blackwell: 236–48.

Said, E. 2003. *Orientalism*. 25th Anniversary Edition. New York: Vintage.

Sen, A. 1999. *Development as Freedom*. Toronto: Random House.

Sparke, M. 2005. *In the Space of Theory: Postfoundational Geographies of the Nation-state*. Minnesota: University of Minnesota Press.

—. 2007. Geopolitical Fear, Geoeconomic Hope and the Responsibilities of Geography. *Annals of the Association of American Geographers*, 97: 338–49.

Springer, S. 2008. The Nonillusory Effects of Neoliberalisation: Linking Geographies of Poverty, Inequality, and Violence. *Geoforum*, 39: 1520–5.

—. 2009. Renewed Authoritarianism in Southeast Asia: Undermining Democracy Through Neoliberal Reform. *Asia Pacific Viewpoint*, 50: 271–6.

—. 2010. *Cambodia's Neoliberal Order: Violence, Authoritarianism, and the Contestation of Public Space*. London: Routledge.

—. 2011. Violence Sits in Places? Cultural Practice, Neoliberal Rationalism and Virulent Imaginative Geographies. *Political Geography*, 30: 90–8.

—. 2012. Neoliberalism as Discourse: Between Foucauldian Political Economy and Marxian Poststructuralism. *Critical Discourse Studies*, 9: 133–47.

—. 2013. Illegal Evictions? Overwriting Possession and Orality with Law's Violence in Cambodia. *Journal of Agrarian Change*, 13: 520–46.

—. 2014. Neoliberalism in Denial. *Dialogues in Human Geography*, 4: 154–60.

—. 2015. *Violent Neoliberalism: Development, Discourse and Dispossession in Cambodia*. New York: Palgrave Macmillan.

Uvin, P. 2003. Global Dreams and Local Anger: From Structural to Acute Violence in a Globalizing World, in Tetreault, M.A., Denemark, R.A., Thomas, K.P., and Burch, K., eds. *Rethinking Global Political Economy: Emerging Issues, Unfolding Odysseys*. London: Routledge: 147–61.

Wacquant, L. 2009. *Punishing the Poor: The Neoliberal Government of Social Insecurity*. Durham: Duke University Press.

Wade, R. 2003. Is Globalization Reducing Poverty and Inequality? *International Journal of Health Services*, 34: 381–414.

Wainwright, J., and Kim, S.-J. 2008. Battles in Seattle Redux: Transnational Resistance to a Neoliberal Trade Agreement. *Antipode*, 40: 513–34.

Willis K., Smith A., and Stenning A. 2008. Introduction: Social Justice and Neoliberalism, in Smith A., Stenning, A., and Willis, K., eds. *Social Justice and Neoliberalism: Global Perspectives*. London: Zed: 1–15.

14

NEOLIBERALISM AND THE BIOPOLITICAL IMAGINATION

Nicholas Kiersey

The continued success of neoliberalism, as a global ideology of economic governance, is all the more stunning if one considers that the history of its disasters already stretches back quite far. Much of the wayward behaviour claimed to be at the heart of the current crisis would simply not have been possible without successive waves of neoliberal or 'supply-side' deregulation, dating back at least as far as the 1970s (Surin 2009: 70). Its principles have been applied unevenly, however, promoting the privatization of great swathes of publically-owned wealth in certain instances, while extending social safety nets to the wealthy wherever the demands of systemic stability require it. True to form, regulators have, in the course of the current crisis, demanded relatively little by way of reparation (Harvey 2011). And, notwithstanding the rise recently in Europe of parties like Syriza and Podemos, electorates have largely shied away from holding the world's financial movers and shakers to account. Indeed, to pick one extreme case, the 2010 election in Ireland returned a centrist coalition, fully committed to austerity and one of the most spectacularly unjust and undemocratic transfers of wealth from taxpayers to foreign bondholders in history (McCabe 2011).

Such acquiescence suggests forcefully the role of neoliberal 'ideas' in shaping public expectations not only about how markets function, but also about the moral premium they must be afforded relative to other arenas of social life. No surprise, therefore, that a range of scholars interested in culture and political economy, from Constructivists to so-called Poststructuralists, have turned their attention to this question. Surveying the landscapes of neoliberal austerity, Constructivists present neoliberal *theory* as a powerful mechanism of cultural normalization, describing and proscribing the norms and values which not only lured thinkers, policy-makers and practitioners alike to pursue market deregulation in the first place, but which also induce in them even now a hubristic confidence that the vicissitudes of contemporary global finance can somehow be mastered. Thus, for example, the classic neoliberal expectation, that markets tend more or less automatically to correct their excesses, is thought to be a factor leading governments to erroneously confident appraisals of the risks of financial deregulation. Mark Blyth (2013), whose work exemplifies this approach, describes at length how 'theory-driven' financial innovation drove the development of the esoteric products that actually collapsed in the meltdown (see also Wigan 2010). Ultimately, then, for these scholars, neoliberalism is something like a discourse of legitimation – that is, a discourse of human affairs which, forgetful of its own reflexivity, is susceptible to unrealistic expectations of economic behaviour.

As plausible as it may seem that neoliberal theory might have been a factor guiding the mindsets of policy-makers and practitioners, Constructivism nevertheless offers little hope in terms of our efforts to understand how everyday populations are themselves so willing to go along with austerity. In this regard, a potentially more powerful account of the role of neoliberal ideas comes from work influenced by the French poststructuralist, Michel Foucault. Invoking Foucault's notion of biopolitics, and the closely associated concept of neoliberal subjectivity, this body of scholarship argues that neoliberalism is actually much more than a system of rules for managing the economy. Rather, following Dardot and Laval, it is a regime of 'practical normativity' (2014: 9), which sees itself quite self-consciously as a strategy of everyday subjectification. Nevertheless, despite the Foucauldian origins of this line of thinking, questions arise concerning the extent to which even this approach can give us much insight into processes of mass neoliberal alignment. Importantly, its proponents focus solely on questions of epistemic power, justifying this move explicitly as a reaction to the reductionist tendencies they perceive in more Marxist approaches. Of course, given the longstanding and unstinting nature of Foucault's complaint against Structuralist forms of social analysis, this justification finds much evidence to support it in his work (see Springer 2012). But there is a danger in reading neoliberalism solely on its own terms. The biopolitical perspective, useful insofar as it grasps the massive anthropological ambition of neoliberal experts and policy-makers, what Mirowski (2013) terms the 'neoliberal thought collective', nevertheless tends to accept neoliberal discourse at face value, reducing it thereby to nothing more than a naive error of thought, a move which is ultimately at odds with Foucault's more bodily ontology of subjectivity.

Crucially, the only evidence we really have of any sustained commentary on Foucault's part on the topic of neoliberalism are transcriptions of his 1978–9 lecture series, published as *The Birth of Biopolitics (2008)*. These lectures are hugely important, insofar as they offer very precise information about the content of biopolitics, nuancing considerably the concept's treatment in his formally published works. Yet neoliberalism was but a fledgling political project at the time of Foucault's engagement with it, and so his lectures could only anticipate the kinds of subjectifying technologies at work on today's neoliberal populations. Thus, while helpful, they also leave a good deal of room for misinterpretation. To remedy this, I invoke Dardot and Laval (2014), and Frederic Lordon (2014), among others, to suggest that biopolitical life cannot itself be fully comprehended apart from the set of material practices that constitute contemporary capitalism. To wit, we may be 'willing slaves' of neoliberal governmentality, but austerity reaches its limits in neoliberalism's capacity to guarantee the survival of capitalism, and the conversion of labour power into actual labour.

An unhappy side-effect of elite epistemology?

'Constructivist' scholars of IPE have focused significant attention on a range of areas where 'everyday' ideas about how markets function, and how they ought to function, appear to have influenced the development of the financial crisis. Questions addressed include how 'theory-driven' financial innovation drove the development of the esoteric products that actually collapsed in the meltdown (Wigan 2010), how epistemic frames helped select instruments for assessing performance in the market (Langley 2010), and how everyday expectations shaped welfare trade-offs in the US subprime mortgage market (Seabrooke 2010). But perhaps the best-known Constructivist critic of the crisis is Mark Blyth. Focusing on the emergence of austerity, Blyth's arguments made a fairly prominent debut in the form of a YouTube video (Brown University 2010; and Mazza 2010). Uploaded in September 2010, and with over 120,000 views to date, the video gives us about five and a half minutes of a tweed-vested Blyth, accompanied by dancing chalkboard-style graphics and symbols, expositing on the difference between debt and leverage, and the idea that while a 'balance-sheet' perspective on the events of 2008 might suggest that it is sovereign debt that should primarily be keeping us up at night, we should in the same breath be wary of what he terms the 'fallacy of composition'. For Blyth, what is good for any one economic actor in a given situation is not necessarily what is good for the whole – this being especially true of cutting government spending in the midst of a global recession.

Expanding on these arguments in a subsequent book, Blyth (2013) argues that a full explanation of the turn to austerity necessarily involves an account of the political power of ideas. Economic theory, he says, is a part of the world we live in, and not just a 'correspondent reflection' of it (ibid: 39). To be sure, the 1999 repeal of the Glass–Steagal Act made possible a panoply of new, complex financial instruments. But the core issue was the 'epistemic hubris' of the US bankers who failed to see the obviously mounting risk in their portfolios (91). In this manner, Blyth appears to suggest that the crisis was essentially an accident. It was a case neither precisely of a lack of regulation, nor of moral hazard, but of a mistaken way of *thinking*. Presenting this case, Blyth presents a genealogy of neoliberal scholarship, from Friedrich von Hayek to Nassim Nicholas Taleb, all thinkers known for their arguments concerning logics of unintended consequences. While Keynesianism was the initial port of call for European policy-makers, Blyth suggests that this was mainly because, at the time at least, most of the world's neoliberal economists were either in a state of complete denial, or had fled the field of debate completely (54). However, neither the European Central Bank (ECB) nor the German government was so easily dissuaded. 'Ordoliberals' by nature, says Blyth, German policy-makers are deeply cautious on the topic of inflation. That is, they are advocates of a *Sozialmarktwirtschaft* model, where the state may intervene to regulate, and provide social safety nets, but only insofar as this might further the 'framework conditions' that 'make the market possible' (57). To this end, order and stability are the premium values, not the rewarding of errant behaviour.

Outgunned in the G20, and with debt-to-GDP ratios soaring on the European periphery, by late 2010 the Keynesian view was in decline. Yet a number of questions remain. The first is how, against the weight of evidence, this German account gained saliency in the first place. After all, as Blyth notes, with the possible exception of the Greek case, there was nothing necessarily catastrophic going on among the PIIGS (Portugal, Ireland, Italy, Greece and Spain). At the end of the day, they were all cases of banking crises *causing* sovereign debt crises (73). In an ideal world, the solution would have been to write down the debts. In other words, effectively, for the PIIGS simply to have printed money. However, as the common currency effectively denied them the autonomy to do this, the task of contriving a genuine solution would necessarily have required the material investment of a host of European partners. Such support was unlikely, says Blyth, primarily because the key policy-makers were beholden to a theory of expansionary fiscal consolidation; a theory first expressed by the so-called 'Bocconi Boys', Alberto Alesina and Silvia Ardagna, and later popularized by the influential economists Carmen Reinhart and Kenneth Rogoff.

Studies carried out by these prominent scholars warned of the growth-suppressing effects of high debt-to-GDP ratios. Moreover, they drew on examples, like Ireland's recovery from recession in the late-1980s, as evidence demonstrating the synergistic effect on growth of cuts in expenditure, wage moderation, and currency devaluation. Blyth cites a barrage of research to debunk these theories, noting ultimately that they conflate correlation and causation. When the ratings agency Standard and Poor's decided on 5 August 2011, to downgrade US debt, the effect was not to chase up the country's bond yields. To the contrary, it was equities that took the hit (3). Thus, far from being worried about government spending, what markets were essentially signalling was an anxiety about the prospects for growth. The point, says Blyth, is not that debt does not matter at all. Rather, it is that the resolution of debt is contingent upon the vicissitudes of the business cycle, and has very little to do with the deficit (12).

For Blyth then, erroneously confident appraisals of the risks of financial deregulation were at the very heart of the crisis. And it is a plausible argument, so far as it goes. However, while one can certainly appreciate how the arguments of neoliberal economists might come to influence policy, it is another question entirely as to how the principles they espouse are so willingly internalized by the populations they govern. Blyth certainly understands that neoliberalism *can* translate to everyday life. After all, as he notes in his YouTube video, austerity has a ring of virtuous commonsense about it. After a decade or more of debt-fuelled growth, recession is all too easily palmed off as the 'pain after the party', recalling to us the true cost of the goods and services we enjoy so much. Neoliberalism, in this sense, is lived as a kind of economic cold turkey. 'Austerity is painful, yes,' goes the refrain of this morality play, 'but it is as natural as a hangover'. Unfortunately, however, Blyth delves no further into these insights. Austerity for him is merely the unhappy side-effect of elite epistemic hubris. And the question of neoliberalism's capacity for everyday normalization is left unaddressed.

Introducing biopolitical economy

By contrast, much recent Foucault-inspired work on the crisis focuses less on the worldview of key elites and intellectuals and more on neoliberalism's history as a project explicitly oriented to the task of producing its own conditions of possibility. Critically, such work marks an interesting expansion on the sorts of questions that Foucauldian scholarship has traditionally been disposed to ask. In the past, such work has tended to fall into one of two categories. One, so-called 'global governmentality' studies, deals specifically with issues of visibility and measurement in regional and global institutions (see Kiersey and Weidner 2009; Joseph 2010). The other, featured mainly in the field of Security Studies, takes its cue principally from Giorgio Agamben's reinterpretation of Foucault's discussion of biopolitics, and focuses principally on the existence of a logic of sovereign exceptionalism in the context of the War on Terror (Dillon and Reid 2001; The Editors 2013). In the wake of the financial crisis, however, a rather different understanding of biopolitics has emerged. Taking its cue from Foucault's *Birth of Biopolitics* lecture series (2008), wherein he explores the emergence of liberal political economy, this literature recognizes Foucault as possibly the first theorist to grasp the full breadth of neoliberalism's anthropological ambition – that is, in Mirowski's terms, its commitment to using markets and governance to completely recast 'the totality of human existence into a novel modality, to be disciplined and punished by structures of power/ knowledge' (Mirowski 2013: 94).

Might such a reading of neoliberalism help us better to appreciate the relationship between ideas and austerity? To answer this question we might first wish to look at a seminal aspect of the broader historical development of governmentality, and the role played therein by the language of political economy. Foucault finds the basic blueprint for this activation of the subject in the early Christian pastoral, which he suggests is 'one of the decisive moments in the history of power in Western societies' (Foucault 2007: 185). But where the Christian pastoral pursued the production of a divine asceticism in the subject, contemporary governmentality pursues the development of a subject of economic life. This subject makes its first appearance in the sixteenth century, roughly around the same time that we see the emergence of the territorially administrative state. At this time, commentators begin discussing a proliferating series of objects, including something referred to as the 'population', which they took somehow to be naturally existing or present in the state of affairs. Moreover, as Foucault elaborates, the 'level of reality', or 'field of intervention', for this population was something called the economy (95). Accordingly, much as in the Christian pastorate, we see a certain naturalization of 'men in their relationships with things like customs, habits, ways of acting and thinking' (96). However, whereas previous modes of rule may have had spiritual goals, the administrative state perceived a need for a measure of *economic* government, to achieve a better arrangement of 'individuals, goods, and wealth' (94).

If, as Foucault describes it, the sixteenth century sees the emergence of the economy as an object of governmental intrigue, by the eighteenth century it has become the 'major form of knowledge' through which government knows and assesses the ethical performance of human life (108). No longer the container or vessel of a soul that must be directed towards heaven, then, the subject is now a creature of economic interests, a *homo oeconomicus*. Thus, suggests Foucault, we find ourselves in the era of Classical Liberalism, where the success of a government is deemed in large part to be contingent on its ability to 'cut out or contrive a free space of the market' for the expression of man's naturally utilitarian impulses (2008: 131). The idea is that there are now certain things which government ought not to do if it is to be economically successful. In this sense, says Foucault, liberal political economy drives 'a formidable wedge' between the powers of the state and the sphere of daily human life (17). In time, however, the idea of a naturally existing *homo oeconomicus* becomes unconvincing, and the era of Classical Liberalism recedes. *Neoliberalism*, its later iteration, is actually founded on a rejection of this idea of a naturally existing economic man. To the contrary, it imagines instead the need to anticipate specific kinds of governance structures which will encourage the emergence of a new kind of subject, the 'entrepreneur of oneself' – that is, one who is constantly balancing the costs and benefits of action not only in the sphere of economic life, but also even in seemingly non-economic spheres.

In Foucault's time, this view reaches its maximum expression with the American neoliberal (or *anarcho*-liberal) strain, associated with the Chicago School. For it is here that we see the neoliberal paradox at its starkest. On the one hand, the foundational myth of this strain is that *every* facet of human life may be read as an ostensibly market-based form of interaction. This logic can be extended to the entirety of human life because, critically, the neoliberal subject is understood as the bearer not of a natural or unitary economic identity but, rather, of something called human capital. Here, because everybody's body is understood naturally to possess an amount of capital, any kind of activity that involves 'substitutable choices', or the application of a 'limited means to one end among others' (222, 268), can be comprehended as labour and, thus, investment. Such labour includes not only the traditional 'job', but also pretty much any kind of activity where the pursuit of some sort of surplus value or future return can be imagined to take place (224). As a result, economic analysis can be applied to activities in a wide range of social arenas: marriage, parenting, discrimination, education, population growth, crime, and even insanity. On the other hand, despite this idea that the entirety of human life can be grasped somehow as a market-based form, the idea of human capital serves effectively to blur somewhat the division between government and market. Because the neoliberal individual is not exactly rational, human capital is made to stand in as a kind of leverage point for the application of market policies in a behaviour-correcting sense. For neoliberalism then, the subject can still be thought of as 'an active economic subject' (223), but only in a much less intentional sense, as one enjoined with its bodily potential, as a kind of assemblage, an 'enterprise unit', a 'machine-stream ensemble' or even a 'capital-ability' (225).

The neoliberal subject is thus one that must be governed if it is to act rationally. Its governability consists in the fact that it will, out of the hope of some return, and in response to the right incentives, modulate itself, changing its basic physical capacities, mental skills, and attitudes

(226, 229). Indeed, says Foucault, for this reason, neoliberals understand the study of economics to be nothing less than the 'analysis of the internal rationality' through which individuals come to their own determination about how they should develop themselves (223). Thus the *market* is viewed explicitly as a mechanism of government, directing this entire process of rational programming from the margins. Only two real questions therefore remain. The first, as Foucault notes, citing the well-known American neoliberal, Gary Becker, is to determine whether there might be any limits to the application of this logic. That is, whether there are any domains where the subject might not be able to 'accept' itself as *homo economicus* (269). The second, however, is to figure out the extent to which entrepreneurial ambitions, once in place, might need restraint. Left to its own devices, for example, the entrepreneurial self might choose to take too much risk and 'live dangerously' (66). And it is in this sense, therefore, that neoliberalism can be said to have a 'consciousness of crisis' (68), understanding 'freedom' as a fragile phenomenon, and one which must be directed if social life is to function optimally (65).

Neoliberalism as 'political project'?

In Lemke's terms, then, contra Blyth, neoliberalism is more than just 'ideological rhetoric'. Rather, it is 'a political project that endeavors to create a social reality that it suggests already exists' (Lemke 2001: 203). Foucault recognizes the paradox in this statement, but he does not connect it with the possibility that neoliberal governance can translate into a politics of austerity. Indeed, nowhere in his commentary on neoliberalism do we find anything like an effort to subject its principles to critique. Instead, we find a diagnostic Foucault, content to describe its contours, but also leaving his views open to interpretation. Thus Mirowski can say, for example, that while it would be 'an absurd counterfactual' (Mirowski 2013: 97) to say Foucault was himself a neoliberal, he nevertheless 'too readily' embraced 'the basic neoliberal precept that the market was an information processor more powerful and encompassing than any human being or organization of humans' (ibid.: 97–8). This position has been joined recently by Zamora, who says that while Foucault self-consciously refused to advocate neoliberalism, he nevertheless 'adopt[ed] all of its critiques of the welfare state' (Zamora 2014). Indeed, citing a number of statements made by Foucault in reference to welfare and healthcare, Zamora finds in Foucault a perspective on public services that would sound not entirely out of place coming from the mouth of Becker himself. In one case we see Foucault even expressing concern about the perverse effects of welfare: 'on the one hand, we give people more security, and on the other we increase their dependence'. Elsewhere, we see him anxious about the patronizing notion of a 'right' to universal healthcare. In these ways, suggests Zamora, Foucault's writings on state services 'actively contributed to [their] destruction', in a manner that was 'entirely in step with the neoliberal critiques of the moment' (similar arguments are elaborated in Behrent 2009).

Of course, the ideal of a single true or essential reading of any thinker is one to be avoided. In the context of the above assertions, however, at least two short points bear mentioning. First, as Kelly (2014) observes, the argument that Foucault was somehow a neoliberal or even crypto-conservative dates back some decades now. Some of this can be attributed to the fact that Foucault did not stint in criticizing actually existing socialist regimes. As he once noted, given that it has only really ever existed either in palliative form, 'within and connected up to liberal governmentalities', or as connected to a 'hyper-administrative' police state, it is impossible to speak of such a thing as an actually existing socialist governmentality (Foucault 2008: 92). In Kelly's terms, however, to interpret this as somehow a backhanded endorsement of neoliberalism is a stretch. Indeed, it is to ignore the simplest of Foucault's lessons about social life, 'that human actions at a micro level combine together at a macro level to produce effects that may be unintended by the participants, but nevertheless shape our society and our lives' (Kelly 2014). Ultimately, while the highly descriptive style of Foucault's writing and lecturing can often make it seem as if he has no political stake in what he is discussing, it is important to remember that nowhere in his work did he back off or retreat from this core intellectual commitment, or suggest that it might not also apply to neoliberalism. Less an opponent of welfare, then, Foucault was arguably encouraging us to try think beyond the blackmail of having to choose between government by the market, or by the state (Frase 2014).

With the above in mind, a second point raised by the debate over Foucault's alleged neoliberal proclivities concerns a general tendency on the part of his contemporary students in assessing the relationship between neoliberalism and capitalism. As noted above, in the context of the 2008 global financial crisis, scholars like Blyth examine neoliberalism as a discourse of legitimation, positioning it therefore as a central ideological variable, explaining both why the crisis happened, and why austerity has become the tool of choice as governments try to resolve it. Foucauldian critics, for their part, tend to be more interested in how the theory expresses a kind of anthropological vision. The subject of neoliberal governance, as Foucault hinted, is highly plastic, but it is also a creature that bears a certain ethical responsibility. In Wendy Brown's terms: 'As human capital, the subject is at once in charge of itself, responsible for itself, yet an instrumentalizable and potentially dispensable element of the whole' (2015: 38).

The 'political project' of neoliberalism, in this sense, is perhaps best captured by Margaret Thatcher's famous axiom, 'Economics are the method but the object is to change the soul' (cited in Hilgers 2012: 82). Neoliberal theory thus expresses the fantasy ideal of an order spontaneously self-organizing around the principles of the market, but the methods of neoliberal practice also bear a pedagogical significance, oriented as they are to the realization of that fantasy.

Indeed, this idea of neoliberalism as a 'political project' is, in fact, ubiquitous in governmentality literature (Davies and Mills 2014; Larner 2003), and clarifies somewhat the methodological contrast with Constructivism. As Will Davies puts it, 'Foucault is a historian of social technologies, material practices, codified routines and texts, and not necessarily of ideas as such' (Davies 2014). Assessing everyday neoliberal practice as well as discourse, in other words, Foucauldian international political economy (IPE) distinguishes itself from Constructivism by taking neoliberalism seriously as a vision of *government*. In Mirowski's terms, neoliberalism cannot be explained by the mere 'consilience' of neoliberal 'doctrine and function' (2013: 154). Rather, through governmental processes, neoliberalism has become 'integrated directly into the makeup of modern agency', and 'fills up the pores of our most unremarkable day' (129). In this sense, then, the critical project of what we might call 'biopolitical economy' addresses, per Jessop's definition, the problem of 'a political project that is justified on philosophical grounds and seeks to extend competitive market forces, consolidate a market-friendly constitution and promote individual freedom' (Jessop 2013: 70)

Neoliberalism and capitalism

If Foucauldian IPE can be said to unify in and around the argument that neoliberalism is more than an ideology, it is not without its share of internal disagreements. Echoing themes in the so-called 'Varieties in/of Capitalism' debate (see Brenner et al. 2010; Bruff and Ebenau 2014), this is especially true when it comes to the question of globalization. Some argue that the idea of a monolithic, globe-spanning neoliberalism is anathema to the spirit of Foucault's work. In reality, these scholars suggest, neoliberal globalization is a highly variegated set of often-contradictory processes. Considering the role of the state, for example, some scholars argue that neoliberalism is necessarily local before it is global, struggling to generate spaces and sovereignties amenable to market-centric logics through context-dependent strategies (Joseph 2009). A task for research, therefore, is to refine our understanding of the specific intellectual influences of these local projects, and to comprehend how local conditions and knowledges have influenced the pathways of neoliberal development (Larner 2003). Others, however, insist that the Foucauldian model of power, properly understood, can easily scale to admit the possibility of a globe-spanning assemblage of neoliberal governance (Legg 2008; Vrasti 2011). Indeed, Bailey and Shibata (2014) cite Deleuze to remind us that the ontological priority of resistance means that the scale question is itself somewhat beside the point; capitalism is necessarily always a project of recapturing the demands and power of labour. Crucially, however, it bears noting that the focus on specificity of the former camp is motivated by a conscious desire to avoid any kind of economic reductionism. Larner cautions, for example, that many critical accounts of neoliberalism remain problematically 'embedded in Marxist or Neo-Marxist theoretical traditions' (2003: 511). With these political cards on the table, then, it is clear that the tension in this debate cannot be reduced to a merely technical dispute over Foucault's ontology.

Of course, the unspoken assumption here is that Foucault was indeed a relentless and unstinting anti-Marxist and, therefore, that the lengthy description of neoliberalism's genealogy offered in his lectures can be read only as an endorsement of this conclusion. However, not only is this a dubious representation of Foucault's work (see Springer 2012), it is also a politically constraining view. For, despite its preoccupation with social technologies and practices, it is still *neoliberalism* that occupies its central point of focus. In this sense, as with Constructivism, it is very difficult to connect the theory with an understanding of what austerity is, or what it is for. 'Variegated' Foucauldians, for want of a better term, ultimately read austerity as nothing more than a rationale of social control through the mechanism of the market. Yet, for many of its victims around the world, the stakes run a good deal deeper than that: neoliberalism's analysis of the current predicaments of capitalism has weighed the survival of a global *economic* system as vastly more important than the dream of a materially enabled human life, decrying the desire for democratic accountability as a kind of moral weakness. The upshot, as Lordon puts it, is that the lives of billions are now overshadowed by a 'scheme of liquidity' which 'irresistibly overflows and spreads throughout the whole of capitalist society, evidently primarily serving those in a position to assert their desire as a master-desire' (2014: 44).

Must a biopolitical account of neoliberalism necessarily reject Marx, and avoid any consideration of capitalism? Dardot and Laval (2014) offer some helpful resources here. In their framing, Foucault's engagement with neoliberalism exposits clearly the neoliberal paradox, its presupposition of the human both as competitive subject and as capital-in-formation. Nevertheless, they suggest, writing in the 1970s, Foucault had no way of anticipating the huge change in the offing for neoliberalism's fortunes that was just in the offing. Reading the earliest formulations of neoliberalism's fantasy, it was clear to him only that it grasped the market as a perfect instrument of governance. Whereas, in reality, the ideal of neoliberalism was itself emerging in a specific context. And, in this sense, its early expressions had to contend with a number of other already ongoing economic realities – namely, as Dardot and Laval observe, the fact that capitalism was itself already experiencing a governmental crisis of sorts.

Dardot and Laval's engagement with neoliberalism brings them into contact with a rather different Marx from the one rejected by the variegated Foucauldians. Their starting point is that capitalism cannot be reduced to a simple logic of bourgeois accumulation. Far from being its master architects, the bourgeoisie are, in fact, a product of its emergence. Neoliberalism, therefore, is not merely the epiphenomenal expression of transhistorical capitalist machinations. To the contrary, the ideational superstructure of capitalism bears no necessary relationship to its base logic; ideology and practice are mutually implicated, with the former informing economic governance 'from within'. Nevertheless, with Foucault's lectures on biopolitics as their principle inspiration, they contend that neoliberalism's biopolitical project 'coincides with the most profound intuitions of Marx, who clearly understood that a system of economic production is also a system of anthropological "production"' (25). Neoliberalism is thus 'unquestionably' capitalist but, nevertheless, constitutes 'a unique form of capitalism that must be analyzed as such in its irreducible specificity' (20–1). Thus, whereas David Harvey (2007) argues that neoliberalism was born of a great crisis of accumulation in the 1970s, characterized by stagflation and falling profits, which drove the bourgeoisie to lay siege to working-class standards of living, for Dardot and Laval none of the contending parties necessarily had a 'true' consciousness of the terms of the crisis, or exactly how it might be resolved.

To the contrary, they suggest, the neoliberal form of knowledge emerged in a situation where it was not already connected to the 'endogenous dynamic' of Fordist capitalism, and where capitalist leaders did not already know the terms and strategies they would adopt to understand and resolve the crisis. Indeed, consulting the historical record, what they find in the early neoliberal debates was discussion not of a crisis of profitability but, rather, something much more along the lines of a crisis of governance. *The Crisis of Democracy*, for example, a report published in 1975 by the Trilateral Commission, spoke fearfully of an 'excess of democracy' in the west, and a rising tide of demand for the political participation of workers, the poor, and other marginal classes (Dardot and Laval 2014: 258). Interestingly, Dardot and Laval's analysis here seems to square with that of Hardt and Negri (2000), who argue that Fordism eventually succumbed to the demands of workers for flexibility and a more democratic division of labour. Thus, the old model, premised on a relatively tight linkage between wages and productivity, which allowed for the emergence of a mass consumerist mode, came up on 'endogenous limits' (Dardot and Laval 2014: 227). This, combined with the economic impact of the two oil shocks, triggered a crisis in the Fordist way of knowing the world. Dardot and Laval add to this story an account of how early neoliberals explained the crisis in moral terms, as a corrosion of social trust caused by the welfare state, thereby opening up avenues of attack on public service. Neoliberalism's solution to the crisis of capitalist governance was to refound society itself in the model of the enterprise, and to cast the state as itself 'an enterprise in service of enterprises' (384).

Thus we can explain 'why, unlike in the 1930s, the crisis of Fordist capitalism resulted in an outcome conducive not to *less capitalism*, but to *more capitalism*' (241, original emphasis). Neoliberalism is a way of seeing and governing the world, true, but it is also the discourse which capitalist leaders came to believe in as their previous way of seeing the world fell asunder. Applied to today's political economy then, we see that the Foucauldian method grasps not only a neoliberalism that transcends mere ideology, but one also which is truly *global* in its scale of application. Foucauldians will agree that what is hidden in neoliberalism is not so much a real condition of labour, or a relation with value that must somehow be recovered. They will also agree that the point is to try to understand neoliberal governmentality on the basis of its specific production of truth, its subsumption of subjective difference within the framework of individual self-interest. To borrow Jason Read's phrasing, 'what has disappeared in neoliberalism is the tactical polyvalence of discourse; everything is framed in terms of interests, freedoms, and risks' (2009: 35). Beyond this, however, we must also recognize neoliberalism as the harbinger of a major transformation in the pace and rhythm of capitalist life. The critique of biopolitical economy is thus the basis not for a reconciliation with value, but for a democratic renegotiation of the terms of life itself. On the strength of this assessment, Lordon is surely right when he says the task of the communist today is to return to the division of labour, and reimagine it in terms of 'equal participation in the determination of a shared collective destiny' (2014: 131).

References

Bailey, D.J., and Shibata, S. 2014. Varieties of Contestation: The Comparative and Critical Political Economy of 'Excessive' Demand. *Capital & Class*, 38.1: 239–51.

Behrent, M.C. 2009. A Seventies Thing: On the Limits of Foucault's Neoliberalism Course for Understanding the Present. In Binkley, S., and Capetillo-Ponce, J., eds. *A Foucault for the 21st Century: Governmentality, Biopolitics and Discipline in the New Millennium*. Newcastle upon Tyne: Cambridge Scholars: 16–29.

Blyth, M. 2013. *Austerity: The History of a Dangerous Idea*. Oxford: Oxford University Press.

Brenner, N., Peck, J., and Theodore, N. 2010. Variegated Neoliberalization: Geographies, Modalities, Pathways. *Global Networks*, 10.2: 182–222.

Brown University. 2010. *Mark Blyth on Austerity* [video file], 30 September. Retrieved from http://youtu.be/FmsjGys-VqA

Brown, W. 2015. *Undoing the Demos: Neoliberalism's Stealth Revolution*. Brooklyn: Zone.

Bruff, I., and Ebenau, M. 2014. Critical Political Economy and the Critique of Comparative Capitalisms Scholarship on Capitalist Diversity. *Capital & Class*, 38.1: 3–15.

Dardot, P., and Laval, C. 2014. *The New Way Of The World*. London: Verso.

Davies, W. 2014. Will Davies Responds to Nicholas Gane's 'The Emergence of Neoliberalism'. In Davidson, A.I., ed. *Theory, Culture Society*. Retrieved from http://www.palgraveconnect.com/doifinder/10.1057/9780230594180 (ebook)

Davies, W., and Mills, T. 2014. Neoliberalism and the End of Politics. *New Left Project*. Retrieved from http://www.newleftproject.org/index.php/site/article_comments/neoliberalism_and_the_end_of_politics

Dillon, M., and Reid, J. 2001. Global Liberal Governance: Biopolitics, Security and War. *Millennium: Journal of International Studies*, 30.1: 41–66.

Foucault, M. 2007. *Security, Territory, Population; Lectures at the Collège de France, 1977–1978*. New York: Palgrave Macmillan.

—. 2008. *The Birth of Biopolitics; Lectures at the Collège de France, 1978–79*. New York: Palgrave Macmillan.

Frase, P. 2014. Beyond the Welfare State. *Jacobin*. Retrieved from https://www.jacobinmag.com/2014/12/beyond-the-welfare-state/

Hardt, M., and Negri, A. 2000. *Empire*. Cambridge: Harvard University Press.

Harvey, D. 2007. *A Brief History of Neoliberalism*. Oxford: Oxford University Press.

—. 2011. *The Enigma of Capital*. London: Profile.

Hilgers, M. 2012. The Historicity of the Neoliberal State. *Social Anthropology*, 20.1: 80–94.

Jessop, B. 2013. Putting Neoliberalism in its Time and Place: A Response to the Debate. *Social Anthropology*, 21.1: 65–74.

Joseph, J. 2009. Governmentality of What? Populations, States and International Organizations. *Global Society*, 23.4: 413–27.

—. 2010. The Limits of Governmentality. *European Journal of International Relations*, 16.2.

Kelly, M.G.E. 2014. Foucault and Neoliberalism Today. *Contrivers Review*. Retrieved from http://www.contrivers.org/articles/12/

Kiersey, N., and Weidner, J.R. 2009. Editorial Introduction. *Global Society*, 23.4: 353–61.

Langley, P. 2010. The Performance of Liquidity in the Subprime Mortgage Crisis. *New Political Economy*, 15.1: 71–89.

Larner, W. 2003. Neolibrealism? *Environment and Planning D: Society and Space*, 21.5: 509–12.

Legg, S. 2008. Of Scales, Networks and Assemblages: The League of Nations Apparatus and the Scalar Sovereignty of the Government of India. *Transactions of the Institute of British Geographers*, 34.2: 234–53.

Lemke, T. 2001. 'The Birth of Bio-politics': Michel Foucault's Lecture at the College de France on Neo-liberal Governmentality. *Economy and Society*, 30.2: 190–207.

Lordon, F. 2014. *Willing Slaves of Capital*. London: Verso.

Mazza, J. 2010. *The Watson Institute at Brown University Presents Mark Blyth on Austerity* [video file], 29 September. Retrieved from https://www.youtube.com/watch?v=FmsjGys-VqA&feature=youtu.be

McCabe, C. 2011. *Sins of the Father*. Dublin: History Press Ireland.

Mirowski, P. 2013. *Never Let a Serious Crisis Go to Waste: How Neoliberalism Survived the Financial Meltdown*. London: Verso.

Read, J. 2009. A Genealogy of Homo-Economicus: Neoliberalism and the Production of Subjectivity. *Foucault Studies*, 6: 1–12.

Seabrooke, L. 2010. What Do I Get? The Everyday Politics of Expectations and the Subprime Crisis. *New Political Economy*, 15.1: 51–70.

Springer, S. 2012. Neoliberalism as Discourse: Between Foucauldian Political Economy and Marxian Poststructuralism. *Critical Discourse Studies*, 9.2: 133–47.

Surin, K. 2009. *Freedom Not Yet: Liberation and the Next World Order*. Durham, NC: Duke University Press.

The Editors, 2013. International Intersections: An Interview With François Debrix. *Interstitial Journal*, May: 1–14.

Vrasti, W. 2011. Universal but not Truly 'Global': An Intervention in the Global Governmentality Debate. *Review of International Studies*.

Wigan, D. 2010. Credit Risk Transfer and Crunches: Global Finance Victorious or Vanquished? *New Political Economy*, 15.1: 109–25.

Zamora, D. 2014. Foucault's Responsibility. *Jacobin*. Retrieved from https://www.jacobinmag.com/2014/12/michel-foucault-responsibility-socialist/?setAuth=822ecd1f989ac753726f872a1378fd34

15

NEOLIBERALISM, SURVEILLANCE AND MEDIA CONVERGENCE

Julie Cupples and Kevin Glynn

Mapping the neoliberal conjuncture

Two decades ago, long before the creation of Facebook, Twitter and YouTube, an incisive and highly seductive mediated critique of neoliberalism was produced from the Lacandón Jungle in Chiapas in southern Mexico and circulated around the globe. The indigenous peoples who lived in that region and called themselves the Zapatistas had had enough of the policies that condemned them to persistent precarity. On 1 January 1994, the day the North American Free Trade Agreement (NAFTA) came into force, they took advantage of the global media presence in Mexico to create their own alternative media spectacle and thus to forge a space through which to articulate their resistance and present their demands. Thanks in part to new media technologies, and in particular rapidly expanding internet connectivity, their ideas spread widely and found resonance not only with other indigenous groups, but also with all kinds of people in Mexico and around the world, including students, environmentalists, farmers, middle-class families, feminists, shantytown dwellers, and others whose lives were similarly characterized by social exclusion and economic insecurity. The Zapatista movement was rooted in the everyday realities of southern Mexico but drew upon and contributed to the development of global counterdiscourses challenging neoliberalism. Through the creative hybridization and rearticulation of the Latin American revolutionary tradition, Marxism–Leninism and Mayan cosmologies, the Zapatistas provided a set of discursive resources that were useful to others whose local realities differed from those of Chiapas but who were up against many of the same destructive global forces. The two decades that have passed since the emergence of the Zapatista rebellion have been a period in which new media platforms and delivery technologies have arisen, and the contestation of neoliberalism has proliferated and intensified.

This chapter develops a form of conjunctural analysis (Grossberg 2010), a method of 'radical contextualism' developed within cultural studies that posits 'conjunctures' as 'problem-spaces' whose illumination 'aims to give people an understanding of the contingency of the present'. Conjuncturalism thus 'presupposes a reconstitution of imagination in the context of its own analysis' (ibid.: 57–8). We start by identifying two key phenomena that we propose as central to the current conjuncture. The first is what we might define as neoliberalism or neoliberalizing processes: a set of discourses, political rationalities, formations of common sense, policy prescriptions and economic practices that took off in the 1980s with heavy support from multinational corporations, international financial institutions, and right-wing politicians, scholars and media commentators. In many ways, neoliberalism is an inadequate concept. As Stuart Hall (2011: 207) writes,

> critics say the term lumps together too many things to merit a single identity; it is reductive, sacrificing attention to internal complexities and geo-historical specificity. I sympathize with this critique. However, I think there are enough common features to warrant giving it a provisional conceptual identity, provided this is understood as a first approximation . . . I would also argue that naming neo-liberalism is politically necessary to give the resistance to its onward march content, focus and a cutting edge.

At its core, neoliberalism involves the intensification of processes of commodification, privatization, individuation and labour flexibilization, and the attempted reduction of social services and social contracts, including healthcare, education, public pensions and public safety nets. The neoliberal state has, however, continued to invest in the expansion of military capacity, intelligence gathering, surveillance activities and data mining.

Neoliberalism has had multifaceted consequences for individuals, households, and communities. On a global scale, we have witnessed a growing increase in social and economic inequality, accompanied by the closing-down of democratic spaces as the rich become richer than ever and those harmed by the system find themselves deprived of political redress. In addition, our planet is in climatic chaos as the neoliberal obsession with economic growth hinders any meaningful political action on global warming (Cupples 2012; Klein 2014). As noted, this state of affairs has met with intense modes of contestation and political activism from a variety of sectors. Neoliberalism's detractors and losers, those harmed or outraged by the unnecessary misery it engenders, have mobilized against neoliberal policies via social media, on the streets, in their communities and workplaces, and through scholarship. At the time of writing, it is not clear whether neoliberalism may be coming to an end, as there is evidence that it is intensifying and giving rise to growing authoritarianism, but also counter-evidence that it is more fragile and contested than ever (Cupples and Glynn 2014; Peck 2012). On the one hand, in the UK, Australia and Canada, as Wilson (2014) writes, neoliberal governments have managed to discursively entrench long-term austerity measures, and, despite their failure to generate prosperity for more than a small percentage of the population, the idea that such measures are necessary has been embraced by the parliamentary opposition and by many ordinary people. In Latin America, on the other hand, we have witnessed the election of several left-wing governments, the so-called pink tide, who have campaigned on anti-neoliberal platforms, although the extent to which neoliberalism is being disrupted in pink tide economies, many of which are based on contradictory forms of neo-extractivism, is debatable (Cupples 2013). The global banking failures of 2008 and the Occupy movements of 2011 seemed to suggest that neoliberalism may be on the way out, but such a prospect seems far more uncertain only a few years later (see Wilson 2016). The recent rise of anti-austerity parties such as Syriza in Greece and Podemos in Spain and the Yes campaign and radical independence movement in Scotland potentially suggests, however, that the setback to anti-neoliberal forces might be temporary.

The second key dimension of the current conjuncture that we identify involves media convergence. Just as conjunctures are conceptualized as problem-spaces structured around core contradictions, media convergence is a contradictory phenomenon that entails both a consolidation of dominating forces and the development, expansion and mobilization of grassroots counterforces. Convergence names a key set of processes that are core to the emergence of a highly elaborated and complex contemporary media environment marked by rapid technological development, digitalization, and new forms of interactivity, connectivity, participation and mobilization. Media convergence is a highly multidimensional phenomenon that scholars have theorized in a range of different ways. Two of the most prominent themes associated with media convergence in scholarly analyses are, on the one hand, ongoing processes of conglomeration that have led to ever greater concentrations of capital and power within the media industries and, on the other, ongoing collisions of 'old' and 'new', digitalized media that shift power relations between producers and consumers and enable media content and discourses to cross technological platforms in highly unpredictable ways. As Henry Jenkins (2008: 18) writes, media convergence,

> is both a top-down corporate-driven process and a bottom-up consumer-driven process. Corporate convergence coexists with grassroots convergence. Media companies are learning how to accelerate the flow of media content across delivery channels to expand revenue opportunities, broaden markets, and reinforce viewer commitments. Consumers are learning how to use these different media technologies to bring the flow of media more fully under their control and to interact with other consumers.

Media convergence is therefore a phenomenon with complex cultural, political, economic and technological dimensions that make the contemporary media environment quite distinctive. Radio, television and newspapers persist and in many places are thriving, and are likely to do so for the foreseeable future. But the ways in which their content is created, delivered, consumed and contested are changing. As Daniel Dayan (2009) observes, rarely have representations of situations and events 'simultaneously involved so many conflicting versions and so many competing media' as in the contemporary environment, where 'the activity of displaying has become a globally sensitive battlefield' to the extent that 'what is today at stake is the authority invested in the act of showing' (ibid.: 20). Once the attacks of 9/11, for example, were instantaneously shown by 'the media of the center' to the bulk of the world's population and thereby 'established as the foundation of a new historical reality', images of these very same attacks were almost as instantaneously rearticulated and mobilized across a myriad of media platforms as a means of challenging the official narratives of 9/11 (ibid.: 27; also see Glynn 2015).

Both contestation and fragmentation are central to contemporary mediascapes. The economy of media attention is fragmented as audiences are increasingly dispersed across a growing assortment of proliferating platforms that include both commercial and bottom-up, alternative and activist media, including many that originate from the global South and from indigenous nations and communities. As Jesús Martín-Barbero (2011: 42, emphasis original) observes, new media forms and technologies 'are increasingly being appropriated by groups from lowly sectors, making *socio-cultural revenge* or a form of *socio-cultural return match* possible for them, that is, the construction of a counter-hegemony all over the world'. Such forms and technologies include indigenous TV and video production, community as well as internet radio and television stations, YouTube and Vimeo channels, and volunteered geographic information. The dynamics of this complex media landscape pose significant challenges for the study of media convergence, which disrupts boundaries between consumption and production to an unprecedented degree. Citizens, activists and conventionally marginalized populations are forging new media literacies and participatory practices and devising new modes of connectivity and expression for engaging with and challenging neoliberal strategies and agendas. For example, media 'prosumers' use Twitter, Facebook, YouTube, blogs, internet forums and crowd-sourced and volunteered geographic information to respond to political events, government policies, corporate initiatives and mainstream media texts. In many cases, government agencies, corporations and commercial media are forced to respond in one way or another to such grassroots practices.

The lived experiences of vast populations today are thus incessantly 'framed by, mitigated through, and made immediate by pervasive and ubiquitous media' (Deuze 2009: 18), so that contemporary 'prosumers' move across multiple platforms and engage with a diverse array of content types. Contemporary citizenship has therefore become 'monitorial' (Schudson 1999), insofar as it involves 'scanning all kinds of news and information sources – newspapers, magazines, TV shows, blogs, online and offline social networks, and so on' (Deuze 2009: 18). The same person that may use Twitter to announce an anti-austerity march or be an avid viewer of *Democracy Now* might also regularly watch Hollywood movies, reality TV shows, soap operas and CNN. At a time of the proliferating saturation of our cultural lives by media texts, our principal focus as analysts must be 'the whole textual environment – how it operates and how readers negotiate it' (Couldry 2000: 67, 76; also see Cupples 2015). In the present media environment, 'in terms of media production processes, we continue to witness a mix of "one-size-fits-all" content made for largely invisible mass audiences next to (and infused by) rich forms of transmedia storytelling including elements of user control and "prosumer"-type agency' (Deuze 2009: 25–6).

Some left-wing academics are dismissive of many forms of contemporary media activity, such as voting in reality TV shows or spending time on Facebook (see, for example, Harvey 2014: 278). But, as Jenkins (2008) recognizes, even in spaces of popular fandom and gaming, media users develop skills of digital participation and collaboration (such as the cultivation of collective intelligence) that can, potentially at least, be put to more overtly politicized and democratizing uses. Not only is it generally easier today for many people to make their own media, but many more are able to share, remix, edit and comment on the media made by commercial producers (Jenkins *et al.* 2013). Hence, while ordinary people increasingly make their own media in ways that challenge top-down control over such processes, many more are remixing and sharing the media produced by corporations with diverse and unpredictable consequences. Consequently, Jenkins *et al.* (2013) have urged us to disrupt the scholarly and industry focus on virality and to look as well at what they call *spreadability*, which facilitates the formation of new collectivities and spaces of public engagement.

While the dynamics of media convergence provide citizens with a powerful set of new tools, there are nevertheless, of course, serious barriers to bringing about meaningful social and political change. In this regard, it is important to recognize the complex spatial and temporal convergences and complicities between the 'corporate-driven' or 'top-down' and the 'user-driven' or 'bottom-up'. Within what Mark Andrejevic (2013) calls the 'digital enclosure', our participatory media activities are being appropriated by states and corporations in the form of 'big data' that can be harnessed towards the advancement of neoliberal agendas. While corporations strive to ever more precisely chart consumer profiles and preferences by exhaustively mining social media sites, the NSA and other agencies subject citizen activists to extensive surveillance and criminalization. Thus, although the internet enables us to access once unimaginable volumes of information and forms of connectivity, it simultaneously renders us vulnerable to algorithmic control exerted by the forces of predictive analytics, commodification and securitization. As Christian Fuchs (2011: 304) writes, web 2.0 users are 'producers of information (produsers, prosumers), but this creative communicative activity enables the controllers of disciplinary power to closely gain insights into the lives, secrets, and consumption preferences of the users'. Indeed, the participatory practices of media users sometimes mimic disciplinary and securitizing control in the mode of what Andrejevic (2005) calls 'peer-to-peer' or 'lateral' surveillance.

The complexities of the contemporary moment are captured by Nick Couldry (2014), who attempts to deconstruct what he calls the 'myth of us': an emergent 'myth of natural collectivity' (ibid.: 885) online that underwrites the idea that '*this* is where we now come together' (ibid.: 882, emphasis original). Against this myth, Couldry argues for the importance of remembering that this new formation of 'us' is itself constituted by the very platforms to which we are drawn, and which the myth asserts was already there all along. These platforms are at present actively reconstituting social relations through the profit-driven serial tracking of users 'as they cross the media landscape' (ibid.: 886). Couldry (ibid.: 885, emphasis original) argues that 'we must be wary when our most important moments of "coming together" *seem* to be captured in what people happen to do on platforms whose economic value is based on generating *just such* an idea of natural collectivity' as that which is promoted by the emergent 'myth of us'.

The neoliberal surveillance state's deep fearfulness and anxiety in the face of the threat posed by 'the power of the imagination, dissent and the willingness to hold power accountable' (Giroux 2015: 132) advance its desire to develop sophisticated statistical profiling techniques that might facilitate the pre-emptive identification of activists and others deemed to threaten the social order. Fiske (1998: 72) argues that the 'function of surveillance is to maintain the normal by disciplining what has been abnormalized', including especially racialized others and dissidents. The fears and anxieties of the neoliberal security state have motivated the exceptional confinement and demonization of those who challenge, disrupt or endanger the operations of the surveillance apparatus, such as Chelsea Manning, Julian Assange, Edward Snowden and Barrett Brown. While the state's extreme responses to the actions of these dissidents might seem to suggest that we have entered a chilling new phase of neoliberal totalitarianism, it is important to remember that there are many historical and contemporary examples of state-sponsored racial terror, oppressive surveillance and the criminalization of dissent in what Franz Fanon refers to as the Zone of Non-Being (see Grosfoguel 2011) – including in Chile during the Pinochet dictatorship, Guatemala during the 1980s (when every Mayan Indian was a suspected guerrilla fighter), the USA during the civil rights struggles, and colonial and postcolonial New Zealand, where the criminalization of indigenous activists has a long history. Indeed, the Zapatistas have been subject to ongoing surveillance and harassment by the Mexican government for the past two decades, and arguably protected from total annihilation primarily by online expressions of solidarity that we might understand as an instance of global counter-surveillance directed against the security state. What is striking today is the magnitude of the extension of (racially asymmetrical) digital monitoring across the entire terrain of neoliberal society, such that it is virtually impossible for *anybody* to avoid pervasive surveillance regimes as governments, corporations, multilateral organizations and even universities jump on 'big data' and 'smart cities' bandwagons despite their limitations and serious implications for human rights (see Deen 2015; Kakaes 2015).

Nevertheless, an analysis of mediated citizen engagement with neoliberal processes reveals heightened discursive contestation around questions of our shared political futures. At the level of transformationally oriented social movements, recent decades have thrown up 'a resurgence of decentralized, networked organization and utopian visions of autonomy and grassroots counterpower' based upon 'emerging network forms and imaginaries [that] have been greatly facilitated by the rise of new digital technologies' (Juris 2008: 10). More ordinarily, many corporations are forced to monitor their Twitter accounts 24/7 as their attempts to use social media to their advantage are subverted or otherwise backfire frequently. Companies such as JP Morgan, British Airways, Ryanair, British Gas, Tesco, Waitrose, Starbucks, McDonalds, Burger King and Coca-Cola have all seen their brands and reputations damaged (at least temporarily) by 'hash tag hijackings' via Twitter due to poor customer service, customer deception, exploitation of employees, unreasonable price hikes, fraud, market manipulation and tax avoidance. Large online communities in both the UK and the USA have used Facebook to contest neoliberalism. Some, such as UK Uncut, organize around anti-austerity agendas, while others, such as 38 Degrees, develop progressive, issues-based campaigns.[1] Some develop from humorous or satirical political reflections on current events. 'Make "Ding-Dong! The Witch is Dead" number 1 the week Thatcher dies' (Make… n.d.) was a Facebook-led campaign created in an attempt to elevate the *Wizard of Oz* song to the top of the charts in time for the 'Iron Lady's' funeral in 2013. In 2015, it remains a thriving, 8,000-member page that describes itself as a site to 'share information and ideas to fight against the ongoing destruction of the country by Thatcherism and greed'. Its focus is on the UK government's current austerity agenda, which it understands as one of Thatcher's destructive legacies. Similarly, during the 2012 US presidential debates, Republican candidate Mitt Romney used the phrase 'binders full of women' in his response to a question about gender-based pay inequities. His remark attracted widespread ridicule and online commentary via Facebook, Twitter and Tumblr, where sites named for Romney's strange turn of phrase have persisted as forums for debate around the impacts of neoliberalism in the USA. In 2015, there remain several active 'Binders Full of Women' Facebook pages (see, for example, BFOW n.d, which has more than 300,000 likes).

Private companies' capacities to exert power across networked space are thus highly contingent on the forms of discursive interactivity that develop around corporate practices and media figures, texts and events as they unfold upon the broader terrain that defines media convergence. The ensuing struggles can be understood in Gramscian terms as skirmishes within ongoing wars of position that offer no guaranteed victories on either side (Hall 1996). To illustrate the kinds of struggles currently underway, we turn now to a discussion of the articulation, disarticulation, rearticulation and contestation of and over the austerity agenda in the UK as it spills across media forms, texts and platforms that include both 'old' media such as tabloid newspapers and newer forms like reality TV shows and social media.

'Poverty porn' and neoliberal common sense

In the UK, a particularly harsh form of neoliberal austerity was implemented by the Conservative-Liberal Democrat coalition that came to power in 2010. Inequality steadily increased, the rich got richer than ever, and UK corporations found themselves sitting on mountains of uninvested capital that was estimated to have grown to £750 billion by July 2012 (Stewart 2012; see also Burke 2013). Huge multinational corporations such as Amazon, Starbucks, Vodafone and Google faced minimal taxation on staggeringly large profits (see Connell 2014). The government looked the other way while the Swiss arm of HSBC enabled wealthy British account holders to hide money and so avoid/evade income taxes (Leigh *et al.* 2015). Yet the same government implemented brutal attacks on welfare spending, and slashed benefits for and applied punitive sanctions on the poorest and most vulnerable sectors of society. While there was widespread concern about government surveillance of all of our private communications, UK beneficiaries were subjected to humiliating forms of surveillance that undermine and threaten well-being and self-esteem. The consequences have been extreme. While the wealth of Britain's richest families has doubled in just five years, half a million British children do not have access to minimally adequate nutrition (Cooper *et al.* 2014). In addition, suicide rates in the UK have started to increase and are disproportionately high among those sanctioned by the Department of Work and Pensions (Platt 2014; Cowburn 2015). Neoliberalization is advanced through state-led discursive strategies that seek to blame and punish the victims of neoliberal policies as if these victims were morally responsible for the misery inflicted by the policies (Slater 2012; Tyler 2013). In a 2010 speech, British Prime Minister David Cameron encouraged hard-working low-income labourers to turn against the undeserving unemployed rather than against the super-rich:

> When you work hard and still sometimes have to go without the things you want because times are tough it is maddening to know that there are some people who

could work but just don't want to. You know the people I mean. You walk down the road on your way to work and you see the curtains drawn in their house. You know they could work and they chose not to. And just as maddening is the fact that they seem to get away with it.

(Quoted in Rose 2011)

Such discourses circulate widely through a range of media. Right-wing tabloids such as *The Sun* and *Daily Mail*, both owned by austerity-endorsing media barons, carry many articles that warn, for example, that 'hundreds of thousands of scroungers in the UK are robbing hard-working *Sun* readers of their cash', thus amplifying and further extending into ordinary common sense a vernacular translation of the government's austerity policy agenda (Sloan 2010). As Hall (see, e.g., 1996) has long argued, the struggle for common sense within a social formation is a crucial component of processes of hegemonization and counter-hegemonization, and therefore an important object of conjunctural analysis.

In recent years, those on benefits have been the focus of a number of reality television shows that some have dubbed 'poverty porn' (e.g., Jensen 2014), including *Benefits Street, Benefits Britain: Life on the Dole, Britain on the Fiddle, We all Pay Your Benefits, Skint, The Future State of Welfare, Britain on Benefits,* and *On Benefits and Proud.* Imogen Tyler (2013) argues for what she calls a 'figurative method' that traces the 'fabrication and repetition of abject figures across several different sites – popular culture, news media, policy documents, political rhetoric, academic discourses – and within a range of social spaces including the communicative practices of everyday life'. Tyler's 'figurative method' helps her to 'ascertain the ways in which national abjects are employed to incite and legitimize "tough" economic measures and punitive governmental responses' (ibid.: 10). Such an approach calls to our attention the reiteration and movement of the figure of the 'lazy benefit scrounger' across a range of discursive terrains stretching from parliament to popular media, and enables us to name the processes of abjection that make such figures into 'ideological conductors mobilized to do the dirty work of neoliberal governmentality'. These figures of 'poverty porn' thus become 'symbolic and material scapegoats' that mediate and legitimize 'the social decomposition effected by market deregulation and welfare retrenchment' (ibid.: 9). The 'poverty porn' programmes thus extend neoliberal surveillance to the realm of the abject figure of the 'undeserving poor', whose visibility and abnormalization thereby function as 'formative factors' in the normalization of the legitimate citizen/consumer (Fiske 1998: 72).

In this way, neoliberal surveillance, in the form of reality TV shows that make up the subgenre of 'poverty porn', plays a constitutive role in the formation of neoliberal common sense. Such an analysis adds to the substantial body of existing scholarship that demonstrates reality television's discursive role in the production of neoliberal subjectivities and governmentalities and the promotion of practices of entrepreneurial self-responsibilization in a period marked by the ongoing disavowal of such responsibilities by the state (see, e.g., Couldry and Littler 2011; Hill 2015; McCarthy 2007; Ouellette 2009; Ouellette and Hay 2008; Weber 2010). McCarthy (2007: 17), for example, writes that 'the reality program – produced (unlike fiction TV) without union labour and proposing the makeover (rather than state assistance) as the key to social mobility, stability, and civic empowerment – is an important arena in which to observe the vernacular diffusion of neoliberal common sense'. And as Hall and O'Shea (2013, n.p.) argue, 'after forty years of a concerted neoliberal ideological assault, this new version of common sense is fast becoming the dominant one'. Hall and O'Shea are also at pains to point out, however, that while 'common sense feels coherent', it is nevertheless 'strangely composite' and thus 'fundamentally contradictory'. They assert the importance of recognizing that 'common sense' is itself 'a site of political struggle' rather than something that is fixed and unitary. Moreover, they note that it is crucial to acknowledge the 'affective dimensions that are in play, and which underpin common sense'. Hall and O'Shea find, therefore, all around us both evidence of 'individualised disaffection' as well as 'many signs of resistance'. In particular, they analysed online comments posted to *The Sun*'s blogs in response to that newspaper's coverage of the Conservative Party's proposal to cut benefits. Hall and O'Shea found that people are far more uncertain about these matters than some polls suggest, and that the ongoing articulation, disarticulation and rearticulation of an array of different discursive elements are generating instability and 'an unresolved struggle over common sense within the individual as well as between individuals and groups'. As Mark Pursehouse (2008[1991]: 287) notes, understanding how the discursive currents at work in a right-wing tabloid, such as *The Sun*, enter into 'real areas of lived culture' requires the analyst to identify some of the affective and ideological investments made by actual readers. In their analysis of responses to *The Sun*'s report on the proposed benefit cuts, Hall and O'Shea thus found that:

> while neoliberal discourse is increasingly hegemonic and setting the agendas for debate, there are other affective and sensemaking currents in play – empathy for others, a liking for co-operation rather than competition, or a sense of injustice, for example.

Thus 'White Dee', arguably *the* central character on *Benefits Street*, is available to be read as the abject figure of the 'dole scrounger' whose life is subject to audience scrutiny and therefore potential appropriation in defence of neoliberal measures. Nevertheless, Allen *et al.* (2014) note that she is also represented as a good mother who is happy, witty, compassionate, caring, articulate and charismatic. Dee is a paradoxical figure that invites identification as well as abjection and provides resources of hope or resistance to neoliberalism as well as acceptance of neoliberal ideologies. After her appearance on *Benefits Street*, she received a range of offers of employment, holidays and media appearances (Aitkenhead 2014), suggesting that, for many, Dee's problem is not her own inadequacy, but rather a lack of decent opportunities. Dee became a minor celebrity, was interviewed in newspapers and appeared on TV shows such as *Newsnight* and *Celebrity Big Brother*. She became the subject of extensive discussion and debate across a range of media. She was vilified and attacked, admired and praised. The coalition government tried to use Dee to justify its neoliberal policies, as when one Tory MP commented that she served as 'a reminder to people of the mess the benefits system is in and how badly' necessary are the Conservative Party's proposed reforms (quoted in Allen *et al.* 2014: 1). At the same time, *The Guardian* editorialized that *Benefits Street* was 'not as bad as the dreadful title suggested', and was, indeed, 'redeemed by the warmth of several residents, especially the single mother styled as White Dee. Smoking but sober, loud but loving, Deirdre Kelly was shown doing the best she could for her kids in straitened circumstances' (*The Guardian* 2014: n.p.). She similarly elicits frequent positive (as well as negative) reactions on social media (see Figure 15.1). Dee produced such diverse modes of popular and official mediated engagement that her status as a figure of fecklessness and abjection could never be stabilized, and she thus served to generate significant public debate about austerity. In light of these debates, White Dee (2014) herself writes:

> I'm not working at the moment, so I don't have to pay rent or council tax. I'd say my income averages about £200 a week. Now I know quite a few working people that haven't got £200 a week – and they're working hard all day. That's not right. I've read about teachers who have to use food banks. That's not right. But I'm not the one who

Figure 15.1   Tweeting the love for White Dee

set up the system. I can see why some people are angry. But I didn't ask for those people who keep coming to my door, offering loft insulation or a boiler for free because I'm on benefits. Why can't people who are working, and struggling be enti-tled to free loft insulation as well?

The public debates over austerity that erupted around the figure of White Dee, *Benefits Street*, and other 'poverty porn' programmes, and the struggle for common sense within the contemporary conjuncture of which these debates were both symptomatic and constitutive, also broke out elsewhere within the convergent mediasphere. For instance, in 2014, High Street greeting card retailer Clinton Cards began selling a Christmas card that ridiculed and stigmatized Britain's poor by offering 'ten reasons why Santa must live on a council estate'. Twitter users who were outraged by the card shared it widely and disapprovingly, which quickly forced Clinton to

Clintons apologises over '10 reasons why Santa Claus must live on a council estate' Christmas card after Twitter and Facebook storm - what's your view?

Keep in touch with local news

Sign up for email alerts

Send your news, pictures & videos

Most Popular

Figure 15.2   Social media smackdown on Clintons

withdraw the item from their line and issue a public apology (see Figure 15.2). The story and Clinton's apology were then recirculated through broadsheet and tabloid newspapers, and other national and local media (see, e.g., Carter and Osborne 2014; Jackson 2014; Wiles 2014). In this way, the grassroots rebellion against Clinton's abjection of poor Britons reached new media consumers who may not be social media users. The event thus extended further the conjunctural struggle over neoliberal common sense, provoking many to vow that they would henceforth boycott Clinton Cards.

This vignette that refocuses visibility away from the stigmatized poor and onto Clinton Cards illustrates a key strategy in the struggle over neoliberalism: the reversal of the relations of surveillance that are enacted through poverty porn. As Fiske (1998) writes, 'countersurveillance may be the most immediately available means of resistance in a surveilled society'. Its significance stems from its contestation of 'the management of visibility' (ibid.: 78), and thus it has potential as a way of intervening into the formation of common sense around neoliberal agendas and priorities. Reality programming that scrutinizes the excessiveness (of all sorts) of the lives of the spoiled and affluent, and that interrogates the logics and discourses of trickle-down economics, such as *Made in Chelsea* and *The Super-Rich and Us*, also moves in the direction of counter-surveillance and the construction of counterknowledges. By the same token, grassroots organizations such as UK Uncut use connective media to circulate material that monitors the costs to the British public of tax avoidance and evasion by the wealthy. As the tweet captured in Figure 15.3 shows, while benefit fraud may cost Britons £1.2 billion a year, lost public revenues from tax avoidance, evasion and noncollection amount to £120 billion per year, by one estimate. By recontextualizing and rearticulating the issue of benefit fraud, such messages suggest that the austerity government's campaign against what it calls a 'something for nothing culture' (see Figure 15.4) has chosen the wrong target. This reversal of visibility aimed at the 1 per cent has helped to animate a growing strand of what Gramsci called 'good sense' (Hall 1996) concerning expanding economic inequality in the age of austerity. By thus making visible the practices of the 1 per cent, connective media have helped bring into view and into popular knowledge the ways in which the major effect of austerity is not the reduction of government deficits but rather

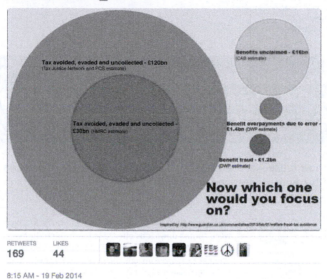

Figure 15.3 Exposing tax evasion on Twitter

the further concentration of wealth in the hands of the already wealthy. This in turn helped make it possible for revelations in February 2015 of HSBC bank-assisted tax evasion by wealthy Britons to generate heavy discussion and debate across the convergent mediasphere. At UK Uncut's Facebook page, for example, the HSBC scandal is articulated to the government's austerity programme and thus used to rearticulate the common sense underpinnings of neoliberalism (see Figure 15.5).

There is nothing inevitable about the establishment of hegemonic neoliberal common sense as a fixed and final outcome. Rather, hegemonization is a process replete with instabilities and contingencies; it is an ongoing war of position. While 'poverty porn' can be read as an instance of what Andrejevic calls 'lateral surveillance', the convergent mediasphere is both facilitating the exertion of new forms of mediatization and disciplinary digital control, and opening up new opportunities for reversals of surveillance, for the establishment of new strategic connectivities, and for the circulation of counterdiscourses and the disarticulation and rearticulation of existing discourses in ways that contribute to the formation and advancement of alternative formations of common sense. While neoliberal discourses produce and circulate the abject figure of the 'undeserving poor' as part of an overall strategy for the normalization of the 'legitimate consumer', some audiences instead affectionately embrace those targeted for neoliberal demonization such as White Dee, while others participate in the counter-scrutinization of the 1 per cent and the interrogation of its trickle-down trickery. Opponents of neoliberalism must understand the instabilities and contradictions that are active in the current conjuncture as opportunities to

GOV.UK

Search 🔍

Departments Worldwide How government works Get involved
Policies Publications Consultations Statistics Announcements

Press release

Benefit sanctions – ending the 'something for nothing' culture

From: Department for Work and Pensions
First published: 6 November 2013
Part of: Employment and Welfare reform

This news article was published under the 2010 to 2015 Conservative and Liberal Democrat coalition government

Latest figures show Jobseeker's Allowance claimants who failed to do enough to find work had their benefits payments suspended 580,000 times.

Jobseeker's Allowance (JSA) claimants who have failed to do enough to find work, turned down jobs offered to them, or not turned up to appointments have had their benefits payments suspended 580,000 times since new tougher rules were introduced in October last year, new figures published today (6 November 2013) show. In each month this is roughly 5% of the number of people claiming JSA.

The new JSA sanctions regime, which was introduced in October 2012, encourages people to engage with the support being offered by Jobcentres

Figure 15.4   Tory attack on the poor

Figure 15.5   Facebooking protest against banksters

participate in the production of social imaginaries capable of envisioning how to harness 'the market to the needs of its people, rather than letting it dictate how we have to live' (Hall and O'Shea 2013: n.p.).

Acknowledgement

This research is supported by the Marsden Fund of the Royal Society of New Zealand, grant number MAU1108.

Note

1 38 Degrees is named after the critical angle at which human-triggered avalanches are most likely.

References

Aitkenhead, D. 2014. Deirdre Kelly, aka White Dee: 'I Would Never Watch a Show Called Benefits Street'. *The Guardian*, 7 March. Retrieved from http://www.theguardian.com/tv-and-radio/2014/mar/07/deirdre-kelly-white-dee-never-watch-benefits-street

Allen, K., Tyler, I., and De Benedictus, S. 2014. Thinking with 'White Dee': The Gender Politics of 'Austerity Porn'. *Sociological Research Online*, 19.3. Retrieved from http://www.socresonline.org.uk/19/3/2.html

Andrejevic, M. 2005. The Work of Watching One Another: Lateral Surveillance, Risk, and Governance. *Surveillance & Society*, 2: 479–97.

—. 2013. *Infoglut: How too Much Information is Changing the Way We Think and Know*. London: Routledge.

Binders Full of Women (BFOW). n.d. *Facebook Group*. Retrieved from https://www.facebook.com/romneybindersfullofwomen?fref=ts

Burke, M. 2013. Companies are Hoarding Cash: That's Why Growth is so Glow. *The Guardian*, 27 October. Retrieved from http://www.theguardian.com/commentisfree/2013/oct/27/companies-hoarding-cash-slow-growth

Carter, C., and Osborne, L. 2014. Clinton Cards Accused of Mocking Working Classes with 'Why Santa Must Live on a Council Estate' Christmas Greeting. *Daily Mail.com*, 7 December. Retrieved from http://www.dailymail.co.uk/news/article-2864211/Clinton-Cards-accused-mocking-working-classes-Christmas-card-Santa-live-council-estate-Christmas-card.html

Connell, P. 2014. *Ending the Free Ride: Making Multinationals Pay their Way*. London: Civitas, Institute for the Study of Civil Society.

Cooper, N., Purcell, S., and Jackson, R. 2014. *Below the Breadline: The Relentless Rise of Food Poverty in Britain*. Oxford: Church Action on Poverty, The Trussell Trust and Oxfam.

Couldry, N. 2000. *Inside Culture: Re-Imagining the Method of Cultural Studies*. London: Sage.

—. 2014. Inaugural: A Necessary Disenchantment: Myth, Agency and Injustice in a Digital World. *The Sociological Review*, 62: 880–97.

Couldry, N., and Littler, J. 2011. Work, Power and Performance: Analysing the 'Reality' Game of 'The Apprentice'. *Cultural Sociology*, 5.2: 262–79.

Cowburn, A. 2015. Suicides Highlight the Grim Toll of Benefits Sanctions in Austerity Britain. *The Guardian*, 3 January. Retrieved from http://www.theguardian.com/society/2015/jan/03/benefits-sanctions-leading-suicides-dwp-depression

Cupples, J. 2012. Wild Globalization: The Biopolitics of Climate Change and Global Capitalism on Nicaragua's Mosquito Coast. *Antipode: A Journal of Radical Geography*, 44.1: 10–30.

—. 2013. *Latin American Development*. London: Routledge.

—. 2015. Development Communication, Popular Pleasure and Media Convergence, in Mains, S., Cupples, J., and Lukinbeal, C., eds. *Mediated Geographies and Geographies of Media*. Dordrecht: Springer.

Cupples, J., and Glynn, K. 2014. The Mediation and Remediation of Disaster: Hurricanes Katrina and Felix in/and the New Media Environment. *Antipode*, 46.2: 359–81.

Dayan, D. 2009. Sharing and Showing: Television as Monstration. *The Annals of the American Academy of Political and Social Science*, 625: 19–31.

Deen, T. 2015. Top UN Official says 'Global War on Terror' is Laying Waste to Human Rights. *Common Dreams*, 8 February. Retrieved from http://www.commondreams.org/news/2015/02/06/top-un-official-says-global-war-terror-laying-waste-human-rights

Department for Work and Pensions. 2013. *Benefit Sanctions: Ending the 'Something for Nothing' Culture*. Employment and Welfare Reform, UK Government. Retrieved from https://www.gov.uk/government/news/benefit-sanctions-ending-the-something-for-nothing-culture

Deuze, M. 2009. Journalism, Citizenship, and Digital Culture, in Papacharissi, Z., ed. *Journalism and Citizenship: New Agendas in Communication*. New York: Routledge: 15–28.

Fiske, J. 1998. Surveilling the City: Whiteness, the Black Man and Democratic Totalitarianism. *Theory, Culture & Society*, 15.2: 67–88.

Fuchs, C. 2011. Web 2.0, Prosumption, and Surveillance. *Surveillance & Society*, 8.3: 288–309.

Giroux, H. 2015. Totalitarian Paranoia in the Post-Orwellian Surveillance State. *Cultural Studies*, 29.2: 108–40.

Glynn, K. 2015. Visibility, Media Events and Convergence Culture: Struggles for the Meaning of 9/11, in Mains, S., Cupples, J., and Lukinbeal, C., eds. *Mediated Geographies and Geographies of Media*. Dordrecht: Springer.

Grosfoguel, R. 2011. La Descolonización del Conocimiento: Diálogo Crítico Entre la Visión Descolonial de Frantz Fanon y la Sociología Descolonial de Boaventura de Sousa Santos, in Vianello, A., Mañé, B., eds. *Formas-Otras: Saber, Nombrar, Narrar, Hacer*. Barcelona: CIDOB: 97–108.

Grossberg, L. 2010. *Cultural Studies in the Future Tense*. Durham, NC: Duke University Press.

Harvey, D. 2014. *Seventeen Contradictions and the End of Capitalism*. London: Profile.

Hall, S. 1996. Gramsci's Relevance for the Study of Race and Ethnicity, in Morley, D., and Chen, K.H., eds. *Stuart Hall: Critical Dialogues in Cultural Studies*. London: Routledge: 411–41.

—. 2011. The Neo-Liberal Revolution. *Cultural Studies*, 25.6: 705–28.

Hall, S., and O'Shea, A. 2013. Common-Sense Neoliberalism. *Soundings: A Journal of Politics and Culture*, 55. Retrieved from http://www.lwbooks.co.uk/journals/soundings/issue/55.html

Hill, D. 2015. Class, Trust and Confessional Media in Austerity Britain. *Media, Culture and Society*, 37.4: 566–80.

Jackson, N. 2014. Twit-Forks and Censorship: A Clinton Cards Christmas Special. *Our Castle's Strength: A Blog about Housing, Home and the Hearth*. Retrieved from https://ourcastlesstrength.wordpress.com/2014/12/09/twit-forks-and-censorship-a-clinton-cards-christmas-special/

Jenkins, H. 2008. *Convergence Culture: Where Old and New Media Collide*, updated and with a new afterword. New York: New York University Press.

Jenkins, H., Ford, S., and Green, J. 2013. *Spreadable Media: Creating Value and Meaning in a Networked Culture*. New York: New York University Press.

Jensen, T. 2014. Welfare Commonsense, Poverty Porn and Doxosophy. *Sociological Research Online*, 19.3. Retrieved from http://www.socresonline.org.uk/19/3/3.html

Juris, J.S. 2008. *Networking Futures: The Movements Against Corporate Globalization*. Durham, NC: Duke University Press.

Kakaes, K. 2015. The Big Dangers of 'Big Data'. *CNN*, 2 February. Retrieved from http://edition.cnn.com/2015/02/02/opinion/kakaes-big-data/index.html

Klein, N. 2014. *This Changes Everything: Capitalism vs the Climate*. New York: Simon and Shuster.

Leigh, D., Ball, J., Garside, J., and Pegg, D. 2015. HSBC Files Show How Swiss Bank Helped Clients Dodge Taxes and Hide Millions. *The Guardian*, 8 February. Retrieved from http://www.theguardian.com/business/2015/feb/08/hsbc-files-expose-swiss-bank-clients-dodge-taxes-hide-millions

Make 'Ding Dong the Witch is Dead'…. n.d. *Facebook Group*. Retrieved from https://www.facebook.com/groups/2807687628/

Martín-Barbero, J. 2011. From Latin America: Diversity, Globalization and Convergence. *Westminster Papers in Communication and Culture*, 8.1: 39–64.

McCarthy, A. 2007. Reality Television: A Neoliberal Theater of Suffering. *Social Text*, 25.4: 17–41.

Ouellette, L. 2009. 'Take Responsibility for Yourself': Judge Judy and the Neoliberal Citizen, in Murray, S., and Ouellette, L., *Reality TV: Remaking Television Culture*, 2nd edn. New York: New York University Press: 223–42.

Ouellette, L., and Hay, J. 2008. *Better Living Through Reality TV: Television and Post-Welfare Citizenship*. Malden, MA: Blackwell.

Peck, J. 2012. Renormalizing Neoliberalism. Paper presented to the In, Against and Beyond Neoliberalism conference, University of Glasgow, March.

Platt, S. 2014. Austerity Led to a Rise in Male Suicide: It Wasn't Inevitable. *The Conversation*, 21 March. Retrieved from http://theconversation.com/austerity-led-to-a-rise-in-male-suicide-it-wasnt-inevitable-23372

Pursehouse, M. 2008[1991]. Looking at 'The Sun': Into the Nineties with a Tabloid and its Readers, in Biressi, A., and Nunn, H., eds. *The Tabloid Culture Reader*. Maidenhead: Open University Press: 287–307.

Rose, D. 2011. There Will be More Protests Like Yesterday's Disability March. *Ouch! It's a Disability Thing*, 12 May. Retrieved from http://www.bbc.co.uk/blogs/legacy/ouch/2011/05/there_will_be_more_protests_li.html

Schudson, M. 1999. *The Good Citizen: A History of American Civic Life*. Cambridge: Harvard University Press.

Slater, T. 2012. The Myth of 'Broken Britain': Welfare Reform and the Production of Ignorance. *Antipode*, 46.2: 948–69.

Sloan, J. 2010. Help Us Stop £1.5bn Benefits Scroungers. *The Sun*, 12 August. Retrieved from http://www.thesun.co.uk/sol/homepage/features/3091717/The-Sun-declares-war-on-Britains-benefits-culture.html

Stewart, H. 2012. Companies 'Should Spend £750bn War Chest' to Kickstart Economy. *The Observer*, 15 April. Retrieved from http://www.theguardian.com/business/2012/apr/15/firms-told-to-spend-cash-to-boost-economy

The Guardian. 2014. Editorial: In praise of… Dierdre Kelly. *The Guardian*, 8 June. Retrieved from http://www.theguardian.com/commentisfree/2014/jun/08/deirdre-kelly-white-dee-benefits-street

Tyler, I. 2013. *Revolting Subjects: Social Abjection and Resistance in Neoliberal Britain*. London: Zed.

Weber, R. 2010, in Desperate Need (of a Makeover): The Neoliberal Project, the Design Expert, and the Post-Katrina Social Body in Distress, in Negra, D., ed. *Old and New Media After Katrina*. New York: Palgrave Macmillan: 175–201.

White Dee. 2014. White Dee's Diary: From Benefits Street to Downing Street? *The Spectator*, 15 February. Retrieved from http://www.spectator.co.uk/the-week/diary/9136981/diary-from-benefits-street-to-downing-street/

Wiles, C. 2014. Red Christmas Card, in*side Housing: News, Views and Jobs in Social Housing*, 8 December. Retrieved from http://www.insidehousing.co.uk/home/blogs/red-christmas-card/7007257.blog?adfesuccess=1

Wilson, J. 2014. The Right has Won Control of the English-Speaking World: Thanks to the Weakness of the Left. *The Guardian*, 14 November. Retrieved from http://www.theguardian.com/commentisfree/2014/nov/14/the-right-has-won-control-of-the-english-speaking-world-thanks-to-the-weakness-of-the-left?CMP=share_btn_tw

—. 2016. Neoliberal Gothic, in Springer, S., Birch, K., and MacLeavy, J., eds. *The Handbook of Neoliberalism*. London: Routledge: 578–88.

16

RESILIENCE

A right-wingers' ploy?

Vlad Mykhnenko

It is often said that cities and regions, their populations, and their governance structures increasingly have to respond to major challenges and a vast range of contemporary risks resulting from environmental change, threats to national and international security, and an array of issues associated with international migration and growing global economic turbulence. In the short term, at least in the global North, local communities, cities, and regions have to tackle and mitigate the impact of the global financial and economic crisis. In the medium term, they ought to be equipped to manage the pressures of an ageing and declining population. In the long run, the capacity and systemic capabilities of the critical urban infrastructure in major population centres must be enhanced to cope with the potentially cataclysmic consequences of climate change. 'Resilience' is a conceptual framework which purportedly offers its adherents a set of mechanisms to confront these monumental challenges of the modern age.

In this chapter, I discuss the impact of resilience as a popular way of thinking about humans and society at large. It is often argued that the market forces unleashed through the neoliberal globalization reforms of the 1980s and 1990s, combined with growing political turbulence following the global financial crisis of 2008, enhanced a sense of personal and collective insecurity, particularly in the West (Birch and Mykhnenko 2010). Consequently, some critics of resilience thinking have linked its supposed ascendance with the perceived desire by the major Western governments, international financial institutions (IFIs), and bilateral donors to respond to such major challenges by shifting the burden of responsibility onto individual citizens and local communities. Within this context, I initially set out differing definitions and approaches to the study of resilience. Consequently, I deal with the somewhat 'elastic' quality of resilience as a political agenda. In turn, I address the question of how influential resilience theory really is in terms of its appeal to academic scholarship as well as public policy-making. In particular, I focus on the failed attempt by the British Conservative Party-led coalition government to enact some of this resilience thinking during its 2010–15 term in office. I conclude this chapter with an overall assessment of resilience, both its strengths and weaknesses.

Resilience: 'fuzzy', functional, formulaic?

'Resilience means different things to different persons': that was the conclusion of the first ever literature review on resilience conducted in 1947 by J.H. Dillon for *Textile Research Journal*

(Hoffman 1948: 141). In what was most probably the scientific community's first attempt to arrive at an agreed definition, Hoffman noticed a paradox involving resilience: the term could easily describe an inherent property of such different substances as rubber, wool, and quartz. To state that these materials were resilient was 'all at least partially true but, at the same time inconsistent' (ibid.). His suggestion of a generalized concept of resilience as rebound elasticity encompassed the focus on stress, strain, and time, so prevalent in physical sciences. This paradigmatic view of the so-called *engineering resilience* as the ability of a material to absorb and withstand compressive stress without suffering permanent deformation has been shaping both theoretical and empirical investigations of the phenomenon ever since. In 1973, the ecologist C.S. (Buzz) Holling was the first to reject the notion of resilience as a 'bounce back' from a shock by developing the so-called *ecological perspective* on resilience, defining it as 'shock absorption' or 'stress resistance'. Holling's research has framed the debates on resilience in ecology and environmental sciences, spilling over into business and economics, public administration, and other social sciences (see Table 16.1). In the early 2000s, psychologists, mental health practitioners, and early education professionals (Folke 2006) proposed a new – social-evolutionary – reading of resilience as 'positive adaptability'. A 'bounce forward' is the metaphor used in describing *evolutionary resilience* as a transformation and attainment of 'good outcomes' under adversity (see Table 16.1). Nevertheless, 65 years after Hoffman's seminal paper in materials science, a fresh review of the literature on the topic declared that 'resilience, we now know, has no agreed definition and is many things', with the only constant in all the elaborate definitions being 'a concern with the response to undesirable changes' (Downes *et al.* 2013: 1–2). Thus, resilience continues to be a sufficiently undefined – 'fuzzy' – concept (see Pendall *et al.* 2010).

Markusen (2003: 702) memorably defines fuzzy concepts as 'characterizations lacking conceptual clarity and difficult to operationalize'; those which possess 'two or more alternative meanings and thus cannot be reliably identified or applied by different readers or scholars'. A number of representative definitions of resilience collated in Table 16.1 illustrate the 'fuzziness' of the term: contradictory opinions about the term are common not just across different disciplines, but within them. The fundamental ambiguity of defining the concept in physical sciences as elastic resilience (or 'bounce-back-ability'), on the one hand, and shock resistance (or 'perseverance'), on the other hand, was uncovered as early as the 1940s. The new paradox of resilience, identified in the 2000s, involves the nature of changes following a shock to the system: a post-crisis recovery understood as a restoration of normality differs from 'positive adaptation' – a transformative process leading, in the words of Martin and Sunley (2015: 13), to a 'new sustainable path characterized by a fuller and more productive use of… physical, human and environmental resources'. Finally, the fourth reading of resilience, which is popular in business studies and disaster management, puts the emphasis not (just) on recovery, but rather on preparedness and anticipatory adaptability. According to one management guru, 'zero trauma' – a culture of automatic, spontaneous, and reflexive responsiveness to shifting circumstances – should become the new ethos of all large organizations, willing to survive (Hamel and Välikangas 2003).

Resilience, thus, emerges as a complex and contradictory multi-disciplinary concept, with multiple meanings. In addition, a large number of fundamental ontological, epistemological, methodological, and ideological conflicts and inconsistences in many readings of resilience have been identified in the literature. Downes *et al.* (2013) provide further ammunition to those critical of applying resilience thinking in social sciences. Finally, Olsson *et al.* (2015) offer the most devastating critique of resilience theory and its complete incommensurability with social sciences. Having conducted a comprehensive review of all the major work on resilience published

Table 16.1 Representative definitions of resilience across disciplines

Research area	What is resilience?	Source
Engineering and materials science	'The capability of a substance to return to its original state at some later time after the removal of a deforming stress... Resiliency is a stress–strain–time property of a material, characterizing the completeness of a recovery from deformation and varying in kind with the modulus of elasticity and the rate of recovery'	Hoffman (1948: 141, 148).
	'The ability to withstand shocks and disturbances and to continue to operate in recognisable form'	Lombardi et al. (2012: viii).
Computer science	'A large-scale, gracefully degradable system can tolerate element failures while providing continued operations... Network resilience... is defined as the maximum number of node failures that can be sustained while the network remains connected with a probability'	Najjar and Gaudiot (1990: 179).
Ecology and environmental studies	'Resilience determines the persistence of relationships within a system and is a measure of the ability of these systems to absorb changes of state variables, driving variables, and parameters, and still persist'	Holling (1973: 17).
	'The capacity of a system to absorb disturbance and reorganize while undergoing change so as to still retain essentially the same function, structure, identity, and feedbacks'	Walker et al. (2004: 5).
	'In the context of communities and settlements, it refers to their ability to not collapse at first sight of oil or food shortages, and to their ability to respond with adaptability to disturbance'	Hopkins (2008: 55).
	'Resilience in our personal lives is about lasting, about making it through crises, about inner strength and strong physical constitution... Resilience can be applied to cities. They too need to last, to respond to crises and adapt in a way that may cause them to change and grow differently; cities require an inner strength, a resolve, as well as a strong physical infrastructure and built environment'	Newman et al. (2009: 1).
	'Community resilience [is] our capacity to both mitigate and adapt to the disruptive implications of climate change, peak oil, and ecosystem decline'	Lewis and Conaty (2012: 19).
	'The ability to absorb disturbances, to be changed and then to re-organise and still have the same identity (retain the same basic structure and ways of functioning)'	Resilience Alliance (2002).
Psychology; medicine and dentistry	'A process whereby people bounce back from adversity and go on with their lives'	Dyer and McGuiness (1996: 276).
	'A dynamic process encompassing positive adaptation within the context of significant adversity'	Luthar et al. (2000: 543).
	'Reduced vulnerability to environmental risk experiences, the overcoming of a stress or adversity, or a relatively good outcome despite risk experiences'	Rutter (2012: 336).

Discipline	Definition	Source
Business and economics	'Think of the boxer who has been floored in the ring. A 'knock-out' may be ignored, since it very rarely happens outside the fable of Atlantis that a whole civilization is completely wiped out. The boxer has a certain resiliency which enables him to resume after a shorter or longer time which is determined partly by his physique and determination, partly by the amount of punishment he has already received. In a somewhat similar way there is what may be called economic resiliency which after a crisis endeavours to recover from the series of shocks which industry and commerce have experienced'	Scott (1930: 291).
	'Strategic resilience is not...about rebounding from a setback. It's about continuously anticipating and adjusting to deep, secular trends that can permanently impair the earning power of a core business. It's about having the capacity to change before the case for change becomes desperately obvious'	Hamel and Välikangas (2003: 53–4).
	'The ability of an economy to (i) recover quickly from harmful external economic shocks; and (ii) withstand the effect of such shocks'	Briguglio et al. (2010,:16).
	'The ability to transform regional outcomes in the face of a challenge'	Chapple and Lester (2010: 86).
	'The region's ability to experience positive economic success that is socially inclusive, works within environmental limits and which can ride global economic punches'	Bristow (2010b, 153).
	'The capacity of a system, enterprise, or a person to maintain its core purpose and integrity in the face of dramatically changed circumstances'	Zolli and Healy (2012: 7).
	'The capacity of a regional or local economy to withstand or recover from market, competitive and environmental shocks to its developmental growth path, if necessary by undergoing adaptive changes to its economic structures and its social and institutional arrangements, so as to maintain or restore its previous developmental path, or transit to a new sustainable path characterized by a fuller and more productive use of its physical, human and environmental resources'	Martin and Sunley (2015: 13).
Public administration; social work	'A capacity to address short-term problems in ways that generate long-term success'	MacArthur Foundation (2007: 2)
	'The capacity to adapt and to thrive in the face of challenge'	World Resources Institute (2008: ix).
	'The ability to adapt to changing conditions and prepare for, withstand, and rapidly recover from disruption,'	Obama (2010: 18).

(Continued)

Table 16.1 (Continued) Representative definitions of resilience across disciplines

Research area	What is resilience?	Source
	'Communities and individuals harnessing local resources and expertise to help themselves in an emergency, in a way that complements the response of the emergency services'	Cabinet Office (2011: 4).
	'The ability of individuals, organizations, systems, and communities to bounce back more strongly from stresses and shocks. Resilience means creating diversity and redundancy in our systems and rewiring their interconnections, which enables their functioning even when individual parts fail'	NYS 2100 (2013: 7).
	'Ability of the community, services, area or infrastructure to detect, prevent, and, if necessary to withstand, handle and recover from disruptive challenges'	Cabinet Office (2013: 66).
	'Resilience is more than what's known as bouncebackability. It includes the ability to self-organise, to maintain balance, and to respond to change... Caricatured as getting volunteers to do the jobs we were once paid for, it really touches on deeper issues of neighbourliness and community, turning the typical reaction to a crisis or injustice of "something must be done" to "we must do something". A socially resilient community doesn't pass the buck'	Dobson (2011).
Other social sciences	'Social resilience is defined as the ability of communities to withstand external shocks to their social infrastructure'	Adger (2000: 361).
	'Urban resilience implies a physical capacity to bounce back from a significant obstacle, much like a rubber ball dropped on the pavement. But cities are not rubber balls, nor is a disaster like an asphalt plane, from which a rebound can be definitely predicted by a set of mathematical equations'	Vale and Campanella (2005: 335).
	'A process linking a set of adaptive capacities to a positive trajectory of functioning and adaptation after a disturbance... Resilience occurs when resources are sufficiently robust, redundant, or rapid to buffer or counteract the effects of the stressor such that a return to functioning, adapted to the altered environment occurs. For human individuals and communities this adaptation is manifest in wellness'	Norris et al. (2008: 130).
	'Rather than viewing resilience as bouncing back to an original state following the external "shock", the term should be seen in terms of bouncing forward, reacting to crises by changing to a new state that is more sustainable in the current environment'	Davoudi et al. (2012: 309).

recently in the top ten natural and social sciences journals, they discovered five major points of contention in the scientific application of resilience. First, they stress *system ontology*: although the notion of 'system' is known in social sciences, it is not as essential, conventional or indispensable to them as it is to resilience theory. Indeed, as Downes *et al.* (2013: 5) convincingly demonstrate, 85 per cent of all social science studies of resilience are conducted at the level of individuals or families, not social systems. Second, critics of the usage of resilience in social sciences emphasize the problem of system boundary: although systems are indispensable to resilience thinking, their boundaries can often be very difficult to demarcate spatially, temporally, or structurally (Martin and Sunley 2015; Olsson *et al.* 2015: 3–4). The third criticism of resilience theory lies in its rather formulaic notions of equilibria, thresholds, and feedback mechanisms. Social systems are driven by human agency at least to the same degree as by structural forces; thus, any systemic 'feedback' is subject to human interpretation and power relations. Fourth, resilience thinking assumes self-organization of the systems understood in complexity theory as a natural propensity. By contrast, in social sciences self-organization refers to a messy societal reaction to power asymmetries and structural inequality, often resulting in the formation of new social movements (Olsson *et al.* 2015: 5). The fifth and final tension between the social and natural sciences' usage of resilience lies in the understanding of function and functionalism – a point raised by many.

Panarchy – a term devised by Gunderson and Holling (2002) to describe evolving hierarchical systems with many interconnected components – is by far the most significant formalized representation of a functioning ecological-social system. According to the book's blurb:

> Panarchy is the structure in which systems, including those of nature (e.g., forests) and of humans (e.g., capitalism), as well as combined human-natural systems (e.g., institutions that govern natural resource use such as the Forest Service), are interlinked in continual adaptive cycles of growth, accumulation, restructuring, and renewal. These transformational cycles take place at scales ranging from a drop of water to the biosphere, over periods from days to geologic epochs. By understanding these cycles and their scales, researchers can identify the points at which a system is capable of accepting positive change, and can use those leverage points to foster resilience and sustainability within the system.
>
> *(Island Press 2012)*

Graphically, the panarchy model is represented by a lemniscate (i.e. a sideways figure 8 sign), mimicking the mathematical symbol of infinity. According to some ecologists, the theory of the adaptive cycle, should only be treated as 'a useful metaphor and not as a testable hypothesis' (Carpenter *et al.* 2001: 766). Yet, given its grand design and purpose of describing the dynamics of how any ecological system, economic system, or political system successively gives way to another and gets transformed (Olsson *et al.* 2015: 5), it is not hard to imagine the model to be taken literally as guidance to future developments. Indeed, a number of social scientists claim the panarchy model – with its four *consequential* and *circular* phases of rapid growth and exploitation, conservation, collapse or release (i.e. 'creative destruction'), and renewal or re-organization – can be used as a set of empirically testable propositions. 'The adaptive cycle model applies well to regions,' argue Pendall *et al.* (2010: 77; cf., Simmie and Martin 2010). Nevertheless, others contend that because of its structural functionalism resilience is incommensurable between the natural and social sciences, whereas core concepts and theories in the latter – 'such as agency, conflict, knowledge, and power – are absent from resilience theory' (Olsson *et al.* 2015: 9). In terms of politics, Martin and Sunley (2015: 8) stress that resilience as a concept can be 'easily captured by neoliberal ideology, to prioritize the status quo, and importance of self-reliance, flexibility and role of "self-correcting" market adjustments'.

Elastic politics of resilience: peak oil, climate change, and neoliberalism

Many of the representative definitions of resilience collated in Table 16.1 and discussed in similar reviews elsewhere (e.g., Brand and Jax 2007; Downes *et al.* 2013; Manyena 2006; Norris *et al.* 2008) invariably differ in terms of coherence, conciseness, and precision. However, the most striking variance may be observed in the philosophical predisposition to resilience. Positivism reigns supreme in physical and natural sciences, medical and mental health research, while normative descriptions of resilience are not uncommon in ecology, environmental studies, and geography, and prevail in business and economics, public administration, and other social sciences. Yet it is the application of the engineering or 'bouncing back' meaning of resilience to social phenomena that has stirred up the biggest controversy. With its appeal to the inherent individual attributes of self-reliance, self-help, and self-organization, the concept of resilience appears vulnerable to abuse by the 'common sense' vulgarity of populist ideologies. To some critics, resilience is an essentially Conservative idea, squarely aimed at the maintenance and privileging of existing social relations of global capitalism in the face of externally derived disorder (MacKinnon and Derickson 2013: 258). Indeed, most frequently, resilience thinking is associated with neoliberalism and Conservative right-wing politics. Walker and Cooper (2011: 144) go further to claim that the success of the panarchy model of adaptive cycle ought to be explained by 'its intuitive ideological fit with a neoliberal philosophy of complex adaptive system... of Friedrich Hayek'. They argue that:

> The emerging consensus on resilient growth... both reiterates and modifies the Darwinian law of natural selection. Relying as it does on the non-equilibrium dynamics of complex systems theory, what the resilience perspective demands is not so much progressive adaptation to a continually reinvented norm as permanent adaptability to extremes of turbulence.
>
> *(Ibid.: 156)*

The number of warnings given by academics to 'watch out' for resilience is rather remarkable (e.g. Martin and Sunley 2015: 8; Olsson *et al.* 2015: 6; Pike *et al.* 2010: 66). Davoudi *et al.* (2012: 331–2) were among the first to emphasize 'the slippery slope to a neoliberal discourse of "self-reliance"', claiming that the resilience theory may be used to 'demonise those people or places who are deemed to be "just not resilient enough"', with vulnerable communities left to fend for themselves.

And yet, I would argue that the main feature of the politics of resilience seems to be its malleability: resilience is an elastic concept, politically. As mentioned by MacKinnon and Derickson (2013: 255), resilience is becoming a popular concept among oppositional groups, green campaigners, anti-capitalist activists, and various anarchist-autonomist movements. Hopkins's *The Transition Handbook: From Oil Dependency to Local Resilience* (2008); Newman, Beatley, and Boyer's *Resilient Cities: Responding to Peak Oil and Climate Change* (2009); Lewis and Conaty's *The Resilience Imperative: Cooperative Transitions to a Steady-State Economy* (2012) – all of these accessible (guide)books to a 'better future' are firmly rooted in the concept of resilience as positive adaptability to the disruptive implications of climate change, 'peak oil', and ecosystem decline. Indeed, many advocates of 'green', 'post-carbon', 'non-capitalist' development trajectories have fully adopted resilience as their main argument against free trade, globalization, and neoliberalism (however defined). Some even commend the controversial 'self-reliance' aspect of resilience, advocating more 'closure' and 'self-containment' in the process of building resilient and self-sufficient local and regional economies (Hudson 2010). Devotees of communitarian beliefs also cherish autonomy and praise the self-organization of local communities. As one enthusiastic newspaper reporter puts it, 'Ultimately, a resilient city has to be one in which, in a crisis, people come onto the streets to help one another, not to riot' (Evans 2014: n.p.).

Resilience: an appealing/appalling proposition

So far this chapter has established that resilience is a multifaceted concept: it is 'fuzzy' in some interpretations; it could be prescriptively formulaic in many adaptations; and it is structurally functionalist to the core. I have also shown how malleable and 'stretchy' resilience can be in its ideological interpretations, appearing as a dangerously reactionary notion to some, and progressively emancipatory in everyday practice to others. The most obvious set of questions to pose here is how influential resilience really is? Are academic scholars increasingly turning to resilience as a research agenda? Is resilience replacing any other long-established areas of scientific interest? For instance, has sustainable development or competitiveness actually lost any following, as predicted earlier (see Bristow 2010b; Davoudi *et al.* 2012)? Furthermore, is resilience public policy relevant? And if so, does resilience theory supply practical answers to policy-makers and practitioners responding to acute exogenous shocks and/or chronic, long-term crises – the so-called slow burns?

First, this section deals with *academic* studies of resilience. For the bibliometric analysis, I have used the new Thomson Reuters Web of Science™, as the world's largest collection of scholarly research and citation data. In particular, the Web of Science core collection of Science and Social Sciences Citation Indices was used to search for journal articles and conference proceedings papers published in English between 1 January 1900 and 15 June 2015, with the following terms and Boolean combinations: (1) topic: (resilienc*); (2) topic: (sustainability or 'sustainable development'); and (3) topic: (competitiveness). The search produced a list of 24,146 publications on 'resilience'/'resiliency', with the first two articles appearing in 1913. 'Sustainability'/'sustainable development' was the most popular topic among the three, though, with 51,425 records; 'sustainability' covered 74 per cent of the total aggregate, first appearing as a scientific research topic in 1974. The first academic paper on 'competitiveness' appeared fourteen years earlier; nevertheless, the topic only generated 13,876 publications within the period concerned.

Figure 16.1 shows the number of papers published each year on these three topics. Looking at the trends, it seems possible to identify certain trigger events in the popularity trajectories of sustainability, resilience, and competitiveness, respectively. For instance, the role of the United Nations Conference on Environment and Development held in Rio de Janeiro, Brazil, in 1992, was paramount in institutionalizing sustainable development as the key idea in the international debate on development, while the UN World Summit on Sustainable Development held in Johannesburg, South Africa, ten years later, served as yet another mega-event promoting the concept. At the same time, one has to mention that the study of sustainability has undoubtedly benefited from ever increasing planetary environmental hazards such as global warming and climate change – the two topics which have generated well over 91,000 articles so far.

Unlike sustainability or competitiveness, resilience is a much more multi-dimensional and trans-disciplinary concept: its rise may be accounted for by very different occurrences. Having being studied for over 100 years, resilience became really popular only in the early 1990s, following a couple of influential papers on childhood development and psychopathology (including Garmezy 1991; Luthar 1991; Masten *et al.* 1990; Werner 2000). The terrorist attacks

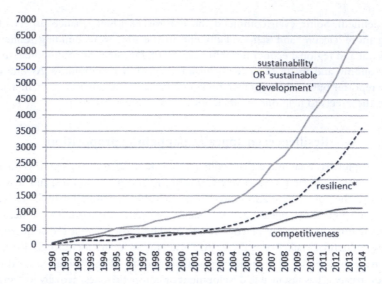

Figure 16.1 Number of articles and proceedings papers published annually on the topics of resilience, sustainable development, and competitiveness

of 11 September 2001 upon the USA, the publication of Gunderson and Holling's *Panarchy* in early 2002, and Hurricane Katrina that hit the southern Gulf of Mexico states in August 2005, all could be considered catalysts for resilience research. The global financial crisis of 2007–8 and Hurricane Sandy in November 2012 provided further impetus. The picture emerging from Figure 16.1 is that resilience is hardly a match for sustainable development as a popular academic research topic; however, it has long surpassed neoliberal competitiveness in terms of popularity – a positive achievement in itself (see Bristow 2010a, 2010b).

The total number of articles published on the three topics between 1900 and 2015 should be handled with caution, however. In a random selection study of 6,548 social science and ecological publications on resilience, Downes *et al.* (2013) found that 40.6 per cent of the entries had to be excluded as irrelevant to the topic. To unpack some of these bibliometric data, Figure 16.2 provides a breakdown of the resilience literature by disciplinary research areas involved (149 in total); publication duplicates were removed from the total count. Environmental sciences, ecology, water sciences, conservation, and the related natural sciences account for almost a half of all research on resilience, with almost a third covered by psychology, psychiatry, and other medical and human health-related sciences; another fifth of all the resilience literature was published in engineering, technology, and materials sciences. By the mid-2015, the share of social sciences in resilience research had only reached 10 per cent.

I have already discussed the ontological, epistemological, methodological, and ideological reasons for the relative unattractiveness of resilience thinking to social sciences (for a comprehensive review, see Olsson *et al.* 2015). The only area of social sciences where resilience has generated some interest includes business and management studies, economics, and their related disciplines. Indeed, 'economic resiliency' was the title of the eighth earliest paper ever published on the general theme (Scott 1930). Despite a lot of interest, however, scholars of business, economics, and economic geography have not been able to agree on a common definition, with some applying the conservative engineering notion of resilience as a 'bounce back', while others are keen on exploring resilience as transformational 'adaptability with better outcomes'.

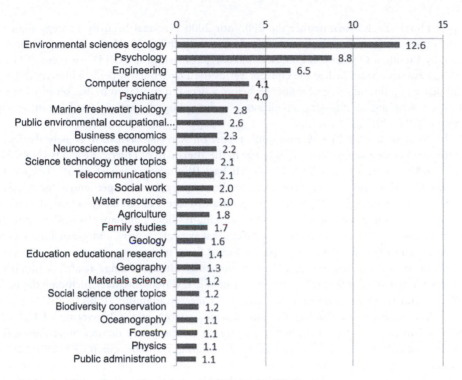

Figure 16.2 Articles and proceedings papers published on resilience

The 'big society': not bouncing back

By far the most contentious application of resilience theory has been in the field of *public administration* and *public policy*. To many critics, this particularly controversial development relates to the emphasis put by the major Western governments, IFIs, and bilateral donors, on the ability of local communities and individuals – both in the rich and poor countries – to 'help themselves' and 'thrive in the face of challenge' (see Table 16.1). As Walker and Cooper argue:

> This is a tacit recognition that 'development' for the post-colonial poor now consists not in achieving First World standards of urban affluence but in surviving – preferably on the land instead of in slums – the after-effects of industrial modernization, the Green Revolution and the financial conditions imposed under the Washington Consensus.
>
> *(2011: 155)*

In the UK, a lot has been made of the entry into the official *Civil Protection Lexicon* in 2009 of 'resilience', seemingly putting the onus of civil contingencies' response on local communities and areas themselves (Cabinet Office 2011, 2013). The term was introduced into the public domain in a package of civil service-related terms and definitions in preparation for the London 2012 Olympic Games. Sporadically, the British government returns to resilience in the context of transport and housing infrastructure damage caused by storms and flooding affecting the UK (BBC 2015; Cameron 2014). Similarly, in the USA, the term was very slow to catch on: resilience did not feature prominently, if at all, in the aftermath of the 9/11 terrorist attacks on New York or post-Hurricane Katrina: neither the 2002 nor 2006 National Security Strategy signed by President Bush mentioned resilience once. It was only the 2010 National Security Strategy signed by President Obama that endorsed resilience, instructing the US Department of Homeland Security to operationalize the concept. Yet, as the Department openly admitted, 2010 was spent discussing the meaning of resilience, before a decision was taken to 'bucket it' within the rubric of 'adapting to changing conditions', 'withstanding disruptions', and 'ensuring rapid recovery' (DHS 2015).

The New York State 2100 Commission report on *Recommendations to Improve the Strength and Resilience of the Empire State's Infrastructure* in the aftermath of Hurricane Sandy (NYS 2100, 2013), and the City of New York Mayor Michael Bloomberg's report on *A Stronger, More Resilient New York* (2013), have gone much further to provide a comprehensive list of actionable recommendations for: (1) rebuilding the infrastructure and buildings in both the city and the region; (2) rolling out a series of 'forward-looking resiliency' initiatives aimed at upgrading the area's costal defences, mechanical and electrical systems, sewers, and green infrastructure floodwalls; and (3) making the city's power, liquid fuels, telecommunications, transportation, water and wastewater, healthcare, and other networks 'climate-change ready'. A number of high-profile charity-funded civil society and academic research initiatives, including the Rockefeller Foundation's $100 million *100 Resilient Cities* programme (100RC 2015), and the MacArthur Foundation's *Building Resilient Regions* network at the University of California Berkeley (BRR 2015), have managed to expand the public policy debates on resilience from disaster management, mitigation, and forward planning, into the spheres of the urban and regional economy, public administration, social policy, and social work. The often-heard criticism of such resilience-building initiatives is that they instil a sense of confidence in finding local technocratic solutions to fundamentally global problems like climate change. While no one would deny the need for New York (or any other global city) to prepare for and bounce back from a human-made disaster, the scale of the environmental challenge facing the city travels far beyond the Empire State's boundary, and the nature of the solution lies in the political sphere.

To investigate the link between resilience and neoliberal policy-making further, I have analysed all 331 publication records on resilience (including articles, book reviews, proceedings papers, and book chapters) which appeared in English between 1900 and 2015 in the following disciplines: Law, Public Administration, Philosophy, Planning Development, Urban Studies, and Political Science. Figure 16.3 identifies the most popular policy-relevant themes developed under the heading of resilience by presenting a 'word cloud' of these titles, with the words 'urban', 'community', 'climate', 'change', 'social', 'building', 'disaster', 'development', 'cities', and 'planning' occupying most of the space.

Overall, this analysis does not seem to support the fear expressed by many scholars and commentators of resilience as some sort of a Trojan horse of neoliberals used to advance their causes. Note the absence of 'public sector' and 'reform' in Figure 16.3. And yet, arguably, it is in the most recent public policy development in the UK that we have witnessed the most far-reaching attempt to utilize the communitarian ideas of resilience through self-organization, self-help, and self-reliance to transform the entire nation. The Big Society programme was launched by Prime Minister David Cameron on 18 May 2010, six days after the coalition agreement was reached between the British Conservative and Liberal Democrat parties to form a government. 'Big society' was the Prime Minister's core idea, ostensibly aimed at giving 'citizens, communities and local government the power they need to come together and solve the problems they face' (Cabinet Office 2010; 2011). The term was coined by Jesse Norman, a newly-elected Conservative Member of Parliament for a rural constituency in the south-east of England. In his book on

Figure 16.3   A Word Cloud of publications with the title on Resilien (including resilience, resiliency, resilient)

the topic, Norman (2010) boldly proclaimed the 'big society' to be 'the most exciting new idea' to 'redefine British politics for a generation'. According to one commentator, however, the 'big society' was the Conservative Party's vaguely concealed attempt to reconcile the contradiction between reducing government spending and maintaining public welfare:

> So whilst Labour's vision of state market relations was beset by the contradiction of increasing expenditure but failing to increase revenue, the Conservatives focused their response around the desire aiming to reduce the deficit rapidly through reducing the role of the state. The Conservative leadership appealed to the Thatcherite desire for small government and an expanded private sector role. Yet, unlike Thatcher the Conservatives were beset by their own contradiction; a commitment to key elements of welfarism in health and welfare. Their attempt to square this circle was based on the notion of the big society but what is yet to be seen is whether a big society can replace the welfare functions of the public sector whilst maintaining quality of service and social justice.
>
> *(Smith 2010: 832)*

The government tried to legitimize the 'big society' as a way to end 'the unhappy social and economic effects of our recent over-reliance on the state' and to 'make the state better… leaner, stronger, and more resilient in responding to shocks' (Norman 2010: 230; cf. Dobson 2011). Yet six months following the launch of the programme, the 'big society' was still seen as 'waffly, unmarketable and disliked by many Tories' (Glover 2010; cf. Pattie and Johnston 2011).

The ruling party members were not the only intellectual sceptical voices: following the rush of academic interest initially, the 'big society' only generated 113 academic papers between 2010 and 2015. Figure 16.4 shows a steep decline in publications on the theme through the course of the 2010–15 Conservative-led government. The 'most exiting idea for a generation' lasted just

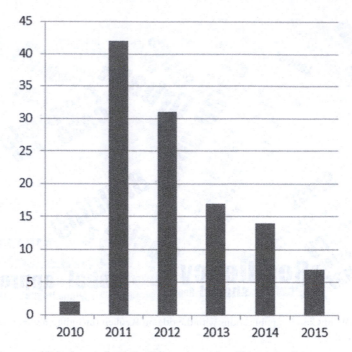

Figure 16.4   Papers published annually in English on the topic of 'big society'

four and a half years. According to an independent investigation, on 27 November 2014 David Cameron's flagship Big Society Network collapsed in debt, having spent *at least* £2.5 million of government funding with no reported records of charitable activity behind this. The number of applications received by the network for local community improvement projects (worth £830,000) reached 0.006 per cent of its target: just 64 groups signed up out of the million initially predicted. The network was subsequently investigated for misused funding and inappropriate payments to its directors (Wright 2014); it left no electronic trace: the network's website http://thebigsociety.co.uk was closed down and made unavailable.

Resilience: what is it good for?

This chapter concludes with a summary assessment of the perceived, potential, and actual merits, flaws, and dangers of resilience thinking. To make this statement meaningful, I have to limit the discussion to social sciences (arts, and humanities), given that the concept of resilience is technically indispensable to engineering, physical, and natural sciences. One of the perceived merits of resilience is the universal and unifying nature of the concept, which could transcend disciplinary boundaries and achieve synergies between natural and social sciences. Another perceived merit of resilience thinking is the opportunity to create a theory of change, which could encompass the sudden shocks to the system as well as the 'slow burns', thus expanding the predictive power of social sciences. Potentially, resilience theory could provide an analytical framework for studying complex socio-ecological systems and bringing the natural and human-made environment firmly back into social science research – an urgent necessity in the context of cataclysmic climate change. Moreover, resilience theory – with its insistence on the value of redundant capacities for shock absorption and stress resistance – has the progressive potential to be realized by local community activists, politicians, and decision-makers in advocating local empowerment and lobbying for the provision of additional resources of all sorts. The actual merits of the resilience thinking we have observed so far include: (1) the steady process of resilience displacing competitiveness as one of the key categories in applied economic research; (2) an increase in our understanding of how local communities and regional economies respond to shocks and disturbances, what determines that response, and how 'better outcomes' can be ensured, interpreted, and narrated; (3) enhanced institutional capacity and a higher degree of preparedness to disasters across many public sector organizations and private firms. A lot of research illustrates how politically charged, symbolic, and necessary the narrative of resilience has always been for society to build anew in the wake of disaster (Vale and Campanella 2005). The fact that resilience thinking has been adopted by various green socialists, anti-capitalist environmentalists, 'slow town' and 'zero carbon' transition movements indicates its potential for progressive change.

The major actual flaws of resilience theory as applied in social sciences concern the system ontology, the system boundary, and the structural functionalism of resilience thinking. Furthermore, the overall technocratic and naturalizing tendencies of resilience theory may cloud one's thinking by providing false hopes and generating erroneous forecasts (e.g. on climate change mitigation). In addition, power, interests, conflicts, and human passions are all perceived to be absent from social science-related resilience theory. There is some evidence of resilience being pushed as an apolitical, even post-political, agenda, especially in US policy circles, where the concept is 'imbued with American values of heroic individualism, self-reliance', and self-help 'in the face of adversity' (Pike *et al.* 2010: 66). Nevertheless, as this chapter has illustrated, the perceived danger of resilience theory to be (ab)used by reactionary political forces and neoliberal ideologues world-wide is highly exaggerated. The potential for passing the buck for dealing with economic crises or environmental disasters to the vulnerable communities themselves *does* exist. However, ideas of the 'invisible hand', *laissez faire*, and 'rugged individualism' – most often invoked by neoliberals and free-marketeers of all sorts – predate resilience thinking by two centuries. In reality, even as simplistic a dichotomy as 'the big society versus the big government' has failed to provide the British Tories with a constructive narrative for their austerity politics. When the high complexity of resilience theory meets the long-established *anti-intellectualism* of the populist Conservative Right, it would appear extremely unlikely that resilience could gain much traction with politicians who are busy protecting the power of monopoly-finance capital.

Acknowledgements

I am grateful to the editors of this volume for their constructive leadership and productive suggestions regarding the text. Consequently, I would like to thank Peter Lee and James D. Sidaway for the many engaging discussions of resilience we have had at the University of Birmingham. This research was supported by Shrink Smart: The Governance of Shrinkage within a European Context (Project no. 225193), funded by the 7th Framework Programme (Socio-economic Sciences and Humanities) of the European Commission.

References

100RC. 2015. *100 Resilient Cities: Pioneered by the Rockefeller Foundation (100RC)*. 100 Resilient Cities 2015. Retrieved from http://www.100resilientcities.org/

Adger, W.N. 2000. Social and Ecological Resilience: Are They Related? *Progress in Human Geography*, 24.3: 347–64.

BBC. 2015. David Cameron says Okehampton Railway Line is 'Most Resilient'. *BBC Local News*, 30 January 2015.

Birch, K., and Mykhnenko, V. eds. 2010. *The Rise and Fall of Neoliberalism: The Collapse of an Economic Order?* London and New York: Zed Books.

Bloomberg, M.R. 2013. *A Stronger, More Resilient New York*. New York: City of New York Mayor's Office.

Brand, F.S., and Jax, K. 2007. Focusing the Meaning(s) of Resilience: Resilience as a Descriptive Concept and a Boundary Object. *Ecology and Society*, 12.1: 23.

Briguglio, L., Cordina, G., Vella, S., and Vigilance, C. eds. 2010. *Profiling Vulnerability and Resilience: A Manual for Small States*. London: Commonwealth Secretariat.

Bristow, G. 2010a. *Critical Reflections on Regional Competitiveness : Theory, Policy and Practice*. London: Routledge.

—. 2010b. Resilient Regions: Re-'Place'ing Regional Competitiveness. *Cambridge Journal of Regions, Economy and Society*, 3.1: 153–67.

BRR. 2015. *Building Resilient Regions: Harnessing the Power of Metropolitan Regions*. Berkeley: The Institute of Governmental Studies at the University of California. Retrieved from http://brr.berkeley.edu/

Cabinet Office. 2010. *Building the Big Society*, 3. London: Cabinet Office.

—. 2011. *Strategic National Framework on Community Resilience*, 28. London: Cabinet Office.

—. 2013. *Lexicon of UK Civil Protection Terminology: Version 2.1.1*. London: Cabinet Office.

Cameron, D. 2014. *Statement by the Prime Minister on the Storms and Flooding Affecting the United Kingdom*. London: Cabinet Office and Office of the Prime Minister.

Carpenter, S., Walker, B., Anderies, J.M., and Abel, N. 2001. From Metaphor to Measurement: Resilience of What to What? *Ecosystems*, 4.8: 765–81.

Chapple, K. and T.W. Lester (2010) The Resilient Regional Labour Market? The US Case. *Cambridge Journal of Regions, Economy and Society*, 3: 85–104.

Davoudi, S., Shaw, K., Haider, L.J., Quinlan, A.E., Peterson, G.D., Wilkinson, C., Fünfgeld, H., McEvoy, D., Porter, L. and Davoudi, S. 2012. Resilience: A Bridging Concept or a Dead End? 'Reframing' Resilience: Challenges for Planning Theory and Practice Interacting Traps: Resilience Assessment of a Pasture Management System in Northern Afghanistan Urban Resilience: What Does it Mean in Planning Practice? Resilience as a Useful Concept for Climate Change Adaptation? The Politics of Resilience for Planning: A Cautionary Note. *Planning Theory & Practice*, 13.2: 299–333.

DHS. 2015. *Resilience*. Washington, DC: United States Department of Homeland Security. Retrieved from http://www.dhs.gov/quadrennial-homeland-security-review

Dobson, J. 2011. *From a Big Society to a Resilient Society*. Sheffield: Urban Pollinators.

Downes, B.J., Fiona, M., Jon, B., Alena, G., and Heidi, E. 2013. How do we Know About Resilience? An Analysis of Empirical Research on Resilience, and Implications for Interdisciplinary Praxis. *Environmental Research Letters*, 8.1: 1–8.

Dyer, J.G., and McGuinness, T.M. 1996. Resilience: Analysis of the Concept. *Archives of Psychiatric Nursing*, 10.5: 276–82.

Evans, J. 2014. Future-Proofing Cities: Bristol Starts Planning for a More Resilient Character. *The Guardian*, 6 March.

Folke, C. 2006. Resilience: The Emergence of a Perspective for Social–Ecological Systems Analyses. *Global Environmental Change*, 16.3: 253–67.

Garmezy, N. 1991. Resiliency and Vulnerability to Adverse Developmental Outcomes Associated With Poverty. *American Behavioral Scientist*, 34.4: 416–30.

Glover, J. 2010. As the Left Falls into a Negative Sulk, the Centre-Right Have Become the Optimists. *The Guardian*, 21 November.

Gunderson, L.H., and Holling, C.S. eds. 2002. *Panarchy: Understanding Transformations in Human and Natural Systems*. Washington, DC, and London: Island Press.

Hamel, G., and Välikangas, L. 2003. The Quest for Resilience. *Harvard Business Review*, 81.9: 52–63.

Hoffman, R.M. 1948. A Generalized Concept of Resilience. *Textile Research Journal*, 18.3: 141–8.

Holling, C.S. 1973. Resilience and Stability of Ecological Systems. *Annual Review of Ecology and Systematics*, 4: 1–23.

Hopkins, R. 2008. *The Transition Handbook: From Oil Dependency to Local Resilience*. Totnes: Green Books.

Hudson, R. 2010. Resilient Regions in an Uncertain World: Wishful Thinking or a Practical Reality? *Cambridge Journal of Regions, Economy and Society*, 3: 11–25.

Island Press. 2012. *Panarchy: Understanding Transformations in Human and Natural Systems*. Washington, DC: Island Press. Retrieved 24 June 2015 from http://islandpress.org/panarchy

Lewis, M., and Conaty, P. 2012. *The Resilience Imperative: Cooperative Transitions to a Steady-State Economy*. Gabriola Island: New Society.

Lombardi, D.R., J.M. Leach, C.D.F. Rogers, and Aston, R. 2012. *Designing Resilient Cities: A Guide to Good Practice*. Bracknell: IHS BRE Press.

Luthar, S.S. 1991. Vulnerability and Resilience: A Study of High-Risk Adolescents. *Child Development*, 62.3: 600–16.

Luthar, S.S., Cicchetti, D., and Becker, B. 2000. The Construct of Resilience: A Critical Evaluation and Guidelines for Future Work. *Child Development*, 71.3: 543–62.

MacArthur Foundation. 2007. *Network on Building Resilient Regions*, ed. E. Poethig. Chicago: John D. and Catherine T. MacArthur Foundation: 2.

MacKinnon, D., and Derickson, K.D. 2013. From Resilience to Resourcefulness: A Critique of Resilience Policy and Activism. *Progress in Human Geography*, 37.2: 253–70.

Markusen, A. 2003. Fuzzy Concepts, Scanty Evidence, Policy Distance: The Case for Rigour and Policy Relevance in Critical Regional Studies. *Regional Studies*, 37.6–7: 701–17.

Martin, R., and Sunley, P. 2015. On the Notion of Regional Economic Resilience: Conceptualization and Explanation. *Journal of Economic Geography*, 15.1: 1–42.

Masten, A.S., Best, K.M., and Garmezy, N. 1990. Resilience and Development: Contributions from the Study of Children who Overcome Adversity. *Development and Psychopathology*, 2.4: 425–44.

Manyena, S.B. 2006. The Concept of Resilience Revisited. *Disasters*, 30.4: 433–50.

Najjar, W., and Gaudiot, J.L. 1990. Network Resilience: A Measure of Network Fault Tolerance. *Computers, IEEE Transactions on*, 39.2: 174–81.

Newman, P., Beatley, T., and Boyer, H. 2009. *Resilient Cities: Responding to Peak Oil and Climate Change*. Washington, DC: Island Press.

Norman, J. 2010. *The Big Society: The Anatomy of the New Politics*. Buckingham: University of Buckingham Press.

Norris, F., Stevens, S., Pfefferbaum, B., Wyche, K., and Pfefferbaum, R. 2008. Community Resilience as a Metaphor, Theory, Set of Capacities, and Strategy for Disaster Readiness. *American Journal of Community Psychology*, 41.1–2: 127–50.

NYS 2100. 2013. *Recommendations to Improve the Strength and Resilience of the Empire State's Infrastructure*, 205. Albany: NYS 2100 Commission.

Obama, B. 2010. *National Security Strategy*, 52. Washington, DC: Office of the President of the United States.

Olsson, L., Jerneck, A., Thoren, H., Persson, J., and O'Byrne, D. 2015. Why Resilience is Unappealing to Social Science: Theoretical and Empirical Investigations of the Scientific Use of Resilience. *Science Advances*, 1.4: 1–11.

Pattie, C., and Johnston, R. 2011. How Big is the Big Society? *Parliamentary Affairs*, 64.3: 403–24.

Pendall, R., Foster, K.A., and Cowell, M. 2010. Resilience and Regions: Building Understanding of the Metaphor. *Cambridge Journal of Regions Economy and Society*, 3.1: 71–84.

Pike, A., Dawley, S., and Tomaney, J. 2010. Resilience, Adaptation and Adaptability. *Cambridge Journal of Regions, Economy and Society*, 3.1: 59–70.

Prime Minister's Office. 2015. *Government Launches Big Society Programme*. London: Office of the Prime Minister. Retrieved from http://www.gov.uk/government/news/government-launches-big-society-programme--2

Resilience Alliance. 2002. Key concepts[web page]. *The Resilience Alliance*. Retrieved 23 June 2015 from http://www.resalliance.org/index.php/key_concepts

Rutter, M. 2012. Resilience as a Dynamic Concept. *Development and Psychopathology*, 24: 335–44.

Scott, W.R. 1930. Economic Resiliency. *The Economic History Review*, 2.2: 291–9.

Simmie, J., and Martin, R. 2010. The Economic Resilience of Regions: Towards an Evolutionary Approach. *Cambridge Journal of Regions Economy and Society*, 3.1: 27–43.

Smith, M.J. 2010. From Big Government to Big Society: Changing the State–Society Balance. *Parliamentary Affairs*, 63.4: 818–33.

Vale, L.J., and Campanella, T.J. 2005. Conclusion: Axioms of Resilience, in Vale, L.J., and Campanella, T.J., eds. *The Resilient City: How Modern Cities Recover From Disaster*. New York and Oxford: Oxford University Press: 335–61.

Walker, B.H., Holling, C.S., Carpenter, S.R., and Kinzig, A. 2004. Resilience, Adaptability and Transformability in Social–Ecological Systems. *Ecology and Society*, 9: 5.

Walker, J., and Cooper, M. 2011. Genealogies of Resilience: From Systems Ecology to the Political Economy of Crisis Adaptation. *Security Dialogue*, 42.2: 143–60.

Werner, E.E. 2000. Protective Factors and Individual Resilience, in Shonkoff, J.P., and Meisels, S.J., eds. *Handbook of Early Childhood Intervention*. Cambridge: Cambridge University Press: 115–32.

WRI. 2008. *World Resources 2008: Roots of Resilience: Growing the Wealth of the Poor*. Washington, DC: World Resources Institute (WRI) with the United Nations Development Programme, United Nations Environment Programme, and the World Bank.

Wright, O. 2014. PM's Office Ignored Official Advice to Stop Funding Failing Big Society Charity. *The Independent*, 27 November.

Zolli, A., and Healy, A.M. 2012. *Resilience*. London: Headline, Business Plus.

PART III

Social tensions

17
RACE AND NEOLIBERALISM

David J. Roberts

More than just a racist eruption: the co-constitution of race and neoliberalism

In 2010, Minelle Mahtani and I published an article challenging scholars of neoliberalism, especially within geography, to approach the connection between race and neoliberalism in a more sophisticated manner. The scholarship on race and neoliberalism, at the time, tended to focus on racialized outcomes of neoliberal reforms – what we called 'the racist eruptions' of neoliberalization (Roberts and Mahtani 2010: 248). We argued that it was problematic to understand and theorize neoliberalism and race as two separate social entities that only sometimes intersect. Instead, we demanded an understanding of race and neoliberalism as co-constitutive. Following Giroux (2005) we argued that while neoliberalism is saturated with race, it also modifies the way that race and racism are understood and experienced in contemporary society. I review and reiterate the main points of our paper below.

Since publication, the article has had significant influence on the theorization of race and neoliberalism, garnering nearly 100 citations at the time of writing this chapter. Here, I revisit the original argument and then proceed to briefly analyse how these arguments have been taken up by other scholars through a literature review of articles and book chapters that have cited the 2010 piece. Towards a conclusion, I work to plot a course as to what I believe to be the future directions in which the scholarship theorizing race and neoliberalism may want to go.

Neoliberal society: a postracial, level playing field?

As a foundational premise, we argued that the logics of neoliberalism have fundamentally reshaped the relationship between the citizen and society with the integration of a market-oriented notion of how one succeeds in society. To this end, we argued that, 'ideally, within a neoliberal theorization of society, the success of the individual is directly related to his/her work output. Modalities of difference, such as race, do not predetermine one's success as each individual is evaluated solely in terms of his or her economic contribution to society' (Roberts and Mahtani 2010: 253). This is the quintessential level playing field – a postracial paradise where everyone is treated equally and each individual is valued and rewarded based solely on her or his ability to contribute to society (or, more specifically, the economy). While this is the ideal that underpins neoliberalism, our work, along with others, exposes the shaky foundation upon which the claims of some sort of achieved level playing ground are based. Specifically, we argue that, in Canada, media discourses about (racialized) immigrants to Canada work to reify a racialized hierarchy in which immigrants are denied complex identities and rendered to be not-quite-real Canadians. We link this reification to the neoliberalization of the Canadian immigration system. I expand on our research findings in the next section.

Our approach to examining the connection between race and neoliberalism follows in a similar vein to numerous amounts of scholarship that has been dedicated to demonstrating the disconnect between the idealism of this level playing field and the lived reality in neoliberal societies. In other words, despite the claims that we, in neoliberalized societies, live in meritocracies, there is overwhelming evidence that race and other modalities of difference continue to be salient in terms of one's social position. Yet, even as many of the scholars critically engaging with neoliberalism recognize this, we argued that, at the time of writing the original article, the scholarship in geography examining the relationship between race and neoliberalism inadequately captured the ways in which these two processes are co-constitutive in nature.

The discourses of immigration in *The Globe and Mail*

The empirical material for our 2010 article, 'Neoliberalizing Race, Racing Neoliberalism: Placing "Race" in Neoliberal Discourses', was obtained through a media analysis of stories about immigrants and immigration within *The Globe and Mail*, a leading Canadian national newspaper. Focusing on the time period spanning 1 October 2002 to 30 September 2006, we created an initial dataset through collecting all articles, letters to the editor and editorials that contained the term 'immigration' in their title, abstract, and/or within their text. This produced a dataset of 3,754 articles. From this dataset, we pared the sample down to 896 articles by eliminating those articles not ostensibly about immigration, immigrants or refugees in Canada. This pared down dataset was then analysed and coded based on the dominant themes in each article, editorial, guest column and letter to the editor. Through this process, 55 sub-themes emerged covering a wide range of topics. These sub-themes were later grouped into major themes focusing on the dominant discourses of immigration being utilized by the authors of the pieces, including immigration as important to increased economic success (14 per cent of the articles) and the linking of immigrants to criminal activities or terrorism (24 per cent of the articles), for example. These sub-themes and major themes significantly influenced our argument, which focused more specifically on the ideas and discourses that seemed to be underpinning much of the coverage of immigration and immigrants in *The Globe and Mail*.

What emerged was a strong tendency to describe immigrants in terms of their utility to Canadian society – both positively, often in economic terms as workers, and negatively, to highlight links to criminality or to describe them as a drain on Canadian social resources. Bauder (2008) found a similar tendency in the German press with regard to immigrants in that country, linking this discourse on immigration to the neoliberal restructuring of Germany's immigration policies. In the process, Bauder (ibid.) highlights the link between discourses focused on the utility of immigration and immigrants and the neoliberal approaches to immigration, and we concur in our findings.

Articles with such titles as 'Labour Shortage Woes Loom, Research Says' (Scoffield 2005), 'New Canadians Can Keep the Lights Shining on the Prairie' (Simpson 2005), and 'Ontario Eyes Brightest Immigrants' (Howlett 2006) are examples of the types of stories that appeared in *The Globe and Mail* in our dataset. Through such pieces, immigrants are depicted as potential solutions to many of the challenges facing the Canadian economy, from low population growth rates to a perceived lack of desire from Canadian-born individuals to work within service industries.

Other aspects of immigrant identities, interests and desires not explicitly linked to some notion of utility are rarely included in the articles that we examined. This tendency to focus on immigrants almost exclusively in terms of their potential utility for Canadian society significantly limits the complexity of immigrant identities within the news media and, we argue, is influential on wider social discourses and perceptions of the appropriate role for immigrants in Canadian cities. Moreover, a focus on immigrant utility is a clear reflection of the neoliberalization of the Canadian immigration policy that focuses on using immigration (and immigrants) as a way to improve the Canadian economy. This is manifested in the points-based system in which immigrants are awarded points for education, employability, etc. as a way of assessing the skills that they will bring to Canada. While there are other potential avenues for individuals to immigrate to Canada, such as through asylum or refugee routes, the primary available slots are through the points-based system. If anything, since the publication of our original intervention, the Canadian government has only increased its commitment to an immigration policy based on treating immigrants as an economic means to an end of an improved economy. For example, the number of temporary foreign workers in Canada tripled in the decade between 2002 and 2012 (Lemieux and Nadeau 2015: 1) largely driven by the expansion of temporary labour migration programmes, especially in care work, agriculture and service industries supporting the resource economies. This has occurred while the state is simultaneously making other, more permanent immigration avenues that are much more difficult to pursue (Goldring and Landolt 2013). The expansion of these temporary labour migration programmes produces a class of non-citizen immigrant workers whose lives and political status are characterized by temporariness and precarity. While immigration policies and the rise of temporary worker programmes were beyond the scope of our original article, it is clear that the expansion of a precarious class of non-Canadian workers in Canada to serve a neoliberal economic agenda works to buttress our observations about the connection between immigration, neoliberalism and race in contemporary Canada.

This media analysis provided the foundation for a larger discussion about the contemporary linkages between neoliberalism and race/racialization. We used this analysis to attempt to intervene in what we saw as the trajectory of scholarship, especially within the discipline of geography about these linkages towards a more nuanced analysis.

Racist eruptions

Several theorists of neoliberalism have recognized the link between the embrace of neoliberalism in policy, and more broadly in society, and the persistence or even exacerbation of racial inequality. At the time of our original article, the most common tendency within this work was to point to the disparate impacts that neoliberal policy interventions have had on certain racialized groups in society. In this type of analysis, scholars generally identified moments of racism (or racially disparate impacts) without providing much in the way of a theorization between the link between race and neoliberalism more broadly. Neoliberalization of policy took place; racialized groups bore the brunt of the negative social outcomes of this neoliberalization. In short, this type of scholarship identifies eruptions of racism without considering the broader social context in which these eruptions take place (see Wilson 2006 and Theodore 2007 for examples of this type of scholarship). While this type of work lays the foundation of critiquing neoliberalism for its disparate impacts, we argued that this form of

> theorization treats racism as an inevitable result of neoliberalization rather than mutually constitutive with neoliberalizing policies. The racist eruptions that result from neoliberal policies and practices are cited, but race is imagined as a fixed category, where

individual racialized groups are seen as distinct and mapped onto neoliberal policy outcomes.

(Roberts and Mahtani 2010: 240)

However, Mahtani and I argue that it is essential to think of these instances where racialized groups are disparately impacted by neoliberal policies in more complex ways than simply eruptions of racism or racialization resulting from neoliberal approaches. In doing so, we argue that it is essential that research on race and neoliberalism starts with understanding race as a fundamental organizing principle in society (Gilmore 2006; McKittrick 2006; Pulido 2006) and to understand the ways in which race and neoliberalism are co-constitutive. Moreover, we argue that race must not be understood as a fixed set of categories that are unchanging in society. While race is a fundamental organizing principle in society, racial categories, meanings or processes of racialization are not set in stone. Neoliberalism works to reify the importance of race in society as well as impact how it is understood, experienced, and contested. In other words, we argue that 'it is essential to understand neoliberalism as a facet of a racist society that works to both reinforce the racial structure of society, while also modifying the processes of racialization' (Roberts and Mahtani 2010: 250).

Reification of the role of race in society

The reification of race and racial differences is clear in the treatment of immigration in the stories found within *The Globe and Mail*. Immigrants, especially racialized immigrants, are depicted as somehow different from white/standard/domestically born Canadians. While some of the values associated with these differences have changed over time, especially with regard to what qualities make a potential immigrant useful for Canadian society, racialized tropes are largely left intact. In highlighting this, we argued that,

> Racism and its accompanying stereotypes associated with immigrants (high fertility, non-professional aspirations) are effectively mobilized as desirable whereas historically these were seen as negative attributes of immigrants. These presumed features of the potential immigrant population are part of a racist lexicon that was previously employed to denigrate immigrants.

(Roberts and Mahtani 2010: 251)

Thus, both the immigration policy that reduces immigrant identities to their contributions to the economy and the media discourses that largely do the same thing work to reinforce already existing racial hierarchies in society. Quite simply, it is a way of marking who is a real Canadian and who is a not-quite-real Canadian. The theoretical, neoliberal, even playing field is not fully available to racialized immigrant Canadians.

Modifying the experience of race in society

This is not the end of the story, however. In addition to reifying racial hierarchies, neoliberal policies, logics, and discourses also work to modify the way in which race is experienced in society. In part, this is a consequence of the argument that neoliberalism is colour- or race-blind. As Davis (2007: 350) explains,

> Under neoliberal racism the relevance of the raced subject, racial identity and racism is subsumed under the auspices of meritocracy. For in a neoliberal society, individuals are

supposedly freed from identity and operate under the limiting assumptions that hard work will be rewarded if the game is played according to the rules. Consequently, any impediments to success are attributed to personal flaws. This attribution affirms notions of neutrality and silences claims of racializing and racism.

Neoliberalism 'effectively masks racism through its value-laden moral project: camouflaging practices anchored in an apparent meritocracy, making possible a utopic vision of society that is non-racialized' (Roberts and Mahtani 2010: 253). Consequently, lack of success in society – either by an individual or group – is understood as a result of individual or group failure or inadequacy. For immigrants to Canada, this is reflected in a perceived inferiority of foreign degrees and credentials and the consequential failure to recognize these in terms of employment, as embodied by the deskilling process (Gardiner Barder 2008). It is also reflected in other, broader, tropes about certain immigrant cultural practices or beliefs as potentially providing an explanation for group failure. This echoes one of Goldberg's (1993) central contentions 'that modern racist culture is marked, fundamentally, by its refusal to acknowledge the role that racism plays in everyday structures of society and how these structures work to fundamentally disguise and, simultaneously, reify the power of racism within society' (Roberts and Mahtani 2010: 253).

The embrace of neoliberalism does more than simply disguise the workings of race as an organizing principle; it essentially mutes contestations of institutional or structural forms of racism (Giroux 2008). The argument that we have entered into a postracial era in North American society is symptomatic of this silencing (Omi and Winant 2014). Under such a logic, racism is now exclusively within the realm of the abhorrent behaviours of a few bad apples in society – hold-overs from previous, more racist times. As such, it should be understood and dealt with on a case-by-case basis, rather than through mechanisms that may address larger systems of racialization and racialized privilege. As such, such underlying structures are essentially left intact.

Given all of this, we argued that neoliberalism is thoroughly 'saturated with race' (Duggan 2003: xvi). Race and neoliberalism are not distinct social processes that sometimes collide in the outcome of particular neoliberal policy reforms, but rather should be understood as co-constitutive.

The reception of this argument

Since the publication of our original intervention in 2010, the reception of this challenge, to develop a more sophisticated approach to analysis and theorizations of the linkages between race and neoliberalism, has been substantial. The list of publications that cite and engage with our work continues to grow. At the time of writing this chapter, there were nearly 100 publications, in print, citing the original piece, ranging from books and book chapters to journal articles to Master's and PhD theses. As the original piece was intended to be a provocation encouraging scholars writing about race and neoliberalism to add sophistication to their treatment, it is interesting and encouraging to see the various ways that our work has had an impact on scholarship.

Not surprisingly, a majority of the articles citing our original intervention have been published in journals focused on research in geography and cognate areas of study (such as urban studies). We still work in an academic world in which disciplinary boundaries have meaning and, despite efforts to engage in issues and interventions that span disciplinary divides, analysis of issues such as the linkage between race and neoliberalism tends to happen in siloed parallels along these divides. This unfortunately creates an uneven landscape of scholarship. That said, while the majority of pieces citing the original article are found within geography journals, there is a wide range of other disciplines and subject areas represented in the work (and journals) that references our work. These include early childhood education (Nxumalo 2012), sociology of sport (Atencio *et al.* 2013), and racial and ethnic studies (Andrews and Mower 2012), to name a few. This indicates a budding cross-disciplinary conversation that can, in my mind, only work to add sophistication and nuance to all of our discussions of the links between race and neoliberalism as insights from different disciplines are brought into conversation. Given that neither the study of race or neoliberalism can or should be contained within geography, the discipline stands to benefit from how others approach the subjects.

In many (most) cases, there was seemingly only minimal engagement with the initial intervention, with the reference to our piece being listed in a string of references to other articles and chapters making arguments about the connections between race and neoliberalism. Thus, while our article is clearly widely read, in these cases it is unclear how our arguments, specifically, have influenced thinking, analysis, or methodology around issues of neoliberalism and race. This is not to say that the articles and chapters are not tackling concerns in ways that are sympathetic to ours; just that it is unclear what influence the original intervention had on this work.

That said, perhaps the most well-developed and nuanced theme that runs through many of the pieces focuses on ways in which neoliberalism has altered understandings and discourses of race in contemporary North American society (see Anderson and Sternberg 2012). Several pieces explore and contest the ways in which claims of racism or structural racial inequality are effectively silenced through a neoliberal appeal to meritocracy (Mele 2013). In part, these can be read as a rejection of the notion that the USA (or Canada) has evolved to a point where 'overt forms of racial discrimination are a thing of the past, and that the United States is in the midst of a successful transition to a "postracial" society' (Omi and Winant 2014: 257). The fantasy of a postracial society is just simply that, a fantasy appealing to perhaps the aspirations of a meritocracy, but one that refuses to address the historical and contemporary foundations of inequality that continue to exist along racial lines.

Despite the growing number of publications adding nuance to the analysis of the connections between race and neoliberalism, there is still room to add greater sophistication. In particular, there continues to be a need to add nuance and complexity to theorizations and scholarship examining the co-constitutive relationship between neoliberalism and processes of racialization. By way of some concluding thoughts for this chapter, in the next section, I discuss the challenge of researching this relationship.

Researching the process of racialization

While there has been greater attention paid to developing a more nuanced articulation of the relationship between neoliberalism and race, this work seemingly still continues to grapple with how to move beyond treating race as a set of fixed, immutable categories. Despite the widespread (and now rather longstanding) acceptance that race is a socially produced phenomenon (with material consequences), there is still a tendency to discuss it as a set of distinct, fixed, groupings. In part, this is a consequence of language and a lack of adequate vocabulary to really capture race as process, but this cannot be the only explanation. I believe that methodology also plays a significant role.

In writing about a feminist methodological approach in geography 18 years ago, Rose notes that,

> The feminist task becomes less one of mapping difference – assuming a visible landscape
> of power with relations between positions ones of distance between distinctly separate

agents – and more one of asking how difference is constituted, of tracing its destabilizing emergence during the research process itself.

(Rose 1997: 313)

The challenge, then, for feminist and feminist-inspired scholarship, is precisely one of researching processes in light of difference and diversity; processes through which socially constructed differences, like race, gender, ability, etc., come to be constituted and to have meaning. While we can see the influence of feminist, anti-racist, indigenous, post-colonial and other critical scholarship on the links between race and neoliberalism, we still have work to do in regard to methodology – in particular, methodology that is focused on processes – racialization as opposed to race and gendering as opposed to gender, for example.

In the original intervention, Mahtani and I were attempting to challenge scholars to understand race as much more complex than fixed categories you may find on the census – categories that we can place onto a landscape of power and that highlight the ways in which neoliberal reforms have disparate impacts. The mapping of race in this way might be interesting and evocative, but it also works to concretize and reify racial categories and social locations. We hoped, through our argument, that we might push scholarship (on race and neoliberalism specifically, but on race and space, more broadly) to move, both analytically and methodologically, towards understanding the social construction of race as an ongoing, evolving project. In other words, critical scholarship should ask how race and other aspects of difference are constituted rather than just map the differences. Taking seriously the notion that race and neoliberalism are co-constituted requires such a move as it necessitates examining how race and neoliberalism are fundamentally linked with each operating to create and give meaning to the other in contemporary society.

In many ways, I see our original intervention has having had the desired impacts. Scholarship such as that of Bonds (2013), Mele (2013), and Inwood (2015) is squarely focused on racialization and the processes through which race comes to have meaning and is experienced. The piece is being read and cited and likely having impacts that are not fully knowable or quantifiable through the methods I use in this chapter. This is encouraging and, hopefully, provides the basis for ongoing research supporting the struggle to dismantle the structures of inequality that so doggedly persist in society.

References

Anderson, M.B., and Sternberg, C. 2012. 'Non-White' Gentrification in Chicago's Bronzeville and Pilsen: Racial Economy and the Intraurban Contingency of Urban Redevelopment. *Urban Affairs Review*, 49.3: 435–67.

Andrews, D.L., and Mower, R.L. 2012. Spectres of Jordan. *Ethnic and Racial Studies*, 35.6: 1059–77.

Atencio, M., Beal, B., and Yochim, E. C. 2013. 'It Ain't Just Black Kids and White Kids': The Representation and Reproduction of Authentic 'Skurban' Masculinities. *Sociology of Sport Journal*, 30.2: 153–72.

Bauder, H. 2008. Neoliberalism and the Economic Utility of Immigration: Media Perspectives of Germany's Immigration Law. *Antipode*, 40.1: 5–78.

Bonds, A. 2013. Racing Economic Geography: The Place of Race in Economic Geography. *Geography Compass*, 7.6: 398–411.

Davis, D.A. 2007. Narrating the Mute: Racializing and Racism in a Neoliberal Moment. *Souls*, 9.4: 346–60.

Duggan, L. 2003. *The Twilight of Equality? Neoliberalism, Cultural Politics, and the Attack on Democracy*. Boston: Beacon Press.

Gardiner Barber, P. 2008. The Ideal Immigrant? Gendered Class Subjects in Philippine–Canada Migration. *Third World Quarterly*, 29.7: 1265–85.

Gilmore, R.W. 2006. *Golden Gulag*. Berkeley: University of California Press.

Giroux, H. 2005. The Terror of Neoliberalism: Rethinking the Significance of Cultural Politics. *College Literature*, 32.1: 1–19.

—. 2008. *Against the Terror of Neoliberalism: Politics Beyond the Age of Greed*. London: Paradigm.

Goldberg, D.T. 1993. *Racist Culture: Philosophy and the Politics of Meaning*. Oxford and Cambridge: Blackwell.

Goldring, L., and Landolt, P. 2013. The Conditionality of Legal Status and Rights: Conceptualizing Precarious Non-citizenship in Canada, in Goldring, L., and Landolt, P., eds. *Producing and Negotiating Non-citizenship: Precarious Legal Status in Canada*. Toronto: University of Toronto Press: 3–27.

Howlett, K. 2006. Ontario Eyes Brightest Immigrants. *The Globe and Mail*, 11 October: A7.

Inwood, J.F. 2015. Neoliberal Racism: The 'Southern Strategy' and the Expanding Geographies of White Supremacy. *Social & Cultural Geography*, 16.4: 407–23.

Lemieux, T., and Nadeau, J.-F. 2015. Temporary Foreign Workers in Canada: A Look at Regions and Occupational Skill. *A Report of the Parliamentary Budget Officer of Canada*. Retrieved from http://www.pbo-dpb.gc.ca/files/files/TFW_EN.pdf

McKittrick, K. 2006. *Demonic Grounds: Black Women and the Cartographies of Struggle*. Minneapolis: University of Minnesota Press.

Mele, C. 2013. Neoliberalism, Race and the Redefining of Urban Redevelopment. *International Journal of Urban and Regional Research*, 37.2: 598–617.

Nxumalo, F. 2012. Unsettling Representational Practices: Inhabiting Relational Becomings in Early Childhood Education. *Child & Youth Services*, 33.3–4: 281–302.

Omi, M., and Winant, H. 2014. *Racial Formation in the United States*. 3rd edn. New York: Routledge.

Pulido, L. 2006. *Black, Brown, Yellow, and Left*. Berkeley: University of California Press.

Roberts, D., and Mahtani, M. 2010. Neoliberalizing Race, Racing Neoliberalism: Placing 'Race' in Neoliberal Discourses. *Antipode*, 42.2: 248–57.

Rose, G. 1997. Situating Knowledges: Positionality, Reflexivities and other Tactics. *Progress In Human Geography*, 21.3: 305–20.

Scoffield, H. 2005. Labour Shortage Woes Loom, Research Says. *The Globe and Mail*, 29 September: B7.

Simpson, J. 2005. New Canadians Can Keep the Lights Shining on the Prairie. *The Globe and Mail*, 23 November: A19.

Theodore, N. 2007. Closed Borders, Open Markets: Day Laborers' Struggle for Economic Rights, in Leitner, H., Peck, J., and Sheppard, E., eds. *Contesting Neoliberalism: Urban Frontiers*. New York: Guilford: 250–65.

Wilson, D. 2006. *Cities and Race: America's New Black Ghettos*. New York: Routledge.

18

GENDER AND NEOLIBERALISM

Young women as ideal neoliberal subjects

Christina Scharff

Gender intersects with neoliberalism in various ways and it is not my intention to provide an overview of these complex entanglements here. Such an overview would depend on our under-standing of 'gender' and 'neoliberalism', which are concepts that have been defined and used differently, depending on disciplinary orientation, political outlook, and spatial and temporal context, to name just a few. In addition, existing research on the manifold intersections between gender and neoliberalism demonstrates that the theme can be explored in a range of contexts, including, but not limited to: education (Davies 2005; O'Flynn and Peterson 2007), parenting and maternity (de Benedictis, 2012; McRobbie, 2013), embodiment and beauty norms (Elias *et al* forthcoming; Evans and Riley 2013; Luo 2012); contemporary work cultures (Ikonen 2013; Swan, 2008; Walkerdine and Jimenez 2012); development (Cornwall *et al.* 2008; Koffman and Gill 2013; Pedwell 2012; Wilson 2013); the postfeminist media culture (Butler 2013; Gill 2007; McRobbie 2009), and the ways in which neoliberalism intersects not only with gender, but also with race, class and neo-colonial dynamics (Allen 2014; Ringrose and Walkerdine 2008; Roberts and Mahtani 2010; Scharff 2011; Tyler 2013; Walkerdine *et al.* 2001; Williams 2014).

Instead of attempting to provide an overview of the various ways in which 'gender' and 'neoliberalism' have been analysed and theorized, this chapter will hone in on recent feminist research on contemporary western societies. This body of work has suggested that women, and in particular young women, have been constructed as ideal neoliberal subjects. Public, media and policy discourses have positioned young women as subjects of capacity who can lead responsibilized and self-managed lives through self-application and self-transformation. Based on empirical research, I will explore these subjectivities. In particular, the chapter draws on over 60 in-depth interviews with young, female classical musicians. Female musicians are chosen because, as I will demonstrate, they may be neoliberal subjects par excellence. By focusing on the ways in which the research participants negotiated playing-related injuries, which were prevalent but often hidden, the chapter will shed light on some of the contradictions, exclusions and politics of neoliberal, gendered subjectivity.

Young women as ideal neoliberal subjects

As discussed in this handbook, neoliberalism is a contested concept and conceptualized variously. This chapter is informed by Foucauldian approaches (Foucault 2008) that regard neoliberalism as a mentality of government (Barry *et al.* 1996). Here, neoliberalism is understood as more than a set of free market principles; amid other dynamics, neoliberalism extends to the organization of subjectivity (Brown, 2006). Under neoliberalism, individual citizens are construed as entrepreneurs of themselves and their lives (Brown 2003, 2006). Neoliberal subjects are entrepreneurial subjects who calculate about themselves and work on themselves in order to better themselves (du Gay 1996). In the literature, both terms – neoliberal and entrepreneurial subject – are used; therefore, I will employ them interchangeably here.

Feminist research has demonstrated that women, and young women in particular, are increasingly positioned as ideal neoliberal subjects (Gill and Scharff 2011; McRobbie 2009; Ringrose and Walkerdine 2008). As Angela McRobbie (2009: 15) has shown, young women have become 'privileged subjects of social change' who capably maximize newly won opportunities such as access to the labour market and control over reproduction. This hopeful positioning of young women is well captured in the slogan of the Nike-sponsored, and globally disseminated, project 'the girl effect – the unique potential of 600 million adolescent girls to end poverty for themselves and the world' (Girl Effect, n.d.; for a critical discussion, see Koffman and Gill 2013). According to Bronwyn Davies (2005), the neoliberal self is defined by its capacity to consume, which further privileges the feminine through the long-standing association between women and consumption. The neoliberal incitement to self-transformation is also associated with femininity (Ringrose and Walkerdine 2008). It is mainly women who are called on to transform themselves, which becomes particularly visible with regard to the management of the body and sexuality (Gill and Scharff 2011).

There are stark contradictions between women's hopeful positioning as subjects of capacity, on the one hand, and intensifying forms of governmentality, on the other. This raises a range of questions relating, for example, to the exclusions that neoliberal subjectivities (re-)produce. As several researchers have pointed out, the neoliberal self, closely tied to the ability to consume, is predominantly middle-class (Ringrose and Walkerdine, 2008). In addition, the empowered, female neoliberal self is often constructed in opposition to allegedly powerless 'other' women. When I conducted research on how a diverse group of young, British and German women engaged with feminism and gender (in-)equalities, I found that they often presented themselves as empowered and that they did so by constructing the figure of the oppressed, 'other' woman who was a passive victim of patriarchy (Scharff 2011). Arguably, neoliberal subjectivity is formed through processes of abjection (Tyler 2013), which position empowered and self-managing subjects as morally superior (Brown 2003). The 'other' of the neoliberal subject – vulnerable, powerless, passive, and dependent – is often constituted along all too familiar hierarchies of power. Despite its inclusionary rhetoric – all 600 million adolescent girls have the potential to change the world – formations of neoliberal subjectivity seem to reproduce classed and racialized exclusions.

And how can we make sense of the privileging of the feminine under neoliberalism? How do neoliberalism's subjects of capacity, namely young women, negotiate their positioning? In order to answer this question, and to gain a deeper understanding of the interplay between gender and neoliberalism, I conducted 64 in-depth interviews with individuals who may be the quintessence of neoliberal subjectivity. I interviewed young, female musicians because they are twice positioned as entrepreneurial: as young women and as individuals who work in the cultural sector. As Rosalind Gill and Andy Pratt (2008: 2) have shown, cultural workers are 'hailed as "model entrepreneurs" by industry and government figures' and, to use Andrew Ross's (2008: 32) words, are 'paradigms of entrepreneurial selfhood' due to the emphasis on autonomy, self-application, and competition in the cultural sector. By drawing on the accounts of young female cultural workers, my study did not focus on a group that is readily associated with entrepreneurialism and neoliberalism; nevertheless, it provides insight into the accounts of individuals who may be entrepreneurial subjects par excellence.

Interviews lasted an average of 75 minutes and the majority of respondents were in their late 20s/early 30s. I spoke to musicians who played a range of instruments (string, woodwind, brass, piano, organ, percussion), as well as singers, conductors, opera directors and composers. While based in London (n = 32) or Berlin (n = 32), the research participants came from a range of countries and, reflecting the under-representation of working-class as well as black and minority-ethnic players, most identified as white and middle-class.[1] In order to identify recurring discursive patterns in the talk of the participants, and to grasp the rhetorical function that they fulfil, I drew on discourse analysis (Potter and Wetherell 1987; Taylor and Littleton 2012) to analyse my data. As I hope to demonstrate, discourse analysis offers useful analytical tools to trace how the research participants talk about and negotiate playing-related injuries.

Hiding injuries

Many musicians experience health problems from the high physical and psychological demands of their profession (Bennett 2008; Zaza *et al.* 1998). More than half of the research participants interviewed for this study had suffered from a playing-related injury, ranging from hearing problems, postural issues and repetitive strain injury to focal dystonia and more instrument-specific illnesses such as vocal problems among singers. Liz, a pianist, told me about the first time she had had an injury:

> I was playing so much, and I got a wrist injury. So at the time I thought that everything was over and I wouldn't play again, just because I went through a phase where I couldn't turn taps or door handles. I had a brace on my arm for a while. It was like a very – it was tendonitis. And I really lost hope at that point.

Equally, Annabel told me that she had back pain from carrying her instrument around, and then went on to say:

> And I once had a really bad breakdown where I got Tinnitus. A lot of musicians get that… It went away. But I really thought 'Now I have to do something completely different.' Even though it was a really quiet tone. But it drove me insane.

And when I asked Zola whether she had ever had an injury, she said:

> Yes, I can show you a very nice scar. Yeah, I had this thing that they called tennis elbow. It actually appeared when I was in college in my last year, right before I was supposed to do my last exam, my recital.

In other, more severe cases, research participants had to stop playing their instrument for a sustained period of time. When I interviewed Esmeralda in October, she told me that she had had to stop playing the viola several months before because of tendonitis:

> I still cannot do any gigs or concerts, if they ask me. Because now all I'm doing is practising every day, now I'm doing like 30 or 40 minutes and then I have to stop because I'm getting tired. You know, I have to build it up gradually. So I cannot play. All I can do is teach.

Lena and Elena also could not play the violin for several months following injury. Lena had tendonitis when she was 16 and 'couldn't play for three months'. Equally, Elena told me:

> You commonly call it a 'played-through finger' and that tends to mean that the nerve in your finger is inflamed because of the pressure of your finger on the string. And it hurts. If it was only numb, it would not be so bad, but it really hurts. And then you can't play for a time so that the nerve can calm down again and then you can play again. And I had it and it just did not go away. I could not play for three months.

As these statements illustrate, playing-related injuries are common and can impact on musicians' ability to play their instrument and pursue their profession.

The extracts also demonstrate that the research participants discussed their injuries in the interview. Many, however, pointed out that injuries were not openly talked about among musicians. When I asked Lauren whether she had ever had any injuries, she told me about her experiences and went on to say:

> Part of the problem with my industry – one of the problems of my industry – is that there is a massive stigma attached to injury, so people don't talk about it as much as they should. People will… musicians will keep on playing on injuries, rather than admit that they are having trouble, because they don't wanna lose their work or they don't wanna be seen to be unreliable.

Numerous research participants shared this sentiment. Kim told me that musicians did not discuss injuries openly and explained:

> It's because there's so many of us going for the same work. And there's always that competition, and you know, we all need money, and we can't just be dropped because of that. So yeah, you have to keep it under cover. And yet, you know, the strain of it creates injuries.

Equally, Linda stated that it's best to keep injuries hidden: 'I suppose you might be worried otherwise that if someone thinks you are injured they won't give you concerts or ask you to do anything.' These statements suggest that musicians do not discuss injuries openly out of fear of losing employment opportunities. As in other cultural sectors (Gill and Pratt 2008), employment opportunities in classical music tend to be scarce and the working lives of musicians are precarious. As a report by the Musicians' Union (2012) has demonstrated, many musicians have portfolio careers, which are marked by low incomes (less than £20,000 a year for 56 per cent of those surveyed), uncertainty, and lack of workplace benefits such as pensions. An analysis of the earnings of freelance cultural workers in Germany has documented similar trends (Schulz *et al.* 2013). The precarious nature of the profession, itself linked to neoliberalism (Kalleberg 2009), makes it difficult to address injuries.

Repudiating vulnerability: injuries as normalized but not politicized

In this section, I want to take my argument further by showing that injuries remained hidden not only because of fears of losing work, but also because they were constructed as a personal weakness. Summing up musicians' attitudes towards injuries, Susan stated that 'they'll talk about how to look after yourself, but people don't really talk about their own problems, because it then shows weakness'. When I asked Esther why musicians did not really discuss injuries, she responded: 'It's a weakness, isn't it and then you might not be asked [to work]. That's the problem.' June shared Esther's sentiment and emphasized that musicians – singers in her case – did not discuss injuries for fear of being seen as 'faulty': 'Singers fear for [sic] being looked at as a – for being slightly, you know, [a] faulty product. They don't wanna be seen as faulty.' In this context, it is notable that June uses the expression 'product' to talk about singers. Indeed, many research participants referred to themselves as products that had to be sold and marketed, suggesting that subjectivity itself is economized under neoliberalism (McNay 2009; see also Scharff 2015). Here, however, I want to focus on the negation of injuries and suggest that it is not merely linked to the fear of losing employment opportunities, but also to a wider repudiation of vulnerability under neoliberalism. As Micki McGee (2005) has pointed out in her research on self-help culture, vulnerabilities tend to be denied in neoliberal culture:

> Not only is it the labour of others, and the value of labour itself, that must be denied by the masterful self, but also it is the vulnerabilities of our bodies. In the model of the self-mastering self, the forms of selfhood that 'fail' to be self-efficient, self-reliant, and self-authoring are seen as somehow defective (Ibid.: 174).

McGee's description of 'failed' forms of selfhood as 'defective' resonates with June's statement that singers do not want to be seen as 'faulty'. Arguably, injuries remain hidden because they puncture the image of the autonomous, neoliberal self and instead evoke the spectre of weakness and failure.

While research participants represented injuries as something that is best kept under cover, they also normalized them. According to Anke, 'almost everybody has something' and Elena pointed out 'there are specific things for every instrument which mean that it's unhealthy'. When I asked Kristina whether she had ever had an injury, such as tendonitis, she replied: 'No, fortunately no tendonitis. But I have back pain. But I think everybody has something.' Jasmin answered the same question in a similar fashion and normalized injuries by stating:

> Yes, so everybody has chronic back pain, really crazy. I also do. So, I notice – I mean I have not yet had any treatment, and I have not been to the doctor because of it, but something is definitely funny with my right-hand side. But that's totally normal.

Despite the acknowledgement that injuries were common, only a few research participants linked the prevalence of injuries to work conditions. Kim stated: 'if you are playing in a very cold hall that can cause injuries'. Saaga, too, reflected on her experiences of playing for an orchestra full time for a year, stating that the rehearsal and concert schedule was 'a little much', having led to several players developing injuries. When told by the orchestral management that the tight schedule was normal, Saaga disagreed: 'It depends on what you are doing, which orchestra even, there is a huge difference in the workload between different orchestras and different countries.' In making this statement, Saaga links the prevalence of injuries to the wider issue of workload. Generally, however, the research participants did not reflect on the more structural causes of injuries. Injuries were normalized, but not contextualized. This also meant that there was no scope for politicization. None of the research participants were angry about the prevalence of injuries. Indeed, anger, as an affect that can give rise to politicization, was remarkably absent from the research participants' accounts. This observation ties in with wider accounts of neoliberalism that regard depoliticization as one of its features. As Lois McNay (2009: 66) has argued, 'the organization of society around a multiplicity of individual enterprises profoundly depoliticizes social and political relations'.

Individualizing injury and emphasizing self-care

Instead of regarding injures as linked to the high demands of the profession, the research participants constructed them as an individual issue. In this way, they could acknowledge the prevalence of injuries without linking them to structural causes. Gesche told me that 'actually, most
musicians have back pain or something', but subsequently pointed out that it is basically 'one's
own fault' if one is or gets injured. Arguing along similar lines, Emilia stated 'it's usually just like
a bad technique if you've got… I mean that sounds really awful, but it is often the reason why
you get tension problems.' Equally, Isabella pointed out that if musicians did something wrong,
they had to teach themselves the right technique to avoid injuries: 'You have to be clever
enough to understand, to understand you are doing something wrong, because even if you were
taught wrongly, in the end you have a mirror and you can teach yourself.'

In these statements, the responsibility to avoid and manage injury is firmly placed on individual
players. The impact of wider forces, such as work conditions or the intensity of training, is disavowed and wellbeing presented as achievable through appropriate self-management. As Nikolas Rose has pointed out, 'reality and destiny' have become 'matters of individual responsibility'
under neoliberalism (Rose 1992: 142). Equally important, the argument that 'you can teach
yourself' constructs the individual as capable of addressing the source of injury, and of changing
it. The individual is thus represented as an autonomous being who, through responsible self-
management, can cope with various demands. Structural constraints are elided and the capable,
self-mastering neoliberal subject is reinstated. Thus, the discourse that injuries can be avoided
through successful self-management not only responsibilizes individuals, but also reinstates neoliberal subjectivity; injuries do not highlight vulnerabilities, but instead serve as an incitement to
self-management.

The construction of injury as a personal shortfall also reflects wider trends in neoliberalism
where failure is individualized (Burchell 1993). According to Mark Banks (2007: 63), '[f]aced
with a multiplicity of discourses that reinforce the autonomy, and thus potential culpability, of
the "enterprising self"', success and failure are understood as triumphs and tragedies of individual
design'. The individualization of failure is well captured by Saaga's reflections on the prevalence
of injuries and why musicians do not discuss them:

> I think people are not so willing to say the real truth about it because it feels that always
> something is wrong with me, it feels like everyone is so strong and that I am not as
> good a player, or something is wrong with my technique if it keeps happening.

Saaga's claim 'something is wrong with me' illustrates that neoliberal subjects only have themselves to blame. Similarly, Astrid observed that injuries were common at the conservatoire she
trained at, but went on to say that they were not discussed and 'half a taboo'. When I asked her
why this was the case, she replied: 'Well, because it shows you obviously did something really
wrong.' In these statements, the individual is represented as the sole source of injury. Annegret
told me that it was easy to get tendonitis, but then went on to say: 'It usually shows you that
you did something technically wrong. Because, actually, it's not designed that you get it.' Arguably, sources of pain and injury that are outside the individual are unintelligible, at least in the
context of the research participants' accounts. Based on this logic, difficulties can only be
regarded as individual failure.

Resonating with the research participants' individualized approach to injuries, the solutions
and coping mechanisms they suggested were all limited to individual acts. More specifically,
several research participants emphasized the need to take 'care of the self' in order to deal with

the prevalence of injuries. According to Amy, 'you just have to be kind of sensible and try and be fit and look after your body and be healthy and stuff'. Similarly, Faith told me about her approach to managing injuries, stating: 'And I'm very aware of taking care of my body. And like having to go for massages, or like exercising and stretching.' Discussing the consequences of her injury at 16, Lena said: 'I'm very aware now of what I need to do to take care of myself. I know the warning signs for when I'm getting too tense or overworked and I have techniques now that I can use to stop that.' As these statements illustrate, the risk of having an injury is transformed into a problem of self-care. Amy, Faith and Lena are responsibilized and 'aware' of the need to look after their physical health. In neoliberal fashion, wider risks – such as musicians' exposure to playing-related injuries – are placed in the individual domain (Lemke 2001). Instead of attempting to change workloads or work conditions such as playing in cold environments, the research participants' strategies revolve around self-management.

Conclusion: better to be sick than angry

In this chapter, I drew on over 60 interviews with young, female, classical musicians to shed light on neoliberal subjectivity. Having argued that the research participants were twice positioned as entrepreneurial – by being young women and cultural workers – I drew on their accounts of playing-related injuries to offer one perspective on the interplay between neoliberalism and femininity. As I have demonstrated, injuries are common among musicians and yet, they often remain hidden. The unspeakability of injuries can be attributed to the precarious nature of the classical music profession. However, I also suggested that injuries remained hidden because vulnerabilities tend to be repudiated under neoliberalism. Sickness punctures the image of the capable, autonomous neoliberal subject and may best be kept under cover. Apart from being hidden, injuries were normalized and their cause was often attributed to individual failure. Wider social factors, such as work conditions, were rarely evoked; instead, individual musicians were responsibilized and called upon to prevent and manage injuries. By exploring the research participants' negotiation of playing-related injuries, I thus shed light on a range of processes that characterize neoliberal subjectivity, such as responsibilisation, an incitement to self-care, and the individualization of failure.

To be sure, the research participants did not exclusively exhibit a neoliberal outlook. As has been demonstrated in detail elsewhere (Doolin 2002), neoliberal rhetoric does not hold absolutely and individuals draw on competing discourses, including 'acceptance, modification or resistance to the entrepreneurial self' (Halford and Leonard 2006: 657–8). While I found that the research participants' negotiation of playing-related injuries was predominantly couched in neoliberal rhetoric, I demonstrated elsewhere (Scharff 2015) that the interviews were marked by competing discourses. A neoliberal outlook was common, but it was not the only one. In tracing the different ways in which the research participants' negotiation of injuries reflected a wider neoliberal perspective, I did not mean to suggest that neoliberalism determined their sense making. Instead, I used the musicians' engagements with injuries to illustrate the workings of neoliberal subjectivity and to foreground some of its key features.

In conclusion, I hope to have demonstrated that young women's positioning as neoliberal subjects comes at a cost. Indeed, the prevalence of injuries among the research participants resonates with Angela McRobbie's (2009) wider argument that being 'culturally intelligible' as a young woman in the current postfeminist and neoliberal moment makes one ill. Speaking more specifically about young women's engagements with feminism, McRobbie argues that feminism is disarticulated in a postfeminist context. According to McRobbie, young women are gender-aware – they have all bumped into feminism – but feminist awareness has to be given up in the era of postfeminism, turning it into an object of loss. This loss becomes opaque and gives rise to a melancholia with attendant patterns of self-beratement, and in a context where pathologies become treatable and normalized. Instead of opening up spaces for asking critical questions about masculine domination and heteronormativity, the postfeminist era forecloses such critical engagements, giving rise to a range of disorders.

While my chapter did not focus on the research participants' engagements with gender issues, there are interesting parallels between McRobbie's argument and the research participants' accounts. In both cases, wider social awareness is replaced with an individualist outlook, and pathologies become normalized. This observation highlights that young women's positioning as neoliberal subjects is characterized by various tensions. Apart from reproducing existing exclusions along the lines of race and class, neoliberal subjectivity seems to entail a repudiation and yet also normalization of injuries that is coupled with a heightened sense of individual responsibility. Of course, my observations may not only apply to young women but also to other groups; further research is needed to explore how these dynamics play out among different demographics. The research does, however, suggest that the privileging of the feminine under neoliberalism, at least in the context described here, comes at a cost because it heightens the pressures associated with neoliberal governmentality.

Note

1 Forty-four musicians in my sample identified as middle-class, seven as working-class, and two as lower middle-class. Eleven were not sure how to describe their socio-economic background, which resonates with broader arguments that popular awareness of class seems to wane. Four described their racial background as mixed-race, 56 as white, one as black, one as Asian and two as East Asian.

References

Allen, K. 2014. 'Blair's Children': Young Women as 'Aspirational Subjects' in the Psychic Landscape of Class. *The Sociological Review*, 62.4: 760–79.

Banks, M. 2007. *The Politics of Cultural Work*. Basingstoke: Palgrave Macmillan.

Barry, A., Osbourne, T., and Rose, N. 1996. *Foucault and Political Reason: Liberalism, Neo-liberalism and Rationalities of Government*. London: Routledge.

Bennett, D. 2008. *Understanding the Classical Music Profession: The Past, the Present and the Future*. Farnham: Ashgate.

Brown, W. 2003. Neoliberalism and the End of Liberal Democracy. *Theory & Event*, 7.1.

—. 2006. American Nightmare: Neoliberalism, Neoconservatism, and De-Democratization. *Political Theory*, 34.6: 690–714.

Burchell, G. 1993. Liberal Government and Techniques of the Self. *Economy and Society*, 22.3: 267–282.

Butler, J. 2013. For White Girls Only?: Postfeminism and the Politics of Inclusion. *Feminist Formations*, 25.1: 35–58.

Cornwall, A., Gideon, J., and Wilson, K. 2008. Introduction: Reclaiming Feminism: Gender and Neoliberalism. *IDS Bulletin*, 39.6: 1–9.

Davies, B. 2005. The (Im)Possibility of Intellectual Work in Neoliberal Regimes. *Discourse: Studies in the Cultural Politics of Education*, 26.1: 1–14.

de Benedictis, S. 2012. 'Feral' Parents: Austerity Parenting Under Neoliberalism. *Studies in the Maternal*, 4.2: 1–21.

Doolin, B. 2002. Enterprise Discourse: Professional Identity and the Organisational Control of Hospital Clinicians. *Organisation Studies*, 23.3: 369–90.

du Gay, P. 1996. *Consumption and Identity at Work*. London: Sage.

Elias, A.S., Gill, R., Scharff, C. eds. Forthcoming. *Aesthetic Labour: Rethinking Beauty Politics in Neoliberalism*. Basingstoke: Palgrave Macmillan.

Evans, A., and Riley, S. 2013. *Technologies of Sexiness: Sex, Identiy and Consumption*. New York: Oxford University Press.

Foucault, M. 2008. *The Birth of Biopolitics*. Basingstoke: Palgrave Macmillan.

Gill, R. 2007. *Gender and the Media*. Cambridge and Malden, MA: Polity Press.

Gill, R., and Pratt, A. 2008. In the Social Factory? Immaterial Labour, Precariousness and Cultural Work. *Theory Culture & Society*, 25.7–8: 1–30.

Gill, R., and Scharff, C. eds. 2011. *New Femininities: Postfeminism, Neoliberalism and Subjectivity*. Basingstoke: Palgrave.

Girl Effect. n.d. *Girls are the Most Powerful Force for Change on the Planet*. Retrieved from http://www.girleffect.org/

Halford, S., and Leonard, P. 2006. Place, Space and Time: Contextualising Workplace Subjectivities. *Organisation Studies*, 27.5: 657–76.

Ikonen, H.-M. 2013. Precarious Work, Entrepreneurial Mindset and Sense of Place: Female Strategies in Insecure Labour Markets. *Global Discourse: An Interdisciplinary Journal of Current Affairs and Applied Contemporary Thought*, 3.3–4: 467–81.

Kalleberg, A. 2009. Precarious Work, Insecure Workers: Employment Relations in Transition. *American Sociological Review*, 74: 1–22.

Koffman, O., and Gill, R. 2013. 'The Revolution Will be Led By a 12 Year Old Girl': Girl Power and the Global Biopolitics of Girlhood. *Feminist Review*, 105: 83–102.

Lemke, T. 2001. 'The Birth of Bio-politics': Michel Foucault's Lecture at the Collège de France on Neo-liberal Governmentality, Economy and Society. *Economy and Society*, 30.2: 190–207.

Luo, W. 2012. Packaged Glamour: Constructing the Modern Bride in China's Bridal Media. *Asian Women*, 28.4: 83–115.

McGee, M. 2005. *Self-Help, Inc.: Makeover Culture in American Life*. Oxford and New York: Oxford University Press.

McNay, L. 2009. Self as Enterprise Dilemmas of Control and Resistance in Foucault's The Birth of Biopolitics. *Theory, Culture & Society*, 26.6: 55–77.

McRobbie, A. 2009. *The Aftermath of Feminism: Gender, Culture and Social Change*. London: Sage.

—. 2013. Feminism, the Family and the New 'Mediated' Maternalism. *New Formations*, 80: 119–37.

Musicians' Union. 2012. *The Working Musician*. Commissioned by the Musicians' Union. Researched and produced by DHA Communications.

O'Flynn, G., and Peterson, E.B. 2007. The 'Good Life' and the 'Rich Portfolio': Young Women, Schooling and Neoliberal Subjectification. *British Journal of Sociology of Education*, 28.4: 459–72.

Pedwell, C. 2012. Affective (Self-)Transformations: Empathy, Neoliberalism and International Development. *Feminist Theory*, 13.2: 163–79.

Potter, J., and Wetherell, M. 1987. *Discourse and Social Psychology: Beyond Attitudes and Behaviour*. London: Sage.

Ringrose, J., and Walkerdine, V. 2008. Regulating the Abject. *Feminist Media Studies*, 8.3: 227–46.

Roberts, D., and Mahtani, M. 2010. Neoliberalizing Race, Racing Neoliberalism: Placing 'Race' in Neoliberal Discourses. *Antipode*, 42.2: 248–57.

Rose, N. 1992. Governing the Enterprising Self. In Heelas, P., Morris, P., and Morris, P.M., eds. *The Values of the Enterprise Culture: The Moral Debate*. London: Routledge: 141–64.

Ross, A. 2008. The New Geography of Work: Power to the Precarious? *Theory Culture & Society*, 25.7–8: 31–49.

Scharff, C. 2011. Disarticulating Feminism: Individualization, Neoliberalism and the Othering of 'Muslim Women'. *European Journal of Women's Studies*, 18.2: 119–34.

—. 2015: doi: 10.1177/0263276415590167. The Psychic Life of Neoliberalism: Mapping the Contours of Entrepreneurial Subjectivity. *Theory, Culture & Society*.

Schulz, G., Zimmermann, O., and Hufnagel, R. 2013. *Arbeitsmarkt Kultur: Zur Wirtschaftlichen und Sozialen Lage in Kulturberufen*. Berlin: Deutscher Kulturrat.

Swan, E. 2008. 'You Make Me Feel like a Woman': Therapeutic Cultures and the Contagion of Femininity. *Gender, Work and Organisation*, 15.1: 88–107.

Taylor, S., and Littleton, K. 2012. *Contemporary Identities of Creativity and Creative Work*. Farnham: Ashgate.

Tyler, I. 2013. *Revolting Subjects: Social Abjection and Resistance in Neoliberal Britain*. London Zed.

Walkerdine, V., and Jimenez, L. 2012. *Gender, Work and Community After De-industrialisation: A Psychosocial Approach to Affect*. Basingstoke: Palgrave Macmillan.

Walkerdine, V., Lucey, H., and Melody, J. 2001. *Growing Up Girl: Psycho-social Explorations of Gender and Class*. Basingstoke: Palgrave.

Williams, R. 2014. Eat, Pray, Love: Producing the Female Neoliberal Spiritual Subject. *The Journal of Popular Culture*, 47.3: 613–33.

Wilson, K. 2013. Agency as 'Smart Economics': Neoliberalism, Gender and Development. In Madhok, S., Philips, A., and Wilson, K., eds. *Gender, Agency and Coercion. Thinking Gender in Transnational Times*. London: Palgrave Macmillan: 84–101.

Zaza, C., Charles, C., and Muszynski, A. 1998. The Meaning of Playing-related Musculoskeletal Disorders to Classical Musicians. *Social Science & Medicine*, 47.12: 2013–23.

19
NEOLIBERALIZING SEX, NORMATIVIZING LOVE

Sealing Cheng

[S]ex is always political. But there are also historical periods in which sexuality is more sharply contested and more overtly politicized. In such periods, the domain of erotic life is, in effect, renegotiated.

(Rubin 1984: 267)

As jubilant crowds hail victories of freedom and equality in legalizing gay marriage (most recently in Ireland in May 2015), reproductive rights activists lament the intensifying campaigns to undercut the right to abortion. HIV/AIDS activists raise concerns about both the dangers of a subculture of 'barebacking', and the institutional pressure to oppose prostitution before receiving funding. Meanwhile, 'sex trafficking' has become the unequivocal embodiment of 'bad sex' that attracts not only surging waves of social and moral condemnation, but also the full force of the state apparatus of law enforcement. At first sight, these disparate concerns may have little to do with each other, or with broader political, economic, and cultural politics. I propose that they are part and parcel of what Gayle Rubin called the 'renegotiation of the domain of erotic life', pertinent to the making of neoliberalism, pertaining to the construction of a regime of truth about sexuality, and a new way in which people become subjects.

This chapter considers the relationship between neoliberalism and sexuality, manifest in national and transnational contexts, and its attendant paradoxes, from two interrelated operations of power: neoliberalism as a mode of governmentality and a mode of subject-making. After providing an overview of how sexuality is fundamental to the constructivist project of neoliberalism, I will examine the intimate effects of these processes from the vantage point of what I call the 'sexual limits of neoliberalism' (Cheng 2013): namely the moral panic, social and cultural anxieties, and political responses to what is popularly known as 'sex trafficking'. To examine the relationship between neoliberalism and sexuality through the lens of 'sex trafficking' is to understand how a renegotiation of erotic life (Rubin 1984) has been taking place at this historical juncture to produce a 'neoliberal sex hierarchy' (ibid.; Cheng and Kim forthcoming).

Neoliberalism, heteronormativity, and homonormativity

Scholars have argued that neoliberalism is about the subsumption of capital into everyday life such that there is nothing outside capital (Read 2009). Thereby, individual interest and competition become the guiding principle not just in the economic sector, but also all aspects of social life. Furthermore, the fantasy of free trade (Dean 2008) comes to constitute the neoliberal actor as rational agents engaged in the market of everyday exchanges, celebrating the consumer as a political subject while banalizing the citizenry (ibid.: 54–63). Posing as a system of rationality and universality that fosters the continuous expansion of a free market inhabited by competitive and responsible individuals, neoliberalism constructs itself as a regime of truth about society and human nature. Neoliberal transformations thereby shape not only the world we live in, but also the idea of being human – and thereby, being sexual.

The privileging of heterosexuality as the unmarked assumption in a set of institutions, structures of understanding, and practical orientation has been identified by Michael Warner as 'heteronormativity' (Warner 1991). The good life offered by this vision of normative intimacy is premised on an ethos of privacy that effectively replaces 'state mandates for social justice with a privatized ethics of responsibility, charity, atonement, and "values"' and enforcing boundaries between 'moral persons and economic ones' (Berlant and Warner 1998: 554). Heteronormativity is not the same as heterosexuality nor heterosexual individuals. A perfect example is how the gay marriage movement has championed ideals of domesticity and privacy under narrowly defined ideas of equality and freedom, over other ways of organizing intimacy and sexuality, and sidelining progressive politics of social and economic justice. As Lisa Duggan explained, this 'new homonormativity' upholds and sustains heteronormative assumptions and institutions, and continues to promote 'privacy, domesticity, and family values in place of progressive politics of social and economic justice, depolitizing racial and class hierarchies' (Duggan 2002: 182).

A 'gay moralism' championing monogamous marriage and condemning 'promiscuity' has therefore come to redefine meanings of 'equality' and 'freedom' accessible only to the privileged few who could exercise their right to privacy. Mario Pecheny and Rafael de la Dehesa discussed similar contradictions in Latin America, pointing out that, despite the growth of the sexual rights movement and a more inclusive politics, the governance of desires have continued to be 'mapped onto broader ideologies of political and economic development' (Pechey and de la Dehesa 2013: 111). Specifically, the integration of sexual and reproductive health paradigms into 'narrow sector-specific policy demands' (ibid.: 103) have the effect of medicalizing and depoliticizing the issues, contributing to new forms of competition and reinforcing various forms of social exclusion. For example, HIV/AIDS activists have lobbied for state support to increase healthcare access for men who have sex with men and *travesti*, while lesbians remain largely invisible to policy-makers and funders in most countries, 'to a certain extent reinforcing the historic gendering of the public/private divide' (ibid.:104).

As we will see in the discussion of 'sex trafficking', these forms of normativity that privilege particular identity groups and proffer a middle-class standard of respectability and propriety have repercussions transnationally through both formal diplomatic manoeuvres and humanitarianism. Significantly, couched in the universalistic language of human rights and civil liberties, this reconfiguration of moral values and the moral self assume the guise of '*amorality*' by taking distance 'from conventional moral discourse in its affirmation of a wholly instrumental rationality' (Brown 2006: 711 fn5).

The sexual subject: *homo economicus* and erotic capital

As a regime of truth, neoliberalism naturalizes the market logic in all of society and as part of human nature. (As Margaret Thatcher famously said, 'There is no alternative.') The neoliberal subject in this form of governmentality is aptly described by Foucault as *homo economicus*: an 'entrepreneur of himself' (Foucault 2008: 226). The human is no longer just a creature of exchange but a creature of competition. Individuals governed by self-interest and competition do not represent an ideology but 'an intimate part of how our lives and subjectivity are structured' (Read 2009: 35). In this system of knowledge production, the market becomes part of human nature (Jameson 1991: 263), and 'capital' comes to mark one's capacity to compete. The worker is no longer 'labour' but 'human capital'.

In this context, becoming a 'sexual subject' is part of modernization and democratization – processes that are never homogeneous and generate 'a plurality of subjects' (Laclau and Mouffe 2001: 181). Yet the 'deployment of sexuality' (Foucault 1979[1976]) operates in very different ways across context: Amuchastegui and Parrini (2012) state that sexual behaviours do not necessarily become a central marker of identity in the global South, unlike that in the global North. Nevertheless, sexual desires and identities have become an increasingly important basis for making claims within the frameworks of human rights and citizenship.

One of the attempts to understand how the market logic penetrates sexual interactions is the concept of 'sexual/erotic capital' (Hakim 2010; Green 2013), extending Bourdieu's idea of the different forms of economic, social, and cultural capital that is convertible to other forms of capital and institutionalized powers (Bourdieu 1986). In this perspective, the structures of desire shape the currency of desirability – sexual capital is derived from both social attributes such as race, class, gender, age and physical attributes, and also acquired through consumer practices such as plastic surgery, fashion, and makeover. The configuration of sexual capital varies across contexts – cultural, social, and spatial settings known as 'sexual fields' (Hakim 2010; Farrer 2010, Green 2013). This theory draws on ideas of market value, self-interest, and competition to analyse intimate interactions between individuals who subscribe to the same brand of rationality (a kind of neoliberal model on neoliberal sexualities). However, in actual practices, the neoliberal logic may work in very different ways to produce 'irrational' behaviours.

These 'irrational' behaviours include those that violate the expectation of 'self-care' that has been an important part of neoliberal ethics. In his account of Foucault's analysis of neoliberal governmentality, Thomas Lemke stated that neoliberalism aspires to produce 'responsible subjects whose moral quality is based on the fact that they rationally assess the costs and benefits of a certain act as opposed to other alternative acts' (Lemke 2001: 59). By this logic, HIV/AIDS campaigns in North America in the 1990s achieved success in reducing infection rates by 'responsibilizing and normalizing' sexual regulation through self-governance as well as through criminal law and public health policing (Kinsman 1996). Yet a 'barebacker microculture' – gay and bisexual men who no longer practised safer sex, especially those who are HIV-positive – has emerged in the new millennium, raising concerns that such irrational behaviours are undermining HIV/AIDS prevention efforts. Rather than any intention to transmit HIV, Barry Adam (2005) found that the neoliberal rhetoric of personal responsibility and consent have constructed HIV-negative men as the main target of 'safer sex' – using condoms is to take responsibility for themselves 'in a marketplace of risks' (ibid.: 340), allowing HIV-positive men to find themselves exempted from the practice, fostering a subculture of 'barebacking'.

Therefore, neoliberal transformations may generate structures, processes, and language that have cross-cultural reverberations, yet their impact on individual subjectivities and experiences may be diverse. Following Zizek's understanding of ideology, Jodi Dean argues that we need to look at 'actual practices; these practices, what people actually do, are the location of ideological beliefs' (Dean 2008: 55). In the following, I give an account of my research on migrant Korean women working in the intimate sector in the USA, specifically how one woman sees her sexual labour and state efforts to criminalize her through the rhetoric of 'sex trafficking'.

Sexual commerce, sex trafficking, and paradoxes of neoliberalism

Elizabeth Bernstein (2007) argued powerfully in her study of contemporary sex markets in San Francisco, Amsterdam, and Stockholm that the boundaries between intimacy and commerce have been radically reworked. Forms and meanings of sexual labour have fundamentally transformed in postindustrial economic and cultural formations. Changes in the labour economy, family and kinship, residential patterns, as well as technological, spatial, and social developments have led to a rapid diversification of sexual commerce. In particular, she identified the form of sexual labour, known as 'Girlfriend Experience' (GFE), as emblematic of the sexual ethic of late capitalism. In contrast to commercial sex that focuses on sexual release in modern capitalist societies, relational meaning within the prescribed time and space of the market transaction is at the centre of the postindustrial context. This 'bounded authenticity' allows cost-efficient intimate relations that are entanglement-free, flexible, and detachable, compatible with the ideal of the autonomous, unfettered, and mobile individual (ibid.: 175).

Yet Bernstein also found a proliferation of state efforts to police sexual commerce under the rubric of 'sex trafficking', and showed that the formally distinct policy frameworks (criminalization of clients in Sweden, legalization of sex work in Amsterdam, and criminalization of all aspects of sex work in San Francisco) in the three sites have disturbingly similar effects of delegitimizing and marginalizing sex workers, particular migrant women sex workers. A whole gamut of law enforcement powers have been mobilized in the name of trafficking to police the mobility and sexuality of women (Agustín 2007). For example, in April 2015, the US Senate passed the Justice for Victims of Trafficking Act with abortions restrictions (Siddiqui 2015). The deployment of anti-abortion language to address victims of 'sex trafficking' is not only part of a larger political project to curb women's reproductive rights in the new millennium, but also a rearticultation of the public/private divide in the neoliberal context (Grewal 2006).

Therefore, I propose to see how 'sex trafficking' operates as a discursive device anchored in a particular way of thinking about and managing licit/illicit sex and lawful/unlawful migration with specific gender/class/racial effects (Cheng and Kim 2014). My research on sex work and migrant women in South Korea and the USA since 1997 has further illuminated some of paradoxes of neoliberalism. While global discourses of 'sex trafficking' have adamantly identified these migrant women in sex work as 'victims of trafficking' (rather than the more silenced category of 'criminals' that many of them end up in), my research showed these women to be migrant and sexual subjects who make the often unsafe journey overseas to pursue their projects of aspiration, unwilling to align themselves with the anti-trafficking agenda of NGOs and the state that are often focused on criminal justice and immigration control (Cheng 2010).

'Sex trafficking': between the technologies of subjection and subjectivity

It is within the neoliberal paradigm of deregulation and risk-taking that Eunjung Kim and I (2014) explore the subjectivity of South Korean women migrating into the US intimate services sector and examine the burgeoning initiatives to combat 'sex trafficking'. Both are products of neoliberal state practices and techniques that span the Pacific. Starting with the 2000 UN Protocol to Prevent, Suppress, and Punish Trafficking in Persons, Especially Women and Children, and the 2000 US Victims of Trafficking and Violence Protection Act, there has been an expansion at both global and local levels to introduce legislation, strengthen law enforcement, and offer victims protection and rehabilitation in order to combat the 'traffic in women'. In South Korea, the Act on the Punishment of Procuring Prostitution and Associated Acts (or the Punishment Act) and the Act on the Prevention of Prostitution and Protection of Victims Thereof (or the Protection Act) were passed by the National Assembly in March 2004. The new laws claimed to protect the human rights of women in prostitution. Yet the crackdowns and arrests that followed spurred a dramatic response in late 2004. For the first time in South Korea's history, thousands of women in prostitution rallied in mass protests, held sit-ins, and picketed in the capital city of Seoul. A dozen or so staged a two-month hunger strike in front of the National Assembly, demanding recognition of their right to live and to work.

From the perspective of the South Korean and the US governments, as well as concerned groups in Korean civil society, women in sex work are potential 'victims of sex trafficking'. The high-profile crackdowns every year since 2004 have reaffirmed the state's commitment to curb 'violations of women's human rights' and restore social and moral order. Yet the laws fall far short of their goal of protecting the human rights of women in prostitution. Those who do not satisfy the conditions that make them victims – such as women who are employed in brothels and room salons despite having no debts, or work independently outside brothels, or manage other sex workers and sell sex at the same time – are considered criminals. Reinforcing the stigma of prostitutes, the new laws offer protection only for 'authentic' victims – those whose sexual purity has been violated.

Nevertheless, the new laws gained South Korea an enviable position in the global competition to combat trafficking. After a one-year spell as a 'Tier 3' country in the first *Trafficking in Persons Report* issued by the US Department of State (2001), indicating its failure to comply 'with the minimum standards of combating trafficking in human beings', South Korea has been a 'Tier 1' country ever since 2002. In fact, in 2005 South Korea was named an example of 'international best practices', as the 2004 laws were cited as a global model for combating trafficking in women and children.

It is therefore interesting to see in the same period a mounting number of reports about Korean women in the USA who either had been trafficked into sexual exploitation or were spa and brothel owners sexually exploiting their compatriots. Since 2005, a few high-profile successful raids against 'sex trafficking' have targeted Korean-run spas and massage parlours. The best known of them was Operation Gilded Cage, which first identified more than 100 Korean women in San Francisco in July 2005, with 27 arrests, and then led to the arrests of 42 Korean women in Dallas (Gambacorta 2007). Many wondered how South Korea, one of the biggest economies in the world, could be among the countries exporting female 'sex slaves' (in the mounting conflation of sex work with sex trafficking and sex slavery in media, NGO, and state responses). In 2007, a Korean NGO with private funding commissioned a global research project on these Korean victims of trafficking. I was part of this project and had to interview Korean women in the sex trade on the East Coast.

Jin was the first woman I interviewed for the project. She was working in a massage parlour in Queen's. She came to the USA after Korean police arrested her in her own home just outside Seoul and charged her for prostitution under the new 2004 anti-prostitution laws, since she was not considered a victim of trafficking and was fined 600 dollars for prostitution. Jin realized that the heavier penalty and police crackdowns meant that she had to look for a way out. She talked about her work in the USA:

Jin:	Some people only come in for table showers, massage, and chats.
Interviewer:	Are they the good clients?
Jin:	No, they are not.
Interviewer:	So who are the good clients?
Jin:	Those people who finish quickly, they are the good ones. Those who have shower and then have sex and go. They are the best.

This response exploded the entire premise of the project and its assumptions about the inherently victimizing nature of sexual labour for women. Those who demand sex rather than conversations are the good clients – if they finish quickly, get themselves cleaned before having sex, and leave immediately after sex. Jin situated sex squarely within a repertoire of labour performance, along with other physical and emotional work, and identified sex as more efficient ('quick') in providing return to her labour. She made between $11,000 and $22,000 per month. Together with the other 58 interviewees from the USA, Australia, Japan and Korea interviewed for the project, Jin refused to identify as a victim of trafficking. Furthermore, she was critical of the anti-trafficking law enforcement efforts and humanitarian interventions that claimed to protect their 'human rights'. Jin said,

> I am working hard and making money for myself… I am not dependent on the government or my family. I am not harming anyone even though this is not a job to boast about. I don't understand these women's human rights. These activists don't understand us. They are people from good background. I am not saying the anti-prostitution laws are wrong. But do they have to go so far?

In light of stories like Jin's that I have repeatedly encountered in my research on migrant sex workers since 1997, I have come to see the global anti-trafficking initiatives as they have taken shape in the twenty-first century as part of neoliberal governance, and 'sex trafficking' as a discursive device for managing illicit sex and unlawful migration with specific gender, class, and racial effects. I have proposed, with Eunjung Kim, to understand Jin's struggles in terms of the effects of neoliberalism as a set of three paradoxes, specifically its a/morality, its de/politicization of risks, and its non/humanitarianism (Cheng and Kim 2014).

Paradox 1 is neoliberalism's assumption of the guise of amorality by affirming an instrumental rationality and market competitiveness, while promoting a conservative sexual agenda that buttresses the family, the market, and the state. In Korea, with the 2004 laws, prostitution is no longer a problem of sexual morals and 'fallen women', but an issue of women's human rights and 'prostituted women'. To protect the 'rights' of women in prostitution, the state supports a network of women's NGOs to help 'prostituted women' through 'self-sufficiency' programmes like access to formal education (mostly for young women) and vocational training to clean, cook, drive, and be hairdressers etc. The neoliberal regime presents them with the opportunities to become 'honest workers' who need not depend on the state (through detention or welfare). Yet the discourse of victimization reinforces the moral values of female chastity and the heterosexual family unit, buttressing the moral hierarchy that marginalizes sex workers in the first place.

Paradox 2 involves the depoliticization of social risks and the hyperpoliticization of national security in neoliberal governance. As an ethic of risk-taking is promoted, the social risks of poverty, illness, and unemployment are displaced onto the individual. These Korean women's migration to the USA embodies the neoliberal ethic of risk-taking that justifies the retrenchment of the state from the social sphere, but they then confront the increased state surveillance through border control and criminalization. Activists continue to call for stricter law enforcement to stop trafficking. The emphasis on policing over welfare could be seen in the fact that five times the amount of money was spent on policing than on welfare provision for 'prostituted women' with the introduction of the new anti-prostitution laws 2005 (Women's Development Fund 2006: 6).

Paradox 3 addresses how neoliberal developments create vulnerable populations by increasing disparities in resources and wealth, while at the same time supporting a set of humanitarian responses from the state and the NGO sector. As a result of the structural readjustments that began with Korea's financial crisis in 1997, policies of deregulation, privatization, and labour flexibilization were implemented with significant gender and age effects. According to OECD statistics, Korea has the highest gender wage gap in OECD countries at 40 per cent (OECD 2011). Unemployment is highly gendered: in the 2008 economic crisis, 98 per cent of the jobs cut were held by women, most of them in their 30s. Unemployment disproportionately affects the young: the 20–9 age group made up 40 per cent of the total unemployed population in 2006 (National Statistics Office 2007). Some of these younger women have chosen to work overseas, often unsafely. Anti-trafficking policies and advocacy promote a racialized and sexual agenda that reproduces the social, moral, and global divide between Western, middle-class female advocates and the 'third world women' for whom they advocate (Agustín 2007; Dozema 2001), without addressing the exacerbation of structural inequalities that is compelling certain groups of women and men to opt for risky migration. In other words, these anti-trafficking measures, like many other humanitarian 'solutions' we see around the world today, symbiotically nourish the problems they are putatively addressing.

It is my observation that these migrant sex workers both embody and contest neoliberal discourses. Even though they are self-sufficient, self-enterprising women who strategize their immigration and labour as sex workers and refuse to depend on state welfare, they violate the neoliberal ideals of relational sexuality, domesticity, and middle-class femininity. As sexual subjects, they need to be restored through rehabilitation programme ('victims') or penalized by criminal law ('criminals'). Even though the anti-trafficking movement hails women's human rights, justice, and protection, it operates predominantly through the crime frame and reinforces gender, class, and racial inequalities. Migrant sex workers therefore embody the sexual limits of neoliberalism.

A polarization of worlds is thereby created. In South Korea, where prostitution has strong echoes with Japanese colonialism (during which prostitution was legalized) and American occupation (when R&R camps were set up near US military bases), commercial sex has come to signify all that is wrong with gender inequalities, capitalism, and foreign intrusions, while non-commercial sex now bears the mark of freedom, independence, and self-determination. The sovereignty of the zone of privacy – in distinction from the public and commercial sphere – now serves as 'a model for freedom or liberty' (Berlant 2002: 117).

The sanctity of the private realm has been constructed in two decades of challenges to a range of sexuality-related criminal laws in Korea, leading to the recognition of rape (including marital rape) in place of 'crime against chastity', and the decriminalization of seduction as well as adultery. These legal changes attest to a liberalization of sexuality that bespoke increasing gender equality, recognition of sexuality as a private matter, and the withdrawal of state intervention from private lives. Both women and men are considered capable of exercising their sexual self-determination right – that is, except for women in sex work.

Sex for money has come to capture the legal imagination of what Gayle Rubin called 'bad sex' regardless of consent. Consent is impossible in prostitution because it's about sex for money, and 'debauched' women's consent does not count. Gayle Rubin has pointed out that 'Within the law, consent is a privilege enjoyed only by those who engage in the highest-status sexual behaviour. Those who enjoy low status sexual behaviour do not have the legal right to engage in it' (Rubin 1984: 168). In the neoliberal sex hierarchy, sex between consensual partners means sex free from monetary exchange, and therefore private and an expression of the self-determination. Sex for money violates the ideal of free will and love, immediately qualifying it as a public issue because it is the epitome of unfreedom.

Gayle Rubin's seminal idea of the sex hierarchy 'grants virtue to the dominant groups, and relegates vice to the underprivileged' (ibid.: 153). The historically shifting divide between good and bad sex has been shaped by ongoing debates about 'where to draw the line'. And the line now lies with explicit economic transaction for sex. Previously criminalized sexual transgressions outside the marital context such as seduction and adultery have moved out of the purview of criminal law, while prostitution has moved front and centre to embody 'bad sex'. Cheng and Kim (forthcoming) emphasize that it is the explicit transfer of money that marks sex work because intimate relations have always been embedded in different forms of economic transactions, as Zelizer has eloquently argued (2005). The law thus comes to embody the 'hostile worlds and separate spheres' (ibid.) understanding of the rigid boundaries of intimate social relations and economic transactions. Sex work thereby becomes what Gayle Rubin called the 'erotic DMZ' [demilitarized zone] (Rubin 1984: 152): the barricade against sexual chaos, family ruins, national demise and other unknown tragedies.

Conclusion

The right for same-sex couples to get married and have families like 'everyone else' has been celebrated as a measure of sexual progressiveness in the twenty-first century. For some, however, such jubilation was premature and, in fact, reproduces some of the fundamental inequalities in neoliberal structures. On the one hand, such celebration neglects the heteronormativity and the system of privileges that remain embedded in the institution of marriage (Warner 1999; Health 2013), in ways that continue to marginalize same-sex couples and alternative intimacies. On the other, the jubilation endorses the expansion of state powers in *both* conferring legitimacy and criminalizing forms of sexual beings and sexual practices, such as abortion and sex work as profoundly antithetical to ideals of equality and freedom.

This short chapter demonstrates that neoliberal transformations reshape ideas and ideals about the self and erotic life, marriage and the family, that are fundamental to changing regimes of governance including citizenship, national security, and global order. While neoliberalism variously presents itself as nonpolitical (Duggan 2002) and amoral (Brown 2006), it is necessary to understand the heteronormative and homonormative currents in neoliberal sexual politics. I further invoke the concept of the 'sexual limits of neoliberalism' as a way to expose the moral and sexual prescriptions of this new sexual order, through a case study of 'sex trafficking' between South Korea and the USA. In doing so, this chapter raises questions about the making of a 'neoliberal sex hierarchy', the notion of consent and free will, and the structures of inequalities and unfreedom that it sustains.

References

Adam, B. 2005. Constructing the Neoliberal Sexual Actor: Responsibility and Care of the Self in the Discourse of Barebackers. *Culture, Health & Sexuality*, 7.4: 333–46.

Agustín, L. 2007. *Sex at the Margins: Migration, Labour Markets and the Rescue Industry*. London and New York: Zed.

Amuchastegui, A., and Parrini, R. 2012. Sexuality, Identity, and Citizenship in Contemporary Mexico, in Aggleton, P., and Parker, R., eds. *Routledge Handbook of Sexuality, Health and Rights*. London: Routledge: 370–8.

Berlant, L. 2002. The Subject of True Feeling: Pain, Privacy and Politics, in Brown, W., and Halley, J., eds. *Left Legalism/Left Critique*. Durham, NC: Duke University Press: 105–33.

Berlant, L., and Warner, M. 1998. Sex in Public. *Critical Inquiry*, 24.2: 547–66.

Bernstein, E. 2007. *Temporarily Yours: Intimacy, Authenticity, and the Commerce of Sex*. Chicago: University of Chicago Press.

Bourdieu, P. 1986. The Forms of Capital, in Richardson, J., ed. *Handbook of Theory and Research for the Sociology of Education*. New York: Greenwood: 241–58.

Brown, W. 2006. American Nightmare: Neoliberalism, Neoconservatism, and De-democratization. *Political Theory*, 34.6: 690–714.

Cheng, S. 2010. *On the Move for Love: Migrant Entertainers and US Military in South Korea*. Philadelphia: University of Pennsylvania Press.

—. 2013. Embodying the Sexual Limits of Neoliberalism. Scholar & Feminist Online 11(1–2). Retrieved from http://sfonline.barnard.edu/gender-justice-and-neoliberal-transformations/embodying-the-sexual-limits-of-neoliberalism/

Cheng, S. and Kim, A. (forthcoming) Virtuous Rights: Violence, Morality and Woman's Sexuality in Korea, in Miller, A. and Roseman, M. eds. *Beyond Virtue and Vice: The (mis)use of the criminal law to regulate gender sexuality and reproduction*. Stanford, CA: Stanford University Press.

Cheng, S., and Kim, E. 2014. Paradoxes of Neoliberalism: Migrant Korean Women and 'Sex Trafficking'. *Social Politics*, 13.3: 1–27.

—. Forthcoming. Virtuous Rights: Violence, Morality, and Women's Sexuality in Korea, in Roseman, M., and Miller, A., eds. *Using Criminal Law to Regulate Gender, Sexuality and Reproduction: Human Rights Perspectives*. Philadelphia: University of Pennsylvania Press.

Dean, J. 2008. Enjoying Neoliberalism. *Cultural Politics*, 4.1: 47–72.

Dozema, J. 2001. Ouch! Western Feminists 'Wounded Attachment' to the 'Third World Prostitute'. *Feminist Review*, 67: 16–38.

Duggan, L. 2002. The New Homonormativity: The Sexual Politics of Neoliberalism, in Castronovo, R., and Nelson, D., eds. *Materializing Democracy: Toward a Revitalized Cultural Politics*. Durham, NC, and London: Duke Univesity Press: 175–94.

Farrer, J. 2010. A Foreign Adventurer's Paradise? Interracial Sexuality and Alien Sexual Capital in Reform era Shanghai. *Sexualities*, 13.1: 69–95.

Foucault, M. 1979[1976]. *The History of Sexuality Volume 1: An Introduction*. London: Allen Lane.

—. 2008. *The Birth of Biopolitics: Lectures at the College de France, 1978–1979*. Senellart, M., ed. Burchell, G., trans. New York: Palgrave Macmillan.

Gambacorta, D. 2007. Busted – for 19th Time. *Philadelphia Daily News*, 19 January.

Green, A.I. 2013. *Sexual Fields: Toward a Sociology of Collective Sexual Life*. Chicago, IL: University of Chicago Press.

Grewal, I. 2006. 'Security Moms' in the Early Twentieth-Century United States: The Gender of Security in Neoliberalism. *Women's Studies Quarterly*, 34.1 and 2: 25–39.

Hakim, C. 2010. Erotic Capital. *European Sociological Review*, 26.5: 499–518.

Health, M. 2013. Sexual Misgivings: Producing Un/Marked Knowledge in Neoliberal Marriage Promotion Policies. *The Sociological Quarterly*, 54: 561–83.

Jameson, F. 1991. *Postmodernism, or, the Cultural Logic of Late Capitalism*. Durham, NC: Duke University Press.

Kinsman, G. 1996. 'Responsibility' as a Strategy of Governance: Regulating People Living with AIDS and Lesbians and Gay Men in Ontario. *Economy and Society*, 25.3: 393–409.

Laclau, E., and Mouffe, C. 2001. *Hegemony and Socialist Strategy: Towards a Radical Democratic Politics*. London: Verso.

Lemke, T. 2001. The Birth of Bio-politics: Michel Foucualt's Lecture at the College de France on Neoliberal Governmentality. *Economy and Society*, 30.2: 190–207.

National Statistical Office. 2007. *Labor Force Participation Rate by Age*. Seoul: National Statistical Office. Retrieved from http://www.donga.com/fbin/output?n=200705300352

OECD. 2011. LMF1.5: Gender Pay Gaps for Full-time Workers and Earnings Differentials by Educational Attainment. *OECD Family Database*. Retrieved from http://www.oecd.org/social/family/database

Pecheny, M., and de la Dehesa, R. 2013. Sexuality and Politics in Latin America: An Outline for Discussion, in de la Dehesa, R., and Parker, R., eds. *Sexuality and Politics: Regional Dialogues from the Global South Volume I*: 96–135. Retrieved from http://www.sxpolitics.org/sexuality-and-politics/volume1.html

Read, J. 2009. A Genealogy of Homo-Economicus: Neoliberalism and the Production of Subjectivity. *Foucault Studies*, 6: 25–36.

Rubin, G. 1984. Thinking Sex: Notes for a Radical Theory of the Politics of Sexuality, in Vance, C.S., ed. *Pleasure and Danger: Exploring Female Sexuality*. London: Pandora: 267–319.

Siddiqui, S. 2015. Abortion Measure in Human Trafficking Bill Shows Republican Focus Unchanged. *The Guardian*. Retrieved from http://www.theguardian.com/world/2015/mar/20/abortion-measure-human-trafficking-bill-republicans

US Department of State. 2001. *Trafficking in Persons Report 2001*. Washington, DC: Department of State.

Warner, M. 1991. Fear of a Queer Planet. *Social Text*, 29.1: 3–17.

—. 1999. *The Trouble with Normal: Sex, Politics, and the Ethics of Queer Life*. Cambridge: Harvard University Press.

Women's Development Fund. 2006. *The General Report of the Women's Development Fund for the Year 2005*. Seoul: Women's Development Fund.

Zelizer, V. 2005. *The Purchase of Intimacy*. Princeton, NJ: Princeton University Press.

20

HEALTH AND THE EMBODIMENT OF NEOLIBERALISM

Pathologies of political economy from climate change and austerity to personal responsibility

Matthew Sparke

Neoliberalism is commonly understood in terms of the expanding global influence of disembodied market forces and rationalities. However, unlike the invisible hands and competitive calculations it unleashes on the world, neoliberalism's implications for health are neither intangible nor abstract. Instead, they are materially embodied in ways that are deeply consequential for life and death (Navarro 2007). Evoked in book titles such as *The Deadly Ideas of Neoliberalism, Dying for Growth, Sickness and Wealth, Infections and Inequalities, Pathologies of Power, Blind Spot*, and, in the aftermath of the 2008 financial crisis, *The Body Economic: Why Austerity Kills*, neoliberalism and associated forms of inequality, austerity and precarity have been tied by health scholars to a vast variety of embodied suffering, disease-vulnerability and low life expectancy right across the planet (Rowden 2009; Kim *et al.* 2000; Fort *et al.* 2004; Farmer 2001, 2005; Keshavjee 2014; Stuckler and Basu 2013). Rallying against these lethal links, a gathering of the World Social Forum in Tunis in 2015 recently concluded that today's global crises in health, health services and social protection are 'in fact the consequence of neoliberal politics globally' (WSF 2015). Meanwhile, amid all the crises, individuals are also now routinely told that their health is simply their own responsibility, a form of resilience that will only endure if they invest in it with the same individualistic and entrepreneurial prudence that is the trademark of personalized neoliberalism more generally (Brown and Baker 2012). As a result, all sorts of embodied health challenges – hunger and obesity being two especially physical examples – are repeatedly recoded as personal management problems even as they embody neoliberal socio-economic developments in society at large (Carney 2015; Guthman 2009).

How then can we better theorize the processes through which neoliberalism becomes embodied in health? While the ill-effects of neoliberal policies and practices have been spreading across borders like an infectious outbreak, neoliberalism is clearly not a biological disease agent itself. Even if it is conceptualized as an epidemic in terms of transnational health impacts, its extraordinarily diverse sequelae do not constitute a singular medical syndrome (Schrecker and Bambra 2015). The etiologies of illness involved are extremely complex, multi-causal and as geographically uneven as they are historically and economically interconnected (Labonté *et al.* 2009). Whether it is the global consequences of the cutbacks in health care caused by neoliberal austerity, or the impact of business deregulation, privatization and user fees introduced in national neoliberal reforms, or the everyday destabilization of communities caused by increasing income inequalities, social insecurity and environmental deterioration, the varieties of experiences, processes and time-space scales to consider are extremely heterogeneous. And then, on the other side of the ledger, there are the health benefits claimed by the privileged for neoliberal innovations in personal risk management, customized medicine, medical tourism and pharmaceuticals – benefits that also sometimes come with increased risks for others such as organ donors and experimental subjects recruited for drug trials in poor countries (Parry *et al.* 2015; Sparke 2014). Across such a wide range of economic, political and social life, 'neoliberalism' – the term – means many different things. Thus before proceeding here to offer a survey of research on the health outcomes that can be diagnosed as embodiments of neoliberalism, this chapter begins by first unpacking what the term means and how we can best theorize its ties to health.

Defining neoliberalism in relation to health

Put most simply, neoliberalism names a way of governing capitalism that emphasizes liberalizing markets and making market forces the basis of economic coordination, social distribution, and personal motivation (Sparke 2013). At a macro scale these developments can be seen as comprising 'neoliberal governance', a set of governmental norms including privatization, business deregulation, and trade liberalization, that reconstitute politics in the shape of the market and repurpose the state as an entrepreneurial actor that governs through proliferating public–private partnerships in the interests of business classes and global investors (Brown 2015; Harvey 2005). At a more intimate scale of personal behaviour it becomes 'neoliberal governmentality', a suite of practices in which individuals across a much wider set of social classes are enlisted into becoming competitive agents who invest in their human capital as entrepreneurs and who reimagine the meaning of their lives, citizenship and individuality – including their personal health – as calculating consumers constantly comparing metrics of ownership, mobility and social ranking (Brown 2015; Dardot and Laval 2013; Lemke 2001). And at once enabling and mediating developments across these different scales, neoliberalism is also a set of economic-turned-political ideas: ideas (like von Hayek's view of health as just another consumer choice) that keep evolving as adaptive and protean yet hegemonic common-sense about market norms and necessities, and ideas that thereby continue to inspire both the macro policies and micro practices of neoliberalization in different ways in different places (Gaffney 2014; Mirowski 2013; Peck 2010). All these accounts of neoliberalism are useful, but, as has been widely cautioned (including by many of the authors cited above), each one risks turning the term into a singular and seemingly inevitable metanarrative when divorced from attention to the historical-geographical circumstances in which neoliberal ideas and discourses actually shape assemblages of neoliberal governance and governmentality (Ong 2006; Sparke 2006; Springer 2012). This is precisely where studying neoliberalism in terms of embodiment becomes so critical, offering a way of coming to terms with how all the global-to-local processes of neoliberalization come together materially to condition and, too often, to shorten and diminish human life.

Not surprisingly, scholars of health have already led the way in reconceptualizing neoliberalism in terms of embodiment. They are not all necessarily informed directly by the account of illness as ecosocial embodiment offered by epidemiologist Nancy Krieger (2001, 2005; but see Birn *et al.* 2009). All sorts of other ecologies and 'epidemiologies of inequality' have been charted as well (Heggenhougen 2005): some stressing the ties between ill-health and the high in-country inequalities created by neoliberal reform (Wilkinson and Pickett 2009; De Vogli, Schrecker and Labonté 2013); others surveying the severe constraints placed on poor country primary health care, health services and, more recently, on health systems strengthening by the structural adjustments and neoliberal austerity imposed by international finance and its political representatives (Birn and Dmitrienko 2005; Gloyd 2004; Kim *et al.* 2000; Pfeiffer and

Chapman 2010); others highlighting in turn the complex biosocial mechanisms through which everything from dam-building to user fees, curtailed drugs programmes, and other structural adjustments materialize as structural violence on the poor (Farmer 2005; Farmer *et al.* 2013); and yet others identifying the particular routes through which poor people's bodies, blood and biological material have been turned into new molecular frontiers for capitalist growth amid the crises and speculative leaps of neoliberal globalization (Cooper 2008; Crane 2013; Rajan 2007). These varied epidemiologies are informed in turn by varied analyses of the pathways through which neoliberalization comes to be embodied. Some stress the transfer mechanisms of neoliberal ideas through international financial institutions, free trade deals and NGOs (Labonté and Schrecker 2007; Rowden 2009; Keshavjee 2014). Others emphasize the class interests and policy reforms of neoliberal governance, including health services privatization (Navarro 2007; Schrecker and Bambra 2015; Schwiter *et al.* 2015). And yet others address the prudential risk-management practices of neoliberal governmentality, whether as they are practiced by consumers of personalized medicine in privileged contexts (Brown and Baker 2012; Lupton 2015), or as they are extended, however unevenly and incompletely, to aid enclaves of therapeutic citizenship in desperately poor contexts (Ngyuen 2010).

The main focus in what follows is on the pathways that can be addressed in terms of *conditionalization*, including under this heading the diverse developments through which neoliberalism in macro political-economic governance has become embodied in various forms of premature mortality and morbidity. Given limited space, less attention is paid here to the various forms of personalized *responsibilization* through which more micro modes of neoliberal governmentality have come to be embodied in individual experiences of risk and biomedical self-management. However, by way of a conclusion, the last part of the chapter points to how both *conditionalization* and *responsibilization* are increasingly coming together to shape contemporary global health *formation*: the formation of a field of research, intervention and outcomes in which we see micro neoliberal innovations in personalized health risk management frequently being advanced as answers to the destructive legacies of macro neoliberal structural adjustment. It is a field in which neoliberal market failures are at once acknowledged and contested even as neoliberal assumptions still strongly shape the ways that corrective counter-measures to the legacies of neoliberal structural violence are imagined, assessed and defended (Kenworthy 2014; Mitchell and Sparke 2016). But to understand the global health problems in poor countries that corrective global health interventions are designed to address we first need to come to terms with the ways in which embodied experiences of health have been structured by neoliberal conditionalization.

Neoliberalization as global political-economic conditionalization

Last year, our imperfect world delivered, in short order, a fuel crisis, a food crisis, and a financial crisis. It also delivered compelling evidence that the impact of climate change has been seriously underestimated. All of these events have global causes and global consequences, with serious implications for health. They are not random events. Instead, they are the result of massive failures in the international systems that govern the way nations and their populations interact. In short: they are the result of bad policies.... In far too many cases, economic growth has been pursued, with single-minded purpose, as the be-all, end-all, cure-for-all. The assumption that market forces could solve most problems has not proved true.

(Margaret Chan 2009)

She did not use the word neoliberalism itself, but, in 2009, in one of the most critical speeches ever made by a Director General of the World Health Organization, Margaret Chan delivered a damning diagnosis of the effects of neoliberal policy-making on health outcomes around the world. At the centre of the 'bad policies' she targeted for critique in this way was the single-minded pursuit of economic growth, and her subsequent references to globalization, market forces, and trade liberalization indexed, in turn, wider neoliberal developments as the underlying causes of the widening global crises. Coming on the heels of the 2008 global financial crisis, Dr Chan thereby summed up a widespread realization that the neoliberal norms tied to market-led global growth were creating massive problems of inequality, volatility and precarity. 'Something,' she said, 'has gone horribly wrong.'

Dr Chan's diagnosis was by no means just a rhetorical response to a bad year. It built upon a comprehensive assessment of the WHO's own Commission on the Social Determinants of Health, which had already reached similar conclusions collected together in a report that was published in 2008 before the full scope of the global financial crisis even became clear (WHO 2008). 'Social injustice is killing people on a grand scale,' announced this report (ibid.: 26). And, as well as presenting voluminous data to buttress their critique, the commissioners also sought to chart some of the pathways of causal connection linking high mortality and morbidity around the world to the structural force of neoliberal policies and associated economic imperatives. The report also did not use the term 'neoliberalism'. It only showed up once in a reference to an online paper on uneven health outcomes and neoliberalism in Africa (republished as Bond and Dor 2007). But as they endeavoured to describe the market-made and market-mediated 'structural drivers' that set the conditions in which people 'are born, grow, live, work, and age', and as they documented how these political-economic forces are experienced and thus embodied as ill-health, the commissioners effectively underlined a form of conditionalization linked to globalization that others would clearly recognize as neoliberalization. 'This toxic combination of bad policies, economics, and politics', they argued, 'is, in large measure, responsible for the fact that a majority of people in the world do not enjoy the good health that is biologically possible' (WHO 2008, 26).

Irrespective of the terminology used, one of the most useful lessons of the analyses offered by the WHO chief and the 2008 WHO report on the social determinants of health is their focus on the processes of *conditionalization* through which global structural forces become embodied in health outcomes. 'Conditionalization' is a useful term to employ here for two reasons. First of all, it indexes the many indirect ways through which neoliberalization around the world has set the basic conditions in which people strive to live their everyday lives. Conditioning connects in this way to vital processes of social reproduction, as well as communicating as a verb – 'to condition' – how living conditions, in turn, become embodied in people's health. Inequality, financial volatility, and the so-called 'race to the bottom' tendencies associated with the relentless global competition for investment and jobs are all important aspects of neoliberal health conditioning in this respect, as too are the massive challenges of climate change, pollution, and food and water insecurity, all of which have been further exacerbated by market liberalization and associated efforts to attract and accommodate business interests globally. More directly, the second reason for using the term 'conditionalization' is that it also points to the very specific neoliberal policies known as 'conditionalities' comprising the rules imposed on poor countries around the world by the IMF, World Bank and US Treasury Department as conditions for support with debt management from the debt crises of the 1980s onwards. Also known as the 'Washington Consensus', the rules of conditionality – rules that included privatization, trade liberalization, financial deregulation, austerity, cuts to health programmes, user fees for health services, cuts to food and fuel subsidies, and diverse experiments in export-led development – constituted the main components of the so-called Structural Adjustment Programmes or SAPs administered by the three agencies based in Washington, DC. These same SAPs have subsequently become the subject of a powerful set of critical studies documenting the structural violence and suffering that structural adjustment imposed on societies across the global South, violence and suffering that has, in turn, been embodied in a whole series of diminished health outcomes (Pfeiffer and Chapman 2010). Let us now examine these contextual and structural patterns of health conditionalization in more detail, starting with the most generalized and global conditioning affect of all: namely, climate change.

Neoliberalism and the contextual conditioning of health

Climate change is viewed by many health scholars as 'the biggest global health threat of the 21st century' (Costello *et al.* 2009). Even if the ties to neoliberalization are not always noted, the health risks of climate change can also, in turn, be examined as being increased and intensified by neoliberal developments globally (Goodman 2014). The freeing-up of market capitalism has undoubtedly freed-up additional carbon as gas and put it straight into the atmosphere, creating the basic conditioning effect – the greenhouse effect – needed to create anthropogenic climate change. The liberalization in neoliberalization takes on a whole new meaning in this regard. As Naomi Klein puts it, 'the liberation of world markets, a process powered by the liberation of unprecedented amounts of fossil fuels from the earth, has dramatically sped up the same process that is liberating Arctic ice from existence' (Klein 2014: 20–1). These liberalization links noted, it would be mistaken simply to blame neoliberalism alone for climate change. The Keynesian welfare-state capitalism of the *pre*-neoliberal West was itself the world's greatest greenhouse gas generator until market-led globalization brought developing countries into the club of big carbon emitters. Looked at like this over longer time-spans, economic development based on energy supplied largely in the form of fossil fuels was always going to lead to the greenhouse effect. Neoliberalism has undoubtedly accelerated the process and enabled recent phenomena such as fracking and tar sands exploitation by blunting government regulation of energy corporations and legitimating new norms for extractive development (Finewood and Stroup 2012; Preston 2013). But, many other older aspects of global development have been contributing to carbon build-up for far longer.

Pre-neoliberal pollution noted, when it comes to how climate change impacts human health, and how societies might mitigate or adapt to the dangers, neoliberalism makes a very big difference indeed (Fieldman 2011). As Klein underlines, 'we have not done the things that are necessary to lower emissions because those things fundamentally conflict with deregulated capitalism' (Klein 2014: 18). Mitigation has thereby been repeatedly mitigated, leading to a series of dead-ends in global climate negotiations from Kyoto to Copenhagen to Cancún to Durban (Bond 2012a). The same economistic appeals to the inevitability of market logics that have helped to naturalize neoliberal globalization have also helped in this way to make shifts away from carbon-intensive energy production seem impossible to political elites. As a result, whatever worries endure about climate change are generally transformed into new market-friendly and market-mediated 'adaptive' opportunities through developments such as carbon credit markets, weather derivatives, patented climate-ready crops and public forest land grabs privatized as carbon sinks (Bond 2012b; Cooper 2010; Dempsey and Robertson 2012). Thus the dominant neoliberal response to climate change has been to focus on the depoliticizing development of so-called resilience, turning market tools and techniques for risk management into new climate adaptation products for those who can afford to invest in insurance and insulation from the most health-threatening implications of climate change (Bracking 2015; Felli 2015; Gilbertson and Reyes 2009; MacNeil and Paterson 2012; Parr 2015). And far from the centres of financialized climate adaptation, the bodies of the poor are simultaneously left vulnerable under neoliberalism to the floods, storms, desertification, droughts, heat waves, and disease outbreaks that the International Panel on Climate Change describes as being created or worsened by climate change, as well as all the associated shortages of reliable food and secure water supplies (IPCC 2014).

The hazardous contexts for human life created by deregulated risk-evading industry impose risks on human health through more than just greenhouse gas emissions (e.g. Mudu 2009). There are many other health-damaging ecologies ensuing from the ways in which the neoliberal competition to attract and retain investment globally has led to diminished controls over corporate activities ranging from power generation to farming, fishing, logging and mining to chemical and pharmaceutical production to the management of food and workplace safety. Ocean acidification, aquifer depletion, overfishing, biodiversity loss, and carcinogenic chemical exposure all threaten the ecological systems that support the reproduction of healthy human bodies, and they are all intensified by neoliberalization (Castree 2010). Similarly, the 'race to the bottom' on (and for) factory floors created by the creation of the increasingly neoliberal global division of labour (i.e. competitive, contingent and highly precarious 'flexible' labour markets) has led to the sidelining of occupational health and safety protections as well as to the undermining of unions and the historic health and pension benefits secured by collective bargaining (Mogensen 2006). The deaths and injuries of workers through hyper-exploitation, suicide, factory fires, building collapses and other industrial disasters are, in this sense, just the most egregious embodiments (indeed disembodiments in some cases) of more pervasive tendencies towards increasing work-related stress, vulnerability and ill-health (Baram 2009; Ngai and Chan 2012). Most vulnerable of all, the precarious sub-citizenship of poor migrant workers in today's global economy – many of them forced into migration by the impact of neoliberalization on domestic economies – leads directly to broken bodies, painful insecurities and, as Megan Carney puts it in her powerful analysis of the food insecurity facing women migrants on both sides of the US–Mexican border, unending hunger (Carney 2015; see also Holmes 2013).

While many workers suffer injury and deprivation in labouring to produce food and other consumer goods and services for the global economy, another way in which workers' bodies come to embody neoliberal precarity is as consumers too. The free market deregulation of corporate activity and other policy shifts away from social welfare protection put populations at increased health risks by exposing consumers, and especially poor and poorly educated consumers, to an increasingly inescapable 'corporate-consumption complex' (Freudenberg 2014). Freudenberg's name for this hybrid assemblage of business interests and networks also underlines – with its echo of the military-industrial complex – the huge importance of public health research into the dangers posed to consumers by industries ranging from alcohol, tobacco and fast food to firearms, petrochemicals and pharmaceuticals (Mercille 2015; Wipfli and Samet 2009). With the increasing globalization of the corporate consumption complex we also return to a form of public health conditionalization highlighted by WHO Director Chan in her account of the rising chronic disease and non-communicable disease dangers associated with market-led development. Unfortunately, though, such structural conditioning is simultaneously being downplayed in individualistic approaches to behavioural responsibilization in public health, approaches that focus on cultivating healthy consumer 'choices' and which constitute a form of neoliberal governmentality that is now travelling transnationally to many of the same consumers being chased by global corporations themselves (Cairns and Johnston 2015; Hughes Rinker 2015; Ormond and Sothern 2012; Parry 2013; Sun 2015). While these micro neoliberal approaches have been theorized as bringing opportunities for customized medicine at the molecular level, and while it is suggested that this new biological citizenship comes without the racial exclusions and other biases of national twentieth-century biomedicine, empirical studies show that they often contribute to personal shame and guilt that leads in turn to the denial of structural conditioning and related forms of vulnerability and dependency (compare Rose 2007, with Eliason 2015; LeBesco 2011; Peacock *et al.* 2014; and Wehling 2010). Thus, insofar as this personalized neoliberal individualization of risk management obscures the socialized neoliberal production of heath risks, it presents what Sara Glasgow and Ted Schrecker usefully refer to as 'the double burden of neoliberalism' in global public health (Glasgow and Schrecker 2015).

Notable among the long list of chronic disease dangers posed by neoliberal development is the lethally embodied obesity threat that corporate food and drink industries have managed to turn from a non-communicable disease into something that is communicated very easily through the trade ties of market-led globalization, branded beverages and fast food. As a recent critic of 'Coca-Cola capitalism' has put it, the sweetened drink industries effectively turn bodies everywhere into silos of high-fructose corn syrup, setting off epidemics of adult-onset diabetes and heart disease that are spreading across borders even further (and in more enduring embodied ways) than acute infectious diseases such as SARS and flu (Elmore 2015). Meanwhile, biological researchers of flu itself indicate that the way neoliberalization has led to more intensive factory farming around the world is now also helping to create the perfect ecology for breeding newly virulent and pathogenic influenza viruses (Wallace 2009). Freed by deregulated meat production and corporate globalization, these viruses are increasingly able to become more lethal and more globally mobile than influenzas of the past because of the spread of so-called 'confined animal feeding operations' or CAFOs and associated global supply chains. These operations stack sick and healthy animals so close to one another that the lethality of viruses is no longer held in check by the evolutionary need (for viruses) to keep one host alive long enough to move on to another. And often located near the millions of factory workers they are raised to feed, the super-vulnerable animal hosts can, in turn, quickly pass on the newly lethal viruses to the super-exploited humans labouring at the heart of the neoliberal world's globalized commodity chains (Davis 2005). It should be noted, in this respect, that one political danger that haunts responses to new infectious disease outbreaks more generally is the cultural formation of what Paul Farmer calls 'geographies of blame': geographies of blame that pathologize certain regions and countries as disease origins without ever examining the global ties that account for disease emergence and cross-border spread (Farmer 2006). Farmer found this to be the pattern with the erroneous blaming of Haiti as the origin of HIV/AIDS entry into North America, and it was a pattern that repeated again with the H1N1 influenza outbreak, when Mexico and Mexicans were blamed for bringing a form of swine-flu into the USA when it already had origins tied to factory farming right across the free trade consolidated North American Free Trade Agreement (NAFTA) region (Sparke and Anguelov 2012). To understand how free trade agreements tend to condition health outcomes more generally, we need now to turn to the ways in which conditionalization works through the structural force of neoliberal rule-setting.

Neoliberalism and the structural conditioning of health

NAFTA, CAFTA, MERCOSUR, the EU and other regional trade agreements (such as the new TPP or Trans Pacific Partnership), along with the global trade rules to which all signatories of the World Trade Organization commit, illustrate another set of more legal mechanisms through which neoliberal governance comes to have ill-effects on health, even though the economic growth associated with trade liberalization has also been advertised as beneficial for life expectancy in immodest arguments that 'wealthier is healthier' (Pritchett and Summers 1996; for a critique, see Sparke 2009). Three main neoliberalization mechanisms account for the negative health outcomes associated with free trade agreements: namely, competition, harmonization and monopolization. The cross-border competition that is deliberately unleashed by the removal of tariff barriers is what enables industry to move to where the costs of production are cheapest while still exporting back into formerly protected markets. It is the resulting market efficiencies so eulogized in economic theory that simultaneously force the 'race to the bottom' and deunionization developments noted above, with FDI and new factories moving to where labour is cheaper, where workers have fewer health and safety protections, and where environmental protections are less stringent or less well-enforced.

Beyond the well-known competition dynamics, the other two neoliberalization mechanisms of harmonization and monopolization also commonly have health-damaging implications too. As the WHO 2008 report on the social determinants of health underlined, this is principally because of the ways in which they shrink the policy space for government and undermine national regulatory authority, something that more recent reviews have also shown to be key in linking trade agreements with unhealthy nutrition too (Friel *et al.* 2013). Harmonization is the legal jargon used to describe how trade agreements work to remove non-tariff barriers to trade. Such barriers can include environmental, food and road safety rules that have been established in one country but which are viewed by businesses in other countries as barriers to entering the foreign market. Bans on carcinogenic pesticides and GMOs, controls on pollution, demands for dolphin- and turtle-safe fishing, and rules about vehicle safety checks have all been targeted for removal and reduction in this way by trade lawyers arguing that they constitute non-tariff barriers to trade (Wallach and Woodall 2004). And then there are the monopolization possibilities, which are also expanded by free trade agreements. Specifically, these involve the increasing extension of patent rights over intellectual property through regimes such as the WTO's TRIPs (Trade Related Aspects of Intellectual Property) agreement. Drug companies argue these intellectual property (IP) monopoly protections provide the necessary profit-making incentive to justify new investments in new drug research and development. But as the WHO 2008 report made very clear, IP protections simultaneously strait-jacket national governments, shrinking the policy space in which the free or subsidized provision of generic medicines can be advanced, and frequently pre-empting the possibility of issuing compulsory licences for essential medicines (Craddock 2007; Heywood 2002). This pattern of pre-emption, it should be underlined, persists despite the 2001 Doha Declaration and other declarations that developing countries ought to be able to opt out from the WTO's enforcement of patent monopolies and intensifying neoliberal harmonization (Alessandrini 2009; Beall and Kuhn 2012; Owen 2014).

Conditionalization through debt management, so-called debt-relief, and global financial discipline has been still more damaging to health and health systems than trade rules. The SAP conditionalities imposed in the 1980s on highly indebted countries as the condition of debt rescheduling and debt management by the IMF, World Bank and associated international financial institutions (such as the Inter-American Development Bank) share much with the conditionalization effects of neoliberal trade agreements. But SAPs shrank the policy space of governments still more directly and dramatically by imposing sweeping neoliberal discipline from the outside, including direct demands to cut health services, cap the wages for health care workers, and impose user fees for medicines as well as more general structural adjustments ranging from austerity to privatization, trade liberalization, and the further expansion of IP protections. The timing and impact of the SAP conditionalities in the 1980s was all the more devastating for two further reasons. First of all, they coincided with the global pandemic of HIV/AIDS as well as with other re-emerging infectious diseases such as TB. Due to a set of complex biosocial feedback dynamics (that included conditionality's cutbacks in medical services), SAP conditionality ended-up becoming biologically embodied in the spread and, in the case of drug resistant TB, the molecular evolution of the diseases themselves (Farmer *et al.* 2013; Hickel 2012; Shahmanesh 2007). Second, the timing of the SAPs in the 1980s was such that they simultaneously changed the trajectory of governmental health policies globally. They came into effect soon after governments from all over the word had pledged in 1978, at Alma Ata, to work for 'Heath for All' by 2000, a plan to expand access and improve health outcomes that rested fundamentally on commitments by national governments to invest in systems of universal primary health care (PHC). And it was this plan and the associated governmental commitments that were effectively ripped to shreds by the neoliberal conditionalities of structural adjustment (Rowden 2009).

Due to its double-acting combination with the other complex biological and political forces, it remains extremely difficult to evaluate SAP conditionality as a stand-alone independent variable in epidemiological analysis (yet see Cornia *et al.* 2009; and Stuckler *et al.* 2008). Nevertheless, pathways of causal connection between structural adjustment and increased morbidity and mortality rates have still been charted with care, including: through the connective thread of increasing in-country inequality (Kawachi and Wamala 2007; Hammonds and Ooms 2004); through their political-economic intersection with social unrest, *coups d'état*, and drug wars, as well as free trade deals (Kim *et al.* 2000); through the links between conditionality and the vulnerability of women and children (De Vogli and Birbeck 2005; Hickel 2012); through the conditionality-compensating NGO-ization and resulting fragmentation of health systems (Pfeiffer 2003); and through the impacts of privatized health services and user fees – which, as Salmaan Keshavjee (2014) shows in his extraordinary account of the impact of Bamako initiative ideas in Tajikistan, travelled from the context of SAP conditionality in Africa to other parts of the world through NGO networking (see also Foley 2009; McCoy *et al.* 2008).

The conditionality of neoliberal structural reforms continues into the present in a variety of ways. SAPs have been replaced by so-called Poverty Reductions Strategy Papers (PRSPs). These supposedly involve more country 'ownership', but they still often impose wage ceilings and other service-reducing rules in the health sector under the policy guidance of the IMF (Ooms and Schrecker 2005). Likewise, the debt relief announced by European government leaders at Gleneagles in 2005 is still being managed by the IMF in ways that impose neoliberal conditions on recipients (Sparke 2013). And, after the financial crises of 2008, Europe, in turn, has come to be haunted itself by the spectre of debt-based discipline, casting a shadow of austerity across the continent and notably increasing suicides and morbidity in countries such as Greece where people's everyday lives have come to embody the structural violence of overnight neoliberalization at its most extreme (De Vogli, Marmot and Stuckler 2013; Stuckler *et al.* 2015; and Stuckler and Basu 2013). Then, at the World Bank, hopes that Jim Yong Kim (the co-editor of *Dying for Growth* and co-founder of Partners in Health) would be a transformative president who would deliver global health from the damaging legacies of conditionality are now also haunted by concerns that the Bank will go on conditioning the meaning and management of 'delivery' in neoliberal ways (Bond 2012c). This connects, in turn, to wider concerns about how contemporary global health efforts to respond to the health-damaging legacies of macro neoliberal reform look set to be compromised by micro neoliberal governmentality going forward.

Conclusion: neoliberalism and global health formation

Global health is a field in formation – an academic field, an epidemiological field of health metrics measurement and mapping, a field of institution-building and policy-making, a field comprised of diverse health interventions and outcomes, and a moral field of humanitarian concern and action. It is also a field where multiple forms of neoliberalization and its discontents come together. As such, global health makes manifest how the ideas, practices and policies of neoliberalism relate and respond to one another, as well as how their outcomes are unevenly embodied.

For the same reasons, it is a field where we need to be especially sensitive to how neoliberaliza-tion as a set of embodied processes is also often deeply contradictory as well as context-contin-gent. The contradictions created in the complex middle ground between a) *global health responses to neoliberal legacies* and b) *neoliberal global health responsibilization* are numerous and here only the briefest of overviews is possible.

At the broadest level of global health policy the switch away from the old neoliberal logic of 'wealthier is healthier' is clear (Sparke 2013). Many policy-makers around the world have come to the same conclusion as Margaret Chan, and argue that it is a grave mistake to believe that economic growth on its own will lead directly to healthier human lives. But neoliberal market logics and language nevertheless still orchestrate the replacement refrain which can be roughly summarized as 'healthier is wealthier'. More specifically it is becoming clear that the dominant global policy-making response to ill-health in poor communities around the world is to argue that they need investments in their health so that they can integrate and grow in the global economy. In the micro-economic calculations and neoliberal prudentialism of this newly domi-nant view, and in the words of *The Lancet 2035* report, the bottom-line is that: 'There is an enormous payoff from investing in health. The returns on investing in health are impressive' (Jamison *et al.* 2013: 1). One particularly prominent co-author of this 2035 report was former US Treasury Secretary Lawrence Summers, the former proponent also of 'wealthier is healthier', and a Washington official closely allied with the old Washington Consensus conditionalities. To the extent that Summers is now advocating the financialized investment logic of healthiness leading to wealthiness, it seems useful to name this new orthodoxy a New Washington Consen-sus. As critics have pointed out in *The Lancet*, the investment languages and logics, the associated double standards, and the inattention to injustice are all continuous with the World Bank neo-liberalism of the 1990s, and, just as with the old Washington Consensus, there is clearly much global dissensus with the new orthodoxy by those who care about health as a basic human right (Chiriboga *et al.* 2014). But, given the association with huge new global institutions that are actually implementing the return on investment logics (e.g. the Global Alliance for Vaccines and Immunizations), and given the allied influence of new public–private–philanthropic (3P) part-nerships – including most prominently those funded out of Washington State by the Gates foundation – the nomenclature of the New Washington Consensus helps name the assemblage of the new neoliberal prudentialism within global health (Mitchell and Sparke 2016).

At another more material level, often indeed at the level of micro-biological material itself, critics have also highlighted the extractive logics of global health research as examples of neolib-eral embodiment too. Johanna Crane (2013) has shown in this way how much grant-funded research in global health simultaneously relies on the health inequalities bequeathed by earlier rounds of neoliberal conditionalization in order to provide opportunities for western scholars to advance their careers as responsibilized researchers securing results-based support in the com-petitive grant cycles organized by 3P governmentality. When we turn to the patchiness and unpredictability of the resulting interventions, other scholars suggest further that health citizen-ship is neoliberalized anew in poor country settings where access to health services increasingly depends on having the right fundable disease in the right place at the right time, as well as being able to tell stories about recipiency and recovery that can travel (Nguyen 2010). 'What results', argues Nora Kenworthy (2014: 12), 'is a vast disruption of political landscapes already marred by earlier incursions of colonialism, development, and structural adjustment. Recipiency replaces entitlement; biopolitics and the administration of promises replace the social contract.'

Of course, none of these developments should take away from acknowledging the many global health improvements that are outlined in the 2035 report as a prelude to the authors' prediction of a great global health *convergence* around longer, healthier lives for all by 2035. But the repeated return of neoliberal responsibilization in global health investment practice, and the way the associated outcomes complicate the basic effort to respond to the legacies of prior eras when neoliberalism conditioned health so damagingly now look set to diminish the chances of real health for all. For the same reason, they also, in turn, underline the importance of the concluding call for solidarity and organization in the Tunis World Social Forum statement noted at the very start of this chapter. This was not an actuarial health convergence predicated on investment logics and languages. Instead, and in conclusion, it called for a new health rights activist convergence to tackle the many social determinants of ill-health globally, including all the diverse neoliberal determinants described in this chapter. 'Let us strengthen the actions for a convergence,' the statement read, 'with movements acting on social determinants of health, such as climate, trade, austerity, debt, working conditions, and gender equality' (WSF 2015).

References

Alessandrini, D. 2009. Making the WTO 'More Supportive of Development'? The Doha Round and the Political Rationality of the WTO's Development Mission. *Law, Social Justice and Global Development Journal*, 1: 2–17.

Baram, M. 2009. Globalization and Workplace Hazards in Developing Nations. *Safety Science*, 47.6: 756–66.

Beall, R., and Kuhn, R. 2012. Trends in Compulsory Licensing of Pharmaceuticals Since the Doha Declaration: A Database Analysis. *PLoS Med*, 9.1: 129.

Benatar, S.R. 2005. Moral Imagination: The Missing Component in Global Health. *PLoS Medicine*, 2.12: 1207–10.

Benatar, S.R., Gill, S., and Bakker, I. 2011. Global Health and the Global Economic Crisis. *American Journal of Public Health*, 101.4: 646–53.

Biehl, J.G. 2007. Pharmaceuticalization: AIDS Treatment and Global Health Politics. *Anthropological Quarterly*, 80.4: 1083–126.

Birn, A.E., and Dmitrienko, K. 2005. The World Bank: Global Health or Global Harm? *American Journal of Public Health*, 95.7: 1091–2.

Birn, A., Yogan, P., and Holtz, T. 2009. *Textbook of International Health: Global Health in a Dynamic World.* New York: Oxford University Press.

Bond, P. 2012a. *Politics of Climate Justice: Paralysis Above, Movement Below.* Scottsville: University of Kwazulu-Natal Press.

—. 2012b. Emissions Trading, New Enclosures and Eco Social Contestation. *Antipode*, 44.3: 684–701.

—. 2012c. Why Jim Kim Should Resign From the World Bank. *Counterpunch*, 16 April. Retrieved from http://www.counterpunch.org/2012/04/16/why-jim-kim-should-resign-from-the-world-bank/

Bond, P., and Dor, G. 2007. Uneven Health Outcomes and Political Resistance Under Residual Neoliberalism in Africa, in Navarro, V., ed. *Neoliberalism, Globalization, and Inequalities: Consequences for Health and Quality of Life.* New York: Baywood: 345–67.

Bracking, S. 2015. The Anti-Politics of Climate Finance: The Creation and Performativity of the Green Climate Fund. *Antipode*, 47.2: 281–302.

Brown, B., and Baker, S. 2012. *Responsible Citizens: Individuals, Health and Policy under Neoliberalism.* London: Anthem Press.

Brown, W. 2015. *Undoing the Demos: Neoliberalism's Stealth Revolution.* New York: Zone.

Cairns, K., and Johnston J. 2015. Choosing Health: Embodied Neoliberalism, Postfeminism, and the 'Do-Diet'. *Theory and Society*, 44.2: 153–75.

Carney, M. 2015. *The Unending Hunger: Tracing Women and Food Insecurity Across Borders.* Berkeley: University of California Press.

Carter, E. 2015. Making the Blue Zones: Neoliberalism and Nudges in Public Health Promotion. *Social Science & Medicine*, 133: 374–82.

Castree, N. 2010. Neoliberalism and the Biophysical Environment: A Synthesis and Evaluation of the Research. *Environment and Society*, 1.1: 5–45.

Chan, M. 2009. Steadfast in the Midst of Perils. Keynote address at the 12th World Congress on Public Health Istanbul, Turkey. Retrieved from http://www.who.int/dg/speeches/2009/steadfast_midst_perils_20090428/en/

Chiriboga, D., Buss, P., Birn, A.E., Garay, J., Muntaner, C., and Nervi, L. 2014. Investing in Health. *The Lancet*, 383.9921: 949.

Cooper, M. 2008. *Life as Surplus: Biotechnology and Capitalism in the Neoliberal Era*. Seattle: University of Washington Press.

—. 2010. Turbulent Worlds Financial Markets and Environmental Crisis. *Theory, Culture & Society*, 27.2–3: 167–90.

Cornia G.A., Rosignoli, S., and Tiberti, L. 2009. An Empirical Investigation of the Relation Between Globalization and Health, in Labonte, R., Schrecker, T., Packer, C., and Runnels, V., eds. *Globalization and Health: Pathways, Evidence and Policy*. New York: Routledge: 34–62.

Costello, A., Abbas M., Allen A., Ball S., Bellamy R., Friel S., ... and Patterson C. 2009. Managing the Health Effects of Climate Change. *The Lancet*, 373.9676: 1693–733.

Craddock, S. 2007. Market Incentives, Human Lives, and AIDS Vaccines. *Social Science & Medicine*, 64.5: 1042–56.

Crane, J. 2013. *Scrambling for Africa: AIDS, Expertise, and the Rise of American Global Health*. Ithaca, NY: Cornell University Press.

Dardot, P., and Laval C. 2013. *The New Way of the World: On Neo-Liberal Society*. New York: Verso.

Davis, M. 2005. *The Monster at Our Door: The Global Threat of Avian Flu*. New York: New Press.

Dempsey, J., and Robertson, M. 2012. Ecosystem Services: Tensions, Impurities, and Points of Engagement within Neoliberalism. *Progress in Human Geography*, 36.6: 758–79.

De Vogli, R., and Birbeck G.L. 2005. Potential Impact of Adjustment Policies on Vulnerability of Women and Children to HIV/AIDS in Sub-Saharan Africa. *Journal of Health Population and Nutrition*, 23.2: 105–20.

De Vogli, R., Marmot M., and Stuckler D. 2013. Strong Evidence that the Economic Crisis Caused a Rise in Suicides in Europe: The Need for Social Protection. *Journal of Epidemiology and Community Health*, 67.4: 298.

De Vogli, R., Schrecker, T., and Labonté, R. 2013. Neoliberal Globalization and Health Inequalities, in Gabe, J., and Monaghan, L.F., eds. *Key Concepts in Medical Sociology*. London: Sage: 32–6.

Eliason, M. 2015. Neoliberalism and Health. *Advances in Nursing Science*, 38.1: 2–4.

Elmore, B.J. 2015. *Citizen Coke: The Making of Coca-Cola Capitalism*. New York: Norton.

Farmer, P. 2001. *Infections and Inequalities: The Modern Plagues*. Berkeley: University of California Press.

—. 2005. *Pathologies of Power: Health, Human Rights, and the New War on the Poor*. Berkeley: University of California Press.

—. 2006. *AIDS and Accusation: Haiti and the Geography of Blame*. Berkeley: University of California Press.

Farmer, P., Kleinman, A., Kim, J., and Basilico, M. 2013. *Reimagining Global Health: An Introduction*. Berkeley: University of California Press.

Felli, R. 2015. Environment, Not Planning: The Neoliberal Depoliticisation of Environmental Policy by Means of Emissions Trading. *Environmental Politics*, 24.5: 641–60.

Fieldman, G. 2011. Neoliberalism, the Production of Vulnerability and the Hobbled State: Systemic Barriers to Climate Adaptation. *Climate and Development*, 3.2: 159–74.

Finewood, M., and Stroup, L. 2012. Fracking and the Neoliberalization of the Hydro Social Cycle in Pennsylvania's Marcellus Shale. *Journal of Contemporary Water Research & Education*, 147.1: 72–9.

Foley, E. 2009. *Your Pocket Is What Cures You: The Politics of Health in Senegal*. New Brunswick, NJ: Rutgers University Press.

Fort, M., Mercer, M., and Gish, O. 2004. *Sickness and Wealth: The Corporate Assault on Global Health*. Cambridge: South End Press.

Freudenberg, N. 2014. *Lethal But Legal: Corporations, Consumption, and Protecting Public Health*. New York: Oxford University Press.

Friel, S., Hattersley, L., Snowdon, W., Thow, A.M., Lobstein, T., Sanders, D., and Walker. C. 2013. Monitoring the Impacts of Trade Agreements on Food Environments. *Obesity Reviews*, 14.S1: 120–34.

Gaffney, A.W. 2014. The Neoliberal Turn in American Health Care: The Failings of the Affordable Care Act are Rooted in a Long Shift Away from the Idea of a Truly Universal Health Care. *Jacobin*, 15 April. Retrieved from https://www.jacobinmag.com/2014/04/the-neoliberal-turn-in-american-health-care/

Gilbertson, T., and Reyes, O. 2009. Carbon Trading: How it Works and Why it Fails. *Uppsala: Dag Hammarskjöld Foundation Occasional Paper Series*. Retrieved from http://www.carbontradewatch.org/publications/carbon-trading-how-it-works-and-why-it-fails.html

Glasgow, S., and Schrecker, T. 2015. The Double Burden of Neoliberalism? Noncommunicable Disease Policies and the Global Political Economy of Risk. *Health and Place*, 34: 279–86.

Gloyd, S. 2004. Sapping the Poor: The Impact of Structural Adjustment Programs, in Fort, M., Mercer, M., and Gish, O., eds. *Sickness and Wealth: The Corporate Assault on Global Health*. Cambridge, MA: South End Press: 43–54.

Goodman, B. 2014. The Debate on Climate Change and Health in the Context of Ecological Public Health: A Necessary Corrective to Costello et al.'s 'Biggest Global Health Threat', or Co-opted Apologists for the Neoliberal Hegemony? *Public Health*, 128.12: 1059–65.

Guthman, J. 2009. Teaching the Politics of Obesity: Insights into Neoliberal Embodiment and Contemporary Biopolitics. *Antipode*, 41.5: 1110–33.

Hammonds, R., and Ooms, G. 2004. World Bank Policies and the Obligation of its Members to Respect, Protect and Fulfill the Right to Health. *Health and Human Rights*, 8.1: 26–60.

Harvey, D. 2005. *A Brief History of Neoliberalism*. Oxford: Oxford University Press.

Heggenhougen, H.K. 2005. The Epidemiology of Inequity: Will Research Make a Difference? *Norsk Epidemiologi*, 15.2: 127–32.

Heywood, M. 2002. Drug Access, Patents and Global Health: Chaffed and Waxed Sufficient. *Third World Quarterly*, 23.2: 217–31.

Hickel, J. 2012. Neoliberal Plague: The Political Economy of HIV Transmission in Swaziland. *Journal of Southern African Studies*, 38.3: 513–29.

Holmes, S. 2013. *Fresh Fruit, Broken Bodies: Migrant Farmworkers in the United States*. Berkeley: University of California Press.

Hughes Rinker, C. 2015. Creating Neoliberal Citizens in Morocco: Reproductive Health, Development Policy, and Popular Islamic Beliefs. *Medical Anthropology*, 34.3: 226–42.

Hunter, M. 2010. *Love in the Time of AIDS Inequality, Gender, and Rights in South Africa*. Bloomington: Indiana University Press.

IPCC. 2014. *Climate Change 2014: Synthesis Report. Contribution of Working Groups I, II and III to the Fifth Assessment Report of the Intergovernmental Panel on Climate Change*. IPCC: Geneva. Retrieved from http://www.ipcc.ch/report/ar5/syr/ (last accessed 24 October 2015).

Jamison, D.T., Summers, L.H., Alleyne, G., Arrow, K.J., Berkley, S., Binagwaho, A., and Yamey, G. 2013. Global Health 2035: A World Converging within a Generation. *The Lancet*, 382.9908: 1898–955.

Kawachi, I., and Wamala, S. 2007. *Globalization and Health*. Oxford: Oxford University Press.

Kenworthy, N. 2014. Global Health: The Debts of Gratitude. *Women's Studies Quarterly*, 42.1 and 2: 69–85.

Keshavjee, S. 2014. *Blind Spot: How Neoliberalism Infiltrated Global Health*. Berkeley: University of California Press.

Kim, J.Y., Millen, J.V., Irwin, A., and Gershman, J. 2000. *Dying for Growth: Global Inequality and the Health of the Poor*. Monroe: Common Courage Press.

Klein, N. 2014. *This Changes Everything: Capitalism vs the Climate*. New York: Simon & Schuster.

Krieger, N. 2001. Theories for Social Epidemiology in the 21st Century: An Ecosocial Perspective. *International Journal of Epidemiology*, 30.4: 668–77.

—. 2005. Embodiment: A Conceptual Glossary for Epidemiology. *Journal of Epidemiology and Community Health*, 59.5: 350–5.

Kulkarni, S., Levin-Rector, A., Ezzati, M., and Murray, C. 2011. Falling Behind: Life Expectancy in US Counties From 2000 to 2007 in an International Context. *Population Health Metrics*, 9.1: 16.

Labonté, R., and T. Schrecker. 2007. Globalization and Social Determinants of Health: Introduction and Methodological Background, Part 1 of 3. *Global Health*, 3.5: 1–10.

Labonté, R., Schrecker, T., Packer, C., and Runnels, V. 2009. *Globalisation and Health: Pathways, Evidence and Policy*. London: Routledge Press.

LeBesco, K. 2011. Neoliberalism, Public Health, and the Moral Perils of Fatness. *Critical Public Health*, 21.2: 153–64.

Lemke, T. 2001. 'The Birth of Bio-politics': Michel Foucault's Lecture at the Collège de France on Neoliberal Governmentality. *Economy and Society*, 30.2: 190–207.

Lupton, D. 2015. Health Promotion in the Digital Era: A Critical Commentary. *Health Promotion International*, 30.1: 174–83.

MacNeil, R., and Paterson, M. 2012. Neoliberal Climate Policy: From Market Fetishism to the Developmental State. *Environmental Politics*, 21.2: 230–47.

MacKendrick, N.A. 2010. Media Framing of Body Burdens: Precautionary Consumption and the Individualization of Risk. *Sociological Inquiry*, 80.1: 126–49.

Mansfield, B. 2012. Environmental Health as Biosecurity: 'Seafood Choices,' Risk, and the Pregnant Woman as Threshold. *Annals of the Association of American Geographers*, 102.5: 969–76.

McCoy, D., Bennett, S., Witter, S., Pond, B., Baker, B., Gow, J., Chand, S., Ensor, T., and McPake, B. 2008. Salaries and Incomes of Health Workers in Sub Saharan Africa. *The Lancet*, 371.9613: 675–81.

Mercille, J. 2015. Neoliberalism and the Alcohol Industry in Ireland. *Space and Polity*, August: 1–16.

Mirowski, P. 2013. *Never Let a Serious Crisis Go to Waste: How Neoliberalism Survived the Financial Meltdown*. New York: Verso.

Mitchell, K., and Sparke M. 2016. The New Washington Consensus: Millennial Philanthropy and the Making of Global Market Subjects. *Antipode*. 48: 3. http://online library.wiley.com/doi/10.1111/anti.12203/abstract.

Mogensen, V. 2006. *Worker Safety Under Siege: Labor, Capital, and the Politics of Workplace Safety in a Deregulated World*. Armonk: M.E. Sharpe.

Mooney, G. 2012. Neoliberalism is Bad for Our Health. *International Journal of Health Services*, 42.3: 383–401.

Mudu, P. 2009. L'evasione del Rischio: La Produzione Della Dipendenza, in Saitta, P., ed. *Spazi e Società a Rischio, Ecologia, Petrolio e Mutamento a Gela*. Napoli: Think Tanks.

Navarro, V. 2007. *Neoliberalism, Globalization and Inequalities: Consequences for Health and Quality of Life*. Amityville, NY: Baywood.

Ngai, P., and Chan, C.J. 2012. Global Capital, the State, and Chinese Workers: The Foxconn Experience. *Modern China*, 38.4: 383–410.

Nguyen, V.K. 2010. *The Republic of Therapy: Triage and Sovereignty in West Africa's Time of AIDS*. Durham, NC: Duke University Press.

Ong, A. 2006. *Neoliberalism as Exception: Mutations in Citizenship and Sovereignty*. Durham, NC: Duke University Press.

Ooms, G., and Schrecker, T. 2005. Expenditure Ceilings, Multilateral Financial Institutions, and the Health of Poor Populations. *The Lancet*, 365.9473: 1821–3.

Ormond, M., and Sothern, M. 2012. You, Too, Can be an International Medical Traveller: Reading Medical Travel Guidebooks. *Health & Place*, 18.5: 935–41.

Owen, T. 2014. The 'Access to Medicines' Campaign vs Big Pharma. *Critical Discourse Studies*, 11.3: 288–304.

Parr, A. 2015. The Wrath of Capital: Neoliberalism and Climate Change Politics – Reflections. *Geoforum*, 62: 70–2.

Parry, B. 2013. Knowing Mycellf™: Personalized Medicine and the Economization of Prospective Knowledge of Bodily Fate, in Meusburger, P., ed. *Knowledge and the Economy*. Dordrecht: Springer: 157–71.

Parry, B., Greenhough, B., Brown, T., and Dyck, I. 2015. *Bodies Across Borders: The Global Circulation of Body Parts, Medical Tourists and Professionals*. Farnham: Ashgate.

Peacock, M., Bissell, P., and Owen, J. 2014. Dependency Denied: Health Inequalities in the Neo-liberal Era. *Social Science & Medicine*, 118: 173–80.

Peck, J. 2010. *Constructions of Neoliberal Reason*. Oxford: Oxford University Press.

Pfeiffer, J. 2003. International NGOs and Primary Health Care in Mozambique: The Need for a New Model of Collaboration. *Social Science & Medicine*, 56.4: 725–38.

Pfeiffer, J., and Chapman, R. 2010. Anthropological Perspectives on Structural Adjustment and Public Health. *Annual Review of Anthropology*, 39.1: 149–65.

Preston, J. 2013. Neoliberal Settler Colonialism, Canada and the Tar Sands. *Race & Class*, 55.2: 42–59.

Pritchett, L., and Summers, L.H. 1996. Wealthier is Healthier. *The Journal of Human Resources*, 31.4: 841–68.

Rajan, K.S. 2007. *Biocapital: The Constitution of Postgenomic Life*. Durham, NC: Duke University Press.

Rose, N. 2007. *Politics of Life Itself: Biomedicine, Power, and Subjectivity in the Twenty-first Century*. Princeton, NJ: Princeton University Press.

Rowden, R. 2009. *The Deadly Ideas of Neoliberalism: How the IMF has Undermined Public Health and the Fight Against AIDS*. New York: Zed Press.

Schrecker, T., and Bambra, C. 2015. *How Politics Make us Sick: Neoliberal Epidemics*. Basingstoke: Palgrave Macmillan.

Schwiter, K., Berndt, C., and Truong, J. 2015. Neoliberal Austerity and the Marketisation of Elderly Care. *Social & Cultural Geography*, July: 1–21.

Shahmanesh, M. 2007. Neoliberal Globalisation and Health: A Modern Tragedy. *Critique*, 35.3: 315–38.

Sparke, M. 2006. Political Geographies of Globalization (2): Governance. *Progress in Human Geography*, 30.2: 1–16.

—. 2009. Unpacking Economism and Remapping the Terrain of Global Health, in Kay, A., and Williams, O., eds. *Global Health Governance: Transformations, Challenges and Opportunities Amidst Globalization.* New York: Palgrave Macmillan: 131–59.

—. 2013. *Introducing Globalization: Ties, Tensions and Uneven Integration.* Oxford: Blackwell.

—. 2014. Health, in Castree, L.N., Kitchin, R., Paasi, A., Radcliffe, S., Withers, C., eds. *Handbook of Human Geography.* Thousand Oaks, CA: Sage: 684–708.

Sparke, M., and Anguelov, D. 2012. H1N1, Globalization and the Epidemiology of Inequality. *Health & Place*, 18.4: 726–36.

Springer, S. 2012. Neoliberalism as Discourse: Between Foucauldian Political Economy and Marxian Poststructuralism. *Critical Discourse Studies*, 9.2: 133–47.

Stuckler, D. and Basu, S. 2013. *The Body Economic: Why Austerity Kills.* New York: Basic.

Stuckler, D., King, L.P., and Sanjay, B. 2008. International Monetary Fund Programs and Tuberculosis Outcomes in Post-Communist Countries. *PLoS Medicine*, 5.7: e143.

Stuckler, D., Reeves, A., Karanikolos, M., and McKee, M. 2015. The Health Effects of the Global Financial Crisis: Can we Reconcile the Differing Views? A Network Analysis of Literature Across Disciplines. *Health Economics, Policy and Law*, 10.1: 83–99.

Sun, W. 2015. Cultivating Self-health Subjects: Yangsheng and Biocitizenship in Urban China. *Citizenship Studies*, May: 1–14.

Wallace, R. 2009. Breeding Influenza: The Political Virology of Offshore Farming. *Antipode*, 41.5: 916–51.

Wallach, L., and Woodall, P. 2004. *Whose Trade Organization? A Comprehensive Guide to the WTO.* New York: New Press.

Wehling, P. 2010. Biology, Citizenship, and the Government of Biomedicine: Exploring the Concept of Biological Citizenship, in Bröckling, U., Krasmann, S., and Lemke, T., eds. *Governmentality: Current Issues and Future Challenges.* New York: Routledge: 225–46.

WHO. 2008. *Closing the Gap in a Generation: Health Equity through Action on the Social Determinants of Health.* Commission on Social Determinants of Health, World Health Organization. Retrieved from http://www.who.int/

Wilkinson, R., and Pickett, K. 2009, *The Spirit Level: Why More Equal Societies Almost Always Do Better.* London: Allen Lane.

Wipfli, H., and Samet, J.M. 2009. Global Economic and Health Benefits of Tobacco Control. *Clinical Pharmacology & Therapeutics*, 86.3: 272–80.

WSF. 2015. *Final Declaration.* World Social Forum/Forum Social Mondial. Retrieved from http://www.phmovement.org/en/node/9939

21

NEOLIBERALISM AND WELFARE

Julie MacLeavy

The worldwide ascendancy of neoliberalism as a political economic orthodoxy has seen a widespread commitment to the reshaping of social institutions on the model of the market. Across the developed world, and elsewhere, we can trace a series of (often counter-productive) impulses towards deregulation, privatization, and welfare state retrenchment to the growing influence of 'neoliberal' ideas (Peck 2010). Starting in the 1970s and early 1980s, emerging conflicts between the complex of policies we call the welfare state and the current stage of capitalism – in which markets in capital, goods, information, culture and even labour are spread across national borders – have led to calls for the revision of the post-war consensus in which the state's role is to counter the adverse effects of market forces through economic intervention and redistribution (Piven 2015). Influenced by the neoliberal conviction that the state should instead implement strategies that seek to facilitate market activity, parties at either end of the political spectrum have introduced policies that subordinate social policy to the needs of labour market flexibility, aiming to put downward pressure on the social wage and the cost of international production (Jessop 2002). As a result, welfare provision has been transformed. Time limits for financial support have been introduced, and activation requirements designed to mobilize the 'economically inactive' to compete for limited employment positions imposed.

The growing influence of neoliberalism is reflected in the establishment of a market-based approach to social policy, in which welfare programmes are primarily intended to encourage self-reliance rather than seek to ameliorate the condition of oppressed or marginal groups through efforts to equalize life chances or address unemployment. In recent years, this process has been driven by austerity measures involving symbolic cuts to welfare budgets and a broader dismantling of social programmes (MacLeavy 2011). But while emphasis placed on self-sufficiency and individual requirements to work has seen the withdrawal of the state from the poor as far as distribution is concerned (Smith (2007), the implementation of neoliberal work-farism (understood – after Jamie Peck (2001) – to comprise work-based welfare reform) has necessitated concerted state intervention to assist welfare recipients in moving from welfare into employment. This has taken the form of programmes that support prevailing capitalist social relations by mobilizing the unemployed through the introduction of stringent conditionality checks for state support, increased surveillance of welfare recipients' work-seeking behaviours, and the promotion of an anti-welfare ideology that seeks to encourage welfare recipients to assume personal responsibility for systemic problems such as unemployment.

This chapter considers the process of policy development that epitomizes a neoliberalized approach to welfare. It starts by reviewing the decline of the post-war welfare state and the emergence of a market-based approach to social policy. Following this, it establishes what constitutes neoliberalism and the defining features of a 'workfare state' in general terms. Recognizing that keystones of the welfare state as 'safety net' continue to underpin the regulation of local labour markets, it then examines the extent to which neoliberal workfarism is reliant upon ongoing state spending and intervention. Developing an argument first articulated in an edited collection under the title 'Remaking the Welfare State: From Safety Net to Trampoline' (MacLeavy 2010), it considers (1) state strategies that support the flexibilization of the labour market and the maintenance of low-wage work, (2) the mechanisms that ensure the integration of welfare recipients into consumer culture, and (3) the long-standing methods of discipline that coerce people into behaving as market actors. The chapter concludes by contemplating the implications of austerity measures introduced in the aftermath of the 'Great Recession', which articulate and reiterate a neoliberalised approach to the broader political economy.

The decline of the post-war welfare state

For many years, governments of both the right and left have been involved in debates over the best way to deliver public services. Whereas during the post-war period it was widely accepted that state provisioning of infrastructure, health, education and social services was the best way to ensure wellbeing, today markets are understood as a better way of delivering public goods and services because they are associated with competition, economic efficiency and consumer choice. For scholars such as Jamie Peck and Adam Tickell (2002) this express commitment to market (or market-like) rule is understood to transform state strategies, modes of governance and political subjectivities through the destruction and discrediting of Keynesian welfarist and social-collectivist institutions (broadly defined) and the construction and consolidation of neo-liberalized state systems, forms of intervention and regulatory reform. This political shift is predicated on the promotion of a minimalist state infrastructure, which is framed as a reaction to the Keynesian and/or collectivist strategies that prioritized demand-side management at a national scale (e.g. stimulating jobs by encouraging mass production and consumption). It requires the promotion of structural or systemic competitiveness through supply-side policies, which aim to increase labour market flexibility, by putting downward pressure on the social wage and thereby reducing the cost of international production (Jessop 2002). Crucially, it also entails a qualitative shift in welfare provision, whereby welfare is based less on a model in which the state counters the market and more on a model where the state serves the market.

In many western post-industrial nations this shift is observed through a move from flat rate to graduated benefits and from universalism to greater means testing. 'Activation' policies form part of this approach, placing work requirements on welfare recipients as a condition of their benefit payments. In the anglophone model, governments have increasingly promoted individual responsibility through work incentives, welfare disincentives, and the privatization of service provision. The welfare state is no longer viewed as a 'safety net' for people with low or no incomes, but has been restructured to support training and the use of compulsions in relation to welfare-to-work programmes.

In support of this restructuring process, a free-market ideology has been marshalled, alongside a (moral) discourse of welfare that warns of the dangers of welfare 'dependency'. This builds on conservative discourse that presents welfare recipients as 'naturally' deficient in the characteristics that make responsible citizens and good workers, and frames welfare as a system in need of reform, not least for its propensity to harbour joblessness and inactivity in the lowest socio-economic sectors of society. This anti-welfare rhetoric is frequently directed at the discursive (and material) body of the young/single/minority-ethnic/inner-city mother, unable to support herself and her children through 'a lack of gainful employment' – a claim which has been expanded and used in some instances to depict the welfare system itself as an enlarged maternal system, spawning offspring that are not only a drain on the public purse, but who also constitute a threat to society through their links with rising crime, juvenile delinquency and myriad other social problems (England 2008).

Rhetoric of this kind points towards the embedding and extension of neoliberalism through the imposition of a new form of governance and is said to signal the end of the post-war welfare state (Powell and Hewitt 1998). In contrast to this claim, however, the ascendancy of a set of neoliberal processes, rules and institutions requires a form of statecraft that retains rudiments of the Keynesian welfare state. Flexible labour markets are underwritten by (conditional) welfare provisions. Social cohesion is maintained through means-tested payments that enable citizens with no or low incomes to participate in society as low level consumers. Furthermore, in spite of frequent allusions to the establishment of 'active citizenship' through the restructuring of social benefits to support training and enterprise, the use of compulsions in relation to state-supported labour market programmes acts to create 'docile bodies' who discipline themselves in the name of individual initiative and responsibility, in a move that parallels the individual self-regulation that was previously achieved through Fordist organizational forms and management practices (see Fraser 2003; Hartman 2005).

Although neoliberal discourse emphasizes the retrenchment of state social provision to make space for market regulation, the neoliberal approach sees social programmes being not simply retrenched, but (also) redeployed. Delivered in varying modes of conditionality, they aim to transform the subjectivities and identities of citizens through the promotion and enforcement of market-compliant behaviour (Larner 2000; Peck 2010). In the case of welfare, this involves new programmes geared towards getting people to accept personal responsibility for getting by in a time of low economic growth, high unemployment and rising poverty, and poses a particular challenge to the sections of the population that are most frequently reliant on state support. This includes younger people with low or obsolete skill sets, families with small children and/or elderly dependents trying to reconcile work with caring responsibilities, and women working in part-time posts or building portfolio careers (MacLeavy 2011).

Neoliberalism and the workfare state: key features

Neoliberalism is a distinctive political economic theory that, at broad level, proposes that 'human well-being can be best advanced by liberating individual entrepreneurial freedoms and skills within an institutional framework characterized by strong private property rights, free markets and free trade' (Harvey 2005: 2). Based on the monetarist theories and research of Milton Friedman (1962; Friedman and Schwartz 1963), it places primary emphasis on the maintenance of (macro)economic stability as opposed to the Keynesian goals of full employment and the alleviation of poverty. Its political philosophy builds on Friedrich von Hayek's (1944) critique of the interventionist state and asserts that the only legitimate role of the state is to safeguard individual and commercial liberty, and strong private property rights. As such, it advocates a 'rolling back' of the state and the creation of a society governed by market mechanisms. While the market is traditionally defined through an absence of state intervention, it is acknowledged that markets are not naturally occurring phenomena, but need to be made, steered and policed. To this extent, neoliberalism maintains a self-contradicting theory of the state as laissez-faire policies cannot be implemented without government intervention. The mantra of 'less state' is thus illusory as neoliberalism compels rather than reduces state action (O'Neill 2004: 259), albeit in different ways to that of more openly interventionist forms of political economy.

In recent times, the principles of marketization, privatization and deregulation associated with neoliberalism have been extended across policy arenas in the global North and global South. Emanating from the political projects of Thatcher and Reagan, this form of statecraft has progressed the qualitative reordering of state–economy relations through an experimental repertoire of policies. The ubiquity of market-orientated politics positions neoliberalism as universal, yet neoliberalism is not a monolithic or entirely homogeneous entity. While recognizing that neo-liberalism is variegated (Peck and Tickell 2002), constellations of core values can be identified in anglophone versions of this political economic phenomenon: as Wendy Larner (2003) notes, there are different variants of neoliberalism, each of which result from the general assertion that market mechanisms are the optimal way of organizing all exchanges of goods and services.

Wendy Brown (2006), for instance, identifies the particular formulation of neoliberalism in the USA, which accords full citizen rights only to those who are autonomous individuals, whereby autonomy is construed as independence from the state or other institutions. This idealized conception of the American citizen with the ability to provide for their own needs and service their own ambitions whether as welfare recipients or workers in ephemeral occupations devalues or misplaces the role of social relationships in promoting autonomy. This produces a culture in which political problems are transformed into individual problems with market solutions. As neoliberalism produces the citizen on the model of the entrepreneur and consumer, it simultaneously makes citizens available to a heavy degree of governance and authority (ibid.: 705). The state is remade on the model of the firm, with entrepreneurial and managerial functions, and this, in turn, facilitates and legitimates significant state intervention in personal, social and economic affairs.

Yvonne Hartman (2005), commenting on the Australian context, notes a contradictory commitment to a libertarian economic philosophy combined with morally conservative view of family, in addition to an appeal to nationalism. The privatization of public assets, the outsourcing and contracting-out of government services (through competitive tendering), and the private provision of economic and social infrastructure have helped to replace state interventionism with market-guided regulation. At the same time, reforms to the Australian welfare system have privileged better-off two parent families, while expanding the scale and scope of regulation for single parents without an employment wage, and asylum seekers (Hancock 2002). These covert forms of government intervention comprise policies (such as mutual obligation and work-for-the-dole), which attempt to construct particular subjectivities on which to impose market disciplines (Dean 2002).

In the UK, neoliberalism has been articulated with social democratic principles and given rise to a philosophy of governance that embraces a mix of market and interventionist philosophies. This starts from the premise that, as relatively closed national economies no longer exist, there is little scope for national-level economic management; however, if decisions are left purely to market forces, then failures will result. Thus, it follows that 'a new democratic state' is needed, in which progress and market innovations are promoted alongside supply-side objectives to permit the pursuit of equity and the improvement of efficiency in contemporary circumstances (Giddens 1998; see also MacLeavy 2007, 2011).

In each of these different national contexts, then, neoliberal discourse tends to castigate welfarism as economically inefficient as well as morally dubious. With competitive mechanisms seen to herald the key means through which states can achieve economic progress, systems that 'discourage' competition in the labour market through the provision of a basic level of income to the unemployed are seen as problematic and in need of revision. Altering this, there is now a 'tough love' approach in which people are 'helped and hassled' back to work (*The Guardian* 2010). Whereas welfare has negative connotations of inactivity, workfare embraces a more punitive approach that emphasizes self-sufficiency and individual requirements to work. The role of civil society has also been recast through the establishment of a new relationship between citizens and the state, in which there is an expectation of increased participation in the socio-political realm: in neighbourhoods, communities and complementary arenas of local governance.

Workfare as a framework of welfare provision

Accounts of the transition from Keynesian welfarism to neoliberal workfarism should note the extent to which the workfare state is subtended by the continued operation of the welfare state as a safety net. While significant, this trajectory of development ought not to frame the welfare state as immobile and thus outmoded, but rather should be used to unpack the different forms of welfare that have emerged in the contemporary period. Indeed, there has been fundamental yet complex restructuring of welfare across western post-industrialized nations, through, for instance, the reduction of cash benefits to the unemployed and the 'underemployed' (who do not qualify for unemployment insurance but instead are eligible to receive means-tested welfare payments), as well as the introduction of new labour market measures that are subordinate to market forces (e.g. the increased private sector involvement in the delivery of state services). As Hartman (2005: 61) observes,

> [al]though welfare may now be leaner and meaner for some, the welfare state has not shrunk; rather different forms of welfare have arisen coupled with new modes of administration and underpinned by a theoretical rationale that has shifted from entitlement to obligation.

There is a need, then, to make visible the extent to which Keynesian welfarism underwrites neoliberalism. In the present era of post-Fordist globalization, welfare has three key functions: first, it underwrites the peripheral labour market by ensuring a minimum level of income to those switching between welfare and work in line with fluctuations in the economy and changing personal circumstances; second, it allows those with low or no pay to maintain (at least) an impression of social integration through consumer activity, because welfare payments are discretely made and blame is allotted at the level of public debate; third, it provides education and training to help (re)connect welfare recipients to work that legitimates a level of (self)regulation, which is reminiscent of the social control established through the disciplinary apparatuses of the post-war period (for instance, social services, public health measures, and therapeutic practices) (on this, see Foucault 2003).

Regulating the labour market

The welfare states of the anglophone or market-based model of capitalism (including Australia, Canada, New Zealand, the UK and the USA) are fundamentally labour market institutions, which condition the rules and dynamics of the job market, particularly with regard to low-wage employment relationships (Piven 1999). As 'liberal welfare regimes', they have long attempted to restrict government intervention in the market by targeting welfare assistance to those in greatest need. This reflects an underlying assumption that the market will be able to provide for most, if not all, who are willing to participate in it. As Gøsta Esping-Andersen (1990: 26) observes, '[b]enefits cater mainly to a clientele of low-income, usually working-class, state dependents' and those on welfare are often stigmatized as unproductive and lacking in work ethic. In recent years, although anti-welfare rhetoric has increased, state provisions have continued to support the (low-wage) labour market through a combination of welfare payments made to those on low or no wages and tax breaks introduced to ensure that 'work pays' for people in minimum-wage jobs (Brewer 2001).

With deregulation of the labour market creating a periphery of workers who engage in precarious employment, the provisions of the welfare state might even be becoming more rather than less important (Hartman 2005). Low-wage workers cannot usually survive on what they earn from work alone, so welfare provision is crucial in allowing this end of the labour market to flourish. Through the granting of tax credits through earned income, government buttresses the working poor and furthers the establishment of a dual labour market which is comprised of a core of stable well-paid jobs, and a periphery of precarious employment (ibid.). This indicates that flexible labour markets, which are seen to have been established through laissez-faire economic policy, are not naturally occurring phenomena, but instead must be constructed, regulated, and policed (Peck 2002). This requires an interventionist strategy to underwrite the operation of contingent labour markets and to socialize the working poor for flexible employment (Peck and Theodore 2000).

The normalization of the flexible labour market and worker insecurity is achieved through the undermining of union organization and experimentation in active welfare and workfare programming. As Peck (2002) outlines in the US context, this re-regulation intensifies competitive pressures by expanding the labour pool, keeping wage inflation low, and facilitating an increased rate of worker exploitation. With the macro-orientation of policy towards full 'employability' rather than full employment, a concordant privileging of individual responsibility over social rights is achieved through the pastoral activities of government operated on individuals so that they work upon and monitor themselves (for example, through further education and training and/or participation in welfare-to-work schemes).

Maintaining social cohesion

Workfarist policies are promoted on the basis of a three-fold political economic critique of the welfare state. This contends that long-term unemployment depletes skills and damages motivation, adversely affecting future chances of getting a job; that people remain unemployed for longer than is necessary because of the level of benefit payments that are made available to them; and that reconnecting people to the labour market through mandatory welfare-to-work programmes will put downward pressure on wage inflation, thereby permitting the economy to operate at a higher level of employment (Peck 2001). Workfare, by contrast, seeks to (re)attach people to the labour market through temporary work placements; to restructure benefit payments in order to remove the 'welfare trap' that effectively sanctions limited non-participation in the labour market; and, through welfare retrenchment, to induce and enforce new rules of engagement with the paid labour market that will animate latent market forces (Peck 2002).

This neoliberal politics is invoked through public discourse, which articulates the doctrines of the individual and the free market (Brown 2006). In the UK, for example, a commentary on welfare reform has accompanied the explicit focus on paid work in government policy. 'Help to Work' is the latest in a line of government schemes – including the 'Work Programme', the 'Community Activity Programme', and 'Mandatory Work Activity' – intended to improve welfare recipients' job prospects (through training, rehabilitation and work experience) and deliver socio-economic gains (by improving expertise and efficiency in the labour market and improving local community arenas through voluntary contributions).

Further legislative reforms of the benefits system have also been implemented in the context of very high levels of economic inactivity through sickness and disability (including those suffering from mental illness). Indicative of this, the UK's 'Employment and Support Allowance' was introduced to bring existing social insurance and social assistance schemes for people incapable of work through long-term illness or disability under the rubric of a single system. This has helped to tighten the basis on which people's capacity for work is assessed, with fit-for-work tests to decide how a person's illness or disability affects their ability to work and new arrangements for supporting their (re)entry to the labour market, through personal action plans and financial sanctions for failure to engage in work-related activity.

The logic of welfare-to-work is complex and hybrid in nature, comprising a problematic combination of 'human capital development' and 'work first' approaches (Dean 2006). While policy rhetoric signals the empowerment of claimants, their preparation and ownership of action plans and the utilization of untapped skills, the strong emphasis on compulsion, participation and the application of benefit penalties or sanctions for non-compliance indicates a different notion of responsibility that obscures the state's failure to meet people's non-material needs, including their need to work. Thus, as job insecurity becomes increasingly common for those who do contingent work or work in low-paid service positions, the requirement for all to look for work, train for work or face sanctions is applied alongside cash transfers to sustain those at the bottom end of the labour market. In contrast to rhetoric about 'hand ups' not 'hand outs', such payments allow recipients to get by and get on at the more mundane level of everyday life, in spite of the scapegoating that appears at the level of public debate. In this sense, workfarist policies seek to promote social cohesion by helping to reduce the income inequalities between workers and the unemployed, and allowing the latter group to conform to societal norms as citizen consumers (for a useful discussion of the building blocks of social cohesion, see Forrest and Kearns 2001).

Preserving social control

By making welfare payments conditional upon recipients' willingness to seek employment, undertake training and/or volunteer for work in the local community, workfare programmes enforce the civic responsibilities of citizens to sustain themselves. This assault on the spectre of dependency culture is intended to draw individuals into accepting responsibility for aspects of social protection once governed by the welfare state by codifying rules of conduct (such as independence and a preference for paid employment to welfare benefits as a source of income) and making them the basis for government intervention (Dean 2002). As poverty is associated with individual irresponsibility or the failure to manage risk, work assumes the form of a moral obligation. This moral obligation entails compliance with the social order in the workfare state era.

The fostering of a shared sense of morality and common purpose is an important element of social control. While anti-welfare discourse operates to legitimate an increased level of control over welfare recipients' lives, it simultaneously ensures that expectations regarding citizen entitlements will be dampened. Thus measures are introduced to make the receipt of welfare payments more onerous for some groups, with broad public support (Hartman 2005). In the anglophone model, the state promotes a general shift away from a culture of state support of the economy, business and society to a new ethos of self-help, enterprise and individual initiative. This occurs through the provision of self-esteem training and job-search skills in a quasi-market. Such quasi-markets of public and private service providers are intended to educate the unemployed into exercising choice in relation to their own economic development. They are further used to promote the neoliberal assumption that the delivery of welfare services and benefits through the market is not only efficient, but also in the interests of individual liberty in the sense of giving the welfare 'consumer' the freedom to choose.

To make certain that choice is exercised at a micro-level, the UK's welfare-to-work programmes, by way of illustration, allot a case manager to individuals to ensure they enrol for courses and training activities tailored to meet their 'specific needs'. This micro-regulation is at variance with the interpretation of welfare reform as a kind of market deregulation, because it reveals that declining support for social welfare is part of a punitive policy development in which the state has a substantial and active role (Beckett and Western 2001). In the wake of Victorian penal policies that reflected the individualist, laissez-faire philosophy of free-market capitalism, the post-war welfare state was built on the assumption that government intervention could and should reform and integrate the socially marginal (Garland 1985). This has since been undermined by new conceptions of social marginality that imply the need for more exclusionary and security-minded responses to marginal groups and individuals. Hence, there is a shift in governance towards workfarist programmes that emphasize the undeserving or un-reformable nature of welfare recipients that tend to stigmatize and separate them from society as a whole. These programmes feature less generous welfare benefits and more punitive anti-crime policies as a result of political discourse about individual responsibility for social problems, and simultaneously welfare programmes and the 'culture of dependency' as important causes of crime (Beckett and Western 2001).

Once again, however, this transformation should not be interpreted simply by counterposing an interventionist to a non-interventionist state. As Nikolas Rose and Peter Miller (1992) make clear, neoliberal political initiatives entail the adoption of a range of devices, which seek both to create a distance from the formal institutions of the state and other social actors, and to act upon policy subjects 'at a distance'. This ought not to be viewed as the disintegration of the disciplinary apparatuses of the post-war period, but as a transformation in the mechanisms of control that are pivotal to the governance of social life. An array of organizational forms and technical methods now impel citizens to conform to particular codes of behaviour through the utilization, instrumentalization and mobilization of techniques and agents other than the 'state' (for example, the calculative personnel of the jobcentre that impel individuals within that locale to work out 'where they are', calibrate themselves in relation to 'where they should be' and devise ways of getting from one stage to the next).

Workfare in the aftermath of the 'great recession'

The expansion of work-based welfare reform in the context of rising unemployment and deep recession poses a challenge to the promotion of self-provisioning, prudentialism and an individualist ethic of self-responsibility. In contrast to the buoyant economic climate of late 1990s, when the first workfare programmes were established in the UK, financial-economic conditions in the years following the global financial crisis have posed a discrete challenge to the neoliberal philosophy of a smaller (welfare) state, the primacy of the market, and the renewed significance of labour flexibility. With businesses shedding jobs and households struggling to pay debts, more skilled workers are coming onto the job market with the effect that the most excluded have to compete even harder to get work. As Richard Johnson, managing director of welfare-to-work for Serco Civil Government (a UK organization that works with government to deliver front-line public services) says: 'Think of it like a conveyor belt: as unemployed numbers rise, those at the front of the queue get pushed lower down' (quoted in *The Guardian* 2008). Against this background, the renewed commitment to a market-based approach to social policy is geared towards changing people's expectations of the labour market, rather than creating jobs or changing the lives of the poor. Its objective is to make low-paid, non-unionized jobs socially acceptable by declaring those who refuse to take such posts as lacking in basic civic virtues, including the propensity for self-help.

Because workfare sidesteps the low rewards for many low-skilled and part-time workers, its ambition to 'solve the wider problems associated with worklessness' (Iain Duncan Smith, former UK Secretary of State for Work and Pensions, quoted in *The Globe and Mail* 2010) is particularly significant for young people, women and those with low skills. It also affects those for whom participation in the formal labour market is difficult because of the ongoing challenges of balancing work and family life. Middle-class parents struggling to reconcile work and caring responsibilities suffer a loss of income from lower limits for tax credits, while unemployed single parents face heightened expectations to participate rather than withdraw from the paid labour market while performing care (MacLeavy 2011).

While it is argued that austerity has 'long been part of the neoliberal repertoire' (Peck 2012: 629), the alleged dangers of debts and deficits have been used in the aftermath of the 'Great Recession' to discipline citizens in politically and economically expedient ways. Contra to evidence that workfare fails to increase the likelihood of people finding work (Crisp and Fletcher 2008), there has been little, if any, serious discussion of how job creation can be achieved through deliberate policy measures or the propensity for austerity to increase pressure on the most vulnerable members of society. In the USA, deficit-reduction plans include sharp cuts in tax rates on corporations and the wealthy alongside moves to remove healthcare and nutritional aid for the poor. In the UK, austerity is linked to a desire to reduce the overall size of government and, especially, spending on social insurance, with Prime Minister David Cameron proclaiming that austerity is a means to make the state 'leaner... not just now, but permanently' (quoted in Krugman 2015). In this respect, it seems, the restructuring of contemporary welfare states might actually be accelerated in the context of austerity – at the very point at which the deepening of a market-based approach to social policy is arguably anathema to social cohesion and the wellbeing of the most vulnerable members of society.

References

Beckett, K., and Western, B. 2001. Governing Social Marginality: Welfare, Incarceration and the Transformation of State Policy. *Punishment and Society*, 3: 43–59.

Brewer, M. 2001. Comparing In-Work Benefits and the Reward to Work for Families with Children in the US and UK. *Fiscal Studies*, 22: 41–77.

Brown, W. 2006. American Nightmare: Neoliberalism, Neoconservatism and De-democratization. *Political Theory*, 34: 690–714.

Crisp, R., and Fletcher, D.R. 2008 A Comparative Review of Workfare Programmes in the United States, Canada and Australia. London: DWP. Retrieved from https://www.shu.ac.uk/research/cresr/sites/shu.ac.uk/files/review-workfare-usa-canada-australia.pdf

Dean, H. 2006 Activation Policies and the Changing Ethical Foundations of Welfare. Paper presented at the *ASPEN/ETYI Conference*, Brussels, 20–21 October. Retrieved from core.ac.uk/download/pdf/93498.pdf

Dean, M. 2002. Liberal Government and Authoritarianism. *Economy and Society*, 31: 37–61.

England, K. 2008. Welfare Provision, Welfare Reform, Welfare Mothers, in Cox, K., Low, M., and Robinson, J., eds. *The Sage Handbook of Political Geography*. London and Thousand Oaks, CA: Sage.

Esping-Andersen, G. 1990. *The Three Worlds of Welfare Capitalism*. Cambridge: Polity Press.

Forrest, R., and Kearns, A.J. 2001. Social Cohesion, Social Capital and the Neighbourhood. *Urban Studies*, 38: 2125–43.

Foucault, M. 2003. *Society Must Be Defended*. Macey, D., trans. London: Penguin.

Fraser, N. 2003. From Discipline to Flexibilization? Rereading Foucault in the Shadow of Globalization. *Constellations*, 10: 160–71.

Friedman, M. 1962. *Capitalism and Freedom*. Chicago, IL: University of Chicago Press

Friedman, M., and Schwartz, A.J. 1963. *A Monetary History of the United States 1867–1960*. Princeton, NJ: Princeton University Press

Garland, D. 1985. *Punishment and Welfare: A History of Penal Strategies*. Aldershot: Gower.

Giddens, A. 1998. *The Third Way: The Renewal of Social Democracy*. Cambridge: Polity Press.

Hancock, L. 2002. The Care Crunch: Changing Work, Families and Welfare in Australia. *Critical Social Policy*, 22: 119–40.

Hartman, Y. 2005. In Bed with the Enemy: Some Ideas on the Connections between Neoliberalism and the Welfare State. *Current Sociology*, 53: 57–73.

Harvey, D. 2005. *A Brief History of Neoliberalism*. Oxford: Oxford University Press.

Hayek, F. 1944. *The Road to Serfdom*. London: Routledge.

Jessop, B. 2002. *The Future of the Capitalist State*. Cambridge: Polity Press.

Krugman, P. 2015. The Case for Cuts Was a Lie: Why Does Britain Still Believe It? The Austerity Delusion. *The Guardian*, 29 April. Retrieved from www.theguardian.com/business/ng-interactive/2015/apr/29/the-austerity-delusion

Larner, W. 2000. Neo-liberalism: Policy, Ideology, Governmentality. *Studies in Political Economy*, 63: 5–26.

—. 2003. Neoliberalism? *Environment and Planning D: Society and Space*, 21: 509–12.

MacLeavy J. 2007 The Six Dimensions of New Labour: Structures, Strategies, and Languages of Neoliberal Legitimacy. *Environment and Planning A*, 39: 1715–34.

—. 2010. Remaking the Welfare State: From Safety Net to Trampoline, in Birch, K., and Mykhnenko, V., eds. *The Rise and Fall of Neoliberalism: The Collapse of an Economic Order?* London: Zed.

—. 2011. A 'New Politics' of Austerity, Workfare and Gender? The UK Coalition Government's Welfare Reform Proposals. *Cambridge Journal of Regions, Economy and Society*, 4.3: 355–67.

O'Neill P.M. 2004. Bringing the Qualitative State Back into Economic Geography, in Barnes, T., Peck, J., Sheppard, E.S., and Tickell, A., eds. *Reading Economic Geography*. Oxford: Blackwell: 257–70.

Peck, J. 2001. *Workfare States*. New York: Guilford Press.

—. 2002. Labor, Zapped/Growth, Restored? Three Moments of Neoliberal Restructuring in the American Labor Market. *Journal of Economic Geography*, 2: 179–220.

—. 2004. Geography and Public Policy: Constructions of Neoliberalism. *Progress in Human Geography*, 25: 445–55.

—. 2010. *Constructions of Neoliberal Reason*. Oxford: Oxford University Press.

—. 2012. Austerity Urbanism. *City*, 16: 626–55.

Peck, J., and Theodore, N. 2000 'Work First': Workfare and the Regulation of Contingent Labour Markets. *Cambridge Journal of Economics*, 24: 119–38.

Peck, J., and Tickell, A. 2002. Neoliberalizing Space. *Antipode*, 34: 380–404.

Piven, F.F. 1999. Welfare and Work, in Mink, G., ed. *Whose Welfare?* Ithaca, NY: Cornell University Press: 83–99.

—. 2015. Neoliberalism and the Welfare State. *Journal of International and Comparative Social Policy*, 31: 2–9.

Powell, M., and Hewitt, M. 1998. The End of the Welfare State? *Social Policy and Administration*, 32: 1–13.

Rose, N., and Miller, P. 1992. Political Power Beyond the State: Problematics of Government. *British Journal of Sociology*, 43: 173–205.

Smith, A.M. 2007. *Welfare Reform and Sexual Regulation*. Cambridge: Cambridge University Press.

The Globe and Mail. 2010. Tearing Apart the British Welfare State: Tories Impose Jobs on the 'Workshy'. *The Globe and Mail*, 11 November. Retrieved from http://www.theglobeandmail.com/news/world/tearing-apart-the-british-welfare-state-tories-impose-jobs-on-the-workshy/article1314833/

The Guardian. 2008. How the Financial Crisis Will Affect Welfare-to-Work. *The Guardian*, 7 October. Retrieved from http://www.theguardian.com/society/2008/oct/08/credit.crunch.welfare

—. 2010. Does Getting Tough on the Unemployed Work? *The Guardian*, 16 June. Retrieved from www.theguardian.com/society/2010/jun/16/lawrence-mead-tough-us-welfare-unemployed

22

NEOLIBERALISM, LABOUR AND TRADE UNIONISM

Ben Jackson

An important consequence of the rise of neoliberalism to political power in many nations has been a significant erosion of corporatist industrial relations arrangements and labour market regulation. How have neoliberals made the case for such radical reforms? This chapter examines the analysis of labour and collective bargaining developed by neoliberals during their long years in the political wilderness and which subsequently emerged as an influential policy discourse after the 1970s. It first seeks to pinpoint precisely what is distinctive about the neoliberal understanding of labour and then traces in more detail the various dimensions of this radical ideological innovation, encompassing neoliberals' understanding of the economic relationship between trade unions and employment, inequality and inflation; of the distinction between the state and civil society; and ultimately the neoliberal attempt to dissolve the language of class altogether through the sponsorship of alternative discourses about 'human capital' and producer and consumer interests.

The rejection of the classical inheritance

The most influential classical and neo-classical economists believed that the buying and selling of labour was a distinctive sort of economic transaction. In *The Wealth of Nations*, Adam Smith famously observed that workers were more vulnerable than the owners of capital when it came to bargaining over wages:

> We have no acts of parliament against combining to lower the price of work; but many against combining to raise it. In all such disputes the masters can hold out much longer. A landlord, a farmer, a master manufacturer, a merchant, though they did not employ a single workman, could generally live a year or two upon the stocks which they have already acquired. Many workmen could not subsist a week, few could subsist a month, and scarce any a year without employment. In the long run the workman may be as necessary to his master as his master is to him; but the necessity is not so immediate. We rarely hear, it has been said, of the combinations of masters, though frequently of those of workmen. But whoever imagines, upon this account, that masters rarely combine, is as ignorant of the world as of the subject. Masters are always and everywhere in a sort of tacit, but constant and uniform combination, not to raise the wages of labour above their actual rate.
>
> *(Smith, 1904[1776]: 68)*

Many years later, Alfred Marshall's seminal *Principles of Economics* echoed Smith by enumerating several respects in which the sale of labour usually differed from the sale of other goods in a market economy. These included: a pervasive inequality in access to marketable skills because of factors beyond the worker's control, chiefly differences in parental economic and cultural resources; the fact that it was necessary for a worker to be present in the workplace to sell their labour, thus creating preferences about the nature of the workplace environment and setting limits to labour mobility; and the length of time needed for workers to acquire skills and training, even though unforeseen changes in the market might very quickly render those same skills outdated. Fundamentally, Marshall agreed with Smith that the sellers of labour often faced 'special disadvantages' because of 'the closely connected group of facts that labour power is "perishable", that the sellers of it are commonly poor and have no reserve fund, and that they cannot easily withhold it from the market'. As a result, said Marshall, it was 'certain that manual labourers as a class are at a disadvantage in bargaining' (Marshall, 1920[1890]: 322–8, quotes at 326, 327).

All of this led Marshall and the other founding fathers of economics to take a nuanced view towards trade unions. For example, most classical economists believed that trade union activity was necessary to prevent short-run wages being depressed by employer power below the equilibrium level; to raise wages during periods of high profits; and to balance the dominant social and economic power of employers (O'Brien, 2004: 341–2). To be sure, this sympathetic stance was often balanced by anxieties about unions becoming too powerful or encouraging acts of violence or social disruption. But the tradition of market economics that had coalesced by the middle of the twentieth century was nonetheless one that broadly accepted the need for workers' combinations to counterbalance the asymmetries of power and wealth that were produced by market forces.

One of the distinctive features of neoliberal economic thought, as it emerged from the middle of the twentieth century, was that it denied that the sale of labour constituted a special sort of transaction and, accordingly, espoused a much more uncompromising view of the ethics and economics of trade unionism (and of labour market regulation more generally). This break from the market economics of an earlier era was sometimes consciously articulated by neoliberal theorists, for example by the South African-British economist, W.H. Hutt, whose pioneering volume, *The Theory of Collective Bargaining* (1975[1930]), explicitly set out to critique the view of the labour market and workers' combinations articulated by older liberal authors such as Smith, John Stuart Mill and Marshall. Hutt argued that these earlier analyses rested on 'vague phrases' about 'the "disadvantage" of uncombined labour' and the 'indeterminateness' of the price of labour which a more rigorous and consistent application of market principles could dispel (ibid.: 24, 79). In other works of neoliberal theory, this historical departure from market liberal tradition was downplayed or left undiscussed and a searching criticism of trade unions was presented as entirely in keeping with an enduring liberal lineage that could be traced back to Adam Smith.

Nonetheless, the novelty of this analysis of the nature of labour represents one of the most important respects in which we can speak of a 'neo'-liberal ideology taking shape during the 1950s and 1960s and emerging as an influential political discourse during the 1970s and 1980s (see Jackson 2011 and 2015 for more detailed discussions, which this chapter draws on; see also Steiner 2009). Neoliberals denied that unions equalized the bargaining power of labour and capital, since they believed that the owners of capital were in principle as vulnerable to competition as workers. Employees, they argued, in fact enjoyed considerable choice and mobility with respect to employment opportunities, while employers found themselves confronted by powerful labour interests willing to use coercive force to achieve their goals. The key political implication of the neoliberal denial that labour was a special sort of commodity was that legislative intervention to equalize the bargaining power of employers and employees in fact privileged trade unions, creating mighty state-sanctioned interest groups that hampered the operations of the market and threatened the very legitimacy of the state. Unions were re-described as monopolies that sought to control the price of labour in order to charge a price for it in excess of its competitive level. This characterization of union activity sought to debunk the perception, fed by the popular historiography of the labour movement, that unions had emerged organically from the struggles of ordinary workers to protect themselves from the exploitative power of big business. This attempt to disenchant labour history encompassed several distinct criticisms of workers' combinations.

Unions, unemployment and inequality

The fundamental economic criticism of trade unions made by neoliberals, and its wider political significance, is often obscured amid the general cacophony of the debate between left and right over industrial relations. The essential point that leading neoliberal economists sought to drive home in their analysis of collective bargaining was that, far from protecting workers' interests, unions increased unemployment and income inequality. Although this was largely an empirical claim, this argument tended to be couched in more abstract terms as a logical outcome of the application of basic economic principles. Since unions raised the wages of those already in a certain job, it followed that employers would control their costs by employing fewer workers and would be reluctant to take on additional workers (raising unemployment). This would increase the pool of labour available for lower paid, non-union jobs, driving down wages in these sectors of the economy. Unions were therefore, on the neoliberal account, primarily devices whereby privileged groups of workers advantaged themselves relative to other groups of workers. As Friedrich Hayek put it:

> The interest of those who will get employment at the higher wage will therefore always be opposed to the interest of those who, in consequence, will find employment only in the less highly-paid jobs or who will not be employed at all.
>
> *(Hayek 1960: 270)*

The empirical evidence to support this claim was much less well explored in neoliberal writings compared to its grounding in economic theory. Yet this did not prevent figures such as Hayek from venturing their own empirical conclusions. The British unions, Hayek wrote, 'have become the chief cause of unemployment' and of 'the falling standard of living of the working class'. Unions, he added, 'are the main reason for the decline of the British economy in general' (Hayek 1984[1978b]: 62, 52). Hayek also predicted 'that the average worker's income would rise fastest in a country where relative wages are flexible, and where the exploitation of workers by monopolistic trade union organisations of specialised groups of workers are effectively outlawed' (Hayek 1984[1978b]: 54). But these claims were not supported by the systematic investigation of empirical evidence. Hayek did not explain how he knew that the unions were 'the chief cause of unemployment' in Britain (Richardson 1997; Jackson 2011: 277–9). Empirical economic studies have, in fact, painted a more nuanced picture of the impact of trade unions on labour markets and income inequality. A robust cross-national statistical finding, for example, is that unions narrow pay dispersion within workplaces and industries, and reduce income differentials between middle-class and working-class jobs, all of which empirically dominate the disequalizing effect of unions stressed by neoliberals, namely that unions raise the wages of certain groups of workers relative to others (Card *et al.* 2003; Viser and Checchi 2009). Likewise, what is termed the 'collective voice' functions of unions – their role in providing employee input into workplace conditions and organization – can also have a positive impact on economic efficiency – for example, by reducing staff turnover (Freeman and Madoff 1984).

While these aspects of the neoliberal critique of unions are open to economic debate, its political implications have nonetheless been highly consequential. Politicians sympathetic to neoliberalism appropriated the purported connection between unemployment and unionization in an effort to reassign responsibility for employment levels from the state to the labour movement itself. If it is primarily labour market 'rigidities', such as high union density, that prevent employers from taking on more employees, then promoting higher levels of employment will naturally require efforts to break down such barriers to the efficient buying and selling of labour. Conversely, on this account much less attention would then need to be devoted to the promotion of employment through traditional Keynesian remedies aimed at supporting aggregate demand. In political terms, this offered neoliberal politicians an important argument for a more aggressive stance towards the powerful unions of the post-war period (Tomlinson 2012).

Unions and inflation

The relationship between trade unions and inflation has been the cause of doctrinal disagreement within neoliberalism. Neoliberals are, broadly speaking, committed to the monetarist insight that inflation is a result of excess growth in the supply of money and can therefore only be controlled by restricting the expansion of the money supply. This makes the reduction of inflation squarely the responsibility of the state, as the only institution capable of controlling the growth of the quantity of money. How, then, do trade unions fit into the neoliberal account of inflation? One influential answer, articulated with particular vigour by Milton Friedman, is that they do not. Friedman argued that, by aiming to control price rises via wage negotiation with unions, states, in fact, seek to divert attention from their own responsibility for inflation. In Friedman's view, union wage bargaining had no effect on the overall price level in the economy; it was only through control of the money supply that inflationary pressures could be reduced (Friedman 1966). Other neoliberal theorists offered a more complex story. Hayek, for example, agreed with Friedman about the monetary roots of inflation, but argued that the reason states were so willing to relax their monetary discipline was because of the colossal political pressure placed on them by powerful trade unions. In Hayek's view, this revealed a political fix at the heart of Keynesian economics. Hayek argued that Keynes had started:

> from the correct insight that the regular cause of extensive unemployment is real wages that are too high. The next step consisted in the proposition that a direct lowering of money wages could be brought about only by a struggle so painful and prolonged that it could not be contemplated. Hence he concluded that real wages must be lowered by the process of lowering the value of money. This is really the reasoning underlying the whole 'full employment' policy, now so widely accepted.
>
> *(Hayek 1960: 280)*

The basis of Keynesian economics was therefore (in Hayek's view) a capitulation to the power of organized labour and a recourse to an inflationary fiscal policy to reduce the real value of wages instead. In contrast to the 'Friedmanite' perspective on inflation, the 'Hayekian' one presented governments as fearful of the social and political power of unions and, accordingly, sought to integrate organized labour into the causal chain that forced up prices. The difference was not a large one, since both sides agreed that unions caused unemployment and exacerbated social conflict, and both denied that traditional Keynesian remedies were capable of tackling inflation (see Haberler 1969 for a discussion of where the similarities and differences lie). But Hayek's account of the relationship between organized labour and Keynesian theory offered a more fleshed-out political economy of inflation than Friedman's more technocratic approach, and delineated a more confrontational prospectus for action to mitigate union power. It was therefore seen by some political actors and commentators as a profound diagnosis of the social tensions inherent in the Keynesian settlement, finding a ready audience among political elites during the acrimonious industrial relations of the 1970s and 1980s (see, for example, Jay 1974).

The strong state

Neoliberal scepticism about trade unionism was not just animated by economic considerations. It was also underpinned by political fears about the threat that unions posed to the authority and legitimacy of the state (see Gamble 1994 for an analysis of this point in relation to the emergence of Thatcherism). As Hayek's discussion of the inflationary consequences of strong trade unions illustrated, neoliberals believed that the growth of powerful labour interest groups would corrupt government policy and ultimately weaken state sovereignty. In principle, neoliberals were enthusiastic about the importance of spontaneous, voluntary associations (as opposed to coercive state activity) in fomenting a vibrant liberal society. But they made a sharp distinction between voluntary and coercive forms of association, and firmly assigned modern trade unionism to the latter category. While neoliberals always stressed that trade union organization was not in itself impermissible, they were sharply critical of the specific form that it had taken in the twentieth century. The problem with modern trade unions, neoliberals believed, was that they forced individuals into taking collective action that they did not personally consent to; they used tactics such as strikes, boycotts and closed shops that were coercive and sometimes violent; and they were artificially sustained in these activities by labour legislation enacted by the social democratic state. As Hayek put it in an interview in 1978:

> Oh, I have no objection against unions as such. I am for – what is the classical phrase? – freedom of association, of course, but not the right to use power to force other people to join and to keep other people out. The privileges which have been granted the unions in America only by the judicature – in England by law, seventy years ago – that they can use force to prevent people from doing the work they like, is the crux, the dangerous aspect of it.
>
> *(Hayek 1978a: 90)*

Neoliberals therefore saw unions as presenting a challenge to the liberal state that was quite distinct from that presented by other forms of organization (Wedderburn 1989: 8). As a result, their focus on the problems caused by trade unionism could appear disproportionate and neglectful of similar issues that arose in relation to, for example, business corporations or local government, both of which neoliberals strongly endorsed, and neither of which were obviously non-coercive or lacking in special legislative protection. Nonetheless, neoliberals pressed the argument that it was unions, in particular, that threatened the fundamental ability of the state to act as a neutral arbiter in economic affairs, standing apart from sectarian interests in the economy and enforcing general rules of competition for all to abide by. Protected by law, unions were at liberty to force governments to accommodate their special demands and to drag the state into areas of decision-making that were better left to market forces than government fiat.

Human capital

A further strand of neoliberal thought took the radical step of attempting to abolish altogether the distinction between labour and capital. Economists such as Theodore Schultz and Gary Becker argued that the skills and knowledge acquired by workers should be conceptualized as a form of capital investment, aimed at increasing the future income flow to an individual from their labour, and analogous to the spending on machinery and equipment undertaken by owners of more traditional forms of capital. Schultz and Becker sought to demonstrate that this growth of 'human capital' had been underestimated by economists and accounted for a considerable portion of twentieth-century economic growth (Schultz 1961; Becker 1993[1964]). This notion that 'people invest in themselves and these investments are very large' was in part a fruitful economic theory that opened up a range of interesting research questions for economists of various partisan stripes (Schultz 1961: 2). Indeed, there was an obvious respect in which such an analysis could even be turned in a social democratic direction, since it could be used to argue that substantial public investment in education and healthcare would enhance economic dynamism and efficiency.

Nonetheless, the language of human capital could be – and was – deployed in a fashion that was more congenial to specifically neoliberal imperatives. Understood not as an economic hypothesis that captured one aspect of the labour market, but rather as a comprehensive description of the drivers of human behaviour, human capital theory pictured the individual, in the words of Michel Foucault, as 'an entrepreneur of himself' (Foucault 2008: 226). On this account, individuals are chiefly focused on a competitive struggle for economic advantage, constantly seeking to increase the value of their 'assets' and thus enhance their future flow of income; other domains of life are relentlessly subordinated to this overriding purpose and eventually colonized by the language of capital and competition (Brown 2015: 36–7). Perhaps the most radical implication of human capital theory, however, is that the category of labour, and associated ideas of class, are displaced from social analysis altogether by the expansion of the concept of 'capital' to include the very economic interests that purportedly stand in opposition to it.

Producers and consumers

In a similar vein, neoliberals asserted that it was through advancing consumer interests rather than producer interests that individual freedom and economic efficiency would be most thoroughly realized. As one of the pioneers of the Chicago School, Henry Simons, put it:

> All the grosser mistakes in economic policy, if not most manifestations of democratic corruption, arise from focusing upon the interests of people as producers rather than upon their interests as consumers, i.e., from acting on behalf of producer minorities rather than on behalf of the whole community as sellers of services and buyers of products.
>
> *(Simons 1944: 2)*

The 'public interest' was therefore construed by neoliberals as being synonymous with the aggregated interests of consumers, whereas producer groups were regarded as seeking to advantage themselves at consumers' expense. Drawing on public choice theory, neoliberals argued that the intensity of the interest felt by producer groups in their own affairs would, without safeguards, lead them to dominate policy-making on their trade, since consumers' interest was usually much more fleeting and less well organized. 'The public interest is widely dispersed,' argued Milton Friedman,

> in consequence, in the absence of any general arrangements to offset the pressure of special interests, producer groups will invariably have a much stronger influence on legislative action and the powers that be than will the diverse, widely spread consumer interest.
>
> *(Friedman 1962: 143)*

'Producer interests' of course encompasses both corporate and labour interests. A lot of work within the broad field of public choice theory has focused on both, with, for example, Mancur Olson concluding that large companies and trade unions are equally damaging to economic growth (Olson 1965: 141–8; 1982: 143–4). But while some of the early writings of neoliberals had taken a similar stance, by the 1950s and 1960s neoliberalism focused its attack on producer interests solely on organized labour. The post-war exponents of a revitalized market liberalism were convinced that business was embattled in the face of the new social democratic state and its allies in the labour movement (Jackson 2010: 141–5; 2011: 268–9). Gottfried Haberler summarized this view: 'in our times industrial "monopolies" and "oligopolies" do not have the same power, strength and iron discipline that many unions have developed in many countries' (Haberler 1972: 34).

The liberal society envisaged by neoliberals was therefore one in which individuals were able to exercise their free agency as consumers, choosing between the variety of goods and lifestyles offered by a market economy. As producers, however, a strict managerial hierarchy was to prevail: the choice that individuals exercised as workers was whether to accept an offer of employment or to leave an existing job in search of a new one. Neoliberals anticipated no further formal role for the exercise of free choice in the day-to-day running of businesses, which were to be subject to the authoritative decisions of managers. This vision of choice within the labour market ultimately underestimated the structural barriers within a capitalist economy to finding and keeping jobs and the extent to which the hierarchical control of the firm constituted a constraint on liberty (Ciepley 2004). But it was a vision that appeared attractive to some politicians, business interests and, ultimately, voters during the 1980s and 1990s, as neoliberalism took on powerful trade unions in the name of breaking the producer interests that purportedly held back economic progress.

Conclusion

There are many reasons for the decline in the status and power of organized labour in the industrialized nations over the last few decades: the changing structure of mature capitalist economies, notably the large rise in service sector employment; the expansion of the world's labour supply triggered by globalization; the increased unemployment levels in the advanced economies after the end of the social democratic 'golden age'. While neoliberalism can be connected to all of these economic developments, and thus to their boost to the power of employers to hire and fire, its impact has been most palpable in shaping a cultural shift that has remade the fabric of industrial relations in many places. The neoliberal ideas discussed in this chapter have reframed the way in which political and economic elites conceptualize the labour market, fostering greater hostility on the part of both the state and employers towards collective bargaining and labour regulation. The old analysis that the labour market systematically favours the interests of employers over employees and so requires the state and unions to act as countervailing powers to protect employees from exploitation – a view that, as we have seen, can be traced back to Adam Smith – has been significantly weakened at elite level by the rival neoliberal discourse of sectional producer interests threatening the consumer. The result has been legislation that hampers the ability of unions to organize and reduces social protections, and the emergence of a more self-confident, uncompromising business class that is much less interested in collaborating with workers' organizations and the state in a corporatist model of capitalism. Yet, as powerful economic analyses of the rise of economic inequality after the 1970s have made clear, it is these political choices as much as structural economic shifts that have led to the greater concentration of income and wealth in the hands of higher earners, as they have significantly reduced the bargaining power of employees in the workplace and in the formulation of public policy (Krugman 2007; Piketty 2014; Atkinson 2015). Any putative new political economy that emerges from the 2007–8 global financial crisis will therefore require a reckoning with the neoliberal vision of labour if it is to seriously challenge the ascendancy of the 1 per cent.

References

Atkinson, A.B. 2015. *Inequality: What Can be Done?* Cambridge, MA: Harvard University Press.

Becker, G. 1993[1964]. *Human Capital.* Chicago, IL: University of Chicago Press.

Brown, W. 2015. *Undoing the Demos: Neo-liberalism's Stealth Revolution.* New York: Zone.

Card, D., Lemieux, T., and Craig, W. 2003. Unions and the Wage Structure, in Addison, J.T., and Schnabel, C., eds. *International Handbook of Trade Unions.* Cheltenham: Edward Elgar: 246–92.

Ciepley, D. 2004. Authority in the Firm (and the Attempt to Theorize it Away). *Critical Review,* 16: 81–115.

Foucault, M. 2008. *The Birth of Biopolitics.* Basingstoke: Palgrave.

Freeman, R., and Medoff, J. 1984. *What do Unions do?* New York: Basic.

Friedman, M. 1962. *Capitalism and Freedom.* Chicago, IL: University of Chicago Press.

—. 1966. What Price Guideposts?, in Shultz, G., and Aliber, R., eds. *Guidelines, Informal Controls and the Market Place.* Chicago, IL: University of Chicago Press: 17–39.

Gamble, A. 1994. *The Free Economy and the Strong State.* Basingstoke: Macmillan.

Haberler, G. 1969. Wage Push Inflation Once More, in Streissler, E., ed. *Roads to Freedom: Essays in Honour of Friedrich A. Von Hayek.* London: Routledge: 65–75.

—. 1972. *Inflation and the Unions.* London: IEA.

Hayek, F.A. 1960. *The Constitution of Liberty.* Chicago, IL: University of Chicago Press.

—. 1978a. *Transcript of an Interview Conducted in 1978 Under the Auspices of the Center for Oral History Research, Young Research Library, UCLA.* Retrieved 6 February 2016 from https://archive.org/details/nobelprizewinnin00haye

—. 1984[1978b]. *1980s Unemployment and the Unions.* London: IEA.

Hutt, W.H. 1975[1930]. *The Theory of Collective Bargaining.* London: IEA.

Krugman, P. 2007. *The Conscience of a Liberal.* New York: W.W. Norton.

Jackson, B. 2010. At the Origins of Neo-liberalism: The Free Economy and the Strong State, 1930–47. *Historical Journal,* 53: 129–51.

—. 2011. An Ideology of Class: Neo-liberalism and the Trade Unions, c. 1930–79, in Griffiths, C., Nott, J., and Whyte, W., eds. *Classes, Cultures and Politics: Essays on British History in Honour of Ross McKibbin.* Oxford: Oxford University Press: 263–81.

—. 2015. Hayek, Hutt and the Trade Unions, in Leeson, R., ed. *Hayek: A Collaborative Biography, Part V.* Basingstoke: Palgrave: 208–28.

Jay, P. 1974. The Good Old Days of Stop-go Economics. *The Times,* 1 July.

Marshall, A. 1920[1890]. *Principles of Economics.* 8th edn. London: Macmillan and Co.

O'Brien, D. 2004. *The Classical Economists Revisited.* Princeton, NJ: Princeton University Press.

Olson, M. 1965. *The Logic of Collective Action.* Cambridge: Harvard University Press.

—. 1982. *The Rise and Decline of Nations.* New Haven, CT: Yale University Press.

Piketty, T. 2014. *Capital in the Twenty-first Century.* Cambridge: Harvard University Press.

Richardson, R. 1997. Hayek on Trade Unions: Social Philosopher or Propagandist?, in Frowen, S.F., ed. *Hayek: Economist and Social Philosopher.* Basingstoke: Macmillan: 259–80.

Schultz, G. 1961. Investment in Human Capital. *American Economic Review*, 51: 1–17.

Simons, H. 1944. Some Reflections on Syndicalism. *Journal of Political Economy*, 52: 1–25.

Smith, A. 1904[1776]. *An Inquiry into the Nature and Causes of the Wealth of Nations Volume I*. London: Methuen.

Steiner, Y. 2009. The Neo-liberals Confront the Trade Unions, in Mirowski, P., and Plehwe, D., eds. *The Road from Mont Pèlerin: The Making of the Neoliberal Thought Collective*. Cambridge, MA: Harvard University Press: 181–203.

Tomlinson, J. 2012. Thatcherism, Monetarism and the Politics of Inflation, in Jackson, B., and Saunders, R., eds. *Making Thatcher's Britain*. Cambridge: Cambridge University Press: 62–77.

Viser, J., and Checchi, D. 2009. Inequality and the Labor Market: Unions, in Salverda, W., Nolan, B., and Smeeding, T.M., eds. *Oxford Handbook of Economic Inequality*. Oxford: Oxford University Press: 230–56.

Wedderburn, L. 1989. Freedom of Association and Philosophies of Labour Law. *Industrial Law Journal*, 18: 1–38.

23

THE COMMONS AGAINST NEOLIBERALISM, THE COMMONS OF NEOLIBERALISM, THE COMMONS BEYOND NEOLIBERALISM

Max Haiven

I am typing these words in the Learning Commons of a local university library, a space defined less by a scholarly atmosphere of contemplation and debate and more by the gently arcing rows of brushed steel computer workstations and the proliferation of corporate brand icons. There, emblazoned on the wall, is the name of a local property developer, renowned for pushing a gentrification agenda, who donated the money to create the Learning Commons. Glowing Apple insignias beam out from students' laptops. Flatscreen TVs announce various policies regarding food and drink on two-thirds of the screen; the last third is reserved for advertisements for debt relief and spa treatments. These help pay for the screens themselves. Long-discarded fast food wrappers clutter wood-laminate tables (cutbacks have led to a scarcity of custodial staff). On the floor lie an array of brand-name designer backpacks and handbags. While this space was allegedly designed to foster the realization of the latest buzzword-driven trends (from collaboration to synergy to cross-pollination to leadership) most of its denizens sit alone and stare transfixed at their respective screens: writing papers or preparing presentations for tomorrow's class, chatting with friends a world away or mere feet away, watching YouTube clips of cute animals, or playing elaborate multiplayer strategy games.

If this is our 'commons' of learning I can safely say I want no part of it. But my complaint has little to do with the press-ganging of a once-radical term into service to the neoliberal university. In an age where the word 'revolution' has been used to sell everything from heating and air-conditioning systems to anti-dandruff shampoo, we can hardly take umbrage at the subjugation of language to neoliberal commercialism. The experience of the 'learning commons' reveals something more profound: the purported acrimonious opposition between the idea of the commons and the phenomenon of neoliberalism, while sometimes rhetorically and politically expedient, is inaccurate and misleading.

This brief chapter narrates how the notion of the commons, evolved within and against neoliberalism in two streams, one explicitly anti-capitalist, the other more reformist in orientation. I seek to show that while the idea and ideal of the commons still promise an antidote, or at least an alternative, to the power and ideology of neoliberal capitalism, the commons has in many ways itself been co-opted and made to serve the reproduction of neoliberalism(s) both rhetorically and materially. In this sense it has been partially enclosed. As such, we are at a moment in which we must transcend innocent enthusiasm for the commons, and instead begin to make key critical, analytic and strategic distinctions.

The commons and neoliberalism

The rise of the idea of the commons in the contemporary moment cannot be separated from the simultaneous rise of neoliberalism as a material process, an ideological orientation and a political-economic period. Whereas neoliberalism implies the relentless capitalist instrumentalization of all aspects of life (de Angelis 2007), the idea of the commons suggests a form of elective coopera-tion and collectivism, one distinct from and superior to the allegedly disastrous forms of state-led cooperation and collectivism attempted under the heading of state-led communism. If neoliber-alism boils social reality down to the bitter marrow of individualist self-seeking and competition (Harvey 2005), the idea of the commons offers us a way to speak of the wealth of community, of mutual aid, and of sharing (see Bollier and Helfrich 2012, 2015). If neoliberals insist that the market is the most efficient and just means to govern social resources (Brown 2015), the idea of the commons promises that we can devise more humane, democratic and egalitarian structures from the grassroots up (see P2P Foundation 2015). If neoliberalism signals the transformation of all the world – everything from sex to sand dunes, from dances to data – into commodities whose value is to be determined by the laws of supply and demand (McMurtry 2012), the idea of the commons offers us visions and practices to reclaim and revalue social wealth and build human relationships outside the market logic (Linebaugh 2014).

In this sense, the commons has become something of a floating signifier, a shared flag of con-venience for scholars and activists the world over who would challenge neoliberalism with a radical imagination that sees beyond the horizon of the state. If, as the Zapatistas put it (see Khasnabish 2008), there is a global movement of 'one no, many yeses', then perhaps when those many 'yeses' sound at once we will hear the word 'commons'.

Such a flexible term has its uses. It implies and sometimes helps cohere a transnational alliance of actors and what might be termed, borrowing from Benedict Anderson (2006), a radical anti-neoliberal imagined community. For example, at international gatherings like the People's Social Forum, the commons, in a vague, idealized sense, can be cited as the unobjectionable common platform for a wide diversity of initiatives and tendencies. But the mutability of the term also has its risks. Not least of these is the ease with which neoliberal institutions co-opt it, as in the above example of the corporatized 'learning commons', or as in the case of the 'creative commons', which, although initially a platform to encourage collaboration and creativity out-side the strictures of capitalist intellectual property regimes, has of late been harnessed as a means to reconfigure corporate strategy and marshal the free or devalued labour of digital and cultural workers (see Murray *et al.* 2014).

Further, as George Caffentzis (2012) notes, we have seen the idea of the commons seized upon with great enthusiasm by a recent crop of international development gurus and NGO-sector leaders, who see in it a potential to foster, encourage and 'empower' communities to become 'self-sufficient' and 'self-reliant' and thereby reduce their 'dependency' on what remains of the eviscerated welfare state. Certainly the Left has enthusiastically greeted the experiments with urban farming in poor, racialized neighbourhoods of Detroit (Boggs 2009; Weissman 2013), or the grassroots development of schools, community centres and clinics in austerity-ravaged Greece or Spain (see Azzellini and Sitrin 2014). But so too has the Right pointed to these as evidence of human adaptability to 'market failures' and 'disruptive innovation' in the absence of what is perceived to be the claustrophobic swaddling of the nanny state (Holcombe 2005). The incredible success of Anthony Williams and Don Tapscott's (2008) book *Wikinomics*, which advises that capitalist enterprises recalibrate based on the power of mass collaboration (modelled on the success of the Creative Commons licence), demonstrates the enthusiasm with which certain notions of the commons are received today.

This is all to say that while we might be tempted to envision the idea(l) of the commons as the horizon that transcends neoliberalism, we need to historicize it as evolving within neoliberalism. This does not exhaust the potential of the commons, but it does open new pathways for our analysis of the neoliberal system and for our struggles within, against and beyond it.

To understand how we arrived at this point, it is worth examining two recent anglophone articulations of the commons, and the different places they potentially lead us. Though both emerged in response to the ravages of neoliberalism, they each have very different motivations and implications.

Global commons?

Before tracing these two streams and their tributaries, it is worth sounding the historical aquifer that feeds them both. The original commons were those lands in medieval England and elsewhere in Europe that were legally reserved for peasants to use and tend in common (Neeson 1993; van Zanden 1999). These lands became the backbone of peasant life, a shared space to grow vegetables, graze animals and hold festivals, markets and meetings. The commons were spaces where peasants developed value practices (de Angelis 2007) for the reproduction of society and social life outside the market and the direct authority of social elites. The commons were tied to the hard-won laws and customs of land tenure that forbade feudal lords from simply evicting peasants or dictating the uses of the land (Perelman 2000).

For Marx and subsequent historians, the birth of capitalism was enabled by the dispossession of the commoners of their lands and livelihoods through 'primitive accumulation': a legal, military and social campaign by the ruling class that stripped peasants of their common rights and transformed formerly common land into the private property of landlords (Marx 1992; Perelman 2000; Thompson 1968). The procedures of enclosing, privatizing, marketizing and securitizing common lands preceded the emergence of capitalism (see Goldstein 2013) and, as we shall see, continued throughout capitalism's history in various forms. Marx saw this process of primitive accumulation as essential to kick-start the further accumulation of capital, the development of a fully capitalist economy, and the legal and institutional structures germane to the bourgeois state. It also dispossessed peasants of their autonomous means of social reproduction, rendering them dependent on waged labour, a process which, over the span of centuries, drove millions into cities to become the proletariat. Furthermore, it created a flood of surplus humanity to be exported to colonies to further dispossess indigenous peoples there of their lands and livelihoods.

There is debate concerning the extent to which we might describe the processes of colonization – especially in colonial-settler states – as a process of enclosure of the commons (see Maddison 2010). Certainly we can make strong analogies between the commons-oriented cultures of European peasants and similar features in many indigenous civilizations in the Americas, Oceania and Africa. And certainly the process of colonialism depended on the transformation of common lands and resources into private property. However, we should be wary of too simple a correlation (see Greer 2012). For one, to marshal all indigenous civilizations under the banner of the commons is to reduce a wide diversity of social formations under a Eurocentric term, one that is, ultimately, Eurocentric. Second, such a position would reinforce a romantic idealism towards both the notion of the commons and indigenous civilizations. In the case of the former, such idealism slides all too easily into platitudes about the inherent benevolence of human nature, suggesting that the commons is somehow our genetic destiny, given that it is evidenced in such a wide range of human civilizations. In the case of the latter, by transplanting our idealized yet Eurocentric notion of the commons onto indigenous civilizations, we risk participating in the rehearsal of myths of the 'noble savage' living in a more 'natural' commons-based state in 'simple' societies. Beyond its blatant racism, this approach would also obscure the fact that commons, even when centred around ecological wealth, are always actively and intentionally communally governed through complex (usually egalitarian) social mechanisms (see Ostrom 1990).

The application of the idea of the commons and of enclosure to the non-European context elides an important historical point: dispossessed European commoners often became colonial actors, agents and beneficiaries (Greer 2012). For instance, those 'common lands' on the outskirts of New England settlements that once provided colonists with game, firewood, room to expand and other necessities were land seized from indigenous people. The use of pasture animals on these lands helped disrupt and deplete the ecosystems on which indigenous people depended. Land grants promised to dispossessed European commoners in return for years of indentured service or simply fealty were, likewise, stolen.

In some senses, the 'commons' as we have come to use the term today is a placeholder or a promissory note for all those rich, nuanced, complex and sophisticated forms of relationality and value practice that have been obliterated within capitalist societies where a huge proportion of social relations have been subjugated to the market. In this sense, the term the 'commons' names a haunting cultural absence. In indigenous and other societies that have maintained non-capitalist forms of relationality and value practice, that thing we name the 'commons' often goes by other, older names. Thus universalizing the term not only risks a Eurocentric flattening of cultural and political diversity, it also risks desensitizing those of us who do emerge from a neoliberal culture to how much we have to learn from cultures that have withstood capitalism and colonialism, both in their historic formations and in their contemporary manifestation in the neoliberalism era. For instance, in the territories where I live, Mi'Kmaq people use the term *Netukulimk* to speak to the active, cyclical reciprocity between humans, community and the earth (see Stiegman and Pictou 2010). It has no sufficient English translation, and while we might be tempted to translate it as 'commons' this would actually reduce the precision, complexity and potential of the term.

More radical commons

In any case, it was the European historical record of the commons and their enclosure that became a resource for contemporary scholars to draw on as a means to explain today's struggles against the forces we would come to know as neoliberalism. In the post-war period, historians like Christopher Hill (1972), E. P. Thompson (1968) and others associated with the production of 'history from below' began to research and publish fairly popular books on the history of the commons and of enclosure, as a means to narrate the origins of class relations in the UK (see Linebaugh 2011). The effort here was to develop a framework for understanding the changing dynamics of class conflict in ways that highlighted the continuities of working-class resistance and refusal, as well as in ways that opened up possibilities for imagining social change and socialist revolution beyond the model provided by the Soviet Union.

Later commons thinkers took inspiration from the Italian Autonomia movement, from the Marxist-feminist movement, from radical post-Trotskyist workerists like the Johnson Forest Tendency (including the work of theorists like C.L.R. James and Runya Dunayevskya) and, later, from the Zapatista uprising (Midnight Notes 2001). This approach framed the commons as a potent metaphor for describing those shared elements of life in today's societies. From this perspective, articulated by thinkers including George Caffentzis, Silvia Federici, Peter Linebaugh, Massimo de Angelis, Harry Cleaver and others associated with the publication of the periodicals *Midnight Notes* and *Zero Work*, rivers, communities, online networks and even natural resources might be understood as commons. Conversely, the process of 'primitive accumulation' was seen not as merely something occurring at the origins or periphery of capitalism, but as its fundamental *modus oparandi* (Midnight Notes 1990). Moving away from an interpretation of industrial labour as the source of all value, these thinkers took a firm interest in the *reproduction* of capital, drawing on Marxist-feminist thinkers who stressed an understanding of capitalism as dependent on 'women's work' in the home (Weeks 2011). Capitalism was reframed as a system that was fundamentally based on the production of disciplinary techniques throughout the field of social life (Federici 2005, 2013; Fortunati 1995; Mies 1986). From this perspective, communities create common value (in the form of socialized wealth) and cooperative energies upon which capitalism vampirically preys, enclosing the commons again and again.

But these thinkers were also critical of the standard set of socialist prescriptions for this crisis, from Leninist vanguard parties to social democratic strategies. Rather, they envisioned the possibility of a society built upon the values of the commons from the grassroots up, seeded in community self-sufficiency and the refusal of capitalist discipline. Hence the idea and ideal of the commons in this valence offered a potent antidote to neoliberalism: the commons promises a form of decentralized political and economic collectivity beyond the welfare state based on – and generative of – autonomy and solidarity. Conversely, historical philosophers like Silvia Federici (2005 and 2013) have located the birth of modern systemic patriarchy in the enclosure of the commons, noting the way the enclosures both relied on and drove the subjugation of women's community-based power, notably through the witch trials of the fifteenth to seventeenth centuries. Hence, for Federici and others, the reclamation and rebuilding of the commons today is both a feminist and an anti-capitalist project, one that is immanent and iterative: we build new common structures, platforms and communities today that in some way prefigure or foreshadow the post-capitalist, post-patriarchal world we aim to create.

This approach is fundamentally based on the question of how the commons, as living actualities as well as a political horizons, might empower and enable the proletarianized classes (a category considerably broader than merely the industrial working class) to escape the capture and enclosure of capital (Caffentzis 2012). From this approach the value of the commons lies not only in its abstract potential to pose alternatives to capitalism but also in its efficacy as a platform and tool of class struggle. Hence these critics are supportive of, but sceptical towards, many of the initiatives and organizations that today claim the language of the commons, from community gardens or social centres to digital tools and platforms to the earth's climate itself.[1] For Caffentzis and company, these should not be seen as good in and of themselves but, rather, assessed on the basis of how they enable anti-capitalist resistance towards a revolutionary horizon.

More liberal commons

This orientation, then, should stand in contrast to more reformist but vitally important efforts to recuperate and recover the idea of the commons, a frame of thinking indebted primarily to the work of heterodox economist Elinor Ostrom. Her approach to the commons was intended to help recuperate the term from the infamy associated with it since Garrett Hardin's 1968 article 'The Tragedy of the Commons', the title of which has become an article of faith for neoliberal thinkers, implying that any form of common resource ownership or management leads inevitably to resource exhaustion, poverty, waste and despair. Hardin makes little reference to actually existing commons past or present, but instead makes a Malthusian argument for humanity's allegedly inherent propensity to allow individual self-seeking activity to undermine the wealth of the whole (Angus 2008). While Hardin's argument was largely a conservative legitimation of state planning, it became a key reference point for neoliberal economists eager to champion the inherent benevolence and natural supremacy of the invisible hand of the market.

Ostrom's work, then, emerged as a romantic counterpoint to this neoliberal adoption of the generic narrative of the tragic commons, pointing out, instead, the creative, considered and often highly democratic ways in which communities stewarded shared resources like water systems and forests. For Ostrom (1990), the commons was to be taken as an alternative or third term beside the all too common binary relationship of 'public' and 'private'. The commons here was to be seen as another means of managing scarce resources that obeyed neither the top-down bureaucratic logic of the state nor the individual competitive logic of the market. But for Ostrom and her later followers, the commons was never imagined in a revolutionary frame. Rather, this work stressed the need to recognize and honour the commons as an antidote to the failures or oversights of states and markets – at worst a supplement, at best an equal partner with the state and market in the reproduction of modern economic life (see Caffentzis 2012; Ostrom *et al.* 2012).

This approach has both neoliberal and anti-neoliberal tendencies. On the one hand, the commons could legitimately be pointed to by neoliberal advocates of the retreat of the welfare state as a non-governmental means of supplying necessities in areas of market failure. Hence the recent neoliberal enthusiasm for ideas of 'community' and even for the organization form of the cooperative, as might be demonstrated by the Cameron government's enthusiasm for so-called 'big society' in the UK (see Dowling and Harvie 2014): a system of incentives that aim to offload welfare state responsibilities onto private, community-based and not-for-profit groups as a means to slash government expenditures.

For anti-neoliberals working in Ostrom's tradition, the commons provides a means to rebuild community and a sense of collective wealth in the wake of their neoliberal destruction (see Bollier and Helfrich 2012, 2015). Here, the commons is imagined predominantly as a small-but-beautiful means for citizens and communities to reclaim power and self-sufficiency within and against the general neoliberal current and, as such, might serve as a platform for a more robust systemic challenge to that paradigm. From free and open software initiatives (see Benkler 2007) to community-managed watersheds to worker-reclaimed enterprises, the commons in this valence is imagined as a form of survival and human dignity fundamentally counterposed to the free-market fundamentalism associated with the neoliberal model, as well as to the (sometimes lethal) paternalism of the welfare state.

There is no clean line between the perspectives outlined here. They share an optimism and enthusiasm for the commons as an antidote to neoliberalism's order of new enclosures and a faith that these must be the pivot of broader social transformation. Yet the distinction between the two, such as it can be made, provokes a series of critical questions which are difficult for any advocate of the commons to answer (some of which are well posed by Srnicek and Williams 2015): could the proliferation of actualized commons (from reclaimed factories to urban gardens to social centres to housing or care collectives to new models of information sharing) in aggregate be sufficient to overcome capitalism in its current neoliberal manifestation? If so, what overarching forms and structures of collaboration, conspiracy and cooperation would be necessary to achieve such power? Is some form of centralized planning or governance necessary either in the present moment of commons-based struggle or in the presumed commons future? What should the role of markets and money be: are they inherently antithetical to a commons-based approach? And if they are to be abolished, how (in the absence of central state planning) can the commons organize a technologically complex society dependent on a highly specialized and global distribution of labour (it's hard to imagine that the same ethos that guides the conduct of a housing cooperative could 'scale up' to oversee the fair and equitable production of a smartphone or MRI machine). How might we even conceive of running the global energy industry as a commons? Should we seize, reorient or replace the global capitalist logistics empire? If so, how (see Bernes 2013)? Or does a movement towards the commons based on ecological principles necessarily demand a winding down (or redefinition) of the scale of human technological and industrial capacity? To what extent, and under what circumstances, do the commons in the present moment actually lead to a broader systemic transformation and to what extent does it simply alleviate the strain or pressure of the system's inherent contradictions and anxieties? To what extent might the enthusiasm for the commons as inherently equitable, egalitarian, open and participatory occlude the perpetuation of racism, sexism, ablism, colonialism and other systems of oppression and exploitation? Ought public, state-run services (e.g. healthcare, housing, schooling) remain as such or be transformed into commons, and would the demand for the latter inadvertently contribute to neoliberal calls for privatization and the downloading of social risk and care onto society at large?

Enclosure 3.0

While I have attempted to parse out several valences of theorization of the commons, the reality is that the term circulates in our neoliberal moment with an increasing currency and vagueness that all too often trade such important political distinctions for a warm, ecumenical euphemism. Hence the 'learning commons' where we began this chapter, or the vague use of the commons as the taken-for-granted horizon in many recent philosophical or political critiques of the new regimes of austerity.

Yet we should be careful not to allow our ire to be drawn towards yet another example of what we might term the 'enclosure' of language, wherein a common term of liberation and possibility is privatized and made to render up new forms of (symbolic) capital. Rather, or in addition, we should focus our attention on the structural uses and abuses of the idea and ideal of the commons under neoliberal capitalism. That is, we should insist that, the diametric opposition between the commons and neoliberalism is not quite as politically or analytically reliable as we might hope.

We have, for instance, already spoken of the UK Conservative government's 'big society' platform which, while it does not explicitly marshal the idea of the commons (somewhat surprising, given the nationalistic, if hypocritical, claim the British government could make to the term's origins), does rest on the idea that volunteerism is the proper vehicle to provide forms of social care which cannot be made profitable by the market. We can also note the way various ideas of the commons have been taken up in the world of international development as the appetite for large-scale economic stimulus and modernization programmes gives way to an enthusiasm for community-level strategies of quotidian capitalism like microfinance lending (Bateman 2010; Federici 2012; Moragan and Olson 2011). The idea here is that 'commons' are a natural and benevolent feature of most human societies, but that they sorely lack capitalization and the capacity to 'scale up' and join the global competitive marketplace. Hence the supposition that loans, incentives and 'capacity building' at the level of individuals and communities will somehow leverage community capacities into an entrepreneurial spirit, which will reduce dependency and lead to economic growth (Roy 2012).

Essentially, as global neoliberal capitalism fails to provide the necessities of life or sustainable happiness to an ever-greater proportion of the world's population, and as the capacities of what remains of the welfare state are further depleted, the commons are cited as the means to provide the basis of life support for abject or surplus populations. Worse still, the commons here become laboratories for future sites of capitalist enclosure or profit generation.

The most telling example is perhaps the birth of the so-called 'sharing economy,' which has risen to prominence in the wake of the 2008 financial crisis thanks in part to the widespread use of smartphone and portable electronic technology. From car-share platforms (Uber, Lyft) to applications that allow individuals to rent out rooms in their house to travellers (Airbnb) to tapping the knowledge of hard-to-reach experts and autodidacts (Quora) to micro-task employers (TaskRabbit, Amazon Mechanical Turk) to applications that allow one to share tools, leftovers and skills, this has been heralded by leading business newspapers and liberal periodicals as the wave of the future. In an era of unrelenting artificial scarcity, new technology can enable us to access the common wealth all around us, to reconnect to community and to generate an income without dependency on either the state or a formal employer. The underlying assumption is one broadly in keeping with a neoliberal narrative of competitive human behaviour and the supremacy of economic rationality. Sharing here is monetized and overseen by the simulacrum of community in the form of user-generated rankings and feedback mechanisms. Such platforms are lauded for their capacity to marketize and therefore recognize, value and render efficient 'resources' that might once have been left idle: a spare room, an unused drill, a parked car or a knowledgeable recluse (Scholz 2014a, 2014b; Morozov 2013). Such initiatives are fundamentally predicated on (and help reproduce) a distorted notion of 'sharing' that can only be germinated and sustained within a relentlessly individualistic and competitive society, wherein the collective wealth and productive capacity of humanity are fathomed as private property to be rented out for profit. Worse still, under the euphemistic banner of the 'sharing economy', labour is reorganized towards a hyper-neoliberal model where each individual is a competitive entrepreneur, responsible for selling their human capital to the highest bidder through proprietary systems, compounding tendencies towards economic and social precarity (Asher-Shapiro 2014).

This is an example of what we might call enclosure 3.0.

Internet gurus speak retrospectively of Web 1.0 as the first generation of internet interfaces: the basic webpages and other online utilities that users navigated towards, as if sailing between different distinct islands in an archipelago. Web 2.0 refers to the rise of social networking sites (Facebook, Twitter), user-generated content (blogs, user reviews), and personalized web experiences, wherein users essentially create their own private islands and set the parameters through which various services and information arrive at the docks. Web 3.0 is speculated to be an (imminent or already-underway) evolution of the previous form, but one empowered and energized by the incredible (and incredibly disturbing) new capacities of algorithmic computing to cultivate user data (based on everything from health records to consumer behaviour to browser histories to past social media activity) and deliver highly customized, highly specific products and information directly to the user based on some alchemy of these occult criteria. Here, we private islanders need only make the most minute of gestures (or no gestures at all) and have the content we desire (but may not have known that we desired) airdropped to our reclining beach chair.

We might understand enclosure 1.0 as the original spatial process, which began in the medieval period and accelerated through the early modern, whereby capitalism, through legal adjustments and brute force evicted commoners from their lands and seized their resources, laying waste to community and self-sufficiency. In essence, as de Angelis (2007) and John McMurtry (1999, 2002) note, this was a process of violence and theft that created the preconditions for critical spheres of social and economic life to be brought under the discipline of capital and made to obey its overarching logic of value: the accumulation of capital for its own sake. This process of enclosure continues today as global extractive capitalism displaces millions of peasants and indigenous people around the world. It might even be said to be occurring in already capitalist urban spaces as the processes of urban displacement (such as gentrification) destroy communities of mutual aid and solidarity in the name of speculative real estate gains. All of these rely on the expansion of surveillance, securitization and militarization. In essence, enclosure 1.0 demonstrates and sets the groundwork for other forms of enclosure: (a) the severing of people from autonomous means of social reproduction, thus rendering them dependent on a capital (b) the replacement of autonomous value practices with capitalist models including the commodification of land, labour, social care and community.

Thus enclosure 2.0 might be said to refer to the broader paradigm of 'enclosure' and the myriad ways in which capitalism has created and continues to create value by seizing on elements of common, cooperative labour and life. For instance: the intellectual property regimes that foreclose the distribution of knowledge, from life-saving pharmaceuticals to academic writing; the privatization of those elements of the welfare state (schools, hospitals, utilities, etc.) that were the residual products of common struggles (Haiven 2014); the destruction of ecosystems in the name of capitalist profit which has the effect of robbing communities of their means of subsistence; and the privatization of social life as public space is securitized and as culture writ large is commodified. To return to the language of value, here capital seeks to expand in a moment of neoliberal crisis (notably the crisis of what Cleaver 2005 calls the 'Keynesian Planner State') by claiming spheres of life once held, for various reasons, outside the market. Under the ideological, political and economic processes of neoliberalism, various aspects of social life come to be directly disciplined or organized by the market, a process Hardt and Negri (2000, 2004) call the 'real subsumption' of labour to capital and which their Autonomist predecessors descried as the rise of the 'social factory' where the logic of capital spread throughout all manner of social institutions (Thorburn 2003).

Enclosure 3.0, like web 3.0, is not a clean break from the past, but an evolution, complexification and intensification of what came before, one that makes full use of the revolutionary technological capacities of computerized, globalized neoliberal capitalism. The sharing economy, as well as the adoption of the 'commons' as a key term of neoliberal economic development and governmental programmes (micro-finance, 'big society') represents the leveraging of torqued technology and institutions to pry open the field of daily life and the final frontiers of non-capitalist cooperation and collaboration and transform these into either (a) means to generate profit or (b) means to maintain bare human life amid relentless market failure. Enclosure 3.0 in this sense signifies capital's seemingly accidental but actually highly convenient 'discovery' of the wealth of social life and its mobilization of the idea and the actuality of the commons as the means of its own survival and reproduction.

As with previous forms of enclosure, we should not see this as simply a top-down, one-way un-nuanced process. Enclosure is driven, in part, by the tragically extorted ingenuity and ambition of dispossessed commoners searching for means to survive and thrive in the absence of forms of collective care and support. Enclosure 3.0 encourages each of us to become an entrepreneur, eagerly searching out ways to monetize those not-yet monetized aspects of our lives. Essentially, capitalism is developing the structural capacity for distributed forms of micro-enclosure. This process occurs in many stages. For instance, the birth of the monetized and commercialized Airbnb platform, which allows individuals to rent out rooms in their private homes on a short-term basis, took inspiration and 'improved' upon more grassroots 'couch-surfing' platforms that were based upon peer-to-peer, free mutual aid (Bialski 2012; Rifkin 2014). In many jurisdictions barter networks or community gardens initially designed to offer free or commons-based platforms for collaboration have been commercialized, or used as selling points to attract new (upwardly mobile) residents to once abandoned neighbourhoods (Markham 2014; see also Harvey 2012). In the bankrupt city of Detroit, for instance, community groups are amid a battle to maintain the urban agricultural commons they have built from corporate enclosure by land speculators and would-be 'philanthrocapitalists' (Liu 2012; Learning from Detroit 2013). We have seen the ways in which the free and open software movement has been oddly embraced and in some cases co-opted by corporate interests keen to harness the voluntary labour of thousands of collaborative coders, designers and others (see Kleiner 2010).

In sum, Enclosure 3.0 represents not merely the theft and subsumption of the material world but also the imagination itself (Haiven 2014). Here the imagination means both the inner world of the individual as well as the shared landscape of possibility and potential shared in common among people in their interwoven and interlocking social spheres. According to Franco Berardi (2012), the capitalist cooptation of the imagination oversees the proliferation of loneliness and anxiety, depression and a sense of endless futility. To the extent that capitalism today has developed the means to tap, shape and harness our capacities for sociality, empathy, creativity, connectivity, communication, community and generosity, it does so within a context of, and in order to reproduce, a regime of commercialization, competition, spectacle and existential and economic precariousness. We must resist the urge to privatize and enclose these affective responses as personal woes, and instead recognize them as structural elements of hyper-neoliberal capitalism and integrate their effects and potentials into our strategies for confronting and overcoming it (see Plan C 2014).

Commons as actuality, spirit and horizon

In providing an overview of the conceptual and political relationship between the idea/ideal of the commons and neoliberalism (as ideology, as process, and as period), I have sought to demonstrate that, while often mobilized as diametric opposites, these two terms in fact reflect and refract each other in complex theoretical and material ways. I've outlined a theory of 'enclosure 3.0', a neoliberal form of enclosure that reaches expansively across the globe and intensively into daily life and the imagination. But I do not wish to echo or amplify a cynicism, so germane to neoliberal times, that would dissuade us from commitment or action. In spite of these new challenges, those who would oppose neoliberal capitalism must hold fast to the commons in at least three valences, all the while recognizing, in dialectical fashion, that none are pure or uncompromised.

First, we must hold fast to the actuality of the commons. By this I mean both the commons of the 'natural' world (watersheds, oceans, forests, climate) and the 'built' commons (community gardens, housing cooperatives, reclaimed factories, certain forms of free and open source software and peer-production systems, etc.). They are the bedrock of resistance to and transcendence of neoliberalism because in their use, care and defence we cultivate, express and render militant non-capitalist values (de Angelis 2007; Haiven 2014). These also provide the necessities and pleasures of life within, against and beyond the capitalist order and, as such, reduce our dependency on exploitative and oppressive systems.

Second, we must recognize that commons do not simply exist but are always under intentional cultivation. This is why Linebaugh (2014) and others insist we see commons as spaces or times animated by acts of *commoning*: the intentional and strategic development of common values, practices and forms. Hence, what separates a commons-based project from a sharing economy-based project is that the former is instilled with and renders militant the values of collaboration, horizontalism, direct democracy, member-participation, egalitarianism, anti-oppression, and the radical imagination, whereas the latter simply mobilizes these principles piecemeal to commodify another aspect of life. Recognizing the spirit of the commons also demands we acknowledge that all our relationships and social institutions are, in fact, undergirded and, indeed, dependent on what Stefano Harney and Fred Moten (2013) call the 'undercommons': that network of insurgent, unruly commoning activity that is occurring even in the most oppressive and enclosing of institutions, where we mobilize mundane solidarities and creative cooperation to struggle within, against and beyond exploitation. As such the spirit of the commons must also always be the spirit of refusal: the rebellion against the reorientation of our energies, time and cooperative capacities towards the reproduction of oppression, exploitation and a destructive system (see Holloway 2002).

Finally, we must continue to envision the commons of the future as a receding horizon. If we understand the commons not as a noun but as a verb it is an activity without end, without limit. Even after we avenge ourselves on neoliberalism (as is patently necessary), the work of building and rebuilding the commons throughout the field of social life will be a continual process and project. That is, all social institutions, even ones already deemed 'commons', will need to be constantly revolutionized to maintain their living dynamism, democratic character, egalitarian ethos and participatory, grassroots character. They will also need to be constantly and actively defended against re-enclosure and more subtle forms of conscription within the reproduction of capital, which we know to be endlessly adaptive, especially amid crisis. Such a recognition need not lead to fatalism but rather should focus our attention on the prefigurative (Day 2005) and iterative qualities of struggle against the neoliberal despair machine.

In a sense, the commons are and have always been our fate. The question now is: who will organize them and on what terms? Presently, the commons risk being conscripted to and subsumed under a vicious and systemically suicidal neoliberal globalization that relies on grassroots participatory forms to 'externalize' the costs of its reckless, endless expansion (de Angelis 2007; McMurtry 1999, 2002). Already, fascistic and reactionary forces around the world are responding by conscripting the commons to serve nationalist, religious or ethnic fundamentalism and provide a means of reproduction in the ruins neoliberalism leaves behind. Thus it is more urgent than ever that we define and develop militant theories, practices and networks of the commons capable of envisioning and bringing about egalitarian democratic and peaceful futures.

Acknowledgements

The author is grateful to Wes Cameron, Baruch Gottleib, Jon Grant, Eli Meyerhoff, Martha Rans, and Fern Thompsett for their critical feedback.

Note

1 A wealth of such analyses can be found in the annals of the journal *The Commoner*, edited by Massimo de Angelis, at www.commoner.org.uk

References

Anderson, B. 2006. *Imagined Communities*. London and New York: Verso.

de Angelis, M. 2007. *The Beginning of History: Value Struggles and Global Capitalism*. London and Ann Arbor: Pluto.

Angus, I. 2008. The Myth of the Tragedy of the Commons. *Climate & Capitalism*. Retrieved from http://climateandcapitalism.com/2008/08/25/debunking-the-tragedy-of-the-commons/

Asher-Schapiro, A. 2014. Against Sharing. *Jacobin*. Retrieved from https://www.jacobinmag.com/2014/09/against-sharing/

Azzellini, D., and Sitrin, M. 2014. *They Can't Represent Us! Reinventing Democracy from Greece to Occupy*. London and New York: Verso.

Bateman, M. 2010. *Why Doesn't Microfinance Work?: The Destructive Rise of Local Neoliberalism*. London: Zed.

Benkler, Y., 2007. *The Wealth of Networks: How Social Production Transforms Markets and Freedom*. New Haven and London: Yale University Press.

Berardi, F.B. 2012. Emancipation of the Sign: Poetry and Finance During the Twentieth Century. *E-Flux*, 39. Retrieved from http://www.e-flux.com/journal/emancipation-of-the-sign-poetry-and-finance-during-the-twentieth-century/

Bernes, J. 2013. Logistics, Counterlogistics and the Communist Prospect, in *Endnotes 3: Gender, Race, Class and Other Misfortunes*. Retrieved from http://endnotes.org.uk/en/jasper-bernes-logistics-counterlogistics-and-the-communist-prospect

Bialski, P. 2012. Technologies of Hospitality: How Planned Encounters Develop Between Strangers. *Hospitality & Society*, 1.3: 245–60.

Boggs, G.L. 2009. *Detroit: City of Hope. In These Times*. Retrieved from http://www.inthesetimes.com/article/4247/detroit_city_of_hope

Bollier, D., and Helfrich, S. eds. 2012. *The Wealth of the Commons: A World Beyond Market and State*. Amherst: Levellers Press.

—. eds. 2015. *Patterns of Commoning*. Amherst, MA: Commons Strategies Group.

Brown, W. 2015. *Undoing the Demos: Neoliberalism's Stealth Revolution*. New York: Zone.

Caffentzis, G. 2012. A Tale of Two Conferences: Globalization, the Crisis of Neoliberalism and the Question of the Commons. *Borderlands*, 11.2. Retrieved from http://www.borderlands.net.au/vol11no2_2012/caffentzis_globalization.pdf

Cleaver, H. 2005. Work, Value and Domination. *The Commoner*, 10: 115–31.

Day, R. 2005. *Gramsci is Dead: Anarchist Currents in the Newest Social Movements*. London: Pluto Press.

Dowling, E., and Harvie, D. 2014. Harnessing the Social: State, Crisis and (Big) Society. *Sociology*, 48.5: 869–86.

Federici, S., 2005. *Caliban and the Witch: Women, Capitalism and Primitive Accumulation*. New York: Autonomedia.

—. 2012. *Revolution at Point Zero: Housework, Reproduction, and Feminist Struggle*. Brooklyn and Oakland: Common Notions, PM Press.

—. 2013. Commoning Against Debt. *Tidal: Occupy Theory, Occupy Strategy*, 4: 20.

Fortunati, L. 1995. *The Arcane of Reproduction: Housework, Prostitution, Labor and Capital*. New York: Autonomedia.

Goldstein, J. 2013. Terra Economica: Waste and the Production of Enclosed Nature. *Antipode*, 45.2: 357–75.

Greer, A. 2012. Commons and Enclosure in the Colonization of North America. *American Historical Review*, 117.2: 365–386.

Haiven, M. 2014. *Crises of Imagination, Crises of Power: Capitalism, Creativity and the Commons*. London and New York: Zed.

Hardin, G. 1968. The Tragedy of the Commons. *Science*, 162.3859: 1243–8.

Hardt, M., and Negri, A. 2000. *Empire*. Cambridge: Harvard University Press.

—. 2004. *Multitude: War and Democracy in the Age of Empire*. New York: Penguin.

Harney, S., and Moten, F. 2013. *The Undercommons: Fugitive Planning and Black Study*. New York: Autonomedia.

Harvey, D. 2005. *A Brief History of Neoliberalism*. Oxford and New York: Oxford University Press.

—. 2012. The Art of Rent, in *Rebel Cities*. London and New York: Verso: 89–112.

Hill, C. 1972. *The World Turned Upside Down: Radical Ideas During the English Revolution*. London and New York: Penguin.

Holcombe, R.G. 2005. Common Property in Anarcho-Capitalism. *Journal of Libertarian Studies*, 19.2: 3–29.

Holloway, J. 2002. *Change the World Without Taking Power*. London and Ann Arbor: Pluto.

Khasnabish, A. 2008. *Zapatismo Beyond Borders: New Imaginations of Political Possibility*. Toronto: University of Toronto Press.

Kleiner, D. 2010. *The Telekommunist Manifesto*. Amsterdam: Institute for Network Cultures.

Learning from Detroit: Land, Life, Liberation. 2013. *Tidal*, 4. Retrieved from tidalmag.org/issue4/detroit/

Linebaugh, P. 2011. Forward, in Thompson, E.P., ed. *William Morris: William Morris: Romantic to Revolutionary*. Oakland: PM Press.

—. 2014. *Stop, Thief!: The Commons, Enclosures, and Resistance*. Oakland: PM Press.

Liu, Y.Y. 2012. Detroiters Rally to Stop 'Corporate Land Grab' of Vacant Lots. *In These Times*. Retrieved from http://inthesetimes.com/uprising/entry/14278/detroiters_decry_corporate_land_grab_of_vacant_lots

Maddison, B. 2010. Radical Commons Discourse and the Challenges of Colonialism. *Radical History Review*, 108: 29–48.

Markham, L. 2014. Gentrification and the Urban Garden. *The New Yorker*. Retrieved from http://www.newyorker.com/business/currency/gentrification-and-the-urban-garden

Marx, K. 1992. *Capital I: A Critique of Political Economy*. New York: Penguin.

McMurtry, J. 1999. *The Cancer Stage of Capitalism*. London and Ann Arbor: Pluto.

—. 2002. *Value Wars: The Global Market versus the Life Economy*. London: Pluto Press.

Midnight Notes. 1990. *New Enclosures, Vol. 10*. Retrieved from http://www.midnightnotes.org/newenclos.html

—. ed. 2001. *Auroras of the Zapatistas*. Oakland and Edinburgh: AK Press.

Mies, M. 1986. *Patriarchy and Accumulation on a World Scale: Women in the International Division of Labour*. London: Zed.

Moragan, J., and Olson, W. 2011. Aspiration Problems for the Indian Rural Poor: Research on Self-help Groups and Micro-finance. *Capital & Class*, 35.2: 189–212.

Morozov, E. 2013. The 'Sharing Economy' Undermines Workers' Rights. *Financial Times*, 24 October. Retrieved from http://www.ft.com/intl/cms/s/0/92c3021c-34c2-11e3-8148-00144feab7de.html#axzz3SrWiOT68

Murray, L.J., Piper, S.T., and Robertson, K. 2014. *Putting Intellectual Property in its Place: Rights Discourses, Creative Labor, and the Everyday*. Oxford: Oxford University Press.

Neeson, J.M. 1993. *Commoners: Common Right, Enclosure and Social Change in England, 1700–1820*. Cambridge and New York: Cambridge University Press.

Ostrom, E. 1990. *Governing the Commons: The Evolution of Institutions for Collective Action*. Cambridge and New York: Cambridge University Press.

Ostrom, E., Chang, C., Pennington, M., and Tarko, V. 2012. *The Future of the Commons: Beyond Market Failure and Government Regulation*. London: Institute on Economic Affairs.

P2P Foundation. 2015. *Commons Transition: Policy Proposals for an Open Knowledge Commons Society*. Retrieved from http://commonstransition.org/wp-content/uploads/2015/03/Commons-Transition_-Policy-Proposals-for-a-P2P-Foundation.pdf

Perelman, M. 2000. *The Invention of Capitalism: Classical Political Economy and the Secret History of Primitive Accumulation*. Durham, NC, and London: Duke University Press.

Plan C. 2014. *We Are All Very Anxious: Six Theses on Anxiety and Why It is Effectively Preventing Militancy, and One Possible Strategy for Overcoming It*. Retrieved from http://www.weareplanc.org/blog/we-are-all-very-anxious/

Rifkin, J. 2014. The Sharing Economy on the Collaborative Commons. *Common Dreams*. Retrieved from http://www.commondreams.org/views/2014/04/29/sharing-economy-collaborative-commons

Roy, A. 2012. Ethical Subjects: Market Rule in an Age of Poverty. *Public Culture*, 24.1: 105–8.

Scholz, T. 2014a. Platform Cooperativism vs the Sharing Economy. *Medium.com*. Retrieved from https://medium.com/@trebors/platform-cooperativism-vs-the-sharing-economy-2ea737f1b5ad

—. 2014b. The Politics of the Sharing Economy. *Collectivate*. Retrieved from http://www.publicseminar.org/2014/06/the-politics-of-the-sharing-economy/#.VqkHwCqLTIU

Srnicek, N., and Williams, A. 2015. *Inventing the Future: Postcapitalism and a World Without Work*. London and New York: Verso.

Stiegman, M., and Pictou, S. 2010. How Do You Say Netuklimuk in English? Learning through Video in Bear River First Nation, in Choudry, A., and Kapoor, D. eds. *Learning from the Ground up: Global Perspectives on Social Movements and Knowledge Production*. London and New York: Palgrave Macmillan: 227–42.

Thompson, E.P. 1968. *The Making of the English Working Class*. New York: Pantheon.

Thorburn, N. 2003. The Social Factory: Machines, Work and Control, in Thorburn, N. (ed.) *Deleuze, Marx and Politics*. London and New York: Routledge: 69–102.

Weeks, K. 2011. *The Problem with Work: Feminism, Marxism, Antiwork Politics, and Postwork Imaginaries*. Durham, NC and London: Duke University Press.

Weissman, T. 2013. Detroit's Edible Gardens: Art and Agriculture in a Post-Environmental World. *Third Text*. Retrieved from http://www.thirdtext.org/detroit%E2%80%99s-edible-gardens-arc

Williams, A.D., and Tapscott, D. 2008. *Wikinomics: How Mass Collaboration Changes Everything*. New York: Atlantic Books.

van Zanden, J.L. 1999. The Paradox of the Marks: The Exploitation of Commons in the Eastern Netherlands, 1250–1850. *The Agricultural History Review*, 47.2: 125–44.

24

RETOOLING SOCIAL REPRODUCTION FOR NEOLIBERAL TIMES

The example of the social economy

Peter Graefe

Early analyses of neoliberalism, adopting an alarmist tone, emphasized the retrenchment of state social provision to make space for market regulation. With time, these added the nuance that programmes were not just retrenched, but also redeployed. It was not just a question of changing the balance of state and market, but of transforming the logics and re-orienting the goals of state provision, and of attempting to transform the subjectivities and identities of citizens (see Larner 2000; Peck 2010).

Analysis of the social economy and neoliberalism has followed a similar arc. At first, the question was one of the social economy as a site for privatization and state offloading. Then, as a site of institutional and policy experimentation, it has sustained the interest of those analysing neoliberalism more dynamically. For more Foucauldian analyses, there is interest in the technologies that align non-state service providers with governmental programmes, as well as the manner in which social economy organizations govern clients. For analysts more versed in the tradition of the regulation school, the interest has been tied more to how this innovation relates to the temporality of neoliberalism. Are we witnessing the roll-out of new institutions and governmentalities so as to extend market metrics deeper into social provisions, and indeed into organizations previously marked by non-market cultures and rationalities, or is the attention to the social economy more akin to creating flanking mechanisms to compensate for problems in social reproduction that might hobble the neoliberal project?

Both the Foucauldian and the regulationist accounts provide useful critical entrées to understanding the development of the social economy, but they share similar structuralist shortcomings. In looking for how the social economy translates or relates to a broader neoliberal project or programme, there is a tendency to overstate processes that reproduce neoliberalism, and to ignore the potentials for the social economy to serve as an element of a settlement that might break with neoliberalism. The way forward would seem to demand an approach with a finer sense of agency. This is not so much a strategy of introducing agency so as to then adopt an excessive voluntarism, as one of keeping an analytical door open to possibilities of change.

What is the social economy?

The social economy, as used here, really entered the international policy discourse in the 1990s, the European Commission's General Directorate Employment and Social Affairs having created a special unit to consider social economy issues in 1989 (Westwood 2009). As a term, it attempted to seize the role of a set of organizations that operated outside of the formal state and for-profit private sectors, and which had some form of collective benefit orientation. There was also interest in capturing how these organizations married social and economic objectives: a community-based training and job placement service could serve traditional labour market objectives, but also with the social participation and inclusion of individuals and groups facing compounding discriminations and barriers. A community restaurant might train the unemployed in food services, while providing affordable meals and a place of sociality for people with limited financial resources. A women's shelter might be considered mostly as a response to the social problem of endemic violence, but a holistic view would also see it as an economic resource both in terms of employing a number of people, but more broadly in allowing women to rebuild their lives and relationships with the labour market. The challenge for any definition is therefore at least two-fold. First, it needs to capture the non-state/non-market character of the organization, the collective benefit orientation, and the imbrication of social and economic contributions, all in one go. Second, it needs to relate that definition to nationally specific sets of organizations and institutions that overlap imperfectly.

A review 15 years ago unearthed at least five definitions (Lévesque and Mendell 1999), and these definitions continue to be presented in more contemporary publications attempting to pin-down the concept (e.g. Borzaga and Tortia 2007; Evers and Laville 2004). A common starting point is a definition by components (cooperatives + mutuals + associations + foundations). The European Council adopted this definition in 1997 (Westwood 2009). It has the benefit of providing a rapid way to tally the economic and employment weight of the sector, but ignores whether it captures the dimensions of social and economic imbrication or even the collective benefit orientation. Large cooperatives or credit unions have distinct property structures, but their actual operation may not look very different from their for-profit competitors. Other definitions focus on the rules used to link an association of individuals to a firm producing goods and services, on the mixing of economic logics (the hybridization of market, non-market and non-monetary logics), or on the diverse logics of action occurring within associations.

With time, definitions have come closer to a definition adopted in Wallonia and then Quebec, which sees social economy activities as those respecting the principles of: service to members or the collectivity as an end; autonomous management; democratic decision-making; the primacy of people and labour over capital in dividing surpluses; and participation, empowerment and individual and collective responsibility (Laville *et al.* 2007). This definition is ultimately one based strongly in values, and so faces the opposite problem of the definition by components, namely in empirically delimiting what organizations fit within its perimeter.

For the purposes of this chapter, it is, maybe, more helpful to use Amin *et al.*'s (1999) definition of the social economy as 'centred around the provision of social and welfare services by the not-for-profit sector'. While it loses the fine touch around the values at play, it does place the social economy in a space between the state and the market economy, while recognizing that it is, in particular, non-profit organizations providing welfare services that fall within the ambit of the sector. For Amin *et al.*, the social economy breaks the binary of the market and the state as sources of welfare provision, and reflects the entrepreneurial and creative activities of relatively dominated actors, seeking to create welfare in a period of labour market and welfare state changes that have created misery for many (1999; see also Westwood 2009). Analytically, if our interest is in how the sector relates to a broader set of political and economic strategies, it has the additional benefit in implicitly visualizing the sector in relationship to the state and its social and welfare services. As such, the social economy exists less *sui generis*, but is in part a co-construction between the non-profit sector and state strategies around service delivery.

It is worth taking a moment to consider why the definition remains so messy. A decade ago, one might have presumed that this reflected the novelty of the field of enquiry (e.g. Graefe 2002: 248). The persistence would seem to suggest that the social economy is an essentially contested concept, and that the definitional morass may also be explained by certain theoretical positions taken below. Those who think of neoliberalism as a process of extending neoliberal rationalities into new domains would see the 'social economy' as necessarily messy, as the term itself denotes a space beyond the mainstream economy and the welfare state that presumably looks different in different countries. In this view, actors caught up in the process of neoliberalization package existing bits of alternative economies into an object susceptible to mobilization through policy strategies. Here they would likely agree with institutionalists that the forms taken in specific countries will be quite variable. For instance, where an encompassing welfare state is in place, as in the Nordic countries, one is likely to encounter voluntary organizations turned towards advocacy, compared to a greater service-delivery orientation in liberal welfare states (Boismenu 2001). For more post-structuralist renderings of the social economy, the issue may be more ontological. As Larner suggests (2014), the social economy is usually defined with respect to public and capitalist sector employment and organizational strategies. As these forms become ever less rigid and come to overlap and blend into each other, it becomes epistemologically problematic to render a social economy that stands in contradistinction to these categories.

Studying the social economy with neoliberalism

Given the topic of this volume, our interest is on relating the social economy with neoliberalism, but it is worth noting at the outset that the vast majority of the work on the subject does not do so. The dominant theoretical framework in the field might be called one of 'governance'. In other words, it describes and traces changes in the institutionalization of state-society interactions, paying attention to the roles that social economy organizations are called on to play (e.g. Ascoli and Ranci 2002; Evers and Laville 2004). Most national literatures have their set of studies on the social economy, or on cognate constructions like the voluntary sector, the non-profit sector or the not-for-profit sectors. The terminology nevertheless changes quickly. Whereas this governance at one time might be tied to considerations of social cohesion or social inclusion, more recently, it is about how non-profits and mutual associations might fit in an ecology of social innovation or social enterprise (Borzaga and Santuari 2003). These studies of governance point to the importance of legal traditions of recognizing/limiting voluntary action, the development of welfare states, and the push of new social movements for explaining the particular form that these relationships take in different places. The difficulty of removing the social economy from national contexts is evident in an international literature that privileges discrete national case studies over comparative analysis and theorization (Amin 2009).

This institutionalism is problematic for scholars working with the concept of neoliberalism because the latter's temporality is rarely worked into analyses, at least not at much depth: it may mark a change in governance but there is not much interest in emphasizing how it specifically reworks rule, policy or governmentalities. It is also useful, however, because it protects against an overly reductive application of theorization about neoliberalism. Whatever the social economy's relationship to neoliberalism in theory, in practice it needs to be thought out against a backdrop of distinct histories and institutions that shape how this relationship plays out. And, at its best, this mainstream work studies phenomena such as marketization or the privatization of social services (e.g. Ascoli and Ranci 2002), of direct interest to students of neoliberalism.

The first contributions to cross the study of neoliberalism with the concept of the social economy came early, and generally took the form of ideological critique. In essence, they took some of the purportedly positive outcomes that social economy organizations were felt to produce, and positioned them as handmaidens to a neoliberal project understood as the wrecking of social protections that had shielded citizens from the market. Thus, if champions of the social economy pointed to innovations in labour market insertion, or to the creation of socially useful jobs, critics would ask if this was just an extension of neoliberal labour market policy. Did these insertion measures simply leave community organizations as participants in workfare? Were they simply feeding more people into the low-end of the service sector labour market? Were the socially useful jobs secure or well-paid jobs? (Boivin and Fortier 1998; Browne 2000)

Similarly, if champions of the social economy emphasized the creativity and innovation of communities in meeting pressing social needs in hard times, and in ensuring people were looked after despite state retrenchment, the critics were unimpressed. They instead saw an instrumentalization of the community sector as a means of cutting the welfare state while maintaining some semblance of a safety net. The social economy thus allowed neoliberals to square a policy of state retrenchment while ensuring some basic social reproduction occurred. In the process, it created a neoliberalized citizenship. Instead of social rights as citizenship rights, the use of the social economy led to a narrower conception of access to services based on needs. Presumably the middle-class could purchase higher-quality services, leaving the social economy as a threadbare welfare state for the poor, delivered by the poor, and even there delivered unevenly based on the capacity of communities to organize. In the process, the social economy organizations themselves would lose their capacity to represent and advocate for at least two reasons. First, service delivery imposed state definitions of clienteles and their needs, thereby choking off the ability to identify new needs and solutions to them. Second, service delivery changed organizations by making them more reliant on the state (and thus less likely to criticize it), and by requiring professionalization (grant writing, contract management, accounting) that reduced democratic management practices (these arguments are described by Eisenschitz and Gough 2011; Shragge *et al.* 2001).

It should be noted that this critical literature, which came in national variants, has largely died out. The questions it asks about job quality in the sector or the impact of state contracting on the capacity of organizations to advocate for their members continue to be difficult ones for promoters of the social economy. Studies continue to show, for instance, that the sector has difficulty creating good work (although some contest that the definition does not capture some goods that individuals draw from this kind of work, see Larner 2014), and in achieving sufficient scale and mass to have large employment effects (see Amin *et al.* 2003; Buckingham and Teasdale 2013). Nevertheless, few specifically relate it to neoliberalism *per se*.

There is a large missed opportunity here as a result. Certainly, the early critiques were almost mechanical in the linkages they drew between observed practices and presumed neoliberal intent, and they clearly used neoliberalism as much as a foe to denounce than as a meaningful analytical category. But if one adopted a more sophisticated stance, the analysis of linkages could be quite rich. For instance, take Peck and Tickell's (2002) attempt to distinguish a roll-back neoliberalism, focused on removing the market-limiting institutions of the Fordist era, from a roll-out neoliberalism, where new institutions and governmentalities are rolled out to stabilize the neoliberal project and extend market and market-like processes into new areas. One obvious entrée into the social economy would be to understand it as a project of roll-out neoliberalism. It would be one way of making sense of the governance research referenced above, and, indeed, the set of reflections coming from the OECD (e.g. Noya 2009) and government ministries on the institutions needed to finance the sector, best practices for partnering and contracting with voluntary organizations and the like.

The application of this sort of analysis nevertheless would need to confront two shortcomings. First, there is the question of agency: the roll-back/roll-out theorization imports some of *régulation* theory's problems of structure and agency. One starts from a neoliberal accumulation regime, and then looks for institutions and governmentalities (read modes of regulation) that reproduce it, leaving a functionalist aftertaste. While careful empirical analysis can open spaces to appreciate agency, and therefore variation across space and time, the analytical proclivity is still focused on forms of agency that reproduce neoliberalism.

The second problem is that the concept of roll-out neoliberalism may be too broad. On the one hand, it points to institutions that stabilize an otherwise chaotic and destructive neoliberalism, while, on the other, it points to the extension of markets and market-like mechanisms ever deeper into the lifeworld. These may be quite different processes. The first points to the issue of possible crises of social reproduction under neoliberalism. Whether we speak in terms of capitalism requiring degrees of socialization in order to sustain accumulation (e.g. Eisenschitz and Gough 2011), or in terms of neoliberalism wearing down extra-economic inputs for competitiveness (such as trust, social cohesion) faster than they are reproduced (Jessop 2000), we might see innovations like the social economy as a response. Indeed, it is the capacity of the social economy to perform this socialization function with limited politicization that Eisenschitz and Gough (2011) see as one of the reasons for its popularity with policy-makers in the current context.

Nevertheless, the institutions that would perform this function well may not be the same institutions that roll out market mechanisms. Among the 'dilemmas of the welfare mix' for Ascoli and Ranci (2002) are trade-offs between mechanisms that maximize competition and those that ensure service quality, or between mechanisms that limit competition to develop high-performing organizations and those that encourage new entrants of unknown quality. As such, there might be value in distinguishing between the use of the social economy as a 'flanking mechanism', to adopt Jessop's terminology, and the active roll-out of market-like mechanisms, such as competitive contracting regimes or social impact bonds.

Engaging neoliberalism in order to place the social economy outside of it

If work directly on neoliberalism and the social economy has been limited and has largely dried up, neoliberalism did provide a foil early on for the alternative view that not everything was neoliberal. This view came originally out of certain strands of *régulation* theory, which argued that the emergent state form could not be reduced to neoliberalism, and, indeed, that neoliberalism was but one post-Fordist possibility among others. Thus, Bob Jessop (2002) wrote of a Post-national Schumpeterian Workfare Regime, with a variety of non-neoliberal possibilities including neo-statist and neo-corporatist trajectories for most European welfare states. Jessop did include a 'neo-communitarian' variant that focused on community mobilization and the social economy, particularly in marginalized areas. Here an emphasis on social use values would act as a spur to development, while extensive local networking and partnerships would ensure the benefits of economic development would be re-embedded locally through skilling, labour market insertion and investment in social infrastructure.

This led others, also with regulationist histories, to place the social economy as part of an alternative, non-neoliberal model of development. For instance, state investment in social economy enterprises was seen as a refusal of an 'everything to the market' logic. Along with initiatives like community economic development, workplace partnerships, peak-level social partnerships, and the co-construction of social services between the state and community organizations, the social economy is a piece of an alternative model that pursues economic democratization (Amin 2009; Laville 1994; Lévesque and Mendell 1999).

This position about the diversity of forms of economic organization in the current moment, not all of which are neoliberal, was restated in a stronger form by the post-structuralist reading provided by Gibson-Graham (2008). Here any talk of the social economy as neoliberal was viewed as defeatist. In importing a top-down and status quo vision of economic relations, it foreclosed the possibility of deconstructing dominant views on economic development, and of resignifying these terms drawing on the broad range of possibilities that exist in the diverse economies that we live in (Graham and Cornwell 2009).

This view has also been developed by Wendy Larner (2014; Larner and Butler 2005). Unlike Gibson-Graham, Larner's critique is less a whole-cloth rejection of structural political economy critique, and more of an engagement with critical political economy accounts of neoliberalism. The critical stance is nevertheless much the same: mainstream theorizations of neoliberalism make it into an invincible foe, and empty any analytical space for thinking about resistance, contradictions, or, indeed, relationships with other projects, as these are seen as too small to make any difference. Like Gibson-Graham, she finds this theorization to be disempowering, pessimistic, and, ultimately, a disincentive to imagining and experimenting with alternatives.

As such, Larner (2000) is more ensconced in the language of neoliberalism, but invested in the understanding of its governmentalities: through what technologies and assemblages do elites try to enact neoliberal programmes of government? If neoliberalism is tied up in projects of partnership, how does this create demand for new types of leaders, with different sets of skills required to do partnerships and relationship building? How are actors in the social sector pushed through 'best practice guides' to adopt specific approaches to funding, contracting and partnership (Larner and Butler 2005)? In doing so, she also tries to capture the ways in which the project of neoliberalism runs up against the projects of other actors, such that recognizing the voices of stakeholder communities or delivering services in culturally sensitive ways get worked into state-community sector relationships. This stance has been picked up by others working on the relationship of neoliberalism with actors working in community-based organizations. For instance, in challenging claims that feminism has been a handmaiden to neoliberalism, Newman (2013) looks at how community-based organizations emerging from feminist organizing and the women's movement in their own way changed neoliberalism, by pushing it to integrate a number of new concerns and perspectives such as reflecting on job quality or the quality of services when engaged in contracting with local authorities.

The neo-Foucauldian literature on neoliberalism and the social economy has nevertheless been two-headed. On the one hand, there has been what we might call a 'global governmentality' literature. In some ways, this takes us back to the early work on neoliberalism and the social economy. In enquiring into the processes whereby state policies create effects, it comes to emphasize the manner in which the social economy serves to ensure the reproduction of a larger neoliberal governmental project. For instance, some researchers have considered how voluntary organizations take on governmental functions as they are contracted to deliver state services. Particular attention is paid to the manner in which they attempt to police and shape the subjectivities of the individuals receiving services. For instance, Cope (2001) emphasized how non-profits delivering employability services worked to depress the short-term expectations and aspirations of clients, while Murray *et al.* (2006) looked at how state policies created a 'community' field, populated with community professionals, to deal with 'problematic people' who are never likely to benefit from inclusion in the economic mainstream. Working at the level of state policy, McDonald and Marston (2002) considered how neoliberal governance in Australia has involved a repositioning of community services in a manner that remakes understandings of social citizenship, and citizens' subjectivities related to welfare and work more generally. Along similar lines, Ilcan and Basok (2004; Ilcan 2009) underline how community organizations come to play governmental roles in responsibilizing their clients to mould them into 'responsible citizens' (Ilcan and Basok 2004: 135). While developed in opposition to the more critical realist work on neoliberalism, such as Peck and Tickell's (2002), in the end these critiques share the weakness of emphasizing the reproduction of neoliberal governance. For all the language of the fragility and imperfection of these assemblages, the emphasis remains on how they create effects, and not on how they fail or leave room for alternatives (Leitner *et al.* 2007; Newman 2013).

The Foucauldian and post-structuralist literature associated with Gibson-Graham and Larner manages to avoid this trap of falling back into a fairly deterministic reading of the social economy serving to reproduce neoliberalism. It might nevertheless swing too much towards indeterminacy, however. Eisenschitz and Gough (2011) characterize Gibson-Graham (2006) as providing an institutionalist political economy dressed up in post-structuralist language. In treating the different spheres of the economy as distinct in their logics, they underplay the manner of their interaction, including possible relationships of hierarchy arising from differential access to capital and the differential ability to accumulate and control capital.

There is a long-standing literature on the pressures of institutional isomorphism for not-for-profit organizations, pushing them to mimic either state organizations or for-profit firms. There is also a large literature on the specific ways that funding regimes and legal frameworks in specific contexts affect how groups organize and function or the overall institutional ecology. Do regimes of competitive contracting or competition for grants create more hierarchical or professionalized organizations, reliant on grant-writers, service managers and accountants? Do they privilege large charitable organizations over smaller grassroots initiatives?

This literature does tend to share the pessimism of the larger neoliberal literature, in emphasizing how state policies limit the space for organizations to represent and advocate for the people that they serve, let alone maintain spaces of democratic dialogue and reflection. But even treatments that are sensitive to this bias, and seek to understand how organizations occupy interstitial spaces and might negotiate how state agendas interact with the goals and priorities of clients (e.g. Trudeau 2008), only seem able to bend the stick back so far. They leave us in a place close to the one sketched out by Newman (2013), where other logics manage to transform neoliberalism as they interact with it, yet where, for the time being, it is neoliberalism that sets the organizing logic of the system.

Moving forward on neoliberalism and the social economy

It would seem that the literature on neoliberalism and the social economy is struggling with questions of structure and agency, on the one hand, and of imagining possibilities beyond neoliberalism, on the other. Both the Peck and Tickell tradition and the neoliberal governmentality work seem to err on the side of emphasizing the reproduction of neoliberalism. Without a lot of space to devote to political agency, and thus to the potential to develop alternative projects, the literature does run the risk of being politically defeatist (Leitner *et al.* 2007). While the post-structural work has a point on this, its emphasis on the agency of social economy groups creates a naive voluntarism. There is a lack of structure to its analysis, and therefore an impoverished understanding of political strategy. Promising practices are celebrated, but in the process they are disembedded from their particular contexts that both sustain them and limit their spread.

What this seems to call for is an analytical stance that can, in Peck's (2004: 396) words, 'make meaningful part–whole connections between localized and institutionally specific instances of reform and the wider discourses and ideologies of neoliberalism', but that at the same time avoids the reduction of reform to the reproduction of neoliberalism and which recognizes the possibility of agency that might transform neoliberalism or develop projects outside of it. One way to do so would be to follow Leitner *et al.*'s (2007) prescriptions to decentre neoliberalism and watch for alternative social imaginaries.

In the case of the social economy, this would involve starting from the projects of actors themselves. Some of these actors would be community organizations seeking to build alternative economic models (e.g. Graham and Cornwell 2009), while others might be social reformers looking to limit the ravages of economic and state restructuring, while yet others might be neoliberals looking for new investment outlets in social finance and social enterprise. Following our discussion of Peck and Tickell (2002) above, we might try to sort these projects into three different ideal-typical boxes in order to relate them to neoliberalism.

On the one hand, there might be projects seeking to *roll-out neoliberalism* in the sense of creating institutions and governmentalities to deepen market relations and to extend market metrics to new realms of social life. Examples in the social economy might include creating quasi-markets through state contracting practices, or the more recent turn to social impact bonds. Alternatively, we might see projects of creating *flanking mechanisms* to shore up neoliberalism by dealing with its contradictory relationship with socialization or social reproduction. The social economy presents an interesting solution in this context by offering non-market policy solutions that might be cheaper and more innovative than the welfare state. However, in this context, the issue is less one of creating competition, than in providing reliable services of at least acceptable quality (e.g. see Ascoli and Ranci 2002). Finally, keeping an eye open for alternative social imaginaries, we might find actors bearing *countervailing strategies* that attempt to undo or move beyond the neoliberalization process. While this could take the form of specific kinds of prefigurative practice embraced by Graham and Cornwell (2009) or Larner (2014), it could also take more politically programmatic forms. For instance, it could involve attempts to democratize local economic and social development policy-making through new channels of popular participation, or attempts to transform the value assigned to different forms of paid and unpaid work and care (e.g. Amin *et al.* 2003).

While this strategy suggests decentring neoliberalism, it also suggests emphasizing political conflict, and particularly the state. The bias towards studying the reproduction of neoliberalism is not unrelated to an analysis that assumes neoliberal policy logics, and then locates politics and resistance at the interface of the state and social economy organizations. However, if we instead depart from actors and their projects for the social economy, we can give more space to assessing concretely how these projects get taken up by actors within the state, and how social mobilization and class pressures make the state more or less receptive of particular projects in given times and places. It also provides a useful terrain for analysing how discourses and projects in global circulation, be they neoliberal or alternative, are appropriated and translated into concrete policy debates (e.g. Graefe 2006).

The other benefit of this stance is to reject a pessimistic and defeatist reading of neoliberalism, on the one hand, without falling into a pure voluntarism, on the other. In recognizing how these diverse projects are embedded in the state, one can begin to map out the institutional footholds that might be available to launch and sustain alternatives to neoliberalism, either within narrow policy areas, or as new projects that stretch across the state.

To conclude

The social economy provides a useful vantage point for assessing neoliberalism, since the changes to state social provision and to labour markets that we associate with neoliberalism are ones that opened space for thinking about the contributions of an oft-neglected third sector to social well-being and economic development. Moreover, neoliberal statecraft itself, whether assessed in *regulationist* terms or Foucauldian ones, seems to include attempts to either activate the social economy or to govern through it in order to achieve varied ends.

Despite this vantage point, critical work on the social economy that draws on thinking about neoliberalism is sparse, certainly compared with the mainstream, problem-solving literature. One step in moving this work forward would be a less mechanistic theorization that would decentre neoliberalism and leave space for alternative imaginaries. What is proposed here is to not presume the neoliberalism of the state and governmental authorities, but to instead look at how the projects of political actors relate to neoliberalism, and how these projects are embedded in the state and its institutions. We could then assess how projects of further rolling out neoliberalism relate to those of creating flanking mechanisms to shore up the existing order and to those that propose countervailing strategies.

References

Amin, A. 2009. Locating the Social Economy, in Amin, A., ed. *The Social Economy: International Perspectives on Economic Solidarity*. London: Zed: 3–21.

Amin, A., Cameron, A., and Hudson, R. 1999. Welfare as Work? The Potential of the UK Social Economy. *Environment and Planning A*, 31: 2033–51.

—. 2003. *Placing the Social Economy*. London: Routledge.

Ascoli, U., and Ranci, C. 2002. Changes in the Welfare Mix: The European Path, in Ascoli, U., and Ranci, C., eds. *Dilemmas of the Welfare Mix: The New Structure of Welfare in an Era of Privatization*. New York: Kluwer Academic: 225–43.

Boismenu, G. 2001. L'Économie Sociale et le Traitement Politique des Sans-emplois, in Giroux, G., ed. *L'État, la Société et l'Économie: Turbulences et Transformations en Période de Décroissance*. Paris: L'Harmattan: 175–214.

Boivin, L., and Fortier, M. eds. 1998. *L'Économie Sociale: L'Avenir d'une Illusion*. Boucherville: Fides.

Borzaga, C., and Santuari, A. 2003. New Trends in the Non-profit Sector in Europe: The Emergence of Social Enterprise, in OECD. *The Non-profit Sector in a Changing Economy*. Paris: OECD: 31–59.

Borzaga, C., and Tortia, E. 2007. Social Economy Organizations in the Theory of the Firm, in Noya, A., and Clarence, E., eds. *The Social Economy: Building Inclusive Economies*. Paris: OECD: 23–59.

Browne, P.L. 2000. The Neo-Liberal Uses of the Social Economy: Non-Profit Organizations and Workfare in Ontario, in Fontan, J.-M., and Shragge, E., eds. *Social Economy: International Debates and Perspectives*. Montréal: Black Rose: 65–80.

Buckingham, H., and Teasdale, S. 2013. *Job Creation Through the Social Economy and Social Entrepreneurship*. Paris: OECD.

Cope, M. 2001. Between Welfare and Work: The Roles of Social Service Organizations in the Social Regulation of Labor Markets and Regulation of the Poor. *Urban Geography*, 22: 391–406.

Eisenschitz, A., and Gough, J. 2011. Socialism and the Social Economy. *Human Geography*, 4.2: 1–15.

Evers, A., and Laville, J.-L. 2004. Defining the Third Sector in Europe, in Evers, A., and Laville, J.-L., eds. *The Third Sector in Europe*. Cheltenham: Edward Elgar: 11–42.

Gibson-Graham, J.K. 2006. *A Postcapitalist Politics*. Minneapolis: University of Minnesota Press.

—. 2008. Diverse Economies: Performative Practices for 'Other Worlds'. *Progress in Human Geography*, 32: 613–32.

Graefe, P. 2002. The Social Economy and the State: Linking Ambitions with Institutions in Quebec, Canada. *Policy and Politics*, 30: 247–62.

—. 2006. The Social Economy and the American Model. *Global Social Policy*, 6: 197–219.

Graham, J., and Cornwell, J. 2009. Building Community Economies in Massachusetts: An Emerging Model of Economic Development?, in Amin, A., ed. *The Social Economy: International Perspectives on Economic Solidarity*. London: Zed: 37–65.

Ilcan, S. 2009. Privatizing Responsibility: Public Sector Reform Under Neoliberal Government. *Canadian Review of Sociology*, 46: 207–34.

Ilcan, S., and Basok, T. 2004. Community Government: Voluntary Agencies, Social Justice and the Responsibilization of Citizens. *Citizenship Studies*, 8: 129–44.

Jessop, B. 2000. The Crisis of the National Spatio-Temporal Fix and the Tendential Ecological Dominance of Globalizing Capitalism. *International Journal of Urban and Regional Research*, 24: 323–60.

—. 2002. Liberalism, Neoliberalism and Urban Governance: A State-Theoretical Perspective. *Antipode*, 34: 452–72.

Larner, W. 2000. Neo-Liberalism: Policy, Ideology, Governmentality. *Studies in Political Economy*, 63: 5–26.

—. 2014. The Limits of Post-Politics: Rethinking Radical Social Enterprise, in Wilson, J., and Swyngedouw, E., eds. *The Post-Political and Its Discontents: Spaces of Depoliticisation, Spectres of Radical Politics*. Edinburgh: Edinburgh University Press: 189–207.

Larner, W., and Butler, M. 2005. Governmentalities of Local Partnerships: The Rise of a 'Partnering State' in New Zealand. *Studies in Political Economy*, 75: 79–101.

Laville, J.-L. 1994. Services, Emploi et Socialisation, in Eme, B., and Laville, J.-L., eds. *Cohésion Sociale et Emploi*. Paris: Desclé de Brouwer: 115–55.

Laville, J.-L., Levesque, B., and Mendell, M. 2007. The Social Economy: Diverse Approaches and Practices in Europe and Canada, in Noye, A., and Clarence, E., eds. *The Social Economy: Building Inclusive Economies*. Paris: OECD: 155–87.

Leitner, H., Sheppard, E., Sziarto, K., and Maringanti, A. 2007. Contesting Urban Futures: Decentering Neoliberalism, in Leitner, H., Peck, J., and Sheppard, E.S., eds. *Contesting Neoliberalism: Urban Frontiers*. New York: Guilford Press: 1–25.

Lévesque, B., and Mendell, M. 1999. L'Économie Sociale au Québec: Éléments Théoriques et Empiriques pour le Débat et la Recherche. *Lien Social et Politiques*, 41: 105–18.

McDonald, C., and Marston, G. 2002. Patterns of Governance: The Curious Case of Non-profit Community Services in Australia. *Social Policy and Administration*, 36: 376–91.

Murray, K., Lo, J., and Waite, A. 2006. The Voluntary Sector and the Realignment of Government: A Street-Level Study. *Canadian Public Administration*, 49: 375–92.

Newman, J. 2013. Spaces of Power: Feminism, Neoliberalism and Gendered Labor. *Social Politics*, 20: 200–21.

Noya, A. ed. 2009. *The Changing Boundaries of Social Enterprises*. Paris: OECD.

Peck, J. 2004. Geography and Public Policy: Constructions of Neoliberalism. *Progress in Human Geography*, 28: 392–405.

—. 2010. *Constructions of Neoliberal Reason*. Oxford: Oxford University Press

Peck, J., and A. Tickell. 2002. Neoliberalizing Space. *Antipode*, 34: 380–404.

Shragge, E., Graefe, P., and Fontan, J.-M. 2001. The Citizenship Building Consequences of Quebec's Social Economy, in Jenson, J., ed. *Building Citizenship: Governance and Service Provision in Canada*. Ottawa: Canadian Policy Research Networks: 91–113.

Trudeau, D. 2008. Towards a Relational View of the Shadow State. *Political Geography*, 27: 669–90.

Westwood, A. 2009. Community Capacity Building and the Local Economy: Private, Government and Non-profit Approaches, in Noya, A., Clarence, E., and Craig, G., eds. *Community Capacity Building: Creating a Better Future*. Paris: OECD: 87–130.

PART IV

Knowledge productions

25

EDUCATION, NEOLIBERALISM, AND HUMAN CAPITAL

Homo economicus as 'entrepreneur of himself'

Michael A. Peters

Neoliberalism is a changing dynamic phenomenon crystalizing as an idea and ideology in the inter-war period, becoming internationalized and institutionalized as a credo for the Mont Pelerin Society (originally the Acton-Tocqueville Society) in 1947, and a set of policies in the service of economic liberalism with the ascendancy to power of Margaret Thatcher and Ronald Reagan in 1979–80 to develop as the supreme reigning economic paradigm of the major world policy agencies and the Western world-view in the last 35 years (Peters 2011). It has demonstrated its remarkable capacity for survival in light of world events, even strengthening its dominance after the global financial crisis (GFC). Against the grain of core ideological beliefs, neoliberal officials and politicians intervened directly in the market using vast amounts of public money to bail out struggling banks on the basis of the slogan 'too big to fail'. Some critics suggested that this central contradiction did little to injure the policy status of neoliberalism. Indeed, financialization and the growth of finance capitalism that led to the global financial meltdown were largely a result of the repeal of financial regulation, especially the so-called Glass–Steagall Act in 1999 that had originally limited commercial bank securities activities' and affiliations.

The GFC drew attention to market volatility, to knock-on effects of 'too big to fail' entities, the dangers of high levels of public debt and the risks associated with the massive growth and expansiveness of the finance sector vis-à-vis the real productive economy. Suddenly, the role of the state and other extra-state agencies was back on the policy agenda as governments explored the scope of new regulatory tools designed to restructure banks, introduce new capital reserve levels and monitor professional standards. Greater thought has been given to the threats that the finance sector pose to the economy as a whole, and European governments in particular have sought to deal with these problems by pursuing austerity measures designed to cut levels of unsustainable public debt. Even with the deepest recession since the 1930s – followed by the slowest economic recovery for more than a century, nationalization of banks and historically high unemployment – neoliberalism survived calls to return to new forms of Keynesian economics and today there is little evidence of paradigm change.

In the aftermath of the crisis neoliberalism has grown stronger. Philip Mirowski (2013) argues that the true nature of neoliberalism has gone unrecognized by its critics because they have failed to understand the movement's intellectual history, the way it has transformed everyday life, and what constitutes opposition to it. Michel Foucault was one of the very first to explore both the conceptual genealogy of neoliberalism and neoliberalism as one of the four main forms of economic liberalism emerging in the early twentieth century with links back to the late sixteenth century. Foucault's account of neolberalism linking it to forms of governmentality provides an understanding of its inherent longevity, its tenacity and resistance to all counter-evidence, and its dynamic ever-changing character. The other major long-term historical tendency (of capitalism), not mentioned by Foucault because it only became evident in the years after his death, is the dominance of finance culture, financialization and the increasing formalization, mathematicization, autonomization and automation of finance markets (Peters *et al.* 2015).

One of the four main forms of economic liberalism analysed by Michel Foucault (2008) in his historical treatment of the birth of neoliberalism in *The Birth of Biopolitics* was American neoliberalism, represented by the late Gary Becker. It was Becker (1962) who, on the basis of Theo Schultz's work and others, introduced the concept and theory of human capital into political economy, privileging education in his analysis. This chapter traces the inception of human capital theory and analyses it in terms of Foucault's analysis of how Becker developed an approach that is not a conception of labour power so much as a 'capital-ability'. Foucault captures this point in the following comment: 'the replacement every time of *homo economicus* as partner of exchange with a *homo economicus* as entrepreneur of himself, being for himself his own capital, being for himself his own producer, being for himself the source of his earnings' (Foucault 2008: 226).

Foucault and governmentality

Foucault's overriding interest was not in 'knowledge as ideology', as Marxists would have it, where bourgeois knowledge – say, modern liberal economics – is considered as false knowledge or bad science. Nor was he interested in 'knowledge as theory', the construction of classical liberalism that erects the notion of disinterested knowledge based on inherited philosophical distinctions from the Greeks, including Platonic epistemology, that is endorsed by the Kantian separation of schema/content, distinguishing the analytic enterprise. Rather, Foucault examined *practices* of knowledge produced through the relations of power. He examined how these practices augment and refine the efficacy and instrumentality of power in its exercise over both individuals and populations, and also in large measure helped to shape the constitution of subjectivity. Fundamental to Foucault's governmentality studies is the understanding that Western society professed to be based on principles of liberty and the Rule of Law and is said to derive the legitimation of the state from political philosophies that elucidated these very principles. Yet, as a matter of historical fact, Western society has employed technologies of power that operate on forms of disciplinary order or were based on biopolitical techniques that bypassed the law and its freedoms altogether. As Colin Gordon (2001: xxvi) puts it so starkly: 'Foucault embraced Nietzsche as the thinker, who transforms Western philosophy by rejecting its founding disjunction of power and knowledge as myth'. By this, Gordon means that the rationalities of Western politics, from the time of the Greeks, had incorporated techniques of power specific to Western practices of government, first, in the expert knowledges of the Greek tyrant, and second, in the concept of pastoral power that characterized ecclesiastical government.

Foucault's lectures on governmentality were first delivered in a course he gave at the Collège de France, entitled *Sécurité, Territoire, Population* (2004a), during the 1977–8 academic year. While the essays 'Governmentality' and 'Questions of Method' were published in 1978 and 1980, respectively, and translated into English in the collection *The Foucault Effect: Studies in Governmentality* (Burchell *et al.* 1991), it is only in the last few years that the course itself has been transcribed from original tapes and published for the first time (Foucault 2004a), along with the sequel *Naissance de la biopolitique: Cours au Collège de France, (1978–1979)* (Foucault 2004b). The governmentality literature in English, roughly speaking, dates from the 1991 collection and has now grown quite substantially (see, for example, Miller and Rose 1990; Barry *et al*. 1996; Dean 1999; Rose 1999).[1] As a number of scholars have pointed out Foucault relied on a group of researchers to help him in his endeavours: François Ewald, Pasquale Pasquino, Daniel Defert, Giovanna Procacci, Jacques Donzelot, on governmentality; François Ewald, Catherine Mevel, Éliane Allo, Nathanie Coppinger and Pasquale Pasquino, François Delaporte and Anne-Marie Moulin, on the birth of biopolitics. These researchers working with Foucault in the late 1970s constitute the first generation of governmentality studies scholars and many have gone on to publish significant works too numerous to list here. In the field of education as yet not a great deal has focused specifically on governmentality.[2]

In these governmentality studies from the late 1970s Foucault held a course on the major forms of neoliberalism, examining three theoretical schools: German ordoliberalism, the Austrian school characterized by Hayek; and American neoliberalism in the form of the Chicago school and characterized by Gary Becker. Among Foucault's great insights in his work on governmentality was the critical link he observed in liberalism between the governance of the self and government of the state – understood as the exercise of political sovereignty over a territory and its population. He focuses on government as a set of practices legitimated by specific rationalities and saw that these three schools of contemporary economic liberalism focused on the question of too much government – a permanent critique of the state that Foucault considers as a set of techniques for governing the self through the market. Liberal modes of governing, Foucault tells us, are distinguished, in general, by the ways in which they utilize the capacities of free-acting subjects and, consequently, modes of government differ according to the value and definition accorded the concept of freedom. These different mentalities of rule turn on whether freedom is seen as a natural attribute as with the philosophers of the Scottish Enlightenment, a product of rational choice-making, or, as with Hayek, a civilizational artefact theorized as both negative and anti-naturalist.

Foucault's account of German ordoliberalism, examines a configuration based on the theoretical configuration of economics and law developed at the University of Freiberg by W. Eucken and F. Böhm that views the market contingently as developing historically within a judicial-legal framework. The economy is thus based on a concept of the Rule of Law, anchored in a notion of individual rights, property rights and contractual freedom that constitutes, in effect, an economic constitution. German neoliberal economists (Müller-Armack, Röpke, Rüstow) invented the term 'social market economy' which shared certain features with the Freiburg model of law and economics but also differed from it in terms of the 'ethics' of the market (as did Hayek in *The Constitution of Liberty*, 1960). This formulation of the 'social market economy' proved significant not only in terms of the postwar reconstruction of the (West) German economy through Erhard, as Minister and Chancellor, but also as the basis of the European Union's 'social model'.

In the last form of neoliberalism he examines American neoliberalism and, in particular, the form he attributes to Gary Becker under the description of human capital theory that privileges an analysis of investment in education. Foucault (2008) asks the question 'what does it mean to form human capital, and so to form these kinds of abilities-machines which will produce income, which will be remunerated by income?', and he responds to his own question with the following account:

> It means, of course, making what are called educational investments. In truth, we have not had to wait for the neo-liberals to measure some of the effects of these educational investments, whether this involves school instruction strictly speaking, or professional training, and so on. But the neo-liberals lay stress on the fact that what should be called

educational investment is much broader than simple schooling or professional training and that many more elements than these enter into the formation of human capital? What constitutes this investment that forms an abilities-machine? Experimentally, on the basis of observations, we know it is constituted by, for example, the time parents devote to their children outside of simple educational activities strictly speaking. We know that the number of hours a mother spends with her child, even when it is still in the cradle, will be very important for the formation of an abilities-machine, or for the formation of a human capital, and that the child will be much more adaptive if in fact its parents or its mother spend more rather than less time with him or her. This means that it must be possible to analyse the simple time parents spend feeding their children, or giving them affection as investment which can form human capital. Time spent, care given, as well as the parents' education because we know quite precisely that for an equal time spent with their children, more educated parents will form a higher human capital than parents with less education – in short, the set of cultural stimuli received by the child, will all contribute to the formation of those elements that can make up a human capital.

(2008: 229)

Responsibilization of self

The 'responsibilization of the self' – turning individuals into moral agents and the promotion of new relations between government and self-government – has served to promote and rationalize programs of individualized 'social insurance' and risk management. By defining Foucault as part of the critical tradition we can get some purchase on his theoretical innovations – particularly his impulse to historicize questions of ontology and subjectivity by inserting them into systems or structures of thought/discourse (an approach that contrasts with the abstract category of the Cartesian–Kantian subject). His notion of governmentality was developed and played out against these tendencies.

Foucault's account of classical liberalism is related to a set of discourses about government embedded in the 'reason of state' (*ragione di stato*) literature of the later Italian renaissance, beginning with Giovanni Botera and Machiavelli, and later in the emergence of the 'science of police' (*polizeiwissenschaft*) in eighteenth-century Germany, where it was considered a science of internal order of the community. Reason of state reinforces the state by basing the art of government on reason rather than God's wisdom or the prince's strategy. It is, essentially, a set of techniques that conform to rational principles that are based on new forms of expert knowledges about the state – its measurement and so-called 'political arithmetic' – and issues in a kind of pastoral care that teaches social virtues and civil prudence. This new art of government represents a break with Christian doctrine as it progressively becomes concerned with the emergence of civil society based on rights. Foucault's genealogy of the emerging political rationality grafts reason of state onto the 'science of police' (*polizeiwissenschaft*), which comes to prominence with the rise of market towns. The police are a condition of existence of the new towns and co-extensive with the rise of mercantilism, in particular, regulating and protecting the market mechanism. They are a correlate of the rise of capitalism and the new science of political economy.

On Foucault's account liberalism stands in ambiguous relation to this literature and tradition; it is both heir and critic. Within liberalism the notion of 'economy' enters into political science in two ways: it refers to a form of government informed by the precepts of political economy, on the one hand, and on the other, to a government concerned with economizing its own efforts and costs, where government has become its own problem. It is in the latter sense, which

Adam Smith identified as a distinctively modern form or style of government, that we can speak properly of the critique of state reason.

Foucault, in historicized Kantian terms, spoke of governmentality as implying the relation of the self to itself (and to others), referring explicitly to the problem of ethical self-constitution and regulation. Governmentality is thus defined as the set of practices and strategies that individuals in their freedom use to control or govern themselves and others. Such an enquiry into power bypasses the subject of law, or the legal concept of the subject, that is demanded by an analysis of power based upon the institution of political society. Foucault's point is that if you can conceive of the subject only as a subject of law – that is, as one who either has rights or does not – then it is difficult to bring out the freedom of the subject and the ethical self-constitution inherent in games of freedom.

On this basis I accept the theoretical promise of the problematic made explicit by these so-called Anglo-Foucauldians (e.g. Barry *et al.* 1996). First, a neo-Foucauldian approach to the sociology of governance avoids interpreting liberalism as an ideology, a political philosophy, or an economic theory, but instead reconfigures it as a form of governmentality that emphasizes the question of how power is exercised. Second, such an approach makes central the notion of the self-limiting state, which, in contrast to the administrative (or 'police') state, brings together in a productive way questions of ethics and technique through the 'responsibilization' of moral agents and the active reconstruction of the relation between government and self-government. Third, it proposes an investigation of neoliberalism as an intensification of an economy of moral regulation first developed by liberals and not merely or primarily as a political reaction against 'big government' or the so-called bureaucratic welfare state of the postwar Keynesian settlement. Indeed, as Barry et al. (ibid.) point out, some who adopt this view approach the era of postwar welfarism as an aberrant episode that has little to do with liberalism as such. Fourth, the approach facilitates an understanding of neoliberalism's distinctive features. For instance, it understands neoliberalism in terms of its replacement of the natural and spontaneous order characteristic of Hayekian liberalism with 'artificially arranged or contrived forms of the free, entrepreneurial and competitive conduct of economic-rational individuals' (Burchell 1996: 23). And, further, it understands neoliberalism through the development of 'a new relation between expertise and politics' (ibid.), especially in the realm of welfare, where an actuarial rationality and new forms of prudentialism manifest and constitute themselves discursively in the language of 'purchaser-provider', audit, performance, and 'risk management'.

Neoliberalism can be seen as an intensification of moral regulation resulting from the radical withdrawal of government and the responsibilization of individuals through economics. It emerges as an actuarial form of governance that promotes an actuarial rationality through encouraging a political regime of ethical self-constitution as consumer-citizens. Responsibiliza-tion refers to modern forms of self-government that require individuals to make choices about lifestyles, their bodies, their education, and their health at critical points in the life cycle, such as giving birth, starting school, going to university, taking a first job, getting married, and retiring. Choice assumes a much wider role under neoliberalism: it is not simply 'consumer sovereignty' but rather a moralization and responsibilization, a regulated transfer of choice-making responsi-bility from the state to the individual in the social market. Specifically, neoliberalism has led to the dismantling of labour laws that were an important component of the welfare state and to increased reliance on privatized forms of welfare that often involve tougher accountability mechanisms and security/video surveillance.

A genealogy of the entrepreneurial self reveals that it is relations that one establishes with oneself through forms of personal investment (including education, viewed as an investment) and insurance that become the central ethical and political components of a new individualized, customized, and privatized consumer welfare economy. In this novel form of governance, responsibilized individuals are called upon to apply certain managerial, economic, and actuarial techniques to themselves as citizen-consumer subjects – calculating the risks and returns on investment in such areas as education, health, employment, and retirement. This process is both self-constituting and self-consuming. It is self-constituting in the Foucauldian sense that the choices we make shape us as moral, economic, and political agents. It is self-consuming in the sense that the entrepreneurial self creates and constructs him- or herself through acts of consumption.

Foucault on American neoliberalism: enter Gary Becker

In *The Birth of Biopolitics* Foucault (2008) provides an account of how American neoliberalism is a form of governmentality based on the production of subjectivity, and, in particular, how individuals are constituted as subjects of 'human capital' (Read 2009). Seven of the 12 lectures are devoted to German and American neoliberalism. In the ninth lecture he looks explicitly at American neoliberalism to focus on its differences with the German versions and its claim to global status, turning immediately to human capital theory as both an extension of economic analysis including the classical analysis of labour and its imperial extension to *all* forms of behaviour (those areas previously considered to belong to the noneconomic realm). In this context Foucault examines the epistemological transformation that American neoliberal effects in the shift from an analysis of economic processes to one that focuses on the production of human subjectivity through the redefinition of *homo economicus* as 'entrepreneur of himself'. In this same context, he examines the constitutive elements of human capital in terms of its innate elements and genetic improvements and the problem of the formation of human capital in education and health that together represent a new model of growth and economic innovation.

In the tenth lecture again he discusses American neoliberalism, including the application of the human capital model to the realm of the social and the generalizability of the enterprise form to the social field. In this lecture he also discusses aspects of American neo-iberalism in relation to delinquency and penal reform, *homo economicus* as the criminal subject and the consequences of this analysis for displacing the criminal subject and 'disciplinary society'. In the 11th lecture he returns to the question of how *homo economicus* in American neoliberalism becomes generalizable to every form of behaviour. This is the genealogy of *homo economicus* that begins as the basic element of the new governmental reason that appeared in the eighteenth century, before Walras and Pareto. In Hume and British empiricism we witness the 'subject of interest' that is differentiated from the legal subject and juridical will, representing contrasting logics of the market and the contract. He also charts and discusses the economic subject's relationship with political power in Condorcet and Adam Smith, the link between the individual's pursuit of profit and the growth of collective wealth. In this environment political economy emerges as as critique of governmental reason.

In the course of discussion, Foucault mentions Gary Becker 12 times, as the Vice-President of the Mont Pelerin Society in 1989, winner of the Nobel Prize in 1992 and author of 'Investment in Human Capital: A Theoretical Analysis', published in the *Journal of Political Economy* in 1962, and considerably expanded into *Human Capital: A Theoretical and Empirical Analysis with Special Reference to Education* in 1964. He regards Becker as 'the most radical of the American neo-liberals' and writes:

> Becker says: Basically, economic analysis can perfectly well find its points of anchorage and effectiveness if an individual's conduct answers to the single clause that the conduct in question reacts to reality in a non-random way. That is to say, any conduct which responds systematically to modifications in the variables of the environment, in other words, any

conduct, as Becker says, which 'accepts reality,' must be susceptible to economic analysis. Homo economicus is someone who accepts reality. Rational conduct is any conduct which is sensitive to modifications in the variables of the environment and which responds to this in a non-random way, in a systematic way, and economics can therefore be defined as the science of the systematic nature of responses to environmental variables.

(Foucault 2008: 269)

The importance of this 'colossal defintion' is to make economic analysis amenable to behavioural techniques, defined in its purest form by B.F. Skinner, where conduct can be understood 'simply in seeing how, through mechanisms of reinforcement, a given play of stimuli entail responses whose systematic nature can be observed and on the basis of which other variables of behavior can be introduced' (Foucault 2008: 270). This speaks to Becker's analysis which inherently points to manipulation and control of the subject. But there is another more important aspect in which Foucault is interested. In the eighteenth century,

Homo oeconomicus is someone who pursues his own interest, and whose interest is such that it converges spontaneously with the interest of others. From the point of view of a theory of government, homo oeconomicus is the person who must be let alone.

(Ibid.)

Yet, in Becker's definition,

homo oeconomicus, that is to say, the person who accepts reality or who responds systematically to modifications in the variables of the environment, appears precisely as someone manageable, someone who responds systematically to systematic modifications artificially introduced into the environment. *Homo oeconomicus* is someone who is eminently governable.

(Ibid.)

Thus, Foucault argues, 'From being the intangible partner of *laissez-faire, homo ceconomicus* now becomes the correlate of a governmentality which will act on the environment and systematically modify its variables' (ibid.: 270–1). This is Becker's major innovation and Foucault leaves us in no doubt that the grim methodology of human capital leaves little room for human freedom. As Jason Read (2009) argues:

The nexus between the production of a particular conception of human nature, a particular formation of subjectivity, and a particular political ideology, a particular way of thinking about politics is at the center of Michel Foucault's research. As much as Foucault characterized his own project as studying '…the different modes by which, in our culture, human beings are made subjects,' this process has always intersected with regimes of power/knowledge. Thus, it would appear that Foucault's work takes up exactly what writers on neoliberalism find to be so vexing: the manner in which neoliberalism is not just a manner of governing states or economies, but is intimately tied to the government of the individual, to a particular manner of living.

(26–7)

In an extraordinary interview, the near unimaginable happens at the University of Chicago on 9 May 2012 with an encounter between Gary Becker, who held the position of University

Professor in Economics, Booth School of Business, and Sociology at the University of Chicago and is the Chair of the Becker Friedman Institute for Research in Economics, and François Ewald who is titular Professor and Chair of Insurance Studies at the Conservatoire National des Arts et Métiers and Director of the Ecole nationale d'assurances. The conversation was chaired by Bernard E. Harcourt, who is the Julius Kreeger Professor and Chairman of the Department of Political Science at the University of Chicago. I say 'nearly unimaginable' for two reasons. First, because François Ewald is considered by some the closest person to a living Foucault (who died in 1984) and worked as his primary assistant interlocutor at the Collège de France from 1976–84, as well as currently being the founder of the Michel Foucault Centre. Second, because Gary Becker died some two years later, on 3 May 2014.[3]

In this engagement, to my utter astonishment, Ewald describes Foucault lectures as the place 'where he (Foucault) made the apology of neoliberalism – especially the apology of Gary Becker, who is referred to … as the most radical representative of American neoliberalism' (Ewald, in Becker *et al.*, 2012: 4).

François Ewald was Foucault's assistant in the 1970s and applied his notion of governmentality to the welfare state in works like 'L'état providence' (1986). Michael C. Behrent (2010) describes Ewald as an 'antirevolutionary' Foucault in his work on the French welfare state and goes on to describe Negri's response to Ewald as someone who repudiates his master:

> Calling Ewald a 'right Foucauldian,' Antonio Negri, the Italian philosopher, chided Ewald for believing that 'the law of the market could function without the guarantee of the state,' predicting the ultimate vindication of the 'true Foucault,' who followed Marx in his analysis of power.
>
> *(586)*[4]

Behrent (2010) makes the additional useful observation:

> Negri's characterization of the 'true Foucault' rests on a plausible and pervasive view of Foucault's significance. Perhaps Foucault's most enduring achievement was his single-minded insistence on the centrality of power to any serious analysis of history and society. He challenged traditional conceptions of power through a number of bracing displacements. Rather than asserting the primacy of economic structures (as did his Marxist contemporaries), he argued for the irreducibility of power relations; instead of identifying power with the state, he probed power's 'microphysics' – that is, the ways it is transmitted through such apparently apolitical institutions as schools, prisons, and asylums; and rather than opposing knowledge to power, he revealed their hidden complicities.
>
> *(586)*

He concludes that while Foucault's thought has been a radical challenge to liberalism and modernity, his influence has been taken up differently by different authors; Ewald represents a conservative, reformist Foucault that has more in common with Becker than one could imagine, and therefore also with neoliberalism and human capital theory.

By comparison Mitchell Dean (2014) suggests:

> Rather than an apology for neoliberalism, let us say that Foucault belonged to a present in which neoliberalism was shifting from a militant, if marginal, thought collective to a regime of the government of the state.
>
> *(13)*

At the same time he is keen to point out:

> [Foucault's] work is unable to move beyond the analysis of the rationalities and techniques of neoliberalism and the attempted production of the neoliberal subject to transformations of capital themselves. While Foucault's analysis can examine how human capital theory enables a rationalization of public authorities, and how the enterprise acts as a paradigm for subjectivity, it fails to capture the intersection of capital and value with such rationalities and technologies.
>
> *(Ibid.)*

As I commented at the beginning of this chapter, the development of finance culture as it has dominated neoliberalism in the 2000s through mathematical modelling and other formalizable procedures escaped Foucault's attention for obvious reasons; it is only since the development of the internet, mobile and sophisticated algorithmic high-frequency trading beginning in the late 1990s that finance culture bloomed, well after his death. Dean is surely correct to remind us about Foucault's 'present' and the shifting nature of neoliberalism but what certainly remains to be analysed is the relation of human capital to finance capitalism, in particular to the huge growth of student loans which, in the USA, total some $1.2 trillion as the second most common form of mortgage – not the entrepreneurial self but the 'indebted self' – and its political consequences, both for the values of freedom and 'freedom of enquiry'.

Conclusion

Foucault provides us with a useful genealogy of neoliberalism in its historical development of three main schools and a framework for analysing human capital theory – its shifting emphases towards privatization and responsibilization that have come to characterize a dynamic and moving set of policies and practices. The recent discussion between Ewald and Becker demonstrates conflicting interpretations of Foucault and therefore of neoliberalism.

In its latest phase under the imperatives of finance culture and financialization, neoliberalism and human capital has tended to shift the analysis of responsibilization to notions of debt financing, especially student debt loading, and attendant notions of the 'indebted self' that now demand greater attention and the most careful scrutiny.

Acknowledgements

This chapter, especially the second section, draws on earlier work including Peters 2005b and http://educationalfoundations.pbworks.com/f/BesleyPeters2007Seven.pdf, used with permission and in terms of the principles of fair copy.

Notes

1 The governmentality literature has grown up around the journal *Economy and Society*, and includes the work of Cruickshank, Hindess, Hunter, Larner, Minson, O'Malley, Owen, and others, as well as those referred to above, most of who have published in *Economy and Society*.

2 See Peters 2005b. My work on Foucault's governmentality dates from Peters 1994, with additional work in Peters 1996, 2001, 2003a,b, 2005a,b, 2006 and 2011.

3 These notes of the meeting are based on the vimeo and transcript of the vimeo available at http://vimeo.com/43984248 and 'Becker on Ewald on Foucault on Becker: American Neoliberalism and Michel

Foucault's 1979 Birth of Biopolitics Lectures: A Conversation with Gary Becker, François Ewald, and Bernard Harcourt' at http://www.thecarceral.org/cn7_Becker_Ewald_Conversation.pdf

4 Antonio Negri makes the remark in 'C'est la lutte des talibans du dollar contre les talibans du pétrole', interview with Caroline Monnot and Nicolas Weill, *Le Monde*, 4 October 2001.

References

Barry, A., Osborne, T., and Rose, N. eds. 1996. *Foucault and Political Reason: Liberalism, Neoliberalism and Rationalities of Government*. London: University College London Press.

Becker, G. 1962. Investment in Human Capital: A Theoretical Analysis. *Journal of Political Economy*, 70.5.2: 9–49.

—. 1964. *Human Capital: A Theoretical and Empirical Analysis with Special Reference to Education*. New York: National Bureau of Economic Research; distributed by Columbia University Press.

Becker, G., Ewald, F., and Harcourt, B. 2012. *Becker on Ewald on Foucault on Becker: American Neoliberalism and Michel Foucault's 1979 'Birth of Biopolitics' Lectures*. Coase-Sandor Institute for Law and Economics Working Paper No. 614, University of Chicago Law School.

—. 2013. *Becker and Foucault on Crime and Punishment*. Coase-Sandor Institute for Law and Economics Working Paper No. 654, University of Chicago Law School.

Behrent, M.C. 2010. Accidents Happen: François Ewald, the 'Antirevolutionary Foucault', and the Intellectual Politics of the French Welfare State. *Journal of Modern History*, 82.3: 585–624.

Burchell, G. 1996. Liberal Government and Techniques of the Self, in Barry, A., Osborne, T., and Rose, N. eds. *Foucault and Political Reason*. London: University College London Press.

Burchell, G., Gordon, C., and Miller, P. eds. 1991. *The Foucault Effect: Studies in Governmentality*. Chicago and London: University of Chicago Press and Harvester Wheatsheaf.

Dean, M. 1999. *Governmentality: Power and Rule in Modern Society*. London: Sage.

—. 2014. Michel Foucault's 'Apology' for Neoliberalism. Paper presented at the Conference, Remembering Foucault, Department of Law, London School of Economics, 25 June. Retrieved from https://www. academia.edu/8018446/Michel_Foucaults_apology_for_neoliberalism._Lecture_given_at_the_ British_Library_on_the_30th_Anniversary_of_Foucaults_death_25_June_2014

Ewald, F. 1986. L'Etat providence [compte rendu]. Rudelle Odile. *Revue française de science politique*, 36.5: 695–7.

Foucault, M. 1991. Governmentality, in Burchell, G., Gordon, C., and Miller, P., eds. *The Foucault Effect: Studies in Governmentality*. Chicago and London: University of Chicago Press and Harvester Wheatsheaf: 87–104.

—. 2004a. *Sécurité, Territoire, Population: Cours au Collège de France (1977–1978)*. Ewal, F., Fontana, A., and Senellart, M., eds. Paris: Éditions Gallimand et des Éditions du Seuill.

—. 2004b. *Naissance de la Biopolitique: Cours au Collège de France (1978–1979)*. Ewal, F., Fontana, A., and Senellart, M., eds. Paris: Éditions Gallimand et des Éditions du Seuill.

—. 2008. *The Birth of Biopolitics: Lectures at the Collège de France, 1978–1979*, Burchell, G., trans. London: Palgrave.

Gordon, C. 2001. Introduction, in Faubion, J.D., ed. Hurley, R., trans. *Power: Michel Foucault – The Essential Works 1954–1984*. London: Penguin: xi–xli.

Hayek, F.A. 1960. *The Constitution of Liberty*. Chicago: University of Chicago Press.

Miller, P., and Rose, N. 1990. Governing Economic Life. *Economy and Society*, 19.1: 1–31.

Mirowski, P. 2013. *Never Let a Serious Crisis Go to Waste: How Neoliberalism Survived the Financial Meltdown*. London: Verso.

Mirowski, P. and Plehwe, D. 2009. eds. *The Road from Mont Pèlerin: Making of the Neoliberal Thought Collective*. Cambridge, MA: Harvard University Press.

Negri, A. 2001. Interview. *Le Monde*, 3 October. Retrieved from Libcom.org/library/interview-le-monde-negri

Peters, M.A. 1994. Governmentalidade Neoliberal e Educacao, in da Silva, T.T., ed. *O Sujeito Educacao, Estudos Foucaulianos*. Rio de Janeiro: Editora Vozes: 211–24.

—. 1996. *Poststructuralism, Politics and Education*. Westport and London: Bergin and Garvey.

—. 2001. *Poststructuralism, Marxism, and Neoliberalism: Between Theory and Politics*. Lanham and Oxford: Rowman & Littlefield.

—. 2003a. Truth-Telling as an Educational Practice of the Self: Foucault, Parrhesia and the Ethics of Subjectivity. *Oxford Review of Education*, 29.2: 207–23.

—. 2003b. Why Foucault? New Directions in Anglo-American Educational Research. Paper presented at the conference, After Foucault: Perspectives of the Analysis of Discourse and Power in Education, University of Dortmund, 29–31 October.

—. 2005a. Foucault, Counselling and the Aesthetics of Existence. *The British Journal of Counselling and Guidance*, 33.3: 383–96.

—. 2005b. The New Prudentialism in Education: Actuarial Rationality and the Entrepreneurial Self. *Educational Theory*, 55: 123–57.

—. 2006. Neoliberal Governmentality: Foucault on the Birth of Biopolitics, in Weber, S., and Maurer, S., eds. *Gouvernementalität und Erziehungswissenschaft: Wissen, Macht, Transformation.* Wiesbaden: Springer: 37–49.

—. 2011. *Neoliberalism and After? Education, Social Policy and the Crisis of Capitalism.* New York: Peter Lang.

Peters, M.A., Paraskeva, J.M., and Besley, T. eds. 2015. *The Global Financial Crisis and the Restructuring of Education.* New York: Peter Lang.

Read, J. 2009. A Genealogy of Homo-Economicus: Neoliberalism and the Production of Subjectivity, *Foucault Studies*, 6: 25–36.

Rose, N. 1999. *Powers of Liberty.* Cambridge: Cambridge University Press.

26

PEDAGOGIES OF NEOLIBERALISM

Sheila L. Macrine

We live in difficult times, in times of monstrous chimeras and evil dreams and criminal follies.

(Joseph Conrad, *Under Western Eyes*)

This chapter responds to Giroux's (2006) call to all public intellectuals to take action and to develop democratic emancipatory projects that challenge neoliberalism's power, dominance and oppression, and to defend democracy, democratic public life and the public sphere in these uncertain times. In response, academics, scholars, and activists are asked to be seen and to see themselves as public intellectuals who provide an indispensable service to the world, and to resist the narrow confines of academic labour by becoming multi-literate in a global democracy in ways that not only allow access to new information and technologies, but also enable us to become border-crossers.

Not being a political scientist, historian, or sociologist, I am approaching this political project from the lens of a critical educator. So, from this perspective, it is proposed that one way to respond to the aforementioned challenge is to develop a comprehensive conceptual framework for naming, organizing and evaluating/critiquing the broad range of neoliberal pedagogical tools that mediate constructions of consent and coercion among the neoliberal centres of power, nation-states, citizen-subjects and in all forms of social life. While pedagogy is essential to teaching and learning inside the classroom, pedagogy in the broader sense plays a key role in transmitting dominant ideologies, as well as notions of national and cultural identity through the reproduction and maintenance of particular discourses and languages (Bernstein 1999). Many neoliberal ideologies, values, economic polices and practices are shaped, conveyed and adopted through networks or constellations of top-down and bottom-up hegemonic tools by way of the media, politics, education, and policy institutes, etc.

The vigorous claims of market superiority have not only moved nation-states closer to neo-liberalization, but have also resurrected nineteenth-century Social Darwinism in terms of valuing competition, efficiency and entrepreneurialism. As a result, this neoliberal turn (Brown 2003) transforms and acquiesces societies, spaces, subjectivities, and modes of organizing towards 'an increasingly broad range of neoliberal policy experiments, institutional innovations and politico-ideological projects' (Brenner and Theodore 2002: 28). These neoliberal turns are achieved through various pathways (i.e. think tanks, policy briefs, political agendas, universities, schools, etc.).

On top this, neoliberalization has been responsible for the widespread dismantling of the welfare state, the weakening of public education systems, decimation of the middle/working classes and perpetuation of the grotesque inequalities of wealth. Neoliberalization also demeans and devalues gender and identity while advancing class/racial injustices by absorbing the democratic practices of civil society within narrow political-economic spaces (Giroux 2004: 106).

This type of market fundamentalism is enabled through a myriad of neoliberal governments, corporations, media and society that inculcate citizen-subjects into believing the Thatcherite motto, that 'there is no alternative' (TINA) to our current market-driven society. As a result, the belief is that the only way for the poor and working classes to succeed is to become entrepreneurs and to adopt the neoliberal ideology and rhetoric of individual freedoms and personal responsibility through meritocracy (Rose 1998) sans public safety nets.

Still, the outward attractiveness of neoliberalism's individual freedom, prosperity, and growth makes it challenging (Smith 2012) for the public to realize that neoliberalization is designed to benefit only a very small class of people and nation-states (Harvey 2005). A worldview such as this makes it easier to justify the thought that some people deserve much more than others because, after all, the neoliberal refrain is that we are all responsible for our own destinies (1).

These pedagogical 'lessons' teach citizen-subjects and nation-states alike that their place in this new world order is to either comply and tow-the-line or suffer the consequences of failure and abject poverty, with no one to blame but themselves. Rather than the promise of democratic citizenship, neoliberalization's uncritical lessons promote profits over people (Chomsky 2011) and values of economic dominance, exploitation, enterprise and entrepreneurship at all costs (McCafferty 2010: 543).

To that end, this chapter introduces a discursive analytic framework aimed at unpacking the bricolage of neoliberalization (Mullen *et al.* 2013) called the 'pedagogies of neoliberalism'. This conceptualization helps to compile the various neoliberal constructions of: knowledge production, reproductions and recontextualizations. Within the neoliberal frame, these pedagogies are selected, disseminated, appropriated and repositioned to become new knowledges (Bernstein 1991) that teach the essence of the new world order while positioning the learner: citizen-subjects/nation-states as reifications of economic capital (Patrick 2013). By connecting the dots, it is theorized that this new framework can help to name, expose and critique the hegemony of neoliberalism's pedagogical tools that both teach and give rise to new social imaginaries in the economy, the public sphere, popular sovereignty and rights (Taylor 2004). Finally, a framework such as the pedagogies of neoliberalism can help to expose how the pedagogies of neoliberalism are insidiously manifested in all walks of life, including education, media, economy, labour market, etc., and explain how these implications hinder our rights to democracy and social justice.

Neoliberalism

Neoliberalism has been accepted as the dominant ideology shaping our world today (Robertson and Dale 2009), making it the most successful and ruthless ideology in world history (Anderson 2000). The guiding principles of neoliberalization are based on Hayek (1973) and Friedman's market-based ideas, which then became the driving force of the economic 'reforms' of the Reagan administration (Harvey 2005). While the wealthy 1 per cent and financial markets have touted and embraced neoliberalism, its wave of destruction has encompassed

> institutional reform and discursive adjustments, entailing much destruction, not only
> of prior institutional frameworks and powers, but also of divisions of labor, social

relations, welfare provisions, technological mixes, ways of life, attachments to the land, habits of the heart, and ways of thought.

(Harvey 2006: 1)

According to Brown (2015) neoliberalism has 'inaugurated democracy's conceptual unmooring and substantive disembowelment'(9). Today individuals and multinational corporations who promote a neoliberal agenda wield such financial power that they 'wreak havoc on much of the world's population by not only ruthlessly destroying resources, nature, and the working classes but also by creating human cast-offs by pushing social groups and whole nations into collective neglect' (Harnecker 2007: 1). The embedded financial orthodoxy was built by 'a monolithic rationalist cult, hell-bent on liberalization and the sweeping aside of all impediments to the thoroughgoing penetration of market forces into all spheres of social activity, regardless of the costs' (Cerny 2000: 226). As a result, neoliberal ideology, and its resultant polices and practices, have been made all more dependent on the market for existence and livelihoods, thus more subject to market disciplines; and disrupted the Left politically by marginalizing non-market-based democratic alternatives from the space of politics (Harnecker 2007).

However, neoliberalism concerns more than globalization, financialization, privatization, deregulation, international competition, de-industrialization, economic crises, and new communication technologies (Bellamy *et al.* 2011); rather neoliberalism is also about the exertion and distribution of political, economic and cognitive power and discourse. Neoliberalism has moved beyond a set of hegemonic discourses and practices to achieve the status of a doxa, or an accepted worldview (Bourdieu 1999; Patrick 2013). This 'doxa' is what Chopra (2003) refers to as, 'an unquestionable orthodoxy that operates as if it were the objective truth' (419). In this manner, neoliberalism realizes its ultimate goal – the monetary and psychological enslavement and subjugation of nation-states and citizen-subjects alike. Warning prophetically about the tyranny of a market-driven society, Karl Polanyi (1944) envisioned the ominous state of neoliberalism, writing that 'To allow the market mechanism to be sole director of the fate of human beings and their natural environment… would result in the demolition of society' (73). Polanyi's words predicted the ideological tsunami of neoliberalism as a potent signifier for the free-market thinking that has dominated politics for the past three decades (Peck 2013).

In fact, after the US financial crisis of 2008, many thought that neoliberalism was hearing its 'death knell'. Yet, in spite of this, the so-called doomed neoliberalism has mutated and persisted in response to the crisis of 2008 and earlier crises. This continuous adapting and self-reconstructing is directly relevant to comprehending neoliberalism's unexpected and continuous evolving strength (Mirowski 2013; Peck 2013). Instead of neoliberalism going completely under and loosing its footing, the financial crises became the one of its modus operandi and the crisis itself becomes one of neoliberalism's preferred courses of action for creating a fuzzy disequilibrium that allows neoliberalism to flourish (Brenner 2006; Klein 2007; Peck 2013; Saltman 2007). The neoliberal pedagogic tool here is 'chaos through crises' which 'offers more latitude for [the] introduction of bold experimental "reforms" that only precipitate further crises down the road' (Mirowski 2013: 53). As a result, the roll-out of crises after crises puts the public and nation-states in a trance-like state of acquiescence by using 'disorientation following massive collective shocks – wars, terrorist attacks, or natural disasters' (Klein 2007: 160) to achieve control by rolling out austerity policies and other economic shock therapies (Peck 2013).

The very term 'neoliberalism' has become contentious. Venugopal (2015) argues that neoliberalism has become a deeply problematic and incoherent term that has multiple and contradictory meanings, and thus has diminished analytical value (1). Stuart Hall (2011) adds that neoliberalism is not one thing or one concept but that it continuously evolves and diversifies. Jamie Peck (2013) contends that neoliberalism is more of a 'rascal concept' that has multiple and varied mongrel formations that can only exist in a mixed forms. For Plehwe *et al.* (2006), neoliberal philosophy is a 'plural' set of ideas rather than as a singular 'pensée unique' (Ramonet 1995). In other words, there is no such thing as a singular neoliberal concept/system; rather neoliberalism has to exist in a parasitical relationship with other systems (Peck 2013). It is better understood as an ethos or a pattern of restructuring that continuously rolls out and rolls back as it adapts and transforms (ibid.).

Barnett (2010) asserts that, if neoliberalization is assumed to work through the naturalization of market rationalities and the normalization of individualistic egoism:

> [T]hen the critical task becomes one of exposing the various dimensions of neoliberalization as social constructs... motivated [a] shift away from public and collective values towards private and individualistic values... that reinforce the image of there being a clear-cut divide between two sets of values – those of private, individualistic self-interest on the one hand, and those of public, collective interests on the other. (271)

Springer (2014) argues for a better understanding that insists on hybridity and variegation rather than a one-dimensional essentialized polemic view of neoliberalism (158). However, for all its multiplicity, neoliberalism has become ingrained in our everyday lives, yet many still do not understand what neoliberalism is all about, or understand how their own lives, their stations in life and thought processes have been manipulated and shaped by it. Therefore, the question becomes, how can the public come to know or for that matter reject something which, for them, 'putatively lacks spatio-temporal solidity, or at minimum, must they themselves consciously understand their beliefs as part of a coherent intellectual tradition?' (Mirowski 2013: 34).

While we know that it is impossible to reject something that is not understood because ideology is embedded, whether Marxist or neoliberal, and acts to naturalize, historicize, and eternalize (Lye 1997), the question is: how might we as public intellectuals and critical pedagogues work within, against, and beyond the unbridled neoliberal market-driven pedagogical strategies? One approach is to develop a language of critique to uncover and explicate the inequitable, unethical, and ultimately inhumane pedagogies of neoliberalism as tools of power in late capitalism.

Pedagogy

General notions of pedagogy include the teaching/learning events in the classroom; however, there is a broader notion of pedagogy that identifies any intentional and/or systematic enterprise, usually outside traditional or formal schooling, in which content is adapted to unique needs and situations to maximize learning (Kleis 1973: 6). According to Basil Bernstein (1991), pedagogic discourses or 'devices of transmission' are relayed through symbolic modalities of practice that construct different forms of consciousness and identity for different categories of learners. A pedagogic device is a discourse of interaction that not only constructs 'particular knowledge and skills to be acquired, but also particular social identities and orientations to meaning for learners... in this way, the outside knowledge becomes inside knowledge' (ibid.: 94). For Bernstein, pedagogic discourse is produced through three hierarchical constructs: the field of production, re-contextualization and reproduction. For example, he notes that certain institutions, such as universities, research institutes, etc., produce newly specialized and complex forms of knowledge which constitute the fields of production that are then interpreted and turned into pedagogical knowledge in order to be accessible and appropriate for different contexts.

So while production involves new knowledges, other pedagogic tools involve selecting from existing forms of knowledge, and converting them for use in very different societal and institutional settings (Bourne 2008). In this sense, Robertson *et al.* (2004) and her colleagues link pedagogy to wider cultural practices and social structures that can be viewed as cultural relays (Bernstein 1996). These relays according to Robertson et al. (2004) are said to be governed by particular regulative structures and practices that take place in and through elements like space, place, time and discourse which work together to regulate all social life (166). They further add that, the relay and relayed are not neutral; that is '…neither set of rules is ideologically free' (Bernstein, 1996: 41). Rather, particular 'rules' act selectively (to restrict or enhance) the meaning potentials and thus what is available to be realized and pedagogized' (4).

For Bernstein (1996) and Gramsci (1971), dominant ideologies such as notions of national and cultural identity are transmitted through the hegemonic production, reproduction and maintenance of discourse and knowledge. The state or the apparatuses of power construct 'boundaries between: different subject areas; between different types of pedagogic institutions; and between different categories of learner, offering each access to selected forms of knowledge' (Bourne 2008: 1). As a result, these ideologies and notions of identity not only impact policies and practices, but also offer 'different forms of specialized consciousness', thus helping 'to construct different identities for different categories of learners' (ibid.), in this case citizen-subjects/nation-states, etc.

Therefore, pedagogy, in this broader sense, plays a key role in hegemonically (Gramsci 1971) transmitting dominant ideologies of society through the reproduction and maintenance of particular discourses and language, as well as knowledge production through which notions of national and cultural identity are transmitted. So, beyond its utility as a metaphor for the current political-economic zeitgeist, what do we know about neoliberalism's pedagogic devices/tools and how are they constructed and transmitted?

Pedagogies of neoliberalism

As already argued, the broad notion of pedagogy must extend far beyond matters of schooling and include those spaces, practices, knowledges, discourses and maps of meaning and affect produced through a range of cultural and pedagogical technologies (Giroux 2011). That said, the conceptualization of the pedagogies of neoliberalism, as tools for description and critique, is concerned with the ways in which specific knowledge structures are produced, reproduced and disseminated through hegemonic networks that underlie and promote neoliberal discourses and practices. The networked machineries of neoliberalism, such as think tanks, policy briefs, political agendas, universities, research institutes and schools, etc., are dedicated to the making of political, intellectual and moral leadership in and through these knowledge technologies (Jessop and Oosterlynck 2008).

Susan Strange (1988) cites four sources of structural power within the current international political economy, including military, production, finance and knowledge structures, that are disseminated through various networked advocacy groups. Yet, according to Strange, power derived from the knowledge structure is the most overlooked, underrated, less well understood when compared with other sources of structural power. Strange writes:

> This is partly because it [knowledge structure] comprehends what is believed (and the moral conclusions and principles derived from those beliefs); what is known and perceived as understood; and the channels by which beliefs, ideas and knowledge are communicated – including some people and excluding others.
>
> *(Ibid.: 115)*

These networks are so pervasive, that, 'no force has emerged that can match the neoliberal networks in terms of organizational capacities, knowledge, production and dissemination on a wide range of policy issues' (Plehwe *et al.* 2006: 41). The seduction of the various neoliberal organizing devices, here conceptualized under the umbrella of the pedagogies of neoliberalism, is both political and hegemonic, not simply because of the dialectical relationships of the neoliberal project vs citizen-subject/nation-state, a sort of quasi power/masses relationship, but also because it is both reciprocal and mutually interacting in a pedagogic way. This is because each pedagogy of neoliberalism emerges from and gives rise to the other, and each is informed by the interest and culture of the other. These dialectical relationships are shared, mutually defined and are precisely pedagogic, hegemonic, and political (Fontana 1993: 26; Freire 1978). For example, pedagogies of neoliberalism's free-market ideologies activate an intuitive but seductive rhetoric of 'freedom', 'choice' and 'entrepreneurship', while at the same time, they underestimate the degree to which contemporary governance-talk is all about 'delivery', 'participation' and 'empowerment' and 'entrepreneurialism' (Smith 2010).

Yet, we know little about neoliberalism as pedagogy or pedagogies. In response to the seemingly rational notion of how neoliberal propositions emerged as the only recourse (Harvey 2005; Graeber 2002), Table 26.1 depicts some of the topics/subjects propagated by the current-day Mont Pelerin Society's think tanks' subject list, adapted with permission from Plehwe *et al.* (2006: 43). It further delineates the various pedagogies of neoliberalism and how these neoliberal technologies/trends are manifest.

Table 26.1, of course, is not a comprehensive list, but reveals some of the subjects propagated by one of neoliberalism's most effective knowledge production mechanisms: think tanks (Djelic 2014). These subjects are then linked to the various pedagogies of neoliberalism which act as hegemonic levers: knowledge production and reproduction, discourses and teachings found in scholarly writings, research, media, think tanks, policies, institutes, universities, schools, politics, etc. Within this critical analysis, the pedagogies of neoliberalism illustrate the conditions in which these hegemonic pedagogies operate, and how citizen-subjects and nation-states learn their places, their roles and their responsibilities as economic pawns in the neoliberal financial global chess match. The impact of some pedagogies of neoliberalism creates spaces in which deeply indebted countries, nation-states, their natural resources and workers, find themselves without a voice or recourse with which to challenge and battle their oppressors against their subjugation and enslavement. These neoliberal pedagogies also create new regimes from the federal level, to the state and county level, resulting in a paternalist regime of poverty governance for disciplining the poor, women and people of colour (Soss *et al.* 2011).

Understanding the tactics used to perpetuate the various pedagogies of neoliberalism will enable us to better understand neoliberalism's pervasive ideology as well as the ways in which it has indoctrinated much of the world (Saunders 2013). Naming the various pedagogies of neoliberalism can help to expose the insipid logic of the neoliberal regimes and expose how these predatory practices teach us to accept our oppression and also accept the decoupling of collective interests from individuals/workers who are left without any option or protective rights of citizenship and are ultimately left without a safety net.

Table 26.1 Neoliberal pedagogies and corresponding trends

Subjects propagated by MPS free-market think tanks*	NL pedagogical trends: how they are manifest/ authors
Economic policy/support/growth	International free trade and freedom of investments
Globalization	(Bandelj *et al.* 2011)
Deregulation/privatization	Assault on labour/unions (Harvey 2010).
Dismantling welfare state	Constructs indebted subject, predatory lending
Labour/wages/employment	(Lazzarato 2012; Paraskeva and Macrine 2015)
European Union/monetary system	Right-wing ideologies (Mirowski 2013)
Consumer protection/risk	Triumph of late-stage capitalism (Bourdieu 1999)
Development/politics of transition	Abolition subsidies/tariffs (Peters and Roberts 2000)
Law and society	Rearrangement of legal regimes and contractual
Legal protection/institutional protection	obligations (Harvey 2010; Mahmud 2013)
of private economic activity	Limiting government protection of individual rights
Rule of law/order of market economy	(Plehwe and Walpen 2006)
Criminal law/crime	Dismantling of public welfare state (Bourdieu 1999)
	Naturalizes the prison-industrial complex, carceral
	sphere (Giroux 2011; Mirowski 2013)
Government/social/economy	Values competition and efficiency, free of govern-
Efficiency/limitation of government	ment, adopts Social Darwinism (Bourdieu 1999;
Taxes/state budget	George 1999; Martinez and García 2000)
Social security/welfare/philanthropy	Market triumphalism infuses its ideology into
Family/moral values	political, social, and cultural institutions at the
Gender/feminism/racism	state level (Harvey 2005)
Pensions/health politics	Promotes a moral code by religious right and
Transport/infrastructure/telecommunication	neo-cons (Mirowski 2014)
Energy politics/ecology/protection	Creates new paternalist/authoritarian regimes of
Regions/federalism	poverty governance for disciplining the poor,
	women and people of colour (Giroux 2009;
	Soss *et al.* 2011)
Education and media	Attacks on higher education, high stakes testing;
Education/market economy	inadequate education funding (Hursh 2012;
Science/technology	Robertson and Dale 2006)
Media/public discourse/culture	Emphasizes knowledge-based, bio-economy
Philosophy/ideological fundamentals	(Jessop 2005)
Theoretical fundament/theory history	Advances enterprising-self (Rose 1998)
Monitoring (of left-wing activities)	Market mechanisms and discourses saturating
	public education (Giroux 2009; Lipman 2011;
	Saltman 2007).
	Limiting protest (Hedges 2013)
Foreign policy/military	Expanding international relations, foreign
Networking/cooperation of think tanks	interventionism (Plehwe and Walpen 2006).
	Disseminate ideas; domestic, international
	and supra-national think tanks (ibid.)
	Deriving power from the knowledge, military,
	production, and finance structures in the
	international political economy (Strange 1988)

Source: Mont Pelerin Society's think tanks' subject list, adapted with permission from Plehwe *et al.*2006: 43.

Therefore, the pedagogies of neoliberalism, first and foremost, need to be understood within the current and continued ascendance of neoliberalism. In this view, neoliberalism enacts a series of pedagogies across institutions and social settings. Some of these pedagogies of accountability, austerity, decentralization, audit, privatization, etc., as well as the extension of economic rationality to cultural, social, and political spheres, have helped to redefine the individual from a citizen-subject to an autonomous economic actor (Baez 2007; Lemke 2001; Turner 2008; Saunders 2013). These pedagogies of neoliberalism take place in particular ways in particular sites – for instance, public education, higher education, corporate America, media, and the industrial-prison complex. Others take place in the public where the pedagogies of neoliberalism serve to rupture public interests and replace them solely with private interests, guided by the market. These neoliberal pedagogies have increasingly shaped individuals' common sense guided by the 'invisible hand' of commodification, commercialization, and marketization. This extension of market logic and the prioritization of economic outcomes have come to redefine the purpose and role of social, cultural, and political institutions (Apple 2001; Giroux 2006; Harvey 2005; Slaughter and Rhoades 2004, Saunders 2013).

If citizen-subjects and nation-states do not understand the impact of the various pedagogies of neoliberalism, how can such a pervasive and dominant ideology exist? The answer to this apparent paradox is found in the characteristics and tactics of neoliberal pedagogies and their hegemonic ideologies. These include alternatives and rival forms of thought that legitimize neoliberal structures and outcomes while they obfuscate the negative impacts of neoliberalism (Eagleton 1991; Saunders 2013). Neoliberalization and its pedagogies have so saturated our consciousness that theydefine our common sense beliefs and become indivisible from our basic ideas and fundamental assumptions (Apple 2004).

One of the problems with this onslaught of neoliberalism is the way in which we are continually pushed to read and accept the neoliberal turn without critical examination of its context in the world, without the context of who or what is communicating that word or message or how this ideology achieves hegemony or how this hegemony is maintained, and what happens when the claims of an ideology are contradicted by reality (Bello 2009). So theorizing and attending to the complexities and dangers of the various pedagogies of neoliberalism as assemblages or constellations (Peck 2013) rather than as a singular entity helps us to better understand the various neoliberal practices that create associations among corporate centres of power, the citizens and nation-states. It is argued that this type of hegemonic dissemination of knowledge becomes one of the trends/mechanisms of the pedagogies of neoliberalism. Conceptualizing the pedagogies of neoliberalism as purposeful and directed knowledges can help us understand how the particular neoliberal views of power are influenced, redefined and reinforced. And yet, the only way we can accurately explain and uncover the predatory nature of neoliberalism in terms of how it defines and shapes culture is if we also illustrate its mechanisms, methods and, most importantly, its pedagogies. Neoliberalization does not follow coherent directions, therefore it is important to consider the different kinds of methodological and research approaches necessary for examining the fluid and nonlinear movements of neoliberalization and neoliberalism as connected assemblages

As such, conceptualizing the pedagogies of neoliberalism can help expose how neoliberalism's disparate strategies are adopted and co-opted in different contexts (Ong 2005), and how neoliberal practices and policies have enabled powerful financial corporations to run roughshod over nation-states and citizen-subjects alike. Naming, conceptualizing and viewing the different trends of neoliberalization through a pedagogical metaphor allows for the creation of new lenses to evaluate and critique the devastating consequences of unregulated financial flow and market-driven ideologies and values.

Conclusion

In short, conceptualizing and naming the pedagogies of neoliberalism is useful in two ways: first, it provides a framework for uncovering the hidden curriculum, social silences, and the cognitive mapping of neoliberal policies and practices as they ensnare nation-states and citizen-subjects alike in collective indoctrination and coercion. Second, understanding the various pedagogies of neoliberalism can teach citizen-subjects to critically think about the different values and beliefs held and perpetuated by think tanks and other neoliberal technologies and organizations that have become purveyors of the neoliberal turn. Third, identifying the pedagogies of neoliberalism can help nation-states and citizen-subjects to recognize that their cognitive maps have been manipulated in relation to their space and place in society. As a result, this framework can be understood as part of the counter-hegemonic praxis of social and political change aimed at challenging and dismantling the neoliberal stranglehold. This can result in action aimed at the greater good by contesting the vagaries of power inherent within these neoliberal pedagogies. In this process, deeply indebted countries, nation-states, and citizen-subjects-workers may realize and take both individual and collective action to refute oppression and to challenge their oppressors against subjugation and enslavement and gain strength from their collective efforts.

Finally, the project of the pedagogies of neoliberalism needs to be further explicated. One of the things public intellectuals can do immediately is to work to uncover and expose the hidden mechanisms that function to keep neoliberalism's practices, policies and influences so entrenched in the public's psyche through prescribed methods of hegemony. Drawing on a wide range of literature across the cultural studies and critical social sciences, and with particular emphasis on the political economy, the explication of the pedagogies of neoliberalism can help us to identify and evaluate the consequences of neoliberal polices and practices, the proliferation and expansion of hegemonic political and economic inculcation that diminishes democracy and freedom.

Finally, this chapter seeks to disrupt neoliberalism's hegemonic practices and policies by naming and theorizing some of its most effective weapons: its pedagogies that increase poverty as they eliminate individual and nation-state sovereignty, while at the same time, increase political and economic subordination and dissolve democracy. In addition, the chapter also explored the way that the various pedagogies of neoliberalism serve to signify and reproduce the divide between rich and the poor. So, by offering a language to name, uncover and critique the inequitable, unethical and ultimately inhumane economic power structures, the pedagogies of neoliberalism stand as descriptive pedagogical tools that argue against the current neoliberal turn in which the interest of capital comes at the expense of human life, democracy, dignity and responsibility towards the future. It is through the articulation of these pedagogies that we can give nation-states and citizen-subjects the tools necessary to live, in the Freireian (1993) sense, with hope and the possibility of a more just and democratic society.

References

Anderson, P. 2000. Renewals. *New Left Review*, 1 (January–February). Retrieved from http://newleftreview.org/II/1/perry-anderson-renewals

Apple, M.W. 2001. *Educating the 'Right' Way: Markets, Standards, God, and Inequality*. New York and London: Routledge and Falmer.

—. 2004. *Ideology and Curriculum*. 3rd edn. New York: Routledge.

Barnett, C. 2010. Publics and Markets. What's Wrong with Neoliberalism?, in Smith, S.J., Pain, R., Marston, S.A., and Jones, J.P. III, eds. *The Sage Handbook of Social Geographies*. London: Sage: 269–96.

Baez, B. 2007. Neoliberalism in Higher Education. Paper presented at the meeting of the Association for the Study of Higher Education, Louisville, Kentucky, November.

Bandelji, N., Shorette, K., and Sowers, E. 2011. Work and Neoliberal Globalization: A Polanyian Synthesis. *Sociology Compass*, 5.9: 807–23.

Bellamy Foster, J., McChesney, R.W., and Jamil, J. 2011. The Global Reserve Army of Labor and the New Imperialism. *Monthly Review*, 63.6: 1–31. Retrieved from http://monthlyreview.org/2011/11/01/the-global-reserve-army-of-labor-and-the-new-imperialism/

Bello, W. 2009. Neoliberalism as Hegemonic Ideology in the Philippines. Paper presented at the plenary session of the National Conference of the Philippine Sociological Society, Quezon City, 16 October. Retrieved from http://mrzine.monthlyreview.org/2009/bello051109.html

Bernstein, B. 1991. *Class, Codes and Control Vol IV: The Structuring of Pedagogic Discourse*. London: Routledge.

—. 1996. *Pedagogy, Symbolic Control and Identity: Theory, Research, Critique*. London: Taylor & Francis.

—. 1999. Vertical and Horizontal Discourse: An Essay. *British Journal of Sociology of Education*, 20.2: 157–73.

Bourdieu, P. 1999. Neo-Liberalism, the Utopia (Becoming a Reality) of Unlimited Exploitation, in Bourdieu, *Acts of Resistance: Against the Tyranny of the Market*. New York: New Press: 94–105.

Bourne, J. 2008. Official Pedagogic Discourses and the Construction of Learners' Identities, in Hornberger, N., ed. *Encyclopedia of Language and Education*. New York: Springer: 798–809.

Brenner, R. 2006. 'What Is, and What Is Not, Imperialism?' *Historical Materialism*, 14.4: 79–105.

Brenner, N. and Theodore, N. 2002. Cities and the Geographies of Actually Existing Neoliberalism. *Antipode*, 34.3: 349–79.

Brown, W. 2003. Neo-liberalism and the End of Liberal Democracy. *Theory Event*, 7.1: 1–28.

—. 2015. *Undoing Demos: Neoliberalism's Stealth Revolution*. Cambridge, MA: MIT Press.

Cerny, P. 2000. Political Agency in a Globalizing World: Towards a Structural Approach. *European Journal of International Relations*, 6.4: 453–63.

Chomsky, N. 2011. *Profit Over People: Neoliberalism and Global Order*. 6th edn. New York: Seven Stories Press.

Chopra, R. 2003. Neoliberalism as Doxa: Bourdieu's Theory of the State and the Contemporary Indian Discourse on Globalization and Liberalization. *Cultural Studies*, 17.3–4: 419–44.

Djelic, M.L. 2014. Spreading Ideas to Change the World: Inventing and Institutionalizing the Neoliberal Think Tank, in Garsten, C., and Sörbom, A., eds. *Political Affair: Bridging Markets and Politics*. Cheltenham: Edward Elgar: 1–41.

Eagleton, T. 1991. *Ideology: An Introduction*. London: Verso.

Fontana, B. 1993. *Hegemony and Power: On the Relation Between Gramsci and Machiavelli*. London and Minneapolis: University of Minnesota Press.

Freire, P. 1978. *Pedagogy in Process: The Letters to Guinea-Bissau*. New York: Seabury Press.

—. 1993. *Pedagogy of the Oppressed*. New York: Continuum.

George, S. 1999. A Short History of Neo-Liberalism: Twenty Years of Elite Economics and Emerging Opportunities for Structural. Paper presented at Economic Sovereignty in a Globalising World, Bangkok, 24–26 March.

Giroux, H.A. 2004. Public Pedagogy and the Politics of Neo-liberalism: Making the Political More Pedagogical. *Policy Futures in Education*, 2.3–4: 494–503.

—. 2006. Higher Education Under Siege: Implications for Public Intellectuals. *Thought & Action Journal*, Autumn. Retrieved from http://www2.nea.org/he/heta06/

—. 2011. *Zombie Politics and Culture in the Age of Casino Capitalism*. New York: Peter Lang.

Graeber, D. 2002. The New Anarchists. *New Left Review*, 13: 61–73.

Gramsci, A. 1971. *Selections from the Prison Notebooks of Antonio Gramsci*. New York: International.

Hall, S. 2011. The Neoliberal Revolution. *Soundings*, 48.1: 9–28.

Harnecker, M. 2007. *Rebuilding the Left*. London: Zed.

Harvey, D. 2005. *A Brief History of Neoliberalism*. Oxford: Oxford University Press.

—. 2006. Neo-Liberalism as Creative Destruction. *The Annals of the American Academy of Political and Social Science*, 610.1: 21–44.

—. 2010. *The Enigma of Capital: And the Crises of Capitalism*. London: Profile.

Hayek, F.A. 1973. *Rules and Order, Vol. 1 of Law, Legislation, and Liberty: A New Statement of the Liberal Principles of Justice and Political Economy*. Chicago: University of Chicago Press.

Hedges, C. 2013. *The World As It Is: Dispatches on the Myth of Human Progress*. New York: Nation.

Hursh, D. 2012. Rethinking Schools and Society/Combating Neoliberal Globalization, in Kumar, R., ed. *Education and the Reproduction of Capital*. New York: Palgrave Macmillan: 101–12.

Jessop, B. 2005. Gramsci as a Spatial Theorist. *Critical Review of International Social and Political Philosophy*, 8.4: 421–37.

Jessop, B., and Oosterlynck, S. 2008. Cultural Political Economy: On Making the Cultural Turn Without Falling into Soft Economic Sociology. *Geoforum*, 39.3: 1155–69.

Klein, N. 2007. *The Shock Doctrine: The Rise of Disaster Capitalism*. Toronto: Knopf.

Kleis, R.J. 1973. *Non-Formal Education: The Definitional Problem*. East Lansing: Michigan State University Press.

Lazzarato, M. 2012. *The Making of the Indebted Man: An Essay on the Neoliberal Condition*, trans. Jordan, J.D. Los Angeles: Semiotext(e).

Lemke, T. 2001. 'The Birth of Bio-Politics': Michel Foucault's Lecture at the College de France on Neo-Liberal Governmentality. *Economy and Society*, 30.2: 190–207.

Lipman, P. 2011. Neoliberal Education and a New Social Order: Dangers and Opportunities of the Present Crisis. *Monthly Review*, 63.3.

Lye, J. 1997. *Ideology: A Brief Guide*. Brock University blog [webpage]. Retrieved from http://academic.uprm.edu/laviles/id218.htm

Mahmud, T. 2013. Debt and Discipline: Neoliberal Political Economy and the Working Classes. *Kentucky Law Journal*, 101.1: 1–54.

Martinez, E., and García, A. 2000. What is 'Neo-liberalism'? A Brief Definition. Retrieved from http://www.globalexchange.org/resources/econ101/neoliberalismdefined

McCafferty, P. 2010. Forging a 'Neoliberal Pedagogy': The 'Enterprising Education' Agenda in Schools. *Critical Social Policy*, 30.4: 541–63.

Mirowski, P. 2013. *Never Let a Serious Crisis Go to Waste: How Neoliberalism Survived the Financial Meltdown*. New York: Verso.

Mullen, C., Samier, E., Brindley, S., English, F., and Carr, N. 2013. An Epistemic Frame Analysis of Neoliberal Culture and Politics in the US, UK, and the UAE. *Interchange*, 43.3: 187–228.

Ong, A. 2005. Ecologies of Expertise: Assembling Flows, Managing Citizenship, in Ong, A., and Collier, S.J., eds. *Global Assemblages: Technology, Politics, and Ethics as Anthropological Problems*. Malden, MA: Blackwell: 337–53.

Paraskeva, J., and Macrine, S.L. 2015. Neoliberal Pedagogy of Debt vs Debtor Pedagogy: Commodity in Education, in Peters, M., Paraskeva, J., and Beasley, T., eds. *The Global Financial Crisis and Educational Restructuring. Series: Global Studies in Education, Vol. 3*. New York: Peter Lang.

Patrick, F. 2013. Neoliberalism, the Knowledge Economy, and the Learner: Challenging the Inevitability of the Commodified Self as an Outcome of Education. *ISRN Education*, 108705: 1–8.

Peck, J. 2010. *Constructions of Consent*. Oxford: Oxford University Press.

—. 2013. Explaining (with) Neoliberalism. *Territory, Politics, Governance*, 1.2: 132–57.

Peters, M., and Roberts, P. 2000. Universities, Funding and Globalization. *Discourse: Studies in the Cultural Politics of Education*, 21.2: 125–217.

Plehwe, D., and Walpen, B. 2006. Between Network and Complex Organization: The Making of Neoliberal Knowledge and Hegemony, in Plehwe, D., Walpen, B., and Neunhöffer, G., eds. *Neoliberal Hegemony: A Global Critique*. London: Routledge: 150–77.

Plehwe, D., Walpen, B., and Neunhöffer, G. eds. 2006. *Neoliberal Hegemony: A Global Critique*. London: Routledge.

Polanyi, K. 1944. *The Great Transformation: The Political and Economic Origins of our Time*. Boston, MA: Beacon Press.

Ramonet, I. 1995. La Pensée Unique. *Le Monde Diplomatique*. Retrieved from http://www.monde-diplomatique.fr/1995/01/RAMONET/6069

Robertson, S.L., and Dale, R. 2006. Changing Geographies of Power in Education: The Politics of Rescaling and its Contradictions, in Kassem, D., Mufti, E., and Robinson, J., eds. *Education Studies: Issues and Critical Perspectives*. Buckinghamshire: Open University Press.

—. 2009. The World Bank, the IMF and the Possibilities of Critical Education, in Apple, M., Au, W., and Gandin, L., eds. *International Handbook of Critical Education*. New York: Routledge: 23–35.

Robertson, S.L., Shortis, T., Todman, N., John, P., and Dale, R. 2004. ICT in the Classroom: The Pedagogical Challenge of Respatialisation and Reregulation, in Olssen, M., ed. *Culture and Learning: Access and Opportunity in the Classroom*. Greenwich, CT: Information Age.

Rose, N. 1998. *Inventing Our Selves: Psychology, Power, and Personhood*. Cambridge: Cambridge University Press.

Saltman, K.A. 2007. *Capitalizing on Disaster: Taking and Breaking Public Schools*. Boulder, NC: Paradigm.

Saunders, D. 2013. Neoliberal Ideology and Public Higher Education in the United States. *Journal for Critical Education Policy Studies*, 8.1: 41–77.

Slaughter, S., and Rhoades, G. 2004. *Academic Capitalism and the New Economy: Markets, State and Higher Education*. Baltimore, MD: Johns Hopkins University Press.

Smith, C. 2012. A Brief Examination of Neoliberalism and Its Consequences. *Sociology Lens*, 2 October. Retrieved from http://thesocietypages.org/sociologylens/2012/10/02/a-brief-examination-of-neoliberalism-and-its-consequences/

Smith, S. 2010. Introduction: Into the Black Box, in Smith, S.J., Pain, R., Marston, S.A., and Jones, J.P. III, eds. *The Sage Handbook of Social Geographies*. London: Sage: 197–204.

Soss, J., Fording, R.C., and Schram, S.F. 2011. *Disciplining the Poor: Neoliberal Paternalism and the Persistent Power of Race*. Chicago: University of Chicago Press.

Springer, S. 2014. Neoliberalism in Denial. *Dialogues in Human Geography*, 4.2: 154–60.

Strange, S. 1988. *States and Markets*. London: Pinter.

Taylor, C. 2004. *Modern Social Imaginaries*. Durham, NC: Duke University Press.

Turner, R.S. 2008. *Neoliberal Ideology: History, Concepts and Politics*. Edinburgh: Edinburgh University Press.

Venugopal, R. 2015. Neoliberalism as Concept. *Economy and Society*, 44.2: 1–23.

27

FINANCIAL ECONOMICS AND BUSINESS SCHOOLS

Legitimating corporate monopoly, reproducing neoliberalism?

Kean Birch

Economics is not neutral knowledge or practice, despite claims made about it in academic or popular debate. This statement should go without saying, but it is important to emphasize, considering that economics, as a form of knowledge, has extraordinary power to shape the world (Fourcade *et al.* 2014). I do not want to argue that economics is 'performative' – see Glass (2016) – but rather that the production of knowledge and its practice are bound up with one another. For example, while economics has an obvious influence in policy and business circles, it is also important to unpack economics as a specific language and set of assumptions that are produced and learned, and thereby shape people's behaviour, decision-making and beliefs about the world and how people should act in the world (Ferraro *et al.* 2005). It is crucial, in this sense, to examine how knowledge (e.g. economics) is produced in the world *and* how it comes to (re)make the world (e.g. in business practice).

Neoliberalism represents an interesting topic to understand this relationship between knowledge and practice. As Peck (2010) argues, this does not mean restating the history of neoliberalism as an explanation (or, *the* explanation) for everything that has happened in the world over the last few decades; it means taking neoliberalism as the thing we need to explain and understand. This task necessitates problematizing neoliberalism as a social reality *and* an analytical concept – see Barnett (2009), Weller and O'Neill (2014) and Birch (2015a) for examples. One area that highlights several key contradictions with both the reality and critique of neoliberalism is the area of corporate power and corporate monopoly, since these forces contrast sharply with the underlying emphasis on (free) markets in both the epistemic basis of neoliberal thought *and* the understanding of neoliberalism by critical scholars, activists and suchlike. However, these criticisms and contradictions need not lead us to throw out the 'analytical' baby with the 'reality' bathwater in our task of understanding neoliberalism (Springer 2014).

My aim in this chapter is to unpack neoliberalism as a market-centred epistemology *and* practice by examining financial economics as a specific form of economic knowledge that legitimates corporate monopoly by resolving the contradiction in neoliberalism between monopoly and free markets. Financial economics, as it is recognized today, emerged in the 1960s and 1970s with the work of people like Eugene Fama and Michael Jensen, and is not usually associated with neoliberalism (cf. Styhre 2014; Birch 2015a, Birch 2016). It has developed in business schools, rather than economics departments, and focuses on the pricing of investment assets and business finance – specifically as these relate to corporate governance and control (i.e. shareholding).

Similarly, business schools are not usually associated with neoliberalism (cf. Harney 2009; Nik-Khah 2011). In focusing on financial economics and business schools, this chapter aims to highlight the importance of two things to the reproduction of neoliberal order: on the one hand, new business and financial knowledges legitimate the expansion of corporate monopoly through the reworking of the 'firm' as a 'nexus of contracts'; and, on the other hand, business schools are key sites of the production of this knowledge, and therefore of neoliberal order.

I start the chapter with an outline of neoliberalism as a market-centred order, highlighting how critical scholars have presented neoliberalism as underpinned by a market ethic or market principles; however, this characterization of neoliberalism is problematized by the expansion of corporate monopoly and the fact that neoliberalism now sits comfortably with the rise of monopolies. After this I provide a brief background on changes in corporate governance and form over time in order to situate better the discussion of financial economics within its historical context. I then discuss the reproduction of neoliberalism through the emergence and spread of financial economics and the sites of its reproduction, business schools. I then conclude.

Neoliberalism as market-centred order

Neoliberalism and markets

Neoliberalism is an ambiguous *thing* to define and identify. There are several reasons for this. First, neoliberalism has a complex and evolving intellectual history involving diverse schools of liberal thought – for example, Austrian, German or Freiburg, British, first Chicago, second Chicago, Virginia (Birch 2015a, 2015b). Second, and just to confuse things further, people we now identify as neoliberal – examples would include Friedrich Hayek, Wilhelm Röpke, Milton Friedman, Gary Becker and James Buchanan – rarely self-identified as 'neo-'liberals themselves; many preferred other terms like 'classical liberal' or 'libertarian' (Peck 2010). Third, there are now numerous analytical definitions of neoliberalism, most of which are critical of neoliberalism both as a set of knowledge claims (e.g. markets are efficient) and as a set of policy practices (e.g. liberalization, privatization, marketization) (Boas and Gans-Morse 2009). In relation to the latter, the identification of neoliberal practice or implementation is, necessarily, always constituted by the analytical approach or perspective taken in the examination of neoliberalism; e.g. institutionalism, Foucault, state theory, geographical, Marxist, etc. (see Birch 2015b). The introduction and other chapters in this handbook demonstrate this diversity of perspectives perfectly.

Despite these difficulties in defining and identifying neoliberalism, it is possible to find one commonality that crosses all these differences; that is the emphasis placed by 'neoliberals' on markets as the best – and most ethical – institution for organizing the economy as well as society. For example, both Hayek (1944[2001]) and Friedman (1962) emphasize the importance of competitive markets in their writings. Similarly, critics like Bourdieu (1998) and Harvey (2005) highlight the central role of the market and market ethic in neoliberal thinking and practice, especially in contrast to collective action. In this sense, neoliberalism can be characterized as a market-centred epistemology *and* set of practices. Although neoliberalism, in these terms at least, implies the installation of the market as the sole institution for organizing society, this does not mean that neoliberalism is anti-statist. For example, the Mont Pelerin Society – identified as the central organizing structure of the 'neoliberal thought collective' by Mirowski (2013) – includes the following in its statement of aims: 'The redefinition of the functions of the state so as to distinguish more clearly between the totalitarian and the liberal order.' Critics of neoliberalism further emphasize the important relationship between markets and the need for the state as the creator *and* regulator of those markets (Birch and Mykhnenko 2010; Peck 2010).

Contradictions of neoliberalism and corporate monopoly

The state plays a key role in markets by ensuring the rule of law, without which markets would not exist and would cease to function. In particular, markets require the protection of private property and the enforcement of contract (Hayek 1960). Another important function of the state, according to most early neoliberals, is the enforcement of anti-trust regulation to stop and/or erode the build-up of corporate (and other) monopolies (Birch 2015a). While certain schools of neoliberalism (e.g. German/Freiburg) retained this negative approach to monopoly, others like the second Chicago School jettisoned it in the 1950s and afterwards. Recently a number of scholars have researched this evolving and ambiguous relationship between neoliberalism and corporate monopoly.

In their work, in particular, Robert Van Horn and Philip Mirowski argue that there was a transformation in the perception of monopoly by Chicago neoliberals after the 1950s (Van Horn 2009, 2011; Van Horn and Mirowski 2009). Before the 1950s, neoliberals were almost universally opposed to corporate monopoly since monopolies of any sort interfere with the proper functioning of market competition and prices – that is, monopolies limit competition and distort market prices, meaning that markets cannot function efficiently in the allocation and distribution of resources (Crouch 2011). This attitude to monopoly was evident across a range of neoliberal schools of thought, including the Austrian, German, Chicago and British schools, with neoliberals like Hayek, Friedman and Röpke all denouncing corporate monopoly (Birch 2015a). However, Van Horn (2009, 2011) and Van Horn and Miroskwi (2009) argue that during the 1950s this attitude changed in the (second) Chicago School as the result of several studies carried out at the University of Chicago, including the Free Market Study and Anti-Trust Project.

Apart from denying claims that corporate monopoly was increasing, what these studies in the 1950s led to were numerous attempts to reconcile markets and monopoly – this is especially evident in the law and economics movement originating in the school of law at the University of Chicago. According to Davies (2010), of particular importance to this project of reconciliation was the adoption of Ronald Coase's (1937) theory of transaction costs – this enabled a wholesale redefinition of the relationship between the firm and market, as well as reconsideration of the distorting impacts of monopoly. In his theory, for example, Coase characterized markets and firms as part of the same continuum, meaning that the firm and the market can be treated as part the same process or system – this proved highly influential in the way financial economics defined the firm as a nexus of contracts (see below). Moreover, it meant that monopoly could be redefined as only temporary and subject to being competed away through market competition, and therefore an unimportant issue (Crouch 2011). The role of knowledge, especially financial economics, in this transformation is critical, as is the emergence of new forms of business organization and practice (Birch 2016). It is these issues that I turn to next.

Background: the evolution of corporate governance and form

In order to understand the relevance of financial economics and business schools in the story of neoliberalism, it is important, first, to get some sense of the transformation of the corporation over time (Birch 2016). This necessitates understanding how corporate governance – as a set of knowledge claims about how corporations should be managed – and corporate form – as the organization and practices of corporations – come to constitute each other in different ways at different times. As Whitley (1999) suggests, this does not mean that the corporation has become more (economically) efficient over time, merely that forms of governance and organization are constituted by changing knowledge claims *and* social practices.

The first thing to note is that capitalism and the corporation have gone through at least three main historical phases since the early nineteenth century. The first two phases have been called 'proprietary capitalism' and 'managerial capitalism' by scholars like Bowman (1996) and Whitley (1999), while I call the most recent phase 'neoliberal capitalism' for convenience (Birch 2016). I have outlined the specific characteristics of each phase in Table 27.1.

According to scholars like Bowman (1996) and Whitley (1999), *proprietary capitalism* was centred on Britain in the nineteenth century, and constituted by ideas derived from political and economic liberalism – or *laissez-faire*. For example, it was based on notions of individual private property and individual competition in self-regulating markets, where effort and decision-making were rewarded or punished by market effects (e.g. bankruptcy) (Ireland 2010). In this era the key business entity was the partnership comprising owner-managers whose livelihoods rose and fell with those of their business. The joint-stock company (or corporation equivalent), in contrast, was seen as a gift (or grant) of government, conferring illegitimate monopoly privileges that inhibited the functioning of the market (Barkan 2013). Direct governance and control were the order of the day when it came to business practice.

Towards the end of the nineteenth century, however, proprietary capitalism was eclipsed by *managerial capitalism* as a result of the so-called 'corporate revolution' (Fligstein 1990; Roy 1997). Corporations were no longer gifts of government; instead they could be established through general incorporation and were run by professional managers. As a result they were able to concentrate significant market and economic power through mergers, vertical integration and economies of scale, all underpinned by shifting modes of ownership and governance (Bratton 1989). Corporations benefited from the ability to attract a large number of distributed shareholders who, in turn, relied on managers to run corporations on their behalf; consequently, securities law became a critical mechanism for coordinating this relationship (Berle and Means 1932). However, managerial capitalism – as the name suggests – was dominated by a new breed of managers, trained in professional business schools in new management techniques and practices, and with enormous leeway in the decisions they made (Khurana 2007).

Table 27.1 Phases of capitalism

	Proprietary (pre-1900)	Managerial (1900–70s)	Neoliberal (1970s onwards)
Corporate governance (epistemology)	Market as self-regulating	Market as transaction costs	Market as (nexus of) contracts
	Corporation as fiction, concession	Corporation as real entity	Corporation as aggregation of contracting parties
	Transactions based on market price	Transactions based on historic cost accounting	Transactions based on contracts
Corporate form (practice)	Key businesses are small or medium-size partnerships	Key businesses are large, oligopolistic corporations	Key businesses are large, monopolistic corporations and others
	Businesses controlled through private property	Businesses controlled by securities law	Businesses controlled by contract law
	Business governance based on ownership	Business governance based on separation of management and ownership	Business governance based on shareholder primacy

By the 1970s, however, this managerial capitalism came under attack from a new breed of neoclassical economists. While some, like Milton Friedman (1962), decried the notion that corporations had any responsibility other than the pursuit of profit, others sought to re-orient corporate governance and control around the notions of shareholder value and shareholder primacy. According to Lazonick and O'Sullivan (2000), this shift reflected dissatisfaction with the management of corporations, especially their poor performance during the 1970s, and the rising power of institutional investors (e.g. pension, mutual and insurance funds) in corporate finance. A growing emphasis on presenting the market – in this case the financial market – as the arbiter of value, as opposed to management or government, led to significant changes in the running and valuation of corporations, as well as behaviour, decisions and practices of senior management (Dobbin and Jung 2010). The reasons for this shift include the emergence of new forms of economic knowledge (e.g. financial economics) and economic practice (e.g. financial accounting), as well as the transformation of key sites of (practical) knowledge production and training (e.g. business schools).

Analysis: legitimating corporate monopoly and the reproduction of neoliberalism

Financial economics: legitimating corporate monopoly

I now turn to financial economics as a form of knowledge that has managed to reconcile the contradictions between markets and corporate monopoly. Financial economics, in its current guise, emerged in the 1960s and 1970s with the work of neoclassical economists on theories of the firm; many of these economists were (and are) working in business schools rather than economics departments. As a branch of economics, financial economics focuses on the issue of pricing investment assets (e.g. share values) and corporate finance (e.g. sources of capital). It is, to all epistemological and practical purposes, focused solely on increasing the value of shares for investors through the actions of a firm's managers; as such, it is built on the assumption that capital owners (i.e. investors) are the best people to determine the allocation of capital investment, and not managers (Styhre 2014). This assumption is somewhat tautological, in that it assumes the market is the best mechanism for capital allocation because capital owners are the best allocators. However, financial economics has come to form the epistemological basis for corporate governance (see Shleifer and Vishny 1997), and is one constitutive element in a significant shift in corporate structure and ownership. It has led to what Stout (2012) and others have called an ideology of 'shareholder value' maximization (Lazonick and O'Sullivan 2000; Engelen 2002), which has helped to legitimate corporate monopoly.

There are two important components of financial economics that help in this legitimation process. First, in his work, Eugene Fama (1970: 383) argued that markets are inherently efficient, in that 'prices provide accurate signals for resource allocation'. This 'efficient market hypothesis' (EMH) underpins the later theoretical contributions of people like Jensen and Meckling, among others. What it implies is that market prices are, by definition, accurate reflections of the underlying value. Thus a corporation's share price reflects all the information that investors know about it, which reflects their (accurate) knowledge of its real value (or earnings potential). As Whitley (1986: 176) points out, however, 'No empirical "finding" about investor behaviour could demonstrate the truth or falsity of the EMH because it does not state what "all relevant information" consists of.' Second, the work of Jensen and Meckling (1976) on the theory of the firm proved highly influential in promoting particular forms of corporate governance (see Shleifer and Vishny 1997 for a review). They argued that there is a 'principal-agent problem' – leading to the term 'agency theory' to describe their perspective – in which corporate managers need to have their interests (e.g. remuneration) aligned with shareholder interests (e.g. share price) (Dobbin and Jung 2010). What this theory stresses is that there should only be one goal for managers – that is, share value – since it is difficult to balance more than one aim in managing a business (Jensen and Meckling 1976).

Writing in the 1970s, Jensen and Meckling (ibid.: 310) were concerned with determining 'the equilibrium contractual form characterizing the relationship between the manager (i.e., agent) of the firm and the outside equity and debt holders (i.e., principals)' – that is, with the *agency costs* (e.g. Fama 1980). These costs relate to the separation of ownership from management (i.e. corporate governance); managers, for example, can exploit their insider knowledge to their benefit and owners disadvantage. Agency theory, however, provides the corrective to this problem, although it depends upon certain assumptions – namely, that the firm is merely (and only) a nexus of contracting parties (e.g. manager, investor, worker, supplier, etc.).[1] This idea that the firm is a nexus of contracts builds on the work of Coase (1937) on transaction costs mentioned earlier. For example, it helped Jensen and Meckling (1976: 311) to frame the firm as (basically) a market in another form: 'In this sense the "behavior" of the firm is like the behavior of the market; i.e., the outcome of a complex equilibrium process.' From this perspective, the firm has no responsibilities since it does not really exist, except as a 'legal fiction'. This refocusing of attention and concern onto corporate decision-making and investor returns enables Jensen and Meckling to argued that 'the existence of monopoly will not increase agency costs' and competition 'will not eliminate the agency costs' (ibid.: 330). Consequently, the focus on agency costs means that corporate monopoly becomes irrelevant, since agency costs are characterized as the only real problem since they stop investors (i.e. capital owners) from re-allocating their money efficiently – that is, from lower-value investments to higher-value ones. Shifting emphasis from the firm to the investor means that corporate monopoly becomes an irrelevant issue, since investors will always pursue those investments that ensure the most efficient returns, whether or not they are monopolies.[2]

As should be evident, financial economics is bound up with the valuation of investments and assets; this means it is intrinsically bound up with (corporate) accounting principles and practices. As Styhre (2014: 63) notes, political-economic actors (e.g. executives, analysts, investors, etc.) need training in financial economies, especially when it comes to understanding value as market price and how to evaluate tangible but especially intangible assets. What is interesting here is that Whitley (1986: 175–6) argues that the rise of financial economics, and specifically Fama's efficient market hypothesis, 'says remarkably little about market valuation processes' (also see Power 2010). Whitley (1986) goes on to argue that the threat of legal action against corporations by shareholders – based on agency theory and ideology of shareholder value – led managers to seek new forms of valuation to legitimate their claims, which helped to stimulate the massive expansion of financial intermediation, analysis, brokerages, and so on. All of this has led to new asset valuation models like *fair value accounting* (Ronen 2008; Zhang *et al.* 2012). However, while these new models may claim to be 'market-based', what this actually means is very different from market transacting and pricing (i.e. sale). In fact, according to Power (2010), the notion of market-based valuation underpinning fair value does not actually entail a market valuation per se (i.e. sale). Instead, it involves an expert judgement of value, thereby 'shifting the focus from transactions to economic valuation methods', which helps to 'embed further the principle of fair value accounting as the "*mirror*" of the market' (my emphasis) (ibid.: 201, 205). This point is supported by Bignon *et al.* (2009: 11), who suggest that fair value 'is based more on the estimates of certified experts than on the current market price'. What this means is that 'Values do not passively reflect the "objectivity" of the market, but are the product of a measurement technology that, by demarcating and measuring resources, assists in the construction of the marketability of assets' (Napier and Power 1992: 87). Here we can see a similar legitimation of corporate monopoly since it is no longer necessary to actually derive value from market transactions (i.e. sale); value and evaluation can be done via expert and *as if* calculations of 'market' value side-step the distorting power of corporate monopoly.

The reason this is important to our understanding of neoliberalism is that it moves the analytical focus away from economics and sterile economic debates to the business school and the training and practices of executives, managers, analysts, traders, market experts, etc. In this sense, it demands a much needed analysis of the sites of the reproduction of economic knowledge and practice.

Business schools: reproducing neoliberalism

The transformation of business schools occurred over several decades and stretches back to the late 1950s when the Ford Foundation sought to instil greater intellectual rigour in business schools by encouraging the integration of neoclassical economics in business curricula (Khurana 2007). While it is possible to see the later re-orientation of business schools as a neutral project based on new forms of economic knowledge, the resulting focus on pushing both free markets and corporate interests was not done in political isolation. For example, the now (in)famous 1971 Lewis Powell Memo to the US Chamber of Commerce, titled *Attack on American Free Enterprise System*, specifically suggested that the 'Chamber should enjoy a particular rapport with the increasingly influential graduate schools of business' in order to support Corporate America. While this enrolment of business schools in support of corporate power is not the focus of this chapter, it does highlight the need to examine the role of the business school as both a site of knowledge production and a social institution for the reproduction of neoliberalism. While there are a number of scholars who have and are doing this important work (e.g. Khurana 2007; Dunne *et al.* 2008; Harney 2009; Henisz 2011; Locke and Spender 2011; Nik-Khah 2011; Styhre 2014), there is a need for more work in this area.

Business schools first emerged in countries like the USA at the end of the nineteenth century as the corporate revolution was transforming capitalism. Khurana (2007: 4) argues that these new business schools played an important role in legitimating corporations and their activities through the creation of a 'managerial class that would run America's large corporations in a way that served the broader interests of society rather the narrowly defined ones of capital and labor'. Hence, business schools supported and legitimated the shift from proprietary to managerial capitalism (Bowman 1996; Whitley 1999). This led to what Locke and Spender (2011: x–xi) – and others – have called *managerialism*, or the emergence of a professional group (i.e. managers) who seek and acquire systematic control over (corporate) decision-making to the exclusion of others (e.g. shareholders, workers). What differentiates managerialism from *laissez-faire* is that the former is not centred on cut-throat market competition; rather, managerialism is concerned more with cost and resource efficiencies in the pursuit of productivity, all based on supposedly technocratic and scientific decision-making (ibid.: 6). During this period, and up until the mid-twentieth century, business education and knowledge was dominated by these practical goals; hence, it was taught more by 'practitioners' than academics (Fourcade and Khurana 2011).

This managerial perspective dominated business education until the late 1950s, when there was a concerted effort to transform business and management studies into more technical and academic disciplines, based primarily on the incorporation of statistical modelling and quantitative methodologies. This move came about as a result of, on the one hand, the demands of state planning: first, with operations research during World War II and, second, with the alliance between state and corporations in response to Cold War fears (Locke and Spender 2011). On the other hand, it also resulted from the actions of philanthropic foundations like the Ford and Carnegie foundations, which sought to 'professionalize' and 'scientize' business school education through funding specific research and teaching programmes (Khurana 2007; Henisz 2011). These demands led to the incorporation and integration of neoclassical economics into business school curricula, which has had several important consequences.

First, Chicago is often represented as an important site to the reproduction of neoliberalism. Usually, the economics department is presented as the most important site, as are other economic departments in other universities (e.g. Peck 2010). However, it is important to consider the role of business schools in the reproduction of neoliberalism, especially places like Chicago's Graduate School of Business (Fourcade and Khurana 2011; Nik-Khah 2011). Business schools are dominated by forms of economic knowledge, especially financial economics discussed above, that reproduce specific epistemic claims and train people in specific business practices. According to Henisz (2011: 302), for example, 'agency theory and models of asset pricing' that underpin financial economics have isolated other social scientific approaches in business schools. Moreover, business schools have 'reinforced and diffused the belief system [in efficient markets, shareholder value, etc.] to traders, fund managers, analysts and managers' around the world (ibid.: 304). This process starts with the integration of neoclassical economics into business schools in the 1950s, but gained a real hold in the 1970s with the emergence of new branches of economics like financial economics and associated fields like corporate governance. Henisz (2011) argues that this work embedded a 'culture of selfishness' in business schools.

Second, business schools not only produce knowledge, they also train students in business practices, embedding the culture and assumptions that underpin disciplines like financial economics. This has become increasingly important to the reproduction of neoliberalism because the number of students trained in business schools – at both undergraduate and graduate level – has risen considerably. For example, Harney (2009: 318) claims that 'one in eight university undergraduates in Britain [are] studying business and management'. Khurana (2007: 338) provides data on the number of MBA programmes in the USA, which rose from 138 in 1955–6 to 955 in 2003–4. As Khurana notes, the range in quality of these programmes is often significant, as are the benefits to students in their careers. In terms of total student numbers, those graduating with a business degree reached 266,000 undergraduates in 2001 and 120,000 MBAs in 2006, according to Fourcade and Khurana (2011). The huge increase in numbers of students taking business degrees is also reflected in the growing proportion of all students who study business and management courses at university.

Finally, the expansion of student numbers has meant that a growing number of people in the workforce, not just in management, have been exposed to specific forms of economic knowledge that promotes specific business practices – for example, beliefs about agency costs, shareholder value and aligning management incentives with share values (Dobbin and Jung 2010). The range of careers that these students go into has diversified significantly since the 1960s according to Khurana (2007). By the 1980s, for example, over 50 per cent of students graduating from Harvard Business School went into consulting and finance, rather than general management (ibid.: 328). The growth in areas like consulting, analysis, finance, investment banking, etc. reflected broader trends in the growth of institutional investment, according to Whitley (1986), which led to an expansion in the demand for business school-trained employees, binding together the expansion of business schools and finance. However, what this has meant, according to Dobbin and Jung (2010), is that business practices based on financial economics – and its neoliberal tenets – that are internal to the corporation have been (and still are) reinforced by the investment practices, again based on financial economics, of external social actors who judge, analyse and value the performance of businesses. In particular, framing corporations as maximizers of shareholder value provides external analysts with a single, simple indicator on which they can focus to the exclusion of other concerns (e.g. social responsibility, employment creation, quality, etc.).

Conclusion

My aim in this chapter has been to understand, on the one hand, the relationship between specific forms of economic knowledge and the legitimation of corporate monopoly, and, on the other hand, the reproduction of neoliberalism in specific sites of economic knowledge production, namely business schools. The overall point I want to stress is that although neoliberalism is generally characterized as a market-based epistemology – in that neoliberal thinkers laud the benefits of (free) market interaction over any other – what this representation of neoliberalism obscures is how neoliberalism is reproduced, especially in a world dominated by large, monopolies that rarely want or seek market competition. This contradiction, as I see it, is resolved through the reworking of the economic understanding of corporations as merely another form of market, and therefore no epistemic or practical threat to neoliberal claims; this emerges in the subfield of financial economics. In turn, this new perspective of corporations is promulgated in business schools as the basis for understanding the business world; students adopt these views and reinforce them in their various employment positions (e.g. executive, manager, analyst, broker, trader, investor, etc.). Thus this economic knowledge comes to inform and shape the world, although not always as initially imagined.

Notes

1 Jensen and Meckling (1976) and other financial economists are rather ambivalent about differentiating between the firm and the corporation, frequently conflating the two when their theories are (largely) only relevant to the latter.
2 An issue not addressed by Jensen and Meckling (1976) – probably because it was not as relevant in their time – is the growing concentration of investment funds in the hands of institutional investors (e.g. pension, mutual and insurance funds). As Davis (2008) highlights, around 75 per cent of the US stock market is now owned by institutional investors rather than individuals; moreover, only three funds represent around 30 per cent of total institutional investment. This suggests that investment has become a form of monopoly, alongside the corporations themselves.

References

Barkan, J. 2013. *Corporate Sovereignty*. Minneapolis: University of Minnesota Press.
Barnett, C. 2009. Publics and Markets: What's Wrong with Neoliberalism?, in Smith, S., Pain, R., Marston, S., and Jones III, J.P., eds. *The Sage Handbook of Social Geography*. London: Sage: 269–96.
Berle, A., and Means, G. 1932. *The Modern Corporation and Private Property*. New York: Macmillan.
Bignon, V., Biondi, Y., and Ragot, X. 2009. *An Economic Analysis of Fair Value*. Cournot Centre for Economic Studies, Prisme no.15.
Birch, K. 2015a. *We Have Never Been Neoliberal: A Manifesto for a Doomed Youth*. London: Zero.
—. 2015b. Neoliberalism: The Whys and Wherefores… and Future Directions. *Sociology Compass*, 9: 571–84.
—. 2016. Market vs Contract? The Implications of Contractual Theories of Corporate Governance to the Analysis of Neoliberalism. *Ephemera: Theory & Politics in Organization*, 16(1): 107–33.
Birch, K., and Mykhnenko, V. eds. 2010. *The Rise and Fall of Neoliberalism: The Collapse of an Economic Order?* London: Zed.
Boas, T., and Gans-Morse, J. 2009. Neoliberalism: From New Liberal Philosophy to Anti-Liberal Slogan. *Studies in Comparative International Development*, 44: 137–61.
Bourdieu, P. 1998. The Essence of Neoliberalism. *Le Monde Diplomatique*, December.

Bowman, S. 1996. *The Modern Corporation and American Political Thought.* University Park, PA: Pennsylvania State University Press.

Bratton, W. 1989. The New Economic Theory of the Firm: Critical Perspectives from History. *Stanford Law Review*, 41: 1471–527.

Coase, R. 1937. The Nature of the Firm. *Economica*, 4: 386–405.

Crouch, C. 2011. *The Strange Non-death of Neoliberalism.* Cambridge: Polity Press.

Davies, W. 2010. Economics and the 'Nonsense' of Law: The Case of the Chicago Antitrust Revolution. *Economy and Society*, 39: 64–83.

Davis, G. 2008. A New Finance Capitalism? Mutual Funds and Ownership Re-concentration in the United States. *European Management Review*, 5: 11–21.

Dobbin, F., and Jung, J. 2010. The Misapplication of Mr Michael Jensen: How Agency Theory Brought Down the Economy and Why it Might Again, in Lounsbury, M., and Hirsch, P., eds. *Markets on Trial.* Bingley: Emerald: 29–64.

Dunne, S., Harney, S., Parker, M., and Tinker, T. 2008. Discussing the Role of the Business School. *Ephemera*, 8: 271–93.

Engelen, E. 2002. Corporate Governance, Property and Democracy: A Conceptual Critique of Shareholder Ideology. *Economy and Society*, 31: 391–413.

Fama, E. 1970. Efficient Capital Markets: A Review of Theory and Empirical Work. *Journal of Finance*, 25: 383–417.

—. 1980. Agency Problems and the Theory of the Firm. *Journal of Political Economy*, 88: 288–307.

Ferraro, F., Pfeffer, J., and Sutton, R. 2005. Economics Language and Assumptions: How Theories can Become Self-fulfilling. *Academy of Management Review*, 30: 8–24.

Fligstein, N. 1990. *The Transformation of Corporate Control.* Cambridge, MA: Harvard University Press.

Fourcade, M., and Khurana, R. 2011. *From Social Control to Financial Economics: The Linked Ecologies of Economics and Business in Twentieth Century America.* Harvard Business School: Working Paper 11-071.

Fourcade, M., Ollion, E., and Algan, Y. 2014. *The Superiority of Economists.* Paris: MaxPo Discussion Paper No.14/3.

Friedman, M. 1962. *Capitalism and Freedom.* Chicago, IL: University of Chicago Press.

Glass, M.R. 2016. Performing Neoliberalism: Practices, Power and Subject Formation, in Springer, S., Birch, K., and MacLeavy, J., eds. *The Handbook of Neoliberalism.* London: Routledge: 337–48.

Harney, S. 2009. Extreme Neo-liberalism: An Introduction. *Ephemera*, 9: 318–29.

Harvey, D. 2005. *A Brief History of Neoliberalism.* Oxford: Oxford University Press.

Hayek, F. 1944[2001]. *The Road to Serfdom.* London: Routledge.

—. 1960. *The Constitution of Liberty.* Chicago, IL: University of Chicago Press.

Henisz, W. 2011. Leveraging the Financial Crisis to Fulfill the Promise of Progressive Management. *Academy of Management Learning and Education*, 10: 298–321.

Ireland, P. 2010. Limited Liability, Shareholder Rights and the Problem of Corporate Irresponsibility. *Cambridge Journal of Economics*, 34: 837–56.

Jensen, M., and Meckling, W. 1976. Theory of the Firm: Managerial Behavior, Agency Costs and Ownership Structure. *Journal of Financial Economics*, 3: 305–60.

Khurana, R. 2007. *From Higher Sims to Hired Hands.* Princeton, NJ: Princeton University Press.

Lazonick, W., and O'Sullivan, M. 2000. Maximizing Shareholder Value: A New Ideology for Corporate Governance. *Economy and Society*, 29: 13–35.

Locke, R., and Spender, J.-C. 2011. *Confronting Managerialism.* London: Zed.

Mirowski, P. 2013. *Never Let a Serious Crisis go to Waste.* London: Verso.

Napier, C., and Power, M. 1992. Professional Research, Lobbying and Intangibles: A Review Essay. *Accounting and Business Research*, 23: 85–95.

Nik-Khah, E. 2011. George Stigler, the Graduate School of Business, and the Pillars of the Chicago School, in Van Horn, R., Mirowski, P., and Stapleford, T., eds. *Building Chicago Economics: New Perspectives on the History of America's Most Powerful Economics Program.* New York: Cambridge University Press: 116–47.

Peck, J. 2010. *Constructions of Neoliberal Reason.* Oxford: Oxford University Press.

Power, M. 2010. Fair Value Accounting, Financial Economics and the Transformation of Reliability. *Accounting and Business Research*, 40: 197–210.

Ronen, J. 2008. To Fair Value or Not to Fair Value: A Broader Perspective. *Abacus*, 44: 181–208.

Roy, W. 1997. *Socializing Capital.* Princeton, NJ: Princeton University Press.

Shleifer, A., and Vishny, R. 1997. A Survey of Corporate Governance. *Journal of Finance*, 52: 737–83.

Springer, S. 2014. Neoliberalism in Denial. *Dialogues in Human Geography*, 4: 154–60.

Stout, L. 2012. *The Shareholder Value Myth*. San Francisco: Berrett-Koehle.

Styhre, A. 2014. *Management and Neoliberalism*. London: Routledge.

Van Horn, R. 2009. Reinventing Monopoly and Corporations: The Roots of Chicago Law and Economics, in Mirowski, P., and Plehwe, D., eds. *The Road from Mont Pelèrin: The Making of the Neoliberal Thought Collective*. Cambridge, MA: Harvard University Press: 204–37.

—. 2011. Chicago's Shifting Attitude Toward Concentrations of Business Power (1934–1962). *Seattle University Law Review*, 34: 1527–44.

Van Horn, R., and Mirowski, P. 2009. The Rise of the Chicago School of Economics and the Birth of Neoliberalism, in Mirowski, P., and Plehwe, D., eds. *The Road from Mont Pelèrin: The Making of the Neoliberal Thought Collective*. Cambridge, MA: Harvard University Press.

Weller, S., and O'Neill, P. 2014. An Argument with Neoliberalism: Australia's Place in a Global Imaginary. *Dialogues in Human Geography*, 4: 105–30.

Whitley, R. 1986. The Transformation of Business Finance into Financial Economics: The role of Academic Expansion and Changes in US Capital Markets. *Accounting, Organizations and Society*, 11: 171–92.

—. 1999. *Divergent Capitalism*. Oxford: Oxford University Press.

Zhang, Y., Andrew, J., and Rudkin, K. 2012. Accounting as an Instrument of Neoliberalisation? Exploring the Adoption of Fair Value Accounting in China. *Accounting, Auditing and Accountability Journal*, 25: 1266–89.

28

NEOLIBERALISM EVERYWHERE

Mobile neoliberal policy

Russell Prince

The 'everywhereness' of neoliberalism

One of the remarkable features of neoliberalism is its ubiquity: it 'seems to be everywhere' (Peck and Tickell 2002: 380). As this volume demonstrates, at all levels, from the local to the supranational, and across international space, from the richest global cities of Europe and America to the poorest communities of Africa, the presence of neoliberalism has been announced. But when we look closely, there is remarkable diversity across time and space between regimes otherwise apparently being reasonably described as neoliberal. Indeed, this diversity has made the status of neoliberalism as a useful descriptor of the current political moment increasingly tenuous (Clarke 2008; Venugopal 2015). If neoliberalism is to remain a worthwhile analytical concept, then we need to square claims about its 'everywhereness' with its apparent spatial diversity. So how might we go about grasping how neoliberalism did, or did not, get everywhere? And what might this mean for how we conceive it?

This chapter approaches this task through one of the key manifestations of neoliberalism: policy. Identifying its policy forms and tracing where these have been instituted would seem to offer a straightforward way of empirically studying the everywhereness of neoliberalism. Political science has a long tradition of analysing policy diffusion, mapping how particular policies get taken up in one state after another, and assessing if this will result in eventual policy convergence (Dobbin *et al.* 2007). Such models can be criticized for overstating the similarity of policy programmes in different states and for reducing explanation to generalized theoretical models, such as economic competition or rational learning, while ignoring the actual processes involved. The policy transfer literature seeks to overcome these shortcomings through a closer focus on the actors and institutions that make policy transfers happen (Dolowitz and Marsh 1996), and with the goal of understanding some of the tectonic shifts occurring in the state system such as globalization and Europeanization.

Central to this has been a consideration of the way that global power dynamics are expressed through transfer processes that will fall on a spectrum between coerced and consensual (Benson and Jordan 2011). One critique of these literatures, coming from geography in particular, is that the formalism of these analyses, based on assumptions of rational actors, has difficultly engaging satisfactorily with the dynamism inherent in transfer processes or with the constitutive socio-spatial contexts in which it occurs (Peck 2011; McCann 2011). The emerging policy mobility literature emphasizes these aspects, and makes a case for studying policy movement in ways that are more critical and constructivist than normative and formalized.

The policy mobility literature, in particular, has consciously tried to engage with the question of neoliberalism as it has made the case for its perspective, so what follows draws largely from this tradition. Three different narratives about the travel of neoliberal policy are told. Each is differentiated by time and scale, but each also offers a different perspective on how neoliberalism proceeds through policy movement. In each case, it is clear that the way we talk about how policy proceeds across space will shape, and be shaped by, what we think neoliberalism is. The chapter will conclude by reflecting on the politics of our analysis.

Consent and coercion

Neoliberalism, especially in its earliest forms, has been associated with a particular set of policies that have been instituted in different combinations and to different extents in much of the world. These include, but are not limited to, the privatization of publically owned assets, the flexibilization of the labour market, the flattening of personal and corporate tax rates, the lowering of border protections on goods and services, the removal of capital controls on investment flows, and a broadly monetarist approach to fiscal discipline and inflation (Harvey 2005). These policies are founded on intellectual work conducted through much of the second half of the twentieth century by such neoliberal scholarly communities as the Mont Pelerin Society (Mirowski and Plehwe 2009), the Centre for the Study of Economic and Social Problems (CESES) (Bockman and Eyal 2002), and the economics programme at the University of Chicago. The latter trained the so-called 'Chicago Boys' who instituted arguably the earliest example of this kind of neoliberal economic reform in Pinochet's Chile in the 1970s (Peck 2010).

The rapidity with which these emblematic neoliberal policies circulated around the world in the 1980s and 1990s has seen this period retrospectively labelled as the neoliberal revolution (Robison 2006; Hall 2011; Dumenil and Levy 2004). Although, at the time, the restructuring that was occurring was often given personalized epithets after some figurehead, such as 'Thatcherism' for Prime Minister Margaret Thatcher in the UK or 'Rogernomics' for Finance Minister Roger Douglas in New Zealand, the institutionalization of neoliberal policy, albeit in different forms and to varying degrees, was common across much of the developed world. But these epithets do reflect the way that the policies were associated with particular people: not just the figureheads but cabals of well-positioned elites, politicians and technocrats who worked together to embed neoliberal thinking in their respective state apparatuses (see, for example, Kelsey 1995). These actors were internationally linked through state and non-state networks to their counterparts overseas and to the various research centres and think-tanks that had emerged to provide the case for neoliberal economics, and it was often across these that neoliberal policy can be seen to travel (Goldfinch and Roberts 2013; Peck and Tickell 2007; Peet 2007).

Although many in the populace of the neoliberalizing developed world might disagree that this neoliberalization was in any way consensual, significant proportions of them voted for it repeatedly. This contrasts markedly with the experience of the developing world and the former Soviet states of Eastern Europe where powerful international agencies, most notably the International Monetary Fund, are generally seen as forcing neoliberalism upon them. The economic crises that had occurred in parts of Latin America and Africa in the 1970s and 1980s led to the creation of what became known as structural adjustment programmes (SAPs), in which the IMF and World Bank, in league with the US Treasury, would provide relief in return for those countries meeting certain conditions. By 1989, those conditions had coalesced as the 'Washington Consensus', the ten-point programme for achieving good governance that featured many of the neoliberal policies referred to above (Peet 2007). Despite the apparent failure of these programmes to achieve growth, similar programmes were put in place in Eastern Europe and South-East Asia in the 1990s in more dramatic form as neoliberal 'shock therapy'. These too failed (Stiglitz 2002), but largely remain in place.

This history of neoliberal policy transfer, where internationally networked elites take control of wealthier states to put in place collectively developed policy programmes which are simultaneously foisted upon poorer nations through institutional pressure, lends itself to two types of analysis in particular. One is a class analysis, such as that offered by Harvey (2005). Here neoliberalism is about the restitution of elite class power that had been eroded by several decades of Keynesian welfare economics dominating policy discourse (see also Peet 2007). The other is a 'top-down' analysis of neoliberalism as a global hegemony that descends on different places and people to the point that the latter are constituted as relatively passive victims or, at best, defined by the extent to which they resist neoliberalism. But neither really escapes the diffusionist analytical imaginary, through which we could conceivably argue that the 'global' context of a political economy of class, or the social construction of a hegemonic discourse, explains policy convergence around the neoliberal agenda. Furthermore, given the transformations we have seen in and around neoliberal policy in the last couple of decades regularly point to a distinct lack of convergence, we need a different analytic that allows us to grasp exactly what policy *is* in relation to neoliberalism and so to rethink some of this history. The emergence of the policy mobility literature in geography, which emphasizes not only the movement of policy across space but its related transformation and mutation as it does so (Peck 2011; McCann 2011), offers such an analytic.

Experimentation and mutation

As has already been intimated, the fact is that there has been a lot of variety in the neoliberal project from the 'beginning'. Different countries and cities have followed often very distinctive and idiosyncratic paths to quite different neoliberalisms which are not easily explained in the terms outlined above (Fourcade-Gourinchas and Babb 2002; Brenner and Theodore 2002; North 2007; England and Ward 2007; Jessop 2016). Moreover, the last two decades are increasingly understood as having seen some clear transitions in the nature of what we describe as neoliberalism (Sheppard and Leitner 2010; Peck and Tickell 2002; Peck 2010; Lewis *et al.* 2008; Sidaway and Hendrikse 2016). After the often figuratively and literally violent 'retreat' of the state from its Keynesian role in the economy, characterized by Peck and Tickell (2002) as 'rollback neoliberalism', the 1990s and early 2000s saw much of the stated ideology toned down. New forms of 'third way' policy emerged, intended to make markets more feasible in ever more parts of day-to-day life while ameliorating some of the harder edges of the new political settlement. This 'roll-out neoliberalism' (Peck and Tickell 2002) was also apparent in developing contexts as the Bretton Woods institutions sought to rectify the failures of the Washington Consensus with reformed, but still neoliberal, policy models (Sheppard and Leitner 2010). Even more recently, the austerity politics that have emerged after the 2008 financial crisis have led others to suggest a new, more aggressive, neoliberalism has arisen (Hendrikse and Sidaway 2010; Sidaway and Hendrikse 2016; Peck *et al.* 2012).

These shifts have been more complex than can be characterized here, but we can see the way that the policy form of neoliberalism has changed when we examine some of the recently popular and fast-moving policy models that speak to its market narrative. I will briefly outline three widely studied examples. First: 'workfare' policies link benefit payments to readiness and willingness to work, extending the neoliberal demand for a flexible workforce into the welfare arena (Peck 2002; MacLeavy 2011; MacLeavy and Peoples 2010). This approach has been taken up across much of the world, although with quite self-conscious variations to suit local institutional, economic and social conditions (Peck and Theodore 2001; Peck and Theodore 2010; MacLeavy and Peoples 2010).

Second: business improvement districts, or BIDs, are areas of a city in which responsibility for taxation and spending is devolved to business interests in the area for the purposes of making them work better for those very businesses. This kind of non-state, private-sector friendly regulation appeals to neoliberal sensibilities (Ward 2006). The BID 'model' has been exported from the USA to other parts of the world, including the UK, Europe and South Africa, where how it has been taken up has varied depending on local political and economic circumstances (Cook and Ward 2012; Peyroux *et al.* 2012; Ward 2006). The BID in Cape Town in post-apartheid South Africa, for example, has focused nascent social development aspects on access for disadvantaged black communities by drawing on traditions of faith-based charities providing work and housing in the BID space (Didier *et al.* 2013).

And third: the 'creative city' is a policy narrative that captures a range of interventions purportedly intended to increase the economic and social impact of the urban population's latent 'creativity' (Evans 2009; Zimmerman 2008). It became a popular refrain through the 2000s for cities in all parts of the world to emphasize creativity, whether it was through developing their own native and imported 'creative industries' (Cunningham 2009), or through attracting more of Richard Florida's (2002) fabled 'creative class' to their inner cities (O'Callaghan 2010). Despite the diversity, they rarely offered more than the kinds of city boosterism, regeneration projects and supply-side supports that did not fall outside of the neoliberal script (Peck 2005, 2012).

Each of these policy models speak to certain neoliberal themes, but each also has a lot of variation across its global geography. The emerging policy mobility literature engages directly with these tendencies by emphasizing mobility and mutation in policy as two sides of the same coin. Additionally, policy itself not only changes as it travels, its movement is linked to the reshaping of the very landscape it moves across. Peck *et al.* (2013; see also Brenner *et al.* 2010a; 2010b; Peck *et al.* 2012) deploy this insight to argue for a perspective on neoliberalism that does not link it to any *particular* set of policies but to a mode of 'market-disciplinary regulatory restructuring' (Peck *et al.* 2013: 269) in which experimentation and the rapid transfer of policy across space is the norm. The mobility of policy – what they call 'fast policy transfer' by coordinated communities of politicians, technocrats, consultants and other policy actors – is central to understanding the political dynamic that constitutes neoliberalism, or, as they prefer, neoliberalization. For these authors, this helps us to explain why policy models like the creative city and the BID are the progeny of 'older' (but still very alive) neoliberal policies like privatization and free trade. But it also explains why they vary so much across space and time as they are made to fit a variety of circumstances. They argue that the post-ideological and often highly technocratic nature of these kinds of policies, purportedly founded on 'evidence' and a pragmatic predilection for 'what works', enables this constant experimentation and mutation, but that it all still occurs within institutional parameters that remain staunchly neoliberal.

The restless policy landscape that this evokes certainly challenges the notion of neoliberalism as a top-down process, foisted on state actors with little choice in the matter. This is partly because neoliberalism is never, in policy terms, one thing: 'systemic geoinstitutional differentia-tion' is understood as one of its defining features (Peck *et al.* 2013: 269). But this is also because it leaves room for new policy models developed outside of the traditional 'heartlands' of neoliberalism (the UK and USA) to circulate back, further reinforcing its apparent openness (Peck and Theodore 2010). Nevertheless, this approach remains open to a class analysis through an ongoing focus on policy elites, albeit one that nuances those analyses more firmly grounded in a Marxist critique of capitalism.

Assemblages and topologies

Another approach which challenges the top-down narrative, but in a different way and with different implications for our understanding of neoliberalism, considers policy formation and mobility through an analytic of assemblage, a concept that plays on its status as both verb and noun (Allen 2011; Anderson and McFarlane 2011; Collier 2006; Marcus and Saka 2006; McCann and Ward 2012). Peck and his colleagues have tended to emphasize circuits that join up different territories in new ways and adorn them with a new suite of policy injunctions and circumscriptions. In contrast, an assemblage approach weaves territories into analyses of policy assemblages that bring together diverse and variable elements in contingent combinations (Phelps *et al.* 2014; Jacobs 2012; Robinson 2011, 2013). Neoliberalism is understood here less as the explanatory structuring narrative and more as a specific set of individualization and marketization technologies that get selectively deployed in different circumstances alongside other governing logics and techniques (Ong 2007).

Rather than thinking about policy as something that gets 'applied' to a territory, an assemblage approach to policy means thinking about how that territory is reassembled, in more or less significant ways, through the assemblage of the policy. Thinking about policy mobility means thinking about how connections to other territories are constructed as a part of this process, and what the consequences of this are. One of the key ways that this occurs is through specific techniques of measurement. Larner and Le Heron (2002), for example, talk about the way the technique of benchmarking by governmental and non-governmental organizations has the effect of drawing their comparators into close proximity, making the practices of those comparators more likely to be emulated in this new relational assemblage of comparison. This has implications for how we might think about which policies from which territories will be considered in practices of policy learning (McCann 2008). For instance, this can help us to understand the circulation of 'creativity'-based policies, which have tended to be founded on the invention of quantitative measures of creativity – from Richard Florida's (2002) city-ranking tables of creativity indices to the more conventional statistical measurement of the so-called 'creative industries' in relation to GDP (see DCMS 2001). The measurement techniques are reproduced in other places, in the process assembling 'creativity' as a universal, and knowable, aspect of cities and economies, and it is across this 'global assemblage' (Collier 2006) that policies which speak to these measurements are mobilized by policy actors (Prince 2010, 2014).

Another way territories are relationally reassembled is through the circulation of knowledge across them. Forms of knowledge produced in one territory can be extracted and made mobile in both textual and embodied forms. In the process, representations of territories circulate and can become a part of other assemblages (Roy 2012). This often happens with 'policy models', such as in the representation of certain cities in ideal terms to shape policy formation in another (Pow 2014; McCann and Ward 2010). And it can happen with people. Experts from places that appear to fit a set of policy aspirations, or who seek out new territories for their own purposes, can connect policy narratives between one place and another. The way they connect these narratives is likely to produce unexpected outcomes in policy form, and can help us to understand some of the disjunctive and surprising ways that policy gets assembled (Larner 2009; Larner and Laurie 2010; Roy 2012).

Neoliberal policy mobility is more circumscribed from this perspective. Indeed, understanding neoliberalism as an overarching structural logic is anathema to this approach. Rather, ideology is subordinate to the work of assemblage. Particular technologies of governing that we might identify as neoliberal, such as those that individualize and responsibilize the citizenry, or that marketize social relations, will often be quite mobile and so a part of policy assemblages that are transnationally constituted (Ong 2007). But to assume that these are their most important components is to understate the significance of other rationalities and logics that emerge to shape policy from changing political constituencies and their expectations and demands (Barnett 2005). Conversely, this can overstate the relative novelty of many of the technologies and policies associated with neoliberalism, which often have much longer and more complex histories than such a designation would suggest (Clarke 2009).

Taking account of the myriad ways that a policy assemblage might be connected to other territories and places, and the shifting significance that might be ascribed to any set of these according to the accident of a given moment, left Robinson (2013) arguing for a different understanding of policy mobility. Rather than think about how policy 'arrives' at a destination, she advocates thinking about how policy is 'arrived at' in place, and so understanding how certain influences loom larger over decision-making while others are pushed to the background. This approach provincializes policy-making, so is opposed to a reading of neoliberalism 'upwards' as universal, global or structural in the way it shapes policy. Instead, it makes the case for more specificity, and thinking about neoliberalism in ways that undermine its dominance in the narrative, rather than cementing it.

Conclusion: everywhere neoliberalism?

I suggested in the introduction that tracing policy should be a straightforward way of grasping neoliberalism's everywhereness. The three discussions above show that it is anything but. While each of them overlaps with the others in certain ways, they tend to sit in tension with one another over the ontological status of neoliberalism. While one is happy to see neoliberalism as a top-down, class-driven global policy project, another describes it as a form of regulatory restructuring that parameterizes and directs market-based policy-making, while the third understands it as a specific set of technologies that get deployed in what are often otherwise highly divergent policy assemblages. Arguably, anyone with much familiarity with recent debates about neoliberalism could recognize the way these can roughly map onto particular conceptions of neoliberalism, such as political economy (e.g. Carroll and Sapinski 2016), regulationist (e.g. Jessop 2016), and governmentality (e.g. Lewis 2016) conceptions respectively. A focus on policy mobility, then, may not resolve these debates, but it nevertheless helps to further nuance each perspective.

But, more than this, a focus on neoliberal policy can make us think about the politics of how we conceive neoliberalism. For example, thinking of it as a top-down project places neoliberal policy at the centre of a fundamental global class conflict, and so something to be necessarily opposed at every step by progressive forces. An approach that considers it a regulatory regime brings the focus more to the way that policy-making institutions are aligned within and across states, and points to effective politics being directed towards reshaping such rule regimes. In contrast, treating neoliberalism as a specific set of technologies that can be parts of complex policy assemblages suggests that a politics opposed to neoliberalism needs to be more carefully specified to not only distinguish what is neoliberal and what is not, but even what may be distinguished as neoliberal that might still be progressive and worth working with (Lewis 2009; Ferguson 2010). Whichever of these is more useful for contending with neoliberal policy is debatable, but it reminds us that neoliberalism is not simply a descriptive and analytical category, it is a political one. What it offers to or closes down for political possibilities needs to be considered whenever we use it.

References

Allen, J. 2011. Powerful Assemblages? *Area*, 43: 154–7.

Anderson, B., and McFarlane, C. 2011. Assemblage and Geography. *Area*, 43: 124–7.

Barnett, C. 2005. The Consolations of 'Neoliberalism'. *Geoforum*, 36: 7–12.

Benson, D., and Jordan, A. 2011. What Have We Learned from Policy Transfer Research? Dolowitz and Marsh Revisited. *Political Studies Review*, 9: 366–78.

Bockman, J., and Eyal, G. 2002. Eastern Europe as a Laboratory for Economic Knowledge: The Transnational Roots of Neoliberalism. *American Journal of Sociology*, 108: 310–52.

Brenner, N., and Theodore, N. 2002. Cities and the Geographies of 'Actually Existing Neoliberalism'. *Antipode*, 34: 349–79.

Brenner, N., Peck, J., and Theodore, N. 2010a. After Neoliberalization? *Globalizations*, 7: 327–45.

—. 2010b. Variegated Neoliberalization: Geographies, Modalities, Pathways. *Global Networks*, 10: 182–222.

Carroll, W.K, and Sapinski, J.P. 2016. Neoliberalism and the Transnational Capitalist Class, in Springer, S., Birch, K., and MacLeavy, J., eds. *The Handbook of Neoliberalism*. London: Routledge: 25–35.

Clarke, J. 2008. Living With/In and Without Neoliberalism. *Focaal*, 51: 135–47.

Clarke, N. 2009. In What Sense 'Spaces of Neoliberalism'? The New Localism, the New Politics of Scale, and Town Twinning. *Political Geography*, 28: 496–507.

Collier, S.J. 2006. Global Assemblages. *Theory, Culture and Society*, 23: 399–401.

Cook, I.R. and, Ward, K. 2012. Conferences, Informational Infrastructures and Mobile Policies: The Process of Getting Sweden 'BID Ready'. *European Urban and Regional Studies*, 19: 137–52.

Cunningham, S. 2009. Trojan Horse or Rorschach Blot? Creative Industries Discourse Around the World. *International Journal of Cultural Policy*, 15: 375–86.

DCMS. 2001. *Creative Industries Mapping Document*. London: Department for Culture, Media and Sport.

Didier, S., Morange, M., and Peyroux, E. 2013. The Adaptative Nature of Neoliberalism at the Local Scale: Fifteen Years of City Improvement Districts in Cape Town and Johannesburg. *Antipode*, 45: 121–39.

Dobbin, F., Simmons, B., and Garrett, G. 2007. The Global Diffusion of Public Policies: Social Construction, Coercion, Competition, or Learning? *Annual Review of Sociology*, 33: 449–72.

Dolowitz, D., and Marsh, D. 1996. Who Learns What from Whom: A Review of the Policy Transfer Literature. *Political Studies*, 44: 343–57.

Dumenil, G. and Levy, D. 2004. *Capital Resurgent: Roots of the Neoliberal Revolution*. Cambridge, MA: Harvard University Press.

England, K., and Ward, K. 2007. *Neoliberalization: States, Networks, Peoples*. Oxford: Blackwell.

Evans, G. 2009. Creative Cities, Creative Spaces and Urban Policy. *Urban Studies*, 46: 1003–40.

Ferguson, J. 2010. The Uses of Neoliberalism. *Antipode*, 41: 166–84.

Florida, R. 2002. *The Rise of the Creative Class: And How It's Transforming Work, Leisure, Community and Everyday Life*. New York: Basic.

Fourcade-Gourinchas, M., and Babb, S.L. 2002. The Rebirth of the Liberal Creed: Paths to Neoliberalism in Four Countries. *American Journal of Sociology*, 108: 533–79.

Goldfinch, S., and Roberts, V. 2013. New Public Management and Public Sector Reform in Victoria and New Zealand: Policy Transfer, Elite Networks and Legislative Copying. *Australian Journal of Politics and History*, 59: 80–96.

Hall, S. 2011. The Neo-Liberal Revolution. *Cultural Studies*, 25: 705–28.

Harvey, D. 2005. *A Brief History of Neoliberalism*. Oxford: Oxford University Press.

Hendrikse, R.P. and Sidaway, J.D. 2010. Neoliberalism 3.0. *Environment and Planning A*, 42: 2037–42.

Jacobs, J.M. 2012. Urban Geographies I: Still Thinking Cities Relationally. *Progress in Human Geography*, 36: 412–22.

Jessop, B. 2016. The Heartlands of Neoliberalism and the Rise of the Austerity State, in Springer, S., Birch, K., and MacLeavy, J., eds. *The Handbook of Neoliberalism*. London: Routledge: 396–407.

Kelsey, J. 1995. *The New Zealand Experiment: A World Model for Structural Adjustment?* Auckland: Auckland University Press.

Larner, W. 2009. Neoliberalism, Mike Moore, and the WTO. *Environment and Planning A*, 41: 1576–93.

Larner, W., and Laurie, N. 2010. Travelling Technocrats, Embodied Knowledges: Globalising Privatisation in Telecoms and Water. *Geoforum*, 41: 218–26.

Larner, W., and Le Heron, R. 2002. The Spaces and Subjects of a Globalising Economy: A Situated Exploration of Method. *Environment and Planning D – Society and Space*, 20: 753–74.

Lewis, N. 2009. Progressive Spaces of Neoliberalism? *Asia Pacific Viewpoint*, 50: 113–19.

—. 2016. Governmentality at Work in Shaping a Critical Geographical Politics, in Springer, S., Birch, K., and MacLeavy, J., eds. *The Handbook of Neoliberalism*. London: Routledge: 59–69.

Lewis, N., Larner, W., and Le Heron, R. 2008. The New Zealand Designer Fashion Industry: Making Industries and Co-constituting Political Projects. *Transactions of the Institute of British Geographers*, 33: 42–59.

MacLeavy, J. 2011. Reconfiguring Work and Welfare in the New Economy: Regulatory Geographies of Welfare-to-Work at the Local Level. *Gender, Place and Culture: A Journal of Feminist Geography*, 18: 611–33.

MacLeavy, J., and Peoples, C. 2010. War on Terror, Work in Progress: Security, Surveillance and the Configuration of the US Workfare State. *GeoJournal*, 75.4: 339–46.

Marcus, G.E., and Saka, E. 2006. Assemblage. *Theory Culture & Society*, 23: 101–6.

McCann, E.J. 2008. Expertise, Truth, and Urban Policy Mobilities: Global Circuits of Knowledge in the Development of Vancouver, Canada's 'Four Pillar' Drug Strategy. *Environment and Planning A*, 40: 885–904.

—. 2011. Urban Policy Mobilities and Global Circuits of Knowledge: Toward a Research Agenda. *Annals of the Association of American Geographers*, 101: 107–30.

McCann, E.J., and Ward, K. 2010. Relationality/Territoriality: Toward a Conceptualization of Cities in the World. *Geoforum*, 41: 175–84.

—. 2012. Policy Assemblages, Mobilities and Mutations: Toward a Multidisciplinary Conversation. *Political Studies Review*, 10: 325–32.

Mirowski, P., and Plehwe, D. 2009. *The Road from Mont Pèlerin: The Making of the Neoliberal Thought Collective*. Cambridge, MA: Harvard University Press.

North, P. 2007. Neoliberalizing Argentina?, in England, K., and Ward, K., eds. *Neoliberalization: States, Networks, Peoples*. Malden, MA, and Oxford: Blackwell: 137–62.

O'Callaghan, C. 2010. Let's Audit Bohemia: A Review of Richard Florida's 'Creative Class' Thesis and Its Impact on Urban Policy. *Geography Compass*, 4: 1606–17.

Ong, A. 2007. Neoliberalism as a Mobile Technology. *Transactions of the Institute of British Geographers*, 32: 3–8.

Peck, J. 2002. Political Economies of Scale: Fast Policy, Interscalar Relations, and Neoliberal Workfare. *Economic Geography*, 78: 331–60.

—. 2005. Struggling with the Creative Class. *International Journal of Urban and Regional Research*, 29: 740–70.

—. 2010. *Constructions of Neoliberal Reason*. Oxford: Oxford University Press.

—. 2011. Geographies of Policy: From Transfer-diffusion to Mobility-mutation. *Progress in Human Geography*, 35: 773–97.

—. 2012. Recreative City: Amsterdam, Vehicular Ideas and the Adaptive Spaces of Creativity Policy. *International Journal of Urban and Regional Research*, 36: 462–85.

Peck, J., and Theodore, N. 2001. Exporting Workfare/Importing Welfare-to-work: Exploring the Politics of Third Way Policy Transfer. *Political Geography*, 20: 427–60.

—. 2010. Recombinant Workfare, Across the Americas: Transnationalizing 'Fast' Social Policy. *Geoforum*, 41: 195–208.

Peck, J., and Tickell, A. 2002. Neoliberalizing space. *Antipode*, 34: 380–404.

—. 2007. Conceptualizing Neoliberalism, Thinking Thatcherism, in Leitner, H., Peck, J., and Sheppard, E., eds. *Contesting Neoliberalism: Urban Frontiers*. New York and London: Guilford Press: 26–50.

Peck. J., Theodore, N., and Brenner, N. 2012. Neoliberalism Resurgent? Market Rule After the Great Recession. *South Atlantic Quarterly*, 111: 265–88.

— 2013. Neoliberal Urbanism Redux? *International Journal of Urban and Regional Research*, 37: 1091–9.

Peet, R. 2007. *Geography of Power: The Making of Global Economic Policy*. London: Zed.

Peyroux, E., Pütz, R., and Glasze, G. 2012. Business Improvement Districts (BIDs): The Internationalization and Contextualization of a 'Travelling Concept'. *European Urban and Regional Studies*, 19: 111–20.

Phelps, N.A., Bunnell, T., Miller, M.A., and Taylor, J. 2014. Urban Inter-referencing Within and Beyond a Decentralized Indonesia. *Cities*, 39: 37–49.

Pow, C.P. 2014. License to Travel: Policy Assemblage and the 'Singapore Model'. *City*, 18: 287–306.

Prince, R. 2010. Policy Transfer as Policy Assemblage: Making Policy for the Creative Industries in New Zealand. *Environment and Planning A*, 42: 169–86.

—. 2014. Consultants and the Global Assemblage of Culture and Creativity. *Transactions of the Institute of British Geographers*, 39: 90–101.

Robinson, J. 2011. The Spaces of Circulating Knowledge: City Strategies and Global Urban Governmentality, in McCann, E.J., and Ward, K., eds. *Assembling Urbanism: Cities and Policy-Making in the Global Age*. Minnesota: University of Minnesota Press.

—. 2013. 'Arriving at' Urban Policies/The Urban: Traces of Elsewhere in Making City Futures, in Söderström, O., Randeria, S., Ruedin, D, D'Amato, G., and Panese, F., eds. *Critical Mobilities*. London: Routledge: 1–28.

Robison, R. 2006. *The Neoliberal Revolution: Forging the Market State*. Basingstoke: Palgrave Macmillan.

Roy, A. 2012. Ethnographic Circulations: Space-time Relations in the Worlds of Poverty Management. *Environment and Planning A*, 44: 31–41.

Sheppard, E., and Leitner, H. 2010. Quo Vadis Neoliberalism? The Remaking of Global Capitalist Governance after the Washington Consensus. *Geoforum*, 41: 185–94.

Sidaway, J.D., and Hendrikse, R.P. 2016. Neoliberalism Version 3+, in Springer, S., Birch, K., and MacLeavy, J., eds. *The Handbook of Neoliberalism*. London: Routledge: 560–8.

Stiglitz, J. 2002. *Globalization and its Discontents*. London: Penguin.

Ward, K. 2006. 'Policies in Motion', Urban Management and State Restructuring: The Trans-Local Expansion of Business Improvement Districts. *International Journal of Urban and Regional Research*, 30: 54–75.

Venugopal, R. 2015. Neoliberalism as Concept. *Economy and Society*, 44.2: 165–87.

Zimmerman, J. 2008. From Brew Town to Cool Town: Neoliberalism and the Creative City Development Strategy in Milwaukee. *Cities*, 25: 230–42.

29

SCIENCE, INNOVATION AND NEOLIBERALISM

David Tyfield

Neoliberalism and science

Science and innovation have changed profoundly during the neoliberal period, generating massive and diverse literatures on specific themes (for overviews see Mirowski and Sent 2002, 2008). But what is systematically missing from most of this literature is any attention to the specificities of the context of *neoliberalism*, let alone to the detailed ways in which developments in science and innovation (and their respective institutional forms) have contributed to and been co-produced with neoliberalism. Seeking to grapple with precisely that question, a growing body of work has begun to appear in recent years and from multiple disciplinary origins (e.g. Busch 2011; Jessop 2005; Lave *et al.* 2010; Mirowski 2011; Moore *et al.* 2011; Pellizzoni and Ylonen 2013; Tyfield 2012a, 2012b; Tyfield *et al.* 2017). It is to this literature, therefore, that the chapter will introduce the reader.

What all this literature has in common is its critical and empirical interest in matters of science and innovation as they are developing as socio-political phenomena, together with a commitment to an explicit attention to issues of political economy and political economic context. The former thus means that much of this work, from whatever discipline it originates, tends towards an engagement with science and technology studies (STS), while the latter concern for political economy, and especially of a critical variety, is what brings with it the interest in neoliberalism. What divides the literature, by contrast, is the specific *way* in which these two – often quite different and even incompatible – intellectual traditions are brought together, and the implications of that theoretical choice. These include whether 'neoliberalism' is taken as a given and highly structured context for knowledge production or is seen itself in relational terms as something that is co-produced in parallel with developments in the political economy of knowledge: hence also the extent to which neoliberalism is cast as irredeemably negative and monolithically powerful or, conversely, normatively complex (if not ambivalent) and/or ontologically dependent on other social conditions, limited and vulnerable. This, in turn, conditions profoundly different judgements regarding a key question today, namely the prospects of the collapse of neoliberalism and what, if anything, is going to replace it. Moreover, these are not two neat camps. For instance, both Mirowski (2011) and Popp Berman (2014) adhere to a concept of both neoliberalism and science as performed, active and social, not given, structural and/or pristine. Yet their normative conclusions are far apart, deeply critical and sceptically untroubled respectively.

The emergence of a literature united by syntheses of STS and political economy, but also that contains a multitude of different perspectives and normative dispositions, however, arguably illustrates something more fundamental about neoliberalism. It suggests that the lens of knowledge production is a particularly insightful one for understanding neoliberalism itself, as well as the concrete trajectory of social change in the neoliberal period. In particular, it is in the identification of neoliberalism as a *political project of fundamentalist market epistemology* (Mirowski 2011) – a definition that complements and illuminates, rather than displaces, other major definitions (e.g. Harvey 2005; Peck and Tickell 2002; Rose 2007; Crouch 2011) – that this may be explained. For this definition (explained below) seems uniquely able to accommodate both of two striking features of neoliberalism. These are its political radicalism and its epistemic radicalism *and* how these are inter-related: respectively, in terms of the *epistemic* nature of its market fundamentalism and the *strategic political* (and hence guiltlessly a-rational but highly 'productive' and destructive) nature of its programme for, and use of, 'knowledge production'. In short, studying neoliberalism through the lens of how knowledge production has changed suggests that it is in the radical substitution or subjection of the Enlightenment project of 'reason' by the project of the 'market' – itself *as* the project of 'reason' – that neoliberalism may be best understood.

Knowledge, politics and their radical reconnection

The history of the relation between (the formation of) neoliberalism and the (changing forms of) knowledge production – as scientific research, 'technological' innovation and (higher) education – thus presents this key aspect of neoliberalism most clearly. This can be studied in two ways. First, consider neoliberalism's political radicalism, which is primarily epistemic and anti-political in character. This follows directly from it being a political project of market fundamentalist epistemology, by which we mean two key points.

First, that (for neoliberalism) the market must be understood not as an economic mechanism of optimal allocation but as an *epistemic mechanism of optimal decision-making*. The market, on this conception, aggregates the individually limited choices and information of market players in ways that then automatically reach the best possible outcome in terms of, respectively, both maximal realization of human negative freedom and aggregated knowledge, with the latter the priority.

Second, therefore, the market and its outcomes *cannot, in principle*, be bettered. This thus makes impossible by definition all attempts to generate what may seem more 'rational' or 'acceptable' outcomes than those generated by markets. Indeed, it robs of all epistemic legitimacy even attempted *criticisms* of markets and market-organized processes. In short, therefore, neoliberalism as market fundamentalist epistemology becomes a pro-market political project that is incalculably more profound than the more familiar doctrines of *laissez faire* classical liberalism. There are at least five ways in which this is so.

First, if the market is the best of all possible decision-makers, it stands to reason that *all* practices involving or susceptible to decision processes would be optimized if arranged as markets. It seems fair, even today, to say this is a radical political programme, but it was undoubtedly and obviously so at the moment of neoliberalism's ascendancy in the late 1970s and early 1980s. In that period, the 'core' capitalist societies from which neoliberalism most strikingly emerged were arranged as Keynesian welfare states, with significant and explicitly carved-out spheres of social life publicly provided; a development that was itself emergent from the turbulent attempts to preserve capitalism against both fascism and communism in the early/mid-twentieth century. Neoliberalism as a project of unbounded marketization, therefore, entailed (and still entails) the fundamental reconstitution of socio-political order.

Second, the relation between neoliberalism and state power signals another aspect of its political radicalism, and one that demands understanding in terms of its (purported) relation with knowledge. For the radicalism of its project of marketizing society inevitably raises significant and heated objections, together with arguments regarding the allegedly catastrophic nature of such reforms. The result, therefore, is that markets must be *forcibly* constructed, in the face of what, by definition from a neoliberal perspective, is 'irrational', 'partial' and/or 'short-sighted' opposition. Yet the primary agency for such forcible construction is the apparatus of state power. State coercion of projects of marketization, however, remains fundamentally legitimated in epistemic terms: insofar as it serves the market, state power is rational and is so without limit. Again, the political radicalism of this position is in marked contrast even with classical liberalism. For the latter, markets, conceptualized as spontaneously and 'naturally' emergent forms of social organization, provide the rational argument for the *limitation* of state power. Moreover, to the extent that a specific market appears to 'fail', for neoliberalism this is simply evidence for the need for more state intervention to ensure the market 'works'. Conversely, for classical liberalism, market failure is the crucial limit case of the rationality of markets; the exception in which a specific good or service is constituted such that its rational optimal allocation depends on state provision.

Third, since the market can neither be rationally gainsaid, nor reach a sub-optimal outcome, there are necessarily no limits to their rational optimal application. Thus, not only should the provision of all things be arranged into markets but also, as primarily *decision-making* processes, all processes involving socially significant judgements should be thus arranged. Furthermore, with no limits to markets, there are no 'real' limits imposed by the (more or less scientifically knowable) 'natures' of particular goods, services or valued phenomena that would render their provision and management incompatible with marketization (cf. the Polanyian argument, 1944/1957, regarding how markets tend to the destruction of social bonds and stewardship of 'nature'). Indeed, neoliberalism – again as market fundamentalist *epistemology* – is fundamentally dismissive of all such apparent ontological limits, seeing these simply as the contingent *epistemic* limits of (at best) current '(scientific) knowledge' that credulous and limited humans dress up in ontological costume. To the contrary, therefore, it is only through the active experiment of subjecting a phenomenon to market-based entrepreneurship that we may find out what that thing is, or rather, what it may become.

Fourth, therefore, neoliberalism has a compelling and world-making, not merely abstract and critical, response to the obvious question of what should be done when confronted with unwanted outcomes from projects of marketization. For in its active commitment to such projects and associated (particularly technological) entrepreneurship, exploiting investment opportunities in a fundamentally uncertain search for personal profit, neoliberalism's epistemology counsels and legitimates a specific form of activity that often proves to be self-confirming: the successful entrepreneur has undoubtedly introduced something new into the world (whether trivial or profound) that thereby both legitimates the neoliberal credo that the naysayers were wrong *and* generates the only relevant criterion of such 'success', namely profit from sales on the market. Indeed, from this perspective it becomes clear that the emergence of problems that projects of marketization *themselves* produce are, for neoliberalism, simply the frontier of opportunity for further Promethean entrepreneurship (cf. Klein 2007, Pellizzoni 2011). In this way, neoliberalism's epistemic fundamentalism – that is, its apparently flagrant *irrationalism* – proves (in many, but not all, circumstances) to be strategically self-empowering and not, as many 'rational' critics of neoliberalism have hoped, simply transparently contradictory and self-defeating. In short, the *epistemic* character of neoliberalism's political radicalism helps us understand how neoliberalism emerges and is sustained, even as its explicit disregard for 'limits' necessarily generates proliferating crises.

Finally, and perhaps of most significance for the remainder of this chapter, the epistemic nature of neoliberalism's political radicalism entails that projects of knowledge production, and the reframing of their institutions as markets, assume a centrality to the broader political project. This follows directly from the redefinition of the market as a primarily epistemic device, a 'marketplace of ideas' in which both terms deserve equal emphasis (Mirowski 2011). For, as such, 'ideas' or knowledges become the privileged medium of politically reconstructing societies, particularly in two key forms of the novel mediation of social relations by profit-seeking technological innovations and/or market-supporting government regulation and coercion. Moreover, 'ideas' themselves become a key sphere of social life to be subjected to marketization. The result is, respectively, the construction of ever-greater systemic demands for, and fetishization of, 'innovation' together with the tendential conflation of science with ('hi-tech') commercialized innovation, where the latter is prioritized. In short, the commercialization of science emerges as a central project and/or front-line in the ongoing project of deepening neoliberalism.

This leads, however, directly to the other face of neoliberalism: its explicitly political and *anti*-epistemic epistemic radicalism. This refers to the way in which, as a market fundamentalist epistemology, neoliberalism necessarily wears the garb of rational legitimacy but also hands questions of rational judgement over to the market, rather than preserving them within the field of rational argument itself. Neoliberalism, therefore, is a project that is not only foundationally inimical to institutions of knowledge production that claim for themselves intrinsic criteria of rational argument – arguments that may well (often, if contingently) contradict the judgements of marketized outcomes and so represent intransigent critical outposts against the rule of the market. More specifically, by vesting the construction of legitimate knowledge *not* in critical, rational and (quasi-)public debate, or an idealized 'republic of science' (Polanyi 1962), but in the outcomes of market-based entrepreneurialism, neoliberalism is also thereby foundationally opposed to the structures and professionalized institutions of modern scientific research and education in the 'public good' form they had taken in the post-war period. While often prosecuted in the language of economics, efficiency, optimized 'output' etc.... the neoliberal commercialization of science is thus primarily a political project, and one founded upon the destruction of existing scientific institutions and their replacement with the 'marketplace of ideas'.

So much, then, for a sketch of how knowledge production illuminates neoliberalism. Let us now consider the history of their co-production in some greater detail.

Science and the emergence of neoliberalism

Science and innovation featured significantly in the emergence of neoliberalism to political dominance. This centrality takes several overlapping and mutually affecting forms. First, consider the critical importance of the neoliberal reform of the political economic structures of knowledge production. Of totemic importance in this regard is the TRIPs (Trade Related Intellectual Property Rights) agreement of the World Trade Organization. This global legislation is a pillar of the neoliberal Washington Consensus and was a highly controversial treaty that was nonetheless implemented despite having been drafted by, and overwhelming beneficial to, only a handful of (primarily US-based) corporations who, not being sovereign governments, were not even signatories. As Sell (1999, 171; see also 2003) described this unprecedented global coup, 'twelve corporations made public law for the world'.

To understand this extraordinary development, one must attend to its political economic context, and in particular to the rise of neoliberalism. The crises of the post-war Keynesian welfare state demanded new spheres of socio-economic life to be opened up to profitable capitalist enterprise. This involved projects of privatization and marketization, a distinctively neoliberal (and financialized) 'globalization' and a seemingly unanimous political consensus supporting new technological innovations. At the overlap of these three developments, and thus at the core of the neoliberal restructuring of the regulatory architecture of global capitalism, lay the 'globalized construction of knowledge scarcity' (May 2006: 53) through accumulation by dispossession (Harvey 2005), subjecting 'knowledge' production to private appropriation in search of profit in the form of strong and global intellectual property rights (IPRs).

In particular, allegedly wondrous, and massively hyped, new prospects of innovation that were supposedly dependent on the private appropriation of knowledge through IPRs and on a global scale were deployed to argue for a global knowledge 'enclosure' movement (Boyle 2003; Lessig 2001; Zeller 2008). The key example, and political agent, in this regard was an emerging coalition of massive pharmaceutical firms, start-ups and elite universities all interested in 'biotech' and all dependent, if in different ways, on private ownership of research results in the form of patents (Tyfield 2008). Justified, thus, in terms of needed and life-saving innovation, TRIPs was primarily the means for this key neoliberal project of constructing a global regulatory architecture suitable for the marketization of knowledge.

Alongside these actual knowledge-focused transformations to the political economy, the *concept* of 'science' was also crucial to formulation of discourses that served to legitimate neoliberal transformations. Particularly in economics (see Nik-Khah and Van Horn 2016), work through the post-war period in American economics, centred on the Chicago School, investigating the 'economics of science' laid the groundwork for the reconceptualization of the 'market' as the ideal information processor; concepts that ascended from *academic* respectability, if unorthodoxy, to *political* dominance in the late 1970s.

This work in economics has not just been crucial to constructing knowledge-power technologies of *legitimation* of the neoliberal project. It has also been crucial in providing key arguments that have shaped the regulatory framework for a specific model of innovation that fetishizes 'innovation' *per se* – itself identified with (high) 'technology' – and particularly in certain 'cutting-edge' industries. Alongside the state-sponsored knowledge enclosure, therefore, this model of innovation privileges innovation that:

- promises high, short-term returns, especially as financial(izable) assets
- focuses on products that service the market demands of corporate/individual consumers, as opposed to publics or states
- supports projects of corporate enclosure of bodies of knowledge and so promises to maximize global corporate control of particular (technoscience-intensive) markets
- is constitutively dismissive of ontological limits and risks.

The quintessential example here of this broader neoliberal innovation model is GM agriculture (Kinchy 2012; Bronson 2009; Levidow and Carr 2009; Bonneuil *et al.* 2014). For genetically modified food staples that are genetically owned (both via global IPRs and, more effectively, through complex technologies that may only feasibly be developed at great expense in well-funded corporate laboratories) by major trans-national corporations present a paradigm case of a commodity that can achieve almost universal and unquestionable individual consumer demand together with all-but-unbreakable monopoly control of supply. Moreover, this was an industry associated with (what, contemporaneously, were apparently) the most 'promising' breakthroughs in science, namely in genomic biotechnology; while, conversely, the industry also systematically belittled any and every objection, regarding not just the potential risks but also undeniable and irreducible uncertainties and unknowns involved in the introduction of these technologies: to complex ecologies, food chains, food quality and human health, social relations of farming, (traditional) farming knowledge, control of seeds and food sovereignty – and all these over the long term. Together with medical or 'red' biotech, this has also generated official discourses of 'knowledge-based bio-economies' as instances of the neoliberal fetishization of innovation (Birch *et al.* 2010).

A key third example of the neoliberal remaking of knowledge political economies concerns the commercialization of science and the academy, particularly in the USA and UK, but increasingly also across the rest of the world. This has taken multiple forms, including (Tyfield 2012a: 11; Slaughter and Rhoades 2004; Radder 2010):

- increased privatization of research funding
- commercial 'accountability' and 'relevance'/'impact' criteria in competitive public funding
- growth in university–industry relations and direct incorporation of science into commerce
- growth in patenting, especially at universities and especially in life sciences
- commodification of higher education.

While the general direction of change is not disputed, debate focuses on the *extent* of these changes and their positive or negative effects, hence also the extent to which they should be deepened or repudiated. Shapin (2008), for instance, argues convincingly that there is no clear *ex ante* reason why the increasing prevalence of scientific research done within or funded by private industry should be seen as problematic. Publicly funded university labs can do 'applied' research, just as, conversely, corporate labs have attained Nobel prizes for their fundamental scientific insights. Such objections, nonetheless, miss the point regarding much of what is seen to be troubling about the commercialization of science. These include various concerns regarding the effects of a deeper penetration of commercial logics into scientific decisions (whether regarding pressures to interpret or even massage data in specific ways), research agendas, sharing findings (or not, against demands of commercial confidentiality) and other conflicts of interest, and the resulting dangers of loss of social trust in and epistemic authority of science more broadly (Radder 2010: 14).

High-profile examples of all the objections have undoubtedly emerged, though it also clearly the case that the institutions of 'science' have not (yet) collapsed beneath the weight of these contradictions. Focusing exclusively on supposed evidence of an abstract incompatibility between the logics of 'business' and 'science', however, paradoxically serves to miss what is arguably most troubling about the neoliberal restructuring of science. For, in conceptualizing 'science' as a pristine sphere of knowledge production entirely for its own sake, one is unable to explore empirically two key questions. First, how what appears or counts as 'science' is itself a political battle-ground in which diverse, if often tacit, political commitments are always in play, hence affording the potential for distinctively *neoliberal* science to emerge (Lave 2012; Lave *et al.* 2010; Busch 2011). And, second, how the foundationally inimical (as instrumental) relation of neoliberalism, as epistemic project, to the 'Republic of Science' can also be seen in various developments in recent decades that are both deeply problematic (from the perspective of a concern) for science and rational public debate thus conceptualized, *and* both *un*problematic and, indeed, positively productive for neoliberalism and the construction of a social acceptance of its epistemology.

Examples of the latter process abound, and especially in the USA. For instance, neoliberalism has deliberately cultivated public suspicion regarding the undisclosed 'political' motives underlying all discourses of rational objections, and especially to projects of marketization and ontological 'limits'. This has produced a cultural discourse intolerant of scientific conclusions that identify the emergence of potentially existential systemic threats, especially on ecological issues such as climate change. Moreover, such popular mistrust is largely *justified* given the emergence of a 'marketplace of ideas' that, now 'legitimately' deploying 'science' as purely strategic means, necessarily includes the proliferation and profitable professionalization of ignorance-production, deliberate obfuscation and sowing of doubt (Oreskes and Conway 2010; Davies and McGoey 2012).

Furthermore, the popular distrust of science is paradoxically heightened further by the neoliberal instrumental deployment of science in the attempted *depoliticization* of political debate, leaving instead the field of political decision-making free for a seemingly 'objective' government by the market. Again, GM agriculture is a classic case in this regard. For, as described by Levidow *et al.* (2007), the trans-Atlantic controversy thrown up by how, or if, to regulate GM crops took the paradigmatic neoliberal form of pro-GM (American) denunciations of (European) objections as based on 'junk', not 'sound', science and the argument, before the WTO, that this was thus an illegitimate basis for an obstacle to free global trade. This thus constitutes an attempted 'scientification' of politics, transforming questions of technological risk purely into answerable scientific questions of risk assessment. But, going further, it is also an attempted 'scientization' of politics and the political process *per se*, attempting to bypass and neutralize with 'sound' (i.e. neoliberal-supportive) science all *public and political* objection to the commercial introduction of new innovations. Inevitably, the attempt to foreclose political debate with science simply leads to the *politicization* of science. Yet this hardly entails a defeat for the neoliberal project. Indeed, to the contrary, as with the other examples just mentioned, by fragmenting further the 'Republic of Science' and the (largely overlooked) social preconditions for its epistemic authority, this is precisely to inoculate the project of ever-deeper marketization from even the *possibility* of concerted and 'reason-based' objection.

Science and the crises of neoliberalism

Neoliberalism and knowledge production have thus been intimately intertwined through the emergence and dominance of the former. But empirical analysis of the latter, as a socially conditioned process and not a 'pure', so-called 'Mertonian' sphere (Mirowski and Sent 2002), also offers key insights into the limits and current crises of neoliberalism, the current response to those crises and their possible outcomes. Let us consider these issues briefly.

First, the limits and crises of neoliberalism. The combination of a cultivated ontological agnosticism regarding 'limits', a fundamental imperative for corporate-owned and privately consumed high-technology innovations and systemic celebration of the key figure of the Promethean entrepreneur, forging worlds out of fiery chaos, constructs neoliberalism as a power-knowledge regime that systematically produces systemic risks. Yet, to the extent neoliberalism's ontological denial is wrong, the creation of global risks (and of increasing scale and depth) tends towards the likelihood of ever-greater systemic crises and crashes (Biel 2012). Evidently, the clearest example of this process, and the one that has cost neoliberalism itself dearest so far, has been the debt-fuelled financialization and securitization of the global economy, which nearly brought on its collapse in 2008. However, by encouraging and technologically enabling, through forms of neoliberal innovation, cultures of heedless mass consumption, particularly of energy, and the globalized growth that has been built on this model, neoliberalism has greatly accelerated and exacerbated numerous global ecological crises, including (but by no means limited to) climate change (cf. Rockström *et al.* 2009).

Moreover, the specifically neoliberal organization of knowledge production has been centrally implicated in the economic crisis. Pagano and Rossi (2009), for instance, have highlighted the crucial role in the economic crisis of a deepening 'investment strike' in technological innovation related to the 'anti-commons' problem of the over-privatization of knowledge production (Heller and Eisenberg 1998; Heller 2008). This is perhaps best exemplified by that acme of neoliberal innovation, the pharmaceuticals industry, which has simply adopted an innovation model that devotes billions to legal chicanery to protect and extend existing patent protection, while the pipeline for development of new drugs has increasingly dried up (Mittra *et al.* 2011).

A similar dynamic is visible regarding the key neoliberal institutional innovation of the university technology transfer office (TTO). For, with only a few exceptions among the most elite universities, TTOs are loss-making while their actual productive effect is to transform the culture and economics of university science and deepen the problems of strangling scientific productivity, whether through administrative red tape, corporate-style audit or anti-commons issues. In both cases, therefore – IPRs and TTOs – the neoliberal transformation of science, like its financialized transformation of the global economy more broadly, effectively constructs inherently unstable, exploitative and fraudulent institutions of knowledge production that maintain the charade of extraordinary economic return only by siphoning ever-increasing sums from the bottom to the top – that is, Ponzi schemes (Mirowski 2012).

The emergence and deepening of these crises, however, whether sudden and dramatic or creeping and invisible, poses significant and enduring challenges to the neoliberal project. This is so in several respects. First, the crises themselves elicit increasing popular demands, including from some erstwhile neoliberal champions of the 'free market' (such as cleantech venture capitalists (Goldstein 2014)), for both positive policy action and rational planned responses. In both respects, however, these are admissions that are fundamentally anti-neoliberal, gainsaying the wisdom of the market regarding 'optimal' outcomes, as an abstract possibility and an urgent necessity respectively. Second, though, the neoliberal response to such crises is conceptually clear and neat, hugely well-resourced and still capable of being strongly marshalled: 'more market', and specifically more market-disciplined (by which is meant corporate, profit-seeking) innovation. Yet the neoliberal innovation model has proven itself spectacularly incapable of responding to these crises meaningfully, even as the fetishized policy term of 'innovation' is the obvious answer 'to hand' for how the neoliberal system will cure itself in all these dimensions. Indeed, all attempts to 'unleash' innovation (and science) in various ways in response to the 'great financial crash' have simply ended up exacerbating the problems. For, in all cases, they serve, at best, only to entrench the *dominant model of innovation*, which is precisely the underlying cause of the economic paralysis.

Moreover, perhaps the most striking example of the latter is the forefront of current 'hi-tech' (or simply 'tech') innovation, namely the replacement and/or disciplining measurement of various forms of knowledge work. At the heart of these whirlwinds of change is the university. This involves subjecting the university more keenly to the disciplines of the market, hence specifically to its various 'consumers': business-sponsors of its research; business-employers of its graduates; and employment-seeking students. In the UK, for instance, this has resulted in the Browne reforms of higher education, which have all but introduced a free market in higher education. Moreover, as students face increasing fees and associated debts, they are themselves increasingly attuned to the (supposed) demands of these would-be-employers as to what constitutes a 'valuable' (and what a 'useless') degree (Collini 2012) – with foreign-language departments seemingly the first casualty.

Moreover, while masquerading as various forms of anti-neoliberal and anti-proprietary innovations in knowledge production, circulation and teaching, the emerging project of open science, open data, open access publishing (Royal Society 2012; Nielsen 2012) and 'massively open online courses' (MOOCs) is actually exactly the same process (Tyfield 2013). Equivalent to a shift from Microsoft to Facebook, knowledge is now to be produced entirely without compensation, but offered spontaneously, voluntarily and to all, while the (massively profitable) platforms and meta-data are to be owned by a tiny handful of (largely American) giant internet and/or data management firms whose practices are even more proprietorial and secretive than those of the IPR-intensive industries previously at the core of neoliberal projects. For what all these internet-based services offer is the corporate-owned measurement and disciplining of what has hitherto – despite the growing assault of commercialization, privatization and pseudo-markets of bureaucratic audit over three decades – remained a relatively intransigent and market-*un*disciplined workforce: researchers/lecturers and their students.

Conclusion: where next?

Where might all this be leading at present? In confronting an epistemic workforce that is no longer so determined to defend a mythical 'Republic of Science' and, conversely, is increasingly comfortable with its irreducibly socio-political role, however, it is far from clear that neoliberalism continues to hold the strategic upper hand in this contest. Indeed, the forms of, and evidence for, a deepening rejection of neoliberalism and its agenda for knowledge production are clear in both socio-political and academic theoretical developments. As regards the latter, in the crucial discipline of economics, the deepening challenges and socio-political demands for 'innovation' coming to the rescue (again, an expectation that neoliberalism has both directly fostered and makes impossible to deliver) are increasingly taken to demonstrate not just what is to neoliberalism impossible, namely 'market failure', but rather a 'system failure' – that is, a *socio-political* and *institutional* arrangement that is 'locked-in' to various ways of doing innovation and thus 'locked-out' of being able to develop technological innovations for different forms of society, presupposing lower energy use, reduced consumption etc. (Unruh 2000; Geels 2005).

A growing prestige is thus being accorded to economic theories of innovation that break with the straightforwardly 'economic' and market-based definition of this process that a neoliberal analysis demands and instead are introducing increasingly complex and sophisticated frameworks that include precisely the elements a neoliberal understanding seeks to deny and exclude: for example, the irreducible importance of specific forms of knowledge, social norms, habits, cultures, social relations, institutions, forms of public-sector support and even power (e.g. Geels 2014; Smith *et al.* 2010; Kern 2011; Tyfield 2014).

Equally, in the academy as in a growing set of fields of socio-political life and around the world, the current reforms attempting to 'complete' the neoliberalization of the university through deepening marketization of higher education and the internet-enabled measurement of researcher 'productivity' (Holmwood 2014), while still undoubtedly ascendant, are also being met with significant resistance, from faculty and students alike, and even some significant defeats, as in the abolition of university tuition fees across Germany in 2014. In this key domain of the neoliberal project, therefore, it is still far from clear that neoliberal reforms will succeed or rather, in the context of broader crises of neoliberalism, prove a crucial undoing of the neoliberal project more broadly.

But explicit protest in the academy is arguably not the most significant issue here. Rather, it is likely in the *work*, and not the explicit political action, of universities and their people that the greatest insights into the prospects for neoliberalism lie. For what the work on neoliberalism and science has unequivocally demonstrated is that actual concrete instances of research and innovation – as the development of new knowledge-power technologies mediated by existing social structures, political agencies and cultural discourses – will remain central processes in the co-production of knowledge, politics and regimes of capital accumulation. Innovation and research responding – slowly, inadequately, pragmatically – to the multiple crises of neoliberalism thus again appear as a privileged window, here on what happens next. In any case, innovation and science will – and must – become increasingly core issues of broader political contestation.

References

Biel, R. 2012. *The Entropy of Capitalism*. Boston and Leiden: Brill.

Birch, K., Levidow, L., and Papaioannou, T. 2010. Sustainable Capital? The Neoliberalization of Nature and Knowledge in the European 'Knowledge-Based Bio-Economy'. *Sustainability*, 2: 2898–918.

Bonneuil, C., Foyer, J., and Wynne, B. 2014. Genetic Fallout in Bio-cultural Landscapes: Molecular Imperialism and the Cultural Politics of (not) Seeing Transgenes in Mexico. *Social Studies of Science*, 44.6: 901–29.

Boyle, J. 2003. The Second Enclosure Movement and the Construction of the Public Domain. *Law and Contemporary Problems*, 66: 33–73.

Bronson, K. 2009. What We Talk About When We Talk About Biotechnology. *Politics and Culture*, 2. Retrieved from http://www.politicsandculture.org/issue/2009-issue-2/

Busch, L. 2011. *Standards, Recipes for Reality*. Cambridge, MA: MIT Press.

Collini, S. 2012. *What are Universities For?* London: Penguin.

Crouch, C. 2011. *The Strange Non-death of Neoliberalism*. Cambridge: Polity.

Davies, W., and McGoey, L. 2012. Rationalities of Ignorance: On Financial Crisis and the Ambivalence of Neoliberal Epistemology. *Economy and Society*, 41.1: 64–83.

Geels, F. 2005. The Dynamics of Transitions in Socio-technical Systems. *Technological Analysis and Strategic Management*, 17.4: 445–76.

—. 2014. Regime Resistance Against Low-carbon Transitions: Introducing Politics and Power into the Multi-Level Perspective. *Theory, Culture and Society*, 31.5: 21–40.

Goldstein, J. 2014. *Planetary Improvement: Discourses and Practices of Green Capitalism in the Cleantech Space*. Doctoral dissertation, City University of New York. ProQuest, UMI Dissertations, 3641836.

Harvey, D. 2005. *A Brief History of Neoliberalism*. Oxford: Oxford University Press.

Heller, M. 2008. *The Gridlock Economy*. New York: Basic.

Heller, M., and Eisenberg, R. 1998. Can Patents Deter Innovation? The Anticommons in Biomedical Research. *Science*, 280: 698–701.

Holmwood, J. 2014. Turning the Audit Screw: The Degradation of Higher Education. *Global Dialogue, Newsletter of the International Sociological Association*, 4.4. Retrieved from http://isa-global-dialogue.net/turning-the-audit-screw-the-degradation-of-higher-education/

Jessop, B. 2005. Cultural Political Economy, the Knowledge-based Economy, and the State, in Barry, A., and Slater, D., eds. *The Technological Economy*. Abingdon: Routledge.

Kern, F. 2011. Ideas, Institutions, and Interests: Explaining Policy Divergence in Fostering 'System Innovations' Towards Sustainability. *Environment and Planning C*, 29: 1116–34.

Kinchy, A. 2012. *Seeds, Science, and Struggle*. Cambridge: MIT Press.

Klein, N. 2007. *The Shock Doctrine*. London: Penguin.

Lave, R. 2012. *Fields and Streams: Stream Restoration, Neoliberalism and the Future of Environmental Science*. Athens and London: University of Georgia Press.

Lave, R., Mirowski, P., and Randalls, S. eds. 2010. Special Issue on 'STS and Neoliberal Science'. *Social Studies of Science*, 40.5.

Lessig, L. 2001. *The Future of Ideas*. New York: Random House.

Levidow, L., and Carr, S. 2009. *GM Food on Trial: Testing European Democracy*. London: Routledge.

Levidow, L., Murphy, J., and Carr, S. 2007. Recasting 'Substantial Equivalence': Transatlantic Governance of GM Food. *Science, Technology and Human Values*, 32: 26–64.

May, C. 2006. The Denial of History: Reification, Intellectual Property Rights and the Lessons of the Past. *Capital and Class*, 88: 33–56.

Mirowski, P. 2011. *ScienceMart: Privatizing American Science*. Cambridge, MA: Harvard University Press.

—. 2012. The Modern Commercialization of Science is a Passel of Ponzi Schemes. *Social Epistemology*, 26.3/4: 285–310.

Mirowski, P., and Sent, E.M. eds. 2002. *Science Bought and Sold*. Chicago, IL: University of Chicago Press.

—. 2008. The Commercialization of Science and the Response of STS, in Hackett, E., Wacjman, J., Amsterdamska, O., and Lynch, M., eds. *The Handbook of Science and Technology Studies*. Cambridge, MA: MIT Press: 635–90.

Mittra, J., Tait, J., and Wield, D. 2011. From Maturity to Value-added Innovation: Lessons From the Pharmaceutical and Agro-biotechnology Industries. *Trends in Biotechnology*, 29: 105–9.

Moore, K., Kleinman, D., Hess, D., and Frickel, S. 2011. Science and Neoliberal Globalisation: A Political Sociological Approach. *Theory and Society*, 40: 505–32.

Nielsen, M. 2012. *Reinventing Discovery: The New Era of Networked Science*. Princeton, NJ, and Oxford: Princeton University Press.

Nik-Khah, E., and Van Horn, R. 2016. The Ascendency of Chicago Neoliberalism, in Springer, S., Birch, K., and MacLeavy, J., eds. *The Handbook of Neoliberalism*. London: Routledge: 13–24.

Oreskes, N., and Conway, E. 2010. *Merchants of Doubt*. New York: Bloomsbury.

Pagano, U., and Rossi, M.A. 2009. The Crash of the Knowledge Economy. *Cambridge Journal of Economics*, 33: 665–83.

Peck, J., and Tickell, A. 2002. Neoliberalizing Space. *Antipode*, 34: 380–404.

Pellizzoni, L. 2011. Governing Through Disorder: Neoliberal Environmental Governance and Social Theory. *Global Environmental Change*, 21: 795–803.

Pellizzoni, L., and Ylonen, M. eds. 2013. *Neoliberalism and Technoscience: Critical Assessments*. Farnham: Ashgate.

Polanyi, K. 1944/1957. *The Great Transformation*. Boston, MA: Beacon Press.

—. 1962. *Personal Knowledge: Towards a Post-Critical Philosophy*. Chicago, IL: University of Chicago Press.

Popp Berman, E. 2014. Not Just Neoliberalism: Economization in US Science and Technology Policy. *Science, Technology, and Human Values*, 39.3: 397–431.

Radder, H. ed. 2010. *The Commodification of Academic Research: Science and the Modern University*. Pittsburgh, PA: University of Pittsburgh Press.

Rockström, J., Steffen, W., Noone, K., Persson, Å., Chapin, F. S., Lambin, E. F., … and Foley, J. A. 2009. A Safe Operating Space for Humanity. *Nature*, 461.7263: 472–5.

Rose, N. 2007. *The Politics of Life Itself*. Princeton, NJ: Princeton University Press.

Royal Society. 2012. *Science As An Open Enterprise*. London: Royal Society.

Sell, S. 1999. Multinational Corporations as Agents of Change: The Globalization of Intellectual Property Rights, in Cutler, A., Haufler, V., and Porter, T., eds. *Private Authority and International Affairs*. Albany: State University of New York Press.

—. 2003. *Private Power, Public Law: The Globalization of Intellectual Property Rights*. Cambridge: Cambridge University Press.

Shapin, S. 2008. *The Scientific Life: A Moral History of a Late Modern Vocation*. Chicago, IL: University of Chicago Press.

Slaughter, S., and Rhoades, G. 2004. *Academic Capitalism and the New Economy*. Baltimore, MD, and London: Johns Hopkins University Press.

Smith, A., Voss, J.-P., and Grin, J. 2010. Innovation Studies and Sustainability Transitions: The Allure of the Multi-level Perspective and its Challenges. *Research Policy*, 39: 435–48.

Tyfield, D. 2008. Enabling TRIPs: The Pharma-biotech-university Patent Coalition. *Review of International Political Economy*, 15.4: 535–66.

—. 2012a. *The Economics of Science: A Critical Realist Overview – Volume 1: Illustrations and Philosophical Preliminaries*. London: Routledge.

—. 2012b. *The Economics of Science: A Critical Realist Overview – Volume 2: Towards a Synthesis of Political Economy and Science and Technology Studies*. London: Routledge.

—. 2013. Transition to Science 2.0: 'Remoralizing' the Economy of Science. *Spontaneous Generations: Special Issue on 'The Economics of Science'*, September.

—. 2014. Putting the Power in 'Socio-technical Regimes' – E-mobility Transition in China as Political Process. *Mobilities*, 9.4: 585–603.

Tyfield, D., Lave, R., Randalls, S., and Thorpe, C. eds. 2017. *The Routledge Handbook on the Political Economy of Science*. London: Routledge.

Unruh, G. 2000. Understanding Carbon Lock-in. *Energy Policy*, 28: 817–30.

Zeller, C. 2008. From the Gene to the Globe: Extracting Rents Based on Intellectual Property Monopolies. *Review of International Political Economy*, 15.1: 86–115.

30

PERFORMING NEOLIBERALISM

Practices, power and subject formation

Michael R. Glass

This chapter provides a critical perspective on neoliberalism rooted in theories of 'performativity' – a term in contemporary social theory that argues the use of language is a form of social action with material consequences (Loxley 2006; Glass and Rose-Redwood 2014; Butler 1993). Neoliberalism is considered a defining feature of late capitalist society, serving as a political-economic concept that interprets policies and practices on specific scales from the individual body to the supra-national. Performative discourse holds that, as with any concept, neoliberalism was not discovered as a fully formed subject for scholarly analysis, nor can it 'do' anything without actants – that is, those people, creatures, or objects that play active roles in a process or event. There are multiple actants at play here who produce and perform neoliberalism, including those who define and carry out the political and economic policies considered neoliberal, those recipients of policy who must determine how to respond, and those who assess the influences of neoliberalism and make claims about its value. These sets of actants are discussed with reference to three key issues used by scholars in research on neoliberalism: practices, power, and subject formation. Through this survey, I emphasize how the concept of neoliberalism is produced in scholarly and policy discourse and is transferred and resisted in specific contexts. I conclude by arguing this production can never be completed, creating the space for resistance.

Political performativity and neoliberalism

Neoliberalism is generally defined as a political-economic position maintaining that market-based solutions are the optimal arrangements for political and social life in modern economies. Neoliberal doctrine centres around two tenets: that capitalist markets are beneficial and beneficent, and that state control of economies (for instance, through regulations or direct ownership) must be minimized to enable the full effect of market economies. The entries in this volume make clear that neoliberalism has material consequences for societies across all geographic scales, and these consequences are not consistent – the impacts of neoliberalism are historically and spatially contingent because the ideology and practice of neoliberal doctrine metastasizes in different contexts. A nagging question therefore remains about this system of political and economic governance. If neoliberalism is a pervading and hegemonic discourse that shapes the economic, social, and political world, then how are we to understand its diffusion, metamorphosis and practice? Rossi and Vanolo (2012) point to three ways of understanding neoliberalism: ideologically, economically, and politically. The ideological approach to neoliberalism engages with its philosophical foundations, with research focusing on the presumption that reducing regulatory constraints leads to more efficient socio-political and economic relationships. The economic approach to neoliberalism considers the doctrine as a policy toolkit that promotes the spread of market-based solutions across the globe, and deepens their penetration through increasing commodification through the economy. The political approach to neoliberalism evaluates how political systems and coalitions are formulated around a collective rationality that presumes government regulation inhibits personal freedom and the common good. Inherent within all three of these approaches is a sense of *who* creates neoliberalism, and *how*.

The questions of who and how are important, because neoliberalism cannot do anything by itself. Without agents, neoliberalism couldn't develop into such a significant ideological feature on the landscape of late capitalism. Neoliberalism – whether perceived ideologically, economically, or politically – is the consequence of practices and actions conducted by specific individuals that support or contest its tenets. In other words, neoliberalism is produced by material and non-material actions that are repeated over time and across space by actors and organizations. It is this *iteration* and *reiteration* of neoliberal philosophy and practice that grants power to the discourse, and that reshapes the way neoliberalism manifests in different contexts. The mobility and mutability of neoliberalism is reflected in scholarship such as Aihwa Ong's analysis that uses an assemblage approach to consider the regional variations of neoliberal policy (Ong 2007), or Jamie Peck's state-centric assessment of policy transfer (Peck 2002). This scholarship points out the flaw in considering neoliberalism to be a totalizing or universal project, yet it does less to reveal how neoliberalism is made through discourse, signs and authority. For this, we can turn to performativity for analysis of the economy, and how markets are made.

Performativity describes a post-structural approach to knowledge focusing on how material and non-material practices can sustain or challenge aspects of the world around us. These approaches are related to the mid-twentieth century speech act theory commonly associated with J.L. Austin (1962). In the original form, speech act theory maintained that certain words have the power and opportunity to create new realities, as long as the speaker has the appropriate authority. Classic examples of this approach include the 'I dos' and 'I pronounce you married' statements in a Christian marriage ceremony, or the naming of a newly launched ship by an appropriate dignitary. Neither the marriage act nor the act of naming something would bring about a new reality without the appropriate parties being involved in the act. Rose-Redwood and Glass note that this theory is highly conservative, since the capacity for a speech act to succeed is constrained by the social role of the speaker – those without the sovereign authority lack the ability to influence the declarative utterances of those with power (Glass and Rose-Redwood 2014). While it is true that particular authority grants the ability to name or claim something, it is equally true that these claims may be subverted, or that the speaker's authority might be challenged over time – this is the basis for modern strands of performativity developed by two influential theorists: Judith Butler and Michel Callon.

For Butler, performativity involves examining the 'power of discourse to produce effects through reiteration' (1993: 20). This draws on Jacques Derrida's concept of citationality that states speech acts gain their performative force through repetition of prior speech acts – and that there is no guarantee that the repeated act will succeed (Derrida 1986). Butler developed her ideas about performativity and citationality by considering how normative gender roles are challenged by the embodied discursive practices of actors lacking sovereign authority. She claimed that, agency begins where sovereignty wanes. The one who acts (who is not the same as the sovereign subject) acts precisely to the extent that he or she is constituted as an actor and, hence, operating within a linguistic field of enabling constraints from the outset.

(Butler 1997: 16)

In essence, prevailing social relations and the agency of given actors interact to either reinforce or change the meaning of given concepts. This view of performative agency meant that, for Butler, concepts like gender cannot be understood as neutral or pre-given attributes, but instead are brought about through performative practices; what this means for understanding neoliberalism will be described in later paragraphs.

The economic sociologist Michel Callon developed a more directly economic strand of performativity during the late 1990s and early 2000s. Callon's work on economic performativity is based on the claim that 'economics, in the broad sense of the term, performs, shapes and formats the economy, rather than observing how it functions' (Callon 1998: 2). This framework implies that economic models and rhetoric do more than simply describe the world: they bring about material effects that change or sustain the world. This occurs through processes of framing and claiming aspects of the economic world that can be used critically to stabilize or destabilize the established economic order (Gibson-Graham 2008; Berndt and Boeckler 2009). For instance, describing a market as 'bullish' or 'bearish' is a discursive act that will subsequently affect that market. It remakes the world as a consequence of the performative practices of those associated with the market – such as economic reporters, individual investors, economists, and the programmers who set the parameters for electronic market transactions. Economic sociologists interested in economic performativity consider the extent to which these effects can be observed to have either benign or substantive effects (Mackenzie et al. 2007).

While there are differences between Butler and Callon's approaches to performativity that are based in their respective emphasis on theoretical or empirical content, there are similarities in their use of performativity. Each eschews the notion of essentialism in the observable world; whether discussing gender or the economy, both versions of performativity described above allow for the possibility of effects in the world reflecting discourse (Du Gay 2010). These two approaches have led to a burgeoning interest in performativity across several academic disciplines. Scholars are attracted by the notion that hegemonic or normative categories are not immutable, and that discourse and material practices provide a pathway to challenging social, economic and political structures.

For neoliberalism, in particular, the consequences of performative discourse are profound. First, performativity holds that there is no pre-existing or stable category known as neoliberalism, and that it is instead created and recreated as the consequence of active and embodied practices. Second, given the citational practice of repeatedly bringing about that (neoliberal) subject through practices operating in its name, there is a very slight chance that neoliberalism is transferred across geographic contexts and over time in an unchanged manner – the real potential for conceptual redefinition occurs and means that neoliberalism cannot be considered as a monolithic subject, despite claims to its hegemonic global status. Third, performative effects are only possible through their continual reassertion. As Butler states, '[t]here is no power that acts, but only a reiterated acting that is power in its persistence and instability' (1993: 9). This suggests that neoliberalism, as with any subject, risks subversion by alternate projects or definitions.

The discursive instability of neoliberalism means that proponents and opponents of the ideology must continuously engage in embodied practices that either support or subvert the concept. For proponents of neoliberalism, this means assembling and using policies and practices that can convince stakeholders of the merits of free market capitalism and limited government regulation. The next section uses a performative lens to examine some of these practices, including the rhetoric of neoliberalism disseminated by scholars, consultants and managers, and the spatial reproduction of neoliberal discourse that occurs through the media, legislation, and consumers. Performing neoliberalism also means struggles over power: whether it is the proponents of neoliberalism who claim the merit of the enterprise, or opponents who use the negative consequences of neoliberal policies to highlight its flaws. Neoliberalism also requires the formation of new subjects, through the repetition of neoliberal discourse over time and across space. This is countered by protest actions that continually seek to undermine the apparent stability and hegemony of neoliberal doctrine. In short, performativity can help to reveal those pathways wherein neoliberalism is reproduced, and alternate pathways that might lead to its disruption.

Practices

Neoliberalism cannot do anything by itself, and instead requires an assemblage of actors willing and capable of promoting the discourse through embodied practices. In recent years, research on the agents of neoliberalism has focused on how experts, consultants and managers reinforce the tenets of neoliberal theory through their actions. Weber and O'Neill-Kohl (2013) point out the necessity of focusing on human agency, arguing that aside from some attention paid to the marquee names of mayors and developers, critical political economy accounts of urban policy tended to obscure the role of individual actors behind the veil of highly scripted structuralism. In contrast, their account focuses closely on the experience of real estate consultants in Illinois who advocated for public subsidization of real estate development. The paper focuses on tax increment financing (TIF) – a form of neoliberal 'do-it-yourself' urban policy whereby the financing for local developments is raised by assessments on the affected geographic area, and not by the city at large (Squires and Lord 2012). Weber and O'Neill-Kohl found that the consultants were not passively receiving policies from elected officials, but instead shaped those policies through social and professional interactions, and consequently added to their own power, noting how 'their professional practices provide the mortar that holds together the complex networks governing contemporary urban development' (Weber and O'Neill-Kohl 2013: 198).

Lee provides a finer-scale analysis of consultants by examining the performative practices used by consultants when facilitating public engagements (Lee 2014). She found that different embodied practices were used by consultants to reinforce the validity of their arguments to the audience. Glass also notes the use of embodied practices by planners engaged in a consultative process to garner support for a new form of regional governance in the Midwestern USA (Glass 2014). He traced a series of performative acts that were used to ostensibly create a platform for consultative dialogue between citizens and planners, although they eventually became coopted by the regional narrative promoted by the initiative's leaders. These leaders were associated with the traditional wielders of political power in the region, and so the consultative process was less transformative than it originally appeared. Lansing's research into global commodity logics and practices draws upon Callon's approach to performativity and looks at how international experts verify the presence of carbon offsets in rural Costa Rica (Lansing 2012). Through close analysis of interactions between local and foreign actors, Lansing indicates the instability of what might appear from afar to be fixed or neutral commodities. What links this research is a sense that engaging with the interpersonal practices of actors can provide a sense of how neoliberalism's structures are created or sustained.

Agents are also required to reproduce neoliberal policies and processes – both across space and over time. Some of the key research using performativity examines the reproduction of neoliberal processes from housing policy. For instance, both Smith *et al.* (2006) and Wallace (2008) draw on Callon's theory of the development of markets to discuss how housing markets are understood and enacted by their participants. Smith *et al.* researched the role of actors in the housing market who function as intermediaries, making and remaking housing markets over time (2006). They find that housing professionals embodied the language of economic rationality in their decision-making, yet also engaged in place-specific practices that created and sustained different types of market. Wallace argued that business decisions were based on information accruing from an actors' interpersonal networks, and that these decisions were frequently invested with emotional or psychological components, rather than simply being the consequence of rational economic behaviour. She found through field interviews that:

> '[t]he Market' was always seen as outside the actions of individuals, certainly beyond their control, and more often than not beyond their influence. However, in these examples the market can be seen as a product of multiple actions, market demand and the emergent properties of complementary or undermining behavior of the people managing or operating it.
>
> *(Wallace 2008: 266)*

Wallace notes that study participants felt it necessary to adhere to market models of housing behaviour, even in circumstances where it was unwarranted because of city's economic circumstances. Farías also researches the behaviour of market agents, claiming that they can engage in *economic improvisation* in cases where economic policies require adjustment and no guidelines exist for how to proceed (2014). Testing this concept in the Chilean context, Farías finds that local actors reacted to two moments of great economic uncertainty by improvising courses of action to stabilize the economy. He considers this process of improvisation to be distinct from Callon's performativity because it did not represent the performance of existing economic models, but instead urgent interventions that were subsequently evaluated against prevailing economic knowledge.

Neoliberalism also travels from context to context (McCann and Ward 2011; Peck and Theodore 2010), facilitated by actors that promote and legitimize free market policies across space. One leading mechanism for this transfer are non-governmental organizations such as the World Bank; Henriksen (2013) researches the role performed by the World Bank in developing a new market for microfinance. He does so by drawing on Callon's approach to performativity, arguing that it is 'important in drawing attention to the specific framing of information in a manner which promotes the widespread acceptance and standardization of specific modes of reporting, comparison, and calculation' (ibid.: 407). The value of this analysis is in understanding how market actions are defined and enacted at a 'capillary level', rather than via the exaggerated abstraction of structural accounts. This fine-grain account of networks of practice and rhetoric shows the ecology of practice that leads to the spread of neoliberal policies, and hints at the capacity for new networks that could destabilize this dominant narrative. Lee *et al.* also look at the spread of neoliberal discourse in their research on the deliberation industry (2013). They engage with this industry to look at how consultants employed to offer public forums for deliberation in different communities are selling the notion that deliberation will lead a community to forms of civic engagement that carry inherently neoliberal values (a 'moralized market'). Lee *et al.* conclude that:

> [w]hen communities accept such framings, political empowerment is effectively divorced from organized challenges to structural inequalities. In this sense, deliberation

may be engaging more citizens in more discussion than ever before, but the results of that engagement may be discursively limited and unlikely to produce collective action beyond behavioral accommodations to the harsh realities of retrenchment.

(Ibid.: 101)

thereby effectively contributing to the diffusion of neoliberal policy across contexts.

Power

As a post-structural theory, performativity follows the position that power is not a commodity or a thing that can be possessed, but is rather the active consequence of relations between networked subjects. These subjects constitute the terms of power relations by the discursive force of specific claims they make to authority (Sarup 1993). This position is closely associated with Michel Foucault's work (Foucault 1980), and can be contrasted to structuralist positions in which power is considered the attribute of a hegemonic class that imposes it wherever and whenever possible. Indeed, Barnett makes the strong claim that Marxist and Foucauldian perspectives on neoliberalism should remain distinct, given the different ontological positions of these approaches (Barnett 2005). For instance, rather than focusing on top-down hegemony, performative analysis of power instead attends to the practices and routines that enact or subvert power.

This attention to practices can lead to research on neoliberalism and economies that occurs at a very intimate scale, such as Garmany's ethnographic depiction of the economic lives of residents in a Brazilian favela. Describing the self-reported activities of these residents, Garmany argues that the language and practices of these residents show that the prevailing economic relations is not so much the consequence of repressive state apparatuses, but is instead 'maintained by self-disciplining individuals who enact the state in their daily routines and discourses, producing it through practice as a constituted, socially constructed reality' (Garmany 2009: 729). In other words, rather than the situation of favela residents being the simply consequence of external forces, the residents also shape the conditions they experience.

Similarly, Waquar Ahmed's research on the role of Enron in India emphasizes the discursive production of power through an assemblage of practices since 1991 (Ahmed 2010). He argues that India's 'neoliberal transformation' was the consequence of power exercised by actors including the World Bank, the International Monetary Fund, and the USA. In this context, neoliberal rhetoric valorizing inward foreign direct investment (FDI) led to the local political environment being shaped to favour foreign corporations. Enron exerted influence through direct lobbying and market manipulation in order to shift the Indian energy market in directions favourable to the company, and the co-dependence between Enron and other corporations along with political elites within India led to further entrenchment of neoliberal policies. Rather than claiming a solely structural explanation for this situation, Ahmed concludes that:

[T]he power of economic and policy transformation unleashed by neoliberalism found willing subjects in India because it preserved and protected the subjects' own precarious positions. The willing subjects were able to 'sell' neoliberalism as a policy that would eventually benefit all, in the face of the balance of payments crisis that India had just undergone.

(Ibid.: 635)

The practices of power are also at the forefront of research by Brett Christophers that evaluates how economic models are performative. Christophers' main argument is that models have the power to enact significant political-economic transformation, although the results of these models remain highly contingent. For example, he explains that broader processes of capitalist market relations under neoliberalism influenced the uptake of housing viability models in the UK: '[p]ower flows through these models (some get selected, others do not), structuring their use and allowing them to perform' (Christophers 2014b: 81). In related research, Christophers examined the prevalence of tiered pricing models in the pharmaceutical industry, whereby different market segments are charged separate prices for the same good. Whereas this model did not appear to have economic benefits, he concluded that it remains useful to the industry for its political effects: it is a practice that suggests the pharmaceutical industry has ethical standards and a commitment to balancing profits with human rights to health. Therefore, it is one of many practices that help to protect the power of large pharmaceutical companies against potential criticism (Christophers 2014a).

What links these examples of performative research on the power of neoliberal policies is a focus on the social and technical pathways that make neoliberalism breathe. These researchers do not consider neoliberalism to be a thing that is external from the social context that it is affecting; instead, it is a consequence of agents who adhere to the central philosophical tenets of neoliberalism, yet implement it based on the networks, knowledge and contingencies that exist in specific places. Lasse Henriksen is clear about this focus when he examines the role performed by international organizations like the World Bank that promote policies associated with neoliberal goals. He looks at the agency of this organization, arguing that the power of the World Bank to shape microfinance policy was helped by establishing local offices that could disseminate policy while accumulating information. He argues that performativity is a key framework for understanding this process, as it draws attention to how information is developed, shared, and promoted by particular economic agents, enabling the spreading of 'socio-technical networks of governance' (Henriksen 2013: 407).

Subject formation

A final question that performativity can address about neoliberalism is: where do neoliberal subjects come from? Do the actors that promote neoliberal policies and benefit from them spring forth from the earth or from putative social classes, and do the actors affected negatively by neoliberalism lack any agency to resist or otherwise affect their situation under neoliberalism? Research on subjectivity and subject formation ignores or diminishes such structural presumptions about the composition of society, and accepts the possibility that incremental or radical change through performative acts can challenge normative conditions like neoliberalism. Rejecting notions of stable and pre-discursive sovereign subjects (i.e. autonomous actors with the authority and recognition to act), scholars including Judith Butler and Merje Kuus argue that subjects do not arrive as fully formed actors, and are instead the consequence of past and present mediations of power structures and context (Butler 1993; Kuus 2007). As with other post-structuralist perspectives, performative discourse argues that there is no such thing as a stable, pre-discursive subject: there is only the repeated performance of subjects-in-formation that continually reiterate their agency and identities through rhetoric, policy, and everyday practices (Jackson 2004). This raises the prospect that most people are intentionally or unintentionally responsible for the replication of neoliberalism – not necessarily because of their social class, but rather because of the practices we perform every day. Without this reiteration, subjects could replace society with an alternative vision. This also means that, regardless of how dominant a position like neoliberalism might appear to be, the space for resistance can always occur.

In her more recent work, Judith Butler recognizes the potential counter-performances that challenge hegemonic discourse regarding citizenship. For instance, in *Who Sings the Nation-State?* (Butler and Spivak 2007), Butler evaluates the 2006 demonstrations by illegal immigrants in Los Angeles. At different protest locations the demonstrators sang the US national anthem in Spanish, marking an attempt to redefine what is seen as normative about citizenship by repeatedly making an alternative statement. The demands for freedom made by a subaltern group in the city is picked up by Amin and Thrift, when they suggest the significance of urban citizenship for the enactment of democracy:

> [The city] offers a practical and material means of meeting social needs ('use value'). And more. It is a place of becoming, and the fulfillment of social potential, of democratic experimentation through the efforts of citizens themselves, as free and socialized agents… [t]his is the sense of urban citizenship we wish to develop: the idea of democracy as access, mutuality, fulfillment of potential. We see the city, more specifically its institutions, providing the opportunity for citizens to become something else and for mutuality to be strengthened.
>
> *(Amin and Thrift 2002: 143)*

For Amin and Thrift, fulfilling social potential arises through confident citizens using urban areas as sites for practising a more participatory, rights-based, and experimental democracy. This type of participation is exemplified in a different context by Carolin Schurr's research on political emancipation in Ecuador. Schurr (2014) examines a situation where speakers of the native *kichwa* language use it for what she terms performative practices that create the space for a new politics. This activism de-naturalizes hegemonic conditions standing in the way of more participatory political geographies, hence opening up a space for change. Whereas it is unclear whether this discursive resistance will have lasting consequences for the material condition of this community, Schurr sees value in performative acts that can articulate new collective demands and bring about alternative imaginaries to existing power structures.

One of the clearest expressions of how performative practices might enable resistance to neoliberal economic principles is given by J.K. Gibson-Graham's influential paper on 'performative practices for other worlds'. In this paper, the author describes a personal transition from a structuralist prescription of 'understanding the world in order to change it' towards a post-structuralist perspective that theorized 'the contingency of social outcomes rather than the unfolding of structural logics' (Gibson-Graham 2008: 615). It considered the work of Callon, Butler, and others to be effective means for reconsidering the seemingly intractable logics of neoliberalism, and reframed their questions to challenge those aspects of society that were considered unjust or unsustainable. The research indicated three dimensions (transactions, labour, and enterprise) along which alternative market and non-market transactions were challenging neoliberal capitalism; for instance, through barter transactions, reciprocal labour arrangements, or communal forms of enterprise. Through a global scan of practices, Gibson-Graham indicated the possibilities for resistance, regardless of whether the agents saw their roles as such:

> We would imagine that not all of these people see themselves engaged in a performative ontological politics – such a politics is a potentiality we are attempting to call into being. But all are contributing in some way to making economic diversity more credible. They are resisting the discursive erasure threatened by neoliberal theory, drawing

attention to and thereby strengthening a range of economic practices that exist outside the purview of this paper.

(Ibid.: 620)

These practices are expanded upon in *A Postcapitalist Politics*, where Gibson-Graham consider challenging neoliberal hegemony through creating a new 'language of economic diversity' seen as a 'crucial prerequisite to the project of cultivating different subjects of economy' (Gibson-Graham 2006: 56). This research approach has generated considerable attention, including work on how scholar-activism can function (Taylor 2014; Delaney 2014) as well as case studies on alternative systems of economics and governance (Wright 2014; Brownlow 2011).

Conclusion: perpetually incomplete neoliberalism

This chapter has presented performativity as a theory that has a lot to say about the production, reproduction, and subversion of neoliberalism. Performative approaches based upon a classic poststructuralist stance (such as Judith Butler) or from science and technology studies (such as Michel Callon) each speak to the power of discourse to bring about material effects that are necessarily incomplete and always being brought into being. Neoliberalism would not exist as a hegemonic structure in the contemporary world without agents considered to have the requisite authority to act, and who are capable of declaring a particular rationality and performing it through words and deeds. Similarly, the performative declaration of neoliberal proponents must be performed by other agents willing to engage in the ensuing power relationships constructed by neoliberal practice.

Performative approaches to knowledge stress that a single utterance is not sufficient to bring about a new social reality. Instead, such a reality is only possible so long as repeated performances reiterate the nature of that reality. In theoretical terms, Derrida and others define this as citationality: without the repeated reinforcement of particular claims, any structure (regardless of its apparent solidity or permanence) runs the risk of falling prey to counter-narratives and alternatives that may supplant it. This circumstance can explain the historical ebb and flow of philosophical positions including classic liberalism, Keynesianism, and neoliberalism, and it also predicts that neoliberalism does not reflect the end of history. Without the potential for discursive closure, the door is always open for alternative visions for society to arise.

References

Ahmed, W. 2010. Neoliberalism, Corporations, and Power: Enron in India. *Annals of the Association of American Geographers*, 100.3: 621–39.

Amin, A., and Thrift, N. 2002. *Cities: Reimagining the Urban*. Cambridge: Polity Press.

Austin, J.L. 1962. *How to Do Things with Words*. Cambridge, MA: Harvard University Press.

Barnett, C. 2005. The Consolations of 'Neoliberalism'. *Geoforum*, 36.1: 7–12.

Berndt, C., and Boeckler, M. 2009. Geographies of Circulation and Exchange: Constructions of Markets. *Progress in Human Geography*, 33.4: 535–51.

Brownlow, A. 2011. Between Rights and Responsibilities: Insurgent Performance in an Invisible Landscape. *Environment and Planning A*, 43.6: 1268–86.

Butler, J. 1993. *Bodies That Matter*. New York: Routledge.

—. 1997. *Excitable Speech: A Politics of the Performative*. New York: Routledge.

Butler, J., and Spivak, G. 2007. *Who Sings the Nation-State?* London: Seagull.

Callon, M. 1998. *The Laws of the Markets*. Oxford: Blackwell.

Christophers, B. 2014a. On the Performativity of Pill Pricing: Theory and Reality in the Economics of Global Pharmaceuticalization. *Antipode*, 46.4: 1054–71.

—. 2014b. Wild Dragons in the City: Urban Political Economy, Affordable Housing Development and the Performative World-Making of Economic Models. *International Journal of Urban and Regional Research*, 38.1: 79–97.

Delaney, J. 2014. Reassembling Policy Through Research: Reflections on Situating Policy Advocacy Through Research and Practice. *Professional Geographer*, 66.1: 18–24.

Derrida, J. 1986. Declarations of Independence. *New Political Science*, 7.1: 7–15.

Du Gay, P. 2010. Performativities: Butler, Callon and the Moment of Theory. *Journal of Cultural Economy*, 3.2: 171–9.

Farías, I. 2014. Improvising a Market, Making a Model: Social Policy in Chile. *Economy and Society*, 43.3: 346–69.

Foucault, M. 1980. *Power/Knowledge*. Gordon, C., trans. New York: Pantheon.

Garmany, J. 2009. The Embodied State: Governmentality in a Brazilian Favela. *Social & Cultural Geography*, 10.7: 721–39.

Gibson-Graham, J.-K. 2006. *A Postcapitalist Politics*. Minneapolis: University of Minnesota Press.

—. 2008. Diverse Economies: Performative Practices for 'Other Worlds'. *Progress in Human Geography*, 32.5: 613–32.

Glass, M.R. 2014. 'Becoming a Thriving Region': Performative Visions, Imaginative Geographies, and the Power of 32, in Glass, M.R., and Rose-Redwood, R., eds. *Performativity, Politics, and the Production of Social Space*. New York: Routledge: 202–25.

Glass, M.R., and Rose-Redwood, R. 2014. *Performativity, Politics, and the Production of Social Space*. New York: Routledge.

Henriksen, L.F. 2013. Performativity and the Politics of Equipping for Calculation: Constructing a Global Market for Microfinance. *International Political Sociology*, 7.4: 406–25.

Jackson, A.Y. 2004. Performativity Identified. *Qualitative Inquiry*, 10.5: 673–90.

Kuus, M. 2007. *Geopolitics Reframed*. New York: Palgrave Macmillan.

Lansing, D.M. 2012. Performing Carbon's Materiality: The Production of Carbon Offsets and the Framing of Exchange. *Environment and Planning A*, 44.1: 204–20.

Lee, C. 2014. Walking the Talk: The Performance of Authenticity in Public Engagement Work. *The Sociological Quarterly*, 55: 493–513.

Lee, C.W., McNulty, K., and Shaffer, S. 2013. 'Hard Times, Hard Choices': Marketing Retrenchment as Civic Empowerment in an Era of Neoliberal Crisis. *Socio-Economic Review*, 11.1: 81–106.

Loxley, J. 2006. *Performativity (The New Critical Idiom)*. New York: Routledge.

Mackenzie, D., Muniesa, F., and Siu, L. 2007. *Do Economists Make Markets? On the Performativity of Economics*. Princeton, NJ: Princeton University Press.

McCann, E., and Ward, K. 2011. *Mobile Urbanism: Cities and Policymaking in the Global Age*. Minneapolis: University of Minnesota Press.

Ong, A. 2007. Neoliberalism as a Mobile Technology. *Transactions of the Institute of British Geographers*, 32: 3–8.

Peck, J. 2002. Political Economies of Scale: Fast Policy, Interscalar Relations and Neoliberal Workfare. *Economic Geography*, 78.3: 331–60.

Peck, J., and Theodore, N. 2010. Recombinant Workfare, Across the Americas: Transnationalizing 'Fast' Social Policy. *Geoforum*, 41.2: 195–208.

Rossi, U., and Vanolo, A. 2012. *Urban Political Geographies*. Thousand Oaks, CA: Sage.

Sarup, M. 1993. *Post-Structuralism and Postmodernism*. Athens: University of Georgia Press.

Schurr, C. 2014. Performativity and Antagonism as Keystones for a Political Geography of Change, in Glass, M.R., and Rose-Redwood, R., eds. *Performativity, Politics, and the Production of Social Space*. New York: Routledge: 95–120.

Smith, S.J., Munro, M., and Christie, H. 2006. Performing (Housing) Markets. *Urban Studies*, 43.1: 81–98.

Squires, G., and Lord, A.D. 2012. The Transfer of Tax Increment Financing (TIF) as an Urban Policy for Spatially Targeted Economic Development. *Land Use Policy*, 29.4: 817–26.

Taylor, M. 2014. 'Being Useful' After the Ivory Tower: Combining Research and Activism with the Brixton Pound. *Area*, 46.3: 305–12.

Wallace, A. 2008. Knowing the Market? Understanding and Performing York's Housing. *Housing Studies*, 23.2: 253–70.

Weber, R., and O'Neill-Kohl, S. 2013. The Historical Roots of Tax Increment Financing, or How Real Estate Consultants Kept Urban Renewal Alive. *Economic Development Quarterly*, 27.3: 193–207.

Wright, S. 2014. Quantitative Research Performing Other Worlds: Lessons from Sustainable Agriculture in the Phillipines. *Australian Geographer*, 45.1: 1–18.

31

NEOLIBERALISM *AS* AUSTERITY

The theory, practice, and purpose of fiscal restraint since the 1970s

Heather Whiteside

Austerity through fiscal restraint – government debt reduction and deficit elimination – is *en vogue* once again. As of 2012, all but four members of the G-20 have declared this to be a leading policy priority and one which is scheduled to take precedence well into the current decade (see G-20 2012). At the extreme, dealing with an acute sovereign debt crisis in Greece has meant the application of seven austerity packages between 2010 and 2013 alone, each one employing some combination of public sector freezes and cuts applied to budgets, services, programmes, and employment. Worldwide, social reaction to austerity runs the gamut, from marches, demonstrations and protest to general strikes and political party organizing around anti-austerity platforms. Though its promoters tout austerity's tools as technocratic imperatives for resolving debt and budgetary disequilibrium, accompanying structural reform of the public sector, affecting both employees' livelihoods and the welfare of society in general, suggests there is clearly much more at stake than a narrow interpretation of austerity will allow. The politics of austerity are entrenching and (re)asserting processes of neoliberalization at global, national, and urban scales, much as they did during earlier iterations of fiscal restraint beginning in the 1970s. In this sense, the history and hegemony of neoliberalism is intrinsically intertwined with that of austerity, and the recent return of fiscal consolidation is both unique to its context and part of a longer historical trend. Austerity is a signature of the neoliberal era much as neoliberalism can be understood *as* austerity.

This chapter examines the decades-long connection between neoliberalism and austerity, with a particular emphasis on its recent return to prominence. Attention is paid to temporal dynamics (the appeal of and to austerity over time), spatial effects (the scalar impact of austerity, particularly downloading onto municipal or local authorities), and socio-institutional reforms (policies and programmes). Neoliberal-era fiscal restraint works in league with other key attributes of its political economy such as financialization and privatization; however, as an overview of the relevant discursive, institutional, and material attributes of austerity, this chapter is able only to briefly discuss this complexity. Given the interconnection between austerity and neoliberalism more broadly, themes raised in other chapters of this book are germane here as well, including Plehwe on hegemony, Craig on development, Springer on violence, and MacLeavy on welfare reforms. This chapter proceeds in two parts, divided, with obvious overlap and interrelation, between the economics and politics of austerity over the neoliberal period.

Austerity economics

Austerity budgets are those which reduce the cyclically adjusted fiscal deficit, achieved by raising revenue (through taxation and growth) and/or cutting government spending. The resurgence of austerity today is unique to its context – the 2008 global financial crisis and its aftermath – but is equally part of a longer historical trend. Mark Blyth (2013a) traces austerity's classical origins in the liberal political and economic tradition from John Locke to Adam Smith and beyond. Blyth sums up the Lockean liberal dilemma as being that while the public good necessities private activities be free from government intrusion – including private property being safe from expropriation via taxation – such safety comes at the cost of sufficiently funding the state so it is capable of protecting freedom and private property (ibid.: 106). The inherent tension and liberal distaste for the accumulation of public debt leads Adam Smith to advocate for 'parsimony over prodigality', claiming that parsimony is both an engine of growth in capitalism and a way for government to avoid inflation, excessive taxation, and debt default (ibid.: 110–13).

More directly, austerity policies today repackage and re-employ pre-existing (pre-2008 crisis) neoclassical strategies initially aimed at resolving stagflation in the 1970s; fiscal austerity as of late is but the most recent episode of public sector belt tightening over the neoliberal period. During the post-war Keynesian era, countercyclical government spending was held as an important tool of aggregate demand stimulation during economic downturns. These ideas were replaced in the neoliberal era with the notion that fiscal restraint can be a driver of economic growth and prosperity. Austerity gained prominence in the late 1970s/early 1980s as a solution to the problem of 'stagflation' which vexed the established Philips curve-derived policy orthodoxy at the time[1] by providing a simple explanation: government spending on the welfare state in the global North was hurting growth by 'crowding out' private spending and creating inflation through excess government borrowing in order to finance budget deficits.

In the 1990s the neoclassical rationale was further refined by orthodox economists. Under the 'expansionary fiscal consolidation thesis' (associated with the Bocconi School) it was argued that austerity was not only a solution to macroeconomic problems, but also had a positive impact on expectations which generated its own virtuous cycle. The elimination of public sector deficits, though potentially painful in the short run, would boost investor confidence, reduce borrowing costs, stimulate private sector growth and lead to lower unemployment (e.g. Alesina and Perotti 1995; Alesina et al. 1998; Alesina and Ardagana 1998; Giavazzi and Pagano 1990). This hypothesis has also been referred to as 'expansionary austerity' (Guajardo et al. 2011). Whereas Keynesian theory dealt a critical blow to Say's Law (that notion that supply produces its own demand) and supported several decades of demand-driven growth policy formulation, fiscal consolidation supplies an argument in favour of austerity: supply creates demand and investor confidence is what drives growth. Controlling and reducing government spending, austerians argue, will tame inflation and improve investor confidence.

It is within the context of this received wisdom that a 2010 study by Harvard economists Carmen Reinhart and Kenneth Rogoff was marshalled as a 'common sense' rationale for terminating a widespread but short-lived experiment with quasi-Keynesian stimulus spending following the global financial crisis of 2008. Using a 40-country 200-year dataset, Reinhart and Rogoff (2010) found that where government debt exceeds 90 per cent of GDP, the average rate of economic growth is adversely affected.

The ideas being circulated by elite economists were seized upon in 2010. Blyth (2013a) describes this as originating with German authorities and within the European Central Bank in the lead-up to the June 2010 G-20 meeting. Irwin (2013) locates its return slightly earlier at the

G-7 finance ministers' meeting in February 2010. The end of stimulus and return to austerity was equally foreshadowed by comments such as those by Canada's Finance Minister Jim Flaherty:

> We'll continue to stimulate the economy this year but what is the plan and the Canadian situation to get back to balanced budgets. We're working on that. I know that… thought is shared by other members of the G7, including the United Kingdom and the United States.
>
> *(Curry and Carmichael 2010: n.p.)*

With the idea that austerity is necessary and beneficial (re-)launched in 2010, it was soon applied to varying degrees and in unique ways within national contexts. Austerity measures in the UK, for example, are comparatively severe, with the British government being described as '[leading] the way in voluntary deficit reduction' (Giles and Bounds 2012: n.p.), with all but a few departmental budgets cut by 25 per cent. In Canada, by contrast, the politics of austerity are not strictly fiscal in nature, given that the federal government aims to balance the budget 'without raising taxes, cutting transfers to persons, including those for seniors, children and the unemployed, or cutting transfers to other levels of government that support health care and social services' (Government of Canada 2011: n.p.) and, indeed, overall (nominal) government spending had increased by 2013. Instead, a climate of austerity is being used to justify privatization and structural reform to public sector programmes, pensions, benefits, and civil service employment. Within the USA we see stark examples of the impact of scalar downloading where 'austerity urbanism' involves foisting the costs of a global banking and financial crisis and national deregulation onto municipalities and local authorities who are in no position to shoulder these burdens and costs (Peck 2012). Municipal bankruptcies, the theft of workers' savings (pensions), and the erosion of social programmes compound all manner of pre-existing social disparities (see Beatty and Fothergill 2014; Davidson and Ward 2014; Peck 2014).

Austerity's return has thus been cast as a response to the 2008 financial crisis, the 2009 temporary experimentation with Keynesian stimulus, and 2010 eurozone debt crisis.[2] Longevity thus far has meant dodging or denying evidence that fiscal consolidation is at least partially responsible for poor growth/recession and social malaise since 2010 (Wolf 2013). Whether imposed (e.g. Greece) or voluntary (e.g. Canada), the implementation of the austerity agenda witnessed across the OECD as of 2010 is leading to dramatic restructuring in the form of more miserly social programmes, cuts to public sector employment, and an expansion of privatization – in other words, enhanced neoliberalization (more on this connection to follow).

As an ahistorical retrospective, within economics circles it is common to now see examples of austerity 'success-stories' from the 1980s and 1990s being used to justify fiscal restraint today. For its reduction of government debt from a peak of 117 per cent of GDP in 1986 to 25 per cent of GDP by 2007, Ireland is frequently turned to as an example of how expansionary austerity can lead to robust growth. Yet Kinsella (2011: 16–18) shows Celtic tiger growth and debt reduction to be due not to austerity exclusively or even primarily, but instead to a host of other historically contingent factors. This includes: growth in the international economy, fiscal transfers from the EU, the opening up of a single market, a 14 per cent increase in the average industrial wage between 1986 and 1989 and similar public sector wage increases, an income tax amnesty in 1988, and a well-timed currency devaluation in August 1986. In a similar vein, Dellepiane and Hardiman (2012: 13) argue that Ireland's 'success' with austerity was not the result of greater investor confidence, as the expansionary fiscal consolidation literature suggests, but due to currency devaluation (which is now impossible with the euro) and growth in the global economy which produced demand for Irish exports (which is now absent given virtual economic stagnation since the 2009 great recession).

Dellepiane and Hardiman (ibid.) raise an additional and related concern with the economics of austerity: the need to consider 'politics in time' when analysing the results of fiscal consolidation. As they describe, the treatment of austerity through formal mathematical modelling breaks down country experiences into multiple discrete episodes so that changes in a state's fiscal condition may be examined from one period to the next. This is problematic given that it ignores the highly varied ways in which countries went from large deficits in the 1980s to balanced budgets by the early 2000s. There are, in fact, a range of possible reasons for balanced budgets such as economic growth, increased demand (domestic and international), tax increases, and fiscal restraint. In Canada, austerity in the 1990s was disproportionately angled in favour of cuts to public spending rather than raising revenue through higher taxes. Posner and Sommerfeld (2013: 152) calculate the composition of austerity measures to be 87 per cent spending cuts, 13 per cent revenue increases. In Britain, fiscal consolidation under the Conservatives (1980s–97) occurred mainly through revenue measures (taxation), not restraint (spending cuts); under Labour, austerity took the form of spending and cost control (Dellepiane and Hardiman 2012: 13). In Australia we see the Labor Party initiating the 1990s era of austerity in 1994 through revenue-based measures, but when the Liberal Party took over in 1996 this switched to expenditure cuts, namely health and social security (Posner and Sommerfeld 2013: 151).

However tenuous these 'success' stories may be, they do not render austerity economics a 'failure'. A clear connection between fiscal restraint, economic growth and widespread prosperity remains elusive but the restructuring of state and society through austerity has been highly successful and is, indeed, its long-lasting outcome, perhaps even its intent. In the face of unique crises and contexts, the target of austerity today remains the same: the size of the public sector (as employer and economic actor) and generosity of social programmes. Further, when compared with earlier periods, there is remarkable consistency across time: the notion that austerity solves economic problems, that government excess is somehow at fault or to blame for capitalist crises, that government spending is unsustainable; the solution being more marketization not less. Taming government growth and trimming back the public sector is now, as it was in the past, the aim and implication of fiscal consolidation. The profligacy of government was seldom the underlying cause of public sector deficits and debt accumulated since 2008 – these were, instead, the by-products of the global financial crisis, and subsequent bailouts (auto and finance sectors), stimulus spending, and a period of protracted low growth/recession. Those actors and institutions most responsible for public sector budgetary crises are least burdened with its remedy. This mirrors the situation in the eurozone: a crisis of the euro and of pre-existing EU integration strategies is shifted from bond markets into sovereign debt through taxpayer funded bailouts, and shifted from surplus trading partners (like Germany) to debtors (like Greece).

Ultimately, austerity has less to do with achieving economic growth (on which its track record is abysmal) than it does with shifting blame for economic conditions from market actors to government departments and displacing the burden of adjustment downward within the state, from capital to labour, and from the wealthy to the already-precarious. The economics of austerity thus extend far beyond mere budget balancing. Under the guise of fiscal restraint, austerity effectively redistributes the 'costs, risks, and burdens of economic failure onto subordinate classes, social groups, and branches of government' (Peck 2014: 4). Austerity, over the neoliberal period, has been less a reaction to crises or deficits than it has been a governance strategy spatially displacing risk and reward, costs and benefits.

Austerity's displacement activities also involve shifting the responsibility for financing a capitalist crisis onto labour and taxpayers (within regressive taxation systems) almost exclusively.

In this vein, critical accounts of fiscal austerity often focus on how it is used to punish labour and/or public service recipients for the follies of capital (e.g. Callinicos 2012). Budget cuts and privatization are thus a tool for controlling labour or, as Sam Gindin (2013) writes, for creating a state more autonomous from popular pressure, and the costs associated with the recent capitalist crisis are being socialized in the process. Intrinsically political, the economics of austerity find their counterpart in the politics of neoliberalism – now and over the past four decades.

Austerity politics

Clarke and Newman (2012) describe the significance of contemporary austerity as being its enabling of greater market-oriented restructuring of the welfare state. This observation holds over time as well. Consider the following quotes:

- 'The Government will exercise restraint in its own expenditures with particular emphasis on improving effectiveness and efficiency in its existing operations while controlling expansion of new activities…'
- 'To create the climate necessary for [recovery] the Government will continue to practice fiscal restraint… the Government remains committed to a reduction in the growth of the public sector… All federal programmes will be reviewed to identify those government activities which could be transferred to the private sector.'
- 'The objectives of imposing more severe restraint on government spending are… to encourage a more vigorous expansion of the private sector by reducing government's share of the nation's wealth… to create a leaner and more efficient government… The government is committed to reducing the size of the federal public service… (and) to continued wage restraint in the public sector.'

It would be easily assumed that these are declarations made since 2010. Instead, they were taken from Canadian federal government budget speeches (also known as Speeches from the Throne) dated, respectively, 30 September 1974, 12 October 1976, and 11 October 1978 (taken from Table 4.5 in McBride 1992: 87). Far from a Canadian phenomenon, this moment signalled the start of a concerted and widespread effort to overturn Keynesian hegemony and redefine the role of the state in society.

In a review of 24 OECD countries from 1978–2007, Guichard *et al.* (2007) find that there were 85 episodes of fiscal consolidation. In Australia, for example, these episodes ran from 1979–80, 1986–8, 1994–9, 2002–3; and in the UK from 1979–82, 1988, 1994–9 (ibid.). More broadly, Pierson describes the 1990s as a period of intense pressure within the global North to pursue austerity (2001: 411). Cutbacks were quite rapid in pioneering neoliberal countries such as the UK, though elsewhere, in Canada (as hinted at above through protracted declarations), for example, austerity involved *relatively* cautious or targeted cost containment measures throughout the 1980s and 1990s (ibid.: 434). For instance, 1980s and 1990s austerity policies included transforming universal into selective programmes, tightening eligibility requirements to qualify for some benefits like unemployment insurance, imposing ceilings on programme costs, forcing programmes to be self-financing or subject to 'clawbacks' over a certain benefit level (Houle 1990). Reforms and restraint varied over time, by policy area, and jurisdiction (Banting 2005), tempered by how much popular support a given programme enjoyed. In contrast to austerity in the 1980s, which featured incremental erosion of the social safety net rather than outright dismantling, by the mid-1990s deficit reduction was clearly prioritized. Federal funding to Canadian provinces dropped, provinces cut their budgets accordingly, social programmes were redesigned to fit with the reality and vision of austerity, and social assistance recipients bore the full brunt of fiscal restraint (McBride and Whiteside 2011). Parallel patterns can be found elsewhere, such as Australia, where the mid-1980s Keating government sought to balance the books through relatively moderate fiscal reforms like deferring personal income tax cuts, adding user fees in education, tightening unemployment benefits, and eliminating a medicare rebate. By the mid-1990s, the Howard government was enacting deep budget cuts and union-busting reforms of riotous proportions (literally: in August 1996 an Australian Council of Trade Unions demonstration led to an attack on Parliament House in Canberra). 'Repairing' the 1996 budget meant privatization, cuts to services, taxes and the bureaucracy, and brought 'the most significant reorganisation of labour market assistance arrangements since the establishment of the Commonwealth Employment Service (CES) in 1946' (Costello 1996: n.p.).

Despite differences in pace and target, neoliberal policy paradigms since the 1970s have been emphasizing budgetary austerity, the implementation of regressive taxation, tax cuts for corporations, de-/re-regulation in a wide range of areas previously subject to regulation, privatization in forms ranging from sale of assets to the implementation of public–private partnerships, public sector reform through adopting market-like processes such as New Public Management, and liberalization of the economy, in part through the adoption of free trade agreements. Virtually every substantive policy area – from industrial relations and social welfare policy, to employment insurance, education, and health care – reveals some impact of neoliberal changes in fiscal policy.

Using Peck and Tickell's (2002) familiar 'roll-back' and 'roll-out' neoliberalization framework, we see austerity at work throughout the neoliberal era.[3] Initially an intellectual project, neoliberalism as a critique of the post-war Keynesian orthodoxy was launched and secured through austerity and monetarism as a 'solution' to stagflation. Policy programmes of Ronald Reagan, Margaret Thatcher, Brian Mulroney and other right-wing leaders then led to the 'roll-back' phase of neoliberalization: gutting the state and tearing down the Keynesian policy system through painfully high interest rates, 'slash and burn' budget balancing and cuts to social spending, regressive taxation, privatizing government entities and activities through asset sales, and granting enhanced investor rights through free trade and deregulation applicable to many key sectors.[4] From roughly the mid-1990s, policies associated with neoliberal 'roll-out' begin to emerge. This includes social programme reform (rather than simply programme cuts), tax expenditures as new forms of the welfare state (rather than removing all support), establishing partnerships with the private sector (rather than full-scale privatization), and re-regulation (rather than deregulation). Evolution was driven not only by new forms of neoliberal policy experimentation, but also out of a need to deal with the contradictions and dislocations that result from austerity. This includes problems of legitimacy, social reproduction, and social and economic instability.

The roll-back and roll-out description of neoliberal transformation is joined by others in the early 2000s – 'inclusive liberalism' and the 'social investment approach' being two of them. Porter and Craig (2004) and Mahon (2008), for example, argue that global institutions such as the OECD and World Bank began to modify their policy position in the 1990s to favour 'inclusive liberalism'. Inclusive liberalism shares important features with neoliberalism (such as an emphasis on the individual, an allegiance to a capitalist market economy and the protection/expansion of private property, an emphasis on supply-side measures such as taxation, and flexibilization of the labour market), however Mahon (ibid.: 262) argues that these two approaches draw on different elements of classical liberalism, with inclusive liberalism being more oriented towards social liberalism and thus focused more on redesigning the welfare state than on dismantlement. These new reforms emphasize assistance and support services, especially with respect to taxation and benefits received, and investment in human and social capital. These ideals were absent from neoliberal paradigm in its early stages (Graefe 2006).

Porter and Craig (2004: 390) call this a 're-embedding, securing phase in contemporary liberal hegemony'. A defensive component to this new phase is evident as neoliberalism failed in many ways to develop the components necessary to produce the social fix needed to promote widespread prosperity and stability following the global accumulation problems that began in the 1970s (see Jessop 2006). Often due to deep austerity measures, the result was a 'lost decade' of international development in the 1980s, debt and financial crises, the erosion of social support, and the rise of violent protests against spending cuts and free trade – all of which created serious social instability and a failure of neoliberalism to gain widespread legitimacy (relative to Keynesianism, at least) (Porter and Craig 2004: 391).

Similarly, with domestic policy transformations, Jensen and Saint Martin (2003) argue that growing concern with the social cohesion problems induced by earlier neoliberal reforms prompted an evolution of social policy in the 1990s. They call this new line of thinking the 'social investment approach', which adds an emphasis on social investment and human capital formation to older neoliberal policy elements. In their words,

> high rates of inequality, low wages, poor jobs, or temporary deprivation are not a serious problem in and of themselves: they are so only if individuals become trapped in those circumstances or if they foster anti-social, exclusionary behaviours, such as criminality, dropping out, and so on. They become important when they affect future life chances or social cohesion in the present.
>
> *(Jensen and Saint Martin 2003: 92)*

Thus the social investment approach is not only a departure from the post-war era distributive or consumption-oriented welfare state, but it is also a modification of the neoliberal paradigm; it is selective austerity.

Of course, inequality was not eradicated in this later neoliberal phase; far from it. Income distribution has become ever more unequal (whether measured in terms of market incomes or after tax incomes), there has been over three decades of wage stagnation for all but the most affluent, and wealth has become increasingly concentrated and unequally distributed (McBride and Whiteside 2011). Trends such as these have been linked to capitalist development itself (Marx 1977; Piketty 2014), yet austerity and neoliberalism are also implicated in the enhancement of social and economic inequality.

Concluding remarks

The return of austerity within global policy-making discourse and at various scales within OECD countries as of 2010 involved mobilizing pre-existing neoclassical and neoliberal reasoning and rhetoric favouring fiscal consolidation. Publications by elite economists and consensus among public and private policy promoting institutions and actors globally gave the return to austerity the nudge it needed to make a significant comeback. Jamie Peck (2014) argues that austerity has to be continually 'pushed' discursively, given that it is not self-evidently desirable or necessary. However, the appeal of austerity must also be understood within the context outlined by Mark Blyth (2013b): there is now a generation of economists and policy-makers for whom Keynesianism is but 'a footnote' in textbooks and in practice. With the notable exception of some vocal New Keynesians/Post-Keynesians like Paul Krugman and Martin Wolf, the relegation of alternative economic paradigms (even those as prominent historically as

Keynesianism) to literal or figurative footnote status suggests a myopia in orthodox economics today and helps explain the 'common sense' appeal to austerity.

The appeal of austerity, as explained throughout the chapter, is revealed through its connection with neoliberalism writ large – indeed, the economics of austerity are its politics. More than mere budget balancing, a near global push for fiscal restraint since the 1970s has enabled significant structural reform along neoliberal lines. Key policies and practices associated with austerity include privatization, more miserly social programmes, and financialization, as well as a shift in the social relations of power, a restructuring of the state, and the redistribution of burdens and benefits in society. Often cast as crisis management, austerity surely produces at least as many contradictions as it resolves.

Notes

1 The Philips curve depicts inflation and unemployment as inversely related. Stagflation – simultaneous economic stagnation (which included high unemployment) and inflation – provided an opportunity for neoclassical economists like Milton Friedman to overturn the dominance of Keynesian- and post-Keynesian-inspired macroeconomic policy.
2 For more on austerity's 'shape changing', see Clarke and Newman (2012) for their description of the alchemy of austerity and its manipulation of the concept of crisis.
3 This framework should be understood as a heuristic and not strictly speaking a chronology, yet for the purposes of this chapter it will be applied in a stylized, linear manner.
4 Overtly ideological/right wing-driven efforts such as these were pre-staged in the 1970s by proto-neoliberal or early neoliberal reforms introduced by the likes of James Callaghan (UK) and Jimmy Carter (USA) (see Swarts 2013).

References

Alesina, A., and Ardagna, S. 1998. *Expansionary Fiscal Contractions in Europe: New Evidence.* Working Paper Number 675, European Central Bank.
Alesina A., and Perotti, R. 1995. Fiscal Expansions and Adjustments in OECD Countries. *Economic Policy*, 21.
Alesina, A., Perotti, R., and Tavares, J. 1998. The Political Economy of Fiscal Adjustments. *Brookings Papers on Economic Activity*, 1.
Banting, K. 2005. Canada: Nation-Building in a Federal Welfare State, in Obinger, H., Leibfried, S., and Castles, F., eds. *Federalism and the Welfare State.* Cambridge: Cambridge University Press: 89–137.
Beatty, C., and Fothergill, S. 2014. The Local and Regional Impact of the UK's Welfare Reforms. *Cambridge Journal of Regions, Economy and Society*, 7: 63–79.
Blyth, M. 2013a. *Austerity: The History of a Dangerous Idea.* Oxford: Oxford University Press.
—. 2013b. *Power & Prejudice: The Politics of Austerity.* New Left Project, 14 August. Retrieved from http://www.newleftproject.org/index.php/site/article_comments/power_prejudice_the_politics_of_austerity_part_1
Callinicos, A. 2012. Contradictions of Austerity. *Cambridge Journal of Economics*, 36: 65–77.
Clarke, J., and Newman, J. 2012. The Alchemy of Austerity. *Critical Social Policy*, 32: 299–319.
Costello, P. 1996. *Budget Speech 1996–1997.* Commonwealth of Australia. Retrieved from http://budget.gov.au/1996-97/speech.asp
Curry, B., and Carmichael, K. 2010. Informal Setting Will Help G7 Reach Consensus, Flaherty Contends. *The Global and Mail*, 5 February.
Davidson, M., and Ward, K. 2014. 'Picking up the Pieces': Austerity Urbanism, California and Fiscal Crisis. *Cambridge Journal of Regions, Economy and Society*, 7: 81–97.
Dellepiane, S., and Hardiman, N. 2012. *Fiscal Politics In Time: Pathways to Fiscal Consolidation, 1980–2012.* UCD Geary Institute Discussion Papers. December.
G-20. 2012. *Policy Commitments by G20 Members.* Los Cabos Summit, 18–19 June. Retrieved from http://www.g20.utoronto.ca/summits/2012loscabos.html

Giavazzi, F., and Pagano, M. 1990. Can Severe Fiscal Contractions Be Expansionary? Tales of Two Small European Countries. *NBER Macroeconomics Annual*. Cambridge, MA: MIT Press.

Giles, C. and Bounds, A. 2012. Brutal for Britain. *Financial Times*, 15 January. Retrieved from http://www.ft.com/intl/cms/s/0/5cc73ea0-3e04-11e1-91ba-00144feabdc0.html?siteedition=intl#axzz2eRZcSxXb

Gindin, S. 2013. Beyond the Economic Crisis: The Crisis in Trade Unionism. *The Bullet*, 16 September. Retrieved from http://www.socialistproject.ca/bullet/878.php#continue

Government of Canada. 2011. *Budget in Brief*, 6 June. Retrieved from http://www.budget.gc.ca/2011/glance-apercu/brief-bref-eng.html

Graefe, P. 2006. The Social Economy and the American Model. *Global Social Policy*, 6: 197–219.

Guajardo, J., Leigh, D., and Pescatori, A. 2011. *Expansionary Austerity: New International Evidence*. IMF Working Paper, July. Retrieved from http://www.imf.org/external/pubs/ft/wp/2011/wp11158.pdf

Guichard, S., Kennedy, M., Wurzel, E., and Andre, C. 2007. What Promotes Fiscal Consolidation: OECD country experiences. *OECD Economics Department Working Papers*, No. 553, OECD. Retrieved from http://www.oecd-ilibrary.org/docserver/download/5l4nrhk97tr7.pdf?expires=1393902812&id=id&accname=guest&checksum=C7F630C58C139FE291B9AA3631322A00

Houle, F. 1990. Economic Renewal and Social Policy, in Gagnon, A.-G., Bickerton, J.P., eds. *Canadian Politics: An Introduction to the Discipline*. Peterborough: Broadview: 424–45.

Irwin, N. 2013. *The Alchemists: Three Central Bankers and a World on Fire*. New York: Penguin.

Jensen, J., and Saint Martin, D. 2003. New Routes to Social Cohesion? Citizenship and the Social Investment State. *Canadian Journal of Sociology*, 28: 77–99.

Jessop, B. 2006. Spatial Fixes, Temporal Fixes and Spatio-Temporal Fixes, in Castree, N., and Gregory, D., eds. *David Harvey: A Critical Reader*. Oxford: Blackwell: 142–66.

Kinsella, S. 2011. *Is Ireland Really the Role Model for Austerity?* UCD Geary Institute Discussion Papers. September.

Marx, K. 1977. *Capital*, Volume 1. New York: Vintage.

McBride, S. 1992. *Not Working*. Toronto: University of Toronto Press.

McBride, S., and Whiteside, H. 2011. Austerity for Whom? *Socialist Studies*, 7: 42–64.

Mahon, R. 2008. Babies and Bosses: Gendering the OECD's Social Policy Discourse, in Mahon, R., and McBride, S. *The OECD and Transnational Governance*. Vancouver: UBC Press: 260–75.

Peck, J. 2012. Austerity Urbanism. *City*, 16: 626–55.

—. 2014. Pushing Austerity: State Failure, Municipal Bankruptcy, and the Crises of Fiscal Federalism in the USA. *Cambridge Journal of Regions, Economy and Society*, 7: 17–44.

Peck, J., and Tickell, A. 2002. Neoliberalizing Space. *Antipode*, 34: 380–404.

Pierson, P. 2001. Coping with Permanent Austerity: Welfare State Restructuring in Affluent Democracies, in Pierson, ed. *The New Politics of the Welfare State*. Oxford: Oxford University Press: 410–56.

Piketty, T. 2014. *Capital in the Twenty-First Century*. Cambridge, MA: Harvard University Press.

Porter, D., and Craig, D. 2004. The Third Way and the Third World: Poverty Reduction and Social Inclusion in the Rise of 'Inclusive' Liberalism. *Review of International Political Economy*, 11: 387–423.

Posner, P.L., and Sommerfeld, M. 2013. The Politics of Fiscal Austerity: Democracies and Hard Choices. *OECD Journal on Budgeting*, 13: 141–74.

Reinhart, C., and Rogoff, K. 2010. *Growth in a Time of Debt*. National Bureau of Economic Research: NBER Working Paper No. 15639. Retrieved from http://www.nber.org/papers/w15639

Swarts, J. 2013. *Constructing Neoliberalism: Economic Transformation in Anglo-American Democracies*. Toronto: University of Toronto Press.

Wolf, M. 2013. Austerity in the Eurozone and the UK: Kill or Cure? *Financial Times*, 23 May. Retrieved from http://blogs.ft.com/martin-wolf-exchange/2013/05/23/austerity-in-the-eurozone-and-the-uk-kill-or-cure/

32

THE HOUSING CRISIS IN NEOLIBERAL BRITAIN

Free market think tanks and the production of ignorance

Tom Slater

What if that machinery were reversed? What if the habits, problems, actions, and decisions of the wealthy and powerful were daily scrutinized by a thousand systematic researchers, were hourly pried into, analysed, and cross referenced, tabulated and published in a hundred inexpensive mass-circulation journals and written so that even the fifteen-year-old high school drop-outs could understand it and predict the actions of their parents' landlord, manipulate and control *him*?

(Martin Nicolaus 1969)

In late 2014 an important social movement, FOCUS E15,[1] was born on the Carpenters Estate in the east London borough of Newham. Two young mothers, Sam Middleton and Jasmine Stone, occupied an empty flat on the estate in late September that year. They were soon joined by several other young mothers who had all experienced the same trauma: being served eviction notices by an emergency hostel (or 'sheltered accommodation', as it is known in the UK) after the funding stream to that council-run hostel was cut. The Carpenters Estate is adjacent to the 2012 Olympic Park, and in 2010 it was cleared of its residents as Newham Council, affected by central government cuts to all local authority budgets, tried to sell the land to cash in on the rent-seeking mega-event bonanza. The deal fell through, leaving nearly 300 council homes empty for four years, and the Council wanted to send the families it had displaced into hostels to Birmingham or Manchester, where rents are considerably cheaper. The FOCUS E15 protest armed itself with a very simple message: 'Social Housing, Not Social Cleansing'. Under the current Conservative government, the context for such a protest is not going to disappear any time soon: social housing all over England is being bought out by private developers, councils are trying to divest themselves of what sparse stock they have left, wages do not even cover social rents (let alone private sector rents), and, most galling of all, thousands of affordable homes lie empty 'in preparation for the billions their destruction will bring in' (Williams 2014). On 2 October, Newham Council failed in its attempt to use the draconian power of 'interim possession order' to evict and silence the mothers, who then left the homes they occupied on their terms while continuing their campaign.

In December 2014 there was a significant victory for residents of another east London housing estate, New Era, when they successfully fought plans by US land investors to evict dozens of families and more than double rents. Westbrook Partners, under huge public pressure because of a campaign against its profiteering motives (again led by mothers on the estate), sold the land upon which the New Era estate sits to the Dolphin Square Charitable Foundation, an affordable housing charity committed to delivering low-cost rents to Londoners on low to middle incomes. These protests in a capital city with grotesquely inflated housing costs across all tenures generated massive attention (helped by celebrity support on social media), and triggered a national debate on housing affordability and similar protests in other UK cities.[2] Above all, the movements demonstrated that, when too many people are unable to afford shelter, it becomes a political problem, and a major basis for social mobilization.

Unsettling supply and demand

Against this backdrop – and particularly against the 2015 General Election backdrop of the (since defeated) Labour Party taking high housing costs more seriously than in its recent history and proposing an upper limit on rent increases within tenancies in the private rented sector – the Institute of Economic Affairs (IEA), a free market think tank and a pivotal institution in the birth of neoliberal ideology in the UK and beyond, published a report entitled *The Flaws in Rent Ceilings*[3] (Bourne 2014). A declamatory crusade against all forms of rent regulation anywhere, from what it called the 'crude rent controls' of the (twentieth-century) inter-war period to 'second-generation rent ceilings', the report began by stating that there is a 'rare consensus' among economists that rent control 'leads to a fall in the quantity of rental property available and a reduction in the quality of the existing stock' (10). A quick inspection of a footnoted URL reveals that the source of this 'consensus' is, in fact, a small survey of 40 neoclassical economists in the USA. Nonetheless, the report continued to argue that 'under rent control there is less incentive for families to reduce their accommodation demands, therefore exacerbating the shortage of properties for others' (16). The tenor of the document reaches a crescendo a few pages later in the spectacular assertion that 'the truth would appear to be that tenants are unwilling to pay for increased security' (25), leading to the conclusion that any 'extra security' for tenants 'comes at the expense of reduced economic efficiency' (35). Instead of rent regulation, the report calls for another round of deregulation in the form of 'planning liberalisation', which is described as a 'welfare enhancing policy' (36) that would lead to the construction of new housing on land currently shielded from development by government red tape. For the IEA, the housing crisis is a basic economic conundrum – too much demand and not enough supply – and its solution is thus to increase supply by stopping all government interference in the competitive housing market, which (true to neoclassical beliefs) must be allowed to operate free of cumbersome restrictions to provide incentives for producers and consumers to optimize their behaviour and push the market towards equilibrium (so that there are no shortages of housing), while yielding the maximum amount of utility for the maximum number of people.

The IEA immediately went about the task of circulating sound bites from the report as widely as possible. Its 'solution' certainly caught the attention of newspapers and commentators supporting a conservative agenda, one illustration being the *Daily Telegraph* printing a feature under the headline, 'Think-tank Criticises "Pointless" Labour Rent Cap Scheme' (6 September 2014). It also caught the attention of the editors of *Channel 4 News*, a widely respected national television news programme, who invited the author of the report, Ryan Bourne (the IEA's Head of Public Policy) to discuss the issue of rent control alongside Jasmine Stone.[4] Even after Stone described her and her neighbours' experiences of struggling to make rent due to various profiteering schemes, Bourne maintained that the 'fundamental reason' for very high rents was not 'greedy landlords'. According to Bourne, the 'real' reason is that, 'Over years and years we haven't built new homes and have restricted supply artificially[5] through greenbelts and other planning restrictions.' When Stone answered positively to the interviewer's question of whether she would like to see rent controls introduced in London, Bourne immediately retorted that she was wrong because 'economists agree' that such 'crude' controls are 'absolutely disastrous'. It did not appear to matter at all to Bourne that Stone was speaking from the experience of poverty, housing precarity and repeated evictions. If economists like him agree, then the debate over rent regulation should end.

The Flaws in Rent Ceilings is a pure exemplar of the way in which free market think tanks function as footsoldiers of, and mouthpieces for, the neoliberal creed. When that creed is under scrutiny or being challenged directly, think tanks scramble to produce 'evidence' (in the form of authoritative reports distilled into accessible sound bites) defending the free market and attacking state intervention in economic affairs. In this IEA case, structural causes of the housing crisis were swept out of sight by appeals to 'sound economics' and by recourse to the easily decipherable logics of supply and demand. Whether by intent or not, reports such *The Flaws in Rent Ceilings* serve to divert attention away from the harsh realities of the housing crisis which lay bare the catastrophic consequences of over three decades of neoliberal housing policies. There is no space here for a full portrait of these realities, merely some brief pictures:[6] by 2014, for the first time since the late 1960s, there were more UK households renting homes privately than in social housing; since 2000, the largely unregulated private rented sector has doubled in size to well over 4 million households; buy-to-let mortgages soared during this period, facilitated by insecure 'shorthold tenancies' and a get-rich-quick scheme for landlords, until mid-2015, subsidized by the state via tax breaks; 1.8 million households (and counting) are on the waiting list for social housing; homelessness is on the rise (there was a 31 per cent increase in rough sleeping from 2010–12), despite the existence of over 750,000 empty homes in the UK; 'affordable rents' in social housing in England are now set at 80 per cent of market levels (up from 50 per cent) – and almost never affordable; 1.6 million households are spending over half their income on housing costs; and the very poorest households have approximately £60 per week left after housing costs are met.

The infamous Right to Buy scheme, introduced in 1980 to encourage direct sales of council housing at large discounts to tenants (to expand home ownership at the expense of the public housing stock) is one direct and major cause of the lack of affordable housing today, yet it is now being extended to tenants in housing association properties.[7] It has been the largest but by no means the only economic deregulation and privatization[8] scheme vis-à-vis housing in Britain. Many remaining council housing stocks have been transferred to housing associations ('stock transfer') as part of a pervasive political desire to end municipal management altogether, accounting for a further 1.5 million public dwellings. Year upon year there is a dwindling public subsidy for housing associations, which have been forced to rely on commercial borrowing to balance the books, putting upward pressure on rents (Hodkinson 2012). On top of this, along with the current erosion of housing assistance in the cruellest way imaginable via the 'Bedroom Tax',[9] urban 'regeneration' policies continue to provide expensive accommodation 'choices' while bulldozing affordable housing. These sobering snapshots all point to the absolute necessity of rent regulation to protect increasing numbers of people trapped by a housing market that offers frequently staggering returns only to those with the financial means to access them, not to mention trapped by a hostile, precarious entry-level labour market into which the most vulnerable are being funnelled by workfarist reforms. Young people (under the age of 40) are most affected: unable ever to save for a deposit to acquire a mortgage loan, a new phrase, 'Generation Rent' (see McKee and Hoolachan 2015), has emerged to capture the plight of those at the mercy of landlords across all sectors. Recently, a 'Living Rent' campaign[10] has emerged in Scotland, taking cues from the remarkable advances of the Living Wage movement to argue for urgent government action to ensure truly affordable rents in the private rented sector.

In sum, it is arguably around the housing question where the contrast between the rhetoric of these think tanks and the realities of so many is at its most glaring. Those arguing for housing justice have truly formidable and very well-financed opponents in free market think tanks, whose devotion to neoliberal beliefs is steadfast, zealous, and often ruthless. This chapter therefore focuses on the housing crisis in the UK to trace and elaborate the critical importance of these think tanks in the mobilization of state power vis-à-vis the extension of market rule. To accomplish this I pay attention to how think tanks have been studied, then provide a short historical overview of the rise of free market think tanks in the UK and their methods of argumentation, before concentrating on the question of how think tanks shield the public from grasping the roots of the housing crisis, and how scholarship might respond.

Think tanks: contrasting analytic perspectives

In an outstanding recent sociological analysis of think tanks (of all political stripes) in the USA, Medvetz (2012) traces their rise and enormous influence in that country over several decades, and in doing so helpfully outlines three distinct perspectives on think tanks in the academic literature:

1　*the elite perspective,* which 'depicts think tanks as the intellectual machinery of a closed network of corporate, financial, and political elites', and as 'instruments deployed strategically in the service of a ruling class political agenda'
2　*the pluralist perspective,* undergirded by a refusal to assign any essential character or role to think tanks, which are analysed as 'one kind of organization among many in a wide array of societal groups that compete to shape public policy'
3　*the institutionalist perspective,* where think tanks are viewed as 'epistemic communities, or networks of politically engaged experts and professionals' and the focus is on 'the structural environments in which think tanks are embedded, the rules and norms that shape their behaviour, and the organizational arrangements and processes to which they must respond'. (8–16)

While taking cues from all three, Medvetz found too many shortcomings in each, as the impact of think tanks extends well beyond official politics into other social spheres (academia, business, media), and particularly as the three perspectives fail to take seriously the 'structural blurriness' (16) and ambiguity of think tanks, which he argues is key to their significant influence across these spheres. Correspondingly, Medvetz developed a *relational perspective* on the think tank, using Bourdieu's concepts of social space and field of power to dissect 'the social relations (of hierarchy, struggle, partnership and so on) that surround and make possible the think tank' (35). There is tremendous potential in Medvetz's new perspective to grasp what is distinctive about think tanks from other research organizations, the relationships among think tanks, the influence they cast over public debate, and especially the role of intellectuals in society (he insists that the rise of think tanks must be set analytically 'against the backdrop of a series of processes that have contributed to the growing subordination of knowledge to political and economic demand' (226)). Yet, given the focus of this chapter on free market think tanks in the context of neoliberalization, Medvetz's warning (a critique of the elite perspective) that 'we must be careful not to smuggle into the analysis any essentialist conclusions about a think tank's ultimate political or intellectual proclivities' (12) is less helpful. To be sure, essentialism is always best avoided, but close scrutiny of the (surprisingly small) literature on free market think tanks and neoliberalism finds conclusions about a think tank's 'ultimate political or intellectual proclivities' to be robust and instructive, rather than sweeping and essentialist. The elite perspective, while limited in scope (e.g. it cannot account for the rise of think tanks positioned *against* ruling-class interests), is certainly still of analytic utility in explaining the power wielded by contemporary think tanks of the right.

Free market think tanks in the UK from Thatcher to Cameron

We did all our stuff publicly, in the public domain. We published, we sent the stuff out, had it raised in Parliament.... If you do it in public over weeks, people are prepared for it – journalists and whatever. By the time the minister gets around to the idea, it's already familiar. He's won part of the battle of public acceptance.

(Senior conservative think tank officer, quoted in Peck and Tickell 2007: 42)

In a pugnacious analysis of the role of intellectuals in shaping the process of neoliberalization, Peck and Tickell (2007) pay specific attention to the free market think tanks during the era of Margaret Thatcher, which played a decisive role in 'translating foundational ideas into circulating policy knowledges, fit for governmental practice' (36). It should be recognized that the Fordist–Keynesian climate of the three decades following World War II meant that these foundational ideas had not been in vogue for some time, and were often dismissed as lunacy. It was the free market think tanks that led the way in changing mindsets, and in 'stretching the vocabulary of the politically feasible' (48). How did they accomplish this? Where previous governments had relied almost exclusively on senior civil servants to produce policy briefs, Thatcher wanted to create a 'market' for ideas within the policy process (Desai 1994). This provided the impetus for think tanks such as the IEA, the Adam Smith Institute, and the Centre for Policy Studies to produce a plethora of widely disseminated policy packages that distilled the arguments of Friedrich von Hayek and Milton Friedman (and their Mont Pelerin disciples) into accessible sound bites for ministers and the electorate: '[T]he various products of the think tanks – pamplets, reports, policy briefs, occasionally books – were purposely circulated through the public sphere in order to generate conversation across different segments of the policy community and in the press' (41).

Wacquant (2009) provides an elaborate account of such a 'conversation' with respect to the 1990s diffusion – from the neoconservative think tanks of Washington, DC, to their 'trading posts' (think tanks and policy institutes) in European cities – of a triad of welfare cutback proposals, paternalist 'workfare' programmes, and 'zero tolerance' policing methods. He describes how the 'mental colonization of British policy makers by the United States' (34) was facilitated by the media and think tank sponsorship of visits to the UK by right-wing intellectuals (e.g. Charles Murray, Lawrence Mead). This was quickly followed by a torrent of widely disseminated publications:

It is through the agency of exchanges, interventions, and publications of an academic character, real or simulated, that intellectual 'smugglers' (passeurs) reformulate these categories in a sort of politological pidgin, sufficiently concrete to 'hook' state decision-makers and journalists anxious to 'stick close to reality'... but sufficiently abstract to strip them of any overly flagrant idiosyncrasy that would tie them back to their originating national context. (Ibid.: 47–8)

Powerful and convincing as it is, Wacquant's analysis blends rather different UK governments into the same explanatory account. While undoubtedly neoliberal in both rhyme and reason, and sporting prominent politicians (e.g. Frank Field, Jack Straw) enamoured with the prophets of punitive governance, the New Labour (1997–2010) government operated in a quite different way with respect to think tanks than the preceding Conservative governments. This period was characterized by a pragmatist 'What Works?' approach to public policy, where centrist think tanks came to dominate all government research activities, and, subsequently, the policy process. The Institute for Public Policy Research and DEMOS, to take the two most Blairite examples, left market rule unquestioned while they commissioned grant-hungry academics to trawl through the 'evidence base' for examples of policies that might soften the sharp edges of supply-side, inflation-busting economic management, and as they conducted focus groups with randomly selected pundits from all walks of life to evaluate policy packages on the table. But at precisely the time the Blairite think tanks were at their influential apex in 'explicating the terms of the politically deliverable' (Peck and Tickell 2007: 48), two new think tanks were born with dramatic implications for the British welfare state in particular.

What distinguishes the free market Centre for Social Justice and Policy Exchange from the think tanks before them is the central involvement of (then opposition) frontline politicians in their initial formation. The former was the brainchild of Iain Duncan-Smith (latterly Work and Pensions Secretary) and the latter that of Michael Gove (currently the Justice Secretary) in collaboration with other Tory politicians. Duncan-Smith and Gove are two staunch Thatcherites and close allies of Prime Minister David Cameron, and the think tanks they created have not only become the go-to sources of comment and 'evidence' arming those of a neoliberal persuasion, but continue to provide the intellectual impetus behind the ongoing Conservative assaults on the public sector and on the welfare state in Britain under the banner of 'cutting the deficit' (austerity). Supported by the press releases and noisy interjections of other free market think tanks such as Reform and The Taxpayers' Alliance, what Owen Jones (2014) calls the 'outriders' have been instrumental in connecting together the worlds of politics, business and the media to defend the neoliberal society they and their predecessors have helped to create, and to keep the national political conversation on terms/categories favourable to ruling elites. But it would be erroneous to view them simply as mere servants of the powerful:

> It might seem tempting to view the outriders as nothing more than tools of the wealthy elite. But they are not cynical charlatans, simply pumping out propaganda at the behest of powerful businesspeople. They are true believers, zealots even. They speak from genuine, unshakeable conviction. Businesspeople are grateful for the work the outriders do in popularising these ideas, and believe donating to them is a wise investment. (38–9)

Jones's central point is crucial: even if the influential think tanks of the moment in the UK are generously funded by large corporations and wealthy individual benefactors, they are first and foremost deeply *political* creations that then attract business support – not the other way round. These think tanks always claim political independence (and seek respect by frequent appeals to their charitable or 'educational' status) but so evangelical is their devotion to market rule and loathing of big government that it serves as a honey pot for substantial financial donations from business interests. They are now so well financed (and thus well staffed) that it makes it very challenging indeed for think tanks opposing free market logics and neoliberal nostrums to produce equivalent volumes of output.

Decision-based evidence-making (and other traits)

If the structural conditions for the creation of think tanks bear close scrutiny, so too do their methods and styles of argumentation. Take, for instance, Create Streets, which describes itself as 'a non-partisan social enterprise and independent research institute focusing on the built environment', with a mission to 'encourage the creation of more urban homes with terraced streets of houses and apartments rather than complex multi-storey buildings'. The brainchild of Nicholas Boys Smith, a director at Lloyds Banking Group, it hit the UK headlines in January 2013, when it published its first report in conjunction with Policy Exchange. Boys Smith co-authored the report with Alex Morton (who has since left Policy Exchange to become David Cameron's special advisor on housing and planning policy) and together they argued that high-rise social housing blocks in London should be demolished to make way for low-rise flats and terraced housing:

> London has a large amount of social housing built as large multi-storey blocks from the 1950s to the 1970s. This housing is unpopular with the public. Nor, ironically, is it particularly high density. Replacing it with proper terraced housing would transform London, making London more attractive, benefitting residents, and potentially allowing a large increase in housing in the capital. Create Streets has therefore been created to encourage and facilitate the replacement of London's multi-storey housing and the development of brownfield sites with real houses in real streets. (Boys Smith and Morton 2013: 5)

Leaving aside the high probability that those living in 'large multi-storey blocks' feel that their houses and streets are already 'real', a call for demolition and displacement on this scale – during a serious housing crisis – cannot be made without some sort of moralizing justification. This is to be found in the language and symbols deployed in Chapter 3 of the report, entitled 'Multi-Storey Housing is Bad for its Residents' (including the subtitle 'Multi-storey housing is more risky and makes people sadder, badder and lonelier'). Some illustrations:

> Other studies have found children in high-rises suffering from more bedwetting and temper tantrums and that the best predictor of juvenile delinquency was not population density but living in blocks of flats as opposed to houses. (30)
> [T]he evidence also suggests that tower blocks might even encourage suicide. Without wishing to be glib, tower blocks don't just make you more depressed. They make it easier to kill yourself – you can jump. (30)
> Multi-storey buildings can create a myriad of opportunities for crime due to their hard to police semi-private corridors, walkways and multiple escape routes. (32)

The 'evidence' for such claims, contrary to being 'unambiguous' and 'overwhelming' (a word used multiple times), is drawn from a few highly questionable studies in the fields of architecture/urban design and psychology, from some journalistic memoirs, and hammered home via obligatory and hagiographic nods to the writings of modernist-bashers Jane Jacobs, Oscar Newman and Alice Coleman. The very few social scientific studies that are mentioned have been mined for quotations entirely wrenched out of their historical, social and geographical contexts. Furthermore, the authors falsely claim that high-rise housing is 'bad for you' regardless of income or social status (avoiding the question of how to account for the explosive growth and appeal of luxury condominium towers in many large cities), and the

obvious and pressing question of how to account for any 'social problems' in low-rise or terraced housing is studiously ignored. Perhaps anticipating some challenges to their drastic
manifesto for a 'London that is more pleasant for everyone', they conclude, 'This agenda is
pro-housing and pro-growth, and would create a more beautiful and better London. We
cannot allow a minority with vested interests to defeat it' (69). This report, resting on the
stigmatization of working-class people and the places where they live, should not be dismissed as a right-wing bourgeois fantasy. At the time of writing, Create Streets has had two
major policy impacts; first, the March 2014 UK Budget followed its recommendations, cited
its work, and created a £150 million Estate Regeneration Fund; and second, in April 2014
the UK Government commissioned Savills (a global real estate corporation with expertise in
elite residential markets) to investigate the potential of its proposals (which informed the
controversial Housing Bill currently working its way through parliament).

In the Create Streets/Policy Exchange report, and in the 2014 IEA report against rent ceilings,
we can find many of the hallmarks or character traits of free market think tanks as they deliver
their arguments. These are summarized in Table 32.1 and are drawn from an extensive reading of
numerous such think tank publications, and the scholarship on them. The final point in Table
32.1 is arguably the common denominator of all free market think tank publications. One of the
catchphrases of the policy process during the Tony Blair years, for better or worse, was 'evidence-
based decision-making'. Yet writers employed by free market think tanks, in particular, have
mastered the craft of *decision-based evidence-making*, tailored to the needs of policy elites and politicians on the lookout for accessible catchphrases to woo a jaded electorate. Politicians very rarely
consult published social science research unless it supports the policies they want to pursue (witness, for instance, the fact that it is virtually impossible to find a social scientist trained outside the
field of neoclassical economics who writes for, or who has ever been consulted by, a free market
think tank). Instead, they depend on neat sound bites and statistics drawn from think tank surveys
or literature reviews that measure nothing more than the worldview of the institution that commissions them, where policy 'researchers' set out to resolve false problems even though they have
already been 'implicitly settled in the way research questions are formulated' (Wacquant 2009:
48). These methods provide the 'evidence base' for the mobilization of state power in the extension of conservative dogma; they actively manufacture ignorance to appease and ultimately sustain their funding sources, buffering politicians and their audiences from viable alternatives and
inoculating them against the critique of autonomous scholarship. The moral authority in the
delivery of conclusions and policy recommendations made by free market think tanks is best

Table 32.1 Key traits of free market think tank argumentation

- Purity of belief in free market and/or 'trickle down' economics
- Intensity of belief (zeal), unwavering conviction
- Abstraction and ahistoricity
- Results from opinion polls, selective literature reviews and rigged surveys presented as 'irrefutable
  evidence'
- Despite widely available counter-evidence, an insistence that, over the long run, they will be proved
  right
- Self-appointed in a particular (neoliberal) ideology, the dismissal and denigration of opposing views as
  'ideologically driven'
- Decision-based evidence-making, yet repeated claims of independence, objectivity, lack of bias, and,
  especially, 'rigorous research' (accepted by mainstream media, so *opinion* quickly morphs into *fact*)

Source: Building on Desai 1993: 40. I am grateful to Tracey Jensen for some suggestions here.

captured by Peck (2006), when he observes that their conservative intellectuals, despite speaking the language of the dominant, 'portray themselves as *lonely voices of reason*, as principled outsiders in a corrupt, distracted, and wrongheaded world' (682, emphasis added).

Charting and challenging the production of ignorance

Free market think tanks of the right in the UK continue to increase in power, and their influence is hard to avoid in any assessment of how the contemporary neoliberal state is aided and augmented. Their glossy and authoritative publications, their fast channels of access to authority and opinion-makers, their speechwriters and backroom 'researchers' have successfully deflected attention away from the neoliberal causes of the miserable housing realities endured by people living at the bottom of the social and spatial order. Take the question of rent control that is the target of the IEA's full wrath. Its assertion that the high cost of all forms of housing in the UK (currently consigning the poor to financial ruin) is a case of too much demand and not enough supply is immediately stranded by evidence judiciously ignored in the report: the startling amount of empty homes in the UK, the amount of land being hoarded by domestic and foreign investors with what Harvey (2010) calls 'speculative landed developer interests' in cities (attracted by low taxation), and the existence of abundant mortgage credit[11] (the lending frenzy set in motion by Thatcher's deregulatory crusade in the 1980s). In short, it is rentier capitalist extraction and the circulation of interest-bearing capital in land markets – facilitated by the neoliberal state – that has resulted in the high cost of housing in the UK (cf. Aalbers and Christophers 2014). Land value (so often ignored in discussions of housing costs) is not created from owning land – it is created from collective social investments in land, which landowners capture as unearned income via private property rights (Sayer 2014). Land speculation and monopoly land ownership, on top of abundant mortgage credit, is actually what makes housing unaffordable. Instead of building decommodified shelter for people in dire housing need, the political-economic system encourages rentier capitalists to 'compete over who can best use their land-banking skills to anticipate the next housing bubble and survive the last one' (Meek 2014: 223). Rent regulation is an urgently required short-term measure to protect against evictions and homelessness, alongside a long-term programme of decommodified housing provision. But the IEA conjures up the threat of economic and housing disaster if any such regulation is imposed, arguing that landlords would not generate enough revenue to maintain their properties or simply withdraw them from the rental market. But in numerous countries and cities where rent controls are long established, there is thin or no empirical evidence in support of these arguments. It is also worth noting that under no rent regulation, one third of all private rented sector tenants in the UK are living in structurally inadequate housing (Lansley and Mack 2015).

The influence and activities of free market think tanks point to the necessity of shifting research questions away from 'what people know' about the society in which they live towards questions about what people do *not* know, and why not. These questions are often just as important, usually far more scandalous, and remarkably under-theorized. This requires a rejection of appeals to 'epistemology' and 'knowledge production', and instead, an analytic focus on the production of *ignorance* instead (see Davies and McGoey 2012, for a timely intervention on 'rationalities of ignorance' vis-à-vis 2008 financial crisis, and Mirowski, 2013, for a compelling dissection of the mass ignorance produced by neoclassical economic theory). There is a word for this focus, *agnotology*, coined by Robert Proctor, a science historian, and meaning 'the study of ignorance making, the lost and forgotten' where the 'focus is on knowledge that could have been but wasn't, or should be but isn't' (Proctor and Schiebinger 2008: vii). It was while investigating the tobacco industry's efforts to manufacture doubt about the health hazards of smoking that Proctor began to see the scientific and political urgency in researching how ignorance is made, maintained and manipulated by powerful institutions to suit their own ends, where the guiding research question becomes, 'Why don't we know what we don't know?' As he discovered, the industry went to great lengths to give the impression that the cancer risks of cigarette smoking were still an open question even when the scientific evidence was over-whelming. Numerous tactics were deployed by the tobacco industry to divert attention from cancer risks, such as the production of duplicitous press releases, the publication of 'nobody knows the answers' white papers, and the generous funding of decoy or red-herring research that 'would seem to be addressing tobacco and health, while really doing nothing of the sort' (ibid.: 14).[12]

It would seem that the actions of free market think tanks are well suited to such agnotological analyses (for an initial attempt, see Slater 2014). It matters because these think tanks are now so powerful that their reports and proposals – littered with dubious assumptions and fabricated evidence, and shot through with zealous devotion to a failed economic experiment responsible for social suffering on a grand scale – *directly shape public policies*. Officially non-state agencies that are never subject to democratic accountability (Denham and Garnett 1999), these think tanks continue to have profound and far-reaching state effects. Wacquant (2010) goes so far to say that they have 'irrevocably altered the institutional matrix through which policy knowledge perco-lates' (442). Whether this is truly *irrevocable* is open for debate, but it would seem that tracing the production and circulation of ignorance by free market think tanks and exposing the class power that undergirds it is essential if the skewed vision of the world presented by these institutions is to be countered.

Notes

1 http://focuse15.org/
2 Due to devolution there are considerable differences in housing policies between England and Scotland. But welfare reform is UK central government legislation that is not devolved, and this has major impli-cations for housing and for cities. So, whilst I acknowledge that the arguments of this chapter are skewed by the experiences of England, particularly south-east England, I argue that it would be a political mistake to jettison 'Britain' as a frame of reference.
3 This is not the first time the IEA has waded into the debate on rent control. Founded in 1957 by Anthony Fisher, an ex-RAF pilot, wealthy chicken farmer and personal friend of Friedrich von Hayek, in 1972 the IEA published a savage tirade against state intervention in housing markets entitled 'Verdict on Rent Control', co-authored by none other than Hayek himself with another archdeacon of neolib-eralism, Milton Friedman.
4 Available to view here: http://t.co/ZLzoiHp2Su [video file].
5 The use of the word 'artificially' is revealing: neoclassical economists are especially prone to viewing a competitive market as a natural evolution that is best left alone if equilibrium and growth is to be achieved.
6 My sources here are Dorling (2014), Meek (2014) and Lansley and Mack (2015).
7 In a cynical appropriation of past language, the Tories have recently launched the 'Help to Buy' pro-gramme to assist first-time buyers purchase residential property. It has thus far had two phases: (1) buyers contribute a 5 per cent deposit and the government provides an equity loan for up to 20 per cent of the property value, and buyers must provide the remaining funds themselves (from a mortgage). This is available only for new-build properties under a certain price (less than £600,000) and the loan is interest-free for the first five years; (2) 5 per cent deposit mortgages are available from ten different lenders with the government acting as a guarantor for the mortgage. This phase is not restricted to those buying new-build: anyone wanting to buy any home in the UK worth less than £600,000 is eligible for the scheme. Even the IMF has warned George Osborne, Chancellor of the Exchequer, about this scheme creating another catastrophic housing bubble.
8 Right to Buy actually failed on its own privatizing terms, as many who exercised their Right to Buy sold on to private landlords, who rented them to tenants at double or triple the levels of private rent,

which required tenants to apply for housing benefit from the state. So Right to Buy actually ended up costing the state far, far more in housing benefit than it ever did in maintenance and management of council homes.

9 Since 1 April 2013 the allocation of Housing Benefit takes into consideration the number of rooms occupied by tenants in local authority (council) and social-rented (housing association) accommodation, and restricts payments to allow for one bedroom per person or per couple. If it is deemed by the state that there are too many rooms in such a dwelling for the number of occupants, the 'under-occupancy penalty' is applied. This reduces housing benefit payments by 14 per cent for one extra bedroom and by 25 per cent for two or more extra bedrooms. Politicians attempt to defend the indefensible by referring to the 'need' to reduce welfare spending as part of their current fiscal austerity agenda. There is also defensive reference to the many thousands of tenants across all sectors in overcrowded accommodation; it is claimed that the 'reallocation effects' of the policy will reduce council housing waiting lists. However, this argument is immediately stranded once it is recognized that people being evicted from their homes due to rent arrears is not going to reduce council housing waiting lists.

10 http://www.livingrent.org/

11 76 per cent of all bank loans in Britain now go into property (64 per cent of that into residential mortgages). Mortgage market 'liberalization', typically framed as making homeownership accessible, has resulted in a debt explosion rather than in more accessible homeownership – especially via 'interest-only mortgages' (a glorified form of renting). I am very grateful to Manuel Aalbers for some timely reminders here.

12 The tobacco industry actually produced research about everything except tobacco hazards to exploit public uncertainty (researchers knew from the beginning what they were supposed to find and not find), and the very fact of research being funded allowed the industry to say it was studying the problem. Since the 1980s, as the cancer risks have become more widely accepted, the industry's goal has been 'to control the history of tobacco just as earlier they'd controlled the science of tobacco' via the employment of historians (through substantial consultancy payments) to write articles and reports documenting the supposedly 'beneficial' effects of nicotine through the ages.

References

Aalbers, M., and Christophers, B. 2014. Centring Housing in Political Economy. *Housing, Theory and Society*, 31: 373–94.

Bourne, R. 2014. *The Flaws in Rent Ceilings*. IEA Discussion Paper No. 55. London: Institute of Economic Affairs. Retrieved from http://www.iea.org.uk/publications/research/the-flaws-in-rent-ceilings

Boys Smith, N. and Morton, A. 2013. *Create Streets, Not Just Multi-Storey Estates*. Retrieved from http://www.policyexchange.org.uk/images/publications/create%20streets.pdf

Davies, W., and McGoey, L. 2012. Rationalities of Ignorance: On Financial Crisis and the Ambivalence of Neo-liberal Epistemology. *Economy and Society*, 41.1: 64–83.

Denham, A., and Garnett, M. 1999. Influence Without Responsibility? Think-tanks in Britain. *Parliamentary Affairs*, 52.1: 46–57.

Desai, R. 1994. Second Hand Dealers in Ideas: Think-tanks and Thatcherite Hegemony. *New Left Review*, 203 (January/February).

Dorling, D. 2014. *All That is Solid: The Great Housing Disaster*. London: Allen Lane.

Harvey, D. 2010. *The Enigma of Capital and the Crises of Capitalism*. London: Profile.

Hodkinson, S. 2012. The New Urban Enclosures. *City*, 16.5: 500–18.

Jones, O. 2014. *The Establishment (And How They Get Away With It)*. London: Verso.

Lansley. S., and Mack, J. 2015. *Breadline Britain: The Rise of Mass Poverty*. London: One World.

McKee, K., and Hoolachan, J. 2015. *Housing Generation Rent: What Are The Challenges for Housing Policy in Scotland?* St Andrews: Centre for Housing Research. Retrieved from http://ggsrv-cold.standrews.ac.uk/CHR/Uploads/Edit/file/Carnegie%20Final%20Report_June2015.pdf

Medvetz, T. 2012. *Think Tanks in America*. Chicago, IL: University of Chicago Press.

Meek, J. 2014. *Private Island: Why Britain Now Belongs to Someone Else*. London: Verso.

Mirowski, P. 2013. *Never Let a Serious Crisis Go to Waste: How Neoliberalism Survived the Economic Meltdown*. London: Verso.

Nicolaus, M. 1969. Remarks at ASA Convention. *American Sociologist*, 4.2: 154–6.

Peck, J. 2006. Liberating the City: Between New York and New Orleans. *Urban Geography*, 27.8: 681–783.

Peck, J., and Tickell, A. 2007. Conceptualizing Neoliberalism, Thinking Thatcherism, in Leitner, H., Peck, J., and Sheppard, E., eds. *Contesting Neoliberalism: Urban Frontiers*. New York: Guilford Press: 26–50.

Proctor, R., and Schiebinger, L. eds. 2008. *Agnotology: The Making and Unmaking of Ignorance*. Stanford, CA: Stanford University Press.

Sayer, A. 2014. *Why We Can't Afford The Rich*. Bristol: Policy Press.

Slater, T. 2014. The Myth of 'Broken Britain': Welfare Reform and the Production of Ignorance. *Antipode*, 46.4: 948–69.

Wacquant, L. 2009. *Prisons of Poverty*. Expanded edn. Minneapolis: University of Minnesota Press.

—. 2010. From 'Public Criminology' to the Reflexive Sociology of Criminological Production and Consumption. *British Journal of Criminology*, 51: 438–48.

Williams, Z. 2014. Housing: How Many Have to be Unable to Afford it Before it Becomes a Political Problem?' *The Guardian*, 26 September.

PART V

Spaces

PART V

Spaces

33

URBAN NEOLIBERALISM

Rolling with the changes in a globalizing world

Roger Keil

In the late 1980s Frankfurt, Germany's global city, had become one of the early laboratories of the incipient urban neoliberalization which we have now experienced as a globe-sweeping reality for more than a generation. In a much publicized image, the then mayor, Wolfram Brück, a devout believer in the possibilities afforded by the opening of world markets to his city's industries – trade, transport, banking, fairgrounds – and New York developer Jerry Speyer look on as Frankfurt Fairgrounds director Horstmar Stauber puts the model of an iconic highrise building into a sandbox style display of development areas. The highrise, designed by Helmut Jahn for Tishmann/Speyer, was meant to mark the awakening of Frankfurt to a new era of postmodern architecture, economic expansion and global reach. A big smile on his face, Brück was certain in his conviction that nothing said runaway economic success and international appeal more than a skyscraper skyline. Making Frankfurt's land and airspace available to global investors and 'starchitects' was a prime strategy of a set of policies that were recognized as the sign of a new era of the entrepreneurial city (Harvey 1989). In hindsight, these elements were also the starting point of a pervasive neoliberalization in cities and through urbanization.

For local activists at the time – full disclosure: I was one of them – the planting of the model in the sandbox of global city development and the public–private coalition of municipality, public company and international developer signalled what Keil and Lieser at the time called an 'attack of the neoliberal conservative city government of Frankfurt on the local post-war Social Democratic mode of regulation' (1992: 53). Yet, in 1980s Frankfurt, the neoliberal phantasmagoria were just that. There were still alternatives: in the experienced past of a social democratic city of public collective consumption services and democratic urbanist discourse; and in a possible future in which the right to the city would be extended to the city's immigrant population – a sizeable third of the entire city – that was disenfranchised, and to local communities threatened by deindustrialization and urban policy agendas; in addition, the debate about urban futures was just about to be expanded to include fundamental socio-ecological concerns as green (protest) politics was at an all-time high in response to the building of the Runway West at Frankfurt's international airport. Given these strong counter-tendencies, neoliberalism in the city still seemed like a partisan pipe dream, its policies not yet realized, its opponents not yet wiped off the terrain of political possibility, its process still considered an outside, foreign, intervention.[1]

Figure 33.1 Frankfurt's Mayor Wolfram Bruck, Horstmar Stauber, head of the Fairgrounds Corporation 'Messe Frankfurt', and Jerry Speyer, President of Tishman-Speyer Properties, check out the model of the planned Messeturm highrise building designed by Murphy/Jahn, on March 21, 1988, in Frankfurt/Main. (Reproduced by permission from DPA/Landov – Photo by Kai-Uwe Wärner)

No image captured this sense of alien aggression more than Tommy Lee Jones's American developer rolling into a Newcastle, UK, ballroom in Mike Figgis's 1988 film *Stormy Monday* under the smiling images of Ronald Reagan and Margaret Thatcher. Cosmo's gigantic redevelopment scheme for Newcastle – fought against valiantly on the ground by Sting's jazz musician-entrepreneur Finney, his humble Irish assistant Brendan, played by Sean Bean and his girlfriend Kate (Melanie Griffith) – appeared positively outlandish at the time. Resistance to such corrosive megalomania still marked the possibility of a different narrative of urban everyday life and economy. This story has since been replayed a thousand times as neoliberal capitalism is remaking our cities in its image. While communities of artists and activists continue to fight gentrification, social injustice, environmental degradation brought upon their cities in the neoliberal age, the terrain of their engagement has shifted dramatically. No longer a fantasy, the neoliberal city has become a brutal reality to many around the world. How did we get to this point?

Urban neoliberalism as discussed in this chapter refers to the interaction of processes of neoliberalization and urbanization. Accordingly, this chapter will trace the histories of the intersection of urbanization and neoliberalization. It provides a clear working definition of the operational terms of neoliberalization and neoliberalism as they relate to urban matters. The moments of roll-back, roll-out and roll-with-it neoliberalization will be explained. It will be argued that there are distinctive schools of thought that provide insights on neoliberalism and that can be mobilized for a critical understanding of the process of neoliberalization. The chapter proceeds to discuss the history, geography and ideological origins of urban neoliberalism with a brief glance at the current crisis and the emergence of post-neoliberalism. A concluding section deals with the pervasive materiality of neoliberal urbanization. Throughout, the chapter will assume that the current 'urban age' – often portrayed as an almost natural demographic, morphological and economic force – has, in many ways, been a product of, and has been productive of neoliberalization. Urban neoliberalism is not a mere consequence of larger scale or upper level processes or dynamics but it is itself a workshop of neoliberalization (Keil 2000, 2002). While 'urbanism' and 'neoliberalism' are mostly open-ended ideological formations, urbanization and neoliberalization are material and discursive processes that lead to real (and imagined) constellations through which modern capitalist societies are being reproduced. Roll-back and roll-out neoliberalization through urbanization have led to what Brenner *et al.*, among others, have called 'variegated' forms of neoliberalization (2010). I am adding the notion of 'roll-with-it neoliberalization' here to denote the inevitability of forging today's political strategies inside an immanent logic created by a generation of neoliberalization (Keil 2009). I treat these three aspects as both moments and periods of neoliberalization and as heuristic devices to explain their significance for cities.

At the outset, we need a working definition of neoliberalization and neoliberalism. I follow Sebastian Schipper here, who has recently identified two 'lines of development' along which we can observe neoliberalization: first, this includes the role of the state in facilitating market rule and, second, this entails an expansion of market mechanisms and thinking to extra-economic sectors – in fact, ultimately, 'all social relations' (Schipper 2014: 238). It must be noted, in particular, that the first line of development suggested here marks a clear departure from early representations of (urban) neoliberalism as a retreat of the state. That was an important aspect of early phases of neoliberalization, which Peck and Tickell (2002: 388) have named 'roll-back' neoliberalism, the transition from neoliberal ideas into practice, often accompanied with a destruction of existing forms of social regulation, such as trade unionism, tenant rights, etc. By contrast, the state has more recently been seen as a facilitator, not victim, of neoliberalization. It has played an especially important role in 'roll-out' neoliberalism, defined by Peck and Tickell (ibid.: 389) as a phase characterized by 'new forms of institution-building and governmental intervention' during which 'neoliberalism is increasingly associated with the political foregrounding of new modes of "social" and penal policymaking, concerned specifically with the aggressive reregulation, disciplining, and containment of those marginalized or dispossessed by the neoliberalization of the 1980s'. The second line has become ever more prominent in recent times as we can barely differentiate any more in everyday life between the rule of market logic and other dynamics.

We can broadly differentiate two main modes of explanation of urban neoliberalism: one is the Foucault-inspired critique of urban neoliberalism that focuses on the recalibrated relationships of the citizen/client/taxpayer to the state and the corporate economy, or its 'governmentality'. The idea of 'governmentality' originates from the work of French theorist Michel Foucault. Following Wendy Larner, governmentality refers to the changing roles of political subjects in neoliberalism that allows 'governing at a distance', meaning increased reliance on people seeing 'themselves as individualized and active subjects responsible for enhancing their own well-being' rather than relying upon direct state intervention (or repression) (Larner 2000: 13; see also Magnusson 2011). In the neoliberal city we can then expect a governmentality that incites 'the subjects to conduct themselves after the model of the enterprise and the general norm of competition' (Dardot and Laval 2009: n.p.).

A second mode of explanation derives from the neo-Marxist critique of neoliberal reason as a capitalist project based on and fuelling the neoliberalization of cities and communities, that is more or less a hegemonic ruling-class project to create a new 'ecological dominance' of neoliberal modes of operation over capitalist cities. The notion of 'ecological dominance' is derived from Bob Jessop, who defines it as the capacity of one system to impose itself onto other systems (Jessop 2000) – which is what urban neoliberalism has done over the past generation.

The predominance of neoliberal ideology in all areas of social life goes along with an increased intensity of capital accumulation processes, the near complete commodification and financialization of urban life and space; it includes a reinforcement of exchange value-oriented activities, a general liberalization as well as the strengthening of the coercive power of competition and a reinforcement of shareholder value in the economy. Everything is now competitive. Brand and Sekler (2009) call neoliberalism a theory and intellectual movement as well as an elite strategy to reconfigure the Fordist compromise. It is ultimately a social practice.

Combining both Foucauldian and Marxist approaches, Schipper postulates that 'the manifestation of the neoliberal or entrepreneurial city can be interpreted as a political rationality that is based on a double inscription of economic thinking into urban politics' which combines an external representation of any place as a 'competitive entity in a global space of competition' and an internal implementation of 'market and competitive mentalities' through new management and similar practices (Schipper 2014: 238). The first dimension has historically always been a key element in the emergence of the neoliberal policies that drive cities, their governments, business and civic organizations as well as individuals and consumers alike. Everyone wants to be a winner and the city is the screen and the red carpet at once. That is, of course, largely a zero-sum game. Some will inevitably be losers in the game. Still, even by minimal standards, some municipal governments fail miserably at putting together a plausible set of representations that make them successful actors in the (now mostly international) arena. That may have to do with their historical circumstances (such as deindustrialization, shrinkage, etc.) but it may also be because the responsible politicians, business representatives and civic leaders regress to a tunnelled inward perspective where the strategic goals of 'internalized globalization' and neoliberalization are at odds with the tactical spontaneous combustion of a local elite in crisis. Toronto, under hapless mayor Rob Ford, would be in that category. During Ford's tenure, Toronto's administration made little effort to connect (or compete) with other cities, the mayor's trips to Austin and Chicago notwithstanding. The big themes of environmental modernization, creative economies, cultural excellence, diversity management and the fight against climate change that had characterized Toronto's international stature under Ford's predecessor David Miller, once the director of the influential C-40 alliance of cities, all but disappeared in favour of restrictive fiscal populism and visionary stasis.

The historical origins of urban neoliberalization

The emergence of neoliberalism as a force through which urban processes could be affected and ultimately determined, reaches back to the late 1970s and early 1980s. David Harvey (2005) dates the onset of neoliberalism to the end of the 1970s with the fallout of the crisis of Fordism/Keynesianism, the experiment of neoliberal government in Chile after the putsch against elected president Salvador Allende, the election of the Thatcher and Reagan governments in what turned out to be the 'heartlands' of neoliberalization in the UK and the USA. At a larger scale, urban policy-makers in the UK and in the USA deployed state spatial strategies such as 'urban enterprise zones' – envisioned as import substitution gateways to higher-profit, less regulated regimes of accumulation – to liberate accumulation and markets and to free them from the fetters of the welfare state. Conservative economic dogma, increasingly influenced by neoliberal thought, posited that Keynesian demand-side economics and ubiquitous state intervention had created immobile and inflexible economies that sucked energy out of the market and overburdened the consumer with unnecessary taxes. The alleged outcome was a society hooked on state transfer instead of individual initiative. Neoliberalization, as a centrally hatched plan, often associated with the long-marginalized members of the Mont

Pelerin Society and the Chicago School of economics, focused on the crisis-ridden cities of the late Keynesian period.

Reagan's neoliberal economic policies in the USA and Thatcher's campaigns in the UK worked as disciplining strategies against the urban working class who occupied *factually* (as shown in the uprisings of Brixton and Toxteth in 1981) or *potentially* uncontrollable spaces of violent contestations or just general discontent. Campaigns against collective consumption, considered the hated hallmark of the Fordist–Keynesian city, became a particular target of Tory and Republican political candidates and their think tanks in the 1980s. The crisis of mass housing, whether in the form of large-scale suburbanization or 'inner city' social housing, of mass automobilization after the first oil crisis, and the American model overall can be counted as influential in the emergence of a mode of urban regulation that was built on self-reliance, responsibilization and market provision of basic services propagated by neoliberal economists and politicians (Peck 2015).

In the early 1980s, some characteristics of what we now recognize as neoliberalization in cities appeared in plain sight. The (inner) cities, all but given up after the economically disastrous and riotous 1960s and 1970s, slowly became the object of desire for investors in real estate who stood to benefit from the huge 'rent gap' afforded by their deterioration (Smith 1987). While it had been observed as early as the 1960s in the UK, gentrification came into its own as the signature process of neoliberalization in inner city neighbourhoods of crisis-ridden American cities such as New York and San Francisco. We witnessed then the ubiquitous use of the term 'yuppie' to describe a new and dynamic generation of urban professionals who 'return' to the city in an age of rampant suburbanization. Gentrification worked particularly smoothly in those jurisdictions where deregulation of rental properties and 'revanchism' against poor and racialized populations were rampant. Those carrot and stick-type policies – or, in other words, policies that oscillated between incentives for capital accumulation and the ostensible maintenance of law and order – became central pillars of neoliberalization in cities around the world.

Postfordism – an emerging regime of accumulation based on flexible production processes – and world city formation – the process of creating urban decision-making centres for global capitalism – can be seen as concrete arenas through which neoliberalization proceeded in the 1980s and 1990s (Keil 1998). These processes created new landscapes (Sassen 1994), some of which were urban, some sub- or ex-urban (meaning new and self-propelling urbanizing formations beyond the classical centre–periphery dialectics; Orange County, California is often cited as the prime example of this development, which has also been called 'postsuburban'). Eventually all coalesced into a sprawling constellation of increasingly de-nationalized, often deregulated spaces, characterized by 'horizontal strategies of surveillance, dispersal, and consumption' (Quinby 2011: 139). The demise of the Keynesian–Fordist model in some of the larger capitalist countries of Europe and North America triggered the roll-out of new just-in-time economies of horizontally disintegrated production processes.

The geographical origins (and spread) of urban neoliberalization

The neoliberal push in the Anglo-Saxon core countries against welfare state Keynesianism was perhaps a case of 'early adopters' of what proved to be a pervasive phenomenon in the decades since. The late 1970s also saw the ominous rise to power in China of Deng Xiaoping, who set his country on a course of liberated market capitalism under tight state control. In that country, the emergence of a neoliberal regime of capitalism has been associated strongly with new forms of urban and suburban expansion: between 1978 and 2013, the urban population there grew by 196 per cent (Vanderklippe 2014).

In some parts of the world, the onward march of neoliberalization was also seen in step with urbanization more broadly and the ascendancy of urban policy more specifically. Ananya Roy notes:

> The urban question has not featured prominently in the plans that have guided the many decades of development in postcolonial India. It is the liberalization of the Indian economy, enthusiastically adopted by the Indian state, in the 1990s, that cast attention on India's cities.
>
> *(2011a: 260)*

This elevation of the urban dimension in development during neoliberalization occurred predominantly through 'three socio-spatial technologies to implement the world class city: slum evictions, Special Economic Zones, and peri-urban towns' (ibid.: 261). Importantly, the Indian example highlights two things about urban neoliberalization. First, the neoliberal turn in Indian cities demonstrates the endogenous development of many path-dependent variants of neoliberalisms. Roy (ibid.: 262) speaks, accordingly, of 'homegrown neoliberalism' in this context. The homegrown neoliberalisms of the rapidly sub/urbanizing global South are simultaneously subject to far-reaching 'inter-referencing' through which local politicians across the globe share a toolbox of possible mechanisms for the neoliberalization of their individual city (Roy 2011b). Second, this development signals a major re-arrangement of the 'geographies of theory' – that is, a challenge to the 'canonical tradition where theory is produced in the crucible of a few "great" cities: Chicago, New York, Paris, and Los Angeles – cities inevitably located in EuroAmerica' (Roy 2009: 820). Neoliberalism in a world of inter-referencing cannot any more be viewed as the distribution of certain (western) models across the globe but a multi-headed affair with a wide range of variations. We have, therefore, seen multiple forms of emergent, endogenous and 'experimental' neoliberalization in cities across Eastern Europe (Bodnár 2001; Hirt 2012), throughout parts of Africa (McDonald 2008), China (He and Wu 2009) and Asia more generally (Park *et al.* 2012; Roy and Ong 2011). In Istanbul, for example, the local AKP party has built the model for a particular brand of neoliberalism that works through the 'the combination of shopping malls and mosques' (Harvey 2014). Urban neoliberalization in Latin America has been seen as a fertile ground for the development of new political constellations and citizenship claims between municipal neoliberalism and municipal socialism (Centner 2012; Goldfrank and Schrank 2009).

The ideological origins of urban neoliberalization

The rise of neoliberalism has been depicted as a freak development of fringe thinkers who have gained control of the global public discourse not least due to a set of accidental sub-plots and historical circumstances. As Harvey (2005) noted, the core beliefs of neoliberals have to be taken seriously as they are based on hard-to-refute appellations to 'freedom' both individual and systemic. The tremendously successful career of marginal ideologues in capturing the imaginations of the powerful – and the powerless – through talk of opportunity and order, liberty and low taxes – was pushed not least by right-wing think tanks and institutions such as the American Reason Foundation and the Manhattan Institute. Of the latter, we know, for example, that it was instrumental in 'turning intellect into influence' from the fiscal crisis of the New York local state in the 1970s to the types of public policy demolitions that came into full relief in the wake of 2005's Hurricane Katrina's devastation in New Orleans (Peck 2010: 134–91). The tendency for urban neoliberalization to ride high on 'disaster capitalist' machinations has been pervasive from the transitional Eastern European cities of the 1990s to the post-war urban centres of Iraq after militarization and privatization of space became the ordering principles there (Klein 2007).

The moment of crisis

Hurricane Katrina in August 2005 confirmed the worst fears people had expressed about the consequences of neoliberal urban policies on communities everywhere: the de-coring of social welfare programmes, the intensification of socio-economic differences and the hardening of socio-spatial divisions had led to a weakening of state capacity; in turn, the events triggered by the deadly winds and floods encouraged yet another wave of neoliberal experimentation that made things even worse on the ground (Peck 2010). Not that disaster was alien to the spread of neoliberalism. In fact, Naomi Klein (2007) attributes a central role to what she calls 'disaster capitalism' to the spread of neoliberalism under American hegemony. As early as in the 1980s, Thatcher's reforms in Britain's water sector had left many without affordable safe access to the piped resource. In Ontario, the neoliberal disembowelling of the public sector and compromise of municipal powers by Mike Harris's 'common sense revolutionaries' (Keil 2002) contributed to the province's worst public health crises during an E.coli outbreak in the rural community of Walkerton in 2000 (Ali 2004; Prudham 2007); and to the SARS crisis in Toronto in 2003 when an infectious disease punctured the eroded public health system and killed 44 patients across that global city's suburban expanse (Ali and Keil 2008). But the worst was yet to come for the neoliberal city during the 2008 financial crisis, as much as the meltdown originated in and unfurled its furore over the world's urban landscapes: both suburban expanses littered with foreclosure signs and central city financial economies that saw the failure of some of the erstwhile most important flagship enterprises of the financial industry (and the miraculous salvation of others) and the loss of tens of thousands of jobs in the ostensible growth sectors of the deregulated neoliberal urban economy (Aalbers 2012; Harvey 2012).

It is indeed not accidental that urban neoliberalism thrives and dies with the perennial urban crisis it has unleashed. The (virtuous) cycle of 'crisis-induced restructuring' of the late Fordist city has now been turned into the (vicious) 'restructuring-induced crisis' that has gripped the entrepreneurial city everywhere. While many observers assumed that after the financial crisis of 2008/9 – in which the contradictions of the neoliberal model became apparent, especially in urban contexts – would lead to a weakening of its destructive power, we saw instead an unleashing of 'the power of neoliberal subjectivity and knowledge production that has enabled the local political elites to frame the greatest crisis of capitalism since the 1970s predominantly within a neoliberal rationality' (Schipper 2014: 237).

This persistence of the neoliberal model as the leading philosophy of capitalist praxis can at least partly be credited to the power of the system to internalize its contradictions in new and innovative ways. As noted above, Peck and Tickell first identified two – sometimes simultaneous, sometime consecutive – moments of neoliberalization, roll-back and roll-out neoliberalism (2002: 388–9). In addition to this separation, we have also seen a progression from the erstwhile 'common sense revolutionaries' of the 1990s – a term coined to (self)identify Ontario's radical neoliberal reformer Mike Harris – to a new crop of softer, gentler neoliberals, third-way social democrats and creative economy gurus. Particularly, Richard Florida's 2002 book about the creative class set off a decade of enthusiasm for 'urbanist' programmes of economic development that were urban to the core but often rubbed the 'familiar neoliberal snake-oil' into the dried-out and needy economies of restructuring-ravaged urban areas around the world (Peck 2010: 192–230).

More recently, as urban neoliberalism has meandered on through a variety of crises, two possible scenarios have been considered: roll-with-it neoliberalization and post-neoliberalism. Both have immediate utility in the urban context. 'Roll-with-it' neoliberalization entails:

> the normalization of neoliberal practices and mindsets, the (frequently contested) acceptance of the 'conduct of conduct' of neoliberalism.... Roll-with-it neoliberalization refers straight to 'ecological dominance' as a 'natural' and often unquestioned condition of life under capitalism today.... To 'roll-with' neoliberalization means that political and economic actors have increasingly lost a sense of externality, of alternatives (good or bad) and have mostly accepted the 'governmentality' of the neoliberal formation as the basis for their action.
>
> *(Keil 2009: 232)*

Roll-with-it neoliberalization provides a conduit for understanding the intricate ways in which neoliberalism has now colonized the very political processes that had long opposed its ascent and establishment. The ecological dominance of neoliberalism in the contradictory landscape of the capitalist city has effected a certain defeatism among its critics. Even those who would be structurally opposed and negatively affected by the ravages of the neoliberal onslaught have sometimes succumbed to the pressures and promises of responsibilization, individualization and entrepreneurialism that have characterized the neoliberal creed. In some progressive urbanist circles, the call for urban revitalization and resilience has a less than uneasy rapport with urban neoliberalism's agenda of pacification of unruly and potentially delinquent working-class districts and poor neighbourhoods. In this respect, roll-with-it neoliberalization points to some of the same phenomena that are subject to a postpolitical critique of urban contestations (Swyngedouw 2009; Leitner *et al.* 2007).

Post-neoliberalism (see Brand in this volume) has been seen as a useful framework to denote 'a perspective on social, political and/or economic transformations, on shifting terrains of social struggles and compromises, taking place on different scales, in various contexts and by different actors' (Brand and Sekler 2009: 6). No argument is made here that neoliberalism as a set of ideas and practices is simply going to vanish. The focus of the post-neoliberal proposition is on charting possible ways of thinking differently about ways in which political action (and policy) can shift the overall structural conditions of neoliberalized states and economies. In the urban context, we can think here about local and regional climate change mitigation and adaptation policies that explode the common ecological modernization frameworks that have heretofore been identified with neoliberal policies (in the sustainability and resilience domains) but also in the invention of new forms of collective consumption, housing and urban infrastructure services (Keil 2009). The 'Right to the City' movement has built some momentum around the world for concrete struggles that point towards post-neoliberal conversations and possibilities (Brenner *et al.* 2012); whether they can coalesce into an 'urban revolution' in the 'rebel city' will have to be seen (Harvey 2012).

The materiality of urban neoliberalization

In the meantime, urban neoliberalism is still the most important game in town, whether it rules through classical 'hard' forms of economic liberalization and penal and revanchist state action (as happened in many cities during the last two decades) (Boudreau *et al.* 2009), or in its more 'third-way' form that includes 'softer' modes of neoliberal regulation (Keil 2000).

A major factor in the imbrication of neoliberalization and urbanization has been the intro-duction of new and changing infrastructures. Since the beginning of the new millennium, we have begun to speak about a 'splintering urbanism' of sharply segregated, class-divided, priva-tized and access-controlled infrastructures in cities and suburbs (Graham and Marvin 2001). In fact, the explosion of infrastructures in water, transportation, communications and other urban services has since remade urban landscapes in an unrecognizable fashion. Those landscapes have built out new grids and networks of hard wires, pipes and transmission towers, but also a fundamentally altered set of modes of production and consumption of urban networked infra-structure services. The latter are particularly striking in the internet-based smart phone revolu-tion that has introduced new forms of urban interaction as much as new modes of often privatized and splintered delivery of such services. Often summarized under the heading of 'smart cities', the digital aspect of urbanization has been a tremendous success story in neoliberal urbanism. Not only did it demonstrate a particular techno-economic strategy which laid the groundwork for novel constellations of firms and workers in 'creative economies', it also prompted heretofore unseen techno-social and techno-spatial constellations, often associated with the generation of the so-called 'millennials', whose reliance on tech labour markets and (fast-moving, yet often precarious) turbo-consumerism has fed a deregulated explosion of inner city urbanism, sometimes coupled with processes of displacement and gentrification in former inner city working-class neighbourhoods. The mobilization of real estate capital, mobility innovation (such as the widely unregulated private transportation service Uber, which poses fundamental questions to the delivery and regulation of urban services and their administration (Sadowski and Gregory 2015)) and corporate investment for the production of this new infra-structure-based landscape of urban creativity comes with a governmentality of self-rule, differ-entiation and individual autonomy which is often seen as strongly divergent from the Keynesian infrastructural ideal.

The continuing tendency towards 'splintering urbanism' (Graham and Marvin 2001) makes mobility, water, health and other critical infrastructures more accessible to urban dwellers with resources and power and harder to access for poor and marginalized communities. As we know now, these differentials are not temporary but rather here to stay as social mobility more gener-ally appears to be more difficult and more differentiated in the neoliberal city, just as the policies that harden the divides have become more mobile (McCann and Ward 2011; Watt and Smets 2014). New forms of segregation appear as the poor are driven from the gentrified centres of the neoliberal city and reassemble in the 'in-between' spaces of inner and outer suburbs. Age differentiation ('the millennials') recombines with emergent class formations and novel ethnic constellations in the neoliberal city.

A particular role in the materiality of the neoliberal city plays the further differentiation of imploding and exploding spaces in the metropolitan region (Brenner 2014). Suburbanization was a major part of the urbanization process in the twentieth century overall but it has, arguably, taken on a new role with a global reach during the most recent period of neoliberalized explo-sive urban growth that created landscapes of often gated and enclaved 'freedom' and homeown-ership with a particularly 'vulgar' appearance and social structure (monster homes and conspicuous consumption of space and resources) (Keil 2013; Peck 2015; Knox 2008). Its life-style and resource use has been inscribed as central tenets of American empire (Keil 2007). Focusing on (sub)urban condensations, we can safely say that the entire model of suburbaniza-tion has been on overdrive since market liberalization and financialization have become main-stays of urban development under neoliberal regimes. Globally, the infrastructure–neoliberal–real estate nexus is a chief contributor to the phenomena of 'home-grown neoliberalism' and 'inter-referencing', both terms popularized in critical interventions by Ananya Roy (2011a, 2011b) as neoliberalized developmental states strive towards realizing ambitious projects of 'smart' cities or university compounds that appear as liberated islands of splendour on a 'planet of slums' (Davis 2006).[2]

Conclusion

In the winter of 2015, a former Ontario attorney general, Michael Bryant, urged the government in which he once served to repeal the province's Safe Streets Act, which was introduced by the pioneer neoliberal government of Conservative Mike Harris in the late 1990s and used extensively by police since 2000 to deal with panhandlers, 'squeegee kids' and homeless people. Understood at the time by both its authors and its critics as an aggressive neoliberal intervention into urban affairs, an attempt to clean up the city for better business and to penalize the poor at the same time, it was now time, in the words of Bryant, to 'right a wrong' as it has become apparent that the law served to 'arrest the poor for being poor'. The initiative, supported widely in the expert community of poverty and homelessness advocates and carried by popular appeal during a time when poverty policies were redirected into a less revanchist direction, also serves as a reminder of the maturation of urban policy in an age of roll-with-it neoliberalization. In this period, the terms of reference are thoroughly set by the foundational values of neoliberalism itself. One of the chief arguments put forth by opponents of the law is a fiscal one and speaks to a core governmentality of neoliberalization: accountability and efficiency. Branded as a '"waste" of the justice system's resources', the law was estimated to have 'cost Toronto police almost $1 million in time to hand out $4 million in tickets between 2000 and 2010 – 99 percent of which are never paid because homeless people cannot afford the fines that range between $60 and $500' (Benzie 2014: n.p.). The *Toronto Star* daily newspaper quotes one expert: 'That is a waste of time and a waste of services'! Does this mean that urban neoliberalism is now a closed system of no options for resistance and social change? Of course not, but while, during the early periods of roll-back and roll-out neoliberalization, activists were able to decry the 'fabulations' of the urban revolutionaries as phantasmagoria, the pathways of critical engagement must now – largely – accept the factuality of the disciplining and defining realities of the neoliberal city in order to play in the system. This does not mean there is no alternative to urban neoliberalism but the players in those cities where its governmentality reigns ignore the weight of its ecological dominance at their peril. Solutions to the contradictions of urban neoliberalism will ultimately have to be sought outside its boundaries.

A word of warning at the end: urban neoliberalism is now a fact of life, as neoliberalization has both built on and furthered the hollowing out of urban societies for the sole purpose of capital accumulation and profit maximization; the financialization of everything has, indeed, been most visible at the level of everyday life in cities, the policies of local states have often been most revanchist in the pursuit of gentrified homogeneity and pacified creative city cores. Yet, this generalization of the neoliberal also must give us pause in at least four respects. First, when everything is 'neoliberal', the term loses its bite, its explanatory power. Not everything in the city can be assumed to be or credited to neoliberalization and neoliberalism. Second, we must beware of presupposing the neoliberal condition as a defining characteristic of our age and see everything in its light. We might deceive ourselves and miss out on the continued diversity and variegation of the capitalism that shapes our cities. This leads, third, to the admonition that, while we need robust theoretical frameworks to understand the city and while we can count the debate on urban neoliberalization among its sharpest tools, we must continue to look closely at the real existing urban processes at hand in order to understand the prevailing mechanics of difference in today's urban regions. With that, finally, comes the recognition of struggle and resistance at the core of the neoliberal city. As the immanent contradictions of roll-with-it neo-liberalization mount, and as we see strands of post-neoliberalization emerge in the 'rebel cities' (Harvey 2012) of today, we might be surprised how quickly urban neoliberalism, still solid today, melts into air.

Notes

1 More up-to-date analyses of Frankfurt's neoliberalization will show that it has taken almost a generation for the city's decision-makers and citizens to fully 'internalize' the demands and claims of the neoliberal city (Keil 2011; Schipper 2013).
2 See, for example: http://www.thehindu.com/news/national/telangana/dubai-keen-to-develop-hyderabad-as-smart-city/article6691068.ece; http://www.indiatvnews.com/news/india/state-govt-dreams-up-21st-century-smart-ap-45204.html

References

Aalbers, M.B., ed. 2012. *Subprime Cities: The Political Economy of Mortgage Markets*. Oxford: Wiley-Blackwell.

Ali, S.H. 2004. A Socio-Ecological Autopsy of the E. Coli O157:H7 Outbreak in Walkerton, Ontario, Canada. *Social Science Medicine*, 58.12: 2601.

Ali, S.H., and Keil, R. 2008. *Networked Disease: Emerging Infections in the Global City*. Oxford: Wiley-Blackwell.

Benzie, R. 2014. Michael Bryant Urges Repeal of Law that 'Criminalizes Homelessness', *The Toronto Star*, 15 December. Retrieved from http://www.thestar.com/news/queenspark/2014/12/15/michael_bryant_urges_repeal_of_law_that_criminalizes_homelessness.html

Bodnár, J. 2001. *Fin de Millénaire Budapest: Metamorphoses of Urban Life*. Minneapolis: University of Minnesota Press.

Boudreau, J.A., Keil, R., and Young, D. 2009. *Changing Toronto: Governing Urban Neoliberalism*. Toronto: University of Toronto Press.

Brand, U., and Sekler, N. 2009. Postneoliberalism: Catch-all Word or Valuable Analytical and Political Concept? Aims of a Beginning Debate. *Development Dialogue*, 51.January: 5–13.

Brenner, N. ed. 2014. *Implosions/Explosions: Towards a Study of Planetary Urbanization*. Berlin: Jovis.

Brenner, N., Marcuse, P., and Mayer, M. eds. 2012. *Cities for People, Not for Profit: Critical Urban Theory and the Right to the City*. London and New York: Routledge.

Brenner, N., Peck, J., and Theodore, N. 2010. Variegated Neoliberalization: Geographies, Modalities, Pathways. *Global Networks*, 10.2: 182–222.

Centner, R. 2012. Microcitizenships: Fractious Forms of Urban Belonging after Argentine Neoliberalism. *International Journal of Urban and Regional Research*, 36.2: 336–62.

Dardot, P., and Laval, C. 2009. Vers un Krach du Sujet Néolibéral? *Le Monde*, 3 April.

Davis, M. 2006. *Planet of Slums*. London: Verso.

Florida, R. 2002. *The Rise of the Creative Class: And How It's Transforming Work, Leisure and Everyday Life*. New York: Basic.

Goldfrank, B., and Schrank, A. 2009. Municipal Neoliberalism and Municipal Socialism: Urban Political Economy in Latin America. *International Journal of Urban and Regional Research*, 33.2: 443–62.

Graham, S., and Marvin, S. 2001. *Splintering Urbanism: Networked Infrastructures, Technological Mobilities and the Urban Condition*. London and New York: Routledge.

Harvey, D. 1989. *The Condition of Postmodernity: An Enquiry into the Origins of Cultural Change*. Cambridge, MA: Blackwell.

—. 2005. *A Brief History of Neoliberalism*. Oxford: Oxford University Press.

—. 2012. *Rebel Cities: From the Right to the City to the Urban Revolution*. London: Verso.

—. 2014. The Crisis of Planetary Urbanization, in Gadanho, P. ed. *Uneven Growth: Tactical Urbanisms for Expanding Megacities*. New York: Museum of Modern Art. Retrieved from http://post.at.moma.org/content_items/520-the-crisis-of-planetary-urbanization?utm_content=buffer95f9c&utm_medium=social&utm_source=twitter.com&utm_campaign=buffer

He, S., and Wu, F. 2009. China's Emerging Neoliberal Urbanism: Perspectives from Urban Redevelopment. *Antipode*, 41: 282–304.

Hirt, S.A. 2012. *Iron Curtains: Gates, Suburbs and Privatization of Space in the Post-socialist City*. Oxford: Wiley-Blackwell.

Jessop, B. 2000. The Crisis of the National Spatio-temporal Fix and the Ecological Dominance of Globalizing Capitalism. *International Journal of Urban and Regional Studies*, 24.2: 323–60.

Keil, R. 1998. *Los Angeles: Globalization, Urbanization, and Social Struggles*. Chichester: John Wiley & Sons.

—. 2000. Third Way Urbanism: Opportunity or Dead End? *Alternatives*, 25.2.

—. 2002. 'Common Sense' Neoliberalism: Progressive Conservative Urbanism in Toronto, Canada. *Antipode*, 34.3: 578–601.

—. 2007. Empire and the Global City: Perspectives of Urbanism after 9/11. *Studies in Political Economy*, 79: 167–92.

—. 2009. The Urban Politics of Roll-With-It Neoliberalization. *City: Analysis of Urban Trends*, 13.2–3: 231–45.

—. 2011. The Global City Comes Home: Internalized Globalization in Frankfurt Rhine-Main. *Urban Studies*, 48.12: 2495–518.

—. ed. 2013. *Suburban Constellations: Governance, Land and Infrastructure in the 21st Century*. Berlin: Jovis.

Keil, R., and Lieser. P. 1992. Frankfurt: Global city – local politics. *Comparative Urban and Community Research, An Annual Review*, 4: 39–69.

Klein, N. 2007. *Shock Doctrine: The Rise of Disaster Capitalism*. New York: Metropolitan.

Knox, P.L. 2008. *Metroburbia, USA*. New Brunswick, NJ: Rutgers University Press.

Larner, W. 2000. Neo-liberalism: Policy, Ideology, Governmentality. *Studies in Political Economy*, 63.Autumn: 1–25.

Leitner, H., Peck, J., and Sheppard, E. eds. 2007. *Contesting Neoliberalism: Urban Frontiers*. New York: Guilford Press.

Magnusson, W. 2011. *Politics of Urbanism: Seeing Like a City*. London: Routledge.

McCann, E., and Ward, K. eds. 2011. *Mobile Urbanism: Cities and Policymaking in the Global Age*. Minneapolis: University of Minnesota Press.

McDonald, D.A. 2008. *World City Syndrome: Neoliberalism and Inequality in Cape Town*. New York: Routledge.

Park, B.-G., Hill, R.C., and Saito, A. eds. 2012. *Locating Neoliberalism in East Asia: Neoliberalizing Spaces in Developmental States*. Oxford: Wiley-Blackwell.

Peck, J. 2010. *Constructions of Neoliberal Reason*. Oxford: Oxford University Press.

—. 2015. Neoliberal Suburbanism: Frontier Space, in Hamel, P., and Keil, R. eds. *Suburban Governance: A Global View*. Toronto: University of Toronto Press.

Peck, J., and Tickell, A. 2002. Neoliberalizing Space, in Brenner, N., and Theodore, N., eds. *Spaces of Neoliberalism: Urban Restructuring in Western Europe and North America*. Oxford and Boston: Blackwell: 33–57.

Prudham, S. 2007. Poisoning the Well: Neoliberalism and the Contamination of Municipal Water in Walkerton, Ontario, in Heynen, N., McCarthy, J., Prudham, S., and Robbins, P., eds. *Neoliberal Environments: False Promises and Unnatural Consequences*. London and New York: Routledge: 163–76.

Quinby, R. 2011. *Time and the Suburbs: The Politics of Built Environments and the Future of Dissent*. Winnipeg: Arbeiter Ring.

Roy, A. 2009. The 21st-Century Metropolis: New Geographies of Theory. *Regional Studies*, 43.6: 819–30.

—. 2011a. The Blockade of the World-Class City: Dialectical Images of Indian Urbanism, in Roy, A., and Ong, A. eds. *Worlding Cities: Asian Experiments and the Art of Being Global*. Oxford: Wiley-Blackwell: 259–78.

—. 2011b. Urbanisms, Worlding Practices and the Theory of Planning, *Planning Theory*, 10.1: 6–15.

Roy, A., and Ong, A. eds. 2011. *Worlding Cities: Asian Experiments and the Art of Being Global*. Oxford: Wiley-Blackwell.

Sadowski, J., and Gregory, K. 2015. Is Uber's Ultimate Goal the Privatisation of City Governance? *The Guardian*, 15 September. Retrieved from http://www.theguardian.com/technology/2015/sep/15/is-ubers-ultimate-goal-the-privatisation-of-city-governance

Sassen, S. 1994. *Cities in a World Economy*. Thousand Oaks, CA: Pine Forge Press.

Schipper, S. 2013. *Genealogie und Gegenwart der 'Unternehmerischen Stadt': Neoliberales Regieren in Frankfurt am Main*. Münster: Westfälisches Dampfboot.

—. 2014. The Financial Crisis and the Hegemony of Urban Neoliberalism: Lessons from Frankfurt am Main, *International Journal of Urban and Regional Research*, 38.1: 236–55.

Smith, N. 1987. Gentrification and the Rent Gap. *Annals of the Association of American Geographers*, 77.3: 462–65.

Swyngedouw, E. 2009. The Antinomies of the Postpolitical City: In Search of a Democratic Politics of Environmental Production. *International Journal of Urban and Regional Research*, 33.3: 601–20.

Vanderklippe, N. 2014. The Other Chinese Revolution: Meet the People Who Took Deng's Economic Great Leap Forward. *The Globe and Mail*, 12 December. Retrieved from http://www.theglobeandmail.com/news/world/dengs-children-success-stories-from-china-reflect-on-the-spiritual-cost-of-doing-business/article22067565/

Watt, P., and Smets, P. eds. 2014. *Mobilities and Neighbourhood Belonging in Cities and Suburbs*. London: Palgrave Macmillan.

34

NEOLIBERALISM AND RURAL CHANGE

Land and capital concentration, and the precariousness of labour

Cristóbal Kay

This chapter analyses the key features of neoliberalism as related to rural change. During the 1970s the statist development paradigm followed by most developing countries came increasingly under fire from neoliberal thinkers. The statist development strategy prioritized industrialization, often neglecting the development of agriculture and the rural areas. The debt crisis of the 1980s, which affected several developing countries, provided the opportunity for multilateral institutions like the World Bank to push for the adoption of 'structural adjustment programmes' (SAPs) as a condition for receiving loans and development aid. The SAPs contained key elements of the neoliberal policy proposals which aimed to reduce the role of the state in the economy and give free rein to market forces by removing protectionist measures and opening the economy to the competitive forces of the world market. These neoliberal policies, referred to in the late 1980s as the 'Washington Consensus', morphed, a decade later, into the 'post-Washington Consensus' as social policies were added to the neoliberal policy package so as to ameliorate the devastating consequences of the initial neoliberal shock which had seen a steep rise in poverty. Neoliberalism profoundly restructured the agricultural sector and rural spaces. The analysis starts by discussing the key propositions of the neoliberal paradigm with reference to rural development. The main section provides a relatively detailed examination of the major impacts of neoliberalism on rural development. It is followed by a discussion of some rural counter-movements contesting neoliberalism. The chapter ends with some conclusions.

The neoliberal paradigm of rural development

The debt crisis and the harsher world economic climate of the 1980s led to the spread of neoliberal ideas and policies. Powerful institutions such as the International Monetary Fund (IMF) and the World Bank spread neoliberal ideas to all four corners of the world. While indebted countries had little choice but to swallow these prescriptions in order to obtain the loans from international financial institutions, others which had the ability to resist these pressures nonetheless often willingly adopted these policies.

A key pillar of the neoliberal economic paradigm is to let markets rule, meaning that they should be 'free' from political interference or manipulation by powerful economic groups. Hence government policy should be directed towards this aim as neoliberals are against sectorial policies which either favour or discriminate against a particular economic sector such as agriculture. They believe in developing a stable, uniform, general macroeconomic framework in which the same rules apply to everybody. In general, neoliberals are against state intervention in the economy as this will inevitably distort prices, thereby leading to a less optimal allocation of resources with a negative impact on efficiency and growth. Free market prices should rule and governments should only intervene to secure the free operation of the market. Indeed, with the spread of neoliberalism worldwide and the opening up of economies domestic prices should mirror international prices.

'Urban bias' and the 'plundering of agriculture'

While the neoliberal paradigm does not advocate any specific sectorial policies it does, however, fiercely criticize all those rural development paradigms which proposed discriminatory policies against the agricultural sector. In particular, neoliberals singled out the structuralist and similar inward-directed development paradigms for advocating an import-substitution-industrialization (ISI) development strategy, accusing them of 'urban bias'. The protectionist policy in favour of domestic industry created a series of distortions in the economy, thereby leading to a misallocation of resources and limiting the country's growth rate. This 'bias against agriculture' or 'plundering of agriculture' takes place through a variety of mechanisms such as turning the domestic terms of trade between the various economic sectors against agriculture and in favour of industry, allocating government resources in favour of industry and the urban sector, and so on (Schiff and Valdés 1992). This leads to a 'low rate of return' in agriculture and hence acts as a deterrent to investment, dampening agricultural output. The opposite happens in industry, where favourable government policies lead to overinvestment in industry, which is wasteful of resources. The low rate of return thesis argues that agriculture's stagnation or its inability to achieve its full potential growth rate is due to government discriminatory domestic price and foreign exchange policy against agriculture which thereby reduces farmers' profitability. Capital will thus not move into agriculture and might even move out of it into more profitable sectors with the consequent negative impact on agricultural investment and growth (Bautista and Valdés 1993). For Lipton (1977) this is just one aspect of his more general 'urban bias' thesis, which, in his view, explains 'why poor people stay poor'.

Even when it can be established that there was urban bias in government policy in a certain period, it is necessary to prove that this bias is the main cause of the unsatisfactory performance of the agricultural sector. In my view if there was any bias against the rural sector it mainly affected the peasantry and rural labourers as capitalist farmers and landlords were partly or fully compensated for any discriminatory price and foreign exchange policy by the generous provision of state subsidies to credit, fertilizers, machinery imports, and technical assistance of which they were the main, if not the sole, beneficiaries. Furthermore, landlords paid hardly any land tax and they were also the beneficiaries of the low bargaining power of rural wage labourers as governments made it generally difficult for them to organize and left them largely unprotected against the abuses of employers. I would argue that the poor performance or underachievement of agriculture was partly due to the unequal land distribution, which allowed landlords to exploit their power by extracting high rents from their tenants, paying low wages to their workers and capturing various subsidies and benefits from the state. Landlords thus did not experience major pressures to improve productivity as the existing state of affairs afforded them a good living, influence and power. However, peasants had too little land and insufficient resources to invest and prosper in agriculture due to the various mechanisms of exploitation and discrimination which they faced.

In short, while price and foreign exchange policies pursued during the protectionist ISI period might have had a negative impact on agriculture, it is largely the peasant sector which carried the burden of these discriminatory policies. Thus, instead of using obfuscating phrases like 'bias against agriculture' or 'urban bias' as neoliberals and neopopulists tend to do, it is more elucidatory to refer to 'landlord bias', 'corporate farming bias' or 'bias against peasant farming' (Kay 2009).

Impact of neoliberalism on rural development

Neoliberals pursue macroeconomic stabilization, fiscal discipline, trade liberalization, financial liberalization, privatization, deregulation, labour market liberalization and secure property rights, among other policies. I will now give a brief overview of some of these policies and their impact on rural development on the understanding that the changes described below cannot always be exclusively attributed to neoliberalism. Some of these changes might have happened anyway sooner or later but neoliberalism certainly accelerated some of them. Its main impact was the reversal of some earlier changes, like land reforms, labour rights and supportive measures for peasant farming. Full liberalization of the land, labour and capital markets has not been achieved, if indeed it can ever be achieved. Nor has foreign trade been completely liberalized. In my discussion I refer mainly to the developing countries as they were the main target of the neoliberal reforms. Powerful developed countries were largely able to retain their protectionist agricultural policies while preaching the pro-free-market rhetoric to the rest of the world (Oya 2005). Far from disappearing, state intervention has merely changed in character to a 'new interventionism' of a neoliberal kind, although in some countries it has downsized.

The neoliberal shift to non-traditional agricultural exports (NTAE)

One of the central tenets of neoliberalism is the liberalization of all markets, including international trade. Developing countries are seen as having a comparative advantage in the production and export of primary commodities. Thus they should specialize in the exploitation of natural resources such as minerals, agriculture and forestry. As this would be the most efficient way of utilizing their resources it would allow them to achieve higher rates of growth than hitherto. In this export-driven growth process they would have a strong incentive to improve their efficiency so as to remain competitive in international markets.

With the implementation of neoliberal SAPs a series of policies were introduced to stimulate agricultural exports. Farmers began to shift their output to the now profitable export market and, over time, to change their production patterns. On the one hand, with the liberalization of foreign trade imports of certain foods rose as they were cheaper than domestically produced foods. Hence farmers reduced or stopped cultivating those crops which had become less profitable or even unprofitable due to foreign competition. On the other hand, some crops and, in particular, the so-called 'non-traditional commodities' became more profitable. They were called 'non-traditional' because they were mostly new agricultural export products derived from horticulture, floriculture, fruit growing, aquaculture (inland fisheries) and new crops like soybeans, which gradually contributed a larger proportion to exports as compared to the traditional agricultural exports such as coffee, tea, sugar, bananas, and cocoa. Thus farmers shifted their land use towards cultivating these more profitable agricultural commodities (Borras *et al.* 2012a: 853).

The impact of the neoliberal-driven agro-export growth on the peasantry, according to Carter *et al.* (1996: 37–8), 'depends on at least three factors: whether small-scale units participate directly in producing the export crop and enjoy the higher incomes generated from it (which we call the 'small farm adoption effect'); second, whether the export crop induces a pattern of structural change that systematically improves or worsens the access of the rural poor to land (the 'land-access effect'); and third, whether agricultural exports absorb more or less of the labour of landless and part-time farming households (the 'labour-absorption effect')'. Most agro-exports, like soybeans, favour large farms, advance land concentration and encroach on more labour-intensive crops with negative employment effects. This leads to 'a highly exclusionary growth trajectory that leaves peasants out as both producers and workers' (ibid.: 58) as the 'labour-absorption effect' and the 'land-access effect' turn against peasants. But in some instances, where the new export crop is vegetables, this could favour smallholders (the 'small farm adoption effect') because of its labour intensity (the 'labour-absorption effect') and other factors. As smallholders expanded production and reaped the benefits of their new export earnings they were able to become more competitive and expand their land base or at least hold on to it ('land-access effect'). Thus all three factors operated in favour of smallholders in this particular case thereby leading to an inclusionary growth process. Intermediary situations can also arise.

In brief, while in some particular instances peasant farmers have benefited from the agro-export boom, neoliberal policies have generally strengthened the development of commercial capitalist farmers. Capitalist farmers have reaped the benefits of this thriving NTAE business, having the ability and resources to adjust relatively quickly to neoliberal trade and macroeconomic policy reforms. For peasant farmers, the export market is often too risky and the required investments too large and costly. Nevertheless, through contract farming with agro-industrial businesses, some smallholders are engaged in production for export. But most of the benefits of these contract farming arrangements accrue to agribusiness due to its greater negotiating power.

Concentration of land, natural resources and capital

Neoliberal land policies reversed state-led land reforms where these had been implemented and instead proposed market-led land reforms, if any at all. However, the few market-led land reforms that were attempted generally failed to prosper (Borras *et al.* 2008). More effective were the neoliberal efforts at privatization, decollectivization, land registration and land titling. The main purpose of neoliberal policy is to create a more flexible and active land market. The guiding principle was that land should be privately farmed. Collective or state farming were seen as less efficient forms of farming because of the lack of incentives, bureaucratization, corruption, and so on. With the development of a competitive market, those private farmers who did not invest and modernize their farms would not survive and would be forced to sell their land to more efficient farmers. Thus the free workings of the market forces would attract other investors, even foreign investors, who, by introducing modern technologies and better management and work practices, would increase resource use efficiency and lead to higher rates of agricultural growth (Deininger 2003).

For this purpose legislation was introduced in some countries to facilitate the individualization of property rights of members of indigenous communities so that those who wished to rent or sell their individual plots of land could do so. In those countries which had implemented agrarian reforms and which had promoted the formation of cooperatives, collectives or state farms, the neoliberal reforms in some cases partially reversed the agrarian reforms, returning some of the expropriated land to the former owners or selling it. Indigenous organizations sometimes managed to mobilize in defence of communal property rights, gaining wider national and international support, leading to changes in legislation which protected their communal land rights.

A significant proportion of farms lacked clear and secure property titles over the land in developing countries. This was mainly the case in smallholder areas, but some larger farms also had dubious property titles. The World Bank (2001) launched a major initiative in the 1970s and 1980s to regularize and register land titles, particularly for smallholders. Besides the World Bank, several international donors, such as USAID, provided funding for this land registration process. Many farms either had no property title at all, or there were multiple claims over the same piece of land, which sometimes led to disputes and violent conflicts. In general, these land registration processes faced greater problems than originally envisaged, making for delays and often remaining incomplete. The process sometimes opened new conflicts and allowed some large landlords to gain illegal property titles through corruption.

Some aspects of the neoliberal land titling projects had a progressive element as they attempted to give equal property rights to women by means of joint titling arrangements to the household couple. Implementing this equity agenda was particularly difficult in indigenous areas as (male) leaders gave priority to defending their customary communal practices over women's individual rights (Deere and León 2001). Nor was it easy to enforce in non-indigenous areas as men were aware that joint titling might empower women and hence did not always welcome such arrangements (Razavi 2003).

Overall, land titling has had a mixed outcome. In some instances it allowed peasant farmers to gain legal titles to their land while in other cases it led to 'modernizing insecurity' and further conflicts, if not dispossession of peasant lands by more powerful capitalist forces.

Land grabbing

Since the beginning of the new millennium increasing concern has been expressed about large-scale land acquisitions or deals which are often referred to as 'land grabbing' (Borras and Franco 2012). The new neoliberal global context provoked an enormous expansion of financial capital and opened up new opportunities for investment worldwide. Land and the exploitation of natural resources in general became increasingly attractive for global capital. Various factors account for the rising global interest in farmland such as the new demand for food and raw materials by the rapidly growing (at the time) BRIC countries (Brazil, Russia, India and China), the Gulf states and other middle-income countries; the energy crisis which, at the time, led to very high fuel prices thereby stimulating investment in land for biofuels or agrofuels; and climate mitigation policies which encourage reforestation and investment in national reserves or parks, dubbed by some as 'green grabbing' because of their supposedly environmental objectives (Fairhead *et al.* 2012).

Global investment in land received a major boost as a consequence of the 2007–8 food crisis which led to huge increases in food prices which many analysts argued would remain relatively high in the future. This whetted the appetite of global finance capital, which designed special financial instruments for investments in land, attracting pension funds, sovereign funds and other funds from countries with surplus capital looking for a better return on their capital. But the food crisis also raised concerns about food security in many countries (Akram-Lodhi 2012). China, South Korea and the Gulf states, among others, have signed contracts with governments, mainly in Africa and Asia and to a lesser extent in Latin America, to buy or lease long term tens and hundreds of thousands hectares of land mainly for the cultivation of food which is then exported to the investing country (Oya 2013). Although campaigners against land grabbing may have hyped up the extent of the actual rush for land (Edelman *et al.* 2013; Kaag and Zoomers 2014), there has been an unprecedented infusion of foreign capital, and in some instances also domestic capital, into the rural sector, leading to the 'financialization' of agriculture and nature in several developing countries (Visser *et al.* 2015).

The issue of land grabbing and its associated (virtual) water grabbing has generated a lively debate and produced a growing literature (Borras *et al.* 2011). Initially, this focused on some African and a few Asian countries, but further research and a wider characterization of the meaning of land grabbing have now revealed it to be more common than at first assumed in Latin America; to the surprise of some researchers, it also affects some East European countries (Franco and Borras 2013). Those authors who favour large-scale land acquisitions or investments argue that such arrangements provide much needed investment resources for modernizing agriculture, incorporate new land and more profitable crops, provide improved technologies and better farm management practices, and achieve economies of scale, thereby increasing efficiency, production and profitability. It is also claimed that land grabbing provides new employment and income opportunities for rural workers. Furthermore, it affords a source of revenue for the government (Deininger and Byerlee 2011).

Critics of land grabbing argue that such land deals often displace local people as lands, which governments claim are vacant and belonging to the state, have, in fact, been in use by people seeking a livelihood for decades or even generations. Thus instances of evictions and violent clashes have occurred. These deals are also criticized for endangering food security as well as food sovereignty as local food cultivators are displaced, the food produced by the new investor exported to the investing country or elsewhere, or crops are grown for non-food purposes such as agrofuels (biofuels) or animal feeds, according to whichever is more profitable. This is the case with so-called 'flex crops': sugar cane can be used for making sugar, alcohol or ethanol for biofuel; soybeans can be used as animal feed, food or for making biodiesel; palm oil for food, biodiesel and other industrial uses; and maize or corn for food, feed or ethanol; that is, the 'food-feed-fuel complex' (Borras *et al.* 2012a). It is not uncommon for the promised employment and income gains not to materialize, especially if the crop is highly mechanized as is often the case with soybeans. Last, but not least, land grabbing often leads to monocropping and the use of genetically modified seeds (GMS), as well as industrial farming technologies based on petrochemicals which can have deleterious effects on the environment (White *et al.* 2013). This is also the case with the large-scale industrial production of agrofuel, which can lead to soil degradation and water pollution (Borras *et al.* 2011; Dietz *et al.* 2015).

Land grabbing in Latin America presents some peculiarities which differentiate it from other regions of the South, with the possible exception of southern Africa. A much larger proportion of large-scale land transactions in Latin America take place on private land as compared to public state-owned land and are often driven by regional 'translatino' capital sometimes allied to capital from outside Latin America (Borras *et al.* 2012b). Paraguay is an extreme case as about a quarter of farms over 1,000 hectares are largely owned by Brazilian and Argentinian capital, and over two-thirds of land cultivated with soybeans in Paraguay, which is the country's principal crop, is in their hands (Galeano 2012).

These large-scale land investments have spatial implications. Some land grabbing has occurred in colonization and frontier regions where indigenous peoples often live and property rights are ambiguous. Such external encroachment has led to conflict as the indigenous people are driven further into marginal areas. Owing to the conflictual nature of some land grabbing, a variety of civil society organizations, governments and international organizations have tried to regulate land grabbing by drafting codes of conduct (Wolford *et al.* 2013; Margulis *et al.* 2014). A few institutions have attempted to go further and propose an alternative investment strategy for rural development which is centred on reclaiming public investment in agriculture by developing public–peasant investment synergies (Kay 2014).

In sum, land grabbing has been facilitated by the neoliberal transformation. It is a process which simultaneously widens and deepens industrialized capitalist agriculture on a global scale.

While it may have enhanced agricultural production and productivity, it has allowed capital to gain increasing control over land as well as water and other natural resources, often at the expense of peasants and rural communities and also of the environment. This empowerment of capital through increased control over nature and space has brought with it greater influence and dominance over social and political affairs nationally as well as internationally.

Labour transformed

The neoliberal turn and the increasing control of agribusiness over agriculture have furthered a process of socio-economic differentiation among the peasantry and brought about a structural shift in the composition of the rural labour force. Generalizing, only a small proportion of peasant farmers could grasp the new opportunities afforded by the new neoliberal context and capitalize their farms and prosper. These are the 'viable' peasant farmers in the neoliberal jargon. Other less fortunate peasant farmers became 'semi-proletarians' as their principal source of income came from the sale of their labour power instead of from productive activities on their household plot of land. Finally, a significant proportion of peasant farmers became fully proletarianized, losing all access to land and having to search for wage work in rural or urban areas in the country or abroad. These were the losers or victims of the neoliberal turn, the 'non-viable' smallholders in the neoliberal jargon, as they were unable to hold on to their land with the new competitive market forces and the withdrawal of state support measures.

Thus a growing proportion of the peasantry has come to rely to varying degrees on wage income to make a living. This shift to wage labour has gone hand in hand with the growth of temporary or seasonal wage labour. In many countries the employment of permanent wage labour in the countryside has declined, even in absolute terms, while in most countries temporary wage labour has increased. The growth of temporary wage labour is particularly evident in those countries which have taken advantage of the dynamic export market for soy, fruit, vegetables, flowers and forestry products. These seasonal wage workers face difficult working conditions, being largely employed by agribusiness. They are often paid on a piece-rate basis; usually have no employment protection; and often their entitlements to social security benefits are not respected, if they exist at all. This flexibilization and casualization of labour has extended employers' control over labour by reducing workers' rights and increased their subordinate and precarious circumstances (Bryceson 2000).

This expansion of the temporary labour force has also been accompanied by a marked gender division as there has been a feminization of agriculture (Deere 2005). Agro-industries largely employ female labour since women are held to be more readily available for seasonal work, to be more careful workers, to have lower wage expectations, and to be less organized than men. The scarcer permanent employment opportunities, however, tend to be the preserve of men. For many young women these jobs represent an opportunity to earn an independent income and to reduce patriarchal control over their lives, even though these jobs are seasonal and low paid. However, this greater participation of rural women in the wage labour market has often led to conflicts in the household and violence against women as well as increasing women's work burden.

The neoliberal transformations also have geographical implications regarding labour and the rural–urban divide. A 'new rurality' is emerging as a consequence of the process of 'deagrarianization' (Kay 2008). Rural households become 'multifunctional' by increasingly engaging in diverse economic activities, sometimes referred to as 'pluriactivity', so as to make a living. In pursuit of a livelihood an increasing proportion of their income is derived from on-farm non-agricultural activities such a rural tourism, home processing of agricultural products or set-ting up a small shop, but, more particularly, from off-farm work in rural or urban areas such as in construction, domestic services and other wage work ('multi-local livelihoods'). Remittances from migrant family labour, either from within the country or abroad, are also becoming a major source of income for some households. An increasing proportion of temporary workers come from urban areas, being recruited by labour contractors. Workers straddle with greater fluidity than in the past different spaces owing to better communications and information, cheaper transport costs and improved education, among other factors. This indicates both the ruralization of urban areas, as a result of high rates of rural–urban migration, as well as the urban-ization of rural areas with the mushrooming of rural shanty-towns, thereby blurring the urban–rural divide (Chase 2002). Furthermore, due to enhanced mobility rural residents have increasingly to compete with urban labourers for agricultural work, and vice-versa, leading, in some instances, to less segmented labour markets and to more uniform wage levels. This diver-sification of activities and income is for the majority of the peasantry a strategy for survival but for some better-endowed peasants it has become a strategy for accumulation, thereby fostering processes of social and economic differentiation (Kay 2008).

In conclusion, neoliberal policies have transformed agriculture in developing countries and beyond and have given rise to 'classes of labour', in Bernstein's (2010) terminology. They have not resolved the problems of rural poverty, exclusion and landlessness. It was only in the 'post-dogmatic' or 'pragmatic' post-Washington Consensus phase of neoliberalism, with the implementation of social policies directed at poor households, that poverty levels began to fall. But the precarious conditions of labour remain.

The food crisis of 2007–8 and beyond

During 2007 and 2008 food prices increased sharply with disastrous consequences for poor people throughout the world, leading to a severe rise in hunger and poverty. Prices of key sta-ples like wheat, rice and maize doubled. Food-importing countries witnessed huge increases in the cost of food imports. The impact of this spike in prices was uneven as poor people and net food-importing countries were particularly negatively affected. Poor people spend a much higher percentage of their income on food as compared to richer people and poorer countries are much more affected by such price hikes, given that a much larger proportion of their population are poor compared to richer countries. Unsurprisingly, this spike in food prices led to food protests and riots in several countries (Bush 2010). Thus the global food crisis is, at root, a crisis of equality between and within countries leading to a new geopolitics of food (Sommerville *et al.* 2014).

There has been much debate about the reasons for this enormous rise in food prices and their higher volatility. The most common early explanation was that world food supplies had not kept up with the rising world demand for food. Some authors began to question this demand and supply narrative and argued that it could not fully explain the degree of the crisis (Busch 2010; Ghosh 2010). In their view the liberalization of financial markets contributed significantly to the food crisis. It is difficult to ascertain the precise impact of this financial dimension owing to its complexity, abstract character and opacity. But it is this financial dimen-sion that creates a more direct link between neoliberalism and the food crisis. Whereas previ-ously various financial instruments like agricultural derivatives and future contracts had been regulated, limiting financial speculation, under neoliberalism financial markets and agricultural commodity markets were deregulated. With the massive expansion of finance in recent decades investors began to look for more profitable and stable returns and created a variety of agricultural commodity index funds. This resulted in the financialization of food and the further commodification of agriculture, thereby increasingly exposing agricultural commodities to the vagaries of global financial markets and to speculative activities (Clapp 2012).

The world food crisis has brought about a paradoxical 'neoliberal geopolitics' as countries have become concerned about their food security and their own domestic political stability in the face of food protests and riots. Some countries introduced measures to protect their food supplies by limiting or banning certain food exports. Similarly, some capital-rich countries with relatively scarce farmland have tried to ensure their food supplies by undertaking large-scale land investments in relatively farmland rich countries – that is, engaging in land grabbing. In some countries this has raised concerns about national sovereignty and led to accusations of neocolonialism. In the last decades the dominant northern agro-food powers have seen the emergence of some southern countries that have significantly increased their share of world agricultural production and trade. This heralds a shift towards a polycentric global agro-food system but one under the control of corporate capital North and South (Margulis 2014).

Finally, who benefits from food price increases? Some large food exporting countries like the USA and Brazil have gained. But do farmers benefit? The power of TNCs (agropower) on global agricultural markets and over the agricultural commodity value chain enables them to capture most of the benefits of rising food prices. The global subsistence crisis reveals a crisis in the world food system with the rise of agribusiness and the processes of concentration and financialization driving many vulnerable smallholders off the land and out of farming.

Contestations of the neoliberal transformations

The neoliberal agenda and the transformations it has brought about in the rural world have not gone uncontested. There are a myriad of everyday struggles of peasants and rural workers for a fairer society which generally go unreported and only reach a wider audience when major violent clashes occur. To what extent neoliberalism has provoked an intensification of conflicts and violence in the countryside I am unable to judge. But it has provoked a new social countermovement which explicitly challenges neoliberalism – *La Vía Campesina* (or the Peasant Way or Peasant Road). Neoliberalism was perceived as a strategic threat to the 'lives and livelihoods by many landless and land-poor peasants, wage labourers and small farmers in southern and northern countries' (Borras 2004: 3). It was founded in 1993 and has become the largest and most active global peasant movement, bringing together rural organizations from the North and the South. Vía Campesina is opposed to corporate industrialized agriculture and its increasing control over natural resources and technology. Instead it promotes peasant and family farming, sustainable and agro-ecological farming, local or 'nested' markets, co-operation and solidarity and human rights for the people of the land (Desmarais 2007; McMichael 2008; Martínez-Torres and Rosset 2010).

Vía Campesina is best known for proposing 'food sovereignty' as distinct from food security. By food sovereignty it means:

> that food be produced through diversified, farmer-based production systems… [It] is the right of peoples to define their own agriculture and food policies, to protect and regulate domestic agricultural production and trade in order to achieve sustainable development objectives.… [It] promotes the formulation of trade policies and practices that serve the rights of peoples to safe, healthy and ecologically sustainable production.
>
> *(Quoted in McMichael 2009: 294)*

The food sovereignty proposal of Vía Campesina has generated much debate as discussed by Jansen (2015).

In sum, while there are many other rural social movements, I have focused on Vía Campesina due to its strong anti-neoliberal stance and international reach. By asking the question 'What is to be done?' it has contributed some proposals for addressing the neoliberal global subsistence crisis (Akram-Lodhi 2013). It has gained an increasing influence in national and international debates on rural issues, but the extent to which it has been able to shape rural development policies is another matter.

Conclusions

Neoliberalism marks a watershed in history as it is a global transformative project. Under the cloak of free markets, emerging neoliberal capitalist interests sought to achieve changes in agricultural policies and markets which would enhance their economic, social and political power. The neoliberal transformation of land, capital, labour, financial, foreign trade and other markets has created new and enhanced existing processes of concentration and unequal development in rural areas. The process of commodification of nature has reached new corners of the world leading to what some authors refer to as the 'new extractivism' (Veltmeyer and Petras 2014). Capitalist relations of production have spread further through processes of dispossession and proletarianization of the peasantry as well as being intensified by new production processes and technologies.

Contrary to the neoliberal free market agenda of 'getting prices right' and that 'markets should rule', historical experience shows that only through state intervention are the required structural transformations achieved (Byres 2003). In agriculture this may include land reform, support for peasant farming, major investments in irrigation and other rural infrastructure, the widespread dissemination of new sustainable technologies, regulation of markets, and the adoption of environmental and social measures (Chang 2012). It will also require the creation of a fairer international trade and financial system. In brief, a major historical lesson from successful development experiences is that only a developmentalist state is able to set a country on a relatively equitable and sustainable development path by creating the conditions for the achievement of synergies between agriculture and industry and between the rural and urban sectors (Kay 2009).

Finally, indigenous and peasant movements have been in the forefront, challenging market neoliberalism. Some countries are seeking to create a post-neoliberal development strategy which comes closer to satisfying the aspirations of the majority of the population. It remains to be seen if such a post-neoliberal path is able to consolidate itself within the current neoliberal world order and whether it can, indeed, reach the promised goals in a sustainable manner.

References

Akram-Lodhi, A.H. 2012. Contextualising Land Grabbing: Contemporary Land Deals, the Global Subsistence Crisis and the World Food System. *Canadian Journal of Development Studies*, 33.2: 119–42.
—. 2013. *Hungry for Change: Farmers, Food Justice and the Agrarian Question*. Halifax: Fernwood.
Bautista, R.M., and Valdés, A. eds, 1993. *The Bias Against Agriculture: Trade and Macroeconomic Policies in Developing Countries*. San Francisco: International Center for Economic Growth, University of California and IFPRI.
Bernstein, H. 2010. *Class Dynamics of Agrarian Change*. Halifax: Fernwood.
Borras Jr, S.M. 2004. La Vía Campesina: An Evolving Transnational Social Movement. *TNI Briefing Series, No. 2004/6*. Amsterdam: Transnational Institute.

Borras Jr, S.M., and Franco, J.C. 2012. Global Land Grabbing and Trajectories of Agrarian Change. *Journal of Agrarian Change*, 12.1: 34–59.

Borras Jr, S.M., Franco, J.C., Gómez, S., Kay, C., and Spoor, M. 2012a. Land Grabbing in Latin America and the Caribbean. *The Journal of Peasant Studies*, 39.3–4: 845–72.

Borras Jr, S.M., Hall, R., Scoones, I., White, B., and Wolford, W. eds. 2011. Forum on Global Land Grabbing. *The Journal of Peasant Studies*, 38.2: 209–98.

Borras Jr, S.M., Kay, C., Gómez, S., and Wilkinson, J. 2012b. Land Grabbing and Global Capitalist Accumulation. *Canadian Journal of Development Studies*, 33.4: 402–16.

Borras Jr, S.M., Kay, C., and Lahiff, E. eds. 2008. *Market-led Agrarian Reform: Critical Perspectives on Neoliberal Land Policies and the Rural Poor.* London: Routledge.

Borras, Jr, S.M., McMichael, P., and Scoones, I. eds. 2011. *The Politics of Biofuels, Land and Agrarian Change.* London: Routledge.

Bryceson, D.F. 2000. Disappearing Peasantries? Rural Labour Redundancy in the Neo-liberal Era and Beyond, in Bryceson, D., Kay, C., and Mooij, J., eds. *Disappearing Peasantries? Rural Labour in Africa, Asia and Latin America.* London: Practical Action: 299–326.

Busch, L. 2010. Can Fairy Tales Come True? The Surprising Story of Neoliberalism and World Agriculture. *Sociologia Ruralis*, 50.4: 331–51.

Bush, R. 2010. Food Riots: Poverty, Power and Protest. *Journal of Agrarian Change*, 10.1: 119–29.

Byres, T.J. 2003. Agriculture and Development: The Dominant Orthodoxy and an Alternative View, in Chang, H.-J., ed. *Rethinking Development Economics.* London: Anthem, Press: 235–53.

Carter, M.R., Barham, B.L., and Mesbah, D. 1996. Agricultural Export Booms and the Rural Poor in Chile, Guatemala, and Paraguay. *Latin American Research Review*, 31.1: 33–65.

Chang, H.-J. 2012. Rethinking Public Policy in Agriculture: Lessons from History, Distant and Recent, in Chang, H.-J., ed. *Public Policy and Agricultural Development.* London: Routledge: 3–68.

Chase, J. 2002. Introduction: The Spaces of Neoliberalism in Latin America, in Chase, J., ed. *The Spaces of Neoliberalism: Land, Place and Family in Latin America.* Bloomfield, CT: Kumarian Press: 1–21.

Clapp, J. 2012. *Food.* Cambridge: Polity Press.

Deere, C.D. 2005. The Feminization of Agriculture? Economic Restructuring in rural Latin America. *Occasional Paper 1.* Geneva: UNRISD.

Deere, C.D., and León, M. 2001. *Empowering Women: Land and Property Rights in Latin America.* Pittsburgh: University of Pittsburgh Press.

Deininger, K. 2003. *Land Policies for Growth and Poverty Reduction.* New York: Oxford University Press for the World Bank.

Deininger, K., and Byerlee, D. 2011, *Rising Global Interest in Farmland.* Washington, DC: World Bank.

Desmarais, A.A. 2007. *La Vía Campesina: Globalization and the Power of Peasants.* London: Pluto Press.

Dietz, K., Engels, B., Pye, O., and Brunnengräber, A. eds. 2015. *The Political Ecology of Agrofuels.* London: Routledge.

Edelman, M., Oya, C., and Borras Jr, S.M. 2013. Global Land Grabs: Historical Processes, Theoretical and Methodological Implications and Current Trajectories. *Third World Quarterly*, 34.9: 1517–31.

Fairhead, J., Leach, M., and Scoones, I. 2012. Green Grabbing: A New Appropriation of Nature? *Journal of Peasant Studies*, 39.2: 237–61.

Franco. J., and Borras Jr, S.M. 2013. *Land Concentration, Land Grabbing and People's Struggles in Europe.* Amsterdam: Transnational Institute.

Galeano, L.A. 2012. Paraguay and the Expansion of Brazilian and Argentinian Agribusiness Frontiers. *Canadian Journal of Development Studies*, 33.4: 458–70.

Ghosh, J. 2010. The Unnatural Coupling: Food and Global Finance. *Journal of Agrarian Change*, 10.1: 72–86.

Jansen, K. 2015. The Debate on Food Sovereignty Theory: Agrarian Capitalism, Dispossession and Agroecology. *The Journal of Peasant Studies*, 42.1: 213–32.

Kaag, M., and Zoomers, A. eds. 2014. *The Global Land Grab: Beyond the Hype.* London: Zed.

Kay, C. 2008. Reflections on Latin American Rural Studies in the Neoliberal Globalization Period: A New Rurality? *Development and Change*, 39.6: 915–43.

—. 2009. Development Strategies and Rural Development: Exploring Synergies, Eradicating Poverty. *The Journal of Peasant Studies*, 36.1: 103–37.

Kay, S. 2014. Reclaiming Agricultural Investment: Towards Public–peasant Investment Synergies. *TNI Agrarian Justice Programme Policy Paper.* Amsterdam: Transnational Institute.

Lipton, M. 1977. *Why Poor People Stay Poor: A Study of Urban Bias in World Development.* London: Temple Smith.

McMichael, P. 2008. Peasants Make Their Own History, but Not Just as They Please, in Borras Jr, S.M., Edelman, M., and Kay, C., eds. *Transnational Agrarian Movements Confronting Globalization*. Oxford: Blackwell: 37–60.

—. 2009. Food Sovereignty, Social Reproduction and the Agrarian Question, in Akram-Lodhi, A.H., and Kay, C., eds. *Peasants and Globalization: Political Economy, Rural Transformation and the Agrarian Question*. London: Routledge: 288–312.

Margulis, M.E. 2014. Trading Out of the Global Food Crisis? The World Trade Organization and the Geopolitics of Food Security. *Geopolitics*, 19.2: 322–50.

Margulis, M., McKeon, N., and Borras Jr, S.M. eds. 2014. *Land Grabbing and Global Governance*. London: Routledge.

Martínez-Torres, M.E., and Rosset, P.M. 2010. La Vía Campesina: The Birth and Evolution of a Transnational Social Movement. *The Journal of Peasant Studies*, 37.1: 149–75.

Oya, C. 2005. Stick and Carrots for Farmers in Developing Countries: Agrarian Neoliberalism in Theory and Practice, in Saad-Filho, A., and Johnston, D., eds. *Neoliberalism: A Critical Reader*. London: Pluto Press: 127–34.

—. 2013. The Land Rush and Classic Agrarian Questions of Capital and Labour: A Systematic Scoping Review of the Socioeconomic Impact of Land Grabs in Africa. *Third World Quarterly*, 34.9: 1532–57.

Razavi, S. ed. 2003. Agrarian Change, Gender and Land Rights, *Journal of Agrarian Change*, 3.1/2: 1–288.

Schiff, M., and Valdés, A. 1992. *The Plundering of Agriculture in Developing Countries*, Washington, DC: World Bank.

Sommerville, M., Essex, J., and Le Billon, P. 2014. The 'Global Food Crisis' and the Geopolitics of Food Security. *Geopolitics*, 19.2: 239–65.

Veltmeyer, H., and Petras, J. 2014. *The New Extractivism: A Post-Neoliberal Development Model or Imperialism of the Twenty-First Century?* London: Zed.

Visser, O., Clapp, J., and Isakson, S.R. eds. 2015. Symposium on Global Finance and the Agrifood Sector: Risk and Regulation. *Journal of Agrarian Change*, 15.4.

White, B., Borras Jr, S.M., Hall, R., and Wolford, W. eds. 2013. *The New Enclosures: Critical Perspectives on Corporate Land Deals*. London: Routledge.

Wolford, W., Borras Jr, S.M., Hall, R., Scoones, I., and White, B. eds. 2013. *Governing Global Land Deals: The Role of the State in the Rush for Land*. Chichester: Wiley.

World Bank. 2001. *Land Policy and Administration*. Washington, DC: World Bank.

35

THE HEARTLANDS OF NEOLIBERALISM AND THE RISE OF THE AUSTERITY STATE

Bob Jessop

My chapter explores the genealogy and development of neoliberalism in its heartlands. What happens here is closely entangled with events, processes and forces elsewhere in the world market, the world of states and global society. I first consider the meaning of heartlands and note some paradoxes in its use in geopolitics, geoeconomics and critical studies of neoliberalism. Second, I present a typology of neoliberalism, note its hybrid forms, and offer a periodization for its instantiation in the 'heartlands', where its dominant form is *principled* neoliberal regime shifts. The best-known cases are the USA and the UK. I then note that *pragmatic* neoliberal policy adjustments can cumulate, through ratchet-like effects, to produce *de facto* regime shifts. Here I briefly consider Germany, the leading example, especially given its central position in the European Union. I conclude with brief comments on the implications of such regime shifts in the heartlands for (1) core–periphery relations in the heartlands themselves, associated with its intensification of uneven development and (2) the overall dynamic of a world market organized in the shadow of neoliberalism.

Where are the heartlands?

This term has five meanings that are relevant here. First, for the British geopolitical theorist Halford MacKinder (1904), it denotes the Eurasian Heartland, which comprises nearly 60 per cent of the world land area. MacKinder claimed that 'Who rules East Europe commands the Heartland; who rules the Heartland commands the World-Island; who rules the World-Island commands the world' (1919: 106, italics removed). Beyond the heartland, he argued, lies a less important hemisphere (comprising the Americas and Australia), plus outlying smaller islands (including, for example, Japan and the UK) and the oceans. To limit Eurasian power, it was necessary to fragment the central landmass and control its rimlands, especially its western and eastern poles. The USA achieved this after 1945 thanks to the Iron Curtain (and, later, the Sino-Soviet split), through its hegemony in Western Europe and Japan, and its dominance in Eurasia's soft Middle Eastern underbelly. Thus seen, apart from an abortive neoliberal system transformation after the collapse of the Soviet Union, which had occupied a significant part of the Eurasian heartland, it is a paradox that the outer crescent now forms the heartlands of neoliberalism and has been using neoliberalism to destabilize the rimlands in Eastern and Central Europe.

Second, a radical international relations scholar, Kees van der Pijl, distinguishes a liberal, Lockean heartland from a series of 'contender states'. The former is characterized by disembedded markets and strong civil societies that underpin the inter-state system; the latter are dominated by a strong political apparatus with centralized control of resources mobilized to challenge the leading economic powers and their inter-state system (van der Pijl 1998). Thus viewed, the Lockean heartland has been transformed into the neoliberal heartland and, under US hegemony, is seeking to integrate or undermine new contenders through hard, soft, and smart power – including a series of global neoliberal initiatives together with efforts to achieve full-spectrum dominance militarily. This can be seen in the pivot to the East to contain a semi-neoliberal China and the launch of the Third Cold War against Russia based on neoliberalism and NATO.

Third, for theorists like Jamie Peck and Adam Tickell (2002) or Philip Mirowski and Dieter Plehwe (2009), the neoliberal heartland is understood in terms of a core–periphery relation. Whereas the first two accounts imply a latent or open antagonism between heartland and periphery, Peck and Tickell explore the diffusion of neoliberalism from its intellectual or political heartlands into successive zones of extension. However, as it travels to particular cities, regions, or nation-states in Latin America, Africa, Asia, and Eastern Europe, it mutates in response to local conditions (Peck and Tickell 2002). So, rather than assuming a self-identical neoliberal*ism*, they highlight processes of variegated neoliberal*ization* as neoliberal ideas and policies undergo hybridization.

Fourth, Wendy Larner (2003) has criticized this core–periphery diffusion thesis on the grounds that the neoliberal project was relatively marginal in the Lockean heartlands until its feasibility was demonstrated in Chile and elsewhere in Latin America. It then migrated back to the 'ideological heartlands' as an apparently successful policy paradigm. Larner, a New Zealander, also notes that ex-politicians and technocrats from her homeland were key advisors to Eastern European governments on their privatization strategies. Indeed, she argues that 'developments in the "periphery" may be as significant, if not more so, as those in the "core" in explaining the spread of neoliberalism' (ibid.: 510).

Fifth, and finally, the term is sometimes merely a geographical and historical descriptor that regards the heartlands of neoliberalism as comprising, at a minimum, the USA and UK, with optional references to Canada, Australia, and New Zealand. Together these countries comprise the Anglo-Saxon heartlands of neoliberalism. Some add Western Europe, although, as noted below, this conflates societies that engaged in neoliberal policy adjustments with the neoliberal regime shifts that occurred in the real heartlands. Even here, however, Kean Birch has recently argued that the heartlands 'have never been neoliberal'. More precisely, and less provocatively, he means that the pure theory of neoliberalism was never really implemented in the USA, Canada and the UK (his three case studies), but served as a rhetorical cloak for policies that promoted, not free markets, but the freedom of monopolistic corporations to limit competition, derive superprofits, and colonize the wider society (Birch 2015: 18 and passim). He adds that many of the symptoms of the financial, economic, debt, and austerity crises attributed to neoliberalism preceded the alleged ascendancy of neoliberalism – and that there is nothing new about financial crises, which have occurred regularly since the sixteenth century. I return to these claims below.

So what is neoliberalism?

Given the polyvalence of the core term, diverse typologies of neoliberalism exist. Here I present one concerned with the economic and political dimensions of neoliberalism and its changing fortunes. Neoliberalization is a distinctive economic, political, and social project that tends to judge all economic activities in terms of profitability and all social activities in terms of their contribution to differential capital accumulation. This might suggest that neoliberalism promotes the primacy of the economic but, because its extension and reproduction require continuing state support and, indeed, often involve what Weber (1975) called 'political capitalism', one might well argue that it entails a primacy of the political. I now offer a baseline definition and identify four forms of neoliberalism; relate neoliberalism to the world market, geopolitics and global governance; and address the role of the political in promoting neoliberalism and handling its contradictions and crisis-tendencies.

Four main historical forms of neoliberalism can be distinguished, although hybrid forms also exist. The most radical form was *neoliberal system transformation* in post-Soviet successor states. Russia and Poland provide two contrasting cases: Chicagoan 'creative destruction' induced by neoliberal shock therapy and a more ordoliberal 'market therapy without shock' respectively. Such cases concern the Eurasian heartland, however, not the heartland of neoliberalism.

The latter is characterized by *neoliberal regime shifts*. Breaking with the post-war Atlantic Fordist settlements, based on an institutionalized compromise between capital and labour, neoliberal policies were pursued in order to modify the balance of forces in favour of capital. The neoliberal policy agenda has six key planks: liberalization, deregulation, privatization, market proxies in the public sector, internationalization, and cuts in direct taxation. These policies have largely succeeded: witness stagnant real wages; cuts in welfare; increasing personal debt to invest in housing, pensions, education, and health or, indeed, to maintain a previous standard of living; and a growing share of income and wealth going to the top decile (especially the top percentile) of their respective populations. Well-known cases are Thatcherism and Reaganism but similar shifts occurred in Australia, Canada, New Zealand, Eire, Iceland, and Cyprus. While often identified with right-wing parties, neoliberal regime shifts have also been initiated, maintained or supported by centre-left parties, often under a 'Third Way' label (e.g. the Clinton administration or New Labour). Moreover, as noted, with help from northern friends and/or military dictatorships, neoliberal regime shifts were actually pioneered in the outer crescent in Latin America.

The third type comprises economic restructuring and regime shifts that were mainly imposed from outside by transnational economic institutions and organizations backed by leading capitalist powers and partners among domestic political and economic elites. It involves neoliberal policies in line with the 'Washington Consensus' as a condition for financial and other aid to crisis-ridden economies outside the heartlands in parts of Africa, Asia, Eastern and Central Europe, and Latin America. While policies in types two and three often overlap in the (semi-) periphery of the global economy, they involve analytically distinct roots, lessons learnt, and likely forms of resistance.

Fourth, neoliberalism can involve a more pragmatic, partial, and potentially reversible set of neoliberal policy adjustments. Not all of the six neoliberal economic policies listed above have been adopted in such cases. They involve more modest and piecemeal changes deemed necessary by governing elites and their social base(s) to maintain existing economic and social models in the face of specific crisis-tendencies and the challenges created by globalization. Nordic social democracies and Rhenish capitalism provide examples. However, such adjustments can cumulate despite the fluctuating political fortunes of the parties that back them and, almost by stealth, can lead to neoliberal regimes (witness Germany in the last 25 years). Moreover, with the contagion of the North Atlantic financial crisis (NAFC) and the distinctive problems rooted in the eurozone crisis, these changes have become harder to reverse. Indeed, as I note below, there are attempts to institutionalize neoliberalism in a succession of pacts and crisis-management responses in the eurozone economies. This creates the paradox that an ordoliberal Germany, which has made regular neoliberal policy adjustments to secure its neo-mercantilist export-led growth model, is backing the austerity demands of transnational financial capital that effectively impose a technocratic neoliberal regime shift on Greece and Spain.

It should be noted that none of these forms of neoliberalism (or neoliberalization) result from the spontaneous operation of market forces: they all involve the exercise of political power to establish and consolidate them and, when confronted with crisis, to rescue them. This illustrates the importance of Max Weber's three types of political capitalism: unusual deals with political authority, accumulation through force and domination, and predatory economic activities. Financialization and what Birch (2015) calls 'assetization' are crucial aspects of the development of neoliberal regime shifts; so are the lowering of taxes on rich households, big corporations, and too-big-to-fail financial institutions. This shows again that neoliberal regime shifts do not conform to the 'theoclassical' account of the free market.

Neoliberalization in the heartlands has involved four main stages to date. First came the rollback of the institutions and institutionalized compromises associated with the Atlantic Fordist post-war settlement. Second, there were efforts to roll forward neoliberal institutions, consolidate the shift in the balance of forces, and constitutionalize neoliberal principles nationally, regionally, and globally – making them harder to reverse even if the political conjuncture temporarily favours socialist or populist right-wing parties and movements. The third stage was blowback as the unintended but inevitable effects of a one-sided emphasis on serving the interests of export-oriented and/or interest-bearing capital led to growing resistance, boom and bust cycles, and recessions. This is the moment of the 'Third Way' and analogous attempts to provide flanking and supporting mechanisms to maintain the momentum of neoliberal regime shifts. Fourth, after the erruption of the NAFC, which is the product of finance-dominated accumulation (see below), central banks and states in the neoliberal heartlands intervened massively to rescue banks at the expense of households, public debt, and industrial capital. Efforts were made to transform the politics of austerity into a permanent state of austerity. Indeed, notwithstanding a brief period when the global financial crisis was construed as a crisis *of* rather than *in* neoliberalism, massive state intervention has since created conditions for a return to neoliberal 'business as usual' in the neoliberal heartlands. Elsewhere in Europe it has prompted ordoliberal policy adjustments alongside efforts to maintain free trade, extend it to services, facilitate non-speculative capital flows, and find market solutions to climate change and other global challenges.

The economic significance of neoliberalism

To establish why neoliberalisms and neoliberalization have been and, despite their respective crisis-tendencies, remain so influential, leading to the renewal of neoliberalization rather than its retreat, we must look beyond its intellectual appeal and its domestic and international political backing. It is also related to the logic of capital and the distinction between the use-value and exchange-value aspects of the commodity. In the first instance, the commodity is both a use-value and an exchange-value: without use-value, it would not be purchased; without exchange-value, it would not be produced. Analogous properties are found in other dimensions of the capital relation. The worker is both a concrete individual with specific skills, knowledge, and creativity *and* an abstract unit of labour power substitutable by other such units (or, indeed, other factors of production); the wage is both a source of demand *and* a cost of production; money functions both as a 'national' currency circulating within a monetary bloc and subject to state control *and* as an international money exchangeable against other monies in currency markets; productive capital is a more or less concrete stock of time- and place-specific assets undergoing valorization *and* abstract value in motion (notably as realized profits available for re-investment); land is a gift of nature *and* a monopolistic claim on revenues; knowledge circulates as part of the intellectual commons *and* can also become the object of intellectual property rights; and so forth. In each case, neoliberalism privileges exchange-value over use-value. It emphasizes cost reduction and cost recovery and subjects all economic activities to the treadmill of matching or exceeding the prevailing world market average rate of profit.

Such one-sided treatment can only disguise, but not suppress, the significance of the use-value aspect of these relations. Eventually, its importance to the reproduction of capitalism (and social life more generally) is reasserted and, in the absence of appropriate ways to handle the contradictions between use- and exchange-value, crises emerge that forcibly re-impose the unity of the capital relation. Accompanying this, however, as elaborated below, is the rise of a permanent politics of austerity and a tendential shift to an enduring state of austerity that is characterized by the 'constitutionalization of austerity' (Bruff 2014) as a political principle and an increasing attack on the institutions and practices of liberal democracy (see the penultimate section of this chapter).

The neoliberal policy paradigm not only privileges capital over labour, but also privileges some fractions of capital over others. For it is capital in its exchange-value aspect that is most easily disembedded from broader socio-spatial-temporal contexts and thereby freed to 'flow' relatively smoothly through space-time. In this sense, compared to the largely intermediary role of finance in Fordist regimes and in a productivist, post-Fordist knowledge-based economy, neoliberalism promotes a finance-dominated accumulation regime. This tends to privilege hypermobile financial capital at the expense of capitals that are embedded in broader sets of social relations and/or that must be valorized in particular times and places; it creates the conditions for differential accumulation in favour of the financial sector based on financial innovation and speculation; and it increases inequalities of income and wealth, limiting the impact of the wage as a source of demand (cf. Dore 2008; Krippner 2005). Its destructive impact is reinforced through the neoliberal approach to accumulation through dispossession (especially the politically licensed plundering of public assets and the intellectual commons) and the dynamic of uneven development (enabling financial capital to move on when the disastrous effects of financialization weaken those productive capitals that have to be valorized in particular times and places). It is also a powerful mechanism of world market integration, for good or ill, affecting different varieties of capitalism in different ways and transmitting crisis-tendencies through diverse mechanisms.

Finance-dominated accumulation

Against Kean Birch's argument that financial crises have occurred over four centuries and are too frequent to be attributable to neoliberalism (at least in its textbook form), I argue that neoliberalism has created a very special kind of financialization with distinctive forms of crisis and crisis-management. Much work on financialization focuses on the role of finance in the circuits of capital. Four relevant definitions are:

- the transformation of future streams of (profit, dividend, or interest) income into a tradable asset like a stock or a bond;
- a 'pattern of accumulation in which profit making occurs increasingly through financial channels rather than through trade and commodity production' (Krippner 2005: 174);
- an increasing tendency towards autonomization of the circuits of finance capital as property (or fictitious capital) from finance capital as functioning capital within the circuits of the 'real economy' (Meacci, 1998: 191–5); and

- the systemic power and importance of financial markets, financial motives, financial institutions, and financial elites in the operation of the economy and *its governing institutions*, nationally and internationally (Epstein 2005: 3).

The third and fourth definitions are especially relevant for my analysis. The neoliberal form of world market integration greatly benefits interest-bearing capital because it controls the most liquid, abstract, and generalized economic resource and because it has also become the most integrated fraction of capital (cf. Demirović and Sablowski 2013). Interest-bearing capital (which differs from traditional usury capital) can facilitate the accumulation of profit-producing capital and it can also function as property, when it is simply one revenue-generating asset among others. In this latter context it underpins a finance-dominated accumulation regime. This is an extreme form of marketization of economic relations in which fictitious money, fictitious credit, fictitious capital, and, indeed, unsustainable fictitious profits play an increasing role in shaping economic performance and crisis-tendencies (Marx 1967[1894]; de Medeiros Carneiro et al., 2015; Jessop 2013). Such regimes emerge to the extent that the circuits of interest-bearing capital become increasingly autonomous from those of profit-producing capital. Of course, financial capital as property cannot become fully and permanently detached from the need to valorize profit-producing capital. On the contrary, because continued expansion depends heavily on the pseudo-validation of highly leveraged speculative and Ponzi debt, this regime has its own inherent crisis-generating mechanism. Elsner (2012) explains this as follows: financial capital in a finance-dominated regime has a target rate of return that is several times greater than the historic norm for profit-producing capital and, worse still, in seeking to achieve it, massively levers fictitious credit and capital. In aggregate, the eventual validation of this capital would demand a total volume of surplus-value that far exceeds the productive and exploitative capacity of existing profit-producing capital.

This explains the emergence of financial crises that develop relatively independently, at least initially, from crisis-tendencies rooted in capitalist production. Indeed, the greater and longer the seeming independence of financial capital and the greater the resulting parasitism of finance as property, the greater and longer the crises required to re-impose the organic unity of the circuits of capital. Attempts to overcome the contradiction identified by Elsner depend on three equally unsustainable strategies. One is to create and manage bubbles, the main redistribution mechanism in finance-dominated accumulation, and then bail out (or get bailed out) at the right moment (ibid.: 146–7; also Hudson 2012). This requires the complicity of central banks and government in finance-dominated economies. Another is to invoke a system-threatening 'financial emergency' that justifies efforts to reduce individual and social wages, impose internal devaluation and financial repression, and privatize public services and assets to pay off the public debt incurred in massive bailouts (cf. Mirowski 2013). States have key roles here and this strategy has reinvigorated neoliberalism and supported the politics of austerity (see below). The third approach involves state-sponsored primitive accumulation (e.g. land-grabbing, capitalizing nature and its services, and enclosing the intellectual commons). Albeit in different ways, all three strategies are implicated in the politics of austerity, whether as its cause and/or one of its mechanisms.

Austerity

We can understand the relation between neoliberalism and austerity if we consider the latter in terms of the relations between the economic and political fields, including their basic forms and institutional architecture, and their mediation through the changing balance of forces.

The conventional distinction between policies, politics, and polity is useful here. It indicates that austerity can take three forms. First, there are *conjunctural austerity policies* that are introduced initially as temporary measures in response to short-term or immediate problems. As the conjuncture becomes favourable again, these policies are suspended or reversed. Second, there is the *enduring politics of austerity* (often called 'permanent austerity') that is promoted in response to a 'chronic' crisis, real or manufactured, in the fisco-financial domain and/or in the economy more generally. This is intended to bring about a more lasting reorganization of the balance of forces in favour of capital rather than to make policy adjustments to safeguard existing economic and political arrangements. Third, there is the *austerity polity*. This results from a continuing fundamental institutional reorganization of the relations between the economic and political in capitalist formations. It can be a possibly unintended cumulative result of the enduring politics of austerity, especially where this aggravates the underlying causes of fisco-financial crisis. It can also result from a deliberate strategy to subordinate the polity more directly and durably to the 'imperatives' of 'globalization' as these are construed in neoliberal discourse with its one-sided emphasis on the logic of exchange-value. And, given the political, ideological, hegemonic, and organic crises that have developed in the context of the financial, economic, and fisco-financial crises, they can also develop as an authoritarian response to growing popular unrest (including right-wing extremism) about the technocratic and plutocratic nature of crisis responses.

Conjunctural policies are found in the pattern of neoliberal policy adjustment (the fourth type of neoliberalism discussed above) and are associated with targeted cuts in specific areas. In contrast, an enduring politics of austerity is characteristic of neoliberal regime shifts and assumes the form of general fisco-financial restraint, putting downward pressure on most areas of expenditure, especially discretionary ones (Pierson 2001; Ferrera 2008; Seymour 2014). This pattern can occur in normal forms of politics, in states of economic emergency or in lasting states of exception. It can be triggered by a genuine crisis, one that is deliberately exaggerated, or one 'manufactured' for political purposes. Indeed, in neoliberal regimes, whatever the state of the economy, it seems that it is always the right time to reduce public expenditure (except for corporate welfare) through an appropriately crafted (and crafty) politics of austerity. This involves more than quantitative cuts in spending because it is also intended to have transformative effects that restructure, recalibrate, and reorient state expenditure. These measures are pursued to consolidate and extend the power of capital, especially interest-bearing capital, and to subsume ever wider areas of social life under the logic of differential accumulation.

Seymour (2014) argues that austerity is now the dominant *political* articulation of the global economic crisis in Europe and North America. In addition, with others, he notes that the politics of permanent austerity is a response not just to economic crisis but also to political and ideological crises and, indeed, an organic crisis of the capitalist social order (ibid.: 4; Bruff 2014; Kannankulam and Georgi 2012; Jessop 2015; cf. Gramsci 1971). This is used to justify a state of economic emergency that is presented initially as a 'temporary' response to immediate or chronic problems but then acquires a more permanent form through cumulative and mutually reinforcing institutional change, routinization of exceptional measures, and habituation.

Seymour identifies seven aspects of this strategy: (1) rebalance the economy from wage-led to finance-led growth; (2) redistribute income from wage-earners to capital; (3) promote 'precarity' in all areas of life as a disciplinary mechanism and means to reinforce the financialization of everyday life; (4) recompose social classes, with increasing inequality in income and wealth and greater stratification within classes; (5) facilitate the penetration of the state by corporations; (6) accelerate the turn from a Keynesian welfare state based on shared citizenship rights to a workfare regime that relies on coercion, casual sadism, and, especially in the USA, penality; and (7) promote the values of hierarchy and competitiveness (Seymour 2014: 2–4).

In many respects, these aspects were already inscribed in the politics of neoliberal regime shifts (as described above) but, for Seymour, they have been heavily reinforced following the 2007–9 financial and economic crisis (cf. Fumagalli and Lucarelli 2011). This occurs in part because the painful measures already taken to consolidate budgets in the 1990s and early 2000s were wiped out by the impact of the North American financial crisis and the eurozone crisis as governments took on more debt to bail out banks and/or engineer stimulus packages (Rasmus 2010; Hudson 2012).

The politics of austerity can be interpreted as a long-term strategic offensive that continues and extends the neoliberal project to reorganize the institutional matrix and balance of forces in favour of capital. It aims to rearticulate relations between (1) the social power of money as capital and of capital as property and (2) the political power of the state. Inter alia, this involves a politics aimed at *disorganizing* subaltern classes and *reorganizing* the capitalist power bloc around interest-bearing capital (in neoliberal regimes) and export-oriented profit-producing capital (in economies where neoliberal policy adjustments prevailed). In the eurozone, for example, the central goal of authoritarian crisis constitutionalism is to deepen EU integration on neoliberal terms and to govern through the treadmill dynamics of competitive austerity. Its aims include socializing bank losses, exploiting the sovereign debt crisis to restructure welfare states and labour markets (including further measures to weaken trade union bargaining power) and to impose shock therapy in the periphery (witness Cyprus and, currently, Greece). In finance-dominated regimes in the heartlands of neoliberalism and export-oriented regimes in the northern European eurozone economies, the overall approach can switch between offensive and defensive tactics (the latter is exemplified by the 'Third Way', with its flanking and supporting mechanisms to maintain the overall momentum of neoliberal transformation). This is an important feature of variegated neoliberalization, which is flexible, adaptable, and resilient, tending, as Peck (2010) writes, to 'fail forward' – that is, to exploit threats to its survival as opportunities for expansion. The successful pursuit of this strategy, which is not guaranteed, leads to an *austerity state* embedded in a political system (polity) that institutionalizes a 'permanent' politics of austerity.

Critics from the right as well as the left have noted this trend and described it in various ways. For example, Albo and Fanelli (2014) refer to a bipartisan or pluripartisan 'disciplinary democracy' as the political form of 'permanent austerity' (cf. Rasmus 2010; Stützle, 2013). Likewise, Bruff (2014) refers to authoritarian neoliberalism; Solty (2013) identifies an authoritarian crisis constitutionalism oriented to the economic governance of competitive austerity; and Oberndorfer (2015) describes the development of authoritarian competitive statism. From a social democratic perspective, Streeck (2014) highlights a move from the welfare state to the consolidation state; and a (former) Fabian Socialist, Crouch, describes the transition to post-democracy (2004). On the libertarian right, there is condemnation of the strong and repressive state that emerges from allegedly unconstitutional intervention to shore up finance capital and to police dissent (e.g. Stockman 2013). Critics also note that the scope for material concessions to subaltern groups has shrunk and, faced with growing resentment and sometimes open resistance, capitalist states are also becoming less open and democratic and increasingly coercive. It also creates different kinds of state and representational crisis that weaken the state even as its powers seem to expand (Poulantzas 1979; Bruff 2014).

Debt–default–deflation dynamics in the USA and UK

The one-sided pursuit of neoliberalization in the USA and UK created the conditions for a debt–default–deflation dynamic that has worsened public finances as well as the private sector (Rasmus 2010). This possibility is inherent in finance-dominated accumulation and was actualized first in the USA and then in the UK. The features of the crisis in both are typical of finance-dominated accumulation but the financial sector is more significant in the UK and, in addition, the USA has the 'exorbitant privilege' of the dollar as world money and a labour force that has suffered stagnant real incomes for 30 years – longer than in the UK.

In the USA, the crisis passed through several stages: credit crunch, liquidity crisis, financial insolvencies, a generalized financial crisis, a recession that risked becoming an epic recession or great depression, and then a manufactured 'public debt' crisis reflected in a surreal fiscal cliff debate in 2010–13. The initial response to the NAFC was the bailout of 'too big to fail' banks, mainly as a covert strategy to recapitalize the banking system and socialize losses. This massively increased public debt and reinforced government dependence on bondholder confidence and 'Mr Market' more generally. Although there was also a federal stimulus package, it could not compensate for falling demand due to wage cuts plus austerity measures introduced at state and local level (where governments must balance their budgets). A scissors effect occurred as public expenditure and debt rose and GDP fell, so that debt increased as a proportion of GDP (the same tendency occurs elsewhere too). This fuelled the neoliberal hysteria around the long-term costs of Medicaid, Medicare, and Social Security and the broader 'fiscal cliff' debate. Yet of the projected $7 trillion deficit, some $4 trillion was due to consolidation of tax cuts introduced by the George W. Bush administration and $1 trillion to an increased defence budget (Solty 2013). The accompanying proposals for deficit reduction never seriously examined cuts in defence spending, ending unfunded wars, halting subsidies to a broad spectrum of corporate interests (often with large reserves, often held offshore), or restoring tax rates on the rich to Reagan era levels, despite stagnant wages and increased wealth inequalities to match those of the roaring 1920s (Piketty 2014).

The UK also experienced a neoliberal regime shift, continued after the Thatcher years under the successive Conservative, New Labour, Conservative–Liberal Democratic coalition, and now (June 2015) Conservative majority regimes. The UK is even more dominated by international financial capital than the USA thanks to the economic dominance of the City of London and the concentration of power in London, which has also entrenched a pattern of uneven development that favours London and the rest of the South East. Thus the NAFC had a greater and more lasting impact in the UK and this has been exacerbated by the more rigid politics of austerity pursued under Osborne's neoliberal Chancellorship, with its procyclical commitment to balanced budgets (a prospect moving into an ever more distant future as the debt–deflation spiral continues), its Ricardian approach to workfare, and its preferential tax treatment of corporations and the wealthy that is not reflected in renewed investment in profit-producing capital in the UK economy (see Seymour 2014). Without the exorbitant privilege of the dollar and the recent trend in the USA towards energy independence, the UK has been lagging behind with its recovery based on new asset bubbles fuelled by quantitative easing and vulnerable to secular stagnation in the eurozone.

These developments help to situate the continuing attempts led by the USA and UK to pursue 'trade agreements' as a stimulus to crisis-ridden economies, such as the Transpacific Partnership (TPP), Transatlantic Trade and Investment Pact (TTIP), and Trade in Services Agreement (TiSA). If implemented, these treaties will limit state sovereignty to challenge transnational capital. One effect could be to enforce a neoliberal project of 'total privatization' of state-owned non-financial assets. Some $9 trillion of government land and buildings has been identified in OECD countries, equivalent to some 18 per cent of their gross general government debt (*The Economist*, 2014). According to neoliberal budgetary and new public management principles, these should be monetized through public–private partnerships, contracting-out and leasing opportunities or even full privatization.

The eurozone crisis and the constitutionalization of austerity

European economic space is organized in the shadow of the German export-led growth regime that, despite significant and cumulative neoliberal policy adjustments in the labour market, has remained firmly inside the 'co-ordinated market economy' camp (Bellofiore *et al.* 2010; Cesaratto and Stirati 2010; Streeck 2009). Its influence in this regard is reinforced by the extension of the German space economy to include elements of other Rhenish economies in Northern Europe. The prime strategic goal is to maintain Germany's export competitiveness and the regional and international stability on which its exports depend. The development of Economic and Monetary Union (EMU) was expected to enhance the competitiveness of French and German industrial capital, especially when reinforced by direct wage restraint, a reduced social wage, and lowered domestic consumption. Reflecting the banking tenets of *das Modell Deutschland*, EMU operated on two key principles: first, the European Central Bank (ECB) may not act as lender of last resort to insolvent banks or indebted states; and, second, sovereign debts may only be discharged by their respective member states (Varoufakis 2013). However, as the crisis tendencies inherent in neoliberalism interacted with uneven development in Europe, the rigidities of EMU, and the faulty institutional design of economic governance in the European Union (absent a banking union, a fiscal union, and an EU welfare regime based on solidarity), it has produced an even more serious crisis than we find in the heartlands of neoliberalism (Jessop 2014).

The contagion effects of the NAFC led to the virtual insolvency of many of Europe's big banks and required urgent measures to recapitalize them and nationalize toxic assets. As in the USA, this led to further concentration in banking. It also threatened a domino effect of sequential bankruptcy of vulnerable member states and their respective banking systems, starting with Greece and Eire and with the systemically important cases of Spain, Italy, and France looming on the near horizon. Without the right to exit the eurozone and regain competitiveness through devaluation (among other measures), the intensification of the eurozone crisis exposed the peripheral economies to domestic debt–default–deflation dynamics as well as to austerity measures mistakenly adopted by other member states and European institutions in the belief that they would limit or resolve the wider crisis. Crisis-management responses premised on deep cuts in spending and regressive taxation actually proved procyclical, provoking a mutually reinforcing downward spiral of actual or feared private and sovereign debt–default–deflation dynamics in the periphery. This is now spreading to the core of the eurozone as contagion effects reverberate.

Conclusions

Despite the continuing crises and bubble dynamics, the neoliberal project still dominates world society thanks to the path-dependent effects of policies, strategies, and structural shifts that were implemented during its highpoint and further measures introduced since to preserve its corrosive dynamic. This is linked to crisis-management in support of finance-dominated accumulation and accumulation via dispossession. These path-dependent effects are political and ideological as well as economic. They derive from the global weight of the US economy (including its pathological co-dependence with China) and the US state's role in shifting the contradictions of neoliberalism elsewhere and/or into the future. Thus neoliberal policies have shaped the forms, timing, and dynamics of economic crises (broadly understood) even in countries where they were *not* willingly embraced, coercively imposed, or unwittingly cumulated. For, in addition to the legacies of neoliberalism where it directly shaped politics and policies, it has also tended to disrupt the structured coherence of modes of regulation and/or governance where alternative policies prevailed. This can be seen in the wider geoeconomic and geopolitical effects of failed neoliberal system transformation and structural adjustment programmes and in the uneven terrain on which struggles over the economic, political, and social effects of neoliberalism are being contested.

The destabilizing consequences of budget-cutting in North America, Europe, and elsewhere are worrying even the high priests of neoliberalism in the International Monetary Fund, the World Bank, the World Economic Forum, and so on. In a joint report with the ILO, the IMF documented serious problems in labour markets reflected in rising unemployment worldwide. It warned that 'high and long-lasting unemployment… represents risks to the stability of existing democracies and hinders the development of new democracies in countries undergoing political transitions' (IMF/ILO 2010: 4). It added that premature fiscal retrenchment could harm growth and lead to even larger deficits and debts. Furthermore, abrupt shifts in fiscal policy stances, in many countries at the same time, could destabilize recovery and weaken future growth. It concluded that 'a credible and gradual return to fiscal stability over several years is likely to be a more successful strategy, not only for recovery and growth, but also for deficit and debt reduction… Social dialogue is essential to avoiding an explosion of social unrest' (IMF/ILO 2010). The IMF issued a similar warning in 2015, in the context of the crisis in Greece (IMF 2015). Likewise, in its 2014 *Global Risks*, the World Economic Forum identifies growing inequalities in wealth and income as the biggest single potential source of global instability. These are three of many similar examples of an impotent recognition of the limits to the politics of austerity.

References

Albo, G., and Fanelli, C. 2014. Austerity Against Democracy: An Authoritarian Phase of Neoliberalism? *Toronto: Socialist Project Canada.* Retrieved from www.socialistproject.ca/documents/AusterityAgainstDemocracy.pdf

Bellofiore, R., Garibaldo, F., and Halevi, J. 2010. The Great Recession and the Contradictions of European Neomercantilism. *Socialist Register 2011*: 120–46.

Birch, K. 2015. *We Have Never Been Neoliberal: A Manifesto for a Doomed Youth.* Alresford: Zero.

Bruff, I. 2014. The Rise of Authoritarian Neoliberalism. *Rethinking Marxism*, 26.1: 113–29.

Cesaratto, S., and Stirati, A. 2010. Germany and the European and Global Crises. *Journal of International Political Economy*, 39.4: 56–86.

Crouch, C. 2004. *Post-Democracy.* Cambridge: Polity.

de Medeiros Carneiro, R., Rossi, P., Santos Mello, G., and Chiliatto-Leite, M. 2015. The Fourth Dimension: Derivatives and Financial Dominance. *Review of Radical Political Economics*, 47: 641–62.

Demirović, A., and Sablowski, T. 2013. *The Finance-dominated Regime of Accumulation and the Crisis in Europe.* Berlin: Rosa Luxemburg Stiftung.

Dore, R. 2008. Financialization of the Global Economy. *Industrial and Corporate Change*, 17: 1097–112.

Elsner, W. 2012. Financial Capitalism – At Odds with Democracy: The Trap of an 'Impossible' Profit Rate. *Real-World Economics Review*, 62: 132–59.

Epstein, G.A. 2005. Introduction, in Epstein, G.A., ed. *Financialization and the World Economy.* Cheltenham: Edward Elgar: 3–14.

Ferrera, M. 2008. The European Welfare State: Golden Achievements, Silver Prospects. *West European Politics*, 31: 82–107.

Fumagalli, A., and Lucarelli, S. 2011. Instability and Uncertainty in Cognitive Capitalism, in Gnos, C., and Rochon, L.-P., eds. *Credit, Money and Macroeconomic Policy.* Cheltenham: Elgar: 313–34.

Gramsci, A. 1971. *Selections from the Prison Notebooks.* London: Lawrence & Wishart.

Hudson, M. 2012. *The Bubble and Beyond: Fictitious Capital, Debt Deflation and the Global Crisis.* Dresden: Islet.

IMF. 2015. *Greece. An Update of IMF Staff's Preliminary Public Debt Sustainability Analysis.* IMF Country Report no. 15/186. Retrieved from https://www.imf.org/external/pubs/cat/longres.aspx?sk=43080.0

IMF/ILO 2010. *The Challenges of Growth, Employment and Social Cohesion.* Retreved from http://www.osloconference2010.org/discussionpaper.pdf

Jessop, B. 2013. Credit Money, Fiat Money and Currency Pyramids, in Pixley, J., and Harcourt, G.C., eds. *Financial Crises and the Nature of Capitalist Money*. Basingstoke: Palgrave Macmillan: 248–72.

—. 2014. Variegated Capitalism, Modell Deutschland, and the Eurozone Crisis. *Journal of Contemporary European Studies*, 22.3: 248–60.

—. 2015. *The State: Past, Present, Future*. Cambridge: Polity.

Kannankulam, J., and Georgi, F. 2012. Die Europäische Integration als Materielle Verdichtung von Kräfteverhältnissen: Hegemonieprojekte im Kampf um das 'Staatsprojekt Europa'. *Arbeitspapier Nr. 30*. Marburg: Phillips-Universität.

Krippner, G.R. 2005. The Financialization of the American Economy. *Socio-Economic Review*, 3: 173–208.

Larner, W. 2003. Guest Editorial. *Environment and Planning D: Society and Space*, 21: 509–12.

MacKinder, H.J. 1904. The Geographical Pivot of History. *Geographical Journal*, 23: 421–37.

—. 1919. *Democratic Ideals and Reality: A Study in the Politics of Reconstruction*. New York: Henry Holt & Co.

Marx, K. 1967[1894]. *Capital, Vol. 3*. London: Lawrence & Wishart.

Meacci, F. 1998. Fictitious Capital and Crises, in Bellofiore, R., ed. *Marxian Economics: Essays on Volume III of Capital. Vol. 1*. Basingstoke: Macmillan: 189–204.

Mirowski, P. 2013. *Never Let a Serious Crisis go to Waste*. London: Verso.

Mirowski, P., and Plehwe, D. eds. 2009. *The Road from Mont Pèlerin: The Making of the Neoliberal Thought Collective*. Cambridge: Harvard University Press.

Oberndorfer, L. 2015. From New Constitutionalism to Authoritarian Constitutionalism, in Jäger, J., and Springler, E., eds. *Asymmetric Crisis in Europe and Possible Futures*. London: Routledge: 185–205.

Peck, J. 2010. *Constructions of Neoliberal Reason*. New York: Oxford University Press.

Peck, J., and Tickell, A. 2002. Neoliberalizing Space. *Antipode*, 34: 380–404.

Pierson, P. 2001. Coping with Permanent Austerity, in Pierson, P., ed. *The New Politics of the Welfare State*. Oxford: Oxford University Press.

Piketty, T. 2014. *Capital in the Twenty-first Century*. Cambridge: Harvard University Press.

Poulantzas, N. 1979. The Political Crisis and the Crisis of the State, in Freiburg, J.W., ed. *Critical Sociology*. New York: Halsted Press: 373–93.

Rasmus, J. 2010. *Epic Recession: Prelude to Global Depression*. London: Pluto.

Seymour, R. 2014. *Against Austerity: How We Can Fix the Crisis They Made*. London: Pluto.

Solty, I. 2013. Is the Global Crisis Ending the Marriage Between Capitalism and Liberal Democracy? In Lakitsch, M., ed. *Political Power Reconsidered*. Berlin: LIT: 161–204.

Stockman, D. 2013. *The Great Deformation: The Corruption of Capitalism in America*. New York: Public Affairs.

Streeck, W. 2009. *Re-forming Capitalism: Institutional Change in the German Political Economy*. Oxford: Oxford University Press.

—. 2014. *Buying Time: The Delayed Crisis of Democratic Capitalism*. London: Verso.

Stützle, I. 2013. *Austerität als Politisches Projekt*. Münster: Westfälisches Dampfboot.

The Economist. 2014. State-Owned Assets: Setting Out the Store. Retrieved from http://www.economist.com/news/briefing/21593458-advanced-countries-have-been-slow-sell-or-make-better-use-their-assets-they-are-missing

van der Pijl, K. 1998. *Transnational Classes and International Relations*. London and New York: Routledge.

Varoufakis, Y. 2013. From Contagion to Incoherence. *Contributions to Political Economy*, 2: 51–71.

Weber, M. 1975. *Economy and Society*. New York: Bedminster Press.

World Economic Forum. 2014. *Global Risks*. 9th edn. Cologny and Geneva: WEF.

36

PERIPHERIES OF NEOLIBERALISM

Impacts, resistance and retroliberalism as reincarnation

Warwick E. Murray and John Overton

In this chapter we will consider the nature, adoption and impacts neoliberalism has had on and in the periphery; how it has created new peripheries and perpetuated old ones; how the periphery has both 'answered back' and led reform through resistance and regulation; and, how the resultant socio-economic geographies at various scales have become ever more complex.

As is exemplified by the breadth of this very collection of chapters, the meaning and definition of neoliberalism are contested and multiple. Although semantics are, indeed, very important, this is not *merely* such a point. One's definition of neoliberalism will both betray and influence real political, social, environmental and geographic perspectives and patterns. It is, therefore, important for us to define what we understand by neoliberalism before postulating as to its impacts in and on the periphery. We consider neoliberalism an economic, political and cultural paradigm which is hegemonic among governments across the world. Neoliberalism, based on ideas from Adam Smith, argues that governments crowd-out economic activity, therefore lowering economic growth. A privatized deregulated economy will address this and will allow resources to flow where they are best utilized through the pursuit of Ricardian comparative advantage. By opening up economic spaces for the free flow of capital and goods along these lines, global welfare will be maximized. This economic Darwinism will lead to an evolution so that the strongest and most efficient survive. In many ways it is the revitalization of ideas in the neoclassical political economy of the early 1800s. In a contemporary sense it is tied to the rise of globalization as currently practised (Murray and Overton 2014) and has been the main driver of the adoption of capitalist principles, especially in the global South. For some, neoliberalism and globalization have become synonymous, but this presupposes only one definition of globalization – a position which is erroneous. However, this rolling together of the concepts has seen the ostensible inevitability of globalization used as a incentivizing mechanism to promote the rolling out of neoliberal policies in the global periphery (as well as, to an extent, in the core). These policies effectively combine four strategies: 1) *downsize* government; 2) *privatize* state-owned assets; 3) *deregulate* to allow the free market to operate, and 4) *globalize* to stimulate competition through scalar effects in export and investment flows. In truth, neoliberalism is much more than just a developmental recipe – it is societal philosophy that is predicated on peripheries and cannot exist without their creation and perpetuation (Larner 2000; Harvey 2005; Murray 2009).

Notwithstanding this 'definition', the first and most important point to make is that neoliberalism varies across space, social groups and social sciences. It varies according to where we are talking about. The neoliberalism exported to and adopted in the periphery of the world economy has been very different from neoliberalism of the core. In the latter, it has indeed been associated with downsizing, privatization and deregulation, but in terms of globalization the main objective has been to influence politics to allow the speeding up and growth of the outflow of capital in order to accumulate more. At the same time it has been accompanied by continued high levels of government expenditure, welfare/social security protections and economic protectionism. This is particularly the case in Japan, Australia, the UK and parts of Europe. On this basis one might question whether neoliberalism has ever been applied in its pure form in the global North. Democratic politics has not allowed it. This is different in the periphery, however, where at the principal time of its roll out (the 1980s and 1990s) many countries were not democratic. Latin America, Africa, and later on parts of the Pacific, were characterized at the time by regimes who could apply neoliberal principles with much more 'purity' without fear of overt resistance. In Latin America, then, we have seen much stricter forms of neoliberalism that follow the general definitions much more closely. This reached a zenith in Chile in the late 1980s and was continued into the 1990s, as we will see. Of course, we can conceptualize the multiple unfoldings of neoliberalism as part of the same geopolitical system. Neoliberalism requires an open periphery in order to allow the penetration of subsided and protected government-backed capital that emanates from the elites of the core. In an Orwellian sense, liberal economics and free trade as recommended and perpetuated by Chicago School neoliberalism have been anything but free – being structured and designed to favour the global North and the elites that control the political economy there. Neoliberalism has never been about freedom – but the illusion of it has been profoundly mythologized and deeply influential in terms of real territorial and social space.

We also need to consider what we mean by 'periphery'. In brief, peripheries can be both spatial and social. In the case of the former they might be territorially definable areas that are marginalized; they may be isolated; they may be 'far away'. Of course, all of these concepts are in themselves relative and socially constructed – marginal to what? Isolated from what? Far away from what? In this sense peripheries – though sometimes neatly mappable – should not be thought of as closer to the outside of the system. Dependency theory has long argued such a point – seeing peripheries and cores as two sides of the same coin (Frank 1969). However, today's peripheries are even more complex than this neat spatial configuration first discussed in the 1960s. Late neoliberalism has become characterized by intricate crystallizing of space whereby cores exist within peripheries and peripheries within cores. This was never rejected by early world systems theory but it does seem to be more apparent in the contemporary world. In this sense peripheries are inherently social and spatial at the same time. We might also think of cultural, political and psychological peripheries which may also not be neatly territorially demarcated. Further complicating this is the possibility of virtual or cyber-peripheries which may have no – or very little – territorial geography at all. Neoliberalism has certainly stimulated and been stimulated by the latter and much work remains to be done to understand the implications of this.

Neoliberalism and the periphery: six geographical themes

We can consider the relationship between neoliberalism and the periphery through six geographical themes:

1. The export of neoliberalism to the periphery
2. The impact of neoliberalism in the periphery – the new peripheries it has created and old ones it has perpetuated

3. The macro, meso and micro geographies of neoliberalism – peripheries within cores and cores within peripheries

4. The peripheralization of other development ideas through the rise of neoliberalism and the peripheralization of everything to market logic (including environment, culture, and society)

5. The forms of resistance to neoliberalism that have arisen in the periphery

6. Reincarnations of neoliberalism in the periphery and the rise of retroliberalism.

The export of neoliberalism to the periphery

The theory of neoliberalism was crystallized through the late 1960s and early 1970s, principally in the USA, led by Milton Friedman based at the University of Chicago. However, it is in the periphery where the ideas were first applied, in particular in Chile following the coup that led to the 17-year-long Pinochet dictatorship (1973–90). Pinochet seized power vowing to eradicate the 'cancer of socialism'. Being economically unschooled himself (he studied military geography and was influenced by Nazi-favoured concepts such as *lebensraum*), he had little in the way of an economic plan and turned to economists from La Universidad Catolica who had studied in Chicago with Friedman under the Alliance for Progress scholarships of the Kennedy era. The 'Chicago boys', as they became known, and Friedman himself who visited on occasion, welcomed the opportunity to try out strict monetarist ideas. As had been the case before and has been since, Chile became a social laboratory for economic and political ideas (Gwynne and Kay 2004; Kay 1989). Within a few short years the country became the most open economy the modern world had ever known. This led to enormous inflows of foreign investment which took advantage of low wages and comparative advantages in sectors such as forestry, fruit and fisheries and led to an unprecedented boom in exports. Despite creating deep social divisions and ecological costs that exist to this day, and although the policy locked the country into a primary product export trap that has proven impossible to shake off, the model was hailed an economic success, and Chile became the neoliberal model for the periphery. The concept was exported all across the global South with the World Bank and IMF giving loans based on the adoption of neoliberal policies wrapped up in Structural Adjustment Programmes (SAPs) as they were then known. The oil and consequent debt crises of the late 1970s and early 1980s represented a watershed in this sense and by the end of the 1980s nearly every country in Latin America, Africa, the Pacific Islands and much of Asia (although models here were much more mixed and state developmentalist – as discussed elsewhere) had had SAPs effectively forced upon them. As we discuss below, the ideas were also adopted in the core. Of course, this phenomenon was not just economic – it was also geopolitical and there was a strong Cold War logic at work, intended as it was to diffuse capitalism and keep socialism from spreading across the periphery. Non-conformist governments such as that of Cuba and, at various points, Venezuela, Mozambique, Angola, Vietnam and others were punished with economic sanctions and international ridicule at best and military intervention at worst.

Although specific country models of neoliberalism have varied across time and space, to a large extent, the underlying principles have become immutable and neoliberalism persists in various forms across the global periphery (Larner 2003; Peck *et al.* 2010). The World Bank, IMF and the WTO have played a major role in perpetuating this diffusion through conditionalities. The deeply undemocratic WTO has led the push towards so-called 'free' trade agreements that have washed across the periphery of late, at the same as it has become increasingly difficult to challenge protectionism in North America and Europe. SAPs are long gone, but they were replaced by Poverty Reduction Strategy Papers under the neostructural regime and, as we discuss later, in the current era new tools are being used to export the latest variant of neoliberalism to the periphery.

The impacts of neoliberalism in the periphery

Opinion on the impacts of neoliberalism in the periphery is deeply divided. Often arguments for and against the model are ideological and rhetorical; using no appreciable empirical evidence to back claims. The adoption of neoliberal ideas in the 1980s came in and of itself to be a measure of success. Implicit in this was the motto that short-term economic pain would be required for long-run structural gain (hence the term SAP). It was almost religiously adhered to in neoliberal circles so that short-term structural impacts such as unemployment, underemployment, inequality, balance of payments deficits, environmental damage and so forth would be replaced by a sustainable model of growth eventually. There were some success stories at the macro-economic level and again Chile was perhaps the principal of these – but other countries were held up as models too such as Peru, Tanzania and Fiji. Neoliberal advocates went as far to try and claim success in terms of the Asian Tigers, arguing that it was free market reform that explained their rapid growth in the 1980s. Others pointed to geopolitical factors, such as the Colombo Plan of the 1950s and 1960s and the role of the developmental state as explanatory, contrasting this to the lack of growth in Latin America. This debate continues in the light of reactions to the global financial crisis (GFC).

Based on their 'success', neoliberal ideas were also adopted in the core. In 1979 in the UK under Margaret Thatcher, in 1980 in the USA under President Reagan, and in 1984 in New Zealand, oddly, under the Labour Party, such principles were applied to reform what were argued to be over-bloated statist economies based on Keynesian principles that had dominated in the North since the end of World War II. As noted previously, however, government expenditure and welfare were not cut to the extent that they were in the South – in fact, under both Reagan and Thatcher governments expenditure rose and protectionism was increased, although the direction of policy towards middle-class constituents did rise. In New Zealand a purer form was pursued, state collectives were sold off and protectionism was reduced very rapidly so that by the late 1980s it became the least protected of all agricultural economies (Kelsey 1995). The main point here is that the adoption of such policies led to social differentiation and inequality that effectively created new peripheries within the core. The legacy of this is being felt today in the politics of all of these countries. New Zealand still attracts much international attention in hyperglobalist circles as a model of neoliberal reform, and it is not uncommon to see foreign delegations from countries as diverse as Cambodia, Indonesia and Colombia visiting in order to learn about public sector reform at its supposed hearth. Under the current National Party these reforms have been and are being deepened, despite clear signs that marginalization and peripheralization of the indigenous and the poor continue unabated.

By the early 1990s and following the end of the Cold War the purist arguments from the World Bank and the IMF had been reduced (Stiglitz 2002). They even admitted to some policy errors. But this was in style rather than substance and subsequent policy regimes, as suggested above, followed similar principles while adjusting them at the margins. To a growing number of academics, to civil society and increasingly populations in the global South itself, the impacts of neoliberalism in the periphery were considered nothing short of devastating. The long-run growth had not been delivered and societies were left economically divided, political fragile, culturally threatened and environmentally exploited. There is a vast amount of evidence from Africa, Latin America, the Pacific and Asia that supports this sceptical view of neoliberalism and the promises it made (see Desai and Potter 2013 for an entrance point). Anti-development ideas and, to an extent, post-development ideas came out of a critique of the impacts of neoliberalism in the periphery. In part, these critiques miss the point: it is not 'development' per se that is the problem but the type of development pursued – modernizing neoliberalism – and the concept of development arguably has always contained critiques of the orthodoxy implicit within it, even if it has been obscured by the mainstream (Cowen and Shenton 1996).

Scalar geographies of neoliberalism in the periphery

The idea of a level playing field is a powerful myth that has been rolled out with missionary zeal in order to placate the masses and persuade them to embrace globalization. Neoliberalism has redrawn the global centre–periphery map, largely in favour of the former. The geometry of the world's socio-economic map is much less state-based or defined by north–south or east–west frames: most of the world's poor now live in middle-income countries (this is the China effect) and peripheries (and centres) are being constructed in more complex ways within states, regions, and cities. This is not to say nation-states are not important – they are containers of culture and economic policy. Nation-state governments in the core are complicit in the system that allows the diffusion of capital across the word in the interests of globalized elites. Geography has become increasingly complex, not flattened, and this has occurred in different ways on different scales.

The rise of new peripheries in the core is a meso- and micro-level impact of the continued influence of neoliberalism. In the case of New Zealand, for example, whole regions – such as the east coast of North Island and west coast of South Island, as well as urban areas – such as Porirua and parts of South Auckland – have been socially and economically distanciated from the neoliberal core. Similar processes are evident across the global North – in the UK and Europe, for example. But the new geographies of neoliberalism are no more evident than in the USA. A journey from Colorado to the California coast, as the authors recently undertook, would clearly illustrate this. Contrast the gleaming wealth of Denver with the grinding poverty evident in the Native American reserves of Navajo country where outside latrines and shacks exist side by side with rusty campervans strewn across the desert. The latter is juxtaposed with the neoliberal hypereality of Las Vegas and Hollywood – in many ways the cultural hearth of late neoliberalism. But the rise of new peripheries in the core has had a major impact in terms of the consciousness of society and, to an extent, the Occupy movement can be seen as a product of this. The so-called GFC of 2007–8 seems to have created new geographies on different scales and, within this, a new seed of the undoing of neoliberalism seems to have been sown. Whether civil society will grasp this and push for new reforms remains to be seen: the political inertia and vested interests in the neoliberal system are profound and often lethal when awoken – witness the oppression of protest across the world by police regimes and the growing monitoring of cyberspace, as well as military interventions that ostensibly promote freedom yet in reality search natural resources to sustain the over-consumption of neoliberalism.

In sum, neoliberalism has perpetuated and stimulated peripheralization at different scales in two ways. It has made many peripheral countries even more peripheral in economic terms – although there has been some shift in the geography of this (and the GFC has actually closed that gap, a little, for now). It has also created new peripheries within peripheral countries as certain groups and places are bypassed by the neoliberal superhighway. This has created new macro, meso and micro geographies. Nowhere is this more evident than in Latin America, where the crystallization of inequity is visible in the juxtaposition of shanty towns and sparkling Manhattan-like areas that are evident in virtually every world city in the region such as Santiago,

Lima, Rio de Janeiro, Sao Paulo, Mexico City, Bogota, and Buenos Aires. But there are also new cores in the periphery where capital and wealth are concentrated in new circuits as a result of the opportunities afforded by neoliberalism, as evidenced in terms of innovation ventures such as Ciudad Empresarial just north of Santiago de Chile's centre.

Peripheralization of development ideas and concerns

Neoliberalism is based on an ideology of free markets and globalization, yet this is manifested differently across space in ways which marginalize alternative 'liberalisms' on the periphery and privilege certain markets and market-based ideas at the centre of the global economy. Most critically, neoliberalism reifies the economy as the central mechanism for change. The logic of the market and its liberalization is central. This acts to obscure the non-economic: society, the environment and culture in particular. Notions of liberal societies or free cultural expression or protection of fragile environments – particularly of relevance in the periphery where customary, non-capitalist or non-commodified forms continue to exist – are relegated within a discourse that promotes market-mediated relationships. This narrow interpretation of freedom within neoliberalism gives primacy to certain market freedoms so that, for example, social relations are captured and restructured through labour-wage markets (rather than customary protocols) and resource management decisions are increasingly determined by new market mechanisms such as that for carbon, rather than by state regulation or customary collective ownership. Not only is this more severely felt on the periphery where market penetration has been hitherto more limited, but it also serves to 'peripheralize' culture, society and the environment vis-à-vis the market in discourses of development and change both within and beyond cores.

Neoliberalism is the dominant development ideology. Yet other ideas and critiques have emerged, many from the periphery. While some of these have gained attention and some appeal in the academy globally, they have been generally overlooked, belittled or dispensed with within the wider political and policy domains. For example, structuralist ideas of the 1950s, associated with the United Nations Economic Commission for Latin America and the Caribbean (ECLAC, CEPAL in Spanish), offered a critique of free trade and promoted alternative capitalist models of development, just as dependency theory in the 1970s offered a more radical set of criticisms of the liberal foundations of what became neoliberalism. Despite some enthusiasm in the past, as with the adoption of structuralist-inspired import substitution industrialization strategies, these have been swept aside with neoliberalism, consigned to a 'failed policy' category and denigrated as anti-liberal. It has been convenient to categorize these theories – and the more recent neostructuralist approaches (see below) – as belonging to the periphery (particularly Latin America) and therefore not in the mainstream.

Yet, perhaps most tellingly, neoliberalism has framed development policy in ways which marginalize alternative conceptions of liberalism from the periphery. Neoliberalism has promoted globalization. It has been very successful with regard to the liberalization of trade, investment and tourism and the global protection of property rights (Sheppard and Leitner 2010). This, of course, has favoured capitalist enterprises at the centre: the investment funds and corporations seeking to extend their operations to new markets. And in the workings of the World Trade Organization we can see how even these forms of market liberalization have favoured the centre: later entrants to the WTO from the periphery have had to agree to much more stringent terms and requirements to liberalize their economies than the founding members from the centre.

However, one form of market liberalization that would, arguably, favour economies on the periphery has been noticeably absent from the neoliberal discourse: labour migration.

While international labour mobility has increased markedly, especially with regard to skilled or business migration, most Northern states have been careful to retain strict controls over immigration from the South. They have needed a continued supply of cheap labour and allowed limited movement but, simultaneously, have introduced some of the heaviest forms of state regulation and border controls in order to restrict and control such labour movement. Yet from the perspective of many individuals and communities on the periphery of the global economy, this is the one form of liberalism that might offer some opportunity, given the demise of local protected industries and deregulation of local labour markets. Millions on the periphery have sought ways to engage in labour migration that would connect them to economies at the centre. Labour migration, coupled with remittances of substantial shares of their incomes back to kin on the periphery, has become a highly visible and significant feature of many peripheral economies. Thus, labourers from Pakistan and Bangladesh are the workers who have supported the construction boom in Dubai; workers from central America or the Philippines tend to the gardens and domestic needs of households in the USA or Hong Kong; nurses from the Philippines or Ghana are found in the hospital wards or rest homes of the UK or New Zealand; and Nepalese Ghurkhas and Fijians serve in the British Army. Their remittances now comprise a major share of national income in countries such as Samoa (21 per cent), Haiti (21 per cent), Nepal (25 per cent), and Lesotho (25 per cent), according to World Bank estimates for 2012 (World Bank 2013).[1] Overall, the largest recipients of officially recorded remittances in 2013 were India ($71 billion), China ($60 billion), the Philippines ($26 billion), and Mexico ($22 billion) (ibid.).

The attraction of such earnings has led people from the periphery to seek access to labour markets in the centre either legally (by exploiting family connections or special migration concessions) or illegally (through overstaying tourist visas or entering countries illicitly). To an extent, we can see these strategies of people on the periphery as demonstrating considerable initiative and skill in identifying and exploiting fissures in the global economy. The Tongan writer, Epeli Hau'ofa, for example saw this as an example of the strongly positive and enduring element of Oceanic peoples, in contrast to the negative depictions of Pacific smallness, vulnerability and passivity by commentators from outside the region (Hau'ofa 1993). However, these voices from the periphery espousing a world open to the movement of people and ideas and the facilitation of 'transnational corporations of kin' are not accommodated in a selective neoliberal discourse of globalization. Neoliberalism and the politicians in the West who promote it are happy to talk of free trade and investment but they simultaneously speak of the illegal movement of immigrants and the threat to local ways of life. From this perspective from the periphery, then, neoliberalism is not open and free but rather selective, self-serving and exploitative. George Orwell saw it coming.

Forms of resistance to neoliberalism in the periphery

Resistance to neoliberalism, and capitalism in general, has been ongoing for much time. The Zapatista movement based in Chiapas, Southern Mexico, is often credited as the starting point of the 'anti-globalization' or the 'contra-neoliberalism' movement. It was certainly an important watershed in the movement and led to global recognition and diffusion. Resistance to neoliberalism as we know it actually began in Chile in the 1970s – as this was the first place where it was applied with such force and purity. The student occupations and rock-throwing protests undertaken at Universidad Metropolitana's Pedagogy campus (which had been separated from the wider University of Chile by the dictatorship to break its power and, in a humorous play on the Spanish word for rock, came to be known as the *Piedragogia*), the Chilean new song movement (that began in the late 1960s led by Victor Jara and Violeta Parra, among others, and flowered among the exiled communities led by groups such as Inti Illimani, Illapu and Los Jaivas) and the small but determined armed resistance embodied in such groups as the Manuel Rodriquez Front all formed different aspects of early resistance to neoliberalism when it was combined with murderous oppression. As already noted, the purity of Chile's neoliberal experiment would never have survived without that oppression – and when the dictatorship finally fell in 1990 neoliberalism morphed into a more human form – neostructuralism – to which resistance has continued right up the present day, leading most recently to the globally significant student protests of the so-called *Invierno Chileno* ('Chilean Winter') from 2012 to the present.

The anti-neoliberal movement, of course, has been active all across the global South and in many forms, and comes out of earlier resistances to modernization and capitalism and colonialism in general. This amorphous nature has been – to some – its very downfall. The overgeneralized nature of the anti-globalization movement has perhaps reduced its effectiveness. Furthermore, the war in Iraq and more recent concerns with terror in the Middle East have deflected attention from the movement in ways that might suggest that capitalist governments have encouraged this refocusing, worried by the growing challenge presented by such a movement. There have been other forms of resistance – state-centred alliances – for example, such as the G77, the Banco Sur, the left-leaning Latin American governments of the 2000s, but these are often painted as troublesome in a northern-controlled monopolistic media which exist to peripheralize alternatives and, to use Chomsky's phrase, manufacture consent. The rise of neostructuralism in Latin America seemed to suggest an organized resistance to the dominant models; and the alignment of Argentina, Chile, Ecuador, Bolivia, and Venezuela, together with their mutual empathy to Cuba in the 2000s, seemed to suggest a new direction for a while (Petras 1999). But, predictably, this has been undermined by the media and even nation-states (US involvement with Venezuela, for example). Elsewhere we contest that weak forms of neostructuralism have become nothing but neoliberalism in slightly more palatable clothing in an electoral sense.

One example of resistance to neoliberalism in the periphery involved protests against attempts to privatize communal land. Following from the ideas of de Soto and others, reform packages in several countries in the 1990s sought to release land held under customary communal tenure and convert it to individual tradable title. Such a change, it has been argued, would allow land owners to free up land for development, provide the incentive for individual investment and gain access to credit markets. In areas where such communal tenure still prevails – in the Pacific Islands, South America and Africa – many groups have a strong historical, cultural and spiritual connection to the land: the home of their ancestors and the means of survival. In Papua New Guinea, after strong pressure from aid donors such as Australia, the IMF and World Bank, the government moved to introduce laws that would help privatize land (as well as a wider programme of privatization of state assets). In 2001 this led to student and local protests and a police crackdown, which left several dead. There was eventually an electoral backlash and the policy change was dropped.

Resistance at the periphery has also taken on less overt or political forms. Work by post-development theorists such as Gibson-Graham has pointed to the way some communities in the Philippines, for example, have built 'diverse economies'. These are local systems that do not entirely reject capitalism but build on a strong foundation of communal self-reliance and reciprocity in ways which help preserve social forms and cultural norms. They are conscious efforts to opt out of some of the perceived more harmful aspects of capitalism. In this way these local economies develop resilience against external shocks and preserve systems of mutual support as a counter to the creative destruction that the market brings. Such forms of organization are not centrally organized or coordinated, nor do they represent a serious threat to the neoliberal project. Yet, in the multiplicity of such diverse efforts to insulate communities at the periphery and elsewhere from the dangers of the market, while retaining access to some of its opportunities, these local movements may point to the limits of neoliberalism on its margins.

Even in the face of the GFC – the worst capitalist crisis in eight decades if not in history – the anti-neoliberal movement – which re-emerged as the Occupy movement – has not managed to break the monopoly on power enjoyed by the very elites that created the conditions leading to the crisis in the first place. The GFC led to the widespread condemnation of neoliberalism, but, ironically, a retrenching in its strength and a re-export of the model across the world have occurred as powerful vested interests managed to overturn any meaningful reform and twist the argument so that it appeared that the reason for the collapse was 'imperfect markets'. This will create ongoing resistance in the periphery for many years to come (Altvater 2009). Tensions between China, Russia and the West, and indeed the current ISIS battle which came out of the occupation of Iraq and false dawn of the Arab Spring, are associated with the GFC and the failure of neoliberalism to deliver global prosperity and democracy as was believed in the heady days of the late 1970s and early 1980s.

The reincarnations of neoliberalism in the periphery: the rise of retroliberalism

Neoliberalism has proved to be resilient, changing its course and appearance over the past 30 years. In many ways, these changes have been felt particularly strongly on the periphery, the structural adjustment policies of the 1990s being perhaps the most glaring example of the export of a particularly virulent strain of neoliberalism. More recently, and in the aftermath of the GFC, a new form has appeared, a variant we term 'retroliberalism' (Murray and Overton forthcoming).

The GFC hit the economies of Europe and North America particularly hard. Those countries on the periphery that had close trading connections with these regions, such as Argentina or South Africa, also experienced economic reversals (Murray and Overton 2014). However, other economies fared batter and continued economic growth in China helped them bounce back: the GFC thus helped to reconfigure the periphery and align many more towards East Asia – especially China – rather than North America or Europe. Yet at a more fundamental level, the GFC led to a metamorphosis in neoliberalism. Forced to bail out many large corporations and introduce Keynesian-style stimulus packages to avert deep economic crisis, Western economies began to adopt a new economic strategy that seemed a far cry from the fundamental early versions of neoliberalism. Neoliberal states appeared to be much less averse to supporting private enterprises, first through immediate crisis-inspired stimulus packages and then, later, by attempts to export such stimulus in more covert ways (Mawdsley *et al.* forthcoming).

As with earlier forms, this new variant of neoliberalism was transferred from the centre to the periphery via aid (as well as conditional loans). In the decade prior to the GFC, international aid had both increased significantly in volume and sharpened in focus, guided by the launch of the Millennium Development Goals (MDGs) in 2000 and agreements such as the Paris Declaration of 2005 (Mawdsley *et al.* 2014). Elsewhere we have termed this the 'neostructural period' (Murray and Overton 2011) as it was influenced by earlier structuralist ideas from Latin America but combined these with outward-oriented models that would favour the free market and stimulate globalization. There was a focus on poverty alleviation and a recognition of the need to support recipient states to develop effective systems of governance in order to pursue these development strategies. There was still a strong concern to continue to liberalize markets and promote global trade and investment. After the GFC, aid levels from Western donors surprisingly did not diminish – some, such as the UK, even increased their aid budgets. But the nature of aid changed. For many donors, the explicit concern for poverty alleviation was replaced by notions of promoting 'sustainable economic development' and, later, the catchphrase of 'shared prosperity' was adopted, a none-too-subtle device to allow for more articulation of donor self-interest in aid. Part of this self-interest was constructed around geopolitical concerns, such as the interventions in Afghanistan, but much was economic: the active promotion of the private sector and the commercial interests of companies in donor countries as they sought to build operations overseas. Retroliberalism in this way has many expressions in the aid world. The UK aid agency, the Department for International Development (DFID), now works in conjunction with City of London financial institutions to promote financial services in sub-Saharan Africa; the New Zealand aid agency has an agreement with Fonterra, a large dairy conglomerate, to – for example – help develop dairy supply chains in Sri Lanka, and Canada has seemingly directed some of its aid to countries where its own mining companies are seeking to expand. Interestingly, these approaches of Western aid donors now resemble somewhat the approach of China to 'South–South cooperation', whereby Chinese state funds are loaned or granted to recipients who then engage Chinese firms to build highways or public buildings.

This retroliberal approach has pitched the notion – the myth – of shared prosperity as a new aid regime. It echoes, to an extent, the 'trickle down' mantra of early neoliberalism (poverty would only be tackled through economic growth), but it goes further to suggest that promotion of one's own prosperity is allowable and desirable. However, because it moved away from an explicit concern for poverty and inequality, in effect it promoted an approach which shared the benefits of economic growth among the elites of donor and recipient countries and further marginalized the poor.

Conclusion

Neoliberalism remains as powerful in the periphery today as it was when first applied in the 1970s. It continues to reorder space along lines that are attractive to capital and, although the geographies shift and become more intricate and complex, the rationale remains the same. The forces that back it also remain much the same.

This is evidenced by the retrenchment of neoliberalism after its obvious failure in the GFC and the rise of the latest version, retroliberalism. Neoliberalism has and will continue to exploit, create and perpetuate peripheries in both a territorial sense and social sense at micro, meso and macro scales across the world. This is because neoliberalism is predicated on differentiation – inequality is not just a consequence of the system, it is the system.

We urgently require new geographical theories to untangle the new geometry of neoliberalism. A new dependency combined with post-development ideas that are realist rather than naively relativistic might be the place to start. As such, until other ideas emerge from the periphery, both spatial and social, and until these are captured by the political classes, neoliberalism will continue to re-write global geographies in ways that entrench peripheries in order to foster the continued exploitation of society and the environment in the name of capital accumulation for an elite minority.

Note

1 Rates of remittances are also high for countries on the margins of Europe (Tajikistan, Moldova, Amenia or Kosovo).

References

Altvater, E. 2009. Postneoliberalism or Postcapitalism? The Failure of Neoliberalism in the Financial Market Crisis. *Development Dialogue*, 51: 73–86.

Cowen, M., and Shenton, R.W. 1996. *Doctrines of Development*. London: Taylor & Francis.

Desai, V., and Potter, R.B. 2013. *The Companion to Development Studies*. London: Routledge.

Frank, A.G. 1969. *Capitalism and Underdevelopment in Latin America*. New York: New York Monthly Press.

Gwynne, R.N., and Kay, C. 2004. *Latin America Transformed: Globalization and Modernity*. 2nd edn. London: Arnold.

Harvey, D. 2005. *A Brief History of Neoliberalism*. Oxford: Oxford University Press.

Hau'ofa, E. 1993. *A New Oceania: Rediscovering Our Sea of Islands*. Suva: School of Social and Economic Development at the University of the South Pacific in association with Beake House.

Kay, C. 1989. *Latin American Theories of Development and Underdevelopment*. London: Routledge.

Kelsey, J. 1995. *The New Zealand Experiment: A World Model for Structural Adjustment?* Auckland: Auckland University Press.

Larner, W. 2000. Neo-liberalism: Policy, Ideology, Governmentality. *Studies in Political Economy*. 63.

—. 2003. Neoliberalism? *Environment and Planning D*, 21.5: 509–12.

Mawdsley, E., Savage, L., and Kim, S.-M. 2014. A 'Post-aid World'? Paradigm Shift in Foreign Aid and Development Cooperation at the 2011 Busan High Level Forum. *Geographical Journal*, 180.1: 27–38.

Mawdsley, E., Murray, W.E., Overton, J., Scheyvens, R., and Banks, G.A. Forthcoming. Exporting Stimulus and 'Shared Prosperity': Re-inventing Aid for a Retroliberal Era. *Development Policy Review*.

Murray, W.E. 2009. Neoliberalism and Development, in Thrift, N., and Kitchen, R., eds. *International Encyclopaedia of Human Geography*. London: Routledge.

Murray, W.E., and Overton, J. 2011. Neoliberalism is Dead, Long Live Neoliberalism: Neostructuralism and the New International Aid Regime of the 2000s. *Progress in Development Studies*, 11.4: 307–19.

—. 2014. *Geographies of Globalization*. second edition. New York and London: Routledge.

—. Forthcoming. Retroliberalism and the New Aid Regime of the 2010s. *Progress in Development Studies*.

Peck, J., Theodore, N., and Brenner, N. 2010. Postneoliberalism and its Malcontents. *Antipode*, 41.1: 94–116.

Petras, J.F. 1999. *The Left Strikes Back: Class Conflict in Latin America in the Age of Neoliberalism*. Boulder, CO: Westview Press.

Sheppard, E., and Leitner, H. 2010. Quo Vadis Neoliberalism? The Remaking of Global Capitalist Governance After the Washington Consensus. *Geoforum*, 41.2: 185–94.

Stiglitz, J.E. 2002. *Globalization and Its Discontents*. London: Penguin.

World Bank. 2013. *Migration and Development*. Brief 21. Washington, DC: World Bank.

37

NEOLIBERAL GEOPOLITICS

Susan M. Roberts

Neoliberalism, taken to indicate social practices that enact multiple extensions of market logics, may be presumed to signal a kind of anti- or post-geopolitics. After all, the most famous adjective to describe the desired global space of neoliberalism is 'flat' (Friedman 2005; Ohmae 1991). The flatness indicates the eroded significance of national boundaries and of differences of most sorts between people and places across the planet (Brown 2006: 699). Geopolitics, by contrast, relies on a world whose surface is not flat. It is, rather, a world exhaustively divided into differentiated territorial states. Moreover, geopolitics understands each state as having its own interests and as pursuing these with force when and where it is expedient.

In geopolitics the capacitated actors defining the world's surface are taken to be states acting on behalf of their own (national) societies. The goals are (national) security and (relative) power. However, in a neoliberal flat world, the capacitated actors are identified as capital. Most obviously this includes corporations, acting on behalf of their investors and managers. But, since neoliberalism re-casts society as individuals understood as human capital, then individuals (who may be employees/employers, consumers, producers, investors, etc.) are individuated capitals themselves too. Instead of states and their respective national societies, the flat neoliberal world is populated by corporations and by individuals understood as, and who understand themselves as, 'little specks of capital' (Brown 2014a). Both firms and individuals are organized by, and themselves organize, market logics. And, they relate to one another through market logics (of price, choice, enterprise and, above all, competition) rather than geopolitical logics (of identity, territory, force, war). This thumbnail sketch of the differences between geopolitical and neoliberal rationalities and logics, though crude and overstated, serves to highlight the point that one might expect that, as neoliberalism has become an increasingly salient feature of life across the globe, geopolitics as a mode of state practice would fade away.

This chapter argues that there has, indeed, been a change in how geopolitics works, but that this is better understood as a reworking of geopolitics than its redundancy. Geopolitical imperatives remain salient, but their content and conduct are being constantly reworked as political and social life move in neoliberal directions. Geopolitics and economics have never been separate pure logics (see Mercille 2008 on the Vietnam War, for example), so the point is not so much that they are intertwined, but that contemporary neoliberal market-based logics are coming to rework the nature and practice of geopolitics. Geopolitics can be thought of as one 'technology of rule' and neoliberalism can be thought of a parcel of market-based 'technologies of rule' and, as many analysts of neoliberal governmentality have shown, it is not a case of either/or. It is not state (or plan) *or* market (Teivainen 2002; Lemke 2013; Brown 2014b). Geopolitical logics and techniques work with, rework, and are reworked by, market-based logics and techniques, meaning we need to 'attend to the co-existence, complementarity and interference of different technologies of rule' (Lemke 2013: 41) or their 'hybridization' (Essex 2012). Moreover, these interactions and meldings of geopolitical and neoliberal technologies of rule are highly contingent outcomes of social and political practices of all sorts. So, as Clive Barnett noted, this entails viewing 'political rationalities as emergent qualities of dynamic interactions' (Barnett 2009: 284). The result of these contingent intersections may be a set of practices that we might identify as neoliberal geopolitics. But this is a highly contingent and variable outcome, not some necessary corollary of an epoch-change, nor of some singular logic of the state or of the market.

The actual trends and examples discussed in much (though not all) the literature on neoliberalism and also in this chapter are, it should be noted, drawn mainly from the global North, and from the USA and Europe in particular. These are not selected because they are to be construed as some kind of leading edge, or as in some ways exemplary, but rather simply because they are familiar to the author. As many have pointed out, the direction neoliberalism takes is highly contextual and there is no singular neoliberal geopolitics that can be identified as operating everywhere in the same way (see, for example, Brenner *et al.* 2010 on 'variegated neoliberalization', and Springer 2011 on 'articulated neoliberalism').

Taking cues from the theorization and diagnosis of neoliberalism offered by Michel Foucault in his 1978–9 lectures, and from the contemporary work of scholars such as Wendy Brown and Thomas Lemke, I treat a neoliberal geopolitics as one facet of a complex situation in which 'the market, competition, and so the enterprise', emerge 'into what could be called the formative power of society' (Foucault 2008: 148). This is not to say that with neoliberalism there occurs a replacement of the political with the economic; and it is not to say that the state is merely positioned as a servant of economic interests. It is more a case of proliferating and diverse situations in which there is a re-making of the political (of the state and of citizens) through market logics. As Wendy Brown has put it:

> more than simply facilitating the economy, the state itself must construct and construe itself in market terms, as well as develop policies and promulgate a political culture that figures citizens exhaustively as rational economic actors in every sphere of life.
>
> *(2006: 694)*

She elaborates:

> The state itself is enfolded and animated by market rationality, not simply profitability, but a generalized calculation of cost and benefit becomes the measure of all state practices. Political discourse on all matters is framed in entrepreneurial terms; *the state must not simply concern itself with the market but think and behave like a market actor* across all of its functions, including law.
>
> *(Brown 2003: n.p., emphasis in original)*

To explore the content and conduct of neoliberal geopolitics, this chapter proceeds by tracing the fortunes of the concept 'geoeconomics' as a term deployed to capture the changed orientation and operation of geopolitics. The term itself can be easily critiqued as a crude one, relying on a realist conception of the state, but it can usefully be examined as a kind of indicator of how neoliberal geopolitics coalesces and functions, at least in the USA and selected states in Europe.

After a brief history of the deployment of the idea of geoeconomics, the chapter turns to consider examples that may be taken to indicate various aspects of a neoliberal geopolitics.

Geoeconomics

US-based military strategist and writer Edward Luttwak, in a 1998/1990 article on *National Interest* and in a subsequent book (1998[1990], 1993), made the case for 'geoeconomics'. He noted that 'as the relevance of military threats and military alliances wanes, geoeconomic priorities and modalities are becoming dominant in state action' (1998[1990]: 127). This was a time in the USA when there was considerable anxiety about the implications of globalization, about the relative rise of Japan as an economic power, and about changes to come from the end of the Cold War. Popular analyses by authors such as Paul Kennedy (1989), Kenichi Ohmae (1991), Francis Fukuyama (1992), and Samuel Huntington (1993) variously proclaimed the dawn of a new phase in world politics. Luttwak's description of a new era defined by geoeconomics, distinguished from the previous era of geopolitics, drew on many of the same motifs of globalization and, though it did not sell as many copies as these other popular narratives, it struck a chord.

In fact, Luttwak did not claim a simple model of history in which a pure form of geoeconomics completely erased a previously prevailing pure geopolitical form of inter-state relations. Unlike many popular analysts, he argued that states' capacities to act were not diminished in the face of globalization. Instead, he proposed 'a much less complete transformation of state action' (1998[1990]: 127) in which states still were significant geopolitical actors with fundamentally unchanged (realist) goals. To achieve these goals, though, Luttwak argued that states (especially the more powerful) were changing their strategies and tools, looking more to the geoeconomic rather than the geopolitical. He wrote of an 'admixture of the logic of conflict with the methods of commerce – or, as Clausewitz would have written, the logic of war in the grammar of commerce' (ibid.: 126). In the USA in the late 1980s and early 1990s, especially during the first Clinton administration, there was much debate over globalization, national competitiveness, the value of free trade, and the utility of strategic trade policies. Luttwak's views reflect this period, to be sure, but his work did identify that, for some states, economic rationalities and market-based modes of calculating and acting were coming to 'trump' any other rationalities (including geopolitical). He stated decisively that 'there is *no superior modality*' to geoeconomics (ibid.: 128, emphasis original).

As Matthew Sparke has noted, Luttwak's idea of geoeconomics is useful inasmuch as it 'gets at the way in which a more or less geopolitical phenomena (of imagining territory as a mode of political intervention and governance) is closely articulated with a whole series of economic imperatives, ideas and ideologies' (Sparke 1998: 69–70). Luttwak himself claimed that the geoeconomic modality arose from two dynamics: first, the needs of state bureaucrats to find a new post-Cold War rationale for themselves, and, second, the 'instrumentalization of the state by economic interest groups that seek to manipulate its activities on the international scene for their own purposes' (Luttwak 1998[1990]: 126; see also Aligica 2002). This points us towards the potential utility of examining exactly which bureaucrats and which 'economic interest groups' find the resources of state power useful, in what ways that happens, and with what effects.

However, by the turn of the millennium, the term geoeconomics had faded away. Then the events of 11 September 2001, the military operations by the USA and allies in Afghanistan from October 2001, and the 2003 US-led invasion and occupation of Iraq seemed to signal the apparent return of geopolitics and the logic of war, and geoeconomics seemed much less relevant. It appeared that geoeconomics had been 'a creature of the early and mid-1990s' only

(Thirlwell 2010: 9). Nonetheless, after a period of dormancy, the term has been revived, making something of a comeback in more recent years (Aligica 2002; Thirlwell 2010).

Thus, in 2011 Robert Youngs wrote, from his perspective in a European think tank that 'A concept that found itself out of favour in the more optimistic and less ribald 1990s has been dusted off', explaining that 'the euro crisis and shifts in global power require a more assertive focus on immediate economic interests' and have prompted 'a "return of geo-economics"' (Youngs 2011: 13). Geoeconomics maintained some currency in the world of US think tanks too. For example, in 2000 the Council of Foreign Relations established a Center for Geoeconomic Studies, using geoeconomics to indicate an interest in 'how economic and political forces interact to influence world affairs' (CFR 2015). Meanwhile, in France, economist Pascal Lorot and colleagues at the think tank Institut Choiseul have promoted geoeconomics as an area of enquiry, founding the journal *Géoéconomie* in 1997 (see Lorot 1999, 2001: 46).

In the borderlands between popular business school approaches to understanding the world economy and policy-wonkdom, Swedish management professor, Klaus Solberg Søilen, has recently promoted geoeconomics reconceptualized along the lines of another influential analysis of the early 1990s, that of the 'competitive advantage of nations' advanced by Michael Porter (Porter 1990). Competition, for Søilen, is the key to understanding geoeconomics. He states, 'What has changed in the 21st century is that the aim is no longer to fight a political ideology with another one, but to become more practical, to develop the most competitive society. The difference is paramount' (2010: n.p., see also 2012).

More recently, a deeper attempt to engage with geoeconomics has been made by Paul Dragos Aligica and colleagues based at the Mercatus Institute, a pro-free market think tank hosted by George Mason University in the USA (Aligica 2002; Aligica and Tarko 2012). Aligica and Tarko, for example, have asked whether geoeconomic actions on the part of states (especially those characterized by so-called state capitalism) can be explained as contingent outcomes of rent-seeking behaviours. So, for example they see how states might use state-owned enterprises, national oil companies, or sovereign wealth funds to generate revenue when tax regimes are weak, not as a grand strategy, but as a result of rent-seeking by individuals and institutions.

The earlier 1990s formulations of geoeconomics were reactions to a time in which the rise of Japan and the problems and possibilities of trade were key, while the more recent formulations tend, inevitably, to focus on the rise of China and on the problems and possibilities of finance. In more recent work, the 2008 and onward economic crisis, and the problems of the eurozone, are featured frequently. The recent works using the term 'geoeconomics' are not, by and large, informed by either political economy or governmentality approaches to neoliberalism. Nonetheless, there are several ways in which they point to features of the contemporary character and operations of political and economic life that are identified as significant by scholars of neoliberalism.

In geography, Matt Sparke has offered analyses of contemporary states' strategies in which he has mobilized a modified understanding of geoeconomics that highlights the ways in which global-local relations are re-imagined (Sparke 2005, 2007; Sparke and Lawson 2003; see also Hyndman 1996; Coleman 2007). In a similar vein, recent work by Sami Moisio and Anssi Paasi has explicated how changing geoeconomic considerations and 'market calculations' 'increasingly govern the social in the state's [internal] welfare policies' (2013: 268). The relationship between geoeconomics and neoliberal governance was a central concern of Deborah Cowen and Neil Smith in a 2009 paper. Picking up on Sparke's earlier analyses, they linked the 'rise of the geoeconomic' and the 'erosion of geopolitical calculation' to pervasive concerns with security. They pointed to 'an emerging geography of economy and security' with 'attendant social forms' (Cowen and Smith 2009: 22–3). In related work, Jamey Essex focuses on the productive discursive elements of both geopolitics and geoeconomics in his study of USAID. He stresses the 'overlaps and tensions' between them (2013: 8) and the way institutional actors strategically select elements of each discursive resource. In 2003, Roberts *et al.* investigated the way elements of neoliberalism were 'interarticulat[ed] with certain dangerous supplements, including, not least of all, the violence of American military force' in shaping and carrying out the US-led invasion and occupation of Iraq (2003: 887). They noted the 'more open, systematic, globally ambitious, and quasi-corporate economic style' of US war-making (ibid.: 888) and how it was legitimated in terms of a neoliberal insistence on integration into the world economy. The work of John Morrissey (2008, 2011) has focused on the role of neoliberal technologies, such as risk assessment, in the US military's interventions in the Middle East. Simon Springer has carefully attended to how, in some times and some places, neoliberalism intersects with Orientalism and colonialist/racist mappings of global spaces and their populations, to promote and legitimize forcible integration as 'civilizing' (Springer 2009, 2013). Whether or not these developments are labelled 'neoliberal geopolitics', each of these geographical analyses raises questions about the nature of the contemporary neoliberalized state and about the reconfigured relations between states, capital, and subjects/citizens.

Some recent geographical analyses of neoliberalism draw upon Foucault's lectures on neoliberalism. For the purposes here, Foucault's observation that 'The market economy does not take something away from government. Rather, it indicates, it constitutes the general index in which one must place the rule for defining all governmental action' (2008: 121) is a significant starting point. While earlier investigations of neoliberalism tended to regard the extension of state activities as a contradiction within neoliberal logic (see Barnett 2009 for a critical overview), more recent work is more in line with Foucault's idea that market logics come to define, rather than diminish, governmental action. Relatedly, Foucault's stress that neoliberalism is characterized by a market logic that is *not* based on supply and demand and on trading, but rather *is* based on competition and enterprise, is important. Foucault said: 'the market that the neoliberals are thinking about is a society in which the regulatory principle should not be so much the exchange of commodities as the mechanisms of competition' (2008: 147), a point he summed up by saying this is 'Not a supermarket society, but an enterprise society' (ibid.). Wendy Brown (2014a, 2014b), in particular, has traced the implications of the enterprise form, and, as Jason Read has noted:

> The shift from exchange to competition has profound effects: while exchange was considered to be natural, competition is understood by the neoliberals of the twentieth century to be an artificial relation that must be protected against the tendency for markets to form monopolies and interventions by the state. Competition necessitates a constant intervention on the part of the state, not on the market, but on the conditions of the market.
>
> *(2009: 28)*

Several researchers have taken this so-called governmentality approach, inspired by Foucault's ideas, and focused on how subjectivity gets reworked under these conditions (see, for example, Larner 2000; Walker *et al.* 2008). Here, though, my interest lies in how the 'regulatory principle' of competition relates to states' foreign policies: in how such forms of neoliberal geopolitics might be operating in the contemporary world.

The US-led invasion and occupation of Iraq (and to an extent the US-led war in Afghanistan) has been treated by many analysts as exemplifying a form of neoliberal geopolitics (Roberts *et al.* 2003; Cowen and Smith 2009). Indeed, the spectacularly bald manner in which the economic interests of the USA and US-based firms were promoted and secured through military force in Iraq cannot be ignored. From the privatization of force itself (Gallagher 2012) and the pervasive role of contractors in all aspects of the occupation (Roberts 2013) to the explicitly geoeconomic aim and calculus of the 2003–4 Coalition Provisional Authority (CPA) in Iraq (Morrissey 2008, 2011), the market, indeed, provided the 'general index' for the occupation's technologies of rule.

The rule of the CPA in Iraq might stand as an historically pivotal moment in the geohistory of neoliberal geopolitics, but there are a proliferating number of phenomena that one can identify as entailing neoliberal geopolitics. One could point, first, to the ways in which development has been re-cast as a project saturated with the logics and technologies of competition and enterprise. For example, US foreign assistance for development (as a subset of foreign aid), relies much more now on private corporations and organizations which, in many cases, bid to win contracts to 'deliver' development programmes as technologies of rule through 'soft Power' (Roberts 2014). The USA's Millennium Challenge Corporation, established in 2004 to operationalize performance-based funding for economic development projects, evinces neoliberal development in a corporate form, as a facet of neoliberal geopolitics (Soederberg 2004; Mawdsley 2007; Roberts 2013). A second example of the ways organizational forms and practices of geopolitics have shifted more fully to the index of the market could be drawn from the area of intelligence. Like development assistance, US intelligence is more and more carried out by private corporations. More significantly, through the use of volunteered information and open source processes, intelligence is relying on market-indexed technologies of rule and risk developing around and through the phenomenon of big data (Crampton *et al.* 2013). To develop these points a little further I turn now to a different example of geopolitics indexed to the market: a recent series of high-profile trade missions to India undertaken by the British government.

The 2013 British trade mission to India

> My first priority as Prime Minister is to do everything I can to ensure that Britain succeeds in the Global Race. I know we have the great businesses and entrepreneurs to make that possible. But I also know that success in business does not just happen. We cannot rely merely on sentiment and shared history with our trading partners. We have to get out there, make the case for Britain and open doors for British business.
>
> (Cameron 2013)

With these words, the British Prime Minister framed his second visit to India as leader of a large trade delegation (the first one had taken place in 2010). '[M]aking the case for Britain' and 'open[ing] doors for British business' is an activist agenda, very much in line with Foucault's identification of an interventionist neoliberal state, working to secure the conditions to 'make the market possible' (2008: 146) but enacted and extended on the basis of a geopolitical imagination (of Britain, of India, of British business and so on). But the Prime Minister, here as in many other speeches and writings, frames the imperative in terms of a race; in fact, *the* 'Global Race' (capitalized in the original). It is hard to think of a metaphor more directly invoking mandatory competition as the condition framing both Britain and 'British business' and hence the work of the state:

> Rushed into use shortly after the 2012 Olympics, by a party whose key figures went to expensive schools that fetishise sport and general competitiveness, 'the global race'

is hardly the most subtle or socially sensitive of rhetorical devices. But it has the advantage of flexibility.

(Beckett 2013: n.p.)

The historical and deeply complex social resonances of the race metaphor lend it plausibility and efficacy, no doubt. It brings with it a host of associated ideas that can be invoked by those wishing to legitimize the practices it is used to describe and sell. Hence:

> Britain, the Tories tell us, needs to 'win' it, 'succeed' in it, and get 'to the top' in it; 'compete' in it, 'thrive in' it, and be 'strong' in it; 'fight' in it; or merely, 'equip' itself for it and 'get fit for' it. If Britain fails to do some or all of these things, it will 'sink', 'lose', 'fall behind', be left in 'the slow lane', or let 'others take over'.

(Ibid.)

More generally, these terms apply equally to the individual's project of being an entrepreneur of him- or herself, responsible for getting into good condition to run the race, investing in their own future (through education, going to the gym, eating healthily etc.) to succeed in the competition (see Lemke 2001; Oksala 2013: 65). The Prime Minister's delegation to India, framed thus, is drawing on the 'race's' multiple valences to cohere this more recent version of the long-standing practice of the trade mission. A closer look at the composition of the large delegation makes its thoroughly neoliberal character clear. Accompanying the Prime Minister on the 2013 trip was a group comprising: three ministers (the Minister of State – Foreign and Common-wealth Office; the Minister for Universities and Science; and the recently created Minister for Business Engagements with India); over 100 'business delegates' (a group that included many major corporations' CEOs and more than a half dozen prominent university vice chancellors); eight MPs; plus several diplomats and various other officials (HM Government 2013). These delegates' work complemented the routine work of diplomatic staff to promote the business interests of their compatriots. A recent research project found that diplomats report spending an increasing proportion of their time on issues broadly construed as 'commercial diplomacy' (Kostecki and Naray 2007). The Prime Minister's delegation brought together high-profile emissaries from the worlds of the state, capital, and academe to join forces in an effort to run the global race on behalf of 'Britain', 'projecting [the principles of a market economy] on to a general art of government' (Foucault 2008: 131).

More specifically, the Prime Minister hoped he could use the trade delegation's visit to clinch one of the biggest arms deals in history. He was keen to secure a major deal for aircraft to replace India's aging MiG-21 fighter jet fleet with the so-called Eurofighter (developed by a consortium of British, German, Italian, and Spanish firms – led by Airbus) and thus win the competition with the Rafale fighter produced by France's Dassault. In this regard, the visit to India was not unusual. Representing the interests of weapons systems manufacturers is a major part of what the highest-level elected officials do when they visit 'partner' countries. In his earlier visit, Cameron had secured a £700 million deal for Hawk training jets, benefiting British-based manufacturers BAE Systems and Rolls-Royce, and during his visit to India in July 2014 the UK's Foreign Secretary William Hague again promoted the Eurofighter with the newly elected Modi government.

Arms deals have long been components of the geopolitical economy; they are 'major strands in the warp and woof of international affairs' (Pierre 1981/2: n.p.). But now it is not just big weapons systems that national leaders undertake to sell. With the rise of the security industries, specializing in everything from counter-terrorism to surveillance and risk analysis, and with the blurring of the defence, policing, private security, big data analysis and intelligence domains, commercial diplomacy now also entails promoting firms across these sectors. In the case of the UK–India relationship, for example, it was reported that, a few weeks before Cameron's huge delegation arrived in India, the UK's Minister for Security, James Brokenshire, had been there, leading a delegation of 'homeland security' firms (Statewatch 2013).

Arms deals are often represented in the language of partnership rather than, or alongside, the commercial interests of the firms involved. Indeed, Prime Minister Cameron told his audience in India 'Britain wants to be your partner of choice'. Partnership conjures the enterprise aspect of market rationality and reworks the relationship between places, in this case between Britain and India. (On the uses of the 'partnership narrative' in neoliberalism more generally, see Davies 2007 and Larner and Craig 2005.) The partnership idea is also aligned with the logic of competition, since Britain's trade mission has, of course, to be seen in the context of a world economy whose most dynamic cores are in Asia and in which the relatively troubled economies of Europe and North America are anxious to 'partner' with rising powers – including India. Britain's 2013 delegation followed high-level visits to India from the USA, Germany, and France, each seeking to be India's favourite partner.

The trade mission also highlights the melding of state and corporate interests and identities. As Luttwak noted in his formulation of geoeconomics, there is an 'instrumentalization' of the state which can pre-empt questions about its political implications. Wendy Brown has observed:

> Thus, from the 'scandal' of Enron to the 'scandal' of Vice President Cheney delivering Iraq to Halliburtion to clean up and rebuild, there is no scandal. Rather, there is only market rationality, a rationality that can encompass even a modest amount of criminality but also treats close state–corporate ties as a potentially positive value – maximizing the aims of each – rather than as a conflict of interest.
>
> *(2003: n.p.)*

Conclusions

The lurching and highly unevenly distributed contemporary world economy and the foreign policy of the world's states are intertangled and co-constitutive. Older conceptualizations and typologies of states and markets seem no longer relevant. China, in particular seems to confound categories. Is it best understood as 'state capitalism', 'socialism with Chinese characteristics', or 'neoliberalism with Chinese characteristics', or a new version of a 'developmental state'? But, as this chapter has touched upon, the British and US states are no less confounding for those seeking to fit them into simple typologies. Some would look to the term 'geoeconomics' to signal the tendency for states to craft and carry out foreign policy based on economic goals and using market-based strategies, and while the term has not enjoyed much currency in more critical scholarly circles, it does signal some significant aspects of the shifting imagination and practice of geopolitics.

When the desired global space of states is described in terms of partnerships, with states teaming up for a race that is a competition, but one presumed to be a win–win scenario, the market is the rationality holding this contradictory image together. The market is imagined as an arena in which calculating individuals, firms, states, compete, but in which it is possible for even the last one to cross the finish line to have gained in some manner. As Luttwak noted, 'war is a zero-sum encounter' but 'commercial relations need not be, and indeed rarely have been' (1998[1990]: 130). States are both competitors in the race and the coaches/trainers/facility builders/award givers for 'their' (and here there are multiple negotiations and inclusions and exclusions over who belongs) firms and citizens, each themselves competing. Such are the conditions in which neoliberal logics rework state practices, including foreign policy. Contemporary forms of neoliberal geopolitics are neither stable nor coherent. Rather, they are a diverse ('variegated') mixture of rationalities and strategies, with some succeeding and some failing. But variously neoliberalized states formulate and conduct foreign policy based on and assessed in terms of the 'Great Race', of competition and enterprise, mixed with concerns for security and risk.

To more fully understand what is happening, and to resist the easy (but meaningless) diagnosis of everything as neoliberal, it will be important for those interested in the contemporary geopolitical economy to trace how exactly market calculations and the logics of competition and enterprise get reworked by states and rework those states themselves in the process. This does not mean that older ideas, such as crony-capitalism or rent-seeking, are no longer relevant. But seeing how such phenomena interlink with broader social and political (and, even psychological) shifts, as the market becomes the regulatory principle for everything, can help us connect the dots somewhat.

References

Aligica, P.D. 2002. Geo-economics as a Geo-strategic Paradigm: An Assessment. *American Outlook Today*, Hudson Institute, 9 August.

Aligica, P.D., and Tarko, V. 2012. State Capitalism and the Rent-Seeking Conjuncture. *Constitutional Political Economy*, 23.4: 357–79.

Barnett, C. 2009. Publics and Markets: What's Wrong with Neoliberalism? In Smith, S., Marston, S., Pain, R., and Jones III, J.P., eds. *The Handbook of Social Geography*. London: Sage: 269–96.

Beckett, A. 2013. What is The 'Global Race'? *The Guardian*, 22 September. Retrieved from http://www.theguardian.com/politics/2013/sep/22/what-is-global-race-conservatives-ed-miliband

Brenner, N., Peck, J., and Theodore, N. 2010. Variegated Neoliberalization: Geographies, Modalities, Pathways. *Global Networks*, 10.2: 182–222.

Brown, W. 2003. Neo-liberalism and the End of Liberal Democracy. *Theory and Event*. 7.1: no page numbers.

—. 2006. American Nightmare: Neoliberalism, Neoconservatism, and De-Democratization. *Political Theory*, 34.6: 690–714.

—. 2014a. Free Speech is Not for Feeling Safe. *Contribution to The Operation of the Machine Panel*, University of California Berkeley, 1 October. Retrieved from http://utotherescue.blogspot.com/2014/10/free-speech-is-not-for-feeling-safe.html

—. 2014b. Undoing the Demos: Neoliberalism and Political Life. *2014–15 Phi Beta Kappa Visiting Scholars Lecture*, University of Kentucky, 11 November. Author's notes.

Cameron, D. 2013. Foreword. *Prime Minister's Delegation: Visit to India, February 2013, Delegation overview*. London: HM Government. Retrieved from http://www.businessgreen.com/digital_assets/6344/February_2013_trade_mission_delegates_booklet.pdf

Coleman, M. 2007. A Geopolitics of Engagement: Neoliberalism, the War on Terrorism, and the Reconfiguration of US Immigration Enforcement. *Geopolitics*, 12.4: 607–34.

Council on Foreign Relations (CFR). 2015. Mission Statement. *Greenberg Center for Geoeconomic Studies*. Retrieved from http://www.cfr.org/thinktank/cgs/mission.html

Cowen, D., and Smith, N. 2009. After Geopolitics: From the Geopolitical Social to Geoeconomics. *Antipode*, 41.1: 22–48.

Crampton, J.W., Roberts, S.M., and Poorthuis, A. 2013. The New Political Economy of Geographical Intelligence. *Annals of the Association of American Geographers*, 104.1: 196–214.

Davies, J.S. 2007. Against 'Partnership': Toward a Local Challenge to Global Neoliberalism, in Hambleton, R., and Gross, J., eds. *Governing Cities in a Global Era: Urban Innovation, Competition, and Democratic Reform*. New York: Palgrave Macmillan: 119–201.

Essex, J. 2012. Idle Hands Are The Devil's Tools: The Geopolitics and Geoeconomics of Hunger. *Annals of the Association of American Geographers*, 102.1: 191–207.

—. 2013. *Development, Security, and Aid: Geopolitics and Geoeconomics at the US Agency for International Development*. Athens, GA: University of Georgia Press.

Foucault, M. 2008. *The Birth of Biopolitics: Lectures at the Collège de France, 1978–1979.* Burchell, G., trans. New York: Palgrave Macmillan.

Friedman, T.L. 2005 *The World is Flat: A Brief History of the Twenty-First Century.* New York: Farrar, Straus and Giroux.

Fukuyama, F. 1992. *The End of History and the Last Man.* New York: Free Press.

Gallagher, C. 2012. Risk and Private Military Work. *Antipode*, 44.3: 783–805.

HM Government. 2013. *Prime Minister's Delegation: Visit to India, February 2013, Delegation overview.* London: HM Government. Retrieved from http://www.businessgreen.com/digital_assets/6344/February_2013_trade_mission_delegates_booklet.pdf

Huntington, S.P. 1993. The Clash of Civilizations? *Foreign Affairs*, 72.3: 22–49.

Hyndman, J. 1996. International Responses to Human Displacement: Neo-Liberalism and Post-Cold War Geopolitics. *Refuge*, 15.3: 5–9.

Kennedy, P. 1989. *The Rise and Fall of the Great Powers.* New York: Vintage.

Kostecki, M., and Naray, O. 2007. Commercial Diplomacy and International Business. *Discussion Papers in Diplomacy, Netherlands Institute of International Relations Clingendael.* Retrieved from http://www.clingendael.nl/sites/default/files/20070400_cdsp_diplomacy_kostecki_naray.pdf

Larner, W. 2000. Neo-liberalism: Policy, Ideology, Governmentality. *Studies in Political Economy*, 63: 5–25.

Larner, W., and Craig, D. 2005. After Neoliberalism? Community Activism and Local Partnerships in Aotearoa New Zealand. *Antipode*, 37.3: 402–24.

Lemke, T. 2001. 'The Birth of Biopolitics': Michel Foucault's Lecture at the Collège de France on Neo-liberal Governmentality. *Economy and Society*, 30.2: 190–207.

—. 2013. Foucault, Politics and Failure, in Nilsson, J., and Wallenstein, S.O., eds. *Foucault, Biopolitics and Governmentality.* Huddinge, Sweden: Södertörn Philosophical Studies: 35–52.

Lorot, P. 1999. *Introduction à la Géoéconomie.* Paris: Economica.

—. 2001. La Géoéconomie, Nouvelle Grammaire des Rivalités Internationales, *L'information géographique*, 65.1: 43–52.

Luttwak, E. 1998[1990]. From Geopolitical to Geo-economics, Logic of Conflict, Grammar of Commerce, in Tuathail, G.Ó., Dalby, S., and Routledge, P., eds. *The Geopolitics Reader.* New York: Routledge.

—. 1993. *The Endangered American Dream: How To Stop the United States from Being a Third World Country and How To Win the Geo-Economic Struggle for Industrial Supremacy.* New York: Simon and Schuster.

Mawdsley, E. 2007. The Millennium Challenge Account: Neo-liberalism, Poverty and Security. *Review of International Political Economy*, 14.3: 487–509.

Mercille, J. 2008. The Radical Geopolitics of US Foreign Policy: Geopolitical and Geoeconomic Logics of Power. *Political Geography*, 27: 570–86.

Moisio, S., and Paasi, A. 2013. From Geopolitical to Geoeconomic? The Changing Political Rationalities of State Space. *Geopolitics*, 18.2: 267–83.

Morrissey, J. 2008. The Geoeconomic Pivot of the Global War on Terror: US Central Command and the War in Iraq, in Ryan, D., and Kiely, P., eds. *America and Iraq: Policy-Making, Intervention and Regional Politics.* New York: Routledge: 103–24.

—. 2011. Closing the Neoliberal Gap: Risk and Regulation in the Long War of Securitization. *Antipode*, 43.3: 874–900.

Ohmae, K. 1991. *The Borderless World: Power and Strategy in the Interlinked Economy.* New York: McKinsey.

Oksala, J. 2013. Neoliberalism and Biopolitical Governmentality, in Nilsson, J., and Wallenstein, S.O., eds. *Foucualt, Biopolitics and Governmentality.* Huddinge, Sweden: Södertörn Philosophical Studies: 53–72.

Pierre, A.J. 1981/2. Arms Sales: the New Diplomacy. *Foreign Affairs* Winter, 60.2 Retrieved from http://www.foreignaffairs.com/articles/35847/andrew-j-pierre/arms-sales-the-new-diplomacy

Porter, M.E. 1990. *The Competitive Advantage of Nations.* New York: Free Press.

Read, J. 2009. A Genealogy of Homo-Economicus: Neoliberalism and the Production of Subjectivity. *Foucault Studies*, 6: 25–36.

Roberts, S.M. 2013. Worlds Apart? Economic Geography and Questions of 'Development', in Barnes, T., Peck, J., and Sheppard, E., eds. *The Wiley-Blackwell Companion to Economic Geography.* Malden: Blackwell: 552–66.

—. 2014. Development Capital: USAID and the Rise of Development Contractors. *Annals of the Association of American Geographers*, 104.5: 1030–51.

Roberts, S.M., Secor, A., and Sparke, M. 2003. Neoliberal Geopolitics. *Antipode*, 35.5: 886–97.

Soederberg, S. 2004. American Empire and 'Excluded States': The Millennium Challenge Account and the Shift to Pre-Emptive Development. *Third World Quarterly*, 35.2: 279–302.

Søilen, K.S. 2010. The Shift from Geopolitics to Geoeconomics and the Failure of our Modern Social Sciences. Paper presented at the TELOS Conference, From Lifeworld to Biopolitics: Empire in the Age of Obama, New York. Retrieved from http://www.bth.se/fou/forskinfo.nsf/all/e4656e3cadf723 c7c12576e0003befac/$file/Telos%20full%20conference%20paper.pdf

—. 2012. *Geoeconomics*. Bookboon.com. Retrieved from http://bookboon.com/en/geoeconomics-ebook

Sparke, M. 1998. From Geopolitics to Geoeconomics: Transnational State Effects in the Borderlands. *Geopolitics*, 3.2: 62–98.

—. 2005. *In the Space of Theory: Postfoundational Geographies of the Nation-state*. Minneapolis: University of Minnesota Press.

—. 2007. Geopolitical Fear, Geoeconomic Hope and the Responsibilities of Geography. *Annals of the Association of American Geographers*, 97: 338–49.

Sparke, M., and Lawson, V. 2003. Entrepreneurial Geographies of Global–Local Governance, in Agnew, J., Mitchell, K., and Toal, G., eds. *A Companion to Political Geography*. Oxford: Blackwell: 315–34.

Springer, S. 2009. Culture of Violence or Violent Orientalism? Neoliberalization and Imagining the 'Savage Other' in Post-transitional Cambodia. *Transactions of the Institute of British Geographers*, 34: 305–19.

—. 2011 Articulated Neoliberalism: The Specificity of Patronage, Kleptocracy, and Violence in Cambodia's Neoliberalization. *Environment and Planning A*, 43.11: 2554–70.

—. 2013. Neoliberalism, in Dodds, K., Kuus, M., Sharp, J., eds. *The Ashgate Research Companion to Critical Geopolitics*. London: Ashgate: 147–64.

Statewatch. 2013. UK: Secret Mission? UK 'Homeland Security' Firms Were in India Three Weeks Before David Cameron's February Trade Mission. *Statewatch article RefNo# 32253*. Retrieved from http://database.statewatch.org/article.asp?aid=32253

Teivainen, T. 2002. *Enter Economism, Exit Politics: Experts, Economic Policy and Damage to Democracy*. London: Zed.

Thirlwell, M.P. 2010. The Return of Geo-economics: Globalization and National Security. Lowy Institute for International Policy (Australia). *Perspectives*. Retrieved from http://www.lowyinstitute.org/files/pubfiles/Thirlwell%2C_The_return_of_geo-economics_web_and_print.pdf

Walker, M., Roberts, S.M., Jones III, J.P., and Frohling, O. 2008. Neoliberal Development Through Technical Assistance: Constructing Communities of Entrepreneurial Subjects in Oaxaca, Mexico. *Geoforum*, 39: 524–57.

Youngs, R. 2011. Geo-economic Futures, in Martiningui, A., and Youngs, R., eds. *Challenges for European Foreign Policy in 2012: What Kind of Geo-economic Europe?* Madras, Spain: FRIDE: 13–18. Retrieved from http://fride.org/descarga/Challenges_for_European_Foreign_Policy_in_2012.pdf

38

IN THE SPIRIT OF WHITENESS

Neoliberal re-regulation, and the simultaneous opening and hardening of national territorial boundaries

Joseph Nevins

On 22 October 2014, José Palazón, a photographer with a human rights group in Melilla, a Spanish (semi-)enclave of 12 square kilometres in north Africa that borders on Morocco, took a photo of a dozen or so individuals who appeared to be unauthorized migrants. They were stuck atop a 6-metre-high fence, the last of three layers of barricades that divide the territory from Morocco. Taken from Spain's side of the international boundary, the photo shows the migrants looking down on white-clad golfers on a verdant course. Meanwhile, one of the golfers looks at the would-be intruders at a distance while his partner gets ready to hit the ball and a Spanish border guard on a ladder tries to beckon the men to climb down so he and his fellow police officers can arrest them (see Kassam 2014b).

The photo went viral. The image of the stark, heavily policed divide between white golfers and black migrants and spaces of privilege and deprivation captures what many have come to characterize as global apartheid (e.g. Dalby 1999; Nevins 2008, 2010, 2012; Sharma 2006). At the same time, it speaks to the particular dynamics of Morocco's boundary with Melilla – as well as that with Ceuta, another Spanish semi-enclave, approximately 400 kilometres east of Melilla: both vestiges of Spanish colonialism are the sites of much conflict as migrants frequently storm their fortified divides in large numbers to gain access to the space of the European Union (see Carr 2012; DiCintio 2013; Johnson 2014). As Palazón explained to the Spanish newspaper *El País* in regard to Melilla, 'The photo reflects the situation really well – the differences that exist here and all the ugliness that is happening here' (quoted in Kassam 2014b).

The image, to the extent it demonstrates the growing hardening of boundaries between the relatively powerful and disadvantaged, also reflects the neoliberal moment in which we live. As a newspaper article from 2007 stated, 'whole countries are fencing up' (Dyer 2007). Referring to the growth in territorial boundary barriers and related policing infrastructure that nation-states across the globe have erected in the name of (among other reasons) stymieing unauthorized migrants and fighting terrorism, the article's central assertion has only become more salient since its publication (see, e.g., Jones 2012).

Policed divides between nationalized spaces of privilege and disadvantage are hardly new. The mid- to late 1800s saw the emergence of the beginnings of immigration restriction between what used to be called 'white men's countries' and the rest of the world (with the exclusion of people from Asia being the central concern; see McKeown 2008) – a development indicative of the newness of national immigration controls broadly. It was also a time when the notion arose that mobility was a universal human right, but only for those of European descent (see Lake and Reynolds 2008). This is indicative of what Matthew Sparke refers to as 'liberalism's own inaugural double standards – with rights for whites in Europe and often utter inhumanity in the colonies' (Sparke 2006: 175).

Rather than casting these seemingly conflicting 'ways of seeing' and being as simply contradictions, we should see them as manifestations of co-productive, and sometimes complementary, processes that reflect and reproduce a world of gross inequalities between peoples and places (see McKeown 2008). What makes the neoliberal era unique in this regard is the depth to which these historical-geographical origins are buried – making it seem as if the past truly is past – and the strength of contemporary boundary policing regimes. These regimes are officially based on distinctions that are non-racial and instead discriminate on the basis of legality – that is, one's nation-state-granted right (or lack thereof) to enter, reside, or work in a particular nationalized space.

The lack of overt racial criteria has led some to assert that race – as a central criterion for determining mobility across global space – is extinct. Historians Marilyn Lake and Henry Reynolds, for instance, suggest that racial exclusion in the realm of immigration is a relic of the past. Indeed, they say, with the demise of South Africa's apartheid regime, 'the last bastion of white supremacy' has disappeared (Lake and Reynolds 2008: 356).

Neoliberalism is many things. Herein, I argue that central to it is whiteness – whiteness of a different form than existed in the era of 'white men's countries' – one that is more difficult to see only because the violence that underlies and produces it has become so normalized, and its socio-territorial expressions (in the form of national boundary policing regimes) so well established. It is a type of 'difference' that complements the various ways in which a number of scholars have analysed neoliberalism in relation to territorial boundaries – the focus of the next section.

Neoliberal boundaries

Neoliberalism has attracted the attention of many scholars interested in territorial boundaries. Initially, it was those swept up by capitalist triumphalism in the aftermath of the fall of the Berlin Wall that seemed most captivated. Seemingly inspired by Francis Fukuyama's (1989) assertion of the 'end of history', business management scholar Kenichi Ohmae (1995), for instance, proclaimed the coming end of the nation-state, arguing that economic globalization and the concomitant growing liberalization of national economies had made national boundaries redundant. It became obvious rather quickly, however, that nation-states, as sociologist Michael Mann (1993) puts it, were not dying, but diversifying as they developed.

Political scientist Peter Andreas (2009), in focusing on the boundary policing regime in the US–Mexico borderlands, makes a similar argument. He asserts that the strengthening of border control apparatuses demonstrates that the economic liberalism and the associated redesign of instruments of government are 'less about reducing the regulatory state than about retooling and redeploying it'. Among the ironies of this development, Andreas contends, is that it illustrates how the most economically advanced countries 'remain most resistant to economic liberalism' as manifested by their 'building up their protective walls against two of the developing world's leading exports: drugs and migrant labor' (ibid.: 141).

It is many of these very same countries – for example, Australia, Canada, the USA, and those of the European Union – that tend to champion neoliberal economic policies as a universal prescription via so-called free trade mechanisms. While this might seem like a contradiction, given the simultaneous 'hardening' of their own territorial boundaries, it reflects a more complex relationship, one involving the reworking of the state–citizen nexus that increasingly embodies the twinning of what Sparke (2006: 153) calls 'securitized nationalism' and 'free market transnationalism'. In this regard, he writes, 'borders are consequential condensation points where wider changes in state-making and the nature of citizenship are worked out on the ground' (ibid.: 152). As the state redesigns itself, it also changes its relationship to, and redefines (in part by enhancing the differences within), the citizenry. Thus, boundary and immigration restrictions are not simply about limiting movement, but also status. As border and migration scholars Anderson, Sharma and Wright (2009: 6) point out, 'restrictive immigration policies have enabled states to shift the status they accord migrating people'. This has led, they assert, to fewer individuals who have migrated without having a status accompanied by rights within the new national spaces in which they find themselves.

In trying to explain the emergence of neoliberal boundaries – particularly the rise of 'walled states' – political theorist Wendy Brown (2010) builds on the work of sociologist Saskia Sassen (1996). Brown asserts that the combined forces of de-regulated, increasingly globalized capital and the increasing power of transnational politico-legal institutions challenge nation-state sovereignty; it is the very undermining of the nation-state that gives rise to the hardened boundaries – walled ones being the most obvious expression. Yet, as Andreas (2009) points out, it is too simple to see states as merely reactive given that they have helped to produce, discursively and materially, the very conditions – in the form of a border 'out of control' – to which they have responded via enhanced policing.

In the case of the US–Canada borderlands, where one sees the implementation of an expedited boundary crossing regime (for some) and heightened state violence in the form of expedited deportations (for others), there is, Sparke asserts, a 'neoliberal double standard' – one 'like liberalism's own inaugural double standards' referred to earlier. In the context of the US–Canada borderlands, this double standard is manifest via eased trans-boundary mobility for the business elite and highly restricted mobility (at best) for those deemed as outsiders.

This is enabled by a boundary crossing apparatus that is far more orderly (and ordered) than that which existed not too long ago. As in the case of the various Israeli-administered 'border crossings' or 'international terminals' – that is, checkpoints – between the occupied Palestinian territories and Israel (see Braverman 2011), the trappings of modernity are present: for example, sophisticated sensors and scanners, biometric identification cards, and electronic databases – all managed by what is presented as a sophisticated, highly rational and professional bureaucracy.

The bureaucracy is expansive – or at least its champions seek that it should be so – in that it tends to spread to realms where it has hitherto not existed. In the process, individual bodies become increasingly categorized, marked (via identity documents, for instance) and regulated (see, for example, Nevins 2014). As such, they effectively become embodied manifestations of territorial boundaries. This speaks to the mobility of boundaries under neoliberalism. As such, the locations of the boundaries – institutionally, socially and geographically – are increasingly difficult to pin down. Boundaries both thicken (in that the policed zone of exclusion goes beyond the official boundary line and spreads into the interior) and migrate – inward to bodies and locales and outward, pre-emptively, to other nation-states – thus making more precarious the lives of migrating persons (Flynn 2002; Coleman 2007; Varsanyi 2008; Ashutosh and Mountz 2011; Mountz 2011; Miller 2014).

Finally, neoliberal boundaries are characterized by discourse infused with the logic of capital. In the case of Israel's new border regime, Palestinian crossers become consumers, Israeli regulators of mobility become service providers (Braverman 2011). In the case of the US–Mexico border region, neoliberal rhetoric similarly emphasizes the needs of consumers and producers – but at a more macro level. In this regard, the 'securing' of the borderlands is presented as central to the needs of capital – in terms of both investors in the region and in relation to the smooth flow of goods and people (of a privileged sort) – so as to produce an economic prosperity that will benefit all. This is the topic that the next section examines in relation to the US–Mexico borderlands in particular.

Re-ordering the US–Mexico borderlands

Since the mid-1990s, the US–Mexico borderlands have undergone a dramatic transformation in terms of the policing apparatus. To give one example, the number of US Border Patrol agents (the vast majority of whom are deployed along the US–Mexico divide) expanded from 4,287 in fiscal year (FY) 1994 to almost 21,000 in FY 2014.[1] In FY 2012, the combined budget of US Customs and Border Protection, the parent agency of the Border Patrol, Immigration and Customs Enforcement, or ICE (which focuses on immigration policing in the US interior), and a biometric tracking system called US VISIT, totalled almost $18 billion (Meissner *et al.* 2013).

This transformation began to unfold in the context of the debate preceding the approval of the North American Free Trade Agreement (NAFTA) and its coming into force on 1 January 1994. According to Robert Bach, who served as the Executive Associate Commissioner for Policy and Planning for the US Immigration and Naturalization Service in the mid- to late 1990s, the policy of the Clinton administration (which Bach helped to design) was such that it perceived the US–Mexico border region as an opportunity, a place, and an anchor.[2] The border is an opportunity in that its proper organization allows trans-boundary, regional integration and NAFTA to occur and allows for economic progress on both sides. The border is a place in the sense that its socio-cultural patterns are geographically unique – an important factor to consider so that federal policy works for families, workers, and employers on both sides of the international divide. And, although border policy is only one piece of a much larger strategy of immigration enforcement, the border is an anchor, primarily for the purposes of law enforcement. To realize its vision, the Clinton administration sought to build an institutional framework within and upon which the 'market' could flourish. As a set of institutional relationships based on the law, this market is taken to be one in which everyone can participate, and from which people on both sides of the boundary can and will benefit (Bach 1997).

The Clinton administration and many NAFTA backers assumed (or at least argued) that the simultaneous implementation of stronger immigrant enforcement measures and the development of a relatively barrier-free boundary to goods and capital would lead to greater levels of prosperity for people on both sides of the boundary. As an assistant to Alan Bersin, the Clinton administration's 'border czar', explained to me in 1997 in relation to the boundary build-up in the San Diego area,

> [N]o one says that the immigration initiatives [of the Clinton administration] are the unilateral answer to economic problems [that exist in Mexico and drive unauthorized immigration]. But they are one way of responding to it and managing the problems so we can have this region that flourishes. That you decrease the amount of illegal activity and bring the benefits to the people that are law-abiding – the majority of the people. People want to come and see the Padres [San Diego's professional baseball team], they

want to come and see the Chargers [San Diego's professional football team]. The types of joint programs that we could be doing are numerous, but we need a little bit more certainty.

(Cobian 1997, personal communication)

It is through the creation of a regime of law and order in the border region that this vision will supposedly be realized. And in a part of San Ysidro (southern San Diego) that used to be an area of heavy (unauthorized) migrant traffic and Border Patrol chases, one abutting the boundary, it seems to have come to be. Since 2001, Las Americas Premium Outlets (originally called the Shops at Las Americas) – a shopping mall that features dozens of stores such as those of Banana Republic, Calvin Klein, Ralph Lauren, and Nike, and whose southern perimeter of its parking lot is the steel boundary wall – has been open to well-resourced shoppers from the USA and Mexico. In October 2014, the Outlets at the Borders, another mall, opened next door (Harvey 2014). Such 'success' has led some to dub San Ysidro – a largely Latino area with a high concentration of poverty and where per capita annual income is less than half of that of San Diego as a whole – 'a shopping mecca' (e.g. Mannes 2012).

Of course, the cost of buying the products in the stores of this shopping mecca, or a ticket for a Padres or Chargers game, is far beyond the means of the vast majority of people in Tijuana, a city where the average daily wage of a factory worker (in 2014) is less than $15 (Zaragoza 2014). Furthermore, it is not possible for a significant proportion of Tijuana's residents – given their modest means and lack of participation in the formal economy (and thus possessing no proof of steady employment, among other criteria they would need to satisfy) – to gain permission to visit the USA.

The build-up of the boundary and its NAFTAization are also linked in another, more nefarious, manner. Growing liberalization of the Mexican economy has facilitated a significant exodus from Mexico's countryside (see, for example, Warnock 1995). Numerous studies suggested that the implementation of NAFTA would only intensify this process. Research suggested that the rural exodus, combined with the resulting intensifying links between the two countries, would lead to a significant increase in migration from Mexico to the USA (Massey and Espinosa 1997; Andreas 1998) – a development of which the Clinton administration was very much aware, even though it publicly argued that NAFTA would lessen migratory pressures and thus serve as a boundary control tool (see, for example, Reno 1993).

As INS Commissioner Doris Meissner admitted during testimony to Congress in November 1993, she foresaw that NAFTA would most likely lead to an *increase* in unauthorized immigration from Mexico to the USA in the short and medium terms, leading her to state, 'Responding to the likely short-to-medium-term impacts of NAFTA will require strengthening our enforcement efforts along the border, both at and between ports of entry' (US Congress 1994: 36). In other words, the liberalization of Mexico's economy would increase migratory pressures among those displaced in the name of economic efficiency, which, in turn, would require an increase in boundary policing. Meissner's words proved to be prescient (see Massey *et al.* 2002; see also Delgado-Wise and Márquez Covarrubias 2008; Nevins 2007 and 2010).

It would be far too simple to reduce the build-up of the boundary policing apparatus to the neoliberal trade agreement (and neoliberalism more broadly) – indeed, there were myriad factors that brought about this change (see Andreas, 2009; Dunn 2009; Nevins 2010). Nonetheless, there is a significant relationship, one that demonstrates how, in some regards, 'opening' and 'closing' the boundary complement one another. At the same time, to the extent that the liberalization of the boundary has allowed for easier movement into the USA for the relatively elite in Mexico and beyond, while the simultaneous growth in restriction has made international mobility markedly more difficult for people on the socio-economic margins of Mexico and elsewhere, it illustrates the two-tiered system of humanity inherent in a neoliberal political-economic era (see Sparke 2006).

Thus, the alleged problem of illegal immigration, as it relates to the US–Mexico boundary, is, to a significant degree, made in the USA. By increasing the porosity of the US–Mexico boundary through trade liberalization, the state must strengthen this boundary in other ways. This seeming paradox is consistent with the observation that globalization does not necessarily lead to a decline in nationalism. In fact, globalization can actually serve to enhance the differences between citizens and so-called aliens (Manzo 1996). In this way, rising boundary-related illegality (such as unauthorized immigration) is an integral part of the NAFTAization of the US–Mexico border region.

This dialectical process dovetails with the 'gatekeeper' state, the task of which is to provide extraterritorial opportunities for national territory-based capital (thus intensifying the destabilizing process of globalization, meaning here the increasing, trans-boundary flow of people, goods and capital) while, somewhat paradoxically, providing security against the perceived social costs unleashed by globalization – especially (unwanted) immigration. This task of security provision becomes all the more necessary in the face of the effects of a neoliberal-fuelled form of globalization which intensifies competition between localities, weakens social safety nets, and generally increases socio-economic instability (see Peck and Tickell 1994; Nevins and Peluso 2008). Yet, rather than fighting the national-based sources of socio-economic instability (largely corporate and financial interests) whose very interests the state disproportionately represents, the neoliberalized state casts its gaze beyond the nation's socio-territorial boundaries, focusing on the alien as a principal source of social problems. The alien takes the form of the criminal, the poor, and the foreigner who are often one and the same.

From the perspective of US officials, the growth of illegal or criminal activity is one of the most significant costs of an increasingly interconnected world, requiring the state to respond with efforts to create order. And a key source of the disorder is the unauthorized immigrant, the transgressor of the law of the boundary and, thus, a criminal, one who is inextricably tied to a socio-geographical zone of violence. It is violent in the sense that the migrant's very 'criminal' status requires the power of the state to arrest and expel him. And it is violent in that the unsanctioned migrant – at least the ones who enter US territory without authorization (as opposed to those who enter *with* authorization but overstay their visas) – must pass through an increasingly militarized and foreboding landscape, one they share not only with US authorities but also with smugglers of contraband, such as illicit drugs, who those authorities are trying to apprehend. One result is a growing number of migrant deaths in the US–Mexico borderlands (see Nevins 2008 and 2010) and beyond.

Conclusion: whiteness of a different colour

On 6 February 2014 hundreds of unauthorized migrants, largely from sub-Saharan Africa, tried to storm the land barrier between Morocco and Ceuta, only to be repelled by Spanish authorities. Later that same day, a large group of migrants tried to enter Ceuta by sea, by swimming around the artificial breakwater that separates the Mediterranean waters of Morocco from those of Spain. Spanish authorities tried to deter them by firing rubber bullets in their vicinity. At least 15 of the migrants ended up drowning (Kassam 2014a).

In a report issued in September 2014, the International Organization for Migration (IOM) estimated that upwards of 3,072 migrants had already died that year throughout the Mediterranean in trying to reach European territory (IOM/OIM 2014). The organization conservatively estimated that 4,077 migrants worldwide had lost their lives during that same period in trying to traverse the space between places of insecurity and those of relative privilege. Taking a longer view, the IOM estimated at least 40,000 migrant deaths across the globe since 2000, the majority of them in the Mediterranean (ibid.). While the IOM report is silent on the matter of race and class – as are the officials from the countries and entities working hard to repel the migrants – it should be hardly surprising that those dying are almost exclusively people of colour and low-income (ibid.).

It is not that travel towards Europe from without is inherently a problem from the perspective of the European Union and its member-states. It is the mobility of those deemed as the wrong kind of people – given their socio-economic status and from where they come – that is deemed problematic – and threatening. Thus, in the case of Melilla's Club Campo de Golf, it is a territory in need of policing, one to be secured from unauthorized persons from 'outside'. As one writer wryly commented, 'No room in paradise. We need the space for golf courses' (Jones 2014).

Such logic helps explain why the Club Campo de Golf received official assistance in the form of a subsidy of €1.1 million from the European Regional Development Fund (an agency of the European Union) in the 2000s. A commissioner of the EU explained why, in justifying the denial of a petition calling into question the subsidy, by noting the golf club's objective was to 'increase tourism, create jobs and promote sport and sporting values' (quoted in Kassam 2014b). In other words, tourists – the well-heeled and the disproportionately white – are to be welcomed, while persons trying to enter Spanish territory from Morocco via the golf course receive the antithesis of a welcome. Indeed, in Melilla on that day of 22 October 2014 referred to in the opening of this chapter, a number of Spanish police officers beat at least one of the migrants with their batons to the point where the man appeared to be unconscious (Kassam 2014b).

A central principle of international boundary walls, physical and metaphorical, is what the great human and civil rights activist W.E.B. Du Bois once called 'the problem of the color line' – the global racial divide that he powerfully decried in his epic 1903 book *The Souls of Black Folk* (2007) as 'the problem of the Twentieth Century'. Du Bois was writing at a time when most of the modern techniques used to classify peoples and regulate territorial boundaries were born – the 1880s to 1910s, according to McKeown (2008) – as part of an effort to exclude those hailing from Asia from migrating to white-settler nations (e.g. Australia, Canada, South Africa, and the USA).

Today that line is one that still divides those who have the benefit of racial and national privilege from those who possess the obverse to which that privilege is inextricably tied: the disadvantage of the global majority. That disadvantage translates into less access and control over the planet's resources, less political power on the world stage, and restricted mobility between countries. It concerns whiteness and blackness in ways that a strict focus on pigmentation and other physical markers does not allow. This helps explain why, almost two decades after writing of the colour line, Du Bois (1975: 16) characterized whiteness as first and foremost about power, not mere phenotype, or 'the ownership of the earth forever and ever. Amen'.

Those who travel precariously in a world of profound inequality, who are compelled to risk their lives in order to reach spaces of relative social and biophysical security, are the 'owned'. Their mobility across territorial boundaries – especially those dividing the rich and poor, the white and non-white, 'owners' and the dispossessed – is highly limited. Indeed, it is often violently repulsed. By contrast, the 'owners' are members of the global minority, i.e. those who benefit from 'whiteness' in Du Bois's terms; they can generally traverse the world's space without serious obstacle or threat, and at the moment of their choosing.

If neoliberalism is, among other things, a regime characterized by the liberalization and de-regulation of national economies and increasing 'flows' of capital and commodities between them, it is also marked by intensifying regulation of immigration and boundary controls. Thus, while the neoliberal era has seen a marked increase in trans-boundary mobility by the relatively affluent, it has also seen a simultaneous hardening of territorial boundaries for those migrating bodies deemed less than desirable by receiving countries. As David Delaney (2007) observes, territories both reflect and produce the social orders to which they are tied. In this regard, the growing filter-like aspect of national territorial boundaries – one that increasingly regulates, among others, the non-white due to marked growth in state policing capacity – is inextricably tied to the neoliberal era.

Notes

1 See http://www.cbp.gov/sites/default/files/documents/BP%20Staffing%20FY1992-FY2014_0.pdf
2 Bach (1997) referred to this policy as the 'Meissner doctrine' – named after then INS Commissioner Doris Meissner and her late husband Charles Meissner (who died in 1996), the former head of international commerce at the Department of Commerce.

References

Anderson, B., Sharma, N., and Wright, C. 2009. Editorial: Why No Borders? *Refuge*, 26: 5–18.

Andreas, P. 1998. The Escalation of US Immigration Control in the Post-NAFTA Era. *Political Science Quarterly*, 113: 591–615.

—. 2009. *Border Games: Policing the US–Mexico Divide*. Ithaca and New York: Cornell University Press.

Ashutosh, I., and Mountz, A. 2011. Migration Management for the Benefit of Whom? Interrogating the Work of the International Organization for Migration. *Citizenship Studies*, 15: 21–38.

Bach, R. 1997. Perspectives on US–Mexico Border Policy. Presentation at the Immigration Control Panel Workshop. Center for US–Mexican Studies, University of California San Diego, 17 October.

Braverman, I. 2011. Civilized Borders: A Study of Israel's New Crossing Administration. *Antipode*, 43: 264–95.

Brown, W. 2010. *Walled States, Waning Sovereignty*. New York: Zone.

Carr, M. 2012. *Fortress Europe: Dispatches from a Gated Continent*. New York: New Press.

Coleman, M. 2007. Immigration Geopolitics Beyond the Mexico–US Border. *Antipode*, 39: 54–76.

Dalby, S. 1999. Globalisation or Global Apartheid? Boundaries and Knowledge in Postmodern Times, in Newman, D., ed. *Boundaries, Territory, and Postmodernity*. London: Frank Cass: 132–50.

Delaney, D. 2007. *Territory: A Short Introduction*. Malden, MA: Blackwell.

Delgado-Wise, R., and Márquez Covarrubias, H. 2008. Capitalist Restructuring, Development, and Labor Migration: The US–Mexico Case. *Third World Quarterly*, 29: 1359–74.

DiCintio, M. 2013. *Walls: Travels Along the Barricades*. Berkeley, CA: Soft Skull Press.

Du Bois, W.E.B. 1975. *The Souls of White Folk: Darkwater: Voices from Within the Veil*. New York: Kraus-Thomas.

—. 2007. [1903] *The Souls of Black Folk*. New York: Oxford University Press.

Dunn, T.J. 2009. *Blockading the Border and Human Rights: The El Paso Operation that Remade Immigration Enforcement*. Austin: University of Texas Press.

Dyer, G. 2007. Whole Countries are Fencing Up. *The Brunei Times*, 14 February.

Flynn, M. 2002. Dondé Está la Frontera? *Bulletin of the Atomic Scientists*, 58.4: 24–35.

Fukuyama, F. 1989. The End of History? *The National Interest*, Summer: 3–18.

Harvey, K.P. 2014. Outlets at the Border Brings Some Firsts. *San Diego Union Tribune*, 22 October. Retrieved from http://www.utsandiego.com/news/2014/oct/22/outlets-at-the-border-opening/

IOM/OIM. 2014. *Migration Trends Across the Mediterranean: Connecting the Dots*. Retrieved from https://publications.iom.int/books/migration-trends-across-mediterranean-connecting-dots

Johnson, H.L. 2014. *Borders, Asylum and Global Non-citizenship: The Others Side of the Fence*. Cambridge: Cambridge University Press.

Jones, J. 2014. Golfers and Asylum Seekers: A Clash of Realities. *The Guardian*, 23 October. Retrieved from http://www.theguardian.com/world/2014/oct/23/migrants-golfers-metaphor-refugees

Jones, R. 2012. *Border Walls: Security and the War on Terror in the United States, India and Israel*. London: Zed.

Kassam, A. 2014a. Spain to Raise Security Around Morocco Territories Over Immigration Fears. *The Guardian*, 6 March. Retrieved from http://www.theguardian.com/world/2014/mar/06/spain-security-morocco-territories-immigration

—. 2014b. African Migrants Look Down on White-clad Golfers in Viral Photo. *The Guardian*, 23 October. Retrieved from http://www.theguardian.com/world/2014/oct/23/-sp-african-migrants-look-down-on-white-clad-golfers-in-viral-photo

Lake, M., and Reynolds, H. 2008. *Drawing the Global Colour Line: White Men's Countries and the International Challenge of Racial Equality*. Cambridge: Cambridge University Press.

Mann, M. 1993. Nation-states in Europe and Other Continents: Diversifying, Developing, not Dying. *Daedalus*, 122: 115–40.

Mannes, T. 2012. Why is San Ysidro Such a Shopping Mecca? *San Diego Union Tribune*, 19 March. Retrieved from http://www.utsandiego.com/news/2012/mar/19/why-san-ysidro-such-shopping-mecca/

Manzo, K.A. 1996. *Creating Boundaries: The Politics of Race and Nation*, Boulder, CO: Lynne Rienner.

Massey, D.S. and Espinosa, K.E. 1997. What's Driving Mexico–US Migration? A Theoretical, Empirical, and Policy Analysis. *American Journal of Sociology*, 102: 939–99.

Massey, D.S., Durand, J., and Malone, N.J. 2002. *Beyond Smoke and Mirrors: Mexican Immigration in an Era of Economic Integration*. New York: Russell Sage Foundation.

McKeown, A.M. 2008. *Melancholy Order: Asian Migration and the Globalization of Borders*. New York: Columbia University Press.

Meissner, D., Kerwin, D.M., Chisti, M., and Bergeron, C. 2013. *Immigration Enforcement in the United States: The Rise of a Formidable Machinery*. Washington, DC: Migration Policy Institute.

Miller, T. 2014. *Border Patrol Nation: Dispatches from the Frontlines of Homeland Security*. San Francisco, CA: City Lights.

Mountz, A. 2011. Specters at the Port of Entry: Understanding State Mobilities through an Ontology of Exclusion. *Mobilities*, 6: 317–34.

Nevins, J. 2007. Dying for a Cup of Coffee? Migrant Deaths in the US–Mexico Border Region in a Neoliberal Age. *Geopolitics*, 12: 228–47.

—. 2008. *Dying to Live: A Story of US Immigration in an Age of Global Apartheid*. San Francisco, CA: Open Media and City Lights.

—. 2010. *Operation Gatekeeper and Beyond: The War on 'Illegals' and the Remaking of the US–Mexico Boundary*. New York: Routledge.

—. 2012. Policing Mobility, Maintaining Global Apartheid – From South Africa to the United States, in Lloyd, J.M., Mitchelson, M., and Burridge, A. eds. *Beyond Walls and Cages: Bridging Immigrant Justice and Anti-prison Organizing in the United States*. Athens: University of Georgia Press: 19–26.

—. 2014. Policing the Workplace and Rebuilding the State in 'America's Finest City': Immigration Enforcement in the San Diego, California–Mexico Borderlands. *Global Society*, 28: 462–82.

Nevins, J., and Peluso, N. 2008. Introduction: Commoditization in Southeast Asia, in Nevins, J., and Peluso, N., eds. *Taking Southeast Asia to Market: Commodities, Nature, and People in the Neoliberal Age*. Ithaca, NY: Cornell University Press: 1–25.

Ohmae, K. 1995. *The End of the Nation State: The Rise of Regional Economies*. New York and London: Free Press.

Peck, J., and Tickell, A. 1994. A Jungle Law Breaks Out: Neoliberalism and Global-local Disorder. *Area*, 26: 317–26.

Reno, J. 1993. Consider NAFTA a Border Control Tool. *Los Angeles Times*, 22 October: B11.

Sassen, S. 1996. *Losing Control? Sovereignty in an Age of Globalization*. New York: Columbia University Press.

Sharma, N. 2006. *Home Economics: Nationalism and the Making of 'Migrant Workers' in Canada*. Toronto: University of Toronto Press.

Sparke, M.B. 2006. A Neoliberal Nexus: Economy, Security and the Biopolitics of Citizenship on the Border. *Political Geography*, 25: 151–80.

US Congress, Subcommittee on International Law, Immigration, and Refugees of the Committee on the Judiciary, House of Representatives, 103rd Congress. 1994 *Immigration-related Issues in the North American Free Trade Agreement*. Washington, DC: US Government Printing Office.

Varsanyi, M. 2008. Rescaling the 'Alien,' Rescaling Personhood: Neoliberalism, Immigration, and the State. *Annals of the Association of American Geographers*, 98: 877–96.

Warnock, J. 1995. The Mexican Disaster. *The Canadian Forum*, 73.838: 6–7.

Zaragoza, B. 2014. A Tour of Tijuana's Maquiladoras. *San Diego Free Press*, 23 October. Retrieved from http://sandiegofreepress.org/2014/10/a-tour-of-tijuanas-maquiladoras/

39

HOUSING AND HOME

Objects and technologies of neoliberal governmentalities

Rae Dufty-Jones

For some time housing has been an object of government and governance. It is not surprising therefore that housing is an important focus for analyses of neoliberalization, particularly the socio-spatial implications of neoliberal policies, programmes and processes. Indeed, neoliberalism has become an important explanatory tool when examining the changes to how housing is produced and consumed and the policy settings guiding this economic activity in the twenty-first century. From analyses of privatization processes of social housing, to tracing the precursors and fall-out of the global financial crisis (GFC), the connections between neoliberalization and housing have been made by commentators and academics alike. This chapter seeks to untangle some of the many links made by researchers regarding neoliberalization and housing. It does this in two ways. First, it examines how housing has come to be seen as 'neoliberalized' – specifically, the way housing has become an object of government: a problem requiring neoliberalized solutions. The second way in which this chapter examines the neoliberalization of housing is as a technology of neoliberal forms of government – in particular, the way in which housing is not only an object of neoliberal governance, but also an important tool employed in the pursuit of wider neoliberal governmentalities. The chapter concludes with some reflections on how housing studies has evaluated the consequences of the neoliberalization of housing and how this field of research could engage with the wider theoretical debates around the concept of neoliberalism in future.

The neoliberalization of housing

The effects of the GFC have brought to the fore the way that the links between the micro-scale of the home and the wider economy have changed. Part of the story of this change is the connections between neoliberalization and housing. Since 2008 individuals, communities, businesses and governments have faced a range of housing issues from the large-scale abandonment of homes due to foreclosure processes to worsening problems of homelessness and housing affordability. However, problematizations of housing emerged well before 2008 and what this chapter is interested in is the way that housing problems – how they are understood, explained and what solutions are presented – are (among other things) rationalized through a prism of neoliberalism – that is, the way housing has become an object of and technology in neoliberal governance.

First, clarification is needed as to how the analysis of neoliberalism and housing that I seek to present will proceed in this chapter. Like other studies of neoliberalism, housing research draws on a range of acknowledged and unacknowledged theoretical perspectives. Some studies blend different theoretical approaches, while others adhere strictly to one approach. This chapter will approach neoliberalism and how it relates to housing from a governmentality perspective. This involves understanding processes of neoliberalization as a series of complex economic rationalities and technologies, whereby 'Knowledges about economic processes are colonised and folded back onto themselves to become artefacts and technologies of government applicable to a variety of domains, resulting in various types of activity becoming "economised"' (Prince and Dufty 2009: 1751). Importantly, in this definition the state is viewed as continuing to have an integral, albeit qualitatively different, role in processes of governance (Dodson 2006; Kitchin *et al.* 2012).

Housing is an important field when considering neoliberalism. Despite the differences in how neoliberalism is defined and approached by housing scholars, a common theme among many researchers is the pervasive impact that processes of neoliberalization have had on how housing is produced, consumed and governed (Flint 2004b; Hackworth 2005; Hackworth and Moriah 2006; Beer *et al.* 2007; Forrest and Hirayama 2009; Hirayama 2010; Beer 2012; Hodkinson *et al.* 2013; Kennett *et al.* 2013; McKee and Muir 2013). For instance, Hodkinson *et al.* (2013: 4) argue that the 'privatization of public housing in the United Kingdom is arguably one of the most iconic and significant applications of neoliberal policy worldwide'. Similarly Forrest and Hirayama (2009: 998) point to housing as being 'at the forefront of... neoliberal policy prescriptions in many countries'. Table 39.1 summarizes the various ways in which the neoliberalization of housing has been understood to have occurred. However, the way that this smorgasbord of neoliberalization processes has played out on the ground means that such processes are both path-dependent and spatially contingent (Forrest and Hirayama 2009; Beer 2012). The studies drawn on in this chapter come from an array of national contexts including Australia (Darcy and Rogers 2014; Rogers and Darcy 2014), Canada (Hackworth and Moriah 2006; Hackworth 2008), Chile (Posner 2012), China (Lee and Zhu 2006), Japan (Hirayama 2010), Sweden (Turner and Whitehead 2002; Hedin *et al.* 2012), the USA (Hackworth 2005) and the UK (Hodkinson 2011; Glynn 2012). However, despite this geographical breadth, only a few have undertaken cross-country comparisons (Dodson 2006; Forrest and Hirayama 2009).

Housing as an object of neoliberal governance

The emergence of neoliberalized approaches to housing has its antecedents in the late-1960s and 1970s. In these early years, the fiscal and representational crises that afflicted many nation-states were important contributors to the specific problematization of supply-side housing policies (e.g. the large-scale development of public housing, state regulation and subsidization of mortgages etc.) that had characterized the liberal post-World War II period (Dodson 2006; McKee and Muir 2013). Through such crises, various versions of the argument that the state was ill equipped to solve problems of economic, social and cultural equality were rolled out in relation to these forms of housing policy (Hackworth 2005; Dodson 2006). For instance, in 1973 US President, Richard Nixon, announced the national public housing system to be 'too expensive and declared a moratorium on all new public housing' (Hackworth 2005: 33). Liberal interventions into housing were seen to produce and/or exacerbate economic, social and cultural problems rather than contribute to their solution.

A range of neoliberalized approaches was presented as solutions to these problematizations of housing. Such measures included the removal or subsumption of housing departments and ministers, to approaches that sought to bring the market into the field of social housing such as the sale of public housing (e.g. the Right to Buy (RTB) system in the UK) and the shift to demand-side policy approaches that provided subsidies to those privately renting (e.g. the Commonwealth Rent Assistance in Australia or the Section 8 voucher system in the USA), in effect replacing 'subsidies for concrete' with 'subsidies for people' (Hirayama 2010: 124). Markets were also prioritized through a range of deregulatory measures such as the removal of rent controls and other protections for renters that enabled easier evictions. Such measures were argued as necessary to encourage greater investment in private rental housing.

The principle of the 'market is best' was also extended to encompass how the remaining social housing stock was managed with the devolution and demunicipalization of this role to a range of private contractors such as community housing providers. Similarly, what new funding and/or assistance that was now provided was also oriented towards the private sector. The shift to private contractors in the delivery and management of social housing enabled private finance to take a stronger role in this area and access what little government funding made its way into social housing (Hodkinson 2011). A variety of 'incentives' were also introduced by different governments to bring the private sector into the social housing space. An example of this was the Low Income Housing Tax Credit (LIHTC) programme that was introduced in the USA in 1986. The programme involved 'the allocation of tax credits to qualifying low-income housing builders… builders of [these] units [then sold] the credits to corporations or individuals with high tax liability to create a revenue stream of their own' (Hackworth 2005: 34). What this example also shows is that while markets were considered 'best practice', their very existence depended on the state.

A key consequence was that the increasingly limited supply of public/social housing meant that what housing stock remained had to be targeted on those most in need. The increased targeting of social housing, combined with the original design of many public housing projects – where economies of scale were achieved through large-scale land release and development of large public housing estates – meant that there was an increase in the 'concentration of disadvantage' in social housing spaces (Flint, 2002; Darcy 2010). It is important to note that the problematization of public housing as producing a 'concentration of disadvantage' was not just an effect of the processes of neoliberalization outlined above.[1] However, the impacts of earlier neoliberal responses did exacerbate such problems, which were only made more pressing as cities became globalized and/or began to gentrify. As a result, what was previously undesirable urban space became of much higher value to the state, private developers and individuals (Glynn 2012; Hedin *et al.* 2012; Darcy and Rogers 2014; Rogers and Darcy 2014).

Combined with the declining quality of social housing stock due to declining funding for maintenance (Hackworth 2005; Glynn 2012), one of the ways the problem of the 'concentration of disadvantage' has been resolved is through the neoliberalized response of housing regeneration. Housing regeneration approaches usually involve some level of large-scale demolition of whole social housing estates. Examples include the US HOPE VI programme, which has a mandate to demolish some of the nation's most 'severely distressed' social housing estates (Hackworth 2005). Housing regeneration also serves other neoliberalizing objectives such as facilitating the further privatization of social housing (Hodkinson 2011) and the further erosion of the quantity of social housing stock available (Hackworth 2005; Glynn 2012). Moreover, housing regeneration also results in the displacement, and with that the destruction, of social housing communities, resulting in the further marginalization of those that such programmes were argued to help and the further splintering of urban spaces (Arthurson 2004; Hackworth 2005; Hedin *et al.* 2012; Posner 2012).

Table 39.1 Neoliberalization of housing

Problem/problematization	Result/response

• Fiscal crises:
  - Declining ability of governments to pay for large-scale supply-side responses to housing need
  - Declining capacity of governments to fund state pension systems
• Representational crises:
  - Citizenship and housing rights increasingly (albeit imperfectly) afforded to those who were not male, white, married and employed
  - Governments do not always know what is best/act in the best interests of citizens
	• Reduced government funding to maintain existing public housing stock
	• Significant reduction in building of new public housing
	• Sale of existing public housing stock
	• Available public housing is increasingly targeted on those most in need. Results in a discursive shift from 'public' to 'welfare' housing
	• Homeownership increasingly constructed as 'best' form of housing consumption
	• The removal or subsumption of housing departments and ministers

• Supply-side housing assistance policies are argued to have a distorting effect on the wider housing 'market' as well as restricting the capacities of recipients of those in housing need
  - Supply-side housing policy as 'inefficient'
  - Where government still plays a role in providing a housing 'safety net' such provision should be as 'market-like' as possible
  - Public provision of housing results in a lack of 'choice' for recipients of housing assistance
	• Demand-side housing assistance policies (e.g. Section 8 vouchers and other forms of private rental assistance/subsidy) argued to be a more effective mode of delivery
	• Legislative changes and tax incentives to make it more appealing for private investors to invest in low-income housing
	  - Removal of rent control
	  - Removal of security of tenure
	• Devolution/demunicipalization of responsibility and stock transferred to not-for-profit sector/community housing/registered social landlords
	  - Another discursive shift from 'public' to 'social' housing
	  - Enables role of private finance in the management and delivery of social housing
	  - Contracting out of maintenance services to private sector

• Social housing 'locking away' valuable urban land suitable for urban regeneration • Declining quality of social housing/poor maintenance	• Sell public/social housing stock and argue that profits will be used to replace this stock elsewhere • Displacement/movement of existing social housing tenants out to more peripheral areas of city • Facilitates gentrification-led housing regeneration

• Concentration and residualization of public housing argued to result in:
  - Problematic 'neighbourhood effects'
  - 'Anti-social behaviour' (ASB) of social housing tenants
• Gentrification exacerbates perceptions of and complaints about 'social problems'
	• Deconcentration
	  - Social mix
	  - Tenure diversification
	  - Makes way for (further) gentrification-led housing regeneration
	• 'Responsibilization' of social housing population
	• Tenant participation programmes
	• Stricter screening of 'problem' tenants
	• Improve ease of eviction

Problem/problematization	Result/response
• Capital 'locked up' in homeownership – 'obduracy' of real estate • Slowing of wage increases – how to create demand for consumer goods despite increasing housing costs	• Deregulation of financial and mortgage markets • Financialization and new forms of financial products (e.g. securitization)

• Housing bubbles – bursting or continuing to grow
 • Global financial crisis – the freezing of money markets
 • Worsening housing inequality
  - Tenurial
  - Generational
  - Spatial
 • Rising fiscal burden of demand-side housing assistance
	• Nationalization of bank debt/state guarantee of bank debt
	 • Currency wars – monetary policy set at 0 per cent and policies of 'quantitative easing'
	 • Austerity measures
	  - Reduce generosity of housing allowances
	  - Flexible tenancies for social housing (end of tenure for life)
	  - Devolution of development planning to local communities – financial incentives provided to encourage local communities to allow affordable housing to be built in their area
	 • Stimulus measures
	  - Government spending programmes to build new social housing stock
	  - Subsidies to private investors in new affordable rental housing
	  - Subsidizing costs of new residential development
	  - Cash subsidies to first-home purchasers

It is also important to recognize that housing as an object of neoliberal governmentalities is not limited to the sphere of social housing. Real estate, especially housing, has traditionally been considered a problematic form of capital investment for a number of reasons, including: the capital invested in housing is immobilized for long periods of time; housing as a source of capital is not easily divisible; housing is an illiquid asset; there are high transaction costs associated with housing as a capital good; and the assessment of risk with housing investments had traditionally been highly conservative due to the way it was regulated by the state (Follain and Zorn, 1990; Pryke and Whitehead, 1994; Weber, 2002; Kamel 2012; Wissoker *et al.*, 2014;). Thus another problematization of housing that emerged during this period was how it could be 'made more flexible and responsive to the investment criteria of capital' (Weber 2002: 519). According to Weber (ibid.: 529):

> Since the 1970s… in order to attract capital looking for large, liquid trading markets, the commodity of real estate [including housing] has become progressively demateralized and deterritorialized. [Housing] has… in the process becom[e] more detached from place and more subject to the disciplining power and accelerated schedules of global capital markets.

Wossoker *et al.* (2014: 2788) summarized the change that occurred during this period as the 'way property markets were … woven into the broader financial architecture of "neoliberalization"'.

Like social housing, the problem of the cost of accessing capital to purchase housing and the illiquidity of housing as an asset was seen to be solved through a range of neoliberalized policy solutions which facilitated the introduction of new financial tools. Deregulation of financial markets, among other things, allowed retail lenders (the traditional source of residential mortgage lending) to source capital from the wholesale market. The expansion of the capital market in this way was argued to reduce the costs of accessing capital to purchase housing as it enabled those lending to home purchasers the capacity to offer loans at lower interest rates. Competition in the mortgage market was also heightened through allowing new players into the residential mortgage lending market. As Pryke and Whitehead (1995: 77) pointed out, since the 1970s the mortgage market had 'changed from an "under-supply" of funds ... to one of intense competition to provide mortgage finance'.

The introduction of non-retail lenders to the mortgage market also had a qualitative shift in the way housing markets operated (ibid.). In particular, new lenders introduced the financial tool of mortgage-backed securitization (MBS). Such tools were not solely the brainchildren of those operating in financial markets, but were also intimately tied to the state. For example, in the USA the development of secondary mortgage markets was supported through state institutions such as Fannie Mae and Freddie Mac. As Weber (2002: 529) explained:

> institutions buy mortgages, package them, and guarantee their payments with government backing on mortgage-backed securities held by other institutions such as pension funds. Securitization connects real-estate credit markets to the nation's general capital markets and creates more liquidity in the system... The secondary mortgage market also enables investors in one part of the country to invest in mortgages originated in another region, effectively ending the geographic segmentation of credit... These innovations, mediated by the development of new electronic trading technologies, have increased the pace of financial transactions so that capital does not get grounded for too long.

Thus, the deregulation of the financial market and the introduction of new financial tools such as MBS seemed to solve many of the problems associated with housing as a capital good. However, as Pryke and Whitehead (1994: 78–9) presciently pointed out, while securitization 'opened up the potential for introducing lower cost funds for housing', it did so 'at the price of higher transaction costs and higher risks which themselves require more complex management'. While new financial tools, like MBS, offered neoliberalized solutions to the problems of capital illiquidity associated with housing as a commodity, they also changed the way that risk was identified, calculated and priced in relation to residential mortgage lending.

Housing as a technology of neoliberal governmentalities

While housing is a problematic object of government requiring neoliberalized solutions, because of its ubiquitous nature it is also regularly enrolled as a technology of neoliberal governmentalities. That is, housing is used as a tool to produce neoliberal subjectivities that are seen to address wider problematizations around the relationship of the state and citizens (Flint 2002, 2003; Dodson 2006; Dufty 2007; McKee 2009; McKee 2011b). The neoliberalized 'good' citizen is active, autonomous, empowered and responsible (Flint 2003). The ideal aspired to is that the 'good' citizen no longer passively looks to the state to address their needs. Rather, the role of the state is to provide citizens with the capacity to become reflexive, rational consumers with a concomitant sense of duty to community (Flint 2004b; Dodson 2006; McKee 2011b). Housing performs an integral role in the development of such neoliberal subjectivities. This has been most clearly demonstrated in the realm of social housing but can also be seen to play out in the field of homeownership more widely.

Supply-side policies to housing assistance were not only problematized as inefficient they were also constructed as limiting the choice/freedoms of public/social housing tenants. Changes to how housing assistance was provided were, thus, not just about reducing the fiscal burden on nation-states. They were also designed to introduce 'choice' – and the effort, education and exercise that involved – to the way recipients of housing welfare consumed housing. For example, the RTB policies in the UK provided social housing tenants with the choice of remaining a tenant or becoming a homeowner (McKee 2011a), while in Australia the rapid expansion of the Commonwealth Rent Assistance (CRA) subsidy in the 1980s and 1990s allowed housing assistance to expand recipients' housing choices to private forms of renting (Dufty 2007). This choice was in terms of not just what type of housing was consumed, but also *where* that housing was consumed. As Dufty (ibid.) showed, while the CRA was recognized to be a less fiscally responsible means of distributing housing assistance, it was pursued as a policy because it allowed housing welfare recipients to make both housing *and* locational choices in response to other governmental issues such as unemployment. Housing assistance policy in many nation-states was thus redesigned to 'empower' recipients to direct their own acts of housing consumption (McKee 2011a).

At the same time, as social housing has increasingly become the tenure of last resort in many countries, those citizens who continue to consume public forms of housing have increasingly been constructed as 'flawed consumers' and thus as 'failed citizens' (Flint 2003; Darcy and Rogers 2014; Rogers and Darcy 2014). As Darcy and Rogers (2014; see also Hackworth 2005 and Posner 2012) outline, those who have access to public/social housing find themselves governmentally trapped. Their legitimacy as social housing tenants increasingly relies on their inability to participate in the wider economy. Yet their disadvantage and outsider status is constructed as both (1) the result of individual deficiency rather than the product of government policy – that is, a product of making the wrong *choices*, and (2) used to justify the withdrawal of other citizenship rights – such as their the ability to enact civic rights to self-organize and resist urban regeneration projects that threaten their homes. The 'flawed consumer' and 'failed citizen' trope can also be seen to be deployed in order to justify the redistribution of resources away from homelessness programmes and the physical relocation of the 'chronically' homeless from urban spaces (May *et al.* 2005; Del Casino and Jocoy 2008).

In addition to being 'taught' how to consume in the appropriate ways, housing assistance recipients are also trained in how to be 'empowered' (McKee and Cooper 2008; McKee 2009; McKee 2011b; Darcy and Rogers 2014). An example of this is the various tenant participation programmes that are variously enrolled by the state, social housing managers and urban development companies. At their best, tenant participation programmes will involve 'tenants taking part in decision-making processes and influencing decisions' (McKee and Cooper 2008: 133). At their worst, these programmes 'obviate the self-organising efforts of tenants' and 'attenuate' their rights (Darcy and Rogers 2014: 236). Tenant participation programmes are an example of how social housing tenants are not just provided with new opportunities to 'choose' and 'participate', but – combined with such 'freedoms' – are governmental processes of responsibilization (Flint 2002, 2003, 2004a, 2004b, 2006; Hackworth 2005; Posner 2012). Hackworth (2005: 35–6) argued that the US 'Quality Housing and Work Responsibility Act' did exactly this when it introduced 'community service requirements and stricter screening' with tenants increasingly required to 'behave in "acceptable" ways to continue to receive their housing benefits'.

Key to the rolling out of the above neoliberal governmental technologies is the changed role of housing providers and managers. As Flint (2002: 622) explained,

> increasingly, the role of social housing agencies… involves techniques of identifying and classifying populations to be governed…. Social housing managers may also be seen to be involved in constructing populations through attempts to establish 'balanced' communities in social housing estates.

Combined with the above governmental roles, social housing agencies also assume much of the risk of not only the behaviour of an increasingly marginalized social housing tenant population, but also the financial risks and uncertainties associated with providing and managing social housing stock (Pryke and Whitehead 1995; Flint 2003; Hodkinson 2011). As a number of studies have shown, the multiple roles of social housing providers – of 'responsibilizing' social housing tenants, managing the wider financial risks of social housing stock, and the social purpose of this type of housing assistance – regularly come into conflict, remain unresolved and have the potential to make social housing agencies less effective in their execution of all of the above roles (Pryke and Whitehead 1995; Flint 2003, 2004b; Hackworth and Moriah 2006). This can result in such organizations being both the enactors and the targets of governmental reform (Dufty 2011).

While much housing scholarship has focused on the way in which social housing is used as a technology of neoliberal government, there is also a growing awareness of how homeownership has also increasingly been used in the same way. Housing researchers have argued that the various housing challenges to both capital and the state have coalesced, making homeownership pivotal to the general health of both domestic and international markets (Coakley 1994; Smith and Searle 2008; Kennett *et al.* 2013). As a consequence, housing has become a fundamental tool in the operation of neoliberal forms of macroeconomic policy. This has occurred in three main ways. First, as various nation-states' capacities to directly fund pensions from fiscal policy have declined, homeownership has become an increasingly important mechanism of redistributing the responsibility of funding the costs of retirement onto individual households. McKee and Muir (2013: 3; see also Smith and Searle 2008; Forrest and Hirayam 2009) describe this as the emergence of the 'asset-based welfare state'. Second, as wage inflation has declined in recent decades homeownership has also become an important tool in producing macroeconomic stimulus. Through financial tools that allow housing and mortgage equity withdrawal, households are encouraged to draw down on the equity in their properties to maintain and expand consumption (Smith and Searle 2008; Forrest and Hirayama 2009; Kennett *et al.* 2013). Last, as the state steps away from addressing social and economic needs, family and community are expected to become responsible for addressing the shortfall. This can be seen in the emergence of Japan's 'parasite singles', the UK's 'kippers', and Australia's 'boomerang' generations as intergenerational family dependency becomes an important feature of homeownership (Forrest and Hirayama 2009; Liu *et al.* 2015). As Forrest and Hirayama argue (2009: 1009) 'neoliberalism in the housing sector has been associated as much with refamilization as marketization'.

Evaluations of the neoliberalization of housing

The outcomes of neoliberalization processes of housing are complex and evaluations of these changes have primarily questioned their sustainability along economic, environmental, social and political lines. The GFC exemplifies the question of the economic sustainability of neoliberalized approaches to housing. One highly visible result of the failure of the neoliberalization of housing markets is the emergence of 'ghost estates'. Kitchin *et al.* (2012: 1311) defined 'ghost estates' as developments of 'ten or more houses in which 50% of the properties are either vacant or under construction'. At the end of 2009 they found 620 such estates in Ireland. However, the question of economic sustainability does not just apply to the spectacular failure of the global financial markets in 2008, but also to the growing fiscal burden of demand-driven and monetarist policies. These policies have narrowed the capacity of the state to respond to changes in economic conditions by relinquishing tax revenue through exemptions, and, as economic conditions worsen, exacerbating the fiscal burden through the increasing demand for housing assistance subsidies. For instance, Kitchin *et al.* (ibid.) argued that a contributing factor to the property crisis in Ireland was governments becoming increasingly reliant on the narrow, but lucrative, tax base associated with property development and sales. Similarly, Beer *et al.* (2007) maintained that the removal of supply-side housing policy options forced governments in Australia to increasingly rely on the blunt, and less effective, tool of planning regulation to address issues of housing affordability.

Related to the economic, the environmental sustainability of neoliberalized approaches to housing has also been raised in a number of studies (Weber 2002; Beer *et al.* 2007; Smith and Searle 2008; Glynn 2012). For instance, both Weber (2002) and Glynn (2012) question the logic behind advocating demolition over rehabilitation. Glynn (2012) points out that refurbishment of existing social housing rather than the wholesale destruction of these assets is both economically and environmentally more efficient. Similarly, Smith and Searle (2008: 23) point to how the capacity of homeowners to make mortgage equity withdrawals has the potential to cause a 'risky drain on the quality and condition' of housing stock as households defer the costs of building maintenance to finance welfare needs or more general consumption.

Intertwined with the economic and environmental is the question of the social and political sustainability of neoliberalized approaches to housing problems. An important fissure is the problem of inequality (Lee and Zhu 2006; Smith and Searle 2008; Forrest and Hirayama 2009; Dorling 2014). Specifically, neoliberalized approaches to housing seem to be exacerbating inequalities, not ameliorating them. For instance, examining the role of housing subsidies in Chile, Posner (2012: 68) maintains that this 'mode of social welfare distribution does not offer a long-term solution to the plight of the poor'. Instead, he points to the way that such policies can undermine political stability by undermining the 'cohesion of disadvantaged communities, thus making it difficult for them to work together to improve their welfare and to hold public officials accountable' (ibid.). Inequality as an intrinsic feature of the operation of neoliberalized housing policies and markets is also pointed out by Forrest and Hirayama (2009: 1011), who emphasize the intergenerational nature of this problem:

> Housing conditions of young people in the future will be partly determined by whether or not their parents own a house... Despite the current period of severe asset deflation, there will be an increasing number of families with considerable housing wealth. Low-income renters, whose parents are also renters, will continue to be excluded from housing property-based societies.

As governmentality scholars will argue, the goal of neoliberal approaches to government is to ensure the security of government. For some scholars, the security of neoliberal forms of government in the field of housing appears to be assured, with many noting that failures in the neoliberal approaches to housing post-2008 are being addressed by new rounds of further neoliberalization (Kitchin *et al.* 2012; Kennett *et al.* 2013). Yet, politically, the sustainability of many of the above approaches remains questionable. A number of housing scholars have pointed to the problematic repressive or disciplinary elements of neoliberalized approaches to housing that involve the erosion of citizen rights rather than an augmentation of their freedoms (Flint 2003; McKee 2011b; Kennett *et al.* 2013; Rogers and Darcy 2014). Others also point to the ways in which subjects of these governmental shifts are not passive victims in such processes but actively 'challenge, contest, reinterpret and subvert' neoliberal subjectivities (McKee 2011a: 3410; Dufty 2007, 2011). These evaluations go to a core conclusion of many studies of the neoliberalization of housing: that such programmes are fragile, unstable, contingent and experimental (May *et al.* 2005; Hackworth and Moriah 2006; Kamel 2012).

Future directions: reimagining neoliberal approaches to housing and home?

A number of criticisms have been levelled at the way neoliberalism has been utilized as an epistemological device in recent years (Larner 2003, 2011; Barnett 2005; Castree 2006; Lewis 2009; Collier 2012). As Lewis (2009: 114) outlines,

> The accusation has been that as a critical frame 'neoliberalism' has been deployed as an anchor for a deep political disaffection and specific critical narratives expressed via overly simplistic critiques of power, weak analysis or its operations, casual empirics and naive and ineffectual politics.

A range of responses has also been outlined advocating greater theoretical rigour; tighter definitions; and more nuanced and detailed empirical analyses. Importantly, these criticisms were not about capitulating to a 'big Leviathan' but a call for researchers to be more attuned to the experimental and flexible elements of neoliberal forms of power relations (Foucault 1991; Lemke 2001). This conclusion picks up on two themes from these debates: (1) bringing neoliberalism back down to size; and (2) the productive opportunities (the 'uses') of neoliberalism – and briefly reflects how they relate to and might be applied to future research on housing and neoliberalization.

Bringing neoliberalism back down to size

Collier (2012: 186; see also Lewis 2009; Barnett 2010; Larner 2011) advocates for researchers to approach analyses of 'neoliberalism as though it were the same size as other things, and trace its associations with them' rather than allowing the concept to be simply 'a macro-structure or explanatory background against which other things are understood'. Indeed, Jacobs and Manzi (2014: 218) make a similar call in relation to housing studies, arguing that while 'studies of contemporary housing processes can benefit from an understanding of neoliberalism… caution is required in using this concept to avoid it simply serving as a convenient label or as an alternative to empirical analysis'. Like Collier (2012) and others, Jacobs and Manzi (2014) point to the need for housing research to reveal other expressions of power that can work alongside, contest, or exist independent of neoliberal forms of government.

With these critiques in mind, there are two ways in which housing research can bring neoliberalism back down to size. The first is to recognize that housing has always been a focus of governmental problematizations. Housing, as an object and technology of government, is not solely a neoliberal phenomenon. Instead, housing researchers should be as mindful of the past ways in which housing has been targeted and enrolled into processes of governmentalization, and seek to trace detailed genealogies of how certain problematizations and their solutions emerge, are contested and change (Dodson 2007; Dufty and Gibson 2010). Genealogical approaches, however, are still prone to 'epochal thinking' and a second way in which housing research can bring neoliberalism back down to size is through what McKee (2014; see also Li 2007; Brady 2014) describes as 'ethnographies of government'. 'Ethnographies of government' seek to go beyond discourse analysis of policy and, instead, illustrate how neoliberal governmentalities are variously engaged with and remade through such relationships. This approach also works as an antidote to the tendency in governmentality approaches to neoliberalism to assume that the 'description of political rationalities also describes the actual accomplishment of subject effects' and that such rationalities are only the product of the top-down actions of the state (Barnett 2010: 281).

The productive opportunities (the 'uses') of neoliberalism

The second theme picks up on the productive opportunities, or what Ferguson (2010: 170) calls 'the uses of neoliberalism'. As has been outlined, a core feature of neoliberal forms of government is the way that it is fragile, contingent and experimental. For Ferguson (ibid.; see also Lemke 2001) this feature should be understood not only as vulnerability, but also as an asset to the way this expression of power operates. The question that Ferguson (2010: 174) poses is whether we can find ways of 'not just opposing "the neoliberal project" but appropriating key elements of neoliberal reasoning for different ends'. Indeed, housing research has made important contributions along the lines that Ferguson advocates. The work of Smith and others (Smith 2005; Smith *et al.* 2006) is a case in point. Through a variety of studies they use the example of housing to not just argue 'against markets as they are' but also to make 'a bid for what they might become' (Smith 2005: 1). Arguing that 'critiques of neoliberalism continue to leave the concept of markets more or less intact' (Smith *et al.* 2006: 81), Smith and others (Smith 2005; Smith *et al.* 2006) point out that the constructed nature of (housing) markets makes them fertile ground for questioning their 'economic essence' and reimagining and remaking them through an 'ethic of care'. The repositioning of our analyses of neoliberalism in this way is radical, but seeking to find the 'uses' of neoliberalism offers up important ways of moving our evaluations out of the cul-de-sac conclusions that neoliberalism simply begets more neoliberalism despite its manifest problems and failures. As Larner (2011: 331) points out 'housing is being understood/problematized in new ways, with the consequence that it is now being politicized and governmentalized in distinctive new ways'. Neoliberalism will continue to play an important part in such processes. It is essential, therefore, that we find new ways of bringing this epistemological tool back down to size, along with ways of reimagining and remaking it to serve alternative (progressive) solutions to contemporary and future housing issues.

Note

1 The effect of the 'concentration of disadvantage' was one of the problematizations of housing that emerged alongside the wider fiscal and representational crises of the state during the 1970s. For example, the problematization and, ultimately, the destruction of the Pruitt-Igoe housing estate in the US city of St Louis, Missouri, in the late 1960s and 1970s.

References

Arthurson, K. 2004. Conceptualising Social Inclusions in Estate Regneration Policy: What Part Does Public Housing Play? *Just Policy*, 34: 3–13.

Barnett, C. 2005. The Consolations of 'Neoliberalism'. *Geoforum*, 36: 7–12.

—. 2010. Publics and Markets: What's Wrong with Neoliberalism?, in Smith, S., Pain, R., Marston, S., and Jones, J.P. III, eds. *The Sage Handbook of Social Geographies*. London: Sage: 269–97.

Beer, A. 2012. Housing Governance, in Smith, S., ed. *International Encyclopedia of Housing and Home*. New York: Elsevier: 497–501.

Beer, A., Kearins, B., and Pieters, H. 2007. Housing Affordability and Planning in Australia: The Challenge of Policy Under Neo-liberalism. *Housing Studies*, 22: 11–24.

Brady, M. 2014. Ethnographies of Neoliberal Governmentalities: From the Neoliberal Apparatus to Neoliberalism and Governmental Assemblages. *Foucault Studies*, 18: 11–33.

Castree, N. 2006. Commentary: From Neoliberalism to Neoliberalisation: Consolations, Confusions, and Necessary Illusions. *Environment and Planning A*, 38: 1–6.

Coakley, J. 1994. The Integration of Property and Financial Markets. *Environment and Planning A*, 26: 697–713.

Collier, S. 2012. Neoliberalism as Big Leviathan, or…? A Response to Wacquant and Hilgers. *Social Anthropology*, 20: 186–95.

Darcy, M. 2010. De-concentration of Disadvantage and Mixed Income Housing: A Critical Discourse Approach. *Housing, Theory and Society*, 27: 1–22.

Darcy, M., and Rogers, D. 2014. Inhabitance, Place-making and the Right to the City: Public Housing Redevelopment in Sydney. *International Journal of Housing Policy*, 14: 236–56.

Del Casino, V., and Jocoy, C. 2008. Neoliberal Subjectivities, the 'New' Homelessness, and Struggles Over Spaces of/in the City. *Antipode*, 40: 192–9.

Dodson, J. 2006. The 'Roll' of the State: Government, Neoliberalism and Housing Assistance in Four Advanced Economies. *Housing, Theory and Society*, 23: 224–43.

—. 2007. *Government Discourse and Housing*. Aldershot: Ashgate Press.

Dorling, D. 2014. *All that is Solid: How the Great Housing Disater Defines Our Times and What We Can Do About It*. London: Penguin.

Dufty, R. 2007. Governing Through Locational Choice: The Locational Preferences of Rural Public Housing Tenants in South-Western New South Wales, Australia. *Housing, Theory and Society*, 24: 183–206.

—. 2011. Governing the Experts: Reforming Expert Governance of Rural Public Housing. *Australian Geographer*, 42: 165–81.

Dufty, R., and Gibson, C. 2010. Shifting Welfare, Shifting People: Rural Development, Housing and Population Mobility in Australia, in Milbourne, P., ed. *Welfare Reform in Rural Places: Comparative Perspectives, Research in Rural Sociology and Development*. Brighton: Emerald: 173–97.

Ferguson, J. 2010. The Uses of Neoliberalism. *Antipode*, 41: 166–84.

Flint, J. 2002. Social Housing Agencies and the Governance of Anti-social Behaviour. *Housing Studies*, 17: 619–37.

—. 2003. Housing and Ethopolitics: Constructing Identities of Active Consumption and Responsible Community. *Economy and Society*, 32: 611–29.

—. 2004a. Reconfiguring Agency and Responsibility in the Governance of Social Housing in Scotland. *Urban Studies*, 41: 151–72.

—. 2004b. The Responsible Tenant: Housing Governance and the Politics of Behaviour. *Housing Studies*, 19: 893–909.

—. 2006. Maintaining an Arm's Length? Housing, Community Governance and the Management of 'Problematic' Populations. *Housing Studies*, 21: 171–86.

Follain, J., and Zorn, P. 1990. The Unbundling of Residential Mortgage Finance. *Journal of Housing Research*, 1: 63–89.

Forrest, R., and Hirayama, Y. 2009. The Uneven Impact of Neoliberalism on Housing Opportunities. *International Journal of Urban and Regional Research*, 33: 998–1013.

Foucault, M. 1991. Governmentality, in Burchell, G., Gordon, C., and Miller, P., eds. *The Foucault Effect: Studies in Governmentality*. London: Harvester Wheatsheaf: 87–104.

Glynn, S. 2012. You Can't Demolish Your Way Out of a Housing Crisis: A Scottish Case Study of What Happens when Neoliberalism Becomes Built Into Legislation. *City*, 16: 656–71.

Hackworth, J. 2005. Progressive Activism in a Neoliberal Context: The Case of Efforts to Retain Public Housing in the United States. *Studies in Political Economy*, 75: 29–51.

—. 2008. The Durability of Roll-out Neoliberalism Under Centre-left Governance: The Case of Ontario's Social Housing Sector. *Studies in Political Economy*, 81: 7–26.

Hackworth, J., and Moriah, A. 2006. Neoliberalism, Contingency and Urban Policy: The Case of Social Housing in Ontario. *International Journal of Urban and Regional Research*, 30: 510–27.

Hedin, K., Clark, E., Lundholm, E., and Malmberg, G. 2012. Neoliberalization of Housing in Sweden: Gentrification, Filtering, and Social Polarization. *Annals of the Association of American Geographers*, 102: 443–63.

Hirayama, Y. 2010. Neoliberal Policy and the Housing Safety Net in Japan. *City, Culture and Society*, 1: 119–26.

Hodkinson, S. 2011. Housing Regeneration and the Private Finance Initiative in England: Unstitching the Neoliberal Urban Straitjacket. *Antipode*, 43: 358–83.

Hodkinson, S., Watt, P., and Mooney, G. 2013. Introduction: Neoliberal Housing Policy: Time for a Critical Re-appraisal. *Critical Social Policy*, 33: 3–16.

Jacobs, K., and Manzi, T. 2014. Investigating the New Landscapes of Welfare: Housing Policy, Politics and the Emerging Research Agenda. *Housing, Theory and Society*, 31: 213–27.

Kamel, N. 2012. The Actualization of Neoliberal Space and the Loss of Housing Affordability in Santa Monica, California. *Geoforum*, 43: 453–63.

Kennett, P., Forrest, R., and Marsh, A. 2013. The Global Economic Crisis and the Reshaping of Housing Opportunities. *Housing, Theory and Society*, 30: 10–28.

Kitchin, R., O'Callaghan, C., Boyle, M., Gleeson, J., and Keaveney, K. 2012. Placing Neoliberalism: The Rise and Fall of Ireland's Celtic Tiger. *Environment and Planning A*, 44: 1302–26.

Larner, W. 2003. Guest Editorial: Neo-liberalism? *Environment and Planning D: Society and Space*, 21: 509–12.

—. 2011. C-change? Geographies of Crisis. *Dialogues in Human Geography*, 1: 319–35.

Lee, J., and Zhu, Y.-P. 2006. Urban Governance, Neoliberalism and Housing Reform in China. *The Pacific Review*, 19: 39–61.

Lemke, T. 2001. 'The Birth of Bio-politics': Michel Foucault's Lecture at the College de France on Neoliberal Governmentality. *Economy and Society*, 30: 190–207.

Lewis, N. 2009. Progressive Spaces of Neoliberalism? *Asia Pacific Viewpoint*, 50: 113–19.

Li, T. 2007. *The Will to Improve: Governmentality, Development, and the Practice of Politics*, Durham, NC: Duke University Press.

Liu, E., Easthope, H., Judd, B., and Burnley, I. 2015. Housing Multigenerational Households in Australian Cities: Evidence from Sydney and Brisbane at the Turn of the Twenty-first Century, in Dufty-Jones, R., and Rogers, D., eds. *Housing in 21st Century Australia: People, Practices and Policies*. Farnham: Ashgate: 21–38.

May, J., Cloke, P., and Johnsen, S. 2005. Re-phasing Neoliberalism: New Labour and Britain's Crisis of Street Homelessness. *Antipode*, 37: 703–30.

McKee, K. 2009. The 'Responsible' Tenant and the Problem of Apathy. *Social Policy and Society*, 8: 25–36.

—. 2011a. Challenging the Norm? The 'Ethopolitics' of Low-cost Homeownership in Scotland. *Urban Studies*, 48: 3399–413.

—. 2011b. Sceptical, Disorderly and Paradoxical Subjects: Problematizing the 'Will to Empower' in Social Housing Governance. *Housing, Theory and Society*, 28: 1–18.

—. 2014. Social Housing and the 'New Localism': A Response to the Crisis in the Neo-liberal Project? Paper presented to Centre for British Studies, University of California, Berkeley, 5 December.

McKee, K., and Cooper, V. 2008. The Paradox of Tenant Empowerment: Regulatory and Liberatory Possibilities. *Housing, Theory and Society*, 25: 132–46.

McKee, K., and Muir, J. 2013. An Introduction to the Special Issue – Housing in Hard times: Marginality, Inequality and Class. *Housing, Theory and Society*, 30: 1–9.

Posner, P. 2012. Targeted Assistance and Social Capital: Housing Policy in Chile's Neoliberal Democracy. *International Journal of Urban and Regional Research*, 36: 49–70.

Prince, R., and Dufty, R. 2009. Assembling the Space Economy: Governmentality and Economic Geography. *Geography Compass*, 3: 1744–56.

Pryke, M., and Whitehead, C. 1994. An Overview of Mortgage-backed Securitisation in the UK. *Housing Studies*, 9: 75–101.

—. 1995. Private Sector Criteria and the Radical Change in Provision of Social Housing in England. *Environment and Planning C: Government and Policy*, 13: 217–52.

Rogers, D., and Darcy, M. 2014. Global City Aspirations, Graduated Citizenship and Public Housing: Analysing the Consumer Citizenships of Neoliberalism. *Urban, Planning and Transport Research*, 2: 72–88.

Smith, S. 2005. States, Markets and an Ethic of Care. *Political Geography*, 24: 1–20.

Smith, S., and Searle, B. 2008. Dematerialising Money? Observations on the Flow of Wealth from Housing to Other Things. *Housing Studies*, 23: 21–43.

Smith, S., Munro, M., and Christie, H. 2006. Performing (Housing) Markets. *Urban Studies*, 43: 81–98.

Turner, B., and Whitehead, C. 2002. Reducing Housing Subsidy: Swedish Housing Policy in an International Context. *Urban Studies*, 39: 201–17.

Weber, R. 2002. Extracting Value from the City: Neoliberalism and Urban Redevelopment. *Antipode*, 34: 519–40.

Wissoker, P., Fields, D., Weber, R., and Wyly, E. 2014. Rethinking Real Estate Finance in the Wake of a Boom: A Celebration of the Twentieth Anniversary of the Publication of the Double Issue on Property and Finance. *Environment and Planning A*, 46: 2787–94.

PART VI

Natures and environments

40

RE-REGULATING SOCIOECOLOGIES UNDER NEOLIBERALISM

Rosemary-Claire Collard, Jessica Dempsey and James Rowe

Neoliberalism is a continuation of much older logics and processes. Think of its most sacred principles: private property, individual freedom, a state whose main role is to protect these property rights and freedoms, and a laissez-faire approach to environmental regulation in order to facilitate economic development – essentially, principles that form an 'ongoing effort... to construct a regulatory regime in which the market is the principle means of governance' (Mann 2013: 148). These principles are far from new. They stem, in particular, from classical liberalism, a western political ideology that is classical because it pre-dates the modern age, and liberal because it holds that 'the golden road to collective wealth' is through individual freedom and a society unconstrained by the state (ibid.: 142). Classical liberal ideas – advocated most famously by thinkers like John Locke and Adam Smith – were put to work in colonial centres and peripheries, formalized in laws, enshrined more generally in the make-up of the nation-state. This might seem like ancient history, but when we read definitions of neoliberalism, we see that it has crucial resonances with these longer logics that are about defining the right way to live, not only with other humans, but also with the more than human world.

The objective of this chapter is to consider the relationship between neoliberalism and environments. But we start with liberalism because it was, like its neoliberal antecedent is, very much about transforming environments and how people relate to them. Neoliberalism inherited from liberalism particular ideas about what are the 'right' ways for ecologies and subjects to be governed, the right practices through which humans should relate to and use the environments in which they are situated. For liberals, classical and neo, when all individuals pursue their self-interest economically, when they relate to nature and land through market logic as a resource to be constantly 'improved', all of society will be wealthier. The 'all', of course, must be put in quotes. The liberal and neoliberal projects have always relied on the violent rendering of whole peoples and places as less valuable, making certain people, species, lands, waters available to be sacrificed, developed for the supposed 'common good'. The Canadian tar sands, for example, which are one of the largest industrial projects in the history of the world, are a blight on First Nations land. The enclosure, extraction and pollution endemic to tar sand production are continuous with the colonial dispossession that began in 1670 when large parts of Western Canada were claimed by the Hudson's Bay Company (a fur trading company started by imperial

Britain), with ruinous disregard for the Indigenous peoples whose territories suddenly 'belonged' to a foreign company.

Given these historical continuities, why even refer to neoliberalism at all? From technological developments facilitating a more globalized economy, to the increased political organization and power of economic elites, there are important distinctions between liberal and neoliberal capitalism. Other chapters in this handbook carefully excavate what is distinctive about the 'neo', in particular by pointing to the break with so-called 'embedded liberalism' (see Jessop 2016), as well as to the rise of globalization and finance (see Aalbers 2016). In this chapter we build from previous reviews of 'neoliberal environments' (e.g. Castree 2010; Heynen *et al.* 2007; Himley 2008) to focus on the re-regulations of nature that characterize neoliberalism and that are producing a host of uneven socioecological effects. By re-regulation, we simply mean that under neoliberalism there is a changing regulatory environment – policies and laws are shifting, with varying effects. One of the hallmarks of competitive states jockeying for investment in the neoliberal era involves governments overhauling regulatory environments that govern access to and control of nature. When it comes to these regulatory environments, the favoured approach is one in which markets are king. This means not only that environmental regulation is increasingly reconfigured so that it does not impede economic development (or improvement), but also that environmental regulators are more and more often turning to markets themselves as regulatory tools. This involves shifting regulatory regimes, not merely eviscerating them. We therefore avoid using the term 'deregulation' because, even though environmental regulation is often curtailed in the neoliberal era, what this frequently amounts to is a repositioning of governing bodies and strategies. Overall, the neoliberal era involves creating the regulatory conditions for further exploitation of natural resources; the innovation of private and voluntary forms of governance; and regulations that transform environmental problems into market-like solutions. These three processes are the focus of the chapter. They are continuous with older logics, but also present their own unique challenges and openings for resistance.

Re-regulation for economic development: the cases of agriculture and mining

Neoliberalism involves setting the conditions for economic development, where the state puts its formidable power behind the extension of enterprise (Polanyi 1944). As Nancy Peluso (2007: 90) explains, the regulations that neoliberal states develop do not seek to protect the state's citizens and territories but rather aim 'to gain or maintain a piece of their sale'. States do not work alone in this pursuit. Multilateral trade agreements, a major regulatory shift in favour of markets (McCarthy 2004), have proliferated in the last two decades and continue to be actively sought after by states. These agreements not only ramp up protections for private investors (for example, by protecting against the nationalization of their assets), but also can effectively privatize conditions of production. A prime example of this is the expansion of trade-related intellectual property rights (TRIPs) to include parts of nature, like genetic material, that were previously considered part of the public domain (ibid.). Also, over the past quarter-century, there has been a concerted effort by international financial institutions, such as the International Monetary Fund (IMF) and the World Bank (WB), to use the severe fiscal crises that have occurred in the global South to enforce neoliberal conditions in exchange for debt restructuring (Klein 2008). These conditions include requiring fiscal austerity (reducing state expenditures), trade liberalization (opening up markets to foreign investment), and the privatization of resources (selling national assets). A host of socioecological effects have followed in the wake of these re-regulations.

For example, in exchange for debt restructuring, Bolivia underwent the 'shock therapy' of the IMF and WB, requiring them to undertake 'currency devaluations; road construction; export tax rebates; reduction of import taxes; and suppression of price controls' (Redo *et al.* 2011: 231) – all to attract national and international investment. Policies were enacted to increase export earnings needed to facilitate loan repayment, which led to the increase of foreign actors, particularly in agriculture. The effect of these policies was an increase in deforestation (see Hecht 2005; Redo *et al.* 2011) and unequal land distribution. As Susanna Hecht (2005: 397) describes, 'the rampant deforestation in Amazonia's "arc of fire" that extends from Maranhao to Santa Cruz reflects a powerful economic dynamic, a kind of market and technology triumphalism'. Chile also experienced rapid growth of export-oriented forestry after its forests were privatized and all export restrictions lifted, and there are links between these policy changes and the loss of old-growth forests with widespread conversion to plantation forestry (see Clapp 1998; Liverman and Vilas 2006).

The case of the North American Free Trade Agreement (NAFTA), which came into effect in 1994, is also illustrative. As outlined in Liverman and Vilas (2006) (themselves drawing on a wide range of research in Latin America), NAFTA is built upon the basic notions of neoclassical economics. In agriculture, the theory was that trade liberalization (reduction of subsidies, tariffs) would lead Mexico, the USA and Canada to specialize in the products for which they hold a comparative advantage. Mexico, it was thought, would specialize in labour-intensive vegetables, nuts, coffee and tropical fruits, moving away from 'inefficient' grain production. Mexico reformed its constitution to encourage investment and efficiency in agriculture, and to move away from common property towards private ownership (because private property was considered more economically efficient). Over a decade later, researchers have found that small-scale farmers were negatively impacted by these changes: 'Smaller and poorer farmers have found it more difficult to access the credit, water, and technical expertise to convert to exports and because of low grain prices and difficult economic conditions have actually expanded the area in corn in order to maintain even modest incomes' (ibid.: 349). Additionally, ecological impacts include increased pressure on water supply, heavy use of agricultural chemicals, and deforestation.

Alongside a revamped agricultural sector, a globalized mining industry has been a linchpin of neoliberalism. In the early neoliberal era, as Gavin Bridge (2007: 85) catalogues, over 90 states adopted new mining laws in an effort to, as he colourfully describes, produce the 'underground as a site for the circulation of international capital'. As a demonstration of the new world order of hyper competitive capital, Bridge quotes a Guyanese document worth reiterating:

> From west to east, there is a global preoccupation with advertising one's mineral heritage, revising mining laws and fiscal policy, in some instances, offering fiscal incentives; advertising one's mining culture, infrastructure, educated human resources, etc. as additional attractions to the potential investor. In some ways it's like jostling for attention in a crowded marketplace.
>
> *(Quoted in ibid.: 78)*

Angling for international investment means countries like Guyana strive to become more hospitable places for foreign capital. So, as Bridge outlines, Guyana reworked its institutions and laws that allocate private access to mining exploration and mineral extraction. In 1989, Guyana revised its Mining Act to liberalize exploration – which led to an explosion of new claims, more than doubling in three years (from 1,316 in 1988 to 3,070 in 1991). To attract further international capital into the country, in 1993 the government created a new kind of permit (longer term, larger size). This led to a 20-fold expansion in the area of land claimed or permitted, from 200,000 acres in 1990 to 3 million acres in 1994. Bridge (ibid.: 82) describes this as a 'process of enclosure in which private property rights… were assigned to lands formerly vested in the state'. In some areas of the country 100 per cent of land was claimed for gold and diamond mining.

These examples carry with them a central take-home message: neoliberalism is fundamentally tied to the deeply rooted classical liberal logic that self-interested competition lifts all boats. Neoliberalism is an attempt to create the conditions for such competition to take place, facilitating efficient economic development. What the above examples show is that this involves the creation of further rules and regulations to speed up and extend economic flows of capital with significant socioecological effects. But it would be wrong to suggest that overall 'capital wins', although it surely comes out ahead. Effects of re-regulating socioecologies in favour of markets can be unpredictable and varied. For an example, we can return to the height of NAFTA, when Mexico had just eliminated a federal institution that helped to regulate coffee markets. In the hole left, struggles ensued between political elites, producers and social movements to control the market in coffee. In some cases this led to strong social movements and small producers being able to capture more surplus for themselves, whereas in less organized spaces, elites came to control markets (Snyder 2001). As Liverman and Vilas (2006: 350) comment, 'local and historical factors mediate the effects of neoliberal processes and how the withdrawal of national controls can open up new forms of control and regulation at the local level'. In several sectors (coffee and forestry, for example), too, these trends in environmental governance towards free trade and freer investment flows take place at the same time as the explosion of *fair* trade and certification, to which we now move.

Corporate voluntarism: the fox guarding the henhouse

The rise in prominence of NGOs and other non-state entities has been a major change in global environmental governance since the early 1990s. With states circumscribed in their ability to regulate increasingly transnational industries and trade, NGOs began to circumvent governments and attempt to directly influence corporations. The resulting 'private' governance bodies – certification regimes, in particular – have been described as 'non-state, market-driven' governance (Cashore *et al.* 2004) or 'informal' regulation (Newell 2001). Their authority can be wielded through carrots (promise of access to particular markets or higher prices, for example through certification regimes) or sticks (such as consumer boycotts or shareholder activism). Their unifying characteristic is that state sovereignty is not used to force compliance (Cashore *et al.* 2004), at least not directly. Compliance – and authority – is, instead, rooted in the market. For example, if a forest company fails to comply with a standard required in order to be certified by the Forest Stewardship Council (FSC), FSC can withdraw its certification and the company will lose access to particular markets for FSC-certified wood.

While some of the scholars tracking these trends do not link them to neoliberalism (ibid.), for many others the connection is obvious, particularly because of the way the market is leveraged to achieve political influence and market transactions serve as the seat of authority (Guthman 2007; Newell 2008). For Peter Newell (2008: 522), then, 'marketised environmental governance is a mode of neoliberal governance'. In particular, for him, it is the emphasis on *voluntarism* that betrays a neoliberal disdain for traditional command and control state regulation. For example, voluntary food labels, including everything from 'dolphin-safe' tuna (Baird and Quastel 2011) to organic vegetables (Guthman 2007), have clear neoliberal marks (see McCarthy 2006 for an overview). A mix of state, private, NGO and multilateral bodies govern these labels, which 'attach economic values to ethical behaviors... and "devolve" regulatory responsibility to consumers' (Guthman 2007: 457). As such, voluntary labels not only fall back on the market as the means to regulate; they may also create new markets.

Three points are important to make here. First, the voluntary food label example points to a broader shift: not only consumers are becoming mobilized as political actors, 'shopping to save the planet' (Liverman 2004), but also shareholders and pension holders are using their collective influence to attempt to shift the terrain of investment towards, for example, decarbonized port-folios, as in the recent expansion of fossil fuel divestment movement. Second, to characterize this growth in market- and consumer/investor-based politics as neoliberal is to miss how it can also work to undermine neoliberal and broadly capitalist forces. To go back to food labels, Guthman (2007) points to Karl Polanyi's 'double-movement' at work. Organic labels, she says, both deploy neoliberal techniques and at the same time push back against the abstracting ten-dencies of capitalist trade and perhaps even address the inequities such trade produces. Eco-labels possibly even create new political openings, such as 'novel possibilities for collective action at transnational, subnational, and regional scales' (Foley and Hébert 2013: 2736). The same can be said about other consumer-based movements – boycotts, divestment – that may have a neolib-eral face but also work to undermine neoliberal markets and orders, and curtail their effects (Rowe *et al.* 2016).

Third, the growth of voluntary labelling regimes is consistent with a broader rise in volunta-ristic environmental governance. Voluntary standards and certification regimes have proliferated in fisheries, forestry, and in numerous international standards regimes that pertain to labour and development. Non-profit certification organizations like the Marine Stewardship Council (MSC) (Foley and Hébert 2013) and the FSC (Klooster 2005) are becoming powerful players, setting global environmental standards for harvests of fish and trees, respectively. Research on the environmental impacts of these environmental standards regimes is sparse, even for forestry (Visseren-Hamakers and Pattberg 2013), whose certification regime is the longest standing. The few studies that exist find mixed results. Organic coffee certification in Costa Rica signifi-cantly reduced chemical inputs (Blackman and Naranjo 2012). But the results are less promising for fisheries. Although MSC-certification has expanded considerably over the last decade, 'there is little evidence... that the MSC has contributed significantly to arrest the decline of fish stocks... [and] risks defaulting to a marketing scheme for the seafood industry' (Gulbrandsen 2012: 335). An additional risk, of course, is that if market advantage cannot be demonstrated or sustained, companies may lose their incentive to certify.

Governments are usually not formally involved in certification regimes, and typically they do not legally require that companies comply with them. But governments may advocate that companies adhere to voluntary standards. This is particularly the case with international stan-dards that seek to guide corporate behaviour abroad. For example, Canada does not require its mining companies to follow Canadian regulation when operating abroad, instead leaving com-panies to follow the regulations of the country within which they are operating, even though many of these companies receive financial support from the federal government for their foreign investments (Gordon and Webber 2008). The Canadian government does, though, 'encourage' its mining companies to act in compliance with the International Labour Organization's (ILO) Convention 169, which requires, among other things, that Indigenous people be consulted before any development on their lands. Canada itself has not ratified the ILO, however, and companies' compliance is entirely voluntary; there are no bodies able to enforce ILO 169. What this means is that 'Canadian mining companies are largely left to govern themselves' (Nolin and Stephens 2010: 49).

If the previous section's main message was that neoliberalism involves creating the environmental governance regimes in which self-interested competition and accumulation can flourish (albeit with unpredictable consequences), this section shows how NGOs and other non-state entities have also been hard at work to cultivate voluntary mechanisms like certification, which they hope can fill the regulatory void left by states unable – or unwilling – to create laws governing environmental development. While re-regulating socioecologies is, then, increasingly taking place beyond the state, the motivations of the groups involved vary. So too do the socio-ecological effects of these voluntary regimes.

Solving environmental problems with private property, markets and commodities

This section focuses on a third type of socioecological re-regulation under neoliberalism – that of market environmentalism. It is linked to, but also distinctive from the previous section. Here we focus on the trend in environmental management over the past quarter-century that aims to extend private titles to resources – land, water, forests, fisheries, genetic resources – as well as the trading of these resources and rights. The overall logic is that private ownership of common resources will create economic incentives that will lead individuals and firms to change to 'environmental' behaviour, in the most cost-effective way possible. These market-based approaches are counter to what are known as 'command and control' approaches that simply set limits or regulations on firm behaviour, meaning approaches to environmental governance that require firms to only emit X tonnes of GhG emissions, or disallow firms from certain land use changes (e.g. no draining of wetlands). These market-based approaches argue that command and control is inefficient, and that market-based approaches will allow for the most flexible and cost-effective achievement of environmental goals. The resonances between free market environmentalism and the philosophies of classical economic liberals are deep. According to Mansfield (2006: 30), proponents of these approaches draw their ideas from 'neoliberal economic and political thinkers such as Ronald Coase and Friedrich Hayek, who themselves draw on liberal thinkers such as Adam Smith'.

The 1990 Clean Air Act in the USA is exemplary of the market-based approach to solving environmental problems. It established a cap and trade system to deal with emissions leading to acid rain. The Act capped the source emissions (the cap lowered over time) and distributed rights to pollute to firms, creating a property right in pollution (in sulphur dioxide and nitrous oxide) as well as laying the framework for their trading. Firms most efficient at reducing their emissions could sell their 'right to emit' to those that were not. Proponents argued that this market – the cap and trade system – would lower the cost of pollution reduction for all of society, lower than, say, if the government implemented a law that required all firms to abate emissions. This rationale is directly linked to an Adam Smithian logic, in that it aims to put the 'natural drive' of profit within a competitive market environment to work at reducing pollution (for an excellent overview of the evolution of cap and trade see McNish 2012). And the proponents were right: this and other early experiments in cap and trade are considered successful in improving air quality in the USA at reduced cost (ibid.). The success paved the way for cap and trade's application to other pollutants.

Perhaps most famously, the 1997 Kyoto Protocol, which established binding reductions of GhG emissions for developed countries, followed in the footsteps of the Clean Air Act in its cap and trade approach. But as McNish (ibid.) outlines, it differed from the previous markets in allowing firms to purchase carbon offsets of various kinds, not simply buy allowances from other firms producing the same gas in the same region. Carbon offsets are reductions in

GhG emissions (certified or voluntary) that 'offset' emissions made elsewhere. The Clean Development Mechanism under the Kyoto Protocol, for example, was created to allow countries of the global North to meet their obligations for emissions reductions by investing in an emission-reducing project in the global South (an offset), such as renewable energy or reforestation projects. The Clean Development Mechanism (CDM) validates and measures projects to ensure that they are 'additional' emissions reductions above and beyond business as usual. The argument, again, is that an international carbon market will reduce emissions at lower costs compared to command and control regulation, finding the cheapest way to lower emissions via the profit imperative (the argument is that offset developers will seek out how to make the lowest cost emission reductions, namely reductions in the global South). Countering the notion of elegant markets, McNish (ibid.) characterizes the international carbon market as more akin to a Rube Goldberg-esque process (meaning, more complex and expensive than necessary) (see also Lohmann 2009, 2011).

Overall, the impact of the Kyoto Protocol and the CDM on emissions reductions is 'highly suspect' (McNish 2012: 418; see also Wara 2007; Bond 2015) with cases of fraud, and widespread problems in accounting the 'additionality' that is the basis for a certified offset. As Patrick Bond (2015: 2) summarizes, so far the international cap and trade systems, including the European Trading Scheme, appear 'unable to either cap or regulate GHG pollution at source, or jump start the emissions trade in which so much hope is placed', with the value of these markets dropping year-on-year since 2011. Further, much of the carbon finance flowing for 'clean development' – a major aim of the CDM – is concentrated in only a few countries, bypassing most places on the planet, especially Africa.

Another early environmental market is wetland banking in the USA (Robertson 2004). In this case, the US government capped development of wetlands by adopting a legislative framework of 'no net loss' (of wetlands). This legislative decree is the constraint on development: the cap. However, within this cap, there are provisions for regulators to allow impact to a wetland in exchange for protection or restoration of a wetland in another site. The developers of a suburban housing development, for example, may be allowed to impact a wetland on the condition that they purchase a 'wetland credit' from a firm (or 'bank') that creates government-certified credits in wetlands by restoring or creating new wetlands. This has led to a market in wetland banking, where private actors create credits and sell them to those who impact wetlands (see Lave *et al.* 2008 on stream restoration banking; Pawliczek and Sullivan 2011 on species banking).

Questions about the environmental effectiveness of these ecosystem offsets abound, as even the most advanced ecosystem banking system in the world has not been subjected to serious systematic assessment (Robertson and Hayden 2008) and there is evidence that wetland banking is not working to achieve 'no net loss.' For example, one study found that a majority of projects (67 per cent) that restored or created wetlands were not successful at meeting permit requirements in terms of wetland area (Kettlewell *et al.* 2008). Another study in Ohio found that many of the bank credits were not up to standard when checked against stringent scientific criteria (in spite of the fact that they had been studied and monitored by the Army Corps and the Environmental Protection Agency) (Mack and Miacchion 2006). Only three banks scored in the 'successful category', while five passed in some areas and failed in others. The remaining four failed nearly every assessment, with wetlands functioning more like 'shallow dead pools' than wetlands (ibid.). There is also growing evidence that compensation and offsetting are taking priority over other aspects of most banking schemes, which require proponents to avoid and minimize impacts prior to offsetting (Clare *et al.* 2011; Hough and Robertson 2009). This means that offsets such as wetland banking may be working, perversely, in some cases as incentives that support developments that may be ecologically problematic. And despite arguments that market approaches are a more cost-efficient approach to environmental policy, researchers raise serious questions about the reality of that claim (Kroeger and Casey 2007; Muradian *et al*. 2010; Walker *et al*. 2009).

There are important questions to ask of these trends in carbon and ecosystem conservation: who is being awarded rights to resources, who is being excluded, are new enclosures created, and do they work to solve the crises they set out to solve in the first place? Patrick Bond (2015) argues that these tactics – particularly of the international sort like the carbon market – tend to '*shift* problems around spatially, without actually solving them' (2), and 'stall a genuine solution to the problems' via promises of future market and financialized solutions, further allowing the North to 'steal more of the world's environmental carrying capacity – especially for greenhouse gas emissions – and perhaps pay a bit back through commodification of the air… while denying climate debt responsibilities' (18). And if the evidence leans towards the ongoing failure of market solutions to achieve their goals – then the question we need to ask is: how and why do they persist as the dominant approach to environmental policy-making options?

Conclusion

The three neoliberal re-regulations of the environment that we have just charted are not smooth. As we point out, the motivations and outcomes of neoliberal governance are unpredictable and varied. In part, this is because, as Sundberg (2007: 269) writes, '[d]espite the efforts of powerful elites to privatize natural resources and enrol individuals into the market economy… people resist, policies go awry, and contradictions emerge' (e.g. Bakker 2013; Harris and Roa-García 2013; St Martin 2007; Wolford 2007). The world is alight with such recalcitrance today – just think of the ongoing debates over new rounds of free trade liberalizations and investment agreements such as the Trans-Pacific Partnership agreement, geopolitical resistance to austerity conditions imposed from financial institutions in Greece, and the rise of Climate Justice movements that reject false solutions like carbon offsets and, instead, stress the imperative to 'keep the oil in the soil, the coal in the hole, the tar sands in the land'.

Meanwhile, though, states continue to bend over backwards to facilitate investment and economic development in their country, leaving international regulation to voluntary agreements and NGO certification schemes. 'Green' economic development promises go unfulfilled, especially when it comes to some of the global environmental issues of our time – climate change and ecological impoverishment. In many ways, it seems hard to imagine a worse way of organizing an effort to temper ecological crises. This begs the question – why? One explanation for this trend is found in the work of David Harvey: falling rates of profit lead to a need to find new fixes for capital. This means opening up new markets: agriculture in Bolivia, mining in Guyana, plantation forests in Mexico – all new ways to let capital circulate through socioecologies. Carbon and biodiversity markets are, too, framed as new sites of accumulation, this time green accumulation (Arsel and Büscher 2012; Brockington and Duffy 2010; Büscher *et al*. 2014; Smith 2007). Such policies aim to fix environmental, 'development' and capitalist crisis, together, but leave status quo relations of power and wealth unchanged (and, as we have charted, they fail to address the environmental problems they set out to address). Certainly the rise of neoliberalism involves actively seeking to protect these status quo relations – for example, by pushing back against growing labour and environmental and global South power (Harvey 2007; see also Mann 2013).

Yet, these kinds of schemes are not solely animated by logics of accumulation or resource capture. As Wendy Brown (2015) points out, neoliberalism is about more than accumulation;

it is 'a governing rationality within which everything is economized... a governing form of reason, not just a power grab by capital'. Neoliberalism redefines the right way to live, cultivating competitive, market-like relations throughout the social sphere. In the world of global biodiversity politics, for example, the promise of economic and market-based approaches for solving global biodiversity is often more political than economic, animated more by desires to improve liberal democratic rule than profit (Dempsey 2016). Ecosystem service accounting, especially, attempts to render the qualities of ecosystems, and rich socioecological relations, into representative forms that can be compared, ranked, and ordered quantitatively. But this effort is not always about the 'tions': privatization, commodification, accumulation (ibid.). Rather, these accounting schemes often set out to make biodiversity tractable for modern liberal governance, to include it in cost benefit analyses and risk assessments, and to guide investments in green infrastructure.

Is there a unifying end-game for re-regulations of socioecologies under neoliberalism? These re-regulations, we argue, are ultimately reassertions of already existing, classical liberal principles in society: the sacrosanct nature of private property, individual and firm freedom, and state commitment to economic development and free trade, attributes thought to lead to greater societal wealth. Noting how neoliberalism is, in this way, a 'continuation of a more deeply historical process' (Heynen *et al.* 2007: 10) is politically important. It means we cannot explain socioecological issues by simply pointing to neoliberalism as the culprit. When it comes to the question of 'what we should do' instead, we cannot simply seek to reverse the trends of the last 25 years, but rather must consider the way that neoliberalism deepens liberal tendencies and ask ourselves if political opposition should be oriented towards the most recent variant, or rather to tackle some of the root foundations.

References

Aalbers, M.A. 2016. Regulated Deregulation, in Springer, S., Birch, K., and MacLeavy, J., eds. *The Handbook of Neoliberalism.* London: Routledge: 549–59.

Arsel, M., and Büseher, B. 2012. Nature™ Inc.: Changes and Continuities in Neoliberal Conservation and Market-Based Environmental Policy. *Development and Change,* 43: 53–78.

Baird, I., and Quastel, N. 2011. Dolphin-safe Tuna from California to Thailand: Localisms in Environmental Certification of Global Commodity Networks. *Annals of the Association of American Geographers,* 101: 337–55.

Bakker, K. 2013. Neoliberal versus Postneoliberal Water: Geographies of Privatization and Resistance. *Annals of the Association of American Geographers,* 103: 253–60.

Blackman, A., and Naranjo, M. 2012. Does Eco-Certification have Environmental Benefits? Organic Coffee in Costa Rica. *Ecological Economics,* 83: 58–66.

Bond, P. 2015. Climate's Value, Prices and Crises Geopolitical Limits to Financialization's Ecological Fix. Discussion paper. Retrieved from http://thestudyofvalue.org/wp-content/uploads/2015/01/WP9-Bond-Climates-value-prices-crises.pdf

Bridge, G. 2007. Acts of Enclosure: Claim Staking and Land Conversion in Guyana's Gold Fields, in Heynen, N., McCarthy, J., Prudham, S., and Robbins, P., eds. *Neoliberal Environments: False Promises and Unnatural Consequences.* New York: Routledge: 74–88.

Brockington, D., and Duffy, R. 2010. Capitalism and Conservation: The Production and Reproduction of Biodiversity Conservation. *Antipode,* 42: 469–84.

Brown, W. 2015. What Exactly is Neoliberalism? Wendy Brown interview by Timothy Shenk. *Dissent Magazine.* Retrieved from http://www.dissentmagazine.org/blog/booked-3-what-exactly-is-neoliberalism-wendy-brown-undoing-the-demos

Büscher, B., Dressler, W., and Fletcher, R. eds. 2014. *Nature™ Inc: Environmental Conservation in the Neoliberal Age.* Tucson: University of Arizona Press.

Cashore, B., Auld, G., and Newsom, D. 2004. *Governing Through Markets: Forest Certification and the Emergence of Non-State Authority.* New Haven: Yale University Press.

Castree, N. 2010. Neoliberalism and the Biophysical Environment: A Synthesis and Evaluation of the Research. *Environment and Society: Advances in Research*, 1: 5–45.

Clapp, R. 1998. Waiting for the Forest Law: Resource-led Development and Environmental Politics in Chile. *Latin America Research Review*, 33: 3–36.

Clare, S., Krogman, N., Foote, L., and Lemphers, N. 2011. Where is the Avoidance in the Implementation of Wetland Law and Policy? *Wetlands Ecology Management*, 19: 165–82.

Dempsey, J. 2016. *Enterprising Nature*. Boston: Wiley-Blackwell.

Foley, P., and Hébert, K. 2013. Alternative Regimes of Transnational Environmental Certification: Governance, Marketization, and Place in Alaska's Salmon Fisheries. *Environment and Planning A*, 45: 2734–51.

Gordon, T., and Webber, J. 2008. Imperialism and Resistance: Canadian Mining Companies in Latin America. *Third World Quarterly*, 29: 63–87.

Gulbrandsen, L. 2012. Impacts of Nonstate Governance: Lessons from the Certification of Marine Fisheries, in Dauvergne, P., ed. *The Handbook of Global Environmental Politics*. Northampton: Edward Elgar: 330–40.

Guthman, J. 2007. The Polanyian Way? Voluntary Food Labels as Neoliberal Governance. *Antipode*, 39: 456–78.

Harris, L., and Roa-García, M. 2013. Recent Waves of Water Governance: Constitutional Reform and Resistance to Neoliberalization in Latin America (1990–2012). *Geoforum*, 50: 20–30.

Harvey, D. 2007. *A Brief History of Neoliberalism*. Oxford: Oxford University Press.

Hecht, S. 2005. Soybeans, Development and Conservation on the Amazonian Frontier. *Development and Change*, 36: 375–404.

Heynen, N., McCarthy, J., Prudham, S., and Robbins, P. eds. 2007. *Neoliberal Environments: False Promises and Unnatural Consequences*. New York: Routledge.

Himley, M. 2008. Geographies of Environmental Governance: The Nexus of Nature and Neoliberalism. *Geography Compass*, 2: 433–51.

Hough, P., and Robertson, M. 2009. Mitigation Under Section 404 of the Clean Water Act: Where it Comes From, What it Means. *Wetlands Ecology and Management*, 17: 15–33.

Jessop, B. 2016. The Heartlands of Neoliberalism and the Rise of the Austerity State, in Springer, S., Birch, K., and MacLeavy, J., eds. *The Handbook of Neoliberalism*. London: Routledge: 396–407.

Kettlewell, C., Bouchard, V., Porej, D., Micacchion, M., Mack, J., White, D., and Fay, L. 2008. An Assessment of Wetland Impacts and Compensatory Mitigation in the Cuyahoga River Watershed, Ohio, USA. *Wetlands*, 28: 57–67.

Klein, N. 2008. *The Shock Doctrine: The Rise of Disaster Capitalism*. New York: Vintage.

Klooster, D. 2005. Environmental Certification of Forests: The Evolution of Environmental Governance in a Commodity Network. *Journal of Rural Studies*, 21: 403–17.

Kroeger, T., and Casey, F. 2007. An Assessment of Market-Based Approaches to Providing Ecosystem Services on Agricultural Lands. *Ecological Economics*, 64: 321–32.

Lave, R., Robertson, M., and Doyle, M. 2008. Why You Should Pay Attention to Stream Mitigation Banking. *Ecological Restoration*, 26: 287–89.

Liverman, D. 2004. Who Governs, at What Scale and at What Price? Geography, Environmental Governance, and the Commodification of Nature. *Annals of the Association of American Geographers*, 94: 734–8.

Liverman, D., and Vilas, S. 2006. Neoliberalism and the Environment in Latin America. *Annual Review of Environment and Resources*, 31: 327–63.

Lohmann, L. 2009. Toward a Different Debate in Environmental Accounting: The Cases of Carbon and Cost–Benefit. *Accounting, Organizations and Society*, 34: 499–534.

—. 2011. The Endless Algebra of Climate Markets. *Capitalism, Socialism, Nature*, 22: 93–116.

Mack, J.J., and Micacchion, M. 2006. An Ecological Assessment of Ohio Mitigation Banks: Vegetation, Amphibians, Hydrology and Soils. *Ohio EPA Technical Report WET/2006-1*. Ohio Environmental Protection Agency, Division of Surface Water, Wetland Ecology Group, Columbus, Ohio.

Mann, G. 2013. *Disassembly Required: A Field Guide to Actually Existing Capitalism*. Oakland, CA: AK Press.

Mansfield, B. 2006. Assessing Market-Based Environmental Policy Using a Case Study of North Pacific Fisheries. *Global Environmental Change*, 16: 26–39.

McCarthy, J. 2004. Privatizing Conditions of Production: Trade Agreements as Neoliberal Environmental Governance. *Geoforum*, 35: 327–41.

—. 2006. Rural Geography: Alternative Rural Economies – The Search for Alterity in Forests, Fisheries, Food, and Fair Trade. *Progress in Human Geography*, 30: 803–11.

McNish, T. 2012. Carbon Offsets are a Bridge Too Far in the Tradable Property Rights Revolution. *Harvard Environmental Review*, 36: 387–418.

Muradian, R., Corbera, E., Pascual, U., Kosoy, N., and May, P.H. 2010. Reconciling Theory and Practice: An Alternative Conceptual Framework for Understanding Payments for Environmental Services. *Ecological Economics*, 69: 1202–8.

Newell, P. 2001. Environmental NGOs, TNCs, and the Question of Governance, in Stevis, D., ed. *The International Political Economy of the Environment: Critical Perspectives*. Boulder, CO, and London: Lynne Rienner: 85–107.

—. 2008. The Political Economy of Global Environmental Governance. *Review of International Studies*, 34: 507–29.

Nolin, C., and Stephens, J. 2010. 'We Have to Protect the Investors': 'Development' and Canadian Mining Companies in Guatemala. *Journal of Rural and Community Development*, 5: 37–70.

Pawliczek, J. and Sullivan, S. 2011. Conservation and Concealment in Speciesbanking.com. *Environmental Conservation*, 38: 435–44.

Peluso, N. 2007. Enclosure and Privatization of Neoliberal Environments, in Heynen, N., McCarthy, J., Prudham, S., and Robbins, P. *Neoliberal Environments: False Promises and Unnatural Consequences*. New York: Routledge: 51–62.

Polanyi, K. 1944. *The Great Transformation: The Political and Economic Origins of our Time*. Boston: Beacon Press.

Redo, D., Millington, A., and Hindery, D. 2011. Deforestation Dynamics and Policy Changes in Bolivia's Post-Neoliberal Era. *Land Use Policy*, 28: 227–41.

Robertson, M. 2004. The Neoliberalization of Ecosystem Services: Wetland Mitigation Banking and Problems in Environmental Governance. *Geoforum*, 35: 361–73.

Robertson, M., and Hayden, N. 2008. Evaluation of a Market in Wetland Credits: Entrepreneurial Wetland Banking in Chicago. *Conservation Biology*, 22: 636–46.

Rowe, J., Dempsey, J., and Gibbs, P. 2016. The Power of Fossil Fuel Divestment (and its Secret), in Carroll, W., and Sarker, K., eds. *Contemporary Social Movements and Counter-Hegemony*. Winnipeg: ARP.

Smith, N. 2007. Nature as Accumulation Strategy. *Socialist Register*, 43: 16–36.

Sundberg, J. 2007. Researching Resistance in a Time of Neoliberal Entanglements, in Heynen, N., McCarthy, J., Prudham, S., and Robbins, P. *Neoliberal Environments: False Promises and Unnatural Consequences*. New York: Routledge: 269–72.

Snyder, R. 2001. *Politics After Neoliberalism: Reregulation in Mexico*. Cambridge: Cambridge University Press.

St Martin, K. 2007. Enclosure and Economic Identity in New England Fisheries, in Heynen, N., McCarthy, J., Prudham, S., and Robbins, P. *Neoliberal Environments: False Promises and Unnatural Consequences*. New York: Routledge: 255–68.

Visseren-Hamakers, I., and Pattberg, P. 2013. We Can't See the Forest for the Trees: The Environmental Impact of Global Forest Certification is Unknown. *GAIA-Ecological Perspectives for Science and Society*, 22: 25–8.

Walker, S., Brower, A., Stephens, R., and Lee, W. 2009. Why Bartering Biodiversity Fails. *Conservation Letters*, 2: 149–57.

Wara, M. 2007. Is the Global Carbon Market Working? *Nature*, 445: 595–96.

Wolford, W. 2007. Neoliberalism and the Struggle for Land in Brazil, in Heynen, N., McCarthy, J., Prudham, S., and Robbins, P., eds. *Neoliberal Environments: False Promises and Unnatural Consequences*. New York: Routledge: 243–55.

41

NEOLIBERALISM'S CLIMATE

Larry Lohmann

> The climate system is natural capital... capital created by nature, not us... an asset that is... valuable because it generates a flow of services over time.
>
> (Geoffrey Heal 2015)

Is it useful to label the current political era 'neoliberal'? Those of us who think that it is are in roughly the same predicament as periodizing historians of music. We have to explain not only what is importantly new about the period we single out as significant, but also how it grew out of what went before. This chapter defends the term 'neoliberal' as a significant category of historical analysis by arguing that what has been made of climate through a range of practices to which the label is attached is deeply novel, yet also multiply dependent on the ways in which climate has been co-constructed during preceding eras of imperialism and regulated industrial capitalism. Just as important musical eras reconstruct what music is in terms of, for example, its tonal organization or social embeddedness, so neoliberalism creatively reworks the capitalistic organizations of climate that it has inherited. Conversely, the construction of a planetary ecosystem service economy that includes climate plays a part in constituting and developing neoliberalism (see also Collard *et al.* 2016).

In investigating what count as climate and climate change for neoliberalism, then, a first step is to consider what they mean for capital. A crude, oversimplified analogy may help pave the way for a more extended analysis: capital tends to experience deleterious climate change in somewhat the same way that it experiences the degraded well-being of workers. What is this well-being, how much is really needed and by whom, and how might it be secured? That is, when, where, how, and to what degree must capital be restrained from 'externalizing' costs onto the bodies and subsistence activities of workers? As negotiations unfold amid conflicting traditions of well-being and diverse medical transformations, new varieties of health become defined and entrenched in countless bureaucratic and regulatory actions and reactions. It is objects such as these that are subsequently privatized and converted into standardized, appropriable, deliverable 'units' under neoliberalism.

This chapter will begin its own particular tale of continuity in change by touching on various inherited aspects of neoliberalism's climate. In particular, it will review some of the circumstances in which, since colonial times, climate and society have been made to seem external to each other as part of larger movements towards organizing nature/human binaries and a 'global environment' (Ingold 2000). Concrete ways of externalizing climate, it will suggest, have provided materials for the neoliberal innovations of climate rent and climate commodities in much the same way that concrete ways of externalizing land from human activities have played a part in widening land and labour markets. Climate as object of colonial management; as external determinant of or limit to human activities and biotic systems; as average weather which is nevertheless subject to change; as molecules and radiation; as chaotic but modellable global circulation system capable of independent agency – all have all been enlisted as material for characteristic neoliberal operations. Among the end results have been the following:

- Regulatory 'boundaries' limiting the excesses of the accumulation process have been globalized, pollution made more abstract, and an expanded palette of compensations and equivalences pressed into service to help override local barriers to extraction, production and circulation.
- Climate change action has been transformed, largely through the agency of the state, into the generation of tradable, priced and ownable units of molecular 'mitigation'.
- New forms of territory and rent have been created by the state and distributed to assorted elites.
- Industrial and financial powers have been both deresponsibilized and handed extended powers to define social choices.
- Meteorological forces have been enlisted in exploitation, oppression and capital accumulation in fresh ways.

Persisting histories of conflict

It has only been through discontinuous, varied, contested and fairly recent historical processes that some intellectual classes have come to be able to conceive of and propose climate as an internally coherent worldwide physical system impinging on separately constituted societies, economies and ecosystems and susceptible to being changed globally through external 'forcings' or external technocratic management. The climate that many elites talk about today has been 'extracted from the matrix of interdependencies that shape human life within the physical world, then, once isolated, elevated to the role of dominant predictor variable' (Hulme 2011: 247).

At most times in the past – as in most places today – what is currently referred to as the 'climate' by environmentalists, national states, the UN and climatologists as a whole would likely have been regarded as an aspect of an exotic, newly exploitative kind of politics. From this point of view, climate is neither natural nor social nor a hybrid of the two, but bound up with 'substantial, living forms' and part of the 'active formation of the lived environment' (Taylor 2015: 39). For example, in Tibet, when weather, there regarded as part of a complex of specific qualitative relations among humans and nonhumans, encountered postwar Euro-American climatology (Huber and Pedersen 1997), what resulted was not an adversarial 'politics of knowledge' or disagreement about how to interpret an external world, but rather a

> staggered transformation of the socio-ecology of the Tibetan plateau in which lives and livelihoods were slowly drawn into a new field of relations with different forms of political authority, organizations of labor, changing social hierarchies and new means of ordering the landscape.
>
> *(Taylor 2015: 39)*

Such encounters are emblems of a persisting history of friction over the complex nets of relationships that influence what weather or climate are supposed to be. This history is extremely heterogeneous and contingent. Even within the relatively small world of climate science, for example, huge shifts have taken place over the past 150 years. At first, climate science was a geographically oriented study 'describing the collective effect of local atmospheric phenomena on human senses' (Fleming and Jankovic 2011). To describe 'climate' *was* to describe differences among different locations; 'global climate' would have been close to a contradiction in terms (Heymann 2011). Later on, in part through the varied and idiosyncratic agencies of globally linked measurement bureaucracies, flight and space technologies, and computers, climatology became almost exclusively a physically oriented study treating not only large-scale weather systems, but also oceans, mountain uplift, photosynthesis and the rest of a unified 'earth system' considered as an isolatable mechanism. Focusing less on variations across space, it concentrated increasingly on variations over time.

Such changes – and there are many more in the history of climate – are resistant to having any simple pattern imposed on them. Yet, over the long term, numerous processes of externalization and abstraction of climate and society from each other are discernible. These processes have both reflected and helped to constitute capitalist and colonialist interests. They have also played a deep role in political conflict. For example, the earlier view that climates and latitude zones were interchangeable – ultimately traceable at least as far back as Hippocrates – became, by the eighteenth century, a tool that, from a distance, 'enabled an entrepreneur to wield expertise in the geography of colonial investment' (Jankovic 2010: 204) and comparative advantage by explaining the different kinds of 'productiveness' or profitability of different regions – in addition to justifying the dominance of imperialist societies through an association of climate with social attributes ('heat encourages laziness and backwardness') that has survived down to the present even among liberal thinkers (e.g. Galbraith 1979). Through fitful processes involving globalization and 'real subsumption' of space and time, climate was gradually becoming one of the so-called 'abstract' natures characteristic of societies dominated by the imperatives of capital accumulation (Moore 2015).

Early colonial discussions and actions on observed *changes* in climate can also be seen as important steps in the abstraction of climate from culture that has provided a foundation for neoliberalism's innovations, whether climatic shifts were seen as potentially manageable threats to colonial production (as on various island colonies and in India) (Grove 1997); the benign result of civilizing European influence and the displacement of indigenous peoples (as in North America) (Vogel 2011); or the dire outcome of a Spanish imperialism insensitive to the balance of nature (as in the discourse of Alexander von Humboldt about the drying up of regions of Venezuela and Peru) (Cushman 2011). The climate that was seen as changing in all of these instances had not yet been separated out into the pure, integrated, three-dimensional worldwide physical agent or force that intellectuals and politicians talk about today. Yet these earlier efforts to isolate or manage it frequently involved a kind of oppression that continues in the neoliberal age in parallel forms (see below: Three aspects of neoliberalism's climate).

Systems and contexts

The eighteenth and nineteenth centuries saw the development of many technologies of industrial control that ultimately also proved crucial to neoliberal construals of climate. Automatic feedback control devices ranging from steam engine governors to thermostats and gyroscopes had to be applied to industrial machinery. Malthus (2014[1798]) described a population servo-mechanism that would keep returning human societies to a condition resembling the brutal transitional capitalism of his day. Fossil-fuelled steam and electrical power, in addition to opening a new era in labour discipline and productivity, further encouraged conceptions of communication as a dynamic, complex form of dominion, in which responses to management could be reduced to feedback for eliciting control adjustments (Beniger 1986).

Early in the twentieth century, European colonies nourished the developing science of ecology and ecosystems, as they had nourished forestry before it, resulting in investigations into energy flows in various habitats and connections between climate fluctuations. Later on, the Second World War became a crucible of forced interdisciplinarity that gave rise to intricately interlinked innovations including systems analysis, cybernetics, game theory, nuclear weapons, modern computers and artificial intelligence, all of which greatly elaborated the control systems that had accompanied the increased material and energy flows of the industrial revolution. As continued military funding encouraged the development of new kinds of human–machine couplings, ranging from computerized flight simulators to interactive computing, the bloodline of postwar cybernetics crossed with that of earlier, imperialism-infused ecosystem thinking. Organisms, animal societies and ecosystems alike were theorized by eminent ecologists such as E.P. and H.T. Odum and E.O. Wilson as command–control–communication systems involving multiple feedback loops (Elichirigoity 1999: 33–6; Haraway 1991: 62–8). Meanwhile, Second World War artillery-targeting analogue servomechanisms morphed not only into giant digital nuclear weapons command and control systems encompassing the North American continent, but also into James Lovelock's NASA-backed models of Gaia, the 'living planet'.

Economics and management sciences, always susceptible to the charm of machine metaphors, were meanwhile undergoing their own cyborg makeovers, challenged by the postwar expansion of industrial society and influenced by Cold War systems thinkers like John von Neumann and Jay Forrester (Mirowski 2002). It was, again, around the time of the Second World War that quasi-cybernetic concepts like 'economic model', 'simulation' and 'price signal' really began to take hold, and that Friedrich von Hayek began to try to configure economic relations across society as an information-processing device superior to conventional statistics-based attempts to predict and control (Cooper 2011). It was not entirely a coincidence, in short, that some of the innovations foundational to neoliberalism and to climate modelling emerged roughly in parallel.

The channelling of expertise into the modelling of systems helped update older nature/society, fact/value and science/policy dichotomies into a 'systems/context' dualism – linked, like its ancestors, to capitalist production, management and, to a certain extent, property creation. If conventional scientists continued to work hard to give the 'untidy world of the laboratory the appearance of perfectly regulated order' (Collins and Kusch 1999: 141), systems experts began to arrange computer-housed multiple feedback simulations in ways that also allowed tendencies towards 'balance' or 'resilience' to be attributed to external natures. Shaped partly by computer evolution and other institutional developments, climatology underwent an accelerated hypertrophy of physical data collection, simulation and theorization accompanied by a continuing atrophy of political, historical and geographical analysis. Just as what mainstream economics laboured to isolate – aided by an institutional hypertrophy of statistics-creating techniques and sophisticated mathematical modelling procedures that tended to pass over labour exploitation, say, or the political ecology of fossil fuels – was a discrete 'economic system' that an external 'state' interfered with at its peril, so too global circulation models and integrated assessment models helped limn a binary comprising, on the one hand, a coherent global 'climate system' and, on the other, an external, residual 'context' or 'social system' category into which everything else was implicitly unloaded, including political decisions, individual preferences, class struggle, oil company strategy, an 'expanding range of ideologies' (Hulme 2008: 9), and other matters seemingly less modellable, predictable or controllable. 'The global knowledge that the Intergovernmental Panel on Climate Change produces', as Fogel puts it, 'helps governments erect and then justify their simplified constructions of people and nature, and the institutions based on them' (2004: 109).

In one sense, this way of treating the whole planet – whether seen as stocks of resources, flows of ecosystem services, or low-cost natural infrastructure – as a 'system amenable to management' (Elichigoity 1999: 37) merely carried forward older appropriationist traditions. Nature was still an ahistorical something-or-other that was subject to prediction and control and that offered specifiable external limits to economic managers bent on profit. It remained relatively constant and self-repairing, given proper oversight (O'Neill 2001). As such, its supposed existence continued to serve as a rationale for the enclosure of commons and a riposte to commoners' claim of the right of all to survival in environments that were typically assumed to require a safety-first approach. While anthropologists trying to 'restore' various human groups to some past, supposedly static condition, or to maintain them in their current status, were increasingly forced to confront charges of racism, restoration ecologists and ecosystem stabilizers seldom faced parallel accusations, except from indigenous peoples (Cruikshank 2005). Yet the systems approach did represent something new, at least in that it helped neoliberals develop their trademark claim of being able to tackle all social issues largely through price discovery. In this neoliberal vision, capital's unstoppable creation of new externalities, as well as increasingly unequal thermodynamic exchange (Hornborg 2012), disappeared in a shimmering spectacle of a late twentieth-century perpetual-motion machine regulated by green economic feedback mechanisms.

Yet if, as Marx had urged, capital is nothing if it does not accumulate, so the new perpetual-motion 'economy' was nothing if it did not 'grow'. The first big takeoff in the use of the phrase 'economic growth' – now so central to international discourse – occurred between 1948 and 1966 (Google 2015). How could this reality be squared with the new 'closed system' norms? The Club of Rome channelled Malthus in insisting that there were 'limits to growth'. As environmental economics and ecological modernization policies proliferated, other specialists envisaged an ecosystem-like, stable version of capital accumulation in which 'value could conceivably grow forever, but the physical mass in which value inheres must conform to a steady state' (Daly 1980: 6). Many economists and scientists posited entities called 'renewable resources', which were supposed to be indefinitely exploitable as long as a calculable, more or less linear schedule for their replenishment was respected.

Predictably, such conceptions ran up against stubborn contradictions and resistances. Yet rather than simply eroding the systems/context binary in a linear fashion, some of these forced it to develop in ways that helped sustain it for decades. The US environmental movements of the 1960s and 1970s, for example, pressured the country's federal government to enact environmental legislation with some decidedly non-cybernetic aspects. US pollution-control legislation of the early 1970s was not set out in cost–benefit terms, but required 'attainment of national standards' at individual points of emission using particular technologies. By 1975, however, it was possible to say that the Clean Air Act was threatening the expansion of polluting energy and manufacturing industries in many states (Lane 2015: 28), and thus impeded 'economic growth'. The US Environmental Protection Agency duly redefined pollution as something to be aggregated, regulated and traded within larger and larger 'bubbles' using any means available, not something that occurred at particular sites and had to be fought using specified technologies. By changing what pollution was – and indeed what territory and jurisdiction were (Rice 2010) – it made it cheaper for private firms to comply with the laws regulating it. Before long, the Reagan regime was requiring federal environmental legislation to pass cost–benefit tests – a commensuration technique that had already been altering the nature of 'nature' for half a century. By the early 1990s, a nationwide sulphur dioxide trading programme was in operation, relieving pressures for innovation in pollution-control technology.

Climate trading as system

Climate change too soon had to be integrated with the 'economy' and commensurated with other features of the obligatory two-dimensional systems diagrams so that it could be governed 'efficiently' according to investment standards. A new climate had to be discovered to sit alongside other emergent natures of the neoliberal era. From early on in the neoliberal era, some intellectuals were asserting the existence of scarce 'atmospheric resources' whose value could be determined in order to 'decide whether they are worth controlling, and in what way they should be controlled' (Maunder 1970). Others posited the existence of a type of climate that could be 'stabilized' at either high cost or low cost (e.g. Lovins and Lovins 1991). Eventually, many experts converged on the view that states might someday not only be able to suggest optimal global temperature increases, but also to estimate roughly how far greenhouse gas pollution needed be capped to keep temperatures below that level and to limit emissions accordingly.

In the 1990s, climate-as-molecules and prices-as-natural-signals fused in the hybrid system of carbon trading, which proved to be one of neoliberalism's landmark innovations. Under US pressure in Kyoto in 1997, the parties to the UN Framework Convention on Climate Change adopted greenhouse gas markets as an 'economically rational' management response to global warming. In the 2000s, Europe moved into the lead in transforming potentially investment-threatening public concerns about climate into a supposedly 'depoliticized' market for ecosystem services through the European Union Emissions Trading Scheme (EU ETS). Both the Kyoto Protocol's carbon market and the EU ETS combined 'bubble' and 'offset' systems, allowing for the circulation of a huge variety of interchangeable tokens or units of pollution compensation. To quote the words one climate market proponent, Pedro Moura Costa of Brazil's Bolsa Verde, the idea was to 'transform environmental legislation into tradable instruments' (Nicholls 2011: n.p.). After having helped to construct a regulatable, nonhuman climate, in other words, national states and the UN then unitized it and made it circulatable.

The units in question facilitated the creation of a 'climate rent' (Felli 2014) that could be charged by polluting industries to the rest of society. European states were now able to appropriate quantifiable, tradable slices of the earth's carbon-cycling capacity and deliver them to their largest corporate emitters in proportion to their prior use of it. Both inside and outside the Kyoto and EU ETS markets, polluters were also provided with mechanisms to supplement these holdings by cheaply annexing various climate change-mitigating capacities outside the 'bubble' in the form of 'offsets', further reducing their costs. For example, a project which reduced HFC-23 emissions from an industrial plant in Korea beyond the level that consultants specified 'would have been the case without the project' could produce cheap credits for sale to European industries which legally empowered them to use or sell on equivalent entitlements to the earth's carbon-cycling capacity. Similarly, the molecule-based systems fiction that fossil fuel combustion could be 'neutralized' by adapting land, trees and crops for maximum carbon absorption helped perpetuate the technopolitical structures facilitating the disastrous flow of prehistoric carbon out of the ground into the earth's oceans, atmosphere and land surface, where it continued to accumulate. Investor freedom – already long protected by a society/nature divide whose 'nature' component was claimed to be defensible through 'limits' – was further extended by the unitization of the limited territory and a trade in climate services.

True to form, the systems/context dualism inherent in the new markets helped them not only to survive over a two-decade stretch of proliferating failures, but also even to spread to new jurisdictions. The collapse of successive attempts to make carbon markets 'work' as advertised –

for example, delaying auctions to relieve pollution rights oversupply, abolishing certain kinds of offsets, taking action against corruption, promising to auction a greater proportion of permits in the future rather than giving so many away for free – could always be attributed to political context, leaving the postulated 'system' free of blame (e.g. Hahn and Stavins 1995; Hahnel 2012a, 2012b) while facilitating further delays and dispossession. Carbon markets and the regulatory nature on which they were based were also justified, at least provisionally, on grounds of heuristics. It was not that anyone 'really' believed that given the right carbon emissions budget or limits on temperature rise (2 degrees Celsius, say, or maybe 1.5 degrees, or maybe 4 degrees), the earth's climate would maintain equilibrium with a quantifiable degree of certainty (Boykoff *et al.* 2010), or could be relied upon to continue to provide a manageable environment for a certain level of global GDP. Nor did anybody think that the scarcity provided by the weak caps legislated under the Kyoto Protocol or the EU ETS were enough for the economic 'system' to function in a way that could seriously address global warming. But experts did continue to propound the claim that trading in scarce pollution permits fashioned out of state-regulated caps, limits and 'planetary boundaries' (and out of the financial mechanisms required for their circulation) must somehow be a 'step in the right direction'. The existing inadequate caps were, it was implied, merely stand-in or temporary values to get the economic-ecological machine up and running until such time as better numbers from scientist/economist/policy-maker collaborations became politically possible.

The detailed political mechanics of commensuration, however, could not but spell eventual trouble for the new climate. As many observers pointed out, in the science/policy process, models for optimizing climate change had a way of becoming 'truth machines' rather than just heuristics or tools for policy-makers to think with, bringing economists' climate into increasing conflict with that of climatologists (Wynne and Shackley 1994; Randalls 2011). For carbon markets to be seen as environmentally relevant, moreover, some correlation had to be posited between the number of carbon permits in circulation and increments of climate stability, no matter how lax the caps were out of which the permits were made; yet it was obvious to serious analysts that carbon trading was actually exacerbating the climate crisis by, among other things, licensing increased exploitation of fossil fuels. To make matters worse, a second cybernetic wave was eating away at the picture of sustainable appropriation associated with the new market-friendly natures. This wave came partly from the increased mathematical power of computer weather modelling itself, which over time had revealed climate's unpredictability (Cooper 2010, 2011). It was perhaps not coincidental that second-order complex systems and nonequilibrium ecology theory came to prominence in an era in which profit crisis, the demise of Bretton Woods exchange-rate governance, and the decline of Fordism was encouraging new waves of disaster capitalism. Instead of attempting to minimize the role of the unexpected as an 'outlier', many theorists embraced it as an investment strategy; even the debt associated with traditional investments in sites with cheap labour was increasingly linked to esoteric financial products, which, despite having been labelled as 'derivatives', began to dominate economic interactions. Human–nonhuman relations aimed at eliciting sustainable yields from an external nature from which human activity had been erased began to seem actively at odds with relations that encouraged the 'resilience' that was needed to 'absorb and accommodate future events in whatever unexpected form they may take' (Holling 1973: 21; Boykoff *et al.* 2010) – including climate events. Growth itself began to be seen less as steady and predictable than as non-linear, discontinuous and dependent on periodic disturbance, disorder and collapse – together with the adaptability and flexibility that could take advantage of them (Nelson 2015). The right of all to survival in a commons became counterposed less to the vision of a passive and stable nature than to a valorization of *sauve qui peut* in a capricious world.

As mathematical probabilities and linear extrapolations were partly replaced by multiple images of starkly different possible futures, 'scenario planning' came into its own at institutions ranging from the World Economic Forum to the USA's National Intelligence Council, as well as in much scientific practice. Today, Pentagon strategists consult Hollywood screenwriters alongside old-timey systems analysts or compilers of actuarial tables. Quant inventions like the Black–Scholes–Merton option pricing formula are no longer imagined as unproblematic machines for the mass production of financial instruments, but are known to invite catastrophes (albeit potentially lucrative ones for those correctly positioned) unless they are constantly 'repaired' *ad hoc* by human traders with instincts for the incalculable (Haug and Taleb 2010). Companies like Royal Dutch Shell toy with the predictability-dependent aspects of carbon trading not in opposition to, but in combination with, the search for innovative profit opportunities in unpredictable climate disasters (Funk 2015).

Three aspects of neoliberalism's climate

At least three aspects of neoliberalism's reorganization of climate merit brief emphasis. First, the standardized units required for the operation of a cybernetic economic-ecological system tend to be different from the units associated with either a resource or conventional biological system or the elements identified in commons regimes. The contributions of capitalist non-resource nature to capital accumulation, as well as many of the ill effects of resource exploitation on communities, had not usually been a matter for precise quantification. They were not broken down into marginal increments nor their management economically rationalized. The units into which nature was divided (for example, species or molecules) tended to serve other purposes. Conservation efforts tended to have multiple and heterogeneous justifications, including that of maintaining political stability or of preserving some aspect of nature 'for itself'. Pollution and pollution-control mechanisms tended to be associated with particular conventionally defined sites, regions, substances and agents. Neoliberal natures, in contrast, tend to be divided into interchangeable 'ecosystem service' units allowing aggregation, exchange and economic circulation. Just as the biological nature of ecosystem services is made up not only, for example, of species, but also of exchangeable 'species equivalents', so too atmospheric circulation defined as an ecosystem service winds up being made up not only, for example, of molecules, but also of 'molecule-equivalents' (for example, 333 CO_2/8.8 CH_4/1 NO_2/0.06 CFC-11) that are collectively certified to be equally destabilizing to the climate and that can all be traded one for another to provide the 'same' services to an 'economy' (MacKenzie 2009; Forster *et al.* 2007). Hence, a power plant emitting 1 million tonnes of carbon dioxide per year need not be a source of pollution in the neoliberal sense of the term provided that it has contracted for 1 million tonnes of 'offsets' per year from 'carbon-absorbing' plantations in Indonesia or from 'foregone' emissions attributed to refrigerant plant improvements in China; rather, it is said to be 'carbon-neutral'. As the location of pollution expands to a 'bubble' where it can be diluted, or to the radius of a 'bubble'-plus-'offsets' arrangement, so does the location of pollution control, abstracting nature's space yet further away from the daily work of communities or even national states while dis-locating environmental responsibility, usually in the direction of the disadvantaged. An 'aggregate natural capital' (Helm 2014) forms a different kind of 'limit' to industrial expansion than did the old disaggregated nature. The new interchangeable parts, of course, can also be used outside formal ecosystems markets. EU targets for climate-friendly 'renewable' energy, for example, are being met partly by importing wood pellets harvested from US land and shipped across the Atlantic for firing in conventional thermal plants. Overall, a huge range of 'performative equations' (Lohmann 2014) defining a standardized 'climate benefit' unit (tCO_2e, or 'tons of carbon dioxide equivalent') are stretching the spatial, temporal and logical ways of conceptualizing both pollution and climate itself.

Thus, in the colonial era, a 10,000-hectare forest management area could never have been seen as a producer of, say, 500 tonnes of carbon sequestration services per year. This is not to say that many of the same human–nonhuman relationships and mechanisms of land control required for timber extraction or conventional colonialist conservation in such an area were not later pressed into service for extraction of climate services. Many foresters belonging to the tradition descending from nineteenth-century experts such as Dietrich Brandis have found employment in the new carbon service industry, measuring tree diameters and using satellite imagery to estimate sequestration rates. But, at the same time, the new ecosystem services technocracy is, to some degree, split by low-intensity internal strife among 'capitalists, scientists and regulators concerning value', the 'functional interdependence of ecosystems', and so forth, as the imperatives of cyborg economics rub up against those of traditional conservation biology (Robertson 2012). These tensions are exacerbated by the fact that, as Antonio Tricarico (2014) points out, the new ecosystem commodities, unlike more traditional commodities such as wheat or oil, have been highly financialized from the outset, involving the development of complex procedures transforming the activities of nonhumans into financializable asset streams. For example, over 95 per cent of EU ETS transactions are speculative futures trades – not surprisingly, since each installation receives its state grant of pollution rights one year before it has to cover its emissions and must hedge against price uncertainties. The unavoidable conflict between the compliance and financial functions of the market that results renders ludicrous the already insupportable claim that it might someday have a positive effect on weather and climate.

Second, the new nature is no less a nature defined by capitalist appropriation of commons and commons relationships than the older 'resource' and 'conservation' natures – even as it features a number of new twists. In the past, water sources might have been mined, without recompensing either indigenous peoples or the earth, in order to supply industrial plants or maintain industrial wheatfields supplying cheap food to urban workers. Today, they can also be appropriated for ecosystem services aimed at reducing or obviating costs of reproduction as they are defined by environmental regulation. If classical industrial capitalism saw value as created mainly through the initiative, sacrifice or organizing ability of owners and managers rather than through the activities of workers, environmental policy in a neoliberal age sees the value of nature as dependent on applications of environmental-economic expertise to an external, non-human entity rather than the historical interactions of commoners and commons. Thus, for example, specialist-controlled seed banks or biosphere reserves occupy a position of honour as repositories of genetic information needed for biotic reboots of agriculture, while the role of 'unbankings' or outgrowings of seeds to expose them to socionatural change is obscured. Tellingly, the role of indigenous peoples in the new green economy is mainly to work for wages as caretakers of a newly constituted climate, or a newly constituted 'biodiversity', whose salient features have been defined by others who tend to work with an alien conception of nature (Ingold 2000). Offset calculations based on a new generation of storytelling practices, meanwhile, carry forward colonialist traditions of representing non-European societies and polities as a static, passive and predictable background to the creative actions of experts and the property-creating 'improvements' of Europeans: in order to create quantified units of climate benefit for exchange, indigenous or 'backward' polities necessarily have to be reduced to a single 'emissions baseline' against which a variety of 'pollution-saving' alternatives identified by specialists can be calculated, insured and financialized. As Andrew S. Matthews (2015: 209) vividly puts it, 'A nightmare of indigenous people destroying the forest becomes more valuable as it becomes more nightmarish, with an added caveat: the international money will not arrive unless you act to make the nightmare go away' by changing what indigenous peoples do.

Indeed, when viewed from an indigenous, peasant, feminist or ecological Marxist perspective, neoliberal natures look more like an elaboration of their pre-neoliberal industrial forebears than a radical alternative to them. Even the most advanced computer climate models succeed in adding credibility to the threat of catastrophic global warming only in the course of sharpening and enforcing a neo-Malthusian, depoliticizing opposition between a purified, monolithic 'nature' and a purified, monolithic 'society' – a homogeneously defined *anthropos* packaged as an object subject to macroeconomic prediction and state governance. Over the decades, global circulation models have selected and incorporated more and more nonhuman processes ranging from CO_2 and chloroflourocarbon molecule circulation to feedback cycles involving vegetation and cloud formation, adding a great deal of fine grain and density to the sense of an exclusively nonhuman 'nature' while simultaneously obscuring the myriad connections linking such processes with, for example, the use of fossil fuels to discipline and increase the productivity of industrial labour (Malm 2014), international transport's need for refrigeration, and diverse indigenous and industrial land use practices. This movement of sorting and solidifying an 'external' nature has been one with expanding a distinct 'nonpolitical' class of bureaucratic scientists and economists equally 'external' to peasants, workers, factory owners, administrators and indigenous societies; the more scientists have gone to work hunting, classifying, isolating and explicating physical processes in the contexts of laboratories, computer programs or wildernesses that have had human communities edited out of them, the more 'external' that nature has become, and, in turn, the more crucial it has become to recruit specialists to understand it.

Within this set-up, political action is forced to restrict itself to a rudimentary interface between the two structures, which consists of 'anthropogenic emissions', 'policy', 'carbon prices' and the like. Mainstream climate politics becomes a matter of border controls between society and nature, not about questioning either the two entities themselves or the interface that has been constructed between them (Rouse 2002). As in the colonial era, the destructive effects of industrial capital are only allowed to be addressed or contained from 'outside' the blackboxed dynamics of capital itself. This is part of the reason why terms like 'coal companies', 'labour' and 'capital accumulation' (which would complicate the programme of establishing simple, straightforward relationships between molecules and their would-be human managers) never appear in the documentation of the UN climate negotiations, why the international community remains unable to get to grips with the global warming challenge, and why it is so difficult to achieve recognition for climate as a labour, energy or civilizational issue. While oil or auto companies' financing of climate change denialist propaganda has been the more favoured target of middle-class climate activists, dominant intellectual elites' modelling of climate as a 'nature' disaggregated from political relationships has been incomparably more powerful in stymieing effective climate action. It is only when they are forced to acknowledge that there exists no uncontested baseline 'external' to human societies to restore ecosystems to that environmentalists are compelled to concede that their desired states of affairs have to be negotiated among different groups of humans and nonhumans. It is only when they (for example) distinguish 'survival emissions' from 'luxury emissions' (Agarwal and Narain 1991) – two entities that refuse to stay on either side of the nature/society divide – that they recognize that climate cannot be defined by climatologists and policy-makers alone.

Third, the new rents, commodities and markets that help define neoliberalism's climate are constructed and maintained overwhelmingly through the expanded activities of the state and international agencies. Carbon trading law stipulates that the climate system is the state's to manage and intervene in from 'outside' as long as it does not venture too far into determining who produces what in which quantities, for whom, and at what price. State-regulated 'caps', 'limits' and 'carbon budgets' define the scarce material out of which tradable units are constructed. State-driven and state-sanctioned quantification, monitoring, reporting, verifying and insuring techniques make offsetting possible. State police and military units take responsibility for the repression and policing of communities whose presence interferes with the efficient production of ecosystem service tokens (see Gilbertson and Cabello 2015; Kill 2015; Lang 2015 for some representative archives). Indeed, state agendas lie behind the very concept of ecosystems, from its earlier colonial incarnations to the military-financed development of the technologies underpinning general circulation models. In keeping with neoliberal tenets, moreover, the new climate is built in ways that help state as well as corporate actors evade much of the burden of addressing the social problems that markets are now advertised as cheaply solving. With the state underwriting the profits of a galaxy of private-sector partners, contractors, consultants and technocrats who carry out most of the work of producing, circulating, standardizing and regulating the new climate benefit units, conventional dualisms opposing 'state' and 'market' are of as little use in analysing official climate policy as they are in understanding other areas of neoliberal politics. As elsewhere in neoliberalism, the flip side of this expansion in the scope of state agency is a ritualistic or histrionic denial of its existence. The copious interventions of the neoliberal state to protect investor freedom are reinterpreted as, at most, mere caretaker moves safeguarding the integrity of a non-state 'system', and are vigorously contrasted with the alleged blunt-force meddling of 'command and control'. Ecosystem services themselves are treated as if they had always been there, state or no state, awaiting merely the figurative flipping of the switch that would allow the profit motive to be enlisted in their behalf (e.g. Heal 2015).

Achieving a well-rounded understanding of the distinctiveness of neoliberalism's climate – and of its continuity with previous capitalist climates – requires a standpoint of resistance. Putting in perspective neoliberalism's claim that it can provide an alternative, cheaper way of preserving and stabilizing a singular, timeless, nonhuman climate needed by all humanity entails listening to the indigenous, peasant, labour, feminist and commons movements with the experience to perceive the classism, racism and neocolonialism inherent in such construals of nature. At the same time, resistance can benefit from an extended historical understanding that can help pre-empt attempts to identify the development of nonextraction rents or commodities with the defence of commons: attempts to establish, for instance, that movements to keep oil in the soil in the Ecuadorian Amazon are really all about 'caps' and 'biospheric limits'; that Latin American indigenous practices of *sumak kawsay* or *buen vivir* amount to green developmentalism, natural resource management or 'resilience'; that indigenous territories are instances of the abstract spaces co-devised by sixteenth-century European map-makers or twenty-first-century prophets of 'natural capital'; or that Andean visions of *pachamama* are one of the externalized 'natures' of capitalism, whose rights, it is implied, can only be defended by humans considered to be outside it. The most penetrating enquiries into neoliberalism's climate, in short, are likely to be connected not just with efforts to 'reculture' climate (Endfield 2011), but also with the formation and defence of radical political alliances and dialogues.

Acknowledgements

This chapter owes its current form to challenges thrown down by Marcus Taylor, Jutta Kill, Romain Felli, Mareike Beck, Sara Nelson, Rich Lane, Tamra Gilbertson, and Jason W. Moore. The challenges may not have been met, but the author is grateful for them.

References

Agarwal, A., and Narain, S. 1991. *Global Warming in an Unequal World*. New Delhi: Centre for Science and Environment.

Beniger, J.R. 1986. *The Control Revolution: Technological and Economic Origins of the Information Society*. Cambridge, MA: Harvard University Press.

Boykoff, M.T., Frame, D., and Randalls, S. 2010. Discursive Stability Meets Climate Instability: A Critical Exploration of the Concept of 'Climate Stabilization' in Contemporary Climate Policy. *Global Environmental Change*, 20: 53–64.

Collard, R.-C., Dempsey, J., and Rowe, J., 2016. Re-regulating Socioecologies Under Neoliberalism, in Springer, S., Birch, K., and MacLeavy, J., eds. *The Handbook of Neoliberalism*. London: Routledge: 455–65.

Collins, H., and Kusch, M. 1999. *The Shape of Actions: What Humans and Machines Can Do*. Cambridge, MA: MIT Press.

Cooper, M. 2010. Turbulent Worlds: Financial Markets and Environmental Crisis. *Theory, Culture and Society*, 27.2–3: 167–90.

—. 2011. Complexity Theory After the Financial Crisis: The Death of Neoliberalism or the Triumph of Hayek? *Journal of Cultural Economy*, 4.4: 371–85.

Cruikshank, J. 2005. *Do Glaciers Listen? Local Knowledge, Colonial Encounters and Social Imagination*. Vancouver: University of British Columbia Press.

Cushman, G.T. 2011. Humboldtian Science, Creole Meteorology, and the Discovery of Human-Caused Climate Change in South America. *Osiris*, 26.1: 16–44.

Daly, H. 1980. Introduction to the Steady State Economy, in Daly, H., ed. *Economics, Ecology, Ethics: Essays Toward a Steady-State Economy*. San Francisco: W.H. Freeman.

Elichirigoity, F. 1999. *Planet Management: Limits to Growth, Computer Simulation, and the Emergence of Global Spaces*. Evanston, IL: Northwestern University Press.

Endfield, G. 2011. Reculturing and Particularizing Climate Discourses: Weather, Identity, and the Work of Gordon Manley. *Osiris*, 26.1: 142–62.

Felli, R. 2014. On Climate Rent. *Historical Materialism*, 22.3–4: 251–80.

Fleming, J.R., and Jankovic, V. 2011. Revisiting Klima. *Osiris*, 26.1: 1–15.

Fogel, C. 2004. The Local, the Global and the Kyoto Protocol, in Jasanoff, S., and Martello, M.L., eds. *Earthly Politics: Local and Global in Environmental Governance*. Cambridge: MIT Press: 103–26.

Forster, P., Ramaswamy, V., Artaxo, P., Berntsen, T., Betts, R., Fahey, D.W., … and Van Dorland, R. 2007. Changes in Atmospheric Constituents and in Radiative Forcing, in Solomon, S., Qin, D., Manning, M., eds. *Climate Change 2007: The Physical Science Basis*. Contribution of Working Group I to the Fourth Assessment Report of the Intergovernmental Panel on Climate Change. Cambridge: Cambridge University Press.

Funk, M. 2015. *Windfall: The Booming Business of Global Warming*. New York: Penguin.

Galbraith, J.K. 1979. *The Nature of Mass Poverty*. Cambridge, MA: Harvard University Press.

Gilbertson, T., and Cabello, J. 2015. *Carbon Trade Watch* [website]. Retrieved from http://www.carbon-tradewatch.org

Google. 2015. *Ngram Viewer*. Retrieved from https://books.google.com/ngrams

Grove, R.H. 1997. *Ecology, Climate and Empire: Colonialism and Global Environmental History, 1400–1940*. Cambridge: White Horse Press.

Hahn, R., and Stavins, R. 1995. Trading in Greenhouse Permits: A Critical Examination of Design and Implementation Issues, in Lee, H., ed. *Shaping National Responses to Climate Change*. Washington, DC: Island Press.

Hahnel, R. 2012a. Left Clouds Over Climate Change Policy. *Review of Radical Political Economics*, 44.2: 141–59.

—. 2012b. Desperately Seeking Left Unity on International Climate Policy. *Capitalism Nature Socialism*, 23.4: 83–99.

Haraway, D. 1991. *Simians, Cyborgs and Women: The Reinvention of Nature*. London: Free Association.

Haug, E.G., and Taleb, N.N. 2010. Option Traders Use (Very) Sophisticated Heuristics, Never the Black–Scholes–Merton Formula. Retrieved from: http://ssrn.com/abstract=1012075.

Heal, G. 2015. Interview with Via Devoucourtes. *Nature, Le Nouvel Eldorado de la Finance*. Paris: ITW. Retrieved from: https://www.youtube.com/watch?v=2TRwpQkYVfg.

Helm, D. 2014. Taking Natural Capital Seriously. *Oxford Review of Economic Policy*, 30.1: 109–25.

Heymann, M. 2011. The Evolution of Climate Ideas and Knowledge. *WIRES Climate Change*, 1.1: 581–98.

Holling, C.S. 1973. Resilience and Stability of Ecological Systems. *Annual Review of Ecology and Systematics*, 4: 1–23.

Hornborg, A. 2012. *Global Ecology and Unequal Exchange: Fetishism in a Zero-Sum World*. New York: Routledge.

Huber, T., and Pedersen, P. 1997. Meterological Knowledge and Environmental Ideas in Traditional and Modern Societies: The Case of Tibet. *Journal of the Royal Anthropological Institute*, 3.3: 577–98.

Hulme, M. 2008. Geographical Work at the Boundaries of Climate Change. *Transactions of the Institute of British Geographers*, 33: 5–11.

—. 2011. Reducing the Future to Climate: A Story of Climate Determinism and Reductionism. *Osiris*, 26.1: 245–66.

Ingold, T. 2000. *The Perception of the Environment*. London: Routledge.

Jankovic. V. 2010. Climates as Commodities: Jean Pierre Purry and the Modelling of the Best Climate on Earth. *Studies in History and Philosophy of Modern Physics*, 41: 201–7.

Kill, J. 2015. *REDD: A Collection of Conflict, Contradictions and Lies*. Montevideo: World Rainforest Movement.

Lane, R. 2015. Resources for the Future, Resources for Growth: The Making of the 1975 Growth Ban, in Stephen, B., and Lane., R., eds. *The Politics of Carbon Markets*. New York: Routledge.

Lang, C. 2015. REDD Monitor [website]. Retrieved from www.redd-monitor.org

Lohmann, L. 2014. Performative Equations and Neoliberal Commodification: The Case of Climate, in Büscher, B., Dressler, W., and Fletcher, R., eds. *Nature^TM: Environmental Conservation in the Neoliberal Age*. Tucson: University of Arizona Press: 158–80.

Lovins, A., and Lovins, H. 1991. Least-Cost Climatic Stabilization. *Annual Review of Energy and Environment*, 16: 433–531.

MacKenzie D. 2009. Making Things the Same: Gases, Emission Rights and the Politics of Carbon Markets. *Accounting, Organizations and Society*, 34: 440–55.

Malm, A. 2014. Fossil Capital: The Rise of Steam-Power in the British Cotton Industry c. 1828–1840 and the Roots of Global Warming. Doctoral dissertation, Lund University, Sweden.

Malthus, T.R. 2014[1798]. *An Essay on the Principle of Population*, London: Kindle Edition.

Matthews, A.S. 2015. Imagining Forest Futures and Climate Change: The Mexican State as Insurance Broker and Storyteller, in Barnes, J., and Dove, M.R., eds. *Climate Cultures: Anthropological Perspectives on Climate Change*. New Haven: Yale University Press: 199–220.

Maunder, W.J. 1970. *The Value of the Weather*. London: Methuen.

Mirowski, P. 2002. *Machine Dreams: Economics Becomes a Cyborg Science*. Cambridge: Cambridge University Press.

Moore, J.W. 2015. *Capitalism in the Web of Life: Ecology and the Accumulation of Capital*. London: Verso.

Nelson, S.H. 2015. Beyond the Limits to Growth: Ecology and the Neoliberal Counterrevolution. *Antipode*, 47.2: 461–80.

Nicholls, M. 2011. EcoSecurities Co-founder Launches Brazilian Environmental Exchange. *Environmental Finance*, 20 December.

O'Neill, R.V. 2001. Is it Time to Bury the Ecosystem Concept? (With Full Military Honors, of Course!). *Ecology*, 82.12: 3275–84.

Randalls, S. 2011. Optimal Climate Change: Economics and Climate Science Policy Histories (From Heuristic to Normative). *Osiris*, 26.1: 224–42.

Rice, J.L. 2010. Climate, Carbon, and Territory: Greenhouse Gas Mitigation in Seattle, Washington. *Annals of the Association of American Geographers*, 100.4: 929–37.

Robertson, M. 2012. Measurement and Alienation: Making a World of Ecosystem Services. *Transactions of the Institute of British Geographers*, 37: 386–401.

Rouse, J. 2002. Vampires: Social Constructivism, Realism and Other Philosophical Undead. *History and Theory*, 41: 60–78.

Taylor, M. 2015. *The Political Ecology of Climate Change Adaptation: Livelihoods, Agrarian Change and the Conflicts of Development*. New York: Routledge.

Tricarico, A. 2014. *Focusing the Debate on Financialisation of Nature: Three Open Questions to Address for Civil Society Strategic Action*. Rome: Re:Common.

Vogel, B. 2011. The Letter from Dublin: Climate Change, Colonialism, and the Royal Society in the Seventeenth Century. *Osiris*, 26.1: 111–28.

Wynne, B., and Shackley, S. 1994. Environmental Models: Truth Machines or Social Heuristics? *The Globe*, 21: 6–8.

42

NEOLIBERAL ENERGIES

Crisis, governance and hegemony

Matthew Huber

When discussing the shift to neoliberalism a number of scholars focus on a single year: 1973 (e.g. Harvey 2005:12). This is not only the year the soon to be neoliberal reformer Augusto Pinochet was installed in Chile, but it is also the year of the Arab oil embargo. The concomitant quadrupling of oil prices and iconic experiences of petrol shortages in the USA is seen as plunging much of industrial capitalist world into a crisis characterized by both recession and inflation or 'stagflation'. It is this economic context which provided the fertile breeding grounds for neoliberal ideas to take hold; or, as Naomi Klein (2007: 7) famously recounts the words of Milton Friedman, 'only a crisis – real or perceived – produces real change. When that crisis occurs, the actions that are taken depend on the ideas that are lying around.' In one sense, the crisis that ushered in neoliberal hegemony (see Plehwe 2016) was an energy crisis. This, by itself, means there is a need for a careful analysis of the relationship between energy and neoliberalism. Yet, as I will argue in this chapter, the relations between neoliberalism run even deeper than that.

This chapter proceeds in three parts. First, I review the history of the political shifts to neoliberalism in the 1970s and argue that the energy crisis specifically provided neoliberal thinkers with a key empirical example of the problems with political interference in markets. Second, we must also consider how neoliberal policy shifts have affected the fields of energy governance in particular. I argue the Deepwater Horizon oil spill is a prime example of a disaster socially produced according to the logics of neoliberal capitalism. Third, while neoliberalism is often envisioned as applying to specific empirical slices of policy reality (e.g. environment, housing, energy, or whatever), it is less common to theorize the social and ecological relations of neoliberal hegemony itself. In this regard, everyday lived practices of energy consumption – specifically in relation to the privatization of housing and automobility – can be seen as underpinning a variety of populist neoliberal logics (e.g. hostility to taxes). I argue that the geography of life (in often suburban contexts) reinforced what Foucault (2008) isolated as the core of the neoliberal project – the enterprise form. Thus, we need not only think of the neoliberalism of energy, but also how energy fuels neoliberalism.

The phony crisis

The 'energy crisis' is phony and a hoax on the people.[1]

(Letter to Richard Nixon's Energy Policy Office)

In order to understand how the energy crisis of the 1970s provided the conditions for the political ascendancy of neoliberalism, we must first understand how the Keynesian political and economic consensus of the postwar period was blamed as the cause of the larger economic crisis itself. Prior to the oil embargo of 1973, the early 1970s was marked by concern over the rising 'cost of living' or inflation. Polling data suggest that, in a decade with no shortage of crisis narratives, the American public felt inflation was their most pressing concern.[2] In 1971, in addition to abrogating the dollar's relation to gold, President Nixon established the Cost of Living Council, which was tasked with controlling wages and prices across the entire economy. Even though inflation is actually an incredibly uneven process – affecting the poor and moneyed interests far more than the 'general' public – it tended to be constructed as a problem for everyone equally. After all, everyone 'feels' it when the price of bread goes up a dollar.

As many have detailed (Harvey 1989; Jessop 2002), postwar capitalism in the USA and elsewhere was structured by a Keynesian consensus that highlighted the importance of government spending, social programmes, and strong unions. In particular, these forces were seen as keys to avoiding crises and fuelling 'effective demand' for a virtuous growth cycle of mass production for mass consumption. Yet, during the inflation crisis of the 1970s, it was precisely these forces that were blamed for the skyrocketing inflation. Government spending was seen as inflationary in itself by expanding the money supply. As Ronald Reagan put it in a radio commentary in November of 1977, 'Whenever the federal government adds to the national money supply, it produces inflation' (Reagan 1977a). Milton Friedman (Friedman and Friedman 1980: 264) posited the monetarist theory of inflation, 'Inflation is primarily a monetary phenomenon, produced by a more rapid increase in the quantity of money than in output.' He blamed the growth in the money supply on three forces in the USA: 'first, the rapid growth in government spending; second, the government's full employment policy; and third, a mistaken policy pursued by the Federal Reserve' (ibid.). In other words, government-directed efforts at providing welfare and jobs to (some) – including Lyndon Johnson's Great Society programmes – were causing price increases for the public at large.

Perhaps more politically important was the vision of labour unions as inherently inflationary. An ordinary citizen from Tampa wrote to Nixon's energy office to claim that, in addition to the gas scarcities of the energy crisis, 'These citizens are victims already of the runaway inflation that was brought about when the Congress enacted into law the infamous Wagner labor law in the 1930s.'[3] According to the labour historian Jefferson Cowie (2004: 84), 'The 1970s ended up as the first decade in which, according to critics, organized workers simply made too much money and their high rates of pay caused a national crisis.' From a neoliberal view, unions were seen as having unfair 'monopoly' position over the labour market – a centralized power structure that 'set' wages according to their own power rather than competitive market forces. Thus, according to neoliberal thought, unions were increasingly viewed as similar to corporations – special interests using their power towards individual gain at the expense of fair competition. Reagan (1977b) called labour unions, 'The most powerful special interest group in America.'

In short, inflation was seen as generated through *political claims on the market*. Whether it was redistributive efforts at fighting poverty by the state, or unions demanding wage increases, these measures were seen as well-intentioned but distortive interventions of what is supposed to be free market forces. This was neatly summed up through a pamphlet circulated by the Cost of Living Council titled *Inflation: On Prices and Wages and Running Amok*:

> In some activities, big corporations and big unions seem able to push prices and wages up even when demand is steady or going down. They are able to do this because

competition to provide the goods and services is limited or restricted in some way. Economists call this 'market power.'

(Cost of Living Council 1973: n.p.)

For neoliberals, the market was meant to be apolitical: a decentralized, competitive system where no single individual or organization has the power to control the market. From such an ideological perspective, any centralized force in the market was seen as inherently unfair and distortive (except corporate monopoly – see Birch 2016). Moreover, because of President Nixon's wage and price control programmes, the government itself was seen as a centralized force dictating prices. This also reinforced neoliberals like Milton Friedman's critique of 'big government's' role in distorting the free market.

The energy crisis was seen as inflationary in itself. Since oil was a critical input and the transportation fuel behind nearly every commodity, a rise in its price, meant a rise in the price of all commodities. As Nixon's neoliberal Treasury Secretary William Simon put it,

> Petroleum is a unique commodity, entering into almost every facet of our economy, as the fuel for heating our residences and other buildings, as the fuel for transportation of goods and people and as the raw material for a myriad of products like fertilizer and petrochemicals.

(Simon 1975: n.p.)

Yet, in order to understand the insurgent neoliberal logics at play, it is important to examine how the energy crisis was explained and what forces were blamed. As it turns out, it wasn't seen as a 'real' crisis at all, and the villains who engineered it appear similar to those responsible for inflation.[4] Consumers and public commentators consistently blamed three political forces intervening in the oil market – rigging it for their own benefit at the expense of everyday workers. First, obviously, the Organization of Petroleum Exporting Countries (OPEC) is the antithesis of a free market. Even though it modelled itself after the capitalist US oil prorationing policy in the postwar period (Yergin 1991: 259),[5] OPEC announced itself as a cartel with expressly political aims of keeping prices high. Even worse, the embargo itself was seen as using oil as a 'political weapon' against those who supported Israel when 'common sense' ideology demanded it be traded freely on the market. Second, polling data reveals that the US public held the most ire not for OPEC, but for the monopolistic oil companies who were seen as a private international cartel that overcharged consumers and earned mega-profits.[6] It is often forgotten that just as much as neoliberal ideology is a critique of government intervention in the market, it is also a critique of 'monopoly power' (albeit with unions perhaps being their favourite example). Monopolies inhibit competition and the decentralized forces of the price mechanism from working their magic. At the heart of the neoliberal critique of the energy crisis was a concern with *fairness*: as one consumer from suburban Long Island states, 'Give the oil companies a fair margin of profit, but do not allow the monopolistic practices of the major companies to continue.'[7] For many everyday consumers, fairness meant a fair market where no single centralized force held political power over the price of oil.

Finally, the most obvious villain from a neoliberal perspective was 'big government'. While the Nixon administration lifted wage and price controls for most of the economy in 1973, oil price controls persisted until 1981. The admittedly bureaucratic complexity of these controls provided endless fodder for neoliberals who lambasted government officials in their audacity to believe they could allocate goods and services better than a free market. Conservative icon William F. Buckley (1973) reasoned that price controls keeping petrol prices low were ineffective, 'You are much better off reducing the amount of gas spent by raising the price of gasoline than by setting up a giant bureaucracy charged with the impossible job of adjudicating everyone's claim to gasoline.' An editorial in the *Altoona Mirror* (1979) castigated the government control of the energy market. '[Government] actually has helped create the crisis by its unwise environmental laws, its red tape, and refusal to help the oil industry produce gas for American cars.' Perhaps the most famous neoliberal ideologue, Milton Friedman (Friedman and Friedman 1980: 14) put it succinctly, '[Petrol queues were caused by]... one reason and one reason alone: because legislation, administered by a government agency, did not permit the price system to function.' If the price mechanism is supposed to be a product of competitive forces, it cannot be directed by political forces – and the most obviously political force in a capitalist society is the government itself.

Overall, like inflation, the energy crisis was seen as being generated by a set of political forces intervening in the market. This was seen as problematic not only because it made the market unfair, with certain 'special interests' gaming the system for private (or government) gain, but also, more importantly, it allowed for a construction of political forces and decisions harming the everyday freedom and choices of ordinary consumers/drivers. Everyday oil-intensive consumers in the suburbs preferred to be 'left alone' by the machinations of 'big government' (perhaps most famously expressed in the 'tax revolt' in California in 1978). The logic of being left alone appeared to apply equally to private capital.

Deregulation and the social production of normal accidents

The historical shift to neoliberalism in the 1970s involved the energy crisis, but the policies and practices of neoliberalism itself meant a new regime of energy governance in the 1980s and beyond. In the wake of the energy crisis of the 1970s, it became increasingly 'common sense' that the market was the most appropriate mechanism to ensure the adequate production of energy. Ronald Reagan was elected in 1980 on an energy platform best summed up by this pithy phrase, 'Our problem isn't a shortage of oil. It's a surplus of government' (Reagan, cited in Jacobs 2008: 209). One of the first things Reagan did was 'decontrol' the price of oil in 1981, which lifted the maze of government control on oil prices. This set the conditions for the entry of financial markets in the shaping of the price of oil. In 1983, the first oil futures were traded on the New York Mercantile Exchange. If financialization accompanies neoliberalism (Harvey 2005), the oil market is no different.

Yet, the most important interface between neoliberalism and energy is in the actual governance of the production and distribution of energy itself. For this, we need to understand the critical role of competition in shaping neoliberal ideology. As Foucault (2008: 147) states, 'The society regulated by reference to the market that the neoliberals are thinking about is a society in which the regulatory principle should not be so much the exchange of commodities as the mechanisms of competition.' Thus, state policies both aimed at increasing the competiveness of particular territories in terms of attracting capital investment and staying competitive became the driving force shaping corporate discourse and ethics.

This ethos of competition infiltrated the state–capital nexus in energy markets. On the one hand, states and capital both viewed 'regulation' as burdensome threats to competition. This meant the decline in the specific rules and regulations overseeing the energy industry. Perhaps more important, however, was the underinvestment in regulatory agencies themselves. The Environmental Protection Agency and other energy-specific agencies were starved of funds and personnel to actually enforce rules and regulations on the books. As Reagan's first Interior Secretary, James Watt, put it, 'We will use the budget system as an excuse to make major policy decisions' (cited in Faber 2008: 128). On the other hand, it became increasingly clear to energy corporations themselves that increasing innovation and global competition forced capital to enact a regime of relentless cost cutting in order to stay competitive. This cost cutting, of course, included wage and salary cutbacks (see Labban 2014), but it also meant the underinvestment in environmental and other safety procedures. In other words, the neoliberal ethos of increased competition almost guaranteed that capital would seek to externalize environmental costs onto society as a whole and the public sector in order to 'stay competitive'.

The evisceration of public regulatory agencies, combined with competitive cost cutting among energy capital, makes 'accidents' entirely predictable. Using Perrow's (1984) concept of 'normal accidents', Prudham (2004: 344) examines a deadly water well poisoning in Walkerton, Ontario, caused by private farmers as what he calls, 'a normal accident of neoliberalism'. While public officials tried to explain away this crisis as the result of exceptional circumstances and natural hazards, Prudham points to the systematic 'undermining [of] the capacity of regulatory agencies, creating specific regulatory gaps while at the same time placing an overall chill on the regulation of capital's access to and impacts on the Ontario environment' (ibid.). In this case, private agricultural capital, left alone, tended to externalize ecological costs of manure application to be absorbed by the 'public' commons of local groundwater supplies. The failure of regulatory agencies to prevent this kind of systematic externalization of ecological harms on the public is what makes this accident predictable and normal.

The Deepwater Horizon disaster in 2010 – which killed 11 workers and expelled between 3 and 4 million barrels of oil into the Gulf of Mexico – is, of course, the most spectacular occurrence of a 'normal accident of neoliberalism'. It is worth pointing out that, at least as far as British Petroleum (BP) is concerned, this 'accident' was only the latest in a disastrous run of corporate negligence resulting in a refinery explosion in Texas City in 2005, and multiple oil spills and pipeline malfunctions in Alaska (Lustgarten 2012). For BP, disasters were certainly a normal aspect of doing business. Yet, the Deepwater Horizon disaster conforms to the wider conditions of neoliberal deregulation in quite specific ways. First, the Minerals Management Service – the public agency in charge of overseeing offshore drilling – was completely ineffective at serving the public interest of insuring drilling was safe. Of course, there are the obvious and spectacular ways in which the agency was captured by oil capital – stories of parties between regulatory officials and corporate players are quite stunning (Dickinson 2010). Yet, more relevant were the ways in which the agency completely lacked the capacity to oversee a technologically complex and environmentally risky form of oil extraction because of a lack of staff and budget. As the scholar of the offshore oil industry Tyler Priest (2010) explained in the wake of the spill, 'MMS has 55 inspectors for about 3,500 production platforms and 90 drilling vessels. The agency's $342 million annual budget would cover only drilling the two relief wells at the Macondo site.' Second, the reckless cost cutting displayed by BP – courts have now called their behaviour 'grossly negligent' (Gilbert and Scheck 2014) – is typical in the neoliberal era of heightened competition. BP not only underinvested in backup blowout preventers, but haphazardly 'skipped a cement test' and drilled 100 feet deeper when conditions suggested risks were increasing (Gold 2014).

If neoliberalism is characterized by increasing reliance upon the private sector for the public wellbeing, the spill itself revealed the disastrous consequences of such a conceit. In the wake of the spill, government officials bizarrely expressed confidence in BP's ability to cap the well. President Obama said, 'What is true is that when it comes to stopping the leak down below, the federal government does not possess superior technology to BP… BP has the best technology, along with the other oil companies' (cited in Huber 2011b: 196). Admiral Thad Allen, in charge of overseeing the cleanup, went as far as to state, 'I trust [BP CEO] Tony Hayward… They have the eyes and ears that are down there. They are the necessary modality by which this is going to get solved' (ibid.). This 'trust' was woefully misplaced. BP's 'emergency response' oil spill plan was revealed to be a complete waste of paper, featuring a discussion of walruses (Dickinson 2010) and an 'emergency contact' person who had been dead for five years (Wright 2010). Their 'junk shots' (sending trash and golf balls down to the well) and other efforts to cap the well were laughably ineffective and revealed they really had little idea of how to handle a spill. The gushing oil continued for nearly three months before it was finally capped. Completely held hostage by BP's incompetence, our public sector stood by and watched while a highly public disaster unfolded.

Powering neoliberalism: energy and the geography of privatism

> We are all neoliberals now.
>
> (David Harvey 2005: 13)

Much of the way neoliberalism is conceptualized is problematic. It is often seen as a monolithic 'thing' that has the agency to do things to particular communities and objects (Peck and Tickell 2002; Larner 2003). As I have argued previously (Huber 2013), the literature on neoliberal natures also conceptualized an empirical field called 'nature' or 'environment' that has neoliberal things done to it (see Collard *et al.* 2016). As Castree (2008) complained, the neoliberal nature literature comes equipped with its set of case studies (water, wetlands, forests) where the natural 'thing' undergoes neoliberalization. Environment becomes the object of neoliberal policy and reform. Yet, this kind of static and dualistic vision of neoliberalism/environment refuses to understand neoliberalization as not only a 'process', but also as relational in that it is produced through relations between society, resources, ecologies and, for the purposes of this chapter, energy. Rather than see the field of 'energy' as undergoing neoliberal deregulation and privatization (certainly a topic worthy of interest), we can also query how the wider socioecological process of neoliberalization is itself already ecological (cf. Moore 2011). This analytical frame must get to grips with David Harvey's quote at the beginning of this section. How do we understand the wider cultural subjectivities, neoliberal norms and 'common sense' as being produced through the societal relation with energy resources?

This broader understanding of neoliberal politics itself is productively engaged with through a reading of Foucault's (2008) lectures on the subject in 1978–9 called *The Birth of Biopolitics*. These lectures – given during the infancy of neoliberal hegemony – hold tremendous insight into the micropolitics of neoliberal subjectivity. Constituting the 'neo' of neoliberalism, a society regulated through competition requires the generalization of the enterprise form: 'I think the multiplication of the enterprise form within the social body is what is at stake in neoliberal policy' (ibid.: 148). According to Fouacault's account of German strands of neoliberal thought in the postwar period – or 'ordoliberalism' – the materialization of this enterprise form is assured through private property: 'First, to enable as far as possible everyone to have access to private property' (ibid.: 147). Putting property at the centre of social reproduction is central to the multiplication of entrepreneurial subjectivities. 'What is private property if not an enterprise? What is the house if not an enterprise?' (ibid.: 148). Indeed, the private homeowner runs their house like a business. So-called responsible homeowners are supposed to construct a family budget tracking spending against revenue, make investments with savings and pensions, and maintain a healthy long-term relation with credit markets. In this context, '[T]he individual's life itself – with his [sic] relationships to his private property, for example, with his family, his household, insurance, and retirement – must make him into a sort of permanent and multiple enterprise' (ibid.: 241).

Thus, the construction of a propertied mass of homeowners – an ownership society, as George W. Bush called it – creates a situation where your very own life is seen as a product of your entrepreneurial choices. Your entrepreneurial capacities all combine to make a life – to make a living – for yourself. The overall product of a successful life is expressed through the material requisites of oil-based privatism – a home, a car, a family. This cultural politics of life differs markedly from Marx's – and most orthodox Marxist – vision of proletariat life. For Marx, the proletariat was defined by his/her propertlylessness. The question for a propertyless proletariat is: how will I live? The answer was, of course, to desperately sell your labour power in exchange for a wage that usually provided the bare minimum of subsistence (and often not because of the very disposability of wage labour). However, the question for the propertied mass of workers in the USA is not 'How will I live?', but 'What will I make of my life?' Of course, this question is undergirded by the very idea of making something of yourself, which assumes that your life itself is purely a product of atomized choices and individualized efforts. It is only in particular historical circumstances that such a question takes on such popular significance.

The logic of neoliberal hegemony – and its material and cultural basis in a propertied mass of suburban white male middle- to upper-income homeowners – is more understandable (although no less defensible) through the lens of this cultural politics of entrepreneurial life. Again, government welfare was seen as skewing the competitive landscape and unjustly rewarding uncompetitive bodies who were marked for not making the right choices in life. Worse still, government was itself seen as a public taking of private hard-earned money (taxes) that was, again, the product of one's own individual entrepreneurial capacities.

The German strand of ordoliberalism Foucault reviews also stresses the, 'decentralization of places or residence, production and management' (ibid.: 147) which conforms to the actually existing geography of suburbanization in the USA and elsewhere. Yet, decentralization *requires* energy – specifically fuel for transportation – because, by definition, you are increasing the distances between critical spaces of work, leisure and residence. Thus, this particular cultural politics of entrepreneurial life is not possible – is not made common sense – without the material transformation of the everyday life centred upon reproductive geographies of single-family homeownership, automobility and voracious energy consumption. Energy, both in oil-fired auto-transport and electrified homes, produces a particular lived geography that allows for an appearance of atomized command over the spaces of mobility, home, and even the body itself. With all the work (or energy) accomplished through the combustion of taken-for-granted hydrocarbons, individuals could more and more imagine themselves as masters of their own lives severed from ties to society and public forms of collective life. Once high levels of energy consumption became more and more entrenched within the reproductive forces of everyday life, those forces informed a politics of 'hostile privatism' where individual homeowners imagined themselves as autonomous, hardworking subjects whose very freedom was threatened by the ever-extending tentacles of 'big government'.

It is important to particularize this neoliberal class project. Entrepreneurial subjectivities discussed above flourished in the decentralized spaces of suburban geographies; again, the very spaces where high levels of energy consumption became everyday necessities. Yet, it would be a mistake to quarantine this politics in particular geographies. The language of self-made lives, of course, has deep historical roots and resonates throughout society as whole. Yet, for those left out of high-energy living – for example, those living in cities without a car who struggle with underinvested public transit systems, or those who rent from landlords who refuse to fix broken electric or heating systems – urban (or rural) poverty starkly reveals the structural barriers to self-made lives: not only because of systemic racial discrimination and a withdrawal of public services, but also because their lives can only be made and remade through collective social support systems. Many do not live with any of the illusions provided by energized privatism.

Overall, if we are to view, as Harvey (2005: 31) instructs, neoliberalism as a 'vehicle for the restoration of class power' we might look to energized geographies of suburban populism as critical in the popular hegemony of that class project. Any movement beyond neoliberalism must confront these wider popular logics.

Conclusion

This chapter has attempted to review three particular ways in which we can examine the relations between energy and neoliberalism. First, the energy crisis itself provided the fertile political logics for the shift to neoliberal hegemony in the 1970s. Second, we can examine the field of governance over the production and distribution of energy resources as going through a process of neoliberalization characterized by the withdrawal of public regulation. The 2010 Deepwater Horizon is, perhaps, a quintessential example of a neoliberal disaster. Third, energy itself – the forms of consumption that power suburban life – has powered a more populist ideology of privatism. For those who have oil-fired cars and electric-fired homes doing so much work for them, it is easy to imagine that life itself is a product of individual choices and the public realm as a burdensome force meant to take what has been privately achieved. As American politics has been profoundly shaped by a suburban populism since the 1970s – undergirded by ideas of meritocracy and low taxes – we need to examine the broader field of politics itself as being shaped by regimes of energy consumption.

Overall, this means that overcoming the neoliberal relation to energy is about so much more than simply applying more regulation or public sector control of our energy system (a carbon tax, for instance). We must, first, tackle a more entrenched and everyday politics of privatism to convince energized (and atomized) individuals that, although their lives appear to be private affairs, it will take a renewal of ideas of the collective public good to not only save the planet from climate change, but also to make a more livable and just society.

Notes

1 Box 15, White House Central Files, Staff Member Office Files, Energy Policy Office, John A. Love, Richard Nixon Presidential Library, Yorba Linda, CA.

2 For example, see Jensen 1974 and *The New York Times* 1978.

3 Box 8, White House Central Files, Staff Member Office Files, Energy Policy Office, John A. Love, Richard Nixon Presidential Library, Yorba Linda, CA.

4 For example, at the height of the petrol line crisis in February 1974, one Roper poll revealed that only 18 per cent of those polled felt the crisis represented a 'real shortage', whereas 73 per cent believed it was 'not a real shortage' and 9 per cent admitted not to know. Fast forward five years, at the height of the second oil shock in July 1979, and the numbers for each only varied slightly to 24 per cent, 58 per cent and 8 per cent, respectively (Richman 1979).

5 I have examined this system elsewhere, arguing that it tried hard to create the *appearance* of competition through price policy that actually protected a multiplicity of high-cost independent oil producers (Huber 2011a, 2013).

6 In an exhaustive study of various polling data, Richman concludes that, 'the predominant view is that oil shortages have been contrived, particularly by the oil companies, to raise prices and profits' (Richman 1979: 576).

7 Box 17, White House Central Files, Staff Member Office Files, Energy Policy Office, John A. Love, Richard Nixon Presidential Library, Yorba Linda, CA

References

Altoona Mirror, 1979. Editorial. *Altoona Mirror*, 9 May.

Birch, K. 2016. Financial Economics and Business Schools: Legitimating Corporate Monopoly, Reproducing Neoliberalism?, in Springer, S., Birch, K., and MacLeavy, J., eds. *The Handbook of Neoliberalism*. London: Routledge: 306–16.

Buckley, W.F. 1973. Gas Rationing? *Newark Advocate*, 21 November.

Castree, N. 2008. Neoliberalising Nature: Processes, Effects, Outcomes. *Environment and Planning A*, 40: 153–73.

Collard, R.-C., Dempsey, J., and Rowe, J. 2016. Re-Regulating Socioecologies Under Neoliberalism, in Springer, S., Birch, K., and MacLeavy, J., eds. *The Handbook of Neoliberalism*. London: Routledge: 455–65.

Cost of Living Council. 1973. *Inflation: On Prices and Wages and Running Amok*. Washington, DC: Government Printing Office.

Cowie, J. 2004. 'Vigorously Left, Right, and Center at the Same Time': The Crosscurrents of Working-Class America in the 1970s, in Bailey, B., and Farber, D., eds. *America in the Seventies*. Lawrence: University Press of Kansas: 75–106.

Dickinson, T. 2010. The Spill, the Scandal and the President. *Rolling Stone*, 1107. 24 June.

Faber, D. 2008. *Capitalizing on Environmental Injustice: The Polluter–Industrial Complex in the Age of Globalization*. Lanham, MD: Rowman and Littlefield.

Foucault, M. 2008. *The Birth of Biopolitics: Lectures at the College de France, 1978–1979*. Burcell, G., trans. New York: Palgrave Macmillan.

Friedman, M., and Friedman, R. 1980. *Free to Choose: A Personal Statement*. New York: Harcourt Brace Jovanovich.

Gilbert, D. and Scheck, J. 2014. BP is Found Grossly Negligent in Deepwater Horizon Disaster. *Wall Street Journal*, 4 September.

Gold, R. 2014. BP's Decision to Drill 100 More Feet set Disaster in Motion, Judge Rules. *Wall Street Journal*, 4 September.

Harvey, D. 1989. *The Condition of Postmodernity: An Enquiry into the Origins of Cultural Change*. Oxford: Blackwell.

—. 2005. *A Brief History of Neoliberalism*. Oxford: Oxford University Press.

Huber, M.T. 2011a. Enforcing Scarcity: Oil, Violence, and the Making of the Market. *Annals of the Association of American Geographers*, 101.4: 816–26.

—. 2011b. Gusher in the Gulf and the Despotism of Capital. *Antipode*, 43.2: 195–8.

—. 2013. Fueling Capitalism: Oil, the Regulation Approach, and the Ecology of Capital. *Economic Geography*, 89.2: 171–94.

Jacobs, M. 2008. The Conservative Struggle and the Energy Crisis, in Schulman, B.J., and Zelizer, J.E., eds. *Rightward Bound: Making America Conservative in the 1970s*. Cambridge, MA: Harvard University Press: 193–209.

Jensen, M. 1974. Inflation Replaces Energy as Nation's Main Concern. *The New York Times*, 14 July.

Jessop, B. 2002. *The Future of the Capitalist State*. London: Polity.

Klein, N. 2007. *The Shock Doctrine: The Rise of Disaster Capitalism*. New York: Picador.

Labban, M. 2014. Against Value: Accumulation in the Oil Industry and the Biopolitics of Labour Under Finance. *Antipode*, 46.2: 477–96.

Larner, W. 2003. Neoliberalism? *Environment and Planning D: Society and Space*, 21.5: 509–12.

Lustgarten, A. 2012. *Run to Failure: BP and the Making of the Deepwater Horizon Disaster*. New York: W.W. Norton & Co.

Moore, J. 2011. Transcending the Metabolic Rift: A Theory of Crisis in the Capitalist World Ecology. *Journal of Peasant Studies*, 38.1: 1–46.

The New York Times. 1978. Living Costs are Held Top Problem in US, A Gallup Poll Reports. *The New York Times*, 30 July.

Peck, J., and Tickell, A. 2002. Neoliberalizing Space. *Antipode*, 34.3: 380–404.

Perrow, C. 1984. *Normal Accidents: Living with High-Risk Technologies*. New York: Basic.

Plehwe, D. 2016. Neoliberal Hegemony, in Springer, S., Birch, K., and MacLeavy, J., eds. *The Handbook of Neoliberalism*. London: Routledge: 47–58.

Priest, T. 2010. The Ties that Bind MMS and Big Oil. *Politico*. Retrieved from http://www.politico.com/news/stories/0610/38270.html

Prudham, S. 2004. Poisoning the Well: Neoliberalism and the Contamination of Municipal Water in Walkerton, Ontario. *Geoforum*, 35.3: 343–59.

Reagan, R. 1977a. Radio Commentary: Inflation. *Box 13, Pre-Presidential Papers*, 15 August. Simi Valley, CA: Ronald Reagan Presidential Library.

—. 1977b. Radio Commentary: Labor. *Box 13, Pre-Presidential Papers*, 23 March. Simi Valley, CA: Ronald Reagan Presidential Library.

Richman, A. 1979. Public Attitudes Toward the Energy Crisis. *The Public Opinion Quarterly*, 43.4: 576–85.

Simon, W. 1975. Statement of William Simon Before the House Interstate and Foreign Commerce Subcommittee on Energy and Power. *Box 2, Policy Subject Files of Sidney Jones*, 17 February. College Park: National Archives.

Wright, T. 2010. BP Oil Spill Plan Consults Miami Dead Man. *NBC Miami*, 10 June.

Yergin, D. 1991. *The Prize: The Epic Quest for Oil, Money and Power*. New York: Simon and Schuster.

43

NEOLIBERALIZING WATER

Alex Loftus and Jessica Budds

The water sectors in both the global North and the global South have been one of the last areas of public service provision to be subjected to neoliberal reforms. Although many other basic human needs (food, shelter, energy) have been formally bought and sold as commodities for significantly longer periods of time, mediating access to water through exchange is particularly contentious because it places the most essential human need in the hands of private parties, and, in some cases, subjects the management of such an important productive resource to market forces. It is this tension between human needs and private profits that is at the heart of debates about the neoliberalization of water.

While the application of such neoliberal principles – commodification, privatization and marketization – to water is commonly regarded as a relatively recent phenomenon, associated with the political-economic reforms of the UK and USA in the 1980s and the Washington Consensus rolled out in the global South from the 1990s, it is important to remember that the (formal, although also informal) private sector has long played a role in water management and provision in many countries around the world. Indeed, it was the private sector that initiated the development of a water network in the UK in the nineteenth century, and which was subsequently replaced by the state due to the detrimental public health consequences resulting from the provision of water and sanitation services to only those households that could afford it. Since then, it has generally been accepted that the state is the only entity to be trusted with such a fundamental public resource and that also has the scale of financial resources needed to provide for water-related infrastructure and service provision.

This logic, however, was to be put to the test as neoliberal dogmatism swept its way through public service provision and environmental policy from the 1980s. In the UK, the government under Thatcher (1979–90) opted for a particularly extreme form of water privatization with the full divestiture of the regional drinking water supply authorities in England and Wales in 1989. While no other country has followed the UK's example of selling off entire water utilities to the private sector (with the exception of the privatization of the first water authorities in Chile in the early 1990s, which was later followed by a switch to concession contracts), water privatization became part of a leading edge in shifts that swept through both the global North and global South. In the global North, where much of the infrastructure was already in place, the argument for privatizing water was primarily focused on efficiency savings, although the rationalization of labour would soon follow. In the global South, advocates of neoliberalism focused on the failure of states to provide adequately, and the potential resources that the private sector could mobilize to extend networks, improve services, and introduce an element of competition through a tendering process (Winpenny 2003). While applying market principles and mechanisms to raw water management has been slower to follow, this too has been in place historically in some contexts, such as in most western states of the USA, and has been introduced more recently in others, most notably Chile.

However, if the global reach of neoliberalism within the water sector is to be judged solely by levels of privatization, it would appear limited, having reached only 10 per cent of the global population by the early 2000s (Budds and McGranahan 2003). Indeed, in recent years re-municipalization has accelerated in many cities (Kishimoto *et al.* 2015), and the forms of private sector engagement are appearing to change, with greater emphasis on new types of financial models and private–public partnerships. Instead, it is necessary to understand privatization as one of several moments within a broader process of the neoliberalization of water. Thus, in this chapter we consider neoliberalism through four different moments: privatization; corporatization; financialization; and marketization. Within each of these one witnesses the ongoing tension between ensuring the human right to water (recognized by the UN General Assembly and Human Rights Council since 2010) and subjecting water to commercial and market forces just like any other public good.

Privatization

Despite private sector participation having existed in the water supply sectors of many countries and over many years, water privatization rose to the fore during the late 1980s and early 1990s when it was heavily promoted as a key means to redress deficiencies in drinking water supply in the global South (Budds and McGranahan 2003). Advocated strongly by multilateral financial institutions, and often packaged with structural adjustment programmes in indebted countries in Africa, Asia and Latin America, water privatization was promoted as a strategy to delegate the management of water and sewerage provision from 'failing' public utilities to 'efficient' private companies (e.g. Brocklehurst 2004). Companies were presented as the only realistic source of the scale of new investment needed to meet the Millennium Development Goals of halving the number of people without sustainable access to safe and affordable drinking water by 2015, as they would be prepared to exploit huge untapped markets of poor people currently paying exorbitant prices for small amounts of often unsafe water. Water privatization was thus presented as a 'win–win–win' situation for states, companies, and citizens (Winpenny 2003).

In the water sector, the term 'privatization' refers to the transfer of some or elements of water provision from the state to the (formal) private sector. Yet, it covers a wide range of different institutional arrangements with very different durations and levels of responsibility and risk. At the upper end of the spectrum is full divestiture, which involves the permanent transfer of the entire service, including assets from the state to the private provider, as in England and Wales in 1989; and at the lower end is a service contract, whereby private providers are paid to conduct very specific tasks, such as meter readings or billing (Table 43.1). In practice, most experiences described as 'water privatization', especially in developing countries, are concession contracts, whereby a private operator (usually an international water company) assumes full responsibility for managing and investing in a water utility for a significant term of around 30 years. Concessions are designed to front-load investment in the initial stages of the contract, and in the later stages companies are expected to gain the majority of the profits from their investment.

Table 43.1 Allocation of key responsibilities for private sector participation in water supply and sewerage

	Service contract	Management contract	Lease/ affermage	Concession	Build–operate– transfer type	Divestiture
Asset ownership	Public	Public	Public	Public	Public/private	Private
Capital investment	Public	Public	Public	Private	Private	Private
Commercial risk	Public	Public	Shared	Private	Private	Private
Operation/ maintenance	Public/ private	Private	Private	Private	Private	Private
Contract duration	1–2 years	3–5 years	8–15 years	25–30 years	20–30 years	Indefinite

Water privatization typically involves more than the transfer of the responsibility for operating, managing and improving a water utility under a concession contract, however. It requires the transformation of water into a commodity. This is achieved both materially, by assigning exclusive rights to the raw water to the company, often dispossessing the rights of former users, and discursively, by reframing water as an economic good, which should be priced according to the full value of its production rather than at subsidized cost. The latter is the basis for full-cost recovery, which caused great controversy when it was applied on an *individual* basis, rather than *cross-subsidized* among different user groups in some concession contracts, which not only rendered services (new connections and water use tariffs) unaffordable for many low-income groups, but was also grossly unfair as (poor) unserved groups were expected to pay the full costs of the infrastructure and services that (rich) existing customers had received for free (Budds and McGranahan 2003).

Water privatization in the global South peaked in 1997 (Silva *et al.* 1998) and subsequently declined as cracks in the triple-win thesis started to appear. By this time, a process of 'cherry-picking' had become apparent, whereby concession contracts had become concentrated in the wealthiest and most stable regions (e.g. Latin America, South-East Asia) and countries (e.g. Argentina, Philippines), the largest and most populous cities (e.g. Buenos Aires, Manila), and more prosperous and well-served neighbourhoods. With the exception of South Africa, contracts in Africa primarily comprised service and management contracts. The largest and most lucrative contracts were also concentrated among the two largest multinational water companies, which allegedly submitted bids with unrealistically low tariffs in order to win contracts with a view to immediately renegotiating the terms (Budds and McGranahan 2003). While some private concessions did undertake expansion and improvement of water and sewerage services, experiences suggested that low-income areas were the least likely to benefit. For example, in Buenos Aires, lower-income areas designated for investment under the contract were subsequently excluded by the concessionaire on the basis of informal land tenure, which was previously the principal reason for non-provision by the state utility (Hardoy *et al.* 2005). In Manila, one concessionaire would only take responsibility for the trunk pipe to the boundary of low-income settlements, delegating responsibility for provision and revenue collection beyond it to the residents' association (Cheng 2015).

From the water companies' perspective, water privatization was a more complex and costly business than initially envisaged. Water and sewerage facilities were often in a more dilapidated state of repair than suggested by pre-bidding surveys, and non-payment levels usually exceeded those suggested by willingness-to-pay surveys. Serious problems arose with the devaluation of local currencies and the repercussions for the revenue of multinational companies reliant on 'hard' currency. For example, the devaluation of the Argentine peso to 20 per cent of its value against the US dollar in 2001 prompted the main Buenos Aires water company to suspend all its plans for investment and expansion, and its contract was later cancelled. The protests that accompanied water privatization in some contexts paralysed the process, and also helped to generate resistance in other places, such as Dar es Salaam. The most notable protests, the Cocha-bamba 'water war' of 2000, were as much a result of the exclusivity over water resources awarded to the company that illegalized existing users (including peri-urban peasants and com-munity water networks), as the immediate and substantial rise in tariffs before any investment had taken place (Assies 2003).

Sceptics always questioned whether the push towards privatization was really a legitimate means of extending coverage among the world's poor, as opposed to a way of facilitating new investment opportunities for northern water companies (Schulpen and Gibbon 2002). However, in 1999, referring to Zimbabwe, the General Manager of Biwater, Richard Whiting, was quoted as declaring that 'from a social point of view these kinds of projects are viable but, unfor-tunately, from a private sector point of view they are not' (*Zimbabwe Independent*, cited in Budds and McGranahan 2003).

Despite most large concession contracts in the global South having ended prematurely, two trends can be observed. The first is the use of shorter and less risky contracts, including build–own–(operate)–transfer (BO(O)T)-type modes, whereby private operators build new infrastructure and operate it for terms of around 15 years in order to recoup their investment and generate a profit, especially in China; as well as the extension of private contracts to new countries, such in India. The second is a morphing of the forms that private sector participation takes, with increasing emphasis on more explicit forms of 'private–public partnership' than the contracts between the public sector and private sector outlined above, whereby private entities support public provision, as well as corporatization, and state utilities are restructured to function on a commercial basis. It is to the latter that we turn next.

Corporatization

If water privatization has slowed in pace over the last decade and a half and, as some suggest, the process has, indeed, begun to reverse (Kishimoto *et al.* 2015), the emphasis on full-cost recov-ery, which was once thought to be part and parcel of privatization, appears to have intensified. This intensification of full-cost recovery should be seen as one element within a more extensive process of corporatization (McDonald and Ruiters 2005), the second of the two processes that we would like to highlight within processes of neoliberalization. With the unravelling of pro-cesses of privatization in recent years, McDonald (2014) has been careful to distinguish between neoliberal forms of corporatization and other more specific – and, potentially, progressive – variants. Indeed, the variety of different forms, from the municipal socialism of the early twen-tieth century to fascist off-shoots of municipal service providers, is important to bear in mind. Nevertheless, for the sake of clarity we will focus solely on neoliberal corporatization. In so doing, we will focus on three shifts that have taken place under the broad umbrella of corpora-tization: the removal of cross-subsidies; the proliferation of new forms of infrastructure focused on the achievement of full-cost recovery; and an increasing emphasis on commodification.

What McDonald (ibid.) refers to as neoliberal corporatization is best understood as an attempt to ensure that publicly owned and operated entities adopt the underlying values of the private sector, in which the latter has generally been understood to be guided more clearly by the profit motive. Often, this shift has been made possible through the creation of a legally separate pro-vider that runs at an arms-length from the state and achieves a degree of financial, political and operational independence. The appointment of a board of directors, and the introduction of New Public Management principles often accompany this newfound independence (ibid.). With financial autonomy from the state there is increasing pressure on service providers to eliminate all cross-subsidies from other services: water providers become ring-fenced entities unable to draw from other services which might produce a surplus or from general taxation more broadly. Service providers must innovate, so the argument goes, in order to ensure their long-term stability (the ideological backdrop to such a claim is thinly veiled when other crucial services such as healthcare and transportation are still more often than not funded through general taxation). The removal of cross-subsidies, furthermore, has a major influence on the relationship between the service provider and those being served. From being understood as *citizens*, entitled to a basic level of service provision, increasingly households are defined as *consumers*. In one felicitous phrase, Meek (2014) describes how such a process has transformed the citizens of the UK into human revenue streams: 'We are a human revenue stream; we are being made tenants in our own land, defined by the string of private fees we pay to exist here.'

How best to ensure that returns can be guaranteed from this human revenue stream becomes one of the key concerns for neoliberal corporatized entities. The dominant orthodoxy is that sustainability, whether in publicly or privately operated systems, depends on costs being recovered entirely through user charges (McDonald and Ruiters 2005). These charges are expected to include not just operation and maintenance but often also construction. As also noted in the previous section, because of this, individualized full-cost recovery, whereby each household pays the full cost of connection, has been particularly contentious: households already served are often not expected to pay for new infrastructure, whereas unserved, and often historically disadvantaged, residences are frequently expected to bear the full cost of network extensions. Ensuring that all costs are met through user charges has therefore generated challenges in designing the most appropriate billing systems as well as an accompanying assault on what is often considered to be a culture of 'non-payment'. In most cases, this assault on the 'unwillingness' of intransigent households to learn to pay has diverted attention from the *inability* of those with low and unstable incomes to pay user charges. Nevertheless, an array of new and old technologies has been enlisted to ensure that household water consumption can be measured and billed accordingly.

The consequences of these infrastructural forms have sometimes been devastating for the newly defined consumers who are exposed to them. Thus, an outbreak of cholera that swept through KwaZulu Natal in the early years of the new millennium is widely acknowledged to have been fostered by the increasing reliance of low-income residents on untreated sources of water following the implementation of pre-payment technologies that relied on continued payment for constant access (Cottle and Deedat 2002). Elsewhere in South Africa, Loftus (2006) documents how the reliance on flow-limiting technologies, which deliver only a basic lifeline supply of water, has served to regulate the daily lives of residents in Durban's townships. Across South Africa, the introduction of an indigent grant for those struggling with payments for services has led to a more widespread implementation of technologies designed not to ensure that people have access to water but rather that access is limited to a basic level (for one discussion, see Hart 2014).

The South African example is a curious one, for the country has promised to guarantee the right to water to all citizens ever since the publication of its ground-breaking post-apartheid constitution in 1996. And yet, in a context of corporatization, the lifeline free basic water allowance that enables this constitutional guarantee to be met has come under great pressure. Free basic water circulates as something resembling a commodity. In the case of Durban, this is partly a result of the municipal service provider's complicated relationship with its bulk water provider, Umgeni Water. Indeed, the latter entity serves as an excellent example of the four characteristics of neoliberal corporatization for McDonald (2014): the adoption of New Public Management principles; commoditization; myopia; and productivism. With regard to the latter, as a white elephant created in the apartheid years to justify the policy of 'separate development', Umgeni Water is now a corporatized entity that operates under the hackneyed triple bottom line of 'People, Planet, Profit'. In seeking to expand beyond the somewhat limited horizons of the Umgeni river basin, Umgeni Water bid too highly for several of the government's rural water contracts, before losing money when tendering to operate the Port Harcourt water concession in Nigeria. Failing in each of these attempts to expand its operations, Umgeni Water relied on recouping its losses through increased bulk water charges to Durban. Rather than achieving efficiency gains, therefore, the entity has been responsible for a new wave of profligacy and waste, which now means that bills in Durban are roughly 30 per cent higher than they would be were it not for the existence of this corporatized entity.

Financialization

If one begins to unravel the travails of Umgeni Water it quickly emerges that the fate of the company has become increasingly tied to its ability to raise capital within the private markets. Although more evident in other parts of the world, the increasing importance of global financial intermediaries can be witnessed in Umgeni Water's stop–start productivism. Indeed, financialization is one crucial moment in the latest wave of neoliberalization, having exerted a major influence on the water sector in England and Wales. Financialization is defined differently in different contexts and is a term that often lacks conceptual purchase. In this chapter, following Bayliss (2014), we take it to refer to the increasing influence of financial markets on the water sector, along with the growing role of financial actors, elites and institutions, and, finally, we understand it to refer to an apparent shift in the locus of power from the 'real' economy to the 'financial' economy at the same time as any boundaries between these two have become increasingly blurred. In the water sector, therefore, financialization needs to be understood as a shift that is dependent on, and yet is also transformative of, several of the processes outlined in the earlier section on privatization.

Perhaps the clearest example of financialization within the water sector can be found in the case of Thames Water (Allen and Pryke 2013). With the outright divestiture of water infrastructure in England and Wales in 1989, Thames Water transformed from being a Regional Water Board to being a privately owned and managed entity, providing water and sewerage services to households in London and the south-east of England. In 2001, following a similar pattern across England and Wales, Thames was purchased by a larger continental European provider. In the case of Thames, its new owner was the German engineering giant, RWE; nevertheless, in something of a twist, the company was sold only five years later to Kemble Water Limited, which is a collection of investors managed by Macquarie Capital Funds (Europe) Limited. With the Australian investment bank's acquisition of Thames the process of financialization gained pace. Macquarie's interest in Thames can be traced to its pioneering of what some have referred to as an Australian model of infrastructure provision (Torrance 2008). Torrance traces the emergence of this model to Macquarie's growing interest in the 1990s in acquiring equity within private road provision. Later, it became clear that such a model could become a vehicle for packaging risk in different ways and opening up new avenues for the investors whose funds the group managed. This pattern subsequently evolved into one that is geared towards highly leveraged provision of infrastructure and has expanded to projects from water to airports, energy and sewerage networks. More recently, the range of investors involved in Kemble Water Limited has expanded to include the British Telecom Pensions Plan, the Abu Dhabi Investment Authority and the investment arm of the Chinese government.

Importantly, financialization within the water sector seems to have opened up opportunities for a range of institutional investors and sovereign wealth funds to acquire significant stakes within water infrastructure. Because of the close involvement of the regulator OFWAT in price setting, the attraction of the water sector in England and Wales for many of these investors is that it provides opportunities that are stable, inflation protected and tightly regulated. Nevertheless, the opportunities are, to some extent, limited by the scope of the infrastructure projects themselves, and it is possible to read into the apparent return of much more ambitious projects a deepening influence of financialization. The Thames Tideway Tunnel is, perhaps, the most prominent of several examples demonstrating that big infrastructure is back in the context of financialized water provision. Ensuring continued returns on these investments, however, still requires an increase in consumer bills – in the case of the Thames Tideway Tunnel bills are expected to rise by, on average, £80 per year, which will push many more households into water poverty. At the same time, the byzantine corporate structure of Thames Water ensures that profits are off-shored and there is a continual pressure to declare smaller profits to avoid the possibility of taxation.

The influence of financialization on the water sector in other parts of the world has been less keenly felt than in England and Wales. Nevertheless, March and Purcell (2014) chart the influence of financialization on the corporate strategies of Aguas de Barcelona, whose expansion to Chile, Argentina and the UK has been influenced by financialization of an uneven and spatially variegated intensity. The authors pose crucial questions on whether or not the locus of profit-making has shifted, while making a clear argument for the rising influence of financial intermediaries within a process, the outcome of which remains unclear. Elsewhere Bayliss (2014) charts the development of water-related exchange traded funds (ETFs), financial vehicles that track the performance of standardized indexes and funds, in an effort to further internationalize and increase the exposure of capital to the potential financial gains in an 'ever thirstier' world. Going on to note investor frustration at the difficulties in generating a pure market in water, she notes how ETFs are part of a broader effort to deepen and broaden the process of financialization. Nevertheless, as in the case of privatization, water remains an uncooperative commodity, so any future influence of financialization is likely to take specific forms and cannot be assumed from the outset.

Marketization

If the financialization of water utilities demonstrates the deepening of the application of market principles to the water sector, the creation of markets in bulk water represent the extension of such rationale to water allocation among water utilities, agriculture, industry and other users. While in most contexts consumers have typically been charged for water and sanitation services (even if not at a rate that covers operation and maintenance), bulk water allocation in most contexts has seldom been priced (at all or realistically) or permitted to be traded among users. Water markets constitute the final instance of neoliberalization that we will examine in this chapter.

Water markets typically exist in water-scarce contexts, where they are designed to facilitate the efficient transfer of water rights – the entitlement to extract and use a defined flow of water under specified conditions – between different users. Water markets have existed in some contexts for many years, including the western USA and Spain, where they are institutionalized (Simpson and Ringskog 1998), and are also present informally in others, such as India and

Pakistan (Bruns and Meinzen-Dick 2000). However, the most salient example is that of Chile, where neoliberal economic and political reforms undertaken between 1975 and 1989 made water rights markets the mainstay of the country's national water policy, with far less state regulation than any other context.

Alongside the push towards the privatization of water supply utilities from the early 1990s, water markets were also strongly promoted by international financial institutions as the basis of effective water management (Hearne and Easter 1995). Water markets are based upon the premise that water is often allocated and used inefficiently, and that establishing exclusive user rights and applying trading will encourage users who need water (and are willing to pay for it to purchase it) from those who either are not using it or are prepared to sell it (rather than use it themselves), thereby promoting efficiency through the reallocation of water to more (economically) productive uses. Two processes are thus at play: the enclosure of water to specific users, and the potential for users to trade water encourage reallocation to higher-value uses. Water trading can comprise either water *rights* (as defined above) or water *volumes* (specific quantities of water, akin to leasing). In order to be make water tradable in practice, water rights and volumes must be clearly defined to enable potential buyers to know exactly what they are buying, and subject to institutional protection that they will continue to exist into the foreseeable future. The latter is deemed to offer the security necessary to encourage water users to invest in their own water infrastructure rather than rely on the state to provide it. As the quote below illustrates, water markets were deemed to lead to efficiency as well as social benefits:

> This approach has the potential to increase the productivity of water use, improve operations and maintenance, stimulate private investment and economic growth, reduce water conflicts, rationalize ongoing and future irrigation development, and free up government resources for activities that have a public good content or positive externalities. *And it is likely to especially benefit the poor and to help conserve natural resources.*
>
> *(Thobani 1995, emphasis added)*

The asserted social benefits are spurious, however, as they are based on unfounded assumptions, including that state water management favoured wealthier users and so private water rights would benefit poorer users; water rights could provide collateral for credit; revenue from water sales and/or taxes could fund poverty alleviation programmes; and that the resulting efficiency gains from trading would increase the availability of water for poorer users (ibid.). Importantly, such promotion of water markets was heavily influenced by the Chilean model and experience, despite no reliable empirical evidence (e.g. Briscoe 1996).

In Chile, water rights have existed in some form since Spanish colonial times (Bauer 1997). In 1981, the Water Code was reformed to convert existing water rights from state-granted concessions to private property rights, protected by the 1980 Constitution (meaning that they could only be expropriated at full market value). Water rights were rendered tradable (if properly registered), separated from land (so that they could be traded independently from land), regulated by civil law rather than public law (meaning that conflicts must be resolved between private parties), and carried no prioritization among different uses, justification of intended use or even obligation to be used. The function of the state water agency, the National Water Directorate, was curtailed to an administrative, as opposed to regulatory, capacity. Water rights could be obtained in three ways: (1) existing water rights were converted into private property rights; (2) new water rights, if available, were granted free of charge; and (3) water rights could be bought from other holders. Once fully allocated, redistribution was expected to happen through the market.

While initial analyses suggested that the system worked well, especially in the agricultural sector (e.g. Gazmuri and Rosegrant 1996), comprehensive empirical work conducted by Carl Bauer in the 1990s suggested that water rights markets were inactive throughout Chile (Bauer 1998). Bauer (ibid.) attributed market inactivity to factors including high transaction costs to trade water between users; geographical barriers to relocate water rights from one area to another, especially between valleys; and cultural resistance to water trading. One apparent exception was the Limarí river basin; however, water trading here was not in (permanent) water *rights*, but in (temporary) water *volumes*, which, in turn, only emerged due to the existence of a reservoir system that indicated water availability before the irrigation season.

A review conducted by Ríos and Quiroz (1995) assessed the advantages and disadvantages of water markets, and identified, in particular, the potential for speculation and hoarding, given that there is no obligation for rights to be used. Despite these authors describing equity as a 'non-issue', Budds (2004, 2008) found that peasant farmers' surface water rights (irrigation canals) appeared to be relatively unchanged and secure, yet their access to new groundwater rights (wells) was significantly lower than that of commercial farmers. While there was no evidence in Budds's case study that peasant farmers were selling off their water rights, the conversion of their water rights into private property, at least in principle, brought their rights into the market and open to acquisition by other users. The outcome may have been different, however, if users requiring additional water for agricultural expansion had turned to the market rather than seek to circumvent it by acquiring water through other (often illegal) means. In this way, while the 'neoliberal' features of Chile's water rights markets systems – private property and tradability – have attracted most attention, it is simultaneously the lack of state regulation that has permitted unfettered accumulation and dispossession of water rights. In 2005, following a protracted and largely ideological debate over the nature and effects of the Water Code, it was modified to address some of these issues, and included a mechanism to legalize the groundwater rights of peasant farmers (Budds 2013).

Conclusion

As this chapter has shown, the particular shifts in state–society relations that are indicated by the term 'neoliberalism' have played out in several different ways when it comes to the provision, circulation and 'framing' of water as a resource. If the privatization process represented the first of several iterations of the neoliberalization of water, its influence has waned considerably in recent years and shows signs of reversing in some contexts while morphing in others. With the promises of privatization having largely failed to materialize, many countries and municipalities have been forced to look for new ways to ensure that populations have access to safe, sufficient and affordable supplies of water on a continual basis. Corporatization of the public sector has often been promoted as an alternative to privatization, influencing the approaches of municipal water providers, development practitioners and state water departments. Along with the establishment of New Public Management, corporatization has ensured that the goal of full-cost recovery has been promoted as an unquestionable principle at the heart of water provision. At the same time, the disillusionment of the private sector in failing to achieve the expected profits within water provision have been partly assuaged through the development of a range of financial instruments and intermediaries that appear to shift the locus of profit-making away from the material resource and towards the operation of the company. Despite growing empirical evidence around the externalities of water markets in Chile, marketizing bulk water to aspire for efficient allocation and use continues to provoke strong interest among economic sectors and state authorities, even in the UK, where they are being contemplated for East Anglia.

Resistance to such processes, at a range of scales, has achieved some remarkable successes. The termination of the Cochabamba water concession shortly after its inception, the blocking of privatization in cities including Montevideo, Dar es Salaam and Thessaloniki, and the UN General Assembly's recognition of the human right water in 2010 are only a few of many inspiring examples of social mobilization to prioritize human needs over private profits. Yet, these outcomes are not due to social mobilization alone, but are simultaneously due to water's inherent resistance to both commodification and competition. Attempts to simply redefine water as a commodity have almost universally failed to erase the deep public and cultural meanings that people around the world attach to water, leading them to reject the notion that water should be enclosed and sold like other commodities (even other public services). As a resource that approximates a natural monopoly and requires substantial infrastructure and energy to transfer from one place to another, water has remained a surprisingly uncooperative commodity (Bakker 2003). Water's uncooperative nature has thus turned out to be an unwitting ally in the quest to ensure the democratic and equitable provision of water for all.

References

Allen, J., and Pryke, M. 2013. Financialising Household Water: Thames Water, MEIF, and 'Ring-Fenced' Politics. *Cambridge Journal of Regions, Economy and Society*, 6.3: 419–39.

Assies, W. 2003. David versus Goliath in Cochabamba: Water Rights, Neoliberalism, and the Revival of Social Protest in Bolivia. *Latin American Perspectives*, 30.3: 14–36.

Bakker, K. 2003. *An Uncooperative Commodity: Privatizing Water in England and Wales.* Oxford: Oxford University Press.

Bauer, C. 1997. Bringing Water Markets Down to Earth: The Political Economy of Water Rights in Chile, 1976–1995. *World Development*, 25.5: 639–56.

—. 1998. *Against the Current? Privatization, Water Markets and the State in Chile.* Boston, MA: Kluwer.

Bayliss, K. 2014. The Financialization of Water. *Review of Radical Political Economics*, 46.3: 292–307.

Briscoe, J. 1996. Water Resources Management in Chile: Lessons from a World Bank Study Tour. *World Bank Working Paper.* Washington, DC: World Bank.

Brocklehurst, C., ed. 2004. *New Designs for Water and Sanitation Transactions: Making Private Sector Participation Work for the Poor.* Washington, DC: World Bank.

Bruns, B., and Meinzen-Dick, R. 2000. *Negotiating Water Rights.* Washington, DC: International Food Policy Research Institute.

Budds, J. 2004. Power, Nature and Neoliberalism: The Political Ecology of Water in Chile. *Singapore Journal of Tropical Geography*, 25.3: 322–42.

—. 2008. Whose Scarcity? The Hydrosocial Cycle and the Changing Waterscape of La Ligua River Basin, Chile, in Goodman, M., Boykoff, M., and Evered, K., eds. *Contentious Geographies: Environment, Meaning, Scale.* Aldershot: Ashgate.

—. 2013. Water, Power, and the Production of Neoliberalism in Chile, 1973–2005. *Environment and Planning D: Society and Space*, 31.2: 301–18.

Budds, J. and McGranahan, G. 2003. Are the Debates on Water Privatization Missing the Point? Experiences from Africa, Asia and Latin America. *Environment and Urbanization*, 15.2: 87–113.

Cheng, D. 2015. Contestations at the Last Mile: The Corporate–Community Delivery of Water in Manila. *Geoforum*, 59: 240–7.

Cottle, E., and Deedat, H. 2002. *The Cholera Outbreak: A 2000–2002 Case Study of the Source of the Outbreak in the Madlebe Tribal Authority Areas, uThungulu Region, KwaZulu-Natal.* Durban: Health Systems Trust.

Gazmuri, R., and Rosegrant, M. 1996. Chilean Water Policy: The Role of Water Rights, Institutions and Markets. *Water Resources Development*, 12.1: 33–48.

Hardoy, A., Hardoy, J., Pandiella, G., and Urquiza, G. 2005. Governance for Water and Sanitation Services in Low-income Settlements: Experiences with Partnership-based Management in Moreno, Buenos Aires. *Environment and Urbanization*, 17.1: 183–200.

Hart, G. 2014. *Rethinking the South African Crisis.* Athens: University of Georgia Press.

Hearne R., and Easter, K. 1995. Water Allocation and Water Markets: An Analysis of Gains from Trade in Chile. *World Bank Technical Paper No. 315.* Washington, DC: World Bank.

Kishimoto, S., Lobina, E., and Petitjean, O. 2015. *Our Public Water Future: The Global Experience with Remunicipalisation.* Greenwich: Public Services International Research Unit.

Loftus, A. 2006. Reification and the Dictatorship of the Water Meter. *Antipode*, 38.5: 1023–45.

March, H., and Purcell, T. 2014. The Muddy Waters of Financialisation and New Accumulation Strategies in the Global Water Industry: The Case of AGBAR. *Geoforum*, 53: 11–20.

McDonald, D. ed. 2014. *Rethinking Corporatization and Public Services in the Global South.* London: Zed.

McDonald, D., and Ruiters, G. 2005. *The Age of Commodity: Water Privatization in Southern Africa.* London: Earthscan.

Meek, J. 2014. *Private Island: Why Britain Now Belongs to Someone Else.* London: Verso.

Ríos, M., and Quiroz, J. 1995. The Market for Water Rights in Chile: Major Issues. *World Bank Technical Paper No. 285.* Washington, DC: World Bank.

Schulpen, L., and Gibbon, P. 2002. Private Sector Development: Policies, Practices and Problems. *World Development*, 30.1: 1–15.

Silva, G., Tynan, N., and Yilmaz, Y. 1998. Private Participation in the Water and Sanitation Sector: Recent Trends. *Private Sector Viewpoint Note No. 147, PPIAF.* Washington, DC: World Bank.

Simpson, L., and Ringskog, K. 1998. *Water Markets in the Americas.* Washington, DC: World Bank.

Thobani, M. 1995. Tradable Property Rights to Water: How to Improve Water Use and Resolve Water Conflicts. *Finance and Private Sector Development Note No. 34.* Washington, DC: World Bank.

Torrance, M. 2008. Forging Glocal Governance? Urban Infrastructures as Networked Financial Products. *International Journal of Urban and Regional Research*, 32.1: 1–21.

Winpenny, J. 2003. *Financing Water for All: Report of the World Panel on Financing Water Infrastructure.* Marseille: World Water Council, Third World Water Forum and Global Water Partnership: 54.

513

44

THE NEOLIBERALIZATION OF AGRICULTURE

Regimes, resistance, and resilience

Jamey Essex

In January 2010, a powerful earthquake devastated Haiti, killing thousands, causing widespread damage, and prompting an influx of emergency aid. This disaster highlighted the extensive and extreme poverty that has made Haiti the poorest country in the western hemisphere, with food insecurity, limited access to clean water, and lack of basic services and infrastructure marking daily life for millions of Haitians. Former US presidents Bill Clinton and George W. Bush quickly launched an international relief agency for those affected by the quake, the Clinton Bush Haiti Fund, though this monumental effort to direct short-term humanitarian relief and long-term development aid to Haiti prompted Clinton to issue a somewhat surprising apology.

In the 1990s, Clinton had helped secure production and export subsidies for American rice farmers in his home state of Arkansas, and led efforts to get Haiti's government to liberalize its rice markets. With liberalization, the Haitian government slashed protective tariffs originally designed to support poor Haitian farmers from 50 to 3 per cent under the conditions of an IMF structural adjustment programme (SAP). Clinton told a Haitian reporter that, in retrospect, this was a 'devil's bargain', and that he had 'to live every day with the consequences of the lost capacity to produce a rice crop in Haiti to feed those people' (O'Connor 2013: n.p.). These consequences, of course, have fallen much harder on Haitian rice farmers and consumers directly affected by the economic volatility and flood of cheap subsidized rice from the USA that followed. The example of Haitian rice, especially the rapid decline of farmers' ability to provide for themselves under conditions of unevenly liberalized world markets for agricultural commodities, is just one of thousands of similar cases that demonstrate the impact of neoliberalization on agrofood systems. So how best to understand the complicated, contested, and often locally specific processes and outcomes of neoliberalization for the systems on which we all rely for food?

In the most general terms, we can state unequivocally that neoliberalism has profoundly altered agricultural practices and systems since the late 1970s. From the production of food and fibre in innumerable diffuse sites around the world to the highly uneven and, as the Haiti case demonstrates, unequal systems of trade, speculation, and consumption through which the world's population feeds and clothes itself, agriculture has proved a vital but highly contentious arena of neoliberalization. This chapter covers the process of neoliberalization in relation to agriculture by emphasizing how neoliberalism has shaped the metabolic relations and processes of agroecological production, and attempted to bend these to the needs of speculative global capital. Particularly important is what is known as *food regime analysis* for understanding global agriculture, and how this has informed critical assessments of neoliberalism and its impact on agrofood systems. The food regime approach stems from regulation theory, and concentrates on global systems and historic shifts in the regulation of capitalism by states and other social and political forces. In doing so, it provides insight into the development of a global corporate-dominated and market-oriented neoliberal system of agricultural production, trade, and consumption. Critics contend, however, that this approach also can limit our ability to understand the varied and often haphazard nature of agroecological adaptation and crisis under neoliberalism, as well as the diverse forms of compromise, resistance, and resilience that have developed among agrarian movements and alternative forms of agriculture.

Highlighting the theoretical and practical diversity in contemporary assessments of neoliberalism, especially the limits of neoliberal agriculture, requires us to understand agriculture as an integrated agroecological system. Agriculture constitutes a form of metabolic interaction between human society and the physical environment, shaped by scientific and technological achievements and profound manipulation of plant and animal resources, but nonetheless bound by the genetic, ecological, and social limits of those resources and how they are used. Identifying, understanding, and working within these limits, rather than blindly ignoring or attempting to overcome them through quick-fix technological solutions and unsustainable political and economic arrangements, means rigorously assessing the viability, resilience, and robustness of non-neoliberal systems. This includes the wide variety of alternative and resistance movements that have emerged over the last several decades in response to neoliberalization.

The remainder of this chapter examines the food regime approach, including its main arguments and shortcomings, before turning to questions of agroecological resilience. Neoliberalism provides a spatially and socially uneven basis for local–global connection that has increasingly clear agroecological limits under conditions of widespread poverty, inequality, and perhaps irreversible climate change. I examine some examples of non- and anti-neoliberal forms of agriculture to conclude with an assessment of the possibilities for alternatives to current inequities in relation to food and agriculture.

Food regimes

Over the last two-plus decades, food regime analysis has become one of the dominant paradigms in research on the international political economy of agriculture and food, and thus on the process of neoliberalization in global agrofood systems. This approach provides a heuristic framework for examining shifts in national and global regulation of agriculture and food, looking especially at relations of production and trade, and serving as 'a key to unlock not only structured moments and transitions in the history of capitalist food relations, but also the history of capitalism itself' (McMichael 2009b: 281). Using the food regime concept, scholars have examined changes in agriculture and food systems as a window on much deeper and more extensive processes of capitalist development and crisis. Building from regulation theory, which itself focuses on stability and periodic crises in the history of capitalist development, food regime analysis defines a 'regime' as a stable system of economic, social, and political regulation and norms that allows for steady (or at least predictable) capital accumulation. In doing so, the internal dynamics of the regime displace or temporarily resolve capitalism's class antagonisms through formal and informal institutional arrangements, most notably by and within the nation-state but also increasingly by and within local and transnational institutions and governance (Aglietta 1979; Peck 2000; Jessop 2013). As capitalism is a volatile and contradictory system of social, economic, and political organization, and so requires some form of political and regulatory management to avoid or mitigate the social and economic impacts of market fluctuations and crashes, identifying periods and frameworks of stability and crisis allows us to map out regulatory structures and practices across time and space. No regime can fully or permanently displace or resolve the capitalist law of value's contradictions, however, and regimes experience crisis and failure until they are replaced by a new regime.

Food regime theorists position food and agriculture as a key component in the wider development of capitalist circuits of finance, trade, and industrial development. Looking primarily at changes in the international state system, changing modes and practices of business regulation, technological changes linking agriculture to other economic sectors, the industrialization of agricultural production itself, and the national state's changing role in mediating political and economic processes, scholars generally identify three main food regimes in the contemporary history of industrial capitalist development. These are known by different names, but, following primarily from Friedmann (2005), can be identified as the settler–colonial food regime (roughly 1870 to the 1930s), the mercantile–industrial food regime (from the immediate post-World War II period through the mid-1970s), and the neoliberal–corporate regime (from the early 1980s onward). Between each are periods of crisis and transition, in which existing practices and institutions meet the limits of their capacity to regulate agriculture in line with broader systems of capitalist accumulation, political legitimacy, and social reproduction.

The food regime concept has sparked considerable debate among critical researchers since first articulated by Friedmann and McMichael (1989). One of the most contentious points centres on the current neoliberal–corporate regime's stability, and whether it is even a 'regime' at all, or rather an extended period of crisis and reorganization (Araghi 2003; Burch and Lawrence 2009; Campbell and Dixon 2009; McMichael 2009b; Pritchard 2009). The settler–colonial regime was defined by the extension of European settlement and colonialism to new areas of the globe (especially the hinterlands of North America, Australia, and parts of the global South), the development of national commodities markets, and a competitive liberal international trading system, especially for cotton, grains, and other staple crops. Following three decades of crisis marked by two world wars and the Great Depression, the post-World War II mercantile–industrial regime built from an intensification and industrialization of agricultural production methods (including in the global South via the Green Revolution, discussed below), the development of mass markets and standardization for many food commodities, and the creation of specialized agrofood complexes around grains and oilseeds, livestock, and processed foods. Underlying these regimes were, respectively, the hegemony of imperial Britain and the postwar USA, which helped construct international regulatory systems based on market forces. Currency and trade rules based on British and then American economic strengths and interests provided a framework for these regimes.

Oil price shocks and stalled GATT trade talks produced another systemic crisis in the 1970s, and the second food regime came to an end. Since the late 1970s, many states have adopted neoliberalism as a preferred platform for agricultural and food regulation as part of economic restructuring and agricultural policy reform. This has profoundly transformed scalar and geographical relations, producing both intermittent crises and new forms of global capital accumulation in the agrofood sector based on financial speculation in food commodities markets, land grabbing in the global South, and deep but uneven liberalization of agricultural production and trade. Food regime theorists trying to make sense of the neoliberal–corporate regime thus emphasize neoliberalism as an ideology that focuses on market dynamics and the state's role as facilitator of global economic connection. Neoliberalism is, at the same time, a set of practices

Table 44.1 Food regimes

	First food regime (colonial–settler)	Second food regime (mercantile–industrial)	Third food regime (neoliberal–corporate)
Period	1870s to 1930s	Late 1940s to mid-1970s	Early 1980s to present
Political economy	Expansion of industrial capitalism; imperial rivalry and colonial domination of global production and flows; extension of agriculture and white settlement in 'neo-Europes'	State regulation of markets and capital; dominance of industrial capital; Keynesian Fordist, communist centrally planned, and 'Third World' developmentalist variants	Self-regulating markets (monetarism) with an overriding emphasis on international trade; hierarchical international state system with multiple poles of power; recurrent debt crises; dominance of finance capital
Policy mechanisms	Colonial domination in much of global South; cheap land policies in neo-Europes; relative free trade; British pound backed by gold standard	Import substitution and land reform in global South; public investment in infrastructure, energy, and industrial upgrading; US dollar backed by gold standard and Bretton Woods institutions	Export-led growth; privatization and fiscal discipline; competitive specialization; trade liberalization through reduction of tariffs and non-tariff barriers to trade
International agricultural trade	Development of international markets for major grain commodities, colonial control of South–North trade	Limited under GATT rules, European Common Agricultural Policy, and other protectionist national policies; massive exports of US food commodities through aid programmes	Liberalization under WTO rules and regulation; small farmers incorporated into global economy; intense competition amid expansion of global food trade
Role of the national state	Encourage trade and expansion of capitalist production and agriculture; provide cheap land and suppress or remove indigenous peoples; minimal regulation	Promote and protect national industries and agriculture; western-style political and economic modernization; advance trade and development within bipolar Cold War system; national food self-sufficiency	Facilitate trade and internationalization strategies and agro-export specialization; guarantee property rights; provide political stability and social order; manage and contain debt crises
Ecological conditions	Elimination of biodiversity and native species in expansion of agriculture; industrialization to expand yields; soil degradation and invention of synthetic fertilizers	Expansion of chemical-intensive industrial agriculture through intensification in global North and Green Revolution in global South; widespread ecological simplification through monoculture	Widespread intensification of agricultural and livestock production; development and expansion of GMOs; concerns over climate change and impacts on established patterns of agricultural production

supporting forms of capitalist regulation favouring corporate interests and the integration of agricultural and food markets into speculative systems of finance and investment.

The result is an unevenly neoliberalized system of food and fibre production, trade, and consumption based on an expansion of corporate power along the entire commodity chain from farm to plate. Intensifying global ties are managed increasingly by and through financial systems, subordinating social and ecological goals within agrofood systems, such as food security and environmental stewardship, to the economic objective of maximizing profits. An important emphasis of food regime analysis is institutional change forged through crisis and crisis management. In this respect, neoliberalism's advance has proceeded through crises that force restructuring in how the nation-state manages agricultural systems and economies, especially in the global South. This has been supported by the expansion of international rules and regulations regarding trade, intellectual property, food safety, and other aspects of agrofood systems. Neoliberalism has also, however, faced challenges from peasant and consumer movements, the development of localized and fair trade food systems, and growing awareness of industrial agriculture's ties to climate change. We must ask, then, to what extent are the institutions, rules, and relations of the neoliberal–corporate food regime stable enough to ensure continued capital accumulation in the agrofood sector without undermining the long-term viability of agricultural systems, and how are we to understand the organization and limits of corporate and state power under this regime?

The World Trade Organization (WTO), for example, brought agriculture under the umbrella of global trade rules in a comprehensive way for the first time when it began operations in 1995. This advanced a broad-based institutional push for trade liberalization in agriculture, instigating deep changes in how states could support small farmers and pursue goals like national food self-sufficiency, while also strengthening the conditions under which transnational corporations could expand control over commodity chains and intellectual property, including seeds (Shiva 2000; Kloppenburg 2004; Clapp and Fuchs 2009).[1] Using food regime analysis, we can focus on the global and national institutional arrangements that govern the production, trade, and consumption of food under neoliberalism, how these have developed historically, and what tensions and contradictions shape them going forward. McMichael (2009a, 2010, 2012) and Friedmann (2005, 2013) have most recently used this form of analysis to examine: the role of corporate power and processes of land grabbing and agrofuel development; how neoliberal forms of regulation and market pressures erode localized and peasant forms of agriculture; the uneasy adoption of environmental standards and 'greenwashing' in the capitalist food system under rubrics of sustainability; and the development of anti-neoliberal social movements based on peasant rights and food sovereignty.

While food regime analysis thus remains pivotal for understanding the steady but incomplete neoliberalization of agrofood systems, it nonetheless faces significant critiques and limitations. Focused on formal institutional arrangements at the national and global scales, on a particular form of class-based analysis, and on moments of crisis, research using the food regime concept can tend to neglect other forms of social difference and collaboration. In turn, it often underplays continuities, limits, and variability in how neoliberalism has developed in practice. It continues to struggle with identifying the historical and geographical contours of food regimes, and, in particular, with appropriately classifying the contemporary neoliberal moment in the development of capitalist (and non- or anti-capitalist) forms of agriculture. Many researchers therefore favour looking not at relatively rigid systems of institutions and rules that govern capitalist food production and trade, but rather at the highly differentiated and extensive networks of interrelated actors that make up agroecological networks. This includes not only human actors like farmers, officials, business elites, and consumers, but also non-human elements such as the plants, animals, texts, and concepts that animate these networks (Whatmore and Thorne 1997; Goodman 1999).

Other agrofood researchers emphasize local embeddedness and the role of place in agrofood systems, as the insistence on a global-scale view misses much of the geographic and ecological diversity on which food's cultural and social significance are built, and on which food production depends (Winter 2003; Bowen 2011). Guthman (2008) and Pudup (2008) are, in a slightly different vein, critical of the often deeply romanticized views of community and participation that drive many food localization movements and, they argue, reproduce neoliberal subjectivities. They call for much closer attention to the 'micropolitics' of food activism than what food regime analysis can provide, to highlight the importance of social identity in how neoliberalization operates at the local scale and through ostensibly alternative forms of agriculture. For understanding neoliberalism as a force in reshaping agrofood systems, however, food regime analysis remains indispensible. Building on these critiques without losing insights on corporate power, institutional restructuring, and global connections food regime analysis offers can allow us to see the diverse and often hybrid forms of neoliberalism that develop with the social, political, economic, and ecological complexity of agrofood systems. Understanding this through the lens of agroecology can, likewise, assist us in identifying the limits of, and viable alternatives to, neoliberalism as an ideology, a set of practices and policies, and a mode of social, economic, ecological, and political regulation.

Agroecology and neoliberalism

Food regime analysis provides a broad historical narrative of agriculture's place in the development of capitalism, globalization, and neoliberalism, but says little about the details of agriculture's ecological contexts and impacts. A more directly agroecological perspective can help correct for this and build ecological insight into the critical political economy perspectives already outlined. Agroecology is the study and management of 'energy flows, species interactions, and material cycling' that takes into account 'the impact of human activity on processes at continental and global scales… [to] address a complex, dynamic, and increasingly uncertain context of multiple, interacting drivers of land-use change' (Tomich *et al.* 2011:195). Emphasizing agriculture's position as part of broader ecological systems prevents a common but untenable abstraction that places humans and human society outside of these systems and their operation. It helps us conceptualize the use of environmental resources and systems like water, soil, genes, and climate in agriculture as a form of metabolism, the irreversible transformation of ecological systems and resources for human needs. In practical terms, and linking the global and continental scale to the local scale, the functional landscape, and the farm unit, agroecology positions agriculture, and sites of agricultural production and consumption, as a closed loop of energy and materials. This is in contrast to a perspective that treats agriculture, and more concretely, sites of agricultural production, merely as throughput points for increasingly globalized capital circulating in a neoliberalized context of open trade, market imperatives, and economic externalities (Weis 2007). Finally, it points to the potential limits of agricultural production and consumption as fundamentally intertwined with and based in ecological and social dynamics.

Speculative and predatory forms of neoliberal agriculture, built on liberalized trade, the interests and institutions of finance capital, and the reconfiguration of political, social, and ecological systems to narrow economic ends are unsustainable in the long run, especially to the extent that they undermine the conditions of food production and social reproduction. This does not mean, however, that there is one singular form of neoliberal agriculture in the current world-historical moment of capitalist globalization and crisis. Instead, there is a highly differentiated set of interlocking systems shaped strongly by neoliberal principles and frameworks, with dynamic agroecological conditions and limits that therefore also map closely onto neoliberalism's social, economic, and political contradictions and limits. While I have highlighted some of these above in discussing food regime analysis and associated critiques, this section provides context for understanding them in ecological terms. I examine neoliberalized agriculture in relation to food security and climate change, from the post-World War II Green Revolution to the most recent 'global food crisis', before addressing how oppositional movements have articulated non- and anti-neoliberal forms of agriculture.

One of the key challenges for neoliberal agriculture is to ensure food security amid competitive global market dynamics and the uncertainty of climate change. Historically, food security has been articulated at a variety of scales and connected to innumerable other social, political, and economic objectives, but at its root has generally meant that everyone has enough to eat on a daily basis. The term itself is highly contested, linked to debates on basic human rights, the appropriate role of state support and intervention for farmers and consumers, and the productive capacity of agricultural technology and practices. Under the rubric of national development in the four decades following World War II (i.e. the mercantile–industrial food regime, as discussed above), the governments of many newly independent states in what was then called the Third World made national food self-sufficiency a cornerstone of economic development. Political leaders and development experts posited that agricultural modernization would rapidly increase food production and provide a sound footing for urbanization and industrialization. Food security was reckoned primarily at the national level and as part of national aspirations for modernization. This, in turn, meant the development and fine-tuning of measures designed to calculate food security and hunger at finer scales, such as the individual and the household, as well as the identification by western elites of 'world hunger' as a serious problem for global political and economic stability (Vernon 2007; Cullather 2010; Jarosz 2014).

Mainstream approaches to food security emphasized both food availability, which decision-makers, development practitioners, and elites in both the global North and South generally understood as a product of technological capacity and agricultural productivity, and political mobilization, which, in turn, was linked to the Cold War context and bitter struggles over postcolonial independence and development. Many states in Latin America and South and Southeast Asia adopted Green Revolution techniques from the 1950s onward to achieve national food security and development goals. This required taking on massive debt from international creditors and large influxes of foreign aid to modernize agricultural practices and infrastructure, especially for irrigation and the production of chemical fertilizers and pesticides. Through these Green Revolution techniques, developing countries sought to catch up to the industrial agricultural model of the USA, and they borrowed heavily to do so, in both financial and ecological terms. While this did increase agricultural productivity, it facilitated a virtual revolution in the countryside. The Green Revolution eradicated peasant forms of food production and land management and displaced millions of poor farmers in favour of more productive agriculture dependent on chemical inputs, foreign debt, massive infrastructural investment, and international markets (Weis 2007; Latham 2011).

Thus, while the Green Revolution improved food security in many states, with notable successes in India, Mexico, and the Philippines (but largely bypassing sub-Saharan Africa), this was measured by national-scale statistics that masked inequalities at the subnational level, and failed to fully account for the ecological costs of intensified agricultural production methods. Seeking to maintain income to pay for expensive chemical inputs and farm machinery, farmers often took on heavy household debts and used soil and water resources more intensively but not always more efficiently. With widespread economic stagnation lingering throughout the 1970s and the ideological and political shift towards neoliberalism in the USA and Western Europe, debt crises hit developing country economies and farmers especially hard. This undermined and erased food security gains achieved through expanded, industrialized production, while debt servicing requirements and loan conditionalities forced many countries to open their national agricultural sectors to global market integration and competition. Ecological impacts that had begun to develop well before neoliberalism's emergence became more noticeable and severe as many states in the global South underwent neoliberalization through IMF and World Bank-backed SAPs, removing protections for small farmers and encouraging further market integration (Friedmann 2005).

In agroecological terms, peasant and smallholder forms of agriculture and land management continued to decline as monoculture production expanded and many farmers turned to industrial, and often imported, fertilizers, pesticides, and herbicides to augment or repair nutrient cycles and increase yields. Several states adopted agro-export strategies, with agricultural policy facilitating specialized production in high-value farm products targeted for export, though many states continued to specialize in low-value raw commodity exports, such as cocoa or coffee beans, and faced poor terms of trade and low farm incomes (Weis 2007). With deepening neoliberalism, policy-makers and development experts increasingly posited food security as a function of purchasing power and market connection. Similar processes drove agroecological change in the global North, where industrial agriculture was already well entrenched by the end of World War II in the USA, and in Western Europe after the war. Farm debt, intensification, and ecological simplification led to soil exhaustion and an ever-mounting reliance on chemical fertilizers and pesticides, and, finally, the development and widespread adoption of genetically modified seeds since the early 1990s in attempts to maintain yields and farm incomes.

As Moore (2010) argues, the transition from the Green Revolution to neoliberalization can be understood as the search for a return to profitability for global capitalism through the integration of agriculture into global financial networks and debt. Moore (2010: 231) states that, as the Green Revolution's productivity enhancements dissolved into insurmountable debt for farmers and governments, neoliberalism offered 'an extractive strategy that discouraged long-term investments by states and capitals, and encouraged socio-ecological "asset stripping" of every sort', extending 'a cheap food regime *without* a corresponding agricultural revolution'. Genetic engineering has failed to maintain steady productivity gains or yield growth in agriculture, while financial integration and asset stripping has undermined the ecological and social conditions that underlie complex agrofood systems. Though this can be identified as a global trend under the rubric of a single global food regime, these processes have taken different forms in different places.

With the rapid liberalization of agrofood sectors in the 1990s and 2000s, these processes continued but also began to encounter staunch resistance from peasant movements, consumer groups, and environmental activists. Finding common cause, critics saw in the neoliberalization of agriculture the undermining of land rights, the expanding power of corporate actors, and the unchecked destruction of environmental resources. In short, neoliberal forms of agriculture are self-destructive, even 'pathological,' precisely because of their ecological, and thus social, unsustainability (Friedmann 2005). Productivist accounts that laud agricultural modernization and market integration emphasize productivity gains, but, Weis (2013: 101) argues, downplay 'the undervalued costs of energy (both *in situ* and in moving things over space) and ensuing emissions and pollution loads', and ignore 'the far-reaching simplification of environments' associated with industrial agriculture and the global sourcing of food that marks the neoliberal–corporate regime. Weis demonstrates how industrial agriculture, including the high-volume production of meat through extended livestock and animal feed commodity chains, exacerbates the 'metabolic rift' that Marx identified as a crucial component of capitalist agriculture in the mid-nineteenth century. The increasing subjugation of environmental systems and objectives to capitalist value production leads to unsustainable forms of nutrient cycling and soil management that exhaust productivity but open agriculture and ecological systems to new rounds of capitalist appropriation and accumulation (Foster 2000; Moore 2011). Neoliberalism drives the further development of this metabolic rift, but builds local–global connections and integrates agriculture into capitalist circuits of value in new ways.

Neoliberal reforms and approaches, however, constantly run up against the ecological variability and specificity that also shape agricultural systems. As in past instances of severe disruption to the environmental conditions supporting agriculture, some agroecological systems have proved more resilient than others to change. In ecological terms, resilience refers to a particular system's stability and adaptability in the face of internal and external changes. Scholars examining natural disasters and climate change have expanded the concept of resilience to include social systems and factors, and considerations of uncertainty and risk, knowledge, and land-use practices (Berardi *et al.* 2011). The neoliberal–corporate food regime must therefore be assessed in terms of its resilience to shocks and changes that are often initiated or exacerbated by neoliberal policies and practices. Food security and climate change are urgent considerations for the future of neoliberal agriculture, especially in the wake of spiking food prices and a 'global food crisis' that erupted alongside energy and financial crises beginning in 2008 (Jarosz 2009; Sommerville *et al.* 2014). Can neoliberal approaches to land management, agricultural policy, and trade ensure food security, given the highly volatile and corporate-dominated global markets on which consumers and farmers both rely? Can they adequately provide incentives and resources for adapting to changing and unpredictable climate patterns? Can they be expected to mitigate or reverse climate change while also expanding oil-dependent monoculture and industrial livestock production, two major contributors to climate change?

It is now widely recognized that ecological pressures, both localized pressures linked to specific forms of degradation and pollution and global shifts resulting from anthropogenic climate change, have potentially profound impacts on agricultural production. Simple expansion of food production through conventional means is neither adequate nor sustainable. As the UN Environment Programme noted in its own examination of the global food crisis, 'agriculture remains the largest driver of genetic erosion, species loss and conversion of natural habitats', undermining the ecosystem services and agroecological cycles that provide the conditions for humanity's food and fibre production (Nelleman *et al.* 2009: 65). Neoliberal forms of agriculture have therefore proved to be decidedly *not* resilient. Policy-makers, fearful of economic and political crises becoming generalized, work to contain these both geographically and socially through inequitable disciplinary mechanisms linked to debt, poverty, and environmental degradation.

The realities of climate change and the persistence of widespread food insecurity thus help identify the limits of neoliberal agriculture, defined by its lack of resilience and susceptibility to multiple, simultaneous forms of crisis. Many development practitioners, policy-makers, and farmers have sought a technological fix for neoliberalism's agroecological limits in a 'second Green Revolution'. Yet long-term adaptation to and of neoliberalized agriculture is difficult to impossible as unresolvable and compounding stresses intensify and expand throughout systems of social reproduction and agroecological management, and adaptation strategies based on new technologies remain unaffordable for most. Almås and Campbell (2012: 4–5) therefore identify the current threats and shocks to agricultural resilience as threefold: 'the Global Food Crisis of 2008 (and beyond); Climate Change (and related issues around energy and biofuels); and the emergence of "neo-productivist" claims for agriculture seeking to re-establish productivism as the central policy rational for agriculture.' All present fundamental challenges to the logic, sustainability, and resilience of neoliberalism as the basis for agricultural policy and land-use management, and highlight the ecological and social necessity of alternatives to further neoliberalization.

Conclusion: from alternatives to resistance

The geographic variability of agroecological systems and practices on which agriculture depends produces wide variation in how neoliberalization has proceeded, even if we can still point to broader and more general patterns, as identified and critiqued by food regime analysis. This variability sometimes has been co-opted into hybrid and divergent forms of neoliberalism and neoliberal agriculture (see also Collard *et al.* 2016), but can also highlight and strengthen the resilience of localized systems. Alternative anti- and non-neoliberal forms of agriculture that build from agroecological resilience must be thought of as adaptations as well, existing in broader contexts and systems, and forming points of resistance to further neoliberalization. These adaptations can help us chart possible futures that move beyond and overcome the inequities of neoliberal models and practices. Numerous movements and groups have built forms of food production and distribution not dominated by neoliberalism, often in response or challenge to neoliberal policies, practices, and institutions. These often begin from principles and practices of agroecologically sound land-use planning and management, political rights to land and livelihoods, and regulatory models that adapt concepts of sovereignty and security to community and human needs.

Alternative food systems are now commonplace, and include globally extensive fair trade movements (Fridell 2013; Burnett 2014), localized forms of urban agriculture and community gardening (Pudup 2008), and movements seeking economic and social rights for migrant farm workers and fast food workers (Walter 2013). All aim to challenge or reverse aspects of the current neoliberal–corporate regime. Perhaps the most widespread and powerful of these alternatives, however, is the food sovereignty movement. Originating in the political activism of rural and peasant communities across the global South, food sovereignty has, since the mid-1990s, become a widely used, if contested and often ambiguous, concept expressing and enacting rights, community, and agrofood regulation in ways designed to counter neoliberal emphases on global market dependence and technological solutions (Hopma and Woods 2014; Jarosz 2014). The global peasant rights social movement group La Vía Campesina has articulated the concept of food sovereignty most directly, defining it as the collective right of peoples to determine their own food and agriculture policy. Food sovereignty repurposes the concept of national sovereignty in order to claim rights to land, knowledge, culture, and decision-making capacities for rural communities under pressure from decades of neoliberalism, especially through agricultural trade liberalization (Desmarais 2007). The call for food sovereignty, particularly the right to localized forms of land management and food production not subject to the dictates of neoliberalized regulatory systems of production and trade, has become an oppositional platform for not only peasants and small farmers in the global South, but also consumers, family farmers, and even urban agriculture movements in the global North. While these groups continue to struggle over the definition and enactment of food sovereignty, it has nonetheless provided a clear alternative to neoliberalism and placed socially expansive and ecologically centred agriculture at the heart of new forms of local–global connection. The future of these movements, and of neoliberalism, depends on multiple social and ecological factors, but, without more resilient forms of agricultural production and more just systems of food distribution and consumption, the crisis tendency of neoliberal agriculture is unlikely to find a socially or environmentally sustainable resolution.

Note

1 It should be noted that the authors cited here do not necessarily employ food regime analysis, but draw widely on political economy and political ecology approaches and concepts.

References

Aglietta, M. 1979. *A Theory of Capitalist Regulation: The US Experience*. London:Verso.

Almås, R., and Campbell, H. 2012. Introduction: Emerging Challenges, New Policy Frameworks and the Resilience of Agriculture, in Almås, R., and Campbell, H., eds. *Rethinking Agricultural Policy Regimes: Food Security, Climate Change and the Future Resilience of Global Agriculture (Research in Rural Sociology and Development, Volume 18)*. Bingley: Emerald Group: 1–22.

Araghi, F. 2003. Food Regimes and the Production of Value: Some Methodological Issues. *The Journal of Peasant Studies*, 30: 41–70.

Berardi, G., Green, R., and Hammond, B. 2011. Stability, Sustainability, and Catastrophe: Applying Resilience Thinking to US Agriculture. *Research in Human Ecology*, 18: 115–25.

Bowen, S. 2011. The Importance of Place: Re-Territorialising Embeddedness. *Sociologia Ruralis*, 51: 325–48.

Burch, D., and Lawrence, G. 2009. Towards a Third Food Regime: Behind the Transformation. *Agriculture and Human Values*, 26: 267–79.

Burnett, K. 2014. Trouble in the Fields: Fair Trade and Food Sovereignty Responses to Governance Opportunities After the Food Crisis. *Geopolitics*, 19: 351–76.

Campbell, H., and Dixon, J. 2009. Introduction to the Special Symposium: Reflecting on Twenty Years of the Food Regimes Approach in Agri-food Studies. *Agriculture and Human Values*, 26: 261–5.

Clapp, J., and Fuchs, D. eds. 2009. *Corporate Power in Global Agrifood Governance*. Cambridge, MA: MIT Press.

Collard, R.-M., Dempsey, J., and Rowe, J. 2016. Re-Regulating Socioecologies Under Neoliberalism, in Springer, S., Birch, K., and MacLeavy, J., eds. *The Handbook of Neoliberalism*. London: Routledge: 455–65.

Cullather, N. 2010. *The Hungry World: America's Cold War Battle Against Poverty in Asia*. Cambridge, MA: Harvard University Press.

Desmarais, A.A. 2007. *La Vía Campesina: Globalization and the Power of Peasants*. Halifax: Fernwood.

Foster, J.B. 2000. *Marx's Ecology: Materialism and Nature*. New York: Monthly Review Press.

Fridell, G. 2013. *Alternative Trade: Legacies for the Future*. Halifax: Fernwood.

Friedmann, H. 2005. Feeding the Empire: Pathologies of Globalized Agriculture, in Panitch, L., and Leys, C., eds. *Socialist Register 2005: The Empire Reloaded*. Monmouth: Merlin Press: 124–43.

—. 2013. Changing Food Systems from Top to Bottom: Political Economy and Social Movements Perspectives, in Koç, M., Sumner, J., and Winson, A., eds. *Critical Perspectives in Food Studies*. Don Mills, ON: Oxford University Press: 16–32.

Friedmann, H., and McMichael, P. 1989. Agriculture and the State System: The Rise and Fall of National Agricultures, 1870 to the Present. *Sociologia Ruralis*, 29: 93–117.

Goodman, D. 1999. Agro-Food Studies in the 'Age of Ecology': Nature, Corporeality, Bio-politics. *Sociologia Ruralis*, 39: 17–38.

Guthman, J. 2008. Neoliberalism and the Making of Food Politics in California. *Geoforum*, 39: 1171–83.

Hopma, J., and Woods, M. 2014. Political Geographies of 'Food Security' and 'Food Sovereignty'. *Geography Compass*, 8: 773–84.

Jarosz, L. 2009. Energy, Climate Change, Meat, and Markets: Mapping the Coordinates of the Current World Food Crisis. *Geography Compass*, 3: 2065–83.

—. 2014. Comparing Food Security and Food Sovereignty Discourses. *Dialogues in Human Geography*, 4: 168–81.

Jessop, B. 2013. Revisiting the Regulation Approach: Critical Reflections on the Contradictions, Dilemmas, Fixes, and Crisis Dynamics of Growth Regimes. *Capital and Class*, 37: 5–24.

Kloppenburg, J.R., Jr. 2004. *First the Seed: The Political Economy of Plant Biotechnology*. 2nd edn. Madison: University of Wisconsin Press.

Latham, M. 2011. *The Right Kind of Revolution: Modernization, Development, and US Foreign Policy from the Cold War to the Present*. Ithaca, NY: Cornell University Press.

McMichael, P. 2009a. A Food Regime Analysis of the 'World Food Crisis'. *Agriculture and Human Values*, 26: 281–95.

—. 2009b. A Food Regime Genealogy. *The Journal of Peasant Studies*, 36: 139–69.

—. 2010. Agrofuels in the Food Regime. *The Journal of Peasant Studies*, 37: 609–29.

—. 2012. The Land Grab and Corporate Food Regime Restructuring. *The Journal of Peasant Studies*, 39: 681–701.

Moore, J. 2010. Cheap Food and Bad Money: Food, Frontiers, and Financialization in the Rise and Demise of Neoliberalism. *Review*, 33: 225–61.

—. 2011. Transcending the Metabolic Rift: A Theory of Crises in the Capitalist World-Ecology. *The Journal of Peasant Studies*, 38: 1–46.

Nellemann, C., MacDevette, M., Manders, T., Eickhout, B., Svihus, B., Prins, A.G., and Kaltenborn, B.P. eds. 2009. *The Environmental Food Crisis: The Environment's Role in Adverting Future Food Crises.* Arendal: United Nations Environment Programme, GRID-Arendal.

O'Connor, M.R. 2013. Subsidizing Starvation: How American Tax Dollars are Keeping Arkansas Rice Growers Fat on the Farm and Starving Millions of Haitians. *Foreign Policy Online*, 11 January. Retrieved from http://www.foreignpolicy.com/articles/2013/01/11/subsidizing_starvation

Peck, J. 2000. Doing Regulation, in Clark, G.L., Feldman, M.P., and Gertler, M.A., eds. *The Oxford Handbook of Economic Geography*. Oxford: Oxford University Press: 61–80.

Pritchard, B. 2009. The Long Hangover from the Second Food Regime: A World-Historical Interpretation of the Collapse of the WTO Doha Round. *Agriculture and Human Values*, 26: 297–307.

Pudup, M.B. 2008. It Takes a Garden: Cultivating Citizen-Subjects in Organized Garden Projects. *Geoforum*, 39: 1228–40.

Shiva, V. 2000. *Stolen Harvest: The Hijacking of the Global Food Supply*. Boston, MA: South End Press.

Sommerville, M., Essex, J., and Le Billon, P. 2014. The 'Global Food Crisis' and the Geopolitics of Food Security. *Geopolitics*, 19: 239–65.

Tomich, T.P., Brodt, S., Ferris, H., Galt, R., Horwath, W.R., Kebreab, E.,… and Yang, L. 2011. Agroecology: A Review from a Global-Change Perspective. *Annual Review of Environment and Resources*, 36: 193–222.

Vernon, J. 2007. *Hunger: A Modern History*. Cambridge, MA: Harvard University Press.

Walter, A. 2013. 'Immokalee Wouldn't Exist Without Fast Food': The Relational Spatial Praxis of the Coalition of Immokalee Workers. *ACME: An International E-Journal for Critical Geographies*, 12: 380–406.

Weis, T. 2007. *The Global Food Economy: The Battle for the Future of Farming*. Halifax: Fernwood.

—. 2013. *The Ecological Hoofprint: The Global Burden of Industrial Livestock*. London: Zed.

Whatmore, S., and Thorne, L. 1997. Nourishing Networks: Alternative Geographies of Food, in Goodman, D., and Watts, M., eds. *Globalising Food: Agrarian Questions and Global Restructuring*. London: Routledge: 287–304.

Winter, M. 2003. Embeddedness, the New Food Economy, and Defensive Localism. *Journal of Rural Studies*, 19: 23–32.

45

MAKING BODILY COMMODITIES

Transformations of property, object and labour in the neoliberal bioeconomy

Maria Fannin

This chapter reviews scholarship on bodily commodification in light of new technologies in medicine, science and technology. I specifically highlight debates over the making of human bodies and body parts into new and contested forms of 'property' in the life sciences, a domain increasingly identified as the site of new forms of capitalist accumulation by a number of commentators (Sunder Rajan 2006; Waldby and Mitchell 2006; Cooper 2008; Rabinow 1996; Scheper-Hughes 2001). The role of neoliberalism in shaping the discourse and practice of science has thus increasingly been identified as a key element of the contemporary 'bioeconomy', whether this new economic form is characterized as a set of policy initiatives designed to enhance national or regional competitiveness (Birch 2006) or as a more open-ended 'promissory construct that is meant to induce and facilitate some actions while deterring others' (Goven and Pavone 2015: 1). The literature on bodily commodities, or the transformation of bodily materials into research tools and marketable products, brings together analyses of the epistemological significance of modern science and medicine in the late twentieth and early twenty-first centuries, the bodily technologies of discipline, governmentality, and self-making, and Marxist and feminist theoretical insights into the workings of neoliberal capitalism.

Melinda Cooper (2008) highlights the conjuncture of market-oriented political economic structures and scientific epistemologies that emphasize the flexible, competitive, and promissory nature of biological processes. The drive to harness, cultivate, and enhance these processes for the extraction of surplus value increasingly shapes contemporary scientific practice (Nelkin and Andrews 1998; Franklin 2006; Sunder Rajan 2010). Technologies that enable the separation of parts (cells, tissues, organs) from living bodies have generated concerns over the fragmentation, division, circulation, and reincorporation of bodily materials into new destinations (Dickenson 2007; Everett 2007). The storage of the fragments of bodies and body parts, and the information derived from these fragments, marks a key site of bodily commodification. And yet theories of commodification that rely on examples of industrial production often cannot fully account for the particularity of how bodily materials are handled and exchanged in the bioeconomy. For example, the expansion of new reproductive technologies such as *in vitro* fertilization and gestational surrogacy, as well as the efforts of stem cell scientists to develop regenerative therapies all involve 'a reorganization of the boundaries and elements of the human body, the development of new kinds of "separable, exchangeable and reincorporable body parts"' (Rabinow 1999, quoted in Waldby 2002: 308). Developments in the biosciences, the bioeconomy and biotechnology thus require a reappraisal of the familiar terms of political economy in ways that reflect the innovations of genetics and genomic research, regenerative medicine, synthetic biology, biobanking, and new sites of experimental practice. These technologies invite closer consideration of the key economic concepts, processes and logics of capitalism at work in the bioeconomy, including those of the commodity, capital, property, assets, labour, value, markets, and speculation (Fannin 2011; Birch and Tyfield 2013; Cooper and Waldby 2014; Lezaun and Montgomery 2015; Martin 2015; Vora 2015).

This chapter draws on three cases to consider the reworking of bodily commodification in the neoliberal bioeconomy. The first involves the practices of dispossession that underwrite regimes of intellectual property, beginning with a discussion of the landmark John Moore case and turning to debates over the identification of indigenous populations as targets for genetic research. The second explores the collection, use, storage and exchange of bodily tissues for research and therapy, and the increasing scale and scope of biobanking as a key site for the making of new kinds of bodily commodities. Finally, I consider recent feminist theorizations of the political economies of reproductive, regenerative and experimental labour that complicate conventional critiques of commodification. This work highlights how the body's biological processes are put to work in settings where what is commodified is access to the body and its 'living labour'. The process of commodification, following Marx, is often understood as the simultaneous alienation of the worker from his or her labour, the crystallization of this alienated labour in the form of the commodity, and the role of exchange in the creation of value of the commodity. Translating Marx's insights into the contemporary bioeconomy reveals how the formation of bodily commodities proceeds through somewhat different paths: alienation of the body from its parts may be whole or partial; the bodily commodity may be seen as agential, mutable and transformable as it circulates outside the body from which it originated; and both deferred and active forms of circulation and exchange may come to shape the commodity's value.

Bodily property and primitive accumulation

The California Supreme Court's decision in the case of *John Moore v The Regents of the University of California* is considered a pivotal moment in the history of the use of bodies and body parts in medical research. The Moore case has been extensively debated in the academic literature, primarily regarding the role of intellectual property claims in the bioeconomy (Andrews 1986; Gold 1995, 1996; Harrison 2002; Waldby and Mitchell 2006; Rao, 2007). Briefly, in the course of his treatment for cancer in the 1970s at the University of California Los Angeles Medical Center, Moore's doctors collected biological material (e.g. sperm, blood, tissue samples), ostensibly for this treatment. Unbeknownst to Moore, these materials were being used to develop a cell line (a stable population of *in vitro* cells) for experimental use. Moore sued his doctor's employer, the University of California, for using his bodily tissues without his consent in research that was not directly related to his treatment and for the 'conversion' of his bodily property into a commercially successful product derived from his tissues. Moore's case is cited as one of the first and most important legal cases to test the property claims of research participants and research scientists, in part because Moore's claim to a share of the profits generated from his doctor's research was eventually denied by the California Supreme Court. This Court's majority decision clearly framed protection of the intellectual property claims of the scientists whose labour transformed Moore's cancer cells as integral to the future of the bioscience industry, over and above any claim Moore might make to an interest in these cells. For many commentators, this decision confirmed the legitimacy of property claims that derived from the intellectual labour of scientific innovation over a claim to 'ownership' of one's body parts. Furthermore, the Court's decision clearly articulated the reliance of the bioscience research economy on the ability to detach persons from their bodily tissue. Judges in the majority decision against Moore argued that to grant a property claim to those persons whose tissues were utilized in scientific research would so radically transform the landscape of scientific research as to threaten the viability of an entire sector of the US economy.

Moore's case rested on what commentators argue is a key presumption of modern property regimes. Property claims in the human body rely on a Lockean vision of property in which the body – presumed to be given from nature – is the matter to which human labour is applied. This is the standard for the protection of intellectual property, a model enshrined in legal regimes around the world. Yet this model rests on the assumption of the body as 'as an already available biological resource, as *res nullius*, matter in the public domain' (Cooper and Waldby 2014: 9). The assumption of bodily tissue as a 'thing from nowhere', and thus open to taking because it belongs to no one in particular, bears comparison with other economic practices of primitive accumulation and colonial dispossession. Moore's arguments also indicate that he 'seems to relate already to his body as an object and a potential commodity' (Kang 2007: 140). Moore's articulation of his bodily material as 'his' to dispose of signals how notions of the body as a kind of individual property were already at work, reflecting the general presumption of a liberal theory of the subject in which one's identity is deeply bound to notions of private property.

More recent court cases have involved the successful granting of what appear to be property claims to contributors of biological materials by virtue of compensation for damages for the loss of materials – for example, in the decision of the Court of Appeal for England and Wales in 2009 in *Yearworth and others v North Bristol NHS Trust*. In this case, the court argued that six men were entitled to compensation for the loss of semen that was stored in a hospital prior to their cancer treatment and later destroyed. The effects of this judgment on the common law principle of 'no property in the body' remain uncertain, but legal scholars cite the suggestive statement by the court in *Yearworth* that 'developments in medical science now require a re-analysis of the common law's treatment of and approach to the issue of ownership of part of products of a living body' as evidence that this case marks another significant shift in legal perspectives on claims to property in the body (Quigley 2009, 2014; Hawes 2010; Skene 2012).

Controversies over indigenous biological materials

Contestation over the rights accorded to researchers and those who contribute bodily materials to research also characterizes the controversial development of genetic and genomic research projects specifically targeting indigenous people. Research projects that 'geneticize' indigenous identity can render less legitimate other forms of belonging, especially given the authority invested in scientific ways of knowing. In rare contexts, claims to genetic identity have been deployed to shore up, rather than eliminate, claims to indigeneity, and have been used in the legal sphere to demonstrate historical ties – and access to rights – to a particular territory (Kent 2013). More commonly, the commodification of indigenous bodies takes place through the efforts of pharmaceutical companies and genetic researchers to 'mine' indigenous groups for knowledge or materials that could be used to develop new drugs or therapies. Critics note that rarely are the technologies or products developed from this research made accessible to those who provide bodily materials (Andrews and Nelkin 1998; Sharp 2000).

High-profile projects like the Human Genome Diversity Project and the *National Geographic*-sponsored National Genographic Project aim to identify 'rare' genes in indigenous populations and to collect samples for use in genetic and genomic research (Lock 2001; Nash 2012, 2013). Indigenous activists and critics draw parallels between the search for 'rare', and thus highly valued, genetic profiles in the contemporary post-genomic era and the colonial imaginaries of untapped and exotic natural resources to be brought into profitable circulation (Hayden 2003; Parry 2004). Controversies surrounding the Human Genome Diversity Project and its efforts to collect biological materials from indigenous people focus on how the groups targeted by the project are deemed to be at risk of 'extinction', a presumption that figures the future of indigenous people as already unthinkable (Andrews and Nelkin 1998; Nelkin and Andrews 1998; Sharp 2000). This emphasis in the rhetoric of scientific projects is also consonant with colonial anthropological efforts to collect knowledge about indigenous language and culture before a people's demise – a vision that positions the extinction and disappearance of indigenous peoples at the heart of purported projects for enhancing 'life'. These presuppositions are part of what anthropologist Kim TallBear (2013a, 2013b) calls the de-animating/re-animating dynamic of research on indigenous biological materials.

Criticism of the colonial imaginaries accompanying genetic and genomic research projects have led to new protocols for research that are reshaping notions of the value of indigenous biological materials, particularly those collected prior to the establishment of informed consent as a necessary part of scientific research projects. Permission to access historical collections of material in Australia, for example, now requires that researchers demonstrate ongoing maintenance of ties to the communities or descendants of those who contributed biological materials. These conditions now also shape efforts to develop new biological collections. Emma Kowal (2013) identifies these conditions as new forms of 'ethical biovalue' that constrain as well as permit research on indigenous biological material and thus shape the process of transforming bodily materials into scientific objects.

Contemporary biobanking

The collection, storage and exchange of bodily materials are an important feature of the early development of the sciences of biology, anatomy and pathology. Vast collections of preserved material were amassed in eighteenth- and nineteenth-century medical collections, and frequently used for research, teaching, and public display (Lock 2002). Other biological materials have long been collected as part of public health initiatives to diagnose congenital conditions in newborns, to screen for disease, and to ensure supplies of blood for transfusion (Titmuss 1971). In this sense, 'biobanking' is nothing new. What is novel about contemporary biobanking initiatives are the new uses to which biobanked materials may be directed, and the technological developments that shape contemporary practices of collection, storage and exchange. The emergence of cryopreservation to preserve living cells, tissues and organs in a stage of 'latency' (Radin 2013), tissue culture techniques to grow living cells outside the body (Landecker 2007), and, more recently, somatic cell nuclear transfer and other techniques to create stem cell lines has made possible the maintenance and transformation of living tissues under laboratory conditions. Biobanking initiatives have intensified and multiplied, particularly in the wake of the mapping of the human genome and public and private investment in genetic and genomic research. These initiatives include public health efforts to combine data collected in longitudinal studies of health and lifestyle with genetic information gleaned from bodily materials, and the substantial growth in forensic DNA collections for use in law enforcement (Hindmarsh and Prainsack 2010)

In Bronwyn Parry's (2008) analysis of the role of biobanks in processes that she calls, following Joanna Radin, 'incomplete commodification', Parry assesses the multiple ways in which out-and-out markets in bodily materials may be illegal, but other marketization, bartering, and exchanges of tissue occur within and beyond the scientific community. Compensation fees, exchanging or bartering samples to enhance reputation or prestige in the form of co-authorship on academic papers, and receiving options on intellectual property rights in exchange for discounted purchase of samples: all are examples that don't fit the model of an outright market in tissues, but involve the exchange of other kinds of 'capital' (see also Parry 2006; Parry and Gere 2006).

Indeed, bodily commodities may also be informationalized as medical records, but, at the same time, never completely 'decontextualised, dissociated and detached from their human subjects' as Beth Greenhough notes in her analysis of the Icelandic government's decision to make the extensive medical, genetic and genealogical records of its population available to a private company for genetic research (Callon 1999, quoted in Greenhough 2006: 445). In this context, bodily experiences of health and illness are commodified as information through the production and circulation of medical records and datasets. Greenhough documents how the notion of alienation of one's self from one's body parts only partially explains these new forms of commodification made possible by academic–industry partnerships, venture capital investments and technological innovation. Her analysis focuses on new concatenations of human and non-human actors, objects, institutions, regulatory frameworks and markets that populate the landscape of bioinformatics research. The boundaries drawn between proper and improper forms of 'commodification' are at issue: the Icelandic government's fee and promised share of profits from future research were to be directed towards public health initiatives, while the presumption that individuals might opt out, in order to be paid to opt in, troubled government ministers. As Greenhough (2006) writes, state commodification of a population-level 'body' was deemed more acceptable than an individual's efforts to engage in frank transactions around access to one's bodily vitality.

Research to date on biobanking demonstrates the complexity of making biological materials into commodities: biological materials may be transformed into commodities by becoming data, and the data generated by donors and its access the 'object' of exchange. Commodification may not be whole, but partial, insofar as ensuring the contributor remains linked to, rather than detached from, the biological material may actually enhance its value. In the post-genomic era, collections of bodily materials and associated health and lifestyle data have become more like capital resources or assets for hospitals, universities, governments, and forms of public–private partnership between state, charitably funded and commercial entities (Mitchell and Waldby 2010; Cooper and Waldby 2014; Lezaun and Montgomery 2015; Birch forthcoming). Commercial biobanking enterprises offering personal tissue storage directly target individuals to promote banking services for cord blood (Annas 1999; Brown and Kraft 2006; Martin *et al.* 2008; Brown *et al.* 2011; Hodges 2013), eggs (Martin 2010; Waldby 2014), and menstrual blood (Fannin 2013). Developments in biobanking extend the arguments for ensuring the 'wise use' of materials that might now be viewed as potentially 'wasted', if not retained for research use rather than discarded (Hoeyer 2008; Kent 2008; Pfeffer 2009; Tupasela 2011). These transformations have engendered different strategies for enrolling populations into local, regional and national biobanking projects or for repurposing older collections, with implications for the forms of genetic or biological citizenship available to biobank participants (Mitchell 2012).

Clinical labour: commodification of the body's 'living labour'

Recent feminist efforts to think beyond liberal concerns with intellectual property and the ownership of the body remind us that the most trenchant insight into the processes of commodification is that concerned with the commodification of labour. An extensive literature exists on the immaterial dynamics of speculation and 'hype' in the 'knowledge economy' of the biosciences (Martin *et al.* 2008; Kent 2012; Morrison 2012; Haase *et al.* 2015; Petersen and Krisjansen 2015). Accounts of 'value adding' activity in the bioeconomy tend to emphasize the work of scientists accorded the protection of intellectual property regimes by virtue of their application of work and skill to transform biological materials into research tools (Zucker and Darby 1996; Zeller 2007; Birch and Tyfield 2013). However, accounts of innovation in the bioeconomy that focus solely on intellectual or knowledge labour can obscure the role of the embodied labour of research participants, tissue donors, and others whose bodily contributions are 'peripheral in terms of rights, but central in terms of the… value produced' (Foti 2004, quoted in Waldby and Cooper 2008). This form of unrecognized embodied participation in the bioeconomy is what Melinda Cooper and Catherine Waldby term 'clinical labour' (Cooper and Waldby 2014). Clinical labour, in their account, is the characteristic form of labour performed by egg and sperm donors, surrogates, and clinical trial participants to provide access to the *in vivo* or *in vitro* vitality of their living bodies. These forms of labour bear much in common with other conceptualizations of reproductive labour, including the unpaid gendered labour carried out in the home and the transnational caring labour of overseas nannies and domestic workers (Waldby and Cooper 2010).

At the same time, the clinical labour of the surrogate or egg donor invites new relationships to the self and to the body that are distinctive, and signal clinical labour as consonant with the forms of fragmented and flexible labour that characterize neoliberalism more generally. In their discussion of the Indian surrogacy market, Cooper and Waldby (2014: 85) note how women contracted to gestate the genetic offspring of other couples are encouraged to consider their uterus as a kind of 'transactable space' in which 'the surrogacy contract requires both parties to agree that the surrogates' parturient biology can be both (semi)-detached and instrumentalized, in order to be rendered as an exchangeable, quantifiable entity' (see also DasGupta and Dasgupta 2014). Cooper and Waldby's analysis of this phenomenon, and the legal categories that are installed in the surrogacy contract, suggests that surrogacy is not simply a commodification of the body's parts as detached, exchangeable things. Rather, they suggest provocatively that the surrogate body's more closely parallels an asset from which rent may be extracted in the form of a 'lease of parturient conditions', rather than a circulating commodity per se. On the one hand, it is clear that the example of surrogacy bears many of the hallmarks of 'commodification' if this process describes the ways in which the social relations of production are made invisible in the making of a thing (in this case, a child). On the other hand, surrogacy is an example of how bringing the embodied labour of reproduction into the analytical frame reveals the limits of prevailing theories of commodification: the notion of commodities as detachable from the bodies that generate them cannot be applied to embodied practices such as surrogacy.

In addition to surrogacy, other forms of clinical labour, namely egg vending and participation in clinical trials, are all embodied practices that involve compliance with complex medical regimes and a willingness to self-monitor. These practices, like surrogacy, compel participants to become 'entrepreneurs of the self' (Cooper and Waldby 2014; see also Tober 2001; Nahman 2008; Roberts and Throsby 2008; Ikemoto 2009; Widdows 2009). Organ vending, egg vending and the participation in clinical trials 'all… require a direct, often highly experimental, involvement of the body's biology in the creation of surplus value' (Waldby and Cooper 2008: 65; see also Sunder Rajan 2005). Analyses of practices of organ vending also demonstrate that these extreme forms of bodily indebtedness are not exceptions to capitalist accumulation strategies, but rather are necessary to it, and stratify populations according to their 'bioavailability', or the accessibility of their biological vitality to extractive processes (Cohen 2003).

Like other domains of the global economy, outsourcing labour beyond the domains of wealthy nations has reduced clinical labour costs for pharmaceutical companies and other commercial entities (Abadie 2010). The context of this shift in the USA for clinical trials is two-fold: the reduced use of prison populations for drug trials, and the increasing use of drugs and other treatments across the population mean that the search for 'treatment naive' trial subjects offshores the risk of experimentation to more vulnerable populations. Yet little is known about the extent of offshored drug trials. There is no comprehensive database and no global structure or legal body that regulates the conduct of clinical trials. Offshoring is carried out in an effort to reduce costs of trial research and to lessen the ethical constraints related to national complexity in drug, device, or therapy regulation. It has also seen the growth of new enterprises in the form of private research service providers who are part of the geography of offshored clinical trials for drugs, regenerative medicine therapies and medical devices (Petryna 2009; Sunder Rajan 2010). From a regulatory perspective, the most valuable trial participants populations are those most economically and socially vulnerable – that is, those who are not receiving medical treatment or have little history of treatment.

Clinical labour as a concept shifts attention from commodified objects in the bioeconomy, to that of bodily performance and the subjective dimensions of participation in the commercial practices of surrogacy, egg vending, and clinical trial participation. The relationship of one's body to the production of 'commodities' is crucial here: while the industrial model of commodity production is premised on a clear division, and, indeed, alienation of the worker from that which is produced by the worker's labour over a definable time, the labour described by Cooper and Waldby (2014) as clinical labour bears closer resemblance to the forms of 'immaterial labour' that characterize contemporary patterns of work in the digital or cultural economy (Lazzarato 1996; Fumagalli 2011; Cooper 2012; Birch and Tyfield 2013). The performance of immaterial labour bears no necessary relationship to formal working hours or to patterns of spatial differentiation between work and home, and it is characterized by its networked, intermittent, precarious and social nature. Similarly, the commodity model of production is less easily applied to the domain of reproductive labour, partly because of the social differences between the production of an object and the creation of a child, which is the goal of the 'reproductive mode of production' in the IVF industry (Thompson 2005).

The bodily materials described by Cooper and Waldby as central to the production of value in the bioeconomy may be commodified insofar as some are transformed into exchangeable units (cell lines, extracted eggs, embryos, and so on). But the central insight of clinical labour is to suggest how critical attention might more fruitfully be drawn away from the focus on property in the body, and the critique of the 'commodification' and 'marketization' of bodily parts – as well as from the imaginary of reproductive labour indebted to Fordism – and towards the role of experimentation, performance, and the engendering of bodily capacities in the bioeconomy.

Conclusion

Public investment in bioscience and health research continues to be seen as an important social priority for national, regional and local economies. Yet the privatization of knowledge through intellectual property regimes and the making of bodily materials into new kinds of objects, tools and products has tended not to involve the massive expansion of patient or consumer benefit, especially given the pressures to diminish state support for health care and expand the market-orientation of health care institutions. This chapter discussed how the social relations and material cultures of the biosciences and medicine simultaneously shape and are shaped by new forms of bodily commodification.

Analyses of the political economy of the life sciences require a nuanced conceptual vocabulary adequate to the complex transformations of property, objects and labour at work in the bioeconomy. Viewing commodification as the process by which bodies and parts of bodies move from the realm of the 'sacred' gift to the 'profane' commodity is rhetorically powerful, but analytically limited. These claims obscure the more nuanced ways in which separation, circulation and exchange of bodies and body parts take on more or less of the character of market transaction, as the examples discussed above illustrate. They also obscure how legal regimes and contractual arrangements call certain forms of subjectivity into being and thus enable and prefigure forms of commodification before any explicit legislative or regulatory framework exists to delineate what becomes a commodity and what does not. The transformation of a bodily material into a scientific object, as Warwick Anderson (2013) suggests, reconfigures relations and generates new subjects (see Strathern 1992; Kowal 2013; Fannin and Kent 2015). Indeed, shifting focus from the creation of new kinds of bodily commodities to unrecognized forms of bodily labour may further open up the development of new alliances and alternatives to neoliberalism.

References

Abadie, R. 2010. *The Professional Guinea Pig: Big Pharma and the Risky World of Human Subjects*. Durham, NC: Duke University Press.

Anderson, W. 2013. Objectivity and its Discontents. *Social Studies of Science*, 43: 557–76.

Andrews, L. 1986. My Body, My Property. *Hastings Center Report*, 16: 28–38.

Andrews, L., and Nelkin, D. 1998. Whose Body is it Anyway? Disputes Over Body Tissues in a Biotechnology Age. *The Lancet*, 351: 53–7.

Annas, G.J. 1999. Waste and Longing: The Legal Status of Placental-Blood Banking. *New England Journal of Medicine*, 340: 1521–4.

Birch, K. 2006. The Neoliberal Underpinnings of the Bioeconomy: The Ideological Discourses and Practices of Economic Competitiveness. *Genomics, Society and Policy*, 2: 1–15.

—. Forthcoming. Political-Economic Platforms and *Rentiership* in the Bio-Economy. *Science, Technology and Human Values*.

Birch, K., and Tyfield, D. 2013. Theorizing the Bioeconomy: Biovalue, Biocapital, Bioeconomics or… What? *Science, Technology and Human Values*, 38: 299–327.

Brown, N., and Kraft, A. 2006. Blood Ties: Banking the Stem Cell Promise. *Technology Analysis and Strategic Management*, 18: 313–27.

Brown, N., Machin, L.L., and McLeod, D. 2011. Immunitary Bioeconomy: The Economization of Life in the International Cord Blood Market. *Social Science & Medicine*, 72: 1115–22.

Callon, M. 1999. Actor-Network Theory: The Market Test, in Hassard, J.L.J., ed. *Actor Network Theory and After*. Oxford: Blackwell: 181–95.

Cohen, L. 2003. Where it Hurts: Indian Material for an Ethics of Organ Transplantation. *Zygon*, 38: 663–88.

Cooper, M. 2008. *Life as Surplus: Biotechnology and Capitalism in the Neoliberal Era*. Seattle and London: University of Washington Press.

—. 2012. The Pharmacology of Distributed Experiment: User-Generated Drug Innovation. *Body & Society*, 18: 18–43.

Cooper, M. and Waldby, C. 2014. *Clinical Labour*. Durham, NC: Duke University Press.

DasGupta, S., and Dasgupta, S.D. ed. 2014. *Globalization and Transnational Surrogacy in India: Outsourcing Life*. Lanham: Lexington.

Dickenson, D. 2007. *Property in the Body: Feminist Perspectives*. Cambridge and New York: Cambridge University Press.

Everett, M. 2007. The 'I' in the Gene: Divided Property, Fragmented Personhood and the Making of a Genetic Privacy Law. *American Ethnologist*, 34: 375–86.

Fannin, M. 2011. Personal Stem Cell Banking and the Problem with Property. *Social & Cultural Geography*, 12: 339–56.

—. 2013. The Hoarding Economy of Endometrial Stem Cell Storage. *Body & Society*, 19: 32–60.

Fannin, M., and Kent, J. 2015. Origin Stories from a Regional Placenta Tissue Collection. *New Genetics and Society*, 34: 25–51.

Foti, A. 2004. Precarity and N/European Identity. Interview by Merijn Oudenampsen and Gavin Sullivan. *Greenpepper Magazine*. Retrieved from http://www.black-international-cinema.com/BIC05/XX. BIC2005/HTML/articles/article_08.htm

Franklin, S. 2006. Embryonic Economies: The Double Reproductive Value of Stem Cells. *Biosocieties*, 1: 71–90.

Fumagalli, A. 2011. Twenty Theses on Contemporary Capitalism. *Angelaki*, 16: 7–17.

Gold, E.R. 1995. Owning Our Bodies: An Examination of Property Law and Biotechnology. *San Diego Law Review*, 32: 1167–247.

—. 1996. *Body Parts: Property Rights and the Ownership of Human Biological Materials*. Washington, DC: Georgetown University Press.

Goven, J., and Pavone, V. 2015. The Bioeconomy as Political Project: A Polanyian Analysis. *Science, Technology and Human Values*, 40: 302–37.

Greenhough, B. 2006. Decontextualised? Dissociated? Detached? Mapping the Networks of Bioinformatics Exchange. *Environment and Planning A*, 38: 445–63.

Haase, R., Michie, M., and Skinner, D. 2015. Flexible Positions, Managed Hopes: The Promissory Bioeconomy of a Whole Genome Sequencing Cancer Study. *Social Science & Medicine*, 130: 146–53.

Harrison, C. 2002. Neither Moore nor the Market: Alternative Models for Compensating Contributors of Human Tissue. *American Journal of Law and Medicine*, 28: 77–105.

Hawes, C. 2010. Property Interests in Body Parts: Yearworth v North Bristol NHS Trust. *The Modern Law Review*, 73: 119–40.

Hayden, C. 2003. *When Nature Goes Public: The Making and Unmaking of Bioprospecting in Mexico*. Princeton, NJ: Princeton University Press.

Hindmarsh, R., and Prainsack, B. eds. 2010. *Genetic Suspects: Global Governance of Forensic DNA Profiling and Databasing*. Cambridge: Cambridge University Press.

Hodges, S. 2013. Umbilical Cord Blood Banking and its Interruptions: Notes from Chennai, India. *Economy and Society*, 42: 651–70.

Hoeyer, K. 2008. The Ethics of Research Biobanking: A Critical Review of the Literature. *Biotechnology and Genetic Engineering Reviews*, 25: 429–52.

Ikemoto, L.C. 2009. Eggs as Capital: Human Egg Procurement in the Fertility Industry and the Stem Cell Research Enterprise. *Signs: Journal of Women in Culture and Society*, 34: 763–81.

Kang, H.Y. 2007. Identifying John Moore: Narratives of Persona in Patent Law Relating to Inventions of Human Origin, in Glasner, P., Atkinson, P., and Greenslade, H., eds. *New Genetics, New Social Formations*. London and New York: Routledge: 138–54.

Kent, J. 2008. The Fetal Tissue Economy: From the Abortion Clinic to the Stem Cell Laboratory. *Social Science & Medicine*, 67: 1747–56.

—. 2012. *Regenerating Bodies: Tissue and Cell Therapies in the Twenty-First Century*. New York: Routledge.

Kent, M. 2013. The Importance of Being Uros: Indigenous Identity Politics in the Genomic Age. *Social Studies of Science*, 43: 534–56.

Kowal, E. 2013. Orphan DNA: Indigenous Samples, Ethical Biovalue and Postcolonial Science. *Social Studies of Science*, 43: 577–97.

Landecker, H. 2007. *Culturing Life: How Cells Became Technologies*. Cambridge, MA: Harvard University Press.

Lazzarato, M. 1996. Immaterial Labour, in Virno, P., and Hardt, M., eds. *Radical Thought in Italy: A Potential Politics*. Minneapolis: University of Minnesota Press: 133–50.

Lezaun, J., and Montgomery, C.M. 2015. The Pharmaceutical Commons: Sharing and Exclusion in Global Health Drug Development. *Science, Technology and Human Values*, 40: 3–29.

Lock, M. 2001. The Alienation of Body Tissue and the Biopolitics of Immortalised Cell Lines. *Body & Society*, 7: 63–91.

—. 2002. Human Body Parts as Therapeutic Tools: Contradictory Discourses and Transformed Subjectivities. *Qualitative Health Research*, 12: 1406–18.

Martin, L.J. 2010. Anticipating Infertility: Egg Freezing, Genetic Preservation and Risk. *Gender & Society*, 24: 526–45.

Martin, P. 2015. Commercialising Neurofutures: Promissory Economies, Value Creation and the Making of a New Industry. *BioSocieties*, doi:10.1057/biosoc.2014.40

Martin, P., Brown, N., and Turner, A. 2008. Capitalizing Hope: The Commercial Development of Umbilical Cord Blood Banking. *New Genetics and Society*, 27: 127–43.

Mitchell, R. 2012. US Biobanking Strategies and Biomedical Immaterial Labor. *BioSocieties*, 7: 224–44.

Mitchell, R., and Waldby, C. 2010. National Biobanks: Clinical Labour, Risk Production and the Creation of Biovalue. *Science, Technology and Human Values*, 35: 330–55.

Morrison, M. 2012. Promissory Futures and Possible Pasts: The Dynamics of Contemporary Expectations in Regenerative Medicine. *BioSocieties*, 7: 3–22.

Nahman, M. 2008. Nodes of Desire: Romanian Egg Sellers, 'Dignity' and Feminist Alliances in Transnational Ova Exchanges. *European Journal of Women's Studies*, 15: 65–82.

Nash, C. 2012. Genetics, Race, and Relatedness: Human Mobility and Human Diversity in the Genographic Project. *Annals of the Association of American Geographers*, 102: 667–84.

—. 2013. Genome Geographies: Mapping National Ancestry and Diversity in Human Population Genetics. *Transactions of the Institute of British Geographers*, 38: 193–206.

Nelkin, D., and Andrews, L. 1998. *Homo Economicus*: Commercialization of Body Tissue in the Age of Biotechnology. *Hastings Center Report*, 28: 30–9.

Parry, B. 2004. *Trading the Genome: Investigating the Commodification of Bio-Information*. New York: Columbia University Press.

—. 2006. New Spaces of Biological Commodification: The Dynamics of Trade in Genetic Resources and 'Bioinformation'. *Interdisciplinary Science Reviews*, 31: 19–31.

—. 2008. Entangled Exchange: Reconceptualising the Characterization and Practice of Bodily Commodification. *Geoforum*, 39: 1133–44.

Parry, B., and Gere, C. 2006. Contested Bodies: Property Models and the Commodification of Human Biological Artefacts. *Science as Culture*, 15: 139–58.

Petryna, A. 2009. *When Experiments Travel*. New Haven, CT: Princeton University Press.

Petersen, A., and Krisjansen, I. 2015. Assembling 'The Bioeconomy': Exploiting the Power of the Promissory Life Sciences. *Journal of Sociology*, 51: 28–46.

Pfeffer, N. 2009. How Work Reconfigures an 'Unwanted' Pregnancy into 'The Right Tool for the Job' in Stem Cell Research. *Sociology of Health & Illness*, 31: 98–111.

Quigley, M. 2009. Property: The Future of Human Tissue? *Medical Law Review*, 17: 457–66.

—. 2014. Propertization and Commercialization: On Controlling the Uses of Human Biomaterials. *The Modern Law Review*, 77: 677–702.

Rabinow, P. 1996. *Essays on the Anthropology of Reason*. Princeton, NJ: Princeton University Press.

—. 1999. *French DNA: Trouble in Purgatory*. Chicago and London: Chicago University Press.

Radin, J. 2013. Latent Life: Concepts and Practices of Human Tissue Preservation in the International Biological Program. *Social Studies of Science*, 43: 484–508.

Rao, R. 2007. Genes and Spleens: Property, Contract, Privacy Right in the Human Body? *Journal of Law, Medicine and Ethics*, 35: 371–82.

Roberts, C., and Throsby, K. 2008. Paid to Share: IVF Patients, Eggs, and Stem Cell Research. *Social Science and Medicine*, 66: 159–69.

Scheper-Hughes, N. 2001. Bodies for Sale – Whole or in Parts. *Body & Society*, 7: 1–8.

Sharp, L.A. 2000. The Commodification of the Body and its Parts. *Annual Review of Anthropology*, 29: 287–328.

Skene, L. 2012. Proprietary Interests in Human Bodily Material: Yearworth, Recent Australian Cases on Stored Semen and Their Implications. *Medical Law Review*, 20: 227–45.

Strathern, M. 1992. *Reproducing the Future: Anthropology, Kinship and the New Reproductive Technologies*. Manchester: Manchester University Press.

Sunder Rajan, K. 2005. Subjects of Speculation: Emergent Life Sciences and Market Logics in the United States and India. *American Anthropologist*, 107: 19–30.

—. 2006. *Biocapital: The Constitution of Postgenomic Life*. Durham, NC: Duke University Press.

—. 2010. The Experimental Machinery of Global Clinical Trials: Case Studies from India, in Ong, A., and Chen, N.N., eds. *Asian Biotech: Ethics and Communities of Fate*. Durham, NC: Duke University Press: 55–80.

TallBear, K. 2013a. Genomic Articulations of Indigeneity. *Social Studies of Science*, 43: 509–13.

—. 2013b. *Native American DNA*. Minneapolis: Minnesota University Press.

Thompson, C. 2005. *Making Parents: The Ontological Choreography of Reproductive Technologies*. Cambridge, MA: MIT Press.

Titmuss, R. 1971. *The Gift Relationship: From Human Blood to Social Policy*. New York: Pantheon.

Tober, D.M. 2001. Semen as Gift, Semen as Goods: Reproductive Workers and the Market in Altruism. *Body & Society*, 7: 137–60.

Tupasela, A. 2011. From Gift to Waste: Changing Policies in Biobanking Practices. *Science and Public Policy*, 38: 510–20.

Vora, K. 2015. *Life Support: Biocapital and the New History of Outsourced Labor*. Minneapolis: University of Minnesota Press.

Waldby, C. 2002. Stem Cells, Tissue Cultures and the Production of Biovalue. *Health: An Interdisciplinary Journal for the Social Study of Health*, 6: 305–23.

—. 2014. 'Banking Time': Egg Freezing and the Negotiation of Future Fertility. *Culture, Health & Sexuality*, 17: 470–82.

Waldby, C., and Cooper, M. 2008. The Biopolitics of Reproduction: Post-Fordist Biotechnology and Women's Clinical Labour. *Australian Feminist Studies*, 23: 57–73.

—. 2010. From Reproductive Work to Regenerative Labour. *Feminist Theory*, 11: 3–22.

Waldby, C., and Mitchell, R. 2006. *Tissue Economies: Blood, Organs, and Cell Lines in Late Capitalism*. Durham, NC: Duke University Press.

Widdows, H. 2009. Border Disputes Across Bodies: Exploitation in Trafficking for Prostitution and Egg Sale for Stem Cell Research. *International Journal of Feminist Approaches to Bioethics*, 2: 5–24.

Zeller, C. 2007. From the Gene to the Globe: Extracting Rents Based on Intellectual Property Monopolies. *Review of International Political Economy*, 15: 86–115.

Zucker L.G., and Darby, M.R. 1996. Star Scientists and Institutional Transformation: Patterns of Invention and Innovation in the Formation of the Biotechnology Industry. *Proceedings of the National Academy of Science USA*, 93: 12709–16.

46

RETHINKING THE EXTRACTIVE/ PRODUCTIVE BINARY UNDER NEOLIBERALISM

Sonja Killoran-McKibbin and Anna Zalik

Increased geopolitical manoeuvring for resource access and a move into commodities over finance as an outlet for surplus capital has attracted growing public and scholarly attention to the global reach of extractive industries. The organization of extraction transnationally demonstrates the persistence of divisions between global North and South as well as rapid shifts in the extractive economies associated with both financialization and the rise of the BRICS. The extensification and intensification of extraction has increasingly provoked localized conflicts at sites of industrial activity. These changes call for a renewed examination of extractive processes, as they are constituted under neoliberal capitalism.

This chapter begins with an examination of the recent history of extractive economies under neoliberalism to consider the difference between productive and extractive industrial activities. From there, we move on to an examination of new modes of extractivism and their relation to demands for resource sovereignty. Here we draw examples from Latin America, and elsewhere, to explore whether Gudynas' (2010a) notion of 'progressive extractivism' breaks from historic patterns of resource exploitation and processes of neoliberalization. Upon this basis, we advance a reconsideration of the relationship between production and extraction as it has shifted under neoliberalism.

We explore two mutually constituted processes which manifest how the global division of nature is persistent in the organization of political economies viewed as relatively 'productivist' and relatively 'extractivist': (1) the relationship between the organization of productive processes (including labour/nature) in creating more or less amenable extractive environments via more or less sovereigntist regulatory and fiscal structures; and, conversely, (2) the extent to which typically productive enterprises, ranging from agriculture to textiles, take on an extractive character under neoliberalism. On this base, we argue for greater attention to a specifically *extractive* form of neoliberalism and for a broader understanding of extraction as it relates to human labour and the environment as co-constituted categories. Indeed, the extractive frontier, in many ways, embodies practices of neoliberalization: it is a powerful force of commodification of the natural environment and, in its enclosure of territory and association with financialization, exemplifies characteristics of what some understand as contemporary 'accumulation by dispossession' (Harvey 2003).

History and debates on extractive industries

Before presenting our argument about the role of *extraction* in neoliberalism, it is necessary to define the term and explain its value as an analytical framework. The process of extracting from non-human nature and exporting resources to other economies was central to colonization (Frank 1969; Girvan 1978; Amin 1977; Clark and Foster 2009) and has been viewed as the principal barrier faced by state economies of the global South seeking to overcome poverty through national development processes (Prebisch 1950; Sunkel and Paz 1970). The problem of primary resource export has been theorized in numerous ways: from dependency scholars' view of the interaction between core and periphery economies (Baran 1968; Frank 1969), to Latin American structuralist interpretations of the need to develop internal markets (Prebisch 1950; Furtado 1976). Additionally, from within institutional theory and conventional economics, resource curse theorizing suggests that an abundance of natural resources impede national development by promoting rent-seeking behaviour (Auty 1993; Karl 1997).

While these approaches vary widely, they share a state-centred focus and an analysis directed at the domestic economy of the producing country, which naturalize international resource exports. By adopting extraction as an analytical framework, we attempt to move beyond the state to draw attention to the actors that demand resources and the historical political economy and global flows of which they are a part. While the state is central to extractive governance, the common-alities across nations suggest that extraction provokes a shared set of experiences that are not lim-ited to national conditions but to the transnational dimensions of extraction (Campbell 2003). Similarly, a state-centred focus can overshadow local-scale considerations or the materialities of particular resources. An extractive lens shifts attention away from the actions and inactions of particular states towards a multi-scalar analysis that not only considers extractive flows of labour and resources from the global South towards the global North, but also integrates local experiences.

We use 'extractive' here to refer to the over-exploitation of nature (including both human labour and non-human resources) to such an extent that it undermines its conditions of exis-tence over time, in the manner of O'Connor's (1988) 'second contradiction of capitalism'. Such over-exploitation has prompted ecological crises due to the separation of human resource use from the basis of production, or what has been termed the metabolic rift (Marx 1993; Foster 1999; Burkett 1999). Scholars have highlighted that this dynamic extends beyond urban–rural divisions to include spatially distant colonial resource frontiers such as sugar plantations and silver mining in the Americas (Moore 2000, 2003). Various schools of thought point to how industry's ability to externalize ecological costs facilitates intensified extraction while shaping long-term environmental problems, including climate change. For instance, the new institu-tional economics (Coase 1937, 1998) emphasis on inter-firm transactions has contributed to theorizing how firms externalize ecological costs onto the commons (Powell and Di Maggio 2012). This perspective has been employed as the basis for certain forms of neoliberal environ-mentalism. That said, like theories of the second contradiction of capitalism and the metabolic rift (O'Connor 1988; Foster 2002), as well as constructivist analysis of the twentieth-century emergence of the 'economy' as a site for intervention (Escobar 1995; Mitchell 1998) it reveals how extractive activities are 'enclaved' both spatially and in terms of formal policy.

Within Marxist theory, however, approaches that centre on the extraction of natural resources have been critiqued for their attention to trade relations and spatial transfers over labour exploitation. Brenner accused dependency and world systems theories of insufficient attention to labour (Brenner 1977), which earned a thorough critique by Blaut (1994) on the grounds of its eurocentrism. Canadian staples theory, itself informed by dependency analysis and spatial approaches to imperialism, has also endured critique as 'commodity fetishism' due to its attention to frontier extraction over labour exploitation (McNally 1981). In recognition of these views, yet wishing to avoid anthropocentrism and eurocentrism, we suggest that extraction can include certain processes by which labour power is extracted from workers. The epoch of neo-liberal globalization has allowed for the increased extraction of labour power from countries of the global South, through the establishment of export processing zones and the promotion of hyper-exploitative working conditions.

Under neoliberalism, extractive industries have taken on changing characteristics, making them central to global trade dynamics in a form reminiscent of classical imperialism (see Moore 2003 on the latter). With the depletion of rich mineral veins and lower carbon fossil fuels, indus-try has increasingly employed strip mining. Energy intensive and territorially extensive, these processes produce huge amounts of waste and create a large spatial footprint (Bridge 2004). As opposed to the height of coal production, which in its relatively low organic composition of capital facilitated liberal democracy by boosting worker's power vis-à-vis industry (Mitchell 2011), contemporary extractive processes have become more technologically and 'nature' intensive. This trend has been deepened by the high commodity prices of the past decade and the role of resources in speculation and financialization. Alongside this expansion, we have seen a changing transnational character of extraction, with the strategic positioning of extractive capital in countries, like Canada, home to advantageous regulatory frameworks (Deneault and Sacher 2012). Following the economic concept of the 'race to the bottom', corporate strategy under financialization seeks to shape, and subsequently invest in, low-cost environments and to reduce firm risk in extractive settings (Emel and Huber 2008).

Additionally, as critical scholars have pointed out, the maintenance of reduced availability in global markets has been employed to maintain a price floor and cushion otherwise falling profit rates (Mitchell 2002; Bina 2006; Labban 2008; Bridge and Le Billon 2012). In the oil sector for instance, corporate cartel-like arrangements like the Achnacarry Agreement were established to ensure market scarcity. According to critical analyses, the creation of OPEC asserted global South resource sovereignty (Coronil 1997; Mommer 2002), increasing its members' ability to influence global prices and thus secure higher rents. Ultimately, however, high prices also ben-efit the transnational corporations that partnered with parastatal oil companies (Nitzan and Bichler 1995). The recent global drop in oil and gas prices, as the USA moves to hydrocarbon energy independence through shale development, will alter the strategic terrain of oil and gas production and perhaps other extracted commodities.

An extractive form of neoliberalism

We join a range of critical scholars of the extractive industries who are sceptical of the way resource curse theory reifies state institutions and de-emphasizes the role of the corporate form and capitalist economic relations in shaping these dynamics, as well as the latent racism implicit in much of the discourse of corruption and rent-seeking (Watts 2004). However, we acknowl-edge that certain attributes signalled by resource curse theorizing may be traced empirically: for instance, the greater weight of foreign trade over national productive sectors weakens the need for national governments to pursue popular legitimacy for tax collection. Elite power arises from connections to export-driven commodity sectors, which diminishes the role of popular consent in establishing hegemony and paves the way for violations of human and environmental rights to secure resource extraction. Likewise, under global financialization, there is a risk of so-called 'Dutch Disease', where the national currency is inflated in value due to high-priced mineral exports, which may erode the international competitiveness of other sectors of the national economy, including those that are large employers.

Extractive industries are frequently export-oriented activities that induce material degradation to the surrounding ecology. The extent to which these activities are labour or capital intensive alters historically with technological change, and will vary depending on the materiality of specific resources. We draw on Bunker's (1984) vision of modes of extraction which held that extractive economies are distinctive from productive economies and possess unique characteristics, both spatially and in terms of intensity. While he insisted on the mutual interdependence of extractive and productive systems, he contested dominant theories of development which, in his view, paid insufficient attention to the unique nature of extraction and its impact on development. Although production and extraction are necessarily related, Bunker pointed to the manner in which these processes had become geographically divorced, leaving one part of the globe in the realm of extraction while the other concentrated on production. Indeed, over time, global changes in demand for particular commodities would lead to an alteration in the organization of production. Methodologically, however, Bunker sought to avoid ahistorical reification of the relations surrounding these sites, arguing that each local mode of production and extraction had to be treated as discrete (ibid.). As such, his later work with Paul Ciccantell, *Globalization and the Race for Resources*, offers a more relational account centring on the productive dimensions associated with particular natural resources and their transport and alteration over time. Therein extractive economies 'become more dispersed, while productive economies become more agglomerated' (Bunker and Ciccantell 2005: 12). Crucial here is the various ways this work informs an approach to space and time that is de-reified and historicized.

Despite these observations and largely due to the changing character of the global political economy under neoliberalism, the nature of extraction and production have altered and the interdependences between these processes warrant specific attention. We posit some adaptations to Bunker's view of the distinctions to productive and extractive economies. In doing so, we consider how, even with extractive industries, economies can be relatively extractivist or productivist based on their articulations with the global economy, the national consciousness, and the treatment of labour within the regime. Over the past half-century what might be understood as division between production and extraction has shifted: extraction involves specific forms of production of nature, and formerly productive industries have taken on more and more of an extractive character.

While the distinction Marxist critics make between productive and extractive systems is ostensibly based on the role of labour power, an over-emphasis on extraction as wholly separate from productive processes runs the risk of overlooking the labour embedded within the process of extraction, while also entrenching a distinction between the role of humans as actors in non-human nature. To address these deficits, we stress the importance of theorizing the production of nature. Smith (2007) highlights the manner in which resources are similarly produced as commodities for trade, thereby muddying the lines between extractive and productive processes. He underscores that capitalist nature 'has always been commodified' as use-values are taken from one site and moved to another through a process, changing the land and labourers while connecting disparate places through transport and trade (25). As Coronil (1997) argues, production refers to both the material and cultural processes surrounding the creation of commodities and the social agents involved. Upon this basis, commodities stemming from extractive processes are, indeed, produced, but this production is simultaneously material, social and politico-legal in its essence. What are understood as 'extractive' commodities, he describes as 'rent-capturing' or 'nature-intensive' (Coronil 2000) to reflect their composition as highly dependent upon the exploitation of non-human natures. This sector's implications for national and regional economic growth are shaped by its ownership structure (Zalik 2008a), as we discuss further below.

The relations between the extraction of non-human natures and their commodification, transport and marketization over time and space present significant challenges for extractive-dependent economies. Varying conceptualizations seek to address the role extraction plays in the global division of nature and highlight its distinguishing features from productive processes. However, herein we aim to highlight the *interconnection* of productive and extractive processes and that neoliberal production relies on extractive labour relations while resource extraction equally relies upon specific relations of production. Given the significant role of resource extraction and spatial transport in global imperialism and formal colonialism, we consider its theorization as central to conceptualizing neoliberal natures. This foundation is essential to understanding the structural challenges faced by proposals for new forms of extraction, and the contradictions inherent in socially oriented nationalized extractive industries.

Resource sovereignty and neo-extractivism

The concept of new extractivism has opened up debates about the capacity for revolutionary change within an export-oriented extractive model, especially in Latin America. Henry Veltmeyer and James Petras (2014) define the new extractivism as 'the form taken by extractive capital and extractivist imperialism under current and changing conditions of a system (capitalism) and a model (neoliberalism) in crisis'. It goes beyond just mining to incorporate the appropriation of natural resources and use of intensive processing to increase exports in a range of sectors (ibid.: 10). Gudynas (2010a), who authored the term, points to a distinction in what he terms 'classical extractivism' and this 'new' form, identifying the role of the state as the main point of differentiation. He argues that a recent turn in Latin America has positioned strong left-leaning states as extractive actors, seeking rents from natural resource mining for the benefit of social programming. While these states are positioned as contesting neoliberalism, the confines of extractivism and the extent of commodification it necessitates replicates neoliberal mechanisms of exchange.

This work intersects with recent and growing scholarly attention to Latin American neostructuralism and associated forms of neo-developmentalism, a set of left-leaning social policies that have included the state's assertion of resource sovereignty (Leiva 2008). The latter has been achieved through raising rents and royalties paid by transnational firms, as well as through outright nationalization. Bolivia under the Morales government and Chavez's Venezuela have received the most attention in this regard, but parallel examples may be drawn from Ecuador and Argentina. These policies have sought to counter the so-called 'resource curse' by using extractive industries as a means to promote social investment. Although these governments defend their reorientation of extractive rents for social programming, others criticize these processes as perpetuating Northern imperialist dynamics.

Policies that we might describe as affiliated with the new extractivism include those implemented in Bolivia, through its nationalization of the oil and gas sector and its reformed mining law, and Venezuela through an increase in royalties. These involve both the direct pursuit of greater returns from exports in taxes and royalties and increased employment opportunities for residents. In sub-Saharan Africa, the 'African Mining Vision' reflects a similar attempt to accomplish more progressive outcomes following on the rise of global mineral commodity prices (Graham 2013). At first instance, such policies seek to counter the ongoing human and environmental rights violations, including extrajudicial murder, that have accompanied intensified foreign investment in the mining sector in Latin America and elsewhere, with Guatemala, Mexico, Peru, Tanzania and Papua New Guinea among various prominent examples. But as Gudynas (2010a) and others have underlined, and as emerging research demonstrates, the dynamics surrounding a mining industry geared at export markets may remain highly exploitative despite progressive intentions. Whether between national firms or individual miners, these dynamics include competition and 'self regulation', expressing the individualized, socio-economic incentive-structure driving neoliberalism.

The most ardent defender against these criticisms of extractivism has been Bolivian Vice-President Alvaro Garcia Linera (2012). He suggests that those who pejoratively characterize the Movement for Socialism (MAS) programme in Bolivia as extractivist undermine revolutionary governments by constraining their capacity to redistribute wealth and to foster the basis for more equitable social relations and economies outside resource exploitation. Rather, Garcia Linera argues that active state control of primary resource industries could allow for improved living conditions for Bolivians, including improved education to lead processes of domestic industrialization (ibid.: 109). However, the supra-economic character of extractivism and its issues of scale and intensity are not incorporated into his position. The challenge in the Bolivian case is further aggravated by the limited extent of government participation in primary resource sectors, despite its resource nationalist discourse. For example, transnational corporations are responsible for the vast majority of mining revenues but the majority of miners are occupied in artisanal-style cooperative enterprises (Francescone 2015). This provokes a simultaneous dependence on foreign capital to form the backbone of the economy and on precarious, decentralized cooperative mining to provide employment. Such conditions, among others, have led to scholars to question the degree to which the new left Latin American governments fit the labels of 'post-neoliberal', given their similarities with the more conservative extractive regimes of the region (Bebbington 2012). Indeed, Kohl and Farthing (2012) point to the structural constraints of historically extractive economies that limit their capacity for redirecting resource rents to national-level social change. When considering the role of foreign participation and the commodification of the natural world, there appears to be a structural incompatibility of extractivism with the discourses of social transformation and decolonization – particularly in terms of the proposals for *vivir bien* or *buen vivir* that have been taken up by Bolivia and Ecuador, respectively.

The manner in which extractivism takes on social, political, economic, environmental and cultural dimensions speaks to the difficulty of overturning it and provokes contradictions in processes of change by left governments (Lander 2014). We suggest that greater attention must be paid to the multi-faceted character of extractive economies. Svampa (2012) coined the term 'commodities consensus' to refer to the adoption of commodity trading as a post-Washington Consensus economic model. This model surpasses the structural adjustments of the neoliberal era, integrating the flexibilization of the nation-state itself in the promotion of export-oriented natural resource exploitation. Effectively, extraction is not simply a form of production but shapes forms of social organization.

Neo-extractive endeavours employ a resource nationalist discourse through calls for resource sovereignty and the reclamation of rents through the ideal of national ownership, or increased taxation or royalty rates. Nonetheless, this discourse evokes views of ownership that maintain the conception of private property and of minerals necessarily represented as resources ready to be exploited, thereby producing and entrenching a commodified vision of the surrounding environment (Mommer 2002). As Gudynas (2010b) argues, government and extractive enterprises mutually legitimize one another through the generation of social programming funded by extractive industries. This dynamic redefines the arena of debate, 'discussions over extraction are distorted, displaced by arguments about how to use the surpluses, leaving in second place a critical analysis over the role extractive industries play in the strategies of development' (ibid.: 9). Moreover, on a wholly practical level, in many cases these ideals remain at the level of rhetoric and continue to depend upon the participation of foreign capital, albeit in a less visible or reduced role through joint-venture schemes alongside limited nationalizations (Rosales 2013).

Rethinking the extractive/productive binary under neoliberalism

Various works associated with indigenous ecological thought (Berkes 2012), actor network theory (Latour 2007) and critical animal studies (Haraway 2007) call for greater attention to the embeddedness of humans in nature and as part of nature. Recent critiques of Marxist political ecology emphasize the pitfalls of 'Cartesian' reproductions of human–nature binaries (Moore 2011). And, indeed, a neat distinction between extractive and productive systems reproduces this binary. It is this binary, arguably, that has facilitated the 'externalization' of the impact of industrial activities on non-human and human natures. The tricky problem of conceptualizing the inseparability of human labour and ecosystems raises the question of whether distinguishing extractivism as a wholly separate category from productivism remains tenable. To what extent does a distinction between extraction and production simply contribute to fetishizing so-called 'natural resources'?

The structural challenges involved with shifting from an extractive national economy and the perpetuation of exploitation in spite of stated commitments by Latin American new left governments point to some of the characteristics of extraction and its exploitation of both non-human nature and labour (as nature). Above we suggest that extractive environments, nature and resources are actively produced through politico-legal structures. But the dialectical, mutually constituted relationship between extractive industry and productive forms does not end there: production – as brought about through the exploitation of human labour – has similarly taken on more of an extractive character under neoliberalism.

The most evident example of this trend in classical terms could be agriculture which, under contemporary post-Keynesian trends and associated with shifts in land ownership (as per the global 'land grab' debates, see Borras and Franco 2012), has become more extractive. This arises from the deepening role of agricultural markets in serving transnational rather than regional market demands and the depletion in local food availability that may result. Clearly, studies of rubber tapping and the early silver trade are reminiscent of these trends, reflecting ecological imperialism under earlier waves of industrialization (Crosby 1986). The centrality of the export market to large-scale agriculture and approaches that presume an exhaustion of soils, mirror the extractive industries, such as mining or oil exploitation. We take seriously the approach of a kind of post-Cartesianism (Moore 2014), including actor network theory (Castree 2002), by arguing not that extraction as a category is fetishistic per se, but rather that the form of industrial production seen under neoliberalism has taken on an increasingly 'extractive' dimension. This prompts greater attention to capitalism's tendency to undermine its basis of existence as per the 'second contradiction' thesis (O'Connor 1988) – a factor highlighted by contemporary attention to climate change.

As discussed above, these dynamics include over-extraction and the exploitation of human and non-human natures. The 'externalization' of social and environmental costs as understood by institutional and environmental economics and the hyper-exploitation of human labour via global value chains (e.g. in maquiladoras and export processing zones), or the more recent Rana Plaza disaster are exemplary. These are made possible by the spatial distance achieved under globalization, a long-standing attribute of imperialism as a 'spatial fix' (Harvey 2006) – but whose boomerang effect has become increasingly evident from the late twentieth century. Under neoliberalism, the capitalist labour process takes on extractive characteristics through politico-legal frameworks which facilitate export-oriented production. Both enclave manufacturing and frontier extractive sites face reduced labour and environmental obligations and corporate tax rates, exacerbating the destruction of the surrounding environment.

On this point, Wright (1999) describes the altered perception of labour power within maquiladora production when she writes that the Mexican woman's 'labour power is subsequently worth less than the value of her labour in a number of ways, given that her labour is valuable also for its inevitable absence from the labour process' (ibid.: 454). She emphasizes the manner in which women's labour power in maquiladora industries is consumed, with managers developing strategies to extract the maximum amount from the feminized workforce while externalizing all costs of social reproduction. In this manner, the women move from forms of value to waste, and this fluctuation is precisely part of their appeal to employers (470). Wasting human labours parallel the generation of revenues through natural resource waste in extractive process, separating the valued commodity from that which is considered useless. The constriction of the labour process to such a degree that workers themselves move from value forms to waste forms signals the adept processes of extraction at play in securing labour power. Important scholarly attention to waste and its disposal – itself imbued with human labour-value (Gidwani 2013) – further problematizes categorizations of various outcomes of human labour in commodities and helps nuance theoretical and methodological approaches to extraction as a category.

Although theorizing the differences between extractive and productive systems has drawn valuable attention to the particularities of resource exploitation, it may mask the role of human labour within extractive activities and retrench the binaries between human and non-human natures. Conversely, centring discussion of value on human labour without considering how the extraction of spatially distant non-human natures has produced both non-human nature and human labour historically, reinforces anthropocentric understanding of nature. Ultimately, as we argue above, attending to the extractive character of neoliberalism and critiquing how Cartesian approaches to nature have shaped conditions for ecological crises helps problematize neat distinctions between productive and extractive activities. Uniting human labour and nature as mutually constituted categories fosters theory and research that examines the simultaneously social and spatial implications of the categories of production and extraction.

Conclusion

The growing debates around extractive industries stem from a variety of political analyses and advocate an array of political approaches to the practical government of natural resources. In recent years, the field has grown to consider the role of financialization and speculation in promoting extractive industries. It has become evident that questions of resource exploitation cannot be limited to development theorizing or to narrow domestic policy approaches intended to challenge apparently inherent rent-seeking tendencies. Rather, scholarly attention has shed light on the global character of extractive flows and demanded analyses of the geopolitical significance of resources alongside their domestic political, cultural and social connections. Recognizing the expansion of extractive industries and their interconnection with contemporary global political economic and ecological considerations, herein we have examined the mutual constitution of so-called extractive and productive economies so as to allow for multi-scalar insights into global capitalist relations under neoliberalism.

By distinguishing extractive from productive economies, scholarship has, at times, created a false binary, one that overlooks the role of labour in securing resources and relies upon a reified division between human labour and nature. Above, we identify rich possibilities for analysing the co-constitution of productive and extractive structures to shed light on both the classically understood nature-intensive forms of extraction and forms of neoliberal production. Globalized production chains appear to mimic extractive processes by isolating different component parts of a finished product, including human labour, subsequently identifying the most discrete method of securing them. The collective analysis of these chains promoted through approaches like global commodity chain analysis (Gereffi 1999; Bridge 2008; Zalik 2008b) helps unify extraction and production as necessarily conjoint processes. Similarly, as outlined above, the conceptualization of 'natural' resources, and, consequently, extractive industries, as commodities whose distinguishing feature is not associated with their form of production may be erroneously presumed if extraction is presumed to be distinct from the outset. These quandaries demonstrate the need for increased comparative and relational theorizing concerning extractive and productive practices under contemporary neoliberalism.

References

Amin, S. 1977. *Imperialism and Unequal Development*. New York: Monthly Review Press.

Auty, R.M. 1993. *Sustaining Development in Mineral Economies: The Resource Curse Thesis*. London and New York: Routledge.

Baran, P.A. 1968. *Political Economy of Growth*. New York: Modern Reader Paperbacks.

Bebbington, A. 2012. Underground Political Ecologies: The Second Annual Lecture of the Cultural and Political Ecology Specialty Group of the Association of American Geographers. *Geoforum*, 43.6: 1152–62.

Berkes, F. 2012. *Sacred Ecology*. New York: Routledge.

Bina, C. 2006. The Globalization of Oil: A Prelude to a Critical Political Economy. *International Journal of Political Economy*, 35.2: 4–34.

Blaut, J.M. 1994. Robert Brenner in the Tunnel of Time. *Antipode*, 26.4: 351–74.

Borras, S.M., and Franco, J.C. 2012. Global Land Grabbing and Trajectories of Agrarian Change: A Preliminary Analysis. *Journal of Agrarian Change*, 12.1: 34–59.

Brenner, R. 1977. The Origins of Capitalist Development: A Critique of Neo-Smithian Marxism. *New Left Review*, 104.August: 25–92.

Bridge, G. 2004. Contested Terrain: Mining and the Environment. *Annual Review of Environment and Resources*, 29.1: 205–59.

—. 2008. Global Production Networks and the Extractive Sector: Governing Resource-Based Development. *Journal of Economic Geography*, 8.3: 389–419.

Bridge, G., and Le Billon, P. 2012. *Oil*. Cambridge and Malden, MA: Polity.

Bunker, S.G. 1984. Modes of Extraction, Unequal Exchange, and the Progressive Underdevelopment of an Extreme Periphery: The Brazilian Amazon, 1600–1980. *American Journal of Sociology*, 89.5: 1017–64.

Bunker, S.G., and Ciccantell, P.S. 2005. *Globalization and the Race for Resources*. Baltimore, MD: Johns Hopkins University Press.

Burkett, P. 1999. *Marx and Nature*. London: St Martin's Press.

Campbell, B. 2003. Factoring in Governance is Not Enough: Mining Codes in Africa, Policy Reform and Corporate Responsibility. *Minerals and Energy - Raw Materials Report*, 18.3: 2–13.

Castree, N. 2002. False Antitheses? Marxism, Nature and Actor-Networks. *Antipode*, 34.1: 111–46.

Clark, B., and Foster, J.B. 2009. Ecological Imperialism and the Global Metabolic Rift: Unequal Exchange and the Guano/Nitrates Trade. *International Journal of Comparative Sociology*, 50.3–4: 311–34.

Coase, R.H. 1937. The Nature of the Firm. *Economica*, 4.16: 386–405.

—. 1998. The New Institutional Economics. *The American Economic Review*, 88.2: 72–4.

Coronil, F. 1997. *The Magical State: Nature, Money, and Modernity in Venezuela*. Chicago, IL: University of Chicago Press.

—. 2000. Toward a Critique of Globalcentrism: Speculations on Capitalism's Nature. *Public Culture*, 12.2: 351–74.

Crosby, A.W. 1986. *Ecological Imperialism: The Biological Expansion of Europe, 900–1900*. Cambridge: Cambridge University Press.

Deneault, A., and Sacher, W. 2012. *Imperial Canada Inc.: Legal Haven of Choice for the World's Mining Industries*. Vancouver: Talonbooks.

Emel, J., and Huber, M.T. 2008. A Risky Business: Mining, Rent and the Neoliberalization of 'Risk'. *Geoforum*, 39.3: 1393–407.

Escobar, A. 1995. *Encountering Development: The Making and Unmaking of the Third World*. Princeton, NJ: Princeton University Press.

Foster, J.B. 1999. Marx's Theory of Metabolic Rift: Classical Foundations for Environmental Sociology. *American Journal of Sociology*, 105.2: 366–405.

—. 2002. Capitalism and Ecology II: The Nature of the Contradiction. *Monthly Review*, 54.4: 6–16.

Francescone, K. 2015. Cooperative Miners and the Politics of Abandonment in Bolivia. *The Extractive Industries and Society*, 2.4: 746–55.

Frank, A.G. 1969. *Capitalism and Underdevelopment in Latin America*. Rev. and enlarged edn. New York: Monthly Review Press.

Furtado, C. 1976. *Economic Development of Latin America: Historical Background and Contemporary Problems*. 2nd edn. Cambridge: Cambridge University Press.

Garcia Linera, A. 2012. *La Geopolitica de La Amazonia*. La Paz: Vicepresidencia del Estado.

Gereffi, G. 1999. A Commodity Chains Framework for Analyzing Global Industries. *Institute of Development Studies*. Retrieved from http://www.ids.ac.uk/ids/global/pdfs/gereffi.pdf

Gidwani, V. 2013. *Six Theses on Waste, Value, and Commons*. *Social & Cultural Geography*, 14.7: 773–83.

Girvan, N. 1978. *Corporate Imperialism: Conflict and Expropriation: Transnational Corporations and Economic Nationalism in the Third World*. New York: Monthly Review Press.

Graham, Y. 2013. The Africa Mining Vision: Looking beyond the Boom, Bust and Boom of Global Mineral Markets towards Structural Transformation. Paper presented at the Conference on the South in the Global Economic Crisis, Geneva, 31 January. Retrieved from http://www.southcentre.int/wp-content/uploads/2013/08/Ev_130201_YGraham.pdf

Gudynas, E. 2010a. El Nuevo Extractivismo Progresista. *El Observador Del OBIE*, 8: 1–10.

—. 2010b. *The New Extractivism of the 21st Century: Ten Urgent Theses about Extractivism in Relation to Current South American Progressivism*. Washington, DC: Center for International Policy.

Haraway, D.J. 2007. *When Species Meet*. Minneapolis: University Of Minnesota Press.

Harvey, D. 2003. *The New Imperialism*. Oxford: Oxford University Press.

—. 2006. *Spaces of Global Capitalism*. London: Verso.

Karl, T.L. 1997. *The Paradox of Plenty: Oil Booms and Petro-States*. Berkeley: University of California Press.

Kohl, B., and Farthing, L. 2012. Material Constraints to Popular Imaginaries: The Extractive Economy and Resource Nationalism in Bolivia. *Political Geography*, 31.4: 225–35.

Labban, M. 2008. *Space, Oil and Capital*. New York: Routledge.

Lander, E. 2014. *Neoextractivismo Como Modelo de Desarrollo En America Latina y Sus Contradicciones*. Heinrich Boll Stiftung. Retrieved from https://mx.boell.org/sites/default/files/edgardolander.pdf

Latour, B. 2007. *Reassembling the Social: An Introduction to Actor-Network-Theory*. 1st edn. New York: Oxford University Press.

Leiva, F.I. 2008. *Latin American Neostructuralism: The Contradictions of Post-Neoliberal Development*. Minneapolis: University of Minnesota Press.

Marx, K. 1993. *Capital: A Critique of Political Economy, Vol. 3*. Fernbach, D, trans. London: Penguin Classics.

McNally, D. 1981. Staple Theory as Commodity Fetishism: Marx, Innis and Canadian Political Economy. *Studies in Political Economy*, 6: 35–63.

Mitchell, T. 1998. *Fixing the Economy*. *Cultural Studies*, 12.1: 82–101.

—. 2002. McJihad: Islam in the US Global Order. *Social Text*, 73: 1–18.

—. 2011. *Carbon Democracy: Political Power in the Age of Oil*. New York: Verso.

Mommer, B. 2002. *Global Oil and the Nation State*. New York: Oxford University Press.

Moore, J.W. 2000. Environmental Crises and the Metabolic Rift in World-Historical Perspective. *Organization & Environment*, 13.2: 123–57.

—. 2003. The Modern World-System as Environmental History? Ecology and the Rise of Capitalism. *Theory and Society*, 32.3: 307–77.

—. 2011. Ecology, Capital, and the Nature of Our Times: Accumulation and Crisis in the Capitalist World-Ecology. *American Sociological Association*, 27.1: 107–46.

—. 2014. The Capitalocene Part I: On the Nature and Origins of Our Ecological Crisis. Retrieved from http://www.jasonwmoore.com/uploads/The_Capitalocene__Part_I__June_2014.pdf

Nitzan, J., and Bichler, S. 1995. Bringing Capital Accumulation Back In: The Weapondollar Petrodollar Coalition-Military Contractors, Oil Companies and Middle East 'Energy Conflicts'. *Review of International Political Economy*, 2.3: 446–515.

O'Connor, J. 1988. Capitalism, Nature, Socialism a Theoretical Introduction. *Capitalism Nature Socialism*, 1.1: 11–38.

Powell, W.W., and Di Maggio, P.J. 2012. *The New Institutionalism in Organizational Analysis*. Chicago, IL: University of Chicago Press.

Prebisch, R. 1950. *The Economic Development of Latin America and Its Principal Problems*. New York: United Nations Department of Economic Affairs.

Rosales, A. 2013. Going Underground: The Political Economy of the 'Left Turn' in South America. *Third World Quarterly*, 34.8: 1443–57.

Smith, N. 2007. Nature as Accumulation Strategy. *Socialist Register*, 43: 16.

Sunkel, O., and Paz, P. 1970. *El Subdesarrollo Latinoamericano y la Teoria del Desarrollo*. Madrid: Siglo Veintiuno de España.

Svampa, M. 2012. Consenso de los Commodities, Giro Ecoterritorial y Pensamiento Crítico en América Latina. *Observatorio Social de América Latina*, 32. November: 15–38.

Veltmeyer, H., and Petras, J. 2014. *The New Extractivism: A Post-Neoliberal Development Model Or Imperialism of the 21st Century?* London: Zed.

Watts, M. 2004. Resource Curse? Governmentality, Oil and Power in the Niger Delta, Nigeria. *Geopolitics*, 9.1: 50–80.

Wright, M.W. 1999. Dialectics of Still Life: Murder, Women, and Maquiladoras. *Public Culture*, 11.3: 453–74.

Zalik, A. 2008a. Oil Sovereignties in the Mexican Gulf and Nigerian Niger Delta, in Omeje, K., ed. *Extractive Economies in the Global South: Multi-Regional Perspectives on Rentier Politics*. London: Ashgate: 181–98.

—. 2008b. Liquefied Natural Gas and Fossil Capitalism. *Monthly Review*, 60.6: 41–53.

PART VII

Aftermaths

47

THE CRISIS OF NEOLIBERALISM

Gérard Duménil and Dominique Lévy

The implementation of neoliberalism in the late 1970s and early 1980s was a rather painful process, with the multiplication of crises around the world, as in the USA during the 1980s, Japan in 1990, Mexico in 1994, Korea and other countries of East Asia in 1997, and Latin America, notably Argentina in 2001. The expression 'crisis of neoliberalism' is, however, used to designate the major crisis that hit the USA, Europe, and indirectly many other countries in the so-called 'financial crisis' of 2008 and the 'great recession' of 2009. Thanks to the dramatic policies conducted in support of financial institutions and the stimulation of the economies by huge deficits of government expenses, the repetition of a scenario similar to the Great Depression was avoided, but macro policies cannot remedy a structural crisis. As of the 2010s, the 'world' is no longer in crisis, but the USA and, even more, Europe are not out of crisis, with low growth rates – what is now denoted as 'stagnation' – and skyrocketing government debts.

The establishment of neoliberal capitalism cannot be understood as a merely economic phenomenon, a change in policies and institutions. The crisis of neoliberalism is the expression of the inner contradictions of a political strategy supported by basic national and international economic transformations, whose main objectives are the restoration and increase of the power, income, and wealth of upper classes. But the international domination of the USA worldwide was considerably weakened during the most recent decades and profoundly affected by the crisis itself as other countries were forging ahead. The new policies now undertaken in the USA testify to a strong determination on the part of the government and the Federal Reserve to revert this declining trend. If these strategies were successful, US neoliberalism could be retrospectively understood as a stepwise process, with a first episode whose major stake was the restoration of the hegemony of upper classes, and a second episode now targeted to the restoration of US international hegemony. Much remains to be done, however, and the final outcome is far from obvious.

The analysis is conducted in five sections. First, we examine the historical background in terms of relations of production, classes, and class struggle. Second, we attend to the success – according to its own criteria – of the new social order and its, at least, provisional failure in the crisis of 2008 marking the end of a first episode in the neoliberal endeavour. The third section is devoted to the resurgence of traditional Keynesian and Marxian interpretations among leftist academics, which may shed some light on this complex course of events but, in our opinion, fails to address the specific class and imperial features of the chain of events that led to the crisis.

Fourth, we address the significance and prospects of the new policies in the USA that aim to restore the country's international economic hegemony, the second episode that remains to be written.[1] A final section is devoted to broader historical prospects.

Neoliberalism as a successful strategy of class reconquest in the overall dynamics of managerial capitalism

Relations of production are in constant evolution, even within each of the successive modes of production. In this respect, the history of the USA since the independence of the country is quite specific as, from the origin, capitalist relations of production developed on the new continent at a distance from the remnants of feudalism or the transition of the *Ancien Régime*. But reaching the end of the century, the emergence of new managerial features signalled a basic transformation in relations of production, with the three revolutions at the turn of the century, namely the corporate, the financial, and the managerial revolutions. The US capitalism of the early twentieth century was already a hybrid society, a 'managerial capitalism'. A straightforward quantitative expression of this secular tendency is the invasion of the upper segments of the income pyramid by wages compared to capital income (rents, dividends, and interest). Considering the top 1 per cent (the fractile 99–100) of households in the income pyramid, prior to the Great Depression in the USA, capital income still amounted to 1.5 more than wages, emphasizing the capitalist nature of the fractile. In 2012, the ratio had been inverted as wages were four times larger than capital income. Nowadays, even within the top 1/1000th of the income pyramid, wages are twice that of capital income.

The progress of managerial relations of production cannot be separated from the transformation of class patterns. For the traditional bipolar scheme *capitalist-proletarian classes*, one must substitute the threefold pattern *capitalist-managerial-popular classes*. The position of managerial classes was originally that of a new intermediate class, but these classes gradually move to the top, at the conquest of the status of new upper class besides capitalists. (Within both classes, capitalists and managers, a large spectrum of positions obviously exists.) Our interpretation is that a transition is presently under way towards a new mode of production in which managerial classes would be the new upper classes. The hybrid features of managerial capitalism are the expression of this transition.[2]

Concerning the politics of the transition, the pattern of dominations and alliances between the three classes are of crucial import. Since the early twentieth century, we distinguish between three social orders:

1. *The first financial hegemony.* From the beginning of the century to the Great Depression, capitalist classes unquestionably dominated social relations, in alliance with the emerging class of managers, an alliance to the right.

2. *The postwar compromise.* From the New Deal to the 1970s, a new social order was set up.[3] This order was the outcome of the depression itself, in the context of the rise of the worker movement worldwide, and under the threat of self-proclaimed 'socialist' countries for capitalist classes. The new social order was the expression of the alliance between popular classes and managers, an alliance to the left, within 'social-democratic' of 'Keynesian' societies. The main social forces in these movements were popular classes, but managerial classes assumed the leadership in the new management of corporations and the definition of new policies.

3. *The second financial hegemony in neoliberalism.* In the context created by the crisis of the 1970s, the continuing struggle on the part of upper classes, and the weaknesses of the postwar

compromise, the alliance swung to the right, between capitalist and managerial classes. The new trends were already manifest during the 1970s and early 1980s, with the dramatic restoration of the income and wealth of upper classes still on the rise after 2000. The management of corporations was radically transformed to the benefit of shareholders; new policies were defined; free trade and the free movements of capital worldwide placed the workers of all countries in a situation of competition. In the USA, the progress of the purchasing power of the bulk of wage earners was blocked and the old controls that the New Deal had placed on financial institutions were lifted. Note that neoliberalism is a phase of managerial capitalism, not an ideology, though there is obviously a neoliberal ideology, that of 'free-market' economics (limited government intervention), as in classical liberalism. One must, however, keep in mind that neoliberal governments remained strong and played a crucial role in the launching and perpetuation of the new social order.

Figure 47.1 shows the average yearly income in constant purchasing power per household in each fractile of the income pyramid since World War I in the USA. The fractiles are listed under Figure 47.1. (For example, 0–90 refers to all households with the exception of the upper 10 per cent, and the fractile 99.99–100 refers to the top 1/10 000th of households with the most elevated income.) The logarithmic scale provides a clearer view of growth rates. The variables have been rescaled to 100 for the average of the period 1960–73 when the growth rates of purchasing powers were almost the same for the various fractiles. The vertical continuous lines in 1933 and 1974 delineate the three social orders above; the dotted lines in 1960 and 2000 separate two sub-periods within the second and third periods.

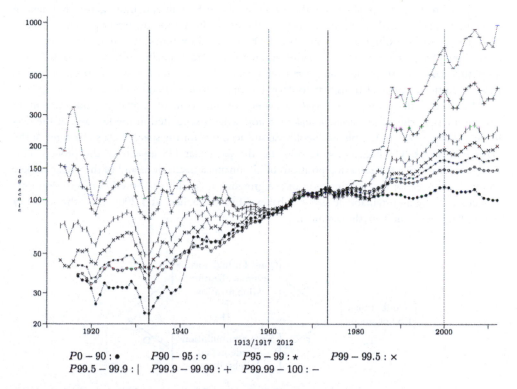

Figure 47.1 Average yearly income per household in seven fractiles
Source: Piketty and Saez 2003

The succession of the three social orders above is clearly apparent in the trends of purchasing power and income inequality. Beginning with the comparatively high levels of inequality prior to the New Deal, a dramatic reduction occurred during the first few decades (up to 1960) of the new compromise to the left; then, all purchasing power grew at similar rates. From about 1974 onward, a new spectacular diverging pattern is apparent, with skyrocketing high income and the income of the 0–90 stagnating (being even reduced). Both the historical profiles of wages and capital income are involved in these profiles.

The following are noteworthy. First, due to their comparative and rising importance, wages are a crucial component of the distinct trends in each period. Second, the income of the top income fractiles was dramatically reduced during the intermediate period, sometimes described as a 'financial repression'. In neoliberalism, upper classes were able to increase both upper wages and capital income. This 'return' of capital income seems to contradict its secular comparative decline but, despite its spectacular amplitude, this movement remained inferior to the rise of wages and confined within very small income brackets at the top.

The structural crisis of the early twenty-first century as class- and national-specific

In the *Communist Manifesto*, Marx compared capitalist classes to apprentice 'sorcerers'. With the aim of increasing their powers and income – and pushed forward by the dynamics of accumulation and competition – these classes boldly innovate and remove all impediments to their action (as in deregulation); they periodically lose control of their magic. Marx described this inclination as a general feature of capitalism, and there is no doubt that credit and, more generally, financial mechanisms, are pushed to and finally beyond the limits during the recurrent phases of expansion. The crisis of neoliberalism is not any of the standard exercises in witchcraft, however, as during the phases of recurrent overheating and recession. Truly specific of the social order is the amplitude taken by these developments over various decades and across countries, as well as their sophisticated interrelations that conferred to the crisis its structural character.

The crisis is the crisis of *neoliberal capitalism*, not any form of capitalism and, even more specifically, the crisis of *neoliberalism under US hegemony*, as suggested in the left part of the diagram in Figure 47.2. In the phrase, 'neoliberalism' accounts for the specific class character of the crisis. The words 'US hegemony' account for the particular US aspects of the process. This hegemony, in which the towering positions of US financial institutions and of the dollar are key elements, allowed for the continuation of the growing disequilibria of the US macroeconomic trajectory to the unsustainable levels of imbalance finally reached after 2000. No other country would have performed anything similar.

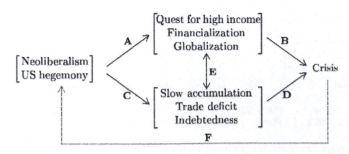

Figure 47.2   A diagrammatic representation

Returning to the chain of events, two basic categories of factors were involved. The upper part of the diagram (following Arrow A) points to the 'quest for high income', meaning the eagerness of upper classes to restore and increase their income and wealth after decades of comparative setback. In a broad context of deregulation, the 1980s were a period of unchecked progress of financialization and globalization, in particular financial globalization. A lot has been written concerning financial instability inherent in the advance of financial mechanisms. Market mechanisms (the stock market, derivative markets, etc.) are centre stage, but also the mechanisms supporting loans (such as securitization or credit default swaps). Important risks were also involved in the process of globalization, in particular the potential imbalance of foreign trade, the flows of short-term capital across the world, and the lost control of credit mechanisms and financial markets.

The lower block of factors (Arrow B) is more specifically typical of the US economy:

1. With the new methods of managements and the rising flows of direct investment towards the rest of the world, the rate of capital accumulation dramatically diminished. The variable in Figure 47.3 is the share in GDP of nonresidential investment of the US private economy. After 1980, a dramatic downward trend was substituted for the earlier rising trend.

2. A crucial determinant of the crisis was the deficit of foreign trade, reaching about 5 per cent of GDP prior to the crisis. The excess of imports over exports results in a deficit of demand towards the enterprises located on national territory. These enterprises are at the origin of the flows of income resulting from production, in the forms of wages and capital income. This income should return to these enterprises when the purchasing power is used to buy goods and services. When, as a result of the deficit of foreign trade, a fraction does not go back to domestic enterprises, a deflationary chain of events is initiated. This is what happened prior to the crisis. Stimulation was required, in the form of a flow of new loans correcting for the deficient demand levels. The new borrowings could come from enterprises, the government, or households. In the USA, in those years, enterprises did not borrow with the aim of investment (another component of demand), only in support of financial activity. An even larger reliance on government deficit was not in line with neoliberal policy options. The new borrowing came from households financed by mortgage loans.

3. A direct consequence of the growing deficit of the US foreign trade was the rise of debts. The 'debt' of the country towards the rest of the world increased mechanically with the deficit. (The flows of financing from the rest of the world can also take the form of the purchase of stock shares, but new loans were the main channel.) The second debt was the rising debt of households, up to the unsustainable levels reached prior to the crisis.

The relationship between the two categories of determinants (Arrow E) is also important. For example, financial deregulation and the rise of financial institutions allowed for the upward trend of the debt of households and its new bold forms of refinancing by private–label issuers (besides securitization by government-sponsored enterprises). The Federal Reserve met with growing difficulties in controlling interest rates, as financial globalization allowed US financial institutions to borrow from foreign (notably Japanese) banks.

The two sets of factors converged (Arrows B and D) during the second half of the 2000s, causing the crisis in the US economy. The crisis was rapidly exported to the rest of the world. First, many countries were themselves engaged to various extents in similar unsustainable practices. Second, a significant fraction of US bad securities had been sold to these countries.

The crisis unfolded step by step. A first phase can be dated to January 2006–July 2007, with the fall of building permits, home sales, home prices, and the beginning of defaults.

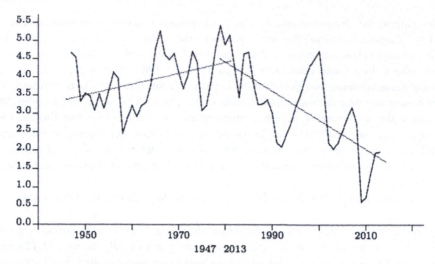

Figure 47.3   Share in GDP of nonresidential investment
Source: Bureau of Economic Analysis, Nipa

The devaluation of the riskiest segments of mortgage-backed securities (MBSs) began. Between August 2007 and September 2008, the situation of US financial institutions deteriorated, with liquidity problems and losses, but the crisis was still a US phenomenon. The most dramatic phase was September 2008–February 2009, with the multiplication of failures (notably Lehman Brothers), the contagion to the rest of the globe, and the contraction of output. The trough of the recession was reached by mid-2009 in the USA, while the default on household debt reached unprecedented levels. Stock-market indices plunged. The reaction of central authorities was rapid and strong: (1) the Federal Reserve engaged massively in the purchase of agency MBSs and supported the financial sector (loans and direct holdings), while federal funds rates had declined to levels close to zero, and (2) government deficits exploded. Since 2010, a rather steady growth rate (about 2 per cent) has prevailed in the USA, supported by the continued strong involvement of the government and the Federal Reserve, while the economy of the European Union (EU) went on stagnating, paralysed by the attempt to correct government deficits in the absence of more profound transformations. Other countries in the rest of the world, like China, were hit by the recession in the old centres and then recovered.

The comeback of traditional Keynesian–Marxian interpretations

The violence of neoliberal capitalism had already been a source of revival of the most critical analyses of capitalism (see Springer 2016). The occurrence of the crisis in 2007–8 prolonged these early assessments. The crisis is explained by basic tendencies inherent in capitalism, like: (1) financial instability; (2 and 3) a mismatch between aggregate supply and demand levels due to either (2) a deficient demand levels caused by a bias in income distribution or (3) excess supply on the part of enterprises; (4) declining profit rates; and (5) the historical recurrence of long waves. The return to the traditional analyses of crises in capitalism is sometimes asserted vigorously, as a refutation of approaches describing the crisis as the 'crisis of neoliberalism' (rather than capitalism). In our opinion, the crisis must be understood in reference to 'neoliberal managerial capitalism', and abstraction should not be made of the specific features of this form of capitalism.

The boundaries are not easy to draw between various trains of thought as, for example, the reference to Keynesian financial instability is directly evocative of Marx's analysis of fictitious capital; similar views concerning deficient demand levels are typical of the two trains of thought, though the particular mechanisms may be distinct.

1. *Financial instability.* There is no surprise in the resurgence to the fore of 'financial instability' as a crucial determinant of crises, a factor whose relevance is unquestionable. Within the Keynesian train of thought, reference is often made to Minsky's analysis of the pattern of cumulative rise, sudden reversal (the Minsky point), and collapse, typical of financial markets. Examples are Paul Krugman (2008) and Paul Davidson (2009), pointing to the rise of financial mechanisms and deregulation. The analysis of Joseph Stiglitz (2010) emphasizes the mistaken macro policy undertaken in response to the 2000–1 recession (and in the wake of the collapse of the stock market). The Federal Reserve drastically diminished the interest rate and, thus, fed the housing bubble that the greed of financial institutions contributed to inflate by resorting to highly risky procedures.

   Among Marxist economists, even if the terminology is distinct, the core analysis hinging around the risks inherent in the accumulation of fictitious capital – that is, financial assets – is in line with the above (Chesnais 2014).

   At a general level of analysis, we have no disagreement with the emphasis on financial mechanisms, deregulation, and mistaken macro policies. They were all part of the 2008 crisis. But the class determinants, accounting for the prevalence of these stubborn trends during more than three decades of neoliberalism, should not be overlooked.

2. *Deficient demand as accounting for the low levels of utilization of productive capacities.* Typical of the Keynesian train of thought but also Marxist perspectives is the reference to deficient demand levels. The origin of the mismatch between supply and demand is located on the demand side, as an effect of the low share of wages and/or its declining trend (Shaikh 2011; Valle 2008). The argument rests on the notion that wage earners spend a larger share of their income than capitalists. Two difficulties are involved: (1) in the USA, the share of wages did not decline prior to the crisis; and (2) as already stated above, a basic feature of the period preceding the crisis was the excess demand (as manifest in the excess of imports to exports), not deficient demand. More sophisticated interpretations are, therefore, required. A substitute for the first objection above could be the consideration of upper income (profits and wages) fractiles, instead of profits alone. Empirical data shows, however, that the recipients of upper incomes diminished their savings prior to the crisis even more than the lower strata (Saez and Zucman 2014). As a reply to the second objection, it is typically answered that the problem was not the lack of actual demand but the lack of demand financed out of income, a deficiency that caused the borrowing spree compensating for the deficient purchasing power of households. (In other words, consumption and investment were high but their financing perilous.) A first counter-argument is that, in the history of capitalism, the needs of the poor segments of the population never pushed banks to lend without sufficient guarantees. Moreover, these interpretations forget that the control of the volume of borrowing is a basic function of monetary policy. Up to the very last moment, the upward trend of household borrowing was a deliberate policy on the part of the Federal Reserve intending to counteract the effect of the deficit of foreign trade (given the refusal to allow the deficit of the government to perform the task). The key role played by the deficit of foreign trade is precisely what is overlooked in these analyses.

3. *Overaccumulation.* Symmetrical, or used in combination with the above, another reading of the crisis points to an autonomous tendency towards overaccumulation (over-supply), a

traditional Marxian contention. US enterprises allegedly went on increasing their productive capacities independently of the actual levels of demand (possibly as a consequence of competition or rapid technical change).[4] It is, however, difficult to imagine why US enterprises maintained this puzzling behaviour over several decades without adjustment. The downward trend of the capacity utilization rate in manufacturing industries is put forward to support this interpretation. We have serious doubts concerning the relevance of this empirical foundation as, taken at face value, the low levels of the capacity utilization rate during the 1990s would imply that overaccumulation was already a feature of the period, when the US economy was growing at rates of about 4 per cent (during the boom of new technologies). Finally, the analysis of delinquencies on loans clearly demonstrates the quite unusual pattern observed prior to the 2008–9 recession, as the delinquencies on industrial loans did not increase before the recession (as in usual cycles) while the delinquencies on mortgage loans exploded.

4. *Declining profit rates.* As the crisis of the 1970s had been a profitability crisis, numerous Marxist economists prolonged this analysis to the new crisis. A crucial issue was therefore the calculation of profit rates, with the usual problems met in the definitions of profits and capital. There is actually a huge gap between: (1) profit rates measured using a very broad definition of profits (total income minus labour compensations) divided by the stock of fixed capital (at replacement cost) and, (2) the 'rate of retained profits' – that is, profits after paying out taxes, interest and dividends, divided by enterprises own funds (Duménil and Lévy 2011; Figure 47.1). The profit rate in the first broad measure partially recovered after the decline that caused the crisis of the 1970s. Subtracting all taxes, the profit rate recovered its levels of the 1960s (as profit taxes were diminished[5]). It is actually the increased flow of dividends in neoliberalism that caused the decline of the retained profit rate – that is, a tendency inherent in neoliberal management procedures. This decline was a crucial factor in the downward trend of investment in Figure 47.3, but did not cause the crisis. (The housing crisis began in 2006 and was later transformed into a recession.) In a profitability crisis, like during the 1970s, capitalism 'sinks' because profits are the oxygen of capitalist corporations, and there is no significant financial component. In a crisis like the 2008 crisis, capitalism 'explodes' as financial mechanisms play an important role.

   A symmetrical line of argument is sometimes put forward by Marxist economists, pointing to a restoration of the profit rate prior to the crisis, pinned on a decline of the share of wages (Moseley 2009; Shaikh 2011; Husson 2012). (See the discussion above concerning the wage share.)

5. *Long waves.* A special emphasis must be put on interpretations hinging around the theory of long waves or Kondratieff cycles, with often a clear reference to the historical framework developed by Fernand Braudel. Capitalism goes through long phases of expansion that culminate in episodes of financialization, as a manifestation of the depletion of profitable opportunities in the nonfinancial sector (Arrighi 1999). Then, a long phase of decline occurs. The causes of the depletion of nonfinancial investment opportunities pinned on various mechanisms evocative of overaccumulation, but not with precise contents. In the case of Emmanuel Wallerstein, the crucial factor is the rise of costs (energy, labour, and the like) whose final outcome will be the extinction of capitalism (Wallerstein 2000).

A broad agenda: exiting the current crisis, avoiding a new crisis, remedying the current stagnating growth, and restoring the US international hegemony

From the viewpoint of its class objectives, namely the restoration of the power and wealth of upper classes, neoliberalism was amazingly successful. Concerning the US economy, the consequences were, however, devastating. (See sections above.) A major crisis occurred, threatening the continuation of the entire endeavour; neoliberal trends were at the origin of a more than three-decade long decline of investment rates on US national territory, when other countries were forging ahead. The already weakened US international hegemony was at risk. Thus, the programme for the coming decades was clearly set out. Macro policies are central, but one cannot remedy a structural crisis only by Keynesian stimulation of demand:

1. Stabilizing the economy – consolidating the aggregate economy (still supported by government deficits) – that is, really getting out of the current structural crisis, and avoiding the repetition of major crises in the future.
2. Stimulating investment and growth, implying forms of re-territorialization of industrial production, notably within key industries.
3. Restoring the US international hegemony (conditioned by the two previous requirements), notably perpetuating the domination of the US network of financial institutions worldwide in the structure of 'Anglo-Saxon neoliberalism' (Duménil and Lévy 2014). This is where the relationship between the class and international components is the closest (a reciprocal relationship). Obviously the role of the dollar is crucial.

A first issue is the political motivation. A sharp difference between the USA and Europe is that, within the EU or the eurozone, there is no national feeling, since there is no European nation. The project of continental integration was the product of the consciousness, after the devastations of the two world wars, of a common cultural heritage and solidarity, but the differences between countries remain of considerable import, as evident in the treatment (or absence of treatment) of the crisis. Policies in Europe are clearly in line with basic orthodox tenets, like the downward pressure on labour costs and the eagerness to 'tranquilize' the banks holding government securities by cutting government deficits: nothing that would allow Europe to move forward. Conversely, in the USA, the 'national factor' plays a central role, and the consciousness of the necessity of safeguarding the international hegemony of the country may provide sufficient grounds for the establishment of a new course. Actually, the process is already under way.

A second issue is the social-political nature of the endeavour, knowing that we refer here to ongoing trends from the viewpoint of upper classes, and not to what 'should', in our opinion, preferably be undertaken. A strong involvement of central authorities, notably the government and the Federal Reserve, is required. No private institution, no 'market' can perform the task, and the conduct of such policies implies a significant break from neoliberal ideology and practices. The new course of events is typical of what can be called 'administered neoliberalism', at odds with the classical liberalism of free markets. Principles and methods are, however, much less important than the class foundations and objectives of the social order – in particular, when the international domination of the country is involved. There is clearly a class component in the definition of these new directions as government officials – a segment of managerial classes and a component in the alliance at the top – play a central role (a new New Deal, politically oriented to the right). The action of high officials within central institutions was and is still central in the treatment of the crisis. They should play a prominent role during the coming decades. If they don't, the objectives will not be reached.

A third issue is the contents:

1. *Regulating financial mechanisms.* A law, the Dodd–Frank Act, was voted in the wake of the crisis to place limits on the action of financial institutions. Its implementation was, to a large extent, blocked by the Republicans. One thing is clear, the volume of transactions on

derivative markets did not diminish with the crisis, and the threat of a new financial crisis is still there.

2. *The competitiveness of the US economy.* The target here is the re-territorialization of industry with, notably, the objective of remedying the deficit of foreign trade. In the lower segments of employment, workers are available to work at a very low cost and deprived of basic social protection. Active policies stimulated the use of shale gas as a source of energy, with dramatic effects on the cost of energy. Given the differences in productivity worldwide (and including the cost of transportation), the costs of one unit of production in manufacturing industries in the USA and China have now converged (Sirkin *et al.* 2014). These new achievements are of utmost importance, since most of foreign trade is in manufactured goods (despite the increase of US exports of services). To these, one must add the new forms of hidden protectionism (notably by the definition of technical norms to which imports are subjected, Evenett 2013), and industrial policies in favour of specific industries (in new technologies). As of 2014, an examination of the latest data shows that the deficit of foreign trade still amounts to 3 per cent of GDP, compared to the 5 per cent observed prior to the crisis.

3. *Macro policies.* Since the 2009 recession, a growth rate of about 2 per cent has been maintained, but the deficit of the government still amounts to 6 per cent of GDP – that is, levels are that are typical of the trough of recessions. The Federal Reserve is fully committed to the restoration of the economy, holding a huge stock of Treasury and government-sponsored enterprise securities with the aim of diminishing long-term interest rates. Nonetheless, the private sector is still paying back its debt instead of borrowing, and the downward trend of investment has not been inverted. To date, no autonomous (unsupported) restoration of the aggregate economy has been achieved. These policies guarantee to the US economy a form of 'reprieve'. The key issue will be the continuing involvement of central authorities in the future and the resistances concerning corporate governance (foreign investment abroad, lavish flows of dividends, extravagant 'compensations' at the top, and the like).

4. *Taxation.* The Foreign Account Tax Compliance Act (FATCA) constrains US citizens (even living outside the country) to report their accounts in the rest of the world, and foreign financial institutions to inform the Internal Revenue Service of the existence of these assets. To what degree the device will be extended to the world and prove efficient remains to be determined. Major countries have signed agreements with the USA, though not Russia or China, but the number of tax havens in the list is impressive. Contrary to the measures above, the new controls could be detrimental to rich individuals forced to pay taxes. But remedies must be found to the deficit of the government.

In the abstract, the potential inherent in the new policies seems unquestionable. Other countries are, however, also active and may improve their own competitiveness as fast as the US economy, or even faster (notably with respect to patents and the price of energy). The class interests inherent in neoliberalism place major limits on policies in most, if not all, of the above respects, and the contradiction between class and territorial objective is acute, as clearly demonstrated during the first neoliberal episode prior to the crisis. Strengthening the situation is really a challenge.

Historical prospects

Returning to the general framework of the first section of this chapter – relations of production and class struggle – the political implications of the above are obvious and of historical import.

At the beginning of the twentieth century, the USA assumed a clear leadership in the transition from the traditional capitalism of the nineteenth century to managerial capitalism (in the corporate, managerial, and financial revolutions). The capability of the USA to lead the path in the establishment of the new institutions of managerial capitalism was the main determinant of the international hegemony of the country during the twentieth century under the new forms of Wilsonian informal imperialism (as opposed to traditional colonial empires).

At stake, in the early twenty-first century, are the political options governing the trajectory towards most advanced forms of managerial capitalism. Two options are opened: (1) a course evocative of the post-depression *path to the left* that commanded the reduction of inequality (the opposite of the rise at the top); and (2) a movement *along the right branch* of the bifurcation, as in neoliberalism. The first option failed during the 1970s. The crisis of neoliberalism was hastily interpreted by analysts on the left, as the failure of the second track. Can the conduct of the second post-crisis episode turn this failure into success, thus demonstrating the compatibility of class and territorial hegemonies? One can have serious doubts, given the amplitude of the task to be accomplished and the obvious resistance to the required adjustments that can be expected on the part of upper classes. These are the domestic contradictions, but the external contractions are also acute. Will Europe remain, staggering, at the cross-road with the consolidation of conservative policies or is there a chance for a left turn on the old continent? And what of China – the other champion of the 'national factor' and the country of the tightest alliance-merger between capitalists and government officials – an obvious candidate for a new global hegemony?

Notes

1 In the remainder of this study, we will only exceptionally refer to our earlier work. Specific contributions are: Duménil and Lévy 2001, 2011, and 2014.
2 We will not discuss here the implications of this 'managerial hypothesis' concerning the struggle for the emancipation of humanity, as necessary as ever and neither less nor more impossible than before.
3 The 'New Deal' is the name given to the set of programmes and policies enacted in the USA under President Franklin Delano Roosevelt after 1933, in the wake of the Great Recession. It is also common to refer to the political groups that supported many of the policies enacted during the first decades following World War II as the 'New Deal coalition'.
4 As in David Kotz's reference to overinvestment (Kotz 2009).
5 Robert Brenner (2009) only subtracts indirect business taxes from profits and, consequently, finds a declining trend of the profit rate, to which the crisis is imputed.

References

Arrighi, G. 1999. The Global Market. *Journal of World System Research*, 5.2: 217–51.
Brenner, R. 2009. *What is Good for Goldman Sachs is Good for America: The Origins of the Current Crisis*. Los Angeles: Center for Social Theory and Comparative History at the University of California.
Chesnais, F. 2014. Fictitious Capital in the Context of Global Over-Accumulation and Changing International Economic Power Relationships, in Bellofiore, R., and Vertova, G., eds. *The Great Recession and the Contradictions of Contemporary Capitalism*. Aldershot: Edward Elgar: 65–82.
Davidson, P. 2009. Alternative Explanations of the Operation of a Capitalist Economy: Efficient Market Theory vs Keynes's Liquidity Theory. *Real-World Economic Review*, 50: 85–100.
Duménil, G., and Lévy, D. 2001. Costs and Benefits of Neoliberalism: A Class Analysis. *Review of International Political Economy*, 8.4: 578–607.
—. 2011. *The Crisis of Neoliberalism*. Cambridge, MA: Harvard University Press.
—. 2014. *La Grande Bifurcation*. Paris: La Découverte.
Evenett, S.J. 2013. Protectionism's Quiet Return. *GTA's Pre-G8 Summit Report*. London: Centre for Economic Policy Research.

Husson, M. 2012. Le Néolibéralisme, Stade Suprême? *Actuel Marx*, 51: 86–101.

Kotz, D. 2009. The Financial and Economic Crisis of 2008: A Systemic Crisis of Neoliberal Capitalism. *Review of Radical Political Economics*, 41: 305–17.

Krugman, P. 2008. *The Return of Depression Economics and the Crisis of 2008*. New York: W.W. Norton.

Moseley, F. 2009. The US Economic Crisis: Causes and Solutions. *International Socialist Review*, 64.

Piketty, T., and Saez, E. 2003. Income Inequality in the United States, 1913–1998. *Quarterly Journal of Economics*, 118.1: 1–39.

Saez, E. and G. Zucman 2014. Wealth Inequality in the United States Since 1913: Evidence from Capitalized Income Tax. *Working Paper #20625*. Washington, DC: National Bureau of Economic Research.

Shaikh, A. 2011. The First Great Depression of the 21st Century. *Socialist Register*, 47: 44–63.

Sirkin, H., Zinser, M., and Rose, J. 2014. *The Shifting Economics of Global Manufacturing: How Cost Competitiveness is Changing Worldwide*. Boston: Boston Consulting Group.

Springer, S. 2016. The Violence of Neoliberalism, in Springer, S., Birch, K., and MacLeavy, J., eds. *The Handbook of Neoliberalism*. London: Routledge: 139–49.

Stiglitz, J. 2010. *Free to Fall. America, Free Markets, and the Sinking of the World Economy*, New York: W.W. Norton.

Valle, A. 2008. La Crisis Estadounidense y la Ganancia. *Razón y Revolución*, 18: 79–93.

Wallerstein, I. 2000. Globalization or the Age of Transition? A Long-Term View of the Trajectory of the World-System. *International Sociology*, 15.2: 250–68.

48
REGULATED DEREGULATION

Manuel B. Aalbers

What is deregulation?

For a while now, I have been suggesting – but not truly argued – that what we commonly label, conceptualize and understand as 'deregulation' could better be understood as 'reregulation' (Aalbers 2008, 2009, 2012, 2013; for related arguments, see, for example, Majone 1990; Synder 1999; Levi-Faur 2005; Igoe and Brockington 2007; Castree 2008). I've never been particularly happy, however, with the label 're-regulation', as it may, incorrectly, suggest that a market becomes regulated *again* after a period of non- or deregulation. Since 2007, most people who use the term 'reregulation' argue for markets to be *more* regulated as they see those markets as *under-regulated*. In other words: reregulation is generally framed as the answer to deregulation – that is, reregulation is a political response that follows from the argument that deregulation of financial and other markets is one of the main causes of the global financial and economic crisis. The logic goes that if the under-regulation of markets resulted in 'irrational exuberance', to borrow Alan Greenspan's widely used phrase, and therefore to crisis, we need more regulation – that is, reregulation – to limit future irrational exuberance and crises. That is not what I would like to suggest.

A large part of the problem, I believe, is that we are generally not very clear about what we mean when we speak of 'deregulation'. Since 'de' is a prefix conveying negation or reversal, deregulation refers to removing or reducing regulation. Deregulation is simply left undefined as it must clearly be the opposite of regulation; so let's see how 'regulation' is commonly defined. In economics and, generally, also in the popular media, regulation is seen as anything that limits the workings of market mechanism and, to most mainstream economists (not just to neoclassical economists), regulation has a negative connotation; it is only deemed beneficial if it addresses market failure.

Heterodox economists and other social scientists generally use a more open definition of regulation that may resemble the following definition from the *Encyclopedia of Political Economy*: 'setting rules and establishing an enforcement mechanism designed to control the operation of the system's constituent institutions, instruments and markets' (Spotton 1999: 971). Here, regulation is not seen in opposition to the market mechanism, and it is common to view markets as depending on state regulation for their stability and growth. In Spotton's terms, deregulation would then refer to removing rules and a reduced role of enforcement mechanisms.

In critical political economy and human geography, deregulation is often discussed alongside terms such as privatization, neo/liberalization, re/commodification, globalization and, increasingly, also financialization, but often the relations between these different concepts are left quite implicit. Frequently, deregulation is seen as neoliberalism-in-action (alongside neoliberal ideology) – that is, as something by which we can empirically *see* neoliberalism. In this conceptualization, when a market is deregulated, there is a clear indication of neoliberalism, but since neoliberalism includes deregulation but is not limited to it, deregulation in itself is not necessarily sufficient to speak of neoliberalism, although neoliberalization is effected through deregulation. My impression is that deregulation, in the writings of many critical political economists and human geographers, often boils down to economic liberalization, a relaxation of government restrictions, instituting or expanding a competitive market system. It is also not uncommon to conflate deregulation and privatization. In other words, deregulation is often reduced to cognate or related concepts, but it is not easy to substantiate this claim as deregulation is generally left undefined.

Bob Jessop is one of the key authors in critical political economy and human geography that does define 'deregulation'. In 2002 he defined deregulation under neoliberalism as the 'reduced role of law and state'[1] (Jessop 2002: 461) – that is, in a similar way to my reading of Spotton's definition. In another paper, Jessop (2003) defines deregulation as 'giving economic agents greater freedom from state control and legal restrictions' – that is, as similar to liberalization. In discussions about deregulation, people have pointed out to me that deregulation should be read in the tradition of the 'Régulation Approach' and that deregulation is not the opposite of regulation but of '*régulation*' – better translated in English as 'regularization' or 'normalization' rather than 'regulation' (Jessop and Sum 2006) – which implies that, in this particular reading of 'deregulation', it should be read as 'deregularization' or 'denormalization'. Although I do not exclude the possibility that some have conceptualized deregulation as opposed to *régulation*, the dominant use of deregulation seems closer to Jessop's definitions, to my readings of Spotton's definition and to 'liberalization'.

Because of the problem – or, if one prefers, confusions – associated with the term 'deregulation', I will propose an alternative concept: *regulated deregulation*. Before explaining what regulated deregulation is and how it relates to deregulation 'as we know it', I will first look into the associated relation between deregulation and neoliberalism. Subsequently, I will discuss three case studies of assumed deregulation as illustrations of my argument that the concept of regulated deregulation captures better than relation between neoliberalism and de/regulation. My aim is to contribute not only to the conceptualization of neoliberalism, but also to stress that regulation is increasingly dense, specialized and juridificated[2] and, therefore, less accessible to society at large and more open to be mobilized by big, powerful and often financialized corporations.

Beyond semantics: the neoliberal cookbook

This has been a very semantic discussion so far, but my argument is not exclusively a semantic one. The point I am trying to make is quite simple: the label 'deregulation' implies less regulation; deregulation is commonly framed as something that frees markets from government intervention, suggesting the rolling out of markets as conceptualized within mainstream economics and mainstream media. Critical analysts within social science see this as evidence of neoliberalization (e.g. Harvey 2005; Brenner *et al.* 2010). This implies that we have criticized the idea of 'free markets' as part of a more general trend towards neoliberalism, but that we have failed to break out of the conceptualization that frames markets as being constrained by government intervention. Although the idea that markets thrive in the absence of state control has been criticized for decades (e.g. Polanyi 1944; Aglietta [1976]1979; Strange 1988; Majone 1994; Evans 1995; Hollingsworth and Boyer 1997; Fligstein 2001; Bourdieu [2000]2005), we have not broken out of the framing of deregulation as something that frees markets from regulatory constraints. In fact, markets were created by, and are maintained through, state intervention. That does not imply that *all* government intervention is there to push marketization, but it does suggest, first, that state intervention is a necessary condition for markets to thrive, and, second, that states often act to facilitate markets rather than to constrain them.

The political process of marketization is deeply embedded in state institutions and practices (Polanyi 1944). Actually existing regulation is not so much market-oriented as it is devoted to the dominance of markets and public life by giant corporations (Crouch 2011). Panitch and Konings speak of 'myths of neoliberal deregulation' because 'Neoliberal *practices* did not entail institutional retreat so much as the expansion and consolidation of the networks of institutional linkages that sustained the imperial power of American finance' (Panitch and Konings 2009: 68, emphasis in original). Neoliberalism is not only 'a self-contradictory form of regulation-in-denial' (Peck 2010: xiii), it is also about facilitating one set of agents in market transactions (Aalbers 2013). Indeed, 'reregulation can thus serve not only as a means to *preserve* power… but also as a way to *expand* power' (Synder 1999: 178, emphasis in original).

To sum up the argument so far: deregulation is not the same as economic liberalization, and deregulation does not necessarily imply neoliberalism at work. Deregulation-as-liberalization is part of the neoliberal cookbook, but the real-life chefs of neoliberalism use selective elements of the regulation spice mix to add flavour to actually existing neoliberal dishes. These chefs know all to well that regulation is a necessary ingredient to prepare these dishes. Their customers, such as the captains of industry, who often claim to prefer a regulation-free diet, simply need regulation to be able to claim the biggest piece of the pie, to enlarge the absolute size of the pie, or to be able to bake a pie in the first place. If you are a captain of industry, a pie simply tastes better if the right mix of regulation spices is added. As a result, agents from a range of economic sectors lobby the state to make some regulatory spices obligatory while ruling out others.

What the preferred and rejected regulatory spices are depends on your position in the market. If you are the incumbent, regulation leading to high entry costs may be a preferred spice. If you run an insurance company and fear that commercial banks may be able to offer insurance policies at more competitive prices, you may prefer regulation that separates insurance from banking. The point is that there is no inherent rejection of regulation *per se*. Deregulation does not necessarily facilitate neo/liberalization, privatization, re/commodification or financialization. Some form of regulation is often needed to facilitate market making, shaping and liberalization. For both 'roll-back' and 'roll-out' neoliberalism (Peck and Tickell 2002), regulation is crucial as a facilitator.

Introducing regulated deregulation

Yet, there remains a tension between neoliberalism and de/regulation, a tension that the concept of reregulation does not take away. Alternatively, I here propose the concept of regulated deregulation, in which the 'deregulation' part refers to deregulation-as-liberalization – that is, giving *some* economic agents greater freedom from state control and legal restrictions (cf. Jessop 2003), while the 'regulated' part refers to 'setting rules and establishing an enforcement mechanism designed to control the operation of the system's constituent institutions, instruments and markets' (Spotton 1999: 971). In other words, under regulated deregulation some economic agents are given greater freedom from state control, but the market framework itself is regulated. In fact, the regulation of the market framework allows for the freedom of some economic agents within that framework (often at the expense of other agents). Regulated deregulation may appear a *contradictio in terminis*, but is intentionally so, an oxymoron, that breaks down the false dichotomy between regulation and deregulation. That is, it problematizes the problematic understanding of deregulation-as-liberalization and of regulation-as-constraining-markets, implying that regulation is not anathema to actually existing neoliberalism.

The notion of regulated deregulation also implies that regulation in the age of neoliberalism does not have to diminish. Typically all these forms of regulation as an oeuvre facilitate markets at least as much as they constrain them. Authors using the term 'deregulation' often focus on the repeal of acts such as Glass–Steagall in the USA, but pay less attention to all the new and expanded regulation that has replaced and repleted it – that is, they have a selective and limited understanding of actually existing regulation. In fact, if we look at the *amount* of regulation in most markets in most countries, we will see that it has only increased – and often increased at a rapid pace – tempting Levi-Faur (2005) to speak of a 'regulatory explosion'. At different scales, it is quite rare for a law or rule to be repealed and, even if this is the case, more laws and more rules generally replace it. Furthermore, new regulation tends to be more specific, more detailed and therefore longer. There is also a tendency for formal laws and acts to be complemented by more and more other types of regulations, such as by-laws, statutes, ordinances, controls, codes (e.g. codes of conduct, honour codes and ethical codes), rules, principles and standards, which are all increasingly institutionalized legally.

Economic historians, sociologists, geographers, anthropologists and political economists of different stripes have all argued, in some way or another, that markets are shaped by the state rather than markets being simply constrained by the state (see Polanyi 1944; Cook 1966; Weber [1922]1978; Aglietta [1976]1979; Durkheim [1893]1984; Strange 1988; Hodgson 1988; Schwartz 1994; Evans 1995; Crouch and Streeck 1997; Hollingsworth and Boyer 1997; Fligstein 2001; Chang 2002; Bourdieu [2000]2005). 'Freer markets, more rules', as Vogel (1996) summarizes the debate. Capitalism is furthered through regulation and the corporatization of the world is a product of regulation, of which the growth of states can be seen as a by-product (Braithwaite 2005; Levi-Faur 2005). It would be easy to take a Polanyian, Bourdieudian, Foucauldian, institutional, international political economy or some other approach to regulated deregulation – and I believe all such perspectives could help to theorize regulated deregulation and embed it into wider arguments about economies and states as well as to put it to the test of empirical scrutiny.

I am not the first to coin the term 'regulated deregulation'. Dalla and Khatkhate (1995) have used the label to contrast slow, moderate and limited deregulation to fast and complete deregulation. Van de Velde and Wallis (2013) never define or even explicitly discuss regulated deregulation, but appear to see regulated deregulation as the opposite of self-regulation in cases of privatization. Their discussion of the privatization and de/regulation of local bus services suggests that their understanding of regulated deregulation fits the understanding advanced here. First's (2002) conceptualization of regulated deregulation is very similar to mine. He argues that, in his case – the market for electric utilities in New York – 'deregulation' is not the best concept because one regulatory system is replaced with another system that 'is more sensitive to economic incentives than was the old… but that the new system is also very much under governmental control [and] state agencies continue to shape the industry' (ibid.: 912).

To illustrate the meanings and implications of regulated deregulation, I will now briefly discuss three cases of what I see as actually existing regulated deregulation: first, the changing regulation of electric utilities (based on First 200); second, the privatization of local bus services (based on Van de Velde and Wallis 2013); and third, the regulation of American and British (housing) finance that enabled securitization (largely based on Gotham 2006, 2009; Wainwright, 2009). I've dropped Dalla and Khatkhate's (1995) discussion of the regulated deregulation of the financial system in South Korea because they simply mean something else when using the phrase 'regulated deregulation'. The three cases I do discuss here are typically seen as instances of neoliberal deregulation: in the first two cases of roll-back neoliberalism and in the third case of roll-out neoliberalism. In these cases we see a regulatory regime shift in favour of the liberalization of some economic agents, creating markets and/or possibilities that hitherto did not exist. Yet, this hardly happens through repealing regulation. These cases demonstrate how regulation is introduced and mobilized to create new, or change existing, markets and how this has selectively benefited some but not all economic agents.

Electric power industry

Harry First (2002) discusses how the new regulatory regime for electric utilities in New York state is not simply a case of deregulation. The New York Public Service Commission (PSC) has often been at the forefront of regulatory reform. The so-called deregulation of the electric power industry started in 1993 with a system of 'flexible pricing' which enabled some industrial and commercial customers to negotiate contracts and prices with suppliers. In the following years the PSC discussed a changing number of 'objectives', 'goals' and 'principles' to guide not only an increasingly competitive industry structure, but also to safeguard environmental purity, affordability and service quality.

These discussions and the documents that came out of them, explicitly stated that competition had to be guided and that competition might not be possible in all circumstances. It was decided to first introduce wholesale competition and only then retail competition. In addition, the existing five major New York utility companies were directed 'to file individual plans for implementing the Commission's vision, including a plan for retail access, rate reductions, and corporate restructuring' (ibid.: 916). Although these utility companies petitioned for court review of the directive, the court approved the directive. As a result, all companies had to draw up their own plans, which were subsequently negotiated with the PSC and all were hereby forced to open up to retail competition.

On the wholesale side, the existing 'New York Power Pool', an organization formed in 1966 as a response to the 1965 blackout in order to improve system reliability, was shored up and transformed into the 'New York ISO'. In 1999 the NYISO took full control of New York's wholesale power system, which included running two auction markets, imposing bidding rules, adopting 'market mitigation measures' (a set of criteria and rules to regulate the market) and monitoring the results.

The competition in the electric power industry was not created through a deregulation that reduced the role of the state. Rather, the state transformed itself, extending its regulatory net to recreate an existing market. Competition was introduced but it did not create a so-called free market – competition was regulated by a set of principles, directives, criteria and rules. As First (ibid.: 925) concludes, the regulatory agencies were not *captured* by the energy companies but rather 'the legislature stepped in to shape the industry'. He continues to argue that,

> No matter how committed the PSC is to marketplace initiatives, it still approaches the problems, first of all, from its institutional perspective as the agency that has been (and will continue to be) responsible for regulating the electric power industry.
>
> *(Ibid.: 926)*

567

Selective economic agents have been liberalized but the 'market power', the power to control prices and exclude competition, lies predominantly with the regulatory agencies PSC and NYISO.

Local bus services

Didier Van de Velde and Ian Wallis (2013) discuss how the privatization of local bus services in Great Britain and Sweden was not simply a case of deregulation to let the market take over.

In Great Britain (outside London) local and regional bus transport has been provided on the basis of a market-initiated regime since 1986. This was initially enabled by the Thatcher era 1985 Transport Act in which all main bus companies owned by the state were privatized. To keep service levels up, two types of subsidies were introduced alongside the selling off of transport services. Van de Velde and Wallis speak of a dogmatic approach to deregulation that wasn't very successful in reaching its goals, which were primarily defined as cost reduction and passenger increase. Almost all forms of coordination between operators were considered anti-competitive, which made it very difficult to establish 'fare integration, timetable coordination, information integration, etc.' (ibid.: 24).

In the early 2000s we start seeing several changes to the existing regulation with the implementation of the Transport Act 2000, including Statuary Quality Partnership Schemes and Quality Contracts that specify the agreements between transport companies and local authorities. In 2006 an official review of the deregulation pointed to several problems in the practices and regulation of transport companies. This resulted in the Local Transport Act 2008, which significantly expanded the regulatory net of the state, providing more tools and flexibility for local authorities. To increase coordination and shore-up monitoring, the existing 'passenger transport authorities' are transformed into 'integrated transport authorities', which are given 'full responsibility for local transport plans, including the road network and not just public transport' (ibid.: 23).

Since the 1990s Sweden has also moved from a model of fully public transport to a privatized yet publicly regulated transport system. The resulting Swedish model, as put into the 2010 *Lag om kollektivstraffik* (Public Transport Law) relies on two pillars: first, the combination of subsidized services with free market initiative; and, second, a strong regionally organized coordinating authority. The Swedish counties, typically in association with their municipalities, each created a 'common planning company' to cooperate not only in urban and regional planning, but also in tendering their transport services. The common planning companies are responsible for drafting and implementing a Regional Transport Supply Programme that covers both commercial services and services to be contracted and includes measures to protect the environment and keep services up throughout the region as well as for target groups such as mobility-impaired people.

Transport companies who want to initiate commercial services must register with the authority, who will then guide the operators in their business plans and can make specific requirements, so-called 'public service obligations', to the operator. Where no operator registers to initiate commercial services, the regional authority can use the set public service obligations to organize a competitive tendering process. Van de Velde and Wallis speak of a hybrid regime that includes strong elements of both deregulation-as-privatization and continued regulation-as-coordination by public authorities.

Mortgage securitization

Kevin Fox Gotham (2006, 2009) discusses how mortgage securitization in the USA has been created by government intervention and has subsequently been expanded through an active redrawing of the boundaries between different parts of the housing and financial sectors. Some of these changes can be characterized as deregulation-as-liberalization, but since significant regulation-as-rulemaking was required at each step of the rolling out of securitization, it is another case of regulated deregulation. Mortgage securitization in the USA dates back to the late 1960s and early 1970s when new legislation allowed the two so-called 'government-sponsored enterprises' (GSEs), Fannie Mae and Freddie Mac, to securitize the mortgages and loans they were legally obliged to buy from local banks and thrifts, and to sell the bonds issued on the back of these assets to private investors. This became known as 'public label securitization' (Gotham 2006, 2009; Ashton 2009).

During the 1970s, these GSEs were involved in a large-scale experiment of constructing a smoothly running securitization machine, which ground to a halt in the late 1970s because of disadvantageous macro-economic conditions. The political response was to introduce additional deregulation to roll out securitization nationwide. In the mid-1980s a package of legislative measures was initiated to increase the accessibility of the primary mortgage market for an ever-larger slice of US households (Gotham 2009; Aalbers 2012). What has happened since is a gradual transformation of local legislative frameworks, techniques, expertise and relationships into a 'private label securitization machine' (Lewis 1989) – that is, securitization by investment banks rather than by the GSEs. This resulted in a step-by-step extension of the securitization technique to other assets, markets and jurisdictions.

Subsequently, Thomas Wainwright (2009) demonstrated that the transfer of US securitization techniques to the UK required multidimensional organizational, institutional and legal adaptations, which were actively negotiated by market insiders and regulators. Wainwright describes how Salomon Brothers established a specialized structuring firm in London in 1986, called the Mortgage Corporation, which issued mortgage-backed securities and sold them to UK-based investors (Lewis 1989; Wainwright 2009). Wainwright stresses that the technique of securitization did not travel well across borders: its wide-scale application in the UK required fiscal, legal and accounting adaptations, which, in turn, required extensive negotiations between market insiders and regulators. Wainwright's paper counters, head on, the mainstream economists' view of financial markets by pointing out that securitization did not develop in an institutional void but required institutional, organization and cultural preconditions for which state intervention was crucial.

Conclusion

There is a complex relation between regulation, deregulation, liberalization and neoliberalism. At the Colloque Walter Lippmann in Paris in 1938 – often considered the birthplace of neoliberalism – neoliberalism was defined in terms of the priority of the price mechanism, free enterprise, the system of competition, and a strong and impartial state (Plehwe 2009), but not yet associated with deregulation, privatization, inequality and the withdrawal of the state (Audier 2008). The problem with the label 'deregulation' is that it implies less regulation and that deregulation is commonly framed as something that frees markets from government intervention, suggestive of neoliberalization. In reality, state intervention is a necessary condition for markets to thrive. Neoliberals do not seek to completely eliminate the state, but rather to redefine the nature and functions of the state (Mirowski 2009). Actually existing regulation and neoliberalism are not so much market-oriented as they are devoted to the dominance of markets and public life by financialized corporations (Crouch 2011; Aalbers 2013).

I have discussed three very different cases of what I label regulated deregulation: the electric power industry in New York state, local bus services in Great Britain and Sweden and mortgage securitization in the USA and UK. All three cases are commonly labelled as deregulation, but I have tried to show how these cases all have elements of deregulation-as-liberalization (cf. Jessop's 2003 definition above) but not of deregulation as defined by a reduced role of law and the state (cf. Jessop's 2002 definition above). If anything, the liberalization has been enabled, managed and controlled by re/setting rules and re/establishing 'an enforcement mechanism designed to control the operation of the system's constituent institutions, instruments and markets' (Spotton 1999: 971). Neoliberalism is not simply the roll-back of the state. Neoliberalization may involve the roll-back of the *welfare* state, but at the same time neoliberalism leads to a regulatory explosion (Levi-Faur 2005), indicative of the state widening its net (Cohen 1985), embedding market principles more deeply in the fabric of society (Panitch and Konings 2009).

The concept of regulated deregulation enables us to see how liberalization of selective economic agents was only made possible by introducing a new regulatory system that replaced or amended the existing regulatory system. Regulated deregulation allows for the combination of competition and economic incentives, on the one hand, and coordination and the regulation authority-led making and shaping of different economic sectors and industries, on the other – that is, regulated deregulation negates the ostensible contradiction between liberalization and state control. Under regulated deregulation some economic agents are given greater freedom from state control, but the market framework itself is regulated. By problematizing the dominant narrative of deregulation-as-neoliberalization, the concept of regulated deregulation stresses that regulation is not anathema to actually existing neoliberalism. By actively mobilizing regulation, neoliberal agents are creating the conditions of neoliberalization through the state.

Coda

By relabelling the trend towards the increased regulation of markets alongside the favouring of some economic agents from deregulation to regulated deregulation, I expect to be criticized for misunderstanding the critical version of the deregulation argument. My critics will argue that the concept of deregulation focuses exactly on the facilitation of markets by states and that we do not need a new term to understand this process. My critics are correct that many authors who have used the term 'deregulation' have focused on how states have facilitated markets, but I feel that they often misrepresent actually existing market regulation as deregulation as they cannot break out of the free market framing that they seek to criticize. They criticize states for facilitating big corporations at the expense of entire populations, but they fail to take seriously the idea that markets work the way they do *because* they are increasingly regulated by states. Some see deregulation as the freeing of markets from constraints, but what has actually happened in most markets in most countries is that the state has facilitated one set of agents as the expense of other sets of agents. Markets have not been freed of regulation to create a level-playing field; markets have increasingly become regulated by the state and its many institutions to create anything but a level playing field. To call this deregulation is a travesty.

Even if one claims to understand this process but to have analysed it within the deregulation framework, the issue remains that the critical concept of deregulation has not been sufficiently divorced from the deregulation arguments of mainstream economists and mainstream media, and therefore run the risk of being easily confused. Moreover, also many critical social scientists use the word 'deregulation' to refer to liberalization, the freeing up of markets. We can continue to label actually existing regulation as deregulation but accept the wider notion that it entails, but I suggest it would make more sense to break out of the framing of the deregulationist perspective and its ambiguities by systematically referring to the increasing regulation of markets to facilitate one set of agents over other sets of agents by the label regulated deregulation. At the least, this will minimize the chance that the label deregulation is misunderstood as freeing up markets from government regulation. But I hope the relabelling will also facilitate a more widespread understanding of actually existing regulation as increasingly dense, specialized and juridificated and therefore less accessible. Indeed, regulation has been mobilized by economic elites in part enabled through juridification (see note 2). As a result, regulation is increasingly facilitating one set of markets agents over others, typically but not necessarily aiding big, powerful corporations at the expense of less powerful small enterprises and the population at large.

The socio-political question is not one of 'more regulation' or 're-regulation', as has been the typical left-wing and to some extent also right-wing response to the financial crisis, but one of better regulation that does not facilitate so-called 'free markets' and privilege big powerful corporations along with big law firms at the expense of everyone else, but rather regulation that protects small enterprises and entire populations from the cannibalizing of markets by a few big players who often do not even pay most of their taxes in the countries they have pushed to reregulate markets to their benefit. The concept of regulated deregulation also opens up a research agenda that could focus on socially and politically relevant questions related to how a select number of agents have been able to shift regulation both ideologically and practically in their direction. This would call for case studies of different markets and different countries. In more plain terms: how have the 1 per cent used state institutions and their regulatory power to further their own interests at the expense of the 99 per cent?

Notes

1 Which, ironically enough, could also be a definition of anarchism.
2 Juridification refers to the law's expansion and differentiation, resulting in increased judicial power as well as the dominance of legal discourse (for a discussion, see Blichner and Molander 2005).

References

Aalbers, M.B. 2008. The Financialization of Home and the Mortgage Market Crisis. *Competition & Change*, 12: 148–66.

—. 2009. Geographies of the Financial Crisis. *Area*, 41: 34–42.

—. ed. 2012. *Subprime Cities: The Political Economy of Mortgage Markets*. Oxford: Wiley-Blackwell.

—. 2013. Neoliberalism is Dead… Long live Neoliberalism! *International Journal of Urban and Regional Research*, 37: 1083–90.

Aglietta, M. [1976]1979. *Régulation et Crises du Capitalisme: l'Expérience des Etats-Unis*. Paris: Calman-Lévy.

Ashton, P. 2009. An Appetite for Yield: The Anatomy of the Subprime Mortgage Crisis. *Environment & Planning A*, 41.6: 1420–41.

Audier, S. 2008. *Le Colloque Lippmann, aux Origines du Néo-Libéralisme*. Lormont: Le Bord de l'Eau.

Blichner, L.C. and Molander, A. 2005. *What is Juridification?* Oslo: ARENA.

Bourdieu, P. 2000[2005]. *Les Structures Sociales de l'Économie*. Paris: Seuil.

Braithwaite, J. 2005. Neoliberalism or Regulatory Capitalism. *RegNet Occasional Paper No. 5*. Retrieved from http://ssrn.com/abstract=875789

Brenner, N., Peck, J., and Theodore, N. 2010. Variegated Neoliberalization: Geographies, Modalities, Pathways. *Global Networks*, 10: 1–51.

Castree, N. 2008. Neoliberalising Nature: The Logics of Deregulation and Reregulation. *Environment and Planning A*, 40: 131–52.

Chang, H.-J. 2002. Breaking the Mould: An Institutionalist Political Economy Alternative to the Neo-Liberal Theory of the Market and the State. *Cambridge Journal of Economics*, 26.5: 539–59.

Cohen, S. 1985. *Visions of Social Control*. Cambridge: Polity.

Cook, S. 1966. The Obsolete 'Anti-Market' Mentality: A Critique of the Substantive Approach to Economic Anthropology. *American Anthropologist*, 68: 323–45.

Crouch, C. 2011. *The Strange Non-Death of Neoliberalism*. Cambridge: Polity.

Crouch, C. and Streeck, W. eds. 1997. *Political Economy of Modern Capitalism: Mapping Convergence and Diversity*. London: Sage.

Dalla, I., and Khatkhate, D. 1995. Regulated Deregulation of the Financial System in Korea. *World Bank Discussion Papers 292*. Washington, DC: World Bank.

Durkheim, É. [1893]1984. *De la Division du Travail Social: Étude sur l'Organisation des Sociétés Supérieures*. Paris: Alcan.

Evans, P.B. 1995. *Embedded Autonomy: States and Industrial Transformation*. Princeton, NJ: Princeton University Press.

First, H. 2002. Regulated Deregulation: The New York Experience in Electric Utility Deregulation. *Loyola University Chicago Law Journal*, 33.4: 911–32.

Fligstein, N. 2001. *The Architecture of Markets: An Economic Sociology of Twenty-First-Century Capitalist Societies*. Princeton, NJ: Princeton University Press.

Gotham, K.F. 2006. The Secondary Circuit of Capital Reconsidered: Globalization and the US Real Estate Sector. *American Journal of Sociology*, 112.1: 231–75.

—. 2009. Creating Liquidity Out of Spatial Fixity: The Secondary Circuit of Capital and the Subprime Mortgage Crisis. *International Journal of Urban and Regional Research*, 33.2: 355–71.

Harvey, D. 2005. *A Brief History of Neoliberalism*. Oxford: Oxford University Press.

Hodgson, G.M. 1988. *Economics and Institutions: A Manifesto for a Modern Institutional Economics*. Cambridge: Polity.

Hollingsworth, J.R., and Boyer, R. eds. 1997. *Contemporary Capitalism: The Embeddedness of Institutions*. Cambridge: Cambridge University Press.

Igoe, J., and Brockington, D. 2007. Neoliberal Conservation: A Brief Introduction. *Conservation & Society*, 6: 432–49.

Jessop, B. 2002. Liberalism, Neoliberalism and Urban Governance: A State-Theoretical Perspective. *Antipode*, 34: 452–72.

—. 2003. From Thatcherism to New Labour: Neo-Liberalism, Workfarism, and Labour Market Regulation, in Overbeek, H., ed. *The Political Economy of European Employment: European Integration and the Transnationalization of the (Un)Employment Question*. London: Routledge: 137–53.

Jessop, B., and Sum, N.-L. 2006. *Beyond the Regulation Approach: Putting Capitalist Economies in Their Place*. Cheltenham: Edward Elgar.

Levi-Faur, D. 2005. The Global Diffusion of Regulatory Capitalism. *The Annals of the American Academy of Political and Social Sciences*, 598.1: 12–32.

Lewis, M. 1989. *Liar's Poker: Two Cities, True Greed*. New York: Hodder & Stoughton.

Majone, G. ed. 1990. *Deregulation or Re-Regulation? Regulatory Reform in Europe and the United States*. London: Pinter.

—. 1994. The Rise of the Regulatory State in Europe. *West European Politics*, 17.3: 77–101.

Mirowski, P. 2009. Defining Neoliberalism, in Mirowski, P., and Plehwe, D., eds. *The Road from Mont Pèlerin: The Making of the Neoliberal Thought Collective*. Cambridge: Cambridge University Press: 417–55.

Panitch, L., and Konings, M. 2009. Myths of Neoliberal Deregulation. *New Left Review*, 57: 67–83.

Peck, J. 2010. *Constructions of Neoliberal Reason*. Oxford: Oxford University Press.

Peck, J., and Tickell, A. 2002. Neoliberalizing Space. *Antipode*, 34: 380–404.

Plehwe, D. 2009. Introduction, in Mirowski, P., and Plehwe, D., eds. *The Road from Mont Pèlerin: The Making of the Neoliberal Thought Collective*. Cambridge: Cambridge University Press: 1–42.

Polanyi, K. 1944. *The Great Transformation: The Political and Economic Origins of Our Time*. Boston, MA: Beacon.

Schwartz, H.S. 1994. *States vs Markets: History, Geography, and the Development of the International Economy*. New York: St Martin's Press.

Spotton, B. 1999. Regulation and Deregulation: Financial, in O'Hara, P.A., ed. *Encyclopedia of Political Economy*. London: Routledge: 971–4.

Strange, S. 1988. *States and Markets*. London: Pinter.

Synder, R. 1999. After Neoliberalism: The Politics of Reregulation in Mexico. *World Politics*, 51: 173–204.

Van de Velde, D., and Wallis, I. 2013. 'Regulated Deregulation' of Local Bus Services: An Appraisal of International Developments. *Research in Transportation Economics*, 39: 21–33.

Vogel, S.K. 1996. *Freer Markets, More Rules: Regulatory Reform in Advanced Industrial Countries*. Ithaca, NY: Cornell University Press.

Wainwright, T. 2009. Laying the Foundations for a Crisis: Mapping the Historico-Geographical Construction of RMBS Securitization in the UK. *International Journal of Urban and Regional Research*, 33.2: 372–88.

Weber, M. [1922]1978. *Wirtschaft und Gesellschaft: Grundriss der Verstehenden Soziologie*. Tübingen: Mohr Siebeck.

49

NEOLIBERALISM VERSION 3+

James D. Sidaway and Reijer Hendrikse

Reconfiguring neoliberalism

This chapter charts the dynamics and features of a reconfigured and rejuvenated neoliberalism emerging out of the financial crisis that enveloped most Western countries over the last decade. It expands our prior designation of a neoliberalism 3.0 (Hendrikse and Sidaway 2010) that, we argued, was reworking earlier phases of neoliberalism and a longer history of what Block and Somers (2014) term 'market fundamentalism'. Our reflections here are offered as a heuristic, rather than definitive statement. We offer the statement, however, in the light of our own research on the aftermaths of crisis from two European sites, a Dutch university (Engelen *et al.* 2014) and a German city (Hendrikse and Sidaway 2014), whereby public institutions have become tangled up with derivatives and subject to financial markets. We are also mindful of wider questions about the periodization and nature of neoliberalism. Such questions have long been debated, among a range of positions on what neoliberalism is, how we study it, where it is to be found and where it came from.[1] Although some argue that neoliberal accumulation patterns never assumed very stable characteristics, and have been 'a "plural" set of ideas rather than a singular "pensée unique"' (Plehwe *et al.* 2006: 2) and notwithstanding variegated outcomes and extents, neoliberalism might be defined as a programme of resolving problems of, and developing, human society by means of purportedly competitive markets (Patomäki 2009: 431), with financial markets leading the way.

For a moment during the 2007–8 crisis, there was a tendency to talk about neoliberalism in the past tense. But what Crouch (2011) termed *The Strange Non-death of Neo-liberalism* turned out to be not that strange at all, but a function of neoliberalism's combined endurance and malleability. We argue that diagnoses envisioning the end of neoliberalism that appeared in the immediate wake of the bailouts accompanying the financial crises mistook the reworking of neoliberalism as an end. Yet in the immediate aftermath of the bailouts and stimulus packages, there was briefly much media, blog, and bulletin board talk about the decline or end of neoliberalism, sometimes anticipating or designating a new Keynesian moment. Reflecting this, the introduction to a valuable set of essays entitled *The Rise and Fall of Neo-liberalism: The Collapse of an Economic Order?* opens by noting how:

> Writing about neoliberalism in 2009 is a challenge. On the one hand, the credit crunch and banking crisis have exposed the fault lines in the neoliberal economic order that has been dominant for the last three decades… On the other hand, the different impacts and implications of the recent economic crises illustrate the diversity in the implementation and embeddedness of neoliberalism in many countries.
>
> *(Birch and Mykhnenko 2010: 1)*

References to diversity and embeddedness, signifying the scalar unfolding and path dependency of neoliberalism across institutional, national, regional, urban, and local sites, became the starting point of the voluminous geographical literature on neoliberalism. A landmark paper on 'neoliberalizing space' that is invariably cited in this literature did much to encourage attention to detail (Peck and Tickell 2002). That paper identified two broad, successive phases of implementing neoliberalism. Brenner *et al.* (2010: 182) also discern successive waves of neoliberalization. Arguably, phase 1 comprised the emergence of proto- and implementation of *rollback* neoliberalism. Proto-neoliberalism was the intellectual project shaped by the likes of Lippmann, Hayek and Friedman (e.g. see Dardot and Laval 2013; Mirowski and Plehwe 2009), which then underwrote rollback, via austerity, monetarism, and privatization, undertaken by Pinochet (through force of arms), Thatcher, Reagan, Lange and their fellow travellers. Subsequently, during phase 2 of *rollout* neoliberalism:

> gradually metamorphosed into more socially interventionist and ameliorative forms, epitomized by the Third-Way contortions of the Clinton and Blair administrations… in which new forms of institution-building and governmental intervention have been licensed within the (broadly defined) neoliberal project. No longer concerned narrowly with the mobilization and extension of markets (and market logics), neoliberalism is increasingly associated with the political foregrounding of new modes of social and penal policy making.
>
> *(Peck and Tickell 2002: 388–9)*

Thinking of neoliberalism in terms of waves or phases is intriguing. Waves break in circular motion and it might seem that we are experiencing a return to rollback neoliberalism. Simultaneously, there appears to be a new phase, as this wave unfolds within novel settings. While we are mindful of complexity and contingency, it seems worth setting out some theses on where neoliberalism is now going – and taking us.

Natively neoliberal

We posit what has emerged since the crisis might be understood as a *neoliberalism 3+*. We are aware of references to capitalism 3.0 (Barnes 2006) or even 4.0 (Kaletsky 2010). However, what we describe here is more specific. Our reference to a figure that was coined to refer to the semantic and mobile web, more deeply connecting people, machines, and code, might be taken as a literal reading of Ong's (2007) description of neoliberalism as a mobile technology. But we draw equally on Rogers's (2009) characterization of a shift from the digitized to the natively digital that has featured in the evolution of the internet and associated technologies. For Rogers, there is a distinction between the objects, content, devices and environments born in the new medium (natively digital), as opposed to those that have migrated to it (digitized).

In similar terms, neoliberalism 3+ works with an already quite thoroughly neoliberalized space; it substantially extends it and seeks new paths, bonds, appeal, and power. Neoliberalism 3+

is, to adapt Rogers' words, an emerging shift from the neoliberalized to the natively neoliberal. Neoliberalism 3+ thus reworks and draws on the results of earlier phases of neoliberalism, but has deepened the agenda of applying market solutions shared among the range of neoliberal theories. In our view, on the thorny question of periodization, the incremental transition can be located between the burst of the dot-com bubble in 2000 and the epic unwinding of America's consumption and real estate boom in 2008. What some anticipated as a return to Keynesianism was piecemeal and turned out to be mostly limited to printing money, rescuing banks, corporations and, more generally, supporting financial assets – bonds, stocks and real estate (Patomäki 2009: 437).

Instead, a reformatted neoliberalism 3+ emerged out of the ashes: with the sobering realization that change implied more of the same. For the core economies in Europe and North America, neoliberalism 3+ has been expressed and unfolds via:

1. A *fiscal crisis of the state*, whereby crises 'represent a continuation… of neoliberalism as an adaptive regime of socioeconomic governance' (Springer 2015: 8). The consequences of recession, write downs, and bailouts (accentuating debt) were used to justify *sudden and significant cuts to public expenditure* on collective goods. Debt crises were forerunners to the development of an earlier phase of neoliberal development policies in the Third World in the 1980s. Debt is again the precursor (Lazzarato 2012, 2015) to neoliberalism 3+. The interpretation of fiscal crises relate to the words and actions of central banks, governments, media and credit rating agencies (Kelly 2001; Sidaway 2008) and the construction of a hegemonic discourse about what can/cannot be afforded (Castree 2010). Such framing became most evident in Europe, but was also central to many state-level strategies in the USA as well as Harper's government in Canada. A complex reworking of the state–economy relations ensues. Public sector agencies are dismantled and the services they provided are fulfilled by for-profit firms or (frequently corporatized) charities. This may not necessarily reduce state spending in the long term, but it redirects it from public to corporate bodies. These shifts are also invariably and frequently expressed unevenly. In the jargon of geography: they are scaled. They have the longer-term result and means of:

2. *Further marketization of remaining social/state assets*, including – paradoxical as it may at first seem – the troubled banks that were nationalized in emergency moves. This belies the old ideological claim that neoliberalism is a simple case of less state, more market. It is rather *the reconfiguring of both, so that they become more thoroughly intermeshed*, in part through their subjection to financial logics (Aalbers 2009). In doing so, like the effect of a Trojan virus, political-operating systems can become subsidiaries of the financial system. Indeed, one observer justifiably described this development for which he proposes the term 'hybrid neoliberalism':

in which market logic is not only regulated and lightly directed by government, but increasingly incorporated into the sphere of state-run economic activities. This has been made possible through the development of a new role for governments, by taking stakes in key financial firms, have started acting in much the same way as activist investors.

(Caprotti 2010: 83)

Notwithstanding his aversion to theory, the French economist Thomas Piketty (2014) has done much to expose the mounting inequality that has accompanied decades of neoliberalization. Across the Channel, Tom Clark and Anthony Heath (2014) focus on the more recent 'divisive toll' of the post-2008 crisis in the UK and USA and, across the Atlantic, Mark Blyth (2013) focuses on the idea and impacts of austerity. However, such startling analyses and empirics (see too Dorling 2015 and Stuckler and Basu 2013) should be read in conjunction with Dardot and Laval's *The New Way of the World: On Neoliberal Society* (2013, originally published in French in 2009), which offers a major finessing of the cultural–historical–political approach to neoliberalism pioneered by Foucault. To Dardot and Laval neoliberalism encompasses the total transformation of the human subject: we will return to this below. They also argue that, 'the Market/State opposition is one of the main impediments to an accurate characterization of neo-liberalism' (ibid.: 5). The range of marketizations hence demands critical scrutiny. In the words of Kean Birch and Matti Siemiatycki (2015: 18) this requires us 'to consider how and why markets and the state are entangled in new rationalities, instruments and agencies'.

3. *Practices of audit and the rhetoric of accountability and enterprise established during rollout neoliberalism are being modified.* The culture of audit has been integral to rollout neoliberalism, often read as a shift from government to governance (Power 1999, 2007). This is being finessed. For example, the London-based National Endowment for Science Technology and the Arts (see Nesta, n.d.) posited shifts from audit to assurance and how public spending cuts produce creativity or radical efficiency – a policy since embraced by British governments. Beyond such rhetoric of value, however, social costs proliferate while the state, the social, and nature (While *et al.* 2010) are reconfigured. This remoulds subjectivities, for the 3+ variants of neoliberalism further:

an extension of market logic far beyond the strict boundaries of the market, notably by generating an 'accountable' subjectivity by systematically creating competition between individuals. One thinks, in particular, of the generalization of the methods of evaluation derived from enterprise in public education.

(Dardot and Laval 2013: 14)

4. The pursuit of *social affinities, rationalities and alliances* in support of these strategies. This was symbolized by Obama s rhetoric of inclusion and the formal alliance between the Liberal Democrat and Conservative parties that established a new government in the UK in the spring of 2010 (Watkins 2010) that lasted until 2015. Both were symptomatic of wider phenomena, whereby neoliberal capitalism does not simply atomize social life, but, in Konings's terms, requires the creation of new social connections, cultural affinities and political capacities (2010: 6). A new generation of firms and consultants inhabit this space. As recently as six years ago, Raymond Plant (2010: 270) argued that:

It may be indeed that there is no stable doctrinal place on the spectrum of political positions for neo-liberalism [since], most of that space is colonized by social democracy with the radical liberalism of Nozick marking a categorical difference at the outer edge.

Today, however, and arguably more than ever: 'far from being [merely] an ideology or economic policy, [neoliberalism 3+] is firstly and fundamentally a rationality, and as such tends to structure and organize not only the action of rulers, but also the conduct of the ruled' (Dardot and Laval 2013: 4).

Such tendencies contain multiple contradictions, posing considerable political challenges. However, they are eased by the fact that organized resistance has generally been at low ebb or takes populist forms that can either be outmanoeuvred or incorporated. Examples of both strategies are evident in responses to the right-wing populism of occasionally influential movements such as the *Partij voor de Vrijheid* (PVV) in the Netherlands, the Tea Party in the USA and the United Kingdom Independence Party (UKIP). Especially in the interactions of features 1 and 2, moreover, we detect an element of what Klein (2008) termed *The Shock Doctrine* whereby geopolitical, natural, or economic crises are drawn upon by elites to cash in on chaos and remake societies in ways that favour profit and power. The combination lends credence to Harvey's (2005a) claim that the neoliberal project is, in substantial measure, about a deepening and reconfigurating of elite power. Thus, the American case, where:

three decades of growing inequality and stagnant wages came to exist in a relationship of mutually reinforcing interaction with neoliberal governmentality. Neoliberalism represents a shift in the modalities and instruments through which the integration of the American middle and working classes into the financial system was effected. This provided financial elites with a world of opportunities.

(Konings 2010: 24)

Since class is partially expressed through race, the racialization of neoliberalism has been visible in the making of the American subprime crisis (Dymski 2010; Wyly *et al.* 2012; see Dymski *et al.* 2013). Likewise, Europe's fraught monetary union has divided the continent in two classes: northern creditors and southern debtors. However, another key way that race, class, state power, and neoliberalization have interacted is through what has been labelled *The New Imperialism* (Harvey 2005b) – in particular, the American-led wars in Afghanistan and Iraq and associated reconfigurations of militarism, security, development and economy that reworked and rearmed systems and logics from the Cold War (Masco 2014).

5.   Hence, there has been a *tightening nexus (unleashed since 9/11) of security, geopolitics, nature and neoliberalism*. A military-industrial complex is not new (Ledbetter 2011). Nurtured by the neocons, military and security operations themselves were increasingly subject to lucrative contracting out (Singer 2004) during the first decade of the 'Global War on Terror'. Moreover, a corrupt strand of neoliberal policies was especially evident under conditions of military occupation. While segregation (green zones and forts), theft, and fraud flourished in Afghanistan and Iraq, it bears noting how both occupied countries underwent privatizations. Privatization of security is also mirrored in many other southern cities and enclaves plugged into global markets (Paasche and Sidaway 2010; Paasche *et al.* 2014; Sidaway 2007; Sidaway *et al.* 2014). The privatization of security is not only found in the periphery, for security also 'imbues itself on all social relations and attaches itself to almost all commodities' (Rigakos 2011: 63). Online, for example, as Edward Snowden's revelations embody and illustrate, American intelligence agencies established relationships with many firms, in an expanding surveillance grid, further fracturing already blurred distinctions between the public and the private, state, security, and profit (Greenwald 2014). We therefore would contest Paul Amar's (2013: 239) claims that, in recent years, 'liberalization was gradually replaced by securitization as the hegemonic project of global governance and of state administration' by stressing the interconnections between security and neoliberalism. Or, to put this in other terms (following Boy 2015), we stress the linkages between privatized

and state securitization (in the military–security domain) and financial securitization (the pooling of tangible assets, mortgage payments and other income streams into tradable financial products). The ways in which discourses on planetary security, climate change and market-making intersect around carbon economies are another pathway for neoliberalism (Klein 2015). As Corbera and Martin (2015: 2024) note how:

> carbon-offsetting activities constitute a process of commodification through which a given good that formerly existed outside the economy – in this case a tonne of carbon dioxide equivalent (CO_2e) that is not emitted into the atmosphere – enters the world of money, markets and thus of potential speculation and financialisation.

However, we also need to be mindful of a sixth trend that also relates to the grand chessboard of global power, especially the place and roles of Europe and America.

6. While crises since the early 1980s were most evident outside the Atlantic heartland, the most recent phase of crisis had its origins and was felt most acutely in the West (Sidaway 2008). Neoliberalism 3+ therefore also *accompanied a sense of shifting geopolitical and geoeconomic power South and East*: witness the discourse and claims that were made on behalf of the BRICs (Brazil, Russia, India and China, latterly plus South Africa) as new motors of accumulation (Sidaway 2010). Such shifts are markedly partial and uneven, liable to ebb and flow (Starrs 2014), but there is a widespread sense that they reconfigure relationships among the great powers as well as the geography and meanings of development (Ravallion 2009). Moreover, capital surplus states, such as the petro-sultanates of the Persian Gulf as well as China (whose surplus derives from manufactured exports) that have long played a role in engendering financialization became more central to the global reproduction of capitalism (Hanieh 2011, Hung 2009) in the lead-up to and immediate aftermath of the 2007–8 crisis. Their key roles in recycling and bolstering financial circuits connect these capital surplus states with the trans-Atlantic heartlands of neoliberalism, even though their own 'internal' polities may be more hybridized.

    Meanwhile, back in the USA, Hayek's *The Road to Serfdom* (originally 1944) and Anne Rand's *Atlas Shrugged* (originally 1957) enjoyed several years among the bestsellers at Amazon.com. These seductive voices inspired a new wave of vocal conservatism (Foley 2010: 39) whose neoliberal agenda and influence might be obscured by the progressive advances around race, gender, culture and sexuality. Disciples of Hayek long advocated a 'nightwatchmen' state in which all but defence, justice, and police were allocated to the market. These too offer rich potential for marketization. Under neoliberalism 3+, therefore, the nightwatcher might become a private security contractor or a joint venture between an intelligence agency and digital service provider. Where security becomes both natively digital and neoliberal, Foucault or Orwell might be better guides to the future than Hayek.

Reworking and resistance?

What is in store for the two European cases we cited early in this chapter: a Dutch university and German city that speculated on real estate and complex financial derivatives linked to it? The once-celebrated German model, which oversaw post-war recovery, funded European integration, and represented a variety of capitalism that informed state–economy relations elsewhere, is now deeply challenged. Dutch politics remains fractured, and the fiscal basis for higher education there uncertain. In Europe, the outcome of progressive political resistance – most notably in Greece, as well as movements like *Podemos* in Spain (as well as far-right resistance in places like France and the populist right elsewhere) – remains uncertain. Elsewhere, however – in Britain and Ireland, for example – calls for alternative economic strategies were outmanoeuvred and largely defeated. Of course, the post-war British state, it was often said, had the task of the orderly management of decline. That Britain's geopolitical decline was accompanied by chronic relative economic decline (Coates 2014) produced a few disorders on the way, and fed into the making of earlier phases of neoliberalism there (Davis and Walsh 2015; Needham 2015).

While it has certainly been profitable for some, the jury is still out on how successful these policies were in restoring anything other than phases of further crisis-prone and relatively slow growth or, indeed, halting that relative decline. Contrary to the hopes of many, the great crash of 2008 ended up consolidating neoliberalism. This has been most marked in the eurozone, where goals of a knowledge-based economy became subdued to a finance-centred one, wracked with crisis (Birch and Mykhnenko 2014). But the operating system of neoliberalism 3+ works across a wide variety of polities, articulating with and configured by those that are not (at first glance) thoroughly neoliberal (such as China and the Persian Gulf sultanates). 'Articulation' both invokes a literature on how forms or modes of production interface and suggests a more active process than notions of 'variegation' invoke. In a related fashion, articulating/articulated neoliberalism has been used to interpret post-socialist contexts in Europe and Asia (Smith 2007; Springer 2008, 2011), though arguably many of these are markedly illiberal (Szelényi 2015). Either way, these articulations are full of imbalances and loaded with geoeconomic and geopolitical tensions. In Europe, as elsewhere, future crises, contests and shifts might offer fresh paths to roll up and discard neoliberalism 3+. Equally, however, we face the troubling prospects of neoliberalism's mutation and further reworking, through collisions with popular demands, contrasting social visions and calamity. Born out of force, the neoliberal age may die with it.

Acknowledgements

An earlier version of the arguments in this chapter appeared in Hendrikse and Sidaway (2010). We are grateful to Pion for permission to rework and republish it here. We also both thank Simon Springer and the Politics, Economies and Space Group at the Department of Geography, NUS, for their comments on earlier drafts.

Note

1 We are grateful to Neil Coe for this formulation.

References

Aalbers, M.B. 2009. Neoliberalism is Dead… Long Live Neoliberalism. *International Journal of Urban and Regional Research*, 37.3: 1083–90.

Amar, P. 2013. *The Security Archipelago: Human-Security States, Sexuality Politics, and the End of Neoliberalism*. Durham, NC: Duke University Press.

Barnes, P. 2006. *Capitalism 3.0*. San Francisco: Berrett-Koehler.

Birch, K., and Mykhnenko, V. eds. 2010. *The Rise and Fall of Neo-liberalism: The Collapse of an Economic Order?* London: Zed Books.

—. 2014. Lisbonizing versus Financializing Europe? The Lisbon Agenda and the (Un)Making of the European Knowledge-based Economy. *Environment and Planning C*, 32.1: 108–28.

Birch, K., and Siemiatycki, M. 2015. Neoliberalism and the Geographies of Marketization: The Entangling of State and Markets. *Progress in Human Geography*. doi: 10.1177/0309132515570512

Block F., and Somers, M.R. 2014. *The Power of Market Fundamentalism: Karl Polanyi's Critique*. Cambridge, MA: Harvard University Press.

Blyth, M. 2013. Austerity: *The History of a Dangerous Idea*. Oxford: Oxford University Press.

Brenner, N., Peck, J., and Theodore, N. 2010. Variegated Neoliberalization: Geographies, Modalities, Pathways. *Global Networks*, 10.2: 182–222.

Boy, N. 2015. Sovereign Safety. *Security Dialogue*, 7 August.

Caprotti, F. 2010. From Finance to Green Technology Activist States, Geopolitical Finance and Hybrid Neoliberalism, in Lagoarde-Segot, T. ed. *After the Crisis: Rethinking Finance*. Hauppauge, NY: Nova: 81–100.

Castree, N. 2010. The 2007–09 Financial Crisis: Narrating and Politicizing a Calamity. *Human Geography*, 3.1: 34–48.

Clark, T., and Heath, A. 2014. *Hard Times: The Divisive Toll of the Economic Slump*. New Haven and London: Yale University Press.

Coates, D. 2014. The UK: Less a Liberal Market Economy, More a Post-imperial One. *Capital and Class*, 38.1: 171–82.

Corbera, C, and Martin, A. 2015. Carbon Offsets: Accommodation or Resistance? *Environment and Planning A*, 47.10: 2023–30.

Crouch, C. 2011. *The Strange Non-death of Neo-liberalism*. Cambridge: Polity Press.

Dardot, P., and Laval, C. 2013. *The New Way of the World: On Neoliberal Society*. London: Verso.

Davis, A. and Walsh, C. 2015. The Role of the State in the Financialisation of the UK Economy. *Political Studies*. doi: 10.1111/1467-9248.12198

Dorling, D. 2015. *Injustice: Why Social Inequality Still Persists*. London: Policy Press.

Dymski, G.A. 2010. From Financial Exploitation to Global Banking Instability: Two Overlooked Roots of the Subprime Crisis, in Konings, M. ed. *The Great Credit Crash*. London: Verso: 72–102.

Dymski, G., Hernandez, J., and Mohanty, L. 2013. Race, Gender, Power, and the US Subprime Mortgage and Foreclosure Crisis: A Meso Ananlysis. *Feminist Economics*, 19.3: 124–51.

Engelen, E., Fernandez, R., and Hendrikse R. 2014. How Finance Penetrates its Other: A Cautionary Tale on the Financialization of a Dutch University. *Antipode*, 46.1: 1072–91.

Foley, S. 2010. Darling of the Right is Reborn in the USA. *The Independent*, 3 July, 38–9.

Greenwald, G. 2014. *No Place to Hide: Edward Snowden, the NSA and the Surveillance State*. London: Penguin.

Hanieh, A. 2011. *Capitalism and Class in the Gulf Arab States*. New York: Palgrave Macmillan.

Harvey, D. 2005a. *A Short History of Neoliberalism*. Oxford: Oxford University Press.

—. 2005b. *The New Imperialism*. Oxford: Oxford University Press.

Hayek, F.A. 1944. *The Road to Serfdom*. London: Routledge and Kegan.

Hendrikse, R.P., and Sidaway J.D. 2010. Neoliberalism 3.0, Commentary, *Environment and Planning A*, 42.9: 2037–42.

—. 2014. Financial Wizardry and the Golden City: Tracking the Financial Crisis through Pforzheim, Germany. *Transactions of the Institute of British Geographers*, 39.2: 195–208.

Hung, H.-F. 2009. America's Head Servant? The PRC's Dilemma in the Global Crisis. *New Left Review*, 60: 5–25.

Kaletsky, A. 2010. *Capitalism 4.0*. Jackson, TN: Public Affairs.

Klein, N. 2008. *The Shock Doctrine*. London: Penguin.

—. 2015. *This Changes Everything*. London: Penguin.

Kelly, P.F. 2001, Metaphors of Meltdown: Political Representations of Economic Space in the Asian Financial Crisis. *Environment and Planning D: Society and Space*, 19.6: 719–42.

Konings, M. 2010. Rethinking Neoliberalism and the Crisis: Beyond the Re-regulation Agenda, in Konings, M. ed. *The Great Credit Crash*. London: Verso: 3–30.

Lazzarato, M. 2012. *The Making of the Indebted Man: An Essay on the Neoliberal Condition*. Los Angeles: Semiotext(e).

—. 2015. *Governing by Debt*. South Pasadena, CA: Semiotext(e).

Ledbetter, J. 2011. *Unwarranted Influence: Dwight D. Eisenhower and the Military-Industrial Complex*. New Haven and London: Yale University Press.

Masco, J. 2014. *The Theater of Operations: National Security Affect from the Cold War to the War on Terror*. Durham, NC: Duke University Press.

Mirowski, P., and Plehwe, D. eds. 2009. *The Road from Mont Pèlerin: The Making of the Neoliberal Thought Collective*. Cambridge, MA: Harvard University Press.

Needham, D. 2015. Britain's Money Supply Experiment, 1971–73. *The English Historical Review*, 130: 89–122.

Nesta (webpage). N.d. Home page. Retrieved from http://www.nesta.org.uk/

Ong, A. 2007. Neoliberalism as a Mobile Technology. *Transactions of the Institute of British Geographers*, 32: 3–8.

Paasche, T.F., and Sidaway, J.D. 2010. Transecting Security and Space in Maputo. *Environment and Planning A*, 42: 1555–76.

Paasche, T.F., Yarwood, R., and Sidaway, J.D. 2014 Territorial Tactics: The Socio-spatial Significance of Private Policing Tactics in Cape Town. *Urban Studies*, 51.8: 1559–75.

Patomäki, H. 2009. Neoliberalism and the Global Financial Crisis. *New Political Science*, 31.4: 431–42.

Peck, J., and Tickell, A. 2002. Neoliberalizing Space. *Antipode*, 34.3:) 380–404.

Piketty, T. 2014. *Capital in the Twenty-First Century*. Cambridge, MA: Belknap Press of Harvard University Press.

Plehwe, D., Walpen, B., and Neuhöffer, G. 2006. Introduction: Reconsidering Neoliberal Hegemony, in Plehwe, D., Walpen, B., and Neuhöffer, G. eds. *Neoliberal Hegemony: A Global Critique*. Abingdon: Routledge: 1–24.

Plant, R. 2010. *The Neo-liberal State*. Oxford: Oxford University Press.

Power, M. 1999. *The Audit Society: Rituals of Verification*. Oxford: Oxford University Press.

—. 2007. *Organized Uncertainty: Designing a World of Risk Management*. Oxford: Oxford University Press.

Rand, A. 1957. *Atlas Shrugged*. New York: Random House.

Ravallion, M. 2009. Are There Lessons for Africa from China's Success Against Poverty? *World Development*, 37.2: 303–13.

Rigakos, G.S. 2011. 'To Extend the Scope of Productive Labour': Pacification as a Police Project, in Neocleous, M., and Rigakos, G.S. eds. *Anti-security*. Ottawa: Red Quill: 57–83.

Rogers, R. 2009. The End of the Virtual: Digital Methods. Text prepared for the Inaugural Speech, Chair New Media and Digital Culture, University of Amsterdam, 8 May. Retrieved from http://www.govcom.org/rogers_oratie.pdf

Sidaway, J.D. 2007. Enclave Space: A New Metageography of Development? *Area*, 39.3: 331–9.

—. 2008. Guest Editorial. Subprime Crisis: American Crisis or Human Crisis? *Environment and Planning D: Society and Space*, 26.2: 195–8.

—. 2010. Geographies of Development: New Maps, New Visions. *The Professional Geographer*, 64.1: 49–62.

Sidaway, J.D., Paasche, T.F., Woon, C.Y., and Keo, P. 2014. Transecting Security and Space in Phnom Penh. *Environment and Planning A*, 46.5: 1181–202.

Singer, P.W. 2004. *Corporate Warriors: The Rise of the Privatized Military Industry*. New York: Cornell University Press.

Smith, A. 2007. Articulating Neoliberalism: Diverse Economies and Everyday Life in Postsocialist Cities, in Leitner, H., Peck, J., and Sheppard, E.S. eds. *Contesting Neoliberalism*. New York: Guilford: 204–22.

Springer, S. 2008. The Nonillusory Effects of Neoliberalisation: Linking Geographies of Poverty, Inequality and Violence. *Geoforum*, 39.4: 1520–5.

—. 2011. Articulated Neoliberalism: The Specificity of Patronage, Kleptocracy, and Violence in Cambodia's Neoliberalization. *Environment and Planning A*, 43.11: 2554–70.

—. 2015. Postneoliberalism? *Review of Radical Political Economics*, 47.1: 5–17.

Starrs, S., 2014. The Chimera of Global Convergence. *New Left Review*, 87: 81–96.

Stuckler, D., and Basu S. eds. 2013. *The Body Economic*. New York: Basic.

Szelényi, I. 2015. Capitalisms After Communism. *New Left Review*, 96: 39–51.

Watkins, S. 2010. Editorial. Blue Labour? *New Left Review*, 63: 5–15.

While, A., Jonas, A.E.G., and Gibbs, D. 2010. From Sustainable Development to Carbon Control: Eco-state Restructuring and the Politics of Urban and Regional Development. *Transactions of the Institute of British Geographers*, 35: 76–93.

Wyly, E., Ponder, C.S., Nettling, P., Ho, B., Fung, S.E., Liebowitz, Z., and Hammel, D. 2012. New Racial Meanings of Housing in America. *American Quarterly*, 64.3: 571–604.

50

POSTNEOLIBERALISM

Ulrich Brand

Since the outbreak of the economic and financial crisis in 2008 and the deepening of other dimensions of the multiple crisis of capitalism – like climate change and the environmental crisis as well as the crisis of political representation and social cohesion due to increasing polarization and social exclusion within many societies – neoliberalism is losing legitimacy. Now, the contradictions and negative impacts of neoliberalism not only during the current crisis, but also during the years before are more obvious. In Latin America, this crisis of functioning and legitimacy has provoked protests and a search for alternatives since the 1990s and has led to important political and social changes. There, and elsewhere, experiences of anti-neoliberal struggles and criticisms by social movements and NGOs, intellectuals, (social) scientists and critical media have existed since the 1990s.

Within both contexts, contested strategies were developed to deal with the multiple crisis of neoliberal capitalism. Besides business-as-usual strategies, some are more classical Keynesian and neo-developmentalist, others attempt to integrate environmental issues and argue for a Green Economy or Green Growth, and yet others prefer more authoritarian or even openly repressive strategies to overcome the crisis. In Europe, authoritarian ways to deal with the crisis currently predominate. A look at Latin America shows that particular strategies may be successful concerning the economic and financial crisis and also the crisis of inequality; however, those crisis strategies tend to work only in so far as they deepen other crisis dimensions such as those of environment and climate.

This is the broad terrain on which the concept of postneoliberalism emerged. It was introduced by progressive intellectuals and leftist governments in Latin America, especially in Brazil. Their rather political uses of the concept attempt to indicate the end of neoliberalism (Borón 2003; Gutman and Cohen 2007; Sader 2009; Macdonald and Ruckert 2009; Escobar 2010; Springer 2014). By contrast, more analytical uses do not claim the end of neoliberalism but its more or less intense shaping – that is, a break with some characteristics while maintaining others (Brand and Sekler 2009b; Gago and Sztulwark 2009; Candeias 2009; Brenner *et al.* 2010; Buckel *et al.* 2010). A common denominator is that 'postneoliberalism' is a term that reflects the analytical and political-strategic search for alternatives to neoliberalism. Yates and Bakker (2014: 65) condense their approach to postneoliberalism in stating that it:

reflects an attempt to conceptualize the multiple and complex ways in which neoliberal orthodoxy is contested by particular actors (ranging from political parties and national regimes to analysts and civil society groups), via a variety of strategies (ranging from concrete legal and political changes to experiments with alternative ideational projects).

In that sense, postneoliberalism is an epistemic terrain, with different approaches dealing with the (negative) impacts of neoliberalism and its growing inability to deal with the emerging contradictions and crises. It is a political and analytical perspective to understand and change realities. And it is recognized that there is no one ideal type of postneoliberalism.

In the next part of this chapter I argue that the different usages of the term '*post*neoliberalism' have to do with the very understanding of neoliberalism (of course, in *The Handbook of Neoliberalism* I do not go into detail). Two broad approaches can be detected: a more political-strategic understanding of neoliberalism as a new phase of (capitalist) development and a more analytical understanding which tries to capture the continuities and discontinuities of neoliberalism or neoliberali*zation*, respectively. I conclude with some reflections on other possible hegemonies and hegemonic projects and, at the very end, with a question which remains open to me.

Postneoliberalism

In the last 40 years, neoliberal policies were implemented in many societies across the globe. This took place in different forms, resulting in fairly specific 'neoliberal' configurations. Therefore, how to understand postneoliberalism certainly depends on the understanding of neoliberalism. If the latter is understood as policy reforms (as the concept of the neoliberal Washington Consensus suggests, see Williamson 1990), then postneoliberalism means that neoliberalism can be countered by reforming the reforms. Close to this is an understanding of neoliberalism which focuses on regulatory restructurings of the economies (Brenner *et al.* 2010).

Others conceptualize neoliberalism rather as profound societal transformations including the logics of and inscribed in power relations of states, (world) markets and civil society, of class and gender structures, of subjectivities and societal nature relations. The neoliberal counter-revolution since the 1970s, for instance, was a shift not just in economic policies, but also in societal class and power relations, of dominant logics (Gibson-Graham 1996; Hardt and Negri 2000; Harvey 2005; Plehwe *et al.* 2006). Thus, postneoliberalism needs to be linked to these characteristics. Neoliberalism is also understood as regulatory reform, but its basis is the successful formulation of a class project – class understood in a broad sense: articulated with gender and *race* – which was implemented by authoritarian state interventions.

Moreover, neoliberalism was never a homogeneous or coherent world view, strategy or practice; it has always been contradictory (Springer 2014). It was articulated with openly violent means (especially through military dictatorships), with conservative or social democratic strategies and social forces. And it changed over time. This is the reason why some scholars prefer the term 'neoliberalization' (Castree 2008; Brenner *et al.* 2010) in order to indicate, according to specific conjunctures, the differentiated forms of implementing neoliberal policies: 'Neoliberalizing practices are thus understood as necessarily and always overdetermined, contingent, polymorphic, open to intervention, reconstituted, continually negotiated, impure, subject to counter-tendencies, and in a perpetual process of becoming' (Springer 2014: 7).

It is also an analytical question in which elements of neoliberalism are considered to be in crisis. There is a strong consensus that neoliberalism involved an increase of the power of capital, especially financial capital. The terms 'finance-led accumulation' or 'finance market capitalism' express this increasing power, which goes hand in hand with the inability to force capital to be distributed, with overaccumulation and debt economies. Other elements of the crisis are the crisis of the world order (the prolonged Pax Americana) due to increasing conflicts and the emergence of new economic and political powers, especially China; the ecological crisis, which is in principle a crisis of fossilist-industrialist and capitalist-imperial societal nature relations – that is, a particular mode of production and living; the crisis of representation and representative democracy; and the obvious inability of neoliberalism to create social compromises and forms of integration. That non-neoliberal countries like China or postneoliberal ones like many in Latin America produce more capitalist dynamics than most countries under neoliberal rule could be considered as a final element.

The concept of postneoliberalism is not very precise (which is criticized by Yates and Bakker 2014). There is no narrow definition,

> since the term refers to a host of variegated social practices and discourses that strategically engage with contested forms of neoliberal governance and have not yet crystallized into a clearly definable body of material practices, and thus do not present a coherent alternative to neoliberalism.
>
> *(Macdonald and Ruckert 2009: 8)*

However, this is less a lack of clarification, but has more to do with the very historical momentum the concept is applied to – that is, it has to do with the fact 'that the old is dying and the new cannot be born: in this interregnum, morbid phenomena of the most varied kind come to pass' (Gramsci 1996[1930]: 32–3; Candeias 2011).

New phase or focus on (dis-)continuities?

The concept of postneoliberalism emerged in a specific historical conjuncture, namely the struggles against neoliberalism in Latin America and the ascent of leftist governments. Neoliberal strategies faced growing resistance from emancipatory social forces and thus could not be implemented as easily as during the heyday of neoliberal hegemony. Since the middle of the 1990s, and more visibly since the beginning of the new century, governments, parties and social movements in Latin America attracted attention with their explicitly anti-neoliberal discourse (Zibechi 2006; Silva 2009). This led to electoral victories of Hugo Chávez in Venezuela in 1998, Ricardo Lagos in Chile in 2000, Inácio 'Lula' da Silva in Brazil in 2002, Néstor Kirchner in Argentina in 2003, Tabaré Vázquez in Uruguay in 2004, Evo Morales in Bolivia in 2005, Daniel Ortega in Nicaragua in 2006, Rafael Correa in Ecuador in 2007, Fernando Lugo in Paraguay in 2008 and Ollanta Humala in Peru in 2011. Particularly, the term 'postneoliberalism' was introduced at the end of the 1990s by intellectuals close to presidential candidate Lula da Silva. Amid intense anti-neoliberal struggles across Latin America, this term served to indicate that a government of the Workers' Party (PT) would break with neoliberal policies, its political economy, and related power relations as well as respective discourses and subjectivities. Also, within social scientific debates, some used the term to look for progressive alternatives and as an indicator of a new era. For example, Macdonald and Ruckert (2009: 6–7) argue that 'the postneoliberal era is characterized mainly by a search for progressive policy alternatives arising out of the many contradictions of neoliberalism. These progressive alternatives contain remnants of the previous neoliberal model, as neoliberalism does not suddenly disappear.' Here, the term 'postneoliberalism' helps us understand 'the discontinuities within continuity in the policy practices of many progressive governments' (ibid.: 2).

However, it is contested whether we are entering into a new, postneoliberal era in general and what might be criteria speaking against and/or for this assessment. We shall see that the usage in the sense of a new phase of (capitalist) development is often employed by progressive forces in Latin America.

Another use of the concept, which will be the focus of this entry, is more analytical and more context-sensitive. It is proposed to consider postneoliberalism as a perspective on social, political and/or economic transformations, on shifting terrains of social struggles and compromises, taking place on different scales, in various contexts and by different actors.

This has a systematic reason: capitalist development is not one-dimensional. It should rather be seen as a dialectical process of the *unifying* forces of the societies under the dominance of the capitalist mode of production and, at the same time, continuous territorially *differentiating and fragmenting* dynamics. Hence, the analysis of societies with similar economic structures does not prevent 'due to innumerable different empirical circumstances, natural environment, racial rela-tions, external historical influences, etc. from showing infinite variations and gradations in appearance, which can be ascertained only by analysis of the empirically given circumstances' (Marx 1968b[1875]: 331).

In this sense, the term 'postneoliberalism' allows a closer look at the continuities and discon-tinuities of spatially and temporally uneven capitalist development. Different postneoliberal approaches have in common that they break with some specific aspects of 'neoliberalism', cover-ing in its alternative approaches different aspects of a possible postneoliberalism; they vary in depth, complexity, scope etc. and everyday practices and comprehensive concepts.

The existence of two different perspectives – that is, understanding postneoliberalism more in the sense of a new phase or to discern the (dis-)continuities – is not surprising. Political actors or intellectuals close to them wish to change the real world more directly and need to formulate, besides concrete political aims, also alternative imaginaries. To open political space for Keynesian or neo-developmentalist policies and a respective role of the state requires an opposite to neoliberal 'free market capitalism'. Of course, the danger lies in a treatment of neoliberalism as a more or less homogeneous system and, implicitly, as a set of economic policies which, in principle, can be reversed by other policies.

Therefore, one important aspect of a critical analysis is precisely to understand current dynamics and to reflect on possible structural obstacles of real historical attempts to change soci-eties. In that sense, critical analysis stands in a necessary and hopefully productive tension with real-world politics. Therefore, in using the term 'postneoliberalism' analytically, most contribu-tions refer to the challenge of understanding elements or characteristics which persist and others which are, at least, intended to be changed or are, in fact, changed.

Of course, the working of specific (dis-)continuities often has to do with conditions which are external to the social and political forces within the countries. Therefore, postneoliberal *strat-egies* need to be distinguished from postneoliberal *effects*. For instance, in Latin America more or less postneoliberal strategies and historical dynamics have to do with high demand of commodi-ties on the world market and high prices. I will return to this point.

In summary, the presented analytical approaches to postneoliberalism – which cannot be detached completely from political-strategic and normative perspectives – make social enquiry more precise. When the term 'postneoliberalism' is used, the task is mainly to detect which char-acteristics of neoliberalism change and which persist. This task is even more difficult since the neoliberal project and related practices themselves change and are articulated with other ele-ments. Therefore, I concentrate on the region where the concept was used for the first time and where the debate is still most vivid: Latin America. However, many dimensions apply to capitalist societies in general.

Corridors of postneoliberalism: structural problems in moving beyond neoliberal capitalism

The political and analytical driving force of the debate about postneoliberalism is to stop neoliberalism and to overcome the manifold processes of neoliberalization. As we saw, creating barriers and promoting alternatives occurs in highly uneven ways. And respective strategies and perspectives must be developed under historically concrete conditions. 'The post-neoliberal project does not – and cannot – entail a wholesale break from neoliberalism or produce its binary other, since the concrete possibilities for such are filtered out by historically constituted institutional conditions' (Taylor 2009; Yates and Bakker 2014: 65). As Marx prominently put it at the beginning of his 'Eighteenth Brumaire of Louis Bonaparte' (1968a[1852]: 96), human beings 'make their own history, but they do not make it under circumstances chosen by themselves, but under circumstances directly encountered, given and transmitted from the past'.

Sheppard and Leitner (2010: 192) see a 'developmentalist socio-spatial imaginary' at work – that is, a thinking which sees Northern development as the highest form, a one-size-fits-all perspective of development and commodification as the major means of capitalist development (see also Webber 2010).

At a more general level, the state remains oriented between, on the one hand, the creation of favourable conditions for capital accumulation – now under conditions of transnationalized and partly financialized capital – and, on the other hand, its need to be legitimate (Offe 1974). State policies are formulated and performed,

> in the framework set by a post-neoliberal society characterised by the predominance of a wider domination of capitalist relations and transnational capital. This limits the character of the state's intervention and makes it very difficult to reintroduce traditional developmentalism. In fact, while the state appears to have more clout in the economy than before, the boundaries for welfare-policies and for directing the general orientation of capitalist development have been strictly narrowed.
>
> *(Féliz 2012: 120)*

A partially shaped power bloc creates a postneoliberal discursive and institutional field, which itself represents a novel social context for all actors. In that sense, in Latin America the attempts to overcome the functional and legitimation crisis of neoliberalism can be called a 'passive revolution' which was enabled by more radical forces, discourses and strategies and now manages to contain them. One does not have to go as far as Taylor (2009: 35–6), who sees current postneoliberal developments as the culmination of the neoliberal project. However, we saw that the concrete analysis of (dis-)continuities is a key to understanding current constellations.

Postneoliberalism per se is not an anti-capitalist project. However, the question remains whether these continuous and discontinuous dynamics might lead to a non-neoliberal or even post-capitalist mode of production and living (Altvater 2009; Gago-Sztulwark 2009; Katz 2016). Or, as Sheppard and Leitner (2010: 193) put it: 'Challenging the developmentalist sociospatial imaginary, however, will require not just probing the limits of neoliberalism, but exploring imaginaries that exceed capitalism' (see also Springer 2014).

Therefore, we could distinguish more reformist and technocratic approaches to postneoliberalism from more transformative ones. It remains historically open – and an object of research and political debates – whether existing postneoliberalist strategies and policies have the potential to transform the very conditions of actually existing capitalism. And it is up to concrete analysis whether particular political actions cause rather progressive or regressive results (Brand and Sekler 2009a; Modonesco 2015), whether there is a postneoliberalism of capital or a postneoliberalism of the people (Ceceña 2009). Strong social movements and trade unions, as well as critique, are not envisaged in more technocratic approaches; the actually existing state is considered as the central site of change.

A broader look at current transformations emphasizes the question whether the neoliberal mode of production and living, related world views, dispositives, power relations, forms of politics and the state can be shaped (political-strategic perspective) or is – in whatever direction – beyond main neoliberal characteristics (analytical perspective). How can neoliberal policies be changed but also neoliberal societal relations – neoliberalism's main characteristics such as the enormous and rising power of (transnational) capital, the orientation towards competitiveness at all levels of society, individualism and egoism – as accepted forms of social action? How can existing or desired principles like solidarity, social responsibility, equity and democracy (including economic democracy) be strengthened?

A transformative perspective helps to overcome an assumed dichotomy of state and market (highlighted in reformist and technocratic approaches to postneoliberalism) and asks which dominant logics and power relations are inscribed within the state, the markets and other social spheres.

Conclusion, outlook and an open question

So far, three broad arguments have been developed. First, there is no clear-cut definition of postneoliberalism, which has to do with the quite open historical situation. Second, social transformation needs to be thought of as power-driven processes which imply struggles and strategies as well as changing practices and dispositives in very different arenas. This means that moves towards neoliberalism or variegated processes of neoliberalization, as well as the shaping or overcoming of particular characteristics, have to be taken into account. And, third, transformations of any kind take place against the background of the existing historically concrete conditions.

From an analytical perspective, we are able to ask questions such as: where are the stabilities of neoliberal configurations? Where does active consent or at least passive consent remain because there are no viable alternatives or because alternatives are silenced? How and in which (historical, political, cultural, social, economic) contexts have postneoliberal practices, strategies and concepts emerged? What are their main objectives and how do they try to achieve them? What are the main obstacles, limitations and contradictions they have to deal with? Which aspects are questioned and tend to be solved in a postneoliberal manner? What tends to remain 'neoliberal' or unquestioned and why?

To conclude, I am going to highlight some broader and possibly postneoliberal 'hegemony' projects and modes of development to overcome the crisis. Then I mention one question that remains open to me.

A perspective informed by critical social theory can go a step further and detect various hegemony projects which – implicitly or even explicitly – claim to be able to deal with the crisis. One such hegemony project which turned into a more or less socioeconomically and politically viable and accepted hegemonic project (on the terminology, Kannankulam and Georgi 2014) was just outlined: neo-extractivism in Latin America – that is, a mode of production and living embedded in a strong dispositive of 'progress' and 'development'.

The question of the emergence and viability of such hegemony projects can be put into a wider framework: in which directions – through struggles, technological innovations, competition and compromises, inclusion and exclusion, violence and wars, etc. – are the contradictions of capitalism being pushed (Brie 2009; Brand/Wissen 2015)? What are the concrete forms of postneoliberalism? (Springer 2014: 7 argues that even neoliberalization, given its broad character, always includes forms of postneoliberalization.)

The debate about postneoliberalism sharpens the question which ways out of the multiple crisis of neoliberal capitalism are probable. Brie (2009: 16) refers here to Hannah Arendt's diagnosis. According to her, liberal capitalism:

> thus fell into crisis because liberalism found no civilizing answers to the central questions of its time and thus set free tendencies that offered solutions through decivilization, promised certain groups advancement and power or at least a good income, appeared to have clear simple answers in the face of growing uncertainty and, instead of a demoralizing degeneration of the social and political situation, proclaimed a great glorious uprising.

In that sense, the crisis of neoliberalism:

> can be transformed into an opportunity to stop the menacing accumulation of elements of a new catastrophe of global civilization and thus to make sure that it does not become the origins of an unleashed barbarism. The probability of 21st century barbarism is now much greater than that of a 21st century society based on solidarity.
>
> *(Ibid.)*

What follows at the very end is one question that remains open to me but needs to be dealt with from a critical analytical and politically emancipatory perspective.

Neoliberalism was not only a strategy across nation states and national economies; it deepened the tendency of capital to create the world market (cf. Marx 1973[1857–61]: 408). Highly interdependent socio-economic relations and the power of capital, especially financial capital, make it difficult – albeit not impossible – to exit those relations. Additionally, as Poulantzas (2001[1973]) has shown, the 'international' is present within national social formations.

When we bring political-strategic and analytical perspectives together, it might be asked: how do we deal politically with those spheres which are beyond steering and control? That is, the world market and its volatility of demand and prices, in our time especially the role of China, neo-imperial and neo-colonial politics. What are emancipatory postneoliberal 'politics of scale'? Probably, projects of regional integration are important. While the North American Free Trade Agreement (NAFTA) is clearly a neoliberal and US-driven lock-in process at the international level, the Bolivian Alliance for the Peoples of our Americas (ALBA) attempts to formulate an alternative. Mercosur needs to be considered. The European Union is quite 'locked in' with a neoliberal constituency, but this cannot prevent us from asking how this can be changed.

International constellations point at another aspect: in what sense is the room for postneoliberal policies in countries of the global South an expression of the weakening of influence and dominance of countries of the global North? This is quite obvious in Latin America with respect to US influence. In which way is China promoting certain ways of postneoliberalism in the world? There will be a certain variety of postneoliberalisms and, necessarily, a competition among them (Candeias 2009). Which form is this going to take?

These and many other questions are on the agenda, and their precise analysis will be important within social scientific debates, as well as for real-world development.

References

Altvater, E. 2009. Postneoliberalism or Postcapitalism? The Failure of Neoliberalism in the Financial Market Crisis. *Development Dialogue*, 51: 73–88.

Borón, A.A. 2003. El Posneoliberalismo: Un Proyecto en Construcción, in Sader, E., and Gentili, P., eds. *La Trama del Neoliberalismo*. Buenos Aires: CLACSO.

Brand, U., and Sekler, N. 2009a. Postneoliberalism. A Beginning Debate. *Development Dialogue*, 51: 1–5.

—. 2009b. Postneoliberalism: Catch-All Word or Valuable Analytical and Political Concept? Aims of a Beginning Debate. *Development Dialogue*, 51: 5–13.

Brand, U. and Wissen, M. 2015. Strategies of a Green Economy, Contours of a Green Capitalism, in van der Pijl, K., ed. *The International Political Economy of Production*. Cheltenham: Edward Elgar. 508–23.

Brenner, N., Peck, J., and Theodore, N. 2010. After Neoliberalization? *Globalizations*, 7: 327–45.

Brie, M., 2009. Ways Out of the Crisis of Neoliberalism. *Development Dialogue*, 51: 15–31.

Buckel, S., Fischer-Lescano, A., and Oberndorfer, L. 2010. Postneoliberale Rechtsordnung? –Suchprozesse in der Krise. *Juridikum*, 4: 414–24.

Candeias, M. 2009. Die Letzte Konjunktur: Organische Krise und 'Postneoliberale' Tendenzen. *Berliner Debatte Initial*, 20.2: 12–24.

—. 2011. Passive Revolutions vs Socialist Transformation. Background paper for the Commons-Conference, Rome, 28–29 April.

Ceceña, A.E. 2009. Postneoliberalism and its Bifurcations. *Development Dialogue*, 51: 33–43.

Castree, N. 2008. Neoliberalising Nature: The Logics of Deregulation and Reregulation. *Environment and Planning A*, 40.1: 131–52.

Escobar, A. 2010. Latin America at a Crossroads: Alternative Modernizations, Postliberalism, or Post-Development? *Cultural Studies*, 24.1: 1–65.

Féliz, M. 2012. Neo-Developmentalism: Beyond Neoliberalism? Capitalist Crisis and Argentina's Development Since the 1990s. *Historical Materialism*, 20.2: 105–23.

Gago, V., and Sztulwark, D. 2009. Notes on Postneoliberalism in Argentina. *Development Dialogue*, 51: 181–90.

Gibson-Graham, J.K. 1996. *The End of Capitalism (as we knew it): a Feminist Critique of Political Economy*. Oxford: Blackwell.

Gramsci, A. 1996[1930]. *Prison Notebooks, volume 2*. Buttigieg, J.A., ed. New York: Columbia University Press.

Gutman, M., and Cohen, M. ed. 2007. *América Latina en Marcha. La Transición Postneoliberal*. Buenos Aires: Infinito.

Hardt, M., and Negri, A. 2000. *Empire*. Cambridge, MA: Harvard University Press.

Harvey, D. 2005. *A Brief History of Neoliberalism*. Oxford: Oxford University Press.

Kannankulam, J., and Georgi, F. 2014. Varieties of Capitalism or Varieties of Relationships of Forces? Outlines of a Historical Materialist Policy Analysis. *Capital & Class*, 38.1: 59–71.

Kate, C. 2016. Is South America's 'Progressive Cycle' at an End? Neo-Developmentalist. Attempts and Socialist Projects, in *The Bullet* No. 1229, 4 March.

Macdonald, L., and Ruckert, A. 2009. Post-Neoliberalism in the Americas: An Introduction, in Macdonald, L., and Ruckert, A., eds. *Post-Neoliberalism in the Americas: Beyond the Washington Consensus?* London: Routledge: 1–20.

Marx, K. 1968a[1852]. The Eighteenth Brumaire of Louis Bonaparte, in Marx, K., and Engels, F. *Selected Works*. London: Lawrence & Wishart: 96–179.

—. 1968b[1875]. Critique of the Gotha Program. Marx, K., and Engels, F. *Selected Works*. London: Lawrence & Wishart: 315–35.

—. 1973[1857–61]. *Grundrisse, Foundations of the Critique of Political Economy*. London: Penguin.

Modonesi, M. [2015]. The End of Hegemony and the Regressive Turn in Latin America: The End of a Cycle? in *Viewpoint Magazine*, 21 December.

Offe, C. 1974. Structural Problems of the Capitalist State: Class Rule and the Political System. On the Selectiveness of Political Institutions, in von Beyme, K., ed. *German Political Studies, volume 1*. Beverly Hills: Sage: 31–57.

Plehwe, D., Walpen, B., and Neunhöffer, G. ed. 2006. *Neoliberal Hegemony: A Global Critique*. London: Routledge.

Poulantzas, N. 2001[1973]. Die Internationalisierung der kapitalistischen Verhältnisse und der Nationalstaat, in Hirsch, J., Jessop, B., and Poulantzas, N., eds. *Die Zukunft des Staates*. Hamburg: VSA: 19–69.

Sader, E. 2009. Postneoliberalism in Latin America. *Development Dialogue*, 51: 171–80.

Sheppard, E., and Leitner, H. 2010. Quo Vadis Neoliberalism? The Remaking of Global Capitalist Governance After the Washington Consensus. *Geoforum*, 41: 185–94.

Silva, E. 2009. *Challenging Neoliberalism in Latin America*. New York: Cambridge University Press.

Springer, S. 2014. Postneoliberalism? *Review of Radical Political Economics*, 47.1: 5–17.

Taylor, M. 2009. The Contradictions and Transformations of Neoliberalism in Latin America: From Structural Adjustment to 'Empowering the Poor', in Macdonald, L., and Ruckert, A., eds. *Post-Neoliberalism in the Americas*. London: Routledge: 21–36.

Webber, J.R. 2010. Latin American Neostructuralism: The Contradictions of Post-Neoliberal Development. *Historical Materialism*, 18.3: 208–29.

Williamson, J. 1990. What Washington Means by Policy Reform, in Williamson, J., ed. *Latin American Adjustment: How much has Happened?* Washington, DC: Institute for International Economics: 7–20.

Yates, J.S., and Bakker, K. 2014. Debating the 'Post-Neoliberal Turn' in Latin America. *Progress in Human Geography*, 38: 62–90.

Zibechi, R. 2006. La Emancipación Como Producción de Vínculos, in Ceceña, A.E., ed. *Los Desafíos de las Emancipaciones en un Contexto Militarizado*. Buenos Aires: CLASCO: 123–49.

51

NEOLIBERAL GOTHIC

Japhy Wilson

Tales of the neoliberal undead

Neoliberalism remains the dominant economic ideology of our times. For over three decades, economic reforms have adhered to the neoliberal principles of privatization, deregulation, and the dismantling of the welfare state, on the assumption that free competition would ensure the best of all possible worlds. In contrast to this utopian vision, the outcome has been persistent poverty, economic oligarchy, and a whirlwind of financial crises that spiralled around the world before finally entering the heartlands of global capitalism with the financial crash of 2008 and the ensuing 'Great Recession'. Yet in the aftermath of this unprecedented annihilation of its material and ideological foundations, neoliberalism has risen diabolically from the grave and now staggers forward once again, as the only symbolic framework through which Western capitalism appears capable of articulating its increasingly spasmodic and dysfunctional reproduction.

In the absence of a rational explanation for this uncanny persistence, critics have resorted to gothic representations of the undead. Colin Crouch has noted 'the strange non-death of neoliberalism' (Crouch 2011); Mitchell Dean has observed that 'neoliberal regimes persist in an "undead" form' (Dean 2014: 160); and Neil Smith has described neoliberalism as 'dominant but dead' (Smith 2008). Among these morbid metaphors, the figure of the zombie has acquired peculiar prominence. Ben Fine (2008: 1) claims that 'the current phase of neoliberalism [is] zombie-like', in the sense that it is 'both dead and alive at the same time'; Mark Fisher (2013) observes that 'Neoliberalism now shambles on as a zombie', noting that 'it is sometimes harder to kill a zombie than a living person'; and Jamie Peck suggests that

> [Neoliberalism has] entered its zombie phase. The brain has apparently long since stopped functioning, but the limbs are still moving… The living dead of the free-market revolution continue to walk the earth, though with each resurrection their decidedly uncoordinated gait becomes even more erratic.
>
> *(Peck 2010a: 109)*

The newfound appeal of the gothic metaphor in critical political economy has been matched in popular culture, which in recent years has been filled with zombies, vampires, and other monstrous incarnations of the living dead. As Evan Calder Williams has noted, 'In these dark, anxious years, the undead are having their day in the sun: none more so than zombies; the contemporary vision of the walking dead horde has, without doubt, become the nightmare vision of our day' (Calder Williams 2011: 72). This is the case, not only in Hollywood productions like *World War Z* and American television series such as *The Walking Dead*, but also throughout the cultural peripheries of global capitalism, including sub-Saharan Africa, where local culture industries are currently thriving on 'unsettling tales of vampires and zombies and of extraordinary intercourse between the living and the dead' (McNally 2012: 175).

This chapter attempts to cast some light upon these murky matters. The first section explores the relationship between political-economic processes and cultural forms in the case of gothic monsters. Against orthodox Marxist analysis, which reduces Frankenstein, Dracula and zombie hordes to fetishized representations of class relations, I argue for a psychoanalytic critique of ideology, which identifies them as symptoms of a darker Real: the emergence of capital as an abstract form of domination. The second section diagnoses neoliberalism as an anxious form of crisis management, which evolves through its failed attempts to conceal its repressed knowledge of the Real of Capital. Yet, in a classically gothic inversion, these very attempts only serve to strengthen the diabolical power that it denies. The third section develops this narrative through the case of the celebrity development economist Jeffrey Sachs, which I relate to the gothic tale of *Dr Jekyll and Mr Hyde*. Once the notorious 'Dr Shock', the architect of the brutal form of neoliberal restructuring known as shock therapy, Sachs has since been reborn as 'Mr Aid', a prominent anti-poverty campaigner and benevolent saviour of 'Africa'. The curious case of Dr Shock and Mr Aid embodies the mysterious persistence and transformability of the neoliberal project, and illustrates the inability of the neurotic neoliberal to escape from the Real of Capital. I conclude with some final reflections on the nature of zombie neoliberalism.

Spectres of capital

In *Monsters of the Market: Zombies, Vampires and Global Capitalism*, David McNally analyses the relationship between gothic literature and capitalist social relations. Drawing on Marx's extensive use of gothic imagery in his critique of political economy, McNally interprets the key narratives of nineteenth-century gothic fiction as mythical renderings of the class relations of industrial capitalism that were being constituted at that time. Mary Shelley's *Frankenstein*, for example, is read as a metaphor for the role of the capitalist class (Dr Frankenstein) in the creation of the proletariat (the Monster) from the disembodied fragments of a dispossessed peasantry (McNally 2012: 17–111). Vampire stories are also cast in class terms, with the vampires as capitalists feeding parasitically on the blood of the working class (ibid.: 113–73). And zombies, which only emerge in popular culture in the twentieth century, are identified as representations of the reduction of the global working class to alienated labour and mindless consumerism (ibid.: 175–251).

From this perspective, gothic literature is just another ideological representation of the class relationship between capitalists and workers. 'If vampires are the dreaded beings which might possess us and turn us into their docile servants,' McNally concludes, 'zombies represent our haunted self-image' (ibid.: 253). While this interpretation undoubtedly captures an important dimension of the monsters of gothic literature, it nevertheless remains faithful to what Evan Calder Williams calls the 'parodic version' of Marxist ideology critique, according to which 'everything is unidirectionally "about" the economy in a banal and dogmatic way' (2011: 79). In *Combined and Uneven Apocalypse*, Calder Williams draws on the psychoanalytic critique of ideology in an alternative deconstruction of the zombie metaphor. Zombie movies and other gothic forms, he notes, are often self-conscious forms of social critique. George A. Romero's *Dawn of the Dead*, for example, 'with its hordes of blank-eyed shopping mall zombies', is an unambiguous critique of consumerism (ibid.: 78). Yet, of real concern to a psychoanalytic critique is not the obvious ideological message that the author or director may have intended to convey, but 'the effects and sets of meanings whose sources cannot be found in the film [or novel] "trying to say something" about social issues … that rat's nest of historical anxieties … which cannot but inflect the final product' (ibid.: 79).

This approach resonates with the Slavoj Žižek's challenge to the orthodox Marxist division between ideological appearances and material reality. Drawing on the work of Jacques Lacan, Žižek argues that 'reality' is itself ideological, to the extent that it is symbolically structured by a web of social fantasies that protect us from the 'Real'. The Real is a traumatic and unrepresentable presence-absence that is excluded from our symbolically constituted reality, but which makes its existence felt in 'a series of effects, though always in a distorted, displaced way' (Žižek 1989: 163). The task of ideological critique is to identify the symptoms of the Real that appear within a given symbolic universe 'in a coded, cyphered form' (ibid.: 73), in order to drag the Real into the realm of the Symbolic (Fink 1995: 70–2). Here I propose a 'symptomatic critique' (Žižek 1989: 21) of the same gothic stories addressed by McNally. Rather than seeing class as the material reality behind these ideological appearances, I argue that the monsters in these stories are themselves a 'coded, cyphered' expression of a much darker Real excluded from the symbolic universes of both their creators and their critics: the Real of Capital as an abstract form of domination.

This ghostly and traumatic dimension of capital has been most successfully theorized by Moishe Postone. In *Time, Labour, and Social Domination*, Postone follows Marx in arguing that value in capitalist society is constituted by socially necessary labour time, and that capitalist production is undertaken for the sole purpose of extracting surplus value through the exploitation of living labour. The constantly expanding reproduction of capital increasingly compels all capitalists to obey its monolithic logic of self-valorization, and capital comes to exert an abstract form of domination that drives towards 'accumulation for accumulation's sake', regardless of the social or ecological consequences. Postone argues that it is, therefore, capital, rather than the proletariat, that constitutes the true subject of history, a subject that the proletariat itself creates through its own alienated productive activity. As the emergent subject of global capitalism, capital is 'blind, processual and quasi-organic… an alienated, abstract self-moving Other, characterized by a constant directional movement with no external goal' (Postone 1993: 270, 278).[1]

Capital first emerges as an abstract form of domination with the consolidation of what Marx conceptualized as the formal subsumption of labour to capital: the subordination of pre-existing forms of production under the reign of wage labour. Formal subsumption, however, is limited to the production of absolute surplus value. This can only be increased through the extension of the working day, and as such has concrete limits. In its blind desire for endless self-valorization, capital therefore drives the transition from the formal to the real subsumption of labour, through which the labour process itself is transformed in accordance with the requirements of capital. Real subsumption enables the production of relative surplus value, through the deployment of technologies that increase the productivity of labour and the rate of surplus value extraction (Marx 1976: 1019–38). In doing so, it further empowers capital as an abstract form of domination. The transition from the formal to the real subsumption of labour is, therefore, the dynamic that drives the becoming of capital-as-subject (Postone 1993: 283–4).

As an invisible, intangible presence-absence that dominates our reality without being symbolically included within it, capital is Real. Yet, as Žižek argues,

> In the opposition between reality and spectral illusion, the Real appears precisely as 'irreal', as a spectral illusion for which there is no room in our (symbolically constructed) reality... The inert remainder foreclosed from (what we experience as) reality returns precisely in the Real of spectral apparitions.
>
> *(Žižek 2008a: xvi)*

With this in mind, I would argue that it is no coincidence that in England, the birthplace of industrial capitalism, the empowerment of capital-as-subject through the shift from formal to real subsumption coincided precisely with the development of gothic literature, through which the Real of Capital began to appear in 'spectral' and 'illusory' forms. From this perspective, the relation between Dr Frankenstein and his Monster is not between the capitalist and the labourer, but between capitalist society and the Real of Capital, which has 'been endowed by living labour with a soul of its own, and establishes itself opposite living labour as an *alien power*' (Marx 1973: 454, original emphasis). Like Frankenstein's Monster, the Real of Capital is 'an animated monster' that 'confronts the worker as something not merely alien, but hostile and antagonistic' (Marx 1976: 302, 1025).[2]

Equally, vampires should not be understood as mere metaphors for exploitative capitalists, but are instead embodiments of the 'ghostly objectivity' of capital-as-subject (Marx, quoted in Arthur 2004: 153). Real subsumption is conceptualized by Marx as the subordination of living labour to dead labour. Dead labour is the value extracted from past labour and accumulated in the increasingly vast machineries through which relative surplus value is extracted in ever-greater quantities, looming above living labour as a spectral subject that continually 'draws new vital spirits into itself, and realizes itself anew' (Marx 1973: 453). Capital is, therefore, 'dead labour which, vampire-like, lives only by sucking living labour, and lives the more, the more labour it sucks' (Marx 1976: 342). In this context zombies appear, not as the working class exploited by capitalist vampires, as the orthodox Marxist analysis would automatically suggest, but as a further embodiment of dead labour, which rises from the grave and is reanimated by the flesh of the living. If, in the nineteenth century, the solitary vampire was sufficient to convey the emergent power of capital as an abstract form of domination, by the late twentieth century the ever-greater masses of dead labour in relation to the living could only be adequately represented by infinite hordes of zombies swarming across the planet in blind pursuit of all remaining human meat and brains. It is for this reason, I claim, that the zombie movie has become 'the dominant vision of apocalypse in late capitalism' (Calder Williams 2011: 73). Zombie neoliberalism, however, is more complex, and is only the latest twist in the labyrinthine gothic nightmare of the neoliberal project.

The nightmare of neurotic neoliberalism

Neoliberalism is typically represented by proponents and critics alike as a remarkably self-assured and one-dimensional orthodoxy. But close attention to its evolution reveals it as an anxious and contradictory process, which has morphed continuously over the course of its history, while retaining an obsessive commitment to an underlying vision of the world. Neoliberalism differs from other utopian ideologies in the way that it understands its own project. For the neoliberal, the acquisitive individual is the essence of human nature, and market society is the natural order of the social world. The aim is not to create a world that never existed, but rather to liberate a pre-existing reality of 'spontaneous market forces' from beneath the dead hand of the state. Neoliberals, therefore, see their project as 'pragmatic' and 'non-ideological', in contrast to the failed utopian ideologies of the past. According to Žižek, however, 'it is precisely the neutralization of some features into a spontaneously accepted background that marks out ideology at its purest' (Žižek 2008b: 31). Far from being pragmatic and non-ideological, I argue, neoliberalism should be understood as a social fantasy that structures 'reality' against the Real of Capital.

Neoliberal ideology is based on Adam Smith's vision of a natural and harmonious market society, in which the self-interested activities of individual entrepreneurs are mediated by the invisible hand of the market to ensure the optimal allocation of resources. As a system of norms, individuals and institutions, capitalism is incorporated into neoliberal ideology. But the Real of Capital is excluded from this symbolic order. The source of profit in exploitation is concealed by the understanding of economic value as an expression of subjective preferences, rather than a measure of socially necessary labour time. The inherent tendency for capitalism to generate vast economic crises is papered over by the assumption that efficient markets operate under conditions of 'perfectly competitive equilibrium'. And the power of capital as an abstract form of domination is represented as the benign operation of the invisible hand of the market. For the neoliberal subject, market economics is, therefore, not a policy framework that can be easily discarded, but is a structuring principle of social reality, which protects the subject from the traumatic Real of Capital. The failure of the neoliberal fantasy is thus experienced, not as the disproval of a theory, but as the inexplicable violation of reality, in the form of financial crashes, credit crunches, economic depressions, and so on. Rather than responding to such traumatic events by discarding their economic model, neoliberals attempt to hold their sense of reality together by explaining their failures in terms that leave their fantasy intact. Understood in this way, the evolution of the neoliberal project appears not as the Machiavellian implementation of a monolithic 'shock doctrine' (Klein 2008), but as a series of failed attempts to prevent the Real of Capital from disturbing the fantasy of a harmonious market society.[3]

If we consider the history of neoliberal ideology, we can see that it has always been driven by an anxious desire to hide the ugly realities of capitalism beneath a fantasy of harmonious order. Adam Smith's original theory of the invisible hand of the market was born in the midst of the violent establishment of capitalism in eighteenth-century Great Britain, providing Smith with a reassuring vision that 'concealed the harshness of the world around him' (Perelman 2000: 208). The first great experiment with economic liberalism in the nineteenth century led to the Great Depression, the Second World War and the rise of communism (Polanyi 1944). These violent upheavals triggered the formulation of the neoliberal project in the 1940s by a group of right-wing economists led by Milton Friedman and Friedrich Hayek, who described themselves as 'drawn together by a common sense of crisis', and 'huddled together… for warmth on a cold dark night' (cited in Peck 2010b: 50, 66; see also Springer, 2016). In this traumatic confrontation with the Real of Capital, the neoliberal fantasy acquired 'an irresistible attraction… the almost silent hum of a perfectly running machine; the apparent stillness of the exact balance of counter-acting pressures; the automatic smooth recovery from a chance disturbance' (Robinson 1962: 77–8).

Neoliberalism rose to dominance by representing subsequent economic crises as crises of Keyensianism or developmentalism, against which the neoliberal project could be advanced as a return to the natural order of a market society. Yet, ever since it became hegemonic in the 1980s, neoliberalism has been plagued by a return of the repressed, in the form of financial volatility, spiralling inequalities, and innumerable social conflicts. In response, the neoliberal project has evolved from the stripped-down fundamentalism of Reaganomics and the Washington Consensus to the more complex interventionist policies of Third Way social democracy and 'globalization with a human face'. These interventions are aimed not at challenging market society, but at making reality conform to the neoliberal fantasy. The principles of free trade and macroeconomic 'responsibility' remain sacrosanct, and the invisible hand of the market remains the guiding force of economic activity, while the role of the state is restricted to providing the economic infrastructure, human capital, and 'investment climate' required for markets to operate efficiently. In the world of international development, for example, the World Bank and the International Monetary Fund have replaced the Washington Consensus with the 'post-Washington Consensus'. Whereas the Washington Consensus entailed the dismantling of public health and education systems in the name of austerity and privatization, the post-Washington Consensus insists that health and education should be valued, but only to the extent that they improve labour productivity. Poverty should be alleviated, but this should be pursued through philanthropy and corporate social responsibility rather than the mandatory redistribution of wealth. And development must be ecologically sustainable, but only as a means of ensuring the sustainability of economic growth and capital accumulation (Taylor 2004; Sheppard and Leitner 2010).

Through a multi-dimensional process of ideological and institutional modifications of this kind, the neoliberal project has created an ever more elaborate system, in order to cope with the proliferating symptoms of the Real of Capital in such a way that the fantasy of a harmonious market society is preserved. This frenetic activity resembles the behaviour of the obsessional neurotic, who 'builds up a whole system enabling him to postpone the encounter with the Real *ad infinitum*' (Žižek 1989: 192). The resilience and transformability of the neoliberal project can, therefore, be understood in terms of a *neoliberal neurosis*.

Neurotic neoliberals include many seemingly 'reformed' neoliberals, such as Jeffrey Sachs, Joseph Stiglitz and Paul Krugman. Once the architect of neoliberal 'shock therapy', Sachs has reinvented himself as an outspoken critic of the Washington Consensus, while continuing to promote free trade and the intellectual property rights of multinational corporations (as discussed below). Stiglitz has, likewise, made a name for himself as a critic of economic orthodoxy, while remaining wedded to neoliberal fundamentals, serving as Chief Economist of the World Bank from 1997 to 2000, and masterminding its transition from the Washington Consensus to the post-Washington Consensus (Cammack 2004). Similarly, not withstanding his current incarnation as a reborn 'Keynesian', Krugman served as an economic advisor in the Reagan administration, and has played a key role alongside Sachs and Stiglitz in the development of 'globalization with a human face', which has been so central to the legitimation of the neoliberal project (Wilson 2011).

This is not to say that all neoliberals are neurotic. In fact, we could contrast the neurotic neoliberals to unreconstructed market fundamentalists such as Niall Ferguson and William Easterly, by drawing a distinction between neurotic and *psychotic* neoliberals, to the extent that the latter remain utterly unaware of any dissonance between their fantasy and the Real (Leader 2011: 39). The contemporary spectrum of mainstream economic debate is limited to a discussion between neurotic and psychotic neoliberals, with the neurotic neoliberals constituting the leftward boundary of acceptable public opinion. Yet, despite being attacked by psychotic neoliberals for their betrayal of the market, it is Sachs and his fellow neurotics who are the true guardians of the neoliberal project. In their willingness to engage in ever more invasive forms of intervention to sustain the coordinates of their fantasy, the neurotic neoliberals exhibit the peculiar combination of transformability and resilience that has made neoliberal ideology so irrationally persistent in the face of its repeated failures. The evolution of the neoliberal project towards increasingly intensive forms of social engineering should, therefore, be understood not as the meticulous manipulation of social reality by a conspiratorial technocratic elite, but rather as a series of increasingly desperate attempts to hold reality itself together, against the relentless pressure of the Real of Capital.

Paradoxically, the obsessive-compulsive rituals of the neurotic neoliberals have only served to intensify the very contradictions they are struggling to contain. The neoliberal project is defined by the drive to liberate capital accumulation from all 'external' constraints, either by removing all impediments to the efficient functioning of the price mechanism, or by designing interventions to compensate for 'market failure'. But the Real of Capital does not correspond to the neoliberal fantasy of a naturally harmonious market order. No matter what the neurotic neoliberals do, their actions do not result in the smooth tranquillity of 'general equilibrium', but only serve to further empower the Real of Capital as an increasingly volatile and destructive force, which is spiralling beyond the bounds of social control and driving inexorably towards economic and ecological collapse. Their predicament thus recalls Goethe's gothic ballad of the sorcerer's apprentice, who, having summoned the forces of the underworld, finds that he is unable to control them, and that his every attempt to do so only serves to strengthen their diabolical powers.[4]

The strange case of Dr Shock and Mr Aid

The peculiarities of the neoliberal neurosis can be further illustrated by a brief consideration of the curious case of Jeffrey Sachs, whose career has evolved in parallel with the twists and turns of the neoliberal project.[5] Sachs was imbued with the neoliberal fantasy at Harvard in the 1970s, and went on to implement his notorious 'shock therapy' programmes in Bolivia and Poland, based on the rapid and wholesale liberalization of these economies. Despite their high social costs, these brutal reforms were celebrated by the neoliberal policy elite for rapidly opening these countries to global capital, and seemed to confirm the 'reality' of the neoliberal fantasy, by stripping back the state to reveal the spontaneous order of a market society. Sachs then implemented shock therapy in Russia. As the Russian economy slid into crisis, a Nobel Prize-winning economist warned Sachs to 'Recall the story of the creature artificially constructed by Dr Frankenstein', arguing that Sachs was risking the creation of a similar monster. If the pace of reform was not slowed down, and appropriate institutional safeguards not put in place, he concluded, 'Frankenstein's monster may prove to be an applicable cautionary tale' (Edmund S. Phelps, in Lipton and Sachs 1992: 278).

Fatefully, Sachs chose to ignore this warning, and Frankenstein's monster went on the rampage. In Russia, shock therapy resulted in one of the longest and deepest recessions in modern history, confronting Sachs with the Real of Capital as crisis-ridden system that tore Russian society apart with a seemingly uncontrollable destructive fury. Sachs's entire subsequent career can be understood as a series of increasingly desperate and ultimately futile attempts to escape this monster of his own creation. Unable to maintain his neoliberal fantasy in its original form, Sachs has been forced to modify it to account for certain symptoms of the Real of Capital, such as poverty and inequality. Rather than attributing these to the inherent contradictions of capitalism, however, Sachs has attempted to explain them away as 'externalities' and 'market failures' to be addressed with targeted policies that leave his fundamental fantasy intact. The intensification of international inequalities, for example, is attributed not to free trade and privatization trapping post-colonial countries in primary commodity production, but to relative distances to sea-ports and the disease burden of tropical climates, and is to be addressed through infrastructure development rather than policies that promote economic sovereignty. Through this process, Sachs has been reintegrated into the neoliberal policy elite, as one of the key figures in engineering the transition from the Washington Consensus to the post-Washington Consensus and beyond.

Sachs's Millennium Village Project would seem to mark the 'logical' end point of this process. Funded by multinational corporations and Wall Street billionaires, the project aims to prove Sachs's solution to extreme poverty in a series of model villages across sub-Saharan Africa. It retains shock therapy's faith in the market-based and entrepreneurial nature of social reality, but, whereas shock therapy sought to shock this reality into existence, the Millennium Villages Project seeks to engineer it down to its very last detail, through a comprehensive set of interventions in every dimension of the villagers' everyday lives. This, then, is the paradox of neoliberalism, which evolves through a series of neurotic displacement strategies, from the destruction of the interventionist state, to the total social production of a supposedly natural order. Of course, this only serves to further exacerbate the underlying contradictions of the project, and the Millennium Villages are very far from realizing their fantasy of a harmonious market society. Yet, at the level of ideology, they have been a great success, appearing to prove the efficacy of philanthrocapitalism, while providing Sachs with a narcissistic stage upon which to perform his imagined identity as the benevolent saviour of Africa, with the trauma of Russia all but forgotten (Wilson 2014c; 2016).

Jeffrey Sachs's peculiar transformation can be likened to Robert Louis Stevenson's gothic classic, 'Curious Case of Dr Jekyll and Mr Hyde', in which Dr Jekyll, a wise and benevolent gentleman, transforms into the obscene and depraved Mr Hyde. In a peculiar reversal of this process, the dastardly Dr Shock would appear to have been transformed into the magnanimous Mr Aid. Yet as G.K. Chesterton noted in his analysis of 'Dr Jekyll and Mr Hyde', 'The real stab of the story is not in the discovery that the one man is two men; but in the discovery that the two men are one man' (Chesterton 2003: 183). In other words, Mr Hyde is not the antithesis of Dr Jekyll, but the explosion of Jekyll's own repressed desires. In the same way, much as Mr Aid might strive to erase the spectre of Dr Shock, his past identity continues to cloud his 'progressive' and 'ethical' visage. This is revealed in Sachs's momentary lapses of judgement and slips of the tongue, which have grown increasingly frequent since the global financial crisis of 2008, when the Real of Capital surged back into his symbolic universe with all its blind destructive rage. It is as if, gripped by this traumatic return of the repressed, Sachs has suddenly been overcome by his old lust for radical austerity, and cannot resist committing acts of public indiscretion. His continued adherence to neoliberal fundamentals has been repeatedly betrayed by his vociferous attacks on any suggestion of a Keynesian solution to the global economic crisis. Momentarily forgetting his new identity, Sachs now finds himself accidentally insisting that 'deficit cutting should start now', and dismissing the suffering caused by austerity as 'an adjustment to be accepted' (Sachs 2010). As if afflicted by a kind of neoliberal Tourette's syndrome, his critiques of the Washington Consensus are increasingly interrupted by the barking of spasmodic eulogies to Friedrich Hayek and Milton Friedman (see, for example, Sachs 2011: 34, 43, 102, 273). As Robert Louis Stevenson (2003: 77) concludes in the case of Dr Jekyll and Mr Hyde, 'The doom and burden of our lives is bound forever on man's shoulders, and when the attempt is made to cast it off, it but returns upon us with more unfamiliar and more awful pressure.'

The death drive of zombie neoliberalism

We can now return to the metaphor of the undead with which our discussion began. As we have seen, the neoliberal neurosis is characterized by repeated attempts to maintain the coherence of the neoliberal social fantasy against the Real of Capital. Yet, because neoliberalism is premised on removing all barriers to the movement of value, and on extending capitalist social relations to the ends of the earth, it paradoxically intensifies the very contradictions of capitalism that it is attempting to repress. The predicament of the neurotic neoliberal thus recalls that of the private investigator Harry Angel in Alan Parker's gothic thriller *Angel Heart*, who fruitlessly pursues a serial killer through numerous false leads, only to make the final horrific discovery that he himself is the murderer. In a similar way, the neoliberal neurosis compels its agents to engage with the symptoms of the Real of Capital, but in a disavowed form that prevents them from identifying their own responsibility for the exacerbation of these very symptoms… until the moment of breakdown. In the aftermath of the global collapse of the neoliberal project, 'the strange non-death of neo-liberalism' can thus be compared to the disintegration of the symbolic universe characteristic of psychosis, in which the fantasy frame has collapsed, and the subject is gripped by what Freud called 'death drive' – a 'blind persistence which follows its path with utter disregard for the requirements of our concrete life-world' (Žižek 2008a: xvi). This definition of death drive recalls Postone's description of the Real of Capital as a 'blind, processual, and quasi-organic', and as 'characterized by a constant directional movement with no external goal' (Postone 1993: 270, 278). If fantasy is the screen that separates desire from drive (Žižek 1997: 43), then beyond the disintegration of their social fantasy, it is the Real of Capital that continues to animate 'the living dead of the neoliberal revolution', as 'the obscene persistence of that which refuses to die' (Calder Williams 2011: 9). As Žižek argues, 'this paradox of dead objects coming alive… is possible only within the space of the death drive, which, according to Lacan, is the space between the two deaths, Symbolic and Real' (Žižek 1997: 112). Zombie neoliberalism inhabits the limbo state between these different deaths. Symbolically, neoliberalism is already dead, but as a global metabolic system it remains alive, enslaved directly to the death drive of the Real of Capital.

Deprived of his social fantasy, the neurotic neoliberal joins the zombie hordes and lurches spasmodically into the ruins of a crisis-ridden future, hungering for living brains to revitalize his moribund ideology. Perhaps this explains why Sachs, Stiglitz, and Krugman all staggered into Zucotti Park during the Occupy Wall Street protests in 2011. All of them appropriated the discourse of the protesters, delivering pseudo-radical speeches that attacked the selfish behaviour of bankers and corporations, while criticizing the free-market system that they had helped to create. Yet they all anxiously insisted upon the sanctity of a good and pure market economy, transforming greedy bankers and corrupt corporations into the latest symptoms through which the Real of Capital could be disavowed (Yates 2011). If there is a lesson for those struggling against zombie neoliberalism, it must be to keep a close eye on those who appear to be fighting alongside you. As Žižek warned during his own appearance at Occupy, we must 'Beware not only of enemies, but also of false friends who pretend to support us, but who are working hard to dilute our protest' (Žižek 2011). In other words: *Watch out! That zombie wants to eat your brain!*

Notes

1 Starosta (2015: 299) claims that 'this is probably the most important critical insight of the fully-developed Marxian critique of political economy… the discovery of the social constitution of capital as an autonomous self-moving subject amounts to the concretization of the young Marx's account of alienated labour'.

2 As these quotations suggest, Marx's usage of gothic imagery in *Capital* and the *Grundrisse* should not be dismissed as mere incidental literary embellishment, but was crucial to his own attempts to represent the unrepresentable spectrality of capital-as-subject (see Godfrey *et al.* 2004).

3 For a detailed exposition of the theoretical underpinnings of this argument see Wilson 2014a.

4 In *The Communist Manifesto*, Marx and Engels appeal to similar imagery: 'Modern bourgeois society, with its relations of production, of exchange, and of property, a society that has conjured up such gigantic means of production and of exchange, is like the sorcerer who is no longer able to control the powers of the nether world whom he has called up by his spells' (Marx and Engels 2002: 225).

5 This story is told in far greater detail in my book on Jeffrey Sachs (Wilson 2014b).

References

Arthur, C.J. 2004. *The New Dialectic and Marx's Capital*. Boston, MA: Brill.

Calder Williams, E. 2011. *Combined and Uneven Apocalypse*. Ropley: Zero.

Cammack, P. 2004. What the World Bank Means by Poverty Reduction and Why It Matters. *New Political Economy*, 9.2: 189–211.

Chesterton, G.K. 2003. The Real Stab of the Story, in Linehan, K., ed. *Robert Louis Stevenson, The Strange Case of Dr Jekyll and Mr Hyde: An Authoritative Text*. New York: Norton.

Crouch, C. 2011. *The Strange Non-death of Neo-liberalism*. Cambridge, MA: Polity.

Dean, M. 2014. Rethinking Neoliberalism. *Journal of Sociology*, 50.2: 150–63.

Fine, B. 2008. Zombieconomics: The Living Death of the Dismal Science in the Age of Neoliberalism. Paper presented at the ESRC Neoliberalism Seminar, 1 April. Retrieved from http://www.cppr.ac.uk/centres/cppr/esrcneoliberalismseminar/

Fink, B. 1995. *The Lacanian Subject: Between Language and Jouissance*. Princeton, NJ: Princeton University Press.

Fisher, M. 2013. How to Kill a Zombie: Strategizing the End of Neoliberalism. *Open Democracy*. Retrieved from https://www.opendemocracy.net/mark-fisher/how-to-kill-zombie-strategizing-end-of-neoliberalism

Godfrey, R., Jack, G., and Jones, C. 2004. Sucking, Bleeding, Breaking: On the Dialectics of Vampirism, Capital, and Time. *Culture and Organization*, 10.1: 25–36.

Klein, N. 2008. *The Shock Doctrine*. New York: Picador.

Leader, D. 2011. *What is Madness?* London: Penguin.

Lipton, D., and Sachs, J. 1992. Prospects for Russia's Economic Reforms. *Brookings Papers on Economic Activity*, 2: 213–83.

Marx, K. 1973. *Grundrisse*. London: Penguin.

—. 1976. *Capital, Volume 1*. New York: Random House.

Marx, K., and Engels, F. 2002. *The Communist Manifesto*. London: Penguin.

McNally, D. 2012. *Monsters of the Market: Zombies, Vampires and Global Capitalism*. Chicago, IL: Haymarket.

Peck, Jamie. 2010a. Zombie Neoliberalism and the Ambidextrous State. *Theoretical Criminology*, 14: 104–10.

—. 2010b. *Constructions of Neoliberal Reason*. Oxford: Oxford University Press.

Perelman, M. 2000. *The Invention of Capitalism: Classical Political Economy and the Secret History of Primitive Accumulation*. Durham, NC: Duke University Press.

Polanyi, K. 1944. *Origins of Our Time: The Great Transformation*. New York: Farrer and Rinehart.

Postone, M. 1993. *Time, Labour, and Social Domination*. Cambridge: Cambridge University Press.

Robinson, J. 1962. *Economic Philosophy*. London: Penguin.

Sachs, J. 2010. Time to Plan for Post-Keynesian Era. *Financial Times*, 7 June. Retrieved from http://www.ft.com/cms/s/0/e7909286-726b-11df-9f82-00144feabdc0.html#axzz3tEBuwt4V

—. 2011. *The Price of Civilization*. London: Random House.

Sheppard, E., and Leitner, H. 2010. Quo Vadis Neoliberalism? The Remaking of Global Capitalist Governance after the Washington Consensus. *Geoforum*, 41: 185–94.

Smith, N. 2008. Comment: Neoliberalism: Dominant but Dead. *Focaal*, 51.1: 15.

Springer, S. 2016. The Violence of Neoliberalism, in Springer, S. Birch, K. and MacLeavy, J., eds. *The Handbook of Neoliberalism*. London: Routledge: 139–49.

Starosta, G. 2015. *Marx's Capital, Method and Revolutionary Subjectivity*. Boston, MA: Brill.

Stevenson, R.L. 2003. Curious Case of Dr Jekyll and Mr Hyde, in Linehan, K., ed. *Robert Louis Stevenson, The Strange Case of Dr Jekyll and Mr Hyde: An Authoritative Text*. New York: Norton.

Taylor, M. 2004. Responding to Neoliberalism in Crisis: Discipline and Empowerment in the World Bank's New Development Agenda. *Research in Political Economy*, 21: 3–30.

Wilson, J. 2011. Colonising Space: The New Economic Geography in Theory and Practice. *New Political Economy*, 16.3: 373–97.

—. 2014a. The Shock of the Real: The Neoliberal Neurosis in the Life and Times of Jeffrey Sachs. *Antipode*, 46.1: 301–21.

—. 2014b. *Jeffrey Sachs: The Strange Case of Dr Shock and Mr Aid*. London: Verso.

—. 2014c. Fantasy Machine: Philanthrocapitalism as an Ideological Formation. *Third World Quarterly*, 35.7: 1144–61.

—. 2016. The Village that Turned to Gold: A Parable of Philanthrocapitalism. *Development and Change*. 47.1: 3–28.

Yates, M.D. 2011. Occupy Wall Street and the Celebrity Economists. *Monthly Review*, 23 November. Retrieved from http://monthlyreview.org/press/news/michael-d-yates-on-occupy-wall-street-and-the-celebrity-economists/

Žižek, S. 1989. *The Sublime Object of Ideology*. London: Verso.

—. 1997. *The Plague of Fantasies*. London: Verso.

—. 2008a. *For They Know Not What They Do: Enjoyment as a Political Factor*, 2nd edn. London: Verso.

—. 2008b. *Violence*. London: Profile.

—. 2011. Actual Politics. *Theory and Event*, 14.4. doi: 10.1353/tae.2011.0065

52

EVERYDAY CONTESTATIONS TO NEOLIBERALISM

Valuing and harnessing alternative work practices in a neoliberal society

Richard J. White and Colin C. Williams

> The capitalist structuring of life excludes participation from so much of human existence.
>
> (Buck 2009: 68)

Written at a time of profound economic, ecological and social crises, this chapter promotes greater awareness around the pervasive nature of 'alternative' non-capitalist spaces within the 'advanced' economies of the western world. Drawing attention to the geographies of these alternative economic spaces, the aim is to consider how these work practices could be better framed, valued and understood in a more expansive economic ontology, so that they may be harnessed as a means of encouraging more empowered, inclusive and sustainable economic modes of production, exchange and consumption. Despite the dogmatic counter-narratives emanating from the incumbent political-economic elite, the starting point of this chapter is that neoliberalism has never been able – nor ever will be able – to achieve the goals of empowered, inclusive and sustainable economic production, exchange and consumption. There are many reasons for this, not least that capitalism – memorably referred to as an act of 'structural genocide' (Leech 2012) – is an economic system condemned to perpetual crisis. As Peck (2010a: 10) noted:

> For all the ideological purity of free-market rhetoric, for all the machinic logic of neo-classical economics,... neoliberal statecraft is inescapably, and profoundly, marked by compromise, calculation, and contradiction. There is no blueprint. There is not even a map. Crises themselves need not be fatal for this mutable, mongrel model of governance, for to some degree or another neoliberalism *has always been* a creature of crisis.
>
> *(Emphasis added)*

Yet, despite increasingly vociferous criticism of the failure of capitalism, neoliberalism still retains a colonizing presence *across* the political-economic spectrum at this time of crisis (see Peck and Tickell 2002; Peck 2010a, 2010b; Springer 2010) and as such exerts an incredible hold over the economic imaginary as to what is possible, preferable and achievable. To throw off this neoliberal straitjacket, and embrace more expansive, diverse and heterodox post-neoliberal visions of the future of work and organization is thus difficult, even if desirable (see Purcell 2016). Drawing on empirical evidence not only to reject the (mythical) spectre of a monolithic capitalist economic landscape, but also to underpin and map out an 'alternative' economic imaginary is an important intervention. It not only transcends the view that there is some meta-theory which is the 'alternative' to neoliberalism capitalism, but also grounds this alternative as existing in the here and now, in the mundane everyday practices of people all over the world. Indeed, the argument of this chapter is that these alternative forms of work and organization that are ubiquitous are essentially *anarchist* in all but name.

While the chapter is focused on interpreting, valuing and harnessing these alternative economic spaces so as to present a truer representation of the complexity of the economic land-scape, it is sobering to observe how re-reading the current reality sometimes seems far from sufficient to usher in a post-neoliberal society. Of course, opening up the economic imaginary (what is desirable, possible and achievable) to display the seeds of the future as existing in present everyday practice is an important political act. However, whether this is the 'best' way to con-test and challenge neoliberalism *in practice* is perhaps questionable. Others might call for more direct action that openly confronts neoliberalism. However, it is sobering to bear witness to the naked violence that the neoliberal state can draw upon, as has been all too readily deployed to suppress and destroy dissent. This has certainly been evident where popular, bottom-up, and truly democratic demonstrations have emerged across Europe – Spain, Portugal, Greece, Italy, the UK – particularly in response to the toxic impacts of austerity measures, and the neoliberal-ism of higher-education. What neoliberalism cannot do, however, is to do the same with the ubiquitous mundane everyday acts of economic practice and organization found in every house-hold and community. For us, therefore, this everyday site represents a useful starting point for constructing alternative economic spaces.

The structure of the chapter is divided into three sections. The first focuses on the evidence gained through time-use surveys, undertaken by governments in the western world. This method is taken in conjunction with the more nuanced qualitative findings of organization promoted by household work practice surveys carried out in England. This allows both a more accurate understanding of the highly limited and uneven purchase that capitalist practices have actually had across western society to emerge, and also suggests that the dominant trend is one of informalization (i.e. more time being spent in non-commodified alternative work practices). In turn, such a radical re-appraisal of the 'economic', one that recognizes the heterodox nature of our economic landscapes, also requires more complex theoretical representations of the econ-omy to come to the fore. In highlighting the significant limits of capitalism, and the importance of alternative economic spaces, consideration as to how to better represent, value, protect and develop these work practices are made. To this end, it is suggested that naming forms of alterna-tive work practice is important. In casting a critical gaze at these self-organized economic spaces, which draw on mutual aid, reciprocity, co-operation, collaboration and inclusion, it becomes apparent that many of these already-existing economic spaces are recognizably and demonstrably *anarchistic*. This then invites, in the third section, the question of how to respond to the challenge of harnessing and developing (new) anarchic spaces and forms of economic practice. How can these spaces illustrate the ways forward so as to open up our future to more empowering and inclusive economic modes of production, exchange and consumption beyond neoliberalism?

Thinking beyond neoliberalism

Neoliberalism seems to be everywhere.

(Peck and Tickell 2002: 382)

Neoliberalism 'generally refers to a new political, economic, and social arrangement emphasizing (capitalist) market relations, minimal states, and individual responsibility' (Springer 2010: 1025). In the twenty-first century, the hegemonic positioning of neoliberalism, by a mainstream political-economic discourse, has been so successful that neoliberalism has become one of those concepts that proves 'difficult to think *about* them when it has become so commonplace to think *with* them. The conventional wisdom can seem ubiquitous, inevitable, natural, and all-encompassing' (Peck 2010b: xi). To demonstrate its dominance over the economic imaginary Shukaitis (2010: 304) considers a scenario where you:

> Ask someone how an economy would run if not based on private ownership. Ask them how society would operate without a state. Chances are they will find it very difficult to describe, which is odd considering that for thousands of years of human history there was no state or market economy. But yet such has become so normalized that thinking outside of such is nearly impossible for many people.

Thus, to think *properly* about – let alone engage identity with – 'alternatives' to neoliberalism is a considerable task. As Byrne *et al.* (1998, as cited in Williams 2005: 226) observed:

> To re-read a landscape we have always read as capitalist, to read it as a landscape of difference, populated by various capitalist and non-capitalist economic practices and institutions – that is a difficult task. It requires us to contend not only with our colonized imaginations, but with our beliefs about politics, understandings of power, conceptions of economy, and structures of desire.

However, it is strongly emphasized in this chapter that the best chance of encouraging a 'post-neoliberal' space to emerge involves demonstrating how the 'alternative' is not wedded to some utopian future, but rather is embedded in the desirable, practical and enactable informal coping strategies that are known and familiar in the here and now. Happily, the findings here reinforce those made elsewhere (see Shannon 2014). As Fuller *et al.* (2010: xxv) observed: 'The world of diversity is not to be found in Neverland. Instead it is real, actual, material; a world in the making rather than a world of make-believe.' The case for the 'alternative' being hidden in plain sight will be made shortly. Before that, it is important to understand how this may challenge the dominant neoliberal narrative about capitalism, and the future of capitalism. With this in mind, the chapter engages with the powerful narrative of the commodification thesis.

The commodification thesis assumes that the capitalist market, 'is becoming more powerful, expansive, hegemonic and totalizing as it penetrates deeper into each and every corner of economic life and stretches its tentacles ever wider across the globe to colonize those areas previously left untouched by its powerful force' (Williams 2005: 1). Crucially, across vast swathes of academic, policy-making and wider public circles, the empirical foundation that underpins this thesis is never questioned. Rather it is *assumed* to reflect the economic reality/ies of the advanced economies of the western world. To see whether or not the thesis holds up to the evidence, attention is drawn to time-use surveys. Time-use surveys have become an influential method of quantifying different types of economic activity (work-based, paid, unpaid etc.) and comparing how these vary across space (e.g. nationally) and over time. Gershuny (2011: 4) has been particularly influential in developing this unit of measurement from the 1980s. Here he explains what this survey aims to do:

> Time-use... describes the allocation of time among various circumstances and subjective states. It is a key social indicator, which finds particular applications in the

assessment of individuals' material welfare and well-being. It provides the core measure of amounts of work in specific paid occupations ('normal/actual hours per week'),
and for unpaid work in private households or in volunteer groups.

When the findings of the time-use survey are held against the arguments of the commodification thesis, a radically different interpretation of the uneven economic geographies between
'paid' and 'unpaid' work across western society emerges (see Table 52.1).

Without question, taken both individually and collectively, when time is taken into account,
the figures fiercely contradict the suggestion that capitalism (i.e. paid work) is all pervasive.
Rather, the reality of the extent of capitalism is far shorter than would be expected, should the
commodification thesis hold true. Indeed, the average time spent in paid work was just over 90
minutes more than non-exchanged work in more than 20 countries surveyed (see Burns *et al.*
2004). Moreover, when the same evidence base, collated from over 20 countries, is used to
indicate the shift over time (e.g. from the 1970s to the present day) between paid and unpaid
work as a percentage of total work, this shows *more* minutes per day spent engaged in unpaid or
subsistence work (see White and Williams 2012a, 2012b).

A richer, more detailed and meaningful impression of work practices and organization can
be achieved when the time-use survey is considered alongside a household work practice survey.
A particular strength of the latter is that it encourages a richer, complex and predominantly
qualitative understanding of economic participation at the household and community level to
emerge. Table 52.2 shows the UK localities where this approach has been undertaken.

Providing more detail in terms of what is included in household work practice surveys, a
wide range of tasks are considered (see Table 52.3). Typically, participants are asked how they
get everyday tasks completed, and, for each task, the interviewee is asked whether the task had
been undertaken during the previous five years/year/month/week/day (depending on the
activity). If conducted, first, they are asked in an open-ended manner who conducted the task
(a household member, a relative living outside the household, a friend, neighbour, firm, landlord, etc.) and the last time that it had been undertaken. Second, to understand their motives to
get the work done, they are asked why they chose that particular individual(s) to carry out the
work, whether they were the household's first or preferred choice, and, if money was not an

Table 52.1 Allocation of working time in western economies

Country	Paid work (minutes per day)	Non-exchanged work (minutes per day)	Time spent on non-exchanged work as % of all work
Canada	293	204	41.0
Denmark	283	155	35.3
France	297	246	45.3
Netherlands	265	209	44.1
Norway	265	232	46.7
UK	282	206	42.2
USA	304	231	43.2
Finland	268	216	44.6
20 countries	297	230	43.6

Source: Derived from Gershuny (2000: Table 7.1)

Table 52.2 Household work practices: UK localities studied

Locality type	Area	Number of interviews
Affluent rural	Fulbourn, Cambridgeshire	70
Affluent rural	Chalford, Gloucestershire	70
Deprived rural	Grimethorpe, South Yorkshire	70
Deprived rural	Wigston, Cumbria	70
Deprived rural	St Blazey, Cornwall	70
Affluent suburb	Fulwood, Sheffield	50
Affluent suburb	Basset/Chilworth, Southampton	61
Affluent suburb	West Knighton, Leicester	50
Deprived urban	Manor, Sheffield	100
Deprived urban	Pitsmoor, Sheffield	100
Deprived urban	St Mary's, Southampton	100
Deprived urban	Hightown, Southampton	100
Deprived urban	Saffron, Leicester	50

issue, would they have preferred to engage a (formal) professional individual, firm, or company to carry out the task? Third, they are asked whether the person had been unpaid, paid or given a gift; and, if paid, whether it was 'cash-in-hand' or not and how a price had been agreed. Finally, they are asked why they decided to get the work done using that source of labour, so as to enable their motives to be understood.

While acknowledging that there are significant differences evident across the household work practices within the deprived and affluent wards studied (see Table 52.4), the important finding for our purposes here lies in the aggregate percentages. This displays the existence not

Table 52.3 Indicative list of material tasks investigated in the questionnaire

Nature of the task	Individual tasks
Property maintenance	Outdoor painting; indoor decorating (i.e. wallpapering; plastering); replacing a broken widow; maintenance of appliances; plumbing; electrical work
Property improvement	Putting in double glazing; house insulation; building an extension/renovating; putting in central heating; DIY activities (carpentry/putting up shelves etc.)
Routine housework	Routine housework (washing dishes/clothes/cooking meals); cleaning the windows; doing the shopping; moving heavy furniture
Gardening activities	Sweeping paths, planting seeds/mowing lawn
Caring activities	Childminding; pet/animal care; educational activities (tutoring); giving car lifts; looking after property
Vehicle maintenance	Repairing and maintenance
Miscellaneous	Borrow tools or equipment; any other jobs

Table 52.4 Participation rates in different labour practices

% respondents in last 12 months participating in:	Deprived urban	Affluent urban	Deprived rural	Affluent rural
Monetized labour				
Formal paid job in private sector	16	48	19	49
Formal paid job in public and third sector	20	27	18	25
Informal employment	5	7	6	8
Monetized community exchange	60	21	63	30
Monetized family labour	3	6	2	4
Non-monetized labour				
Formal unpaid work in private sector	1	2	1	2
Formal unpaid work in public and third sector	19	28	21	30
Off the radar/non-monetized work in organizations	2	0	2	1
One-to-one non-monetized exchanges	52	70	54	73
Non-exchanged labour	99	100	100	100

Source: Colin Williams's own English Localities Survey

of a neoliberal market society but an economy of difference and diversity. The penetration of the market into the household is shallow and uneven. In terms of challenging capital-centric perceptions and expectations, therefore, there are several particularly important findings here.

Focusing on the urban localities, for example, first, the majority of monetized transactions were not to be conducted by those in formal paid jobs in the private sector. Instead, 60 per cent of monetized exchanges in deprived localities (where the gross household income was less than £250/week), and 21 per cent in affluent localities, were accounted for by monetized community exchange. Burns *et al.* (2004: 32) refer to this type of exchange as 'autonomous' paid informal work, where people engage in paid work mostly for friends, relatives and neighbours, exhibiting strong characteristics of mutual aid. Mutual aid (one-to-one non-monetized exchanges which takes place between households) was also a key informal coping strategy, as was self-provisioning (work that is non-exchanged labour by members of the household for the household).

Far from a commodified world in which the capitalist market is dominant over other spheres of production, what we can clearly identify here in these localities, therefore, are real, dynamic, and meaningful modes of alternative exchange, ones which are neither market-like nor profit motivated (in the narrow monetary sense) (see also White 2011; White and Williams 2012a, 2012b).

Capitalism, having less purchase in the present than is dominantly assumed, is, therefore, but one possible mode of organization. We are, in many important and authentic ways, already living this alternative economic life in the here and now. Ultimately, the evidence that underpins the central arguments of this chapter, when taken to their most radical and logical conclusions, draw new epistemological representations of the economic. Under this critical epistemological gaze, it is capitalism that becomes a *utopian* (im)possibility; an economic *alternative*, a *fantasy*. As Williams (2005: 5) argued, it is 'those who assume the ubiquity of commodification who are living in a dream world rather than facing the stark reality of economic life today'.

Representing and valuing the 'economic'

> Of course, one person's alternative is another person's orthodoxy.
>
> (Parker *et al.* 2007: xiii)

Given the centrality of 'alternative' work practices in the advanced economies of the western world, how should this diversity – and the dynamic economic relationships that underpin different work typologies – be better represented and visualized? Here, a total social organization of labour approach has been particularly instructive (Table 52.5).

What is particularly important to note here is the way hash lines are used to emphasize the fluidity and dynamism between the economic typologies identified. There are no *absolute* economic practices that exist in splendid isolation, and that operate in some pure space independent of 'other' types. In contrast, the table encourages the reader to appreciate the complex economic landscape as existing on spectrums of difference (between paid and unpaid, and between formal and informal).

Collapsing formal boundaries that separate 'formal' (capitalist) and 'informal' work practices calls into question the very concept of 'alternative' economic spaces. Interrogating where the alternative exists, and what it represents (and how it can be preserved and protected against creeping forms of commodification and appropriation) is extremely important. Jonas (2010: 3) captures the danger of a washed down, co-opted 'alternative' here:

> it now seems as if alternatives are proliferating everywhere. Whether it is lifestyle, housing, finance, economies, food, music, politics, language, culture, holidays, gardening, decorating, activism, entertainment or, for that matter also, academic research, we all want to embrace alternatives.

Table 52.5 Typology of forms of community engagement in the total social organization of labour

PAID			
1. Formal paid job in public, private or voluntary sector	2. Informal employment	3. Paid community exchanges	4. Paid household/family work
e.g. formal job in voluntary organization	e.g. wholly undeclared waged employment; under-declared formal employment (e.g. undeclared overtime); informal self-employment	e.g. paid favours for friends, neighbours and acquaintances	e.g. paid exchanges within the family
FORMAL			INFORMAL
e.g. unpaid work in formal community-based group; unpaid internship	e.g. unpaid children's soccer coach without formal police check	e.g. unpaid kinship exchange; neighbourly favour	e.g. self-provisioning of care within household
5. Formal unpaid work in public, private and voluntary sector	6. Informal unpaid work in public, private and voluntary sector	7. One-to-one unpaid community exchanges	8. Unpaid domestic work
UNPAID			

Source: Williams 2009: 216. Fig. 1: Typology of forms of community engagement in the total social organization of labour

Uncritically highlighting non-capitalist 'alternative' possibilities, new visions, new futures of work and organization, clearly is problematic, and a more rigorous discussion is needed as to 'whether or not alternatives are necessarily seen as alternatives to the mainstream per se' (ibid.: 4). For example, focusing on the question of housing, Hodkinson (2012) interprets the alternative(s) to market provision as being 'alternative-oppositional', 'alternative-additional' or 'alternative substitute'. As Hodkinson surmises: 'alternatives can either happily co-exist with or substitute for dominant social configurations, or seek to transform and transcend them' (ibid.: 426).

One significant way of defining and protecting the grounds on which a radically oppositional (anti-capitalist/post-neoliberal) alternative exists is to represent it by another name: *anarchism*. On so many levels, these self-organized, bottom-up, inclusive, free-from-coercion empowering forms of work practice are examples of anarchy in action. Colin Ward (1973[1996]: 8) drew attention to the importance of recognizing the anarchism in the everyday, which he considered as present within:

> common experience of the informal, transient, self-organizing networks of relationships that in fact make the human community possible, rather than through the rejection of existing society as a whole in favour of some future society where some different kind of humanity will live in perfect harmony.
>
> *(Ibid.)*

Elsewhere, there are many further bonds between (many) alternative economies outlined here with an anarchist collective emphasis on the 'social' (see Baldelli 1972; Day 2010; Jun 2012; Landauer 1895[2010]; McKay 2008). For Deleon and Love (2010: 160): 'anarchist theory is informed by the autonomy of the individual, the importance of small and localized communities, the move toward more organic and organizational structures, social justice and the freeing of our desires'. What we would like to emphasize here is a working understanding of anarchism as a theory of organization that considers alternative work practices; 'a description of human organization rooted in the experience of everyday life' (Marshall 2011: 17). Ward, like Kropotkin who inspired him greatly, saw anarchism *in* action. His anarchist perspective was 'mainly concerned with the relations between people and the environments in which they lived, worked and played' (Marshall 2011: 19), and promoted an understanding of anarchism as a theory of organization, in which 'the ideal-typical organizations were voluntary, functional, temporary and small' (Levy 2011: 13).

The next pressing question to be addressed then becomes just 'how' can these *anti*-capitalist anarchic economic spaces be harnessed? This is a significant challenge. As Posey (2011: 299) notes:

> The economic turmoil of the last 2 years has shown that three decades of neoliberalism have failed to produce an economy that is not bubble-prone and that is capable of improving the living standards of most people in the world. Articulating an alternative to neoliberalism is therefore an urgent task.

Despite the crisis of neoliberal state capitalism, which continues to debilitate and destroy many organic life-affirming social, political, ecological and economic spaces, we must recognize the remarkable resilience and resistance embodied in these spaces, as well as in the people that organize and invest in alternative economic strategies. There is a remarkable truth that captures the contemporary realities of economic life that so impressed the Russian anarchist geographer Kropotkin at the turn of the twentieth century. For now, as then:

> Although the destruction of mutual-aid institutions has been going on in practice and theory for full three or four hundred years, hundreds of millions of men [and women] continue to live under such institutions; they piously maintain them and endeavour to reconstitute them where they have ceased to exist.
>
> *(Kropotkin, 1901[1998]: 184)*

The realities of economic life in the contemporary world embody great hope, promise and possibilities for anarchist 'alternative' visions of work and organization to continue to take seed, blossom and flourish.

Conclusions

Moving from a 'capital-centric' reading of economic exchange (Gibson-Graham 1996) and re-positioning capitalism more properly as *one* possible mode of economic exchange is, in one sense, to embark on a radical departure from normalized imaginations, conventions and expectations about what we are told the 'economic' is, and where our economic futures lie. And yet, paradoxically, peering into non-commodified activities is to pay attention to, celebrate and value those types of activities of production, exchange and consumption that all of us are already actively participating in, renewing and creating in the form of a diverse array of vibrant and real, 'alternative' non-capitalist forms of economic and political spaces in our daily activities. In this way, re-reading the/our economic landscape does not require strenuous leaps of imagination and mental gymnastics that result in visualizing some sort of utopian brave new economic world. On the contrary, to look beyond capitalism, is to observe the 'alternative' that plays a central role in our everyday coping strategies. But interrogating the alternative further is necessary should one wish a 'post-neoliberal' future to become more of a reality.

Identifying a great deal of the alternative forms of organization as anarchy in action is an important step in establishing a firm foundation from which to understand and promote these work practices, and ensure that they are not co-opted by creeping commodification. These diverse 'anarchist' alternative economic practices can – and do – provide real opportunities to move society towards truly empowered economic, environmental and socially sustainable futures. It is hoped that the central arguments developed in this chapter will promote further creative discussion as to how 'alternative' non-capitalist spaces can be more fully engaged and promoted. If there is one final thought, it would be: remain conscious of, and sensitive to, the diverse economic landscapes – and the possibilities that they present. Thinking and acting 'beyond neoliberalism' brings sharply into focus an overlooked world of informal work and organization predicated on the values of community self-help: physical, social and emotional worlds that we (co-)create, engage, maintain, harness through our voluntary participation and support. These alternative and uneven spaces – in the final analysis – are intimately known, deeply valued and, we contend, essentially anarchist in all but name.

References

Baldelli, G. 1972. *Social Anarchism*. Harmondworth: Penguin.

Buck, E. 2009. The Flow of Experiencing in Anarchic Economies, in Amster, R., DeLeon, A., Fernandez, L.A., Nocella, A., and Shannon, D., eds. *Contemporary Anarchist Studies: An Introductory Anthology of Anarchy in the Academy*. London: Routledge: 57–69.

Burns, D., Williams, C.C., and Windebank, J. 2004. *Community Self-Help*. London: Palgrave Macmillan.

Byrne, K., Forest, R., Gibson-Graham, J.K., Healy, S., and Horvath, G. 1998. Imagining and Enacting Non-Capitalist Futures. *Rethinking Economic Project Working Paper No.1*. Retrieved from www.arts. monash.edu.au/projects/cep/knowledges/bryne.html

Day, R. 2010. Preface, in Landauer, G., ed. *Revolution and Other Writings: A Political Reader*. Oakland, CA: PM Press.

DeLeon, A., and Love, K. 2010. Anarchist Theory as Radical Critique: Challenging Hierarchies and Domination in the Social and 'Hard' Sciences, in Amster, R., DeLeon, A., Fernandez, L.A., Nocella, A., and Shannon, D., eds. *Contemporary Anarchist Studies: An Introductory Anthology of Anarchy in the Academy*. London: Routledge: 159–65.

Fuller, D., Jonas, A.E.G, and Lee, R. 2010. Editorial Introduction, in Fuller, D., Jonas, E.A.G., and Lee, R., eds. *Interrogating Alterity: Alternative Economic and Political Spaces*. Farnham: Ashgate.

Gershuny, J. 2000. *Changing Times: Work and Leisure in Post-industrial Society*. Oxford: Oxford University Press.

—. 2011. *Time-Use Surveys and the Measurement of National Well-Being*. Oxford: Centre for Time-Use Research, Department of Sociology, University of Oxford.

Gibson-Graham, J.K. 1996. *The End of Capitalism (As We Knew It): A Feminist Critique of Political Economy, with a New Introduction*. Minneapolis: University of Minnesota Press.

Hodkinson, S. 2012. The Return of the Housing Question. *Ephemera: Theory & Politics in Organization*, 12.4: 423–44.

Jonas, A.E.G. 2010. 'Alternative' This, 'Alternative' That...: Interrogating Alterity and Diversity, in Fuller, D., Jonas, E.A.G., and Lee, R., eds. *Interrogating Alterity: Alternative Economic and Political Spaces*. Farnham: Ashgate: 3–30.

Jun, N. 2012. *Anarchism and Political Modernity*. New York: Continuum.

Kropotkin, P. 1901[1998]. *Mutual Aid a Factor of Evolution*. London: Freedom Press.

Landauer, G. 1895[2010]. Anarchism-Socialism, in Landauer, *Revolution and Other Writings: A Political Reader*. Oakland, CA: PM Press: 70–4.

Leech, G. 2012. *Capitalism: A Structural Genocide*. London: Zed.

Levy, C. 2011. Introduction: Colin Ward (1924–2010). *Anarchist Studies*, 19.2: 7–15.

Marshall, P. 2011. Colin Ward: Sower of Anarchist Ideas. *Anarchist Studies*, 19.2: 16–21.

McKay, I. 2008. What is Anarchism?, in McKay, *An Anarchist FAQ*. Edinburgh: AK Press.

Parker, M., Fournier, V., and Reedy, P. 2007. *The Dictionary of Alternatives*. London: Zed.

Peck, J. 2010a. Zombie Neoliberalism and the Ambidextrous State. *Theoretical Criminology*, 14.1: 104–10.

—. 2010b. *Constructions of Neoliberal Reason*. Oxford: Oxford University Press.

Peck, J., and Tickell, A. 2002. Neoliberalizing Space. *Antipode*, 34.3: 380–404.

Posey, J. 2011. The Local Economy Movement: An Alternative to Neoliberalism? *Forum for Social Economics*, 40.3: 299–312.

Purcell, M. 2016. Our New Arms, in Springer, S., Birch, K., and MacLeavy, J., eds. *The Handbook of Neoliberalism*. London: Routledge: 599–608.

Shannon, D. ed. 2014. *The End of the World as We Know It: Crisis, Resistance, and the Age of Austerity*. Edinburgh: AK Press.

Shukaitis, S. 2010. An Ethnography of Nowhere: Notes Toward a Re-Envisioning of Utopian Thinking, in Jun, N.J., and Wahl, S., eds. *New Perspectives on Anarchism*. Plymouth: Lexington: 303–11.

Springer, S. 2010. Neoliberalism and Geography: Expanding Formations. *Geography Compass*, 4.8: 1025–38.

Ward, C. 1973[1996]. *Anarchy in Action*. London: Freedom Press.

White, R.J. 2011. Re-Visiting the Barriers to Participation in Mutual Aid. *International Journal of Sociology and Social Policy*, 31.7/8: 392–410.

White, R.J., and Williams, C.C. 2012a. Beyond Capitalist Hegemony: Exploring the Persistence and Growth of 'Alternative' Economic Practices, in Nocella, A.J., Asimakopoulos, J., and Shannon, D., eds. *The Accumulation of Freedom: Writings on Anarchist Economics*. Oakland, CA: AK Press.

—. 2012b. The Pervasive Nature of Heterodox Economic Spaces at a Time of Neoliberal Crisis: Towards a 'Postneoliberal' Anarchist Future. *Antipode*, 44.5: 1–20.

Williams, C.C. 2005. *A Commodified World? Mapping the Limits of Capitalism*. London: Zed.

—. 2009. Geographical Variations in the Nature of Community Engagement: A Total Social Organization of Labour Approach. *Community Development Journal*, 46.2: 213–28.

53

OUR NEW ARMS

Mark Purcell

This chapter is supposed to be about 'protest and resistance to neoliberalism', but I'm not going to write about any of those things. I think that the Left today, and particularly Left scholars who write for and read a book like this, are suffering from a serious illness. Our illness, which after Nietzsche I will call *ressentiment*, is our obsession with neoliberalism. *Ressentiment* has atrophied our imagination to the point where we are only able to think in terms of *negating* neoliberalism. As theorists we can only sing in the key of critique. We meticulously record and discuss the crimes and contradictions of neoliberalism. When we imagine the world we want instead, we can only speak in terms of not-neoliberalism, of cancelling out the current political-economic regime. When we act, we can only act in the register of protest, resistance, contestation, and refusal – of struggle *against* neoliberalism. We turn our faces and our bodies towards neoliberalism, it occupies the entirety of our vision and our imagination, we bathe in its dark light, and we can think only of blocking it, disrupting it, and, one day, in our fondest dreams, causing it to collapse.

But we don't have to be sick. There is another way to think, another way to be. We can become obsessed with ourselves instead. What do we want to create? What are we capable of producing? Who are we capable of becoming, together? What worlds, what ways of life have we already started to build, and how can we help them grow, spread, and flourish?

We are sick

It's all Marx's fault. He is obsessed with negating capitalism. Obviously, *Capital* is Exhibit A, and it is here that both his brilliance and his unhealthy obsession are most fully on display. Page after page, volume after volume of meticulous analysis of capitalism: its productive power, its contradictions, its pitiless domination. He is by turns admiring, outraged, and resentful. But he is always fully absorbed in the project that consumes everything: a critique of (capitalist) political economy.

The young Marx is much better, but he suffers too. The 'Economic and Philosophic Manuscripts' are mostly a critique of alienation and private property. Most of the text is taken up by a brilliant and utterly convincing analysis of why they are destructive, and why we must try to invent a world without them (1994: 58–68). The text offers much less discussion of what that other world would be like. He does give it a name – communism – and he devotes some pages to it. But he conceives of communism entirely negatively. He defines it as the overcoming or cancellation (*aufgehoben*) of private property. Communism is not narrated as the positive mobilization of our productive capacities; it is, rather, the negation of capitalism's central relation. Even when Marx does focus on the question of communism, he spends much of his time negating the versions of communism he does *not* want (e.g. crude communism where property rights are extended to everyone), and relatively less time describing the communism we *do* want. Only near the end of the section on 'Private Property and Communism' do we get a very brief (though tantalizing) glimpse of ourselves in communism, in which we are restored to ourselves as social beings, beings who are capable of producing freely and in common (1994: 71–9). This is Marx at his best, at his most useful. It is a Marx we rarely see.

Or consider 'On the Jewish Question'. Here Marx entirely dismantles the insidious oppression of the liberal–democratic state, and he shows how its strict separation between public and private spheres actively guarantees that capital will be left free to accumulate profit and immiserate the working class. He develops at length and with great force his argument for why such 'political emancipation' is inadequate and even counterproductive. He says that we must aspire instead to 'human emancipation'. But it is not until the final, dense, thrilling last paragraph of the first section that we get a glimpse of what this might mean:

> Only when the actual, individual man has taken back into himself the abstract citizen and in his everyday life, his individual work, and his individual relationships has become a *species-being*, only when he has recognized and organized his own powers as *social* powers, so that social force is no longer separated from him as *political* power, only then is human emancipation complete.
>
> *(1994: 21, emphasis added)*

So much is going on here, so much that needs to be unpacked. But Marx leaves it latent, unelaborated. He gives us a patient and detailed critique of what is wrong, and really just this single, final, tantalizing sentence to indicate what we should create instead.

Even in 'The Civil War in France' (1871) a series of addresses *to* workers about the most extraordinary attempt *by* workers, perhaps ever, to create a new society beyond capitalism, Marx says far more about the machinations of the powers that be than he does about the innovative new practices that workers in the Commune created. He goes on at length about the treachery of the Thiers government and the barbarism of the Prussians. He seems to have a real taste for the sourness of it all. But his descriptions of the Commune are fleeting, vague, and almost, at times, obfuscating, as though he is trying actively *not* to investigate the details too closely. Of course this was all composed in the moment, during and after the fall of the Commune, and so we should not expect a comprehensive historical account. But yet, still, he is gregarious and painstaking on the details of Thiers, and almost evasive when it comes to the Commune.

Perhaps the text most obsessed with negation is The *Communist Manifesto*. It isn't really about communism at all. It is mostly a screed against the exploitation and domination of capitalism, and, secondarily, against all the false socialisms threatening the anti-capitalist movement. The communists in the *Manifesto* are not members of an association producing freely, rather they are a Communist Party vanguard that sees more clearly than the proletariat and has the resolve to take the necessary action (1994: 169ff). The action that is necessary, of course, is negation. Negate private property, negate class, negate the pillars of the capitalist political economy. Marx and Engels are so absorbed in their will to negate that they seem to have neglected to think seriously about how this negation should be carried out, or who should do it. And so, in the

Manifesto, we get the disastrous plan: the proletariat will form into a class and organize itself into a party, which will seize the state, use the state to abolish private property and therefore capitalist class relations, and then allow the state to wither, at which point we will all witness the emergence of another world, a communist world. Today, of course, it is easy to look back on that program and see the folly.

But, even at the time, Bakunin saw the folly quite clearly. He insisted, loudly, that we are fools if we think we can use coercive state power and dictatorship to free ourselves. He said such a dictatorship, once in power, would not wither away but grow ever stronger. He said we would have a new ruling class of workers-party officials who would dominate society no less disastrously than our current capitalist masters (1972: 330ff). He said that we need to create another way of life not by negating the present one, but by directly creating the new one. And he reminded us that we already possess, within ourselves, the capacity to organize our lives in common, in a functioning society without capitalism and without the state (1973a: 148–9; 1973b: 128–30). Bakunin's wisdom was available to us then, and it is available to us now. We need to heed it.

And, in fact, this wisdom is there in Marx too. To be fair, we can see him struggling, here and there, against his own will to negate. It's probably more Hegel's fault than it is Marx's. Despite Marx's energetic and explicit attempts to critique and move beyond Hegel (e.g. the second half of the 'Economic and Philosophic Manuscripts', 1994: 79–97), the latter's habits of thought were deeply imprinted. Marx often seems trapped, despite himself, in the assumption that negation is productive, that creation can only proceed by way of destruction. And perhaps that is the right way to look at Marx: there are many Marxes, some of whom accept the gospel of negation, and others searching for another way to think and act in the world.[1] So, to be fair, the 'Marx' I have been complaining about is really those Marxes who think in terms of negation. It is entirely possible, and indeed I think we should, re-discover and learn from those other Marxes, those minor Marxes who are able to think beyond or without negation.[2]

The problem is that the Marxes of negation have become the major Marxes, the ones who dominate our contemporary imagination. We think only (or overwhelmingly) with those Marxes, and we ignore the others. As a result, we have become enthralled by neoliberalism.[3] We are utterly fascinated by it, tracking its every move, cataloging its many sins, grudgingly admiring its power to maintain its domination. We write brief histories (Harvey 2005) and primers (Chomsky 1999), we map its geographies (Brenner and Theodore 2003), we dissect its logics (Peck 2010), we chart its spread to other parts of the world (Park *et al.* 2012), we document the way it destroys the environment (Heynen *et al.* 2007), we show how it lurks behind natural disasters (Johnson 2011), how it persists even after the crisis of 2008 (Mirowski 2013), and we examine it up close with every method in our arsenal, both quantitative (Dumenil and Levy 2013) and qualitative (Greenhouse 2012). We are relentless. We are obsessed. And, like Marx in the wake of the Commune, we have developed a taste for this sour discourse. Lewis Hyde once complained about irony that it:

> has only emergency use. Carried over time, it is the voice of the trapped who have come to enjoy their cage. That is why it is so tiresome. People who have found a route to power based on their misery – who don't want to give it up though it would free them – they become ironic.
>
> *(1986: 16)*

We have carried our irony over time, and we have come to enjoy our cage.

Nietzsche: Ressentiment

It turns out that Nietzsche diagnosed our problem before the fact, in his work on morality. What we have been enmeshed in, under the sway of Hegel's negative Marxes, is what Nietzsche called *ressentiment*. *Ressentiment*, he says, is a bad humour, a bitter resentment that has plagued Judeo-Christian civilization throughout its long history. *Ressentiment* arises when those in a society who are oppressed become consumed by thoughts of their oppressors. The oppressed cannot change the conditions of their oppression, and so they console themselves by stoking and stewing in their hatred for their oppressors. They make sense of their world by developing what Nietzsche calls a 'slave morality', a morality that defines the actions and values of the oppressors to be 'evil'. Good is then defined, negatively, as whatever is not evil. So the oppressed are defined as good, but not because of some positive goodness they possess. They are only good because they are *not* the oppressors. The entire logic of this morality revolves around the oppressors. The oppressed are consumed by bitter thoughts of their oppressors, and they rarely consider themselves.

Clearly, *ressentiment* is a destructive rather than a creative energy. The only action it can think to propose is to resist evil. It urges the oppressed to destroy their oppressors, or, at the very least, to cancel their power. In most circumstances this action remains merely a fantasy for the oppressed. But, even in the unlikely event they are able to revolt and seize power from their oppressors, they will have nothing to offer in place of the old society. They lack any positive idea of the good. The only real resource they possess is their meticulous catalogue of the strategies their now-former oppressors used to subordinate them. All they could be expected to do is to systematically negate everything in the catalogue, hoping that this will give rise to the good. Obviously, this story maps right onto the experience of actually existing socialism: seize state power and cancel out the bourgeoisie's primary strategy of oppression (private property) so that the good (communism, which is nothing more than 'private property overcome') can emerge. The acute dangers of *ressentiment*'s destructive energy, and its inability to create anything new, should be abundantly clear.

But Nietzsche suggests there is a related and equally important problem with *ressentiment*, which is that it orients the oppressed in the wrong direction. It focuses their attention on the wrong subject. All of their energy is spent thinking about their oppressors. They understand very well their oppressors' excellence, power, and intelligence. But they *fail to examine themselves*. They never attend to their own excellence, power, and intelligence. They have no idea what they are capable of. They do not know what worlds, what other ways of life, they might already have the power to create together.

We can get well

And so we are working away, sourly, in this rotten groundwork: a stubbornly persistent Hegelian phantasy of creation-through-negation sitting on top of a deeper civilizational predilection for *ressentiment*. It is a dank basement full of foul air. We need a new groundwork, an entirely different way to think about and be in the world. We need to train ourselves to think not in terms of negating what exists, but in terms of producing what we desire. We need to be attentive to and discover our excellence, our power, our ability to imagine and create new objects, new relations, and new forms of life. To steal a line from Henry Miller (1965: 429–30), we need to:

> cease pouring it out like a sewer, however melodious it may sound to our ears, and rise up on our own two legs and sing with our own God-given voice. To confess, to whine, to complain, to commiserate, always demands a toll. To sing it doesn't cost us a penny.

Deleuze and Guattari, just to take one example

The good news is that the new groundwork we need isn't new at all. We have already invented it. It has existed as a minor current in our thought throughout our long march in the wilderness of Hegelian negation. In the modern era, particularly intense manifestations of this current are to be found in the work of writers like Machiavelli, Spinoza, Nietzsche, Bergson, and Deleuze and Guattari. In this section I will focus on Deleuze and Guattari's collaborative work, but that work should be understood as part of this larger flow that is not obsessed with negation but is focused on our power to produce, to create, and to affect the world around us.

Right from the beginning (1977[1972]), Deleuze and Guattari train their attention on what they call 'desiring-production', which they say is the only force in the world that is capable of creating new things. Most of the powers that be – capital, the state, the family, Oedipus – are secondary, derivative; the only thing they can do is to capture or channel the originary power of desiring-production. These 'apparatuses of capture', as Deleuze and Guattari (1987[1980]) call them, cannot themselves produce anything new. They are wholly dependent on the creative power of desiring-production. Capital, for example, cannot create value. It is a system for organizing the value that is created by living labour.[4] The state, similarly, cannot generate political power. It merely organizes the political power that people choose to surrender to it.[5]

Given this ontological starting point, Deleuze and Guattari don't see any reason to focus our attention on capital, the state, or any of the apparatuses that confine us. Our imperative must be to understand desiring-production, to know how it works, and what it can do. There is a scene in *Anti-Oedipus* (1977[1972]: 45) that crystallizes the problem. The psychoanalyst fails because he insists that the patient accept the Oedipal diagnosis, accept that his troubles (and the solution to them) are contained in the triangle of daddy–mommy–me. The analyst, therefore, never gets at what matters, he never 'says to the patient: "Tell me a little bit about your desiring-machines, won't you?"' For Deleuze and Guattari, it is our desiring-machines that hold the key. They are what is capable of generating new forms of life, new ways of being together. They have not been the focus of our enquiry, but they should be.

I am, perhaps, being a bit too stark. Deleuze and Guattari do not call for us to *entirely* re-orient our attention towards desiring-production, to pay no attention at all to the apparatuses. Rather we need to pay *some* attention to them because they currently imprison desiring-production and prevent it from producing on its own terms. To escape this confinement, desiring-production must invent what Deleuze and Guattari call 'lines of flight', fugitive acts whereby desiring-production frees itself from the apparatuses and begins to create according to its own volition. To launch these escapes, Deleuze and Guattari admit, it is helpful to be attentive to the structure of the apparatuses (which they call 'strata' here).

> This is how it should be done: Lodge yourself on a stratum, experiment with the opportunities it offers, find an advantageous place on it, find potential movements of deterritorialization, possible lines of flight, experience them, produce flow conjunctions here and there... have a small plot of new land at all times. It is through a meticulous relation with the strata that one succeeds in freeing lines of flight.
>
> *(1987[1980]: 161)*

So we need to have relations with the strata, with the apparatuses of capture. And these relations should be thoughtful; we should take care in learning the contours of the apparatuses. But, at the same time, our concern with them is contingent and fleeting. They are only of interest for now, because they are currently capturing our desire. We must pay attention to them only for as long as it takes to escape. The goal is not to destroy the apparatuses, they are none of our concern. Our concern is with ourselves, with our desiring-machines. Our goal is to flee so that they will be able to create as they will.

If we were to mobilize Deleuze and Guattari's more general imagination here in the context of the concrete political economy, we would have no desire to resent capitalist social relations and no taste for their destruction. We would be concerned, instead, to leave, to flee those relations. And we would do so only as part of the main project, which is to discover our *own* capacities for economic production, and learn more about how we might use those capacities effectively in common. Similarly, we would have no interest in smashing the state. The state is not important. Instead, we would be interested in our desire to govern ourselves, to learn our capacity for democracy, and practise using it together wisely.[6]

There is little point in resisting neoliberalism or protesting austerity. It is not necessary to negate them in order to create something new. We need only to flee and set about producing the world we want instead. And so: enough about neoliberalism. We need to stop talking about it now. We have droned on far too long. We need to let go of our obsession with it, turn our face away from it, and move purposefully in another direction. We need to become obsessed with ourselves instead, with the myriad other forms of life we are already capable of creating. We don't need a *Handbook of Neoliberalism*. We don't need any more books about exploitation, injustice, alienation, domination, privatization, enclosure, marketization, or financialization. Instead, we need books (upon books) about the other lives people are already creating instead. We need a *Handbook of Care*, a *Handbook of Democracy*, a *Handbook of the Common*. We don't need to think in terms of struggle, resistance, refusal, protest, and contestation. We need to think in terms of creation, production, innovation, desire, invention, and we need to eagerly begin the project of building another life together.

¡Democracia real YA!

That shift will not be easy because we are not in the habit. We are too steeped in *ressentiment*. And so, in this section, I am going to hold up the wave of movements in 2011, 2012, and 2013 as an example, as an inspiration that can spark our imagination. But I want to do so cautiously, because it is very hard to make generalizations about those events as a whole. It is not possible to reduce them to one desire, one guiding idea. There were many different movements, in many different places with different histories and systems of rule and cultural traditions. Tunis was not the same as Madrid, which was not the same as Tel Aviv, which was not the same as Oakland. To intensify the problem, each movement itself was also multiple, both in terms of the different desires of the different people who participated, and in terms of how each movement changed as it unfolded in time. It is misguided to try to reduce this multiplicity to a single logic, to make claims about what the 'true soul' of the movements was, to make an argument about the right way to understand the movements. In every movement, there were *both* clear desires to protest and negate the current system, *and* clear desires to flee and create a different way of being together. What I want to do is only to pick out a cluster of desires that were, in fact, present, to a greater or lesser degree, in every uprising, and give them pride of place in my narrative. I will focus mainly on Spain, not because it is representative of the whole, or because its participants exhibited a greater desire to flee, but simply because it is the case with which I am the most familiar. I am suggesting that we should look for these desires *wherever* they exist, be attentive to them, learn more about them, and discover how we can help them flourish.

Clearly, in all of these movements there was a sense that lots of things were wrong with the current state of affairs. In Spain and Greece, for example, there was an explicit animating emotion of 'indignation' at the way the political elites had fused with the banking elites to promote financialization and austerity (Oikonomakis and Roos 2015). This emotion was strong enough that participants took on the moniker *indignados* (Spain) and *Aganaktisménon-Politón* (Greece). Certainly, there was the desire to march against this political-financial elite, and to *negate* their policy agenda. The slogan in Spain, *no nos representan* ('they do not represent us'), refused the idea that the representatives in the Spanish government effectively represented the Spanish people. And the even stronger hope *que se vayan todos* ('get rid of them all'[7]) expressed a wish that the *whole* of the current regime – both parties of the Spanish state as well as the financial elites in the European Union, European Central Bank, and the International Monetary Fund – should exit the political stage. Even the call for *¡Democracia real YA!* ('Real Democracy Now!'), is in part a rejection; it denies that the current political system, liberal democracy, is *real* democracy. It argues that liberal democracy is false democracy, a broken system that needs to be replaced.

But, despite this desire to negate, the *indignados* were never consumed by it. They did express these negative desires, but they did not spend all their time marching on parliament and demanding that the powers that be govern differently. Much of what they did, instead, was to turn *away* from parliament, away from the broken system, and turn towards each other instead. They set about the work of actually creating a different way to live together. Thus, the cry of *¡Democracia real YA!* was not only or even primarily an implicit critique of the existing liberal-democratic system, it was also an explicit declaration by the *indignados* that they intended to begin – now – the work of imagining and practising real democracy instead. And so they experimented, extensively, with ways of being together (Oikonomakis and Roos 2013). They established institutions (for food distribution, information/communication, education, first-aid, sanitation, etc.), shared information, discussed key issues, set meeting agendas and schedules, facilitated discussions, negotiated disagreement, and made decisions collectively. They drew on and reinvigorated methods like general assemblies, consensus processes, *acampadas* (encampments), and *encuentros* (encounters) in order to both discuss what kind of world they wanted instead, and begin the work of actually building that world, now. They decided they favoured a leaderless and horizontal community, and so they worked on how to prevent the emergence of hierarchy and centralization in their midst. They aspired to make decisions by consensus so that the majority did not outvote and alienate the minority, but they struggled with what to do when many diverse values made consensus difficult.[8] None of what they created was ideal, and there were many mistakes made. But that is precisely what one should expect from people who have not practised. The important point is that these activities to produce another way of life were what preoccupied participants, and they were, in the main, less interested in protest, resistance, and opposition. Throughout the long hours of meetings, discussion, and deliberation, they were not turned towards the state or the European financial powers. They were turned towards each other, literally, and they struggled to learn together what they wanted, what they were capable of, and who they wanted to be.[9]

This orientation was reinforced by the much-discussed tendency among most of the movements in 2011 not to make any demands. They tended to eschew the typical model whereby a movement draws enough people and makes enough noise to get the attention of the authorities, and then demands certain changes in how those authorities govern. In many places – Greece, Spain, New York – there was a palpable sense that the current order was a lost cause, that there is no point in trying to fix it, and so there is no reason to demand changes in the way it governs. The most spectacular example of this turning away from power was when the Mayor of Denver decided Occupy Denver had become significant enough that he should meet with their leaders and hear their demands. Occupy Denver agreed to the meeting, but they sent a border collie named Shelby to represent them.

The same kind of orientation could be seen in the much-discussed tactic of occupation. In almost every case in 2011, movements occupied and inhabited an important and central urban space, usually for a period of weeks or even months. But the occupations were not military. They were not done to confront the state or engage it in a test of strength. Occupation was done to acquire and hold a space in order to *use* it, in order that participants could set about the work of creating another society, the work of governing themselves. They were occupying the *agora* of the *polis*,[10] and they did what citizens of the *polis* are supposed to do there: they governed themselves. In the state's mind, of course, these occupations *were* military, territorial seizures that directly challenged the state's sovereignty, and so they had to be cleared. In every case, the state sent police and/or military forces to clear the square, usually violently. But the response by the occupiers was typically *not* military; they did not engage in a violent struggle with the state. In Spain, confronted by lines of heavily armed police in riot gear, occupiers raised both hands in the air and chanted *estas son nuestras armas*, 'these are our arms'. They blocked entry into the square, tried to hold the square as long as they could, but not really in order to confront or defeat the state. They occupied the square in order to have a space in which they could govern themselves. They did not hope the state would notice them so much as they hoped the state would leave them alone so they could get on with their work.

Conclusion

There is much more to say about the movements of 2011 and after, of course, but I hope the point is clear that they were strongly marked not only by a conviction that the current state of affairs is broken, but also by a strong desire to get started producing a different way of living together. And they not only expressed that desire, they actually began the work of creating that new way of life. The movements of 2011 are, therefore, one promising model of what we might be like if we were to get well, if we were to wean ourselves off of our *ressentiment* and move beyond our debilitating obsession with negating neoliberalism. We have developed so many tools of negation, and we are so practised at using them, that it would be natural to feel a fair amount of apprehension, and even fear, at giving them up. The good news is that we already *also* have considerable tools for producing another way of life, even if we are not as experienced at using them. We are skilled at negating, but we will need to practise before we feel confident in our ability to create instead. So we need to start practising, and we need to start now. We need to turn away from neoliberalism and towards ourselves, to begin the difficult – but also joyous – work of managing our affairs for ourselves. Negation, critique, protest, resistance, struggle – we have been using the wrong tools. They are making us sick. What we need instead are invention, desire, production, creation, delight, joy. Estas *son nuestras armas*.

Notes

1 These latter Marxes, for example, are attracted to Feuerbach's critique of Hegel, and the former's insistence that thought must begin from 'the self-subsistent positive positively grounded on itself' (Marx 1994: 80).
2 Good examples of how to do this really well, I think, are Miguel Abensour (2011) and Deleuze and Guattari (1977[1972]).
3 And its follow-on mutations, like austerity and precarity.
4 Marx draws on David Ricardo (1817) to make this point in *Capital* (1993[1867]: Chapter 10, Section 1).
5 This is absolutely clear in Hobbes, who writes *Leviathan* as a passionate attempt to convince us that we must *continue* to surrender our originary political power to the state, which will keep the peace by terrorizing us into obedience.

6 Clearly, this project, which I have narrated in the language of Deleuze and Guattari, has much overlap with an anarchist idea of prefigurative politics, stemming from classical sources (e.g. Bakunin 1972; Kropotkin 1972[1902]; Proudhon 2005[1864]), modern ones (e.g. May 1994; Bey 2003; Day 2005; Graeber 2009; Newman 2010), and the ongoing project to take up that work in radical geography by authors like Springer (2012) and Ince (2012).

7 Literally: 'would that they all go'. The Spanish is in the subjunctive, and so it is expressing a desire for a state of affairs that is not currently actual. The English rendering I have given is in the imperative mood, and it doesn't quite capture that subjunctive longing.

8 Marianne Maeckelbergh (2012) offers an excellent account of the nuances of these practices, as well as how they were similar to and different from the practices of the alterglobalization movement.

9 Most of the practices in this paragraph were also present in the movement in Athens, the various Occupy movements in the USA and UK, and the movement in Turkey in 2013, to name only a few examples.

10 Quite literally, in the case of Syntagma Square in Athens.

References

Abensour, M. 2011. *Democracy Against the State: Marx and the Machiavellian Moment*. Cambridge, MA: Polity.

Bakunin, M. 1972. Critique of the Marxist Theory of the State, in Dolgoff, S., trans and ed. *Bakunin on Anarchy*. New York: Knopf.

—. 1973a. State and Society, in Lehning, A., ed. *Michael Bakunin: Selected Writings*. London: Jonathan Cape.

—. 1973b. God and the State, in Lehning, A., ed. *Michael Bakunin: Selected Writings*. London: Jonathan Cape.

Bey, H. 2003. *TAZ: The Temporary Autonomous Zone, Ontological Anarchy, Poetic Terrorism*. Brooklyn: Autonomedia.

Brenner, N., and Theodore, N. eds. 2003. *Spaces of Neoliberalism: Urban Restructuring in North America and Western Europe*. Chichester: Wiley-Blackwell.

Chomsky, N. 1999. *Profit Over People: Neoliberalism and the Global Order*. New York: Seven Stories Press.

Day, R. 2005. *Gramsci is Dead: Anarchist Currents in the Newest Social Movements*. London: Pluto.

Deleuze, G., and Guattari, F. 1977[1972]. *Anti-Oedipus*. New York: Penguin.

—. 1987[1980] *A Thousand Plateaus*. Minneapolis: University of Minnesota Press.

Dumenil, G., and Levy, D. 2013. *The Crisis of Neoliberalism*. Cambridge, MA: Harvard University Press.

Graeber, D. 2009. *Direct Action: An Ethnography*. Oakland, CA: AK Press.

Greenhouse, C., ed. 2012. *Ethnographies of Neoliberalism*. Philadelphia: University of Pennsylvania Press.

Harvey, D. 2005. *A Brief History of Neoliberalism*. Oxford: Oxford University Press.

Heynen, N., McCarthy, J., Prudham, S., and Robbins, P. eds. 2007. *Neoliberal Environments: False Promises and Unnatural Consequences*. New York: Routledge.

Hyde, L. 1986. *Alcohol and Poetry: John Berryman and the Booze Talking*. Dallas, TX: Dallas Institute of Humanities and Culture.

Ince, A. 2012. In the Shell of the Old: Anarchist Geographies of Territorialisation. *Antipode*, 44.5: 1645–66.

Johnson, C., ed. 2011. *The Neoliberal Deluge: Hurricane Katrina, Late Capitalism, and the Remaking of New Orleans*. Minneapolis: University of Minnesota Press.

Kropotkin, P. 1972[1902]. *Mutual Aid: A Factor of Evolution*. New York: New York University Press.

Maeckelbergh, M. 2012. Horizontal Democracy Now: From Alterglobalization to Occupation. *Interface: A Journal for and about Social Movements*, 4.1: 207–34.

Marx, K. 1871. *The Civil War in France*. Retrieved from https://www.marxists.org/archive/marx/works/1871/civil-war-france

—. 1993[1867]. *Capital, Volume 1*. New York: Penguin.

—. 1994. *Karl Marx: Selected Writings*. Simon, L., ed. Indianapolis, IN: Hackett.

May, T. 1994. *The Political Philosophy of Poststructuralist Anarchism*. University Park: Pennsylvania State University Press.

Miller, H. 1965. *Sexus*. New York: Grove Press.

Mirowski, P. 2013. *Never Let a Serious Crisis Go to Waste: How Neoliberalism Survived the Financial Meltdown*. New York: Verso.

Newman, S. 2010. *The Politics of Postanarchism*. Edinburgh: Edinburgh University Press.

Oikonomakis, L. and J. Roos, 2013. We Are Everywhere! The Autonomous Roots of the Real Democracy Movement. Paper for the 7th Annual European Consortium for Political Research Conference, Bordeaux, September.

—. 2015. A Global Movement for Real Democracy? The Resonance of Anti-Austerity Protest from Spain and Greece to Occupy Wall Street, in Angelovici, M., Dufour, P., and Nez, H., eds. *Street Politics in the Age of Austerity: From the Indignad@s to Occupy*. Amsterdam: Amsterdam University Press.

Park, B, Hill, R., and Saito, A. eds. 2012. *Locating Neoliberalism in East Asia: Neoliberalizing Spaces in Developmental States*. Chichester: Wiley-Blackwell.

Peck, J. 2010. *Constructions of Neoliberal Reason*. Oxford: Oxford University Press.

Proudhon, P. 2005[1864]. Manifesto of Sixty Workers from the Seine Department, in Guerin, D., ed. *No Gods, No Masters: An Anthology of Anarchism*. Oakland, CA: AK Press: 103–10.

Ricardo, D. 1817. *On The Principles of Political Economy and Taxation*. Retrieved from https://www.marxists.org/reference/subject/economics/ricardo/tax/index.htm

Springer, S. 2012. Anarchism! What Geography Still Ought to Be. *Antipode*, 44.5: 1605–24.

INDEX